Guts & Glory

Guts &

*The Making of the
American Military
Image in Film*

Revised and Expanded Edition

Lawrence H. Suid

THE UNIVERSITY PRESS OF KENTUCKY

Glory

Publication of this volume was made possible in part
by a grant from the National Endowment for the Humanities.

Editorial and Sales Offices: The University Press of Kentucky
663 South Limestone Street, Lexington, Kentucky 40508–4008

06 05 04 03 02   5 4 3 2 1

Frontispiece: George C. Scott as Patton.

Library of Congress Cataloging-in-Publication Data

Suid, Lawrence H.
      Guts and glory : the making of the American military image / Lawrence H. Suid.
      p. cm.
      Includes bibliographical references and index.
      ISBN 0-8131-2225-2 (alk. paper)
      ISBN 0-8131-9018-5 (pbk : alk. paper)
      1. War films—United States—History and criticism. I. Title.
      PN1995.9.W3 S93 2002
      791.43'658—dc21   2001 007630

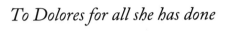

To Dolores for all she has done

We have shared the incommunicable experience of war. We have felt, we still feel, the passion of life to its top. In our youths, our hearts were touched with fire.

Oliver Wendell Holmes

If you glorify war you create a climate for more wars.

Arthur Hiller, director of *The Americanization of Emily*

Contents

 **Acknowledgments**

MY ACKNOWLEDGMENTS IN THE ORIGINAL EDITION of *Guts & Glory* hopefully thanked all the people who provided aid and comfort in one form or another, especially Donald Baruch, Dr. Clarence Cramer, and Gertrude Weiner. This revised, expanded edition owes its existence to the same people and I will allow that acknowledgment to continue to speak to their help. However, many other people have contributed to making this new edition possible and I would require more space than I have to thank everyone. Nevertheless a few people deserve special recognition.

Simply put, without the support of my friend Dolores Haverstick, I could not have written this book. She has read the new chapters, offered cogent criticism, and then read the revised manuscript. The revised edition in every way reflects her special interest and assistance. Likewise, Phil Strub made the new book possible by continuing Don Baruch's policy of providing answers to my many questions about the Pentagon's relationship with the motion picture industry and the films made during his tenure. As with Don, however, this thanks is given less for his information than for his refusal to tell me what to say or how to say it. Instead, he offered only constructive criticism that helped ensure the accuracy of my many articles, of *Sailing on the Silver Screen,* and now this book.

I have never used the word friend lightly and would never assume that because someone would agree to an interview or provide information that he or she had become a friend. Some people, however, have become friends, and for their friendship and staunch support of my work I thank Chuck Champlin and Brig. Gen. Edwin Simmons, USMC (Ret). Likewise, although Norm Hatch kept a professional distance while head of the Audio Visual Division in the Department of Defense, he has become a primary source of information on the Hollywood/military relationship and a friend. The same can be said for Budd Lesser, Delbert Mann, Beth Resko, Kerry Wiessmann, the late Edmund North, and the late Wendell Mayes, who always found time for lunch and good conversation whenever I visited Los Angeles.

Many other people within the Hollywood/military relationship including Kathy Ross, Matt Morgan, Chuck Davis, Melissa Scheurmann, Dale Dye, John Markanton, Mitch Marovitz, Jack Green, Chas. Henry, Ray Smith, Malcolm Wright, and Gary Shrout, have gone far beyond the call of duty in providing me information for this new edition. I fear they will be happy to see the book done so that they no longer have to answer my queries. Similarly, Jim Farmer, Don Bittner, Bob Fyne, writers and scholars in their own right, have regularly provided information and suggestions for improving my writings.

As important, I would like to thank my many personal friends who have been there for me in both the good times and the occasional bad times, all of whom made my survival possible: Paul and Brenda Coran, Chris and Don Sylvester, Chuck Lieman and Jeanne Mullaney, Carleen and Don Rule, Fred Geldon, John Haugen, Jon and Karstin Goldman,

Stuart and Ellen Chasen, and Ginny Shapiro. I have been lucky to have befriended all of them. I only hope they know that.

Madeline Maltz in the Library of Congress Film Studies Department has remained an indispensable source of help in locating information of all sorts for more years than either of us can remember, as has Charles Silver at the Museum of Modern Art. I am also grateful for the generous help from the staff at Collectors Warehouse, Inc. I thank them, Aunt Marcella, cousins Lois and Harvey Swack, and Dent, who all contributed each in their own way to the writing of the book.

Preface

UNTIL THE EARLY 1960S, MOST AMERICANS perceived the nation's armed services as an all-conquering and infallible force that could protect the United States from any threat and project the national interest to any corner of the world. Conveyed in history books, popular literature, and the mass media, this image received its highest expression in the military's overwhelming success in World War II. If Korea did not become another smashing victory, most people believed the fault lay with the politicians in Washington rather than the armed forces in combat. Regardless, during the 1950s, the military retained its aura of invincibility, spearheaded by its growing fleet of aircraft carriers, nuclear submarines, and SAC bombers.

During the 1960s, however, the nation's perception of its armed forces underwent a profound transformation. As the World War II victories receded from memory and the 1962 Cuban Missile Crisis threatened the American people with nuclear holocaust, disenchantment with things military began to develop. The escalation of the Vietnam War and the rise of the antiwar movement after 1965 accelerated the criticism of the armed forces in the print and visual media. Tet, the My Lai massacre, and the ultimate realization that the United States had lost the war politically, if not militarily, completed the savaging of the positive military image which the services had cultivated for so many years.

The original edition of *Guts & Glory* told the story of the symbiotic relationship between the armed services and the motion picture industry from its origins through the burnishing of the military's image in the 1950s, to 1978 when the initial cinematic portrayals of the American involvement in Vietnam were reaching theaters. This revised, expanded edition continues the narrative through the rehabilitation of the armed services' shattered reputations to the present when Hollywood has decided that people are once again willing to pay to watch combat movies, whether the action occurs at Pearl Harbor, in the Middle East, in Bosnia, in Somalia, in World War II, or even in Vietnam.

Neither the original book or this edition questions the legitimacy of the military's relationship with the film industry. Congress has legislated that the armed services should have a public relations operation. Nor does the book consider the cost of military assistance to filmmakers except as it relates to the controversies surrounding the amount of support certain movies received. Government regulations state that assistance must come at no cost to the nation's taxpayers. The degree to which the military establishment adheres to this regulation cannot readily be measured. In any event, the armed services' assistance to commercial films clearly costs less than if the military produced its own "message" films. More important, Hollywood films effectively reach far more people than service-produced documentaries or infomercials.

Unlike the first edition, this book does discuss military comedies, including *Private Benjamin* and *Stripes,* which in their own way have contributed to the message that the armed services have again become socially acceptable institutions in which young people may spend a few years. It even discusses one of the great cinematic musicals that in its first incarnation as a Broadway play in the 1960s made a powerful antiwar, anti-Vietnam statement. It does not discuss foreign war movies except in passing and it does not consider Hollywood's portrayals of pre-twentieth-century American wars except where a service assisted on the production. Nor does it discuss made-for-television movies and miniseries.

The first edition of *Guts & Glory* focused exclusively on war movies and peacetime military stories. For the purposes of this study, I am defining a war movie as one in which men appear in battle or in situations in which actual combat influences their actions. A military movie portrays men in uniform in training situations during peacetime or performing duties intended to preserve the peace. This edition does add one new category, the Vietnam homefront movie, on the theory that Hollywood's portrayal of the American experience in Southeast Asia includes the impact of the war on the civilian population. I do recognize that such films as *Coming Home* and *Running on Empty* contain no visual images of combat and received no assistance from the Pentagon. However, each in its own way helps provide significant images of the war. *Heroes* and *Cease Fire* bridge the gap between the two categories since they focus on the plight of the soldiers who fought in country and each uses a brief combat sequence to explain their post-war suffering.

Virtually all the military movies made up to the early 1960s received assistance from the armed services in their production, and my discussion focuses on the process of obtaining cooperation and describing how the help contributed to the creation of the military image. Beginning with *Dr. Strangelove, Fail Safe,* and the other anti-bomb films of the mid-1960s and the growing protest movement against the Vietnam War, however, the traditional relationship came to an end and the armed services began to reject scripts which they believed contained negative portrayals of their men and activities. The book will describe the changes that took place and how Hollywood's new images of the military contributed to the changes in people's perceptions of the armed services. This edition will pick up the story from the low point of the relationship in the mid-1970s through the rehabilitation of the military image in movies to the present time.

To the extent that the book has a thesis, it postulates that Hollywood's creation of the image of all-powerful, always victorious armed services through the late 1950s contributed to the ease with which Lyndon Johnson and the best and brightest people in government took the United States into the quagmire of Vietnam. The thesis certainly does not provide a complete explanation of how the country found itself in Vietnam. Clearly, the president's character contributed to escalation of the war rather than withdrawal. A visit to the Alamo illustrates why no Texan could retreat in the face of what he perceived were hostile actions directed against his country. Nevertheless, the research on which I have based this book suggests that without the consistently positive image of the American armed services on movie screens, the nation would very possibly have become more skeptical, sooner of General Westmoreland's claim that the light was at the end of the tunnel and he needed only another 100,000 troops to defeat the North Vietnamese peasant army.

Hopefully, then, the new edition of *Guts & Glory* will continue to provide insights into the impact which the images, both positive and negative, of the armed services, created in almost one hundred years of military movies, have had on the American people. The book also continues the examination of the irony of filmmakers' claims that they make only anti-war movies while continuing to portray combat as exciting and as the place where boys become men, where men become heroes, and even role models to the next generation.

I consider this book a work of military history rather than a film history, which I define as a study of directors, producers, actors, screenwriters, studios, and cinematic technology. I have also described the original book as an institutional history, a study of the symbiotic relationship between two of the most powerful organizations in the world. I have suggested that the product of that relationship has helped shape the perceptions that the American people have had of war, of violence, and of its armed services. To the extent that the book does these things, I believe it helps explain how the government and cultural institutions can shape the minds of its population, for good or for evil.

Of course, I would like to think the book can be read simply as a story about how the armed services and the film industry operate. In the good old days before Vietnam, many of the leading directors, screenwriters, and producers had taken part in either World War I or World War II. They understood the military, and military leaders understood filmmakers. Today, few people in Hollywood have served in the armed services and so have little understanding of the military culture. In contrast, government officials and military public affairs officers have a good understanding of the motion picture industry and the mantra that Hollywood makes movies only to make money.

This narrowly focused goal has led filmmakers to claim that they must take dramatic license in transferring history to the screen. More than that, in the name of creativity, most filmmakers ignore the suggestion that truth might be better than fiction. In *Pearl Harbor*, director Michael Bay created a scene in which President Roosevelt learns about the Japanese attack while his valet wheels him down a huge generic hall. In fact, FDR was working on his stamp collection in his study. Likewise, Bay shows the president learning about the probable failure of the Doolittle raid on April 18 in the White House garden where his valet has just cut a rose for him. The author can testify from experience that roses in Washington do not bloom until late May.

Do these deviations from reality matter? Do they change history? Probably not. Truth matters, however, to the extent that truth matters. If films can influence audiences, which I believe is true, then the willingness of Hollywood to play loose with the facts may well contribute to people's apparent lack of concern with truth. Therefore, in the new edition of *Guts & Glory* I have considered the question of the limits of dramatic license in films which purport to portray a historical event and I have tried to provide some answer to the question of whether movies about military events can be used to teach students the history of war and men in combat.

The original book ended before the first significant movies about the war had begun to appear. Having taught the history of Vietnam in 1967, I had come to the conclusion that our national interest had not required that the United States intervene in what had become a civil war between the North and South, and I believed that the nation had suffered its first military defeat. However, as I began to write about the films which portrayed that defeat, my friends in the armed services and the Defense Department continued to argue that the American forces in Vietnam had not lost a significant battle, including the Tet Offensive in 1968. Consequently, I faced the need to define victory and defeat.

The Japanese seemed to have inflicted a great defeat on the United States at Pearl Harbor, but *Tora! Tora! Tora!* showed Admiral Yamamoto concluding that the attack had simply awakened a sleeping giant. In Korea, the Marines claimed they were not retreating in the face of the Chinese onslaught in December 1950, but were simply advancing in another direction. In Vietnam, the United States believed its new helicopter assault tactics had defeated the North Vietnamese regular army in 1965 in the Ia Drang valley. The

North Vietnamese believed they had learned how to defeat the helicopters and so would win the war. Trying to find balance, I have accepted, with reservations, that the American military did not lose the war on the battlefield, but that the United States did lose the war politically. However, if Clausewitz's contention that war is diplomacy by other means, then only one conclusion can be drawn: the United States lost the war in Vietnam.

In any case, I would like to believe that people can read this book and enjoy it without having seen even one of the movies discussed. My best friend and most trustworthy critic refuses to see any war movie, not liking blood and gore. Nevertheless, she has read and edited *Sailing on the Silver Screen* and now this book in its entirety, at least twice. I am very appreciative of that and would hope that the narrative itself helped her go beyond the call of duty.

Finally, I must stress that I am not writing about films as works of art in this book. I have tried to convince a friend that most movies serve simply to entertain and few become art. For what little it may be worth, I believe a good movie whatever the genre should make a comment on the human condition by telling a story with a beginning, a middle, and an end. Further, a great film should be able to stand by itself as a complete entity—independent of its original source. To succeed as art and as entertainment, a movie should also contain people with whom the audience can empathize.

Most war movies, in contrast, attempt to create their dramatic impact through noise, spectacular combat scenes, and violence. Since most Americans like escapist entertainment in the form of action and adventure more than social commentary, the war film has remained, along with the Western, the most enduring of Hollywood genres. But few war films have become works of art. Consequently, *Guts & Glory* does not consider the dramatic quality of the movies under discussion except as that quality may affect the image of the service being portrayed. Instead, it describes how Hollywood and the armed services have conspired, with some few interruptions, to provide the nation with its perception of the military establishment in war and peace for almost one hundred years.

Introduction

IN THE PREFACE TO THE FIRST EDITION of *Guts & Glory*, Lawrence Suid wrote, "The book is not a definitive history of the relationship between the film industry and the armed forces." Perhaps not. But for the first time, a scholar had documented the curious and intriguing story of how Hollywood and the armed services, working from different perspectives and with different goals, cooperated to create stories about the U.S. military in war and peace. These movies became the source of most people's knowledge of the American fighting men and women and the wars in which they fought to protect the nation from any external threat. Whether these films accurately portrayed combat, life in the military, and the history of twentieth-century warfare is another matter.

In the original volume, Suid devoted his primary attention to explaining how the film industry and the armed services have interacted in what he describes as a symbiotic relationship. In this edition, Suid has also explored the limits of dramatic license in war movies, how Hollywood views historical accuracy, and how much latitude the military will allow in portraying its operations and actual events. He disputes filmmakers' arguments that they must often fictionalize portrayals to heighten the cinematic drama and that they are making entertaining movies, not documentaries. Suid suggests that a director's claim that he has captured the essence of an event is often a convenient excuse which hides a multitude of sins, and he points out that the truth is often more interesting and dramatic than the fiction that appears on the screen. He believes that truth does matter and concludes that the theater is probably not the place to learn history.

When *Guts & Glory* appeared in 1978, Hollywood was beginning to release movies which called into question every aspect of the nation's involvement in Vietnam, and the American military found its prestige at its lowest point of the century, if not the nation's entire history. Suid has picked up his story with the release of *The Deer Hunter, Hair*, and the long awaited *Apocalypse Now*. However, he points out that along with the continued battering of the military image, filmmakers also began producing films that started to rehabilitate the reputation of the services. He then has traced the process by which Hollywood returned the armed services to glory.

At the same time, Suid has gone back to the earlier days of the relationship, adding new chapters describing the development and then formalization of the process by which the military provided assistance to filmmakers. He has also created a counter-point to his original discussion of the anti-bomb films of the 1960s by looking at how movies of the post–World War II period glorified the atomic bomb as a weapon to keep the peace. In fact, the bomb did that, validating the Strategic Air Command slogan, "Peace Is Our Profession." However, Suid explains that the military establishment and the film industry faced the same dilemma following the collapse of the Soviet Union: where would each organization find suitable enemies?

The heart of the new *Guts & Glory* remains the same. Suid has described in detail, but without getting bogged down with minutia, the process by which the individual services decided which films, on the basis of their scripts, would receive the use of planes, tanks, locations, and even troops. Until the Vietnam War, most projects received support after negotiations to resolve differences over procedures and actions which the services believed portrayed their men and policies in a bad light. For the most part, the military objected to projects it believed would not reflect proper glory on the services and even on the very ideas of battle and war.

As the Vietnam War became controversial, Hollywood reflected the growing antipathy in the country toward the military, and filmmakers avoided portraying the war—except for John Wayne, who produced, directed, and starred in *The Green Berets*. Suid gives Wayne full credit for playing "John Wayne" by having the courage to put his money where his mouth was and make a movie that reflected his particular political views on the conflict. In contrast, only after the war ended did other filmmakers begin creating images which conveyed their anti-war sentiments, and the military reacted as expected, refusing to provide assistance to any movie portraying its experience in Vietnam negatively. Knowing this, producers often did not even bother to submit their military stories, even ones not about Vietnam, to the Pentagon, realizing their contents were so manifestly anti-brass and anti-war that any approach was doomed to failure.

Nevertheless, except in the immediate post-Vietnam period, the military and the filmmakers continued to enter into negotiations, with each side trying to give as little and obtain as much as possible. Using information from more than four hundred interviews and primary sources, including DoD and studio records, Suid has chronicled this process. However, he has not lost sight of the larger picture or Hollywood's twin goals of entertaining the audience and so making money. He functions as both a military historian and a film fan and film critic. The more controversial a film was in its time or in the longer view of history, the more careful Suid is in rendering a fair and balanced and consistently insightful judgment as to the movie's strengths and weaknesses.

This is no mean accomplishment, especially in the post-Vietnam era when a film such as *The Deer Hunter* contained ambiguous images. Was Cimino's film applauding patriotism and sacrifice when the reunited friends sing "God Bless America" as a kind of dining table grace, or was he suggesting war's irony and futility? Suid then compares this ending with a similar one in *Hair* in which the friends sing "Let the Sun Shine In," suggesting they have learned from the loss of their friend, who died in Vietnam.

Regardless of one's view of the military, war was never again to be so uncomplicated thematically as it was before Vietnam. Those of us who served in World War II had the luxury of knowing why we fought, who the enemy was, and why it was crucial to defeat both Germany and Japan. We did not need Frank Capra's brilliant *Why We Fight* series of documentaries to tell us. Indeed, the revelations that came with the liberating of the concentration camps deepened our conviction about why we were fighting and why all the sacrifices were justified.

It was in the postwar era that the Department of Defense's decision-making grew more difficult and delicate and Suid's findings more interesting and significant. There were at first the films that looked at battle more realistically, but still as heroic and ennobling. There were not many of these war's end films, but the best of them had a documentary flavor: *A Walk in the Sun, Battleground, Twelve O'Clock High,* and *The Longest Day* all received Pentagon assistance.

The fast-lowering temperature of the Cold War and then the onset of the Korean conflict in 1950 launched a new era of ambiguity in our foreign relations and in the national attitudes toward war. The creative decisions of the filmmakers, let alone the judgments of the Department of Defense, were never to be so simple again. This became even more cruelly true when the Vietnam conflict, boiling out of the mid-1960s, divided the country over the question of U.S. involvement.

Stanley Kramer once told me that he wanted desperately to make a Vietnam film. But as he well knew, movies are a mass medium, and a mainstream film almost requires a national consensus. Kramer could not conceive a story that would be acceptable to both the Hawks and the Doves in society. Kramer, of course, was not alone, and the monumental films out of Vietnam came only after the issue had been resolved and the United States had withdrawn. Neither *Apocalypse Now* nor *The Deer Hunter* had Pentagon assistance. Only very slowly did Hollywood and the armed services reach a consensus on how to portray the war, culminating in the Army's providing full assistance to *Hamburger Hill* in 1987. By then, thanks to *Private Benjamin* and *An Officer and a Gentleman*, which did not receive cooperation, and *Top Gun*, which did, the American people again viewed the armed services positively and would soon support the military in the Gulf War.

Suid tells this story well, and the new edition is a major and impressive work of historical research. For the military historian, the book goes behind the scenes of the Pentagon's public relations operations and looks at how the armed services try to represent themselves on the nation's movie screens. For the dedicated moviegoer, it is a memory-flogging checklist of a significant film genre spanning many decades. *Guts & Glory* is also in its own way a kind of graph of the growing evolution of the American film over the years, from the relative innocence of the pre–World War II period through the war itself and into the Cold War and beyond, when the rise of television deprived the theatrical motion picture of three quarters of its audience and nearly all of its calculated naivete. And if not before, I believe the book has now become the definitive study of the relationship between Hollywood and the U.S. military.

Charles Champlin
Arts Editor Emeritus of the *Los Angeles Times*

1 Hollywood and War

WHY WAR MOVIES? WHY MILITARY MOVIES? Why the attraction of war to the American people? Gen. George Patton, through his film reincarnation George C. Scott, provided perhaps the quintessential explanation of the nation's continuing fascination with things military. Standing beneath a huge U.S. flag, Patton-Scott addressed his unpictured audience, the troops, and, implicitly, the nation: "Men, all this stuff you've heard about America not wanting to fight, wanting to stay out of the war, is a lot of horse dung. Americans traditionally love to fight. All real Americans love the sting of battle. When you were kids, you all admired the champion marble shooter, the fastest runner, the big league ballplayers, the toughest boxers. Americans love a winner and will not tolerate a loser. Americans play to win all the time. I wouldn't give a hoot in hell for a man who lost and laughed. That's why Americans have never lost, and will never lose a war: because the very thought of losing is hateful to Americans."[1]

Scott's monologue synthesized several of Patton's exhortations to his officers and NCOs on the eve of the Normandy invasion. In classic terms, he glorified military combat as the highest form of manliness: "You know, by God, I actually pity those poor bastards we're going up against—by God, I do. We're not just going to shoot the bastards. We're going to cut out their living guts and use them to grease the treads of our tanks. We're going to murder those lousy Hun bastards by the bushel." Urging his men not to worry about chickening out under fire, he assured them they would all do their duty: "The Nazis are the enemy. Wade into them. Spill their blood. Shoot them in the belly. When you put your hand into a bunch of goo that a moment before was your best friend's face . . . you'll know what to do."

Patton then reminded his men that they were never to merely hold their positions: "We are advancing constantly and we're not interested in holding onto anything except the enemy. We're going to hold onto him by the nose and we're going to kick him in the ass. We're going to kick the hell out of him all the time and we're going to go through him like crap through a goose." To Patton, these actions would not only assure victory but would allow his men to return home with a sense of pride: "Thirty years from now, when you are sitting around your fireplace with your grandson on your knee and he asks you what did you do in the great World War II, you won't have to say, 'Well, I shoveled shit in Louisiana.'"

If Patton's espousal of combat had appeared on movie screens anytime before the mid-1960s, few people would have raised dissenting voices. *Patton* would undoubtedly have been viewed as simply another Hollywood war film glorifying America's success in battle. Only after the anti–Vietnam War movement caused people to question the morality of combat could even a portion of the populace criticize *Patton* for glorifying the martial spirit in the American people.

Until the mid-1960s, most Americans believed they lived in a peace-loving nation, which went to war only in self-defense and to uphold democratic ideas. To preach peace, however, has never committed the nation to a philosophy of nonviolence. The United States won its independence in a war, fought a civil war to remain united, and has continued to exist through selective but regular use of its military power, not always justified but usually with the approval of its people. Ironically, to return the world to peace following the most horrific of all wars, the United States achieved that worthy goal by unleashing the most terrible weapon mankind had ever seen. Clearly, a contradiction exists between the great emphasis Americans have put on peace and the means the nation has used to preserve itself.

As long as the nation remained unvanquished on the

George C. Scott opens *Patton* (1970) with a salute to his men and a monologue to the audience.

battlefield, this ambiguity in its national character could be safely ignored. Into the 1960s, Hollywood did its part to show war in terms that Patton would have appreciated. Virtually all American films about war and the military followed the pattern established from the earliest days of the motion picture industry, showing only the glamorous side of combat—the excitement, the adventure, the camaraderie. Filmmakers might not always portray combat as a pleasant experience, but they made it clear that ultimate victory did require some pain and suffering. Not until the growing disenchantment with the Vietnam conflict did Americans begin to explore their long-standing love of the martial spirit and their previously unquestioned respect for the military establishment. In this changed environment, Patton's justification of war and the virtues of combat became subject to a different interpretation.

As the antiwar movement grew and television brought the realities of the Vietnam conflict into American homes during the dinner hour night after night, the film industry backed away from military subjects. Following the release of *Patton, M*A*S*H, Catch-22,* and *Tora! Tora! Tora!* during 1970, Hollywood stopped producing war films. With few exceptions, the industry even avoided movies that portrayed the armed forces in a negative light.

In 1976 Hollywood began once again to release movies about the military and combat. The United States was no longer waging a war that might require morale-boosting, patriotic films. Vietnam was finally fading from the American conscience, though the

Lon Chaney, as the archetypal Marine sergeant, along with actors and U.S. Marines, film *Tell It to the Marines* (1927) at the Marine barracks in San Diego.

wounds from that divisive conflict had not yet healed. Supposedly, the trauma of the lost war in Southeast Asia had eroded Americans' interest in things military. Nevertheless, *Midway*, a truly terrible movie, became the sixth-largest-grossing film that year and the first of a growing number of productions that once again began exploring the American military experience.

Walter Mirisch, who produced *Midway*, offered two reasons for making his film. He felt that young people had a nostalgic interest in seeing the period planes that fought at Midway. In addition, he wanted to give the American people a Bicentennial gift. In portraying the victory of the badly outnumbered American task force over the Japanese armada, Mirisch believed he was reminding the nation of a glorious day. The comparison to the American experience in the Revolution was implicit. The United States had, at least in the past, emerged victorious from battle whatever the odds.[2]

Like *Midway*, the films that soon followed it focused on World War II, both in Europe and in the Pacific. By the end of 1977, *The Eagle Has Landed, Cross of Iron, A Bridge Too Far*, and *MacArthur* had all appeared. Even a film depicting other worlds, *Star Wars*, which immediately began to challenge box-office records, contained many elements from the old World War II movies about aerial battles. George Lucas, the director, viewed combat footage from *The Memphis Belle, The Battle of Midway*, and *Twelve O'Clock High* to help him create a sense of authenticity in the dogfight and bombing sequences in his outer space battles.[3]

On late-night television, old Hollywood war movies remained a staple item, and documentary series such as *The World at War* and the venerable *Victory at Sea* appeared regu-

The mock-up of the USS *Arizona* that Twentieth Century Fox built in Hawaii for *Tora! Tora! Tora!* It cost more than $1 million and also represented the other battleships during the sneak attack on Pearl Harbor.

larly. At the same time, the networks turned out new productions portraying the military at work and play. *Baa, Baa Black Sheep* tried to combine elements of *Sergeant Bilko, The Dirty Dozen,* and *M*A*S*H* into a glorification of the World War II flying exploits of Marine hero Pappy Boyington. *M*A*S*H* itself continued to top the television rating charts. In a more serious vein, NBC broadcast the miniseries *Once an Eagle,* based on Anton Myrer's best-selling novel. Focusing on the "necessary wars," the series followed American participation in both world wars through the eyes of its major characters. Although the novel concluded with the early years of the American involvement in Vietnam, the television version chose to ignore the less-appreciated wars in Korea and Vietnam.

Vietnam and its aftermath had, however, become the inspiration for a growing number of Hollywood productions. Francis Ford Coppola, the director of the two classic *Godfather* movies, turned from violence in America to violence in Southeast Asia when he began working on *Apocalypse Now* in 1975. Originally expected to appear in 1977, it became the first major Hollywood film about Vietnam to go before the cameras since John Wayne had released *The Green Berets* in 1968. While Coppola suffered through many difficulties that delayed the premiere of his film until May 1979, other projects about Vietnam and its veterans, including *Good Guys Wear Black, Rolling Thunder, Go Tell the Spartans, The Boys in Company C, Heroes, Hair, Coming Home,* and *The Deer Hunter,* began arriving in theaters.

The renewed production of military films again focused attention on one of Hollywood's most enduring genres. Like the western, war movies offer escapist entertainment that

Swirling fighters grace the cover of a 1927 program for *Wings,* the first Hollywood movie about aerial combat.

Gregory Peck, as General Frank Savage, in the cockpit of a B-17 bomber during the filming of *Twelve O'Clock High* (1950).

appeals to viewers' most basic, most primal instincts. Otto Preminger, the director of the 1965 *In Harm's Way,* observed, "Whether it is a western or a war film, there's lots of action. You have undoubtedly some scenes where people fight and kill each other, where people run or drive fast tanks, ships. . . . It's the basic motion picture thing that one man runs after the other and whoever can run faster kills the other."[4]

Of course, a crucial difference exists between the western and the war film. Far beyond the fate of a mere wagon train, stagecoach, marshal, or town, victory in cinematic combat determines the very survival of the nation and democracy. From the earliest days of the relationship between filmmakers and the U.S. military, war movies have shown the armed forces always winning these victories, whatever the odds.

What Price Glory, Wings, Air Force, Sands of Iwo Jima, The Longest Day, and hundreds of other Hollywood films have also created the image of combat as exciting, as a place to prove masculinity, as a place to challenge death in a socially acceptable manner. As a result, until the late 1960s, American war movies always ended in victory, with our soldiers, sailors, Marines, and fliers running faster than their enemy—whether German or Italian or Japanese. These screen victories reinforced the image of the American military as all-conquering, all-powerful, always right. In a real sense, then, Hollywood war films have helped justify war and the use of violence to achieve national goals.

The contradiction between this justification and the existence of an idealized peace-loving nation may help to explain the difficulty some Americans had in recognizing that the United States had embarked on a disastrous policy in Vietnam. Moreover, the paradox of glorifying war while opposing conflict finds no better expression than in Hollywood itself. Virtually all filmmakers, including John Wayne, have claimed to oppose war and militarism. They maintain that they make only antiwar movies, which convey their antiwar messages by using "war is hell" images.[5]

Better than most, *Patton* illustrates the gulf between the professed goal and the actual results. The movie contains many scenes showing the horrors of war—dead bodies, the mourning friends, battle fatigue, commanders' knowing sacrifice of some soldiers so that more will live. Patton himself comments about the waste of lives of so many young men. However, he acknowledges, "I love it. God help me, I do love it so—more than my life!" And the film documents well the reasons for this love, portraying war as exciting and romantic, as an escape from the mundane world, and as a chance to attempt great feats in

Director Franklin Schaffner and technical advisor Paul Harkins discussing the filming of the Battle of the Bulge sequence in *Patton.*

the companionship of one's peers. Most important, *Patton* ends with victory and a scene of the living Patton at the height of his fame.

Patton contains no women, not even the general's mistress, his niece by marriage, to soothe the soldiers during their respite from battle. However, war movies often include women to serve as objects of men's pursuit, providing calm moments during lulls in the high-risk adventure. They may satisfy men's sexual needs but ultimately cannot compete with the thrill and challenge men experience facing death in combat. For the soldiers, the heat of battle has eclipsed the need for a woman's body.

Discussing his wartime flying experience, which served as the basis for *Catch-22,* Joseph Heller recalled, "There's something sexual about being in a big plane, with a *big* gun and having *big* bombs to drop."[6] Pete Hammill, in commenting on the connection between violence and sex, observed that while reporting on the war in Vietnam, he saw a sexual-like "euphoria" on soldiers' faces as they came out of combat.[7] Planes, bombs, guns, the destruction they cause, the very elements that filmmakers believe show the evil of war ultimately provide the attraction that makes war films so popular.

War films do more than serve as a means for vicariously experiencing the proximity of death, the romance, and the adventure of war. They offer an escape from reality, the same appeal that war itself offers those who are involved in combat. In his autobiography, Leon Trotsky gives a classic explanation of this appeal in describing the celebrations in Vienna at the outbreak of World War I. He wrote: "The people whose lives, day in and day out, pass in a monotony of hopelessness are many; they are the mainstay of modern society. The alarm of mobilization breaks into their lives like a promise; the familiar and long-hated is overthrown, and the new and unusual reigns in its place. Changes still more incredible are in store for them in the future. For better or worse? For the better, of course—what can be worse to [the ordinary person] than 'normal' conditions?"[8]

These "normal" conditions include wives and children. Men may love their families and their women but still feel tied down by the responsibilities of marriage. More than that, in psychosexual terms, a woman's greater capacity for sex can threaten a man's security and ego. Military life and war offer a legitimate alternative to this threat. A soldier can do his duty to his family by being away from them, protecting them from outside danger. He then has the best of both worlds—a woman when he wants her, masculine friendships, and the sexual release of combat.

John Gilbert leaves Renee Adoree behind as he and the American army depart for the front in *The Big Parade.*

John Wayne discussing his portrayal of Sergeant Stryker with Leonard Fribourg, the Marine technical advisor for *Sand of Iwo Jima* (1949).

David Halberstam, who saw combat firsthand in Vietnam as a reporter for the *New York Times* and wrote two books about the war, *The Making of a Quagmire* and *The Best and the Brightest*, observed that "there are a lot of men in the military who are very good at what they do because they prefer it to the normality of life." He explained, "They prefer danger and threat, dislocation, to what we would call normality. They don't really want to be at home." Halberstam concluded that war is liberating to these men. Although they are heterosexual, they really don't like women; they replace sex with war.[9]

While attending war films, viewers may experience the same escape that combat itself provides the participants. John Wayne and the military image he created in his many war movies offered and continue to offer viewers an alternative to their rather dull lives. In his films Wayne seldom has a wife, although he may have been married and may even have a son whom he misses. Marriage, however, only interferes with his more important job of fighting to protect the nation. Often, as in *Sands of Iwo Jima*, a woman may have rejected Wayne because of his commitment to the military. But he retains the memory of his one-time family. By identifying with this Wayne image, men can feel heroic, can have their home life, but can vicariously free themselves from family and responsibility.

Since women make up half the moviegoing population, filmmakers have, of course, included ingredients in their war stories designed to appeal to women: the colorful uniforms, the strong and attractive men, the noble and patriotic wait for their returning soldiers. With very few exceptions, women in war films, apart from serving as convenient sex objects, have become willing martyrs. They wait patiently for the return of their husbands and boyfriends, ready to nurse them back to health if need be, but in all cases standing by them, whatever injuries they have suffered. By clothing war in noble terms, filmmakers have given women a stake in the successful outcome of the battle.

Nevertheless, combat has always occupied a relatively small part of life in the armed forces—however much attention filmmakers have given it. Recognizing the broad appeal of the peacetime military, Hollywood has not ignored dramatic stories about rescues from sunken submarines or training and preparations for the next war. At the same time, filmmakers have created comedies, musicals, or romances, portraying soldiers, sailors, and Marines cavorting in exotic places or finding love with beautiful women. Especially during the 1930s, *Devil Dogs of the Air, Seven Sinners, Submarine D-1*, and *The Singing Marine*, among other films, provided an escape from problems of the Depression.

For women, these movies differed little from similar stories set in other milieus. For men, they showed the lighter side of military life, the fun of travel, the pursuit of women, the humor inherent in good fellowship. For filmmakers, military settings provided alternative locales in which to tell their fables, locales that the average person could not experience, thus adding appeal to the movie.

Hollywood has always believed that for military movies to succeed, whether set in peacetime or the most desperate combat, they must have an authentic ambience. To create such images of reality, filmmakers have regularly sought assistance from the armed forces in the form of technical advice, men, and hardware. The military has seen these films as a superb public relations medium. Consequently, the services have taken great care to assist only on movies that would provide benefit by informing the public and the Congress of their activities, by aiding recruitment, and by boosting the morale of the officers and men who actually participated in the filming. Apart from saving Hollywood thousands of dollars and ensuring visual accuracy, such cooperation has enabled filmmakers to create the illusion of the proximity to death, dramatic action, exotic vistas, and romance, characteristics that contribute to the continued popularity of war films.

In addition to enhancing the movies' chances of success, these combat sequences have offered Hollywood a socially acceptable means of bringing violence to the screen. Undoubtedly more people have died in war movies than in all the conflicts in which American servicemen have ever fought. Though the motion picture industry itself opposed mass slaughter on the screen, its officials have always had a difficult time refusing to approve films in which the military directed violence against the enemies of the United States. Despite all the hand-wringing about media violence, particularly in Hollywood movies, following the high school massacre in Littleton, Colorado, in April 1999, no one cited the extreme violence in *Saving Private Ryan* as a contributing cause of the slaughter. After all, the fighting took place in a necessary war, for a good cause, to defeat Hitler, with whom the teenage killers had become fascinated.

To be sure, over the years, the armed services and film industry officials have made requests to play down scenes of violence and death in military movies. The Navy Department, for example, asked MGM to delete repetitive scenes showing a sailor trapped in a flooding submarine in the 1933 *Hell Below* because the sequence was "unduly oppressive."[10] For its part, the Code Office requested that Darryl Zanuck eliminate some of the blood from his 1962 epic *The Longest Day*. Though recognizing that many men died on D-Day, the office felt that this aspect of the story should be minimized rather than emphasized.[11]

At the same time, Hollywood's special-effects men have always worked hard to make the violence as realistic as possible. Not satisfied with the way actors were "dying" during the shooting of the 1943 *Bataan*, the filmmakers tied ropes to the intended casualties and, on cue, jerked the men into the air to create the illusion of being hit by bullets.[12] The greatest special-effects achievements in creating violence on the screen have come not in "killing" individual soldiers, however, but in combat spectaculars ranging from *Birth of a Nation*, the first great war film, through the 1920s classics *The Big Parade* and *Wings* to the more recent *Tora! Tora! Tora! Midway, A Bridge Too Far, Platoon, Gettysburg, Saving Private Ryan,* and *Pearl Harbor*. In these films, meager plots have served only to move the viewer toward the climactic scenes of death and destruction.

Hollywood's renewed production of war films in the mid-1970s may have reflected, at least in part, the industry's desire to portray violence on the screen without criticism. In recent years, excessive mayhem in movies and on television has come under increasing

(Top) Darryl Zanuck recreates Omaha Beach during the making of *The Longest Day* (1962). (Bottom) German soldiers fighting off a combined French/American assault on the fortified Ouistreham Casino in *The Longest Day.*

attack. Nevertheless, if surveys and box-office revenue offer any indication, audiences continue to enjoy cinematic bloodshed. Only in the war genre, however, can filmmakers justify their use of violence in the name of patriotism and historical reality.

How closely the Hollywood image of war has ever approximated the reality of battle remains a subject of much debate. Military men have always been divided as to the authenticity of combat scenes in war movies. Gen. Maxwell Taylor has written that he stopped going to military films after a few early exposures because he found "little reality in the portrayal of war and military life, either in Hollywood or on TV."[13] In contrast, Gen. David Shoup, who won the Medal of Honor for action on Tarawa, thought the Tarawa landing in *Sands of Iwo Jima* recreated the Tarawa he experienced.[14] Gen. Paul Tibbets, for another, claimed that the 1952 *Above and Beyond* accurately portrayed his experiences in training for and dropping the first atomic bomb on Hiroshima.[15] And whether or not Steven Spielberg's portrayal of the violence on Omaha Beach in *Saving Private Ryan* conveyed absolute reality, it probably captured the horrors of combat as realistically as any soldier or civilian would ever want to experience them.

Irrespective of whether the new wave of war films matched the authenticity of earlier

D.W. Griffith stages the Battle of Antietam for *The Birth of a Nation*.

military pictures, the post-Vietnam movies contain for the most part a far less worshipful attitude toward the military. From *Birth of a Nation* in 1915, through *Patton* (1970), Hollywood films created an image of the American fighting man as brave, determined, and successful. The recent Hollywood spectaculars about World War II may in some ways resemble the old-fashioned combat movies of the 1950s and early 1960s. But even the 1977 *MacArthur*, a respectful homage to the general's career, portrayed his shortcomings—though in the end the film depicted him as successful in battle and respected by his country and peers.

Vietnam, in contrast, presents filmmakers with few happy endings and few opportunities for military men to rhapsodize about their victories, even though they strenuously argue they did not lose the war on the battlefield. The films about the Vietnam experience may show Americans winning a particular engagement, or they may even portray fighting men doing their jobs in a professional manner. Nevertheless, Hollywood will never be able to interpret the war in Southeast Asia as another in a long line of glorious American victories in the name of freedom and the democratic way of life. Nor will the movies contain many happy endings for the heroes. Whether audiences will see films lacking this positive image as the continuation of the antiwar sentiments of the late 1960s or simply consider them an extension of the action-adventure war movies of the pre-Vietnam era remains an open question.

In any event, war films will remain popular as long as men still love war itself above

Japanese planes launch their attack on Hickam Field in *Pearl Harbor*.

their own lives as Patton did, as long as men still find in combat a unique confrontation with death, and as long as war reflects a pervasive sexuality. In his much-praised book *Dispatches*, based on his journalistic experiences in Vietnam, Michael Herr captures these twin emotions as well as any recent writer: ". . . your senses working like strobes, free-falling all the way down to the essences and then flying out again in a rush to focus, like the first strong twinge of tripping after an infusion of psilocybin, reaching in at the point of calm and springing all the joy and all the dread ever known, *ever* known by *everyone* who *ever* lived, unutterable in its speeding brilliance, touching all the edges and then passing, as though it had all been controlled from the outside, by a god or by the moon. And every time you were so weary afterwards, so empty of everything but being alive that you couldn't recall any of it, except to know it was like something else you had felt once before. It remained obscure for a long time, but after enough times the memory took shape and substance and finally revealed itself one afternoon during the breaking off of a firefight. It was the feeling you'd had when you were much, much younger and undressing a girl for the first time."[16]

2 Beginnings

AT BEST, WAR FILMS CAN ONLY CREATE THE ILLUSION of the emotions Herr described. Nevertheless, the continuing popularity of movies about men in combat attests to Hollywood's ability to capture the ambience of battle, usually with the help of one or another of the armed services. Only in the few years following a major war has the motion picture industry avoided using the armed forces and combat as subjects for its cameras. The symbiotic relationship between filmmakers and the military began almost as soon as the new medium itself became part of American life.

The armed forces quickly realized that movies in which they appeared would aid their recruiting campaigns as well as their efforts to inform the public and Congress of their activities and procedures. Over the years, the services developed guidelines requiring that cooperation must benefit them or be in their best interest and must be given at no cost to taxpayers. Within this framework, each branch approached requests for assistance based on its own perceptions of its role in the military establishment.

With its great victories during the war with Spain and the fleet's subsequent world tour, the Navy early on offered filmmakers an exciting, colorful stage on which to create dramatic stories and comedies. The Navy quickly realized the value that motion pictures offered at a time when the service was growing in size and acquiring a more technologically complex fleet, during Teddy Roosevelt's presidency. In recruiting young men from the heartland of the nation, the Navy found that films provided a unique format to explain life at sea to potential enlistees and their families, most of whom had never seen an ocean or a warship.[1]

Initially, newsreels simply showed ships in harbors, sailors marching in parades, and prominent officers, with George Dewey, the victor at Manila Bay, the most photographed. At the 1904 St. Louis World Fair, the Navy exhibited about sixty films made by the Biograph Company of the "life and duties of officers and crews of United States men-of-war, both in peace and war," a display the *Scientific American* found both "instructive and spectacular."[2]

The next year, the Navy exhibited the same films at the Lewis and Clark Exposition in Portland, Oregon, in a theater that held about two hundred people. A catalog of the exposition praised the pictures as "an exceedingly rare treat to visitors" and asserted that "there is nothing missing from these realistic scenes excepting the roar of the cannon and the cheers of the men." Although other government agencies had still photographs on display, the Navy alone offered the excitement of motion.[3]

Dramatic movies featuring sailors or using ships and sailors as background quickly followed. As a result, the Navy Department soon had to address the matter of how it wished commercial filmmakers to portray its equipment, men, and activities in order to achieve the appropriate results and benefits. As requests to film at naval installations and aboard ships increased, the service quickly discovered that it could exercise a surprising level of control over these entertainment films. Consequently, the service began creating regulations governing the process by which it would provide cooperation to the motion picture industry.

The purpose of this control served in part to minimize the disruption at Navy installations and to maintain security. The department also censored movies to ensure that they presented a favorable image of the service. Eventually, requests for photographing Navy facilities became common enough for the department to begin exercising a centralized authorization process. The 1913 edition of Naval Instructions forbade the filming of ships, stations, or equipment without the written permission of the Navy Department. In 1914 the Navy provided more complete instructions for carrying out its policy through General Order 78, which required that all persons "making protracted visits" to a naval vessel must secure a permit from the Bureau of Navigation. Commanding officers of Navy bases could authorize tours of the facilities or ships on their own authority but had to report the names of visitors to the Bureau of Navigation. Filmmakers who used naval facilities were also required to submit copies of the movies for censorship before release. In addition, the department reserved the right to use the film itself for noncommercial purposes.[4]

In practice, the Navy seldom refused to allow the use of its facilities; the rejections that did occur usually involved considerations of security. The department routinely rejected requests to record target practice, in order to protect the designs of range finders and information on the range as well as the accuracy of the fleet's guns. In 1916 the Navy offered newsreel companies nonclassified, official footage of target practice, and several of them accepted the offer. However, the service refused to allow filming of the testing of new technology, rejected requests to shoot such activities as the launching of an airplane from a battleship, the firing of anti-aircraft guns, and the testing of "aeroplane motors at the Washington Navy Yard." Requests to film submarine launchings met quick refusal "in view of the confidential nature of all matters connected with submarines."[5]

Given the popularity of Navy images in newsreels, filmmakers quickly began to create comedies and dramatic stories in which actors portrayed Navy personnel. However, theatrical props and stage sets could not produce an authentic ambience, and producers soon began asking local base commanders for permission to film on naval bases. Naturally, the Navy applied the same orders that governed newsreels to entertainment productions and took care to ensure that the completed movie reflected credit on the Navy. As a result, the service soon began reviewing scripts before granting permission for a production company to shoot on a base or a ship, and it assigned an officer to watch the actual filming.

During the early years of the relationship between the motion picture industry and the Navy, the system worked relatively smoothly for both sides. In 1914, for example, Pathe had no trouble securing the use of a battleship deck for "a little comedy love scene" in the movie *Via Wireless,* in which an officer and a young woman "steal way" from her mother during a visit to the ship, "much to the mother's annoyance." Unlike most of the prewar commercial films, *Via Wireless* had a rather complicated plot centered around the development of large-caliber guns for coastal defense. Apart from the romance, thanks to the Navy, the film contained scenes of the Atlantic fleet cruising, the battleship USS *New York* at dry dock in the Washington Navy Yard and at sea, as well as naval guns being tested at Sandy Hook, New Jersey.[6]

As the relationship developed, the Navy began giving official support to stories involving active participation of the Navy. Nevertheless, the Navy refused to cooperate on some scripts containing subject matter that the service considered unacceptable. *The Son of Nobody,* which portrayed a Naval Academy graduate as a bully and a villain, did not receive assistance because the service felt that the story placed "naval officers before the public in a manner that is very discreditable to them and that [has] no foundation in fact."[7]

The Navy also refused in 1915 to cooperate with producers of a film based on the opera *Madame Butterfly*. Secretary of the Navy Josephus Daniels informed the Famous Players Film Corporation that "it will be impracticable to allow one of the battleships to be used to illustrate a scene in the moving picture story of Madame Butterfly. As the action of the Naval Officer in the story does not reflect credit on the Naval Service, I do not feel that I can properly do anything that will serve to make your production more convincing." Daniels's displeasure with the story did not prevent completion of the film, which starred Mary Pickford as, in the words of the *New York Times*, "a winsome Cho Cho San."[8]

Not all theatrical films featuring the Navy requested assistance—and even for those that did not, the service on occasion tried to regulate productions that did not portray it in a positive light. In late 1914, for example, the Navy turned to the National Board of Censorship for help in an effort to prevent the release of *Neenah the Foster Mother*, which showed sailors in a "house of ill fame" and "dancing with women of low caste and also drinking at the bar." Secretary of the Navy Daniels wrote the board claiming that such portrayals became "an affront to the splendid body of men themselves and to the parents and relatives of men who are honorably serving their country" and "would undoubtedly deter many self-respecting young men who see them from entering the Navy if life in it were as depicted in dissolute and immoral scenes; parents would not want their sons to enlist under such circumstances; many people would become prejudiced against the Navy and its fine and manly body of enlisted men."[9]

In reply, the board explained that it did not have the power to exclude such scenes as sailors in saloons or cafés but suggested that Daniels write directly to film companies to express his concerns. The producers responded to his letter with promises of support. Italia Film Company of America, for one, answered that it was "in sympathy with your views and will do everything possible to keep our productions free from the atmosphere described in your letter."[10]

After the outbreak of World War I in Europe and during the period when the United States remained neutral, the Navy continued to cooperate with film companies but carefully avoided linking the service with prowar messages. Comedies such as *A Submarine Pirate* provided safe settings for making an acceptable appearance. Released in 1915, the film benefited from the notoriety which German submarines had been receiving since the outbreak of World War I. In this instance, Syd Chaplin, Charlie's brother, codirected and starred in the Keystone movie about a bumbling waiter's efforts to thwart the hijacking of a gold-laden freighter by the inventor of a miniature submarine. Ultimately, with the help of a Navy gunboat, he defeats the pirates. Despite the silly story, the Navy Bureau of Navigation, the department that then dealt with requests for assistance, approved the script. As a result, the service provided the use of a submarine, a gunboat, and permission to shoot in the San Diego Navy Yard.[11]

The Navy's assistance lent the film a feel of authenticity that Chaplin could not have created on a set. In particular, the actor's antics on the submarine's deck as it plows through the water and his holding onto the periscope as the craft actually submerges stood in sharp contrast to the farce inside the boat, staged on the studio-built set. Ignoring the slapstick nature of the story, Secretary of the Navy Daniels approved the film, and the chief of the Bureau of Navigation went to New York to arrange with the producers to have *A Submarine Pirate* shown in all naval recruiting stations.[12]

Mack Sennett, head of the studio, appreciated the then unusual privileges which the Navy provided in allowing the production to use the submarine and in granting a two-week extension to complete the filming in Los Angeles Harbor. In turn, Secretary Daniels believed the film would encourage young men to become submariners because of the manner in which it presented the glamour and technology of the new weapon of war. With both parties to the assistance satisfied with the results, the film helped establish closer ties between the Navy and the motion picture industry.[13]

When the United States entered the war in 1917, the Navy, of course, abandoned its reluctance to be associated with prowar messages. However, the Navy had more important things to do than help either newsreel or commercial filmmakers with their projects. Assistant Secretary of the Navy Franklin Roosevelt had to advise Pathe News that the service could not allow it to shoot the trials of a newly completed submarine for "certain military reasons." In fact, the Navy's primary role of convoying ships to Europe during the American involvement in the conflict did not provide many dramatic stories for filmmakers to recreate, either during the war or afterward. As a result, few movies featured the Navy's activities during the war.[14]

In contrast to the Navy, the Army has usually assisted filmmakers more readily than the other military branches, recognizing that as the least glamorous service it needed all the publicity it could obtain. The Army began its cinematic appearances as early as 1911, when Lt. Hap Arnold took his Army biplane by train from College Park, Maryland, the home of the service's first airfield, to Long Island, New York, to fly in an air show. While he was there, a filmmaker persuaded him to perform for his camera and used the resulting footage to make the two-reeler *Military Air Scout*. Arnold, who picked up "a few extra bucks" for his services, became so excited about movies that he almost quit the Army to become an actor.[15]

Fortunately for the United States, he stayed in the service, helped create the Army Air Corps, and during World War II commanded the Army Air Force. Nevertheless, Arnold had quickly recognized the value that motion pictures could have in promoting the military and he developed and maintained close ties with the film industry throughout his Army career. In turn, Hollywood received full access to airplanes and men to regularly make movies about Army aviation in peace and war.

In the meantime, D.W. Griffith turned to the Army for help while filming *The Birth of a Nation* in 1915, when he requested technical advice from West Point engineers in preparing his Civil War battle sequences. Subsequently, the U.S. Military Academy even provided some Civil War artillery pieces for close-up shots. Recognizing the value of such assistance, in 1924 Griffith again approached the Army for more extensive help, during the

Lt. Hap Arnold at controls of the Army biplane he flew in *Military Air Scout* (1911), one of the first films in which an active duty serviceman participated.

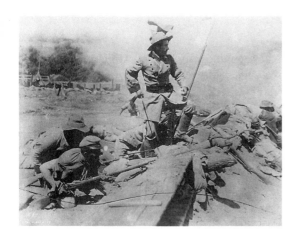

(Top) Henry B. Walthall as "The Little Colonel" in *Birth of a Nation* (1915) prepares to lead a Confederate charge on Yankee fortifications. (Bottom) D.W. Griffith talks to Jonathan Wainwright, mounted, who is about to lead a charge during the filming at Fort Myer, Virginia, of *America* (1942).

filming of *America,* his re-creation of the Revolutionary War.[16]

In response to his request, Secretary of War John Weeks ordered the Army to provide the director with every reasonable help. The service loaned Griffith more than one thousand cavalrymen and a military band to help stage the crucial battles of the War of Independence. Reportedly, the cavalry units loaned to him constituted the largest number ever assembled outside actual war maneuvers. The War Department justified its assistance by saying that the combat sequences gave Army observers the opportunity to study the Revolutionary War battles with a precision never before possible. According to Griffith, he received thousands of dollars worth of help because President Calvin Coolidge and Secretary Weeks believed the film would have a "wholesome and quieting effect" on the American people.[17]

Nevertheless, the Army did not provide significant assistance to filmmakers on either peacetime or World War I stories until the 1920s. Only the Marine Corps helped create a movie portraying its men in combat during the war, motivated by its ongoing concern over threats to its existence as a separate service. To help ensure its survival, the Corps began providing assistance to filmmakers, with the intent of fostering its image as a unique armed force, a few good men who became the first Americans on the battlefield.

The Marine Corps's relationship with the film industry began even before American entry into World War I. The Edison Company's *Star Spangled Banner,* released in early 1917, focused on the peacetime Marines and their training. Nevertheless, by adding a reference to the entry of the United States into the war, the film also served as a medium for rallying the American people to the Allied cause.

Opening in England but taking place mainly at the Marine Barracks at Bremerton, Washington, the movie told the story of how an arrogant English teenager comes to respect the Marine Corps. The boy's mother, an American widow of an Englishman, marries a Marine colonel who has been serving as a military observer in France and returns with him to his next assignment as commander of the barracks. Though actually born in the United States, the son considers himself an Englishman, superior to Americans in general and particularly to the Marines, whom he considers a joke. He knows nothing of American history, and only at the insistence of his mother does he begin to read Bancroft's *History of the United States.*

The movie portrays the boy's adjusting to his new life and learning about his heritage.

It also offered the filmmakers and the Marines ample opportunity to inform the moviegoing public about activities at Bremerton, including marching, drilling, training with boats, and ceremonies. At the same time, the director was able to recite the history of the American military and of the Marines. When the boy falls down a cliff, the whole base undertakes a search-and-rescue mission, even though he has alienated most of the Marines on base. The boy's rescue naturally changes his beliefs, and now that the United States has declared war, he places the Stars and Stripes on his mirror beside the British Union Jack and the French Tricolors, a symbolic merger of the Allied war effort.

With the United States preparing its expeditionary forces for deployment, the Edison Company turned to a portrayal of the Marines in combat. Based on Mary Raymond Shipman Andrews's novelette *The Three Things, The Unbeliever* told the story of Phil, "a rich, young sophisticate," who leaves his life of leisure in Long Island society to enlist in the Marines.[18] The young man, still an elite snob, finds himself stationed alongside Ray, his former chauffeur, at the front in Belgium. In the course of the war, Phil experiences life in the trenches, gives a good account of himself in battle, learns equality from his former employee, finds God as the result of his friend's death and his own serious wound, overcomes prejudice, and wins a bride.

In truth, the Marines never fought in Belgium, and when the filming of the combat scenes took place in November 1917, the only leathernecks overseas were spending their time in training camps.[19] Historical inaccuracies aside, the battle scenes have the feel of actual combat, thanks to full cooperation from the Marine Corps at its Quantico, Virginia, training base.

As has often happened, particularly during wartime, the filmmakers did not find it easy to obtain the assistance they needed in a timely fashion. Writing to the studio from Quantico on November 10, 1917, director Alan Crosland complained to L. W. McChesney, the manager of the Motion Picture Division, about the "obstacles and complications and hardships that stall progress" of the production. He found "a great cloud of conscientious objections" in the Post Headquarters and Quartermaster's Division, which led to a delay in the arrival of helmets necessary for the combat scenes. According to the director, only after Marine headquarters in Washington became involved did the shipment finally arrive. Nevertheless, Crosland felt that "the scenes we are getting are going to be well received and will

Herbert Evans, as Colonel Barron, stands before Marines lined up in front of their barracks at the Bremerton, Washington, Navy Yard during filming of *Star Spangled Banner* (1917).

give *The Three Things* [the production's working title] a fine setting." Consequently, despite the delays, he now felt "a ray of optimism" for the success of the production.[20]

McChesney acknowledged that he had worried about obtaining assistance because "in these camps where everything is done according to military regulation, there is bound to be more red tape and lack of co-ordination and co-operation than even in our own studio." He did advise the director that despite the problems, he hoped to release the film on December 17. He also informed Crosland that the head of the studio felt that *The Three Things* "is a very bad title for advertising purposes" and asked him to suggest an alternative.[21]

Responding on the seventeenth, Crosland reported that despite weather problems, he hoped to finish shooting by the weekend. He said that requests for alternative titles "have not produced remarkable results" and suggested asking the writer for advice. Explaining that even with bright sunlight, filming the trench scenes remained "almost impossible," Crosland said he was rooting for the sun so he could shoot the "over the top" charge the next day using one thousand Marines.[22]

In the completed film, those scenes help provide an ambience of the magnitude of the war then raging in Europe. To be sure, they resembled the trench warfare of the Civil War as much as the contemporary back-and-forth struggle, with men pouring onto the battlefield and advancing in a hail of fire to seize the opposing fortifications. Nevertheless, the combat footage that the Marines helped create remains an impressive piece of filmmaking. Even though the battlefield scenes gave the movie scope, they did not provide it with a personal dimension.

That came from Phil's rite of passage from dilettante to mature young man, which includes taking the initiative with Ray to blow up a German tunneling operation, protecting a young Belgian girl from the German barbarians, and surviving his battlefield wounds. Nor did the Marines' assistance at Quantico provide the propaganda message about the German brutality. That came from scenes filmed on Long Island in a lifelike representation of a Belgium village that the Edison Company created for the production.

There, the heroine serves as a lookout to warn the Belgian Army of the German advance and then sees a German officer, Erich von Stroheim, as evil incarnate, shoot down her mother and younger brother in retaliation. Later, Phil hides the girl in the attic of another house while downstairs von Stroheim kills an old lady, which precipitates his men to mutiny and shoot him. The village and the surrounding area also provide the setting for

Having protected her from the German menace, Raymond McKee sends Marguerite Coutot to his parents in America as he returns to his fellow Marines and combat in *The Unbeliever* (1918).

an urban battlefield in which a Marine unit first retreats in disarray from a German attack and then returns in victory to liberate Phil and his Belgian friend.

After giving the girl a message to his parents and entrusting her to the Red Cross, Phil rejoins his unit and receives a severe wound. While on the verge of death, he sees Christ wandering on the battlefield and experiences a religious conversion. Having learned equality from his now-dead friend Ray and having accepted God, Phil loses his racial prejudice, the third "thing" of Andrews's story, during his recuperation in the hospital. There, while lying in bed between two dying German soldiers, he comes to realize that his enemies do not differ from him as human beings. In the end, he returns home a far better person than when he left and, like so many Marines in so many war movies, receives his just reward, the young Belgian girl, who has found her way to his Long Island mansion.

With all these elements, the retitled film *The Unbeliever* became a box-office hit when it opened in February 1918. The *New York Times,* for one, thought the Marine combat sequences "were effectively worked into the story to give the effect of real war." The reviewer found the patriotic message "clearly sounded without the introduction of provincialism." Addressing the film's anti-German propaganda, he wrote: "Several scenes depict Prussian brutality in realistically ugly form, but rebellion against it by Germans themselves prevents sweeping condemnation of the Teutonic people."[23]

The *Moving Picture World* agreed that *The Unbeliever* "presents a clear picture of what war is really like. The massed scenes for the first time mean something to the audience and they evoke round after round of applause." At the same time, the reviewer felt that the story "acts as a damper on enthusiasm aroused by the splendid showing of the marines and some well-considered appeals to patriotism." Moreover, he thought the actors stood "wholly out of mood with the play. Their easy indifference is a jarring note, but not so serious as the infirmity of purpose in the play itself." In contrast, the reviewer thought the actual fighters on both sides showed "dignity and courage. . . . The enemy is not belittled, though some of his brutality is shown." Likewise, the critic believed the filmmakers effectively used the revolt of the German soldiers against the "Hun despotism" of their brutal officer.[24]

Exhibitors had a more positive view of the production. One congratulated the distributer for "placing before the public such a wonderful picture." Having shown most of the movies about the war, he had concluded that "none of them have equaled *The Unbeliever* either in point of interest, production, photography, and above all, Box-office results." He believed that such movies built business: "Every AMERICAN with a drop of patriotic blood coursing through his veins could not help but appreciate *The Unbeliever.*"[25]

The Marines had even more reason to like the film. In Denver, a theater manager reported that during the first week of its engagement, more than two hundred men enlisted in the Marine Corps at the recruiting booth in the theater lobby.[26] The Kleine branch manager in Pittsburgh sent the company a similar report, writing: "Every one is talking about the Marines. Lieut. Brown, who is in charge of the Marine Recruiting Headquarters in this city, advises us that in his opinion *The Unbeliever* has certainly stimulated enlistments. While he cannot trace the enlistments direct to this picture, he stated that it certainly had a great deal to do with it." To further this success, the manager said that the officer had "supplied us unlimited advertising matter and gives us the use of any of his men whenever possible."[27]

Such reports of the impact that the film had on recruiting justified the Marine assistance during the wartime emergency. Nevertheless, at least one Marine had mixed feelings about the story. Capt. H.C. Daniels, a recruiter in Boston, advised the Edison Company that he found *The Unbeliever* "a wonder and one of the best that I have ever saw and on a par with the *Birth of a Nation.* etc. The parts were well acted, the scenes excellent—I could well imagine that I was actually taking part myself and right in Belgium too." He believed the film "comes the nearest to any one in accurately portraying military conditions and historical action." Nevertheless, he complained that "the scene where the Marines are falling back—this would not be true to fact for a MARINE WOULD NOT RETREAT—under any condition—we are trained differently."[28]

Whatever the validity of the captain's comment on the Marines in combat, the portrayal did not apparently affect recruiting. In May 1918 the director of the Marine Corps Recruiting Publicity Bureau in New York wrote to the Edison Company that recruiting stations throughout the country were reporting that *The Unbeliever* had enjoyed "unprecedented success." As a result, the officer asked if the company could supply three more copies of the film "for inter-family use" so that the service could send them to the fleet at sea and Marine stations "in the far away tropics."[29]

Although showing the film to its men remained important, the Marines saw its primary value as a recruiting and information vehicle and continued to work with the George Kleine System, the distributor, to promote the service's involvement in the production. In particular, throughout the initial release period, the distributor wrote to mayors across the country to inform them that their hometown boys had taken part in the filming of *The Unbeliever* while in training at Quantico and then gone to France to fight. In a typical letter, the Kleine System advised the mayor of Fort Thomas, Kentucky, that the Marine Corps had informed the company about the men who had appeared in the film who had been cited for bravery in Europe. Included on the list was a Marine from Fort Thomas, and the distributor provided the citation, knowing "that you will feel great pride" in his gallantry.[30]

The joint promotion campaign did have a positive effect, as seen in a response from the mayor of Perry, Missouri, to the Kleine System. He wrote that the Marine citation, describing the actions of one of the town's residents, included in the company's letter, was the first information he had received "as to the particular circumstances" of the man's wounding and thanked the distributor for his "thoughtfulness." He also informed the company that when *The Unbeliever* ran in Perry, "it was the unanimous verdict of our people that it was the greatest war picture ever shown here."[31]

The distributor and the Marines may have benefited from their symbiotic relationship in the production and promotion of the film, but not everyone considered *The Unbeliever* a success. James Davis, for one, sent a letter criticizing the film to Hinton Clabaugh, head of the Chicago office of the Secret Service. He began by stating that the film "intentional or not, suggestively and positively gives support to contentions of socialists, pacifists and apathists to such an extent as to make it effective as a German propaganda to retard mobilization and war financing."[32]

He went on to complain that the elitist attitude of the rich toward the poor that Phil and his friends expressed early in the film "tends to confirm the charge frequently made by the German press that our patriotism is sordid; our aristocracy one of wealth, and that the lines of distinction between the classes are in our country more clearly drawn and rigidly observed than they are in their social system." Davis thought this "would affort suggestions to our Bolshevikia for campaign material of possibly considerable influence on the ignorant." Given this perception of the story, he dismissed Phil's espousal of equality as "more akin to a tolerant patronage influenced by propinquity and later by gratitude than a real enlightened consciousness of equal worth socially."[33]

Furthermore, Davis thought the revolt of the German soldiers against their brutal officer would give "support to the opinion held by the pacifist and apathist that a political collapse of Germany in consequence of Army initiated revolution will bring the war to an end without our participating in it." In this regard, the film's anti-Prussian slant served only "to encourage the belief in this country that Prussia is the arch devil of the Empire, the dominating war force, the tyrant, the instigator of the war and developer of all its dreadfulness, and all other Germans are angels with clipped wings ready to revolute but 'dassent.'"[34]

Davis did find the portrayal of the Marines "fine" and the scenes in the trenches "very interesting and inspiring." If they had been "removed from the story they would be very effective as a patriotic exhibition." He did express concern that in *The Unbeliever,* the Marine retreat became "a panic, and a mob-like rout," with victory coming only after the arrival of reinforcements. Moreover, he felt that the filmmakers should have "featured" the victory rather than letting it pass in a "flash." Overall, he concluded that "the many opportunities for dramatic appeal to patriotism are overlooked or only flashed and the portrayal of the Americans in many respects is derogatory to our national spirit and character. Worst of all, Davis thought the film "would be dangerous to a degree which would justify its classification as German propaganda."[35]

George Kleine naturally took issue with Davis's complaints. In a detailed response to Hinton Clabaugh on March 16, the distributor suggested that Davis had "used a microscope to pick out certain details of this film, magnifying the possible crudities when standing alone without viewing the effect of the film as a whole." Noting that many of Davis's complaints focused on technical details, Kleine acknowledged the ongoing debate among filmmakers and critics over the limits of dramatic license. However, he considered moot the question of "whether it is better to maintain absolute accuracy under all conditions at the risk of becoming prolix and uninteresting or whether embodiment of the main idea would be sufficient."[36]

To Kleine, Davis's criticisms about the film's patriotism remained irrelevant, because his conclusions that it supported socialists, pacifists, and apathists lacked any validity. He argued: "If this film were full of blowholes, if it reeked with directorial inaccuracies, if it violated every rule of the film-producing trade, we have nevertheless and beyond question the most tremendous force to arouse patriotism into action and to energize the pacifist into works that has yet been produced." He explained that he had reached this judgment on the basis of the actual reaction of viewers cited in letters from exhibitors.

Kleine said that since the United States had entered the war, he had seen audiences, after watching *The Unbeliever,* "so inspired with patriotism of the kind that leaves you restless and eager to do something, whether enlisting or assisting the government in the other activities that are necessary to win the war. The eagerness of the audience to applaud every telling point was an inspiration." He claimed that the dramatic license and technical inaccuracies that had concerned Davis did not seem to bother viewers. In fact, he argued: "The enthusiasm that swept over the House when our men 'went over the top' would wash away any little doubts that Mr. Davis might have as to the effect of this picture upon the public."[37]

Having thus defended his film, Kleine acknowledged that neither the Edison Company nor he would object to eliminating the title "love your enemies" when practicable. He maintained that Davis's objection on this point "is somewhat turgid but I, myself, believe that the phrase should be eliminated on the ground that it is not in keeping with the spirit that must be engendered to win the war." Nevertheless, the distributor concluded: "I am more in accord with another critic who stated 'there are some enemies who must be licked before they can be loved.'"[38]

From the Marine perspective, the promotion of the film and the images it created remained its primary concern, not parochial debates over the particular elements in the story. To the service, *The Unbeliever* simply became the paradigm recruiting and information vehicle. From its release, the film stimulated recruitment and showed the American people how the Marines intended to fight the evil Germans during the war.

To this end, throughout the conflict, the Marine Corps continued to work with Kleine to spread the film to audiences everywhere. The distributor ultimately decided to create a new introduction for *The Unbeliever,* which would inform the public of the contribution to the war effort of the Marines who had taken part in the film's production. In response to his request for help, Col. A.S. McLemore, the Marines' assistant adjutant and inspector, detailed on October 24 the problem Kleine faced and offered a solution. He explained that the officers and men who had appeared in the movie had served at Belleau Wood and Chateau Thierry, where they had suffered nearly 80 percent casualties. In addition, many others had received citations for bravery. As a result, the colonel said that Kleine would need about a thousand feet of film to run all the names.

Realizing that the distributor could not do this, McLemore suggested using one title stating that the Marines in the film had become heroes in France and a large percentage had been killed, wounded, and recommended for bravery. In addition, he advised Kleine that some of the wounded Marines were recuperating in the Brooklyn Naval Hospital and it might be possible to include pictures of these men in the new introduction. Ignoring any possible antiwar sentiment inherent in such images, McLemore wrote: "Practically all of them have been permanently disabled and such a picture should bring home to the audiences of *The Unbeliever* more vividly than anything else, what these men have gone through, who a few months ago 'played' the game of war before the movie camera."[39]

Kleine created a new introduction using material McLemore had sent him. Writing on December 28, the distributor said he had used the suggestions "with a view to giving the greatest credit to the Marines who took part in the film, and to those who were individually mentioned in the original production." Now that the war had ended successfully, he also congratulated the Corps that the public sentiment "was crystalizing into the judgment that the work of the Marines was the vital factor in turning the war to victory."[40]

Even after the war, the Corps continued to use *The Unbeliever* to reinforce this conclusion. In January 1922 the Marine Recruiting Bureau in Brooklyn wrote to Kleine requesting a copy of the film to screen for the Belleau Woods Post of the Veterans of Foreign Wars. The recruiting officer explained that he was writing at the request of the members of the post who had served in the battalion that had furnished the men and equipment during the making of the film.[41]

Today, of course, *The Unbeliever* and *Star Spangled Banner* seem almost comical in their portrayals. The rite of passage of a young man to maturity through his experiences in the military has become a stereotype at the heart of most movies about the armed forces. Visualizing religious conversions on the battlefield seems trite today. After all, many people have observed that atheists do not exist in foxholes. Moreover, in today's all-volunteer U.S. military, equality among soldiers has assumed the status of an unquestioned truth.

In fact, both movies stand as seminal works that helped create the images that have evolved into cliches. In *Sands of Iwo Jima,* John Wayne's Sergeant Stryker turns his boys into men in combat much the way that Phil becomes a man on the battlefield, albeit without the benefit of a strong father figure. If Stryker dies before he can become a father to his own son, his Marines will carry on to victory thanks to the teaching he has given them. And like Phil in *The Unbeliever,* hundreds of other cinematic soldiers, sailors, fliers, and Marines have subsequently returned home to their girlfriends, wives, and parents.

From the perspective of the Marines, *The Star Spangled Banner* and *The Unbeliever* started the long and honorable relationship with filmmakers, which proved invaluable to the Corps as a vehicle to aid recruiting and to inform the American people of its procedures and activities. Most important, however, for the last eighty years, Hollywood feature films have served as probably the Marines' most significant medium by which to argue the case for the Corps's survival as an independent service: a few good men who remain the first to fight, the first to uphold the honor of the nation.

3 A Standard for the Future

THE COMBAT FILMS WHICH RECREATED THE GLORIOUS American successes in World War I became the focus of Hollywood's portrayals of the military during the mid-1920s. King Vidor, a young, promising director, originally predicted that it "would take ten years to evolve a true War Picture. Propaganda and the passions of the struggle blind the participants from seeing it sanely; then satiety and a cynical reaction follow, no less blinding or distorting." Vidor considered war "a very human thing, and in the ten years' perspective the human values take predominance and the rest sinks into insignificance."[1]

By 1924, however, the director was seeking a worthy subject for his first major film, one that "comes to town and stays longer than a week." He suggested to Irving Thalberg, head of MGM, that "war, wheat, or steel" would provide a suitable subject. Thalberg dismissed steel and wheat but asked if Vidor had a particular war story in mind. Although the director had no clear concept at the moment, he later recalled that he "wanted to make an honest war picture. Until then, they'd been all phoney, glorifying officers and warfare. There hadn't been a single picture showing the war from the viewpoint of ordinary soldiers and privates, not one that was really antiwar." Vidor told Thalberg that he wanted to show the reactions of a typical young American "who was neither overpatriotic nor a pacifist, but who went to war and reacts normally to all the things that happen to him."[2]

Vidor recalled that this approach whetted Thalberg's interest and he immediately directed MGM's story department to send all the synopses of World War I stories it could find to the director. However, he found that "they all looked the same after a while," and he told Thalberg the stories had an "unreal, almost musical-comedy flavor about them" and so lacked any sense of the realism he envisioned for his film. Instead, he wanted the audience to "share the heart beats of the doughboy and his girl and mother and folks." Vidor did not want to ignore "the huge surrounding spectacle" of war, but he did hope to show it through the eyes of the common soldiers. Through this approach, the audience would see how the "human comedy emerges alongside the terrific tragedy. Poetry and romance, atmosphere, rhythm and tempo take their due place."[3]

While Vidor continued to read story ideas at MGM, Thalberg went to New York, where he attended *What Price Glory?* which had opened on September 5, to "some of the wildest applause" Broadway had ever seen. The play impressed him so much that he immediately hired Laurence Stallings, one of the playwrights, to work with Vidor on a screenplay. Stallings, a former Marine captain who had lost a leg at Belleau Wood, arrived in Hollywood with a five-page treatment entitled "The Big Parade."[4]

The scenario focused on three young men, a millionaire's son, a riveter, and a bartender, who join the Army and become friends despite their divergent backgrounds. In France, the rich doughboy sees his two friends die in combat, falls in love with a French girl, and loses a leg in battle. Like *The Unbeliever* and most infantry stories, "The Big Parade" portrayed the lives of ordinary soldiers trying to survive in a hostile environment not of their own making. Stallings created no glory-seeking heroes and no strutting officers winning the war by themselves—it was precisely the kind of story Vidor was seeking, and the studio purchased it immediately.

While writing additional material to flesh out the original treatment, Stallings moved into Vidor's house. The director later recalled that the writer "had more knowledge to communicate—more knowledge for my purpose—than the Committee on Public Information's 750,000 feet of stored films through which my agent pored in Washington." However, despite the obvious help he provided Vidor, Stallings had no desire to remain in Hollywood to write the screenplay, and he soon headed back to New York in the company of Vidor and a young studio playwright, Harry Behn. After reminiscing with Stallings on the trip across country and whenever they could catch up with him during a week in New York, Vidor and Behn headed back to Hollywood, writing the entire way. As a result they were able to turn in a completed script three days after their return to the studio.[5]

Vidor then faced the job of recreating an authentic flavor of wartime Army life. Like virtually every creator of war movies over the years, he believed he had to make each detail as accurate as possible because so many men had taken part in the events he was portraying and could become harsh critics. Since he had not served in the war himself, Vidor spent hours viewing combat footage the Army provided. He also hired two ex-soldiers as technical advisors.

In addition, during the course of the filming, the director often received firsthand information from unexpected sources. In trying to construct a number of German gun emplacements, he discovered that his technical advisors had seen only blown-up gun nests. A laborer listening to the discussion offered to describe the proper alignment based on his own experience as a German noncom during the war. After providing the information, he became an actor in the film commanding the German machine gun position he had helped replicate.[6]

To create the large-scale scenes of whole units advancing to the front, Vidor turned to the War Department for assistance. He asked the Army for two hundred trucks, three thousand to four thousand men, a hundred planes, and other equipment to help portray the troop movement. When the service agreed, Vidor sent a film crew to Fort Sam Houston near San Antonio to shoot the required scenes. The director had wanted the men and trucks to move in a straight line away from the camera and into the horizon with the planes flying over at a specific moment. Unfortunately, the assistant director became caught up in the Army's bureaucracy. He accepted the general's claims that no long, straight roads had existed in the French battlefields and allowed the commanders to stage the maneuver on a curved road. Although Vidor found the performance "magnificent," none of the twenty-five reels of film contained the effect he was seeking.[7]

At night, American soldiers reach a German gun emplacement in *The Big Parade*.

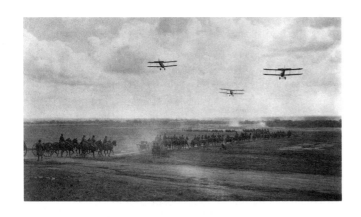

Army troops, equipment, and planes move to the "front" during the filming in Texas of *The Big Parade.*

To create the desired shots, Vidor told Thalberg he wanted to go to Texas, locate a straight road, and stage the march again. Receiving permission, the director went to Fort Sam Houston, found the appropriate road about twenty-five miles from the base, and told the base commander he wanted to reshoot the maneuver there. Not surprisingly, the general strongly opposed the request, citing the Army's original assistance and the distance the soldiers and equipment would have to travel to the new site. Vidor ultimately persuaded the officer to provide the additional help through sheer persistence: "I was firm about my request." By combining the footage taken during both trips, the director was able to create the illusion that he had received more assistance than the Army had actually provided. In fact, the camera crew shot only one day on each trip, using several cameras filming from different angles, to capture the troop movements.[8]

The Army had actually rendered relatively little help, but it proved essential in enabling Vidor to give his film a feeling of openness and size. In acknowledging the importance of this cooperation, the director said the military "cannot be overpraised." Except for the scenes shot in Texas, however, the Army's help consisted only of a small amount of Signal Corps training and combat footage used to create a few battle sequences. Vidor filmed the remaining combat scenes in and around Los Angles, with most of the action taking place on a tract of land about as large as a city block.[9]

Extras, most of whom had served in the Army, though not necessarily overseas, played all the soldiers in these scenes. Their military experience saved the director the expense of training them to act like soldiers, something future filmmakers often had to do when using extras in their war movies. In fact, Vidor had only a limited number of men and trucks at his disposal in Los Angeles. Consequently, to create the illusion of large troop movements, he had the men and trucks move in circles (out of camera range) to sustain the action for the desired length of time. More important, Vidor's immersion in the Signal Corps combat footage, his long discussions with Laurence Stallings, and the advice of his military advisors enabled him to produce the authentic atmosphere of combat in *The Big Parade.*[10]

On occasion Vidor actually came closer to recreating reality by ignoring the advice of his technical advisors. In one instance he chose to photograph soldiers going into battle in columns of two and then had them fan out as they deployed for battle. The advisors argued that these maneuvers had never occurred in France, but Vidor used the scenes anyway. He said he "just figured that nobody could have seen the whole front." He later had his feeling confirmed when he found several sequences in the Signal Corps footage showing troops actually advancing in columns of twos.[11]

In another instance, Vidor ignored expert opinion and filmed the soldiers opening their ranks as they advanced into battle. In the titles, the director labeled the maneuver "Attack Formation." In a letter to Vidor, the War Department itself confirmed the techni-

King Vidor's army marches in the hills above Hollywood during the filming of *The Big Parade* (1925), the first major American film of the 1920s about World War I.

cal accuracy of the action. Although *The Big Parade* contained an antiwar theme, Vidor said the Army never objected to the film's portrayal of war.[12]

The director personally thought the film elicited "an antiwar feeling, definitely. . . . But I don't know if you can call the whole film an antiwar film." Before it opened, he "anticipated an attack from militarist factions. But there were none." The reverse happened. When one of the DuPonts, the manufacturers of large amounts of war materials, visited the set during shooting, he liked what he saw so much that he told Vidor he would supply a tent in which to show the picture if exhibitors refused to handle it. The offer proved unnecessary. The film met with instant acclaim and box-office success.[13]

Even though Vidor would not label his movie "antiwar" in its totality, he did create a feeling within the audience that war has few socially redeeming qualities. Believing that "war has always been a very human thing," Vidor did not feel the Great War had differed from earlier conflicts. He saw it occurring from "a mixed-up sentiment," the culmination of a "long series of human misunderstandings." As a result, he observed: "When a nation or a people go to war, the people go and do not ask why. But in this last war they asked one question at all times. It was, 'Why do we have war?'" In developing that theme in his film, the director said he did not wish to appear as having taken a stand one way or another: "I certainly do not favor [war], but I would not set up a preachment against it. You might as well try to sweep Niagara backward as stop war when people start it. It bursts upon them, and must then be taken as a matter of consequence and a job that requires immediate attention and no argument."[14]

Vidor focused on the common soldiers to capture the feeling "that all people concerned are affected alike, that they are just the same in habit and living, with similar hopes, loves, and ambitions." Moreover, none of his characters become heroes, not even the film's star, John Gilbert, who played the millionaire's son. Vidor's cinematic message emphasized that Gilbert "lost his leg instead of coming home a hero. . . . He laughed at anything heroic, overly patriotic." The director saw Gilbert's character as the common man, "neither a pacifist nor an overpatriot. He just went in and experienced what he experienced and then reacted. You couldn't call him an activist."[15]

Similarly, Vidor did not attempt to create antiwar sentiment by strewing the screen with blood and gore to show that war is hell, as many filmmakers have done over the years. By using violence in this manner, directors have usually produced movies that portray war as an exciting adventure filled with romance and good times. In contrast, Vidor explored the unglamorous side of combat. Gilbert's buddies die; he comes home with only one leg; and the girl he left behind falls in love with another man. This plot twist has remained virtually unique in the history of war films. Even though Gilbert returns to France to claim the girl with whom he has fallen in love, the audience comes away with the impression that war offers few rewards. According to Vidor, in all Gilbert's "war actions, all of the praise and the hospital bit and the killings of his buddies, he is cynical about the war thing. It was a great adventure as far as the girl goes, but not as far as the war goes."[16]

Whatever effect the story had on the martial spirit of the audience, *The Big Parade* did attract record-breaking crowds as a result of Vidor's direction, the quality of the acting, and the authenticity of the combat sequences. According to the film critic of the *Boston Transcript*, *The Big Parade* gains "sweep and pathos and a certain boisterous humour through the directorial acumen of King Vidor. To watch it unroll is to realize anew all the shallow bombast, all the flatulency and all the saccharinity with which previous picture-makers have encumbered the trade of war." The writer noted that Stallings and Vidor "are not content with spectacle. They must have interludes of gusty and sentimental humour." He observed that scenes of the soldiers at rest, doing mundane tasks interspersed with moments of romance, followed by the "intense confusion of the moving up into the line," make the actual attack stand out "the more vividly."[17]

Not all critics found *The Big Parade* totally realistic, especially when compared to *What Price Glory?* One writer argued that Vidor had not created a cinematic equivalent to Maxwell Anderson and Stallings's play: "There is in the picture none of the matter-of-fact bitterness, none of the professional disillusionment, little of the humdrum sordidness that characterizes the spoken play." Despite Vidor's intent to make a realistic movie, the critic further said that audiences would find "sentiment" in *The Big Parade* because filmmakers remain "distrustful of too much realism." Nevertheless, he conceded that the film "goes farther toward honest naturalism than any preceding film of the German war. It indulges in a minimum of affect flagwaving and makes no bones about allowing the unpleasant to intrude."[18]

How close *The Big Parade* or any war movie can ever come to capturing the feel of combat has remained an area of dispute throughout the history of filmmaking. The *New York Times* critic felt that Vidor's treatment of war became "so compelling and realistic that one feels impelled to approach a review of it with all the respect it deserves, for as a motion picture it is something beyond the fondest dreams of most people. . . . The battle scenes excel anything that has been pictured on the screen and Mr. Vidor and his assistants have even seen fit to have the atmospheric effects as true as possible."[19]

The actors' commitment to the film greatly contributed to this feel of authenticity. In particular, John Gilbert changed his characterization from the "dandyisms" of his earlier roles to a down-to-earth doughboy. He refused to use makeup and wore an ill-fitting uniform. Dirty fingernails and a sweaty, grimy face replaced the perfectly made-up character of his "great lover" roles. Although Gilbert at first resisted this change, he became sold on the common-man portrayal after seeing a few of the rushes. As a result he became willing to work day and night on the film. Vidor recalled that after "rolling around in the French farmhouse mud in the daytime, he would crawl on his belly across No Man's Land by night." The director said the actors got their makeup from the "muck. It was laid on with the trowel, not the paint brush."[20]

These efforts by Vidor, his crew, and the actors produced a film that may not have provided a literal reproduction of combat, but at least it created a superb illusion of war. Of course, the ultimate judges of authenticity remained the soldiers who had served in France, who had rolled in the real mud, whom the real bullets maimed, the 2 million men Vidor intended to satisfy when he said, "I did all that was humanly possible to insure accuracy on this picture."[21]

(Top) King Vidor talks to John Gilbert as the director prepares to film a scene from *The Big Parade*. (Below) King Vidor in 1975.

An ex-sergeant who had fought in the trenches agreed after seeing the movie: "It is all there, good people—incredibly real, incredibly tragic, and therefore true to nature." Watching a scene in which the soldiers were eating, this veteran said he "could actually smell those beans and that amazing coffee, so useful in getting gravy or grease off your mess kit." He labeled *The Big Parade* "a war film. And when I say 'war' I do not mean a sham battle in the suburbs of Peekskill either. This means that some folk, and particularly our women folk, won't like it, but it will 'get' them just the same." He believed it presented war "with all its horror and its comedy, its agony and its gayety, its ruthlessness and its infinite love and sacrifice."[22]

A man who watched the movie with the ex-sergeant felt the same way: "This is no picture. This is the real thing." Both men thought the actual war scenes "were so obviously true that if you forgot for an instant you were only looking at a picture you caught your breath and wondered how the Signal Corps ever did it, and how King Vidor ever got these films released for his picture."[23] That soldiers believed they were viewing actual combat footage instead of a re-creation probably pays the filmmaker the ultimate compliment. Nevertheless, for the studio, only the box-office success of *The Big Parade* justified its production. Released in 1925, Vidor's movie ran at the Astor Theater on Broadway for two years, taking in $1.5 million. It played for six months at Grauman's Egyptian Theater in Hollywood. And in a few years, it had grossed over $15 million on an investment of only $245,000.[24] People had clearly demonstrated that they would attend Hollywood re-creations of the Great War.

As its contribution to the cycle of films about the conflict, the Fox Company acquired the rights to *What Price Glory?* for $100,000. Although no studio up to that time had paid that much for any property, critics had hailed the play as the best modern war drama in the English language. The *New York Evening Sun* reviewer Alexander Woollcott wrote, "In the tremendous irony of the comedy and the sardonic laughter which fills in every scene, there is more said about the war than all the editorials on the subject which, if placed end to end, would reach nowhere."[25]

With such praise, the play provided the studio a presold audience in contrast to Vidor's original story. Perhaps more important, the film would feature the Marine Corps with its claim to uniqueness among the military branches, an image that many journalists had enhanced by their accounts of the leathernecks' World War I combat successes. Nevertheless, Stallings's pacifistic messages in *What Price Glory?* and in his script for *The Big Parade* would give the Marines reason to question the honor of becoming involved in the cinematic version of the play.

The Navy Department, in which the Marine Corps then occupied a subordinate position, had other, more fundamental concerns about the play's portrayal of military life and respect for authority. Having received a complaint that *What Price Glory?* brought discredit on the Army and the Marines, the commander of the Corps Area on Governors Island delivered the letter to the Third Naval District Intelligence Office in New York. The intelligence officer then sent a civilian operative to attend the play along with an officer from the Army Intelligence Division and two Justice Department officials.[26]

In his report on September 20, Inspector Peterkin began by quoting from the program, which described *What Price Glory?* as "a play of war as it is, not as it has been presented theatrically for thousands of years. The soldiers (mostly marines) . . . talk and act much as soldiers the world over." Peterkin indicated that this prelude "is of vital importance in this report and acts more or less as an excuse for the play." He then observed that in the opening scene, three Marines reveled in boasting of their conquests of women and remarked "sarcastically" that Marine recruiting posters should change the slogan "Join the Marines and see the World" to "see the girls." He further complained about the continual profanity and use of the words "hell, Jesus, damn, God damn it, etc."[27]

He described the entrance of Captain Flagg, one of the play's leading characters, as "disgusting. He is uncouth in his language and is very familiar with his orderlies who are seated at a table." Worse, Peterkin reported that the men "convey to the audience the lack of discipline in the marine corps, as the top sergeant clearly states that he does not take any orders from his captain and that he does as he 'damn pleases.'"[28]

In summarizing the rest of the play, Peterkin complained about the men's making love to the same girl in turn in front of their subordinates, about the lack of discipline among the Marines, and about the disparaging comments about the Army. According to the inspector, the best scene, "which is not saying much," shows the respect that Flagg has for his men under fire. As a whole, however, he found the scenes of drinking as "very disgusting insofar as they tell all about debauchery and seducing, the language of which is all obscene." He reported that the heroes, Captain Flagg and Sergeant Quirt, have a drinking bout five miles from the front and "gamble in front of the orderlies for the possession of the girl and the Captain is the victor." He then observed: "From a military standpoint, the show clearly demonstrates that there is no system, no discipline, no morale in the U.S. Marine Corps or the U.S. Army."[29]

Given such images, the officer believed that the play "clearly shows that subordinates do not have any respect for superior officers," since this portrayal caused the audience "to believe that the personnel and officers of the USMC are subject at all times to debauchery and seducement." Consequently, he concluded that the play "belittled" the Marines and the Army, "showing that they are drunkards most of the time and that there is a lack of discipline and respect which tend to bring discredit and reproach" on both services.[30]

After reading the report, the commandant of the New York Navy Yard advised the secretary of the Navy that he considered action could be taken against the producers of the play under laws governing portrayal of the Navy. With this in mind, he informed the secretary that he had met on the twenty-fourth with the police commissioner and local and federal prosecutors to coordinate action against the play. Nevertheless, he assured the secretary that "he is not concerned in any manner with the censoring of any plays now or that may hereafter be produced in New York, but is entirely and solely concerned with abating a violation of the law which directly affects the Naval Service in this particular play."[31]

Although the law stated that no play or film could "bring discredit or reproach upon the United States Army, Navy, or Marine Corps,[32] rehabilitation of the perceived negative images in *What Price Glory?* did not come from the courts. Instead, the change came from director Raoul Walsh, who had begun his film career as an actor, including the role of John Wilkes Booth in *The Birth of a Nation.* Walsh had also served as D.W. Griffith's assistant on the film and had amassed a long list of directing credits by the time he received the assignment to transfer *What Price Glory?* to the screen. In handing Walsh the script, Winfield Sheehan, who had just become production chief at Fox's Westwood Studio, simply told the director not to "pull any punches."[33]

After reading the screenplay, Walsh concluded that he had to treat the cinematic version not as a "war play" but as an "anti-war" film: "The action revolved around the combat conditions, but the idea projected by the characters was that war is a farce." He felt that Stallings had "intended the play as an illustration of how war is actually waged" and identified with the officer, on the edge of a breakdown from combat fatigue, who asked of a wounded fellow officer: "What price glory now?" Walsh discerned the play's message as "that war is not only futile but a dirty, bungled mess" and decided to create such images in his film.[34]

Despite his idealistic intentions, Hollywood's mantra—that it produces motion pictures only to entertain and make money—in the end took precedence over any messages inherent in the play, and Walsh turned the film into "the archetypal celebration of war as a game played by roistering comrades."[35] Opening up the action from the confines of the theater, the director created "characteristically sweeping battle scenes" that became a model for future large-scale combat spectaculars. Walsh did pay lip service to the "war is hell" sentiments of the play, diluting the potential impact of the message on the audience by having "weaklings and hysterics who get killed, while military careerists lament 'civilians' being in war at all," speak the words.[36]

True, the hero of the film, Victor McLaglen as Captain Flagg, whom Stallings modeled on Capt. Philip Case, his commander at Belleau Wood, orates, "There's something rotten about a world that's got to be wet down every thirty years with the blood of boys like those." However, the antiwar sentiment fails because Walsh sets it in the context of a wartime comedy and then emphasizes the comedy at the expense of the irony and bitterness of the stage version. As a result of this new focus on romance and excitement, the Marine Corps loved the way the service appeared in the film. The director later recalled that he always stood well with the service after the release of *What Price Glory?* He said the Marines "had more recruits after that picture than they'd had since World War I. It showed the boys having fun, getting broads. Young fellers saw it, they said, 'Jesus, the Army [*sic*] is great.'"[37]

Years later, when Walsh was directing *Battle Cry* (1955), the World War II Marine epic, a general came up to him during shooting in Puerto Rico and said, "Son of a bitch, you got me into this army [*sic*]," explaining that he had joined the Marines after seeing *What Price Glory?*[38] More important for Hollywood, the success of the film reinforced the conclusion that *The Big Parade* had suggested: audiences would pay to see combat stories. It also demonstrated that moviegoers wanted to see war movies simply to watch battle scenes of men fighting and dying, of planes flying, and of men loving during their time away from combat, not because of any antiwar sentiment they might contain.

Ironically, Walsh created most of his images of combat on the Fox back lot, which the Century City office complex now covers. With the sequences set within the confines of a small French town, the director included no large over-the-top battle scenes, and the whole film contains only about nine minutes of combat. Walsh showed the enemy one time, when a German officer comes to the Marine trenches to surrender. As a result, unlike Vidor, Walsh needed little assistance from the Marine Corps. Perhaps most significantly, a Marine barber ensured that the actors sported the proper haircuts for each of the film's locales: China, the Philippines, and France. The director's information on equipment, uniforms, and Marine procedures came from a Marine veteran who had received seventeen wounds in action. Viewing the film seventy-three years after its release, Edwin Simmons, the director emeritus of Marine Corps History and Museums, thought "the best part of the film is that the uniforms, weapons, and drill are absolutely authentic."[39]

Whether Walsh actually captured the essence of the stage play or the ambiance of men in combat became a matter of some debate. In the *New York Herald-Tribune*, Richard Watts Jr. wrote: "If you cherish the original 'What Price Glory' as one of the noble plays of our time, I fear you will have some difficulty in escaping the feeling of sacrilege when you watch the screen version." He did find positive things to say in its favor: "Technically, it is in many ways an admirable production. The war scenes are, I suspect, the finest and most vivid ever shown on the screen. The many photographs of marching troops, too, are so effective that even the painted backdrops behind them are not too offensive." Nevertheless, he objected to the film version "not only because it fails to be the faithful transcription of a magnificent play, but also because it would have been tremendously more powerful had it been loyal to the original." In particular, he complained: "Each time the picture sentimentalizes the characters and the incidents of the play it is weakened thereby." Likewise, some Marines thought Walsh had stretched realism to the breaking point due to the humor and portrayal of men enjoying wine, women, and song, even though Stallings had drawn upon his wartime experiences in France. Others also claimed that the antics of McLaglen and his sidekick, Edmund Lowe as Sergeant Quirt, placed the Marines in a bad light.[40]

For most leathernecks, however, *What Price Glory?* became the paradigm against which to judge all future Marine films. It was to stimulate Hollywood's ongoing interest in the Corps. As important to Walsh and the Fox studio, *What Price Glory?* became a box-office hit and further encouraged the production of films about the American experience in World War I.

With the Army and the Marines already on the screen, the Army Air Corps became the logical subject for the next combat film. Following Walsh's example, *Wings* in 1927 dispensed with all pretensions of a serious plot. Moreover, the prospect of filling the air with planes locked in mortal combat offered Hollywood the opportunity to outdo the battle scenes in *The Big Parade* and *What Price Glory?*

To help William Wellman achieve a breakthrough in filming the spectacular flying and ground combat scenes, the War Department provided him with more assistance for a longer period of time than any subsequent war movie has ever received. As a result of this cooperation, *Wings* stands out as the standard against which all future combat films and all military assistance to Hollywood must be measured.

Despite the Army's commitment to the project, the idea for *Wings* did not originate in Washington. As with virtually all war movies, the concept came from within the film industry and, more specifically, from a writer trying to sell one of his stories. At the same time, the process of creating the story that became *Wings* illustrates the circuitous evolution of a screenplay that the director ultimately films.

In September 1924 writer Byron Morgan approached Jessie Lasky, the vice president of Famous Players–Lasky, a component of Paramount Pictures, proposing that the company do a series of airplane stories. Lasky selected "The Air Mail" for the immediate production as "an ordinary program picture." However, later in the month, Lasky decided that the subject of aviation deserved "a big special" and accepted Morgan's suggestion that he develop an "incident and plot" from the air mail story for the larger production.[41]

"The Menace," the project's working title, focused on the failure of the American aerial effort in the Great War and the effect that the nation's "aviation unpreparedness would have in the next war." During his development of the scenario with William Shepherd, a former war correspondent, Morgan informed Lasky that the first part of the story, a straightforward portrayal of America's air service during the war to end all wars, was growing much bigger than he expected and suggested discarding the "propaganda element." However, Lasky would not agree to simply doing a combat story, saying he wanted D.W. Girffith to direct the film with two parts as originally proposed.[42]

Despite Morgan's efforts to convince Lasky to drop all propaganda from the story, the executive would not give up his hope of keeping the preparedness message. Nevertheless, when Morgan and Shepherd submitted a synopsis of "The Menace" in March 1925, Lasky became worried about the propaganda line and shelved the project. However, Morgan continued to work on the story, the first part of which focused on the experiences of two young American fliers who go to France and fight in the air. In June, Morgan again discussed the project with Lasky, who told the writer that it remained a great idea and said that if he could find a director who "was thoroughly enthusiastic" about the story, the studio would approve the project.[43]

Morgan then discussed the idea with Victor Fleming, a director under contract with Famous Players–Lasky and an aviator. Although he liked the story, Fleming questioned the value of a war film at that time and doubted that the company would spend the money necessary to acquire the number of airplanes a major movie would require. As a result, Lasky told Morgan to shelve the project until he had completed work on his current film. However, the executive then assigned Morgan to write the script for another production rather than resurrecting the aviation story; and he directed the writer to stay with the project during the filming.[44]

While Morgan was involved with the production, *The Big Parade* appeared, and on February 16, 1926, after seeing Vidor's film five times, he wrote to Lasky saying he was "more convinced than ever that there is a great picture to be made around the air service during the war." He contended that the scenario for "The Menace," minus the propaganda, could make as great a film as *The Big Parade.* He added that Sam Wood, a leading director, found the idea "tremendous" and was "more than enthusiastic about the possibilities it offers." Morgan never had the opportunity to find out if his story would have achieved box-office success.[45]

During the same month, while he was finishing his assignment, another writer, John Monk Saunders, brought his own idea for a movie about World War I fliers to Lasky, pointing out that Hollywood still had not filmed the war-in-the-air. Consequently, he said that the sky remained a "virgin-province" for the motion picture camera, with the aerial battlefield offering the opportunity for spectacular combat scenes. He explained that duels between aviators, planes falling in flames, or balloons being shot down could not be presented on a stage or "imprisoned" within the covers of a book. To him, only the screen could serve as the "proper medium" for presenting the war in the air.[46]

Lasky liked the picture Saunders described but expressed concern about the cost. Saunders conceded he was proposing an expensive project: "If it were attempted at all, it must be done on a grand scale. The very magnitude of the subject demanded heroic treatment." Lasky then asked where a filmmaker could obtain the quantity of planes and men needed to stage the action. Since Saunders knew about the military assistance extended to *The Big Parade* and *What Price Glory?* he felt that the War Department would also provide men and equipment to make an Air Corps picture: "We all take pride in our Army, our Navy, our Air Force. Suppose we present a really fine war picture, a picture of historical significance, of national interest, of military importance. Suppose the picture reflects the practice, spirit, and tradition of American aims. Why shouldn't the War Department go hand-in-hand with us?"[47]

Lasky agreed that if the military saw *Wings* in that context and would assist in its production, he would commit the full resources of the studio to the production of the movie. To that end, Saunders immediately left for Washington to discuss the project with Secretary of War Dwight Davis. According to the writer, the merits of the proposed film; help from Will Hays, head of the Motion Picture Producers Association; and the interest of several high-ranking military officers—rather than his own presentation—obtained the War Department's approval. In agreeing to assist on the production, the Army suggested that the action sequences be filmed in the vicinity of San Antonio, Texas, since both flying facilities and Army bases were located close by. Even with cooperation assured, however, the studio required six months to develop a script based on Saunders's story, plan the production, and assemble the film crew in San Antonio.[48]

The screenplay itself became a relatively insignificant aspect of *Wings.* It followed two young men, Buddy Rogers and Richard Arlen, who join the Army Air Corps at the beginning of America's participation in the Great War, become friends while learning to fly, and go off to France to win the war. The dramatic high point of the weakly constructed story occurs when Rogers shoots down his friend, who is attempting to return to his own lines in a stolen German plane after having crashed in enemy territory.

The accidental killing stretches credibility, since Arlen should have been easily able to identify himself to his friend, given the open cockpits and slowness of the World War I planes. Few people noticed such incongruities in the plot, however, since it served primarily to ensure that the true stars of the film, the fighter planes, would appear on the screen as often as possible. To put them there, Paramount hired William Wellman, a young, relatively inexperienced director who, by his own admission, had made one "stinker" as well as one successful film for the studio.[49]

(Above) Clara Bow as she appeared in *Wings* (1927). (Right) Director, film editor, and original author as pictured in program for *Wings*.

Wellman was later to achieve renown not as a creator of great visual compositions but as a director of action and dramatic films, including *Public Enemy* (1931), *Beau Geste* (1939), *The Oxbow Incident* (1942), and *The High and the Mighty* (1953), as well as two of Hollywood's great war movies, *The Story of G.I. Joe* (1945) and *Battleground* (1949). Though he brought to *Wings* little in the way of pictorial style, in the film Wellman did introduce Hollywood to the big boom shot. The sequence in which the camera sweeps through a Paris nightclub to locate the featured actors started a trend as other directors began using a boom to get inside a scene without interrupting the take to move characters or scenery.[50]

Wellman also provided the production two attributes without which *Wings* undoubtedly would have failed. Of all the directors in Hollywood, he alone had flown in combat in World War I. This experience enabled him to know exactly what he wanted to do with his planes and pilots on the screen, even to the extent of actually flying one of the planes to demonstrate the maneuver he was seeking. Perhaps even more important, Wellman brought a no-nonsense attitude to the project and, once on the job, ran the production completely, whether dealing with the military or studio executives.[51]

Wellman's assignment to direct *Wings* undoubtedly influenced the War Department's agreement to support the project to the degree it ultimately did. Until the Defense Department changed regulations during the early 1960s, however, the final decision on the amount of assistance actually provided rested with the local commanders. They could give whatever help they saw fit as long as it did not interfere with normal operations. In essence, this procedure allowed a commander to label any assistance a regular training maneuver if he liked the filmmaker and the project. If a base commander did not want to be bothered with a film company, he could permit the shooting only of scheduled exercises and provide only a minimum of other assistance.

Given Wellman's attitude toward his work, he took the War Department's initial agreement to provide assistance to *Wings* as a blank check. To him, the local commanders existed only "to help me. Nobody else!" He said he "went down to Texas and told the commanders what I needed." Predictably, the director had no problems with this approach to the commanders of the flying facilities. Not only did the Air Corps see the film as a way to boost its branch of the service, but most of the officers knew the director from his flying days.[52]

Arranging use of the infantry for the ground scenes became far more difficult. Wellman later claimed that the infantry commander "had two monumental hatreds: Fliers and movie people." He recalled that he was in the general's doghouse before he "hardly drew a breath." Being only twenty-nine did not help him, either. When the two men had "a hell of an argument" almost immediately, Wellman said he "gently" reminded the general of the War Department's orders and told him, "Look. You're just being a goddamn fool because the government has told me you have to give me all your men and do just exactly what I want you to do." Pointing out to the general that he knew how to obey orders, Wellman said he "straightened himself out" even though "he hated to do it."[53]

With the matter of cooperation settled, the director could devote his full attention to using the military assistance to the best advantage. His first two months in Texas produced little usable footage because he had not yet developed techniques for taking close-ups of fliers in the air or for capturing the sense of an airplane's motion and speed on film. In addition, Wellman discovered that the training facility at Kelly Field did not have enough fighter planes or skilled pilots to perform the dogfights and other aerial maneuvers that formed the heart of the film. Consequently, while shooting early sequences depicting pilot training, the director sent an SOS to Washington for technical help and experienced pilots.

In response, the Air Corps detached six fliers and their planes from the First Pursuit Group stationed at Selfridge Field near Detroit and sent them to Texas. According to one of the pilots, Gen. Clarence "Bill" Irvine, then a young lieutenant and flight engineer, Hap Arnold had told him to "make sure it's a first class job" so that it would not only make money for the producer but also be good for the Air Corps. Irvine served as Wellman's advisor and engineered an airborne camera system that enabled the director to get close-ups of fliers aloft. Irvine helped plan and flew in dogfight scenes, performing one of the major crashes in the film when the chief stunt pilot botched the crackup and broke his neck.[54]

"WINGS" —— the story

WITH the great adventure of the sky as its background, "Wings" is the story of two boys,—Charles Rogers and Richard Arlen—and a girl—Clara Bow. The two boys are American aviators, first enemies, then buddies. The girl is "the girl next door" who, like so many other American girls, answered when the country needed her.

The story opens in a small town of the middle west, introducing Charles Rogers as a boy born with the whir of wings in his ears. It is in 1917 when War, to this country, and especially to this small town, is remote. Rogers is a happy, care-free, lovable chap who is adored by Clara Bow, just "the girl next door," to him, for there is another girl.

There is another boy, Richard Arlen, fine youth of the aristocratic family of the town. The boys are rivals for the affections of the other girl, played by Jobyna Ralston, and because of this there is little fondness on the part of either Rogers or Arlen for the other. The maelstrom of War devours them both and both enlist in the air corps. Rogers leaves thinking Jobyna loves him and takes by mistake a locket meant for Arlen, who understands the situation.

The boys are plunged into training school. Marvelous scenes show every step necessary in the making of a flier: The first days in the air, the first thrill of the "ship" leaving the ground.

It is here that the two boys are bound together in inseparable companionship. Their enmity is buried forever. Their commissions arrive. They are in France as members of the 39th Aero Squadron. Clara Bow, in the meantime, has volunteered and is also at the front as an ambulance driver.

(Continued on Page 12)

Even with all the flying and technical aspects of the project going smoothly, the filming of the aerial sequences dragged on for most of the company's stay in Texas. The early flying footage shot on cloudless days had lacked any visual excitement because the scenes had had no background that would emphasize the plane's movement. Wellman later explained that "motion on the screen is a relative thing. A horse runs on the ground or leaps over fences or streams. We know he is going rapidly because of his relation to the immobile ground." In contrast, the director had difficulty showing a plane high in the sky and in motion relative to the ground or even to another plane. Ultimately, he obtained the proper sense of height and speed by shooting the planes in front of or above cloud banks. The director explained, "They furnished a background that was exactly what we needed for the dogfight, or battle sequences. Against the clouds we could see the planes dart at each other. We could see them swoop down and disappear in the clouds. We could sense the plummet-like drop of a disabled plane."[55]

These new techniques did put the filmmaker at the mercy of the elements, and Wellman admitted, "We waited—while costs surmounted budgets—for the right kind of clouds, heavy banks of them that would show on the screen correctly." This budget-be-damned approach to making *Wings* ensured spectacular shots but an unhappy studio. At one point, Paramount sent an executive to Texas to insist that Wellman shoot the big dogfight scene regardless of the clouds. The director treated the hapless messenger as he had treated the infantry general. He recalled that he gave the executive two choices: a trip home or a trip to the hospital.[56]

Although the delay in filming the aerial sequence lasted more than a month, Wellman did not remain idle. He was also preparing for the climactic ground engagement of the film, the Battle of Saint-Michel. For its great cinematic moment, the infantry had recreated the battlefield down to the last barbed-wire obstacle and trench. In looking over the site, Wellman recalled, "It seemed a shame that we couldn't transplant some of our enemy here and fight out our differences." To guarantee the split-second timing needed to coordinate the planes, special-effects explosions, and troop movements, the director rehearsed the thirty-five hundred infantrymen and five dozen planes for ten days. Seventeen manual and twenty-eight remote-controlled cameras were positioned around the prepared set so that no angle would be uncovered in this one-time performance. Wellman also decided that he himself would operate the control panel that detonated the explosions in front of the advancing men.[57]

In scheduling the shooting date, Wellman became the master of everything—including the weather! Instead of the clouds he needed for the dogfight sequence, he now required bright sunlight for the ground sequences because of the slow film stock then available. The director faced two additional burdens as the shooting date approached. The Air Corps had given the studio an ultimatum after two military planes had crashed during filming with minor injuries to the pilots and major ones to the planes: one more damaged plane

A typical scene from the program for *Wings*.

and the Air Corps would withdraw its participation in the project. With the major aerial dogfights still waiting for proper clouds, Wellman said that the loss of the planes would mean that "the whole damned picture would go down the drain." At the same time, the three major financial backers of Paramount Pictures were coming to Texas to see where all their money had been going. Appropriately, they were supposed to arrive the day of the big battle.[58]

The appointed day dawned cloudy and apparently unsuitable for filming. Describing it as "just as dark as hell," Wellman surveyed the sky with a "hunch" he could get sunshine for the five minutes he needed to complete the shot. As soon as the sun started to break through the clouds, he ordered the planes into the air and told the soldiers to stand by. When the film's production manager yelled that they had no sunlight, Wellman responded, "You get your big ass back and get ready!" With everyone in place, the sun appeared, as if on cue, Wellman shouted "Camera," and he began pressing buttons. According to the director, the first explosion nearly blew him off his platform, and "all hell broke loose, advancing infantry, diving planes, falling men." Concentrating on hitting the buttons in the right sequence, the director could see only what was happening directly in front of him. However, he described what he saw as "majestic."[59]

The "war" continued until Wellman got to button 13, with only six more to go and one more minute of sunshine needed. At that point, he recalled, "Some son of a bitch spoke to me. I pushed the wrong button, and a couple of bodies flew through the air. They weren't dummies." Worse, as Wellman continued to push the buttons, he saw one of the pursuit pilots deviate from his assignment, swoop down almost on top of the soldiers, and threaten to foul up the rest of the advance. When the plane suddenly crashed, Wellman felt "almost glad." Nevertheless, he hit the remaining buttons, and, again on cue, the sun went behind a cloud.[60]

Despite the accidents, the film crew exploded in excitement and relief. The cameramen yelled that they had gotten "sensational" shots. Wellman's only reaction was to head toward the accident sites. He found that he had not killed his "infantry," although the mistimed explosion had caused serious injuries to several men. The crash had demolished the plane, but its pilot had somehow survived. However, his dazed condition had not resulted from the crash. Wellman suddenly realized that in all his planning, he "had forgotten one terribly important factor, the human element. The pilot had flown at the front. He had received decorations. He had flown missions just like this one. For five minutes, he had returned to 1918 from 1926. He just stuck out his hand and said, 'I'm sorry.' C'est la guerre."[61]

Wellman captured this feeling of realism on film so well that audiences found themselves caught up in the movie despite its superficial plot. Once the early romantic antics of the lead characters have played themselves out, the story of men, including a young Gary Cooper, learning to fly and then fighting in the air provided viewers with visual excitement seldom found on the screen—even seventy years later. So successfully did Wellman do his job that later filmmakers have regularly imitated shots such as a plane spinning to earth trailing a cloud of smoke or an aircraft strafing a bridge from which enemy soldiers fall or dive frantically into the water to escape.

These actions moved one reviewer to write, "Nothing in the line of war pictures ever has packed a greater proportion of real thrills into an equal footage. As a spectacle, *Wings* is a technical triumph. It piles punch upon punch until the spectator is almost nervously exhausted." Another critic observed, "The exceptional quality of *Wings* lies in its appeal as

An Army plane strafes German train in *Wings.*

a spectacle and as a picture of at least some of the actualities of flying under wartime conditions." Wellman's re-creation of the dogfights seemed so realistic that a writer looking at the movie forty-five years after its release thought the director had used authentic war pictures in which machines crash to the earth in flames."[62]

Wellman concerned himself primarily with the technical accuracy of the combat scenes, not with the literal reproduction of the World War I period. In contrast to Vidor's careful adherence to detail, Wellman used 1927 clothes and cars in the picture. When asked about this incongruity much later, Wellman admitted he never had thought about it before. Despite such lapses, the movie ran for a year and a half in New York and six months in Los Angeles, made a fortune for Paramount, and won the first Academy Award for best picture of the year.[63]

The Air Corps found the product of its assistance eminently satisfactory. Wellman dedicated the film "to those young warriors of the sky, whose wings are folded about them forever." General Irvine, looking back on *Wings,* said that the film showed the public the kind of people and kind of equipment the Air Corps had and communicated the military's message that "if you are second best, you are dead." He also thought that as a recruiting instrument, the film had an immediate and continuing effect. "Beginning about that time," Irvine noted, "the Air Corps never had problems getting enough people."[64]

The Army Air Corps was to help on only a few other movies before 1940, but the other services began to cooperate regularly with filmmakers following the release of *Wings,* albeit mostly on peacetime stories. But no Hollywood film has ever received as much military assistance for so long a time as Wellman received in Texas in 1926. And very few other films have ever managed to recreate aerial battles as well as *Wings.* As a result, Wellman's movie became the yardstick against which all future combat spectaculars have had to be measured in terms of authenticity of combat and scope of production.

Of course, not all films that received assistance have provided the cooperating service such benefits or succeeded at the box office and with critics as did *The Big Parade, What Price Glory?* or *Wings.* However, each military branch provided the same scrutiny to each request for help, whatever the scope and quality of the project. Over the years, producers regularly sought more help in the form of men and equipment than the military was willing or able to provide. Subsequent negotiations over the content of the script and the amount of assistance a service would give usually led to compromise and approval of cooperation on the project.

This became the case with *The Patent Leather Kid.* Writing on August 12, 1926, to Lt. Harrison Johnson in the Army Signal Corps, then the department that supervised assistance to filmmakers, producer A.L. Rockett of First National Productions asked whether the service could move twenty-five tanks from Fort Lewis, Washington, to Los Angeles to appear in the production. He explained that that number "would give us just about what we would need for our big tank action and attack. I cannot tell you at the present time for how long we would need these, but I do know that we will need four or five tanks for a couple of weeks for intimate shots and closeups."[65]

At that point, Rockett had only a treatment for a film about a "flashy, conceited, cowardly prizefighter who through his service in the war becomes a regenerated character." The producer hoped to obtain approval for the project in a few days, even though he had presented "only the basic idea for our story," which he felt would become "one of the greatest stories ever written, and will make a picture which will be a great credit to the United States government and army."[66]

At the direction of Lieutenant Johnson, Rockett next wrote to Maj. Gen. Charles Saltzman, the chief signal officer of the Army, requesting cooperation on "one of the greatest war stories we have come across. . . . one that will be of great military, educational, historical and patriotic value." In turn, Saltzman advised the adjutant general that "the grimness of war on the battle field and in the hospitals is depicted in very remarkable scenes, which, however, appear characteristic and true. It is not apparent how such a scene could be made less grim and give a true picture." He found the story "clean and wholesome throughout" and said it had "a happy and elevating termination."[67]

Saltzman believed that people would leave the theater with "the idea that the Army and the war had produced a remarkable effect in the regeneration of the principal character and other characters in the picture." Given these images, the general recommended that the Army cooperate on the project and direct the local commander to "extend such facilities as are practicable under existing War Department policy." Saltzman also said that the commander should "designate a suitable officer as representative of the War Department to supervise the filming of all portions of this picture in which troops or materiel pertaining to his corps area appear, with the understanding that such parts of the film will not be used unless, together with all titles and subtitles connected therewith, they are acceptable to the Commanding General . . . to the end that the picture may be entirely acceptable."[68]

Once the Army approved the project on August 31, First National worked directly with the commanding general of the Ninth Corps Area based at the Presidio in San Francisco to arrange for the necessary assistance. Unfortunately, the Army could provide only eight tanks in the district, and the studio tried to arrange for the "tremendous tank attack" sequence at Camp Meade (now Fort Meade), in Maryland just north of Washington. Ultimately, because of possible poor weather conditions there in March, when the studio wanted to shoot the scene, the Army provided the required men and equipment at Camp Lewis in Washington state, where exterior shooting took place from March 19 to April 29.[69]

The filmmakers experienced only one problem, their desire to dress four hundred to five hundred American soldiers in German uniforms in a long shot for the tank-attack battle. Although the studio had received permission in August for the costume switch, the Army had subsequently instituted on January 26, 1927, a regulation forbidding American soldiers from wearing uniforms of any foreign nation. The studio then asked the Motion Picture Producers and Distributors in Washington to intercede on its behalf; its representative, Jack Connolly, wrote to General Saltzman asking him to authorize the use of the soldiers wearing German uniforms. In turn, the Signal Corps officer advised the adjutant general to grant the studio's request. However, after due consideration, the adjutant general refused to violate the spirit of the National Defense Act.[70] Although the War Department itself had not forbidden American soldiers to depict foreign military men, he pointed out that the Ninth Corps Area did have such a provision in its policy. Moreover, he pointed out that the War Department had "never looked with favour upon requests to have the Army portray the roles of foreign soldiers." Finally, he pointed out that the Army had always had a provision that the use of soldiers in filming a picture should never result in the loss of employment for civilian labor.[71]

Whether First National had to hire extras or circumvented the War Department's regulations in shooting *The Patent Leather Kid*, in coming years filmmakers were to dress on-duty American soldiers in enemy uniforms and have planes and ships masquerade as German or Japanese equipment. In the midst of World War II, five hundred soldiers in German garb attacked Humphrey Bogart in *Sahara*. An American fighter impersonated a Japanese Zero in *Air Force*. An American cruiser assumed the role of the German battleship in *Pursuit of the Graf Spee*. An American aircraft carrier launched the Japanese attack on Pearl Harbor in *Tora! Tora! Tora!* And Marines even invaded Omaha beach in the guise of American G.I.s in *The Longest Day*.

In any event, if *The Patent Leather Kid* did not become "one of the greatest stories ever written," its portrayal of tank warfare during World War I and the maturing of the hero did benefit the Army. The *New York Times* reviewer questioned whether the film devoted too much time to the "agony" of the military operations, wondering if the drama "of a surgical operation is an appealing subject." Nevertheless, he found the acting of Richard Barthelmess as the kid flawless and the film "an emphatically human chronicle, one that is filled with incidents that are true to life and some really good comedy."[72]

Unfortunately for the filmmakers, *Wings* premiered three days earlier; and by comparison, *The Patent Leather Kid* did not distinguish itself as any more than another conventional World War I story that added nothing to the portrayal of men in combat. Moreover, by the time the film appeared, Hollywood had well satisfied the desire of the American people to watch serious ground-combat stories. The rise of isolationism during the 1920s also reduced Americans' interest in refighting the Great War on motion picture screens.

Perhaps most important, with the advent of the Depression, people lost their taste for mass carnage in their escapist entertainment. Instead, filmmakers turned to the peacetime military as settings for light comedies, musicals, and love stories, all of which could have taken place in any civilian locale. However, the glamour of the uniforms, the exotic scenery in which the soldiers, sailors, and Marines usually found themselves, and the appeal of the planes and warships continued to attract audiences.

The armed services' limited appropriations and reduced manpower during the 1920s and 1930s prevented them from providing cooperation on the scale that the Air Corps had extended to *Wings*. Nevertheless, the military remained willing to assist on suitable scripts in order to aid recruiting and help inform the nation of the services' peacetime mission. Consequently, from the late 1920s to the outbreak of World War II in Europe, the relationship between the military and the film industry enjoyed a golden age of mutual exploitation.

4 | The Golden Age of Military Movies

UNLIKE THE ARMY, THE ARMY AIR CORPS, AND THE MARINES, the Navy had participated in no major battles during World War I and so offered Hollywood only convoy duty as a subject for cinematic combat. However, ships and sailors and the distant locales to which they sailed did provide opportunities for peacetime stories of romance, comedy, and drama. Since so many Americans lived far from oceans, movies about the Navy also provided audiences with new vistas of a previously unseen and often mysterious world. As a result, these noncombat Navy films returned a profit to the studios and became a powerful recruiting tool, which produced many enlistees from the nation's midlands during the 1920s and 1930s.[1]

Recognizing the value of these movies for recruiting as well as for informing the American people about its activities, the Navy worked diligently to create a positive screen image. Its officers, most of whom had attended Annapolis, regarded themselves as members of an elite organization. As career officers, they usually served a tour in the Navy's public relations office, which gave them the opportunity to help burnish this image. The office, which functioned under the direct supervision of the chief of naval operations, helped ensure that films receiving Navy cooperation would provide accurate or at least complimentary portrayals of the service's activities and men.

Of these movies, the ones that focused on life at the Naval Academy probably provided the greatest benefit to the Navy. Beginning with *The Midshipman,* released in October 1925, Hollywood regularly portrayed the Navy's education of its future officers with virtually the same inconsequential plot line. The filmmakers relied on images of the Academy's beautiful grounds, marching midshipmen, football weekends, dances, and beautiful girls to entertain the audiences. Screenwriters might seek some dramatic tension from a midshipman's small transgression, but never from a cheating scandal, lies, or rape. Any script trying to tell a story of life at Annapolis containing such warts or the reality of a midshipman's four years at the Academy would have brought a swift denial of access to Academy grounds.

None of the stories accurately portrayed the conditions of life at the school—the rigid discipline, the lack of the freedom that most other college students enjoyed, restrictions on travel, and the limited and proscribed social life. Instead, virtually all the movies followed the same formula, in which the midshipman enjoys school; meets the perfect girl, who happens to appear on campus; experiences some minor obstacles in winning the girl and his commission; graduates; and immediately marries. The films did not acknowledge that newly minted officers could not marry for two years after graduation. Nor would the Navy have approved any story which revealed that a midshipman occasionally eloped or that some young officers actually married in violation of the rules. Nor did the stories remind audiences that Navy men took long cruises, sometimes during the arrival of babies or family crises.

If the Academy movies presented a highly sanitized version of how the Navy produced its officers, the glamour of the uniforms, the perfection of the parades, the utter sincerity and patriotism of the cinematic midshipmen, and the highly romanticized boy-girl relationships all conspired to give the movies an appeal that transcended their stories. Nevertheless, the filmmakers often sought more than the simple appearance of authenticity in the scenes they shot on the Academy grounds. For *The Midshipman*, in 1925, the studio received permission to have Ramon Novarro dress up as a midshipman, take his place among the graduating class, and receive a diploma from the secretary of the Navy. Not satisfied, the producer proposed that President Coolidge give out the certificates, a request the Navy readily refused despite the propaganda value the scene might have engendered.[2]

The deceit that did occur caused an Academy alumnus to write an angry letter to the *Army Navy Journal* in which he complained: "The humiliating spectacle of a Secretary of the Navy presenting a fake diploma to a fake Midshipman is reprobated by practically all graduates of that institution. Such a travesty of the solemn ceremony, the crown of four years' hard work, is unpardonable." The writer argued that the Navy and its friends should boycott the "fraudulent" film and Secretary Wilbur should resign because he did not "know he is advertising a film actor and *not* the Naval Academy."[3]

Others did not see the film in this light. Arthur Barney wrote to Secretary Wilburn that he believed movies served as "our greatest educational institution." He also said, "A good picture of the academy portraying those wonderful traditions of the school will do a great deal to win the public to our greatest national academy that is now suffering from the pangs of Public Economy as well as unjust criticism." Barney felt it was just as important that the "publicity received from the picture would do more to promote the friendly spirit towards the Academy than anything that has been done in the past decade."[4]

Whatever the truth of this observation, Annapolis ultimately became disenchanted with the sameness of the stories, and the producer of *Midshipman Jack* did not receive the usual welcome from the Academy superintendent in 1933. Despite the Navy Board's approval of the script, the superintendent expressed his concern to the chief of naval operations "that a photoplay of better caliber has not been proposed." He also pointed out that the story featured a fifth-year "turn back and it is common knowledge in naval circles that men of that category are scarcely representative of the Regiment."[5]

The superintendent "regretted that so much of the plot hinges about boy and girl relations which seems to be the natural gravitation of authors writing about the Academy." Since he believed love stories appeared less in movies about civilian colleges, he wished writers would "break away from that phase of life when they take on the Naval Academy." Though he acknowledged that the film would not "react unfavorably upon the Academy," he expected "the product will be somewhat mediocre" and so failed "to see wherein it can do the institution any benefit."[6]

These concerns did not persuade the Navy to revoke its agreement to provide access to the Academy, and the completed film justified the superintendent's concerns. The *New York Times* reviewer described the film as a "juvenile discussion of the gallant lads at Annapolis and the manner in which the glorious traditions of the Naval Academy are implanted in several recalcitrant students. To adopt a superior metropolitan attitude toward it would be to endow it with intentions which are alien to the producers. To note that its production is without finesse and that its story is on the inventive level of a Frank Merriwell story would be pompous and unfair." Still, the critic believed children "should find it satisfying."[7]

A retired officer recounting his career to a midshipman in *Annapolis Farewell*, one of the many movies about the Naval Academy that Hollywood churned out in the 1920s and 1930s.

Despite such tepid reviews, Hollywood remained enamored of Annapolis throughout the 1930s, producing such indistinguishable and undistinguished movies as *Annapolis Farewell* and *Shipmates Forever* in 1935 and *Annapolis Salute*, *Hold 'em Navy*, and *Navy Blue and Gold* in 1937. By the end of that year, however, the rise of fascism in Germany and Japan was creating a very real threat to the nation. Images of a capable officer corps and a strong Navy that the Annapolis films created would naturally foster a sense of security within the American people. For the most part, however, the ubiquitous Academy films of the 1920s and 1930s simply transported audiences to a beautiful locale in which bright, good-looking boys in uniform experienced their rites of passage.

The nation would certainly need competent officers to stop Hitler and Tojo. But the Navy would also need warships, planes, and well-trained enlisted men, and Hollywood provided the service ample opportunity to show its hardware in action in peacetime from the late 1920s to Pearl Harbor. In particular, Hollywood manifested interest in the peacetime submarine service. Nevertheless, unlike the excitement of undersea wartime combat, aboard a submarine during a training cruise, nothing much happens to interrupt the boredom of routine operations. What is a filmmaker to do? Sink the submarine to create the drama, of course.

Whether another warship, a freighter, or an ocean liner causes the disaster, it usually results from an officer's mistake, not a very good image for the Navy, especially when Charlton Heston is playing the captain, as in *Gray Lady Down*. Despite any reservations that the Navy might have, however, the submarine service has invariably provided full assistance to the projects, beginning with Frank Capra's 1928 *Submarine*. Why?

The Navy simply accepted the reality that submarines do sink accidentally in peacetime, whether the F-4 in 1915, the S-4 or the S-51 in the 1920s, the Squalus in 1939, or two nuclear submarines in the 1960s. If a submarine might sink, then the Navy believed it had to show that it had developed the ability to rescue the trapped crew from the ocean floor. Moreover, by agreeing to assist on the disaster film, the Navy had some hope of salvaging the reputation of the erring officer through negotiations on the script.

Apart from the drama inherent in watching men slowly die while waiting for rescuers to arrive, filmmakers could produce their submarine stories at small cost. The Navy provided the submarine and rescue equipment for the exterior shots at little or no expense to the studio. The service also assigned a technical advisor, who ensured accuracy, if not plausibility, in the actions and procedures of the crew. He also helped the set designer create an authentic-looking interior of a submarine. Given the relatively small complement of men aboard ship, the producer needed only a small number of actors and had to build only a few sets, which the studio often passed on to another studio for the next undersea story.

The limited vistas and the similarity of the stories did have a downside. To impart some originality to their films, writers and directors had to predicate their stories on tensions within the crew, the nature of the accident, and the problems involved in the rescue of the doomed men. Nevertheless, most of the submarine disaster movies from *Submarine* to *Gray Lady Down* resembled each other to a greater or lesser extent, much as did the Annapolis stories. Most important for the Navy, whatever the plot twist, a majority of the crew members needed to survive the accident, albeit not before they had given up all hope of rescue and had breathed virtually the last bit of oxygen.

Although the title does not adequately preview the film's subject, *Submarine* became the model that all filmmakers imitated for the next fifty years. If truth-in-advertising laws had existed in 1928, Columbia should have titled the movie "Navy Diver" or "Submarine Rescue," since the story had almost nothing to do with life abroad a peacetime submarine. Except for the climactic rescue effort, Capra could have used any occupational setting for the "buddy" story of two men and the dance hall floozie who threatens their friendship by marrying one and conducting an affair with the other.

The Navy did not object to the adultery, perhaps because an enlisted man, not an officer, committed the sin and because the film showed how the service was prepared to rescue men from a sunken submarine. To help demonstrate this, the Navy provided Capra with an amphibious plane from the USS *Saratoga* to carry Jack Holt, playing the diver, to the disaster site so that he can attempt to attach an air hose to the stricken submarine, whose crew includes his friend Ralph Graves. More important, actual Navy divers and equipment helped shoot the opening diving scenes and the closing rescue scenes in Los Angeles Harbor. However, the director used a two-foot toy submarine and two-and-a-half-inch toy diver to portray Holt's descent to the sunken submarine.[8]

Despite the Navy's concerns about accuracy in portraying its activities, the service ignored the implausibility of the rescue sequence. The service had spent nine months, including a winter pause, raising the S-51 from a depth of 132 feet. In *Submarine*, Holt dives 400 feet, a depth the film acknowledges that no man had ever reached, and attaches an air hose. Even if a diver could have performed the feat, the film conveniently fails to explain how a team of divers could possibly have worked regularly at such a depth to salvage the submarine before the men died of exposure and lack of food or water. Nevertheless, after Holt attaches the air hose, a cinematic admiral says, "Now we can raise them with pontoons." Pontoons had raised the S-51 and the S-4, but from much shallower water and without the pressure of trying to rescue living sailors. Without explaining how divers had carried out the rescue, the film ends with the buddies reunited, which provided the Navy the message that it could rescue sailors from a stricken submarine.

John Ford's 1930 *Men without Women* told virtually the same story, and as with *Submarine*, the title contains no hint of the plot line. In fact, the studio might well have titled it "Men with Women," since the first half of the picture takes place in Shanghai, where the crew of an American submarine cavorts with assorted loose women at the world's "longest" bar. Such images would undoubtedly aid in recruiting submariners from among midwestern farm boys. However, from the Navy's perspective, the film had to show how the submarine service could rescue the crew if it were to find itself trapped on the ocean bottom following a collision with a destroyer while on a training exercise.

To accurately portray life aboard a submarine and the rescue procedures, the Navy assigned a technical advisor experienced in undersea operations to supervise the military aspects of the production. Then Lieutenant and later Admiral John Will had the authority to correct errors that might slip into the script. He also secured equipment used in the interior scenes shot on a soundstage and arranged for ships during location shooting. This assistance guaranteed that the finished movie would authentically depict life aboard a submarine.[9]

During the shooting, Will succeeded almost too well. In the film's dramatic highlight, a destroyer runs over the submerged submarine, damaging its hull and loosing an avalanche of water into the control room. Watching Ford directing the scene, the technical advisor was so startled by the realism of the action he had helped create that he shouted, "Jesus Christ!" even though the cameras and recording equipment were still running. This spontaneous reaction forced the director to reshoot the whole sequence, since the sound recordings then used could not be edited for extraneous noise.[10]

Hollywood did not create all films equal, of course, and not all submarine films could have the same impact on audiences. Fortunately for Hollywood, the Navy and the other military branches have seldom tried to use artistic quality as a criterion in deciding whether to cooperate with a production seeking assistance. Nevertheless, the Navy ultimately reached a point where the similarity of the submarine stories and the negative images of dying sailors gasping for breath weighed heavily into the decision to provide assistance.

In particular, the debate within the Navy on whether to cooperate with *The Devil's Playground* remains a classic example of the negotiating process between a film studio requesting assistance and a military service trying to decide whether to approve a project. Not surprisingly, the Navy had an adverse reaction to Columbia Pictures' request, on July 28, 1936, for assistance in the production of another undersea disaster movie. At least initially, the Navy's antipathy to "The Depths Below" (the original title) focused as much on the negative images of the sailors themselves as on the obligatory sinking of a submarine.[11]

In reviewing the original script, Capt. H.A. Badt, the senior member of the Navy Motion Picture Board, objected to the portrayal of "the unfaithful Navy wife" and the "enraged Navy husband who drowns his sorrow in drink." Badt thought such images gave "the public false ideas of Navy married life and of the enlisted men of the Navy." At the same time, he expressed concern that the scene in the sunken submarine "is sure to cause unnecessary worry to the families of enlisted men in submarine service. Also the parents of young boys, who desire to enlist in the Navy, will, in a great many cases, be unwilling to consent to the enlistment of their sons." Consequently, he recommended that the service not approve cooperation.[12]

The Motion Picture Board used Captain Badt's memo almost verbatim to advise the chief of naval operations (CNO) on August 12, 1936, that he should deny Columbia Pictures's request for assistance. Upon receipt of the board's recommendation, the CNO wrote to the studio that the service would not assist on the production because of the script's portrayal of naval marriages and "the fact that the proposed photoplay unduly emphasizes and greatly exaggerates the hazzards of service in submarines."[13]

As usually happened when the Navy denied assistance to a project, Columbia Pictures immediately revised the script and had its representative, Sol Rosenblatt, personally deliver it to the CNO. During the meeting, Rosenblatt discussed the project and asked the Navy to consider the new script, which the CNO then asked Captain Badt to "carefully read." Writing to the commandant of the Eleventh Naval District, Adm. Sinclair Gannon, who would provide any assistance to the filmmakers, Badt noted that the revisions did not eliminate the problems that the Navy had found in the original script.[14]

Instead, Badt concluded that the "horrors of doomed and dying Navy personnel; the remarks and craven actions of men who are apparently doomed to a slow and agonizing death; the hysterical scenes of the families of the trapped men; the master diver, who tries to forget his unfortunate marriage in drink, and practically refuses to return to duty and go to the assistance of his doomed shipmates—are not favorable publicity for the Navy and its personnel." Nevertheless, Badt advised the admiral that the CNO did want to work with Columbia Pictures on the project, but that "such cooperation must be in the interest, or at least not to the detriment, of the Service."[15]

Badt went on to explain that the CNO believed "that there is much in this script which, if properly presented, would be beneficial in educating the public." As a result, the CNO had directed that some young officer with submarine experience work with the studio in revising the script and serve as technical advisor during the production. Since Columbia desired to start work on the film as soon as possible, the studio had agreed to pay all expenses involved in such assistance. Nevertheless, Badt told the admiral that the CNO did not want any help given to the filmmakers until they had revised the script "to the satisfaction of the Navy representatives and the objectionable features removed."[16]

According to Badt, the CNO concurred with his objections to the portrayal of the disgruntled diver, particularly in his refusal to report for duty to go to the aid of the men trapped aboard the sunken submarine. He felt that portraying the diver as "going on a prolonged drinking spree, does not truly represent the fine type of petty officer in the Navy today." In addition, the CNO had strong objections to the actions and comments of some of the trapped men and felt the script "can be revised to show these men facing death with courage." Moreover, he maintained that the captain's shooting of one of his men "would not occur in the case of a Navy disaster. Such melodrama is alright for a dime novel story."[17]

One of Admiral Gannon's officers found a more basic problem with "Depths Below" when he read the script. In a memo on September 2, Capt. H.A. Jones pointed out that the studio had simply done a rewrite of Frank Capra's *Submarine*, even giving the characters the same names. Jones recalled that at the time, several studios had submitted stories of submarine disasters inspired by the 1927 sinking of the S-4. He wrote that the Navy had denied all requests for assistance on the same grounds as Captain Badt had cited in his letter to Admiral Gannon. Jones also noted that all studios, except for Columbia, "respected" the Navy's wishes and dropped their proposed films.[18]

Jones pointed out that Capra's film included "in a more offensive form all the objectionable features of 'Depths Below'" and that most of the important sequences remained "practically identical." Although the new story had toned down some of the worst portrayals, Jones felt that the "action is still objectionable from the Navy view point." In addition, he had not mentioned the numerous technical errors that any technical advisor could easily correct. On the positive side, Jones pointed out that "Depths Below" did contain a decompression tank sequence, "which is a desirable addition."[19]

Ironically, Jones had fewer problems with the portrayal of the wife and the diver's relationship with her. He saw her simply as a dance-hall girl who "has tricked a good Navy man who knew little about women into marrying her." As a result, he felt "confident that the public will look upon her in that characterization and not as a 'navy wife.'" In fact, Jones believed that "a further blackening" of her character "would help the story, giving as it would a better reason" for the diver's leaving her so abruptly. Though he suggested that the script not attribute the diver's delay in answering the rescue call to his drunkenness, he acknowledged that his late arrival does add suspense and so helps the story, but it "need not be deliberate."[20]

Jones recognized that the action in the sunken submarine "must necessarily be highly dramatic," since it would become the "high spot" of the film. Nevertheless, he stated that the officers and men "must act according to the best training and traditions of the Navy." He expressed more concern about assisting on a "re-hashed" story, because the studio might simply make a cheap picture using footage from *Submarine*. In this regard, Jones reported on his meeting the previous November with the director assigned to the project. The director had said then that Columbia would like Navy assistance but intended to make the movie without assistance if necessary. Jones thought he had persuaded the director, and through him, the studio, to drop the project because "it was a bad Navy story."[21]

If Columbia had now decided to go ahead with the project, however, Jones acknowledged that the Navy would have a difficult time stopping it. The only grounds for legal action required proof that the film brought the service into disrepute. Jones did not think the Navy could demonstrate that, "especially in view of the many objectionable plays that have been placed on the stage without objections on our part." Consequently, he suggested to Admiral Gannon that the Navy advise Columbia it would not provide assistance because the story remained objectionable and did not give an accurate account of naval training and traditions.[22]

Admiral Gannon wrote to Captain Badt on September 4, detailing his solicitation of reactions to the script from officers in his command. He expressed his agreement with Jones's evaluation of the project but felt "a little more drastic in that I think the picture, if allowed to be made, would be a disgrace." Although he did not find "any particular fault with" the portrayal of the unfaithful Navy wife, he did intend to have one of his officers go to Columbia to point out "with as much emphasis as possible the undesirable features" the Navy found in the script. Saying that all the officers with whom he had spoken agreed with his position, Gannon closed by saying he wished "the whole thing could be given the 'deep six' and forgotten in times limbo."[23]

Despite the opinions of the several officers who had read the script, the Navy Department advised Admiral Gannon on September 8 that he should send a submarine officer to visit Columbia Pictures "to investigate possibility of and to assist in revising script to eliminate undesirable features and if a satisfactory script is produced, to cooperate in filming the picture." The officer discovered that the studio did want to receive assistance and expressed a willingness to revise the script. Less than two weeks later, on September 21, the Navy authorized the Commander in Chief, United States Fleet (CINCUS) to cooperate on "Depths Below," even though Columbia had not yet requested any specific cooperation.[24]

As it turned out, Columbia still had not committed itself to revising the script, even though Lieutenant Young thought he had succeeded in eliminating the offending parts of the story while working with the filmmakers in Los Angeles. The day after he returned to San Diego, Young received a call from screenwriter Jerome Chodorov, saying that the studio had decided to proceed with the production without assistance. According to the writer, Columbia felt that it would spoil the story if the film did not portray the diver being drunk and refusing to report for duty. In addition, with the production costing it ten thousand dollars a day, the studio did not want to wait for the Navy to approve the script. Although Young offered to expedite the process, Chodorov refused to make the requested changes and said the studio did not want a Navy technical advisor. Young informed Admiral Gannon of Columbia's intransigence and then forwarded the information to the Navy Department.[25]

Harry Cohn, the volatile president of Columbia, called Young, "very much agitated" about Gannon's dispatch to Washington, claiming that the studio had not said the things Young had reported to the admiral. Cohn's legendary ability to intimidate his employees did not have the same effect on the lieutenant, who told him that "nothing had been reported to Washington that I had not been told over the telephone by his representative." In response, Cohn asked the Navy to read the revised script and, if the service liked the new version, to approve cooperation. Young agreed and found that the studio had made all the corrections he had recommended during a visit to Hollywood. As a result of Young's review, Admiral Gannon wired to the Navy Department that he recommended the service approve the script for cooperation.[26]

Subsequently, Cohn called Young twice regarding the studio's request for assistance in the form of ships and men, but Gannon's office had not yet received a response from Navy headquarters. As a result, in a letter to a friend in Washington, the lieutenant wanted to know "out of curiosity, how far the Navy Department is going to cooperate." In any case, Young suggested that Cohn's change of direction on script revisions occurred only after the studio discovered that the Navy's August 1932 policy on cooperation to Hollywood stipulated that studios could not use stock footage in their productions without having secured script approval from the Navy.[27]

Ultimately, the Navy did agree to provide limited assistance, primarily in the form of stock footage to lend authenticity to the story. However, the Navy's difficulties with Columbia and the project did not end with the release of the film, now titled *The Devil's Playground*. On February 27, 1937, the new CNO, Adm. William Leahy, wrote directly to Harry Cohn saying that Columbia had violated Navy regulations by not submitting the film for review prior to release. As a result, the CNO said the Navy Motion Picture Board was considering whether to bar the studio from receiving any future assistance from the Navy. Leahy did tell Cohn he would listen to any explanations that Columbia might offer before the board took official actions.[28]

In turn, Cohn wrote to Leahy twice within a week, showing proper contrition for the studio's omission and assuring the Navy that he was taking the steps to ensure that Columbia would not again violate the service's regulations on cooperation with Hollywood. In response, the CNO expressed his appreciation for "the spirit with which you have investigated the filming of your recent photoplay." Leahy also said he had ascertained from Motion Picture Board members that, as Cohn had stated, *The Devil's Playground* did not contain anything objectionable. However, the CNO pointed out that this "might well not apply to future releases" and so expressed his hope that the studio had now become aware of the Navy's requirements for review of movies on which it had provided any form of assistance. By "strict compliance" with the regulations, Leahy suggested, Columbia "will avoid jeopardizing future Naval cooperation."[29]

In fact, *The Devil's Playground* simply did not merit the time and effort the Navy spent to obtain a satisfactory script that would deserve even limited assistance. The *New York Times* reviewer described it as a film "with a completely commonplace idea . . . treated with the detailed care and technical respect of a Hollywood superspecial. It is, in short, B product at its unimportant best." Likewise, *Weekly Variety* called it an "unoriginal and familiar gob drama." What did the Navy assistance achieve? According to the same reviewer, as a fadeout salute, "the customers get an extra glimpse of the fleet at sea and a mass flight of planes overhead."[30]

The Devil's Playground may have contained "fairly effective" shots of "gasping sailors trapped in the sunken sub" and good underwater camera work. However, the Navy needed more than images of ships and planes or a lone brave diver to explain the new developments in the technology of submarine rescues. By 1937 the Navy had solved the rescue problems, at least at moderate depths, thanks to the perfection of the Momson escape lung and the McCann rescue chamber. To demonstrate these new techniques on the screen would require the Navy to lose two more submarines in cinematic collisions with surface ships. Although such accidents obviously did not portray submariners in the best possible light, the Navy recognized the ultimate benefit of assisting on a film that would have informational and recruiting value.[31]

The vehicle to accomplish these purposes, *Submarine D-1*, received virtually unlimited support from the Navy throughout its production. In contrast to the manner in which Columbia had resisted adhering to the Navy's regulations, Warner Brothers had an unquestioning commitment to satisfying the service's requirements and expectations. The three Warner brothers, sons of Polish immigrants, had become strongly committed to the security of the country that had given them the opportunity to become rich and successful. As a result, they saw their movies that glorified the military as repayment for the opportunities they had found in the United States.[32]

The way the studio implemented this commitment in producing *Submarine D-1* became clear in the letter Spig Wead wrote to the Navy, accompanying his initial, July 28, 1936, script, then titled "Submarine Story." Wead explained that the studio wanted to film necessary scenes at the Submarine Base in New London and at West Coast facilities. The writer said he was planning to come to Washington and place himself "at the disposal of the Motion Picture Board for any discussion which may be necessary in connection with the script."[33]

Wead said that if the Navy approved cooperation, Warner Brothers intended "to make this as fine and creditable a picture as is possible. The studio is extremely anxious to meet the wishes of the Navy Department in every detail." To this end, he assured the service: "If any scenes in the script as it now stands are for any reason objectionable, I am sure that they can be eliminated or that other unobjectionable can be substituted for them." Furthermore, he told the Navy that he had full authorization to represent the studio in negotiations.[34]

Wead said that Warner Brothers believed the script "displays the submarine service of our Navy in a more creditable light than any picture yet made or proposed and that it is the first one to truly reflect the training and the spirit of that service." He also wrote that the studio felt moviegoers remained interested in the submarine branch and so "will be grateful for being informed more fully concerning it." To this end, the disabled Navy aviator turned screenwriter assured the service that Warner Brothers would "gladly" make any changes the service requested and that the shooting schedule would cause a minimum of trouble or interference.[35]

Given such obsequiousness, the Navy readily agreed to cooperate despite the dramatic requirement to "sink" two submarines to visualize how the service now carried out underwater rescue operations. The CNO advised the commander of the New London submarine base to give full assistance to the filmmakers when they arrived in May 1937. To facilitate the studio's obtaining the required footage, the CNO subsequently sent a memo on May 14, 1937, to the chief of the Bureau of Construction and Repair and the chief of the Bureau of Engineering, advising them that Warner Brothers "very much" desired to photograph a submarine under construction, subject only to "such special restrictions" as were necessary to "safeguard matters of military secrecy."[36]

With the way cleared, director Lloyd Bacon and his cameramen, assistants, and cast, including Pat O'Brien, George Brent, and Ronald Reagan, arrived in New London the third week in May. Bacon had no difficulty adjusting to the base environment, having served as a naval officer in World War I and later as a reservist, still spending thirty days a year on active duty. Given the director's background, Warner Brothers's eagerness to please the service, and the Navy's own desire for an informational film on its new technologies, Bacon, for all practical purposes, turned the Submarine Base into a movie set, filming all the activities including the launching of a submarine.[37]

However, the director's raison d'être for coming to New London remained the underwater rescue training facility. To explain the new escape techniques that the submarine service had adopted since the loss of the S-51 and the S-4, Bacon and his crew focused their attention on the one-hundred-foot training tank, put into operation in 1930. There, for the camera, ensconced in a miniature diving bell, the Navy demonstrated how men learned to make their way to the surface using an "artificial lung." Bacon felt such scenes, when incorporated into his film, would spell the doom for submarine disaster films, particularly those showing sailors on the verge of suffocation, begging to escape from torpedo tubes à la *Men without Women*. In fact, the submarine service saw the lung as only a last resort now that the service had new rescue bells, the development of which became the film's focus.[38]

During the subsequent filming on the West Coast, Warner Brothers even managed to persuade the Navy to reverse its policy on providing photographs of a submarine's interiors to help the set designers create the insides of an undersea craft on the studio's soundstage. Answering its request for such assistance, the new CNO, William Leahy, informed the studio that the Office of Naval Intelligence would be pleased to select shots of the interiors of the older S type submarines that would enable the studio to create authentic-looking sets on its soundstage. In constructing the "innards" of the movie submarine, however, the set designers had to modify reality in order to satisfy the practical needs of filming action in confined spaces. This cinematic license had the added virtue of satisfying the Navy's concerns about security, since the ersatz sets would confuse a foreign nation hoping to learn American submarine secrets from the movie.[39]

In the end, the Navy's cooperation enabled Warner Brothers to produce a pseudo-documentary on the training of submariners and the development of the rescue chamber. Although the trapped submariners in *Men without Women* had used an early version of the Momson Lung, the film had provided no explanation of its operation. In contrast, *Submarine D-1* detailed the training submariners received in the use of the lung. Moreover, with the sinking of the D-1, the Navy received two benefits for the price of one assistance. Most of the crew escapes using the Momson Lung, and the new diving chamber rescues a badly injured officer. With such images and the exoneration of the captain from any blame for the accident, approval of the film became only a formality.[40]

Submarine D-1 served both as a recruiting vehicle and a means of assuring recruits and their families that if a submarine did sink, it no longer had to become a death trap. However, though reviewers found no problems with the production except the normal carping about the dull romance, the film did engender some complaints from viewers. A Chicago insurance agent, for one, wrote his senator that the Navy and the American people "are the goat" for allowing the filmmakers to use government facilities without extracting payment in return. He suggested that Warner Brothers should have paid at least twenty-five thousand dollars for the assistance it received.[41]

In response, the Navy advised the senator that no law existed authorizing it to charge studios for the use of naval material in making their films. The service also explained that it "carefully" supervised all scenes involving the use of naval locales, equipment, and men and "censored" the completed films before release to the public. Justifying the free assistance, the Navy stated its belief that motion pictures "which include naval scenes taken under the conditions stated, serves [*sic*] to stimulate greater public interest in the Navy and to assist the Government in securing desirable recruits for the naval service and that in this way it is justly recompensed for the use of naval property and facilities which may have been used in the production of such films."[42]

The Navy could not always make that claim, of course. Nor did all film producers give the service the respect and subservience that Warner Brothers gave. In one case a studio obtained footage of naval aviators through deceit. The resulting film well portrayed the power of the service's air arm, but the Navy had actually attempted to avoid involvement in what became one of its more successful cinematic missions, killing a dangerous monster. In December 1932 the RKO Studios location manager, Herb Hirst, wrote to the Navy requesting use of four Navy Hell Divers for one day with a total flying time of two and a half hours per plane in the making of *King Kong*. He explained that since the planes were stationed in Long Beach, they would not have to leave their base. He also noted that the commander of the Eleventh Naval District had assured the filmmakers full cooperation if the Navy Department approved the request.[43]

Following the standard procedures, Hirst said the studio would secure insurance to cover damage or injury to the planes and pilots and would reimburse the Navy for the cost of operating the aircraft. RKO further agreed to conform to all the Navy's regulations covering cooperation and to submit the completed film for preview. Hirst also said that the studio would eliminate any scenes from the final print that the Navy found objectionable.[44]

In response, the chief of naval operations wrote to Hirst on December 21, 1932, that the script did not fulfill the service's requirements for cooperation "in that there is nothing pertaining to the Navy and use of planes as requested would compete with [the] civilian airplane industry." As a result, the CNO was "compelled to disapprove of Naval cooperation in this project."[45] In this instance, however, the studio thwarted the service's rejection by requesting assistance directly from the commanding officer at Floyd Bennett Field on Long Island when the filmmakers went east for location shooting. In return for one hundred dollars to the Officers' Mess Fund and ten dollars to each pilot, the operations officer ordered four Navy biplanes to fly over New York City. Gen. John Winston, then a young Marine flier putting in his required flight time at the naval facility, recalled that he and three Navy pilots stationed on the base received the "mission to go and jazz the Empire State Building."[46]

Winston recalled that everyone responded, "Oh, boy!" since regulations forbade planes to fly below one thousand feet over New York City. He assumed the studio had obtained permission from the authorities: "We didn't know what it was all about. They just said there was some kind of movie being made." In any case, then-Lieutenant Winston and the other pilots did not know where the filmmakers had placed the cameras. They simply made a couple of passes at the top of the skyscraper, which took less than fifteen minutes. Winston remembered that although he did not want to run into the building, he "got close enough to scare my observer."[47]

The general recounted that the mission differed little from other training assignments except for the low altitude and the closeness to the building. For the studio, however, the "attack" provided valuable footage of Navy planes flying in formation, first peeling off, then diving at an imaginary target, then looping and attacking from the other direction. Ultimately, the filmmakers intercut twenty-eight scenes of the Navy aircraft with process shots and miniatures to create the fatal assault on Kong atop the Empire State Building. In the end, however, most people did not hold the Navy responsible for the evil deed. As the capturer of Kong observed, "No, beauty killed the beast."[48]

Complicit or not in King Kong's death, naval aviation enjoyed and surface warfare received much more positive portrayals from Hollywood during the interwar years. Frank Capra's *Dirigible,* released in 1931, attempted to do for naval aviation in general and the lighter-than-air service in particular what *Submarine* had done for submariners. Thematically, *Dirigible* differed little from Capra's earlier film, simply transferring the buddy story from under water to the air and, ultimately, the South Pole. And following the same formula, *Dirigible* graphically portrays the destruction of one of the Navy's prize dirigibles, before a sister ship aids in the climactic rescue.

The filmmakers were drawing on the history of fatal Navy dirigible crashes as their springboard. Consequently, the service had no basis for refusing to provide assistance to the project. Nevertheless, the portrayal of a dirigible flying nonstop from New Jersey to the South Pole to rescue lost explorers stretches plausibility as much as the four-hundred-foot dive and the pontoon rescue in *Submarine.*

Given the rousing reception the cinematic Navy rescuers received as well as Capra's positive military portrayals in *Submarine* and in *Flight,* his 1929 homage to Marine aviation and U.S. policy against the "gooks" in Nicaragua, the service rendered all necessary assistance to *Dirigible.* This included an impressive flying sequence of Navy planes and dirigibles filmed at Lakehurst, New Jersey. The service did receive a telegram from the Professional Pilots Association, claiming that civilian pilots in San Diego "HAVE NECESSARY EQUIPMENT TO HANDLE THIS WORK AND THIS ORGANIZATION STRENUOUSLY OBJECTS TO WAR DEPARTMENT EQUIPMENT BEING USED IF COMMERCIAL PILOTS CAN HANDLE THIS WORK." In turn, the CNO advised the commander of the Eleventh Naval District that Navy policy mandated assistance to filmmakers "only in case of photoplays attempting to depict Naval Activities and only to extent necessary to insure correct pictorialization of such activities."[49]

Nominally a peacetime film, *Flight* portrayed Marines enjoying their time away from combat in masculine camaraderie and pursuit of beautiful women with quasi-wartime battles against Nicaraguan revolutionaries, opponents of the U.S.-backed government. The buddies from *Submarine,* Jack Holt and Ralph Graves, this time find themselves as avia-

A romantic moment away
from aerial combat in *Flight.*

tors supporting their fellow Marines on the ground fighting the rebels. Apart from the action and the romance, the film documented how the Marines were developing the close air-support tactics that would serve the Corps well in World War II.

To help Capra create his story, the Marines put all the facilities and personnel of its base at North Island, San Diego, at his disposal, including a squadron of nine Curtis fighter bombers, two-seater, open-cockpit planes, and top Marine Corps pilots. For the jungle scenes in which the Marines defend a rude fort from a rebel onslaught with close air support from Marine aviators, Capra used a leatherneck battalion. As a result of this unlimited assistance, *Flight* previewed the close air support the Marines would use against Japan in the Pacific less than fifteen years later.[50]

The Marines were to reinforce this tactical development in *Devil Dogs of the Air*, released in 1935. Very much resembling Capra's story, the film remained essentially a romantic comedy, in which Marine fliers Jimmy Cagney and Edmund O'Brien cavort through the air and chase the same beautiful waitress. To create the appropriate atmosphere, Marines provided the primary assistance to the production in the form of planes, men, and locations. However, in a grand, ten-minute documentary-like montage, the Pacific Fleet supports a Marine land, sea, and air assault on a beach south of La Jolla.

In the training maneuver, Navy ships simulated preassault bombardment, and the USS *Saratoga* launched Navy and Marine planes to support the amphibious landing. In fact, *Devil Dogs of the Air* remains the only film Hollywood has ever made showing Marine planes flying off a carrier and serving as a component of naval aviation.[51] As portrayed, the Marine carrier squadrons provided the close air support of landing forces, while Navy units protected the fleet. However, the film did not actually explain the relationship between Marine and Navy carrier units, a subject of ongoing, doctrinal debate between the two services within the Navy Department.

Nonetheless, *Devil Dogs of the Air* did illustrate how the Navy provided the primary, forward strike force in projecting the nation's power. Moreover, as the then superior component in the Navy Department, the Navy had to approve the script before the Marines could provide assistance to the filmmakers. In this case, the service also had to respond to an inquiry from Sen. Elbert Thomas, a member of the Foreign Relations Committee, about the assistance given to the movie. In a letter of January 28, 1935, Navy Secretary Claude Swanson explained that the service provided cooperation only in "rare cases" when the story featured life in the Navy. According to Swanson, the Marines and the Navy assisted in "special" scenes and allowed some shooting of routine exercises.[52]

In regard to the issue of cost to the Navy, the secretary explained that the service "believed that the benefits derived by the Navy in having appropriate scenes of Naval life presented to the public in good pictures, more than compensates for the amount of work involved." In fact, Swanson said that the expense remained "negligible as the Naval background furnished is usually taken from regular routine work." Moreover, he said the service restricted filming of naval scenes to ones the studio could not create itself in order to minimize the loss to civilian employment. In further justifying cooperation, Swanson stressed that the Navy felt its assistance "is more than compensated by the favorable publicity value of the product."[53]

In this instance, the joint cooperation in the production created images of how the Navy in coordination with the Marines would carry any future war to the enemy's homelands. At least to the *Washington Herald* reviewer, the message came across very clearly: "Young American men and women, seeing the actual flying, extra-ordinary courage and skill of American war pilots, will be fired with the ambition to fly, and help conquer man's newly acquired realm, the ocean of the air." At the same time, the reviewer learned from the film "that weak as we are in the air, *weakest among important nations,* the fliers that America develops could subject any hostile air fleet to exceedingly unpleasant experiences."[54]

The reviewer provided an even better indication of the Navy's success in obtaining "favorable publicity value" from cooperation when he observed, "Congressmen, and governors of States, seeing this picture will take pride in the marvelous efficiency of the American flier and will be humiliated by the knowledge that among the world's important nations we stand last in airplane defence." Dismissing the "usual" American love story, the review concluded: "The real picture is in the flying of real American air fighters. Don't fail to see it."[55]

Likewise, the *New York Times* reviewer found himself affected by *Devil Dogs of the Air,* despite describing himself as a "peace-loving citizen at heart" and "no admirer of the films which publicize Uncle Sam's armed forces." He described the movie as "distinguished by the most remarkable stunt flying and aerial photography the screen has seen in years. Even the most determined of the anti-militarists is likely to find his principles rolling under the seat when the photo-play is in the air." If the film itself did not contain any "great surprises," the reviewer did find it "both amusing and exciting." The Marines and the Navy did not, of course, care much about the entertainment value of the movie. Rather, their reward for extending cooperation came in the reviewer's concluding sentence, in which he described *Devil Dogs of the Air* as "loaded with pictorial dynamite, even if it is only an advertisement for the preparedness boys."[56]

What about peacetime portrayals of the Army during the interwar years? An unsigned 1928 memorandum on pictorial publicity advised the service to follow the Marine Corps's example of using motion picture appearances to promote itself. Noting that the American armed forces had resumed the "status of undesirable step-children" since the end of World War I, the writer explained that the Marines had sought to alleviate the problem by becoming "probably the first armed force in history to take up publicity as a means of interesting the people of the United States in the Marine Corps. The success of this move is fairly well known to every student of modern military."[57]

Unfortunately for the Army, it could not provide filmmakers exotic ports of call, the drama of men trapped under the water, floating airships, aircraft carriers launching fight-

The Singing Marine with Dick Powell (1937) created a fanciful image of life in the Marines during the inter-war years and provided escapist entertainment to the American people suffering through the Depression.

ers, or dramatic combat over the jungles of Nicaragua. Like the Marines, the Army did travel to Nicaragua, but only to survey a possible route for another sea-to-sea canal, and slogging through the Central American rain forests did not offer much in the way of drama or romance. Moreover, when the Army Corps of Engineers surveyors tried to help rescue efforts and stop the fires in Managua following the devastating earthquake in 1927, the antigovernment forces accused the Americans of blowing up the capital. Hollywood could do little in the way of positive storytelling in such a situation.[58]

Of the Army's three overseas bases between the wars, the Panama Canal Zone, the Philippines, and Hawaii, only the last might provide interesting locales in which to set a story. Nevertheless, screenwriters faced a challenge in portraying the Army in paradise. Officers and their wives spent their time socializing and playing golf and had virtually no interaction with the enlisted men—low-ranking officers could coach service football and baseball teams but not take part in the action. And as James Jones was to describe in *From Here to Eternity,* the signs in the better bars and restaurants made it clear that enlisted men and dogs were not welcome.

Given the unglamorous nature of the Army's peacetime activities, Hollywood featured that service less often than the other military branches during the interwar years. Not surprisingly, West Point became one of the few safe locales for positive cinematic portrayals of Army life, and as with the Naval Academy, Hollywood visited the Military Academy regularly during the 1920s and 1930s. Using the same locales over and over, directors created a series of generic films that replaced the reality of strict discipline and weekend romance with formula boy-meets-girl stories, all with happy endings. Even so, the Army often had problems with the plots and portrayals, demanding script changes before agreeing to allow film companies onto the campus overlooking the Hudson.

The scenery and the uniforms offered such appeal that filmmakers sometimes found themselves competing for the right to portray Academy life. On January 20, 1927, William Orr, MGM's East Coast representative, wrote to Secretary of War Dwight Davis requesting permission to make a film about the life of a cadet at West Point. He reminded the secretary that he had previously mentioned the project and Davis had thought the film "might be good constructive propaganda for the Academy and the Army." Orr cited previous MGM films about the other military branches that had "completely" satisfied their leaders as having provided "distinct benefit." He assured the secretary that the studio would approach the West Point picture "subject, of course, to any improvements or amendments or additions, either to the general idea or to the contract that you would wish to add."[59]

Davis answered that he was "quite in accord with your views that such a picture would have undoubted value to the Army and the military Academy in bringing visually to the country what is actually being done in the training of cadets to become officers." Nevertheless, the secretary said he had to solicit the views of Brig. Gen. M.B. Stewart, the Academy's superintendent "as to the advisability of undertaking such a project at this time." To this end, Davis said he was forwarding Orr's letter to West Point.[60]

Unfortunately for MGM, Stewart had already entered into an agreement with Grey Productions to make a movie at the Academy. As a result, he advised Maj. Livingston Watrous, the adjutant general, whose office then had responsibility for approving Army assistance to motion picture studios, that he "would much prefer not to have a second company on the grounds until the first has finished and gone." In fact, Grey Productions had completed a film about West Point the previous year using stock footage and then had requested permission to shoot a movie on the Academy grounds that would focus on the development of a cadet. Stewart had found the initial story unappealing because it was not "in keeping with the dignity of West Point." However, when a second synopsis, titled "Raw Material," "appeared suitable," the superintendent had agreed to allow filming at the Academy. Stewart advised the adjutant general that shooting was to begin in July and he "did not intend to turn West Point into a moving picture studio."[61]

Accepting the recommendation of Maj. Walter Prosser in the Signal Corps office, Watrous agreed that Grey Productions should keep its priority. However, he took note of Prosser's concerns about the scenario and advised General Stewart that he found the synopsis for "Raw Material" "totally unsuitable and its use will not be approved." In particular, he objected to the cadet protagonist, "a prize fighter who, according to the script, is an unsavory character when he enters the Military Academy." He acknowledged that West Point draws its cadets from all walks of life, "but it is believed the depiction of such an unsavory character would constitute a reflection upon the members of the corps of cadets in that it would give a false impression as to the standards of young men who enter the Military Academy."[62]

Watrous also objected to a key scene in the scenario in which artillery firing over the heads of cadets during training hits one of the men. While admitting such accidents had happened, he said live firing does not usually take place during peacetime maneuvers. Consequently, he "believed that this would tend to create apprehension in the minds of the public and invite criticism of thoughtful people wherever seen."[63]

When he received the decision, Stewart directed Maj. A.W. Chilton, the coauthor of the story and a member of his staff, to prepare a new synopsis that would address the War Department's concerns. However, Chilton informed Stewart that the Academy no longer had a copy of "Raw Material," explaining that the C.B. de Mille Picture Corporation had bought the screenplay and was working on a revised story. He then voiced his disagreement with Watrous's decision to reject the original version, saying that to him, "the objections seem specious and based upon insufficient knowledge of the story." He claimed that "the central figure is not an unsavory character—unless a prize-fighter is *per se* considered unsavory. The attempt is made, and I think successfully, to show an utterly selfish but likeable youngster turning into an unselfish one." In regard to the artillery scene, he pointed out that firing was not directed over the head of the cadets and that the patrol had wandered into the target area only through "the wilful carelessness of one of its members."[64]

Stewart then sent Chilton's comments and his own reaction to the adjutant general. He said he had found nothing about the principal character's background "inconsistent with his candidacy for cadetship." He agreed with Chilton that the man's rite of passage resulting from his training and the traditions of the Academy reflected "all the more credit on the institution." He also said that "circumstances have made me keenly alive to the regulations about overhead fire, and I would not permit anything that suggested its use. A careful study of the completed script discloses that no such impression is conveyed."[65]

These arguments failed to impress Major Prosser, who advised the adjutant general that the story's protagonist "uses skillful and unscrupulous methods in securing his appointment as a cadet, the appointment having previously been awarded another person." The Signal Corps officer also pointed out that Washington, D.C., and many states banned shipment of prizefighting films across state lines. Furthermore, Prosser claimed that, contrary to the opinion of the author and the superintendent, he and his office believed that the film would undoubtedly create the general impression in the audience that "the military peace-time maneuvers at the United States Military Academy may at times subject cadets engaged to danger from artillery fire."[66]

With a consensus supporting him, the adjutant general advised the superintendent that the War Department still considered the scenario "unsuitable" and that it "might well be the basis of a misconception" within the general public. Given this continuing negative opinion, Chilton went to the source of the discontent, meeting on May 18 with officers from the adjutant general's office, the Signal Corps office, and the General Staff's office. He then revised his original scenario to eliminate the War Department's objections to the script and submitted it to the superintendent with the note that the de Mille Picture Corporation wished to produce the story.[67]

The effort seemed to work. General Stewart advised the adjutant general on June 6 that he had approved the new script, now titled "The West Pointer." On June 15, Lt. Col. John Hemphill, the Signal Corps's executive officer, concluded that the synopsis "is not offensive to the army altho the treatment of the theme in the earlier part of the subject is on too low a plane." Demonstrating an awareness of the process of creating a feature film, Hemphill acknowledged the difficulty of visualizing the completed film from a script: "The picture takes shape in the hands of the director and whether it will be offensive to or in harmony with War Department desires can only be definitely settled by an official War Department preview before release to the public."[68]

Despite this possibility, Hemphill recommended that the adjutant general approve the synopsis with the understanding that the filmmakers would make small changes in the story. He wanted the story to show that West Point selected candidates by competition, which produces "high grade" cadets. He also wanted to make sure the producers knew that it would "not be acceptable to the War Department" if they portrayed the hero as a "tough." Finally, he said the Army would follow existing policies in providing troops during the production.[69]

Accepting the recommendation, Major Watrous endorsed the project. However, before informing the producers of the approval, he took the screenplay directly to Army Chief of Staff Charles Summerall for his personal inspection, perhaps indicative of how little serious business the Army had to conduct during the 1920s. Summerall promptly disapproved the story, telling Watrous the only scenario "dealing with West Point Cadet life which would meet with his approval would be one placed on a very high plane." Under the circumstances, the adjutant general had no choice but to inform Grey Productions and de Mille Pictures to prepare a new script if they wished to pursue the project further.[70]

Within a week, the producers had attempted to address the Army's concerns by submitting two nine-page scenarios labeled "A" and "B," which differed only in the first four pages. Gen. C.M. Saltzman, the service's chief signal officer, found the identical story in the final five pages of each script "remarkable." Perhaps. But Cecil de Mille's involvement in the project undoubtedly had something to do with the decision. In his letter to the adjutant general on June 23, Saltzman concluded: "With the lofty sentiments of 'The Corps' guiding the hero in an emotional struggle, and with the remarkable scene in the Cadet Chapel as a background, the master hand of that remarkable genius of the movies, Cecil de Mille, (who produced "The Ten Commandments" and "The King of Kings") can make a picture which will bring out the noblest and best West Point ideas and which will deeply move every graduate."[71]

Most people appreciate portrayals of their organizations regardless of the artistic merit. However, like Hemphill, Saltzman understood the problems of transferring the written word to the motion picture screen. He cited a short sentence that would "introduce much comedy" in the film but without the guidance of a technical advisor could "take a most unpleasant turn and ruin the picture from the standpoint of the Army." Although concerned about similar situations throughout the script, Saltzman recommended that the adjutant general approve the story.[72]

The adjutant general's office advised Grey Productions that it had selected scenario "A," which used an aviator, not a prizefighter, as the hero. To obtain a satisfactory rendering of life at the Military Academy, the Army would assign a West Point graduate to work with the director throughout the filming. The service also informed Grey Productions that it reserved the right "to eliminate or modify any part of the play or to reject the entire play when it is completed." In view of the recent problems the Army had had obtaining an acceptable story, it further stated that the secretary of war was to "exercise the rights reserved without hesitation."[73]

Meanwhile, in early June, William Orr had sent a scenario titled "West Point" to the Military Academy seeking approval for MGM to film the story at West Point. Despite having approved "The West Pointer" for Grey Productions the day before, the adjutant general's office informed Orr on June 28 that the Army was authorizing MGM to film at the Academy, subject to the same conditions it had listed in its letter to Grey Productions. The same day, the adjutant general's office informed the superintendent that he should determine the matter of priorities between the two film companies.[74]

Schuyler Grey later attributed the War Department's approval of MGM's production to the intervention of Will Hays, the president of the Motion Picture Producers and Distributors of America, probably the most powerful person in the film industry. However, the imminent arrival of a major competitor on location did not seem to intimidate Grey or his collaborator, the de Mille company. In early July, the producer requested and received permission to shoot flying scenes at Mitchel Field on Long Island. Then on August 13 he informed the Signal Corps office that his company was "getting pretty well finished up" at West Point and would be done by the seventeenth, although he had told the MGM production people his company would not be leaving until the end of the month.[75]

The next month, Grey wrote from Los Angeles to Major Prosser in the Signal Corps office to inform him that the de Mille executives liked the rough cut "very much." However, because of the length of the picture, they had decided to discard the aviator sequence, make the hero a farm boy, and have him enter the Military Academy, with the balance of the story remaining the same. In any case, he assured Prosser that he had made "a very fine picture," which he would be bringing to the Academy and the War Department in a week or so.[76]

Probably because of the competing *West Point,* the de Mille company changed the title of its film to *Dress Parade,* and the film opened in New York on October 31. Whether Grey had created as good a film as he claimed, whatever the title, remains in doubt. The *New York Times* reviewer concluded: "It is chiefly noteworthy for its scenes of glorious West Point, for the story itself is a conventional romance wherein the hero finds himself in danger of dismissal from the academy." Although he felt the film had a "haphazard denouement," he thought it did contain "a number of compelling views of West Point, some depicting the parades and others showing the chapel, the cadet rooms and the beautiful walks overlooking the Hudson."[77]

More important, did the Army receive the desired benefit from the effort it expended to obtain a story "placed on a very high plane" as General Summerall had demanded? And did the assistance it rendered, including allowing the director to film the hero "occupying" the room in which Gen. John Pershing had lived when he attended West Point, help create the proper image of life at the Military Academy? The *New York Times* reviewer believed the film emphasized the discipline the cadets experienced and showed that "jealousy and discipline don't go together." The *Variety* reviewer wrote, however, "One gets the impression that the producer is trying to stuff the patriotic and sentimental appeal down one's throat."[78]

In any event, the Army did receive a better portrayal of life at the Academy than MGM's *West Point* provided when it appeared the next January. The service's failure to give MGM's screenplay for *West Point* the same rigorous vetting it had given Grey's story undoubtedly contributed to the making of a film that provided no discernible benefit to the Academy or the Army. The *New York Times* reviewer opened his dissection: "One might search the highways and byways of the United States and never find quite as preposterous youth as Brice Wayne, the insufferable bounder in a picture glorying in the title 'West Point.' And if by chance one could happen upon such a character it is highly improbable that he would be honored by an appointment to the United States Military Academy." He observed that Wayne "is hardly mentally qualified to become a cadet." The reviewer conceded that the film did contain "some impressive scenes" of West Point, "notably those depicting the dress parade of the budding officers." Nevertheless, he concluded, "A story dealing with the fine young men of the United States Military Academy should be plausible and dignified, and these qualities would not make it any the less entertaining. The present offering is tedious and often annoying."[79]

Clearly, neither the Army nor the filmmakers had figured out how to create a positive, inspiring cinematic image that realistically showed West Point transforming boys into men during four years at the Military Academy. Nevertheless, they kept trying in such movies as the 1934 *Flirtation Walk*, which managed to combine the Army's most glamorous outpost, Schofield Barracks in Hawaii; the Military Academy; and some pleasant, diverting music into a reasonably interesting story.[80]

The author of the original story, Louis Edelman, believed that an entertaining film could be made using the West Point canvas as a background: "We felt that the rigidity of their way of life, the code under which they operated, the relationship of honor to duty and the relationships among the cadets, their spirit, was the basis of good dramatic story material that would be entertaining. Frankly, I don't think anything more is necessary as a motive as to why you want to do it."[81]

If Hollywood made such films for pure entertainment and to show the public something that it had never seen before, why did the Army cooperate on films like *West Point* and *Flirtation Walk*? Edelman answered: "Very simple. It felt that the more good things that could be said about it, the better it would like it." In this case, enlisted man Dick Powell realizes that the only way to win Ruby Keeler is to become an officer. So he wrangles an appointment to West Point, sings some songs, and accomplishes his self-serving goals.[82]

To the extent that this rite of passage and glorious scenes on the Academy grounds benefited the Army, it remained in its best interest to cooperate with filmmakers, especially in view of the lean budgets and low troop levels of the 1930s. However, West Point stories and innocuous comedies, which constituted the vast majority of the Army's cinematic appearances during the interwar years, did little to prepare people for the real threat to the nation's security then developing overseas.

Only at the end of the decade did Hollywood return to serious movies about the military, portraying the services defending the nation against possible attack. However, even then, filmmakers continued to slight the Army's ground force. *Sergeant York*, in 1941, did glorify the American foot soldier, but in a story set on the World War I battlefields of

France. Nonetheless, the movie fostered within the American people a patriotic feeling that would help unite the nation against its potential enemies. It did not show how the Army would fight the next war.

In contrast, *Flight Command* (1940), *I Wanted Wings* (1941), and *Dive Bomber* (1941) informed the American people how the Navy and Army Air Corps trained for their anticipated aerial missions. From the motion picture industry's point of view, these essentially documentary movies enabled studios to put popular actors like Errol Flynn and William Holden in military settings where they could combine flying sequences with the obligatory romantic interludes. Whether these films succeeded in their preparedness mission remains open to question.

Flight Command, for instance, focused on the development of navigational aids for Navy pilots. However, Hollywood's portrayal of the ultimate success of the homing device came with a price the service probably should not have paid. Robert Taylor, who has the new equipment in his plane, ignores orders from Walter Pigeon, who is about to crash, to lead his squadron through the fog to base. Instead, Taylor lands and rescues his commander, who has suffered severe injuries. Only then does he use the new homing device to shepherd the lost flight back to base.

Rather than being court-martialed for disobeying a direct order and endangering the rest of the squadron, Taylor becomes a hero. In creating such a positive image, Hollywood glorified ignoring direct orders at a time when war was looming. The filmmakers would have better served the Navy and the other armed services by portraying the reality that a commander must sometimes sacrifice the individual for the good of the many. Discipline and obeying orders become crucial in combat, and following commands may well require more courage than foolhardy bravery. As the Navy had demonstrated in cooperating on submarine disaster movies, however, the portrayal of new equipment and technologies sometimes became more important than the loss of a submarine or the breaking of an order.

Not everyone accepted such priorities even when the service itself believed the film offered significant benefits. Within a conventional Hollywood fictional story, the 1941 Warner Brothers *Dive Bomber* documented how Navy doctors were solving the problem of pilot blackouts. Nevertheless, some viewers saw the movie in decidedly negative terms. E.C. Roworth wrote to Navy secretary Frank Knox on August 21, saying he thought it "very unwise to permit the making and showing" of the film because young men who saw it would "shy away" from becoming Navy fliers. He thought it portrayed flight instructors using "dictatorial methods" and that it put too much emphasis "on the fact that death in its most horrible forms is the portion, sooner or later, of each aviator." Furthermore, he said the film suggested that "fliers are quickly worn out, physically and mentally, after which they become helpless, useless and unwanted."[83]

Arthur Keil also wrote to Knox, saying on December 1, 1941, "If there ever was a picture shown to discourage anyone from joining the Air Corps it is the picture *Dive Bomber.*" The writer thought it would lead every "potential draftee to stay clear of aviation" because the film showed that "every aviator loses his health due to flying. Perhaps this is so, but it seems a queer time to advertise this throughout the country. If this picture was made in Germany and sent here I could see the point." The man could see that the film was intended to educate the public, but he observed that it "sure won't get any recruits in the air service." In response to Roworth, the Navy's Public Relations Office claimed that audiences had had a favorable reaction to *Dive Bomber* and suggested that if the movie had shown only the positive side of the aviation story, "it would not ring true and would be declared propaganda by the public." Nevertheless, the Navy maintained that it was trying to have filmmakers present the service "in the best light possible, and we hope to achieve that aim in time."[84]

Propaganda was exactly the label that the leading isolationists in the Senate, Champ Clerk and Gerald Nye, applied to *Dive Bomber, I Wanted Wings, Sergeant York,* and several other "preparedness" films released in 1940 and 1941. In a radio speech on July 25, 1941, Nye claimed that "for too long now, the silver screen has been flooded with picture after picture designed to rouse us to a state of war hysteria. Pictures glorifying war. Pictures telling about the grandeur and the heavenly justice of the British Empire. Pictures depicting the courage, the passion for democracy, the love of humanity, the tender solicitude for other people by the generals and trade agents and the proconsuls of Great Britain, while all the people who are opposed to her, including even courageous little Finland now, are drawn as coarse, bestial, brutal scoundrels." He accused the eight major Hollywood studios of "trying to make America punch drunk with propaganda to push her into war."[85]

Ultimately the Senate isolationists were able to convene a hearing of the subcommittee of the Committee on Interstate Commerce in September 1941, to investigate the making of these films. They summoned Hollywood's leading filmmakers to Washington to answer charges that they were making propaganda films. With the defeated 1940 presidential candidate, Wendell Wilkie, as the industry's counsel, Harry Warner, Darryl Zanuck, and Barney Balaban, among others, argued that they made movies purely for entertainment and profit. In denying the charges against the industry, Warner, president of Warner Brothers, acknowledged that he was "opposed to Nazism" and told the subcommittee, "I abhor and detest every principle and practice of the Nazi movement. To me, Nazism typifies the very opposite of the kind of life every decent man, woman, and child wants to live."[86]

He denied that his company was producing propaganda films as the senators had alleged. Rejecting Senator Nye's claim that *Sergeant York* was designed to create war hysteria, Warner maintained that the film "is a factual portrait of the life of one of the great heroes of the last war. If that is propaganda, we plead guilty." Likewise, he said that *Confessions of a Nazi Spy* (1939) was a "factual portrayal of a Nazi spy ring that actually operated in New York City. If that is propaganda, we plead guilty." In fact, Warner argued, these films were "carefully prepared on the basis of factual happenings and they were not twisted to serve any ulterior purpose." Most important, he said that "millions of average citizens have paid to see these pictures. They have enjoyed wide popularity and have been profitable to our company. In short, these pictures have been judged by the public and the judgment has been favorable."[87]

Warner acknowledged that his company had during the past eight years made feature films about the armed forces. But he stressed that the studio "needed no urging from the government and we would be ashamed if the government would have had to make such requests of us. We have produced these pictures voluntarily and proudly." Despite this justification, the testimony of Warner and other industry leaders did little but produce acrimonious exchanges with the subcommittee, and the committee adjourned the hearings until December 8.[88]

Pearl Harbor gave lie to the isolationists' claims that the Hollywood antifascist and military-preparedness films were drawing the United States into World War II. The stunning success of the Japanese attack also stood in stark contrast to the cinematic preparedness message that the American armed forces could well defend the nation against any threat. These films therefore did more than entertain the American people. They may have aided recruiting and helped obtain appropriations from Congress. But they also lulled the nation into a false sense of security. The belief that no enemy would dare challenge the might of the American military and attack U.S. territory undoubtedly made Pearl Harbor that much more traumatic.

5 World War II: Fantasy

DESPITE THE VOCIFEROUS CRITICISM FROM THE ISOLATIONISTS inside and outside Congress, Hollywood had continued to put military-preparedness films into production up to December 7. After Pearl Harbor, the studios simply added an appropriate opening and closing message to the completed movies, calling on the nation to win the war. Even so, the 1942 *To the Shores of Tripoli,* the first color Marine movie, remained a peacetime romantic fantasy, albeit one filled with Marines marching and drilling at the Recruit Depot in San Diego and training at Camp Pendleton. The war intrudes only in the opening dedication and the closing comments. Lowell Thomas's voice-over describes the Marine as "the best fighting man on earth" and dedicates the movie to "the immortal band of Leathernecks" trapped on Wake Island, who, when asked what they needed, replied, "Send us more Japs." And at the end, the Marines march aboard their transport to the singing of the Marine Hymn with orders to "Give 'em hell."

Even before Pearl Harbor, Hollywood had begun to create fanciful combat stories using the war in Europe and Asia as locales for *Yank in the RAF, Eagle Squadron, A Yank on the Burma Road, Flying Tigers,* and *Across the Pacific.* Although these films featured Americans fighting the evil Japs and Nazis prior to December 7, 1941, the armed services had provided little or no assistance. Nevertheless, with the appropriate tag lines that acknowledged our entry into the war, the movies showed the nation what it was now facing on the battlefield.

With the United States in the war, any caution the motion picture industry may have had about making combat movies ended. Pearl Harbor, the fall of Wake Island and the Philippines, the British tank battles against Rommel in North Africa, Jimmy Doolittle's raid against the Japanese mainland, and the Battle of Midway were all to provide inspira-

John Payne drills Marines at the Recruit Depot in San Diego in *To the Shores of Tripoli.* Begun as a war preparedness film, when released it contained a support-the-war message.

tional stories intended to stimulate America's patriotic impulse. For the most part, the initial films only loosely followed actual events, since factual accounts often took months to reach the public because of security concerns and the amount of time participants needed to transfer their combat experiences into the printed word. Moreover, given the months studios needed to transform the words into visual images, the early combat films did not begin to reach theater screens until almost a year after Pearl Harbor.

Even then, the fictionalized portrayals usually lacked scenes of large-scale battle, because the armed forces had more important things to do with their men and equipment than to give them to Hollywood. As a result, the early combat stories came from the imaginations of the screenwriters and the storerooms of the prop managers. Although the studios, as always, hoped these initial movies would find success at the box office, the writers and producers consciously designed their images to lift the morale of the nation and stimulate the war effort.

Wake Island, the first attempt to dramatize American servicemen in combat, did not reach theaters until mid-August 1942. It portrayed the brave but doomed struggle of a small garrison of Marines to hold Wake Island against an overwhelming Japanese invasion force, in the first days of the war. Based on the account of the last Marine to leave the island before it fell, a few subsequent radio messages, and the filmmakers' creative visions, the portrayal rekindled the emotions the nation had felt when the Japanese had overrun the few surviving defenders the previous December.

To portray the siege, Paramount shot the film on the shore of the Salton Sea in California, creating the battle scenes with special effects, miniatures, and some stock footage.

Japanese soldiers prepare to shoot a Marine radio operator in *Wake Island,* an early World War II fantasy movie that portrayed the enemy as evil killers.

William Bendix and Robert Preston prepare for a scene in *Wake Island* (1942) filmed on the shore of the Salton Sea in California.

Despite these limitations, the *New York Times* reviewer thought the story of Marines fighting to the last man should "surely bring a surge of pride to every patriot's breast." The film's box-office success proved that Hollywood could combine wartime propaganda with exciting entertainment.[1]

Focusing on a small band of Marines, *Wake Island* needed little, if any, military assistance. *Air Force* did receive a limited amount of help from the Army Air Corps, because Gen. Hap Arnold saw the benefits of a movie that would show the American people the Air Force in action. Jack Warner, executive producer of Warner Brothers, had accepted Arnold's suggestion for this kind of film and initiated the project almost immediately after Pearl Harbor. In writing the script, Dudley Nichols had at his disposal battle reports that the War Department supplied and the technical advice of Capt. Samuel Triffy, an Air Corps pilot who had worked on a couple of "March of Times" reports about the service. The plot, which grew out of the collaboration of Nichols, Triffy, and the director, Howard Hawks, became little more than a vehicle for portraying the Army Air Corps winning the war almost single-handed.[2]

Starting with the historical fact that a flight of twelve B-17s arrived in Hawaii during the Japanese attack on Pearl Harbor, *Air Force* traced the adventures of one bomber crew across the Pacific to Wake Island, the Philippines, an epic sea battle, and finally a crash landing on an Australian beach. While the movie contained the usual mixture of human emotions and comic relief among the crew members of the *Mary Ann*, the lack of any real dramatic conflicts and the loose attention to history contributed to a pseudo-documentary quality in the movie.

Although it used rather obvious propaganda techniques, *Air Force* created for the audience a powerful message of hope for ultimate victory. After the plane's crew briefly expresses its horror at the disastrous results of the sneak attack at Pearl Harbor, the bomber receives orders to fly alone to the Philippines to help stem the Japanese tide. While in the air, the crew listens to President Roosevelt's war message to Congress, with his call for an "absolute victory" over the "treacherous enemy." When the Japanese overrun the Philippines, the *Mary Ann* manages to take off just ahead of the advancing soldiers and heads for Australia.

On the way, the plane comes across a huge Japanese fleet also heading toward the subcontinent and radios the flotilla's position. Despite not having taken on a full load of fuel, the *Mary Ann* then circles overhead—endlessly it seems—until the Air Force arrives like the cavalry. What happens next, in its own way, anticipates the end of Samuel Peckinpah's classic 1969 *The Wild Bunch:* wave upon wave of American planes slaughter the Japanese fleet, thereby turning the tide in the Pacific. As the *Mary Ann* reaches the Australian coast, it finally runs out of gas and crash lands in the surf. At the film's close, the surviving crew members are preparing to make the first large-scale raid on Tokyo to begin the final push to victory.

Air Force, in fact, anticipated history, sometimes by months, sometimes by years. The climactic air-sea battle, created with miniatures and special effects, might have borne a vague resemblance to the Battles of the Coral Sea and Midway. In fact, Warner Brothers had staged and filmed the sequence long before the actual battles had taken place. B-17s did participate in both actions, although not in the manner portrayed in the film. At Coral Sea, three B-17s actually attacked part of the American fleet accidentally, but fortunately without inflicting damage. At Midway, Navy carrier-based planes carried the brunt of the attack to the Japanese fleet. The Air Corps did bomb Tokyo in April 1942, but in a small hit-and-run operation that sixteen two-engine B-25 bombers carried out after taking off from the USS *Hornet* in one of the most daring raids in military history. Regular bombing raids on Japan did not begin until 1944, when B-29 Super Fortresses began attacks from Pacific islands that American forces had only recently captured.

Despite its mythical-cum-historical narrative, however, *Air Force* did more than entertain the American people. The cinematic slaughter of the Japanese fleet provided a catharsis for the setbacks suffered at Pearl Harbor, Wake Island, and the Philippines. Filmmakers also tied into the plot continuous overt and subtle propaganda messages, conveyed in terms that were becoming familiar to wartime moviegoers. The crew of the *Mary Ann* consisted of a heterogeneous cross section of the nation, except for a black, of course. The plane's crew chief, a crusty old sergeant, provided a father figure to the younger men. The pilot's wife and the copilot's girlfriend served as the faithful women, waiting loyally at home. And the mascot, an all-American mutt who raged at the mention of Tojo, provided some comic relief. Although one of the gunners, a washed-out pilot, becomes a temporary malcontent, the "crew takes care of each other," and everyone does his assigned job for the good of the *Mary Ann*. A fighter pilot delivers the final didactic message. Along for the ride to the Philippines, he learns how important bombers are becoming in the war against Japan, and by the time he reaches Australia, he wants to fly a B-17 for the duration.

In contrast, the film characterizes all Japanese as sneaky and treacherous and refers to them in derogatory terms. This message receives constant reinforcement, from the opening scenes onward. On the way to Hawaii, the crew hears a news broadcast that a Japanese peace envoy was planning to meet with Secretary of State Hull on the morning of December 7. When the plane lands at Pearl Harbor, the crew immediately hears stories about Japanese sabotage of American planes before the attack, which had never occurred. Throughout the film, the Japanese fight unfairly, attacking without warning and shooting at a helpless flier as he parachutes from his disabled plane. Not only does the movie demonize the Japanese, but it also portrays them as inferior in fair combat. The *Mary Ann* shoots down Japanese plane after plane, and the Air Force sinks the entire enemy fleet.

The message stands out clearly, putting into visual images President Roosevelt's December 8 speech to Congress: the United States will win the war. We may have lost the first round through deceit, but we will attain ultimate victory. The film expressed this idea most forcefully when the crew's father figure arrives in the Philippines and discovers that his pilot son died in the first attack while trying to take off to join the battle. He receives his son's personal effects in a handkerchief, asks if this is all that is left, sheds perhaps a single tear, and returns to his job, as the American people all must do. Did the audience leave the theater with this same commitment? Given the quality of the production, the first-rate acting, the taut script, the fine photography and special effects, many viewers may well have simply enjoyed the film as escapist entertainment, irrespective of any messages it offered. Nevertheless, the movie's prophecy of victory, repeated enough times, would inevitably have a positive influence on the war effort.[3]

The sense of urgency in presenting this message to the nation manifested itself in the speed with which production of *Air Force* got under way. Even before Nichols completed his script, Warner Brothers's special-effects department constructed a Japanese fleet in miniature and then began bombing it in Santa Monica Bay. As a result, before photography of the principals ever began, the company had spent a half million dollars and filmed the climactic battle of the movie.[4] The War Department acted with all appropriate speed when it finally received a script from Jack Warner in mid-May of 1942. In requesting an "analysis as to military detail and advisability of giving full War Department cooperation," the chief of the Pictorial Branch (a section of the Bureau of Public Relations) asked the Special Service Branch to return the script with comments in twenty-four hours because the film was "a special Air Corps recruiting job." All department offices approved cooperation within this time limit, requesting only minor script changes that related to security matters. The Review Branch, for one, informed the Pictorial Branch that "mention of any blind spots of any aircraft or other indications of vulnerability is restricted. Also no reference may be made to position of turrets, cannon, and machine guns of Flying Fortresses."[5]

The War Department notified Jack Warner of its decision to cooperate on May 22 and reminded him that it would strictly adhere to all regulations governing assistance, including its requirement to review the film prior to any screening. The Air Corps formally assigned Captain Triffy and another officer to be technical advisors on the project. When notifying the commander of Drew Field near Tampa that Warner Brothers would be shooting the film on his base, the War Department said it "desired that you extend such assistance as, in your judgment is deemed necessary to insure the success of the sequences planned." The department placed only one restriction on its cooperation: "It is the policy of the War Department not to allow soldiers or military equipment to be disguised and photographed as representing the personnel or equipment of foreign countries."[6]

Despite this directive, the local commanders ignored the policy when the film crew arrived at Drew Field. Warner Brothers had, in fact, selected the site partially because the studio could not photograph "Japanese fighters" along the West Coast because of the continuing fear of enemy attack. At Drew Field Triffy obtained fighters, had them painted with the Rising Sun insignia, and then flew them in the sequences portraying Japanese attacks on American planes and positions. His ability to arrange this assistance had little to do with Washington's help, however. Triffy recalled that the men on the base did not offer "a hell of a lot of support for the film because everyone was concerned with the war."[7]

The technical advisor was able to accomplish his assignment because he knew most of the officers in charge of planes and equipment around the Tampa area. Also, he had a card on which General Arnold had written "Good idea" after seeing the original script of *Air Force*. With this tacit approval of the film and his friendships, Triffy could usually obtain the planes Hawks needed to film either solo or formation flights. Also, the commanding officer of the bomber facility near Sebring, Florida, provided the B-17 bomber to play the *Mary Ann*.[8]

As with the pursuit planes in *Wings*, the *Mary Ann*, rather than the actors, became the star of *Air Force*, flying from one crisis to the next like any Hollywood heroine. Similar to most actresses, the bomber played a composite character, representing several planes and their crews' actions, including Colin Kelly's heroic, if mythical, sinking of a Japanese battleship off the Philippines in the first days of the war.

To create a proper sense of men in battle, Hawks and the film crew showed little concern for the safety of military equipment. After one flight in a disguised fighter, Triffy nearly had to crash-land because of a balky landing gear. When the director found out, he suggested that Triffy should have made a belly landing—after making sure the cameras were rolling. Not unexpectedly, Triffy described the filmmakers as "ruthless, absolutely ruthless! If they could have damaged a plane in flight so I would have had an accident, they would have done it! Really, I couldn't trust them!"[9]

But Hawks's single-minded pursuit of authenticity did make the career of the *Mary Ann* and her crew seem almost real. The *New York Times* reviewer felt that the director's "boundless enthusiasm and awe" for the American fliers had enabled him to make a "picture which tingles with the passion of spirits aglow. . . . Mr. Hawks has directed the action for tremendous impact. . . . Maybe the story is high-flown, maybe it overdraws a recorded fact a bit. [But I would] hate to think it couldn't happen—or didn't—because it certainly leaves you feeling awfully good."[10]

This "feeling awfully good" about something represents the goal of all effective propaganda. As a result, *Air Force* became one of Hollywood's highest achievements in World War II morale-building, a film to rival the dramatic quality of *Wings,* and one that became a major box-office success. As with the best propaganda, *Air Force* blended some truth with much fiction to create a sense of reality. Hawks made a first-rate adventure movie filled with action, a careful buildup of tensions, and human interest. With the exception of an occasional cliché, Nichols had written a sparse and authentic screenplay, giving the viewer a sense of the war as it was actually fought in the air. The camera work, acting, and editing were of uniformly high quality. The special effects, particularly important because of the limited military help and the lack of combat footage, equaled such 1970s spectaculars as *Tora! Tora! Tora!* and *Midway* in believability, if not in scope.

In contrast to the Marines or the Army's air branch, early in the war, the Army could not offer even small successes or brave holding actions which might inspire filmmakers to create patriotic images and the expectation of future victories. The service had suffered an ignominious defeat in the Philippines, and not even Douglas MacArthur's bravado could disguise the reality of his furtive escape from Corregidor. Nor did American soldiers take the offensive until late in 1942, when they relieved the Marines in Guadalcanal and landed in North Africa. Out of inglorious disaster, however, MGM was to create a stirring portrayal of brave soldiers defending the flag to the last man.

The original idea for *Bataan* came from screenwriter Robert Andrews, who suggested to Dore Schary, the studio's chief of production, a story set in the Philippines along the lines of *The Lost Patrol,* in which Arabs wipe out a British unit lost in the desert. Schary "jumped at the idea. . . . because I wanted to tell the people they were in for a tough fight." He considered the portrayal of the rearguard action by the doomed Americans as pure propaganda that prepared the audience for a long struggle and gave it a morale boost.[11]

Bataan accomplished this by showing the strength and success of the Japanese military while at the same time creating a feeling of pride in the gallantry of the American soldiers as they faced certain death. Andrews wrote a script in which all of the characters had individual identities and traits with which people could empathize. As in *Air Force* and most other war films made during the conflict, the unit included representatives of all ethnic groups. Schary went one step further.

He told Andrews to include one character in the script without describing him. Then, in casting the film, he assigned a black to play the unidentified role. Schary later admitted that "it really was inaccurate, because there were no combat soldiers who were black." Given his political liberalism, Schary did what he felt was right and didn't worry about the many critical letters he later received. More important, the men had identities, even if they were stereotyped ones. As a result their ultimate deaths (including that of superstar Robert Taylor) had a more powerful impact than in the typical war film. The losses became almost personal and helped make the fall of the Philippines more meaningful to the audience.[12]

Focusing on a small group of men interacting within a limited area, *Bataan* duplicated the intimacy of a stage play. Given the film's modest production demands in terms of men and equipment, MGM did not require Army assistance. Nevertheless, the studio submitted

Marines advance through typical Hollywood jungle in *Marine Raiders* (1944).

the script to the War Department in October 1942 "for the record." The Public Relations Office found it "a good story," which "could make a good picture—but not a great picture." The chief of the Feature Film Division did not think the script justified cooperation. Nor did he think MGM needed help, since "the equipment of the personnel involved can all be assembled at the studio; all of the men in the patrol would have to be actors; the Japs, extras. The whole picture could probably be made on the back lot, or on location very nearby."[13]

Even though it did not intend to provide assistance, the Army, as usual, informed the studio it "desired that where officers or soldiers appear in uniform, they be correctly attired, and conduct themselves in a manner consistent with the customs and courtesies of the Service." The Pictorial Branch therefore suggested that the producer hire a retired officer to serve as technical advisor and asked to review the film for military accuracy prior to its release."[14]

Given the wartime restrictions on travel and the film's small-scale combat scenes, MGM decided to shoot *Bataan* entirely on its Sound Stage 16. According to director Tay Garnett, the studio's set designers constructed "a real-as-hell jungle," which had "everything except sixteen foot snakes."[15] Moviegoers who are accustomed to the feel of reality created in recent years by filming on location may be put off by the "made-on-a-set" quality of *Bataan*. In 1943, however, Hollywood had conditioned audiences to accept studio jungles and special effects that helped provide the illusion of reality, and the artificiality of the set did not interfere with the action to any great extent.

To increase the dramatic impact of this action, Garnett used all the tricks of his directorial art. When he became unhappy with the way his actors were reacting when shot, the special effects men tied ropes around the soldiers selected to die and, on cue, the technicians jerked the lines to provide the desired visual effect. Likewise, the director heightened the feel of reality in the film's climactic scene by creating jungle "ground fog," through which the Japanese soldiers advanced toward Robert Taylor, the last survivor of the doomed patrol. In this case, the special-effects men dumped dry ice into tubs of water and blew the resulting vapor across the set. In addition to creating the proper appearance of a misty terrain, the fumes nearly killed two extras who ignored warnings not to breathe as they crawled through the fog. Despite the near tragedy, the visual effect of the vapor added greatly to the power of the closing sequence.[16]

Having buried his men, Taylor digs his own grave, mounts a machine gun in front of it, and prepares to stall the enemy for as long as his ammunition lasts. As the Japanese emerge from the fog, Taylor mows them down, firing nonstop and yelling wildly, "Come on, you bastards, I'm here. I'll always be here." The camera moves forward so that the firing machine gun fills the screen. Suddenly, it falls silent with only a wisp of smoke slowly curling up from its barrel.

As message, the closing sequence had the proper effect. Although noting that *Bataan* had "melodramatic flaws" and technical mistakes, the *New York Times* reviewer thought the film "still gives a shocking conception of the defense of that bloody point of land. And it doesn't insult the honor of dead soldiers, which is something to say for a Hollywood film these days." *Time* magazine thought that the film's drama was "constantly loud and over emphatic. But there are a few stretches when the military situation calls for silence; the noisy sound track quiets down and, for a moment, incredibly enough, Hollywood's war takes on the tense, classic values of understatement."[17]

Like most directors, Garnett undertook the project because he found it a good current story with excellent dramatic possibilities and an excellent cast, including Taylor, Lloyd Nolan, Desi Arnaz, and George Murphy. Garnett also recognized that the film would "arouse a great deal of admiration for the courage of these boys and pride in the American man." This patriotic feeling received reinforcement from characters who represented traditional American stereotypes, enabling audiences to more readily identify with the men, empathize with their bravery, and mourn their deaths. In doing this, *Bataan* contributed to the war effort when victory remained a hope, not yet a certainty.[18]

Hollywood did not limit its stereotypes to Americans, of course. If anything, the characterizations of the enemy in movies made during the war became even more sharply delineated. In movies such as *Wake Island, Air Force,* and *Bataan,* filmmakers portrayed the Japanese as a barbarous enemy who machine-gunned fliers dangling in parachutes as easily as they had attacked Pearl Harbor on a peaceful Sunday morning. The Germans fared better in Hollywood films, possibly because their skin color and cultural heritage more closely resembled American society. As soldiers and sailors, they usually appeared efficient, disciplined, and patriotic, and determined to win the war at all costs. If the German military man seldom delighted in cruelty, Hollywood did show officers committing brutal acts in its early combat films designed to stir up support for the war effort. *Action in the North Atlantic,* which received assistance from the Navy and the Merchant Marines, portrayed a German U-boat cutting Humphrey Bogart's lifeboat in two as an officer filmed the atrocity.

The clash between the Nazi aspiration for world domination and the American determination to stop Hitler's conquests had one of its best expressions in the 1943 *Sahara.* The film carried stereotyping to its logical conclusion by having actors represent whole nations. The hero, Humphrey Bogart, plays a typical American sergeant—tough, resourceful, determined, "probably the best screen notion of the American soldier to date."[19] As commander of an American tank, the *Lulubelle,* which has been fighting alongside the British in Libya, Bogart and his crew battle the desert as well as the enemy in an attempt to reach Allied lines.

The three tankmen first pick up four Britishers, all stereotypes of their respective social classes and their nation. The passenger list grows with the addition of a South African, a Frenchman, and a Sudanese and his Italian prisoner. The Sudanese character provides a legitimate role for a man of color, but his rank as a corporal denotes an inferior position—typical of Hollywood's casting of blacks until the mid-1960s. The *Lulubelle* provides the final addition to the multinational caravan when it shoots down a German fighter that is strafing the tank. The captured pilot epitomizes the typical cinematic Nazi:

Humphrey Bogart with British soldiers and the *Lulubelle* during the making of *Sahara*.

unrepentant, proud, and determined to get the best of his captors. As the filmmakers did with the German submariners in *Action in the North Atlantic*, however, they show the flier in *Sahara* going beyond permissible behavior when he brutally kills his Italian ally.

Bogart and his traveling companions (minus one of his crew, who has died of wounds) finally reach a water hole and defend it against attack from a five-hundred-man German patrol desperately searching for water. In the fierce battle, seemingly hundreds of German soldiers, and all the tank's passengers except Bogart, die. In the end the surviving Germans surrender to the American sergeant and the *Lulubelle*, who convoy them to Allied lines. Apart from the liberties taken with history—American tanks did not fight alongside the British in the desert in early 1942—the soldiers' test of endurance against the desert environment and their fight against a vastly superior German force provided the message that the Allies would ultimately triumph. At the same time, the *New York Times* reviewer said that the film contained a "laudable conception of soldier fortitude in this war and it is also a bang-up action picture cut out to hold one enthralled."[20]

In contrast to the military's disinterest in providing or inability to provide assistance to *Wake Island* and *Bataan*, the Army proved willing and, by the end of 1942, able to give Columbia Pictures full cooperation in creating the combat sequences in *Sahara*. In preparing for production, the director, the writer, and the production staff visited the Army's desert training facilities in California, Arizona, and Nevada. The Army provided briefings

The Army helped stage the opening battle for *Sahara* (1943) in the California desert.

The *Lulubelle* under attack by a "German" plane during the making of *Sahara* (note German marking on the P-40 despite War Department regulations against American equipment portraying enemy materiel.)

and demonstrations of tank operations, agreed to allow the company to shoot the film in an area near Eagle Pass, one hundred miles east of Palm Springs, and donated a tank to the studio for the two months the crew and actors spent on location.

As part of the technical advice during preproduction, the Army had a plane strafe a tank to demonstrate for the special-effects man what bullets looked like kicking up the dirt. The officer in charge offered to repeat the attack for the cameras during filming, pointing out that the tank could take a direct hit without damage. The director graciously rejected the offer and had the special-effects man simulate the bullets hitting the ground by using compressed air forced through buried hoses. Disregarding the long-standing regulations against disguising American equipment to represent foreign matériel, the Army allowed one of its planes to masquerade as a German fighter to play the attacking enemy in the sequence. Likewise, for the German attack on the water hole, the Army allowed the filmmakers to dress five hundred soldiers in German uniforms for the two days it took to rehearse and film the battle.[21]

This assistance enabled Columbia to take the production out of the soundstage and back lot, where most of the early war films had been made, and it gave *Sahara* the feeling of authenticity. However, the movie worked as drama because the contrasts between the stereotyped Allies and their stereotyped enemies mirrored the tensions and differences between the warring nations themselves, not because of the Army's assistance.

Bogart, for example, at first refuses to allow the captured Italian soldier to join the *Lulubelle* passenger manifest because of the scarcity of food and water. American ideals would not, of course, permit such an inhumane act, even in wartime, and Bogart quickly reverses his decision. The Italian soldier has all the mannerisms and background that audiences associated with Italians: he has a relative in the United States; he loves his large family; he is apolitical and has no love of war; he likes Americans. Nonetheless, he avoids becoming a traitor to his country's alliance with Germany by not revealing to Bogart that the German pilot understands English and so knows the American's plans. However, when the Italian ultimately tries to prevent the pilot's escape to his besieging comrades, the German brutally murders his ally, thereby reinforcing the cinematic evil Nazi image. At the same time, the stereotypical Italian image conveys the idea to viewers that one man, Mussolini, not the Italian people, wanted war. This portrayal had obvious value given the number of Italians in the United States.

Although *Sahara* worked as action, drama, and message, it still did not recreate World War II as it was actually being fought. The British could point out that the Americans had had no part in defeating the Germans at El Alamein in 1942, Humphrey Bogart and

Lulubelle notwithstanding. Likewise, the British felt they had a right to be furious when *Operation Burma,* in 1945, had Errol Flynn single-handedly defeat the Japanese—even though no Americans fought in Burma at that time. Nevertheless, in the early days of the war, the United States had few successes to which it could point except on the sea.

There, the submarine service immediately began patrols into the Western Pacific. There, the Navy carried Doolittle, his sixteen B-25s, and their crews to within 624 miles of Japan to launch the first strike against the Japanese homeland. There, the United States turned the tide of the war in the Pacific in June 1942, at the battle of Midway. Studios quickly transformed Navy preparedness films in production into combat stories created from the screenwriters' imaginations.

Although started after Pearl Harbor, *Crash Dive,* released in April 1943, created even more fanciful images of nautical victory, this time against Germany. In hopes of aiding recruiting from the all-volunteer silent service, the Navy allowed Twentieth Century Fox to film virtually all of *Crash Dive* at the Submarine Base at New London, Connecticut. However, the cooperation provided only an authentic background for a portrayal of combat that remained in the realm of pure fantasy.

Tyrone Power plays an avid PT-boat skipper who finds himself assigned as an executive officer on a submarine despite his affection for the plywood raiders. After two cruises in the Atlantic, however, Power develops an appreciation of undersea warfare. Within the framework of this unexceptional story, the filmmakers and the Navy combined to explain, for the first time in color, how the submarine service was training its officers and men for combat. The pseudo-documentary portions of *Crash Dive* did provide information to the American people and undoubtedly aided recruitment.

Conversely, the combat sequences set in the North Atlantic provided no value in showing how the submarine service was waging war under the sea. Given the paucity of German surface ships as targets, the Navy deployed all American submarines to the Pacific Theater from the earliest days of the war, with the exception of one failed sortie to the French coast in 1942. Moreover, the film's dramatic high point, the destruction of a secret German submarine base somewhere in the North Atlantic in a commando-type raid, which Power leads, lacked credibility, either factually or operationally.

Out of concern that Germany might seize Iceland and use it as a base for U-boats attacking the northern shipping lanes, English forces had occupied the island in 1940, and American Marines arrived in July 1941, staying until March 1942. Whether the fear had any foundation, Germany had no choice but to locate its U-boat fleet bases along the European coastline, not on some mysterious island. Likewise, having American submariners conduct commando operations sprang from a screenwriter's fantasy, not from a recorded action. Only in the first week of July 1945 did Gene Fluckey, the captain of the USS *Barb* and a Medal of Honor winner, send a raiding party ashore on the east coast of Karafuto to blow up a railroad bridge. In any event, such actions never became the submarine service's modus operandi during World War II.

The portrayal did cause Bosley Crowther, in his *New York Times* review, to wonder why he should bother criticizing the antics of the film: "*Crash Dive* is one of those films which have no more sense of reality about this war than a popular son." In regard to the raid, he observed: "Well, to call it fantastic would be understating the case, for the sub crew . . . play commandos with a wild and vicious zeal. They blow up oil tanks, ammunition, set fire to barracks and ships and escape through a sea of flaming fuel oil, with the captain steering from the submerged bridge. Such incredible heroics have seldom been seen on the screen. It is Hollywood at its wildest. And in Technicolor, too! Oh, boy!"[22]

Crash Dive, of course, no more accurately portrayed World War II under the sea than Hollywood portrayed Errol Flynn single-handedly beating the Japanese in *Operation Burma,* at a time when no American troops were fighting anywhere near Burma. Such inaccuracies, of course, remained beside the point. The action and adventure in *Crash Dive* served the Navy's needs well as a recruiting tool. The destruction of the German submarine base, however fanciful, showed Americans beating the Nazis at a time when the United States was still fighting an uphill battle against an enemy who remained entrenched on the European continent.

The images of victory alone did not satisfy the filmmakers. Nor did the triumphant return to New London, with the crew, including the now-obligatory black enlisted man, waving to the cheering crowd, provide a fitting end to the film. Instead, Power explains to his admiral/uncle why he will stay in the submarine service. As he begins his heavy-handed recitation on how the Navy was leading the way in the war against the Axis, the scene dissolves to a PT-boat flotilla on the high seas.

To the strains of "Anchors Away" welling up in support of his fervent oration, Power first gives homage to his true love: "The PT boats are swell. They do a grand job. And they'll play their part in winning the war." Then, with a dissolve to a submarine plowing along on the surface, Power's voice-over pays tribute to the entire Navy: "But not without the submarines. They've got their job to do in all the seven seas and boy, how they're doing it." A rapid series of dissolves follows, each to the ship Power is praising: "The carriers that bring the planes that drop the bombs that sink the enemy ships; and the cruisers that protect the airplane carriers, and the battleships, the dreadnaughts and super dreadnaughts, the bigshots of the fleet, they're in there punching too, they're all in there doing their job, working together. I found that out, sir."

Power found out something else, also. With a dissolve from ships to men on parade at New London and then back to the PT boats, the submarines, and all the Navy ships at sea, he continues: "It isn't one branch of the service, it's all branches, and it isn't all ships. It's men. The men behind the guns of the PT boats, and the submarines, and the Coast Guard ships, and the mine layers, and the tenders, and the tankers, and the troop ships, the men that take them out and fight their way over and land them there, that's the Navy, the United States Navy."

Destroyer, also appearing in April 1943, conveyed the same message, that to win the war, ships and men had to work together as a team. Two years in the making, the film had begun as a prewar preparedness Spig Wead story in which he intended to try "to create a personality out of a navy ship and to make the ship one of the main characters in the story." He proposed to include "various human characters, with the dramatic problems and conflicts in their lives" and so create an interaction between the sailors and their ship.[23]

By the time the Navy approved the final script on February 6, 1942, the service had more pressing concerns than cooperating on movies, no matter how much they might benefit from the images of the service in action. As a result, the Navy advised producer Lou Edelman "that due to the stress of the war situation and the needs for ships to operate with the fleet as fighting units," cooperation "will necessarily be cut to a minimum." Nevertheless, the completed film remained true to Wead's original concept of showing how the crew and the destroyer worked together as a team.[24]

Throughout the war, all Hollywood films, whatever the service they portrayed, shared the common themes that defeating Germany and Japan required teamwork of men and equipment and that cooperation was needed between the military and the homefront. The initial combat movies had conveyed these propaganda messages in fictional stories, which actual events had at best only inspired. By the time *Crash Dive* and *Destroyer* appeared, however, news reports and stories from the combat zone had begun to provide Hollywood with ideas for fact-based films. Moreover, as the military situation improved, the individual services found it possible to provide significant assistance to filmmakers. As a result, by late 1943 movies conveyed a greater sense of realism and authenticity in portraying the American fighting man.

Coincidentally, the images of the Japanese and the Germans underwent profound and perhaps more significant changes, even as the war raged unabated in all theaters of operation. On November 5, 1943, the War Department, through its Pictorial Branch, advised the Office of War Information's liaison office in Los Angeles to notify all the studios to stop making Japanese-atrocity movies. The office immediately called its headquarters in Washington to ask whether the change in policy covered only acts of torture or physical mutilation against American prisoners of war and if it included "atrocities against women, starvation of prisoners or conquered populations, machine-gunning and strafing of civilians, bombing of hospitals, sinking of hospital ships, shooting down transport planes, etc."[25]

The film industry also sought to clarify the directive. On November 9, John Flynn, executive secretary for the Society of Independent Motion Picture Producers, informed Roy Disney of the Army's action, stating that "no production companies, by use of picture or dialogue, or any treatment whatsoever, make reference to any Japanese atrocities, that is no specific reference to Jap atrocities, including torture of prisoners of war, and any picture or dialogue to this effect will be passed by the War Department, and letters of export will be withheld." In the following weeks, the War Department tried but failed to fully enunciate how to implement its atrocity policy, perhaps because the issuing authority, the High Command, Chief of Staff George Marshall's operational staff, never provided a reason for the change.[26]

In fact, no one in authority left a paper trail documenting the evolution of the new policy. Without such documents or memoirs, a historian risks a loss of credibility if he speculates on why the Army would ask the film industry to moderate its images of a still powerful enemy in the midst of hostilities. Nevertheless, circumstantial evidence suggests that the November directive grew out of the belief in the highest circles of government that once the war ended, the alliance between the Soviet Union and the West would break apart. From where did this belief come?

In part, of course, the long-standing fear of Communism within the government, the military, and the general population fueled the distrust of Stalin's regime, which the West had joined only in a marriage of convenience against Hitler. The Manhattan Project did not invite Soviet scientists to join the effort to build the atomic bomb although physicists from Canada, Great Britain, and France, as well as émigrés who had fled from Hitler, made significant contributions to the development of the new weapon. Moreover, the government indicated its perspective when it prosecuted the Rosenbergs for spying for an enemy during wartime, although the Soviet Union had fought with the West against Hitler.

Winston Churchill accepted the necessity of joining the Soviet Union to defeat Germany, but he had no illusions about the nature of his ally. President Roosevelt, however, may have thought he could work with Stalin even after the defeat of Germany—at least until April 1943. Then he received a warning to the contrary from Alexander Sachs, known, if at all, only for delivering to the White House in October 1939 the now mythic letter from Albert Einstein about the possibility of building an atomic bomb. In fact, Sachs, a true Renaissance man, had begun advising Roosevelt on economic and foreign policy matters even before Roosevelt became president. He had discussed developments in nuclear power even before delivering the letter he had written with concerned physicists and which Einstein had only signed. He had then served as the liaison between the scientific community and the government and coordinated the early research on the bomb until Roosevelt ordered the Army to take over the program in 1942.

Subsequently, Sachs had advised the president on other subjects, and in April 1943 he delivered a briefing to Roosevelt in which he raised questions about the future of relations between Stalin's repressive regime and the democratic West. He began by noting that "to shed light on today's emerging crisis in Russian-Allied relations, there must be a realization that when we pass to totalitarian systems, the fundamental framework that we take for granted in democracies becomes inapplicable." After analyzing the nature of the Soviet and Nazi systems, he advised the president to prepare for a postwar confrontation with Stalin. The warning may well have contributed to the decision Roosevelt and Churchill made at the Quebec Conference in August 1943 not to inform the Soviet leader about the Manhattan Project.[27]

To be sure, the president and General Marshall knew that Stalin most likely had knowledge of the Anglo-American effort to build an atomic bomb from his espionage network, and they could well anticipate that the decision not to inform the Soviet dictator about the project would only reinforce his distrust of the West. Logic dictated that the United States would have to create a new alliance when the war had ended to counter a postwar confrontation with the Soviet Union. With Great Britain and France greatly weakened, the United States would need additional allies to stop the spread of Communism. From where would they come?

Roosevelt and General Marshall would have had little difficulty realizing that after the Allied victory, Germany and Japan might serve as buffers to Soviet expansion. Before this could happen, however, the United States would have to rehabilitate the negative wartime cinematic images of the enemy that Hollywood had been creating on the nation's theater screens since the late 1930s. Both Marshall and Roosevelt fully understood the power of motion pictures to shape public opinion. The Army chief of staff had initiated Frank Capra's *Why We Fight* motion picture series to explain the war to inductees during basic training. The president had approved showing American movies to Italian prisoners of war held in the United States to help change their views about America.[28]

In this context, therefore, the decision in November 1943, whether directly from Marshall, his immediate staff, or the president, ordering Hollywood to stop making atrocity movies becomes explicable, even without "a smoking gun" document. In any case, the atrocity directive had an immediate impact on the manner in which Hollywood henceforth portrayed the nation's enemies, and the resulting images support the thesis that the Cold War actually had its origins in the Quebec agreements in August 1943.

Although the directive did not explicitly mention portrayals of Germans, a German submarine captain became the first enemy Hollywood rehabilitated. In January 1944 Alfred Hitchcock's *Lifeboat* featured Walter Slezak as a U-boat commander who became the strongest, most interesting character in the movie. He might well have cut Bogart's raft in two like the captain in *Action in the North Atlantic* and by no means qualified as a "good"

77

German. Nevertheless, he became a three-dimensional human being, simply trying to survive as any person would in a similar situation, unlike the Nazi villains of the early World War II antifascist films.

At the same time, in movies about the war in the Pacific, the image of the enemy underwent a profound change from the cinematic recitations of Japan's duplicity in attacking Pearl Harbor and portrayals of Japanese pilots shooting helpless American aviators as they floated to earth and Japanese soldiers shooting unarmed American Marines. The trilogy of movies that chronicled Jimmy Doolittle's raid on Japan, from *Destination Tokyo* in December 1943; to *The Purple Heart,* released the next month; to *Thirty Seconds Over Tokyo,* appearing later in the year, demonstrate how Hollywood made the transition from creating purely negative images of the Japanese to featuring more moderate and even positive portrayals of the current enemy. These films and the ones that followed during the remainder of the war had a far-reaching impact on how Americans viewed their current enemies. Just as important, they illustrate the manner in which motion pictures can influence attitudes and politics.

6 | World War II: Pseudo-Reality

BY THE END OF 1943, THE ALLIES HAD NOT YET ASSURED themselves of victory. Nevertheless, the tide had turned. The Doolittle raid on Japan in April 1942 had done relatively little damage, but it had demonstrated to Japan that it could no longer consider its home islands inviolate. The combined Navy–Air Force operation showed both the Japanese military and the American people that the U.S. fleet had rebounded from its losses at Pearl Harbor and could carry the war to all parts of the Pacific. The subsequent American defeat of a vastly superior Japanese armada at Midway, Allied successes in North Africa, the invasion of Italy, and the regular bombings of Occupied Europe and the German homeland all contributed to a growing feeling of optimism in the United States.

The improved military situation enabled the armed services to again assist filmmakers, thus allowing them to turn out more authentic-looking combat movies than had been possible during the first year of the war. The combat successes also provided sources for a series of movies that portrayed the war with greater historical accuracy, depicting either actual events or a synthesis of several actions that filmmakers combined for heightened dramatic impact. Of all the military operations in the first two years of the war, probably nothing so stimulated the imagination of the American people as Doolittle's raid against Japan. Planned and carried out in absolute secrecy, and revealed to the American people with mystery still shrouding most of the mission, the attack on the Japanese mainland spawned three major Hollywood productions, two of which mixed fact with fiction.

Both *Destination Tokyo* and *The Purple Heart* used Doolittle's raid only as the starting points for fictionalized stories, which gained credibility if not historical accuracy from their references to actual events. In contrast to the earlier *Crash Dive*, the screenwriters said that *Destination Tokyo* attempted "to tell a factual kind of story" about submarine warfare, drawing on incidents from several submarine cruises in enemy waters. In this instance, Doolittle's attack on Japan provided the historical framework in which to set the story. In the script the studio submitted to the Navy in May 1943, the writers explained that the movie would inform the public that submarines "are of much greater value to the Navy and the nation than simply sinkers of ships. We want them to know the high caliber of submarine officers and men, that they are skilled, well-trained, and that they can take it as well as 'dish it out.'"[1]

The filmmakers told the Navy that *Destination Tokyo*, unlike earlier characterizations of the Japanese, intended "to show the Japanese as a tough adversary, an intelligent one." Furthermore, the writers explained that the submarine in their film would not be going "into mythical waters" and would not "sink the whole damned Jap fleet." Instead, the *Copperfin* would perform its mission "quietly and well," and the action would illustrate that both the men and their ship "can take it, that a submarine can take a terrific depthcharging and still come home." Finally, and "most of all," the writers said they wanted

79

"to show the public that the submarine service is doing a great and varied, though silent, job in this war!"[2]

To accomplish their goals, the writers created a relatively simple plot. The Navy has detailed the *Copperfin* to the Aleutians to pick up a Navy meteorologist and deliver him to the shore of Tokyo Bay to gather weather data for Doolittle's raid. While waiting for the officer to accomplish his mission, the submarine itself gathers intelligence data to radio to the attackers. Within this slim framework, the *Copperfin* and her crew experience several adventures that heighten the dramatic impact of the film.

In Alaskan waters, a Japanese float plane attacks the submarine and scores a direct hit. However, the bomb does not explode and the crew shoots down the bomber. The pilot stabs to death the sailor trying to rescue him from the water, reinforcing Hollywood's wartime image of the brutal, fanatical enemy, not the "intelligent" one the screenwriters had assured the Navy they would be portraying. After the crew kills the pilot and disarms the bomb, the *Copperfin* arrives in Tokyo Bay and dispatches the meteorologist.

While the submarine waits for him to complete his mission, a sailor suffers an appendicitis attack. In a sequence based on an actual operation aboard a merchant ship, which inspired several similar operations aboard submarines, the ship's pharmacist's mate removes the diseased organ, although he is inexperienced and lacks proper medical equipment. After the crew retrieves the weather expert and watches the bombing of Tokyo through the ship's periscope, the *Copperfin* sinks a Japanese carrier. Enemy destroyers retaliate with an archetypal depth-charge attack that became the model for all subsequent World War II submarine movies. Surviving the barrage, the *Copperfin* returns to San Francisco.

To bring this story to the screen, Delmer Daves, the screenplay writer, had to withstand the scrutiny of Jack Warner, the Production Code Office's prohibitions on anything it considered of a sexual nature, and the Navy's concerns about security and proper image. After reading the initial script, Joseph Breen, the office's arbitrator of moral and linguistic correctness, warned the studio on June 22, 1943, about the portrayal of one sailor. He complained that "the present characterization of the man, Wolf, as a man of very loose sex habits could not be approved in the finished picture. It would be acceptable to show Wolf as a 'flirtatious' type rather than the present entirely immoral characterization" with "promiscuous and loose sex habits."[3]

The Navy also had problems with Wolf and his doll. One reader of the script observed, "In my 17 years in the Navy I have never seen a sailor with a doll aboard nor expect to in the future—This will put a bad taste in any Navy man's mouth and I should think the general public's also." For the most part, however, the service's concerns focused on technical and operational portrayals. The same officer found the submarine's entering Tokyo Bay by following a Japanese ship through the submarine net "only possible in the movies—too far fetched even for public to follow—already used in *Crash Dive* and was ridiculous. Could never get out. The assignment of a modern fleet submarine to penetrate Tokyo Bay for weather data is wholly unsound."[4]

Daves also ignored history when it served his dramatic needs. Most obviously, the director/writer created a chronological framework for his story which bore no resemblance to history. The film opens with a voice over stating: "After months of secret preparations, a far-reaching combined operation is about to begin." The *Copperfin* then leaves San Francisco on Christmas eve. The year? If it is 1941, then planning for the Doolittle raid had begun before Pearl Harbor. In fact, Capt. Francis Low, an operations officer on the staff of CNO Ernest King, brought the idea for the mission to his boss on January 10, 1942, and

Capt. Donald Duncan, the staff's air operations officer, then took only five days to develop the plan. In the alternative, if the submarine is leaving port on December 24, 1942, then it has no orders to carry out since Doolittle's bombers struck Japan on April 18, 1942.[5]

Whatever the year, the *Copperfin* sails under sealed orders, which the captain is not to open for twenty-four hours, leaving the audience to wonder how he knows which direction to take once he passes under the Golden Gate Bridge. Of course in the real world the submarine would have left from Pearl Harbor, the base of Pacific operations, since it could not carry sufficient fuel to reach Japan and return to the West Coast. Daves does include a brief montage of the Doolittle raid, using actual footage of the launch. However, when the planes arrive over Tokyo, the director portrays them bombing in formation instead of attacking individually as they actually did.

Although the film did not tell the true story of a single submarine or even a completely accurate historical re-creation, most of the fictionalized incidents in *Destination Tokyo* either happened during the war or could plausibly have happened. Bombs did strike U.S. submarines without exploding. The submarine did radio back weather information to Doolittle's raiders, but from off the Japanese coast, not inside Tokyo Bay, and it probably did not contribute much to the success of the raid. Later in the war, American submarines did venture into Tokyo Bay, although not in the manner portrayed in the film. Submarine medics did perform several appendectomies until the Navy issued a directive forbidding such procedures except in a dire emergency. An American submarine did sink a Japanese carrier later in the war. Even more than the authentic-like situations, however, the filmmakers' adherence to detail and concern for accuracy of procedures aboard ship created a sense of reality and believability not found in many later submarine films.[6]

Destination Tokyo did not force audiences to stretch their credibility to any great extent, thanks to the care writer-director Delmer Daves lavished on the film. While working on the script, Daves went to the Mare Island Submarine Base in San Francisco Bay and lived with the submariners for a week, then returned to the studio to incorporate the material into a meaningful story. In one instance, his attention to detail resulted in an almost too realistic reproduction of still-secret radar equipment. When the Navy saw the "radar" set, it demanded to know the source of Daves's information. He was finally able to mollify the service's Security Branch by explaining that he had conceived the prop from

Director Delmer Daves (seated, center), producer Jerry Wald (seated right). and actor John Garfield during filming of *Destination Tokyo*.

his own research. The writer-director further satisfied the Navy's concerns when it realized that the "radar" in the film operated on the principle of an oscilloscope, whereas actual radar scopes used an electronic sweep to project its images. As a result, the Navy was more than willing to allow the Japanese to "learn" from Daves's invention.[7]

The American people learned from the film how men exist aboard submarines during wartime. Cary Grant, "a crisp, cool and kind-hearted gent who is every bit as resourceful as he is handsome and slyly debonair," commands the *Copperfin* and a crew with the typical cinematic mixture of ethnic backgrounds. Unlike later submarine tales in which conflicts among the crew help create the dramatic tensions, *Destination Tokyo* depicts the ship's complement as united in its effort to win the war as quickly as possible, a goal still in the distance when Warner Brothers released the film. The successful mission of the fictional *Copperfin*, juxtaposed with the success of the historical Doolittle raid, undoubtedly helped maintain the morale of the American people as the war entered its third year. This purpose aside, the movie made "a pippin of a picture from a purely melodramatic point of view."[8]

It also contained the requisite pre–November 1943 image of the evil Jap in the pilot's stabbing of Mike, his would-be rescuer. The attack also gives Cary Grant the opportunity to philosophize on the difference between the peace-loving American democracy and its brutal enemy: "As I see it, that Jap was started on the road 25 years ago to putting a knife in Mike's back. There are lots of Mikes dying right now and a lot more Mikes will die until we wipe out a system that puts daggers in the hands of 5-year-old children."

Unlike *Destination Tokyo*, in which one enemy flier committed a senseless act of brutality, *The Purple Heart* focused on the perfidy of the Japanese government and war machine. Using the actual capture of several of Doolittle's fliers only as a springboard, Darryl Zanuck wrote and produced a fictional film about the show trial to which the Japanese subjected the Americans. Although the story itself had no basis in fact, the film, directed by Lewis Milestone, seemed so real that people thought Twentieth Century Fox had been provided secret information about the captured fliers.

By showing American men being tortured, albeit offscreen, and hauled into a Japanese court as war criminals, the film presented an image of American courage and steadfastness in the face of enemy brutality and thus inspired the nation to continue the struggle against its cruel and bloodthirsty foe. To reinforce the anger of its audiences, *The Purple Heart* went even further than the historical reality that the Japanese did execute three of Doolittle's fliers by having the court sentence all eight captured fliers to death. Nevertheless, the Office of War Information found that the portrayal fell within the guidelines of the November anti-atrocity directive, concluding that in the completed film, the "atrocities have been played down to a minimum of sensationalism and emphasis has been placed on the theme of the strength and courage of the people who are fighting Fascism, exemplified in the eight American fliers."[9] Perhaps the War Department felt that the filmmakers satisfied its requirements by not showing the torture or executions on screen.

In contrast to the fictionalizing of history in *Destination Tokyo* and *The Purple Heart*, *Thirty Seconds Over Tokyo*, released in late 1944, had to avoid fictionalized melodrama because of its source. Based on Ted Lawson's book of the same title, the film portrayed the flier's experiences on Doolittle's raid, for the most part as he had described them, and so created its dramatic impact solely from the events that had actually occurred. As with any historical movie, the filmmakers faced the difficulty of bringing suspense to a historical event whose ending the audience already knew.

To overcome this problem, *Thirty Seconds Over Tokyo* introduced the audience to liv-

Lt. Col. James Doolittle wires a bunch of prewar Japanese medals to the fin of one of the 500-pound bombs he and his volunteer fliers were to drop on Japan in April 1942. Spencer Tracy was to re-create Doolittle's pre-launching cer-emony in *Thirty Seconds Over Tokyo* (1944), and the raid was also to figure in the stories of *Destination Tokyo* (1944), *The Purple Heart* (1944), *Midway* (1976), and *Pearl Harbor* (2001).

ing heroes in Ted Lawson, whom Van Johnson played with boyish good humor; in Jimmy Doolittle, whom Spencer Tracy portrayed with appropriate reserve; and the rest of the men who volunteered for the mission. Yet the fliers became more than heroes. The pro-ducers explained to the Army that they wanted "to make a picture in which there are no individual heroes because all are heroes; a picture in which the leading characters are the living symbols of millions of service men and their wives who quietly and gallantly offer to the American people the greatest sacrifice within their power to give." Likewise, the War Department hoped that the "picture will result not in the glorification of one officer, but the heroic exploits of the [whole] Army Air Force" in the raid. The Pictorial Branch fur-ther noted that the Army "has been reluctant to glorify any single individual. As Captain Lawson was one of a great number of men on this particular mission, it is expected that this picture will result in giving equal credit to all, rather than any single member."[10]

The producers indicated in the first script sent to the War Department that they felt "a heavy responsibility" in approaching Lawson's book. They believed a picture based on it would contribute "constructively and dynamically to the public morale. The best propa-ganda, of course, is the truth; and in Captain Lawson's book the truth is presented simply, decently, and dramatically." Also, by dramatizing the close cooperation between the Army and the Navy that made the Tokyo raid possible, the filmmakers sought "to destroy the malingering whisper that a harmful rivalry exists between these two branches of the ser-vice." Finally, they expected that the scenes showing "the devotion and courage of the Chinese people as they smuggled scores of American airmen to safety [would] constitute a genuine contribution to the relations between the American people and their courageous Chinese allies."[11]

Thirty Seconds Over Tokyo was supposed to show all these things factually. But in put-ting across its message, the film did not tell the entire story of the mission. Intended more as a public relations event than a military maneuver designed to inflict heavy damage, the raid did bring the war to the Japanese homeland for the first time. Although the enemy now had to devote some of its resources to homefront defense, the actual bombing did little damage to military or industrial targets but cost every one of Doolittle's planes. As a propaganda document, the film stressed the public relations aspects of the raid, ignoring the lack of military success. Likewise, though it did show Chinese civilians helping the fliers to safety, it failed to identify the rescuers as Communist guerrillas, not citizens loyal to Chiang Kai-Shek. Screenwriter Dalton Trumbo pointed out that everyone knew the truth, "but there was no point in emphasizing this. The object of this film was to establish in the American minds that we had a powerful ally in the Chinese people. And that made the war effort more hopeful."[12]

To transfer Lawson's first-person account to the screen as accurately as possible, Trumbo interviewed the pilot and many of the fliers involved in the raid. The conversations also enabled Trumbo to describe details of the training and flight as thoroughly as security would allow. Among other things, the Navy would not permit the screenwriter to identify the aircraft carrier used to launch the mission. Nor could he reveal that one of Doolittle's planes had landed in Siberia, where the Soviets interned the crew. Within the limits of security and the demands of the war effort, the military cooperated fully with MGM. Trumbo recalled that he flew on a B-25 until "I knew every position on the plane and every job on the plane."[13]

Unlike contemporary director-oriented Hollywood filmmaking, Trumbo worked closely with producer Sam Zimbalist in developing the script and preparing for the film. MGM did not select Mervyn LeRoy to direct the movie until shortly before it went into actual production, and he spent only two weeks working on the script before shooting began. According to Trumbo, very few changes were made on the script during this period, "nothing fundamental."[14]

The movie traces the Doolittle raid through Ted Lawson's eyes. From their training camp at Eglin Air Force Base near Pensacola, the men fly their planes to San Francisco for loading on the aircraft carrier. Although their training has included takeoffs consistent with the length of a carrier flight deck, the fliers do not learn of the purpose of their mission until they are actually on their way to the Western Pacific. After unexpectedly encountering Japanese patrol boats, the bombers have to take off when they are 624 miles from the Japanese coast instead of 400 miles as originally planned.[15] Doolittle leads all sixteen planes off the pitching carrier deck and toward their bombing targets. Afterward, however, the fliers must attempt to reach friendly territory in darkness with their fuel rapidly being exhausted. With the exception of the plane that lands safely in Russia, the crews either bail out or crash-land once they reach the Chinese coast.

Until the takeoff, Lawson shares the film with Doolittle and his fellow fliers as they train for the mission. However, once in the air, Lawson and his crew become the focus of the story. In China, their odyssey through enemy territory assumes heroic dimensions, with the crew suffering various injuries as a result of the plane's crash landing onto a rocky beach. Lawson himself perseveres despite a painfully shattered leg that the doctor who flew on the raid must ultimately amputate. Lawson's homecoming and reunion with his wife recreated the nation's welcome to the fliers for their courageous achievement in bringing the war to the Japanese homeland in the first dark months of the war.

The War Department found Trumbo's version of the raid acceptable for cooperation subject to certain changes that dealt mainly with military procedures and security matters. In a letter to the studio, the Pictorial Board told the filmmakers not to show an enlisted man in an Officers Club scene; to delete the phrase "Singapore itself will fall," because it had "a defeatist implication"; to eliminate all references to the speed of the B-25s; and to disguise the names of several characters who might be in Japanese-held territory.[16]

The Army did make clear that the accuracy of many points "must be the responsibility of Captain Ted Lawson, particularly regarding his personal affairs. If he vouches for the correctness of the scenes involving matters of his own personal knowledge, then there is no War Department objection." The Army suggested, however, that Lawson's operation should be "toned down" or photographed so that "pictorially it will not exhilarate the emotions

Shot of actual takeoff of B-25 from the USS *Hornet*, used in *Thirty Seconds Over Tokyo* and *Midway*.

through these unfortunate situations." The service acknowledged "that there is a certain amount of dramatic value in Captain Lawson's experience, but this action should be handled most carefully and with dignity." Finally, because of the possible repercussions of emphasizing Chinese assistance in getting the fliers out of enemy-occupied territory, the Army suggested that this aspect of the story "should be reduced to a minimum, and only utilized where it is necessary to carry the thread of the story and where assistance by individuals is important to the picture."[17]

In agreeing to provide assistance on *Thirty Seconds Over Tokyo,* the War Department explained that cooperation might present a "problem" because of normal demands on training facilities. By the time the film went into production in early 1944, however, the Air Corps allowed Mervyn LeRoy to do his location shooting at Eglin Air Force Base, the site Doolittle's men had used for their training. During the month in Florida, with a crew of ninety-three people including the cast, LeRoy received technical advice from Ted Lawson and two other raiders. He also had the use of as many as eighteen B-25 bombers when the script called for scenes of the entire squadron preparing for its mission.[18]

The location shooting was only the first step in the film's production. The War Department and the Navy could not provide the planes and a carrier for MGM to photograph scenes of the bombers and crew aboard ship or to actually restage the launching of Doolittle's raiders. The studio was therefore forced to build a section of the USS *Hornet*'s flight deck on its Stage 15 and managed to squeeze four B-25s onto it. To recreate the takeoffs themselves, Buddy Gillespie, head of MGM's special-effects department, built about four-fifths of the deck of the *Hornet* on a scale of one inch to the foot. The sixty-foot miniature was then set in the studio's three-hundred-square-foot water tank. Because of its size in relationship to the tank, the miniature was kept stationary. Gillespie made the carrier rise, pitch, and roll hydraulically as water was moved past the ship with pumps and wave machines. He then photographed miniature bombers, attached to an overhead trolley with piano wire. The planes' "takeoffs" were controlled by means of little synchronous motors. These sequences were then combined with a limited amount of the newsreel footage taken during the actual takeoffs. Gillespie did his job so well that only someone familiar with the newsreel film can distinguish the recreated takeoffs from the actual launchings. To reproduce the raiders' approach to the Japanese mainland, the Air Force flew several B-25s carrying cameras mounted on their noses inland over Los Angeles from the Pacific.

The technique worked so well that later the producer of *Midway* resurrected the footage to open his film, even though the original montage is in black and white and the 1976 re-creation of the Battle of Midway is in color.[19]

This care for detail and visual reproduction resulted in a film that had "the tough and literal quality of an Air Force documentary."[20] In fact, the production may have succeeded too well in this regard. When Trumbo later did a brief stint as an Air Force correspondent in the Pacific, he discovered that B-25 pilots, after seeing the film, felt challenged to imitate the quick, short-distance takeoffs whenever they had the chance. Commanding officers told the writer that the pilots' actions caused an increased number of accidents that might have been avoided if the film had not shown the short takeoffs.[21]

Trumbo himself criticized the movie from a dramatic point of view. In dealing with a historical subject, he explained, a film's climax often came at the end of the second act rather than the third. In *Thirty Seconds Over Tokyo,* the raid itself should have become the climax, the writer acknowledged. However, he said, "We had to go on for another hour." As a screenwriter he had "to go to so many tricks to cover it up. . . . you have to dance." Under the circumstances, Trumbo thought that the success of the picture "depends more or less on the ability, principally of the writer, because he constructs the picture, to fake it and to conceal that enormous defect in the structure."[22]

Although the film may have had this dramatic flaw, as war propaganda each act of *Thirty Seconds Over Tokyo* worked well. Director LeRoy recalled, "It showed the Air Force in a great light which they should be shown in."[23] Volunteering for a secret, implicitly dangerous mission and quickly learning new flying techniques illustrated the spirit of taking chances, of challenging the unknown, that is inherent in American tradition and in the growth of the nation. Flying the almost suicidal mission because it might shorten the war demonstrated the courage of the American fighting man for the nation better than any headlines could do. The journey to safety may have become anticlimactic dramatically, but to Trumbo it demonstrated the determination of the armed forces to persevere despite adversity and physical pain. The movie provided "a fitting tribute" to all the participants in Doolittle's raid and, according to Bosley Crowther of the *New York Times*, "It is certainly a most stimulating and emotionally satisfying film."[24]

Thirty Seconds Over Tokyo satisfied critics and audiences, and it provided a reasonable re-creation of history. However, it portrayed only a limited kind of war. The film showed little combat and no dead bodies. It presented the conflict in the detached way most fliers participate in combat—at a distance, whether over Tokyo, Berlin, or the jungles of Southeast Asia. Even the struggle of Lawson and his comrades to reach friendly territory had little to do with combat as most American participants saw it in the war. Moreover, the film presented a different enemy from the one that the soldiers, sailors, fliers, and Marines were then fighting to the death.

In fact, *Thirty Seconds Over Tokyo* provided the precise images that the War Department had envisioned in its November 1943 anti-atrocity directive. It contains no negative images of the enemy, either visually or verbally. None of the fliers even talk about exacting revenge against Japan for Pearl Harbor, which had occurred only four months before the raid. Instead, the evening before Doolittle's planes are to take off for Japan, two of the pilots discuss their feelings about the enemy in the most innocuous terms.

Van Johnson, as Lawson, tells another pilot, a young Robert Mitchum: "My mother had a Jap gardener once. He seemed like a nice little guy." Mitchum responds: "You know, I don't hate Japs, yet. It's a funny thing. I don't like 'em, but I don't hate 'em." Lawson agrees: "I guess I don't either. You get kind of mixed up. It's hard to figure. I joined the Army in '40 because I figured it was the best way to learn. I wasn't sore at anybody. But, here you suddenly realize you're going to drop a ton of high explosives on one of the largest cities in the world. I don't pretend to like the idea of killing a bunch of people, but it's a case of drop a bomb on them or pretty soon they'll be dropping one on Ellen." "Yea, that's right," Mitchum agrees.

To show how the Navy was making its contribution to ending the war before this happened, *A Wing and a Prayer* combined a historical event, the Battle of Midway, documentary footage taken during the shakedown cruise of the new USS *Yorktown*, and a fictionalized account of life aboard an aircraft carrier before and during the decisive battle of the war in the Pacific. The only American movie made during the war to dramatize the role of carriers in the Pacific, the Twentieth Century Fox production sought to inspire patriotism by focusing purely on combat.[25]

After the writing of a draft screenplay in early January 1943, however, the studio abandoned a documentary approach to the story, which had focused on the heroic but tragic story of Torpedo Squadron 8. The *New York Times* reported that "a certain high Government official" had protested that the proposed approach "would carry a defeatist implication." The sacrifice of 15 of the *Hornet's* torpedo planes in the first few minutes of the battle certainly would not convey a positive image to the American people. Moreover, the cinematic portrayal of the subsequent torpedo bomber attacks would not have done much to instill confidence in naval aviation. The squadron from the *Enterprise* lost 10 of 14 aircraft, and the original *Yorktown* lost 8 of its 12 planes. Even worse, not one torpedo hit a Japanese ship.[26]

For about a hundred seconds, the Japanese believed they had won not only the Battle of Midway but also the war itself. Then, in less than a minute, the Japanese fortunes changed dramatically and irreversibly when Navy dive bombers inflicted mortal damage on two of the enemy's carriers. By the end of the battle, the other two Japanese carriers had met a similar fate, thereby validating the arguments of naval aviators that the future of the Navy rested with carriers rather than battleships. The service itself as well as the "high Government official" would obviously prefer to have Hollywood portray the final victory at Midway, not the initial futile attacks.

To that end, Twentieth Century Fox spent the next several months developing a new screenplay. To help the project along, the Navy agreed to Darryl Zanuck's request to allow a camera crew and a few actors to go aboard the *Yorktown II*, during a portion of its shakedown cruises in May and June of 1943. Finally on October 26, a new writer, Jerry Cady, completed a treatment titled "Wing and a Prayer," which stated in its foreword: "For military purposes, the names of men and vessels in this motion picture are fictitious, but the strategy, the essential incidents and the heroism are a matter of history." The story then opened with a scene of the wreckage at Pearl Harbor, introduced the officers and men of a carrier, and followed the ship as it created deceptions that tricked the Japanese and led to Midway.[27]

In a story conference on November 19, 1943, Darryl Zanuck pointed out that the picture would not depend on a plot. He warned that the filmmakers "must avoid plot, otherwise we will destroy the value of the honesty that we must maintain." To compensate for the absence of a dramatic story, he thought the filmmakers had to rely on three elements: casting, dialogue, and battle sequences.[28]

In regard to casting, Zanuck stated: "We must have characters that an audience will follow and love and root for in lieu of a story. In other words, our story is our characters." He felt the dialogue and "the business" that the characters perform "is as vital as the casting of the characters themselves, especially the elements of comedy." Finally, Zanuck said the filmmakers "must adroitly take advantage of every inch" of the combat footage the studio had obtained from the Navy in order to create the excitement and thrill of authentic battle scenes. This would create "genuine excitement; not melodrama so much as the feeling that our characters are actually in battle."[29]

In a meeting with his staff on January 24, 1944, Zanuck compared the studio's project with the newly released and highly successful *Destination Tokyo*. He thought their story would have an advantage "in that the mission in *Wing and a Prayer* is a genuine, honest mission, while in *Tokyo* it was fictional. However, it was so well done that audiences no doubt accept it as factual." Nevertheless, Zanuck believed their project offered another significant advantage over Warner Brothers's film. He noted that no carrier movie had appeared since Pearl Harbor, whereas *Destination Tokyo* had become the second major wartime submarine film.[30]

Zanuck did acknowledge that this might not provide a real bonus, given people's perceptions about submarines compared to aircraft carriers: "There exists in the public mind the belief that submarine service is the most dangerous of all. Of course it is true that if a sub gets hit that's the end of it—it sinks to the bottom of the ocean. As against this, the public also regards an Aircraft Carrier as the safest place to be, because the Carrier itself looks so substantial and strong, and you do not have the feeling that people are trapped on it as in the case of a submarine. Therefore, since our story takes place on a Carrier, we do not have this element of constant menace, and we have to do whatever we can to enhance our personal plot."[31]

This attention to detail and arduous effort produced a film with an unnamed aircraft carrier, "Carrier X," as its hero. Beginning with Cady's original question, "Where is our Navy?" the story focused on the crew of a squadron of torpedo bombers aboard a carrier cruising the Western Pacific in the months before the Battle of Midway. The carrier had orders to allow the enemy to see it, with its escorts, in widely scattered areas, but it was ordered not to have its planes give battle under any circumstances. The Navy hoped that this would give the Japanese the impression that U.S. forces were weak and afraid to fight.

The cinematic story within this framework contained the stereotypical clash between a rigid veteran commander and his young, inexperienced fliers, who do not initially appreciate that the combat knowledge he is trying to impart may save their lives. In visualizing this clash, *A Wing and a Prayer* performed a valuable service to its audiences. Beyond that, however, the movie offered no insights into the manner in which the Navy was actually conducting carrier operations during the war. Nor did the film in any way present an accurate account of the events leading up to the Battle of Midway and the course of the engagement itself.

The question "Where is our Navy?" and the film's answer, trying to deceive the enemy, remained convenient cinematic fiction. In fact, during the months that *A Wing and a Prayer* portrayed a lone carrier running before an enemy without firing a shot, the Navy was actually waging an aggressive campaign against the Japanese within the limits of its resources. In February the *Enterprise* raided Kwajalein Island and the *Lexington* hit the Japanese-held port of Rabaul on New Britain. In March planes from the *Lexington* and the *Yorktown* attacked Japanese bases on the north coast of New Guinea. In April the *Hornet*, with the *Enterprise* providing air support, sailed to within 624 miles of Tokyo to launch

Doolittle's sixteen B-25 medium bombers. In May the *Lexington* and the *Yorktown* led an Allied force against the Japanese in the Battle of the Coral Seas, the first naval engagement in which no ship of either side sighted a ship of the other.[32]

Clearly, no reason existed to ask "Where is our Navy?" Despite the disaster at Pearl Harbor, the Navy was fighting back during the spring of 1942, not running from the enemy. Moreover, even as fiction, the premise that any commander would conceive a plan that used a precious aircraft carrier as a decoy and would forbid its men and planes to defend themselves when attacked lacked even a modicum of believability. In any war, commanders sometimes must issue orders that put their men in harm's way. However, unlike the Japanese, Americans do not order their men to undertake suicide missions, as the "Carrier X" fliers were ordered to do. Nevertheless, if the story line far exceeded dramatic license, the order and the fliers' reaction to it created dramatic conflict within the confines of the film.

Furthermore, *A Wing and a Prayer* did portray life aboard an aircraft carrier in wartime with some authenticity. It also contained a scene that had never appeared in a carrier movie before and never appeared again. Using perhaps three seconds of Navy footage, the film showed the catapult launching of a bomber from the hangar deck during the height of the aerial battle. The Navy had actually tried to launch a plane from a carrier's hangar deck four times. Three ended ignominiously. There is no way to determine whether the footage in *A Wing and a Prayer* showed the one successful launch.

Unfortunately, the Battle of Midway, as depicted in *A Wing and a Prayer,* became only a generic portrayal of combat created with newsreel footage and models. It did not provide an understanding of or resemblance to the actual course of events during the first day of the fighting. In particular, the film showed "Carrier X"'s torpedo planes scoring several direct hits on the Japanese carriers even though dive bombers had accomplished the damage.

Recognizing early on that the studio would have access to a relatively limited amount of combat footage, Cady resorted to creating a portion of the battle by means of radio transmissions of the fliers to each other, piped throughout the carrier. As the sounds and voices of the fighting came through the speakers, the director focused his camera on the reaction of the carrier's men to hearing the ebb and flow of the battle. Used for the first time in *A Wing and a Prayer,* the device forced audiences to fill in the details with their imaginations and won Cady an Oscar nomination for best original screenplay. It also had a lasting impact on at least one viewer, an actor then making training films for the Army Air Corps in Hollywood who later became Commander in Chief of all U.S. military forces.

Throughout his political career, Ronald Reagan regularly recounted how a B-17 pilot returning home from a mission over Europe refused to bail out of his crippled plane after discovering a wounded gunner unable to abandon the craft. The pilot sat down next to the scared boy and told him: "Never mind, son. We'll ride it down together." According to Reagan, the pilot received the Medal of Honor posthumously for his actions. However, in answer to requests for verification of the story, neither the White House nor the Air Force History Office could find any evidence of such an act of heroism.

Ultimately, a World War II veteran provided the source of the quote. It came not from a B-17 pilot but from a torpedo bomber pilot in *A Wing and a Prayer* talking to his wounded radio operator. When the man informs his pilot that the plane is burning and that he cannot move, the flier responds: "I haven't got the altitude, Mike. We'll take this ride together." Having seen the film, the veteran immediately recognized the strong similarity between the dialogue in the film's Midway battle sequence and Reagan's quote. If the president confused image and reality, the Navy veteran recalled that he and his friends "laughed at" the film's "corniness."[33]

In all fairness to Reagan, *A Wing and a Prayer* did combine the few combat sequences with the soundstage action very well, thanks to the Navy's assistance and Zanuck's ongoing guidance. The film itself also intertwined image and reality when Dana Andrews reprimanded a glory-seeking pilot by telling him, "This isn't Hollywood." Moreover, the United States did award a dozen Medals of Honor to pilots killed while trying to land their planes in order not to abandon wounded crewmen. Therefore, if Navy men considered *A Wing and a Prayer* corny and historians found it lacking any validity as an account of the Battle of Midway, the average viewer could accept the movie as a credible portrayal of carrier operations in wartime.

The *New York Times* reviewer acknowledged that *A Wing and a Prayer* may not always represent the facts "in exact proportion." Nevertheless, the critic felt that director Henry Hathaway "has so skillfully woven documentary film footage into the story that it is difficult at times to spot the ending of an incident out of history and the beginning of an episode fashioned on the typewriter of Scenarist Jerome Cady." At the same time, the writer pointed out that people could easily "dismiss a sizable portion of the happenings in *A Wing and a Prayer* as the products of a fertile Hollywood mind had not so many equally and in some cases seemingly more improbable events been recorded in Navy logbooks."[34]

In the end, however, the reviewer recognized that "it still is more than likely that the development of the trap set for the Japs at Midway is, in the case of this film, more Cady than Halsey, Nimitz or King." From the perspective of a viewer, the writer concluded that the film "misses out on the epic sweep of the actual Midway campaign," in contrast to the Navy's own 1943 documentary, *Battle of Midway,* which John Ford had directed. Still, the critic believed that *A Wing and a Prayer* did provide "a good over-all glimpse of what life is like aboard a floating airfield." As such, the film became "at once a sobering reminder of the perilous conditions under which the American Navy sailed the vast Pacific in the months immediately following Pearl Harbor and a first-rate piece of movie-making to boot."[35]

However good *A Wing and a Prayer* became, like *Destination Tokyo,* it remained more fictional than real, resorting to melodrama, humor, and scenes of combat in order to attract viewers. Moreover, the fantasies the filmmakers created within a broad historical framework could not provide victories. But they could impress the American people with some of the realities of war. Hollywood thereby helped stimulate patriotism and the war effort on the home front, and it offered the message of ultimate victory for the Allies. In any case, the "real" war between 1942 and 1945, the one that finally made a difference, did not take place on the sea or in the air, but on the ground, infantry against infantry, man against man, struggling for every foot of territory. Airplanes and ships might have had more glamour, but only the foot soldier experienced all the grime, discomfort, and blood.

Wake Island, Bataan, and *Sahara* had only hinted at the true nature of this struggle, because they sprang from screenwriters' imaginations. *The Fighting Seabees,* another combat fantasy that gained credibility from its factual origins, had an even more humble beginning when a truck driver at Republic Studio told John Wayne about a new organization that was turning construction engineers and workers into Navy builders. Since the actor did not yet "have enough pull to do what I wanted to do," he sent the man to see a studio producer, who co-opted the idea. Ultimately, Herbert Yates, Republic's president, informed Wayne, "Duke, I've got the greatest idea that's come up so far. We're going to do a story on the fighting Seabees and put you in it."[36]

The Navy had created the Seabees early in the war to serve as construction engineers to build bases and airfields on islands captured from the Japanese. The filmmakers created a purely fictional story which featured John Wayne as a civilian engineer turned Navy officer. Nevertheless, the movie did inform the public about the Seabees' mission, and the combat sequences illustrated why construction engineers had to carry weapons. As a result, the Navy gave Republic permission to shoot, at Camp Pendleton, north of San Diego, a Seabee training exercise, which included the building of an airfield. The filmmakers then wrote those scenes into the story and cut that footage, some of which had the actors strategically placed in the action, into the film.[37]

Despite this assistance, the *Commonweal* observed that although the battles were "made as realistic as possible" with the help of Navy technical advisors, men who had experienced war firsthand would find flaws in the re-creations. Whatever the film's dramatic and technical deficiencies, the Navy benefited from the first, and only, portrayal of the Seabees in action. Moreover, the *Commonweal* reviewer, for one, found it "gratifying that this cinema tribute should be handled in such a straightforward, sincere manner."[38]

The Fighting Seabees had one other distinction. It became the first of only two war movies in which John Wayne is killed, dying in glorious combat as he is routing the Japanese and saving the day. To the Navy, John Wayne and this positive image transcended the mundane plot and made it "probably worth the effort." Nevertheless, although Wayne died for his country, it remained only a symbolic death of an actor, in a Hollywood fantasy. It did not cause audiences to grieve or leave the theater cursing the horrors of war.[39]

The deaths of the five Sullivan brothers in the battle of the Guadalcanal Sea and the Marine leathernecks on Guadalcanal in 1942 had a much more powerful impact. *The Sullivans* did not permit audiences the luxury of dismissing death as a cinematic device promoting patriotism and the war effort. Nor did it matter that the filmmakers took dramatic license in the way they chose to portray the deaths of the five Sullivan brothers in the sinking of their ship during the naval battle at Guadalcanal in November 1942. Nothing could change the reality that all five brothers had died together in real combat.

In becoming the medium for perpetuating the significance of the Sullivan boys for the American people, the film provided at least as much value to the war effort as any combat movie made during the conflict. When *The Fighting Seabees* ended, Wayne and the rest of the actors would go on to their next roles, as did the actors playing the five Sullivans. But nothing could change the reality that the five brothers were not going to return to their family. To be sure, many people did die in war to protect the American way of life, as Cary Grant had explained to his men in *Destination Tokyo*. But the sheer magnitude of that one family's loss, however necessary the war, overrode any positive message the film might offer. Their father might go to work as he had done for thirty-three years. Four of the brothers on their way to heaven might have to wait for their youngest sibling as they had had to wait for him in life. Their mother might christen a new destroyer *The Sullivans* in memory of her sons. However, none of these images could hide the reality that all five brothers had died.

Likewise, the cinematic Marines in the 1943 *Guadalcanal Diary* had their origins in real Marines about whom Richard Tregaskis had written in his book of the same name. The screenwriter did not invent their struggles and sufferings trying to capture the island during long months of fighting. As a result, the film became a pseudo-documentary account of the bloody battles and portrayed the Marine Corps in one of its finest hours. Although the studio originally planned it as a "quickie picture," the Marines agreed to cooperate on the production and provided a ship and men on maneuvers off San Diego to help recreate the landing on Guadalcanal. Actor Lloyd Nolan recalled that most of the filming occurred at Camp Pendlelton, with less than a week back at the studio. The "landing," staged on the tropic, coconut-palmed beach at San Clemente, California, featured the First Battalion, Twenty-fourth Marines, Fourth Marine Division, which shipped out shortly after taking part in the filming and "got shot up pretty bad" thereafter, according to the actor.[40]

With much the same approach and images, *The Story of G.I. Joe,* which did not appear until June 1945, showed the American people the stark reality of World War II ground combat. It did so because it used as its source the reporting of Ernie Pyle, who had experienced combat firsthand and was able to put what he had seen into words. It did so because 150 or so combat veterans served as extras and in some cases as speaking actors, recreating before the camera their combat experiences. Most important, it did so because an old World War I flier, William Wellman, who agreed to direct the film despite his inherent dislike for the infantry, brought his directing skills to a "beautifully written" story.[41]

As the director, Wellman served as a catalyst in bringing together Ernie Pyle, his stories, the actors, and the Army to create a uniquely realistic movie. Nevertheless, *The Story of G.I. Joe* illustrates the extent to which filmmaking used to operate as a collective process, not as a director's medium. Unlike most World War II films initiated by the major studios, the concept for *G.I. Joe* originated with an independent producer, Lester Cowan. As Wellman later recalled, when Cowan started talking, all you could do was "just sit and listen."[42] The producer had started talking with the War Department about an idea for a major Army film as early as September 1943. Though he had no clear concept in mind, he wanted to make a film in the class of *Air Force,* a prospect the service found of "particular interest."[43]

By October 1943, Cowen had reached an arrangement with United Artists for financial backing and distribution and had a scriptwriter talking to Ernie Pyle. As a result of these conversations, Cowan sent the War Department an outline of a story based on a collection of Pyle's columns in *Here Is Your War.* He proposed to feature the infantry, its training, and its actions at the front. The Army Ground Forces Headquarters approved the outline on November 27 but noted, "It must be realized that many modifications will occur before this picture is completed."[44]

The film did not go before the cameras for more than another year, because Cowan had problems in developing a suitable script. In a letter to the Army's Bureau of Public Relations in June 1944, the producer explained the delay: "In our script we are undertaking something quite without precedent. It is a challenge to undertake the writing of a dramatic story about the war and the soldier during the war. As you know, in the past, the best war stories evolved during the ten-year period following the war, when issues and events had become resolved and could be viewed with some perspective." Cowan claimed that the picture would represent the first attempt at a screen autobiography, in the sense that it would use the words of Ernie Pyle. Translating Pyle's words into visual drama had caused for the writers a problem that Cowan said they had solved by approaching Pyle's reporting "as a love story, figuratively speaking, of Pyle and the soldier."[45]

Cowan admitted that it was "an ambitious claim" to now say he had licked the story, since the script seemed to be bogged down in the mud of Corsica along with the war. But the recent D-Day landings had provided the solution. The war was moving to its climax, and the film would show Pyle moving toward victory. As a result of this breakthrough in the evolution of the script, the producer felt he was prepared to commence photographing on August 1, since he would have enough of the script written in two weeks to cover the first four weeks of shooting. Cowan was in fact manifesting wild optimism; the writing continued throughout July. More important, he did not have a director for the film yet.[46]

In early July he sent a telegram to the Pictorial Branch of the War Department to inquire about the possibility of securing John Huston as the director for his film. Although Huston had made only two films before entering the Army, since enlisting he had directed *Report from the Aleutians* and was then completing *The Battle of San Pietro*, a documentary about the Italian campaign. Cowan thought this gave him "irreplaceable experience of living with soldiers under frontline conditions, so that he knows and feels the difference between the real thing and any Hollywood version." Cowan also felt he had the "rare opportunity to make Hollywood's first honest and authentic picture about the infantry soldier" and so wanted to work "with people who know from actual first-hand experience." Unfortunately, though Huston read a draft of the screenplay and made "very constructive and helpful criticisms," Cowan was not able to secure his services.[47]

Turning to another unsolved question, whom to cast as Ernie Pyle, the producer learned that Pyle wanted Burgess Meredith to play the role. Meredith, however, was serving on active duty, and the Army presented Cowan with a choice: either turn over all profits of the film to the Army Emergency Relief Fund (as had been done in other films), or Meredith would have to resign his commission.[48] Eventually, when Meredith accepted the role, he went on inactive status and seemingly became Pyle, "because his impersonation [was] so consummate." Dudley Nichols, who had written *Air Force*, felt that it did not matter "whether Pyle looked like himself or like Meredith; the feeling that Meredith projects into the whole film, illuminating the lifting scenes into high significance, is the feeling that Pyle projected through all his writing. Out of all this ugliness, it seemed to say, out of all this horror, this filth and misery and butchery and waste, comes this—this wonderful thing, man!"[49]

By the beginning of August 1944, however, Cowan had still not found a director, and he decided to approach William Wellman. Walking into his house uninvited, Cowan proceeded to tell the director all about the film. Before running out of breath, Cowan said that both he and Pyle had decided Wellman was the man to direct the picture. Wellman "politely declined the great honor that they would bestow on me," but Cowan refused to accept the rejection. He continued to argue until Wellman told him bluntly, "I was not interested in working my ass off for the infantry." He explained why he "hated the infantry with such a fury . . . that I frightened him into getting the hell out of my house. That was that, I thought."[50]

Not for Cowan, who returned a few days later with a letter from Pyle. Wellman knew Pyle by reputation but "had not bothered to read any of his writings because they touched on but one subject—the infantry—and to me, that was like waving a red flag in front of a bull, so I slammed the door in [Cowan's] face." Again Wellman believed he had ended the subject. However, Cowen did not intend to be denied, and he returned a few days later with presents for the director's five children. "The son of a bitch even knew their names," Wellman recalled. After telling Cowan off in "well-chosen four-letter words," he told the producer to stay away or he would put him in the hospital.[51]

Wellman soon discovered that Cowan was "a persistent bastard." The same night, Pyle himself called the director from his home in Albuquerque, inviting him to visit and listen to his story firsthand. He expressed confidence that the director would change his mind after he realized the great need for such a picture and "what it would mean to the thousands of kids that were fighting for his and my country." Wellman later said that

Pyle almost had him crying on the phone. He went to New Mexico two days later. After another two days of talks, with Cowan in attendance part of the time, Wellman finally agreed to direct the film. Pyle returned with him to Los Angeles to work on polishing the script. According to the director, he and Pyle collaborated to create "a great shooting script. Cruel, factual, unaffected, genuine, and with a heart as big as Ernie's. This was the story of G.I. Joe."[52]

In the conventional sense of Hollywood's dramatic films, *G.I. Joe* had no plot, no story that built up to a grand climax. It simply followed an infantry unit in battle and at rest as it slogged up the Italian peninsula. In documentary style, the film recorded the interactions of the men, their foibles, and their longings to be home or anywhere but in war. *G.I. Joe* succeeded in visualizing Ernie Pyle's newspaper columns. The filmmakers may have changed the men's names, but the film portrayed their experiences. It contained no Hollywood theatrics. Moreover, Wellman avoided the usual formula—

William Wellman, director of *Wings* (1927), *The Story of G.I. Joe* (1945), and *Battleground* (1949), in a 1975 photo.

single-handed heroics, dramatic firefights, and a little romance on the side. In a Hollywood rarity of that time, no women appeared in the film. *G.I. Joe* showed men at war, trying to survive—no more, no less.

The rewriting and polishing of the script ended in mid-November 1944, when Wellman was about ready to begin shooting. Although the Army had promised full cooperation, Wellman required only a limited amount of military hardware. Mostly, he needed experienced soldiers, and the War Department agreed to provide 150 veterans of the Italian campaign who were then in transit to the Pacific Theater. Their stay in California served as a respite from combat, but during the six weeks of filming the officers and men carried on their regular training when not before the cameras.

The Army stressed that since "it is the plan of everyone concerned to have the troops make the best possible appearance in the film both in physical condition and in military techniques, the training program will be rigorously pursued." The Army expected the men to show "exemplary conduct" and warned that it would deal sternly with any trouble in public places. The service allowed the men to let their beards grow, but only "for purposes of realism in combat scenes." Nevertheless, since the soldiers had experienced some of the worst fighting in Europe and were heading to the Pacific, the studio tried to make their stay in Hollywood enjoyable by providing them spending money and entertainment.[53]

Wellman had his own instructions for the soldiers. When they had settled in their quarters, the director asked the officer in charge to assemble them so he could "straighten them out." He wanted to be sure that the soldiers knew what the film meant to them, to him, and to Pyle. Although Pyle had told the G.I.s about Wellman's change in attitude toward the infantry, Wellman wanted to make his feelings clear. He told them, "Look, you have a goddamn broken down old flier who is going to be your boss. Now you have to make up your mind that I'm a tough son of a bitch. I want you to do just exactly what I want you to do. But I'll never double-cross you. I'll never ask you to do something you don't want to do." He told them that *G.I. Joe* would not become just another war picture, "but something that you, Ernie, and I will be proud of. That's a big expensive job, that's why you are here, that's why actors have been training with you, so they will look like you, handle themselves the way you do. That's also why a lot of you fellas will be playing scenes, speaking lines. I want to make this the goddamndest most honest picture that has ever been made about the doughfoot."[54]

To prepare the actors ("as few as possible") for their roles, Wellman insisted that they go through regular training with the soldiers and live with them. He wanted them to act and smell like soldiers, and he made this requirement very clear when he cast them: "Look, you are going to live with the group or you don't get the job." Wellman also selected several of the soldiers themselves for speaking roles. He told them: "All through the picture, when a G.I. has something to say, I want a G.I. to say it, not some bastard G.I. You know the story is good, and it's real, and it's beautifully written by a man whose very life is you." He assured them the camera would not "bite," but it would "pick up everything, and what I want it to pick up is honesty and sincerity." With a little luck, he said, "when it's all over, you'll see something up there that will be more than a picture of the infantry; it might just be a monument, and I am going to make it that if it breaks my ass."[55]

Wellman recalled that the men responded by learning their lines and carrying out their orders: "All those kids that were in it were great, and they all went to the South Pacific, and none of them came home." Nor did Ernie Pyle, who died covering one of the island landings. The director wondered, "How does that make you feel? You, the man that directed the picture, that got to know all of them and liked most of them. How do you feel? [I] felt lousy. . . . but at least we had some fun together. We were shooting, but [with] blanks, and nobody was getting hurt. We had a lot of laughs together, a lot of work, a lot of drinks. . . . It all seems so futile now. It's the one picture of mine that I refuse to look at."[56]

Thanks to the commitment of Wellman and the real soldiers, *The Story of G.I. Joe* provides an image of men in combat which few other American films have created. General Eisenhower called it "the greatest war picture I've ever seen." When the men of the Fifth Army in Italy, some of whom had fought in the campaigns portrayed, saw the film, they reacted with: "This is it!"[57] Lewis Milestone's *A Walk in the Sun*, released in November 1945, created a similar impact by focusing on even fewer men during a single action. Nevertheless, *The Story of G.I. Joe*, of all the films made during the war period, best visualized the nature of the infantrymen in combat, the day-to-day struggles with the elements and a formidable enemy.

Wellman succeeded in doing this by making the faces of his actors and the combat veterans symbolize all the young men about whom the American people had been reading since December 7, 1941. Approaching Ernie Pyle's experiences and writings with a starkly documentary style, Wellman concentrated on the lives of average soldiers, not on the false heroics usually portrayed in Hollywood war movies. Having committed himself to telling the story of Ernie Pyle and his relationship with the infantrymen, Wellman created a film containing an "extreme sensitivity and deep tenderness for manly human beings."[58]

To Dudley Nichols, the inclusion of Pyle as a character in the film elevated *The Story of G.I. Joe* above the level of "an almost monotonous story of a company of foot soldiers." He explained that using Pyle proved a beautiful "device," one that is "used as pure film, what I would call screen-film, and not the kind of stage-film we frequently are given because it is easier to write words than to imagine pure film." Nichols observed that Pyle seldom talked in the movie, and when he did, "there is no eloquence. But in his silences, in his contained compassion, his profound sense of tragedy and waste, there is a continued eloquence that soars beyond the scope of words."[59]

John Huston's documentary *The Battle of San Pietro* (1945) is the only other movie made during the war that contains an equally eloquent statement about the American experience in World War II. Huston created his feeling of war through the use of combat footage that he and his Signal Corps cameraman took during and after the Battle of San Pietro. He does not dwell on individuals, does not develop characters with whom viewers identify as in a dramatic film. Using the camera to report rather than tell the story, Huston captured the sense of the war's impersonality, the individual's insignificance, the impermanence of life itself. Even though *San Pietro* remains a documentary showing real men, the film presents no less an illusion of war than the fictionalized *Story of G.I. Joe*.

All film creates an illusion of reality. The camera sees and captures only what the filmmaker allows it to record. Reality, in contrast, exists only in the continuity of unbroken images. Once a camera stops, once an editor cuts the strip of celluloid, the image projected on the screen becomes the vision the filmmaker chooses to present. For example, the other great documentary of the war, *The Memphis Belle*, ends with the B-17's return from its twenty-fifth mission over Germany. But in fact, William Wyler switched the actual twenty-fifth mission, a relatively easy bombing of submarine pens on the French coast, with the twenty-fourth mission over Germany, because of the greater dramatic impact of striking at the enemy's homeland.[60]

Whether viewing a documentary or a dramatic film, the audience sees an illusion of love, hate, peace, or war. How close any of these images approximate reality depends on the skills of the filmmakers, their scripts, the resources available to them. Even in the best of circumstances, as in the making of *The Story of G.I. Joe*, the filmmaker cannot recreate all the realities of war. Wellman, in reminiscing about his film, touched on the problem of communicating this sense of authenticity, of being there: "The writing, poetry of the doughfoot, cruel poetry but so honest, so tragic, so miserable, so lonely, and so many wonderful kids gone. You can't replace them, ever, but maybe you can stop wars so we don't keep adding to that castigated list. Castigate—'to punish in order to correct.' It's a hell of a punishment, and we haven't corrected a thing."[61]

7 | World War II:
       First Reflections

BY THE TIME WELLMAN'S FILM APPEARED, HOWEVER, the war had ended and people wanted to get on with their lives, not think about the recent horrors or seek ways to eliminate future carnage. The motion picture industry had long anticipated the disinterest audiences would have in revisiting the conflict and had begun to cut back on the number of combat stories in production once battlefield successes in Europe and the Pacific assured imminent Allied victory. Like *G.I. Joe, They Were Expendable* and *Walk in the Sun* appeared after the Japanese surrender and, validating Hollywood's business acumen, languished at the box office, despite their realistic portrayals of men in combat and excellent reviews.

With this antipathy in mind, Warner Brothers suspended pre-production on *Task Force* less than a month after the Japanese surrender, although shooting was about to begin after more than a year's work on the project. Instead, Hollywood focused its attention on stories of the returning veterans, including *Pride of the Marines, Best Years of Our Lives,* and *Till the End of Time,* all of which deal with the transition of servicemen from war to peace. Only occasionally did a studio make a movie having anything to do with the war itself. Even when it did use the recent war as the stage, as in *13 Rue Madeleine,* the film told the story of espionage in the days immediately proceeding D-Day, rather than about men in combat.

The cessation of the production of combat movies after the V-J Day did not, of course, signify the end of Hollywood's interest in war stories. However, as in the years immediately after World War I, filmmakers faced the question of how soon the public would again be ready to spend money to see the war fought on a screen. During 1947 several studios began discussing possible military projects, and by early 1948 two small-scale films had gone into production. MGM's *Command Decision,* based on the 1947 play of the same name, dealt with the strategic bombing of Germany during the buildup of American air strength. The studio shot the picture mostly on its soundstages, integrating some combat footage to set the context, and released it in late 1948.

More ambitiously, Warner Brothers's *Fighter Squadron,* also appearing at the end of 1948, portrayed a P-47 fighter group, which included a young Rock Hudson as one of the fliers, stationed in England in 1944. Combining color gun-camera footage that the Army Air Corps had begun using in June 1944 with limited assistance from the Michigan Air National Guard, Warner Brothers created a visually exciting film about fighter planes during and after the Normandy invasion. Like *Wings,* the story served only to fill the moments between episodes of *Fighter Squadron's* raison d'être, the war in the air. The combat footage provided the film an authenticity and a sense of realism that Wellman's re-creation could only approximate.

In contrast to *Wings,* in *Fighter Squadron* the on-screen aerial combat takes place between real planes and pilots locked in mortal battle. Audiences did not have to pretend

A P-47 Thunderbolt attacks a
German airfield during filming of
Fighter Squadron.

they were watching reality. Real men had flown the fighters. Some had lived and some had actually died on the screen.

These early films and virtually all subsequent World War II combat stories did lack one significant character, the evil German or the evil Jap. To be sure, in *13 Rue Madeleine,* Gestapo officers administer a horrific beating to Jimmy Cagney as they try to elicit information from him about the impending Normandy invasion. As portrayed, however, the Germans were simply doing their jobs. Cagney, as an Office of Special Services operative, would have readily admitted that he would have used the same techniques in trying to obtain information from an enemy agent. By the time the film appeared at the end of 1946, however, the Office of War Information had been out of business for more than a year.

Why did Hollywood continue to moderate its portrayals of the former enemy after the war? What organization had assumed the responsibility for ensuring that these images would contribute to the future rehabilitation of Germany and Japan? What modus operandi accomplished this mission? Hollywood's financial backers certainly recognized that films with negative portrayals of the recent enemies would not have appeal in either country. However, such concerns remained moot until theaters opened again and people had more to occupy their time and resources than simple survival.

In fact, the impetus for the ongoing positive portrayal of Germany in motion pictures came from the same place as the November 1943 anti-atrocity directive. Less than two weeks after V-E Day, the War Department informed Taylor Mills, chief of the Office of War Information's Bureau of Motion Pictures, that the Army was making plans to take a representative group of motion picture executives to Europe. The service's Public Affairs Office stressed that "it is of the utmost importance to the Army that certain key men of the industry be included for the mutual facilitation of the production of certain, immediate films in which the Army has a current and specific interest." It explained that the War Department wanted Harry Cohn, president of Columbia Pictures; Nicholas Schenck, president of MGM; Barney Balaban, president of Paramount; Spyros Skouras and Darryl Zanuck, president and head of production, respectively, at Twentieth Century Fox; and Harry and Jack Warner, president and head of production, respectively, at Warner Brothers, to receive invitations. If any of the men could not accept, the office said their studios could send an alternate, but that "for the purposes of this trip it is not advisable to include writers."[1]

Mills sent the letter to Francis Harmon, executive vice chairman of the film industry's War Activities Committee. He wrote that the War Department wanted to include executives "who might be instrumental in the production of certain important feature pictures which the Army feels might well come out of the war devastated areas in Europe." Mills believed that the War Department foresaw "public pressure developing within the next eighteen or twenty-five months to bear on occupational troops." If Hollywood made appropriate films about the situation in Europe, Mills thought that the American people would better appreciate "the importance of the magnitude of the problem of reindoctrinating eighty million Nazis so that war will not again come to this world in the next twenty years" and so allow the military to keep occupation troops in Europe.[2]

In his formal invitation to Harmon on June 14, Maj. Gen. A.D. Surles, director of the Army's Bureau of Public Relations, said the tour members "will have an opportunity to study various problems affecting the United States Army in Europe, with emphasis upon redeployment, Army of Occupation and the operation American Military Government." Before embarking, the executives, including Cohen, Balaban, Jack Warner, and Zanuck, had lunch with Army Chief of Staff George C. Marshall on June 16 in the Pentagon. Thanking the filmmakers for their contribution to the war effort, Marshall told them: "All other weapons are not worth anything without morale. Your industry has contributed much to morale and you will contribute more."[3]

In the preface to *Western Europe in the Wake of World War II,* the report Harmon wrote following the tour, he explained that movies in all their forms "must now be used to the uttermost in the titanic struggle to cleanse the minds, change the attitudes, and ultimately win the cooperation of the German people. An entire generation of German youth must be trained to live at peace with their fellows in a world so small that any future war will be nothing less than planetary suicide." According to Harmon, General Eisenhower wanted the studio executives "to make a first hand study of ways and means for using films to help accomplish the unfinished tasks which confront us in the transition from war to peace."[4]

Hollywood had, of course, contributed mightily to the war effort, not only with feature films that extolled the virtues of democracy and the evils of the Axis powers but also with endless shorts showing how the home front could contribute to victory. Whether the standard Hollywood fare of westerns, gangster movies, comedies, musicals, and war films could help reeducate the German people, who had lived through twelve years of unrelenting Nazi propaganda, was highly questionable.

Lt. Col. P. Lieven, a Canadian and chief of the Communications Section of the British Military Government in Hamburg, expressed such concerns to the executives. He told them that any movies they exported to Germany should show American life without propaganda and should not include gangster films. He also counseled against releasing the anti-German wartime films, since, he said, they contained "inaccuracies" and would become a source of humor to the discredit of the British and Americans. Instead, he suggested that Hollywood should send entertainment films showing Americans and British "as reasonable people—living happily.[5]

Despite their wartime service, however, once the fighting stopped, the motion picture industry had little interest in serving as an instrument of change in Germany and sent any film abroad that might make money, which has always remained Hollywood's only reason for existence. The ostensive reason for the tour notwithstanding, the Army's implicit goal for the tour quickly became clear. During the trip, from June 17 to July 18, which included stops in England, France, Belgium, Holland, Germany, Poland, Italy, and North Africa, in not very subtle terms, the executives received regular warnings about the threat that the Soviet Union now posed and the concurrent need to cleanse American minds of their wartime anti-German feelings. To impress these concerns upon the executives, the Army arranged for them to meet Field Marshall Bernard Montgomery, a top aide to Winston Churchill, and the Pope. More important, perhaps, they also received regular briefings from lower-level military officers and met anti-Nazi Germans.

Officially, the military expressed the hope that the Allies would be able to resolve their differences over the future of Central Europe. Gen. Mark Clark, then deputy Army commander in Europe, told the executives, "We *must* get along with the Russians." Montgomery echoed this when he told the executives on June 29: "The fighting men have won the war. It is now up to the statesmen to win the peace." For the most part, however, the tour members received less optimistic predictions for future peace.[6]

British Air Marshall Arthur Tedder, for one, warned the executives about the potential confrontation with Russia when he said: "Gentlemen, we are facing an important phase in the history of western civilization. East is East and West is West, but now they have met and that's that! One role which you of motion pictures can play is to give the people back home a true picture of this situation."[7]

Sol Lesser, the producer of the Tarzan movies in the 1930s and 1940s, later recalled: "We were then allies of Russia and most of the commanders who talked to us introduced the subject: 'For God's sake, get the message home. The war isn't over until we get all the territorial things settled with the Russians and the other allies. And so we better stay armed.'" By that time, however, Lesser noted that Americans were already beginning to clamor for demobilization.[8]

This reality made the rehabilitation of the German people that much more urgent from the perspective of both the victors and the vanquished. In his meeting with the executives, Montgomery stressed the need to reeducate the Germans, but he warned: "This cannot be done blatantly. It must be done carefully." To do this, he explained: "What we want today is films! Uplifting and enlightening films are needed in Germany at once. Only last week Zhukoff (Soviet marshal) said to me: '*He who controls the cinema, controls Germany.*'"[9]

In fact, the German people had not yet had time to come to terms with having supported Hitler and the Third Reich. Nowhere did this become clearer than during the meeting in Hamburg on July 2, with Pastor Volkmar Heintricht, a Lutheran minister who had been imprisoned for his hostility to the Nazi regime. He told the executives: "It is hard for you to realize the power of the demonic National Socialist propaganda. National Socialism did away with God and built up the State and man as its ideals. Hitler was worshiped as a god and his words were accepted as a command." Heintricht said he wanted to win back the young Germans from this indoctrination as the Communists had already started to do.[10]

In contrast, he wanted to provide God as "the fountainhead of justice and a just power in the world." He maintained that the German people had no opinion about responsibility for the war because "it is too soon after the fall of the Nazis for any national public opinion to crystallize." He said the people were surprised to hear about the concentration camps and reported that people believed the atrocities resulted from "the mistake of the National Socialists and we had no special part in it."[11]

Heintricht also reported that he had heard a man say he felt no guilt over the death camps because thousands of Germans had died in the Allied bombing. Nevertheless, he did not want the Allies to show documentaries about the bombings of Rotterdam or Coventry or the concentration camp atrocities: "I doubt the curing effect of a negative policy." Instead, he advocated using anti-Nazis to lead the reeducation campaign and said any films sent to Germany should stress positive aspects of life and show man's respect for his fellow man.[12]

Then in Berlin, the executives confronted the ultimate good German–bad German dilemma in the person of Dr. Martin Niemoller, a World War I U-boat commander and highly respected pastor whom Hitler had thrown into prison for his opposition to the Third Reich. Niemoller told the executives that up to 1938, Germans must accept guilt for supporting Hitler, but that afterward the Nazis had the country by the throat. He explained: "I could not stand in a pulpit and tell 'the little people' in my congregation that they, individually, were responsible for events after 1938." He pointed out that many people had joined the party because their friends had, not because of any commitment to Hitler. He did believe the people responsible for the atrocities, whom he limited to the Gestapo and war criminals, should be punished.[13]

Despite his strong anti-Nazi views, Niemoller had volunteered to return to the submarine service after seven years in solitary confinement, but the government turned him down, saving him from the dilemma of having to take the oath of allegiance to Hitler. Trying to justify his actions, he said, "My body belongs to the state though my soul belongs to God." However, he acknowledged that the decision to offer his services to Hitler had left him with "a bad conscience." Francis Harmon recognized that Niemoller personified the German paradox: "A queer mixture of U-boat Captain and German theologian who consulted not only his conscience but his wife and his lawyers."[14]

Yet, he also represented the good German whom the Allies would need to help purge the country from its Nazi past. The loudest voice of the need for films to show the American people that good Germans existed came from Will Rowland, a civilian in charge of films for SHAFE in Bavaria, and an Army medical officer whom Harmon chose not to identify by name. Rowland told the executives that they must show the Germans positively or the Russians would. He also suggested that the filmmakers should show the positive side of American life.[15]

The doctor warned: "You cannot speak against the German people, you can only speak against the Nazis. We are deposing the Nazis but some of them are still going around adding to the black market problems through liberal use of the paper money they still have." He cautioned further: Your films will fail in Germany unless you understand the human situation. *Good art demands good observation and sympathetic understanding.*"[16]

Nowhere did this "understanding" by the film industry become more obvious than in the executives' nonreaction to the concentration camps. Harmon does write that the tour took an "interesting" motor trip to Dachau on July 3, which he described as the "model concentration camp of the Nazis. . . . where their hapless victims were butchered, gassed, and starved to death and their bodies burned in a battery of specially constructed furnaces." He mentions that the tour group received a brochure about Dachau, but he never acknowledges the identity of the vast majority of the people who died. In fact, he never refers to the genocide of the Jews in his report, and not even the head of the Jewish Aid Society mentioned the subject.[17]

Clearly the VIP tour served the War Department well. During and immediately after the hostilities in Europe, the OWI, in concert with the Army, had released newsreel footage of the German death camps. However, most people probably ignored the grizzly scenes, which remained outside their frame of reference, or simply went to the popcorn stand during the screening. Instead, they were to see feature films that portrayed Germans and Japanese in a positive light, since not one of the film executives on the VIP tour returned to Hollywood and made any anti-German or Holocaust movies. Hitler and his cohorts became the only scapegoats. Likewise, only the Japanese warlords receive negative portrayals in movies about the war in the Pacific.

Battleground usually receives credit for initiating the cycle, because of its critical acclaim and box-office success. In fact, it appeared almost simultaneously with *Task Force*, *Sands of Iwo Jima*, and *Twelve O'Clock High*. However, *Task Force* had its origins more than two years before the other three films. When Warner Brothers initiated the project in early 1944, the company anticipated that the war might end before it could complete the film. So it conceived of *Task Force* as both a dramatized history of naval aviation and an account of World War II carrier warfare.

Despite this broadened approach, after V-J Day the studio shelved the project, though allowing producer Jerry Wald and writer-director Delmer Daves to continue developing a screenplay and collecting combat footage. Having written scripts for *Shipmates* and *Shipmates Forever*, and having written and directed *Destination Tokyo*, Daves had established close contacts with the Navy by early 1944, when he had first discussed with Navy officials the possibility of making a major movie about the development of aircraft carriers. By April 1945, he, Wald, and writer Ranald MacDougall had researched the history of naval aviation and compiled an extensive set of story notes. Daves had also begun looking at Navy documentaries and newsreel footage that traced the story pictorially. The Navy helped by tracking down and selecting the best combat footage sent back from the Pacific. In formally assigning junior officers to the task in mid-May, the secretary and the undersecretary of the Navy indicated they were "interested in the successful production" of the Warner Brothers film.[18]

MacDougall turned in a preliminary script at the end of June, a revised script in July, a completed script at the end of August, and a final script in October. All of these 1945 versions, as well as the final script written by Daves in 1948, tell basically the same story of the struggle of Navy officers committed to the development of aircraft carriers and naval aviation. As the composite officer, Gary Cooper flies off the first Navy carrier, the USS *Langley*, during the 1920s. He so strongly advocates the need for a carrier fleet that he has his career sidetracked in the 1930s. During the war, he commands a carrier and soon after retires as an admiral, receiving a salute from Navy jets in a flyover as he departs from one of the new sixty-thousand-ton floating airfields. The fictional story serves primarily as a framework around which the film portrays the historical development of naval air power. As a result, *Task Force* lacks the dramatic impact of other military films that focus on individuals and their efforts to survive during battle. Nonetheless, the combat footage, carefully selected and superbly integrated into the second half of the film, effectively provides the audience with the ambience of carrier warfare.

One line from an early draft screenplay summed up the theme of *Task Force*, the struggle of a small group of naval aviators for planes and carriers: "You might as well know appropriations for aviation are hard to get—that our planes were not designed for carrier operations. We do our best with what we have."[19] In addition, the film contains a strong implicit Navy message: that aircraft carriers won the war in the Pacific and can protect the nation against any future aggression. In fact, the studio advanced the film's release date several months so that it appeared at the height of the Air Force–Navy battle waged in Congress over appropriations for bombers versus aircraft carriers.

Anticipating the contemporary debate, the film's characters debate senators, Army officers, and battleship admirals about the efficacy of carriers over other military hardware.

In one scene a senator observes that the service lost four carriers in the first six months of the war, and a Navy flier asks, "Is it your contention, Senator, that we should abandon *airplanes*—because they've been shot down? Tanks—because they've been knocked out of action? We need to out-produce the enemy in planes, tanks, and aircraft carriers! The only thing wrong with carriers is that we don't have enough of them!" Later in the meeting, Gary Cooper responds to a general's argument in favor of land-based bombers: "The General is right—*if* we have to take every Pacific Island en route to Japan. But two dozen carriers are worth more than 200 enemy-held islands, anchored in one spot! Our carriers won't be anchored—they'll be fast moving islands from which we can launch fighters and bombers against the enemy wherever we choose!"[20]

These arguments clearly represented the position of the Navy's aviation branch. By the time *Task Force* appeared, the advocates of aircraft carriers had received vindication, and the film became a monument to their victory as well as a tribute to the contribution carriers had made to winning the war in the Pacific. Warner Brothers admitted that the decision to advance the release date sprang from a desire to take advantage of public interest aroused by the congressional hearings over the bomber-versus-aircraft-carrier issue. The Navy denied that it had asked the studio to move up the film's release date. The Navy also did not construct the arguments in favor of carriers for the script, however much it later approved of them. The scripts of August and October 1945, which Daves wrote four years before the Army-Navy confrontation, contain virtually the same dialogue as the final screenplay.[21]

To be sure, the Navy had contributed to *Task Force*'s pitch for aircraft carriers. The friendships both Daves and Wald had developed with Navy men while working on earlier films undoubtedly influenced their perceptions of the service. Moreover, during their five years of research, they worked solely with aviators who had a procarrier bias. Finally, the actual history of the war in the Pacific, from Midway onward, clearly demonstrated the importance of carriers in defeating the Japanese.

Message aside, *Task Force* became the first major postwar film made with large-scale military assistance to bring World War II to American theaters. Daves spent many weeks aboard carriers during normal training exercises and then took his film crew to sea to shoot interior scenes. The Navy also permitted him to land and take off vintage aircraft for his cameras. He then combined these sequences with the extensive Navy combat footage he had collected during his initial work on the project to make a movie which portrayed the reality of war in ways no special-effects men could duplicate.[22]

In the dramatic highlight of the movie, a kamikaze attack on Cooper's carrier turns the ship into a flaming wreck. Using color footage taken aboard the USS *Franklin,* the most extensively damaged ship in World War II to return to port, the filmmakers gave the audience a sense of the horror of combat. Real flames are engulfing an American carrier, not a studio set or special-effects miniature. The dead sailors will not get up and walk away. Makeup artists will not wash away the men's burns as they do with actors when they complete a scene. So despite its pseudo-documentary style and lack of a dramatic story line, *Task Force* created an emotional impact unequaled by most war films.

In contrast to the epic dimensions and great sweep of time portrayed in *Task Force,* the next major postwar film, *Battleground,* focused on the actions of a small group of men caught up in a single major battle. Yet, virtually all of the action took place within the controlled environment of a soundstage, not on an outdoor location. The film created its version of war not by using combat footage and great numbers of soldiers but by developing the characters of individual soldiers and their reactions to unexpected adversity.

The struggle to make *Battleground* provides enough material for its own movie. When Dore Schary first conceived the project in early 1947, while head of production at RKO, he received strong opposition from executives who felt that audiences were not yet interested in attending war movies. Schary himself feared that Americans might experience the same sort of disillusionment that swept the country after World War I. To him, therefore, "it was imperative to do a film about World War II that would say the war was worth fighting despite the terrible losses. . . . The men who fought this war were not suckers. They had not been used. There was something at stake. It was the first time, in a long, long time, hundreds of years, that there had been a real danger of a takeover by a very evil and strong force."[23]

To symbolize this threat, Schary looked for a specific situation in World War II in which the Allied cause was in jeopardy. Believing that Hollywood had well visualized the war in the Pacific, he turned to the European Theater, which he believed filmmakers had portrayed during the war in only "a couple of very good pictures." Schary considered the rest to have been "kind of bang-bang pictures" with virtually none showing the fighting during the period after Normandy. He decided that a portrayal of the crucial siege of Bastogne during the Battle of the Bulge would represent the threat to freedom he was seeking. As a result, he called in Bob Pirosh, a writer who had served in Europe, and asked him what he knew about Bastogne. "Know anything?" he responded, "I was there!"[24]

Pirosh had come out of the war with notes on his experiences and a desire to do a movie about the Battle of the Bulge. Consequently, after his meeting with Schary, he began work on the project, but under the title *Prelude to Love* to disguise its subject, explaining that Schary "did not want anyone in the industry to know I was making a war film." In April 1947 Pirosh, in an initial step, returned to the battlefields where he had fought. He quickly decided to content himself "with an attempt to portray the activities of one squad of riflemen—without heroics, without fancy speeches, without a phony romance." He wanted to write "a picture which would ring true to the men [who had fought there] and which would not be an insult to the memory of those we left there." Pirosh felt that the story of one squad "was, in a sense, the story of all squads. I happened to be sent to

William Wellman talks to screenwriter Bob Pirosh (center left) and producer Dore Schary on the outdoor lot used for opening drill scenes in *Battleground* (1949).

Europe, you happened to wind up in the Pacific, somebody else sweated it out in the Aleutians. The important thing is, what did it do to us? How did we feel?"[25]

Although Pirosh had fought in the Battle of the Bulge, he had not served in the 101st Division, which the Germans had surrounded for eight days at Bastogne. He worried that he might not be able to develop a true-to-life script and so sought advice from Gen. Anthony McAuliffe, who had commanded the 101st Division during the siege and whose succinct "Nuts!" to the German demand for surrender had become the symbol of American determination during the war. Pirosh wanted to know whether his not having fought at Bastogne would hamper him in producing an accurate script. McAuliffe, responded with another "Nuts!" He told Pirosh, "You were fighting under the same kind of conditions. You were just as cold, the fog was just as thick, the suspense was just as great. Go ahead and write it the way you feel it."[26]

Meanwhile, Schary was testing the market for a war film by broaching the subject to sales representatives who visited the West Coast. Disagreeing with their negative evaluations, he polled movie exhibitors across the country by phone and by letter. When they indicated that a good war film would draw audiences, Schary formally announced the project, now titled *Battleground*.[27]

Pirosh finished his first draft of the screenplay in mid-January 1948, and by early spring, Schary, who was personally producing the picture, had begun to cast the main roles. At that point Howard Hughes suddenly bought RKO. Initially, he allowed Schary to continue running the studio, but when he told the producer to take *Battleground* off the studio's production schedule, Schary resigned, telling Hughes that he was "too tough" and "too rich" to fight. He requested only that Hughes sell him the script of *Battleground*, to which he agreed.[28]

When Schary became head of production at MGM a few weeks later, he advised Louis B. Mayer, the head of the studio, that he wanted *Battleground* to become his first film. Mayer expressed the same reservations about a producing a war story that Schary had already encountered at RKO. Nevertheless, neither he nor Nicholas Schenck, president of Loew's, the distributing branch of MGM, wanted to oppose Schary too strongly so soon after his return to the studio, especially since they knew how strongly he felt about *Battleground*. Consequently, Mayer suggested that they allow Schary to make the movie, and if it failed, they would be better able to keep him under control. Although Schenck agreed, the project quickly became known as "Schary's folly."[29]

With studio approval in hand, Schary asked Hughes how much he wanted for the screenplay of *Battleground*. Hughes said he wanted only what the studio had spent on writing the script, about twenty thousand dollars, which Schary considered a "bargain." He then brought Pirosh to MGM to complete the screenplay and arranged with General McAuliffe and the Army to provide some veterans of the 101st Division's struggle at Bastogne as extras on the film. Schary also supervised the casting of the principal roles, including Van Johnson, James Whitmore, and George Murphy, all veterans of earlier war films.[30]

The producer kept the film essentially an all-male production, but the script did include one woman, a French farm girl who feeds some of the soldiers during a lull in the battle. For that part, Schary hired Denise Darcel, "a buxom, juicy French girl" who, he said, "sashayed into the office with ample, rounded buttocks and breasts that, as she walked, presented a movable feast." An MGM public relations man later went so far as to suggest that the success of *Battleground* could be attributed to an ad showing Darcel in a tight black sweater. She was cutting a loaf of bread—with the knife coming perilously close to

A helmeted William Wellman rehearses his actors (including James Whitmore to the director's left) and soldiers from the 101st Airborne Division on a soundstage with writer Pirosh (center, also in helmet) listening intently.

Snow-covered Bastogne recreated outdoors in Culver City, one of the few exterior locales for *Battleground*.

her breasts. William Wellman, who directed the film, did not think that a war film should have included "that kind of stuff." He said he would not have put a girl in *The Story of G.I. Joe* "for all the money in the world." Nevertheless, he conceded that cinematically Darcel's breasts proved "wonderful to play with." Actually, given the quality of the picture and the critical acclaim it received, the public relations man undoubtedly gave his ad too much credit for the success of *Battleground*.[31]

Wellman became an obvious choice to direct *Battleground*, given his successful portrayal of infantrymen in *G.I. Joe*. Though he claimed to dislike Schary and did not agree with his desire to put messages in film, Wellman's animosity was naturally directed toward anyone who might interfere with his work. He recalled, "I hate all producers, frankly, if you want to know the truth!" However, he did like Pirosh's screenplay, and when the studio offered him "an awful lot of money to do it," he agreed to direct the film. Nevertheless, he told Schary, "Look, I can't make a *G.I. Joe* out of this thing. I'll make a film about a very tired group of guys."[32]

Both the studio and the military went all out to help the director make *Battleground* as realistic as possible. Since the Battle of the Bulge had taken place over snow-covered terrain, the studio faced a major problem in creating a winterlike atmosphere. To do this, Schary took out a wall between two soundstages and fabricated a huge indoor battlefield, giving Wellman a completely controlled environment in which to work. Apart from the obvious benefit of not having to worry about melting snow, he had a set that facilitated lighting and filming. For scenes in which G.I.s moved across open spaces, Wellman used

Denise Darcel provides the only respite from combat in *Battleground*.

rear-view projection of actual long shots. For large movements of men and trucks, the film editor matched staged action with a limited amount of combat footage. Wellman shot only the opening and closing sequences outdoors. Unlike *Battle of the Bulge*, made in Spain in 1964, in which snow-capped mountains and palm trees appeared in the background and dust replaced snow as the tanks roar into combat, *Battleground* had carefully dressed exteriors that matched both the interior shots and the combat footage.[33]

General McAuliffe and the Army liked the project from its inception. McAuliffe's interest stemmed from his original discussion with Pirosh about the story, and he served as a technical advisor for the writing of the script. He also recommended Lt. Col. Harry W.O. Kinnard, who had served under him at Bastogne, to serve as technical advisor during the shooting. McAuliffe helped arrange for the Army to send twenty members of the 101st Division from Fort Bragg to Los Angeles to serve as extras during the production. Wellman had his actors train with the soldiers, as he had done during the making of *G.I. Joe*, so that they would perform in military fashion. The Army also provided Wellman with a couple of tanks, trucks, and other needed equipment.[34]

"Was the trip necessary?" A chaplain asks the question at the end of the film, after the siege of Bastogne has ended. The rhetorical query served as the instrument for inserting Schary's rationale for making *Battleground*. His message, conveyed through Pirosh's script, responded to the Nazi threat: "Nobody wanted this war except the Nazis. A great many people tried to deal with them, and a lot of them are dead. Millions have died for no other reason except that the Nazis wanted them dead." Their actions gave the Americans no choice but to fight. The chaplain, Schary's mouthpiece, saw in this a great lesson, and "those of us who are learning it the hard way are not going to forget. . . . We must never again let any kind of force dedicated to a super race or a super idea or a super anything get strong enough to impose itself on a free world. We have to be smart enough and tough enough in the beginning to put out the fire before it starts spreading."[35]

The commentary and the film itself reflected the manner in which Hollywood was going to portray Germany during the next two decades. The blame for the war rested with the "Nazis," not the German population as a whole. The narrative explicitly criticized Hitler's philosophy, not the beliefs of the German people. In *Battleground* no evil Ger-

"Was this trip necessary?" asks the chaplain on MGM's winterized soundstage as he verbalized Dore Schary's rationale for making *Battleground*.

mans appear. The film makes no mention of the German army's violation of international law prohibiting soldiers from wearing enemy uniforms or of the German massacre of American prisoners at Malmédy.

Message and rehabilitation aside, *Battleground* justified the efforts put into its production. Wellman did think it became "very movie-picture like," in contrast to *G.I. Joe*, which he felt contained a "real" ambience of men in combat. Although the incidents in *Battleground* actually occurred, Pirosh had distilled them in his screenplay, and the film became essentially a motion picture story, in contrast to the documentary quality of *G.I. Joe*. Wellman felt that the fact the war was still being fought and the soldier extras would be returning to battle at the end of the production underlay the fabric of the film. This sense of impending doom gave *G.I. Joe* a quality that *Battleground*, made during peacetime, could not attain. Nevertheless, Wellman conceded that a lot of people liked the second film better: "I don't know why. I guess because there was a lot of humor, a dirty kind of humor."[36]

This humor helped make *Battleground* a box-office success. A nation at peace could laugh at a big-breasted girl's efforts to cut a loaf of bread without doing herself bodily harm; people could laugh at jokes about a soldier's lost teeth; audiences could enjoy the well-staged combat sequences without having to worry about boys at the front who might be dying. Schary may have made the movie to remind the nation of the reasons men had had to die, but both he and Wellman knew that in peacetime, a war film had to do more than create a patriotic feeling in its audience. *Battleground* also had to entertain, and so the filmmakers had to accept the compromises that separated it from *The Story of G.I. Joe*, the compromises that made it a war movie instead of a pseudo-documentary.

At the same time, *Battleground* offered audiences much more than most Hollywood movies. Thanks to the skill of the studio technicians and the military assistance, Wellman captured the feel of battle, the loneliness of being surrounded by a superior enemy force, the struggle against the elements and against a German force making its last effort to win the war. These feelings resulted from top-notch performances by the actors and soldier-actors, working with a taut, powerful script that only a survivor of the Battle of the Bulge could have written. To Pirosh, the commitment to the project by all those involved had made the film a "dream come true." The audience found it a grim, authentic war drama, one the nation was ready to see, however close in time it might have been to the war itself.[37]

Unlike *Battleground*, in which the soldiers endured almost continuous fire during the film, *Twelve O'Clock High* contains only a short combat sequence at the very end of the movie. The men experience war in a different context, as the film explores the problems of leadership and the terrible effect that responsibility has on a commander. As Gen. Frank Savage, Gregory Peck prepares his men for aerial combat by pushing them to their limit and beyond, setting an example by pushing himself even harder. In wanting his men to survive the air war over Europe, rather than becoming dead heroes, Savage initially alienates his officers by his hard-driving methods and cold exterior. Ultimately, his men come to realize that his teaching offers them the tools to survive and win the war.

Combat novels and movies have seldom dealt with the command-level decisions that commit men to battle and often to death. In war, of course, military officers must think of their men as numbers and impersonal units rather than as human beings, as sons, brothers, husbands, or fathers. To think of them as individuals would produce too great a psychological burden on leadership. So in war, leaders must reduce their fighting men to symbols they move on maps and commit to lists—whether of numbers of battle-ready soldiers or of casualties.

Most war literature, print or visual, has not concentrated on this level of reality or on the burden of command responsibility. The portrayals deal instead with the relationships among officers in the field, between officers and their men, or among the men themselves. Whatever their rank, these men receive orders from commanders that must be carried out without question, because soldiers, sailors, and fliers must act, not think. The dramatic conflict develops from interpersonal tensions between men or between two combating forces. Death, always close at hand, usually becomes a traumatic, individual loss. In contrast, *Twelve O'Clock High* shows the effect of the command decisions on the leaders themselves. (So well does it do so that over the years the film has continued to be used in leadership training seminars to illustrate the problems of decision making for the commander in war, business, or education.)

Even though *Twelve O'Clock High* dealt with a seldom portrayed subject, the film followed the usual complicated path from its inception as a project in the spring of 1947 to its completion in 1949. Twentieth Century Fox originally expressed interest in William Wister Haines's play *Command,* based on his novel *Command Decision.* Its plot represented "a constant and powerful undertone of the inevitable friction between staff and command," the doers versus the planners. Even so, Lyman Munson, a Fox executive, thought Haines was "either off the track or frankly overboard when he touches on the relationships between soldiers and congressmen, officers and men, and so forth." Munson did stress that with easily made revisions, the story "should make a great picture, and someone will certainly make it when the deluge of war films gets underway." Nevertheless, he advised "against touching" it unless Haines modified his financial demands, which Munson termed "utterly ridiculous."[38]

Becoming interested in another Air Force story, an as yet unpublished novel by Sy Bartlett and Beirne Lay titled *Twelve O'Clock High,* Fox did not pursue *Command,* the rights to which MGM quickly bought. Just as quickly, Munson now found the novel *Command Decision* "synthetic and artificial," saying it "does not ring true. Its characters and its situations are almost hysterically overwritten. It has no love story. . . . And unless it is drastically changed, the Air Forces will give neither cooperation nor assistance." In contrast, Munson found the novel *Twelve O'Clock High* "practically photographic in its accuracy. Its characters and its situations are plausible and believable. It has an unusual love story. And the Air Forces obviously will give to the limit with assistance, stock footage, and publicity." He noted also that "the story is jammed with incidents which are generally dramatic but also occasionally delightfully humorous." He hoped the studio would buy it.[39]

Such praise and suggestion notwithstanding, Darryl Zanuck, head of production at Twentieth Century Fox, took his time about deciding to buy the rights to the novel. He had a number of problems to face, including possible charges by MGM of plagiarism of *Command Decision,* the authors' high price for the rights to their novel, the cost of the film's production, and the feeling of Joe Schenck, Fox's president, that people were not yet ready for films about World War II. Harper and Brothers settled the plagiarism issue to Zanuck's satisfaction in September, when the company decided that *Twelve O'Clock High* told a different story from Haines's work and bought the novel.[40]

Since Bartlett already worked for Fox and wanted the studio to turn his novel into a film, he and Lay showed flexibility in their negotiations, particularly when presented with the possibility of doing the screenplay. Studio executives advised Zanuck that they could keep production costs, apart from the salaries of the director and actors, relatively low, since the film would require little set construction and material, assuming that planes and military equipment could come from the Air Force. Finally, though no one knew in 1947 how soon people would be willing to pay to see war movies, Munson told Zanuck that he disagreed with Schenck's feelings. More to the point, he saw the story not as a war movie but "primarily as a clash of personalities, as a highly dramatic, personal story of people."[41]

With these inputs before him, Zanuck decided in early October to buy *Twelve O'Clock High,* indicating to Munson that he felt it "imperative that we be prepared to go into production in late spring or early summer of 1948. He said he had already decided Gregory Peck was "the absolutely perfect choice" to play General Savage because he "has the guts, the age and the deep quality."[42] Despite Zanuck's eagerness, the studio took eighteen months to start the cameras rolling. It first had to arrange to obtain combat footage from the Air Force, not only for use in the film but also to help guide the scriptwriters and the production department. It also had to obtain a suitable script that it could submit to the Air Force as the first step in obtaining cooperation. Once the service agreed to cooperate, it had to locate equipment and find a suitable shooting locale. And Zanuck had to select a director and the rest of the cast.

By November of 1947, the Air Force had read a synopsis of the novel and expressed a willingness to provide assistance. The studio had selected Bartlett and Lay to do the screenplay, albeit with some hesitation, since Zanuck thought that the authors may "have shot

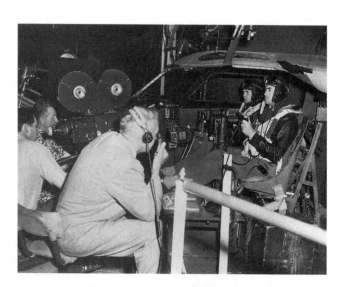

Director Henry King rehearses a scene with Gregory Peck in a B-17 mock-up for *Twelve O'Clock High* (1950).

their wad on the [novel]." Knowing that he would not hesitate to replace them if "they did not pan out early in the game," the writers worked "pretty slowly" throughout the spring and early summer. In July of 1948, Bud Lighton, the film's executive producer, noted that the studio should have expected them to proceed slowly: "They have lived together on the material long enough, between the book and the script, that I begin to gather that the marriage is wearing a bit thin." At the same time, he thought the script was beginning "to fall fairly solidly into place."[43]

Even before the writers completed their work, however, Zanuck began to worry about the Air Force's initial commitment to assist on the film. Ignoring normal channels, as he was wont to do, Zanuck went right to the top, writing on a personal, first-name basis to Air Force Chief of Staff Hoyt Vandenberg in an attempt to ascertain the service's current position. He reminded the general that *Gentleman's Agreement* had won him an Oscar as best picture of 1947 and that he had the film rights to *Twelve O'Clock High*, a best-seller that had impressed all the Air Force men he had met.

Getting down to business, Zanuck explained he was hesitant to invest the $2 million needed to turn the book into a movie given the current situation in the film industry and the need for "so-called sure-fire entertainment." He noted that *Twelve O'Clock High* could not be "classed as orthodox entertainment. It is a powerful, sincere, and dramatic story and a glorification of the officers and men of the Eighth Air Force. There is no doubt in my mind that unquestionably it can serve as tremendous propaganda to stimulate interest in the Air Force." To further his case, Zanuck said he had temporarily assigned William Wellman to direct the film. However, before proceeding, he needed to know if the Air Force wanted the film made and if so, whether he could expect its assistance.[44]

Despite Zanuck's request for an answer within a week, an invitation to the general to visit him in Palm Springs, and some high-powered name dropping (Gen. Mark Clark, Harry Luce, Averell Harriman, and "Ike"), the Air Force took two weeks to prepare a response for General Vandenberg. Saying he found Zanuck's letter "most interesting," the general indicated that his director of public relations, Stephen Leo, would give the request for assistance his personal attention. In his own letter two weeks later, Leo agreed with Zanuck that *Twelve O'Clock High* would "make a most interesting picture. Its effect on the public should be quite favorable to the Air Force." He indicated that the service would be glad to extend cooperation within the limits of regulations and present restrictions. However, he warned Zanuck that the service might have a problem finding a sufficient number of now-obsolete B-17 bombers, although he expected the Air Force would probably be able to locate eight or ten planes. He also explained that the service would have to approve any script for security and policy before it could formally approve cooperation and closed by saying that the Air Force looked forward to reading the completed screenplay.[45]

The script, which finally reached the Pentagon the next week, told the story of Gen. Frank Savage's efforts to rebuild the hapless 918th Bomb Group during the early years of American daylight bombing over occupied Europe and Germany. He is forced to take over command from his friend Keith Davenport, who has looked after his fliers like a brother and so suffered the strain of identifying with them on their near-impossible missions. Savage subjects the depressed fliers to merciless discipline and training to bring them back to fighting peak. In doing so, however, he is caught between his own developing friendships with the men and the inherent inhumanity of ordering them to face death. Gradually earning the respect of his men, Savage comes to know them as comrades; and

The Leper Colony, designated as the home for the incompetents and misfits of General Savage's bomb group, became one of his best planes until it was shot down, thereby contributing to Savage's breakdown.

when they are shot down, he loses not combat crews but friends. Ultimately he breaks down under the same pressure of leadership that Davenport had previously experienced.

In dramatizing this breakdown, Bartlett and Lay portray Savage as becoming irrational and bursting out hysterically. As might be expected, the Air Force had problems accepting this behavior. In commenting on the script, the Air Force suggested to the studio that it would "prefer not to indicate to the public that a commanding general like General Savage became as irrational as indicated.... We do not believe that a man with the strength of character as indicated and of his moral fiber would burst out hysterically or have a complete mental collapse. It seems that he would most likely break down with physical ailments, nervousness, short temper or just plain fatigue."[46]

In the script, Bartlett had tried to explain the burdens of leadership as he observed them during his wartime experiences in the Air Force. He recalled that "there was so much abuse heaped on anybody who was a commander. They were looked upon as people who just waved the wand and sent boys off to die." He explained that few people "understood what a dreadful experience it was for a man to have the responsibility" to order men into combat. To him, Savage's breakdown showed what responsibility "can do to a man who carries that load, that a man made of pig iron can break down under this kind of stress."[47] Nevertheless, to satisfy the Air Force, the completed film transformed the original portrayal of Savage's collapse into a quieter, more subtle breakdown. The climactic scene, one of the most powerful in any war film, if not in any Hollywood film, shows Savage inca-

General Savage is helped from the field after being unable to board his plane for a crucial mission.

pable of pulling himself into his bomber to lead the crucial mission and then sinking into a comatose state until the group returns.

Although the portrayal of a commanding officer failing to fulfill his responsibility had never appeared in a Hollywood film to that time, the Air Force accepted the sequence because the situation seemed plausible in the context of the story. The service did ask for other changes in the script, however, in particular, the portrayal of the seemingly excessive use of alcohol by the officers of the group. The Office of Information told the studio, "We have no desire to portray all Air Force personnel as being teetotalers. However, the use of liquor in innumerable scenes might create an unfavorable public reaction by fostering a belief that the Air Force drank its way through combat, and important decisions were made by officers while under the influence of liquor."[48]

The Office of Information also objected to another scene in the original script, which showed a plane being wrecked deliberately so that mechanics could use its parts to repair battle-damaged planes. Although acknowledging the accuracy of the scene, the service requested a change. Instead of the dialogue "Run a tractor into one so you can report it a total loss," which "might cause unfavorable public reaction," the Air Force wanted the film to suggest that ground crews only cannibalized inoperative planes for their parts. Similarly, the service said it "would prefer not to show the Chaplain actually playing poker. . . . We believe the idea that the Chaplain is one of the boys could be achieved if he is standing watching the game just as well as showing him participating in it." With these exceptions, the requested changes related to technical matters and inconsistencies in the script itself.[49]

Revisions proved to be no problem, and the Air Force quickly began the process of locating the required planes and equipment. Ultimately the service selected two southern bases as shooting locations. For the exterior scenes of the base and its Quonset huts, the studio chose Eglin Field outside Pensacola, Florida. However, the filmmakers could not use its white concrete runways for shooting takeoffs and landings because the wartime fields in England were black, to make them less visible to possible enemy bombers. Consequently, the studio went to Ozark Field, an inactive training base in Alabama, to film the flying sequences.[50]

Ozark offered not only the right landing strip but also surrounding countryside that appeared properly English. The waist-high grass at the edges of the runway hid the airstrip as required for the opening and closing scenes, which took place several years after the war. Once director Henry King shot these sequences, mowers cut the grass for the flying shots. Since the film company recreated battle scenes with actual combat footage, it had to shoot only landings and takeoffs and a few close-formation "training" maneuvers. In these sequences King used twelve B-17s, which the Air Force had collected from the Air-Sea Rescue Service and retrofitted to their World War II combat configurations. However, for the spectacular crash early in the film of a battle-damaged plane returning from its mission, the studio had to buy a B-17 and stage the landing using its own stunt pilot.[51]

For this, Fox hired Paul Mantz, Hollywood's premiere stunt flyer, a man who had performed at least ninety crashes in films. The script called for Mantz to belly-land the thirty-eight-thousand-pound plane and skid it off the runway through a row of tents before it came to a stop. Since he didn't want to risk additional lives, Mantz arranged the controls so that he could take off, fly, and crash the four-engine plane by himself, normally a two-man operation. The pilot could not anticipate every eventuality, however. The night before the crash, the first tent in the row Mantz was to hit blew down. To prevent a recurrence, the prop man replaced the wooden support pole with an iron one. Fortunately,

B-17 at rest following Paul Mantz's spectacular crash that was one of the visual highlights of *Twelve O'Clock High*.

Mantz had a premonition as he landed the plane, and instead of hitting the tent directly, he aimed the plane so that the tent struck it between the fuselage and the inboard engine. The bomber crash remains one of the most spectacular in Hollywood stunt-flying history, and the makers of *Midway* reprieved the sequence for their 1976 epic.[52]

Twelve O'Clock High does not derive its power from these spectacular sequences, however. Even the use of rare combat footage, which gains added impact from being used only as the impetus for General Savage's breakdown, does not become the film's primary attraction. Of the four major films that initiated the cycle of postwar combat movies, *Twelve O'Clock High* tells the best dramatic story. The film's appeal also results from the excellent acting of Peck, Gary Merrill, and Dean Jagger as well as from King's taut directing. Few side issues distract from the plot's primary focus, the rise and fall of General Savage.

What little humor the movie has occurs in Savage's relationship with his driver and the scene in which the general discovers that his overage ground executive (played by Jagger, who won an Oscar for his portrayal), the base doctor, and even the chaplain have flown on a crucial mission. After the bombing raid, Jagger tries to defend himself by saying he thinks he hit a plane. Savage dryly asks whether he hit one of ours or one of theirs. Even here, however, the general reinforces the grim reality of his responsibility, by pointing out that if the Germans had shot down the stowaways' bombers, he would have had to write to their families.

The weight of this responsibility in the end destroys Savage, even though his strength and determination transformed the 918th Bomb Group from its deep state of depression into an effective instrument of war. The focus on one man's psychological as well as physi-

Savage sits comatose, waiting for his group to return from its mission. Meanwhile his friends try to explain his breakdown.

Davenport: It's screwy. I would never think it could happen to him.
Stovall: I did. I watched him sweep his feelings under the carpet long enough. It had to spill out someday.
Davenport: But I never saw him more full of fight than at briefing.
Doctor: Did you ever see a lightbulb burn out? How bright the filament is just before it burns out. I think they call it maximum effort!

cal struggle to survive lifted *Twelve O'Clock High* out of the category of war films to the level of those few movies that make a significant comment on the human condition. Most combat stories have tried to attract audiences with their scenes of battle, men in mass attacks, ships churning through the oceans, planes filling the skies. They give the illusion of authenticity by the use of military hardware, not by delving into the psychological states of men in conflict. In contrast, *Twelve O'Clock High* created its dramatic impact by focusing on an individual with whom the audience can empathize.

In the end, General Savage has broken down, but he has accomplished his goal. As the group's doctor explains, Savage gave his "maximum effort." His men have become well trained and are prepared to carry the battle in the air to German soil. The 1950 audience left the theater enjoying the fruits of victory that men like Savage helped bring about.[53] As *Battleground* had done, *Twelve O'Clock High* reminded the American people that the nation had had to take the trip and suffer the losses so that the United States could again live in peace.

8 | The Image of the Marines and John Wayne

THE MEN WHO HELPED REMIND THE AMERICAN PEOPLE that the trip remained necessary—actors such as Gary Cooper, Van Johnson, George Murphy, James Whitmore, and Gregory Peck—portrayed traditional Hollywood servicemen, whom screenwriters synthesized from their research and experiences and to whom directors gave life. However well they performed their roles, the actors remained only actors, soon moving on to other characterizations. Throughout the history of Hollywood war movies, few actors have created a military presence that carried beyond the immediate film in which they appeared.

Victor McLaglen developed his role of Captain Flagg in *What Price Glory?* into a stereotypical image of the professional soldier in a series of films culminating in *The Professional Soldier* (1936). Lon Chaney became recognized as the hard-bitten sergeant after his starring role in *Tell It to the Marines* (1927). Wallace Beery created the image of a crusty old military man in films such as *West Point of the Air* (1935), *Salute to the Marines* (1943), and *This Man's Navy* (1945). And Randolph Scott, as the star of *To the Shores of Tripoli* (1942), developed a portrait of the wartime Marine, the lean-jawed serviceman doing his duty in the face of adversity. None of these images remained permanently etched in the American mind. None of these actors became the symbolic American fighting man.

Not until John Wayne created the role of Sergeant Stryker in *Sands of Iwo Jima* and then merged his own personality with the character did Americans find a man who personified the ideal soldier, sailor, or Marine. More than fifty years after he appeared in *Sands of Iwo Jima,* Wayne and his military image continue to pervade American society and culture. References to Wayne and his film-made image appear in virtually every book about Vietnam. Television dramas, newspaper and magazine articles, and even beer commercials still regularly bandy about his name and cinematic persona. By the time he died in 1979, after a nearly fifty-year Hollywood career, Wayne had become an American legend, instantly recognized both in the United States and abroad, a member of the "loyal

Lon Chaney, as the tough drill sergeant, forces the raw recruit to grow up quickly in *Tell It to the Marines* (1927).

opposition, accent on the loyal," a narrator of television programs, and the author of *America, Why I Love Her.*[1]

Wayne remained a part of the American culture for so long that occasionally even people in the television film industry forget when his impact actually began. In an episode of the short-lived TV series *Baa, Baa Black Sheep,* while fleeing from Japanese captors, one of Pappy Boyington's rescuers volunteers to hold off the group's pursuers. A fellow rescuer asks, "Who do you think you are, John Wayne?" although Wayne had not begin to develop his movie image as a military man until at least seven years after Boyington's wartime heroics.[2]

To be sure, Wayne had played military roles for many years before the release of *Sands of Iwo Jima* at the end of 1949. He had portrayed a submariner in *Men without Women* (1930), a pilot in *Flying Tigers* (1942), a Seabee in *The Fighting Seabees* (1944), and a PT-boat commander in *They Were Expendable* (1945). Nevertheless, until he became Sergeant Stryker, most audiences thought of Wayne primarily as a western hero in countless horse operas, some of distinction but most less than memorable. Only with his success in *Red River* (1948) and *She Wore a Yellow Ribbon* (1949) and the great acclaim (including an Academy Award nomination) for his Stryker role did Wayne emerge as Hollywood's all-time leading star.[3]

Sands of Iwo Jima did more than propel Wayne to his unique position and help launch the postwar cycle of movies about World War II. It contained the classic portrayal of the Marines' military achievements in the recent war, and it became the most significant movie to result from the Corps's long relationship with the film industry. Of all the armed forces, the Marine Corps has remained the one branch that over the years has best publicized its role in the nation's martial history. Recognizing the potential of the film medium from its earliest days, the Corps made appearances in motion pictures a major part of its public relations operations.

Beginning with *Star Spangled Banner* (1917) and *The Unbeliever* (1918), the Marines had used dramatic films to help create the image of the Corps as an elite organization, one prepared for any eventuality. So well did the service succeed in combining motion pictures with other self-promotion activities that in 1950, Pres. Harry Truman wrote to a congressman that the Marines "have a propaganda machine that is almost equal to Stalin's."[4]

Except for *What Price Glory?* however, most films about the Marines made during the

Raymond McKee and Darwin Karr portray Marines in *The Unbeliever* (1918) filmed in part at the Quantico Marine Base.

1920s and 1930s focused on the peacetime exploits of the Corps, including its actions in Latin America and China. Of these, only Frank Capra's *Flight* (1929) rose above the level of the average Hollywood adventure story or musical comedy set in a military environment. Even during World War II, despite the spectacular successes of the Corps, only *Wake Island* and *Guadalcanal Diary* became more than run-of-the-mill combat stories; the Marines emerged from the war without a film of the critical stature of *Air Force, Thirty Seconds Over Tokyo,* or *The Story of G.I. Joe.*

Nevertheless, even without the benefit of a classic film, the Corps' very survival as an independent military branch during the post-war unification of the armed services provides a testament as to how well the Marines had learned to use motion pictures to explain their raison d'etre to the American people. By late 1946, Marine Commandant General Vandegrift had come to believe the Marines were facing annihilation from the Army, Gen. Douglas MacArthur, and members of Congress. Lt. Gen. Victor Krulak, then a lieutenant colonel stationed at Quantico, "concluded that a film was needed and that its central thrust should be extolling the Air Force, and then showing that it could not have reached the main Japanese islands without the Marines and their skills." *Bombs Over Tokyo* was also to explain that the Marines' capture of Iwo Jima provided a haven for crippled B-29s returning from bombing raids over Japan.[5]

Krulak suggested the animation that illustrated the range of the B-29 Superfortress and found historical combat footage to incorporate into the shot. Norm Hatch recalled that due to time constraints, the Marines were "not overjoyed, technically, with the final product." Nevertheless, he said that the twenty–minute documentary *Bombs Over Tokyo* "hit the target." The Marines screened prints around Washington "with good effect," and the Corps survived the National Security Act of 1947 with three divisions and three aircraft wings.[6]

However, even after Hollywood began to fight World War II on the screen, filmmakers did not immediately look to the Marines for a story. Only after major studios had begun work on *Task Force, Battleground,* and *Twelve O'Clock High* did the Corps draw interest from Edmund Grainger, a producer at Republic Pictures, who ultimately created the classic Marine film. As important, *Sands of Iwo Jima,* with its enduring image of the Corps, also assured the service of its continued existence.

Ironically, unlike the other initial portrayals of World War II, *Sands of Iwo Jima* grew out of a vacuum. Aware of the lack of a Marine story in production, Grainger came up with the title for his proposed film after seeing the line "sands of Iwo Jima" in a newspaper. Joe Rosenthal's picture of the flag-raising on Mount Suribachi suggested the movie's climax. With these two ideas in mind, Grainger wrote a forty-page treatment that told the story of a tough drill instructor and the men he leads into battle. To write the screenplay, he hired Harry Brown, a veteran Broadway playwright, who had previously done the screenplay for Lewis Milestone's 1946 *A Walk in the Sun.* According to Grainger, Brown did "a brilliant job" of translating his concept into a shooting script.[7]

Sands of Iwo Jima focuses on Sergeant Stryker, a tough, outwardly emotionless leader, and his unit. Just as General Savage beats his fliers into fighting shape, Stryker molds his unit into a first-rate fighting force despite personality conflicts much like those portrayed in *Twelve O'Clock High.* Beneath his stoic exterior, however, Stryker bears the pain of a wife who, with their son, has left him because of his single-minded commitment to the Marines. Implicitly, Stryker transfers his feelings of love and loneliness for his son to his men and becomes a father and teacher whom they come to respect, if not love.

The film follows the sergeant and his men through the invasions of Tarawa and Iwo

Jima to the successful capture of Suribachi. As his unit relaxes there, a Japanese sniper shoots Stryker in the back and he dies instantly. His death, of course, inspires the men to further action, and they carry on the battle as they had been taught by their father-teacher.

Edmund Grainger, like Dore Schary, felt that his film told the story of a crucial battle, because Iwo Jima proved to the Japanese that they could not hold their island outposts: "If they had won there, they would have felt that they could have stood off the assault on the mainland of Japan." The defeat on Iwo Jima, in Grainger's opinion, made the Japanese realize they had lost the war and could only fight defensively until peace was negotiated. Ironically, his film portrayed the battle of Tarawa in much more graphic detail. Gen. David Shoup, who received the Medal of Honor for his actions at Tarawa and later became commandant of the Marine Corps, noted this discrepancy: "It was sort of a screwed up thing, really. The sands of Iwo Jima really didn't have anything to do with most of the film."[8]

Title aside, Grainger and his film received the most extensive assistance of any of the four films that began the cycle of movies about World War II. The small size of Republic Pictures and its limited financial and technical resources became the only significant problem Grainger faced in seeking Marine cooperation. But after he spent a week in Washington talking to top Marine officers, he convinced the Corps that the studio could complete a project of the magnitude of *Sands of Iwo Jima*.[9]

As the first step in the cooperation process, the Marines assigned Capt. Leonard Fribourg to serve as the film's technical advisor. His only instruction from the Marine Corps commandant directed him to ensure technical veracity in the film and provide complete cooperation to the studio. Marine Headquarters did recognize that the exigencies of filmmaking might require occasional bending of military procedures. In pursuance of these instructions, Fribourg worked at the studio during preproduction helping to polish the script and selecting combat footage to match with the company's own battle sequences. He also made arrangements with Camp Pendleton for Republic to do all its exterior shooting on the base, where the necessary men and equipment would be available for the action scenes.[10]

This assistance enabled Grainger to carry out his intention of making *Sands of Iwo Jima* "very realistic" rather than simply turning out another "Hollywood version of the Marine Corps." His commitment to accuracy of detail and procedure notwithstanding, the film succeeded primarily because of John Wayne's presence. Grainger originally had envisioned Kirk Douglas as Sergeant Stryker. But in the middle of negotiations with

Preparing to film a scene of *Sands of Iwo Jima* (1949) at Camp Pendleton, left to right: Capt. Leonard Fribourg, the technical advisor; director Allan Dwan; John Wayne; and Lt. Col. Andy Geer, a Marine consultant.

Douglas's agent, Wayne approached the producer requesting the role. He later told Fribourg that he had wanted the part so badly "he could taste it."[11]

Wayne saw *Sands of Iwo Jima* as a "beautiful personal story," one that "made it a different type of war picture." He felt that Stryker's relationship with his men became "the story of Mr. Chips put in the military. A man takes eight boys and has to make men out of them. Instead of four years in college, he's given eighteen weeks before they go into battle." Unlike the 1955 *Battle Cry*, which would tell its story of Marines in World War II in broad strokes, Wayne thought that *Sands of Iwo Jima* showed how "to paint a picture of the whole [war]" from the vantage point of a small unit.[12]

Responding to Wayne's belief that he would make the perfect Stryker and to problems in securing Douglas for the role, Grainger went to Herbert Yates, head of Republic Pictures, to suggest that the studio cast Wayne in the film. According to Grainger, Yates rejected the proposal because he considered Wayne's career to be on "the downgrade." Wayne later disputed this belief, pointing out that he had just completed *Red River* and *She Wore a Yellow Ribbon*. In fact, neither film had yet premiered and they would only reinforce Wayne's image as a western hero. Consequently, only after Wayne's personal visit to Yates and Grainger's continued urging did the studio chief finally allow Wayne to play Sergeant Stryker.[13]

With the casting settled, the script completed, and arrangements made for assistance at Camp Pendleton, the film went into production during the summer of 1949. At the Marine base, the director, Allan Dwan, used a company of Marines as background for the principal actors. For the large assault sequences, Fribourg arranged to have the equivalent of a battalion of Marines as well as various types of equipment and vehicles perform for the cameras. He also ran a modified boot camp for the actors to teach them to act like Marines. The technical advisor recalled that he never had any problems with the cast: "They wanted to do it, wanted to cooperate. They wanted to wear the uniform right, the emblems, wanted to know what the stripes meant, wanted to know Marine Corps lingo, and put the right words in the right places." Dwan himself paid a great deal of attention to detail, and he never rolled the cameras on a scene in which the military was involved without asking, "Does that look okay?"[14]

The director's concern with accuracy and the Marine Corps's own recognition of the need for some dramatic license facilitated Fribourg's relationship with the film company. In the combat sequences, for example, he permitted Dwan to keep the men bunched closer together than they would have been in actual battle, because the cameras of the small-screen era could capture only a limited area on film. Rarely did the technical advisor object to a sequence. His major problem came in a scene calling for Wayne to teach bayonet fighting to a member of his squad who is having difficulty. The script required Wayne to hit the man with a horizontal butt stroke. When he did this in rehearsal, Fribourg remembered, "I almost fell off my chair." He told Dwan that he could not "have your sergeant hit this guy with a rifle butt."[15]

Although Dwan argued that the Marine Corps public affairs office had approved the script and the sequence contained excellent drama, Fribourg refused to budge. However, when he sent the matter to Marine Headquarters to resolve, Washington overruled the technical advisor. Nevertheless, Dwan did tone down the action to which Fribourg had objected. According to Wayne, the Marines allowed the "jaw smashing" to take place because a humorous scene followed it immediately and thus ameliorated the severity of Stryker's "teaching." In the final version, Stryker and the awkward Marine do the Mexican hat dance, which Wayne described as "being the most humorous scene in the script." Nevertheless, he recalled that Grainger apparently remained "afraid of the scene" and tried to have it deleted from the shooting script. Wayne said that he interceded by going directly to Herbert Yates, who ordered Dwan to shoot the sequence.[16]

By his own admission, Wayne became a "sort of 'Richelieu' of Republic" in the behind-the-scenes "struggle and conniving" that took place during the production of *Sands of Iwo Jima*. However, his primary concern was to make himself into a Marine sergeant. He questioned Fribourg and other Marines about all aspects of their work and combat experiences and spent a great deal of time with a warrant officer who seemed to typify Stryker. From all this on-the-spot research, Wayne discovered that the Marines did not train their men to die for their country. Instead, basic training prepared them "to live for their country and to live to fight again. It was survival training. We learned that you didn't get to the bottom of the barrel toward the end of the war. You got to the young fellow who was so damn good that the older fellows couldn't hardly keep up with him."[17]

To realistically portray the Marines in this historical context, Wayne and Grainger received not only Marine Corps assistance but also in-person advice from Shoup and Jim Crowe, another leatherneck hero at Tarawa. The two men helped recreate their actions at the seawall, but only after Shoup insisted that Grainger have the script rewritten to portray events as they had actually occurred. According to the future Marine commandant, the original script did not accurately render some of his dialogue with Crowe over a field telephone, as well as some of his combat actions. Due to his input, the sequence contained the actual words spoken on Tarawa. In addition to this information, the use of military motion pictures, still photos, and newsreel footage enabled the filmmakers to recreate the Tarawa beachhead so realistically that Shoup recalled: "It was a fearsome thing to look at because having experienced the battle, goddamn, I didn't want to go through it again."[18]

For the climactic Mount Suribachi assault, Grainger recruited Capt. George Schrier

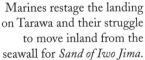

Marines restage the landing on Tarawa and their struggle to move inland from the seawall for *Sand of Iwo Jima*.

Marines land on "Iwo Jima," this time for the camera.

to portray himself leading the patrol that raised the flag. The producer also brought to Pendleton the three surviving members of the flag-raising detail to recreate their actions. (One of them, Ira Hayes, later became the subject of *The Outsider* [1961], which detailed the Puma Indian's life following Iwo Jima.) This concern for detail produced a film that Shoup said reminded him of the actual battle. Other Marines later told Grainger that the film "was the finest Marine Corps picture ever made by the motion picture industry." According to Grainger, this "was because it told the truth about the Marine Corps."[19]

(Above) Felix W. De Weldon, sculptor of the Iwo Jima Monument, advises the actors representing the three survivors of the flag raising, Ira Hayes, John Bradley, and Rene Gagnon, on the proper position to take during the shooting of this climactic scene. (Below) Sergeant Stryker's men turn from his body to watch the flag-raising on Mount Suribachi during rehearsal for the film's climax.

The *New York Times* critic thought the honesty "is marred, and quite seriously by the standardized movie conniptions back in the staging area in New Zealand." Nevertheless, he felt that *Sands of Iwo Jima* contained "so much savage realism . . . so much that reflects the true glory of the Marine Corps' contribution to victory in the Pacific that the film has undeniable moments of greatness." In addition, the reviewer noted that Dwan brought "to the shipboard sequences as the convoys stand off the beaches an overpowering sense of the dread which gripped the men immediately before going over the side into the landing craft." Likewise, the *New Yorker* found *Sands of Iwo Jima* a "worthwhile film. . . . The invasions are represented here in a frighteningly authentic manner, and no attempt has been made to gloss over the squalor and horror that go with war." Despite objecting to the dialogue

that "gets a trifle lofty, and now and then love makes an unlikely appearance," the reviewer thought that "by and large the picture is a whole lot better than many highly touted war films that have gone before it."[20]

Critics found much to praise, and General Shoup called *Sands of Iwo Jima* "the finest military film I've ever seen," but moviegoers became the ultimate judges of the picture. They made it the eighth-largest-grossing movie of 1950, and many people still regard

Sands of Iwo Jima as the film that best portrays the Marines in action. More than fifty years after its release, Marine recruiters claim volunteers still increase whenever the movie appears on television.[21]

Apart from the realistic combat sequences, John Wayne's embodiment of the tough Marine sergeant gave the film its unique staying power. Nonetheless, Marines themselves remain divided in their loyalties between *Sands of Iwo Jima* and *Battle Cry*. Many consider the 1955 film more representative of their service experiences. To them, *Sands of Iwo Jima* tells the story of one Marine, Sergeant Stryker. In contrast, *Battle Cry* tells of the varied experiences of many men, both in military situations and off duty.

Some of these experiences, which Leon Uris portrayed in his novel of the same name, would obviously be of concern to the Marine Public Information Office, particularly the brutal treatment of recruits and the adulterous affair between one young recruit and the wife of an Navy officer. Whatever the images, however, the success of the book and the positive portrayals of the Marines in combat had predisposed the service to work with Warner Brothers on the project. The director of information informed the commandant that with "adequate assistance on the part of the Marine Corps, this picture will be one of the best ever produced about Marines." He also reported that in the initial synopsis the company had submitted, the filmmakers had omitted "certain objectionable parts of book . . . specifically, illicit love scenes and the brutal treatment of recruits." As a result, he recommended that the Marines provide full cooperation at the Recruit Depot in San Diego and at Camp Pendleton.[22]

Uris came to Washington in October 1953 to discuss the film with the Marine Corps. He found "an air of excitement" about the production, for which he was to write the only screenplay of his career. He informed the studio that during a story conference which Claire Towne of the Defense Department's Public Affairs Office and the entire Marine Public Information Office attended, he had reached a complete agreement with the service about what he should keep in the film and what he would have to omit. As a result, he felt that the Marines had shown a "high regard and an outward feeling of comradeship" for the production, "the same as had been shown for the novel." Uris noted that this attitude stood in marked contrast to the Marines' recent relations with Hollywood, which had seen the service refuse to cooperate on any production in more than a year.[23]

The success of *Sands of Iwo Jima* had inspired a series of Marine films, beginning with *Halls of Montezuma*, which appeared in late 1950. It, too, had followed a small group of Marines ashore in a generic landing on an enemy island, where the men had the mission of capturing a Japanese soldier alive to gain information. In contrast to Wayne's film, the Twentieth Century Fox production focused on officers and their particular command-and-control problems. Richard Widmark, the company commander, a former school teacher, must watch his men die in combat. To ward off the migraine headaches resulting from the demands of leadership and his fear of battle, Widmark takes unidentified pills. Karl Malden, the medical Corpsman, tries to minister to Widmark's troubled mind and body, as he drives himself to the limits of endurance.

Despite the fine performances the two men gave, *Halls of Montezuma* did not become the personal story that Wayne's presence had given to his film. Malden probably provided the best explanation when he said he "never" looked at war movies as a unique genre. He said the uniform his character wore, whether a doctor's, policeman's, or street cleaner's, did not "mean a thing to me. The quality of the person is the important thing to me, how he lives, why he lives, relationships between him and people, that's what interests me most."

Sands of Iwo Jima did, of course, focus on relationships. But whereas Wayne *became* Stryker, Malden was simply playing a role, however well he rendered his portrayal.[24]

For this reason, *Halls of Montezuma* lacked the intensity that set *Sands of Iwo Jima* apart from the traditional war movie. Nevertheless, in the battle scenes, the film did come alive, thanks to the full cooperation that the Marines provided, including stock footage, technical advice, and the facilities at Camp Pendleton. The service's only objection to the original script related to the issue of the drug Widmark was taking. Once Marine Headquarters satisfied itself that the film would not imply that he was taking some kind of narcotic, the service went all out to ensure that the completed movie would have the same authentic combat ambience that had distinguished *Sands of Iwo Jima*.[25]

Although the film's excitement and ultimate victory benefited the service's image, *Halls of Montezuma* remained only one more Marine action war movie. Recognizing this and the need to portray other elements of the service, Gen. Clayton Jerome, head of the aviation branch, approached Grainger with the request to make a movie portraying the contribution Marine fliers had made to winning World War II in the Pacific. The producer, now at RKO Pictures, readily agreed, but he decided to set the story in the current war in Korea.[26]

When the Navy had to withdraw the loan of an aircraft carrier to the studio because of the demands the war was making on its resources, Grainger changed the locale to the World War II battle for Guadalcanal. As a result, *Flying Leathernecks* told the story of ground-based Marine pilots flying close air support against Japanese rather than Korean and Chinese soldiers. During the filming in early 1951 at Camp Pendleton, Marine fighters based at the El Toro Air Station regularly flew down the coast to perform the aerial sequences for the cameras. The Corps even provided Grainger with a few airplanes to masquerade as Japanese fighters.[27]

This assistance and the use of Marine gun-camera color footage for the first time in a Hollywood movie enabled the producer and his director, Nicholas Ray, to authentically recreate the excitement of the Corps' exploits in the air during World War II. However, the scenario itself became no more than a tired rehash of earlier Marine war stories. John Wayne, now promoted to major, suffers the same antagonism from his men as other cinematic military disciplinarians. As with Don Ameche's fliers in *A Wing and a Prayer*, Gregory Peck's in *Twelve O'Clock High*, or Wayne's Marines in *Sands of Iwo Jima*, Wayne's fliers learn that in the crucible of combat, strict adherence to orders often becomes the only thing standing between death and survival.[28]

Although Wayne reprieved his role as a teacher to the next generation, the film itself lacked any originality. Moreover, the flying sequences rather than the Wayne persona became the center of attention. Perhaps Wayne sensed this, since his portrayal lacked the depth and nuances of his Sergeant Stryker role. Nevertheless, for the Marines, *Flying Leathernecks* served its purpose admirably, reminding the American people that the Corps had an air arm that had performed with distinction in World War II. By implication, of course, the film also suggested that the Marines were again supporting their men on the ground during the Korean police action then being fought.

By the time *Flying Leathernecks* appeared in July 1951, however, studios had concluded that their World War II films needed more than a laudatory portrayal of past successes to attract audiences. As a result, like the other services, the Marine Corps found itself having to fend off Hollywood's interest in exploring the dark side of military life. The public affairs office turned down MGM's request in 1952 to provide assistance on a script titled "Take the High Ground," a story about the troubles that a drill instructor experienced in training recruits during the Korean War. Dore Schary, head of production at the studio, acknowledged, "We were going to make it a pretty tough picture, not an expose, but a very truthful picture. The Marines would not cooperate. They said they didn't want any part of anything like that."[29]

Likewise, Frank McCarthy, later to produce *Patton*, wanted to make a Marine D.I. film during the same period for Twentieth Century Fox, basing it on the true story of a drill instructor who led his men into a swamp where several had drowned. He said he intended to turn the film into a positive account by showing that "if you train men very, very severely, you prepare them better for the battle that they go into later. And you must train them so severely that occasionally you're going to have a casualty." McCarthy, the wartime secretary to Gen. George Marshall and a retired reserve general, took his story personally to the Marine Commandant, Lemuel Shepherd Jr., a close friend. The commandant told him, "You know I'm not going to help you make this." Although Shepherd acknowledged that the script portrayed everything accurately, he asked why the Marines should advertise this reality. Although McCarthy could have made the film without cooperation, he chose not to pursue the project.[30]

The Marines continued their reluctance to work with filmmakers by turning down a request for limited assistance on the small-scale, independent production *Beachhead*. The script told the story of a four-man patrol ordered to obtain information about Japanese defenses on a Pacific island. During the mission, two of the Marines die. Although the two survivors bring back the intelligence, and Marine Headquarters liked the portrayal of leathernecks carrying out their jobs heroically, the service refused to cooperate. The Public Information Office told the producer that it did not want to become involved with a film showing Marines suffering 50 percent casualties at a time when it was in the midst of a recruiting campaign designed to create a new, less danger-seeking image.[31]

In this instance, the caution backfired. The Pentagon's Public Affairs Office liked the script and thought the film should be made. Since the office did not have the authority to order the Marines to reconsider its decision, it arranged for the Navy, the National Guard, and the Coast Guard to provide the limited assistance producer Howard Koch needed while shooting on location in Hawaii. When Koch screened the completed film in the Pentagon, the Marines "were enthusiastic and loved it" and agreed to provide a Marine band to help promote the film when it opened in February 1954.[32]

The decision to become involved in the production of *Battle Cry* may well have influenced the decision to support *Beachhead*. Uris had informed Warner Brothers after his meetings in Washington in October that he had learned from the Pentagon's Public Affairs Office that the Marines "held *Battle Cry* in such high regard that they are willing to completely reverse their thinking." He quoted Towne as saying that the book is "certainly the turning point in what was beginning to look like a very bad policy."[33]

Uris included a copy of the letter from the director of information to the commandant, recommending full cooperation as long as the filmmakers honored their agreements made in the story conference. He explained that the Marines did not think the illicit love between a young recruit and a married woman belonged in the film: "The Corps feels that Forrester represents an idealistic type of boy . . . the type of youth they hope to appeal to. Showing him, as an eighteen year old, humping a married woman twice his age will have many detrimental aftermaths." Reality might well suggest the very opposite, that the images would have a positive affect on recruiting. Nevertheless, Uris reported that the public information director had told him the commandant would provide a strong objection if the filmmakers did not delete the story line from the film.[34]

Uris himself thought they could keep the affair in the movie, but he noted, "There is a deep feeling of bitterness in Washington and the services about ETERNITY. They feel that Yarborough [the Navy wife] sequences are put in directly as an imitation of that film." Consequently, the author said he would "certainly hesitate to advise it as our cooperation may not be quite as good as the type they are willing to offer now." Therefore, he suggested "that we assure them it will not be in the script." As might be expected, the relationship between another recruit and a prostitute did not bother the service. Nor, as Uris wrote, did either the Marines nor the Defense Department object to the other two significant romantic relationships, finding the "humpings are actually more sexually stimulating and certainly more honest. They found nothing objectionable in them . . . so, it isn't as though they were anti-sex . . . merely anti-illicit."[35]

Otherwise, Uris said the story conference had resolved all the minor issues, including the matter of the number of deaths in the novel. He believed the Marines "were fair in raising this issue and in the screenplay a number of characters who are killed in the book will remain alive in the picture." He even thought the change "will actually improve over the novel." In any case, he expressed astonishment that the military found so little objectionable and saw "absolutely nothing" to hold up the script once he removed the adultery."[36]

As part of the process, on October 16 Towne forwarded to George Dorsey the military's formal comments on the first-draft screenplay and outline, which, if incorporated into the next script, would assure Marine assistance. In contrast to the casualty problem with *Beachhead,* the Marines said, "We should be able to see that at least fifty percent come out of the war alive," and noted that not everyone wounded in combat dies. The service also indicated that the script had to eliminate the idea that all recruits have to get drunk before they can become good Marines.[37]

Echoing Uris's earlier report to the studio, the Marines strongly suggested cutting out the adulterous affair, even though the service acknowledged that the book had made this a story point and it is "not essentially tied to our primary interest in the project, i.e., to assure accurate and authentic treatment of those aspects of the story which have military significance." Nevertheless, the Marines did not like the emphasis on the affair and felt that it distracted "from other very creditable aspects of the story." Consequently, the service recommended the affair "as the first candidate for the scissors." Finally, the Corps suggested that director Raoul Walsh portray air support of ground operations, since it remained an important part of the Marine combat experience: "It need not be too elaborate or time consuming as long as it is there."[38]

With the concerns satisfied and approval received, Warner Brothers filmed the recruit training at the Recruit Depot in San Diego and the New Zealand rest and relaxation sequences at Camp Pendleton. To create its combat scenes, the studio sent the cast and crew to Vieques, a small island off Puerto Rico, for six weeks to shoot regularly scheduled Marine amphibious exercises as background for the scripted action. Since the book had not identified any actual battles, technical advisor Jim Crowe, of Tarawa fame, and Walsh remained free to fabricate the action Uris had set on Guadalcanal, Tarawa, and Saipan for the best visual and dramatic effect, restricted only by the limits of the terrain and plausibility.[39]

Although the action does gain impact from being shot in color for the wide screen, some Marines found the combat sequences overdrawn and unrealistic compared to the visual authenticity of *Sands of Iwo Jima.* Some officers suggested that because Uris served

Filming the forced march sequence at Camp Pendleton for *Battle Cry*.

as an enlisted Marine during World War II, he had not been able to accurately portray officers in his book, and they thought the film had the same problem. However, the training sequences at the Recruit Depot with actual recruits as extras provided the same ambience of Marines in training that distinguished *Sands of Iwo Jima*. In any case, *Battle Cry* shows a side of Marine life lacking in Wayne's film, the drinking and masculine camaraderie, the search for love, and the pain of rejection. Since these aspects of life occupy their thoughts and time as much as training and combat, Marines suggest that Walsh's film presents a fuller portrayal of their lives in the Corps than the singular focus on Sergeant Stryker and his small group of men in *Sands of Iwo Jima*.[40]

As the Public Information Office had trouble dealing with the fuller portrayal of the service during the negotiations with Warner Brothers for cooperation, the Production Code Office had problems with the script and, ultimately, the completed film. At one point during the filming, a studio executive warned Walsh that the Code Office had described *Battle Cry* as "the most gutty script (and they include FROM HERE TO ETERNITY) to pass their inspection." He advised the director that in the beach scene, in which Forrester and his girlfriend consummate their love [in the book], the script has them "in entirely too intimate a position," and to the Code Office, "the suggestion of an illicit sex affair between Danny and Kathy is unacceptable." Consequently, the executive advised that the "studio objective here will be to get as sexy a dissolve as we can" within the limits the code would allow and suggested the director "shoot the scene in two or possibly three ways."[41]

Walsh also faced a complaint from Crowe about a scene in which Colonel Huxley, played by Van Heflin, and Mac, played by James Whitmore, get into an argument. The director informed the studio that the Marines will not stand for "bickering between a noncommissioned officer and an officer." Nor would the service accept a discussion about field equipment being inadequate and out of date. Of course, given the "great cooperation" he had received, including the holding for three days of a bunch of recruits waiting to have their heads shaved and twelve hundred men for the sixty-mile-march sequence, Walsh had no choice but to change the offending scenes.[42]

The pressure to make changes did not come only from the Marines, nor did it end once Walsh completed filming. On July 1, 1954, Joseph Breen, in the Code Office, sent the film editor a list of scenes that he had to shorten or cut out altogether. The office criticized the brawl in the bar as "too lengthy and too brutal." The beach scene remained a sticking point that Breen said "unmistakably suggests a sex affair. As you know, we could not approve such a suggestion in this story." He also complained that the Navy wife is "apparently nude" when she changed into a bathing suit and said that the office considered "the finger," the "thumbing of a nose," and "the so-called Italian gesture" unacceptable in the sixty-mile-march sequence.[43]

As it had done with *Retreat, Hell!* in 1951, the Code Office also objected to the inappropriate use of the word *hell*. If an actual person had uttered the word in a historical context, or if it had appeared as a cliché, the office ultimately would approve the use, albeit with great reluctance. In *Battle Cry*, however, Uris had tried to avoid using the phrase "War is hell" by having a general say to Van Heflin, "Sam, I sometimes think myself it's a hell of a way to make a living." In this instance, Warner Brothers appealed directly to the Motion Picture Producers Association for the right to use *hell* as written and was able to keep the sentence in the completed film.[44]

After Walsh screened *Battle Cry* for the Defense Department and the Marines in November, Don Baruch informed the studio that the Defense Department still considered the beer party "unfavorably" and asked that the sequence be reedited "to eliminate as much of the apparent drunkenness" as possible. His office had no other objections and said the Pentagon was giving its approval whether or not Warner Brothers made the changes. At the same time, he noted: "However, we trust you will make every effort to comply in the best interest of our future relations and especially of those with the Marine Corps."[45]

After the screening, Walsh advised the studio that a Marine friend had expressed concerns about the downbeat ending in which Danny comes home wounded, the lumberjack returns to his New Zealand wife and new baby missing a leg, and many other of the movie's characters have died in action. He suggested ending the film with the scene in which the men debark from the troopship with the band playing and the flags waving: "a mass shot of Marines marching and the George M. Cohan finish." The director also reported that his friend had told him the Marines were saying that "this was the best Marine picture ever made and that they were all real fighting men and not Hollywood actors." Given this and other endorsements, the studio left the original ending in place.[46]

Commandant Shepherd, for one, enjoyed *Battle Cry* so much that he immediately offered Warner Brothers official participation in promoting the film. Then reality struck. Warner Brothers had opted to disregard the service's requests to eliminate the adultery and despite having retained some of the illicit sex scenes had managed to obtain the Code Office's approval. On December 9, Shepherd wrote to Jack Warner "to offer my congratulations upon the skill and accuracy with which the purely Marine Corps aspects of the picture are depicted. The portrayal of recruit camp, wartime field training, and the impact of actual combat all achieved a degree of realism which I have never before seen in a motion picture made for entertainment." Nevertheless, he added, "careful reconsideration of certain aspects of the picture has compelled me to withdraw the offer. This decision is based upon certain reactions that would accompany official Marine Corps participation. Dependence upon a very widespread public approval of all that it does is most important to a volunteer service."[47]

Such concerns aside, *Battle Cry* did show the full range of Marine life in World War II that was lacking in the narrowly focused *Sands of Iwo Jima*. *Weekly Variety* suggested that "amatory rather than military action is the mainstay of this saga."[48] Nevertheless, if many Marines believe *Battle Cry* better captured their wartime experiences, they acknowledged that none of its stars, Van Heflin, James Whitmore, Tab Hunter, or Aldo Ray, personified the Marine Corps. As Mac, Whitmore certainly did his job of turning his kids into fighting machines, but he did it "with the perfect mix of gentleness and discipline."[49] As a result, he did not become a second Sergeant Stryker. Nor did Jack Webb, whose portrayal of a drill instructor in the 1957 *The D.I.* remains the standard against which all cinematic D.I.s will always be measured. Neither man stimulated young men to enlist or served as a model for military skill or courage.

To former and current Marines as well as to most Americans, John Wayne remains the symbolic Marine, even in death, as he did when *Sands of Iwo Jima* first appeared. *Newsweek* thought John Wayne gave "one of his best performances as the rugged top sergeant who bullies and beats his men into a fighting unit." The *New York Times* reviewer thought Wayne became "especially honest and convincing for he manages to dominate a screen play which is crowded with exciting, sweeping battle scenes. . . . His performance holds the picture together." Wayne received an Oscar nomination for his role and felt he was "worthy of the honor. I know the Marines and all the American Armed Forces were quite proud of my portrayal of Stryker."[50]

Edmund Grainger agreed with the reviewers that Wayne's Stryker "dominated the screen." He thought the actor's "innate character, his thinking about life, his philosophy of life" helped create the role. Although conceding that Kirk Douglas would have given a professional performance if he had accepted the part, the producer said Wayne "was a more typical Marine sergeant because he believed in the role. . . . He was so immersed emotionally in this part that it came out. I think it is the best thing he's ever done." Most moviegoers probably think of Wayne as a cowboy first, but to the Corps he became one of them. Speaking for most Marines, General Shoup said Wayne symbolized the "hell for leather, go and get 'em attitude [of the Corps]. . . . When we went into combat, we went after the enemy."[51]

By the time he played Stryker, Wayne had been going after the enemy in films for almost twenty years. But only with *Sands of Iwo Jima* did he become the symbol of the American fighting man, the defender of the nation. As with all images, Wayne's action-hero did not emerge full-blown. His career spanned almost half a century and more than two hundred films. He appeared in more westerns than any other genre, but his military characterizations ultimately established him as America's quintessential fighting man.

This image came to pervade American society and ultimately became a cliché in the late 1990s, when the image of Wayne as a general dressed in fatigues appeared in Coors beer commercials. Nevertheless, it remains a powerful influence on the nation's youth. In fact, Wayne became the model of the action hero for several generations of young males, representing the traditional American ideal of the anti-intellectual doer in contrast to the thinker.

Admittedly, Wayne created his fighting-man image on the motion picture screen rather than through real conflict. Jim Brown, who probably saw himself as a black John Wayne, may have said it best: "Man, John Wayne came off like he could whip anybody's ass. He did it on the screen, pretended he could do it in real life. There were 2 million guys who could kick John Wayne's ass every day of the week. Deep inside, John probably knew it too. So he played to the image."[52] For most Americans in recent years, however, the reality of life and the illusion of the screen have become tightly intertwined. Americans may now find their heroes in cops-and-robbers adventures, James Bond–type exploits, or even in sports. Nevertheless, the image of the action hero remains the same as it was in the days of the Alamo, the cowboy and Indian, the charge up San Juan Hill, or the flaming beachhead.

Although Wayne perpetuated his image through the guise of fictionalized or historical characters, he became just as much a military hero, a frontier hero, and a supporter of

God, country, and motherhood as the Andrew Jacksons, Davy Crocketts, Buffalo Bills, and Teddy Roosevelts of American history. In creating this symbolic, mythical American hero, Wayne incorporated elements of Sergeant Stryker into his characterizations, whatever the role or the locale. He became at once the fighter and the teacher, instructing the next generation how to survive in combat as he taught his men to fight on Tarawa and Iwo Jima. The oil-well firefighter in *Hellfighters* (1969), Colonel Kirby in *The Green Berets* (1968), and the old rancher in *The Cowboys* (1973) all pass along to younger men the knowledge accumulated from their experiences fighting the elements or human enemies. With the possible exception of Rooster Cogburn in *True Grit* (1970), this Stryker/Wayne characterization will remain the one people remember, the one that forever established Wayne as the fighting man who remains ever ready to fight for and defend his country.

Marines have often cited Wayne's portrayal of Stryker as the reason for their attraction to the Corps. Ron Kovic, a Vietnam veteran, recalled in *Born on the Fourth of July:* "The Marine Corps hymn was playing in the background as we sat glued to our seats, humming the hymn together and watching Sergeant Stryker, played by John Wayne, charge up the hill and get killed just before he reached the top. And then they showed the men raising the flag on Iwo Jima with the Marines' hymn still playing. . . . I loved the song so much, and every time I heard it I would think of John Wayne and the brave men who raised the flag on Iwo Jima that day. I would think of them and cry. Like Mickey Mantle and the fabulous New York Yankees, John Wayne in *Sands of Iwo Jima* became one of my heroes."[53]

The appeal of Wayne's heroics spread wherever his films have appeared. Richard Pryor recalled, "My heroes at the movies were the same as everyone else's. I wanted to be John Wayne too. . . . I didn't know John Wayne hated my guts." The man who grabbed the arm of President Ford's would-be assassin in San Francisco said that when he signed up for the Marines, "I didn't really know what war was, but I wanted to fight for my country." Only after a tour in Vietnam did he learn that it "is no John Wayne movie." Wayne's image as a successful fighter has even impressed his long-time foes. Despite his slaughter of thousands of Japanese, or perhaps because of his film victories over the emperor's subjects, Hirohito specifically asked to meet John Wayne while visiting the United States in 1975.[54]

In countless films, Wayne extolled the simple virtues of doing right and feeling useful. The "Duke" and the roles he played became fused in the opinion of the public. Playing Davy Crockett in *The Alamo,* for example, Wayne sermonized: "Republic! I like the sound of the word. It means people can live free, talk free. . . . Republic is one of those words which makes me tight in the throat."[55] To Wayne, as to the character he was playing, *republic* is a word that makes the heart feel warm, something worth fighting for, dying for. It is also a place its people must support—right or wrong. The Colonel Kirby who advocates the virtues of American policy in *The Green Berets* differed little from the John Wayne who told Jimmy Carter and the American people on Inauguration Eve, 1977: "I am considered a member of the opposition—the loyal opposition, accent on the loyal. I'd have it no other way."[56]

Wayne's portrayal and advocacy of patriotism and action enjoy instant recognition in the United States as well as throughout the world. When asked, in 1976, to name their favorite actor, a class of black fourth graders answered "John Wayne," not Jim Brown, O.J. Simpson, or Sidney Poitier. When his doctor told him he was "perishable," a heart attack victim suddenly realized he just could not picture himself as "a brown-edged, sagging sponge of leaves" or "a rotting piece of fruit." His fantasized self-image always remained

"John Wayne in any number of westerns . . . a man with inexplicable charm who over-comes psychological confusion and winds up, in the end, with the girl."[57]

In person, perhaps even more than on the screen, Wayne's character and charisma became all-enveloping, even to those who may disagree with his philosophy and politics. Because of this presence, his son Michael believed his father "would have been an outstanding anything because he has that drive. He has a particular personality. He has charisma. It is just something that differentiates people. He has it. So no matter what field of endeavor he went into, he would have been a star or one of the most important people in that field. That characterized him more than anything else."[58]

That something caused presidents, politicians, and even an emperor to court Wayne as if he were a political figure. His political views became known and debated by his constituency as if he had entered the political arena, and he received welcomes not only from those whose views he shared, but from the "Opposition" as well. He reached that position by visualizing in movies a mythic quality inherent in the American character. According to Dore Schary, Wayne "was a representation of the American image of the soldier, of the frontiersman, of the American who doesn't knuckle down and the American who when things get tough is willing to pick up the gun and fight."[59]

While shooting *The Outsider* at Camp Pendleton in 1960, Delbert Mann asked a group of Marine recruits why they had joined the Corps in light of the strenuous training they had to undergo. Half of them answered that they had enlisted because of the John Wayne movies they had seen. On an *Owen Marshall* television episode, the mother of a deserter asks him why he thought war was right before he joined the Army but not after he had fought in Vietnam. He responded, "I was eighteen and war was something John Wayne fought or we watched on our new color TV."[60]

Why did the screenwriter draw on the Wayne military image? His answer: "Because in the predominantly liberal community that makes up the film industry, Wayne, though not disliked for it, is outspokenly gung ho. He supported the war vocally and his professional image repeatedly made heroic those men who fought wars or used guns and violence to achieve their goals. Wayne . . . is larger than the man himself. An 18-year-old boy saw Wayne fight endless battles on the big screen and the boob tube . . . from *Sands of Iwo Jima* to *The Alamo*."[61]

Countless references in fiction and nonfiction to Wayne and his military roles illustrate his influence in creating an image of life in the armed forces and of combat to young men. In *The Lionheads*, a novel about Vietnam, one of the characters recalls his drill instructor describing how the Japanese attacked in World War II "like in the John Wayne movies: 'Marine, you die.'"[62] The Wayne image appears in nonmilitary novels as well. Lisa Alther describes Hawk, the freaked-out lover of the heroine in *Kinflicks*,

Director Delbert Mann discusses with Tony Curtis his portrayal of Ira Hayes during the filming of *The Outsider* (1961) at Camp Pendleton.

going to Vietnam "in the grip of the basic male thing: Here was this rite that would either make a man of you or destroy you. If you returned alive, you'd somehow conquered Death."[63]

Once in Vietnam, however, Hawk finds that he must concern himself only with enduring the incredible boredom, staying alive, and returning home, all of which require him to do as he is told. While on a patrol, he and four other men abduct a Vietnamese girl. When he protests, his fellow soldiers tell him to shut up. His immediate reaction is to speculate "on pulling a John Wayne and rescuing her." He then pictures the probable result of his effort—being shot in the head: "It was one of those jarring moments when a person realizes that he's stepped out of the familiar everyday world into a realm of primal lawlessness in which anything goes." So Hawk joins in raping the girl, indulges in the reality instead of the movie-made image.[64]

The body of personal literature growing out of the American experience in Vietnam and the firsthand accounts of journalists document both the pervasiveness of the Wayne image and the dichotomy between the Wayne model of masculine behavior and the reality the war itself imposed. In *365 Days,* a doctor's recollection of stories he heard while treating wounded men from the battlefields, an officer describes his training "with the crazies, the tough, role-playing enlisted kids right off the streets of Chicago, Gary, and back roads of Georgia who had gone airborne because of all the John Wayne movies they'd seen."[65]

Ron Kovic recalled that after listening to the Marine recruiters at a high school assembly, he could not wait to run down and meet them: "And as I shook their hands and stared up into their eyes, I couldn't help but feel I was shaking hands with John Wayne and Audie Murphy." Ron Caputo, in *A Rumor of War,* said that even before he talked to recruiters, he saw himself "charging up some distant beachhead, like John Wayne in *Sands of Iwo Jima,* and then coming home a suntanned warrior with medals on my chest. The recruiters started giving me the usual sales pitch, but I hardly needed to be persuaded."[66]

Knowledgeable journalists who covered the Vietnam War, including Bob Schieffer, Ward Just, and David Halberstam, have all attested that the Wayne image profoundly influenced the men who fought in the war. Each reported seeing men fight and talk about fighting as they had seen John Wayne fight the Japanese in his World War II films— without regard to the efficacy of the techniques. As a result, an exasperated old sergeant once reportedly told some careless troops: "There are two ways to do anything —the right way and the John Wayne way." Soldiers' imitations of Wayne even assumed mythic dimensions. David Halberstam recounts a story, perhaps apocryphal, that made the rounds in Vietnam: a soldier threw a grenade into a hut as he had seen John Wayne do, only to have "his ass blown off" because the hut was made of grass rather than the more solid material of a Japanese bunker.[67]

Wayne's influence reached not only enlisted men but also the decision makers and officers in the field. One high-ranking officer who served in Vietnam during the buildup of American forces in the mid-1960s thought the escalation of American efforts to win the war became at least "in a simplistic sense" the response of people "racing around trying to be John Wayne, applying force to a problem which required something else." Josiah Bunting, author of *The Lionheads* and an officer in Vietnam, confirms the journalists' accounts on a more basic level. Drawing on his own military experiences, Bunting observed: "There is no question that the officers in Vietnam, combat infantry officers, especially in the grade of lieutenant colonel, which was *the* rank in Vietnam [were influenced by] this whole aura of machismo. . . . The influence of John Waynism, if you want to call it that, on these people was terribly profound."[68]

To Wayne, this influence arose from his characterizations, which always appealed to the same emotions: "You can call it primitive instinct or you can call it folklore. It has no nuance. It's straight emotions, basic emotions. They laugh hardy and hate lustily. There is a similarity in that. I wouldn't call it primitive as much as I would call it man's basic fight for survival." In response to critics who suggested that these portrayals primarily appeal to adolescents, Wayne answered that he hopes his attraction recalls "the more carefree times in a person's life rather than to his reasoning adulthood. I'd just like to be an image that reminds someone of joy rather than of the problems of the world."[69]

Wayne's hope notwithstanding, the problems of the world, the bullies, and the bad guys, provided the challenge he confronted in virtually all his films. To solve these problems, the characters he played used action and violence in the most direct manner. Action not only speaks louder, but violence leaves a more lasting impression on a majority of viewers. Josiah Bunting visualized Wayne as "a guy constantly kicking over cans, kicking over lamps," as he did in *The Horse Soldiers*. Such men cut through the Gordian knot to get to the heart of the problem. To Bunting, this manner of solving problems has "a fundamentally anti-intellectual kind of appeal" that becomes as attractive to an educated, thinking person as to the "anti-intellectual Archie Bunker temperament. . . . In other words, after three or four hours of trying to solve a problem, here comes this great big strong guy who kicks over a lamp, gets on a horse, and kills a bunch of people. It's so simple. It's fulfilling. It's finite."[70]

Wayne and his roles both reflected and helped create the desire in Americans to solve problems simply and directly. One screenwriter who used the Wayne image as the instrument to convey the idea of war to his male character suggested that this reflection/creation process is "probably symbiotic." To him, the John Wayne fan "is a relatively simple person who is very independent, believes you get out of life what you put into it. . . . that force is the great solver of problems. Certainly, he believes in America and believes in it simplistically. . . . He enjoys the father image. Wayne represents all of this."[71]

Most of all, Wayne represents the use of violence rather than reason to solve problems. In the early days of American involvement in Vietnam, this part of his image became widely admired by the men in the field. Covering the war for the *New York Times* during this period, David Halberstam observed this appeal at close range: "It influenced the officers and men, everyone. The Wayne image of the guy cleaning up the town, the good guy standing alone was there." He saw it in the imitation of Wayne's "swagger, the tough guy walk. . . . there were a lot of guys out there playing John Wayne."[72]

Wayne himself acknowledged the appeal of his "swagger," but he considered it a part of his sexuality: "There's evidently a virility in it. Otherwise, why do they keep mentioning it?" William Wellman, however, attributes Wayne's military appeal directly to his "swagger. . . . He walks like a fairy. He's the only man in the world who can do it." Although sex and combat violence seem to be closely related, Wayne nevertheless denied that his screen violence had a particularly profound impact, pointing out that "children's stories have always included knights and dragons with blood, fire and everything." At the same time, he admitted, "I've shot as many people on screen as anybody." However, he differentiated between his killings and other screen violence: "I haven't shot them—like they do today—with snot running out of my nose, sweating, and with my pants torn open."[73]

Wayne felt that his violence had always remained somehow cleaner, neater, more pristine than other people's: "When I came into this business, it was a medium where we used illusion to set off reality. The bad guy always wore a black hat, the good guy always wore a white hat and gloves and he wouldn't hit first. Someone would always break a chair over his back. When someone threw a vase at me, I always hit right back. That started a different kind of western. But it was illusion. I never used things like animal livers to show someone getting shot. That's just bad taste." Wayne complained, "Today they're trying to make 'em real either by concentrating on turning your stomach with violence or running everyone by nude. Well, I'm too old to play in-the-nude stuff. And I really like the illusion of violence more than putting a squib in a cow's liver and a bunch of catsup on it and blowing it up in slow motion."[74]

Wayne's death in *Sands of Iwo Jima* represents the paradigm of the type of clean violence of whuch he approved. A shot rings out and Sergeant Stryker lies dead. No blood trickles from his mouth or streams down his shirt. Moreover, he would only direct this brand of violence against the bad guys. Given his concern for correctness, Wayne turned down the lead in *Patton*. He told Frank McCarthy that the military characters he portrayed do not go around slapping American soldiers. He felt that he had always tried "to portray an officer . . . or a non-commissioned officer or a man in the service in a manner that benefits the service and also gives a proper break for the man to react in a human manner."[75]

In spite of their admiration for Wayne and his image, young men in Vietnam quickly discovered that their war bore little resemblance to the conflicts he had fought on the movie screens. Survival rather than giving a man the opportunity to react in a human manner became the only thing that mattered. As the war dragged on into the late 1960s, it became less and less clear to the American people, and more particularly to the men in Vietnam, that we were, in fact, playing the John Wayne good-guy role fighting the bad guys. Perhaps most disillusioning to them, the soldiers in Vietnam discovered the falseness of the visual model Wayne had provided them of war as clean and bloodless with little suffering. Instead, they saw their buddies torn apart and mutilated for a cause that ultimately seemed to have no socially redeeming features.

In *Home from the War*, Robert Lifton details the anger returning veterans felt at being betrayed by these screen models. Whereas Wayne had once provided them with their images of war, he now became a scapegoat for their frustrations and bitterness. Likewise, in *Born on the Fourth of July*, Ron Kovic spoke for all those who came to see that the reality of war bore little resemblance to the antiseptic battles he had watched Wayne fight in the name of patriotism and justice. His bitterness and anger most clearly illustrate the betrayal he came to perceive in the Wayne image. Paralyzed from the chest down, Kovic rages over his lost manliness: "Now I can't even roll on top of a basketball, I can't do it in the bathtub or against the tree in the yard. It is over with. Gone. And it is gone for America. I have given it for democracy. . . . I have given my dead swinging dick for America. I have given my numb young dick for democracy. . . . Oh God oh God I want it back! I gave it for the whole country. I gave it for every one of them. Yes, I gave my dead dick for John Wayne. . . . Nobody ever told me I was going to come back from this war without a penis. But I am back and my head is screaming now and I don't know what to do."[76]

To Wayne, of course, death or loss of manhood always remained as important as life. Death gave life more meaning. It gave the new generation the opportunity to assert itself. *The Cowboys* (1972) contains the explicit manifestation of Wayne's symbolic role as the transmitter of cultural values from one generation to the next. Playing an aging rancher whose men have deserted him to take part in a gold rush, Wayne gathers a bunch of schoolboys to help drive his herd to market. During the trip, Wayne passes on to them his skills and values. When an outlaw murders him, his boys kill the killer. He has passed the ultimate expression of manhood from one generation to the next.

During the film's production, the studio suggested to Wayne that he did not have to die. He responded that the movie would be "no good if I live. The whole idea of it is what this Mr. Chips teaches the kids. If I'm alive and they recapture the herd of cattle from the rustlers, it doesn't mean as much."[77] Nor does his death matter any more than Sergeant Stryker's death matters. In each case, his disciples will carry on the skills and values he has imparted to them.

Thus, although Wayne's image of war proved deficient during the Vietnam experience, his model of courage and patriotism remained viable to the men who fought in the conflict.[78] The majority of men obeyed their orders, did their jobs, and returned home still loving their country. If most people ultimately rejected Wayne's hawkish view of the war, the message of national preparedness explicit in his movies remains the goal of virtually every citizen. Nevertheless, Wayne denied that his military movies had an undue influence on the American people.[79]

He claimed that he made his movies primarily for "entertainment" and that people had an interest primarily in the personal or provocative parts of the story. To him, the military served only as a device to attract attention to the picture and to its subject matter.[80] From *Sands of Iwo Jima* onward, however, John Wayne, rather than an actual military hero, served as the symbol of America's fighting men for a significant number of American moviegoers.

9 | A Different Image

IF NONE OF THE SUCCESSORS TO *SANDS OF IWO JIMA* produced a hero figure to equal John Wayne, the failure did not result from lack of effort. Following the lead of the successful filmmakers, every Hollywood studio began cranking out its own versions of the war. In addition to the Marine Corps movies, *Operation Pacific* (1951), *Above and Beyond* (1952), and *Take the High Ground* (1953) attempted to duplicate the box-office appeal of the cycle-initiating movies. As often happens, however, the imitators lacked the clarity and insights into war and men in combat that distinguished the original films. They relied instead on spectacular battle scenes, women, and romance to attract audiences. As escapist entertainment, they did attract audiences; but as drama, they lacked the power of *Twelve O'Clock High*, *Battleground*, *Sands of Iwo Jima*, or *Battle Cry*.

For the armed forces, however, the primary consideration remained their appearance in as many films as possible, rather than the dramatic quality of the productions. Recognizing the value of the visual medium as both an informational and a recruiting tool, the individual services began to compete for time on the motion picture screen as soon as it became clear that Hollywood was again regularly making war movies. In particular, the Navy and the Air Force saw films as ideal vehicles in which to carry on their interservice debate over the relative merits of aircraft carriers versus intercontinental bombers. Made with the full cooperation of the services, *Flat Top* (1952), *Men of the Fighting Lady* (1954), *Bridges at Toko-Ri* (1954), *Above and Beyond* (1952), and *Strategic Air Command* (1955) attempted to convey the messages of their sponsors to the American people.

Ironically, this screen rivalry began during unification of the individual services into the Department of Defense under the direction of James Forrestal. As part of the process, Forrestal consolidated all public affairs operations into one office, leaving each service with a limited staff, which was to act only in an advisory capacity and as a line of communication to the field for the Defense Department's director of public information. As part of this reorganization, the Defense Department in 1949 created the Motion Picture Production Office. Under the direction of Donald Baruch, its first chief, the office received the mandate to take over the cooperation process from the individual services and supervise the details of assistance, thereby regulating the armed forces' zealous pursuit of film roles.[1]

After Forrestal's resignation as secretary of defense in March 1949, however, the individual services began to regain control over their public affairs operations, a process that the outbreak of the Korean War in June 1950 further accelerated. As a result, Baruch's office failed to function as originally planned, and until the early 1960s it served essentially as a conduit for requests from Hollywood to the individual services. In this capacity, the office could recommend that a service provide assistance, could help with negotiations between a filmmaker and a service, or could refuse to approve cooperation on a film that did not serve the best interests of the armed forces. However, Baruch could not require a service to assist on a movie, and once his office had approved a project, it had no involve-

Beginning in 1949, Donald Baruch helped arrange cooperation between the military and the film industry in his position as Chief, Motion Picture Production, in the Department of Defense Public Affairs Office.

ment in the cooperation process. Consequently, throughout the 1950s each service had virtually a blank check to provide assistance, much as it had done from the earliest days of its relationship with the motion picture industry. Filmmakers received as much help on any movie as a service's public affairs office in Washington and its commanders in the field decided served its best interest.[2]

Though the Korean War helped abort Forrestal's plans to regulate assistance, the war itself never became a popular subject for filmmakers, most likely because of the nature of the conflict. In contrast to World War II, which was a struggle between good and evil that would be fought until victory was achieved, Korea was a "police action." The fighting still pitted good against a well-perceived evil, but the goal remained a negotiated settlement, not victory. If Americans had a difficult time understanding the conflict as the stale-mate dragged on, Hollywood had as difficult a time portraying a conflict shaded in gray instead of painted in the easily defined black and white of World War II.

To capitalize on the initial wave of interest, filmmakers did immediately seize the war as a new subject. In much the manner of *Wake Island* and *Bataan*, Lippert Pictures, a small independent company, rushed Samuel Fuller's *The Steel Helmet* (1951) into production and hastily completed it, with the resulting back-lot appearance of the early World War II films. Although Fuller incorporated some anecdotes gleaned from early accounts of the fighting in Korea, the combat he portrayed could just as easily have taken place during World War II, and the squad he followed differed not at all from the soldiers who had defeated Hitler and Tojo.[3]

Following the pattern of World War II moviemaking, the armed forces showed an interest in assisting on films about the Korean conflict as soon as the military situation stabilized. In fact in one of the rare instances of the military's solicitation of Hollywood during the entire history of their relationship, the Air Force approached Howard Hughes and RKO Pictures about making a movie showing the close air support its fighter planes were supplying troops on the ground. The resulting film, *One Minute to Zero* (1952) received full cooperation from both the Air Force and the Army during its production at Camp Carson in Colorado. However, despite its origins in the Pentagon and the large-scale assistance it received, the Army refused to approve the completed film because it contained a scene not in the original script, a sequence in which artillery fire is directed against a group of Korean refugees that has been infiltrated by Communist troops. Once Hughes ascertained that the Pentagon would not revoke his extensive military contracts, he refused to delete the scene—the film's dramatic high point—and released it without the traditional acknowledgment of armed forces assistance.[4] Although the controversial scene could be justified under the rules of engagement, the Army did not want to become associated with a film that showed its men killing innocent civilians.[5]

In contrast, the Marines received a positive portrayal in the 1952 *Retreat, Hell!* which portrayed the story of the American withdrawal from the Chosen Reservoir in December 1950 following the massive Chinese attack across the Yalu River. Upon reaching the coast, Gen. Oliver Smith, the commander of the 1st Marine Division on its thirteen-day, seventy—mile breakout from the enemy's encirclement and escape to the coast, purportedly said, "Retreat? Hell! We are just attacking in another direction." Although General Smith denied ever having made the statement, he later pointed out that encircled soldiers cannot withdraw and must attack to break out.[6]

Most people realized such bravado, whoever made the comment, was simply putting the best face on a severe defeat. Gen. Edwin Simmons, director emeritus of Marine Corps History and Museums and author of *The United States Marines,* undoubtedly put it best when he observed that the U.S. military's "advance to the Yalu marked the zenith of America's post—World War II imperialism. The subsequent defeat and retreat signaled the beginning of the waning of American's overwhelming dominance in world affairs."[7]

Despite this reality, the Defense Department had a "favorable" reaction to Warner Brothers' proposal to make a movie about the Marines' retreat to the sea, which the studio's Washington representative, George Dorsey, sent to Lt. Col. Clair Towne in the Pictorial Branch on December 7, 1950. Although the battle was still in progress and the outcome in doubt, the studio explained that it wanted to make a film "based on the savage fight for life being put up presently by the trapped U.S. Marines." While recognizing that the filmmakers did not have "any semblance of a story," the Pentagon's deputy director of public information advised Dorsey that the Army and the Marines "are very interested in seeing this picture made." The public affairs office immediately granted the studio a priority for its project, and Dorsey advised the Pentagon that Milton Sperling, a Marine officer in World War II, would be producing the film.[8]

On January 9, Dorsey forwarded to the Pictorial Branch Sperling's proposal for the project, which drew its inspiration and title from the by then widely circulated description of the Marines' withdrawal from the Chosen Reservoir. In the outline, the producer explained that the film would be "the story of a victory—the story of an American victory over almost insurmountable odds." He assured the Pentagon that the film would not portray "a defeat. The Chinese declared that they would destroy to a man the trapped American forces. Instead, Americans decimated the Chinese ranks and clawed their way out, fit and able to fight again." He explained that film would portray the nature of the enemy, "the miracle of the air lift," and the terrors of "nightmare alley." The story would show the men in adversity and the "effect of the march on their characters and on their relationships with each other. We shall avoid cliches; our story will be virtually plotless. It will be an account, honest, straightforward and as close to the truth as we can discover it."[9]

After working diligently with Sperling to develop a screenplay which would contain these images, the Marines approved the final script on August 9, 1951, saying that the portrayal "is an accurate, gripping story of an outstanding chapter in the history of the Marine Corps." In turn, Warner Brothers submitted a detailed ten-page list of requirements for men and equipment during the anticipated six weeks of shooting at Camp Pendleton. There, in September and October, the Marines provided the film company

Director Joseph Lewis working with actors during filming of *Retreat, Hell!* at Camp Pendleton.

with full cooperation during filming, despite the escalating demands of the Korean War on its resources.[10]

Ironically, General Smith had recently become commanding general of the base and was to express his admiration for "the remarkable job" the filmmakers did in transforming a portion of the grounds into North Korea. He recalled that they appropriated the small Pendleton airstrip and bulldozed a road out of the side of a canyon through which the Marines retreated and then used gypsum sprinkled over both locales to create a suitable image of snow-covered terrain. Although the cinematic snow provided a reasonable facsimile of the conditions in which the Marines had suffered before reaching the coast and safety, the actors, wearing winter parkas and other cold weather gear, suffered through opposite conditions in the warm Southern California climate.[11]

Smith later expressed concern to Commandant Lemuel Shephard Jr. that the Marines might receive criticism for cooperating in the production of *Retreat, Hell!* He pointed out, "What the general public may not realize is that this assistance was worth about $1,000,000 to Warner Brothers. Unfriendly sources could make something of this. Our defense would be that the loan of equipment and personnel was in the interest of public relations."[12]

In fact, the Production Code Office caused the only significant problem to the successful completion of the film by refusing to approve the title because of its ban on the use of the word "Hell." Smith, not known for his use of profanity, wrote a letter to Marine Commandant Clifton Cates objecting to the "pusillanimous title" Warner Brothers was proposing to use to satisfy the Code Office. He later said he felt that *Retreat, Hell!* "was a much better title than the one they proposed and I didn't see anything particularly wrong with the 'hell' there."[13]

Responding to the Marines' complaint, the Pentagon's public affairs office wrote to Dorsey on November 20, 1951: "The Department of Defense and the Marines extended full cooperation on this production in the belief that the title "Retreat, Hell!" would be used. Perhaps the facts are not known to those now dissenting on its use." The office pointed out that Smith's statement "was given public acclaim and is a matter of record along with the historic and gallant Marine action. We believe those words will take their place along with other memorable historical quotes." Consequently, the Defense Department and the Marines said they "will appreciate every effort being made by the studio to change the opinions of the dissenters and to retain the title, 'Retreat, Hell!'" Thanks to the intervention of the Marines, Warner Brothers was able to reverse the Code Office's decision.[14]

If the resulting film portrayed a low point in American military history, it did burnish the Marines' image by showing its men performing bravely in a desperate situation. Nevertheless, when Allied Artists proposed in 1953 to recount virtually the same story, the Marines initially refused to become involved, even though the Corps had recently assisted the studio in the making of *Battle Zone,* a story about Marine combat cameramen in Korea. In his memo for the record on June 23, 1953, Don Baruch reported that the Corps saw the story, based on Pat Frank's novel *Hold Back the Night,* as "*Retreat, Hell!* with a whiskey bottle—nothing new would be told or shown the public and studio wants a great deal for quite some time for the filming . . . it would be a major effort just to give the public a rehash of a story that has been done well by another company."[15]

In his formal turndown the next day, the Marine director of public information advised Baruch that the requested cooperation "is too extensive. The troops and equipment cannot be furnished without unwarranted interruption to training schedules." However, the similarity to *Retreat, Hell!* remained at the heart of the problem, with the Marines explaining that *Hold Back the Night* would follow "the release of that picture so closely in the matter of time as to make the public relations value to the Marine Corps questionable."[16]

In turn, Baruch suggested to Allied Artists that they turn their film into an Army story. However, after reading it, that service noted that the "basic tone of the script is still somewhat Marine instead of Army." Nevertheless, the Army agreed to provide assistance if the studio would use a technical advisor to make necessary corrections to complete the transformation of the script. Instead, Allied Artists chose to temporarily shelve the project and when the studio resurrected the picture the next year, it decided to again court the Marines.[17]

This time around the Corps proved more receptive, with Baruch writing to the studio on December 15 that the Marines "understand and accept your desire to produce the picture with its original Marine Corps background without any ill feeling. However, they hope you will be able to schedule a picture about the Army in the near future." And, after the usual revisions for accuracy, the Marines did provide full cooperation during filming at the service's cold weather training facility at Pickle Meadows, in Northern California.[18]

After reading the book, General Smith had written to the novelist, "I appreciate, of course, that this is literature. But it certainly is not history, because you have us coming out on two roads and we only had one road." Frank had responded that he had simply looked at a map in Marine Corps headquarters and dreamed up the story. Nevertheless, Smith recalled that he liked it better than *Retreat, Hell!,* believing it "was very well done, it looked almost documentary, but it just wasn't." Although filmed in snow and low winter temperatures, *Hold Back the Night* simply lacked the feel of the bitter weather the Marines had

Chinese forces attack dug in Marines during filming of *Retreat, Hell!* on the "snow-covered" hills of Camp Pendleton near San Diego.

experienced in Korea and that *Retreat, Hell!* had managed to recreate on the "painted hills" of Camp Pendleton. Moreover, the later film failed to provide any real sense of the actual desperation that the retreating Marines had felt, perhaps because the war in Korea had been over for three years by the time *Hold Back the Night* appeared in 1956, and because people knew the outcome of the battle and the war.[19]

As a result, even films intending to explain and justify American involvement in Korea could not avoid a pessimistic ending. During the war, James Michener had spent time aboard an aircraft carrier operating off the Korean coast. He first wrote an article for the *Saturday Evening Post* reporting on the men flying the combat missions against the Communist forces and then wrote the best-selling *Bridges at Toko-Ri,* which told virtually the same story in fictional form. MGM bought the rights to the article and obtained a priority from the Defense Department and then approval from the Navy for assistance in the making of *Men of the Fighting Lady.* Subsequently, Paramount bought the rights to the novel and sought assistance from the Navy in making its own movie. After much negotiations, the Navy agreed to assistance on *Bridges of Tokyo Ri,* and the studio agreed not to release its film for six months after MGM's docudrama appeared.[20]

Men of the Fighting Lady focused on the Navy fliers, often identified by name, and their actual exploits in combat, albeit occasionally dramatized for greater impact. In contrast, as a work of fiction, Paramount's film could put messages into the characters' mouths, most particularly Frederic March as the admiral, commanding the carrier task force, and William Holden, playing a lawyer recalled to active duty as a jet pilot. The admiral has lost his pilot son in World War II and "adopts" fliers of his son's age, such as Holden, to become surrogates. Bitter at having to leave his successful law practice and his family, Holden becomes March's sounding board in a dialogue seeking to justify American involvement in a distant war.

Despite full Navy cooperation, which helped create spectacular flying scenes, and superb special-effects work, which used miniatures to produce a realistic bridge-blowing sequence, the film succeeded only in emphasizing the futility of the war. At one point the admiral explains: "All through history men have had to fight the wrong war at the wrong place. But that's the one thing they're stuck with. People back home behave as they do [indifferently] because they are there. A jet pilot does his job with all he's got because he is here. It's as simple as that. Militarily this war is a tragedy. But if we pulled out they'd take Japan, Indo-China, the Philippines. Where would you have us take our stand? At the Mississippi?"[21]

The argument undoubtedly had validity. But in the end, having helped knock out the bridges at Toko-Ri, Holden is forced to crash-land his damaged plane behind enemy lines, where North Korean soldiers shoot him in a muddy ditch where he has sought cover. Even though he has done his job in a tragic, if perhaps necessary war, his death offered no spiritual uplift, as Sergeant Stryker's had. Instead, audiences probably left the theater with only the feeling that the Korean police action had become worse than tragic: it had no redeeming features.

Paradoxically, though the Navy loved the film because it showed the excitement and importance of carrier aviation and thus provided the service with a visual sales pitch to Congress for additional jet planes and the seagoing airfields from which to fly them, *Bridges at Toko-Ri* made the first true antiwar statement in a post–World War II Hollywood film by showing the futility of combat. It did so, however, without distracting from the image of the American fighting man. Like General Savage and Sergeant Stryker and the other

William Holden discusses the crash scene in *Bridges at Toko-Ri* (1954) with Capt. Marshall Beebe, the film's technical advisor who had arranged to transport the wrecked jet to Thousand Oaks, California, for the location shooting.

heroes of Hollywood's war films, William Holden had acted bravely, and if he questioned the conflict in which he was participating, he nevertheless did his job to the best of his ability. And filmmakers, like the population as a whole, blamed the politicians rather than the military for the stalemate with which the war ended. Consequently, the American experience in World War II, the all-conquering Army, Navy, Air Force, and Marines, remained the model on which most directors, producers, and screenwriters based their military portrayals during the 1950s.

To be sure, practical considerations contributed to Hollywood's positive image of the armed services during the decade. Given the high cost of filmmaking, few studios cared to gamble large sums of money on unconventional or controversial films, whatever the subject. Moreover, because of the unique requirements of large-scale movies dealing with military subjects and the expense of trying to fulfill them through civilian channels, filmmakers preferred traditional stories about men in war, ones that would guarantee Pentagon cooperation. At the same time, the political climate of the early 1950s discouraged the production of any movie that might call a filmmaker's loyalty into question. For these reasons, Hollywood seldom had problems with the military during the first few years of the war-film boom.

In contrast to the generally positive visual re-creations of the military, the first major literary works about World War II to appear following the end of hostilities reflected their authors' personal and often unflattering perceptions of their own participation in the events about which they wrote. Unlike the collective artistic and financial compromises inherent in filmmaking, writing requires an individual effort, with the author answering only to himself. Publishing manuscripts represents some financial gamble, but one or two failures do not bankrupt a company. A publisher can usually take a risk on a potentially controversial work, whereas a film studio can only rarely do so. In any case, unlike the cinematic image of the armed forces, the early postwar novels exposed facets of life and command in the military that the services either rejected as inaccurate or preferred to keep out of sight.

Nonetheless, the novels did capture the atmosphere of military life, and their authenticity helped make instant critical and popular successes of Norman Mailer's *The Naked and the Dead* (1948), Irwin Shaw's *The Young Lions (1948)*, James Jones's *From Here to Eternity* (1951), and Herman Wouk's *The Caine Mutiny* (1951). As a result, Hollywood expressed immediate interest in transferring the books to the screen, but the studios invariably showed caution in developing the projects. Given the novels' essentially unflattering portrayals of the military, filmmakers approached the armed forces to ascertain the possibility of receiving assistance before actually committing themselves to any of the novels. As one of the would-be producers of both *From Here to Eternity* and *The Caine Mutiny* pointed out, companies are willing to risk all kinds of money on scripts they think they can ultimately turn into finished motion pictures. But they want to make the final decision on whether they make a film. Where these novels were concerned, the studios feared the decision would be made by the Defense Department or the individual services, not their own production staffs.[22]

Despite the armed forces' opposition to the contents of the novels, their great success with the public ensured that some filmmakers would ultimately adapt them for the screen. Given Hollywood's long-standing reliance on military men, equipment, and locales to provide accurate ambience, efforts continued to win approval for screenplays based on the novels. As it turned out, each production received assistance only after the filmmaker agreed to significantly modify crucial elements in the plots of the novels. These changes illustrated the way the armed forces have always worked to create what they have considered the proper image of themselves through commercial films.

Given the Defense Department's requirement that its cooperation must be in the best interest of or provide benefit to the service being portrayed, a script faithful to *From Here to Eternity* would clearly not qualify for assistance. Picturing Army life in the days immediately before Pearl Harbor, James Jones's novel focused on the stories of 1st Sgt. Milton Warden, Pfc. Robert Prewitt, and the woman each loved. Warden, who runs a company at Schofield Barracks for his weak and pompous commander, Capt. Dana Holmes, knows the Army system and willingly works within its limits. Prewitt struggles as a nonconformist whose determination to maintain his individuality undermines his basic love of the Army. When Prewitt refuses the captain's request to box on the company's team, Holmes initiates his destruction through "the treatment." Despite this abuse of power, the Army ultimately promotes the captain. Around these stories, Jones interweaves subplots of love and infidelity, camaraderie, and the brutality of soldier against soldier that culminate in violence in the stockade of Schofield Barracks.

Although the Defense Department and the Army did not deny the accuracy of the narrative, they argued against the novel's depiction of negative aspects of Army life that they claimed the service no longer tolerated. They felt that the portrayal of a situation that no longer existed would mislead the millions of mothers, wives, and sweethearts of men currently in the service. They maintained that no film based directly on the novel could benefit the Army, and so it did not qualify for assistance under the department's regulations.

Despite its awareness of Pentagon stipulations, Warner Brothers took an option on the book and asked its Washington representative to approach the Pentagon about assistance. When the Army told him it would never assist on the film, the studio dropped its rights to the novel. Twentieth Century Fox met the same reception and likewise backed

Director Fred Zinnemann discusses a scene in *From Here to Eternity* (1953) with Montgomery Clift and Frank Sinatra at Schofield Barracks in Hawaii.

off. Finally, Harry Cohn, president of Columbia Pictures, simply bought the book—without inquiring about the possibility of military assistance.[23]

Daniel Taradash, who wrote the screenplay for the film, said that Cohn bought it "because he was a man with a lot of guts." Taradash believed that the studio head thought he would have a great movie if he could develop a script acceptable to both the military and the Motion Picture Code Office. At the same time, Taradash noted that Cohn bought the book despite "immense protests" from Columbia's New York office.[24]

Aware of the problems he faced transforming the novel into a movie, Cohn asked Raymond Bell, Columbia's Washington representative, for his assessment of problems the studio would face from the Defense Department, from the Motion Picture Code Office, and from state censorship boards and religious organizations. After reading the book, Bell told Cohn, "I feel like I spent the weekend in a whore house." He wrote Cohn a long letter detailing the difficulties he foresaw. He first objected that the book contained "a lot of apparent Communist doctrine" that would cause problems with the American Legion and other organizations.[25]

Taradash strongly disagreed with this analysis, arguing that Jones had written "an honest book" into which no "political doctrine entered." In any event, Bell was sensitive to the Red Scare in Hollywood in the early 1950s, and he felt he had to warn Cohn that the studio might have problems with organizations that would label Jones "either a sympathizer or a dupe" of the Communist party. Moreover, Bell thought the book had an anti-Catholic and anti-Jewish bias.[26]

The most significant problems, however, in Bell's view, centered on Jones's portrayal of life in the pre–Pearl Harbor Army. He noted that the subplot of the "gold-bricking captain" whose top sergeant was carrying on an affair with his wife would not be looked on favorably in the military. Far more serious was the explicit brutality directed against both Prewitt and Maggio throughout the book. Bell recognized that Jones was describing life in an army where tough discipline may have had a place. Nevertheless, he noted in his letter to Cohn that potential recruits or parents would probably not understand that conditions in the Army had changed since 1941.[27]

With all these potential obstacles in mind, Cohn and his producer, S. Sylvan Simon, faced what most people in Hollywood believed were impossible odds against developing an acceptable screenplay. As a first step, at the end of March 1951 Simon went to Washington with a preliminary treatment and discussed Columbia's proposed movie with Department of Defense officials. On April 3, Towne, writing for the Pictorial Branch of the department's Office of Public Information, informed Bell that the reaction was unfavorable: "The basic ingredients of accuracy and authenticity, [of] value to the public information programs of the Department of Defense and Army, and overall benefit to National Defense, are not apparent in the Columbia proposal. The treatment portrays situations which, even if they ever did exist, were certainly not typical of the Army that most of us know, and could serve only to reflect discredit on the entire service." According to Towne, the Defense Department concurred with the comments the Army had forwarded separately. As a result, he concluded that it was "very difficult to conceive of any revisions to the current treatment which would justify reconsideration of this project."[28]

At this point, Columbia hired James Jones to attempt a screenplay. The novelist (who had received eighty-five thousand dollars for the rights to his book), did little serious work during his stay in Hollywood. By his own admission, he ran around, met a lot of starlets, and went to a lot of parties. He said he actually "knew so little about screenplay writing at the time" that he was "helpless," and he described his treatment, written in May 1951, as "very bad." Apart from his lack of experience, Jones explained that he could never lick the problem of "how to have whore houses without having whore houses" in the film. They were an integral part of the novel but could not be mentioned in the movie because of censorship restrictions.[29]

Taradash, who eventually solved the problem by calling a brothel a "social club," said of Jones's effort that he had "never read a worse treatment based on a first-rate novel." He explained that Jones had virtually gutted his own novel of any vitality. Instead of Karen being Holmes's wife, as in the novel, Jones made her Holmes's sister; he had Holmes tell Warden to "take it easy" with Prewitt, the reverse of his orders in the novel; instead of having Holmes initiate the brutality against Prewitt for refusing to box, Jones made the noncoms the villains and Holmes a nice, fair man. Taradash observed, "This is absurd. This isn't *From Here to Eternity*."[30]

While Jones was struggling with his treatment, the producer died. When the novelist's effort ended in failure, the project entered a period of limbo. Finally, in the fall of 1951, Taradash approached Cohn through studio channels with his own concept of how he could transfer the book to the screen. When he had first read *From Here to Eternity* shortly after publication, Taradash "thought it was great" but that "they'd never be able to make it into a movie." However, the story stuck with him, and he ultimately came up with two notions "which suddenly made me see the whole thing."[31]

In his meeting with Cohn, Buddy Adler (the new producer), and other studio executives, Taradash explained that the brutality in the stockade could be suggested rather than literally depicted. In the novel, Maggio, a cocky enlisted man from the streets of New York, fades from view after he is released from the stockade. In the movie Taradash suggested having him escape and die in Prewitt's arms as the result of the bludgeoning he received from Fatso, the brutal sergeant in charge of the jail. This would give Prewitt the opportunity to play taps as the climax to the second act of the screenplay. Taradash also proposed that the novel's two love stories should be intercut from one pair of lovers to the other throughout the film, even though their paths never cross in the novel until the very end. The writer explained that this cutting "solved a major dramatic problem, the structure of how you do this immense story."[32]

Cohn and Adler immediately recognized the merit of Taradash's proposal and gave him the assignment to write the script. It took more than a year, until February 1953, to complete the final draft of the screenplay, obtain military approval and promises of cooperation, select a director, and cast the roles. To begin, Taradash reread the book, took notes, and spent two months writing a 135-page detailed outline. The first draft of the actual script took another three months. To satisfy industry censors, Taradash turned the New Congress Hotel into the New Congress Club, and he described it as "a sort of primitive U.S.O., a place of well-worn merriment. It is not a house of prostitution." He handled the novel's many four-letter words by simply eliminating them rather than replacing them with recognizable substitutes. He did not even consider nudity in the famous beach scene. And he explained Karen's sterility as caused by a miscarriage, not from gonorrhea, as in the book.[33]

By anticipating the Army objections and changing the offensive material himself, Taradash opened the door to military approval of the script and cooperation. His key change was to eliminate the explicit brutality of the stockade, which Jones had made central to his novel. To pacify the Army, Taradash had the dying Maggio explain to Prewitt that he had fallen from the truck during his escape from the stockade: "... shoulda seen me bounce . . . musta broke something." Nevertheless, Maggio continues, in two long speeches, to describe how Fatso hit him repeatedly "in the gut with a billy . . . hit me ten times runnin." He also vividly describes his experience "in the Hole." Consequently, without showing actual brutality and despite the implication that some of Maggio's injuries came after escape, Taradash felt "that the last impression received by the audience is that Fatso and the stockade beatings are what really killed Maggio."[34]

Columbia sent the revised script to the Department of Defense on February 11, 1952. Hoping to smooth its entry, Taradash included in a preface excerpts from several reviews of *From Here to Eternity* to remind the Army that it "was a damn fine novel, not just an anti-Army novel." From the *New York Times,* for example, he quoted, "It will be apparent that in James Jones an original and utterly honest talent has restored American realism to a pre-eminent place in world literature." From the *Saturday Review of Literature* he cited, "This is the best picture of Army life ever written by an American, a book of beauty and power despite its unevenness, a book full of the promise of things to come."[35]

Despite Taradash's efforts, no one in the Pentagon thought the new script would produce a picture that could benefit the military in any way. Within the Public Information Office, some officials felt that though the script was "less objectionable" than earlier versions, it still did "not qualify for cooperation." They argued that the Defense Department "should keep hands off completely. It contains no informational value nor can it be of benefit to the defense effort." Don Baruch, however, felt that by working with the studio it would be possible to remove some of the worst features of the script. Gen. Frank Dorn, the Army's deputy chief of information, agreed with this tactic, since Columbia Pictures had committed itself to make the picture even without cooperation. By providing assistance, Dorn thought any improvements in the finished film would justify cooperation as being in the best interest of the Army.[36]

Reacting to the debate with the Pentagon, Clayton Fritchey, director of the Office of Public Information, wrote to Gen. Floyd Parks, the Army's chief of information, on February 19: "It has always seemed to me that our purpose in cooperating with commercial film companies has been to portray the armed services, their personnel, officers, training, ideals, aims and goals with the general intent of informing the public, of increasing morale among military personnel, and perhaps indirectly to aid recruiting." According to Fritchey, the consensus in his Office and in the Army remained that *From Here to Eternity* would "obtain none of the above-mentioned results." Rejecting the belief that providing Columbia with assistance could "mitigate in some way the unfavorable impact of the filmed story," Fritchey said "it would be difficult if not impossible to explain" any cooperation. Moreover, Defense Department assistance "would be linked to a commercial enterprise upon which it could never look with favor" and so would be setting "an ill-advised precedent." Therefore, he said that neither the Army nor the Office of Public Information should "in any way" cooperate in the production of the film.[37]

Despite this stricture, Fritchey did not cancel a meeting Baruch had scheduled for the next day with Taradash and Adler. He thought General Parks might want to protest his decision and that as long as the filmmakers had come to Washington, they should have their day in "court." He also felt that the session would give all parties the opportunity to present their cases and then decide how they should proceed.[38]

In the meeting, Baruch explained that any definite commitments about cooperation would have to come from the "front office." He pointed out that the military's objections to the screenplay were "personal recommendations," and even if the filmmakers acted on

the suggestions, "they would help the script but might not qualify the picture" for cooperation. He emphasized that the changes "are the intangible ones of making the picture positive rather than filled with negative values." Baruch then told Taradash and Adler that the
Defense Department would read the script after they had further revised it and would
judge it on its own merits apart from the book. He also arranged for the Army to provide
research in Hawaii at Pearl Harbor and Schofield Barracks.[39]

At this point, the studio selected Fred Zinnemann to direct the film. Taradash had
recommended his hiring after watching Zinnemann's *Teresa* (1951), which the writer found
the most "realistic depiction" of soldiers he had ever seen. Zinnemann had also directed
two other movies having a military environment, *The Search* (1948) and *The Men* (1950),
and had received two Oscars for his direction of short films. He and Taradash spent "five
months of intensive work" on the second draft of the script with additional inputs from
Harry Cohn and Buddy Adler. The collaboration produced many changes, "some of them
quite fundamental," according to the director, but the new script maintained the structure
Taradash had created in his initial treatment.[40]

When the revised screenplay reached the Pentagon in early September, Don Baruch
found it did "nothing" for the Army's image, but he felt that it would "not be anti-Army
with a few additional changes." To effect these revisions and discuss cooperation, Baruch,
General Dorn, and other Defense Department officials met with Ray Bell and Adler on
September 11. Among other requests, the Pentagon asked the producer to revise the portrayal of the stockade treatment "to eliminate the impression that the treatment was universal." The officials also wanted the studio to delete Karen Holmes's admission of previous
affairs. If the studio made these changes, the Pentagon told Adler, he could again submit
the script with a request for cooperation. The Army also said that until it saw the completed film it would hold in abeyance whether it wanted the studio to acknowledge in the
screen credits the service's assistance.[41]

Although the Army had tentatively agreed to cooperate as a result of this meeting, it
did so with more resignation than enthusiasm. Baruch still felt that *From Here to Eternity*
was "never going to be a good story for the military." However, by agreeing to assist the
project, he explained that the Pentagon gained the advantage of being able to exert some
leverage to get the screenplay revised and so "make it less objectionable or more present-
able. We didn't destroy any of the dramatic impact on the story values" but modified "the
way it was being presented."[42]

Modifications occurred not only in the manner in which the film dealt with the brutality in the stockade but also in the way Taradash portrayed the Army's treatment of
Captain Holmes, Prewitt's tormentor. In the novel, the Army promotes him despite his
brutality and abuse of authority. From his initial treatment onward, Taradash has Holmes
returned to the United States after he is severely condemned by the officer who discovers
his brutal treatment of Prewitt: "You have no capacity for leadership. What you did was
shameful. The sooner you get demoted in rank to a spot where you won't be in command
of troops, the better for everyone, especially the Army." After his discussions in the Pentagon, Taradash added, "You have your choice of a court martial or resignation."[43]

The Army's image clearly benefited from the removal of Holmes rather than simply
his humiliation. Taradash conceded that dramatically it was "not as good as the book; it's
much more ironic that Holmes be promoted. I like that infinitely more." Nevertheless, he
felt he had to make concessions to the Pentagon: "We had to show that we were not out to
attack the Army." According to Taradash, the military was "delighted" with the change,

with the "idea that the Army had found its rotten apple itself and gotten rid of it rather than this horror, to them, of promoting Holmes."[44]

Fred Zinnemann, who won an Academy Award for his direction of *From Here to Eternity,* agreed that he "would have liked to see the captain being promoted because it was a fine sardonic touch." But he also accepted the change "as a sacrifice that had to be made" to obtain cooperation. Also, Zinnemann's contract limited his creative control of the film, and as he pointed out, Harry Cohn ran the show: "It was his pet project."[45]

Cohn often sat in on script conferences, offering suggestions and attempting to play Taradash off against Zinnemann and Adler, a ploy the writer thought was "part of his game." Ultimately, Taradash and Zinnemann were able to squelch most of Cohn's ideas, which Taradash described as "really dreadful." Wanting the end to be "real sentimental," Cohn first proposed that Prewitt die in Warden's arms. Later, he even suggested that Prew didn't have to die at all. Cohn also adamantly insisted that Aldo Ray should play Prewitt. Zinnemann felt the character needed "spirit, particularly strong, indomitable spirit, a kind of nobility. And Monty had that beyond a question of a doubt, more than anybody I knew." He finally told Cohn that he could not make the film without Clift. After additional objections, the studio head agreed to Zinnemann's selection of Montgomery Clift to play Prewitt.[46]

On the other hand, Cohn would not agree to allowing *From Here to Eternity* to run more than two hours. He told Taradash, "I don't give a goddamn how good it is. I don't care if it's the greatest picture ever made. I don't care if it will gross a fortune. It's not going to run more than two hours." Taradash at first thought the restriction "madness." Although both he and Zinnemann believed the film could have used a few more minutes, Taradash did concede that Cohn's restriction "wasn't madness," and Zinnemann admitted, "Harry made it move."[47]

To Taradash, Cohn's time restriction represents simply one example of the kind of limitations a writer works under when he does a script. Consequently, he did not consider the Army's requested changes a form of censorship. Instead, they became simply another restriction he had to accept, "just as I accepted that I couldn't use the word 'whore' or 'fuck' at that point even if I had wanted to."[48]

In fact, the Code Office proved far more intransigent than either Harry Cohn or the Pentagon. In addition to putting absolute restrictions on language, industry censorship forced the filmmakers to eliminate themes and change situations in developing their script. Besides changing the brothel to a social club and not mentioning gonorrhea, the Code Office forced Taradash to transform Lorene into a club hostess rather than the prostitute of the novel, ignore the book's homosexuality, and punish Warden and Karen for their illicit affair through the expediency of adding a line about the "scheming, sneaking and hiding" their relationship required. Even after the film's completion, the Code Office required changes, insisting that the studio cut the famous beach scene by about six feet, even though the deleted footage contained nothing different from what remained.[49]

In contrast, except for the time restriction and a budget limitation of $2 million, Cohn had little influence on the structure and content of the film. Likewise, apart from Taradash's pragmatic elimination of the stockade violence in anticipation of military objections and the subsequent decision to have Holmes removed from the Army rather than simply transferred, the Pentagon had little direct impact on the final form of *From Here to Eternity.* Nevertheless, the Army continued to suggest revisions almost up to the beginning of actual shooting in Hawaii.

Despite Taradash's firmness in ignoring their earlier requests, as late as January 19 Ray Bell forwarded a list of changes the Army wanted incorporated into the final shooting script. To four of them, Taradash simply said no. He agreed to insignificant changes on two other requests. To the last request, he agreed with the Army's observation that the script still failed to provide proper motivation for Prewitt's failure to halt for the MPs as he tries to return to his unit after the attack on Pearl Harbor. To resolve this problem, the writer inserted several lines to clearly establish the reasons for Prewitt's desperate desire to get back to Schofield Barracks after he had gone AWOL while recovering from wounds suffered when he killed Fatso.

In his cover letter attached to Taradash's responses, Buddy Adler told Bell, "I do hope that both Defense and Army understand we have made every effort to be cooperative so that we could justify their cooperation." He said the studio had studied the suggestions "with great care and with much thought." As a result, the producer explained that the studio's responses represent "firm conclusions that to proceed in any manner other than indicated would work harm to the dramatic effect of our picture."[50]

Despite the changes resulting from the Pentagon's decision to work with Columbia Pictures, the Defense Department still did not consider the completed film a "representative portrayal of the Army or of the typical men and officers who make up its ranks today, or who comprised the pre–Pearl Harbor Army." After looking at the rough cut of *From Here to Eternity*, however, the Pentagon made only one objection to the movie. It wanted the studio to trim one scene in which Sergeant Warden appears acting excessively drunk, staggering around, and stumbling off a porch. In discussing the sequence with Buddy Adler, the Pentagon pointed out that Warden had been presented as an outstanding representative of the Army up to that time and that emphasizing his drunken condition would shock audiences. Nevertheless, the Army did not put its request very strongly ("as much as is possible should be trimmed"), and Columbia left the scene as shot since Warden's condition became a dramatic necessity to subsequent events.[51]

Whatever the changes needed to satisfy the military, Zinnemann believed their cooperation essential to his success in capturing the atmosphere of the story. He said he would have resigned from the project had Columbia not obtained Army assistance allowing the studio access to Schofield Barracks and the use of training planes made up to look like Zeroes to briefly recreate the attack on Pearl Harbor. The Army also assigned a top sergeant to supervise military details, particularly for the leading actors, some of whom had not been in the armed forces. Although actual soldiers appeared in only a few scenes, Zinnemann felt that "being in the authentic barracks and seeing the Army life around us gave the actors a kind of framework that was very useful to them and helped them create characters who were reasonably authentic." According to the director, if extras had been used to play the soldiers, the film would "never have had the feeling of tautness, discipline or any of the other things that were part of the professional American Army. The picture would have been a caricature." Without cooperation, he believed "the film would have been unthinkable."[52]

Zinnemann did not think the compromises, which he saw as imperative in obtaining military assistance, had significantly affected his artistic creativity or the dramatic power of the film. In the context of the 1950s and even without the barracks language of Jones's novel, he thought the film created "quite an impact on the audience." He agreed that if he had made the film in the 1970s without the language and sexual restrictions, it might have become more realistic. However, Zinnemann believed the film reflected the time in which he made

A "Japanese" fighter strafes Schofield Barrack on December 7, 1941, in *From Here to Eternity*. Alvin Sargent, the "machine-gunned soldier," years later wrote the screenplay for Zinnemann's *Julia* (1977).

it and that it remained true to the spirit of the book, "which was not anti-Army. Prewitt is proud to be a good professional soldier, a thirty-year man, 'I love the Army' he says."[53]

Almost without exception, reviewers of the movie agreed with Zinnemann's judgments. According to the *New York Times*, the film "stands as a shining example of truly professional moviemaking." The critic saw the film as a "portrait etched in truth and without the stigma of calculated viciousness." Despite the deletion of the stockade chapters, he thought the film "fundamentally cleaves to the author's thesis."[54]

James Jones did not initially agree that *From Here to Eternity* captured the flavor of his book: "I hated it when it first came out and I thought I would never go to see it again." When he did look at it five years later, however, it impressed him. He explained his change in attitude by saying that when he saw the film the first time he was still too close to the book and was unhappy about the deletions. But after five years, those compromises had had time to fade from his memory. He recalled, "I liked it and I was pleased at how well they had done it."[55]

More than most movies, *From Here to Eternity* demonstrates that to do a film "well" requires a collective effort, not just the genius of the director. Harry Cohn contributed more to the creation of the project than studio heads usually do. Buddy Adler nursed the script through the complex negotiations with the Pentagon and helped to mute Cohn's efforts to impose his ideas on the film. Daniel Taradash's script, which won him an Academy Award, became almost as much a masterpiece, as fine a piece of work, as Jones's novel. And unlike most scriptwriters, Taradash contributed to the production apart from the screenplay, becoming involved in the Pentagon negotiations, the selection of the director, and the casting. Nevertheless, Fred Zinnemann's direction provided the catalyst for bringing all the elements together to give the film its scope, power, and impact.

In contrast to most movies about the armed forces, Zinnemann's direction of his superb cast made the characters, rather than the military organization, the center of attention. Clift, Burt Lancaster, Sinatra, Deborah Kerr as Karen Holmes, and Donna Reed as Lorene—both women cast against type—all created characters with whom the audience could empathize and about whom they could care. Their interactions, their individual struggles to bring meaning to their lives, brought a richness to the story not found in most military movies, which rely on hardware, combat, or the color and romance of the services for their dramatic impact. Zinnemann remained in control of all elements of the film, conveying all the violence of the novel without ever showing it, creating the atmosphere of Army life in pre–Pearl Harbor Hawaii, and giving meaning to a climax that would have had the bathos of a soap opera in lesser hands. As a result, *From Here to Eternity* became

Fred Zinnemann rehearses Montgomery Clift and Frank Sinatra for a scene in *From Here to Eternity*.

one of the few Hollywood portrayals of the armed forces that ranks both as a great military film and a great American movie.

The film did not receive only positive reactions, however. Those who resented the film for what they saw as its antimilitary perspective criticized it in the same manner as those who criticized the novel. A critic in the *Los Angeles Times* wrote that the film "goes all out in making the military situation look its worst, and could probably be used by alien interests for subversive purposes if they happen to want to make capital of this production."[56] Even the president of the United States and the Defense Department received complaints, to which the Public Affairs Office could only answer that a private company had produced the film.[57] The Navy, however, took stronger action. A Board of Admirals banned the film from Navy ships and shore installations because they considered it "derogatory to a sister service." Of course, this criticism ignored the fact that the Army had cooperated in making the film as well as the purchase by both the Army and the Air Force of prints for their motion picture service.[58]

As Baruch had observed, *From Here to Eternity* did not portray the Army in a very good light even though neither Jones nor the filmmakers considered their work "derogatory." Like the novelist, Zinnemann saw the work as a study of an "individual striving to maintain his identity in the face of pressure from a huge organization." To him, the "organization is shown from the worm's eye-view as it were. The soldier in his articulate way says a man has to do what he has to do. . . . And he does it. He absolutely refuses to be a boxer. Eventually he gets killed for wanting to be himself. That is really what it is about."[59]

The military clearly had not seen *From Here to Eternity* as a comment on the human condition. Throughout their negotiations with the studio, the Defense Department and the Army expressed concern only with the image of the service that the film would create for its audiences. For this reason, the negative aspects of the portrayal always outweighed any dramatic or entertainment considerations. Adm. Lewis Parks, the Navy's chief of information, probably spoke for the majority of Pentagon officials when he said, "I enjoyed the movie as a dramatic motion picture. The acting was magnificent. Certainly, *From Here to Eternity* reflects credit on the actors, the writers, the director, and the producer as a dramatic achievement. And it definitely is not as objectionable as the book upon which it was based." Nevertheless, Parks maintained that the film "does not reflect any credit whatever on the Armed Forces of the United States."[60]

For such stories, Hollywood continued to turn to the veterans of the recent conflict who returned home and began putting their experiences onto paper. James Jones, Leon Uris, and Herman Wouk, among many others, produced novels containing characters about whom a reader might care. *From Here to Eternity, Battle Cry,* and *The Caine Mutiny* all became movies that portrayed the military and war with some realism and passion. Ultimately, the Army, the Navy, the Marines, and the Air Force assisted in the transformation of each book into a major motion picture.

If the novels captured the atmosphere of military life, and their authenticity helped make instant critical and popular successes, each in its own way contained images that did not necessarily flatter the services, particularly the officers. Used to receiving positive scripts or scripts that they could modify appropriately, the public affairs office of each military branch struggled to a greater or lesser extent with the filmmakers to achieve a mutually satisfying screenplay. From the studio's perspective, the novels had presold the movies they would produce, and to significantly change the plots might well weaken the completed films. Consequently, the process of turning the great war novels into possibly great war movies sometimes became as dramatic as the combat stories themselves, albeit without the blood and gore.

Whereas the Army had major problems with the portrayal of an incompetent officer, his unfaithful wife, and a brutal senior enlisted man in *From Here to Eternity*, the Navy had only two areas of concern with *The Caine Mutiny*. It objected to the word *mutiny* in the book's title, claiming the service had never had a mutiny. And it found the character of Captain Queeg, the World War II equivalent of Captain Bligh, offensive and derogatory to its officer corps. Consequently, Stanley Kramer, the film's producer, needed more than eighteen months of intense negotiation to resolve the problems and obtain assistance.

Aware of the potential problems inherent in Wouk's novel, Warner Brothers initially asked its Washington representative to submit a synopsis of *The Caine Mutiny* to the Defense Department in April 1951, for an official reaction as to possible Navy assistance on a film. Towne, answering for the Navy and the Pentagon, said that the "consensus of opinion of all concerned is that the development of a screenplay which could be considered acceptable for official cooperation would be a difficult, if not impossible, task for any writer to achieve."[61]

Towne explained that everyone felt that the plot contained a "combination of extremes, both as to characterizations and situations." He then claimed, "Neither the characters portrayed, nor the situation that they became involved in would have been tolerated in the Navy for long." Moreover, he pointed out that the "resolution of conflicts is accomplished after such a lapse of time as to be of no value in redeeming the service, or in offsetting the derogatory and very harmful sequences through which one must wade during the major part of the story."[62]

At the same time, he noted that although the story itself remained "full of errors, as may be expected," the Department of Defense would make no attempt at this time, to "offer constructive criticism in the interests of accuracy and authenticity . . . in view of the nonacceptability of the overall story line." In an attempt to persuade the studio not to undertake the project, Towne concluded, "We do not desire to offer any hope of our being able to work anything out on this project, as far as eventual approval of cooperation of Departments of Defense and Navy are concerned."[63]

Ultimately, however, the Navy would have to face the problem head on in handling Stanley Kramer's request for assistance in transferring *The Caine Mutiny* to the screen. Despite the service's ongoing opposition to cooperation on any film based on the book, Herman Wouk always considered himself a total Navy man. He had even sought technical advice from the service while working on the novel. In contrast to *From Here to Eternity*, *The Caine Mutiny* contained no scenes of physical brutality, no whorehouses, no adultery, and no profanity. In fact, in a note at the beginning of the book, Wouk had written: "One comment on style: The general obscenity and blasphemy of shipboard talk have gone almost wholly unrecorded. This good-humored billingsgate is largely monotonous and not significant, mere verbal punctuation of a sort, and its appearance in print annoys some readers." Moreover, Wouk did not paint an unflattering portrait of the Navy as a whole, and until the military suggested otherwise, he believed he had written a complimentary story.

Despite its title, *The Caine Mutiny* actually focuses, not on a "mutiny" but on Willie Keith, one of the war's typical ninety-day wonders. He has joined the minesweeper *Caine* as a newly commissioned ensign after graduating from Princeton and Officer Candidate School. In the course of his duty aboard the *Caine,* during the war in the South Pacific, Willie matures from a pompous and affected mama's boy to a man who ultimately becomes the ship's captain. The reader observes Captain Queeg and the "mutiny" from Willie's viewpoint as the war matures him. Although the young officer becomes an unwilling participant in the takeover of the *Caine,* he finally reaches manhood not through the mutiny or the court-martial but as a result of his actions when a kamikaze hits the ship in the closing days of the war.

The mutiny and the court-martial constitute the dramatic focus of the novel, but the significance of *The Caine Mutiny* as a war story lies in Wouk's portrayal of life on a minesweeper during wartime. He successfully recreated the experiences of men living in close proximity aboard ship, facing danger together for extended periods. Except for Captain Queeg's extreme behavior and ultimate breakdown, many Navy men have testified to having served under officers of his manner. Likewise, many high-ranking officers have indicated that Lieutenant Maryk's takeover of the *Caine* during the typhoon constituted a legitimate action under the circumstances Wouk created in his book.[64]

These opinions notwithstanding, the title of the novel itself prompted most of the Navy's opposition. Then-Commander James Shaw, who served as technical advisor, later observed, "I hazard a guess that if the book had been named *The Caine Incident,* minus that inflammatory word 'Mutiny,' Navy cooperation would have been obtained speedily." In fact, from the time of Wouk's first discussion of his proposed book with the Navy's Public Information Office in 1948, the service stated that it had never had a mutiny aboard any of its ships.[65]

Whether the history of the U.S. Navy supports that contention remains highly debatable. In preparing himself for his job as technical advisor, Admiral Shaw did considerable research on the subject and uncovered several incidents aboard Navy ships that clearly qualify as mutinies. Perhaps the most famous of these occurred aboard the brig *Somers* in the winter of 1842, when the ship's captain hung Midshipman Philip Spencer for mutiny.

In front of the film's story board, Comdr. James Shaw discusses shooting of *The Caine Mutiny* (1954) with producer Stanley Kramer and his staff.

Whether Spencer's actions consisted only of words or of actual planning, his execution caused a sensation, since his father, John Spencer, was then serving as secretary of war.[66]

Although the Navy tried the captain for murder, the court acquitted him, justifying his claim that he had put down a mutiny. In fact, the sensational affair did have a positive effect, producing national support for a formal training program to replace the traditional method of educating midshipmen aboard ship. Although previous efforts to do this had failed, the *Somers* affair resulted in a mandate to the new secretary of the Navy, George Bancroft, one of America's leading historians, to establish the Naval Academy at Annapolis, in order to ensure high-caliber education for future naval officers.[67]

In any event, whether incidents such as occurred on the *Somers* constituted a true mutiny, the Navy has seldom demanded historical accuracy in the fictional films on which it has assisted. The portrayal of a submarine's contribution to the Doolittle raid in *Destination Tokyo* or the origins of the Battle of Midway in *A Wing and a Prayer* immediately come to mind. Instead, plausibility served as the determining factor in deciding to approve cooperation, with dramatic license providing filmmakers with some flexibility. In military comedies, even probability often goes by the board. In *Jumping Jacks* (1952), for example, the Army permitted the film to show Jerry Lewis parachuting onto Dean Martin's canopy even though if this happened during a real jump, the chute most likely would have collapsed.[68]

Realistic or not, to many naval officers *The Caine Mutiny* obviously brought to mind *Mutiny on the Bounty* and the image of Fletcher Christian setting Captain Bligh adrift in a rowboat. Nothing so dramatic happened on the *Caine*. In his preface, Wouk wrote, "It was not a mutiny in the old-time sense, of course, with flashing of cutlasses, a captain in chains, and desperate soldiers turning outlaws. After all, it happened in 1944 in the United States Navy." As Wouk explained, when he first went to the Navy for assistance in writing his book, the mutiny was a "mutiny of the mind," not of arms.

Most Navy men seemed to understand this distinction, but they did not necessarily trust the American viewing public to do the same. Wouk himself did not help the efforts of the film's potential producers. After the novel appeared, the author explored the mutiny issue in much greater detail in a stage play, *The Caine Mutiny Court Martial*. Like the book, the play became a major success and reinforced the Navy's worries about the adverse effect of a movie.[69]

Despite this obstacle, Wouk's novel continued to lure filmmakers because of the huge audience it had reached. However, when Warner Brothers and other studios met a stone wall with their inquiries about possible cooperation in the spring of 1951, they decided not to pursue the project. At that point, Stanley Kramer, a young independent producer, took an option on the screen rights to *The Caine Mutiny*. By the summer of 1951, Kramer had a financial and distribution arrangement with Columbia pictures as well as a reputation for refusing to compromise his artistic and creative principles. Kramer himself concedes, "I was known as somewhat of a 'rebel' to the military establishment and to the government sources with whom I dealt. If I weren't a 'rebel' then I was considered a radical, a man who was dealing in extremes and in bothersome material."[70]

To be sure, his 1950 film *The Men* focused in a serious and controversial manner on hospitalized World War II paraplegic veterans. By showing the public how the government rehabilitated seriously wounded servicemen, Kramer's film had significant informational value and benefited the armed forces. However, his earlier *Home of the Brave* (1949) portrayed the abuse of a Negro soldier by his fellow G.I.s during wartime and helped establish the producer's controversial reputation. The Daniel Taradash–Buddy Adler–Fred Zinnemann team that made *From Here to Eternity* might have been able to assuage Navy worries about handling the "mutiny" on the screen because of their willingness to work with the military in developing a suitable script. However, given his reputation, Kramer was destined to collide with the Navy as soon as he began to develop a screenplay based on *The Caine Mutiny*.

The producer denied that he had any "soapbox" intentions in producing *The Caine Mutiny*. He saw Wouk's book simply as "a very broad-based novel of the Navy. It's really a cross section of Navy life on a mine sweeper in the Pacific—officers and men and the crazy Queeg." The Navy naturally saw little benefit in having one of its officers characterized as "crazy," irrespective of the mutiny problem. As a result, Slade Cutter, director of the Navy's Public Information Division, said he was ordered "to drag the Navy's feet, so to speak, as long as possible to delay the inevitable and to get the script cleaned up as much as I could."[71]

Although Kramer wanted cooperation in making *The Caine Mutiny*, he started off on the wrong foot with his selection of Stanley Roberts to write the screenplay. According to Cutter, when Roberts came to Washington to discuss the project, the officer recalled that he found it "like talking to Baby Snooks. My pride in the Navy was something absolutely impossible for him to comprehend or accept. He thought I was silly, unrealistic, irrational, and the possessor of that worst of all impediments to progress—the military mind, whatever that is." Roberts had an even more serious deficiency as far as the Navy was concerned. He had been caught up in the Red Scare that swept Hollywood in the late 1940s and early 1950s and had been accused of having ties to the Communist party. Whatever the truth of these charges, Cutter said the Navy Office of Information gave them credence and this "had no small part in the dragging feet operation."[72]

However, Kramer made his most serious mistake in his efforts to win Navy assistance when he decided to approach the Navy directly, which amounted to entering a lion's den unarmed. Both Baruch and Ray Bell, Columbia's Washington representative, attributed most of the producer's problems to his refusal to follow regular military channels in requesting cooperation. According to Bell, Kramer believed that on the strength of his reputation as a filmmaker, he could "probably obtain better and quicker cooperation from the Pentagon than working through me."[73]

The producer, of course, saw the situation differently. He said he wanted no lobbyist whose first responsibility remained with his company and who believed in compromising to obtain military help. This "more adamant viewpoint" with which Kramer admitted he approached the military, perhaps as much as the book itself, forced the producer to spend eighteen months in on-again, off-again negotiations, sometimes in the Pentagon, sometimes publicly in the media, before he obtained assistance in making *The Caine Mutiny*.[74]

Kramer tried, of course, to keep as much control over the script as he could, while still prepared to make some concessions to the Navy in order to obtain assistance. In one early effort to capture the flavor of the novel and perhaps curry favor with the service, Kramer hired Wouk to work with Roberts on the initial treatment. As soon as Wouk realized the depth of the Navy's feelings about not wanting his book transferred to the screen, he urged Kramer not to make the movie and offered to return the money he had received for the film rights. The producer responded with what he described as a "scathing" letter, in which he called the author "some sort of jellyfish."[75]

When Roberts completed his initial script and Kramer sent it to the Navy for consideration, the service found its worst fears fulfilled. Slade Cutter recalled that the "enlisted men were worse than bums, and the admiral was a stupid stuffed shirt." He conceded that it would have ruined "the picture to attempt to portray the 'Caine' as anything but a 'honey barge.' And we didn't object to that. The problem was that there was no indication that the rest of the Navy wasn't as bad as the 'Caine.'" The Navy therefore took the tack of trying to encourage Kramer to develop a script that would indicate the atypical nature of both Queeg and the *Caine*.[76]

Finally recognizing the problems he faced, Kramer hired a highly respected retired admiral to advise Roberts on the script and help bridge the gap to the Navy. In addition, he turned to Ray Bell for assistance at Harry Cohn's insistence. As part of Columbia Pictures's financial arrangement with Kramer, the studio could exercise some control over production through the size of its budget. Ultimately, Kramer also "jumped the chain of command" by requesting a meeting with the secretary of the Navy to make a passionate in-person plea for assistance.[77]

Kramer could have circumvented these problems by focusing on the court-martial and making a small, "interior" film as Wouk had done in the stage play. He also could have resorted to miniatures, special effects, and combat footage for the exterior sequences, as other filmmakers had done when they couldn't obtain real ships. However, as Bell noted, by 1954, when *The Caine Mutiny* appeared, filmmaking "had matured to the point where you could no longer phony something and feel that it was creditable to sophisticated audiences."[78]

The producer explained that *The Caine Mutiny* took place in the "massive environment of the U.S. Navy at war," and "to bring to the picture everything that is inherent in the book" required large-scale military assistance. He believed that to paint "this picture on a smaller scale would be to rob it of its value." Therefore, he pursued Navy cooperation more resolutely than the Navy dragged its feet, until the service finally approved assistance in December 1952.[79]

Kramer's meeting with the secretary of the Navy became moot, since the service had already decided to cooperate on the film. Although Admiral Parks, as chief of information, had bitterly opposed the film, most officers had enjoyed the book and only wanted any movie based on the novel to be as accurate and authentic as possible. Admiral Fechteler, the chief of naval operations, conceded after reading the book, "It's a hell of a yarn." He only wondered how Wouk in only two years of sea duty as a reserve officer had observed "all the screwballs I have known in my thirty years in the Navy." Moreover, Slade Cutter characterized Parks as not giving "a damn for public opinion or any of the media. He felt that doing a good job would be recognized eventually, and if it wasn't, so what?" Consequently, when Parks went to see the CNO about Kramer's impending visit to the Navy secretary, the chief of naval operations told him, "You had no business refusing cooperation in the first place."[80]

Parks himself recalled that Fechteler's comment "pulled the rug right out from under me after all this time," noting that the CNO had never mentioned the matter to him before. In any case, recognizing that he had lost the fight, the chief of information set about to salvage what he could. After Kramer's meeting with the Navy secretary, which now served only to formalize Fechteler's pronouncement, Parks told the producer that the approval did not "mean that you are going to get any extra help from me, because I don't agree with [it]."[81]

As a start, rather than allowing Kramer to use his own technical advisor, Parks assigned James Shaw, an active-duty officer with experience on ships similar to the *Caine*, to serve as the official Navy representative on the film. During the six months Shaw served on the project, he strictly supervised the production, working with writer Michael Blankfort on revising Roberts's script, arranging for Navy assistance at Pearl Harbor and San Francisco, and ensuring accuracy in the portrayals of actions and procedures.[82]

Despite the travails that accompanied Kramer's efforts to obtain assistance, he and his director, Edward Dmytryk, received "total" cooperation during the making of the film. In Hawaii, for example, the Navy put all its dockside derricks into operation simultaneously for one of Dmytryk's shots. As the script required, the Navy also provided use of attack boats, Marines, a carrier, and two destroyer minesweepers (one in Pearl Harbor and one in San Francisco) to play the *Caine*. The service would not, however, permit Kramer to acknowledge its cooperation in the screen credits. Nevertheless, a title stated: "The dedication of this film is simple: To the United States Navy."[83]

In any case, by working with Kramer and assigning one of its best officers to serve as technical advisor, the Navy expected that it could achieve a more positive image of itself in the completed film. In writing to Ray Bell in September 1953, Admiral Parks said, "I am still hopeful that *The Caine Mutiny*, although it will show the seamy side of the Navy, also will include some decency and good and thereby be a good movie reflecting credit upon the armed services and the people in uniform." And perhaps because their initial expectations had been so low, naval officers were enthusiastic about the way Kramer had handled the story when they saw the finished film at a Pentagon screening in January 1954.[84]

In its formal letter of approval, the Department of Defense Public Affairs Office stated: "We consider that Columbia Pictures fulfilled its obligations to the Department of Defense in bringing *The Caine Mutiny* to the screen in such a

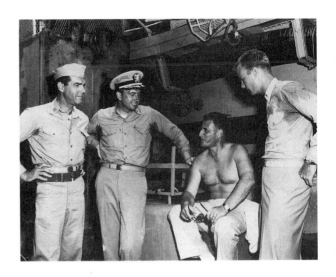

Producer Stanley Kramer (center right) discusses filming of *The Caine Mutiny* with Fred MacMurray (Tom Keefer), Comdr. James Shaw (technical advisor), and Robert Francis (Willie Keith).

Van Johnson, flanked by Stanley Kramer and James Shaw, waves at the camera during production of *The Caine Mutiny*.

commendable manner." On behalf of the Pentagon, Baruch wrote to Kramer: "We do want you to know, officially, that we believe you faithfully carried out your assurance to produce *The Caine Mutiny* in a manner which would be in the best interest of the Department of Defense. We consider the job well done, and will look forward to working with you in the future."[85]

Ironically, given all the smoke and fire that had accompanied the eighteen months of negotiations, the film they were praising did not stray very far from Wouk's book. To be sure, the author himself "thought it was a poor adaptation of my work." However, any artist has difficulty seeing his work altered, and filmmaking necessarily demands that liberties be taken in translating a lengthy book to less than two and a half hours of screen time. In this case, except for the differences in the presentation of Queeg's actions as a naval officer and the rationalization of the mutiny, the film adheres to the novel very closely.[86]

The portrayal of Captain Queeg, however, like the handling of Captain Holmes in the screen version of *From Here to Eternity*, simply illustrates how the military manages to improve its image in any film on which it assists. Although Wouk's book and Kramer's film remain ambiguous in their final treatment of Queeg, both the character and the Navy fare significantly better in the film than in the novel. In his version, Wouk reduces Queeg to virtual insanity and then half-heartedly tries to save him. After the court-martial, Barney Greenwald, the lawyer for Maryk (whom the Navy tried for mutiny), seems to rationalize Queeg's breakdown by suggesting that he helped guard the country during the 1930s, when most Americans ignored the Navy and its dedicated men. In truth, Wouk fails to connect Queeg's prewar service with his unstable behavior aboard the *Caine*. One literary critic pointed out that "Queeg is a goddamn maniac" and further observed that Wouk's justification would have validity only if it could be demonstrated that "Queeg worked himself down to the elbows for six years on this tin can in the North Atlantic and therefore he was crazy." Consequently, as Wouk plays out the story in the novel, the reader ultimately feels that Queeg had become mentally ill and that the Navy had carelessly allowed a potentially dangerous man to command one of its ships.[87]

Likewise, the film portrays Queeg as an obviously disturbed man, who performs in an increasingly irrational manner. Most Navy men have acknowledged that Maryk had real justification for taking over the *Caine*, given the manner in which Wouk structured the events leading up to the crisis during the typhoon. In *The Caine Mutiny*, however, Greenwald's posttrial defense of Queeg focuses on the conflict between a regular Navy officer and civilians turned sailors. In confronting the officers of the *Caine* after Maryk's acquittal, the lawyer argues that they bear the responsibility for Queeg's mental illness.

When Willie points out that Queeg did actually endanger the *Caine*, Greenwald retorts, "He didn't endanger anybody's life, you did, all of you. You're a fine bunch of officers!" When another officer reminds the lawyer that in the trial he had said Queeg "cracked" aboard the *Caine*, Greenwald responds that the captain had come to his officers for help and they had turned him down: "You didn't approve of his conduct as an officer. He wasn't worthy of your loyalty, so you turned on him. You ragged him. You made up songs about him. If you had given him the loyalty he needed, do you think the whole issue would have come up in the typhoon?"

When Maryk acknowledges the truth in Greenwald's comments, Willie realizes that he and his fellow officers really had committed mutiny. Greenwald jumps on that: "Ah. You're learning Willie. You're learning you don't work with a captain because of the way he parts his hair. You work with him because he has the job." Thus, in the film, Queeg remains as disturbed as Wouk shows him in the book, but clearly, as Greenwald points out, "He couldn't help himself." The civilians turned sailors have contributed to the disintegration of the regular Navy man, one who defended the nation when most Americans were comfortably at home making good careers and lots of money. In the film, then, Queeg emerges as a far better officer than Wouk's petty tyrant. Moreover, the film explains his breakdown rationally, whereas the book's captain seems only slightly different from his fellow commanders. The Navy would obviously prefer Kramer's version of the regular Navy officers to Wouk's more critical portrayal.

Kramer himself knew perfectly well that he had improved Queeg's character only to win Navy cooperation. In his pitch to the secretary of the Navy, he had said, "Fellows, you just aren't acquainted with dramatics. You cannot make white unless you make black. . . . Look, Captain Queeg was an officer who had battle fatigue and was going off his rocker. He did these things. Why did he do them? He did them perhaps because some of his officers were not patient enough with him and did not realize he was a sick man." In order to win cooperation, therefore, Kramer promised to show "simply that [Queeg] was an officer in the Navy who had gone off his rocker." Years later, though, Kramer conceded that the ending he devised "was immoral." He said that a year after he completed the film, he convinced himself that Maryk "should have taken over command."[88]

The success of the Navy and the Defense Department in modifying Captain Queeg's behavior probably had little effect on the public's perception of the Navy. They knew perfectly well that the service did not usually staff its ships and bases with unstable officers. The United States could never have won the war if a Queeg had captained many Navy ships or if a Holmes or a Fatso had abused their men. At the same time, audiences realized that a Frederic March or a Gary Cooper did not command all the Navy's carriers. Nor did John Wayne or Gregory Peck provide crucial leadership to their men. In fact, James Jones believed that the military might well benefit more from realistic portrayals like *From Here to Eternity* than from the more typical, sanitized war films. He suggested that audiences recognize a falsely positive image as pure propaganda and reject it out of hand.[89]

Perhaps. Nevertheless, *From Here to Eternity* and *The Caine Mutiny* remained aberrations. Robert Altman's 1956 *Attack!* did show an enlisted man shooting his incompetent officer, and the Army refused to cooperate. However, with very few exceptions, Hollywood's portrayals of the armed services for the rest of the decade contained few images that would

Dick Powell, director of *The Enemy Below* (1957), discusses the film with Capt. Herbert Hetu, the technical advisor, Frank McCarthy, Twentieth Century Fox executive, and the commanding officer of the destroyer on which shipboard shots for the film were made. In contrast to *The Caine Mutiny*, *The Enemy Below* was a "good" film for the Navy, showing a destroyer locked in mortal combat with a German submarine.

cause the Pentagon significant concern even if the story stretched the limits of credulity or showed officers at odds with each other.[90]

Run Silent, Run Deep (1958), based on a highly praised adaptation of Edward Beach's popular novel, examined an ongoing conflict between the captain and the executive officer and still received substantially more material assistance from the Navy than earlier submarine films. This cooperation and a highly detailed, actual-size, studio mock-up of a submarine's interior gave the film a better visual sense of what life was like aboard a World War II submarine than even *Destination Tokyo*. Nevertheless, as with most war movies, many of the incidents depicted leave the audience confused or incredulous.

In the opening sequence, a Japanese destroyer launches a depth-charge attack and apparently sinks the American submarine. The sub's captain somehow finds his way onto a life raft, avoids capture in Japanese waters, and makes his way in short order back to Pearl Harbor. The story itself is built on the premise that a Japanese submarine can torpedo an American craft while both are submerged. In actual World War II combat, however, the only submarines torpedoed had been cruising on the surface. While not denying the possibility of a successful attack on a submerged sub, former submarine commanders suggest that its likelihood would be remote. Likewise, although conceding that a submarine could torpedo an attacking destroyer with a straight-on "down-the-throat" bow shot as shown in the movie, submariners say it was done only rarely. (The captain who perfected the technique later disappeared on a cruise.)[91]

Nevertheless, *Run Silent, Run Deep* resembled a documentary; it highlighted submarine warfare techniques and command decisions. Moreover the movie featured two leading stars, Clark Gable as the captain and Burt Lancaster as the questioning, troubled "exec" officer, both overaged for their submariner roles. The *New York Times*'s Bosley Crowther praised director Robert Wise's skillful filmmaking that "did not waste movement, time, or words."[92]

Most combat movies of the decade simply imitated the seminal works, retelling the same stories of both World War II and the Korean War, with few new insights into the nature of men in combat. Likewise, Hollywood seldom produced a peacetime military drama or comedy that could not have been set equally well in a civilian environment. Even the Cold War preparedness films such as *Strategic Air Command* and *Bombers B-52* struggled to find ways of making life in the military interesting or attractive.

From the perspective of the Pentagon, scenes of planes, ships, or ground forces doing their jobs usually justified the time, energy, and cost of providing assistance. Given the ongoing threat that the Soviet Union posed, filmmakers showed great reluctance to create negative portrayals of the military, challenge its procedures, or question its competence to defend the nation. Only Stanley Kramer's 1959 *On the Beach* sought to warn the American people of the potential danger of nuclear war. And in recognition of the need for allies against the Communist menace, virtually all Hollywood films set in World War II showed America's enemies, if they appeared at all, as dedicated fighters, simply doing their jobs, with little reference to the nature of the political system for which they were fighting.

10 | The Most Ambitious Undertaking

THE REHABILITATION OF THE FORMER ENEMIES, which had begun before World War II ended, continued unabated into the 1960s. In the 1948 *Fighter Squadron,* a German pilot does shoot at Edmund O'Brien as he parachutes to earth. However, one of his men promptly shoots down the enemy plane with only the comment: "Burn, you crumb, burn." No recriminations, no reference to Hitler or the Third Reich. Even that portrayal remained an aberration.

The novel *Twelve O'Clock High* contained a similar scene, based on an actual event. General Savage's B-17 suffers fatal damage on the climactic mission over Germany, and he finally crash-lands the plane in the English Channel. The whole crew successfully evacuates the bomber, only to have a German fighter commence a strafing run on their lifeboat. The scene could have appeared in any Hollywood movie made during the first two years of World War II, and the book reinforces the reader's outrage against the atrocity when Savage's driver–waist gunner dies after reentering the sinking bomber to drive off the attacking fighter. That sequence, which helped bring on Savage's breakdown, appeared in the original screenplay that Twentieth Century Fox submitted to the Air Force. It did not appear in the completed film.[1]

Few, if any, other scripts, even in their initial version, portrayed an enemy war crime. Instead, Hollywood worked assiduously, in concert with the Pentagon, to picture Germans in a positive light. *The Big Lift,* appearing in 1950, focused upon the efforts of the U.S. Air Force to thwart the Soviet blockade of Berlin. In advising Air Force headquarters in Wiesbaden, Germany, of writer-director George Seaton's visit to collect information for his screenplay, the Directorate of Public Affairs said it believed the film "is an opportunity to really tell the public what the Berlin airlift is made of." The service's director of public relations wrote directly to Gen. Lucius Clay, commander in chief of the European Command, asking him to provide all possible assistance to Seaton and meet with him personally during his visit.[2]

Upon his return from Germany, Seaton wrote to the Air Force Public Affairs Office that the "effect of the operation on Berlin, on the Germans, would be of even more dramatic value than the lift itself." He explained that he wanted audiences to "identify themselves with some of the characters in the operation" and said he was "most enthusiastic" about the possibilities for making the film. He also reported: "I have had long discussions with Mr. Zanuck and he has given the project the green light, high priority as to purse strings, and is determined to get the best and most popular cast available."[3]

Seaton later explained, "Our theme will be what to do with the Germans? It will exemplify the two opposing viewpoints—don't let 'em work, let 'em starve versus, Hitler's gone, why make the people suffer? If we can teach them democracy we can't grind 'em in the gutter all the time, crying revenge, revenge, revenge! But we can't, we mustn't, forget either."[4]

To help create this story, the Air Force provided full cooperation to the production, including transporting the motion picture equipment from Los Angeles to Germany. There, Seaton filmed all aspects of the Berlin Airlift, which enabled him to include a pseudo-documentary portrayal of how the United States carried aid to the city's residents with clocklike precision. However, as Seaton had suggested earlier, he focused on human relationships, with Paul Douglas loathing the Germans with a bitterness stored up from his years as a POW, whereas Montgomery Clift naively seeks friendship from the Berliners and particularly from a calculating girl who wants to get to America to be reunited with her German boyfriend.

Although the film conveys both sides of the argument, the message that ultimately comes through focuses on the need to develop friendship with the German people so that they can serve as a counterbalance to the Soviet threat. In contrast, Leon Uris's novel *Armageddon*, which told the same story of the Berlin Airlift and good Germans within the broader scope of postwar de-Nazification, never attracted attention from filmmakers, perhaps because it raised questions about the German people's complicity in Hitler's genocide against the Jews.

In truth, the Army and the American public did not always find these revisionist portrayals of the recent enemy appropriate even as the Cold War heated up and Germany was rapidly becoming our ally. Nowhere did this become clearer than with the 1951 *Desert Fox*, an account of Field Marshall Edwin Rommel's North African campaign. Unlike Erich von Stroheim's overblown portrayal of Rommel as a pompous egomaniac in *Five Graves to Cairo*, James Mason was to play the general and his ultimate defeat in a restrained and positive manner.

In response to Twentieth Century Fox's request for combat footage and information about the 1944 strafing of Rommel's staff car, the Army advised the Defense Department's public affairs office that the script "glorifies Rommel and may be a sensitive story." The Army also reported that the State Department considered that the film "would be disastrous" and the service's decision to provide the requested footage "would be guided by the decision of State Department." In contrast, General Marshall did not seem bothered by the film. In writing to Darryl Zanuck, the studio's head, in February 1951 about the Pentagon's screening of *Why Korea?* Marshall, then the secretary of defense, mentioned without comment information he had received about the production of *The Desert Fox*.[5]

However, Harry Green, a former chief historian of the Adjutant Generals Department and a member of the American Expeditionary Forces in World War I, expressed a decidedly different view in a long, rambling letter to Eric Johnston, president of the Motion Picture Association. Green first presented a litany of criticisms of Rommel's actions in North Africa. He claimed that Rommel had ordered "his subordinates to deliberately mistreat captured American prisoners," had some of the Afrika Corps dressed in Allied uniforms, which was "forbidden by the Geneva convention," and ridiculed "the capabilities of American generals and soldiers in a most insulting and degrading manner."[6]

Green then said that Rommel's reputation as "the Desert Fox" resulted from "his open cruelly deliberate and continuous violation of every rule of international warfare. He also reported that a leading American historian was writing a book "that will completely annihilate the attempt by Rommel-worshipers to depict this inhuman military and personal monster in the favorable and heart-warming light they [the filmmakers] seem so foolishly determined to put across." He then cited a number of editorials that had criticized the making of the movie and concluded with an attack on Nunnally Johnson, the producer-writer of *The Desert Fox*.[7]

In contrast, Johnson believed that the threat of fascism had become sufficiently dif-fused to justify "objectivity toward a dramatic figure" and promised that every scene would have a historical basis. He recognized the criticisms that the production was receiving but said he was "as concerned with the welfare of my country as the ordinary man. I think we can say about the Germans: 'Now that the war is over, we will do what we can to judge you individually, without prejudice.'" Johnson acknowledged that if Rommel had not turned against Hitler, he could not be making the film and claimed, "Circumstances allowed Rommel to be a pretty good fellow because there were no civilians involved in the North African campaigns."[8]

Johnson said he was not trying to solicit sympathy for Rommel "except in the final sequence. There, the circumstances as he says goodbye to his wife and son to go to his death would undoubtedly create sympathy for any man." He thought Rommel had the problem of a conflict of loyalties: "He followed a false god, and when he found out he risked the role of a traitor." Finally, in support of creating a positive portrayal of the field marshal, Johnson cited Winston Churchill's praise of Rommel in the House of Commons in January 1942.[9]

There, the prime minister had said, "We have a very daring and skilful opponent against us, and, may I say across the havoc of war, a great general." In *The Grand Alliance*, Churchill later acknowledged that his remarks had brought "some reproaches from the public" but refused to retract them. He explained that although Rommel's "ardor and dar-ing inflicted grievous disasters upon us," the general had deserved the salute he had ren-dered. Churchill also reminded his readers that "although a loyal German soldier, he came to hate Hitler and all his works, and took part in the conspiracy of 1944 to rescue Ger-many by displacing the maniac and tyrant."[10]

Johnson did not convince Harry Green, who wrote the writer-producer a long dia-tribe on March 31, 1951, concluding that he should abandon the project for the "welfare of your country" and make a movie about an American war hero rather that about "one of the worst Nazis of them all." Nor did the completed film, which closed with Churchill's assessment of Rommel from *The Grand Alliance*, impress Sidney Orenstein after he saw *The Desert Fox* in December 1951. Writing to President Truman to ask that he prevent *The Desert Fox* from being shown in Germany, he claimed, "This film is an insult to all who have ever worn an American uniform. It tends to glorify the career of a Nazi General. These Nazis butchered, gassed, and killed—Let us not forget this—Nor give them the chance once again."[11]

In response, Towne, in the Pentagon's Motion Picture Section, explained to Orenstein that *The Desert Fox* had received no official cooperation from the Pentagon and "is not subject to any action on the part of this office." He also reported that the producers had agreed not to release the film in Germany "at least for the time being." Nevertheless, Americans saw a movie that turned Field Marshall Rommel into a hero and helped create the idea that good Germans had existed in Nazi Germany.[12]

The apex of this process occurred in the 1957 Twentieth Century Fox film *The Enemy Below*, which became the quintessential rendering of the former enemy in Hollywood films, focusing on the desperate battle between an American destroyer and a German U-boat. Humanizing the conflict, director Dick Powell created three-dimensional combat-ants, skilled warriors in arms, not hated enemies. Each captain matches the other's tactics, maneuver for maneuver, with neither man gaining an advantage until Curt Jurgens man-ages to mortally wound the American destroyer. In turn, Robert Mitchum rams the sub-marine, leaving the two ships entangled in a death grip.

In the original script, the captains die when their ships explode as Mitchum reaches for Jurgen's hand in a failed rescue attempt. In the completed film, Mitchum's rescue effort succeeds, allowing the two warriors to praise each other's courage and professionalism aboard an American destroyer, which picks up the surviving crew members. Given the context of the Cold War shift in alliances, the duel, which neither man wins, suggests that whatever the system for which they fought, nobility exists between comrades-in-arms.[13]

Probably true and certainly more realistic than showing a submarine run over Humphrey Bogart's lifeboat in *Action in the North Atlantic*. Nevertheless, *The Enemy Below* makes it easy for viewers to forget the true nature of Hitler's Germany. Jurgens only alludes to the nature of the government for which he wages war, with his primary concern being the welfare of his crew. The juxtaposition of the honor among warriors and the loss of good men's lives does create a significant antiwar statement in the film, and *The Enemy Below* remains one of the very best movies about World War II and about cinematic naval warfare.[14]

The U.S. Navy expressed enthusiasm for the script and requested only minor technical changes in language and procedure from Twentieth Century Fox before approving full cooperation to the production during filming in Hawaii. To ensure the accuracy of the portrayals, the service detached a destroyer captain from his command to work with the screenwriter and director and assigned another officer as liaison to the filmmakers at Pearl Harbor to coordinate the use of a destroyer in the exterior combat sequences.[15]

The Navy even fired two training torpedoes at the destroyer to create the sequence in which Mitchum outguesses Jurgens by turning his ship at the last minute to avoid being hit. Filmed from the air, the scene dramatically shows the two torpedoes straddling the destroyer. In contrast to such realism, the studio used miniatures to film Mitchum's ramming the submarine. Although the difference between the live-action and the special-effects photography becomes obvious, the sequence passes so rapidly that it distracts only marginally from the realism of the rest of the movie or the image of the noble enemy.[16]

As presented on the screen, *The Young Lions* also comments on the futility of war and posits the existence of good Germans. To create those messages, however, the filmmakers had to radically revise Irwin Shaw's 1948 novel, the last of the great World War II novels to reach the screen. Director Edward Dmytryk explained: "We just felt that it was that long after the war—more than ten years by the time the film came out—and that people weren't looking at the war in the same way they were then. The book was written right after the war, in white heat. Nazis were complete heavies. All Germans were Nazis, and everybody hated everybody." However, by the late 1950s, the director said, people were "looking at the whole situation a little more honestly and we realized that not all Germans had been bad Germans. We didn't excuse Nazis. There were always bad Nazis. But there were many people fighting on the German side who weren't Nazis and who weren't cutthroats and who weren't murderers and Jew Haters."[17]

To effect this change in portrayal, the filmmakers turn Christian Diestl's persona inside out. In the novel, he starts out as an intelligent, moderate man who does not even belong to the Nazi Party and sees Hitler as giving Germans back their pride. As he gets involved in the war, his brutal side comes out and he becomes more and more brutal, turning on his own men and murdering people, until by the end he has become, according to Dmytryk, "really the worst brute imaginable." In contrast, as played by Marlon Brando, Diestl comes to recognize the evil he has supported, particularly after he has stumbled upon a concentration camp. However, the filmmakers failed to avail themselves of the opportunity to portray the horrors of the extermination factories, since they include no images of gas chambers or emaciated inmates.[18]

Instead, the focus remains on the good German, not the Third Reich. Why? According to Irwin Shaw, Brando, as usual, wanted his character to appear in a complimentary and sympathetic light. Consequently, unlike the novel's character, Brando's officer "is not at the end a man brutalized out of all humanity by the combination of his fundamental philosophic beliefs and the events he has been through, but an innocent wanderer, shocked by the realization of where his behavior and the behavior of his compatriots has finally led him." At the same time, Shaw noted: "The influence of the State Department, which was interested in rehabilitating the image of the Germans at that period, might also be discerned."[19]

The Pentagon had its own problems with Shaw's portrayal of life within the wartime Army, particularly the brutality and anti-Semitism directed against Montgomery Clift's Noah Ackerman during basic training. To obtain the cooperation they needed, the filmmakers toned down the anti-Semitism and reduced the violence to a series of fistfights between Ackerman and the bigots, the last of which he wins. In addition, Shaw noted that at the dictates of the Pentagon, the "brutal, fascist-minded Captain is disciplined at the end by his superiors." Thus, the Army ended up with a portrayal similar to the one it negotiated on *From Here to Eternity*. And people were left with an image of a good German, not an evil Nazi.[20]

Despite this ongoing rehabilitation, nothing could completely mask the horrors of Hitler's Germany, except perhaps expediency. The hand of the Army in shaping the image of a "good" German for its own purposes becomes obvious in the 1960 *I Aim at the Stars*, often uncharitably subtitled "But sometimes I hit London." In fact, the film remains a classic study of expediency overwhelming moral and ethical considerations. Since the United States needed his rocketry expertise, the filmmakers transform Wernher von Braun, a Nazi party member and the creator of the V-1 and V-2 rockets, into an American hero who helps the United States develop its missile program. Ironically, while von Braun was to create the Saturn moon rocket soon after the film appeared, NASA refused to cooperate on the production. According to an official in the agency's public affairs office, NASA still did not want to become associated with "the guy who helped Hitler pump V-1s and V-2s into London and Antwerp—killing all those people." In fact, the official "felt that VB would have worked for the Russians if they had taken him instead of us."[21]

NASA had company in its concern about the transformation of von Braun in *I Aim at*

Wernher von Braun (second from left), Producer Charles Schneer, and Turner Shelton, of the U.S. Information Service, and Army generals at the Pentagon's official approval screening of *I Aim at the Stars* on February 18, 1960.

the Stars. Curt Jurgens agreed to play the rocket scientist only after von Braun acknowledged that the film should frankly admit that the Nazis used some of his inventions for destructive purposes. Jurgens said he did not "want this to be a phony picture. . . . It is quite an important point to be frank because this picture could be pretty dangerous."[22]

The actor also felt that the film had "to show that the man I play invented the V-2 rocket, which almost destroyed London." At the same time, he said, "It is important to show he came here and was almost isolated to do scientific work and that he has advanced to now being almost the No. 1 American scientist. That is drama." The actor had to explain to von Braun that if the film showed only his work on rockets, without including his Nazi past, it would become dull: "It is much more interesting to show that a man has a period of danger in his life and has the power to get rid of it." Despite von Braun's work for the Nazis, Jurgens believed Germans would only ask, "What else could he do?" The actor felt that the film's "main point is not just to show off that he is now an American citizen—but to make friends. And the best way to do that is to bring more persons over here. Maybe we can even do it with the Russians."[23]

Producer Charles Schneer looked at his film in much the same way, saying that he was not attempting to whitewash von Braun. Noting that the rocket scientist agreed that the film had to remain a frank and truthful presentation, Schneer explained: "After all, von Braun is making contemporary history. Since his story is already known to millions of people, any attempt to take undue liberties would quickly be discerned. This, then, is a true story, literally a document of our times. It will of necessity create controversy, but it will also entertain." To do this, the producer selected an American, a German, and a British screenwriter to collaborate in an effort to provide an unbiased point of view of von Braun.[24]

The resulting film may have done that, and the cultural exchanges about which Curt Jurgens talked may have ultimately led to the end of the Cold War. At the time *I Aim at the Stars* appeared, however, the Soviet Union remained an implacable foe and von Braun's rocket expertise was helping the United States maintain the balance of power. As a result, neither the Army nor the Defense Department's public affairs office raised any objections to providing assistance to the filmmakers, despite von Braun's wartime activities. The few problems the Pentagon had with the script focused on technical matters and the interservice missile rivalries. In one instance, the DoD office responsible for arranging cooperation asked the producer to delete von Braun's "remarks accusing the Navy of promising more than they can deliver," since they would "serve no useful purpose, and we believe would create ill feeling with the Navy." The office also reminded the producer to send the script to NASA, which had just come into existence, and include reference to any of the agency's projects relating to space exploration that came under its jurisdiction.[25]

Not everyone was willing to forgive or forget von Braun's past, however. In April 1959, Norman Retchin wrote to the *Daily Variety* to complain about Hollywood's willingness to make movies that pictured a Nazi "as a sensitive human being equipped with the same set of human feelings as anyone else." The writer reserved most of his wrath for the von Braun story, then still in preproduction: "We are now about to glorify for the entire world an ex-Nazi—in this case a scientist, but still a Nazi." He said that while Americans were fighting Hitler, "this ex-Nazi was doing his stuff for the Fuhrer and was almost as much of a hero to The Third Reich as he seems to be to a lot of people in our country." Retchin worried that von Braun "is about to become glorified on the screen and the indirect conclusion will be drawn wherever the picture is seen all over the world that, 'Well, maybe those Nazis weren't such bad fellows after all.'"[26]

The British ultimately expressed the same concerns when *I Aim at the Stars* premiered in London in November 1960. During the protest at the opening, one pamphlet scattered to the audience warned, "The showing of the Von Braun film makes a mockery of the tributes to our fallen dead." Inside the theater, two men burst onto the stage carrying a twelve-foot banner, which read, "Nazi Braun's V-2 rockets killed and maimed 9,000 Londoners."[27]

In the United States, the *Los Angeles Times* reviewer recognized the controversial nature of *I Aim at the Stars* but said that since the film seemed reasonably factual, "the American with no love for the Nazis or any of their works may be willing to remain at least fairly objective while viewing" von Braun's story. Perhaps more important for the filmmakers, the reviewer felt, "It IS fascinating."[28]

Sen. John Sparkman (D-Ala.) agreed, telling the Senate on August 23, 1960, that *I Aim at the Stars* "is probably one of the most forthright stories ever brought to the screen about a living person. And I believe it is safe to say that not many stories in motion picture history have dared be as frank, forthright, and blunt as this." Sparkman did acknowledge the controversy surrounding von Braun and the reality that he had joined the Nazi Party. However, the senator focused on the American military's decision to "corral the Von Braun group" and bring them to the United States to work on the Army's rocket program. He also stressed that the film "tells the story of a man and his dedication in such universal human terms, in his contacts with his family and his coworkers, and even those who oppose him that it will have strong appeal to men and women everywhere as a story alone, during the enjoyment of which they will also learn much of value about important steps on man's road of progress."[29]

Among those who viewed *I Aim at the Stars* less favorably was Bosley Crowther, who observed in the *New York Times:* "In the way of examination of the ethical reasoning by which the fabricator of the Nazi's deadliest missiles is now warmly accepted on our side, the film is conspicuously fuzzy and takes its stand on the none too certain ground that Dr. von Braun's driving interest from boyhood was simply to develop rockets that could reach out into space." The reviewer questioned whether anyone could reach "intently into the depths of his scientist's mind" and comprehend his complex motivations by watching "this poorly written film. Anyone looking for clear, white light on his personal drama will not find it in *I Aim at the Stars.*" In fact, Crowther found "little in this made-in-England drama to interest or convince anyone. Its synthetic brand of hero worship may be annoying and offensive to some."[30]

Von Braun apparently had this reaction, since he did not like the film much, according to the NASA public affairs official.[31] Nonetheless, the film did contain a positive image of von Braun and the work he and his fellow German scientists were then doing for the U.S. Army. It also stands as a paradigm of the debate over the responsibility that Germans should bear for following Hitler.

An American military officer, who serves as von Braun's accuser in the film, argues that the Allies should have tried von Braun as a war criminal. Von Braun says he will accept that charge if the officer agrees that anyone who worked in any munitions factory should be considered a war criminal. To von Braun, however, his only sin was wanting to develop rockets that would travel in outer space. The movie does show that his obsession almost got him executed as a traitor by the German Army and only a last-minute pardon from Hitler himself saved him. In the end, however, a more cynical, less sympathetic von Braun emerges. In answer to her concern over the lethal nature of the weapon he is developing, von Braun tells his fiancée he does not care that civilians may die from his V-2 rockets. As a good German, he simply is helping his country to win. Like Rommel, he turns against his government only when defeat is eminent, not because of the nature of Hitler's Reich. Moreover, he would have the audience believe he simply remained a rocket scientist, doing work that differentiates man from lower animals.[32]

Jurgens's character had made the same point in *The Enemy Below*. Warriors simply pursue their profession, irrespective of the system for whom they are fighting. Missing from such a philosophy, of course, is any recognition that some regimes do not warrant support under any circumstances because of the absolute evilness of their actions.

Likewise, *The Longest Day* ignores the government and leaders responsible for the horrors of World War II. Instead, the film tells the story of the D-Day invasion of France from the perspective of the four combatants who fought each other on the day that determined the future of democracy, of good over evil. Despite the significance of the event, few people in Hollywood could understand why Darryl Zanuck wanted to make *The Longest Day*. Even Zanuck's son Richard begged his father not to undertake the project, recalling: "What scared me was that we were getting into an eight or eight and a half million dollar picture, which at that time was really fantastic."[33] Ultimately, however, Zanuck was to create the largest, most expensive war movie up to that time and it was to become a major box-office success.

Ironically, when he began the project, Zanuck appeared to be washed up as a producer. His son thought *The Longest Day* might become "really the end of the line." He asked his father, "Who cares about World War II?" pointing out that a high percentage of the moviegoing public had not been born at that time. The young Zanuck pointed out that trying to duplicate the battle scenes would be an "awesome" project.[34] Nevertheless, *The Longest Day* recreated the Allied landings on Normandy so faithfully that stills taken during the filming seem nearly indistinguishable from photos taken on June 6, 1944. Many knowledgeable people, including military men who have seen *The Longest Day*, think its visual authenticity resulted from the use of actual combat footage. In reality, Zanuck shot the entire picture in 1961, with the assistance of the U.S., British, French, and German military commands.

Of all the war movies that preceded it, only *Wings* had received assistance of this magnitude, and just as *Wings* set the standard for combat movies up to *The Longest Day*, Zanuck's film became the model for the war spectaculars that followed. But whereas Wellman's 1927 picture opened virgin territory for filmmakers and moviegoers, *The Longest Day* completed the postwar cycle of World War II movies that had begun in 1948. By 1960 the war had been over for fifteen years, and Hollywood had nearly exhausted the possibilities for stories about that conflict. Moreover, World War II–vintage equipment was rapidly vanishing. Not even the U.S. military had much matériel from the pre-1945 period.

Zanuck described the film as the "most ambitious undertaking" since *Gone with the Wind* and *Birth of a Nation* when he announced in December 1960 that he had acquired the film rights to Cornelius Ryan's *The Longest Day*. He had paid $175,000 to French producer Raoul Levy, who had purchased the rights to the 1959 best-seller shortly after the book had appeared. Zanuck said he planned to use no stock footage in the film. Instead, he would recreate the entire invasion of Normandy. Although he had not yet calculated the cost of making a film of this scope, he estimated that he would have to spend $1.5 million just to restage the Allied landings on Omaha Beach. He expected that the greatest expenditure would result from the time needed to arrange logistics and locate equipment. With the exception of gliders, which he would have to build especially for the film, he believed he could round up enough landing craft, amphibious tanks, planes, and other equipment for an accurate re-creation of D-Day.[35]

Zanuck claimed that he was being forced to restage the invasion in its entirety because no footage of the Normandy landings existed in military archives. Actually, a limited amount of footage of the initial assaults did exist. According to Andrew Marton, one of the film's three directors, the twenty-seven feet of film taken on Omaha Beach had "a shockingly dramatic quality." However, he said the footage had poor visual quality, and reprocessing it into CinemaScope dimensions and editing it into newly shot footage would have produced visually distracting results. Moreover, not enough quality footage of all the D-Day landings existed to reconstruct even a convincing small-scale landing. For *D-Day, the Sixth of June* (1956), actually a three-sided love story with only a small-unit assault as part of the film's climax, director Henry Koster staged a landing on a beach north of Los Angeles. Likewise, Arthur Hiller filmed James Garner's one-man landing on Omaha Beach for *The Americanization of Emily* (1964) in the same locale because he could not put together enough footage for even that brief sequence.[36]

Consequently, Zanuck was telling the truth when he said he could not use combat footage to recreate D-Day. And restaging a historical event of the dimensions of the Normandy landings did truly constitute a "most ambitious undertaking." Nevertheless, filming such a large-scale military battle did not qualify as the unique cinematic endeavor Zanuck implied it would become. Filmmakers had been shooting most of their ground combat sequences since the perfection of the wide-screen projection processes in the early 1950s. For such epic stories as *Battle Cry,* directors photographed scheduled military training maneuvers with the help of the Pentagon. For smaller productions like *Pork Chop Hill* (1959), they usually staged their own battles, relying on technical advice from one or another of the services, some equipment, and occasionally a few men for a limited time. The resulting footage may have lacked some of the authenticity of actual combat film, but it presented none of the problems of visual quality that would have resulted from reprocessing the standard-dimension combat footage and then trying to intercut it with the non-combat portions of the movie.

Filmmakers did, however, continue to use old gun-camera film, which they blew up to wide-screen size, when they needed to portray large-scale aerial combat, because of the difficulty of acquiring large numbers of World War II planes. Even so, in *The Battle of Britain* (1969), Guy Hamilton staged all the combat sequences, since he was making a wide-screen, color spectacular, and the available footage had been shot on standard-dimension, black and white film. Fortunately, Hamilton was able to borrow fifty German Heinkel bombers from the Spanish Air Ministry to photograph on the ground and in formation. He also found sufficient numbers of British and German fighter planes in England, on the Continent, and even in Canada, to fill out the ranks of the opposing air forces.[37]

In contrast, only four years after the war Zanuck had had difficulty obtaining B-17 bombers when he made *Twelve O'Clock High.* Since the B-29 Superfortress had made other planes obsolete even during the war, the Air Force had quickly scrapped their fleets of B-17s and B-24s as soon as fighting ended. (The B-24 Liberator bombers never acquired the romantic image of the B-17s, and no major film ever featured them.) Due to the cost of maintaining the large bombers in flyable condition, airplane collectors or dealers could supply only a few bombers to filmmakers. As a result, World War II airplane movies such as *The War Lover* (1964) and *The Thousand Plane Raid* (1968) used a few rebuilt B-17s for shots of individual planes on the ground and for specific maneuvers in the air. For their waves of bombers and sweeping combat sequences filmmakers went to the same Air Force archives that provided black and white footage for *Twelve O'Clock High*. Only after D-Day did the Air Force use color stock in their gun cameras, and then not on a wide scale.[38]

The Navy and the Marines, in contrast, used color film in the Pacific from the beginning of the war. Therefore, most movies about the war against Japan could be made in color if the producer chose, as Warner Brothers did in *Fighter Squadron* and in the second half of *Task Force* and as RKO did in *Flying Lethernecks*. In addition, film companies could also generally shoot aboard Navy ships to obtain authentic locales to intercut with the combat footage and studio dramatizations. But they could not borrow whole fleets to restage their sea battles. For one thing, the composition of task forces and the types of ships in them changed during the 1950s. The Navy put its battleships into mothballs, and its straight-decked carriers became obsolete with the development of jet planes. These changes precluded the photographing of contemporary armadas to represent World War II flotillas. Thus, in making movies about the World War II Navy, filmmakers had the options of reprocessing old combat footage with its attendant sacrifice in the quality of the visual image or of using miniatures and sacrificing authenticity. Walter Mirisch chose the first method with *Flat Top* (1952) and *Midway* (1976), whereas Otto Preminger for *In Harm's Way* (1965) and Elmo Williams for *Tora! Tora! Tora!* (1970) chose the second, all with limited success.

In contrast, Zanuck faced the challenge in *The Longest Day* to recreate authenticity on the land. The lack of suitable combat footage did give him the option of using color film for the production. However, he and Elmo Williams, his associate producer and the coordinator of the battle episodes, found from test shots that color would distract from the gritty, documentary style in which they intended to shoot the film.[39]

If Zanuck could not plan to save money by using combat footage, he had become well versed in the Hollywood practice of cutting expenses by obtaining military assistance. As production chief at Twentieth Century Fox, he had supervised many military films in addition to *Twelve O'Clock High*, including *To the Shores of Tripoli*, *A Wing and a Prayer*, and *Halls of Montezuma*. For *The Longest Day*, however, Zanuck realized he would need more help than he could obtain from any one nation. In his December 1960 press conference, he announced that the NATO Command and the four governments that had fought at Normandy had promised him assistance. To coordinate the actions of these armies, Zanuck said he would use a director from each of the four nations, overseeing their work himself.[40]

Ken Annakin, the British director, described Zanuck as like many American film people who "did not really like or trust Limeys and had only hired me because he'd made the promise that each section would be directed by the national of those armies." Nevertheless, Annakin quickly became part of the production team, which essentially functioned as a collaborative director. Annakin recalled that Zanuck "was a beaver for work" and tried to watch every scene being shot, ready to give suggestions, occasionally interfering with the director's decisions and orders to the actors. As the British director stressed, however, Zanuck's concern always remained "realism and accuracy, at almost any cost. . . . In my opinion, [he] was determined to make the greatest and truest film about the second World War which had ever been made."[41]

Zanuck ultimately claimed he had actually directed 65 percent of his film, but he acknowledged that "if anybody acts in *The Longest Day*, it is unintentional and not a result

Ken Annakin, director of the British sequences in *The Longest Day*, supervises the British landing on Sword Beach.

Ken Annakin discusses a scene in *The Longest Day* with Darryl Zanuck.

of my 'direction.' My job was to *prevent* actors from acting—to encourage them to play their individual roles realistically and without 'camera awareness.'"[42] Zanuck may have given himself too much credit for even this nondirecting. James Jones, one of the writers Zanuck brought in to work on the script, thought the size of the production probably contributed to making *The Longest Day* the most true-to-life war film produced in Hollywood. "Simply because of its magnitude, the filming of it was like conducting a major military campaign. By its very scope it is precluded from concerning itself with basic human character, even as modern war itself is." To Jones, the film became basically a historical documentary. Like history, it recorded the personalities of the generals rather than the privates.[43]

Zanuck did not consider his film a documentary. At his press conference, he admitted that *The Longest Day* would have "no regular plot" as in a dramatic film. However, he asked: "What is a documentary? This is not a picture about World War II, but about actual persons who participated in the Normandy landings." During a subsequent interview, he said that after reading Ryan's book, he had become "convinced that it would make one of the really great war pictures of our time." At his first news conference, though, Zanuck emphasized that "the production would not be a war picture as such." Instead, he said it would be "the story of little people, of the underground and of general confusion." *The Longest Day* would have as its theme "the stupidity of war," and though it would condemn war, Zanuck hoped the film would "be fair about it."[44]

Darryl Zanuck with director Andrew Marton (Foreground) prepares a shot on "Omaha Beach" during the making of *The Longest Day* (1962).

Throughout the course of the production, the producer repeated his belief that *The Longest Day* would do more than simply portray history. He maintained that any picture "made on such a scale and with so much effort must say something." He felt it was important to convey through the film a message about the current world situation and the threat to "our way of life." He wanted his movie to serve as "a reminder to millions and millions of people that the Allies, who once stood together and defeated an evil because they stood together, can do so again in a different situation today which in some ways is similar to what they faced in 1940."[45]

Most filmmakers like to think their motion pictures will make a significant comment on the human condition, and Zanuck's pomposity differed only in degree from that of his colleagues. In any film of the dimensions of *The Longest Day,* themes and messages often become lost in the rush of production demands. Not surprisingly, therefore, Zanuck had to focus primarily on the organization of men and materials needed to recreate D-Day in much the same way as General Eisenhower planned the original invasion. The cost of making the film would have become prohibitive without the cooperation of the four armed forces who were to provide sufficient troops and equipment to recreate D-Day. Of all the planning, therefore, none became so crucial to the success of Zanuck's endeavor as the arrangements with each government for the use of its men and equipment.

Although Zanuck announced in December that he had already obtained cooperation, he had only begun negotiations at that time. As his first step, he wrote to Air Force general Lauris Norstad, then commander of NATO. In the controversy that later arose over the use of American troops in the film, the press described General Norstad as Zanuck's "friend," although both men were to deny the characterization. The producer pointed out that he had met Norstad only twice—the last time in 1952—and that he had never called him about cooperation. He had simply described his plans to make a film and asked Norstad whether he should apply to NATO for assistance or go directly to each of the four governments. Norstad advised him to deal directly with each government, because going through NATO would "complicate things."[46]

Acting on the general's suggestion, Zanuck quickly reached agreements with the British, German, and French military authorities. From the British he received promises of a fleet of World War II–vintage ships and 150 men from the East Anglia and Greenjackets Brigades. The Germans promised matériel and technical advice but no troops. The French military agreed to loan Zanuck 2,000 troops despite its current war in Algeria. Later, when some of the promised American soldiers became unavailable for the final location shooting, the French Defense Ministry provided an additional 1,000 commandos for almost five weeks and even permitted them to wear American uniforms.[47]

Despite the loss of American soldiers, Zanuck later denied having had any real difficulty obtaining assistance from the United States: "The fact is that the Pentagon was very cooperative and we were able, in one way or the other, to use a great many American troops."[48] General Norstad did send a telegram on February 1, 1961, to Assistant Secretary of Defense for Public Affairs Arthur Sylvester advocating support for Zanuck's film. Nevertheless, the producer claimed he "religiously followed" established Hollywood–Defense Department procedures in applying for assistance.[49]

According to Defense Department regulations, Zanuck's initial approach to General Norstad did not constitute "an exception" to standard operating procedures. Nor was the general's telegram to the Pentagon in which Norstad recommended that Sylvester approve any request for assistance on *The Longest Day:* "I feel that this excellent book, brought to the screen with Zanuck's skill, could be very useful to the military services and to the United States. I think the German aspect could be handled in reasonable perspective and, on balance, the film would benefit the alliance." He recognized that the production would require a considerable amount of assistance from the American military at "substantial cost." However, if the secretary approved cooperation, Norstad proposed to have the European Command work directly with the producer to clearly define requirements and ascertain problem areas for the military.[50]

Sylvester had become an assistant secretary only a few weeks earlier, and he had acted primarily on assurances from his predecessor and the public affairs staff that Zanuck was making a routine request for assistance. Later he admitted he had responded "before I knew what in the hell I was doing." Sylvester cabled Norstad on February 8 that he agreed with the general's recommendations. He also asked Norstad to advise Zanuck to channel his requests for assistance directly to the Pentagon. In response to the general's remark about "substantial costs" involved in Zanuck's request, Sylvester quoted the regulations governing military assistance to the film industry: "Cooperation will be at no expense to the Government." He further noted that his telegram did not imply approval of the project or that cooperation would automatically be forthcoming, but that it was merely "a courtesy preliminary survey without commitment."[51]

Following Sylvester's instructions, Zanuck began the process of obtaining assistance through negotiations in Washington and with the American Command in Europe. He was not shy about dropping names in his communications, once quoting a note in which President Kennedy had said, "I am delighted to learn that *The Longest Day* will now be a screenplay. I think that this is one of the finest books dealing with events of the Second World War, and I very much look forward to seeing your dramatization of this book." Despite such high-level support for the project, Norstad's office extended no special treatment to Zanuck, refusing, for example, to switch regularly scheduled amphibious exercises from the Mediterranean to Normandy. Nevertheless, after extensive discussions in the Pentagon and with the military in Europe, Sylvester's office approved full cooperation on May 5, 1961, with the understanding that Zanuck would make certain minor changes in the screenplay he had submitted in April.[52]

Coming up with a workable screenplay often resembled a battle on the magnitude of D-Day. Zanuck recalled that when he first read Ryan's book, "I went absolutely nuts about it." Even before he acquired the film rights, he and Elmo Williams had written a treatment that included the episodes they wanted to portray in the movie. Zanuck said he was "not interested in making a film that is only historically accurate. It just so happens that this one happens to be accurate. I am interested in following the brave, funny, bewildering, human and tragic events of the day." He not only attributed the book's success as a best-seller to its accuracy, but he also said "it gave the public a chance to see our own errors and our own successes, our own confusion and our own clear thinking." However, he also wanted to show the events on the enemy side during D-Day and to avoid "a rosy, star-spangled banner drawing of D-Day," because that would lead to failure. According to Zanuck, the only way to make a film a box-office success would be to "tell audiences *what they do not know about what happened that day.*"[53]

To do this, Zanuck hired Ryan in January 1961 to write the screenplay, a decision that proved to be a double-edged move. Ryan had become an expert on the historical details of D-Day but lacked the expertise to transform them effectively into a screenplay. The author had covered the Normandy invasion for the *London Daily Telegram,* and a return visit to the French Coast in 1949 had rekindled his interest in Operation Overlord, the invasion's code name. For ten years he researched the invasion, conducting more than a thousand interviews with the participants. To him, the resulting book had become a story "not about war but the courage of man."[54]

Perhaps more important, having spent much of his life becoming a part of D-Day, he thought he knew what had happened that day and wanted *The Longest Day* to portray events precisely—as he had written them. However, Ryan did not understand the needs of a filmmaker. Even the military, with its concern for authenticity, appreciated the tyranny of the movie camera, the requirement to move ships and men closer together than they operate in actual battle. Ryan did not recognize this need for compromise to ensure dramatic visual impact. In contrast, Zanuck was experienced in attempting to combine historical reality with Hollywood dramatics. Zanuck's biographer pinpointed the problem that led to virtual war between producer and writer: "One crucial difference between Zanuck and Ryan, it seems, is that Zanuck was usually aware when he was altering a truth for dramatic purposes, whereas Ryan could never admit to an error." Zanuck considered any inaccuracies in the film to be minor: "They are close to the event that occurred. We did land. We did take the beach. We took dramatic license to make it effective. Anything changed was an asset to the film. There is nothing duller on screen than being accurate but not dramatic. There's no violation if you use basic fact, if you dramatize basic fact."[55]

With *The Longest Day,* Zanuck's argument about dramatization may have cinematic validity. Still, one must ask how far a filmmaker can extend dramatic license before a historical movie or a movie set within the framework of actual events loses credibility. Many people in Hollywood argue that as long as a film contains the essence of the actual event, the change of facts or occurrences is acceptable.[56] But what if these changes challenge the assertions of filmmakers that they are telling a "true" story, as stated in the opening credits of *Chariots of Fire?*

Cornelius Ryan (left) and director Andrew Marton talk with Darryl Zanuck (right) about a scene for *The Longest Day.*

Among many other errors of fact, the movie portrays Harold Abrahams beating the clock in a race around the Trinity College courtyard at Cambridge and losing to Eric Liddel in a one-hundred-meter race although the two men only faced each other once, later in the two hundred meters during the 1924 Olympics, something not mentioned in the story. However, the film aspires to explore the human condition through the efforts of two men striving to achieve personal goals by competing in the Olympics rather than becoming a documentary of the athletic achievements of the two runners. Since it succeeds in its goal, the changes in fact, although unnecessary, count for less than if the film sought to document the two men's athletic careers and the 1924 Olympics.

The Gallant Hours, the 1960 story of Adm. Bull Halsey's winning the naval battle of Guadalcanal, makes the same claim of telling a true story. Director Robert Montgomery went even further. He served on Halsey's staff and said he intended to create a film that would faithfully document the two weeks leading up to and including the battle. A reading of the history of the sea battle off Guadalcanal supports Montgomery's claim right up to the defeat of the Japanese fleet on November 13, 1942. Unfortunately, the film then ends with Halsey's staff running from the radio shack with the news that the admiral had capped off the day by succeeding in having Admiral Yamamoto shot down. In fact, the Air Corps did not assassinate the victor at Pearl Harbor until April 1943. Does this error matter? Clearly, the director's claim that he was adhering to fact conflicts with history. Can the audience believe anything that came before, given the egregious error in the final sequence? Montgomery said he was creating a true account of actual events, with entertainment only a secondary consideration. Coming at the penultimate moment, the climax clearly violates the director's stated goal in making the film and so would seem to exceed the limits of dramatic license.[57]

With *The Longest Day,* during the months Ryan worked on the script, he and Zanuck waged war over their different visions of how the film should portray D-Day. Ultimately, the filmmaker was to claim victory in the battle for truth, recounting that Romain Gary, whom he had hired to work on the portrayal of the French contribution to the invasion, uncovered one of the "major errors" in Ryan's book. Zanuck explained that Ryan had described the assault on the Ouistreham Casino, one of the crucial skirmishes between the Germans and the French that had enabled the British to advance from the beach. However, the producer said Gary had discovered that the RAF had demolished the casino two years before D-Day: "There was a hotel still standing in Ouistreham, but no casino." Nevertheless, based on Ryan's description, Zanuck had started to reconstruct the casino, and he said that "because it turned out to be a great sequence, I talked Romain into leaving it in."[58]

This account has only one problem. It has no basis in fact. Contrary to Zanuck's claim that Ryan erred in *The Longest Day* when he described the assault on the casino, the book contains no such description. Ryan only mentions the casino as "now believed to be a strongly defended German command post" and in quoting a French commando as telling his commander, Philippe Kieffer, that he looked forward to the assault with "pleasure. I have lost several fortunes in that place." Moreover, Gary mistakenly credited the RAF with destroying the casino. The Germans had demolished the building and replaced it with a fortified gun emplacement, which commanded Sword Beach, where the British landed.[59]

How then did *The Longest Day* come to portray the assault on the Ouistreham Casino, one of the most dramatic sequences in the movie, albeit on a building that looked nothing like the original casino and filmed in a different location? Ryan had interviewed Commander Kieffer and read *The Green Berets,* his book on the French Green Berets, but inexplicably he did not include the story in *The Longest Day*. In their treatment, Zanuck and Williams blocked out the assault, most likely based on Kieffer's book. When Ryan began work on the screenplay, he simply followed the filmmakers' guidance and fleshed out the story based on his interview and Kieffer's account. Director Ken Annakin then shot the sequence as written; and apart from the geographic and structural differences, the cinematic rendering of the assault closely followed Kieffer's story.[60]

Why then did Zanuck falsely accuse Ryan of describing an assault on a phantom casino, apart from the reality that the two men came to dislike each other intensely during the writing of the script? At the onset, the filmmaker probably misread Kieffer's account of attacking the German fortification in "Casino" square and assumed that the casino still existed. In addition to being visually exciting, the sequence would enable Zanuck to show the French contribution to D-Day. Then looking for some humor in an otherwise grim story, he extrapolated from the commando's comment about losing money at the casino a brief scene in which a soldier machine-guns the nonexistent interior of the nonexistent casino. In the completed film, Zanuck's rendering of the structure did not resemble the original building, having instead the elements both of a French building and of a German fortification. In accusing Ryan of making a mistake in his book, Zanuck was undoubtedly attempting to make the writer the scapegoat in case anyone discovered the truth about the casino as well as some of his other cinematic fabrications.[61]

In any case, Zanuck often became as inconsistent as Ryan, who stubbornly fought to retain his book's account. At one point, for example, Ryan suggested including in the film one or two romantic interludes that had actually occurred on D-Day. Zanuck responded in a blistering memo: "I do not want to badger you or cramp your style, but when you bring up, as you did at luncheon yesterday, an extraneous idea like love scenes between Gille [a French resistance fighter] and his fiancee, I have to speak up. These are just the things that we do not want and are the same things that have killed off so many other war pictures when they have tried to introduce a touch of sex." By the time *The Longest Day* went into production, however, Zanuck had cast his current mistress, Irina Demick, as the fiancée and expanded a minor, purely fictional role that he had created into the only significant female character in the film.[62]

Despite these changes of direction and continuous disagreements, Ryan turned in a thick script on April 5, 1961. Zanuck found many things in it out of proportion for the

Combined French and American military units help Darryl Zanuck reproduce the original Franco-American assault on the Casino of Ouistreham in *The Longest Day*.

story he intended to tell, and he set to work redoing the screenplay to suit his purposes. Very quickly, Ryan's *The Longest Day* became Zanuck's *The Longest Day*. Although Zanuck and Elmo Williams made most of the contributions to the revision, the filmmakers sought additional advice from writers in the four countries involved in D-Day. Ultimately, only Romain Gary and James Jones made significant contributions to the final script.[63]

Zanuck specifically wanted the author of *From Here to Eternity* to make Ryan's G.I. dialogue sound more authentic, without taking into account the effect such language would have on the Production Code Office. When Zanuck submitted the script for approval, the office refused to approve the "casual profanity" and the obvious substitutions for four-letter words that it contained. The censor objected to the use of dialogue like *crap, muck it, motherlover, bastards, damn, hell,* and even lines like "they couldn't sink the clucking can if they tried to."[64]

To make matters worse, the office observed, "We are concerned with what seems to us to be an excessive amount of slaughter in this story. We realize that it is impossible to tell the story of the invasion of Normandy without indicating the staggering loss of human life. We do urge you, in those scenes you stage, to minimize the dramatizations of personal killings. We think that such an effort on your part would avoid the 'bloodbath' effect." For the most part, Zanuck ignored these requests. Jones, however, expressed outrage at such strictures. Writing to the producer, he said, "I was *morally* shocked at . . . their 'concern' over the 'excessive slaughter' in the story. What the fuck do they think war is? What did they think Omaha was, if not a 'bloodbath'? I find it incredible that these ostriches can go on like they do, building fallout bomb shelters, with one hand, and not allowing honesty in combat films with the other. And if they tell me this is what American people *want,* I can only answer that they're full of *bullshit.*"[65]

Faced with these reactions, a continuing dialogue with his writers, and the Pentagon's requests for changes, Zanuck admitted in mid-May that he was "going very slowly" on the final script. At the same time, work on other aspects of the production was proceeding toward an early-summer shooting date. Zanuck brought together a general staff of seventy technical advisors, headed by Ryan for the American sequences, General Pierre Koenig for the French, and Admiral Friedrich Ruge for the German. Most of the experts had participated in D-Day; some had even been face-to-face combatants. (In one instance, only his death shortly before filming began prevented a former German pilot from working as an advisor with the French marine he had strafed on the beach seventeen years before.) Zanuck even verbalized the hope that the original commander in chief, General Eisenhower would consent to speak a few lines for a "faceless" actor in two brief but critical scenes.[66]

Zanuck faced his "biggest problem" in locating actual war equipment, and his staff conducted a vast scavenger hunt across Europe to find obsolete matériel. Spain offered a repository of old German weapons, especially tanks. The sands of Normandy yielded a British tank that had been buried for seventeen years. Guns came from all over Europe. Zanuck located the British piano company that had built the original gliders for the invasion and had two exact replicas manufactured for the film. He also found three British Spitfires in Belgium and two German Messerschmitts in Spain. Fortunately for the producer, thick overcast had obscured the sun over Normandy on D-Day, and he was able to maintain accuracy without recreating an entire Air Force. Uniforms for the Allies proved no major problem, since battle dress had changed little since 1944. However, Zanuck had to order German uniforms specially made, because the West German Army had destroyed all vestiges of its Nazi past.[67]

In all his efforts to recreate D-Day, Zanuck kept in mind that many potential viewers had been there and would recognize any sharp differences between history and its dramatic portrayal. During his preparations, he also adhered to his original concept of the film. "Remember our story is not a military picture," he repeated in mid-May. "It's not a war picture. It's the heartbeats on both sides." Ironically, though, the producer had virtually assumed the role of a supreme commander in assembling his staff, in supervising all aspects of the production, and in all decision making. He organized and planned the filming as carefully as the Allies had prepared for D-Day. Even a similar tense excitement prevailed. As Zanuck noted, "All you can do is to get the buildup ready for the day we say "Shoot." To be sure, unlike General Eisenhower, Zanuck did not have to keep his preparations secret.[68]

But he did have limited resources. Zanuck had hoped to begin production at Omaha Beach, using the promised British fleet to recreate the original invasion task force. When the Admiralty informed him that a three-hundred-thousand-dollar fuel bill accompanied the fleet, he turned to the U.S. Sixth Fleet, which had amphibious maneuvers scheduled at Corsica at the end of June.[69]

To prepare for the filming, the producer sent Elmo Williams, Andrew Marton, and six camera crews to the Mediterranean, with a French LST providing the transport for the men and equipment. When Williams first approached the commander of the Marine assault force for permission to shoot the landing, the officer expressed serious reservations because of his men's inexperience. He also pointed out that the Marines had become an integrated force in contrast to the American assault forces at Normandy, which did not include black soldiers. After considering a response for perhaps two seconds, Williams assured the officer that this would not matter. (During filming, however, he instructed the cameramen to avoid capturing a black face if at all possible.) He then convinced the commander to approve assistance by pointing out that the landings would be more realistic for the men and so better for training purposes if the film company recreated the Normandy beaches and set off explosive charges.[76]

To prepare the location, the film crews built fortifications on Saleccia Beach, where the landings were scheduled to take place. By the time the fleet arrived, the company had built obstacles along a two-mile stretch of beach, buried explosive charges, and simulated machine-gun emplacements so that the shoreline looked like Omaha Beach as it had appeared on D-Day. The twenty-two ships of the Task Force, which represented the Sixth Fleet's largest concentration since it had been stationed in the Mediterranean, provided the background for the landing of sixteen hundred men of the Third Battalion, Sixth Marine Division.[71]

The first wave of Marines, representing G.I.s, land on "Omaha" beach during first filming for *The Longest Day* on Corsica in June 1961.

With his ships and a large-scale landing on film, Zanuck turned his attention to location work in Normandy. Shooting there began in mid-August when Zanuck took over the French town of Sainte-Mère-Eglise to recreate the disastrous American parachute drop of D-Day. For two weeks, seventeen French stuntmen wearing American uniforms made repeated jumps, dropping everywhere except in the town square. Finally, after several injuries but only a couple of successful landings in front of the cameras, Zanuck resorted to the traditional Hollywood method of dropping the parachutists into the square from cranes.[72]

At the same time, filming began on the Normandy beaches. Like Saleccia Beach, they required makeup jobs to return them to 1944 conditions. The filmmakers could not use Omaha Beach at all because its D-Day monument was too large to be camouflaged and it still contained an abundance of buried live ammunition. Zanuck therefore filmed the Omaha Beach landing at Ile de Ré in late October and early November. However, he shot the American struggle to scale Pointe du Hoc a short distance down the shore from Omaha Beach at the original site. Armed with French permission and original D-Day photographs, Zanuck's crew "burned the whole bloody place," fabricated shell holes, built fortifications, removed old mines, and sandbagged the monuments to look like bunkers. The American Command in Germany provided the invading force for the assaults on the German cliff positions, assigning a unit of the 505 Infantry Battle Group and a battalion of Army Rangers.[73]

Numbering about 150, the G.I.s served for almost three weeks as supporting players to four of Zanuck's actor-soldiers in late August and early September. The Rangers trained for both amphibious landings and mountain climbing, and their job at Normandy included preparing the actors for the cliff assault. Zanuck had made their job harder by hiring three rock and roll singers, Paul Anka, Tommy Sands, and Fabian, along with Robert Wagner, a Hollywood veteran, to play soldiers in the four-minute sequence. According to Ryan, Zanuck did his casting with the goal of attracting young people to the film. Nevertheless, Elmo Williams admitted that his boss's choices for the physically difficult roles shocked him.[74]

The associate producer's reaction seemed justified during the early filming, when first a speck of sand in his eye and then a torn fingernail immobilized Anka. One of the Rangers was moved to suggest that the actors didn't "have what it takes." After continued work with the Rangers, however, the four stars went up the cliffs side by side with the soldiers during the filming. By the end of the sequence, Williams had come to view the casting in a different light, observing that the "kids have done everything we've asked them. Anka had to fall off a ladder seventeen times before we got one scene right." If the director of the sequence, Andrew Marton, had any complaint about authenticity, it was that the soldiers were

Filming the assault by U.S. Rangers on Point du Hoc for *The Longest Day*.

sometimes too proficient. Occasionally he had to remind them that things had not gone perfectly on D-Day and he didn't "want it to be perfect now."[75]

Marton's major problem, apart from minor injuries, flubbed lines at thirty-five thousand dollars a day, and unrealistic perfection, became the presence of Darryl Zanuck himself. Whenever the producer came to a location, he would stand behind Marton and breathe down his neck. During one scene, the producer rasped, "There's too much smoke. Cut!" Boss or no boss, the director turned to Zanuck, bellowing, "Nobody says cut! Nobody says action but me when I'm directing. Nobody!" Despite such interruptions, spectators watching the filming at Pointe du Hoc could not help but admire Zanuck's invasion. One observer noted that the explosive charges shook the ground, water spouts soared a hundred feet into the air as landing craft came in off the Channel, and the newly burned-out craters from the original shelling had a "sickening realness to them."[76]

Sgt. Joseph Lowe, who had taken part in the original assault on Omaha Beach, became one of the best judges of the authenticity of Zanuck's D-Day. Participating in the filming at Pointe du Hoc, the veteran thought the re-creation was "very realistic." Did it replicate D-Day? "Oh. No sir, it wasn't anything like this. Nothing will ever be like that believe me, sir." Trying to describe the difference, the sergeant said, "There was a good deal of confusion on D-Day and men were falling into the water or down onto the beach everywhere you looked. There is confusion now. Lots of it. When we fall, it is because we are told to. The danger is not above us this time, it's below."[77]

Having recreated the "general confusion" of Normandy as planned, Zanuck felt he had left behind all the difficulties that had earlier plagued his production. By the second week in September, filming of the parachute drops at Sainte-Mère-Eglise was nearing completion. British and French sequences were being shot or were in the final planning stages. And the producer had already scheduled final location shooting in Normandy for October and November, again using American troops which General Norstad had promised. Even at this stage of production, Zanuck had doubts about the possible success of the film: "I don't think anyone's ever had to spend so much time putting so little on film. Right here we're spending two and a half weeks and half a million dollars for four minutes. . . . Moviemaking costs so much you lie awake all night worrying about it. I'd like this to be the best picture I've ever made. But I don't know."[78]

Without the military assistance, of course, Zanuck would not have been able to film *The Longest Day*. Nevertheless, at the same time he was using American G.I.s from Germany as advisors and extras in Normandy, the Defense Department had been mobilizing Army Reservists and National Guard units and was planning to immediately send forty thousand men to Europe to meet the Communist challenge posed by the building of the Berlin Wall. The direct phone line linking American headquarters in Germany to Zanuck served as a constant reminder that the Army could recall units assigned to his production at the first sign of trouble.[79]

Although the 1961 Berlin Crisis constituted a threat to Zanuck's continued use of troops, the producer saw the Wall as a justification for his film's theme. In his mind, the Communist threat in Berlin emphasized the parallel between the current situation and the one in 1944. He saw his motion picture as fundamentally "the story of David and Goliath, the triumph of the seemingly weak over the seemingly invincible. There were the Allies, weary of long years of war, of humiliating defeats, divided, uncertain, the knife at their throats, uniting in a combined attack that first broke the hold of Nazism and then broke its neck." He compared the defeatists of 1944 who spoke of "the wave of the future" to those currently spouting the better-Red-than-dead line. "But," he said, "I believe that freedom will never be crushed as long as there are men as brave as the men of D-Day. That's what's implied—though not directly stated—in *The Longest Day* and that's why I'm making it and making it now."[80]

Zanuck was not the only person using American troops to convey this message. In early September, Jack Paar, then host of NBC's *Tonight* show, decided to provide his viewers with on-the-spot coverage of the Berlin Crisis. On September 7, with a television crew and four cameras and Pentagon approval, Paar traveled to Friedrichstrasse, a border crossing that had become the scene of several confrontations between East and West during the previous three weeks. Seven officers and about fifty men in seven Army jeeps arrived at the same time. The men took positions on the sidewalk and in a war-damaged building, and Paar filmed his program. When newsmen later questioned the Army about the unusual concentration of troops at the Wall, a spokesperson explained, "There was an operational changeover of units in progress this afternoon. In an effort to be accommodating, we permitted Mr. Paar to film these activities. Mr. Paar took advantage of this situation."[81]

By the next day, Paar's visit to the Wall had made the headlines in Washington, where it caused an immediate outcry in the Senate. Describing Paar as a "TV comic," Majority Leader Mike Mansfield reminded people that the Berlin Crisis should not serve as a TV spectacular. Majority Whip Hubert Humphrey added that the government had other things to do "besides provide a backdrop for television shows." These reactions became a forewarning of Hollywood's difficulty in obtaining future assistance from the military. Most ominously, Clifford Case suggested that "the practice of making facilities of the defense establishment available for any private ownership, for commercialization and commercial profit, is one to be examined, and should be permitted only in a situation in which their use would not in any way endanger the security of the United States."[82]

Ironically, *The Longest Day* did not enter the discussion, although the September 8 issue of *Time* magazine contained an article describing the assistance Zanuck had been receiving from the military since June. After the Army announced on the ninth that it had taken disciplinary action against two Army officers in Berlin, the Senate lost interest in the Paar incident. However, the controversy over Hollywood's use of military personnel had just begun.

David Brinkley, in defending his network colleague from congressional and press criticism, made the connection between Zanuck's use of the military and Paar's activities. By the eleventh, Secretary Sylvester had begun to publicly express his reservations about Pentagon cooperation with the film industry: "I have grave doubts whether this sort of thing is a proper use for military equipment and manpower. It looks to me like a skunk in the military garden party." He said the issue of military assistance had been on his mind for a long time, and he questioned Zanuck's making arrangements with the services at the same time the Army was complaining about a manpower shortage. He further noted, "Zanuck isn't paying for any of the time our troops put in or for the equipment."[83]

The media's continued attention to the Paar incident and to Zanuck's use of troops in Normandy served to rekindle political interest in the matter. Congressman Bob Wilson, head of the Republican Congressional Committee and a member of the House Armed Services Committee, wrote to Secretary Sylvester on September 13, asking a series of questions about the Paar incident and its relationship to *The Longest Day*. His letter was clearly politically motivated, and he lost interest in the subject as soon as Sylvester answered him on the twenty-fifth with the standard public relations justification of military cooperation with Hollywood.[84] When later asked about the controversy, Zanuck commented, "I think that story got out of hand and was exaggerated by people who thought they could get headlines out of it."[85]

From his perspective in France in September 1961, however, Zanuck did not realize that the uproar had aroused Sylvester's concerns about cooperation. The press soon discovered that General Norstad still intended to loan Zanuck seven hundred soldiers for his final shooting at Ile de Ré, a small island two hundred miles south of Normandy. In confirming the assistance, a spokesman for the U.S. Command in Europe said on October 16 that the Defense Department had approved the request. He explained that the Army considered the troops to be on a training exercise involving a movement by vehicles and an amphibious assault. He added that Zanuck would be paying at least part of the cost of transporting troops from their base near Frankfurt.[86]

Responding to inquiries, the Pentagon issued a statement that both the White House and the Pentagon were "reviewing any further cooperation with Darryl Zanuck." The White House, however, refused to take part in the investigation of Norstad's agreement. When questioned about continued cooperation, an aide to Congressman Wilson replied, "What's okay with General Norstad is okay with us." The general believed his decision to assist Zanuck was his own business and declined to act on the Pentagon's "suggestion" that he send fewer soldiers to Zanuck. Ultimately, Secretary of Defense Robert McNamara ordered a cut in the size of the force from 700 to 250 men, and the Pentagon explained, "This decision was based on the fact that the number originally planned was much larger than is normal in military cooperation. The curtailed participation is being authorized on the basis that it is in the national interest to do so and that the U.S. and its allies are cooperating in helping to film a great story of American, British, and French heroism."[87]

Zanuck said the loss of the 450 men would have meant he could not have recreated Omaha Beach without help from the French government, which loaned him 1,000 French commandoes for five weeks. Just as important, the French military allowed them to wear American uniforms. Moreover, the 250 G.I.s whom the Army did provide cost the producer three hundred thousand dollars, because he "had to pay every penny of their expenses" as a result of Sylvester's closer scrutiny of cooperation.[88]

The reduced number of soldiers and Zanuck's payment for their transportation and expenses became the first tangible signs of the secretary's reevaluation of the Pentagon's policy on cooperation. To actually effect significant changes in the regulations, however, Sylvester needed to overcome opposition from both the military and the film industry. His commitment to making these changes received reinforcement by another controversy stemming from the military's help to *The Longest Day*. In November, while filming was in progress at Ile de Ré, the United Press reported that Robert Mitchum, portraying Gen. Norman Cota in the movie, had complained that during a major action scene some of the American soldiers Zanuck was using appeared afraid to board a landing craft in high seas. Reports quoted Mitchum as saying, "I had to hop aboard first myself with some other actors and stuntmen before they gave in." To make matters worse, Mitchum also said he had seen two top officers watching the landing operation from the beach. "Unfortunately they got cold as we were wading in the icy water and asked for a good fire to get warm." Although both Mitchum and Zanuck subsequently denied the inferences drawn from the actor's remarks, the newspaper accounts kept the cooperation issue alive.[89]

To exacerbate the situation further, Sen. Sam Ervin, chairman of the Senate Subcommittee on Constitutional Rights, announced about a month later that some soldiers were

Robert Mitchum, portraying General Cota, lands on "Omaha" beach, at Ile de Re, off the French coast, in November 1961. Mitchum's comments about the Army assistance during this scene added to the controversy surrounding the making of *The Longest Day*.

claiming that the Army had forced them to take part in the filming at Ile de Ré. At first the service insisted that all the men Zanuck used had come from Germany as reported in the press and so were there on regular assignment. In the follow-up report, however, the Army acknowledged that some of the soldiers Zanuck had used came from a transport unit near Ile de Ré and some of these men had refused to participate in the shooting.[90]

If Sylvester needed any more evidence to harden his conviction that he should change the policies, Zanuck himself provided it. When the producer sent *The Longest Day* to Washington for final approval on September 21, 1962, the Defense Department found that the print contained a brief sequence it had specifically requested that Zanuck delete. The action portrayed an American soldier machine-gunning a group of German soldiers who were apparently trying to surrender. The Germans advanced toward the soldier calling "Bitte! Bitte!" (Please), but the American did not understand German and fired. After the screening, the Defense Department Public Affairs Office and the Army reiterated that Zanuck should delete the scene, and Don Baruch informed Twentieth Century Fox's Washington representative of the request. The Pentagon's chief of the Production Branch explained, first by phone and then by letter on September 24, that the Pentagon had approved the original script only with the understanding that Zanuck would change the scene or delete it altogether. In response, the filmmaker had advised the Pentagon that he would do the sequence in a way he felt would satisfy all parties. Nevertheless, Baruch told the studio that "the scene still is objectionable. Unless this objection is overcome the film is not approved for public release."[91]

The subsequent correspondence took on an air of surrealism and finally became moot. By the time Zanuck answered Baruch on October 1, 1962, *The Longest Day* had had its world premiere in Paris with the controversial scene intact, and the studio had made and distributed more than one hundred prints. Zanuck defended the release of the film uncut, saying that the portrayed shooting had actually occurred and he had edited the sequence so that it showed that the G.I. had not deliberately killed soldiers attempting to surrender. He said he had screened a rough cut of the film for many high-ranking officers in Europe and none had objected to the scene. He reported that Gen. James Gavin, a D-Day veteran and currently ambassador to France, had not objected to the sequence; and no one at the Paris opening had objected to it. He further suggested that the problem remained a sincere "difference of opinion," not an attempt to skirt the regulations. He mentioned the number of troops, which the Pentagon had "arbitrarily" reduced, and the problems this had caused him. He then asked that the Pentagon once again screen the film and judge it not on the basis of one scene "but on its overall impression and on its authenticity as a sincere and realistic portrait of D-Day and of the triumph of the combined efforts of the Allied forces."[92]

In responding for the Defense Department, Baruch repeated the Pentagon's objections and cited regulations that required "a film to be approved prior to multiple printing and public release unless otherwise determined." Noting that no such discussions had occurred, Baruch said that Zanuck had taken a calculated gamble in making the one hundred prints before receiving Pentagon approval. He repeated, "The scene still is not considered in our best interest and, therefore, in accordance with the policy under which assistance was extended on this production, we assume it will be deleted."[93]

Of course, Zanuck had no intention of recalling all the prints to delete the offending scene, and the Pentagon had no way of stopping the film's distribution. The sequence itself, running less than seventy seconds, was done realistically and had a strong dramatic impact. It could have had little adverse effect on "the best interest" of the Army or the military establishment. Nevertheless, Zanuck had clearly violated his agreement with the Defense Department. He should have objected to the requested deletion before, not after, he had completed the film. With proper negotiations, Zanuck could have had both this scene and military approval. Instead, his actions only reinforced Sylvester's determination to increase Defense Department supervision of policies governing cooperation.

Clearly, *The Longest Day* had become Zanuck's sacred cow. Neither Cornelius Ryan, nor the military, nor his directors, nor Twentieth Century Fox executives were going to tell him how to make his film. In the end, the movie returned more than $17.5 million in domestic rentals on an investment of close to $10 million, the most expensive black and white film ever made. Usually, foreign sales equal or slightly outdo the American-Canadian market. Given the subject matter, *The Longest Day* undoubtedly did even better overseas, making it one of the most successful black and white films produced and, up to that time, the best war film in box-office terms. Its success meant the rebirth of Zanuck's career and the financial salvation of Twentieth Century Fox.

The film that did all these things presented many faces to its viewers. Perhaps because it attempts to be both a pseudo-documentary history and a commercial drama, *The Longest Day* exhibits a split personality. As James Jones observed, it ultimately worked because its production so closely resembled the combat it was trying to portray. And like the Allies' success on D-Day, the film succeeded in spite of great obstacles, even errors.

If a film should limit its focus to two or three individuals with whom a viewer can empathize in order to achieve a significant dramatic impact, then *The Longest Day* should have failed. It had not one central character but rather a galaxy of historical figures played by stars appearing in cameo roles. If a successful film should relate a story with a beginning, a middle, and an end, building dramatic tension as the plot unfolds, then again, the movie should have failed. It had no plot and portrayed what might be termed only a slice of life, one day lifted out of history. Moreover, every audience knows the story's ending, knows further that D-Day only began eleven more months of struggle in Europe. Finally, like *Tora! Tora! Tora!* and *Midway*, which imitated *The Longest Day* but became dramatic disasters, Zanuck's film spends too much time getting to the action, too much time talking, planning, preparing for battle.

Despite all these burdens, *The Longest Day* provided powerful drama, owing much of its success to the great skill with which Zanuck, Williams, and their co-directors re-created the battles on the Normandy beaches. In his initial *New York Times* review, Bosley Crowther concluded, "It is hard to think of a picture aimed and constructed as this one was, doing any more or any better or leaving one feeling any more exposed to the horror of war than this one does." He reinforced this observation in his second review, saying that he had not seen any other war film in which "the labor and agony of warfare, the sheer, awful business of getting there and going into battle and being blasted with shot and shell while you struggle to kill other people had been shown more lengthily or graphically described."[94]

The Longest Day became this quintessential war film because of the authenticity of the battle scenes and because Zanuck followed the lead of Cornelius Ryan and focused on men on both sides before, during, and after battle. Although none of the characters became fully developed, most of the actors transcended their roles and created believable people who experienced human fears, pride, courage, and misery. In the end the film, like the book, leaves a lasting impression of the human element of war, in which men on both sides do their best to carry out orders and try to survive their own longest day.

Whether *The Longest Day* also provides a reasonably accurate account of D-Day, as Zanuck had hoped, remains another matter. Historians must ask, as they do of any war film set within the framework of actual events, whether *The Longest Day* exceeds the limits of dramatic license to the extent that it cannot legitimately inform people of what actually happened on June 6, 1944. The encounter between a downed RAF pilot played by Richard Burton and an American paratrooper in the film's closing minutes never happened. However, the scene does not distort history and does convey the essence of the day for many of the men who survived.

Zanuck earned the wrath of the Rangers who climbed Pointe du Hoc for not identifying them in the film as Rangers and not explaining the full significance of their action. Still, American soldiers did climb the cliff in much the way shown in the film, and the sequence provided audiences with an appreciation of the exceptional bravery of the men. While debate continues as to whether a Ranger then shot German soldiers trying to surrender, Cornelius Ryan included the account in his book based on information he had gathered. Even though the Army demanded Zanuck delete the incident from the film, not wanting to acknowledge that such things occur, intentional and unintentional shooting of enemy soldiers trying to surrender happens in all wars. Ryan later included a similar incident in *A Bridge Too Far*, and the Pentagon did not object to its portrayal in the movie version.[95]

The Longest Day visually identified all officers by having their insignia embossed on

German soldiers attempt to repulse U.S. Rangers as they scale the cliffs of Point du Hoc during shooting for *The Longest Day.*

their helmets. Officers and men who have experienced combat, whatever the war, regularly point out that the officers who made themselves into targets by so conspicuously wearing their ranks quickly became dead officers However, even if the cinematic convention gives audiences an inaccurate portrayal of officers in combat, it does not change history. In *The Longest Day*, officers lived or died as they had on the battlefields of Normandy, not because of their insignia.

Even if the Casino no longer existed, if Zanuck's structure bore no resemblance to the real building, and if the cinematic assault took place in a different location, the sequence bore some resemblance to the actual assault on the German fortification and certainly gave the French commandos their due. Likewise, Zanuck and his crew did a fine job of recreating the disastrous parachute drop on Sainte-Mere-Eglise, with one significant exception. Although the film shows the paratroopers trying to defend themselves as they fall into the town square in the face of withering German fire, one of the survivors, who otherwise praised the sequence, pointed out that no parachutist could jump holding onto his rifle as portrayed. Technically wrong, of course, but at least from Zanuck's perspective, he had shown the paratroopers dying bravely defending themselves, not helpless in their chutes.[96]

But what about the film's climactic sequence in which Gen. Norman Cota directs the blowing up of the massive tank barrier at the Vierville Draw under intense German fire, enabling the American soldiers to break out of Omaha Beach and move inland? As portrayed, Cota rallied his men, bravely disregarding his own safety when the outcome of the assault on Omaha Beach seemed in doubt, and rides up the draw to victory. Even reasonably close? Not really. It certainly did not deserve even one of the general's ever present cigars for accuracy.

During the actual battle, Cota had ranged the beach ignoring the enemy fire to get his men to move inland, and his leadership had inspired the soldiers to climb the bluffs and drive the Germans back from the dunes. In fact, fighting was taking place inland by the time Noel

American forces break through the sea wall on "Omaha" beach, filmed at Ile de Re, and move inland, assuring Allied success on *The Longest Day*.

Dube's engineer squad blew the concrete barrier blocking the draw late in the day. Dube also pointed out that his men used TNT from two engineer bulldozers, not bangalore torpedoes, whose purpose was to clear barbed wire, not thick fortifications. And, while Cota may have ordered the destruction of the barrier so that tanks and supplies could get off the beach, Dube said he did not see the general or receive the orders directly from him as shown in the film. Nor did any yelling soldiers then charge through the breach.[97]

Does the cinematic version exceed the limits of dramatic license? After all, *The Longest Day* does brilliantly capture the desperate struggle for Omaha Beach and Cota's bravery. And movies do need a visual, exciting climax. Does it matter that the film has gotten its chronology and events wrong, or that the cinematic climax occurred several hours before the actual blowing of the tank barrier, which essentially ended the fight for Omaha Beach? Does it matter that it occurred under less dramatic circumstances with almost no hostile fire raining down on Dube, or that a captain, undoubtedly acting at Cota's direction, not the general in person, gave the order to blow the tank barrier?[98]

In response, Elmo Williams says the film was not actually attempting to recreate Dube's actions at the end of the day. Instead, the producer explained that he had found an intact bunker during filming at Isle de Re and "used it to symbolize the massive allied attack on Omaha Beach for drama." He acknowledged that in making films, sometimes "license is taken to dramatize fact. When you tackle the job of nailing down truth about historical truth, you are on treacherous ground." Why? He said that in researching for *The Longest Day,* he found many conflicting reports from men who had participated in the same action. Citing Tolstoy, Williams also claimed that historians themselves "are notably prone to stretch the truth on their reporting for the sake of dramatizing their writings."[99]

Whatever the validity of the producer's observation or whether people understood the symbolism he thought his cinematic climax created, audiences most likely came away from the theater believing that the Longest Day had ended with a huge explosion, a rousing charge through the rubble, and Cota's victory ride. Of course, even if *The Longest Day* rewrites history, it does recreate the essence of D-day and closely portrays many of the events that took place on a day which changed history. However, it does so filtered through the eyes of Zanuck and his associates. Ultimately, then, the film has the feel of a documentary and reminds people of the significance of what happened on June 6, 1944. However, it does not provide a literal or even a completely accurate historical account of the longest day.

11 A Marriage Ends

THE LONGEST DAY SERVED AS THE MODEL FOR ALL subsequent combat spectaculars. Like Zanuck's film, *Battle of the Bulge* (1965), *Bridge at Remagen* (1969), *Tora! Tora! Tora!* (1970), *Midway* (1976), and *A Bridge Too Far* (1977), among others, told the story of great battles of World War II from the viewpoints of the combatants on both sides. These movies traced the events leading up to a particular battle, with the participants speaking in their own tongues as they did in *The Longest Day.*

However well each motion picture recreated history, the narrative served only as a framework for the film's objective: the spectacular combat scenes. Individuals seldom counted for much in the stories, with leading actors portraying, usually in cameo appearances, the major historical characters. Visual drama, violence, and noise replaced personal drama, the stories of men and their struggles, and the kinds of portrayals that had made *Twelve O'Clock High*, *Sands of Iwo Jima*, and *From Here to Eternity* significant movies irrespective of their genre. That few imitators of *The Longest Day* enjoyed the same box-office rewards suggests that a film must focus on believable human beings with whom the audience can empathize if it is to succeed critically and commercially.

To succeed, of course, a film not only must tell a dramatic story and tell it well, but also it must tell one that interests people. As a biography first and a war movie second, *Patton* did all these things. But in general, the combat spectaculars that followed *The Longest Day* did not tell their stories as well either narratively or visually. Worse, with the exception of *Midway*, which became a major box-office hit despite both a dull script and poor visual effects, the large-scale war movies that imitated Zanuck's epic related stories that failed to interest enough people to make the films financially successful.

Even before Zanuck undertook his project, most Hollywood filmmakers believed the market for movies about World War II had become saturated. The Korean War market had died with *Pork Chop Hill* in 1959, if not earlier. *The Longest Day* succeeded at the box office because it drew its story from a popular book and attained a unique visual and dramatic authenticity. By 1963, however, the Cold War began to thaw following the realization after the Cuban Missile Crisis that the Super Powers could not resort to nuclear war to solve their disagreements. In this atmosphere, people had less interest in reliving past battles. At the same time, the new generation of Hollywood filmmakers had little commitment to the traditional relationship with the military that had produced an almost unbroken string of movies glorifying the armed forces.

In practical terms, by the early 1960s, the problems involved in attempting to recreate World War II on the screen also played a major role in ending the cycle of movies about that conflict. As Zanuck's searches and expenditures for military equipment demonstrated, filmmakers were going to have an increasingly difficult time finding the material needed to authentically restage World War II. *In Harm's Way, Tora! Tora! Tora!* and *Midway* depicted their sea battles primarily with miniatures, mock-ups, and combat footage. However, filmmakers shot most of the ground combat spectaculars that followed *The Longest Day* in Europe, where producers could still find usable World War II equipment and even armies available for rent. Nonetheless, the cost and the logistics involved in these overseas productions limited the number of major projects that Hollywood was willing to undertake.

Paradoxically, then, *The Longest Day* marked the end of the cycle of traditional World War II films that had begun in 1949, while spawning an era of combat spectaculars. Zanuck's epic also brought an end to the free and easy marriage between Hollywood and the military that had existed since the early days of Hollywood. The controversies the film created because of the amount of assistance Zanuck received from the Army and because of the producer's own disregard for Pentagon regulations left the relationship in disarray. As a result, a period of retrenchment took place between 1962 and 1965, during which time the armed services reexamined the process of cooperation. While the Pentagon was rewriting the regulations, filmmakers became wary of approaching the military for any assistance. As a result, the number of films about World War II declined, as did stories about all aspects of the military establishment.

Over the years, an occasional member of Congress or of the media had questioned the armed forces' policy of loaning men and equipment to filmmakers. But nothing much had ever come of these queries. Now, because *The Longest Day* had brought the issue of cooperation before the public, and because Arthur Sylvester became drawn into the controversy on so many occasions, he initiated a reevaluation of Pentagon regulations governing military assistance to commercial filmmakers. As the study progressed, Sylvester became convinced that the Public Affairs Office had to assume tighter control over assistance to the film industry. He had his determination to change the regulations reinforced in February 1962, when a sailor died while preparing explosives for use in *No Man Is an Island,* to which the Navy was giving limited assistance. Although the sailor had taken leave, Rep. Welter Norblad reacted to the incident with a declaration that filmmakers should hire their own extras and employ civilian experts for dangerous special effects.[1]

Arthur Sylvester.

The film industry did have its defenders. Later in February, Senators Vance Hartke and Thomas Kuchel praised the documentary *A Force in Readiness,* which Warner Brothers made at cost for the Marines. On the Senate floor, Hartke gave particular credit to Jack Warner, who "put all the facilities of his company" into the making of the film. Nevertheless, during the first half of 1962, cooperation between the film industry and the military slowed measurably as Sylvester's office continued its policy review.[2]

The Motion Picture Association, unsure of the secretary's intentions, solicited the help of Sen. Hubert Humphrey, who wrote Sylvester in mid-June to inquire about the current status of the relationship between Hollywood and the Pentagon. The secretary responded that he was "cognizant of the benefits of cooperating with the film industry to more fully inform the American public of the activities of the Department of Defense." He also cited criteria that filmmakers would have to meet before the Pentagon could agree to assist them in the future. These included an evaluation of the dramatic quality of the potential movie, the need to assure safety for servicemen working on the films, and the requirement that assistance not interfere with the operational readiness of the armed forces.[3]

Sylvester then informed Humphrey that his office had already developed new guidelines to ensure that these criteria would be met and would "serve the best interests of the taxpayers and the nation." Sylvester also assured the senator that the new guidelines would not stand in the way of continued assistance to filmmakers, citing his office's recent approval of cooperation on *A Gathering of Eagles* and *PT-109*.[4]

In fact, neither of these examples supported the secretary's claim that the film industry could still expect to receive assistance without red tape and inhibiting restrictions. *A Gathering of Eagles*, a direct descendant of *Air Force, Twelve O'Clock High, Strategic Air Command*, and *Bombers B-52*, had the backing of Gen. Curtis LeMay, the father of the Strategic Air Command (SAC) and one of the most powerful men in the Pentagon. Sy Bartlett, the producer, had served as an Air Force officer in World War II and had established his credentials with the Pentagon as a result of his work on *Twelve O'Clock High, Pork Chop Hill* (1959),and *The Outsider* (1961). Also, Universal Studios was producing *A Gathering of Eagles*. Its Washington representative, John Horton, had helped Don Baruch set up the Motion Picture Production Office in 1949 and had become one of the most effective studio representatives.

In line with Sylvester's new requirements, Bartlett had submitted a detailed list of the men and equipment he would need to make the film and a precise schedule of when he would need them. This marked the first time the Pentagon had requested such a strict accounting, and Don Baruch later said he had labeled the list "the Bible." Even so, Sylvester initially had refused to approve cooperation on the film because he considered it simply another Air Force public relations movie.[5]

At this point, General LeMay took a personal hand in the matter. He had become concerned with criticisms of SAC's safety procedures then being raised by both Peter George's 1958 *Red Alert* and Stanley Kubrick's *Dr. Strangelove*, based on the novel, then in the planning stage. In conversations with Bartlett, a longtime friend, the general talked about the possible detrimental effect of the movie on SAC. Bartlett recalled that he "instantly" saw the possibility of doing a film that would explain SAC's function. He wrote the story himself, without any direct request from LeMay, combining the informative aspect of the film with dramatic flying sequences and a plot focused on the tensions under which the wives and families of the fliers lived.[6]

LeMay himself had ambivalent feelings about Hollywood films. He liked Hollywood because people played up to him, but he admitted that he "never did like any movie that came out of Hollywood about our activities. They always had to throw this Hollywood stuff into it, a little sex, the hero had to have a problem he had to surmount and conquer and so forth." He conceded that Air Force people did have problems but said they were not the type that were "of particular interest to a moviemaker," no people "with mental problems and things of that sort." Since Hollywood emphasized those elements to make good stories, LaMay felt their films "really didn't tell the story of what we were trying to do."[7]

At the same time, he appreciated the public relations and recruiting advantages of the films. Consequently, when he discovered that Sylvester had rejected Universal's request for assistance for *A Gathering of Eagles*, LeMay wrote a memo to the secretary saying the Air Force wanted the film made. His aide, Arno Leuhman, hand-delivered it to Sylvester, who approved cooperation almost immediately.[8]

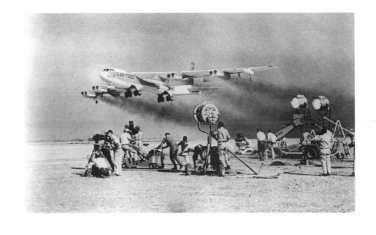

Sylvester's new regulations gave him no more control over the actual assistance extended than he had had under the original guidelines. According to Bartlett, the film company was able to do things about which the secretary "sure as hell" did not know when the cast and crew went on location at Beale Air Force Base in California. The producer said he dug up a runway, had a special training takeoff exercise repeated when a camera malfunctioned, and in general made the film as studios had always made movies

A B-52 bomber roars skyward during filming of *A Gathering of Eagles* (1963), a film about the Strategic Air Command which received full Air Force cooperation despite stricter supervision of the Hollywood/ Pentagon relationship by Assistant Secretary of Defense for Public Affairs Arthur Sylvester.

receiving military assistance. The film company even had access to SAC's underground command center in Omaha, and during their visit, the commander allowed Rock Hudson to actually speak his lines over the SAC worldwide radio alert network.

Given such cooperation as well as a script written by Bob Pirosh and directed by Delbert Mann (both Oscar winners), *A Gathering of Eagles* realistically captured the conflicts and tensions in the peacetime Air Force. More important for the service, it accurately portrayed its fail-safe procedures. Despite Bartlett's need to include the "Hollywood atmosphere" of women and family problems, General LeMay thought it came "the closest any of [the Air Force films] ever came to showing a true picture of what the military was all about."[9]

In contrast, *PT-109* offered little "truth" in portraying military life aboard PT boats in the South Pacific in World War II. In the pre-Sylvester era, the Navy would have routinely agreed to assist on a similar, but fictionalized, story because of the innocuous nature of the script and the limited help needed, much as it had done with John Ford's 1945 *They Were Expendable*, which portrayed PT boats in the first days of World War II. However, if *PT-109* had served as a test case of Sylvester's new policy as he had suggested to Senator Humphrey, he would most likely have turned down the request for cooperation. But the movie was to portray the wartime experiences of an incumbent president, and so the new regulations would have little relevance to any decision to assist Warner Brothers.

The film necessarily portrayed a two-dimensional character. It could not contain the typical war-movie romantic interlude, and it could not very well show a man with warts, since the president would be running for reelection soon after the film's projected release date. Consequently, it offered little in the way of potential dramatic quality—one of Sylvester's criteria for approving a script. Moreover, if the story had not portrayed President Kennedy's wartime heroics, the script probably would not have interested filmmakers. Lewis Milestone, the movie's original director and one of Hollywood's premier makers of war movies (*All Quiet on the Western Front, A Walk in the Sun, Pork Chop Hill*), later observed that the script contained a lot of "cornball jokes" and never became more than "just another adventure story." He believed that if it had told a fictional tale, the studio would have abandoned it: "Why bother? We've got better stories than this." However, Jack

Warner, president of Warner Brothers and a long-time friend of the Democratic party, had liked Robert Donovan's book, *PT-109*. And Brian Foy Jr., the producer, believed the film would make money.[10]

Ordinarily, these political and commercial factors would have reinforced Sylvester's opposition to assisting on any film. But when President Kennedy indicated that he did not object to the Navy's participation, the secretary had no choice but to approve assistance. Even with stricter guidelines on cooperation, Sylvester would have had a difficult time turning down Warner Brothers's request for assistance. Over the years the studio had made more commercial military films with armed forces assistance than any other company. In addition, Warner Brothers had regularly produced military documentaries such as *A Force in Readiness* at little or no cost to the various services.[11]

PT-109 needed relatively little in the way of men or equipment and so satisfied Sylvester's criterion that assistance be on a noninterference basis. Since the Navy no longer had any World War II PT boats, the film company planned to construct reasonable facsimiles. For actual shooting, the studio needed only about a hundred sailors and a few ships and planes for a short time on location near the Key West Naval Base. But even this limited request proved to be too much. Although the controversies surrounding *The Longest Day* undoubtedly influenced the Defense Department's action, White House fears of Republican criticism clearly dictated the Pentagon's decision to cut the amount of assistance.[12]

President Kennedy, while agreeing to allow Navy participation on the film, stated through his press secretary that the service "should not extend a single bit more cooperation to do this movie than it would to do any movie in which it determined that the interests of the Navy as a fighting service were involved." With this advice in hand, the service provided less than a dozen sailors and rejected the studio's request for planes. As a result, Warner Brothers was forced to hire off-duty sailors and to rent the needed aircraft. The Navy did provide a destroyer, six other ships, and some equipment for the filming. In any case, probably no amount of assistance could have improved the quality of *PT-109,* which resembled a dull campaign propaganda film more than a Hollywood commercial release.[13]

Clearly, Sylvester's new regulations had little if any effect on the assistance the military provided to *PT-109* or *A Gathering of Eagles.* Nevertheless, the secretary cited them as positive examples in his letter to Senator Humphrey. He concluded with the hope that his proposed controls would be "a means of assuring the film industry that equitable arrangements can, in fact, be developed between the industry and the Department of Defense."[14]

Neither the letter nor any of Sylvester's actions in formulating a new Defense Department Instruction on military assistance during the next eighteen months was to assure the film industry. Shortly after the secretary's reply to Senator Humphrey, Kenneth Clark, executive vice president of the Motion Picture Association, observed that the industry would manage to work things

Leslie Martinson directs Cliff Robertson, playing a young John F. Kennedy, in *PT 109*, a santized version of the president's wartime experiences.

out, "but cooperation will be more difficult in the future than in the past. The old easy, informal ways are over."[15]

Sylvester's proposals for a new set of regulations offered virtually no changes from the 1954 Instruction, which he intended to replace. Nevertheless, in October 1962, Sylvester repeated that the "United States military can't be rented by anyone. They are not going to be turned over to motion pictures indiscriminately." Although his office would continue to provide assistance, he stressed that in the future, he wanted "all Hollywood requirements spelled out in advance. And whether the training is necessary or merely make-believe, we don't want to be put in the position of writing to any parent that 'your son was killed in making a picture.'"[16]

The film-industry leaders doubted that Sylvester would have a lasting effect on the Hollywood-military relationship. Eric Johnson, president of the Motion Picture Association, wrote to Darryl Zanuck in October 1962, suggesting that Sylvester did not have "the last word. In this case, I would say that he was merely the first word. If we find that the revisions are objectionable and Sylvester is unyielding, we shall carry our case to the highest authorities in the Department of Defense and in the White House." In Robert McNamara's Pentagon, however, the assistant secretaries did have almost complete authority over their own departments. As a result, Sylvester remained the last word as well as the first word in determining new policies on military assistance to Hollywood.[17]

The new regulations issued in January 1964 reflected Sylvester's intention to impose tighter control over the cooperation process. First verbalized in September 1961, at the height of the *Longest Day* uproar, the new Instruction did not stop military assistance to filmmakers in any sense. According to Sylvester, though, "they got it on our terms." Under his new regulations, he said, the military would accept "less ordering stuff all around and more precise definition beforehand of what cooperation was to involve. It was not a case in which we just went whish, come take anything you want."[18]

Initially, the film industry responded to this tighter control with cries of anguish. Stan Hough, a production supervisor at Twentieth Century Fox, wrote to Richard Zanuck in 1964 saying that the new regulations gave the Defense Department "a very strong voice in the creative controls of any film requiring their cooperation." From a production standpoint, he found that the policies had become "quite rigid," with a studio now required to "not only designate equipment and material but also the date, location and the time of day." He conceded that there "would be some 'give' but it is frightening that we must name months in advance the time of day we expect to make a shot of some military equipment or personnel." Hough later admitted that the new regulations "did not prove to be as awkward as they seemed. More practical minds prevailed."[19]

If the new policy ultimately proved workable, its immediate effect was to reduce the number of films made with military assistance. Of these, Otto Preminger's *In Harm's Way* probably received more assistance than it deserved. When the director read James Bassett's novel, he found it "interesting and a good story for a movie. Pearl Harbor was interesting, a lot of action and a good part for John Wayne." However, he claimed he did not make the movie to glorify war: "I would never have done that because I am completely against war."[20]

Whatever the film might ultimately say, Preminger did need military cooperation, particularly if he wanted to use Pearl Harbor as a location. However, his initial effort to obtain assistance showed his ignorance of how the Hollywood/military relationship worked, pure arrogance, simple political naivete, or probably a combination of all three. The director recalled that he asked Bassett, who had worked on Richard Nixon's 1960 presidential cam-

John Wayne on the bridge of the USS *St. Paul* during location filming of Otto Preminger's *In Harm's Way* (1965), which received Navy and Marine assistance immediately after the issuance of new Department of Defense regulations governing cooperation.

paign, to call the former vice president and request that he contact President Kennedy to find out "if we could use the Navy to shoot our picture." Bassett undoubtedly exercised good judgment and the director's inquiry went no further. Preminger then went through normal channels and paid for the assistance he received, as Sylvester's new guidelines required. The director emphasized that he reimbursed the Navy for its time and use of ships and other equipment: "I remember very well that there was never the taxpayer's money involved."[21]

Preminger did not consider war films different from any action films: "Whether it is a Western or a war film, there's a lot of action. You have undoubtedly some scenes where people fight and kill each other, where people run or drive fast tanks, ships. In *In Harm's Way*, all those models chased each other like mad." To the director, the chase went back to silent films and remained the "basic motion picture thing that one man runs after the other and whoever can run faster kills the other."[22]

Given the fictional story and Preminger's view of war films as a subset of the action genre, it was not surprising that the movie stretched the limits of dramatic license. Marines parachute into combat, which never happened in World War II. Wayne, as Admiral Torrey, runs the risk of capture when he accompanies the "paramarines" to the drop zone, despite having devised the battle plan. Enemy sailors or soldiers never appear on the screen, as they had done with good effect in such films as *The Enemy Below* and *The Longest Day*. The larger-than-usual cinematic ships still look like models, not warships. Worse, when the miniature ships fire their broadsides, the guns spit out sparkles, not realistic clouds of smoke. As a result, neither the climactic battle nor very much else relating to combat convey any sense of reality.[23]

The creative and visual problems, of course, remained the responsibility of the filmmakers. Ironically, according to Capt. C.J. Mackenzie, one of the technical advisors on the film, Preminger himself "was very anxious to make this picture very authentic and depended upon me to watch this end of it." As a result, the Navy did what it could to impart a feel for the times and its operations.[24]

In one instance, the technical advisor pointed out that cups from which two ensigns were drinking coffee had clearly come from the crew's mess, not the wardroom mess. Mackenzie said that Preminger thought the heavy cups looked better and so shot the scene with them. In this instance, he then relented and did it "Mackenzie's way." In any case, the technical advisor recalled that he felt the movie would have "mutual advantage" for Preminger and the Navy and that the director had "a great deal of respect for the Navy and he was very anxious to make a picture which showed the Navy in good light."[25]

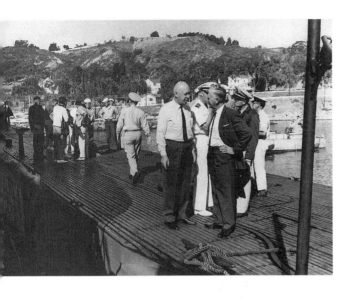

Otto Preminger confers with technical advisor Capt. Colin Mackenzie during filming of *In Harm's Way* aboard a submarine.

Nevertheless, despite an uplifting ending and John Wayne's presence, the film provided little if any positive benefit to the Navy. Apart from Preminger's graphic depiction of Pearl Harbor, the movie resembled nothing so much as a very expensive soap opera. First, Wayne's alcoholic executive officer, Kirk Douglas, and his screen wife embarrassed the service. After making a spectacle of herself at the Officers' Club, she commits adultery with an Army Air Corps pilot, no less, before conveniently dying when a Japanese fighter strafes the beach. Before the film concludes, Douglas drowns himself in self-pity and rapes Wayne's son's girlfriend; Wayne loses two ships and one leg, and his estranged son in combat; and Douglas dies bravely but without redemption, because Wayne refuses to award him a medal.

Despite such negative images, the Navy loaned Preminger a few ships and men and allowed him to film inside the Pearl Harbor port area itself. Good intentions aside, *In Harm's Way* offered only a tired old John Wayne as a positive image for the service and continued Preminger's decline as a director. Nevertheless, he did have defenders of his effort to create an almost-three-hour epic.

Weekly Variety observed that the film contained "a full, lusty slice of life in a time of extreme stress," which Preminger had "artfully guided so that incidents of adultery, rape, suicide, opportunism and stupidity in high command—not to overlook a couple of pungent but typically salty expressions—come across naturally, making their intended impression without battering the audience. This film is as good an example as any of what by now is an old Hollywood adage, 'It's not what you do, but the way that you do it.'"[26]

Time magazine said that with "half a dozen plots to juggle, Preminger keeps all of them interesting for at least two of the three hours spent *In Harm's Way*." However, the reviewer felt the film became "marred by wearisome repetition and by a climactic confused sea battle between miniature U.S. and Japanese fleets. But even toy battleships do not seriously impede the progress of a slick, fast-moving entertainment aswarm with characters who seem quick-witted, courageous, and just enough larger than life to justify another skirmish in the tired old Pacific." Philip Scheuer in the *Los Angeles Times* probably captured the audience's reaction best: "From a quiet fade-out scene at the end the screen cuts to the cast of characters superimposed on raging waves and culminating loudly in the burst of an atom bomb. Preminger may have been making a last-ditch attempt at significance here, but I am afraid most people will already be half-way out of the theater by this time."[27]

The quality of the completed film became important to the armed services only to the extent that people actually saw their men and equipment in action. From Sylvester's point of view, however, *In Harm's Way* showed that his regulations were working, and he was to even approve limited assistance to nonmilitary films such as *Thunderball* and *Goldfinger.* Even so, Hough advised Zanuck that the studio "should weigh very carefully whether it would be feasible to undertake any project which requires intensive military cooperation." John Horton, who had arranged cooperation between Hollywood and the Pentagon for almost twenty years, specifically attributed the decline in films about military subjects to Sylvester's 1964 regulations. And Ken Clark, of the Motion Picture Association, noted that "the new regulations produced decisive changes in the manner and history of cooperation between Hollywood and the American military establishment."[28]

Under the circumstances, some Hollywood producers, apprehensive of Sylvester's new regulations, began making their war stories overseas. Whether in Spain, Finland, or other European locations, *The Victors, The Thin Red Line,* and *Battle of the Bulge* avoided confrontation with the Pentagon by renting equipment from local armies. Unlike previous fictionalized cinematic accounts of the December 1944 surprise German attack into Belgium, the 1965 *Battle of the Bulge* attempted, in one film, to tell the entire story of Germany's last, desperate effort to stop the Allies' advance to the Rhine. By focusing on a single unit surrounded at Bastogne, *Battleground* (1949) had captured the urgency and the desperation of the Battle of the Bulge. But Dore Schary had made his film in the standard screen format and in black and white, and filmmakers in the midsixties believed that only widescreen, color spectaculars would draw people into theaters.

Given this perception, historical accuracy counted for little. As a result, *Battle of the Bulge* bore little relationship to the historical events it purported to portray. More important, as drama it said almost nothing of the human experiences of the pivotal battle. Consequently, it failed to capture the character of the life-and-death struggle for survival between the Germans, who were making their last major effort to stop the Allies, and the Americans, who were suddenly confronted by an overwhelming force.

In fact, *Battle of the Bulge* failed at the box office for more reasons than simply its bloated size and hollowness. Although the movie told the story of a historical event, the filmmakers populated the story with fictional characters who never came to life as believable people, remaining artificial and one-dimensional. Beyond that, because the filmmakers had little concern with historical accuracy, the movie seemed phony.

The producers reinforced this feeling by their choice of location, the time of the year production took place, and the apparent lack of concern for an authentic ambience. The film opens with Henry Fonda playing an intelligence officer flying past snow-capped Belgian Alps in a reconnaissance plane. The dusty plains of Spain simply did not look like the wintery Belgium of December of 1944. Nor did the palm trees in the background, visible in the original cinerama version, serve as suitable substitutes for the snow-covered forests and fields of northern Europe.

Two very practical considerations dictated the decision to shoot the production in Spain, despite the problems it presented to authenticity. The financial backers had money in the country that they could only spend there, and the Spanish Army had a fleet of World War II tanks of both American and German manufacture. Moreover, the Spanish government readily rented its army to filmmakers, since it had little else to do except enforce domestic tranquillity. Given the availability of this equipment and these men, the producers did not need the Pentagon's help. Nevertheless, the film presented an essentially positive image of the American military.[29]

Although caught off guard and initially driven back, the U.S. Army ultimately wins

Robert Shaw prepares to lead a column of German tanks, rented from the Spanish army, in recreation of surprise assault in *Battle of the Bulge.*

Ken Annakin directing James MacArthur and Henry Fonda in a scene for *Battle of the Bulge.*

the battle. Because the film's soldiers remained faceless men, audiences could not care about them, could not believe they were suffering the bitter cold of winter, could not forget that they were merely actors. Ultimately, *Battle of the Bulge* failed not because of its ersatz location, not because of doubts about the validity of its history, but because audiences did not empathize with the characters, did not believe they represented American fighting men.

If Sylvester's new requirements gave impetus to Hollywood's turning away from its reliance on cooperation from the military services and moving to overseas productions, America's changing attitudes toward the armed forces also influenced the content of the combat films the industry made. By 1962 audiences had less interest in reliving past military glories via the movie screen. President Kennedy had proclaimed a new era of peace, the Cold War was apparently thawing, and the Soviet Union was negotiating a nuclear test ban treaty with the United States. Despite the Bay of Pigs, the Berlin crisis, the missile crisis, and a minor war in Southeast Asia, military preparedness seemed less important than it had during the 1950s, when nuclear war posed a continuing threat. In the midst of this semipeaceful interlude, World War II and Korea seemed less appropriate topics for Hollywood films.

In truth, of course, the fear of nuclear holocaust remained ever present in the early 1960s. The military continued to talk of new weapons, of intercontinental ballistic missiles to replace long-range bombers, of nuclear submarines and aircraft carriers. Despite the perceived ebb in the Cold War, the Pentagon was conducting business as usual. The contradictions between the talk of peace and the reality of continued preparedness, as well as the growing distance from the wars of the 1940s and early 1950s, created a new atmosphere, one in which it became possible to voice at least subtle criticism of the military in films.

Meanwhile, in Hollywood the defenders of the traditional relationship between the film industry and the military—Louis B. Mayer, Harry Cohn, Harry and Jack Warner—were disappearing from positions of authority. Only Darryl Zanuck retained his power throughout the 1960s. Television was bringing to an end the old studio system. Hollywood was being taken over by bankers and conglomerates who were more interested in financial returns than in fostering images. The new industry leaders were willing to invest in a project with any kind of story line as long as the proposed film had potential appeal. Often this new generation of independent producers had no contact with or commitment to the traditional relationship with the military. More important, the younger generation of filmmakers considered no subject sacred. They saw film as a medium in which to create drama, and they neither respected nor wished to perpetuate the Production Code's view of sex and the family or the military's view of its own infallibility.

Until the early 1960s, with only a few exceptions, Hollywood had consistently portrayed the American armed forces positively. Admittedly, the historic model, from which the filmmakers drew their inspiration, offered little of a negative nature. In both World Wars I and II, American forces had fought bravely and had emerged from the conflicts with glorious victories. If American history books and movies slighted the Allies' contributions (especially the Russians') to victory in World War II, no one questioned that the United States enjoyed a major share of the responsibility for the defeat of Germany and Japan. If the armed forces had not exactly won in Korea, most people blamed the stalemate on political decisions, not military shortcomings. But in the new climate of the 1960s, Hollywood began to present another view of the services, one that often differed greatly from the image suggested by its earlier collaborations with the military.

Antiwar, antimilitary themes have always had an honored place within the war-film genre. Lewis Milestone's 1930 classic *All Quiet on the Western Front* and Stanley Kubrick's 1957 *Paths of Glory* both expressed strong antiwar themes, and both received critical acclaim. However, neither movie portrayed the American military, and both dealt with World War I. Stanley Kramer's *On the Beach* (1959) did strive for a pacifist message by dramatizing the consequences of nuclear holocaust. But the film showed no destruction, contained little explicit criticism of the American military, and was set for the most part in the remoteness of Australia.

Only an occasional film, like Kramer's *Home of the Brave* (1949) or Robert Aldrich's *Attack!* (1956), dared show American officers and men performing in less than an exemplary fashion. Neither film received Pentagon assistance, and *Attack!* became one of the very few war-movie projects for which military officials refused even to discuss possible script revisions that might have made it acceptable for cooperation. After reading the screenplay, which included an enlisted man killing an incompetent officer, Don Baruch told Aldrich that under no circumstances could he keep that situation in the movie if he wanted assistance. Since the whole story built up to this dramatic high point, Aldrich would have had no movie without the scene. As a result, he made the film without military support, and he created a highly dramatic story that presented another side of military life, albeit a rare one.[30]

Nevertheless, the director made it clear that he was not faulting the military as a whole. The soldier who killed the officer explains at one point: "The Army is not a mockery! The war is not a mockery! It's just this small part!" He also ended up with a movie obviously shot mostly on a soundstage. Visually, the film lacked the authentic feel of men in combat, and without that realism the film failed to attract large audiences, however meritorious its story.[31]

The portrayal of negative human qualities such as cowardice, pettiness, and self-aggrandizement does not necessarily make a movie antiwar or antimilitary. In fact, Hollywood filmmakers have often seemed to lack a precise understanding of what constitutes an antiwar theme. Virtually everyone in the industry, including John Wayne, has purported to oppose war and claim to make only antiwar films. However, filmmakers have usually depicted the brutality and violence as exciting and as a means to win victories against implacable enemies without considering the impact and effect such images and messages may have had on audiences.

Darryl Zanuck, for example, believed that *The Longest Day* conveyed antiwar sentiments because of the manner in which it portrayed combat. Better than most Hollywood productions, the film did create a very real sense of the horrors of war, the waste of lives and resources, the senselessness of attempting to use violence to solve ideological problems. Zanuck's production reinforces these images because it tells a factual story rather than creating simply another fictionalized portrayal of combat. The men who die in the film really existed, rather than being the figment of the screenwriter's imagination. The audience knows that French stuntmen have assumed the roles of the American paratroopers whom the Germans shoot as they drop into the town square at Sainte-Mère-Eglise. Viewers perhaps even know the stuntmen are descending from Zanuck's hired crane. But unlike the stuntmen in a typical war film, they represent real human beings who died on June 6, 1944, precisely as portrayed in the film. The men who "die" in 1961 on the beaches of Corsica, Pointe du Hoc, or Il de Ré, the Germans who "die" because an American soldier does not understand "Bitte! Bitte!" represent soldiers who actually died on D-Day.

Zanuck had expected this reality would have a sobering impact on audiences, hoping they would see the film as a cautionary tale for future generations. In response to the suggestion that the rousing cinematic images of combat and battlefield victory might have the opposite effect, Zanuck said in a 1969 TV documentary made for the twenty-fifth anniversary of D-Day, "I did not agree. I thought that reproducing authentically the brutality and inhumanity of war would have the opposite effect. Obviously, I was wrong." Speaking as the Vietnam War raged, the producer acknowledged that *The Longest Day* "certainly didn't have the effect I had hoped for."[32]

Zanuck's admission mirrored the response of French director Jean Renoir to a ques-

Darryl Zanuck's *The Longest Day* in large measure captured the emotions of what it was like to be under fire in scenes such as the landing on Omaha beach.

Original ending for *The Longest Day* that Darryl Zanuck decided not to use because he thought it was "too downbeat."

tion about the effect of antiwar films: "In 1936 I made a picture named *La Grande Illusion* in which I tried to express all my deep feelings for the cause of peace. This film was very successful. Three years later the war broke out. That is the only answer I can find to your very interesting enquiry." In fact, the antiwar thrust of *The Longest Day* might have had a shattering impact on the traditional cinematic glorification of men in combat if Zanuck had not excised his film's original ending in which a soldier sits on an ammunition box at water's edge, staring at the incoming waves. Rows of bodies and other flotsam of the battle surround him. The script says that "he is sobbing quietly almost without movement. He picks up a stone and tosses it into the water and he picks up another and another and another."[33]

Zanuck found this climax was "too downbeat" and wrote a new, completely fabricated, closing montage. In the first scene, Richard Burton as a downed RAF pilot and Richard Beymer as an American soldier sit crumpled on the ground beside a dead German soldier. Beymer admits: "You know something? I haven't fired my gun all day." Burton responds: "It's funny. He's dead. I'm crippled. And you're lost." Beymer asks: "I wonder who won?" A quick cut to Omaha Beach. Robert Mitchum, having blown the seawall obstacle to the interior, climbs in a jeep and says: "O.K. run me up the hill, son."[34]

Whatever feeling of revulsion the combat sequences may have engendered, Zanuck dissipated them with this upbeat ending. Instead of the vision of mentally and physically exhausted soldiers and dead bodies (unbloodied ones, to be sure, since not one drop of believable blood appears on the screen), the audience leaves the theater with the image of men going "up the hill" to victory. The soldiers have fought their way off the beaches, and the Allies have taken a giant step toward defeating Hitler.

Ironically, if Zanuck had not succumbed to box office exigencies, *The Longest Day* would have provided a powerful ending at the expense of historical accuracy. Ryan had loosely based the scene on two sentences in his book in which Sgt. William McClintock told of encountering a soldier "sitting at the edge of the water, seemingly unaware of the machine gun fire which rippled all over the area. He sat there 'throwing stones into the water and softly crying as if his heart would break.'" In his book, Ryan did not identify the man as an officer, who like others on the beach, believed the invasion had failed. However, the incident McClintock witnessed occurred early in the day, before the outcome had become clear, not at the end of the day as in the script. If Zanuck had put the vignette at the time it actually took place, the scene would have lacked the impact it would have had as the movie's concluding image. So, apart from the desire for an uplifting climax, Zanuck faced the on-going Hollywood dilemma, historical truth or cinematic drama. In this case, of course, he let the box office dictate the ending.[35]

In trying to make their antiwar statements, other filmmakers have also regularly juxtaposed images of war's brutality with war's successes. Violence and excitement, the horrors of war, and its adventure and romance too often cancel each other out. Their efforts to use the motion picture medium to create patriotism and build morale usually end up justifying the costs of war. Likewise, the escapist entertainment that war movies provide their audiences often outweighs the negative images of combat that Hollywood believes it has visualized.

Filmmakers have, of course, understood the difficulty of presenting an "anti" message on the screen, whether about war in general or violence in particular. Norman Jewison said he intended *Rollerball* (1975) to serve as a critique of violence: "The statement of the film is surely against the exploitation of violence. If the film itself is accused of exploiting violence, then I would ask how you make a statement about violence without showing any violence." In translating word pictures to the screen, however, he acknowledged that "the images are so much more vivid that the film may be open to misinterpretation. That's why I just don't know how effective films are. I know certain people will be excited by the violence in *Rollerball*. I just hope they understand why they're being excited, and by the end of the picture perhaps realize that the violence is appealing to their more base instincts."[36]

Audiences usually do not have time to think during a movie, especially one as filled with action as *Rollerball*. For the most part, they came away from the film with an appreciation for the visual beauty of the action. That the action became extremely violent did not seem significant to many viewers, who found the film simply exciting and escapist entertainment rather than a message against violence.

Similarly, films that claim to condemn war produce in the audience a sense of patriotism, of adventure, of camaraderie, but seldom a sense of repulsion. *Paths of Glory* plainly presents a negative picture of the French officer Corps and seeks to provoke horror at the random execution of French soldiers for mutiny in the front lines. Nevertheless, no one in the film (or probably in the audience) questions the validity of the executions as a means of suppressing the revolt. Most military men would argue that despite the incompetence of the French officers that caused the soldiers' uprising, the punishment served as a legitimate means of reestablishing discipline. Moreover, the closing image does not convey the senselessness of war, or even the tragedy of the execution of innocent men. Instead, the surviving soldiers appear drinking and singing, preparing to fight another day for the glories of France, not philosophizing about their dead comrades. They may be drinking to put the executions out of their minds, and Kubrick may have intended to condemn war by juxtaposing the executions with the relaxing soldiers. But sufficient ambiguity exists at the end of the movie to mute the film's antiwar sentiment.

Likewise, Sy Bartlett's *Pork Chop Hill* (1959) suffers from the ambiguity of its conflicting images, the bravery of men who find themselves in an untenable situation because of the irrationality of war. Set in Korea during the final hours of peace negotiations, the film documents the true story of the American capture of Pork Chop Hill, an action ordered only to demonstrate to the Communist negotiators that the United States still had the will to fight on if the negotiators could not reach an agreement. The G.I.s vaguely understand the ultimate meaninglessness of their action, but as well-trained soldiers they go out to fight and die, obeying military orders. To Bartlett, this portrayal clearly represented an antiwar statement, that no man should have "to face a situation like that during his lifetime." Nevertheless, the producer said that the Pentagon strongly approved of the film for two reasons. It showed the Army carrying out its mission. More important, it answered the post-Korean "world-wide gossip that the American soldier broke and ran."

Robert Redford during a respite from combat in *War Hunt* (1962), a film that attempted to make its antiwar statement by showing the corrosive effect war has on its participants.

Consequently, the movie offers diverse perspectives. Whereas Bartlett claimed he had created a "very, very antiwar" story, others saw his film as glorifying the determination of military leaders to win on the battlefield regardless of the human cost.[37]

Only rarely, in films such as *War Hunt* (1962), *The Victors* (1963), and *The War Lover* (1964), did filmmakers attempt to suggest an antiwar message by portraying the futility of combat. *War Hunt* illustrated the destructive nature of combat through a character who loved war because he lived to kill. In the film, his superiors consider John Saxon a good soldier because he has a talent for killing North Koreans. However, after the truce he continues his forays because he likes to kill. His actions, now deviant, no longer serve the best interest of his country because they jeopardize peace. Consequently, Saxon's commander must ultimately dispose of the killer, who cannot adjust to peacetime conditions.

Terry Sanders, the producer of *War Hunt*, sent the script to the Pentagon "on the remote chance that they might not read the script and might give him a few tanks or something." Being realistic, however, Sanders recognized that the Army would probably find the script incompatible with any image it hoped to portray. The Army confirmed his belief when it objected to many elements of the script, including the portrayal of an enlisted man as a professional killer whose officer caters to him because of his killing ability.

Robert Redford in *War Hunt* looks on after his commander has been forced to kill John Saxon, playing a compulsive killer who cannot adjust to peace and has continued his forays despite the cease fire.

The service also objected to the portrayal of an enlisted man as a coward, to a scene in which a captain calls a sergeant an idiot, and to scenes it considered too gruesome to be in good taste. The Army recommended that the producer "explore other avenues of approach to a new story line which would be acceptable."[38]

War Hunt is significant, however, because it illustrates the problems of making even a small-scale war movie without military cooperation. The movie has a valuable comment to make about war and killing, but it lacks the dramatic impact of *The Longest Day*, which had no plot and a known outcome. Unlike Zanuck's film, *War Hunt* did not have authentic military equipment, and it used extras instead of trained soldiers. To help disguise these physical deficiencies, Sanders shot much of the film at night. Despite noisy explosions, the film lacked a realistic atmosphere and authentic-looking battle sequences. The resulting "back lot" feel of the movie at a time when *The Longest Day* offered "reality" continually intruded on the story. The audience cannot suspend disbelief, cannot pretend it is watching war, and so the message is weakened.[39]

Although *War Hunt, The Victors,* and *The War Lover* showed a negative side of war, they tried too hard to make audiences aware of their message. In *The Victors,* Frank Sinatra's crooning of a Christmas carol on the sound track accompanies the execution of an Army deserter, shown in graphic detail. And the final confrontation, in which an American G.I. and a Russian soldier kill each other over an insignificant right-of-way becomes too heavy-handed in its symbolism. Moreover, each film depicted the excitement and the fellowship of men in combat, which further muted the films' antiwar statements.

Some filmmakers have tried to overcome this paradox by showing the futility of death in battle. *All Quiet on the Western Front* (1930) offers the classic example of this kind of antiwar statement. At the film's close, the hero reaches for a butterfly, a symbol of hope and beauty, and a sniper shoots him as the armistice is about to begin. In a more contemporary setting, *Beach Red* (1967) also attempts to create this sense of the futility of war.

The producer-director-star, Cornel Wilde, explained that he had tried to "show people what war was really like whichever side you are on. The enemy is not a faceless extra who gets mowed down while the heroes charge up the beach gung ho, and we feel sorry for those who are hurt." Wilde said he had not created a "war as hell" film in which men are "torn apart by shrapnel, or maimed by 50mm machine guns or cut in half, [or] have an arm blown off." Instead, he "tried to show that war, even without the killing and maiming, just the physical and mental stress is horrifying."[40]

Wilde recognized that "deadly combat is always exciting to people," and so in his ending he attempted to show "that war was terrible and a waste of human life, of youth, and of human relationships and that it accomplishes nothing." In the climax, a Marine and a Japanese soldier burst into a clearing at the same moment and wound each other severely. They lie twenty feet apart, both in agony and incapable of moving. Staring at each other, they recognize their common youth and common pain. The Marine senses the agonizing thirst of the Japanese, who is dying from a stomach wound, and he throws the soldier his canteen. The Japanese cannot even drink, but to reciprocate, he tries to throw the Marine his one remaining cigarette. As he does, an American patrol arrives, sees only that the Japanese is about to throw something, and kills him. According to Wilde, the soldier's meaningless death illuminated the horrors of war without showing any positive value.[41]

Beach Red may still have portrayed aspects of war as an exciting romantic escape. Yet it came closer than most war movies to conveying the absurdity and uselessness of war. Recognizing the thrust of Wilde's script at a time when the Vietnam War was escalating, the Marines extended only limited assistance to the film, in the form of combat footage from the Marine film archives. (The Marines probably benefited more from this assistance than Wilde, since the footage had deteriorated and he had it restored in the process of blowing it up to wide-screen dimensions.) To obtain the men and equipment needed for his battle scenes, Wilde went to the Philippines and arranged to use its armed services for the large-scale action sequences.[42]

Although these re-creations became as realistic as any done in a Hollywood war movie, Wilde managed to avoid picturing combat as adventurous. Instead, he portrays war as a

Marines land on Pacific Island in *Beach Red* (1967), Cornel Wilde's effort to make an antiwar statement by showing combat as it really is, without the typical war film excitement and escapist entertainment.

grim, desperate business. His Marines have no time for typical Hollywood antics. They find themselves in a struggle for survival with an enemy little different from themselves and who are also willing to die for their cause. As shown in the final confrontation, they also possess humanity and compassion. Unlike so many intended antiwar movies, this interpretation of combat conveyed the message the director desired. Wilde reported that at the first sneak preview the audience watched the film in virtual silence. Afterward, a weeping woman came up to him and said, "I want to thank you, Mr. Wilde, for showing people what it's really like. I lost one of my two sons in Vietnam." At another screening, Wilde reported that a serviceman left the movie "sobbing uncontrollably."[43]

The film equally moved reviewers. One critic described *Beach Red* as "a grim, wryly humorous, gripping, and emotion-packed drama of war." In taking a "fresh approach to both the purpose and purposelessness of war," Wilde made a picture in which "neither preachment, chauvinism, nor cynicism gets the upper hand . . . as it explores the human sacrifice that war imposes on both sides." To the reviewer, the film came "close to being the definitive drama on human expendability in war." Similarly, another critic said that *Beach Red* showed "war without glamour; death without glory; hatred without reason. [It] is so frighteningly real in its portrayal of war in the Pacific that it could be a shouting sermon against militancy." A third reviewer noted that although "there are practically no mock heroics as the men writhe and bleed and yell or moan," this "is not what makes it such a powerful antiwar document." Rather, its statement came from showing "that the men don't want to kill, want to live themselves, and that they are frightened most of the time."[44]

Fright, of course, becomes the other aspect of the excitement war offers men who challenge death in combat. By focusing on the negative side of the combat experience, Wilde's antiwar theme did not get lost in a wave of gratuitous violence, adventure, or romance. Nevertheless, the frightened men remained only actors in a fictionalized story. Their emotions originated from their performances. For a movie to convey the full impact of fright, the camera must capture the faces of men who are caught up in actual combat, men who may actually die the next moment.

Such visualizations are of necessity found only in documentaries, and even then only in an honored few. Of these, John Huston's *Battle of San Pietro* remains probably the best motion picture—documentary, pseudo-documentary, or pure fiction—about the experience of men in combat. Although the Army saw the film as the record of a single battle in southern Italy, most viewers have seen it as an antiwar statement, because it so well captured the fear on men's faces as they went into battle, so well showed the meaninglessness of death, so well conveyed that no real glamour exists in actual combat.

Yet *The Battle of San Pietro* succeeded not only because it showed war from the perspective of the men who did the fighting, but also because it showed the victims of war, the men who died and the civilians whose lives were shattered by the battle that swept over them, their homes, and their land. Perhaps in conscious or unconscious recognition of the message these images portrayed, the War Department had Huston delete some of the shots of soldiers dying or being killed. And the film spends a few moments showing civilians returning to their homes; later it shows their land again in bloom. Although *The Battle of San Pietro* ends on this upbeat note, the overall effect remains one of revulsion at war and the horrors it brings to all people, soldiers and civilians alike.[45]

In focusing on the victims of the battle, Huston provides perhaps the best answer to Norman Jewison's question of how to make a statement about violence without showing any violence: focus not on the violence but on the victims, as much as possible. Huston's *Let There Be Light* (1945), makes an even stronger antiwar statement by focusing exclusively on soldiers as victims, men who have returned from war suffering the psychological effects of their combat experiences. They have damage as severe as any physical wounds. Huston's narration in the film describes them thus: "Born and bred in peace, educated to hate war, they were overnight plunged into sudden and terrible situations." Showing the effect that combat has on men without portraying actual combat, *Let There Be Light* documents the horrors of battle much more graphically than any film claiming to condemn the brutality of war by showing scenes of battle, either real or imagined.

Not surprisingly, the Army refused to release *Let There Be Light* to the general public until the early 1990s. Huston claimed that the service suppressed the film for more than thirty years after the end of the war because of its antiwar content. The Pentagon denied the accusation, pointing out that the rights of privacy of soldiers appearing in the film prevented its showing. Huston responded that he had secured releases from all the men who appeared on screen. Nonetheless, *Let There Be Light* might well have had a devastating impact on the men and their families, given the images it contained. In any case, the film remains the prototype of the antiwar movie that conveys its message through the victims of war rather than through combat.[46]

Several Hollywood feature films have tried to convey the negative side of war in similar but less dramatic ways. Delmer Daves's *Pride of the Marines* (1945) portrays a blind Marine's adjustment to civilian life; William Wyler's *Best Years of Our Lives* (1946) features three veterans, one of whom has lost both hands in battle, trying to bring order to their lives after the war. Fred Zinnemann's *The Search* (1948), made in Europe with help from the Army, shows German children as the victims in postwar Germany. Two years later, Zinnemann directed Stanley Kramer's production of *The Men*, which again returned to the soldier-as-victim theme.

John Garfield, as the blinded Al Schmid, receives a medal for his actions in *Pride of the Marines* (1945).

Portraying a group of paralyzed veterans who attempt to adjust to a life of permanent helplessness, the film depicts a story of war victims about whom people seldom talked and whom Hollywood had never portrayed. *The Men* received the full cooperation of the Army and the Veteran's Administration, who saw it as a way to inform the American people of the

government's efforts to rehabilitate terribly wounded soldiers. The images Zinnemann created suggested another message: war destroys human beings and does not provide the glamorous adventure that most other films set on the battlefield conveyed. *The Men* also became the model for two Vietnam-era films, *Coming Home* and *Born on the Fourth of July*, which used the plight of paralyzed Marines to make their antiwar statements.[47]

Although the Army apparently did not see the significance of the victim approach in 1950, the Air Force was quick to recognize it when they saw the script of *Limbo* (1972). The film told the story of POW wives waiting for their husbands to return from North Vietnam or for word that they had died. Director Mark Robson saw *Limbo* as a true antiwar film because it shows the suffering of the women but none of the excitement or adventure usually found in a war movie. The producer, Linda Gottlieb, stated that the Air Force refused to provide even limited assistance because the plot included unfaithful wives. The Air Force felt the movie would adversely affect the morale of fliers in Vietnam, and more so the American POWs, whose captors might somehow treat them to a screening of the film within a few days of its release in the United States. The Air Force further contended that less than 2 percent of POW wives had cheated on their husbands. Without making a judgment on the women, Gottlieb said that her research showed the figure to be much higher.[48]

Of course, the film intended to portray the tragedy of the women's situations, irrespective of who did what, when, and why. However, the Air Force felt that the film would convey an unflattering image of the service and its wives. As a result, the Air Force not only refused to provide assistance but also went out of its way to make sure the Pentagon denied the film company help even of an informational nature. Ironically, the service's concern about the effect of *Limbo* became moot when the POWs began to return at almost the same time the film appeared. With the story irrelevant, few people bothered to see the film, and whatever antiwar message it may have contained failed to attract attention. In any event, the movie illustrated, by focusing on the victims rather than the combatants, a potent means of presenting the negative side of war without portraying any of the glamour or excitement of combat.

In the 1964 *Americanization of Emily*, the filmmakers took a radically different approach in putting their antiwar message on the screen. They rejected the value of combat altogether and suggested that man should perhaps not make the ultimate sacrifice, even for the good of his country. In creating its comment on the absurdity of war and the irrationality of military men, *The Americanization of Emily* became the first major Hollywood production to portray an American serviceman proudly professing the virtues of cowardice. When confronted with such a unique portrayal, many reviewers reacted with stunned outrage. One critic described *The Americanization of Emily* as "so hypocritical—because it dares to call itself funny—so callous, so cruel, and so crass, that it provokes only anger and a feeling of resentment that we, as Americans, have allowed ourselves the 'luxury' of permitting such encroachment against our very heritage as it were."[49]

The Americanization of Emily undoubtedly lacked evenness and presented its thesis too verbosely. Perhaps worst, its message contained inconsistencies and fallacies. Nevertheless, through alternating satire, slapstick, and serious drama, the film attempted to question the glorification of war and to ridicule the idea that to die for one's country was a positive good. Starting out with William Bradford Huie's novel *The Americanization of Emily*, Paddy Chayefsky used a rather conventional love story as the framework in which to reexamine the premises of war. Rather than make his antiwar observations in a traditional dramatic script, Chayefsky used "savage comedy with brash and irreverent situations."[50]

In the biggest change Chayefsky made in transferring the book to the screen, he turned the hero, played by James Garner, into a professed coward, a "charming churl whose principle it is to be without principle." Garner, a junior Navy officer in pre-D-Day London, serves as a "dog-robber" for his admiral, one of the planners of the invasion. In return for the security of a safe position, Garner procures luxuries for his boss—from liquor to food to women. In the course of his assignment, Garner meets an American-hating English war widow, played by Julie Andrews in her first nonsinging and probably best screen role.[51]

Garner woos Andrews with a mixture of charm and his philosophy of cowardice, which takes advantage of her bitterness over her husband's combat death. He tells her, "I preach cowardice. Through cowardice we shall all be saved. . . . If everybody obeyed their natural impulse and ran like rabbits at the first shot, I don't see how we could possibly get to the second shot." He talks about the unreasonableness of waiting to be killed "all because there's a madman in Berlin, a homicidal paranoid in Moscow, a manic buffoon in Rome, and a group of obsessed generals in Tokyo." To be sure, Garner is ignoring the nature of the enemies the United States is then facing and the very real possibility that if he and those like him were to run away, the "paranoids" and "buffoons" would happily take over. Nonetheless, his espousal of cowardice suggested for the first time in a major American movie that one thing people could do toward eliminating war was "to get rid of the goodness and virtue" they usually attribute to combat.

Ultimately, Andrews responds to the American's philosophy: "I am glad you are yellow. It is your most important asset, being a coward. Every man I ever loved was a hero and all I got was death." Ironically, as Garner wins the battle for Andrews's love, his boss's brainstorm threatens his efforts to remain alive. The admiral has decided that a sailor should become the first dead man on Omaha Beach so that the Navy can show it has no peer for bravery among the services. Ultimately, in a scene of comic irony, Garner finds himself forced onto the beach at gunpoint, ahead of the assault force. At this juncture, the filmmakers conspire to save him. Initially reported dead, he reappears in England as a wounded hero and, after first refusing, he agrees to return to the United States to take part in a victory bond drive.

This traditional heroic ending notwithstanding, *The Americanization of Emily* stirred up wrathful criticism not only in the media but also among moviegoers. Director Arthur Hiller reported that he even lost a few friends "because their heroic vision of the goodness, virtue, and nobility of war has been tarnished" by the movie's disrespect for the traditional American view of combat. As a result of the controversies stirred up during the film's sneak previews, Hiller attended the first public screening in New York to hear reactions from an actual audience. He found many people "hopping mad."[52]

One viewer considered it "a pretty deadly joke making a comedy episode out of the D-day landing and having laughs at the expense of an admiral who had a breakdown." Others objected to the film's several messages: war had no virtue or goodness; death in war offered no nobility; women who wear their widow's weeds like nuns help to perpetuate the very wars that gave birth to their sorrows; death in war does not necessarily make men brave or noble, but probably simply the victims of societies that glamorize war. These critics believed that the film perverted some American institutions and misrepresented some human foibles. The consensus suggested that it should have remained unmade.[53]

Hiller responded that he saw dead heroes as simply dead men and that living cowards could achieve more. He emphatically believed that "a wild, satiric, cynical comedy" served as the way to comment "on the lunacy of the attributes we attach to war. . . . Goodness and virtue and nobility are so out of place in the context of war that satiric laughter is the only logical response." At the same time, Hiller argued that *The Americanization of Emily* did not ridicule those who ended up having to go to war. It did not consider all wars. Nor did it deny that a time might exist when a necessary cause might require the sacrifice of lives.[54]

To the director, the film only showed "war for what it is, a barbaric, inhuman act of man—a miserable hell. It says one thing we can do toward eliminating war from our world is to get rid of the goodness and virtue we attribute to war. Be grieved by death, but not proud of it. Stop naming streets after generals, stop erecting statues. It says stop applauding death—stop celebrating war. [These celebrations are] helping to perpetuate circumstances in our world that will bring our heroes, again and again, into situations where they must give their lives." He did not consider war itself a fraud but believed the fraud "is in the virtue and goodness we attribute to war. If you glorify war you create a climate for more wars."[55]

Not everyone agreed with Hiller about the essence of *The Americanization of Emily*. One retired Army officer, who had served in the service's Public Affairs Office in Los Angeles in the early 1950s, answered the director's published remarks with his own essay. He said he did not object to the portrayal of military men as cowards, but he disagreed with Hiller's "didactic preachment about the meaning of the film and his specious or naive reasoning that the deglorification of nobility and virtue in war and the glorification of cowardice will contribute to lessening the climate for future wars."[56]

Melvyn Douglas, who played the eccentric admiral on the film, disagreed with this perspective, seeing value in looking at the military with some irreverence: "I often wish that we were like the British, who have a capacity to laugh at themselves and their own institutions which far exceeds our own." He felt that all organizations "should be able to look at themselves with humor as well as with seriousness." Douglas, who served in both World Wars, said he had "seen first-hand some of the excesses that were exploited in the film," including the part Garner played.[57]

Nevertheless, in 1964 the Navy was not ready to laugh at itself or openly acknowledge the existence of officers even approximating Garner's Charlie Madison. Knowing this, the producer did not even bother to seek the limited military assistance he needed for the brief Omaha Beach sequence. And when the film appeared, the Navy discouraged distribution to its bases because the "story and characterizations do not present the Navy accurately."[58]

Ironically, in the end Garner's Charlie Madison accepts his hero's mantle in the best tradition of the American fighting man. Bowing to his love for Emily, Madison seemingly embraces her argument that "war isn't a fraud. . . . It's very real. . . . We shall never get rid of war by pretending it's unreal. It's the virtue of war that's a fraud. Not war itself. It's the valor and the self-sacrifice and the goodness of war that need the exposing. And here you are being brave and self-sacrificing and positively clanking with moral fervor, perpetuating the very things you detest, merely to do the right thing." But what is doing the "right thing" in this instance—telling the truth about what happened on Omaha Beach, or letting "God worry about the truth" and knowing the "momentary fact" of his love for Emily?

Madison may sell out to the establishment, but Emily also accepts the traditional values of society. When she first meets Madison, she says, "I don't want oranges, or eggs, or soap flakes, either. Don't show me how profitable it would be to fall in love with you,

Charlie. Don't Americanize me!" But she changes. Whereas she previously found Madison's cowardice a virtue, she now finds it a failing if it means he will go to prison for telling the truth about Omaha Beach. Having become Americanized, Emily wants her man home even if he must play the hero, however fraudulently.

In transforming the characters' values so quickly, the movie may have copped out. As Douglas says, the filmmakers "lost their courage at the end. They didn't go as far with it as they could. They tried to sweeten up the end." In fact, Hiller and Chayefsky had three different endings to the film. Hiller wanted Madison to die on the beach a hero and have a statue erected to him. Despite his efforts, Chayefsky could not create all the scenes that this ending would have required to make the same point Garner's actual return makes possible. Hiller said that it "wasn't worth it to have a stronger ending and lose almost a third of the meaning of the film." In any case, if the final sequence weakened the film's message, it did so with such rapidity, so close to the end, that most viewers missed the transformations completely, or found them so ambiguous that they ignored the switches. As a result, the general feeling remained that *The Americanization of Emily* contained an antiwar and pacifist statement.[59]

Bosley Crowther, in the *New York Times*, described the film as "a spinning comedy that says more for basic pacifism than a fistful of intellectual tracts. . . . [It] gets off some of the wildest, brashest, and funniest situations and cracks at the lunacy of warfare that have popped from the screen in quite some time." Other critics noted, however, that the film's "preachiness" sometimes slowed its pace. More important, the film's then unique message and the ambiguity of its apparent change in direction created confusion about the film and caused some people to find it distasteful. Consequently, *The Americanization of Emily* initially enjoyed indifferent success at the box office.[60]

It also had the same effect on American perceptions of the growing war in Southeast Asia as Renoir's *Grande Illusion* had had on the developing threat of war in Europe in the late 1930s. The studio later re-released the film with its title shortened to *Emily* in an attempt to capitalize on Julie Andrew's success in *Mary Poppins* and *The Sound of Music*. Nevertheless, not until the rise of the antiwar movement of the late 1960s did *The Americanization of Emily* find its place as a cult film that voiced the ideals of the Vietnam War protesters. More than any of the contemporary films, *The Americanization of Emily* addressed the antiwar generation's disillusionment with the armed forces and the growing realization that the U.S. military could no longer sweep all enemies before it.[61]

As such, it became a quintessential non-Vietnam Vietnam movie, containing one fundamental idea with which war protesters could readily identify: it is better to become a live coward than a dead hero. Much of the social ferment in the late sixties focused on this issue, and during that period a significant segment of the American population came to reject the long-standing notion that the highest calling a man could have was to die for his country.

12 | The Bomb as Friend and Enemy

UNTIL THE CIVIL WAR IN VIETNAM ESCALATED and became an American quagmire, antiwar messages like the ones that *The Americanization of Emily* espoused had little chance of changing people's views on patriotism and the ability of the armed services to protect the nation from all threats. Ever since August 6, 1945, the atomic bomb had provided that protection, ensuring that the United States could destroy any nation that dared to launch an attack against its sovereignty. Hollywood helped create the perception that the nation had the ultimate weapon and the men to deliver it to the far corners of the earth.

The building and use of the atomic bomb offered filmmakers all the ingredients they needed to create a story with broad appeal, a science-fiction-like setting in which to explore the unknown, the dramatic tension of waiting to see if experiments would work, the test of the completed bomb, and finally the military mission to deliver the new weapon. With its usual hyperbole, the MGM press book noted, "From the moment an atomic bomb dropped on Hiroshima on August 6, 1945, it became the greatest news story ever to break upon the consciousness of the civilized world. To this day, with discussions raging everywhere as to its possible influence on the world's future . . . if any . . . it remains a vital topic to every living person." Given the top-secret nature of the Manhattan Project, the studio faced a daunting challenge to bring the story to the screen in a timely fashion.[1]

MGM began its efforts only three days after the attack on Hiroshima, when the studio's Washington representative, Carter Barron, called the War Department's Bureau of Public Relations to discuss the idea of a movie about the development of the atomic bomb. Barron followed up his conversation with a letter on August 14, confirming the studio's interest. As part of the initial research, MGM requested on November 3 that the Army allow producer Sam Marx to visit Oak Ridge, the uranium-producing facility. On the ninth, the service's Pictorial Branch advised the Bureau of Public Relations that Gen. Leslie Groves, head of the Manhattan Project, supported the production.[2]

After visiting Oak Ridge, Marx came to Washington, where he interviewed Groves and other military people involved with the Manhattan Project and in Army Public Affairs. He was also able to obtain a meeting with President Truman to discuss the decision to use the atomic bomb. Marx later recalled that as the hour's meeting was ending, Truman told him, "Make a good picture. One that will tell the people that the decision is theirs to make . . . this is the beginning or the end." That phrase became the title for the film after Truman verified its accuracy in a letter to Marx on November 26, 1945. Barron later wrote to the chief of the Army's Pictorial Branch that Groves and Truman "were so enthusiastic and inspiring that we then proceeded with confidence and gratification. General Groves' agreement to cooperate was wholehearted but nevertheless always within the security rules established by the War Department."[3]

As a result of Marx's research trip, Spig Wead was able to produce a temporary script by December 26, and the studio proceeded to obtain approval from the people whom the film would portray, including President Truman; Groves; J. Robert Oppenheimer, director of the Las Alamos Laboratory, which fabricated the bombs; Col. Paul Tibbets, who commanded the bomber group and flew the Hiroshima mission; Adm. William Parsons, who armed the bomb in flight; and Army Chief of Staff George C. Marshall. In response to Barron's direct request to Marshall, the general, then in China, advised the War Department that if Groves would be checking the script and the completed film, he saw "no objection." However, he noted: "I do not want any announcement to effect that I personally have cooperated in production of film."[4]

Once MGM had completed the initial screenplay, the studio submitted it to the White House and the War Department and to Groves for vetting and approval. The general found relatively minor problems of fact and language and in his own portrayal. He did note: "Incidentally, all attempts to make me demonstrate emotion, such as getting mad or excited or pacing the floor, which appears from time to time, are entirely untrue to life. The less emotion, etc., the more true to life it will be." He also said he had not even paced while waiting for his children's births.[5]

Correcting factual matters, Groves pointed out that no one at the Trinity test of the plutonium bomb in July 1945 wore goggles or covered themselves with suntan lotion and that his secretary had never sat on the floor. He did wonder where the screenwriters had learned that "I infrequently eat a chocolate or two. I would suggest that one of the two references . . . be eliminated. Mrs. Groves might remember the incident less if the earlier reference were the one left in." For a man concerned with historical accuracy, Groves here manifested more of a concern for his personal image than with truth, since he remained a chocaholic his entire life and was always fighting his waistline. In the end, however, he found no security problems: "No classified information has been given away nor would any individual or group be assisted in guessing at classified information by means of this script." Just as important, he said the depictions of the Army and both real and fictional people do "not in any way reflect discredit on the Army," and he felt that the filmmakers had "done their job well."[6]

With Groves satisfied, the Army quickly approved the script on April 17 and took up the requirements list that MGM had submitted on the sixteenth. The White House also gave its permission for the filmmakers to portray the president making the decision to drop the atomic bomb against Japan. In turn, the studio agreed not to mention that the president had suggested the title and not to refer to Senator Truman or his Investigating Committee, which had unsuccessfully sought information about a mysterious project in Tennessee, thereby causing Groves serious security concerns. The studio also promised to depict the president "only from the rear or from the side in such a way as not to show his countenance in any way. With all these issues resolved, the studio received the use of several B-29s, men, and equipment, as well as permission to film exterior scenes outside secure areas at Oak Ridge. Despite the research and Groves's own involvement, the secrecy then still surrounding the atomic bomb project forced MGM to take many liberties with history and fact in making *The Beginning or the End*. To anticipate criticism, the studio included at the opening of the film the disclaimer: "This is a true story. However, for dramatic license and security purposes, some rearrangement of chronology and fictionalization was necessary."[7]

Did these changes matter? What constitutes legitimate dramatic license in a film that supposedly is providing Americans their first factual account of the development and use of the atomic bomb, restricted only by security issues? Groves and the Army had approved the screenplay as well as the completed film, and the fact remains that the studio was creating a feature film, not a documentary. Apart from its many inaccuracies, however, Admiral Parsons found the film "dangerously *untrue*" because it portrayed key people "all mixed up emotionally." He denied this emphatically: "Any story or film that shows us mixed up is distorting and sugar-coating the truth dangerously." In contrast, one of the scientists who worked on the bomb and served as a technical advisor during the filming concluded, "I have become convinced that it can be expected to give the average person his clearest understanding to date of the most lethal weapon ever devised by man, and the essential problems of atomic energy now confronting the world. That, to me, makes the picture of unique value to all humanity."[8]

Probably not. The filmmakers attempted to lend *The Beginning or the End* credibility by having the cinematic Oppenheimer introduce the story. They do show Enrico Fermi and his associates building a uranium pile under Stagg Field at the University of Chicago and creating the first chain reaction, a crucial step in development of the atomic bomb. Although the film provides a reasonable explanation of how Fermi controlled the reaction, the flashing lights and sound effects in the control panels here and in later portrayals of nuclear reactions, particularly at the Trinity test, bear no resemblance to the actual experiments and the assembly of the atomic bomb.

The film fairly describes the magnitude of the Manhattan Project through a brief, effective montage showing the dislocation of farmers from the site of the plutonium factories at Hanford, Washington, and the building and operating of the facilities at all three bomb-making locations. In this, however, the directors were simply reporting the facts, which required no embellishments. Although the film acknowledges the contribution of private industry, which built and operated the facilities, it does so in a fabricated scene in which the company executives have a meeting with Groves and agree to work at cost to build the bomb. A scientist mouths the truism that "only a war can give us this chance" to split the atom, something that the physicists later conveniently forgot when they began to publicly suffer guilty consciences from having built the bomb. And the MGM special-effects department did a fine job of creating an ersatz atomic explosion. It was so good, in fact, that the Army used the footage in its own documentaries on the bomb. Little else in *The Beginning or the End* comes close to the truth about the development of the bomb.[9]

The very number and significance of the factual errors, fabrications, and distortions subverted history without serving any valid dramatic or security function as claimed in the opening credit. The proverbial monkey pounding away on his typewriter might well have infused the film with more veracity than the filmmakers provided. Why introduce General Groves as the head of the Manhattan Project more than six months after the date he actually took command? Moreover, he enters the story as a general although he did not receive his first star until after he received the assignment to build the bomb. In the name of historical accuracy, the filmmakers only had to have Groves's cinematic boss tell him, "A star comes with the job." In fact, the real general did say that, to assuage Groves's unhappiness over not receiving a combat appointment.[10]

Likewise, the informational value of the film suffers greatly when President Roosevelt starts dictating a letter to Vice President Truman about the Manhattan Project minutes before he suffers his fatal stroke. Whether or not he should have done so, the president did not start such a letter. In fact, the filmmakers failed to avail themselves of the drama surrounding the story of how Truman actually learned about the bomb project. On April 25, thirteen days after Roosevelt had died at Warm Springs, Georgia, Groves had come to the White House, entering through a back door to avoid attracting the attention of reporters. Ushered into the president's office where Secretary of War Henry Stimson was waiting, Groves proceeded to brief Truman about the Manhattan Project. To the general's relief, the president did not bring up his Senate investigating committee's efforts to learn about what was happening in the Tennessee hills. No issue of security would have prevented the filmmakers from portraying the meeting accurately.

Once the location moves to Tinian, the filmmakers show even less concern with historical reality. The fictional young scientist who appears throughout the movie—working with Fermi at Columbia, helping control the first chain reaction in Chicago, meeting with Groves in Washington, living in Oak Ridge—for some unexplained reason, sticks his hands into the access hatch of the already assembled bomb waiting to be loaded for the trip to Hiroshima. Smoke and noise rise from the weapon and he dies of radiation poisoning within twelve hours. Despite the apparent seriousness of the accident, the bomb did not require repairs. This never happened, could never have happened.

Meanwhile, Tibbets briefs the crews headed to Japan on the weather, photography, and delivery planes. To illustrate the power of the bomb, he shows the men a motion picture of the Trinity test of July 16, eliciting a stunned reaction. The briefing did take place, but the projector ate the film and so the men had only the briefer's description of the power. When the fliers reach the flight line, they find that the art department has painted "Enola Gay" on the wrong side of Tibbets's plane. Undeterred, they take off in bright daylight even though the B-29 actually left at 2:45 in the morning. Apparently not worried about visual consistency, the filmmakers rightly used footage of the *Enola Gay* on the ground accurately configured, without the machine-gun turrets, which Tibbets had had removed from the plane to save weight and give the planes more speed. However, the plane that takes off and flies to Hiroshima has turrets in some shots and lacks them in others. And for dramatic reasons, the filmmakers portray Captain Parsons having trouble completing the assembly of the bomb during the flight, something that did not happen.

To the filmmakers, their inaccuracies may have seemed insignificant in the broader context of trying to provide the American people with some understanding of how the United States built and decided to use the atomic bomb. Certainly they needed to compress almost six years of history into two hours and use composite characters such as the young scientist. However, to portray him dying serves no informational purpose, since no

The Enola Gay usered in the atomic age over Hiroshima in 1945. *Above and Beyond* (1953), depicting the story of Col. Paul Tibbets and his mission, became the forerunner of a series of Air Force movies about the atomic bomb as a deterrent to war. Today, Tibbets's plane awaits complete restoration and exhibit at the new Air and Space Museum when it is completed at Dulles Airport outside Washington.

such accident occurred. The continued secrecy surrounding the Manhattan Project certainly required some license, including the art department's rendering of the Hiroshima bomb. However, *The Beginning or the End* lacks even the essence of the flight of the *Enola Gay* to Hiroshima to deliver "Little Boy," the uranium bomb, and so it loses any value it might have had with a greater attention to the facts.

In any case, the film's title, which came from President Truman's comment to the producer, suggested that the filmmakers had a broader agenda than simply telling the story of the atomic bomb. Appearing when it did, *The Beginning or the End* contained the implicit warning that the bomb could end civilization. Thus, it helped set the tone for the developing Cold War. The United States had to remain ever vigilant against the danger that the Soviet Union posed, and the bomb would serve as our weapon of choice to thwart any attack on the country and the capitalist way of life.

The Beginning or the End focused on the development of the atomic bomb, with the delivery of the weapon of secondary interest to the filmmakers. In contrast, the 1952 *Above and Beyond* intended to tell the true story of Lt. Col. Paul Tibbets and his command of the 509th Composite Group, which dropped the atomic bombs on Hiroshima and Nagasaki. In reality, the film contained two different stories. It represented itself as a docudrama that traced Tibbets's military career from North Africa to Hiroshima and the dropping of the atomic bomb. However, it became a virtual soap opera, pitting Tibbets against his wife, who resents that his command responsibility comes before his relationship with her.

Tibbets later acknowledged that he could not be available much of the time he was preparing for the atomic bomb mission; of necessity, this became his priority: "There were times because of the secrecy requirements that not only she, but also my parents couldn't understand why I couldn't give them a logical answer to some of their questions, I became very evasive. I became very misleading. Deliberately, I tried to move anyone off the track of becoming anywhere near understanding what it was I was in fact doing." The movie captures this reality very well, providing a unique insight into the burdens that leadership brings with it. Tibbets had flown the first B-17 missions over occupied Europe from England under the command of Frank Armstrong, the model for General Savage in *Twelve O'Clock High*. Beirne Lay had patterned one of the characters in the movie after Tibbets, who fully understood the pressures under which he labored.[11]

Lucy Tibbets could not or would not recognize that her husband must have a highly important assignment. In most Hollywood films, military wives appear as submissive, supportive women thinking only of their husband's careers and the good of the nation. *Above and Beyond* presents an entirely different image. Lucy becomes bitterly unhappy that Tibbets's duties take up so much of his time and, even worse, that he cannot confide in her what he is doing. She does not seem to even appreciate how lucky she is to have him home at all when most able-bodied men were fighting in some overseas theater of operations. Instead, she sees his secret assignment simply as destroying their relationship. Finally, Tibbets has no choice but to exile her from the training base, and she does not find out about the nature of his assignment until after he drops the bomb on Hiroshima.

In contrast, the wife of Gen. K.D. Nichols, the Manhattan Project district engineer, recalled that she did not expect Nichols to tell her anything about what was happening in Oak Ridge during the more than two and a half years they lived in the secret site whose plants were processing uranium for the Hiroshima bomb. Knowing the identity of the many physicists who regularly visited her husband, she had assumed he was building some sort of death ray. Ultimately, she did ask her husband, who appeared as a composite character in *The Beginning or the End* despite his primary contribution to the Manhattan Project as General Groves's deputy, to reveal to her what he had been doing before the secret became public. Unfortunately, she was busy when a messenger delivered a large envelope on August 6, 1945, and opened it only after her sister (also living in Oak Ridge, married to an officer working on the bomb project) called to tell her about the dropping of the atomic bomb. Then she found all the previously written press releases, which Nichols had sent her as his way of telling her about the bomb.[12]

In any case, Tibbets did have a clause in the contract he signed with MGM that permitted him to reject anything he "thought might be considered degrading, misleading, or anything like that." Beirne Lay, who wrote the original story and worked on the screenplay, recalled, "It surprised me how lenient he was in our taking liberties as long as it wasn't anything that he thought was flagrantly untrue or wrong." If *Above and Beyond* captured the essence of the Tibbetses' wartime marital problems, it also provided a most unflattering picture of their relationship. So why become involved with the project?[13]

As with virtually all films about the armed services, fiction or history, Tibbets's cinematic road to Hiroshima began in Hollywood. While writing the novel that became *Twelve O'Clock High,* Beirne Lay and Sy Bartlett had asked Tibbets to review some of the chapters, since he had been in the Ninety-seventh Bomb Group at the time in which they were setting their story. After reading the manuscript, the men began discussing Tibbets's experiences with the atomic bomb, and Lay observed, "Oh my God, what a screenplay that would make." According to Tibbets, Lay wanted to pursue the idea, because he had connections within the film industry and thought he could sell the project. Nevertheless, development of the story had to wait about three years until Tibbets could obtain a security clearance from the Air Force. Then, after numerous conversations in California and at Eglin Field in Florida, where Tibbets was stationed, Lay formalized a two-and-a-half-page synopsis, which interested MGM. Before the studio finalized the purchase, however, an Air Force friend of Tibbets ascertained that the service would assist with the production.[14]

Apart from the studio's interest, Tibbets explained that the situation within the Strategic Air Command at the time had influenced "to a small extent" his own willingness to cooperate with the film. He said that in the early 1950s, SAC was experiencing "the highest divorce rate ever known anywhere" among its personnel as a result of the continuous rotation of units overseas. He said this was producing "a tremendous morale problem" within SAC. Lay, a close friend of SAC commander Curtis LeMay, believed that the problems of discipline and training that Tibbets had had to deal with in the 509th Composite Group and the resulting family tensions resembled the current situation within SAC. Consequently, he felt that a movie about the atomic bomb mission might help the morale of the servicemen. When LeMay heard about the idea, he responded: "Oh my God. Let's do this. I think it will be one of the greatest morale factors that has ever hit the Strategic Air Command because it will show the women that are complaining today that there have been women in the past who have put up with a lot of things and so the current women are not the great pioneers."[15]

Whether or not *Above and Beyond* actually helped improve the situation within SAC, Tibbets said the relationship with his wife was "reasonably accurate as portrayed. I could live with it and so could she. . . . It is so close to realism that really we would have to be very, very nitpicking to separate what was on the screen from reality." Even so, he acknowledged that the film "really didn't portray the tensions as bad as they were. You would expect that."[16]

Does this dramatic license matter? Given the movie's stated purpose of telling the story of the atomic bomb mission against Hiroshima, did the filmmakers devote too much time to the relationship between the Tibbetses? Since the portrayal intended to show the pressures under which Tibbets labored, the domestic problems had relevance to the story. Toning down the ongoing tensions between him and his wife did not mask his single-minded focus on his assignments, as a bomber pilot, test pilot, or commander of the atomic bomb mission. Moreover, despite the value that Lay, Tibbets, and LeMay saw in revealing the problems in the marriage, the filmmakers had no intention of producing an exposé. Nor would the Production Code have allowed them to reveal that the marriage ultimately ended. Nevertheless, the couple's marital strife did seem to become the focus of the film rather than its raison d'être of providing an account of a singular historical event, the delivery of an atomic bomb to Hiroshima.

Once it turned to Tibbets's military assignments, *Above and Beyond* took on the guise of a docudrama, albeit with typical cinematic visual and dramatic license. He had told the full story of his assignment and the Hiroshima mission to Lay and later talked with the writers and directors Melvin Frank and Norman Panama while they were working on the final screenplay. Col. Charles Sweeney, the pilot on the Nagasaki mission, contributed information to help ensure that the filmmakers told the story as accurately as possible. And Adm. William Parsons, who had armed the Hiroshima bomb, read and critiqued the script.[17]

Despite his commitment to tell Tibbets's story accurately, Lay found himself in conflict with the writers, who he said "really wanted to do something far different than I or Tibbets wanted to do. They wanted to imbue some terrible guilt complex to him and weave the story around that. This doesn't happen to be true, so we wound up somewhere in the middle." Just as important, Lay said Panama and Frank "didn't give a damn whether it was authentic or not. And we fought like hell over certain points that I thought would destroy credibility unless we took some pains to be closer to the truth. We had a lot of battles about that. All they cared about was dramatizing it."[18]

Admiral Parsons also had many complaints about the misrepresentations he found, including the distortion of his arming the bomb aboard the B-29 after takeoff. He had written to the Air Force Public Affairs Office: "I suppose I must bow to atomic mythology." However, he said, "I would prefer 'putting in the key pieces and buttoning up' to 'arming' but I am a purist in this matter." In even stronger terms, he objected to the manner in which the filmmakers created "the brink-of-the-abyss, hysterical impression as to the hazards and uncertainties of the assembly job," noting that this had become "one of the false notes" in *The Beginning or the End.* He explained that the task was exacting, "but not because it was very ticklish, and only a suicidal maniac could have made it dangerous." Tibbets also acknowledged that "Hollywood introduced considerable turbulence to add to the suspense. This wasn't exactly accurate, but it was an effective way to portray the feelings of the crew when the mightiest explosion in the world was coming to life in the bomb bay of their airplane."[19]

Perhaps recognizing the problems he would face trying to convince Hollywood to tell his story accurately, Tibbets turned down the studio's request to serve as technical advisor: "Obviously, I was too close to the forest to see the trees." Instead, the Air Force assigned three officers to work on the production. One, Col. Charles Begg, had served as the Ordinance Squadron commander in the 509th Composite Group, which the Army had formed to deliver the atomic bombs to Japan. Begg had had the responsibility for assembling the Hiroshima bomb, and Tibbets said that thanks to him, the film's recreation of the training sequences at Wendover Field on the Nevada-Utah border "were absolutely accurate."[20]

Before he was able to achieve this portrayal, however, Beggs had his own problems with the filmmakers: "My first reaction to the script was that it was a trivial matter and something that had little to do with reality." He said the original script did not "remotely" capture the training experience: "It touched on the subject and it was a very large subject, of course." He found the story "somewhat comical in places. . . . there was very, very little information other than a personal story of Tibbets." Consequently, he worked with the art director to create words, pictures, and actions "that would depict something suitable" and at least create an authentic ambience."[21]

Despite such inputs from the three advisors, however, *Above and Beyond* stretched and ultimately exceeded the limits of dramatic license even though it purported to tell a true story. Although at first "sensitive" to the changes, Tibbets said he "came to learn that this approach is routine" to "jazz things up a bit to heighten suspense and excitement—but usually within the framework of probability." In particular, the lack of concern for visual reality that Frank and Panama demonstrated in telling their story undoubtedly distracted quick-eyed viewers. Early on, the filmmakers used combat footage of B-17s in flight to show Tibbets leading a mission to bomb the Tunisian seaport of Bizerte. However, when they cut to the dropping of the bombs, they used a shot of a two-engine, B-26 medium bomber releasing its payload before returning to B-17 footage. Twice they inserted footage of B-17 crashes to represent B-29 crashes, even though Air Force footage of actual Superfortress crashes existed, and they transformed into desert and mountain landscapes the actual prairies around Wichita, over which Tibbets flew while flight-testing the new bomber.[22]

The filmmakers did better in presenting the process by which Tibbets became commander of the 509th, beginning with a second mission to Bizerte the same day as the opening combat sequence. The losses his squadron has received from bombing at 6,000 feet cause Tibbets to question the orders and to ask permission to fly the mission at 21,000 feet to reduce casualties. When his commanding general suggests that the request implies cowardice on Tibbets's part or that he is suffering from battle fatigue, he challenges the general to serve as his copilot. The general simply orders him to fly the mission as planned, and Tibbets leaves. A visiting general, seeking an officer to take charge of working out the problems in the new and still experimental B-29 Superfortress, watches the episode play out and later offers Tibbets the assignment. After he accepts, the general phones his superior, Gen. Lauris Norstad, to advise him he has found his man.

Close, but not exact. The film does accurately place Tibbets in North Africa questioning orders to fly a mission at 6,000 feet. However, the confrontation occurred with General Norstad himself in a meeting about bombing tactics. Norstad complained that the bombers were not flying low enough to get satisfactory results, and Tibbets said he would fly at whatever altitude the general wanted if he would serve as Tibbets's copilot on the mission. Norstad did not accept the offer and was to hold a long-standing grudge against Tibbets for his audacity. (Norstad apparently did not learn—or care, if he did learn—that when his plane came under attack from German fighters while preparing to take off after the meeting, Tibbets taxied his B-17 over to the general's transport so that his machine guns could cover Norstad's escape into a ditch.)[23]

Does such dramatic license matter? Dore Schary, then head of MGM, explained that the studio "had to cover up the relationship with a rather fancy Air Force general who was a pain in the ass and Tibbets' superior." At the time, Norstad's career was still on the rise, and he ended up as NATO commander. To show him as Tibbets's antagonist would clearly not benefit Norstad, the Air Force, or Tibbets. Just as important, fictionalizing the character in no way affected the portrayal of Tibbets as a strong leader who had demonstrated his courage as one of the Air Corps's most successful and proficient pilots, his ability to command, his willingness to challenge his superiors when necessary, and his skill in giving and executing orders with speed and efficiency.[24]

A similar use of dramatic license occurs when Tibbets auditions for the command of the 509th Composite Group. The head of security for the Manhattan Project asks him if he has ever been arrested. After a brief pause, Tibbets acknowledges that he spent a brief period in jail after a policeman arrested him as a teenager for driving seventy miles per hour. In reality, the police chief in North Miami Beach arrested the teenage Tibbets in the backseat of his car while enjoying an assignation with a girl. Apart from the fact that the Code Office would not have allowed that admission on the screen, the truth would not have done much to help Tibbets's hero image. The exact nature of Tibbets's indiscretion, the cinematic or the actual, was beside the point, of course. His telling the truth to the security officer won him the assignment.[25]

Such incidents of dramatic license may remain minor distractions. The need to fictionalize some of the characters because of the problem of obtaining clearances raises other questions of credibility. Tibbets's security officer, Maj. William Uanna, also seems to be a fictional character, a cinematic creation who always seems to know the right answers, to do the right things, to be supportive of Tibbets during the training at Wendover. Does James Whitmore play a real person, and does he have the character right? Uanna did exist, but he joined the CIA after the war and for all practical purposes disappeared. Does the Air Force officer in the film, who talks too much and unwittingly reveals secrets, represent an actual person or a fictional character the filmmakers used to illustrate how ruthlessly Tibbets enforced security?[26]

Ultimately, the credibility and informational value of *Above and Beyond* rest on how accurately it portrays Tibbets's military career; his flight-testing, which turned an unreliable, even dangerous experimental plane into the B-29 that carried the war to Japan's home islands; his command of the 509th; and the events leading up to the delivery of the atomic bomb on Hiroshima. The brief montage that shows how Tibbets debugged the Superfortress accurately captures how well he carried out the assignment. Americans may have learned for the first time that the B-29 did not begin life as the powerful weapon it later became. Through the account of Lucy, the film explains that Boeing's lead test pilot for the B-29 died in a crash weeks before Tibbets joins the project and that the plane has developed a reputation as a death trap. She then recites the many problems Tibbets had to fix: engines regularly caught fire, windows blew out, landing gear did not work, and cabin pressurization failed. In the end, thanks to his work, but at the expense of his relationship with his wife and children, the B-29 enters combat as the most powerful bomber the world has seen.

At that point, his mentor, in this case a fictional general, selects Tibbets to create the 509th Composite Group and prepare it to drop the atomic bombs once the Manhattan Project scientists complete their work. However, the writers fictionalized the account of how this happened. Lay acknowledged changing some of what the cinematic general told Tibbets about the project and why he had been chosen. Despite this, Tibbets told Lay, "I'm sure if he'd had a tape recording this wouldn't be exactly what he said or I said, but the gist of it is very close to what actually happened. I'm satisfied."[27]

Nevertheless, the technical advisors fought an uphill battle with the filmmakers, who consciously ignored history or, as Lay pointed out, really did not care about creating an accurate story. The mistakes range from relatively minor ones to serious ones of fact and time. More important, the reality would, if anything, have improved the drama, not distracted from it. In the film version, Tibbets has the name of his mother painted on the B-29 only an hour or so before takeoff, when in fact he actually made the request the afternoon of August 5. The filmmakers do not avail themselves of the opportunity to create drama out of the relationship between Tibbets and Bob Lewis. Although reality dictated that Tibbets would command the first atomic bomb mission, Lewis's surprise and anger when he learns that he will serve as Tibbets's copilot would have added to the tensions of the flight. Likewise, the film does not contain the scene in which Lewis confronts Tibbets for selecting the name for the plane, which Lewis has considered his own. Worse, the filmmakers duplicate the mistake in *The Beginning or the End* by placing the name on the right side of the fuselage under the copilot's window, even though all photographs clearly show the name on the left side under the pilot's window.

Perhaps worst of all, as with the earlier movie, the filmmakers turn night into day, which remains inexplicable. As shown in a historic photo, Tibbets waves good-bye from the *Enola Gay* sitting on the darkened tarmac. During the cinematic briefing, Tibbets fixes the takeoff time as 2:15 A.M. and later walks the darkened flight line, less than an hour before departure. However, the *Enola Gay* takes off in daylight. The filmmakers had no reason to have the scene take place in daylight for filming purpose, since lights brightly illuminated the final moments before takeoff so that cameras could record the mission for newsreels and history. Panama and Frank only had to recreate the actual event to have sufficient lighting for their own cameras.

They then mar the cinematic takeoff by using three clearly different B-29s. The B-29 appearing as the *Enola Gay* on the ground before takeoff has a full complement of turrets, even though Tibbets had stripped all the machine guns except the two in the tail from all bombers in the group configured to carry the atomic bomb. The Superfortress that rolls down the runway has no turrets. The one that leaves the ground has turrets. The switch in planes becomes obvious to any observant viewer.

Within this takeoff montage, the filmmakers miss an opportunity to portray what should have become the dramatic highlight of the flight and illustrate how the tensions that existed between Tibbets and Lewis grew worse on the trip to Hiroshima. During the actual takeoff, Tibbets kept the bomber on the ground as long as possible to gain enough speed to get the plane, overloaded by fifteen thousand pounds, into the air. As the *Enola Gay* neared the end of the runway, Lewis involuntarily reached for the controls, only to have Tibbets order him to "leave it." Once the plane headed to Hiroshima, the two men exchange only necessary information. The filmmakers chose not to portray this coldness or the drama that occurred in the cockpit during the takeoff, however much it would have contributed to the full story of the flight that changed history.[28]

Such straying from historical accuracy aside, the film fails to do justice to its subject because it portrays Tibbets as a man filled with doubts about his mission, one who writes shortly before take off, "Mom, I'm scared." He wonders, "Maybe I'm scared of the idea of dropping one bomb that can kill thousands of people. It's a hard thing to live with, but it's part of my job and I've got to do it." The cinematic concerns Tibbets manifested in the film, which Lay had fought to keep out, bear no resemblance to his actual feelings about dropping the bomb. Never once since August 6, 1945, did the general express doubts or remorse in interviews, speeches, or his own books about the assignment he had received and carried out. To him, the atomic bomb accomplished the goal set for it, the ending of the war against Japan.[29]

Why then did the film contain such an erroneous portrayal of Tibbets during the hours leading up to his flight? In his December 1951 critique of the script, Admiral Parsons had objected to such a representation, noting that *The Beginning or the End* had contained the same inaccuracies. In particular, he insisted that the script did a disservice to the key people involved in the development and delivery of the atomic bomb, that showing them as disturbed or having regrets distorted reality.[30]

In response to his criticisms, Panama and Frank wrote to Parsons on January 15, 1952, explaining changes they would make to the script based on his inputs. They specifically addressed his concerns about the portrayals of people as "all mixed up emotionally." In regard to Tibbets and his supposed "moral conflict about dropping a bomb which will kill eighty thousand people," they stated "that we dare not portray, in an American film today, an American airman killing eighty thousand Asiatics in a flash, and expressing no feelings of conscience about this, without seriously playing into the propaganda hands of the Kremlin."[31]

However necessary such a portrayal might seem diplomatically, it certainly did an injustice to Tibbets and helped contribute to the myth that significant opposition to using the atomic bomb existed within the armed services. Nevertheless, if the film misrepresented Tibbets and failed as a docudrama, it did provide the Air Force and the Defense Department the benefits the military sought. *Above and Beyond* portrayed the determination and competence of Tibbets and his men and the ability of the B-29 to serve as delivery vehicles for atomic weapons, both in history and potentially in a future war against the Soviet Union.

It did not, however, raise questions about the use of the atomic bomb in the future or in contemporary wars such as the one in Korea, where fighting continued at the time the film appeared. Nor did it or the subsequent movies about atomic weapons explain the appeal the bombs enjoyed within the military establishment. Simply put, nuclear weapons provided a cheap deterrent against any aggressors compared to maintaining a huge standing army and the weaponry it would need to fight a ground war.

If *Above and Beyond* looked backward to a historical event that ended a necessary war, the 1955 *Strategic Air Command* and the 1957 *Bombers B-52* focused on the current Cold War and how SAC was prepared to use nuclear weapons to preserve the peace. This time using fictional formats, the two films contrasted the competing needs of the Air Force and military families as the framework in which to portray the nation's air might. In each case, the actors play secondary roles to the true stars of the movies, B-36s, B-47s, and finally, B-52s, which became the bombers for all seasons.

In *Strategic Air Command*, the ostensible story revolves around a big-league baseball player and reserve Air Force pilot, played by Jimmy Stewart, whom the service recalls to active duty because of a shortage of pilots. Here, art was imitating life, since the Marines had recalled Ted Williams from the Red Sox to once again fly close air-support missions from a carrier off the Korean coast. Despite his initial bitterness about the sacrifice he must make at a crucial time in his career, Stewart comes to appreciate that his country needs him more than his baseball team. Unlike Lucy Tibbets, June Allyson, playing the traditional military wife, follows her husband where his assignment takes him with few complaints and much support. Ironically, her life on the SAC air base differs not very much from life as a baseball player's wife: Stewart is often away from home on flying missions just as he previously had to travel from stadium to stadium. After an injury suffered in a crash permanently grounds Stewart and ends his playing career, he elects to remain in SAC in an administrative position rather than return to baseball as a coach or an executive.

The unexceptional story grew out of Beirne Lay's ongoing relationship with the Air Force. As a reserve officer, he did fifteen days of active service, including assignments in SAC commander Curtis LeMay's office. Lay recalled that LeMay would ask him, "When are we going to make a picture about SAC?" With the request "in the back of my mind," Lay ultimately wrote an original story and took it to Stewart, by then a colonel and later a brigadier general in the Air Force Reserve, who agreed to do the film. Despite both men's extensive contacts with the service, LeMay's personal interest in the project was needed to obtain cooperation from the Air Force because of the demands on SAC's personnel and planes in the early days of the Cold War. Lay said that LeMay "felt so strongly that this was

Gen. Curtis LeMay (with author in 1975), the father of the Strategic Air Command, encouraged Hollywood productions about the Air Force.

important for the national understanding of SAC's mission that he was mainly instrumental in getting the Defense Department's cooperation."[32]

Ultimately, SAC provided full assistance to Paramount, initially trotting out B-36s, which had replaced the B-29s as the nation's nuclear delivery force, and by the end of the movie, the new B-47s, the Air Force's first pure jet nuclear bombers. As with all flying movies since *Wings,* the planes taking off, in flight, and landing, sometimes none too softly, become the dramatic center of the movie. Lay said that SAC so much wanted *Strategic Air Command* made that it went to "extreme lengths" to help create the visual excitement, which in the end cost the taxpayers many thousands of dollars.[33]

To facilitate the "enormous amount of cooperation," LeMay assigned Col. Dick Lassiter, one of his top officers, to serve as technical advisor, and Lay did not think the studio could have made the movie without him. Any time the director would request something, Lassiter would answer, "No problem." In one instance, the filmmakers wanted to get some dramatic shots of a B-47 takeoff by loading a bomber with six cameras, each shooting from a different angle. To do this, the ground crew had to strip down the plane and remove the canopy. The base commander told the director, "I won't take the responsibility for flying a B-47 in this configuration just to get the shot." Lassiter responded, "Sir, I'll take the responsibility on the authority of General LeMay and I'll fly the airplane myself." As a result, Lay said the filmmakers were able to get "some magnificent footage."[34]

Not satisfied with this deviation from standard operating procedures, which risked the loss of a valuable plane, director Anthony Mann asked the technical advisor to arrange for a flight of B-47s to take off en masse, since the normal, individual taxiing and taking off lacked drama. Observing that "the pilots were all movie actors," Lay said they were "anxious to do more than they were required to and they wound up taxiing almost tail-to-tail with no regard for the dust and debris the engines were ingesting. Mann obtained the visual images he wanted and did not care whether the taxpayers had to pay hundreds of thousands of dollars to replace the burned-out engines.[35]

Despite the cost, Lay thought the film accomplished its mission: "Absolutely I do. I think it had an enormous effect on the public. For one thing it was a big success. I think it gave people an idea they had never had of what the guys in peacetime are doing to carry out their mission." Bosley Crowther wrote in the *New York Times* that the use of the new VistaVision process gave the film "size, depth and clarity, as well as fidelity of color, to big and detailed outdoor scenes," which gave *Strategic Air Command* visual drama and explained the film's box-office success. The great panoramic shots of airfields, planes on the ground, and planes in the sky helped create the dramatic images that conveyed the idea that SAC was carrying out its mission to safeguard the nation.[36]

As *Strategic Air Command* had portrayed the service's transition from the B-36 to the B-47, *Bombers B-52* focused its attention on the bomber that has remained in service for almost fifty years and fought in three major wars, ironically with conventional weapons. Like the earlier film, a fictional story creates the framework in which the Air Force has the opportunity to show off how the bomber came into service and overcame the normal technical glitches associated with every new plane. In this telling, a senior NCO, Karl Malden, whose wife and daughter want him to leave the service for a lucrative executive job, becomes the human hero. Ultimately, he remains in the Air Force, having decided that he can make a difference there—as a ground crew chief, he can help ensure the success of the new bomber.[37]

SAC naturally saw the virtues of such a message and provided full assistance, including B-47s at March Air Force Base and then B-52s at Castle Air Force Base, both in California. With the help of two technical advisors, the filmmakers had access to the bases for scenes of the ground crews performing maintenance work and then for shooting the airborne scenes of eleven B-47s flying low in formation and later of a flight of B-52s in mass formation, as well as sequences of individual planes landing and taking off to fit the requirements of the story. Despite the dramatic visual images the film contained, the *New York Times* saw the story for what it was: "Put down this frank tribute to Air Force nuclear power, laced together with a familiar service feud, as one that's easy to go along and aloft with. . . . The basic ingredients seem as old as the Wright Brothers' original take-off."[38]

Stories aside, *Strategic Air Command* and *Bombers B-52* did show the full power of SAC without hiding the dangers that SAC offices and enlisted men faced on a daily basis on the ground and in the air. In-flight problems occurred, and planes sometimes crashed. If the cinematic accidents were only scripted drama to advance the story, in *Bombers B-52*, art did interact with reality. Maj. Ben Ostlind had received the assignment to serve as one of the technical advisors on the film while waiting out a mandatory grounding after his plane had blown up behind him during a landing at Castle Air Force Base. He and his copilot had successfully ejected, but the rest of the crew had died. The remains of the crash site appear in the movie out the cockpit window during a landing sequence.[39]

Although the films created positive images of SAC and its fliers, who regularly put themselves in harm's way, they virtually ignored the other side of the story. The omissions stand in stark contrast to the portrayal of atomic weapons as benign protectors of the United States and democracy inherent in each of these four movies. Nowhere in them do the filmmakers raise questions about the possibility of the launching of an accidental nuclear attack by the Cold War adversaries. Except for the fictitious nuclear accident that killed the young scientist and the flashing lights and whirring sounds in the instrument panels in *The Beginning or the End,* none of the films hint at the dangers of radiation. Only the ominous title of *The Beginning or the End* and the fabricated doubts that the filmmakers attributed to Paul Tibbets before his flight to Hiroshima challenge the conventional wisdom of the inherent value and efficacy of nuclear deterrents. Apart from the reference to the concern by a few scientists at the Trinity site that the test might ignite the atmosphere, none of the films raised questions about whether nuclear weapons could ultimately destroy the world. Given the support from the Air Force and the Defense Department and the military's connections to Hollywood, no one should have expected otherwise.

Only in low-budget, science fiction films throughout the 1950s did the atom appear as the enemy, and only on rare occasions did the Pentagon provide assistance. In the classic 1951 *The Day the Earth Stood Still,* an alien arrives on the Ellipse in Washington to warn the world that it must stop the spread of nuclear weapons or face destruction from a more advanced civilization that will not tolerate atomic warfare in the universe. The Army and the National Guard did provide some soldiers and equipment, since the Pentagon acknowledged that the military would confront any threat to the nation's well-being. Of course, the alien did not direct his criticism of nuclear weapons only at the United States, and the armed services would not want to appear as opposing world peace. The soldiers do, however, fire on the peaceful alien and his robot assistant, who then render the military helpless—not an image that would reassure the American people about the ability of its defense establishment to protect it from attack.[40]

The War of the Worlds, in 1953, reinforced the reality that the military would usually find itself ineffectual against alien invaders. Although the Army arrives on the scene en masse shortly after the first Martian capsules land in New Jersey, the aliens quickly dispatch the soldiers and tanks. Perhaps because the later atomic bombing of the aliens fails to dent their defenses, the Air Force expressed reluctance to provide the studio with even a small amount of footage of an experimental flying wing that the filmmakers wanted to use to deliver the atomic bomb. Ultimately, the Pentagon relented to the extent of allowing Northrup to give the studio a short shot of the plane in flight.

The military's effectiveness improved in *Them,* appearing the next year. More importantly, the film became a paradigm of how Hollywood would provide dire warnings of the danger of radiation. In the New Mexican desert, presumably near the Trinity test site, radiated ants grow to a huge size and begin foraging for food, including humans. Although the police and the Army ultimately corner and dispatch the queen ant in the sewers of Los Angeles, the message is clear: the atom may not always be a boon to mankind. The Japanese *Godzilla* movies, *The Beast from 20,000 Fathoms* (1953), *The Incredible Shrinking Man* (1957), and *The Beginning of the End* (1957) all contained characters adversely affected by nuclear radiation. Nevertheless, the impact remains limited and ultimately controlled, often by the military itself. Moreover, even the best and most popular of these films reached a rather limited audience of science fiction devotees, who enjoyed the stories for their entertainment rather than their anti-atom messages.

Stanley Kramer approached the bomb differently when he brought Nevil Shute's end-of-the-world 1957 best-selling novel *On the Beach* to the screen in 1959. He had a message about the threat the atomic bomb posed, and he wanted everyone to hear it, not just a few science fiction buffs. Shute had told a very simple, straightforward, apocalyptic story about the aftermath of an unexplained nuclear war. Now, a cloud of radioactive dust that blanketed the Northern Hemisphere, killing the entire population, is slowly drifting south.

In Australia, the book's setting, Comdr. Dwight Towers, the crew of the American nuclear submarine *Scorpion,* and the civilian population await death. Sent to investigate an indecipherable signal emanating from the coast of Washington state, the *Scorpion* confirms that no one remains alive north of Australia. It also discovers that a Coke bottle and a window frame resting on a telegraph key have been tapping the mysterious signals when the wind blew. By the time the submarine returns to Australia, radiation sickness has increased, and with death imminent, Towers takes his ship to sea and the crew's last dive.

Always a maverick, independent filmmaker Kramer had a reputation for producing controversial movies that sometimes delivered less social significance than expected. In reading *On the Beach,* Kramer said the nuclear scientist's explanation of why the holocaust had occurred "was something I felt deeply then—and now." In dialogue somewhat condensed for the movie, Fred Astaire, as the scientist, describes what happened: "The war started when people accepted the idiotic principle that peace can be maintained by arranging to defend themselves with weapons they couldn't possibly use without committing suicide." In the end, Astaire says, "Some poor bloke probably looked at a radar screen and thought he saw something; . . . he knew that if he hesitated one-thousandth of a second his own country would be wiped off the map, and so he pushed a button . . . and the world went crazy."[41]

To portray the results of this craziness, Kramer focused on a few Australians as they face death within the desolation of the rest of the world. To help create his images, he needed a few shots of a submarine cruising on the surface as well as access to an American nuclear sub so that his art director could build interior sets for the scenes aboard ship. To obtain this, Kramer's production designer, Rudolph Sternad, wrote to Don Baruch's office on May 28, 1958, requesting cooperation to film an "Atomic Type Submarine" docked in Melbourne entering and leaving the harbor, as well as submerging and surfacing in open waters. He also requested research help in the construction of a mock-up of the interiors of a submarine on a soundstage in Melbourne and asked about the possibility of borrowing obsolete equipment such as a periscope unit. He did promise that the filmmakers would not "attempt to use this equipment as other than simulated action by actors."[42]

Even this request for limited courtesy assistance evoked an immediate and angry response from the Navy Office of Information to Baruch: "It is difficult to perceive how cooperation in this production could in any way enhance the U.S. Naval Service or the Department of Defense." Saying the story was only science fiction, the office concluded, "Any service cooperation on such a movie would only serve to dignify the story and add an official blessing to the possibility of such an impending disaster."[43]

The U.S. Information Agency had a similar response, telling Baruch that it believed that "at this time this film with its utterly pessimistic outlook and message does not deserve any cooperation in connection with its production." The agency found that the "entire theme is negative to say the least, and frankly there appears to be a tendency to 'blame America' in much of its presentation." Since it did not feel the film "could conceivably advance the interests of the United States," it did not wish to become associated with the project "in any way."[44]

Combining the two responses, Baruch advised Sternad on July 1 that the request "is not favorably considered for government assistance" since the Pentagon felt "it does not meet the basic stipulation of Defense policy that cooperation had to be 'in the best interest of national defense and the public good.'" Nevertheless, he said the Navy would furnish some informational assistance. For the record, he added that the service would not have been able to provide a nuclear submarine in Australia or at sea "in other waters" during the period when Kramer would be filming.[45]

Sternad then requested as many photographs as possible of the interior of a nuclear submarine as well as unclassified exterior shots of the superstructure. In light of the unavailability of an actual sub, he asked if the Navy had black and white stock footage of an atomic submarine that Kramer could use. In response, Baruch's office sent Sternad eighteen photographs that the Navy had supplied and informed him that the service "will be happy to make a minimum quantity" of film available.[46]

Despite the service's willingness to provide such limited assistance, Kramer put into practice knowledge he had gained from obtaining cooperation in the making of *The Caine Mutiny* and came to Washington on August 25 to meet directly with Pentagon and USIA officials. He helped his cause by bringing with him Navy hero Adm. Charles Lockwood, his technical advisor. As a result, Pentagon officials agreed to allow the director to make shots of a nuclear submarine submerging and surfacing, and the USIA withdrew its objection to government involvement with the production.[47]

In the course of the meeting at the Pentagon, Lockwood said he understood that an American submarine would be coming to Australia on a goodwill tour while Kramer would be there filming. Although the Defense Department said it did not know of such plans, it agreed to allow Kramer to make some unclassified scenes aboard the submarine if one did show up. Kramer further helped his cause by agreeing to make "such changes that were mutually agreed on by the Navy and himself to remove the pessimistic slant of the novel on 'utter annihilation' which might be unfavorably interpreted."[48]

Baruch's office then briefed Navy Chief of Information Adm. C.C. Kirkpatrick on the meeting, and he agreed that the Defense Department was handling the project correctly. However, on October 20 Kirkpatrick informed Baruch that after "careful consideration, it has been definitely determined that the motion picture *On the Beach* would not serve any beneficial purpose for the Navy, and cooperation should not be extended by the Navy for its production." Although the Navy had already given Kramer photographs of the interiors of nuclear submarines and had allowed him to shoot his own pictures aboard the USS *Sargo*, Kirpatrick advised Baruch that the Navy "does not wish to be further identified with this production."[49]

Kirkpatrick's decision to distance the Navy from *On the Beach* had as much effect on Kramer as had Admiral Park's refusal to cooperate with him on *The Caine Mutiny*. In fact, on October 23, the producer-director met with Chief of Naval Operations Arleigh Burke to discuss cooperation on his movie. To receive the help he needed, Kramer agreed to change his script to the satisfaction of the Navy by incorporating into the film Burke's "philosophy." As a result, on October 29, Kirkpatrick had to advise Baruch that he was canceling his October 20 decision.[50] In confirming the Navy's agreement to provide assistance, Baruch advised Kramer on November 4 that the service had not put the philosophy "on paper, as yet, but, meanwhile, there is no reason for you to be concerned about cooperation." He said the Navy would release the stock footage Kramer's representative had selected. It would also make arrangements to provide an appropriate submarine for the director's use in Hawaii.[51]

In return for this assistance, Baruch reminded Kramer that the Navy expected him to change the script to the service's "satisfaction. The philosophy will be the basic matter for re-write." Although the Navy expected to review the revised script, Baruch said the service would not delay providing the submarine until it received the script. He also advised the director that he might want to include an acknowledgment of cooperation in the titles. In addition, he said the degree of assistance Kramer was receiving "justifies it anticipating thirty 16mm prints for use on board ships where no admissions are charged."[52]

In fact, Admiral Burke did not worry about the portrayal of the Navy itself in *On the*

Beach. Instead, in the memo that delineated his philosophy, the CNO said the Navy was supporting the film out of "responsibility for the effect which the film will have on the public. It is assumed that our support gives us some voice in the script. It is important that we use this lever in the national interest." Burke believed the film would create "revulsion against the use of nuclear weapons of any kind and a possible sense of defeatism with respect to the use of armed force as an instrument of national policy." If this happened, the CNO believed it could "seriously reduce the resolution of the American public to take the risks at lower levels of conflict which their security demands. A certain amount of this is inevitable, but the damage will be reduced if the script undertakes to show how the war might have been avoided."[53]

Burke then provided three ideas that Kramer should inject into *On the Beach*. First, the film should explain that the West should have developed the concept of limited war to prevent being "stampeded into inordinate reaction (general war) because they had no other way of dealing with a deteriorating situation." Second, he wanted the Communists to bear primary responsibility for the war. Third, he believed the film must explain that the major powers should have made their nuclear strike forces invulnerable in order to avoid a hasty all-out war: "Instantaneous response of U.S. retaliatory forces had been rationalized as a virtue when it was really an unfortunate necessity to avoid pre-emptive enemy action." Since Burke felt the movie could become highly successful both commercially and in the national interest, he suggested the Navy continue working with Kramer "with a view to furthering both these objectives."[54]

Although Burke had his "philosophy" forwarded directly to Kramer's technical advisor, the Defense Department's Office of Security Review and the USIA found it "unsatisfactory material to pass on to the producer." However, Baruch later noted that his office decided it "would not dispute" Burke's views with the Navy. In any case, however much or little of the CNO's philosophy Kramer did incorporate into *On the Beach*, the completed film could not in any way serve the national interest of the United States.[55]

Like the novel, its message provided a simple and final warning to the world. Mankind had failed. The human race had committed suicide. Civilization had come to an end. In the novel, the few remaining Australians take poison in order to die with dignity, and the American submarine vanishes into the mist on the way to its final voyage. Moira, the woman who could never make Towers forget his wife and children "alive" back in Connecticut, watches from a hill overlooking the sea. Shute closes: "Then she put the tablets in her mouth and swallowed them down with a mouthful of brandy, sitting behind the wheel of her big car."[56]

Despite all his good intentions, Kramer could not leave it at that. Unfortunately, he chose to dilute the warning inherent in the unmitigated grimness of Shute's reality. Instead of Shute's ending or even the film's empty streets in the penultimate scene, Kramer closes *On the Beach* with an upbeat message to the world. A Salvation Army banner proclaiming "It is not too late . . . Brother" fills the screen. In truth, the film had already made it perfectly clear that time has run out for mankind.[57]

The false optimism aside, *On the Beach* became one of the most discussed and thought-provoking motion pictures of the decade, generating the first serious discussion of the value of the bomb. The film gained dramatic power by juxtaposing the results of man's stupidity with portrayals of the essential worth of individuals, who have found the courage to face death with calmness and a certain nobility. All the people, civilians and military alike, have become victims of the madness to which they somehow, in some manner, contributed knowingly or unknowingly. Now they must accept responsibility for their collective actions or inactions. In Gregory Peck, as the submarine captain, and Ava Gardner, as Moira, all these elements of innocence and guilt come together, yet with no apparent character flaws, and so make them even more tragic.[58]

In fact, the Navy could point to Peck with pride as a perfect officer and role model. Likewise, his entire crew performs in a most exemplary manner, voting, at the end, to go home with Peck rather than remain alive on shore for a few more days. Nevertheless, to whatever extent Admiral Burke's "philosophy" found its way into *On the Beach*, its message could not serve the national interest or even the Navy's interest. As a result, after screening the film, the Department of Defense requested that Kramer not include a title giving credit to the Navy for its assistance in order to avoid "any possible misunderstanding in regard to Government endorsement" of its contents.[59]

Ironically, after all the vacillation about whether to provide assistance to Kramer, the Navy had ended up giving the filmmaker only the informational photographs, a limited amount of stock footage, and use of a submarine to film sailing under the Golden Gate Bridge. The Navy had agreed to route a nuclear submarine to Australia for Kramer, but the USS *Segundo* arrived too late to star in the movie. By then Kramer had used the British submarine HMS *Andrew*, with its sailors dressed as Americans. According to the director's assistant, he would have used the American ship if it had arrived earlier. One U.S. sailor complained, "We have come all the way from Pearl Harbor to be film stars and find the British navy has beaten us to it."[60]

Of course, the submarine and the crew, regardless of their country, served only as minor props in a drama that Kramer hoped would alert the world to the reality that the bomb might not serve as the preserver of world peace as the American military had represented it during the 1950s. If he had needed reinforcement for the alternative view, Kramer received it from the captain of a nuclear submarine who told him, "Young fella, you think too much about this H-bomb thing. Millions of people might be killed but it's not the end of the world." Kramer would naturally disagree. *On the Beach* showed the other side of the bomb with its potential to destroy all civilization, not just millions of people. It did more than that, however. *On the Beach*, not the Vietnam War, marked the real beginning, albeit in a very limited way, of a greater scrutiny of the U.S. military establishment by the mass media and the cultural community.[61]

Up to that time, of course, Hollywood had consistently portrayed the American military as all-conquering, its leadership always correct, and its troops brave, competent fighters. Filmmakers had little need to tamper with the history of the U.S. armed forces in the twentieth century. It offered few accounts of losses on the battlefield, of American atrocities committed against enemy troops or civilians, of mutinies, of cowards, or of traitors that might have provided the ingredients for interesting, if unflattering stories. In both World Wars the troops had fought well and emerged from the conflicts with glorious victories, which engendered patriotic feelings within the population as a whole. If Hollywood had slighted the contribution of our Allies, especially the Russians, to victory in World War II, no one doubted that the United States had contributed mightily to the defeat of Germany and Japan.

Only occasionally did filmmakers create less-than-favorable images of American officers and men during peacetime or in combat. Captain Holmes in *From Here to Eternity* remained an aberration, whereas Captain Queeg in *The Caine Mutiny* ultimately became a sympathetic victim rather than the out-of-control officer of the novel. An Air Force officer in the Pentagon did object to *Twelve O'Clock High*'s showing bomber pilots unwilling to fly for their new and demanding commander. Writer Sy Bartlett recalled that the officer asked him, "Colonel Bartlett, you mean to tell me that an Air Force officer like you is actually going to make a film which says and shows that a group refused and would not answer a field order and refused to fly?" In response, the writer said, "Colonel, if that's all you read into the book and that's all you read into the script, I guess that's what I'm going to do." In the end, of course, General Savage wins the respect of the men, who go on to perform bravely in combat.[62]

By the early 1960s, however, commentators had started to question some of the basic assumptions about the ability of the armed forces to protect the security of the nation. The Cuban Missile Crisis had brought a sudden halt to the apparent thaw in the Cold War. The thirteen days in October 1962, covered so thoroughly on television and in the press, forcibly reminded people that the bomb might well pose danger to the future of mankind. Having lived for more than fifteen years under the tensions of a peace maintained through the threat of nuclear destruction, Americans had abruptly confronted the other side of the bomb and its relationship to the future of civilization. Instead of serving as an instrument to preserve peace, the bomb now loomed as the potential destroyer of all mankind. As a result, the U.S. military establishment began to experience increasing scrutiny from the mass media and the cultural community.

This change in perspective among the American people coincided with significant changes within the film industry that would contribute to a new image of the armed services on the nation's motion picture screens. Under the impact of competition from television and the forced divestment of their theatrical chains, the old Hollywood studio system came to an end. In its place, a new generation of young, independent writers, producers, and directors assumed control of the industry. These men had few ties to the political, financial, or military establishments and no compunction about looking for new story lines among previously sacred icons, including the armed services. In recognition of the continuing threat that the Soviet Union posed to the nation's security, the filmmakers were not yet ready to produce stories that cast the armed services as a whole in a negative light. Nevertheless, the climate of opinion about the bomb then developing gave them the courage to disregard the possible wrath of the Pentagon over unflattering portrayals of its nuclear arsenal and the military leadership that controlled its use, especially if the movies would attract audiences.

That seemed very likely. Except for the few science fiction movies and *On the Beach*, the bomb had enjoyed a benevolent press since Hiroshima and Nagasaki. In fact, the malevolent side of atomic weapons offered filmmakers a virgin territory from which to draw new stories suggesting that the bomb's potential to destroy all of modern civilization might well outweigh any military benefits it offered. Consequently, in criticizing a particular weapons system, filmmakers could comment on the horrors of war without attacking the necessity of having a strong military establishment. Moreover, using the impersonal bomb as a symbolic scapegoat avoided the risk that the excitement which combat movies generate would mute the antiwar images inherent in scenes of battlefield horror.

The Air Force, in considering requests from Hollywood for assistance in making movies about the bomb, had always insisted on a serious and factual presentation of its procedures and preparedness as well as the portrayal of the competence of those who had their fingers on the buttons of the nuclear arsenal. It saw these movies as a valuable means of informing the American people not only of SAC's military potential but also of its precautions against accidental launchings of a nuclear attack. As a result, the service remained immutable in its refusal to support any story about the bomb that challenged the images created in *Strategic Air Command* and *Bombers B-52.*

In the aftermath of the Cuban Missile Crisis, however, the message in *On the Beach* became less abstract, and as Hollywood is wont to do, filmmakers began to explore the subject. With several antibomb films under development, General LeMay turned to his friends in the industry with a request to make another SAC movie. Despite the new regulations that Arthur Sylvester was putting into place, Sy Bartlett moved from World War II to the Cold War and produced *A Gathering of Eagles,* which appeared in 1963.[63]

Differing little in substance from the earlier SAC films, it showed the Air Force doing its job in a responsible manner and its fliers acting selflessly and putting patriotism before personal gain for the good of the nation. The film conveyed this message well, reflecting the competence of Academy Award winners Robert Pirosh, screenwriter (for *Battleground*), and Delbert Mann, director (for *Marty*). Nevertheless, despite dramatic flying sequences, the film provided no new insights about the bomb or the nature of the men who were prepared to deliver it if necessary.[64]

In fact, *A Gathering of Eagles* addressed an audience no longer willing to accept the Air Force's story uncritically. Moreover, its pseudo-documentary style and traditional message provided no competition for the brilliance of Stanley Kubrick's *Dr. Strangelove, or: How I Learned to Stop Worrying and Love the Bomb* or the dramatic tensions of Sidney Lumet's *Fail Safe,* both released in 1964. Their portrayals of insane officers, incompetence, and technological breakdown confirmed General LeMay's worst fears that they might have serious negative impact on the image of the Air Force he had so long cultivated in Hollywood films.[65]

Based on Peter George's 1958 novel *Red Alert, Dr. Strangelove* posited the story that a mad Air Force general could order a squadron of B-52 bombers to attack the Soviet Union in hopes of triggering a war that would obliterate the Communist menace. As if one film did not provoke enough questions about Air Force procedures, LeMay also had to face a second picture with essentially the same plot. In *Fail Safe,* based on the Eugene Burdick and Harvey Wheeler novel of the same name, a faulty computer rather than a deranged general launches the strike force. As in *Dr. Strangelove,* neither the United States nor

A Gathering of Eagles (1963) shown being filmed at Beale Air Force Base in California, was made with the service's full cooperation despite Arthur Sylvester's initial refusal to approve assistance. In contrast, *Dr. Strangelove* and *Fail Safe* had to be made in studios using miniatures, mock-ups, and newsreel footage because the Air Force would have nothing to do with either production.

Soviet defense systems are able to stop all the bombers. One plane reaches Moscow and delivers its hydrogen bombs. Both films suggested that despite its claim, the Air Force did not truly control the bomb, and as a result a nuclear accident became inevitable. In reaching this conclusion, however, the two movies approached their common thesis in diametrically opposite manners.

Dr. Strangelove took on not only the bomb but also military and government leaders, American and Russian alike, using satire and black humor to attack virtually everyone and everything. Kubrick peopled the film with incompetents, bigots, and warmongers, with the military characters bearing the brunt of the criticism. In contrast, *Fail Safe* developed its message through a serious, taut melodrama. The filmmakers characterized both government and military personnel as dedicated people who were genuinely stunned by the catastrophe facing the world.

Kubrick did not set out to convey his message comically. Having made one major antiwar statement in *Paths of Glory,* he had for some time "been keen on the theme of a nuclear war being started by accident or madness." When he discovered *Red Alert,* written by a retired RAF pilot in 1961, he decided almost immediately that it would serve as the basis for his statement about the bomb. Although the director tried to follow the serious tone of the novel in beginning to work on the screenplay, he soon found that each time he created a scene, it turned out to be comic. He later recalled, "How the hell could the president ever tell the Russian premier to shoot down American planes? Good Lord, it sounds ridiculous." Consequently, the film turned into a satirical nightmare, a surrealistic portrait of humans blundering through war rooms, carrying on absurd dialogues on a hot line and committing sheer lunacy while the world moved inexorably toward destruction.[66]

Opening with a poetic, rhythmic, sexual scene of a B-52 bomber being refueled in midair, the film unfolds in a rapid-fire sequence of events that leaves the audience breathless. A SAC general orders a squadron of bombers to attack Russia; the president informs the Soviet premier of what has happened; to the leaders' mutual horror, the premier admits that the Soviet Union has built a Doomsday Machine that will destroy the world if a nuclear weapon falls on Russian territory; the crew of the lead bomber prepares for its mission; the governments of both nations attempt to stop the attack both in the air and by trying to capture the insane general; all efforts fail; and one plane reaches its target. At the fadeout, bombs explode like fireworks, filling the screen with mushroom clouds.

In creating his biting denouncement of man's inability to control the ultimate weapon of war, Kubrick used potent visual and verbal imagery. He followed the sexual coupling of the two planes at the opening of the movie with regular shots of a bomber flying gracefully, sensually over a snow-covered landscape toward its target. The beauty of the plane in motion contrasts starkly with the absolute destructiveness of its mission. When the bombs go off, the explosions assume their own sensuality, which Kubrick reinforces ironically with the soothing sounds of a popular World War II ballad: "We'll meet again, don't know where, don't know when, but I know we'll meet again some sunny day."

The director reinforced the symbolic visual effects of the movie with language, from the singing and the music to the names of the characters, which establish their personalities. Jack D. Ripper, the demented SAC commander, orders the attack; Pres. Merkin Muffley tries to save the world, with little help from Premier Dimitri Kissof; Ambassador de Sadesky lurks around the War Room; Chairman of the Joint Chiefs of Staff Buck Turgidson offers Curtis LeMay–type advice; British Group Captain Mandrake tries to abort the bomber attack; while Col. Bat Guano directs the assault on Ripper's headquarters at Burpelson Air

Force Base. Dr. Strangelove, a "rehabilitated" Nazi scientist whose character Kubrick develops both visually and verbally, becomes the heart of the film. Strangelove makes his entrance into the underground war room in a wheelchair, struggling with his artificial right arm, which has a mind of its own. Periodically, Strangelove reverts to his German background, addressing President Muffley as "Mein Fuhrer" while desperately trying to restrain his arm from strangling him or giving a Nazi salute.

In the scene that best captures the tone and outrageousness of *Dr. Strangelove*, President Muffley calls Premier Kissof on the hot line to tell him of the impending disaster. In helping the president track down Kissof at his mistress's residence, Ambassador de Sadesky explains, "Our premier is a man of the people." Muffley launches his conversation with the always unseen Kissof: "How are you? . . . Oh fine. Just fine. Look, Dimitri, you know how we've always talked about the possibility of something going wrong with the Bomb? . . . The Bomb? The HYDROGEN BOMB! . . . That's right. Well, I'll tell you what happened. One of our base commanders did a silly thing. He, uh, went a little funny in the head. You know, funny. He ordered our planes to attack your country . . . let me finish, Dimitri."

But he really has nothing else to say. General Ripper has accomplished his mission. In Ripper, Kubrick has created a caricatured right-wing fanatic, tormented by the "Commie plot" to fluoridate American drinking water and debilitate the people by destroying "the purity and essence of our national fluids." He has severed all communications with the outside world, and only he knows the code for recalling the bombers. What follows resembles a tour through every insane asylum that ever appeared on the motion picture screen.

When General Turgidson starts wrestling with Ambassador de Sadesky over a camera the diplomat has secretly been using to take pictures of the underground command center, President Muffley reproves both men: "You can't fight in here; this is the War Room." In arguing that the president should seize the opportunity and launch an all-out attack, Turgidson admits, "I'm not saying we won't get our hair mussed." Going over their survival kits containing rubles, dollars, gold, Benzedrine, cigarettes, nylons, chocolates, chewing gum, prophylactics, and tranquilizers, one of the crewmen remarks, "I could have a pretty fine weekend with this in Vegas."

Unfortunately, the plane is not headed to Las Vegas but to a Soviet missile base. The Russians might have been willing to accept the accidental loss of one missile site. But the Doomsday Machine will generate enough radioactivity to make the earth uninhabitable for ninety-nine years. Yet for that to have acted as a deterrent to enemy attack, the Russians needed to have publicized the device, as Dr. Strangelove notes with suitable irony: "The whole point of the Doomsday Machine is lost *if you keep it a secret! Why didn't you tell the world, eh?*" The ambassador can offer only the now moot explanation that Kissof "loves surprises" and was going to reveal his secret at the upcoming Party Congress.

The only hope rests in finding a way to recall the SAC bombers or, failing that, to destroy them. Army units besiege Burpelson Air Force Base, and the battle with security forces rages under a SAC billboard proclaiming "Peace Is Our Profession." Inside, Mandrake alternately pleads with General Ripper to recall the planes and tries to figure out the proper recall code based on the general's rantings and doodlings. When he does discover the code after Ripper commits suicide, Mandrake tries to call the president. But he has no money and the White House will not accept collect calls from an unknown group captain. In desperation, Mandrake pleads with Col. Bat Guano to shoot the lock from a Coke machine to get the needed change. But the officer recoils in horror, "That's private property."

In the end, Mandrake gets through to the president, and the Air Force transmits the recall code. The exhilaration that sweeps the war room as planes begin their return ends abruptly when the plotting map shows one bomber continuing on its way. With a damaged radio that prevents it from receiving the recall message, the B-52 eludes all Russian fighters and anti-aircraft missiles and heads toward its target. In a seeming last-minute reprieve, the bomb will not drop from the plane. In *Red Alert,* the bomb itself suffered damage and did not detonate. However, in the final grim moment of truth, Kubrick does not cop out. The pilot, Major Kong, an unreconstructed Texas cowboy, climbs onto the bomb, shakes it free, and rides it downward, yelling wildly and waving his Stetson as if he had mounted a bucking bronco rather than the instrument that will end the world. This paradox of pure joy juxtaposed with the scene of absolute destruction that immediately follows symbolizes the two sides of *Dr. Strangelove.* On one hand, it produces side-splitting laughs; on the other, it creates horror at the ramifications lurking just around the corner.

As surrealistic and comic as the story appears on the screen, the threat of nuclear accident comes across as a plausible reality. Kubrick observed, "The greatest message of the film is in the laughs. You know, it's true. The most realistic things are the funniest." To the director, *Dr. Strangelove* may have seemed realistic. He estimated that he had read seventy books on the subject of the bomb, and he maintained an extensive file of relevant articles. He also had talked to nuclear war strategists, including Thomas Schelling, and to Herman Kahn, the author of *On Thermonuclear War* and *Thinking about the Unthinkable* and one of the models for Dr. Strangelove. Consequently, Kubrick could believe that a psychotic general might have the ability to unleash a squadron of bombers against Russia, and he could argue that "for various and entirely credible reasons, the planes cannot be recalled, [and] the President is forced to cooperate with the Soviet Premier in a bizarre attempt to save the world."[67]

To the Air Force and to General LeMay, however, the film was not a laughing matter. Nor did they think it bore any resemblance to reality. During preproduction, Kubrick had made unofficial contact with the Air Force to discuss possible cooperation. The service told the filmmaker that, apart from the portrayal of its officers as insane, bloodthirsty, and ludicrous, the misrepresentation in the script of the Positive Control safeguards precluded official Pentagon assistance. The Air Force maintained that a SAC base commander cannot order a single plane to undertake a nuclear bomb attack. Furthermore, only the president or his surrogate knows the attack code, and he must relay it to SAC Headquarters, which in turn issues the appropriate orders. As would be expected, officials maintained that no one could subvert the Positive Control System; it remained fail safe.[68]

Kubrick naturally disagreed—he was making *Dr. Strangelove* to warn of the possible dangers in the safeguard system. Consequently, portraying the literal accuracy of Air Force procedures had little relevance to him. He intended to convey a message, not make a pseudo-documentary. With the military's refusal to provide assistance, Kubrick became the film's sole technical advisor, using knowledge gained from a youth spent watching war movies in New York City. He fabricated a B-52 cockpit and cabin from magazine pictures and impressions gained from watching earlier Air Force films. The director and his art director built the war room out of their imaginations, since no one had ever acknowledged the existence of an underground crisis center in the Pentagon, much less released a picture of it. Kubrick produced the sequences of the bomber in flight by placing a ten-foot model of a B-52 in front of a moving matte made up of shots taken over the Arctic. If the end result bore little resemblance to actual Air Force procedures or equipment, most people accepted it as reality in spite of the film's comic motif.

Dr. Strangelove does not, of course, portray reality, Kubrick's intentions notwithstanding. Instead, he produced a black satire, a genre that depends on exaggerated visions of reality to expose humanity's and society's foibles. To succeed, satire, or any social commentary, must reach its intended audience, and *Dr. Strangelove* became highly successful at the box office. Whether its popularity had more to do with its message or its cinematic qualities remains unanswered. In any case, the picture remains one of the highest artistic and social achievements by any filmmaker.

Although clearly an "American" movie which draws its meaning from the American experience with the bomb, Kubrick shot *Dr. Strangelove* in England to accommodate Peter Sellers, who became indispensable to the film. Sellers assumed the roles of President Muffley, Group Captain Mandrake, and Dr. Strangelove, managing to instill in each a unique personality in a tour de force of character acting. George C. Scott as General Turgidson and Sterling Hayden as General Ripper were equally superb. The actors, however, performed within the structure that Kubrick created, manipulated, and directed. His interweaving of the visual and verbal images, the use of sound and music, and the imaginative production all combined to produce a rare film experience, one that retains its impact even though missiles have, for the most part, replaced bombers as the United States's delivery system of choice and people have all but stopped thinking about accidental nuclear warfare.

Dr. Strangelove does have a fault, but one that Kubrick could not avoid if he was to make his movie. Since he based his story on inaccurate premises and factual errors, viewers with a knowledge of how SAC's Positive Control System, the fail safe system, actually functions must suspend their disbelief and allow Kubrick his dramatic license. In fact, a SAC base commander had no means of ordering his bombers to attack the Soviet Union, or any target for that matter. Commanders transmitted the code to the bombers orally, not by means of a black box. And the Air Force's fail safe mechanisms operated on the principle of positive control—the bombers on their missions had to receive a direct order to launch their attack. The absence of such a command would automatically abort the mission.

Alastair Buchan, director of the Institute for Strategic Studies, a nongovernmental research organization, recalled that Kubrick met with him in 1961 to discuss making a film about a nuclear accident. Buchan told the director he thought it would be "unwise because he would not be able to describe precisely what precautions the United States or other nuclear powers take to guard against the danger of accident or false command." He also warned Kubrick that any film would "mislead anxious people." After seeing *Dr. Strangelove*, Buchan said that few viewers "will be aware that the basis of the plot is a series of distortions even of the known facts about United States control and safety procedures."[69]

Unfortunately for the Air Force, few civilians either knew or had the time and interest to ascertain how the system worked. As a result, most viewers readily accepted Kubrick's version of the system as well as its implied deficiencies. At least some viewers therefore emerged from theaters not only entertained but also concerned about the possibility that one crazed Air Force officer might actually start World War III. For most people, however, *Dr. Strangelove* became a comedy rather than a message film, and so relatively few viewers took the movie as seriously as Kubrick had hoped.

Bosley Crowther, in the *New York Times*, found *Dr. Strangelove* "a bit too contemptuous of our defense establishment for my comfort and taste." He found the film "cleverly written and most skillfully directed and placed." Moreover, he conceded that it provided "devastating satire," which contained some "awfully funny" stuff, and he described the initial phone conversation between President Muffley and Premier Kissof as a "simply delicious passage."

Nevertheless, Crowther thought the "sportive speculation about a matter of gravest conse-quence seems more malicious than diverting, more charged with poison than wit."[70]

After watching the movie a second time, Crowther still thought *Dr. Strangelove* did a disservice to the nation. He concluded that the film gave "vicarious fulfillment to the gravest fears that anyone might have about the imminence of nuclear disaster because of reckless and insufficient control of the bomb." He had no problem with Kubrick using the military as a target, believing that he could be "cheered for maintaining a stinging satire on sensitive but legitimate grounds. The mentality of generals and of their subordinates in positions to command has always been valid material for jovial to highly caustic jokes. That is because the rubbing is based upon a modicum of truth. Some military minds are pretty fuzzy, even in the top echelons."[71]

Crowther did object, however, to Kubrick's shooting "far beyond this satiric range. He is firing his blasts of derision and mockery at everyone. He is telling us in this comic fancy, which ends up not a comedy at all but a very adroit and horrendous politico-science fiction burlesque that more than the generals and the majors and the pilots who fly the bombing planes are mentally unstable and reliable." According to Crowther, because Kubrick sug-gests that no one has the ability to control the bomb, he is supporting "the currently fash-ionable notion, to wit, that nothing can be done about the bomb." Such a conclusion "may give satanic satisfaction to those who are so cynical or confused by the dread of what might happen that they can actually enjoy a feeling of revenge." Crowther objects to this view, arguing that "the trouble with it as a thesis for mordant satire in a film is that it is based more on wild imagination than on basically rational truths. Indeed it is a dangerous indul-gence of that emotional condition that derives from extreme anxieties and assumptions about the possible triggering of the bomb."[72]

To those who saw the film as making a serious statement, it did become a focus for discussions about the possibility of an accidental nuclear war. Responding to Crowther's reviews, Lewis Mumford thought the film represented the "first break" in the nation's "cold war trance." He observed: "What has masked the hideous nature of our demoralized strategy of total extermination is just the fact that it has been the work of otherwise well-balanced, responsible men. . . . What the wacky characters in *Dr. Strangelove* are saying is precisely what needs to be said: this nightmare eventuality that we have concocted for our children is nothing but a crazy fantasy, by nature as horribly crippled and dehumanized as Dr. Strangelove himself." Rejecting the criticism that Kubrick had made a "sick" film, Mumford suggested that "what is sick is our supposedly moral, democratic country which allowed this policy to be formulated and implemented without even the pretense of open public debate."[73]

Other reviewers thought the film performed a more positive service. *Newsweek* called it "outrageous" and said it contained "low clowning." But it also found that the film "sug-gests all too clearly that human society is not yet so well organized as to be able to afford such dangerous toys as hydrogen bombs." The reviewer maintained that the use of comedy to convey this message made Kubrick's observation "all the sharper, all the clearer, and that much better a film. . . . Kubrick, and his biting bitter satire, stands as eloquent testimony not only to the possibilities of intelligent comment in film, but to the great freedom which moviemakers have, even if most of them have not dared use it."[74]

If *Dr. Strangelove* failed to impress its message sufficiently on its audiences, the prob-lem probably lay in Kubrick's very success as a filmmaker. Whatever the validity of his warning about the bomb to the American people, the laughter from the audiences may have weakened its ability to persuade them. *Newsweek* noted that the film was "side-splittingly funny." As a result, more viewers undoubtedly remembered the film for its entertainment, its comedy, its acting, and its directing than as a serious treatise on the dangers of the bomb and incompetent leadership.[75]

This complaint cannot be directed against *Fail Safe*, appearing later in 1964 and conveying virtually the same message. It contrast to the cinematic brilliance and comedic comment on the human condition in *Dr. Strangelove*, Sidney Lumet took a grim, gritty, pseudo-documentary approach to filming Wheeler and Burdick's 1962 best-seller. Like Kubrick, Max Youngstein, the film's producer, had had a long-standing interest in the issue of nuclear safeguards. He had become a member of SANE and other groups concerned about the possibility of accidental nuclear war and believed that the government was withholding critical information about the potential for failure of the nation's safeguard system.[76]

Given his interest in the subject, when Youngstein read *Fail Safe* in manuscript form in 1962, he recalled that "it hit a very important nerve with me." Having just become an independent producer after years as an industry executive, he set about to acquire the property for his first picture, even meeting with the authors to convince them that he had the same concerns about nuclear safeguards as they had raised in their novel. To Youngstein, the book, "whether or not it was a fictionalized description of reality . . . was close enough to the information I had come across in my own research so that I could give the film validity."[77]

Wheeler and Burdick considered their book more than a fictionalized novel: "Thus the element in our story which seems most fictional—the story's central problem and its solution—is in fact the most real part. Men, machines, and mathematics being what they are, this is unfortunately, a 'true' story. The accident may not occur in the way we describe but the laws of probability assure us that ultimately it will occur. The logic of politics tells us that when it does, the only way out will be a choice of disasters."[78]

Making this statement in the book's preface may have seemed pretentious. But it did alert readers that *Fail Safe* intended to do more than simply entertain. It also helped make the novel controversial from the moment the *Saturday Evening Post* began serializing it in October 1962, shortly before it was published. This, along with a good publicity campaign, made the book an immediate best-seller and so offered Youngstein good commercial prospects as well as a forum for his antibomb message.

All claims to the contrary, however, *Fail Safe* did not tell a "true" story of the U.S. Positive Control System. In fact, the term *fail safe* had actually become obsolete long before the book appeared. Despite Wheeler and Burdick's claim that their "research was endless," the authors had not bothered to take a trip to SAC Headquarters in Omaha to learn how the Positive Control System really worked. If they had, or if they had used the basic unclassified material readily available from the Air Force or in print, they probably would not have written a novel about the failure of the system.

Technicalities aside, the Air Force maintains that the safeguards designed to prevent a nuclear accident had become virtually foolproof. The president or his stand-in must give SAC the correct code, which is then transmitted to the bombers and missile silos. Whether the orders are issued verbally, as the military maintains, or mechanically, as described in the book, they must be given positively, not by default. Any failure in the system, such as a malfunctioning computer, would automatically result in the recall of the bombers and not in a signal to attack as presented in the novel. Although the military would undoubtedly concede, if pressed, that no absolutes exist, Air Force officials have always maintained that the odds of an accident's occurring remain infinitesimal.

If Wheeler and Burdick had understood and accepted the validity of the Positive Control System, they would have had no story. Nevertheless, they operated on the assumption that if something is not absolutely impossible, it becomes probable, and on this tenuous premise they fabricated their story. The authors claimed their book came close to the truth, but it remained a truth only in the minds of those to whom truth exists as an intellectual creation rather than an approximation of reality. Youngstein said that in his discussions of the book with Wheeler and Burdick, the authors "were the first ones to admit that maybe this is not the exact way it would happen, but there was no question that in principle this is what could happen; that there was a damn good chance of it happening."[79]

In fact, the foundation of their story and of the movie rested on a series of false portrayals. Apart from the crucial misrepresentation of the Positive Control System, their description of SAC's underground headquarters and its operating procedures was erroneous. A single unidentified object could not trigger an alert of the entire SAC fleet. Since attack signals are relayed to the bombers by verbal command, not by electronic computer, no plane has a "black box" receiver as described in the book. Finally, military analysts take into account the current political and diplomatic situations around the world, and absent an ongoing crisis, they would not escalate readiness on the basis of one on-screen anomaly as happened in the novel and film.

Given these realities, facts clearly had little relevance to Wheeler and Burdick. They did not intend to write an informative book about SAC operations but rather to warn the American people about what they perceived as the potential threat of nuclear accident. Since Youngstein had the same agenda, for him, as for Wheeler and Burdick, the story—rather than objective truth—became the primary consideration in transferring *Fail Safe* to the screen. Given this goal, Walter Bernstein's script followed the novel much more closely than most movie scripts based on books. As a result, it contained the same inaccurate descriptions of Air Force operations as the book and was bound to elicit negative reactions from the service when the producer delivered it to the Pentagon with a request for assistance.[80]

Youngstein recognized that the book had "alerted" the Pentagon to the story and so realized that the military would be "doubly alerted to the film" and would have "preconceived notions" about the script. Nevertheless, he apparently had not expected to be "turned down absolutely cold." He recalled, "It was kind of staggering because it meant a revision in the script on certain scenes which from a visual standpoint, a motion picture standpoint, purely a question of quality of the motion picture validity, just had to be rewritten."[81]

The producer did try to negotiate with the Air Force, but he acknowledged that he could see the military had "a very adamant position already established. Apparently, some edict had been handed down about this particular property. And, it had come from very, very important sources. In other words, there was no give or take." Youngstein said he received "two generalized reasons" for the rejection. Not surprising, the Air Force simply said the scenario could not happen because the system was 100 percent fail safe. It also said that the script presented material than ran contrary to government policy and would be "injurious" to the nation. Although Youngstein tried to ascertain the foundation for this contention, he recalled, "I was never able to find out how. I just felt that a democratic form of government should always bring the truth to the public, whether in the military or other department."[82]

Most likely, the producer was tilting with windmills in trying to negotiate with the Air Force, given their diametrically opposite views on nuclear safeguards. Youngstein simply did not accept the military view that fail safe worked: "This I did not believe based on my own personal research which I believe had great validity. Plus, I had talked to many people who were fairly knowledgeable in the field through my relationship with SANE, people in government circles, people I knew through my service during the war years. So I would simply not accept the fact that it could not happen. I don't accept it today [in 1974]. I don't accept the infallibility of fail safe systems as seen by what happened to the astronauts on Apollo 13 and the three who died in the [Apollo One] fire. I don't believe in the computer as a fail safe system."[83]

Whatever his personal beliefs, having received the service's contention that the book and script did not portray the safeguard system correctly, Youngstein went back to see Wheeler and Burdick. They assured him that they had done extensive research. However, they stressed that they made no claim of writing anything but a novel, albeit a novel they hoped would have an impact. To accomplish this, they felt they were not tied to accurate technical descriptions of the system's operation. Instead, they simply wanted people to accept their story because it sounded right, because of their reputations as academics, and because of their research on the subject. As a result of Youngstein's conversation with the authors, the issue became not the accurate portrayal of the Positive Control System but whether any foolproof system existed.[84]

Youngstein said he could never obtain from the Pentagon a description of the way Positive Control procedures actually functioned. In light of the producer's position, however, the refusal is understandable. Youngstein acknowledged that even if the Air Force had told him how the system operated, he would not have made changes in his script. He simply wanted to show how an accident could happen: "If they were telling me I didn't have the correct way, if it couldn't possibly happen this way, in terms of leading up to the accident—not the end result—tell me how it does happen. It was all a very technical kind of objection."[85]

Not really. If the Air Force said an accident could not happen the way Wheeler and Burdick has portrayed it, Youngstein wanted the Air Force to tell him how to create one. The service maintained that it could not describe an impossible occurrence. Moreover, from the military's point of view, it would accrue no benefit, nor would it be in its best interest to have the system portrayed correctly, if the filmmakers still intended to show the system failing. But without showing the accidental launching of a SAC attack, Youngstein would have no story.

With every intention of making *Fail Safe,* Youngstein took steps to find alternatives to the military assistance he had hoped to obtain. In particular, the producer needed shots of bombers on the ground and in the air. He approached several of the large film libraries that maintained collections of stock shots of most subjects. At first, he found them cooperative. But when it came time to furnish the footage, the libraries did not return his calls: "It was like trying to punch our way out of a paper bag when we would inquire if they had found anything. It became a nightmarish thing that you could never pinpoint." Finally Youngstein asked one of the film libraries to explain its reluctance to give him the requested footage. The librarian told him: "I'm probably not supposed to tell you, but orders have come down that we're not to cooperate on the making of this film." When the producer asked if the orders had originated with the government, the librarian responded, "I'm not at liberty to tell you. But they are orders from people that I cannot afford to disregard." Ultimately, a film archive that the order had apparently missed provided Youngstein with about a hundred feet of film showing bombers in formation, and through optical work in a film laboratory, he obtained enough footage to meet the needs of the film. Nevertheless, he had to discard his original plan to show formations of planes flying toward their readiness positions in all parts of the world.[86]

Without military assistance, Youngstein also had problems creating authentic sets. To reproduce the cockpits of the bombers in the picture, the production company rented an old commercial plane at LaGuardia Airport and modified its cockpit. The confined space inside the plane made it necessary to shoot the cockpit sequences through open windows from the outside. In contrast, films that the Air Force approved usually had the use of cockpit mock-ups from the plane's manufacturer, which the filmmakers could disassemble to facilitate shooting interior scenes. The military's refusal to help Youngstein also created problems for him in reproducing the SAC war room in Omaha (as opposed to the Pentagon's fictional war room in *Dr. Strangelove*), one of the movie's main sets. Although the Air Force had already turned down his request for assistance, Youngstein approached the service, asking it to allow him to send his art director on a research trip to SAC Headquarters so that he could recreate the facility as exactly and authentically as possible. The Air Force had recently allowed Sy Bartlett to shoot a sequence for *A Gathering of Eagles* in the war room itself, and the Pentagon had routinely given filmmakers permission to make research trips to military facilities and to ride on planes, ships, even nuclear submarines. Nevertheless, Youngstein received "as cold a turn-down as you ever saw in your life. Under no circumstances would they allow anybody connected with the project to go out there and look at the war room." Consequently, as Kubrick had done, the art director created Youngstein's war room, using suggestions from several people including a man who had once been in the SAC facility.[87]

In the end, *Fail Safe* provided enough semblance of authenticity that the visual images did not intrude on the story. Nevertheless, Youngstein felt that the lack of cooperation "hurt the whole look of the picture. It affected the atmosphere, the size, the validity that you get if you have cooperation." It also affected the budget, especially with the cost of building the war room rather than shooting on location. Although the producer would not attempt to estimate the effect of the lack of authenticity on the film's success, he was "firmly convinced of the fact that if we had gotten the material from the government, it would have enhanced the picture and I am a believer that the better the picture . . . the better the box office, the better the acceptance the picture has from the public."[88]

Most viewers did accept *Fail Safe* as an exciting account of a potential nuclear accident. To be sure, not even the producer considered it a work of art in a class with *Dr. Strangelove*. He thought his company had turned out "a good picture," but Youngstein conceded that Kubrick had "turned out a brilliant picture. It's as simple as that. . . . It was a brilliant type of black humor, so far ahead of its time."[89]

Nevertheless, *Fail Safe* had a greater chance of conveying its message because of its serious tone and seemingly factual depiction of military procedures. Bosley Crowther observed in his *New York Times* review that, unlike *Dr. Strangelove*, *Fail Safe* "does not make its characters out to be maniacs and monsters and morons. It makes them out to be intelligent men trying to use their wits and their techniques to correct an error that has occurred through over-reliance on the efficiency of machines."[90]

Except for the Defense Department and the few people who understood the Positive Control System's actual operation, viewers had little concern about the film's accuracy or with the reality that human beings, not machines, maintained control of the nuclear arsenal and its launch procedures. Even Hubert Humphrey, the Democratic vice-presidential candidate in the 1964 election, had more interest in the film's message than with its "controversial phase as to the possibility of malfunction of 'fail-safe' mechanisms." Ignoring the government's refusal to become involved with the production of the film, Humphrey wrote to Press Secretary Bill Moyers that he was glad *Fail Safe* had been brought to President Johnson's attention: "Many people feel that the more millions of people who might see it in these next few weeks, the better will be their understanding of the crucial role of the Chief Executive in preserving the peace." In turn, Moyers sent Johnson a memo the next day saying that the film "should have pretty good impact on the campaign in our favor, since it deals with irresponsibility in the handling of nuclear weapons."[91]

The film's theme did tie in perfectly with several of President Johnson's television commercials linking Barry Goldwater to the irresponsible use of nuclear weapons. His one-minute campaign ad, broadcast only one time, showing children playing in a field with a mushroom-shaped cloud appearing in the background, made nuclear safeguards one of the central issues of the 1964 presidential campaign. In the sense that *Fail Safe* contributed to that dialogue, it performed a useful function. Nevertheless, it did so through a distorted and inaccurate portrayal of Air Force procedures and equipment.

Ironically, although people were willing to ignore the implausibility of the story, few viewers found the ending believable. Once the president realizes that neither the United States nor the Soviet Union may be able to stop the destruction of Moscow, he orders an American bomber loaded with two hydrogen bombs to circle over New York City. When the Russian capital is demolished, he orders the plane to drop its payload on New York City to prove to the Soviet president that the destruction of Moscow was truly an accident. Crowther did not think the film's resolution was "a sensible or likely one, but it is, at least, a valid shocker that induces the viewer to think." Youngstein said that the climax had "legitimacy to it. But even if I did not believe it was a legitimate situation, I don't think it should be dismissed just because it doesn't coincide with popular thinking."[92]

Such thinking naturally found it difficult to accept a president's ordering the destruction of the nation's largest city under any circumstances. But in the context of the film, or even in the real world, a president would have few alternatives by which to demonstrate good faith. A Soviet leader could not confront his people solely with an American apology or even an offer of reparations and expect to prevent the demands for retaliation, let alone stay in power. In contrast, with the awesomeness of the calamity facing both powers, the film's conclusion, a commitment from the president to meet his Soviet counterpart as quickly as possible to reach a disarmament agreement, has a feel of believability. In fact, the message of the movie may be not that a nuclear accident could happen but that until an accident provides the impetus, the world will not bring itself to disarm.

Even when motivated by the fear of world destruction, many people did not accept disarmament as a viable alternative. Fletcher Knebel and Charles Bailey used the military's dissatisfaction with a crisis-initiated disarmament treaty as the starting point for their novel of an attempted coup against the president of the United States. *Seven Days in May*, published in 1962, details the discovery and the president's successful stifling of a plot by a popular chairman of the Joint Chiefs of Staff and his cronies to seize the government. A disarmament treaty has been hammered out and barely ratified, following a Soviet incursion into Iran that has led to that country's partition and has almost caused a third world war. Air Force general James Scott and other top military commanders have opposed the treaty, believing it indicates a policy of appeasement at a time when President Lyman's 29 percent rating in public opinion polls shows him to be an ineffectual leader. They see his lack of leadership as an invitation for the Soviet Union to cheat on the new treaty (an eventuality that comes to pass as the story unfolds) and further weaken the United States. To prevent this, Scott, several high-ranking officers, a conservative senator, and a right-wing television commentator plan to seize control of key communications, isolate the president, and take control of the government.

Without question, the novel requires the reader to accept as probable a series of events that taken together strain credibility. The conspirators' base of operations occupies enough space to handle the largest Air Force transports, but it remains a secret from the president, Congress, noninvolved military men, and local residents. A Marine colonel stumbles across bits of suggestive information and immediately suspects the coup. Although only a colonel, he secures a meeting with the president within a few hours of discovering the plot. Subsequently, an obscure diplomat recovers a crucial piece of evidence against the conspirators from a plane wreck (one of the events used to heighten the melodrama), recognizes its significance, and brings it directly to the president without telling a single other person. Despite these implausibilities, the book worked because the authors were able to create the atmosphere of the Washington political scene, write a suspenseful story, and dramatize the then-current national concern about the military's role in politics. As a result, *Seven Days in May* remained on the New York Times best-seller list for forty-nine consecutive weeks.

Hollywood, as expected, wanted to turn the book into a movie. The military naturally saw the novel as a virtual travesty because it portrayed the highest-ranking command officers plotting the overthrow of the U.S. government. Arthur Sylvester, then developing the Pentagon's policies on cooperation with the film industry, told Ray Bell, still Columbia's Washington representative, that any film based on the book would never receive Defense Department assistance. Bell, whose studio had obtained an option on the novel, felt that Sylvester had based his decision on his interpretation of the novel as depicting an ineffective government.[93]

Although the book portrays some military men as traitors, it does show the constitutional government surviving. Most people, both inside and outside the Pentagon, continue to respect the tradition of civilian control of the military. To be sure, a film showing military leaders plotting a coup would offer little benefit to the armed forces. And since the plot of the novel would of necessity form the basis of the movie, the military had little leverage in requesting script changes, as it had been able to do with *From Here to Eternity* and *The Caine Mutiny*. Unlike *Dr. Strangelove* and *Fail Safe*, however, *Seven Days in May* did not give the military a strong case on grounds of implausibility.

The story takes place twelve years in the future (1974), in a political climate in which well-meaning military men could conceivably believe the survival of the country requires an immediate change in leadership. Historically, the nation had witnessed two military men defying civilian authority not long before the novel appeared. President Truman had removed Gen. Douglas MacArthur from his command because of the general's public opposition to presidential decisions. More recently, Gen. Edwin Walker had formed an alliance with the far right and had attempted to indoctrinate his men with his political beliefs. Although General Walker remained atypical, the armed services would have been hard-pressed to categorically deny that under the right circumstances a group of military men might plot to seize power. In fact, Ray Bell said that high-ranking officers told him that if the country ever fell asleep, a coup similar to the one described in *Seven Days in May* could very well become a possibility.[94]

With this in mind, Bell asked Pierre Salinger, President Kennedy's press secretary, to read the novel as a personal favor. When Salinger had finished it, Bell related Columbia's problems with the Pentagon and asked if he thought the book contained anything detrimental to the country's best interests. "Hell, no!" said Salinger. Moreover, he could see "absolutely" nothing that would hurt the military. On the contrary, he thought that a few revisions in the script would create a strong document, showing that a plot to overthrow the president would undoubtedly be nipped in the bud, as Knebel and Bailey demonstrated in the book.[95]

Given Salinger's reaction, Bell asked the press secretary to meet with him and Sylvester at the White House to explore further the possibility of military assistance to the film. Bell said he wanted "Sylvester, from an objective third party, to get these views which I hoped would be persuasive." As a result of the meeting, Bell felt certain he had "somewhat modified" Sylvester's perspective. However, before he could formally request military assistance, the studio decided the cost of the project would prove prohibitive and it relinquished its rights to the story.[96]

At that point, Edward Lewis and Kirk Douglas acquired the rights and set out to produce the film. They hired Rod Serling as the screenwriter and John Frankenheimer as director. Lewis said in October 1962 that he "anticipated non-cooperation and stumbling blocks from the Pentagon." At the same time, he expected the executive branch would have a favorable view of the proposed film. In any case, he intended to make the movie despite any objections, believing that "it is important that we have the strength to see that such a problem exists and meet it; this is a patriotic film."[97]

President Kennedy apparently agreed. According to his aide, Ted Sorensen, Kennedy enjoyed the book and joked that he knew a couple of generals who "might wish" to take over the country. With Kennedy's approval, Frankenheimer and his assistants were able to tour the White House so that they could accurately reproduce the living quarters and the Oval Office. The director later received permission to film entrance and exit scenes at the White House and stage a riot between opposing treaty factions in front of the mansion. Ironically, Frankenheimer filmed the demonstration two days after the initialing of the 1963 Nuclear Test Ban Treaty in Moscow, and the police had to move real pickets aside to make room for the fictional riot.[98]

Frankenheimer did not, however, follow up Ray Bell's efforts to obtain military assistance for the movie "because we knew we wouldn't get it." The filmmakers did ask to visit the office of Gen. Maxwell Taylor, then chairman of the Joint Chiefs of Staff, but the Pentagon made permission contingent on the producers' submitting a script. The director refused what he considered a covert form of censorship. His reluctance to even show a script to military officials may have provided him with a sense of creative freedom, but it also generated problems in producing visual authenticity in scenes involving military locales and equipment. Without asking permission, Frankenheimer planted cameras in the back of a parked station wagon to shoot a sequence of Kirk Douglas walking into and out of the Pentagon in his role as the Marine colonel who discovers the planned coup. In editing the film, however, the director cut the segments, finding them extraneous.[99]

Another time, the filmmakers needed to shoot aboard an aircraft carrier for the sequence in which the president's key advisor meets with a nonparticipating admiral to ascertain details of the conspiracy. Lewis and Frankenheimer talked their way aboard the USS *Kitty Hawk* in San Diego Harbor by asking the duty officer to allow them to shoot a small boat from a high vantage point. Once they completed the sequence, they asked permission to film an actor disembarking from the small boat and walking along to the bow of the carrier. Then Lewis asked to shoot a scene of the actor crossing the flight deck and entering the island of the carrier. In this sequence, he even used one of the ship's officers as a messenger. Before leaving the carrier, Frankenheimer was able to shoot still another scene utilizing two sailors as extras and filmed the small boat approaching from a lower angle.[100]

When the Defense Department discovered what had happened, it protested to the Motion Picture Association that Lewis had "acted unethically" in obtaining his footage: "We believe that he was fully aware of our policy covering the assistance on such productions but took the calculated risk that someone in the field might be unaware of the policy and from a seemingly innocent request involved the Navy in a situation that is embarrassing."[101]

Lewis disagreed. He explained that the request to shoot aboard the ship came about as "a simple, unplotted, natural location request" that he made to see if "the wishes of the director could be fulfilled" to obtain a better vantage point. The producer said he had given the ship's office all the information about his project: the name of the book, the studio involved, the stars, and the director. He claimed he had assumed that because *Seven Days in May* had remained a best-seller for over a year, the officer would have full knowledge of the subject matter. Moreover, because he had never discussed possible cooperation with the Pentagon, Lewis questioned the Defense Department's contention that he was "fully aware" of its policy governing assistance. Nevertheless, he conceded that the Pentagon had no obligation to assist on projects with which they do not agree.[102]

The military's involuntary assistance and the White House's willing help gave *Seven Days in May* an authentic visual atmosphere in which to tell the story of General Scott's attempted coup and President Lyman's successful efforts to preserve democracy. To Edmund O'Brien, who played a Georgia senator and close friend of the president, the story needed "to have one tremendous emotion—the survival of the United States. If that can be attained, it will have the same emotional pull as a war picture. In this one, the American ideal must become a living person."[103]

It is impossible to measure how much, if any, damage the film actually did to the military's image. Given the climate of the times and the unfavorable portrayals of the military in contemporary films, *Seven Days in May* undoubtedly engendered a greater awareness of the relationship between the military and the civilian government. For most viewers, however, the film functioned primarily as a gripping suspense thriller pitting the good guys against the bad guys, with the latter just happening to be military leaders.

For those willing to look deeper, the film offered a perceptive comment about the mood of the country in the mid-1960s. President Lyman sadly noted that the motivation behind the coup did not come from the military's lust for power but resulted from the growing fears and anxieties of the nuclear age. That, not General Scott, became the true enemy. In an observation equally appropriate to *Dr. Strangelove* and *Fail Safe*, President Lyman suggested that the bomb "happens to have killed man's faith in his ability to influence what happens to him."

Within this framework, *The Bedford Incident* used the classic theme of an obsessed ship captain to question the military's ability to control its nuclear weapons. Like Ahab and Queeg, who cannot drop their pursuit of white whales or strawberry eaters, the *Bedford's* Captain Finlander, played by Richard Widmark, loses touch with reality as he tracks an elusive Russian submarine. Having detected the Cold War enemy in Greenland territorial waters, Finlander continues to harass the submarine even after it has returned to international waters and apparent safety. His antipathy toward Communism and the continuing

Richard Widmark modeled his portrayal of Captain Finlander in *The Bedford Incident* (1965) on the mannerisms and speeches of Senator Goldwater during the 1964 Presidential campaign.

pressures of commanding nuclear weapons directed against similar enemy weapons prevent him from letting go of his prey once he has begun the chase.

As the pursuit changes from a game of cat and mouse into a virtual war, Finlander's obsession overwhelms rational behavior. No longer involved in just another Cold War confrontation, he sees the Russian submarine as a dangerous enemy that he must force to the surface. Finlander ignores orders to break off the hunt in his personal war, a war which no one on board the destroyer can persuade him to end. Like *Dr. Strangelove* and *Fail Safe*, *The Bedford Incident* offers the warning that man may no longer control the nuclear arsenal he has created.

The film ends with the accidental triggering of nuclear weapons, reinforcing the theses of the two earlier movies. Finlander's explanation to the men on the destroyer's bridge that he does not intend to attack first becomes a misinterpreted command to fire: "The Bedford will never fire first. But if he fires one, I'll fire one!" The weapons officer, hearing only "Fire one," presses the launch button. Picking up the sound of the missile entering the sea, the Russian submarine fires its torpedoes. Suddenly realizing where his obsession has taken him, Finlander refuses to take evasive measures. As the hunter destroys his prey, the explosion of the Russian's nuclear torpedoes destroys the pursuer.

The Navy allowed producer-director James Harris and screenwriter James Poe, as part of their extensive research to prepare the script, to take a five-day cruise aboard a destroyer. The filmmakers also met in November 1963 with military officials at the Pentagon and incorporated the Navy's suggestions into the script. The screenplay then went to an admiral, who made corrections of a technical nature in Navy operations and dialogue. Poe took the script back to the Pentagon in June 1964, at which point the Defense Department and the Navy objected for the first time to the script's cataclysmic ending.[104]

Officials said they did not want an atomic explosion implied in the accidental firing of the ASROC, the antisubmarine missile, even though it was public knowledge that the weapon had nuclear capability. They also objected to Finlander's passivity after the torpedoes were fired, feeling that his "calm stoic acceptance of termination is apt to be misinterpreted by the public." To provide motivation for the captain's zealous pursuit of the Russian submarine, officials suggested having the craft "exhibit an unusual and strange device." Although the Pentagon did not want the American ASROCs in the film armed with nuclear warheads, the military did suggest that the filmmakers "introduce the strong possibility that the Russian submarine's torpedoes are armed with nuclear warheads," then not part of the script. Finally, the Pentagon wanted Finlander to clearly state, "Only if the enemy fires first will we fire."[105]

Poe incorporated the suggestions into his revised script of June 14, which he then sent to Harris, Richard Widmark, and Ray Bell, who had been working on the project for

Columbia Pictures. Harris and Widmark refused to accept the Pentagon's version of the ending. Harris thought the message of accidental nuclear warfare was "worth saying again and again." Since the Pentagon and the State Department did not want an American movie to show the U.S. Navy provoking a nuclear incident, the Department of Defense then rejected the filmmaker's request for use of a destroyer and other assistance.[106]

Harris had recognized the ramifications of the Pentagon's refusal, saying in August 1964 that if necessary, "we'll either use models, miniatures, and process, or fake it with some other kind of destroyer." The deadlock with the Pentagon forced him to resort to all these expedients. Since he had always intended to make the film in England, Harris sought and obtained the use of a British destroyer and helicopter for his opening sequence in which Sidney Poitier, playing an American journalist, arrives aboard the *Bedford* to do a story on Captain Finlander and the new Navy. The British navy also allowed the company to shoot establishing shots with a miniature American-type destroyer in its model test basin on Malta. Harris then filmed the shipboard sequences on a mock-up of a destroyer built in a studio in England.[107]

At the same time, Harris and Widmark hired Capt. James D. Ferguson, a recently retired Navy officer, as technical advisor to ensure as much accuracy in the film as possible. Ferguson himself expressed no concern at the Pentagon's refusal to assist or with the film's ending, although he did feel the climax "was stretching things pretty far. . . . It probably could happen, but it would be really far-fetched." As Harris and Poe structured the story, the dialogue between Finlander and the *Bedford*'s weapons officer accidentally overrode the fail-safe mechanisms built into the destroyer's system of nuclear safeguards. Ferguson claimed that in a normal situation, a captain would not be in a position to have his words misinterpreted, but he acknowledged that the film did not portray a normal situation. The *Bedford* initially had come upon the Russian submarine in territorial waters. While a more stable captain would probably not be likely to force the final confrontation, Ferguson believed that the whole point of the story was showing that Finlander "was driving himself nuts." Harris thought the story could be more accurately described as Finlander "driving everyone else nuts," which caused the weapons officer to misinterpret the captain's comment about not firing first.[108]

The characterization itself, however, had a firm basis in reality. Richard Widmark said he used Barry Goldwater as his model, because the 1964 Republican presidential candidate had become "one of my pet peeves," even though he liked him personally. Widmark said he compiled a rather extensive folder on Goldwater and his statements during the campaign, which was in progress while the film was in preproduction. Admitting that he "enjoyed playing Berry Goldwater," the actor said, "it gave me an added dimension to play with. Actually, his statements were not unlike the captain's actions."[109]

In *Seven Days in May*, President Lyman observes that in the nuclear age man has lost faith in his ability to influence what happens to him. The *Bedford*'s captain has endured long and seemingly fruitless patrols in the North Atlantic, and his frustration, combined with a hatred of the Russians, put him over the edge and turned him into an obsessed man. To Captain Ferguson, Finlander's enforced removal would not have offered a viable resolution to the confrontation.[110]

Although he believed that in *The Caine Mutiny*, Maryk acted correctly in removing Captain Queeg, the technical advisor explained that a "completely different" situation existed aboard the *Bedford*. Finlander's irrational behavior developed only during the pursuit of the submarine, while he was on the bridge, where a captain remains in complete control. In contrast, Queeg's behavior on his bridge during the typhoon crowned a long series of deviant actions.[111]

Whatever his views on the story's plausibility, Ferguson's primary concern focused on efforts to create an authentic military atmosphere. Consequently, although he continued to believe *The Bedford Incident* lacked plausibility, he saw his role as technical advisor as trying to make the film "look like it could happen as much as I could." As a result, his script modifications, both at the beginning of his advisory work and during the shooting, dealt with matters of procedure and dialogue that the filmmakers readily incorporated into the script.[112]

In the end, however, neither Ferguson nor Harris could change the need to use a British destroyer and helicopter to represent American counterparts. The technical advisor pointed out that when the helicopter delivers Poitier to the deck of the ship, "you can see it is a British ship. All Navy men will notice it . . . [but the] only people who would know are those familiar with ships and helicopters." Nevertheless, opening the film with a live shot enabled Harris to establish a sense of reality, which then allowed him to use models and mock-ups without much loss of authenticity.[113]

To prevent possible recognition of the British destroyer in the repeated full-ship shots, the film company photographed a miniature U.S. Navy frigate for the open-sea sequences. By using the British test basin in Malta for these sequences, Harris was able to create waves of the right frequency and size to fit the model. To provide the illusion of being in the North Atlantic, the special-effects men also floated "icebergs" in the water and had the *Bedford* sail between them. Ferguson, who did not go to Malta, felt that a destroyer would have been incapable of these feats. He would have preferred to eliminate the shots. Even so, the basin allowed Harris to shoot the real sea as background and gave more realism to the film than any other available method. Shooting the deck shots and interiors in a studio had little adverse effect on authenticity.[114]

Ray Bell thought the filmmak-

(Above) Filming the *Bedford* at night in the test basin on Malta. (Below) The *Bedford* sails past an iceberg during filming of the story of Captain Finlander's compulsive pursuit of a Russian submarine. (Note the perimeter of the test basin and the Mediterranean Sea in the background.)

ers "did turn out a very credible picture. They maintained the authenticity." He said the Pentagon failed to realize that most people believe what they see on the screen and therefore would conclude that the military had given assistance whether it had or not. To Bell, both *Fail Safe* and *The Bedford Incident* showed "that things could be done authentically by imaginative people who have limited budgets." Captain Ferguson believed that an audience becomes "so engrossed in the action that they don't care whether it is real or not." He thought the movie "had a feel of authenticity even if it wasn't 'real'!" Harris believed that "striving for authenticity is worthwhile only as a supportive base to the drama and the issues dealt with in the film. In other words, if there are glaring errors in authenticity, it could jeopardize the audience's willingness in accepting the more important parts of the overall film. Authenticity for the sake of authenticity alone is merely an exercise and has very little to do with film as an art form."[115]

Unlike a typical military film, *The Bedford Incident* relied less on visual authenticity than on its story for dramatic impact. Ironically, the buildup of tensions during Captain Finlander's obsessive pursuit of the Russian submarine obscured the filmmaker's intended message. In the end, Finlander becomes a Captain Queeg clone, and his mental deterioration, like Queeg's, becomes the heart of the story. As a result, despite Harris's hope that his movie would warn people of the possibility an accidental nuclear confrontation, audiences become more involved with an individual man's irrationality than with mankind's irrational reliance on the bomb to preserve the peace. Moreover, the strong impact the destruction of the two ships creates undoubtedly would have remained even if the mutual extinction had resulted from conventional weapons rather than nuclear warheads.

Nevertheless, the image of nuclear weapons in *The Bedford Incident* and the other antibomb films of the mid-1960s differed greatly from the image of the bomb Hollywood had presented in *Strategic Air Command, Bombers 52,* and *A Gathering of Eagles.* Instead of presenting the bomb as the preserver of peace, the filmmakers now suggested that the bomb might well bring on the Apocalypse. While each story required a significant suspension of disbelief, they became potent vehicles to convey not only antibomb but also broader antiwar statements.

13 John Wayne, *The Green Berets,* and Other Heroes

DESPITE THE POWERFUL ANTIBOMB, ANTIWAR MESSAGE in *Dr. Strangelove, Fail Safe,* and *The Bedford Incident,* in 1965 most Americans still held the armed forces in high esteem, and the military continued to win World War II in such films as *In Harm's Way* and *The Battle of the Bulge.* The fighting in Vietnam was just beginning to draw attention, and the war had not yet become controversial. It did, however, attract the interest of John Wayne, who had always stood for and symbolized the "My Country Right or Wrong" school of patriotism. If he had a goal in his movies, he explained, he wanted "to pass the message of preparedness to the country. No weak nation makes treaties. It's a strong nation that gets things done and we can't allow ourselves to become second rate."[1]

With this commitment, Wayne would naturally see the Vietnam War as a subject for a movie. In fact, in making *The Green Berets,* Wayne was practicing John Waynism, in which a lone individual takes on a far larger number of opponents in an endeavor he considers correct. At a time when no one else in Hollywood would put money behind his beliefs, pro or con, about the increasingly unpopular war, Wayne decided to produce, direct, and star in a movie backing the American effort in Southeast Asia.

Wayne had always supported the government's actions in Southeast Asia, and having recovered from the removal of a cancerous lung, he was ready to fight in the war on the screen. However, he was not the first filmmaker to seek military assistance to produce a movie about the Green Berets. As early as January 1963, Columbia Pictures had written to the Army indicating a desire to make a film about a Special Forces Team. The studio intended "to show the formation, military training, and indoctrination of the men who make up this particular team, stressing, among other things, the importance of the work that the Special Forces are doing." The Army found the proposed film to be "very desirable" and recommended that the Defense Department Public Affairs Office encourage the filmmaker to visit Special Forces training installations. By the end of 1965, however, the studio had failed to come up with an acceptable script, and in June 1966 the Defense Department canceled the studio's priority.[2]

In the meantime, Robin Moore's novel *The Green Berets* had appeared in the spring of 1965. Focusing on the exploits of the Special Forces in Vietnam, the best-selling book angered Pentagon officials because Moore described Green Beret forays into North Vietnam, which the Defense Department denied had ever occurred. In response, Moore claimed he had based his narrative on firsthand knowledge gained when he had accompanied Green Beret units in Vietnam. Moore later said the Pentagon refused to cooperate with filmmakers who wanted to purchase the rights to his book because of the military's unhappiness with the novel.[3]

David Wolper, among others, denied these accusations. He said that although he had expressed a strong interest in acquiring *The Green Berets,* his failure to make the movie had nothing to do with Pentagon intransigence. Wolper explained that Columbia Pictures still

247

held its priority to make a film about the Green Berets when he approached the Defense Department about cooperation for a movie based on Moore's novel. In addition, he said he had not been able to acquire the necessary financial backing for the project.[4]

By then, John Wayne had learned that the film rights to Moore's book remained available, and in December 1965 he wrote directly to President Johnson setting forth his interest in making a film about the Green Berets based on Moore's novel. He explained that although he supported the administration's Vietnam policy, he knew the war was becoming unpopular. Consequently, he thought it was "extremely important that not only the people of the United States but those all over the world should know why it is necessary for us to be there. . . . The most effective way to accomplish this is through the motion picture medium."[5]

He told Johnson he could make the "kind of picture that will help our cause throughout the world." While still making money for his company, he could "tell the story of our fighting men in Vietnam with reason, emotion, characterization, and action. We want to do it in a manner that will inspire a patriotic attitude on the part of fellow-Americans—a feeling which we have always had in this country in the past during times of stress and trouble." To make the film, Wayne explained, he would need the cooperation of the Pentagon, and in support of his request, he cited his long film career and specifically his portrayal of the military with "integrity and dignity" in such films as *They Were Expendable, Sands of Iwo Jima,* and *The Longest Day.* He concluded that his film could be "extremely helpful to the Administration" and asked Johnson to help "expedite" the project.[6]

In advising the president on how to respond to Wayne's request for assistance, presidential aide Jack Valenti wrote, "Wayne's politics [were] wrong, but insofar as Vietnam is concerned, his views are right. If he made the picture he would be saying the things we want said." In fact, Wayne did not need to have made his extended plea to the White House. Ultimately the Pentagon decided to cooperate because they viewed the final screenplay as another Wayne action-adventure film and thought the movie would benefit the services and the war effort. Nevertheless, Michael Wayne, John Wayne's son and the film's producer, required eighteen months to secure approval of a script and begin shooting the film.[7]

Developing a script acceptable to the military became the major obstacle to getting production started. In February 1966, as a first step in this direction, the junior Wayne hired James Lee Barrett, an ex-Marine and a successful scriptwriter, to start work on the screenplay. That choice relieved Pentagon fears that Robin Moore would be asked to adapt his own novel to the screen. Moreover, Michael Wayne assured Don Baruch and DoD public affairs that Barrett would do "what amounts to an original screenplay using only a few incidents from Moore's book."[8]

From the beginning, however, John Wayne's own views on the conflict gave the script and ultimately the movie its focus. Responding to encouragement from the White House, he wrote to Bill Moyers, the president's press secretary, repeating his hope that *The Green Berets* would tell Americans what was happening in Vietnam. He wanted "to show such scenes as the little village that has erected its own statute of liberty to the American people. We want to bring out that if we abandon these people, there will be a blood bath of over two million souls." Wayne said the film would portray the professional soldier "carrying out his duty of death but, also, his extracurricular duties—diplomats in dungarees—helping small communities, giving them medical attention, toys for their children, and little things like soap, which can become so all-important." He thought these things could be inserted into the picture "without it becoming a message vehicle or interfering with the entertainment."[9]

In early April, both Waynes and Barrett visited the Defense Department to discuss details of the film and then traveled to the John F. Kennedy Special Warfare Center at Fort Bragg, North Carolina, on a research expedition. Afterward, John Wayne wrote to Don Baruch thanking him for leading his party through the Pentagon and its bureaucracy. He admitted that they had "arrived with trepidation [but] left with a feeling of confidence that the Department was sincerely sympathetic and would cooperate within any reasonable limits."[10]

The senior Wayne also wrote to Bill Moyers about his visits and commented on the strong impression the men at Fort Bragg had made on him. He attached a copy of a letter he had written to several senators, including Richard Russell and J.W. Fulbright, in which he advocated continued support of the government's policies in Vietnam. He asked Moyers if these views came "reasonably close to the thinking of our Administration." The letter itself amplified Wayne's position on the type of guerrilla activity against which he intended to portray the Green Berets fighting in his film. He asked the senators to remember that if such guerrilla-type warfare proved successful in Vietnam, it could also take place in South America.[11]

Wayne still had a long way to go before actually getting these ideas on film. As one step in his preparations, he made a three-week USO tour of Vietnam, where he was able to see firsthand some of the combat he intended to show. Once, the action came almost too close when Vietcong snipers fired into an encampment where he was talking to Marines. Wayne made light of the incident, saying, "They were so far away, I didn't stop signing autographs." Landing within seventeen yards of where he was standing, however, the bullets did bring war close enough to give him a true feeling of the conflict.[12]

In the meantime, Barrett continued working on the first draft of the screenplay. By the end of May 1966, Michael Wayne informed the Pentagon officials that he hoped to have it finished by mid-July. The producer was also working on the financial and distribution arrangements of the film and by the end of June had reached an agreement with Universal Pictures.[13]

When Barrett finally completed the first rough draft of the screenplay in early August, Michael Wayne informed Baruch that before revising the script he wanted to send the writer to Vietnam for some firsthand information. Like all producers of war movies, Wayne expressed concern about the need to have military assistance to ensure the right ambience. Moreover, television and news coverage had brought the war into American homes, and Wayne explained that he could not "afford to come up with anything less than the real thing." Consequently, he felt the trip was necessary for Barrett "to familiarize himself with all the jargon, attitudes, equipment, and procedures indigenous to the war."[14]

The Defense Department granted the request. But Michael Wayne quickly discovered that although he considered visual and verbal authenticity important to him as a filmmaker, the Defense Department's Public Affairs Office had more interest in the movie's plot. Baruch asked Wayne to submit the rough draft of the screenplay so that his office would have some indication of the direction the writer was taking. When it arrived, Baruch found the story disappointing. The script portrayed a covert mission into North Vietnam to blow up a bridge and power plant and to seize a high-ranking Communist official. Baruch recalled that this plot conflicted with normal Green Beret actions of "reconnaissance, surveillance, and training," which the Army had described to both Waynes during their trip to Fort Bragg. Consequently, Baruch advised Wayne that the fictionalized mission did not represent "one that the Green Berets would participate in."[15]

The Army had an even more negative reaction. It advised Baruch that the "development of plot is not acceptable in that the type of mission evolved is not one which Special Forces would be involved in under present policy." The Army recommended that "the producer be informed that substantial plot changes would have to be made to conform with the mission of Special Forces in Vietnam before cooperation by the Department of the Army could be made."[16]

Barrett began revisions as soon as he returned from Vietnam in September, and he wrote Baruch that he would have no problem making the suggested changes. In light of his experiences in Vietnam, he stressed that he wanted to "write a meaningful, exciting, and enlightening motion picture, portraying our Special Forces as accurately and honestly as possible." Because the film would be the first movie about the Green Berets, Barrett said he wanted it to be "the best" and so was sure his second draft would be done "to the satisfaction of all concerned."[17]

To ensure this, Michael Wayne and Barrett went to Washington on September 29 to discuss the script's problems with Pentagon officials. Amplifying what Baruch had told him, the Army denied that the Green Berets went into North Vietnam as described in the script. The service admitted, however, that Special Forces units would conduct raids across the border if the South Vietnam army requested it. The officials stressed that Green Berets would take part in a specific mission into the North only in conjunction with other actions.[18]

Wayne had felt the script contained a "legitimate" account of events that either had happened or could have happened. In fact, he thought it "was a better script than the film we made in terms of dramatic value for the screen." Nevertheless, at the meeting, he agreed to delete the across-the-border kidnapping, explaining later that he had no choice, since he needed the Army's cooperation to supply required equipment and men. Perhaps more to the point, he did not want to face his father with news that the Defense Department had refused to cooperate on a John Wayne war movie. The younger Wayne said he never told his father that the Army had rejected the initial script: "I was actually afraid to because he would have said, 'You dumb son of a bitch!'" Also, he said that Batjac, the Wayne Production Company, had alreay announced that it was making *The Green Berets*, and he did not want any negative publicity.[19]

Although Wayne told Pentagon officials at the meeting he would have the revised script done by the end of October, Barrett began to fall behind schedule. Finally he finished his draft at the end of December and wrote to the Army Office of Information that he realized the script still had "technical inaccuracies" which were "unavoidable" because of his "ignorance of military matters and procedures." However, he assured the Army that all these errors could be corrected with the help of a Special Forces technical advisor and expressed confidence that the Army would be pleased with the final script.[20]

Despite his hope, the Army found many things in the revised screenplay not to its liking when it finally received the script in February 1967. Some of the problems pertained to technical matters such as the wrong height for a free-fall tower and the wrong type of aircraft. Other matters, however, related to question of image and propriety. The Army suggested, for example, that one character's lines be changed from "Well, sir, I'm a soldier and it's the only game in town" to something like ". . . when I came into the Army a wise infantry sergeant always told us to 'move toward the sound of guns because that's where we'll be needed most.'" The Army felt that the reference to war as a game would "degrade the image we are attempting to project with the movie."[21]

Michael Wayne again readily agreed to the changes requested, and on March 1 he sent copies of a third draft to Baruch with a note saying he was working on a list of requirements the film would need from the Army "if and when the script is approved." Although the Army and the State Department both requested changes in the revised script, the Defense Department formally agreed on March 30 to assist Wayne's Batjac Production Company, provided the modifications were made. In the meantime, the Public Affairs Office suggested that Wayne contact the Army's Los Angeles Information Office for advice in developing his list of requirements.[22]

The Defense Department changes again included both substantive and technical matters. Instead of referring to the war as "North against South," the Pentagon recommended: "We do not see this as a civil war, and it is not. South Vietnam is an independent country, seeking to maintain its independence in the face of aggression by a neighboring country. Our goal is to help the South Vietnamese retain their freedom, and to develop in the way they want to, without interference from outside the country." The Public Affairs Office also pointed out that the brutal treatment of a prisoner by a Vietnamese officer, and its approval by the Americans "is grist for the opponents of U.S. policy in Vietnam. It supports some of the accusations of these opponents against the U.S., and is of course a clear violation of the Articles of War."[23]

On a technical level, the Pentagon noted that it found "objectionable" the incident that causes the journalist to change his views on the war and to begin to support it. The Defense Department said that the writer's seizing a gun and becoming a combatant "violates the rules under which he operates as a news correspondent, and to the extent that the incident is considered realistic by those who might see a film based on this script, might indicate that it would not be unusual for a newsman to perform such violations." Despite its requests for changes, the Defense Department said it looked forward to working with Batjac, the Wayne production company, "on what promises to be a most worthwhile and, we trust, successful production."[24]

On April 10 Michael Wayne sent the Army the revisions the Pentagon had requested. He noted that the script was adding an explanation that would give the Vietcong official "more importance" to better justify the Green Beret operation to capture him. Wayne said he will become "The Man who controls all VC operations in that war zone. He gets all his orders directly from Hanoi, and in fact has just recently returned from there. His capture will cause chaos in the VC war plans, and give us very valuable intelligence, thus saving thousands of lives both American and Vietnamese." He said the writer was "taking remedial steps" to improve the opening BRIEFING sequence and requested that the Army assign a technical advisor to the project.[25]

Although the Pentagon had expressed its satisfaction with the state of the production, Universal Studios became disenchanted with its involvement in a film about an increasingly unpopular war. Michael Wayne recalled that the studio claimed to be unhappy with the proposed budget. But when he and his father sat down with officials to resolve the difficulty, studio executives raised questions about the script. As soon as the senior Wayne realized the studio was looking for a way out of its contract, he said good-bye and walked out of the meeting. Apart from the issue of the Vietnam War, a Universal executive subsequently called the screenplay the worst he had ever read.[26]

John Wayne, as Colonel Kirby, leads his men against a Vietcong attack in *The Green Berets*, filmed at Fort Benning, Georgia.

Even without considering the dialogue and character development, the final screenplay Barrett submitted to the Pentagon did not stand as a dramatic triumph. *The Green Berets* portrayed the activities of Lt. Col. Michael Kirby (John Wayne) during a tour of duty in Vietnam. A liberal journalist, played by David Janssen, arrives in Vietnam to report on Kirby's actions as commander of a Special Forces unit. Janssen at first expresses strong skepticism of American involvement in South Vietnam but later reverses his position and comes to accept the military's point of view from his coverage of Kirby's working closely with his Vietnamese counterparts. During the film, the Vietcong overrun Kirby's Special Forces camp, only to be driven back in a furious attack by American helicopters and planes. In the movie's climax, a small Green Beret force kidnaps a leading Vietcong officer—basically an anticlimatic episode because the battle for the Special Forces camp actually remains the dramatic and visual highlight of the story. If Wayne had placed the covert mission before the battle sequence or left it out altogether, the movie would have had a much stronger dramatic impact, regardless of the artistic aspects of Barrett's script.

Although the Pentagon generally limits its advice to technical matters of one kind or another, Don Baruch did talk to Michael Wayne about restructuring the script to improve its impact. The producer agreed with Baruch's observation but felt it expedient to leave the screenplay as it was—John Wayne's name alone would make *The Green Berets* project attractive to most studios. His son had judged accurately. Batjac found a new financial backer and distributor almost immediately with Warner Brothers in June 1967. Wayne then scheduled filming to begin in early August.[27]

Batjac had begun searching for a suitable site for the exterior filming as soon as the Army had agreed to cooperate on the movie. John Wayne would have preferred to shoot the film in Vietnam but admitted that "if you start shooting blanks over there, they might start shooting back." Okinawa offered tropical terrain and an Army helicopter facility, but on an inspection trip Wayne and his codirector, Ray Kellogg, found that the aircraft would not be available on a regular basis. Moreover, transporting equipment and the logistics of providing for the needs of the film crew raised costs to an unacceptable level.[28]

The Army strongly suggested that Batjac consider shooting the film at Fort Benning, Georgia. At first the company showed little interest in the location, believing that Georgia would not look like Vietnam. But after a scouting trip to the base, assistant director Kellogg called John Wayne to say that the Georgia terrain would serve their visual needs. More important, Kellogg found that the Army regularly had twenty to thirty Huey helicopters in the training program at Benning, and these would be available during filming. Since the

Hueys provided an essential part of the story, this became a crucial factor in their decision. Wayne made his own inspection tour of Benning, then told his son to go ahead with a formal request to use the facility.[29]

In approving the request, the Army indicated that "there will be a minimum of difficulty in acceding to Mr. Wayne's request." As was always the case with military cooperation, however, the final approval of assistance rested with the local commander. In light of the Army's interest in making a film about Vietnam, and with John Wayne producing, directing, and acting in the project, the Fort Benning command provided the filmmaker with most of the assistance he needed. The only major problem Wayne had as director was coordinating his shooting schedule with the base's training schedules and the availability of the helicopters.[30]

Following Arthur Sylvester's new regulations, the Pentagon watched the production closely. Unlike earlier films, which had had one technical advisor who supervised all aspects of military assistance, *The Green Berets* had three contacts with the Army, a technical advisor to supervise actual military procedures; a liaison man with the Fort Benning command, who arranged for equipment and men when needed; and an overall liaison man who informed Baruch's office of progress on the production.[31]

While the Army could no longer provide on-duty soldiers to work as extras or set up special exercises, Wayne was still able to film regularly scheduled training maneuvers. As might be expected, the service stretched the envelope and did as much as possible to ensure the film's visual authenticity. Among other things, the Army brought a platoon of Hawaiians down to Georgia from Fort Devens, Massachusetts, and placed them on administrative leave so that Wayne would have enough Orientals to fill the screen. To help create the proper atmosphere in which both the Green Berets and the "Vietnamese" could perform, Batjac built a Vietnamese-type village at a cost of more than $150,000, which the company later left standing for the Army's use as a training facility. In addition, following the new regulations, the company paid the government $18,000 for fuel and other items used exclusively in the shooting of the film.[32]

Despite the producer's careful efforts and the Army's attempts to implement Defense Department instructions, *The Green Berets* did not avoid controversy. In June 1969, a year after the film opened, Congressman Benjamin Rosenthal of New York launched an attack on Wayne for having made only a "token" payment to the Pentagon; he demanded a General Accounting Office investigation. Although the GAO said Wayne had followed regulations as they were written, Rosenthal charged that the Army had subsidized Wayne in making his hawkish film. In response, Wayne called Rosenthal "an irresponsible, publicity seeking idiot." Denying that he had received more than $1 million worth of weapons and man hours in return for his token payment, Wayne said, "I wish this were the 1800s. I'd horsewhip him."[33]

Wayne's major problem in making *The Green Berets* had nothing to do with government regulations or Congressional criticism, however. He faced the task of portraying the Vietnam War in the manner he had promised the president and senators—as the good guys against the bad guys. However, the conflict in Southeast Asia differed from earlier American conflicts, in which the nation had for the most part enjoyed the support of its people. David Halberstam, author of *The Best and the Brightest,* explained: "Vietnam simply wasn't a very patriotic war. It was a lie." As a result, it became "a terribly difficult thing for John Waynism." To Halberstam, the key ingredients in Waynism are that "all the other guys are richer, more powerful and dominate the town, and you are a part of the smaller group. You are leading the way for the numerically smaller group, weaker, don't have ammunition, guns, whatever. Now you suddenly have to take Waynism and transfer it to a place where you are bringing on the heaviest carnage in the history of mankind, to a peasant nation." Halberstam said that Wayne was able to transfer Waynism to the Vietnam War by singling out a single microcosm within the conflict. By sending a small Special Forces unit to fight with the Montagnards, Wayne created a classic Wayne situation: a few good guys surrounded by a sea of enemy bad guys.[34]

In a sense, Wayne himself was practicing Waynism simply by making *The Green Berets.* Because opposition to the war was becoming increasingly bitter, because television brought its body counts and battles into American homes every night, and because of the continuing negotiations that might end the war at any moment, no one in Hollywood wanted to make a film about the conflict. Even doves who might donate large amounts of money to the antiwar movement refused to finance an anti-Vietnam film that might lose money. Likewise, except for Wayne, the supporters of the war would not make a pro-Vietnam film because they also recognized it would probably not do well at the box office.

Michael Wayne explained, however, that he and his father saw the controversy surrounding the war as "a natural subject for a film." Beyond that, he did not see the story itself as controversial: "It was the story of a group of guys who could have been in any war. It's a very familiar story. War stories are all the same. They are personal stories about soldiers and the background is the war. This just happened to be the Vietnam War." For Michael Wayne, the film may only have told "a fresh story because there were different uniforms, a different unit, and a different war." The Department of Defense may have seen the film as simply another John Wayne adventure film that would benefit the military and the war effort. The White House may have believed the film was saying the things it wanted said. And John Wayne may have played his standard soldier role, carrying out his mission while trying to survive in a hostile atmosphere. But he also saw the movie as "an American film about American boys who were heroes over there. In that sense, it was propaganda."[35]

For his efforts and for his patriotic intentions, Wayne received nothing but criticism from film reviewers. The most extreme attack came from Renata Adler in the *New York Times.* She found *The Green Berets* "so unspeakable, so stupid, so rotten and false in every detail that it passes through being fun, through being funny, through being camp, through everything and becomes an invitation to grieve, not for our soldiers or for Vietnam (the film could not be more false or do a greater disservice to either of them) but for what has happened to the fantasy-making apparatus in this country. Simplicities of the right, simplicities of the left, but this one is beyond the possible. It is vile and insane. On top of that, it is dull."[36]

Even the trade journals, which are usually gentle with the films they review, found *The Green Berets* wanting. The

John Wayne with author (1974).

Hollywood Reporter called the film "a cliche-ridden throwback to the battlefield potboilers of World War II, its artifice readily exposed by the nightly actuality of TV news coverage, its facile simplification unlikely to attract the potentially large and youthful audience whose concern and sophistication cannot be satisfied by the insertion of a few snatches of polemic." The reviewer thought the film was "clumsily scripted, blandly directed, and performed with disinterest" and predicted it would have a "chill-run" domestically and "an even colder reception abroad."[37]

Wayne and his film also had their defenders. Responding to Adler's *New York Times* review, Sen. Strom Thurmond told the Senate that the first paragraph of her remarks "was enough to convince anyone that his was a good movie," suggesting that Adler's calling the film "dull" became the tip-off. Declaring that he found it "hard to believe that John Wayne could ever be dull," the senator called Wayne "one of the great actors of our time. He is a true and loyal patriot and a great American. It is men of his caliber and stripe who have built America and made it what it is today—the greatest country in the world."[38]

Moreover, Green Berets who saw the film seemed to find it authentic. One lieutenant colonel commented that "when Hollywood's doing it, you have to expect dramatization—some exaggeration. But I thought it was a real fine film." Another officer enthusiastically said, "I think it caught the essence." According to a Green Beret sergeant major, the film "was just God, Mother, and Flag. Now who the hell could have any opposition to that? It was a good, low-key, accurate picture.... The accuracy was there, and the photography was real great." Anyone seeing himself or a reasonable facsimile of himself portrayed on the screen admittedly lacks objectivity. General Edwin Simmons, who fought in Vietnam and commanded a Special Forces unit in his area and later served as director of the Marine Corps Historical Center and Museums, undoubtedly put *The Green Berets* in better perspective. He found the film so bad that it almost made him sick. Among other things, he noted that Georgia simply did not look like Vietnam.[39]

If both Waynes had stuck to their stated goal of making an authentic and entertaining film rather than compromising with the military to obtain needed equipment, *The Green Berets* might have had some artistic merit. Instead, it became no more or less than another John Wayne adventure film, and one of his lesser efforts. In many respects, it resembles one of his typical westerns but set in a different locale. Michael Wayne went so far as to say it was a "cowboys and Indians [film]. In a motion picture you cannot confuse the audience. The Americans are the good guys and the Viet Cong are the bad guys. It's as simple as that ... when you are making a picture, the Indians are the bad guys."[40]

In *The Green Berets,* John Wayne relied on Army helicopters rather than a stagecoach or horses to transport the good guys through Indian territory. Nevertheless, the siege of the Special Forces camp literally resembled thousands of Indian sieges that had long been a staple of Hollywood westerns. And, as in those films, the struggle in Vietnam pitted white men against colored men, in this instance, yellow men rather than red men; and as David Halberstam noted, the conflict in Vietnam had produced a switch in roles. Americans no longer universally perceive themselves as the good guys in the struggle. It just might be that we had become the many bad guys surrounding a few good guys. Moreover, the war offered no easy way out for Americans; it had become too complex and impersonal for pat solutions. Consequently, Wayne could not solve the problems of Vietnam with a sudden burst of violence in the last reel of *The Green Berets* as he could in most of his previous roles.[41]

The film's epic size also worked against Wayne's being able to play his typical character. Most of his movies had relied on the Wayne image and his physical presence to carry the story. Trying to direct the film and at the same time act in it, Wayne now had to compete for star billing with helicopters, planes, and all the other instruments of modern war. In the end, he succeeded only in becoming lost in the cast of thousands and military gadgetry. Audiences came away from the film remembering the spectacular firefight and the Vietcong general being snatched by plane far more than any of Wayne's actions. To be sure, like so many of his western characters, Wayne heads off into the sunset at the end of the film. Symbolizing the difficulty he had in finding the proper dramatic direction, however, Wayne's sun is setting in the east, into the South China Sea.

Despite such geographic errors, creative problems inherent in the script, the controversial nature of the subject, and virtually unanimously poor reviews, *The Green Berets* became a box-office hit. Confounding critics and Hollywood insiders who had predicted the film would flop, it brought in $8.7 million in film rentals during the first six months of its run. Against a production cost of $6.1 million, *The Green Berets* generated a total domestic theatrical film rental of $9.75 million, which constituted Warner Brothers's share of the theater box office for the United States and Canada. Foreign distribution and sales to television brought in additional revenues.[42]

The film's success confirmed Wayne's statement that although he had made it "from a hawk's point of view," he had also made it "strictly for entertainment." At the same time he credited the criticism of the movie with helping to make it successful: "Luckily for me, they overkilled it. *The Green Berets* would have been successful regardless of what the critics did, but it might have taken the public longer to find out about the picture if they hadn't made so much noise about it." Irrespective of the artistic merit of the movie, most reviewers directed their criticism more at Wayne's hawkish views than at the film as entertainment. And John Wayne's long-established reputation gave him an advantage over the critics' opinions.[43]

Ironically, the Vietnam War itself was to mark the beginning of the end of America's glorification of war and the virtue of dying for one's country, ideals at the core of the Wayne image. Nevertheless, Wayne and his image emerged from the controversies not only unscathed but seemingly more popular than ever. Despite its box-office success, however, *The Green Berets* did not encourage other filmmakers to use Vietnam as a subject for military movies, given the growing antiwar sentiment in the country during the second half of the 1960s. At the same time, Hollywood did continue to make movies about World War II. Though their numbers declined, the size and cost of the films generally increased as studios attempted to lure people away from their television sets with "spectaculars."

Apart from a few low-budget films such as *Beach Red*, most American-produced combat movies, including *In Harm's Way* (1965), *The Battle of the Bulge* (1965), *The Dirty Dozen* (1967), *The Devil's Brigade* (1968), and *The Bridge at Remagen* (1969), became large-scale projects. Likewise, European filmmakers were turning out spectaculars such as *Operation Crossbow* (1965), *Where Eagles Dare* (1968), and *The Battle of Britain* (1969), which focused on the Allies' fight against Hitler. With the exceptions of *In Harm's Way*, which Otto Preminger shot on location in Pearl Harbor, and *The Devil's Brigade*, partially shot in the United States, the Pentagon provided little or no assistance to the American productions filmed in Europe. The lack of World War II equipment by the mid-1960s, not problems with the stories, limited the participation of the armed services in the projects made overseas.

In most cases, retired officers who had fought in the war could arrange directly with a studio to work as technical advisors on a production. Moreover, following the release of Arthur Sylvester's new regulations in 1964, Hollywood had become reluctant to approach the Defense Department for assistance. A Preminger might ignore normal channels, scream a little, and obtain cooperation. Most filmmakers, however, did not want to submit scripts, do revisions, and go through red tape, preferring instead to negotiate for assistance with countries such as Spain, Italy, and Austria, which had World War II equipment and men available for rent. Spain had even compiled a thick price list covering every type of military hardware; their price for a soldier depended on his rank.

Despite the lack of Pentagon assistance and supervision, the image of the American military in these productions did not radically differ from the earlier portraits: the military always demonstrated competence and patriotism and, of course, always defeated Hitler's Germany. To be sure, *The Dirty Dozen* did not portray a group of soldiers about whom the Army would want to boast. Nevertheless, historical basis existed for a story about a unit made up of soldiers convicted of serious crimes; the men were to perform a highly danger-ous mission in return for their freedom. The military itself had cooperated on films that had portrayed units of misfits who become rehabilitated through their combat experi-ences. In *Twelve O'Clock High,* for example, General Savage ordered one of his planes named *The Leper Colony* and manned with a crew comprised of the squadron's losers and oddballs. Although the men do not resemble in the least the rapists and murderers who form *The Dirty Dozen,* little dramatic difference existed between their becoming one of the best crews in Savage's group and Lee Marvin's suicide squad successfully destroying a German High Command pleasure retreat.

With its more limited scope and identifiable people, *The Devil's Brigade* did not have criminals as heroes. Made with Pentagon assistance, the film portrayed the actual story of a unit of American rejects who join with a highly disciplined group of Canadian soldiers to assault a virtually impregnable German position high on a mountain. Shot near the actual battle site in Italy and in the mountains of Utah, the film received armed forces coopera-tion in Europe and National Guard assistance in the United States. In Utah, a National Guard engineering unit bulldozed a road to the mountain used in recreating the actual assault, helped build the fortress, and then participated in the filming. The resulting com-bat sequence captured the intensity of the struggle to the satisfaction of the commander of the actual unit, who also served as the movie's technical advisor.[44]

The Bridge at Remagen, also based on an actual event, had less success in duplicating history. Although the book's author, Congressman Ken Hechler, wrote a solid work of history based on primary documents and interviews with those who fought on both sides, he acknowledged that the movie could have turned out more accurate. The problem had nothing to do with the lack of Pentagon assistance. David Wolper, the producer and a highly respected documentary filmmaker, chose to fictionalize virtually all the characters. In doing so, he transformed the soldiers into Hollywood stereotypes, and not very inter-esting ones at that. Moreover, Hechler said that the filmmakers "hoked up" some of the scenes with excessive military action that had not occurred during the capture of the Ludendorff Bridge over the Rhine River. He particularly objected to a fictional firefight at the end of the picture that he thought served no purpose. If the film had not been "so Mickey Moused" up, Hechler believed it would have made a more exciting drama.[45]

While he also disagreed with many of the details in the script, Cecil Roberts, the technical advisor and a retired colonel, thought that "the major events were there. The personalities as portrayed in the script were simply fiction for the most part." Roberts did try to hold down the excessiveness of the filmmakers, but he recalled that director John Guillermin regularly disagreed with him over the size of the explosions: "He always wanted one tank round to destroy a complete building." In the face of Guillermin's claim of "dramatic licence," Roberts admitted that he usually lost the arguments.[46]

When active-duty officers such as Gen. Leonard Fribourg (on *Sands of Iwo Jima*) and Adm. James Shaw (on *The Caine Mutiny*) served as technical advisors on Pentagon-assisted films, they usually had significant leverage in supervising the accuracy of the film's military aspects. Filming in Czechoslovakia and, after Soviet troops moved into that country, in Italy, Wolper had not received Defense Department assistance and so did not have to work under Pentagon regulations regarding historical and technical veracity. As a result, Roberts saw his role as concerned primarily "with the uniforms and vehicles and the authenticity of the scenes from a military point of view," rather than matters of story, personality, and literal accuracy.[47]

Frills and fictionalized drama notwithstanding, *The Bridge at Remagen* probably captured the drama of the American dash to the Rhine in March 1945 and the capture of the last surviving bridge across the river inside Germany. The Ludendorff Bridge, which remained standing for ten crucial days after its seizure, enabled the Allies to establish a beachhead in Germany and so bring the war to a quicker ending. Wolper's film fictionalized the characters on both sides to facilitate the drama and avoid problems in obtaining releases from the battle's actual participants. Nevertheless, Hechler said that the filmmakers had patterned most of the cinematic characters on real people, and those who had fought for the bridge or read his book could readily identify perhaps 75 percent of the combatants. Of course, most viewers had not taken part in the battle or read the book and so had no way of judging the accuracy of the film's rendering of history.[48]

Some of the battle's survivors did ultimately object to what they saw as inaccurate portrayals. Even so, Hechler found nothing in the script that he felt would have made Pentagon cooperation impossible in terms of historical veracity. Nevertheless, when Wolper submitted the script for comment to the Army's Public Relations Office in Los Angeles, officers gave him an unofficial opinion that assistance would not be forthcoming as long as the script included a scene in which an American sergeant takes binoculars and a wrist watch from a dead German soldier. Wolper "was not shocked" by the opinion, believing that the military should not assist on a film it finds "violently anti-Army."[49]

While Wolper and the Army might have resolved the problem if the producer had formally requested assistance from Washington, he had no reason to do so, given the film's requirements and his means of satisfying them. Wolper said the movie needed "one thing more important than any men or equipment: a bridge. We found the bridge in Czechoslovakia." Wolper did admit that if he had found a suitable bridge in the United States, he would then have had to deal with the Pentagon to obtain military equipment: "I don't know what would have happened. It would have been difficult."[50]

Finding the bridge had required considerable effort. After a year and a half of searching, Wolper came upon the Davie Bridge, which he felt looked like the Ludendorff Bridge and was located on a site that resembled Remagen, Germany, in 1945. (In fact, the Czech bridge bore no resemblance to the bridge over the Rhine.) Fortunately for him, Czechoslovakia was experiencing the Dubcek reform movement to liberalize the country, and government officials wanted Western contacts and money. Wolper was therefore able to reach agreements with the government to use soldiers to play both Americans and Germans and to have river traffic suspended during the filming.[51]

The selection of Czechoslovakia, more than problems with the script or lack of appropriate equipment, made American military assistance impossible as well as unnecessary.

(Above) David Wolper hastily constructed a bridge set at Castel Gondolfo, Italy, for *Bridge at Remagen* after the film company was forced to flee from Czechoslovakia because of the 1968 Russian invasion. (Right) Director John Guillermin (foreground with cap, next to camera) prepares one of the closing shots in *Bridge at Remagen* as Bradford Dillman and Ben Gazzara study the script.

Wolper could readily obtain American uniforms and weapons from costume rental agencies in Europe and the United States. The producer found German uniforms and weapons available in Czechoslovakia, since its film and television industries often produced films about World War II and Hitler's occupation of the country. For his tanks and other heavy equipment, Wolper turned to the Austrian Ministry of Defense, which rented him World War II matériel, purchased as war surplus from the United States after the war. The production company then shipped the collected arsenal of equipment and supplies into Czechoslovakia in May 1968 without difficulty shortly before filming began.[52]

The dated armaments, trained soldiers, and a reasonable facsimile of the Remagen area enabled the director to depict the essence, if not the complete accuracy, of the capture of the Ludendorff Bridge. In recreating the atmosphere of combat, Guillermin had unexpected assistance from the Soviet Union. With the filming only two-thirds completed, Russian armies moved into Czechoslovakia to crush the liberal Dubcek government. Congressman Hechler, then on location as a part-time technical advisor, managed to leave the

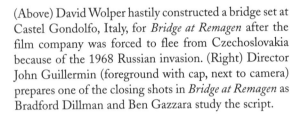

Austrian tanks were rented and brought to Davle, Czechoslovakia, during the filming of David Wolper's *The Bridge at Remagen* (1969).

country on one of the last planes out of Prague. The film company itself left in a fleet of taxis the afternoon of August 22 and walked across the border into Austria that evening in a rainstorm. The producer then negotiated in Vienna with a Russian general and a representative of the Czechoslovakian government for return of the Austrian tanks and heavy equipment, which went by train from Prague back to Austria without incident.[53] Ultimately, Wolper completed the movie at sites in Austria, Germany, and Italy, and a second unit returned to the bridge at Davie, where they filmed some long shots with the tanks, armor, and Czech soldiers as extras, all performing under the watchful eyes of the Russian Army.

Despite the unintentional warlike ambience, the equipment, and the men, all of which contributed relatively realistic atmosphere, *Bridge at Remagen* ultimately failed as drama. To Congressman Hechler, the filmmakers' efforts to expand a singular event into a large-scale spectacular caused the second half of the movie to drag. Wolper disagreed with Hechler's reasoning as to why his film failed at the box office, saying Hechler was "totally incorrect." Instead, the producer blamed the recent release of other World War II films, including *Castle Keep,* as well as the Vietnam War for the lack of interest in *Bridge at Remagen.*[54]

With all due respect to Wolper, the film failed because it did not build up tensions by focusing on the American forces racing against time to capture the bridge before the Germans could blow it up. Instead, the story jumps back and forth between the two sides, and detailing the decisions and actions of the opposing forces so carefully dissipates the drama inherent in the action, and the capture of the bridge becomes anticlimatic. At the same time, individuals become lost in the sweep of events, and the result became an impersonal, two-dimensional visual image that leaves the audience uninvolved in the story.

Patton did not suffer from this deficiency. Like *The Battle of the Bulge,* the film contained spectacular scenes of large-scale combat, also filmed in Spain, using the same tanks and equipment. It even portrayed some of the same history. However, it had a narrower and sharper story than the earlier film. In focusing only on the wartime exploits of Gen. George S. Patton Jr., the film avoided the pitfalls of most cinematic biographies, which tend to clutter the story with unnecessary personal entanglements. An authoritative study of the military career of one of America's great generals, the film never lost sight of its subject. Consequently, George C. Scott became Patton to those people who had never met the general. And to many of the men who knew the general, Scott became more like Patton than Patton himself. Gen. James Gavin, who knew Patton "awfully well," explained that this happened "because the movie seemed to accentuate his idiosyncrasies, and in that way somehow the real Patton was left behind."[55]

Patton succeeded as a biography and as a war movie because of Scott's study of the general and his virtuosity as an actor, because of a superb script, and because of excellent direction that combined Scott's acting with effective use of the Spanish military and locales. Most important, however, the film became more than the sum of its parts because the project represented a labor of love for the producer, Frank McCarthy. McCarthy had served as secretary to Army Chief of Staff Gen. George C. Marshall during the war and eventually rose to the rank of brigadier general. After the war, he became a film industry executive and later a staff producer at Twentieth Century Fox. McCarthy had come to know Patton during the war when he accompanied General Marshall on his trips abroad. Of all the generals McCarthy had known, he believed Patton was "the guy you ought to do a movie about." He thought he could possibly prove mathematically that Patton became the most successful Army field commander of World War II. More important for moviemaking purposes, he said that Patton "was very theatrical and very flamboyant and had several Achilles heels. All these things put together made for fine drama."[56]

Other filmmakers, of course, recognized the potential for a major motion picture about Patton. In October 1950 Columbia Pictures had advised Don Baruch's office of its plans to produce a movie about the general. Clair Towne wrote back to studio representative Ray Bell explaining that Patton's widow had turned over to her brother Frederick Ayer "full authority . . . on all matters pertaining to the use of the General's life in stories, magazine articles, and motion pictures." Consequently, Towne wrote that "it appears desireable [*sic*] for you to contact Mr. Ayer." When Mrs. Patton "indicated an unwillingness to see the picture made," the Army's head of public information wrote a personal letter to her suggesting she should consider the proposal, but she rejected the idea and Columbia dropped the project.[57]

Then, immediately after Patton's widow died in late September 1953, Warner Brothers seized on the moment to request a priority for its project to produce a Patton film, which the DoD Office of Public Information registered on October 1. In a meeting with all the Washington-based studio representatives on October 5, Gen. Frank Dorn, the Army head of public relations, announced that Warner Brothers had obtained an initial priority on the Patton story. He indicated that the Army hoped the studio would at least have the goodwill of the Patton family, if not an actual release, which he acknowledged it would not need legally if the picture did not mention the family. Nevertheless, Dorn said that if Warner Brothers obtained at least the goodwill of the family, the Army would not throw a "monkeywrench" into the deal.[58]

The studio then attempted to reach the family, first through friends and then directly. W.L. Guthrie, Warner's long-time military liaison, advised studio executives including Jack Warner that he had "gone all out on this deal" but had not yet contacted the Pattons since he "figured it would be very bad to call them before, I might say, the body was cold." On October 6 Guthrie did talk with retired general Harry Semmes, to whom Mrs. Patton had given General Patton's diaries so that he could write a biography. Semmes described the diaries as "very exciting" and told Guthrie that Patton's son, now designated George Patton Jr., was going to spend the coming weekend at his house and would discuss the proposed film with him. Then on the ninth, Guthrie reached Patton junior directly.[59]

Guthrie found the young Patton "to be a very much confused young fellow," who wanted to follow his mother's wishes in regard to any film "to the letter." At the same time, while realizing that any story about General Patton might be in the public domain, he indicated that he was having his attorneys look into the legalities of the matter. He also told Guthrie that he did not know a "living actor" who could portray his father "in any dignified motion picture and that he would not desire anything portrayed about his father unless it was dignified." Having heard rumors that the studio was considering John Wayne to portray the general, Patton Jr. told Guthrie he believed "his little baby could portray his father better than John Wayne." In the end, he told Guthrie he would get back to him shortly, and Guthrie advised the studio that he thought the Army and the Defense Department "would state the facts" to Patton when he visited Washington and convince him to agree to the production.[60]

It never happened, in part, according to McCarthy, because Warner Brothers and other studios "had the bad grace" to approach the family even before Mrs. Patton's funeral. In any case, the family objected so strenuously to the making of any film that Warner Brothers soon abandoned the project. Patton's daughter, Ruth Totten, later explained, "The publicity that the press gave him for years was so disgusting and so unfair that we could not imagine a media [*sic*] as vulgar as the movies giving him any kind of a break at all. We had a mental block that they would picture him as a coarse, cursing, nosepicking, belching, gorilla of a man, none of which things he was." Less emotionally, the family was to express its concern that any film would portray the widely publicized slapping incidents in which Patton struck two shell-shocked soldiers in Italy and almost lost his command. Although the worry that any motion picture would reveal Patton's intimate relationship with his niece by marriage remained unspoken, the fear that a film might portray the extramarital affair existed implicitly in the record of the family's ongoing opposition to any production.[61]

Despite the obstacles that the family had thrown up early on, Frank McCarthy had begun his own nineteen-year odyssey to bring Patton to life on the screen in October 1951, when he had sent a memo to Darryl Zanuck, then head of production at Twentieth Century Fox, proposing a film about Patton. Now a reserve officer, McCarthy had wide-ranging contacts within the Army and had produced one critically acclaimed, if not financially successful, war film, *Decision before Dawn* (1950). Although Zanuck quickly approved his proposal, McCarthy met with immediate problems. The Army expressed fear that any story about Patton would necessarily be derogatory in light of the general's reputation as a rebellious man who had slapped soldiers, had remained a difficult subordinate throughout the war, had wanted to fight the Soviet Union once Germany had capitulated, had made anti-Semitic comments, and had refused to de-Nazify Bavaria.[62]

Given the opposition from the Army and the family, Twentieth Century Fox did not pursue the project. Nevertheless, McCarthy continued his interest in doing a Patton film, and over the next decade he explored possible approaches to the family through friends and military acquaintances even though the Pentagon reaffirmed the Warner Brothers priority in January 1956. In response to an inquiry from Twentieth Century Fox, Don Baruch stated that his office had "concluded that there is no reason to vacate the presently held priority by Warner Brothers." At the same time, he advised Fox, "The Department of the Army reiterates its desire to respect the wishes of the Patton family and does not care to consider cooperation without such consent. It is understood that the Patton family does not care to have a film made in which an actor portrays the General. Consequently, the project is at a standstill."[63]

McCarthy thought Baruch was "completely wrong" in his conclusion: "Since Warners have had their priority for two years and more . . . and have only succeeded in lousing the whole thing up, we should certainly have our opportunity to try." Even so, both Warner Brothers and McCarthy continued their pursuit of the family's approval of their projects. In March 1957 McCarthy wrote to Buddy Adler from Washington saying he had learned that Warners had continued to pressure Patton Jr. as recently as two weeks earlier: "He is apparently very sore with Warners but can't get them to leave him alone." He advised the Fox producer that he had learned that Patton and his sister had promised their mother "on her deathbed" that they would "do everything possible to frustrate the production" of a Patton movie. However, McCarthy doubted that she would have "extracted any deathbed promise from her children" even though she "was violent on the subject."[64]

Not surprisingly, therefore, McCarthy resorted to his own brand of pressure on the Patton children. In June 1959 he advised Adler that he had scheduled a meeting with Ruth Totten to discuss the possibility of the family's approving a Patton film, while acknowledging that she had already told him that all members "are dead set against her father's ever appearing as a character in a motion picture." Nevertheless, he believed "there is no harm in having a throw at her anyway. If I tackle each member of the family as and when I can see them, we might some day make a dent." He also told Adler he was doing that with the assumptions that the studio would undertake production as soon as the family gave permission, that the film would portray Patton "in only the most favorable light," that the studio would give the family "very broad approvals," and that Patton Jr. could serve as technical advisor.[65]

Following the meeting, McCarthy penned a memorandum for the record. He reported that Mrs. Totten had said she and her brother remained "strongly opposed" to any film about their father. They were "deeply hurt by the publicity which followed certain of General Patton's war and post-war actions, particularly the slapping incident." McCarthy wrote that they felt "virtually all the publicity toward the end of his life was bad and that this hurt him and hurt the conclusion of his Army career." Mrs. Totten also told him: "If you want a good picture, wait until you get a chance to read the Patton diaries." She said that Scribners had turned them down for publication because they contained seventeen potential libel suits "in the first chapter," including "some spicy facts regarding General Eisenhower." In light of the harassment of the Warner Brothers representatives at the time of their mother's death, she indicated the family had "only contempt" for the studio. However, because the family considered Twentieth Century Fox's *A Man Called Peter* the best film biography they had ever seen, they would only deal with that studio if they ever changed their minds about approving a story about their father.[66]

Despite this positive comment, McCarthy did little more on the project until November 1960, when he wrote to Don Baruch's office inquiring about the old Warner Brothers priority. Baruch advised him that Warner Brothers was no longer interested in the project. He also informed the Army of McCarthy's renewed interest in a Patton biography and suggested that the service should consider cooperating on a film even if the family was still opposed. McCarthy, though, was not yet willing to proceed without the family's approval.[67]

By this time McCarthy had become a brigadier general in the Army Reserves, with his active duty assignment as deputy chief of information in Washington. During his two weeks of duty in 1961, McCarthy spent considerable time convincing his boss that the Army should allow Twentieth Century Fox to make a Patton film. Apart from the obvious fact of his fortuitous Army connections and sympathies, he argued that the Army had no right to oppose the movie, since Patton's military career had entered the public domain. He also suggested that the Army was on shaky ground if its opposition continued only as a favor to Patton's family.[68]

His arguments and the Defense Department's now-favorable position began to "warily" change the Army's stance. In July 1961 the service informed the Patton family that it would probably cooperate with Fox if the studio submitted a suitable script. At a meeting the same month, the Army told McCarthy it could assist on the film and that no legal liability would result if he proceeded without the family's permission. The Army nevertheless encouraged him to seek their "blessing."[69]

The family, however, remained adamantly opposed to any film. Through its attorney, it advised Spyros Skouras, president of Twentieth Century Fox, on September 11, 1961, that its position had not changed from that of the early 1950s. The lawyer wrote that the family objected "not only on the ground of possible invasion of privacy but, equally important, on the ground that it is their considered opinion that such motion picture could not portray the character of General Patton as he actually was." As a result, they regarded "the making of such picture with great distress and assure your company that such motion picture will be most important to them, and further assure your company that they have opposed strenuously and continue to oppose strenuously the production of such a picture so distasteful to each of them."[70]

When the controversy over the Pentagon's assistance to *The Longest Day* erupted in Washington the same week, Arthur Sylvester informed the Army that if cooperation on a Patton film was "going to involve any large use of troops, I would back away from it at this time." And despite the Army's conclusion that the Patton family had no grounds for a court case, he expressed concern over the family's threat of legal action.[71]

With Sylvester's reluctance to commit the Pentagon to another major production and the continued opposition from Patton's family, McCarthy made little headway in the next months. Consequently, in February 1962 he advised Don Baruch that he was experiencing an unexpected delay in developing a script but that the research was progressing on both Patton's military career and the accumulation of appropriate anecdotal material. Because of the studio's own financial problems and its failure to win approval from Patton's family, Fox shelved the project by the summer. When the studio did not answer Don Baruch's June 1963 inquiry about the status of the film, the Pentagon canceled Fox's priority in July. Shortly afterward, McCarthy moved to Universal Studios as a staff producer.[72]

The appearance of Ladislas Farago's *Patton: Ordeal and Triumph* (1964) rekindled Fox's interest in a filmed biography. Darryl Zanuck, now in control of the studio, had been looking for a military subject with which to duplicate the box-office success of *The Longest Day.* Having had a year to digest the Pentagon's new regulations governing cooperation, Zanuck and his son Richard, now in charge of production, bought the rights to Farago's book, and in March 1965 they announced that Frank McCarthy was returning to Fox to produce the "major budget" biography.[73]

Although *Patton: Ordeal and Triumph* served as the basic reference source in developing the screenplay, McCarthy also drew on his original research for the project and, even more important, on his personal contacts, including correspondence and visits with former president Dwight D. Eisenhower. During one meeting in Palm Springs, Eisenhower asked McCarthy why he had chosen to portray Patton rather than Omar Bradley. McCarthy later pointed out that Eisenhower had answered his own question in his book *At Ease,* when he wrote that of all the ground commanders he had known or read about, he "would put Omar Bradley in the highest classification. In every aspect of military command . . . Brad was outstanding . . . Patton was a master of fast and overwhelming pursuit. Headstrong by nature and fearlessly aggressive, Patton was the more colorful of the two, compelling attention by his mannerisms as much as his deeds. Bradley, however, was master of every military maneuver, lacking only in the capacity—possibly the willingness—to dramatize himself." According to McCarthy, Patton's dramatic qualities, his spectacular military success, his flamboyance, and his maverick nature all made him "ideal theatrical material"[74]

In early 1966 General Eisenhower sent McCarthy a "Personal and confidential" letter that provided a "personal evaluation of my old friend." He described a friendship that had "remained strong and close" despite the "many differences of opinion" engendered by Patton's "volatile character, accompanied by a strong trait of exhibitionism." Eisenhower stated that only his intervention on several occasions had kept Patton in positions of command during the war: "Indeed the most serious of these occasions never had any publicity whatsoever."[75]

Eisenhower felt that Patton's "temperament made him a headliner in the press but he was not the kind of all-around, balanced, competent, and effective commander that Bradley was. . . . But he was a genius in pursuit. Recognizing this, I was determined to keep him in my war organization no matter how often the public might scream for his scalp because of some publicized and foolish episode." Eisenhower submitted that Patton "disliked, intensely, the heavy fighting necessary to break through, and because of this I did not even use him during the slugging match that finally brought about the breakout from the beachhead in late July 1944. . . . [But Patton] was a natural to put in for exploiting the weaknesses of the Nazi forces on our right flank" once the Allies had broken through, as he had done in Sicily and as he did after the crossing of the Rhine in 1945. Eisenhower noted that when the Allies "got into dirty ding dong fighting in Moselle and later, when [Patton] was trying to fight his way to the relief of Bastogne, he was apt to become pessimistic and discouraged. In such instances he liked a great deal of moral 'patting on the back.'"[76]

Officers who served with Patton may have disagreed with Eisenhower's judgments, and the film may not have incorporated all of his observations. Nevertheless, his information greatly aided McCarthy's script preparations, and he responded that he agreed "without qualification" with Eisenhower's comments and stated that the script would "reflect General Patton accurately rather than glamorize him unduly or gloss over troublesome incidents which are matters of public record." Acknowledging that Patton's "controversial nature" made him a worthwhile dramatic subject, McCarthy anticipated what was to become the completed film's hallmark: "The best parallel I can think of at the moment—and it is by no means an exact one—is *Lawrence of Arabia*. One left that film intrigued by the character, perhaps understanding him a little better, but certainly not condoning his excesses, which had been amply presented."[77]

In early 1966, however, McCarthy still had a long way to go before he had a screenplay ready to shoot. As a first step after his return to Twentieth Century Fox in 1965, he had begun the process of reestablishing the studio's Defense Department priority for the project. In formally confirming its renewal that July, Don Baruch made it clear that the Defense Department's agreement to grant protection for the project did not constitute a commitment for eventual assistance. He also restated the Army's position that it would "not assist in the making of a film which depicts General Patton in any manner that would detract from the roles and accomplishments of his senior commanders."[78]

Despite the Army's approval of the project, the Patton family's opposition continued. In August their lawyer wrote directly to Secretary of Defense Robert McNamara requesting that the Pentagon "withhold any cooperation or assistance to Twentieth Century Fox or any other motion picture company which may request a priority for the commercial exploitation of the General's life and military career in a motion picture." In responding, the Defense Department's general counsel once again pointed out that Fox did not need consent or cooperation to make the film. He explained that the Pentagon "considers that its cooperation will undoubtedly result in a better picture, since only then will the Department be given the opportunity to review the script for accuracy. . . . [The department] will make every effort to assure that the picture accurately presents the life and military career of General Patton and that it is otherwise in the best interest of the Department."[79]

McCarthy found that producing a script that would satisfy these Defense Department requirements posed a major problem. Although he had initially signed Calder Willingham to write the screenplay in April 1965, nothing came of the effort. By June 1966, he had turned to Francis Ford Coppola, then newly out of the UCLA film school, to write a second draft. McCarthy explained to Richard Zanuck, Fox's head of production, that Coppola "is the most impressive young writer I have met in years. He is standing on the edge of a great screenwriting career, and this view is enthusiastically attested by Ray Stark, who is about to put three of Coppola's scripts into production." The producer said the writer "is intensely interested" in the project and he "impresses me as having the best potential."[80]

Furthermore, McCarthy thought Coppola's youth provided him with an advantage—he would not have recollections of Patton to influence his perspective. Although he did not expect Coppola to finish the new screenplay until early fall, McCarthy also hired William Wyler (*Best Years of Our Lives, Ben Hur*) to direct the film. At the same time, the studio informed Don Baruch that it had budgeted *Patton* at more than $10 million and intended to make it a road show picture in 1967. By November, though, problems with the script and Wyler's availability had combined to push production back at least until the summer of 1967.[81]

In large measure, the delay resulted from disagreements over the script between Wyler and George C. Scott, whom McCarthy had selected to play Patton. Originally, in 1951, McCarthy had envisioned Spencer Tracy in the title role. Later, he considered Burt Lancaster and, despite Patton's son's denigrating comment, John Wayne. In 1962 Darryl Zanuck told McCarthy that he thought Wayne "would be much better than Lancaster," and after seeing him in *The Longest Day* the producer agreed. Then in 1966 Darryl Zanuck screened *The Bible* for McCarthy and told him, "There's your Patton," pointing to Scott, then hidden under the beard of Abraham. Although Scott liked Coppola's script, Wyler didn't. In an attempt to resolve the impasse (conducted through McCarthy, since Scott and Wyler never met or even talked on the phone), McCarthy hired Jim Webb to write a new screenplay by the fall of 1967.[82]

When Webb completed his draft, McCarthy found that he still had the same disagreement between director and star, but this time in reverse. Wyler liked Webb's screenplay, but Scott didn't and said he would not play the part. He wanted to portray Patton "as multifaceted as he really was." Recalling the disagreements over the scripts, Scott explained: "I simply refused to play George Patton as the standard cliche you could get from newspaper clips of the time. I didn't want to play him as a hero just to please the Pentagon, and I didn't want to play him as an obvious, gung ho bully either. I wanted to play every conceivable facet of the man." Scott believed the conflicts during the film's production resulted from "trying to serve too many masters. We had to serve the Pentagon, we had to serve General Bradley and his book, we had to serve the Zanucks. If you ride that many horses at the same time, you're going to have problems."[83]

Frank McCarthy's problem with Scott soon became more exacerbated because of the need to hire a new director. The sixty-four-year-old Wyler decided to resign from the project when he realized that the film, which was to be shot in Spain, would be too physically strenuous for him to do at his age. McCarthy offered the job to Richard Brooks, John Sturges, Henry Hathaway, and Fred Zinnemann, among others.[84] Zinnemann said he turned down the picture because he had already made his military movie (*From Here to Eternity*), was interested in another project, and didn't "have tremendous sympathy and admiration for Patton as a man, aside from his obvious military genius."[85] McCarthy offered Scott's role to Burt Lancaster, Robert Mitchum, Lee Marvin, Rod Steiger, and John Wayne, all of whom turned it down. Although Wayne no longer wanted to be seen hitting a soldier (as he had hit a Marine in *Sands of Iwo Jima*), he later told the producer that he had made a big mistake in that decision. On his part, McCarthy thought that *Patton* would have become a different picture with Wayne in the title role.[86]

At that point, Scott again expressed interest in the role—provided McCarthy would go back to Coppola's script. With this impetus, the producer hired Franklin Schaffner to direct the film and Edmund North to rewrite Coppola's script. North recalled that the script had "brilliant material in it and some brilliant scenes." While saying that Coppola was "a very talented man," North noted he was still "a very inexperienced man at that time." As a result, North explained, "What the script needed was structure and direction. That's really what I was brought in to do. What we tried to do was keep the best of the Coppola material and take off from that and construct a story."[87]

To this end, North began working with Schaffner and McCarthy in mid-June 1968, to tighten the script and add new elements as "necessary or desirable." North, who would never meet with his collaborator, felt that Coppola's original "contribution was as large as it was obvious, and we made every effort to retain the many brilliant things in his script. In addition, his basic approach to the material was the correct one—and that is no mean contribution."[88]

As with any complete rewrite, North said "this one involved a good deal of new creative material. The development of a strong central story line between Patton and Bradley—who served with him, first as subordinate, then as his superior—is one major example." North recalled that the Patton-Bradley story served "as the clothesline, the glue that would hold the whole thing together." The material North needed to achieve this came not only from Coppola's script but also from Farago's book and General Bradley's autobiography, *A Soldier's Story.* He also met daily with Bradley for about a month, going through the script to ensure perfect technical detail.[89]

In October, Bradley, Schaffner, and McCarthy visited the principal battlefields that the filmmakers planned to recreate in the movie. To further ensure accuracy, McCarthy hired retired general Paul Harkins to serve as technical advisor. Harkins, who read five drafts of the screenplay before he agreed to work on the film, had served as Patton's deputy chief of staff from Patton's arrival in Casablanca until his death in 1945. With all this attention to accuracy, McCarthy felt he submitted "an almost perfect" script to the Pentagon in December 1968. With McCarthy readily agreeing to make two minor corrections, the Defense Department approved the script in less than five weeks. McCarthy pointed out, "There wasn't very much they could say," given General Bradley's involvement in and approval of the screenplay.[90]

Although the Pentagon had little to question about the film, other people did ask about the movie's purpose: why was McCarthy making *Patton,* clearly a war movie, while the country was involved in an increasingly unpopular war in Vietnam? When he accepted

George C. Scott, film crew, and military men discuss the re-creation of Patton's landing on Sicily, staged with Pentagon assistance on Crete.

his Academy Award, Edmund North answered, "I hope those who see the picture will agree with me that it is not only a war picture, but a peace picture as well." On his part, Franklin Schaffner saw it simply as an antiwar film.[91]

Even Frank McCarthy, whom North described as being "thoroughly integrated into the military" and as having a different viewpoint, insisted that the film's contents implied an antiwar attitude: "The horrors of war are nothing new. But you can't look at what we shot at Almeria and think of it any other way." McCarthy saw Patton himself as very violent, talking of shooting up the enemy and greasing the treads of tanks with them. Nevertheless, the producer also pointed out that he was "a very genuinely religious man. With women he was very courteous. With people on his immediate staff, he was a martinet, a very tough taskmaster. All of these things put together made a fascinating character for me." *Patton* was clearly a war film, but McCarthy considered that its battle scenes served primarily as the "tapestry in the background," against which the filmmakers could develop Patton's character.[92]

The long process of creating an accurate and dramatic script had not brought about an agreement among McCarthy, Scott, and Schaffner on just how to develop that portrait. With the film his labor of love, McCarthy served as the fulcrum: "I knew Patton and admired him—dramatically, theatrically. I'm not talking about him as a man. Mrs. Roosevelt thought he was a devil with horns. Hedda Hopper thought he was a saint. I wanted to get all the facts into the script." If he succeeded in doing this, McCarthy believed that audiences could judge for themselves the "enigma" that Patton remained long after his death.[93]

Scott created that character through his acting, but he was also concerned with guarding what he considered the authenticity of his portrayal. From books and three thousand feet of film, Scott studied the man he was to interpret: "I watched the way he moved and talked. Some of it I absorbed, some I threw out. For instance, he had a high, squeaky voice, like a football coach. The more excited he got, the higher it got. I didn't use that. People are probably used to my gravel voice and if I tried to use a high little voice it would be silly." His main consideration "was to not distract the audience with eccentric (albeit factual) mannerisms. I didn't want the medium to be more arresting than the message." Scott tried to avoid interjecting his judgments of Patton into his portrayal: "Hell, you get paid for acting, for giving the illusion of believing, not for actually believing. For Chrissakes, no, I didn't believe in what he did any more than I'd believe in the Marquis de Sade or Frank Merriwell! This is a schizoid business to start with. The biggest mistake an actor can make is to try to resolve all the differences between himself and the characters he plays."[94]

Scott did develop an "enormous affection" for Patton, "a feeling of amazement and respect for him," and had as his only goal in his characterization the creation of "a fair and respectful portrait." Given the nature of the man, however, Scott's task sometimes seemed impossible. The ambiguity of Patton's character and actions produced in him mixed feelings about the man, the role, and his own performance: "I studied General Patton as comprehensively as humanly possible. He was a very complicated human being, and I never came to any conclusion about what I wanted the character to say, though everybody thought I did." Scott felt that "Patton actually believed what he was doing was right. . . . But he wasn't a hypocrite. Even though war was all he cared about, it was what he did for a living. It was a profession." Moreover, the actor noted that Patton's war "was unavoidable," not like Vietnam, which the actor called "an obscenity."[95]

In trying to develop the controversial as well as the positive aspects of Patton's character, Scott told McCarthy he did not want to play another Buck Turgidson: "I already

A man of many facets, Patton often took time to pray before and after combat.

played that goddamn part." He also rejected "the glory-hunter cliche. Patton was a mean sonofabitch, but he was also generous to his men." In the end, Scott concluded that he had succeeded in producing a fair portrait: "There are still things about him I hate and things I admire—which makes him a human being, I guess."[96]

To make Patton into a human being, "the point of the whole goddamn thing" in Scott's mind, he had to make himself over externally and keep "screaming" about dramatic aspects of the characterization until he had a script that finally enabled him to capture the "essence" of the man. Although he did not resemble Patton physically, Scott used his body and the art of film makeup to create a realistic impression of the general. He shaved his head daily and used a half-bald hairpiece; he straightened his nose with plastic and net; he had his dentist make false teeth to fit over his own, which lengthened his jaw and simulated Patton's longer, patrician jawline; and he added two moles, even though the one on his left ear was hidden.[97]

The physical transformation was simple compared to developing the character. At one point during the shooting, he complained, "It's an unactable part, and I'm not doing too well. It's an inadequate script, and it's very difficult for me." Scott felt Patton "was misunderstood contemporaneously, and he's misunderstood here—and I'm ashamed of being part of it." As an actor, he said he was doing the best he could "to load the part with pyrotechnics, with smoke screens, with every dirty sneak actor's trick to bring out what I want to bring out, but I'm thoroughly disgusted with the entire project."[98]

Of necessity, Franklin Schaffner had to bear most directly the brunt of Scott's animus against the script and the project. As director, he not only had the responsibility for helping Scott create his role, but also he had to work with the rest of the huge cast while also orchestrating the battle scenes. He was more willing to take dramatic license with certain episodes than Scott, whose only concern was with Patton's character and its visual portrayal. On occasion, Schaffner shot around a controversial scene until Scott had calmed down, or he tried to compromise with him. Scott, who felt Schaffner "did a superb job in an extremely difficult assignment," recalled that the director "was personally kind to me and tolerant of even my worst peccadillos." He said his only real unhappiness with the director resulted from his "apparent lack of clout with Fox."[99]

In fact, *Patton* did not become another 1960s director's film in which the director had total control through the final cut as did *2001: A Space Odyssey* with Stanley Kubrick or *Catch-22* with Mike Nichols. It much more resembled a movie made in the heyday of the Hollywood studio system, a collaboration in which the director's contribution remained only one of several inputs. With *Patton*, inputs also came from Scott, McCarthy, the Zanucks, Generals Bradley and Harkins, and the Pentagon. As a result, Schaffner found it difficult to impose his will on the film, a reality that Scott himself documented.

To illustrate, he cited one key scene in which Patton tells Gen. Lucien K. Truscott Jr., "If your conscience won't let you conduct this operation I will relieve you and let someone else do it." Scott believed that Schaffner was structuring the scene too harshly, which created an image of Patton as a megalomaniac and suggested he had a callous disregard for the lives of his men. The actor also thought it portrayed Patton as vain and self-serving and that it juxtaposed Bradley's humanitarian devotion to his men with Patton's intransigent lack of flexibility and his indifference to the loss of human life. Feeling the scene "was slanderous and false and one-dimensional" and disliking it "so intensely," he refused to play it as written. He said, "My repugnance drove me to the laborious rewriting of the scene, using guidelines of Farago's excellent reconstruction of what actually happened and why."[100]

Frank McCarthy, the producer of *Patton*, checks a shot during filming.

Scott described Schaffner's response as "accommodating, if not enthusiastic," telling the actor that he "did not have the power to alter the text." Scott recounted that McCarthy also "pleaded a similar unfortunate impotence" when he received the proposed changes and "bucked it upstairs to the Zanucks." According to Scott, word came back to "shoot it like it is." In frustration, the actor asked if he could "confer with someone—anyone!" Scott recalled what did not happen next: "Experience has demonstrated a curious phenomenon that years of experience had caused him to label *Executivitis transmigrati*. I have witnessed this grim affliction strike down a number of top brass from time to time. No one can *find* the patient. No one can speak with him on a telephonic communication. The disease sets up a resistance to cablegrams and letters. It induces profound loss of hearing and speech. The hapless victim is too crippled to walk, drive, or fly to the location in an airplane. In fact, he actually *dematerializes* for relatively short albeit harrowing periods of time." Scott went on to explain that the "malodorous symptoms are shortlived. Most cases clear up completely . . . after the crisis of decision has passed, the scene shot, the frustrated and distraught actor (a carcinomic lump in the studio's corporate breast) removed from the premises."[101]

In light of this reality, Scott said he no choice but to speak the lines as originally written. Nevertheless, he found a way to express his displeasure with the scene. With the agreement of Schaffner, he "did it supine. Not only as a private (however impotent) little protest of my own, but in the hope that anyone who ever knew General Patton would recognize the falsity of the technique. To my knowledge, no one ever witnessed Patton lying down either psychologically or physically in a command situation." General Harkins's reaction confirmed Scott's hopes: "Imagine General Patton lying down on a couch. Oh, me!"[102]

Whatever their differences, Schaffner felt that Scott was "the only American who could play the part. He has no strong screen image as a personality and he has the required vigor, anger, and insanity" to become Patton. Schaffner did not begin by admiring the general, but as he read through the research, he found that "one develops an enormous empathy for this man." He saw Patton as "a warrior, a throwback to the 16th century. He was misguided and a man after a headline. He hated peace and wanted to start trouble with the Russians. . . . After the war, he began to fall apart, but we were lucky to have him during the two years that we needed him."[103]

While the script and character development fomented, McCarthy also had to work out the practical aspects of the production. Though the film focused on Patton, the producer realized that it would require visual authenticity. Ironically, despite McCarthy's long negotiations with the Pentagon to get the project approved, the Defense Department actually provided very little assistance during production. Throughout the 1950s, the military's refusal to become involved with a Patton film had effectively prevented any studio from undertaking the project because only the armed forces could then provide the needed tanks and other equipment. By the mid-1960s, the situation had reversed. The services no longer had surplus World War II equipment in any quantity. The Army had changed its position on a Patton film because it knew that a company could now make the movie abroad, and yet the Pentagon could have input into the script only by offering to assist.

McCarthy had decided by June 1966 that Spain offered the only suitable terrain for shooting the bulk of his film. Just as important, given Arthur Sylvester's continued presence as assistant secretary of defense for public affairs, Spain offered for rent the only available army, World War II tanks, and other equipment needed to make *Patton.* The Spanish government had received the tanks in exchange for American air and naval bases there and, unlike other recipients of obsolete equipment, the Spanish military had maintained it in excellent condition. The Spanish Army also had some German equipment dating from Franco's friendship with Hitler.

Seeking the use of these men and weapons, McCarthy took Coppola's original script to Spanish officials, only to have them deny the request for assistance. According to Spanish military authorities, the screenplay defamed Patton and so discredited soldiers everywhere. McCarthy soon discovered that the translation of the script, done at UCLA, was "perfectly terrible." Once he had a new translation made with the help of a retired bilingual Spanish general, military authorities readily agreed to provide help on the film. When he asked about the cost of such assistance, the military replied, "That's easy," and produced a mimeographed memorandum stating rates per day for each soldier by rank. McCarthy also paid for transportation, gasoline for the tanks and other vehicles, and subsistence for the soldiers while they worked on the film. Ultimately, about $6 million of the film's $12.5 million cost went to the Spanish Army. But in return, McCarthy got his combating armies.[104]

Although *Patton* remains first of all a character study, the combat sequences provide the framework within which the actors function and stand in the first rank of Hollywood war movies. As often happens in movie production, Schaffner did not shoot the screenplay

Filming one of the panoramic shots of Patton's advance in Sicily, on location in southern Spain.

in chronological order: he actually filmed the last battle first. In early February 1969, Schaffner and his crew went to Segovia in central Spain to create Patton's daring dash across France to relieve the siege at Bastogne. The film company had to wait a week for enough snow to fall in order for them to duplicate the wintery conditions in Belgium in December 1944. Unlike the soldiers in *The Battle of the Bulge,* Schaffner's army looks cold because the men felt cold. With this sequence done, the crew went to the Pamplona area to shoot Patton's campaign across France into Germany, and then to Almeria in southernmost Spain to film the battles of Kasserine Pass and El Guettar and the Sicily invasion. Schaffner completed the principal photography by the end of May. According to General Harkins, the goal in all this location work was to create as realistic battle scenes as possible.[105]

To accomplish this, Schaffner had practically a whole army at his disposal—in military terms, he filmed *Patton* at infantry battalion strength. The Air Force consisted of four Heinkels, four Messerschmidts, six T-6s, three Nords, and one observation plane, and the armor of thirty-four German Tiger Tanks (converted M-48s) and twenty American M-41s and M-42s. The special-effects crew made its usual contribution, blowing up jeeps, burning tanks, and simulating airplane strafing. Schaffner received additional help from the sultan of Morocco, who loaned him his ten thousand-man honor guard, colorfully uniformed, with horses and camels richly decorated, to recreate the review that the sultan had staged to honor Patton for liberating his country. Schaffner also went to Crete to film with Navy assistance an amphibious landing for the black and white "newsreel" shots of Patton and Bradley coming ashore in Sicily. Finally, the film company went to Knutsford, England, to shoot Patton's controversial speech there in 1944, in which he warned of the threat he perceived Russia posed to the West.[106]

With the exception of the few simulated newsreel segments, Schaffner shot *Patton* in seventy-millimeter, Dimension 150, with color by Delux. The process produced an awesome sense of depth and grandeur, especially in the long, open battlefield shots. Despite the antiwar material, McCarthy found that in these scenes, the very beauty of the pictures tended to dissipate the feeling of horror that the images of death and destruction created. Moreover, because the filmmakers reproduced the battle sequences as giant, impersonal panoramas rather than hand-to-hand, small-unit struggles, the viewer ultimately becomes detached from any sense of war's brutality.

Only when Patton walks through the aftermath of the battle at Kasserine Pass in February 1943, and then through shattered American tanks following a firefight during the advance across Europe in 1944, does the war become personal. However, if any feeling emerges from the sweeping vistas of combat, it is the impression that war can become beautiful, whether fought in the boiling desert or the freezing snow. The vastness of the landscapes reduces to virtually nothing the conflicting armies, the tanks, the civilians caught up in war. As a result, the audience's attention is focused on one man, George C. Scott, who becomes Patton and totally dominates the film in a great screen performance.

To Franklin Schaffner, contributing to the success of this performance, rather than staging the huge battle scenes, became the most impressive task he had to face. He saw *Patton* as "the personal story . . . the intimate story of a man involved in great events." More important, he considered that man "our necessary evil." To Frank McCarthy, Patton remained an "enigma." Karl Malden, who portrayed General Bradley, would not have wanted to serve under Patton, but he felt "it was lucky he was on our side." And within George C. Scott's characterization rest all these interpretations, all these reactions to Patton, the general and the man.[107]

When he began the project, McCarthy had hoped he could present a many-faceted Patton, a man in whom people could see what they wanted, and he believed he had succeeded. Although he considered *Patton* a war film, "because it had battles in it," he also left it up to the viewer to decide whether it should stand as a war film or an antiwar film. He thought people came out having "fulfilled their own wishes as to what they wanted to see. Some people came out saying, 'What an antiwar picture,' meaning wasn't it grueling, wasn't he rough. Other people came out saying 'If we just had somebody like that in Vietnam.'" McCarthy himself disagreed with both North and Schaffner, who thought they had made an antiwar movie.[108]

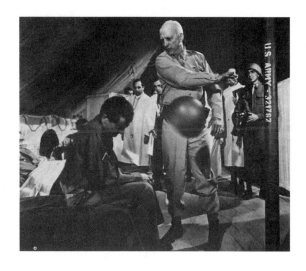

George C. Scott re-creates the slapping incident, Patton's most controversial action.

Ironically, McCarthy himself remained ambivalent about what kind of film he had ultimately created. He contended that his first purpose had been to make an entertainment movie, not a war film. He wanted to depict "a close-up portrayal of this man. Patton was the most explosive commander in the war, or perhaps in military history. He was pious and profane, brutal and kind—and we show him with all his faults as well as virtues." Nevertheless, the producer conceded that once "you say this is a military man and a war, you instantly evoke a feeling of urgency." Although he disagreed with Schaffner and North about the film's thrust, he did insist that the graphic filming could serve as antiwar material: "The horrors of war are nothing new. But you can't look at what we shot at Almeria and think of it any other way."[109]

Even though Edmund North has always seen the film as making an antiwar statement, he admits, "I see other interpretations possible." Patton's own personality, his ambiguities and beliefs, all of which Scott captured, contributed to these divergent reactions. North said he had attempted "to be as objective as I could in whatever contribution I made to the film. The easy thing to do would have been to make a monster. All the material in the world was available." He recalled that he constantly had to catch himself and say, "But, wait a minute. He also did this which was positive and good and necessary." In summing up his feelings, North said he felt that the "strongest comment the picture makes is that war is the kind of business that requires 'this' kind of man. I think this is a commentary of the institutions of war itself, condemnatory of its brutality, mindless glory-seeking, and insensitivity to the value of human life."[110]

Whether people actually came away from *Patton* perceiving this commentary and so seeing the film as an antiwar statement remains another matter. The blood and gore became too beautiful and too remote to create a sense of revulsion. More important, the combat sequences conveyed a sense of the excitement rather than the horror of war. At times, Patton muses on the negative aspects of combat, the death of good men, the waste of energy. However, from his opening monologue onward, Patton sees war as an adventure for himself and his men, a game to be played and won. Despite the losses, he can't help but admit, "I love it. God help me, I do love it so." If the film had ended with Patton's fatal accident shortly after the war's end, his death would have reinforced the images of death and destruction throughout the film. But at the close, *Patton* leaves audiences with the image of a triumphant, if restless, general and a glorious victory in a necessary war.

The film would undoubtedly have made its comments on war and brutality much more powerfully if Darryl Zanuck had permitted Schaffner to shoot two scenes that North had included in his script. In one that George C. Scott described as "beautifully written," Patton becomes so "revolted" by his examination of a death camp that he forces the local citizens to inspect it one by one and clean it up. The hamlet's mayor returns to his office and commits suicide. Scott said, "I had seen Patton's face countless times in the newsreel footage as he emerged from the ovens—his eyes wet, struggling to control his gorge, a handkerchief held to his mouth, and the most chilling expression of revulsion coupled with vengeance I have ever beheld in a human being's eyes. It could easily have been the paramount sequence in the film—perhaps any film." In reply to Scott's inquiry about why the scenes were eliminated, Schaffner told him that Zanuck felt they were inappropriate because "we've seen that sort of thing before."[111]

North's concluding scene, which Zanuck also eliminated, would have created a strong final impact and antiwar statement by focusing on the victims of the conflict. North explained that his script called for a closing shot tight on Patton's grave in the huge American Military Cemetery in Luxembourg: "From his grave the camera was to pull slowly back and upward, finally including the graves of all the 6,000 dead of the Third Army. I thought then—and I think now—that this would have been the right ending, one that would have made a powerful statement. But I couldn't get anyone to agree with me. They said it was too downbeat."[112]

The ending aside, if *Patton* had appeared any time before the mid-1960s, people would have seen it as simply another glorification of a great military leader and a confirmation of America's military superiority in the world. Because it appeared while the Vietnam War still raged, *Patton* offered the viewer other options. Having been exposed to antiwar rhetoric and an increasingly unpopular war, people had new perspectives on war and the military. Perhaps for the first time, they could see the negative aspects in a Patton-type character and his philosophy of combat. In addition, however, at a time when people were beginning to realize that the United States was suffering a defeat in Vietnam, *Patton* offered a ready explanation for the quagmire in which the military found itself caught. If only we had a Patton, we could go through the North Vietnamese and Vietcong as Patton had gone through the Germans. Edmund North provided his own answer to why people saw both explanations in a film he considered antiwar: "I believe it was because each person brought to it his own underlying feelings about the Vietnam war. Those, like Richard Nixon, who regarded Vietnam as a noble enterprise could find comfort and support in Patton's self-righteous and dedicated savagery."[113]

In the final analysis, people left theaters with the power of Scott's performance, a performance which overshadowed all the scenes of combat, all the ambiguities of the film, all the other actors. His portrayal proved powerful enough to dissolve the twenty-year opposition of Patton's family to a movie. Patton's daughter, Ruth Totten, went to see McCarthy's rendering of her father's career "screaming and kicking inside, but, I hope, in a calm and ladylike fashion outside." She expected the worst because of all the negative publicity Patton had received during the war.[114]

After seeing the film, Mrs. Totten had to admit that the family had been wrong to assume that any film would necessarily present a brutal picture. At the same time, she found some virtue in the family's prolonged opposition, believing that if the movie had been made sooner, Scott might not have played her father. She was impressed that the actor "had obviously made a deep study of General Patton both on film and in his writings and books written about him. So many of his gestures, particularly his 'mirthless smile,' were so true to life that it gave me quite a start." According to Mrs. Totten, Scott's deep study also enabled the actor to get under Patton's skin and indicated to the family that Scott "not only liked General Patton, he understood him—which few people did, do, or ever will." She thought his performance was a "tour de force and he has made a great contribution, not to the so-called Patton legend but to film history." More than that, she thought Scott conveyed her father's dedication to his country better than she had ever seen it done before—a dedication that put country before wife and children.[115]

Not everyone, of course, would agree with Patton's priorities. Nevertheless, *Patton* illuminated all aspects of the general's personality and stimulated a wide diversity of reactions to the man and movie. Nowhere did the multiplicity of responses become more evident than among reviewers. Although they universally praised Scott's performance, the critical response to the film ranged from accolades to outrage, sometimes within the same review and even in the same sentence.

In the *New York Times*, Vincent Canby wrote, "The real surprise is that the film, though long (and from my point of view, appalling) is so consistently fascinating." He thought the film "looks and sounds like the epic American war movie that the Hollywood establishment has always wanted to make but never had the guts to do before." The film was "an incredible gas, especially in this time and place." In one long sentence, he then managed to capture the entire flavor of the movie: "*Patton* is a loving, often sentimental, semi-official portrait of a man it characterizes as a near schizo, a man who admitted that he damn well loved war, was surprised and somewhat taken aback when men near to him were killed, who quoted the Bible, believed in reincarnation, had the political acumen of Marie Antoinette, and according to the movie, somehow so touched General Omar Bradley with his folksy honesty ('I'm a prima donna—I know it!') that Bradley went through the war looking always as if he were about to weep."[116]

Canby found that for a "supposedly sympathetic character in a superspectacle" to admit his love of war became, "in a negative way, a refreshing change from the sort of conventional big-budget movie claptrap that keeps saying that war is hell, while simultaneously showing how much fun it really is." Nevertheless, the reviewer did not think that *Patton* marked an advance "in the civilizing processes of our culture," but he thought it remained "a good deal less hypocritical than most patriotic American war movies." Recognizing his contradictory responses to the film, he conceded, "If I sound ambivalent about *Patton*, it's because the movie itself is almost as ambivalent about its hero."[117]

The *New Yorker* reviewer, Pauline Kael, also pointed out the ambiguities of the title character and of the movie. But she had much less trouble deciding what she thought of *Patton*, writing that in its almost three hours, "there is not a single lyrical moment. The figure of General George Patton, played by George C. Scott, is a Pop hero, but visually the movie is in a style that might be described as imperial. It does not really look quite like any other movie, and that in itself is an achievement (though not necessarily an aesthetic one)." She seemed to be unhappiest with the film's refusal to take a position on Patton, which she concluded was probably as "deliberately planned as a Rorschach test. He is what people who believe in military values can see as the true military hero—the red-blooded American who loves to fight and whose crude talk is straight talk. He is also what people who despise militarism can see as the worst kind of red-blooded American mystical maniac who 'believes' in fighting; for them, Patton can be the symbolic proof of the madness of the whole military complex."[118]

Because the film plays Patton "both ways—crazy and great—and more ways than that, because he's a comic-strip general and even those who are antiwar may love comic strips," Kael suspected that people would most likely see in the film what they wanted, with the result that "a lot of them are going to think *Patton* is a great movie." However, she thought the film "strings us along and holds out on us. If we don't just want to have our prejudices greased, we'll find it confusing and unsatisfying, because we aren't given enough information to evaluate Patton's actions." She pointed out that Patton is treated "as if he were the spirit of war, yet the movie begs the fundamental question about its hero: Is this the kind of man a country needs when it's at war?" She further suggested that "every issue raised is left unresolved."[119]

In the snows of northern Spain, Scott portrays Patton's brilliant rescue of the Americans surrounded at Bastogne during the Battle of the Bulge.

Despite their equivocations about the film and its hero, in the end both reviewers revealed their antipathy toward the man in objecting to the movie's subtitle: "A Salute to a Rebel." Kael asked: "Whom does Twentieth Century Fox think it's kidding? What was Patton a rebel against except humanitarianism?" Canby thought Scott dominated the film, "even its ambiguities," and was "continuously entertaining and, occasionally, even appealing," but he concluded that the actor "never quite convinced me that Patton, by any stretch of the imagination, could be called a rebel against anything except the good, gray, dull forces of bleeding heart liberalism."[120]

Perhaps this arch-authoritarianism is what appealed to Richard Nixon. Perhaps the film's appeal to the president came from Patton's rabid anti-Communism, his desire to turn against Russia after the defeat of Germany, his lust for combat and compulsion to emerge victorious from every struggle. Perhaps the president simply appreciated the film's excellent character study of Patton. In any case, Nixon saw the film on April 1, 1970, and again on April 25, just five days before he ordered American forces into Cambodia. In his 1977 interview with David Frost, the ex-president denied that the film had had any effect on his decision to order the incursion. Nevertheless, while the troops still occupied positions in Cambodia, Nixon commented on *Patton* to a group of businessmen and financial leaders he had called to the White House. He talked about Patton's accomplishment in rescuing men trapped during the Battle of the Bulge, an action that other generals said was impossible. He also cited Patton's asking the chaplain to pray for good weather and then decorating him when the sun came out. He said that now every chaplain in Vietnam was praying for early rain so that the Communists could not easily reoccupy the sanctuaries then being destroyed. He observed, "You have to have the will and determination to go out and to do what is right for America."[121]

Why did Nixon find Patton and the movie about him so intriguing? Hugh Sidey, then *Life* magazine's presidential correspondent, suggested that Nixon may have empathized with a man who had lived through criticism, endured rejection, and in the end still remained willing to try what seemed impossible, to take the bold stroke. Sidey also pointed out that like Patton, Nixon had faith in God and was a complex man, one who had as many ambiguities and facets as the general. According to Sidey, Nixon acted like "an insecure man. He had an inferiority complex. . . . He cast around for stronger people. He was fascinated with Kennedy. Part of this was the sureness with which Kennedy moved through his world. He liked Kissinger and Connolly for this reason. And I am sure that he thought that the Wayne model, the old-fashion courage [offered the same strength]. Then the *Patton* film comes along. Here's a man in battle. Here is an argument for boldness, innovation, ready-made. . . . It was just a marvelously articulated argument for precisely what Nixon fancied he was doing in Cambodia."[122]

The film's influence on Nixon went further than his decision to invade Cambodia. Ladislas Farago, author of the book on which *Patton* was based, asked Margaret Mead why she thought Nixon had become so fascinated with Patton. The anthropologist explained that Nixon "thrives on opposition. It is a form of stimulation for him. His enemies should take heed. Any figure who had had to make decisions in the face of opposition as he has done will seem appealing to him." Dr. Mead also observed that the mementos of the president's career became the relics of his fights, his victories. Similarly, his book *Seven Crises* focused on Nixon's challenges and crises, perhaps matching those Patton went through in his career and in the film.[123]

Like Nixon, some people undoubtedly went to see *Patton* to empathize with the man and to find strength to act. Some went to see a major antiwar film, others to learn how war should really be fought. Most, however, went simply to be entertained by a superb actor and an excellent film. Whatever their reasons, people did go to see *Patton,* and it became a smash hit, giving Twentieth Century Fox two concurrent box-office successes about war. Ultimately, McCarthy's film became the most profitable or second most profitable military film of all time, depending on how one classifies *M*A*S*H,* the other Fox hit of 1970.

14 Illusion and Reality of War

WHATEVER ITS MESSAGE, AUDIENCES PERCEIVED *Patton* as a film about war and, more specifically, as a biography of a single man in war. Most people also perceived that *M*A*S*H* and *Catch-22* portrayed men in battle, or at least men's relationship to battle. Although both films comment on relationships in society, neither actually looks at men in combat, external appearances notwithstanding. In contrast, *Tora! Tora! Tora!* does look at combat, more precisely, the failure of the United States to prepare adequately for battle. However, the film's dramatic and visual shortcomings negate much of the impact of its conscious effort to portray men at war. Ultimately, each movie says far less about combat than its military framework suggests or than most audiences probably expected.

Most people viewed *M*A*S*H* as a war film or at least a spoof of war films; some have seen it as a war comedy, others as an antiwar statement. One critic called it "an animated cartoon with the cartoon figures played by real people." Although the filmmakers set the story in the Korean War, many thought its director, Robert Altman, was making a comment about the Vietnam War. One reviewer suggested, "A strong case could be made for *M*A*S*H* as a clinically ambiguous study of the way Joe College and Fred Pre-med adjust—sell out—to a pervasive, corrupting system like War."[1] In fact, *M*A*S*H* is simply a portrayal of people interacting within a structured bureaucracy that just happens to be a military hospital. Altman himself observed, "It's told with war as a background—we hear the firing, but the only gun we actually see in the entire picture is that used by the timekeeper at the football game to mark the end of each half."[2]

The uniforms the characters wear and references to the battles that provide the MASH (Mobile Army Surgical Hospital) doctors with their patients remain the only real connections the film has to combat or the military. The film could just as easily have taken place in any war or even any disaster area or crowded freeway for all the relationship the mutilated bodies have to war. The characters make infrequent comments about combat, but they show no concern for the progress of the war in which they are supposedly involved. As much as anything else, *M*A*S*H* becomes a satire on doctors and the medical profession, closely related to Paddy Chayefsky's *Hospital* or Otto Preminger's *Such Good Friends*. George C. Scott, who starred in *Hospital,* said of *M*A*S*H*: "Half the budget was raw meat. Every time he [Robert Altman] got in trouble he flashed back to the operating room with the blood. Cheap tricks. To me, the worst sin of all is cheapness and shoddiness."[3]

The producer of *M*A*S*H*, Ingo Preminger (Otto's brother), saw no need to create an authentic military atmosphere. After an initial inquiry to the Pentagon about acquiring MASH tents from the Army, he never returned with a script or made further requests for assistance. Instead, he shot the film on the Twentieth Century Fox Ranch outside Los Angeles, renting helicopters and other equipment from commercial sources. Ironically, despite the movie's irreverent portrayal of the relationships between officers, the rowdy military discipline, some of its language, and its explicit sexuality, Don Baruch indicated that the Defense Department might have provided some limited assistance if Preminger had followed up his initial inquiry. His reaction suggests that the Public Affairs Office saw the film primarily as a comedy that implied little, if any, judgment about war and the military, pro or con.[4]

*M*A*S*H* had its origins in a comic novel of the same name by an Army surgeon writing of his experiences in an Army field hospital during the Korean War. Altman ultimately fashioned a screenplay written by Ring Lardner Jr. into a film that portrayed the adventures of three surgeons in a MASH hospital. Lardner felt that the film would have been better if Altman had not changed some things found in the original script. He criticized the movie's opening, saying that "the Keystone Kops spill and slapstick" indicate a "too self-conscious effort to establish the film as a comedy." He faulted the football sequence for being "too long and ending too abruptly," and he thought the barrage of abuse heaped on Major Burns after his "broadcast" lovemaking with "Hot Lips" went on too long. He also regretted the implication that Lieutenant Dish was having an affair with Hawkeye, feeling that it vitiated her supreme sacrifice of giving herself to the impotent dentist to restore his virility.[5]

Lardner's criticism of Altman's portrayal of women in *M*A*S*H* mirrored feminist attacks that condemned his films for "an adolescent view of women as sex objects." Altman, however, defended his treatment of "Hot Lips": "The precise point of that character was that women *were* and *are* treated as sex objects. They can't blame me for the condition because I report it. We're dealing with a society in which most of the significant activity until now has been initiated by males. If you make a western or a sports story or a story about big business or gangsters, it's automatically going to reflect the secondary positions women hold."[6]

Altman has seen himself reporting on society in his films. But he perceives that society and the people who interact within it in a largely unfocused, unstructured manner, and he sees it as a cruel society. He did intend *M*A*S*H* "to be a cruel film. That's what it was. That's what I see constantly. Certainly that time and certainly that situation breeds that." For Altman, the settings he uses to show this cruelty are irrelevant. *M*A*S*H* had no more to do with war than *Nashville* had to do with country and western music. When asked if *M*A*S*H* contained a bitterly antiwar message, he replied: "Do you know anybody who is prowar?" To the charge that some viewers had perceived the film as a prowar statement because it lacked structure and emphasized emotional rather than literal accuracy, Altman assumed that "they are people who need to see children burning to think something is antiwar." He dismissed them as "people who want a political statement rather than an artistic one."[7]

With few exceptions, reviewers and moviegoers accepted *M*A*S*H* as a superior artistic statement and as a movie about men in war. But as with *Patton*, people saw in the film what they wanted to see. To most viewers, the uniforms, the military forms of address, and the military-type equipment made it a war film. These visual and verbal devices remain necessary ingredients in films about war. Nevertheless, a movie about combat or even about the military in general requires more. It must have some visual and dramatic connection to combat or to a military bureaucracy, and it must clearly establish the direct influence of these on the characters' actions. *M*A*S*H* focuses on doctors who happen to be wearing Army uniforms but who show no interest in or concern about the Korean War or any war or about the military establishment. Although *M*A*S*H* may say something about man in an artificially structured society, it makes a comment about men in combat or in the military only insofar as the military reflects society as a whole.

Catch-22, also released in 1970, has little more to do with war than *M*A*S*H*. Based on Joseph Heller's 1961 satiric novel of the same name, it focuses on man versus the system, human relationships, survival, dying. War serves only as the framework for the characters' actions, although the story originated in Heller's own World War II experiences as a B-25 bombardier. Unlike Yossarian, the hero of his novel, however, Heller did not try to avoid combat: "I actually hoped I would get into combat. I was just nineteen and there were a great many movies being made about the war; it all seemed so dramatic and heroic . . . I felt like I was going to Hollywood."[8] Perhaps the gap between the image and the reality inspired him. In any case, Heller wrote one of the most original comic novels of its time. But its images do not deal with men in combat. Nor do the movie's images portray men in actual combat, despite the filmmaker's efforts to ensure visual authenticity of the locales and the aerial sequences.

John Calley and Martin Ransohoff, the producers, acquired a squadron of B-25 bombers, which Frank Tallman restored to their World War II configuration and flying condition. Calley and production designer Richard Sylbert found a site near Guaymas, Mexico, that resembled Heller's fictional airbase in Corsica. They built a runway, a base, and roads to represent the book's island of Pianosa. With the planes and pilots that Tallman brought together, director Mike Nichols staged and filmed the air action in a style befitting *Twelve O'Clock High* or even *Wings*.[9]

Nichols did see a couple of movies about the air war, since his film would have flying sequences. But he found nothing useful, because the book "isn't a literal rendering of what happened. It's a dream." Andrew Marton, who helped stage the flying sequences, said that Nichols had no intention of making a flying epic. Instead, the director saw airplanes in flight as a cliché, representative of most combat extravaganzas, and to have included them might have made *Catch-22* just another aerial war picture.[10]

Even so, the opening montage became one of the great flying sequences in all film history. From total darkness, the screen gradually becomes lighter as the sun comes up through time-lapse photography. The barking of a dog gives way to the sound of plane engines coughing to life. Finding the bombers as they warm up, the camera follows them, seemingly without a cut, as they rumble down the runway, take off into the lightening sky, and pass, one after another, in perfect order, behind a shattered control tower. In a later sequence, filmed with a telephoto lens, the bombers are shown taking off fully loaded. The camera makes the air shimmer as the planes rise, seemingly one on the top of the next, shaking as they climb into the sky. One wonders if men could have fought the war with such machines.

They did, but not in Heller's novel or Nichols's movie. The author himself confessed, "I wrote it during the Korean War and aimed it for the one after that." He had warned that *Catch-22* was no more about the Army Air Corps than Kafka's trial was about Prague, that "the cold war is what I was truly talking about, not the World War."[11] Nichols saw the movie as a story about dying: "And the theme is about when you get off. At what point do you draw the line beyond which you won't go? . . . that you can't live unless you know what you'll stop at."[12]

The characters in *Catch-22* wear uniforms, fly planes that drop bombs, die in combat unseen, receive medals for bravery, and chase women during their free time, as in most traditional war movies. But combat only symbolizes to Yossarian the threat that all of civilization poses to his survival. The continuing visual image of that threat, the dying Snowden, an image that the film repeats in ever greater detail as it progresses, had its basis in actual combat. On Heller's thirty-seventh mission, one of his plane's gunners was wounded and bled copiously into his flight suit. As a consequence, Heller became petri-fied of flight: "War was like a movie to me [until then]. I suddenly realized, 'Good God! They're trying to kill me too.' War wasn't much fun after that." He took a ship home when his tour ended and did not fly again for another fifteen years.[13] Snowden's wound initiates a similar realization for Yossarian. It tells him it is time to get off, to get himself grounded. In the movie, however, Snowden receives his wound from some distant impersonal war, and the recurring scene becomes surrealistic, the images part of a dream.

In trying to draw the line, trying to stop the insanity that confronts him, Yossarian meets his Catch-22: "In order to be grounded, I've got to be crazy. And I must be crazy to keep flying. But if I ask to be grounded, that means that I'm not crazy anymore and I've got to keep flying." In the end, Yossarian does the only thing possible, he deserts: "It's the only sensible thing for me to do." After fighting for his country for three years, he con-cludes, "Now I'm gonna start fighting for myself." When his friends warn him that he will "be on the run with no friends! You'll live in constant danger of betrayal!" Yossarian yells: "I live that way now!" And he takes off, carrying a yellow rubber life raft past the row of bombers, into the sea, inflating it as he goes to paddle to Sweden.

Yossarian represents Everyman, confronting a world that seems to control his destiny and seems to render him powerless. But it remains a universal world, not the distinct world of war or combat. Perhaps Heller's words capture Yossarian's moment of truth better than the movie's dialogue with its visual images of the bombers and the base: "'But you can't just turn your back on all your responsibilities and run away from them,' Major Danby insisted. 'It's such a negative move. It's escapist.' Yossarian laughed with buoyant scorn and shook his head. 'I'm not running away from my responsibilities. I'm running to them. There's nothing negative about running away to save your life. You know who the escapists are, don't you Danby? Not me and Orr.'"[14]

The nature of this message combined with the book's structural complexities made transferring Heller's novel to the screen appear to be an impossible task. Heller himself thought the film sacrificed most of his humor "in a vain attempt to establish a 'story line'— something the novel didn't have to begin with." He had had "virtually no hope" that Catch-22 would become a good film: "And if I had participated in making it, I would have been compelled to care how it turned out." He did get to know Alan Arkin (Yossarian) and Nichols before shooting began and found them "so concerned about doing 'justice' to the book—which is, of course, impossible in any film—that I found myself rooting for them."[15]

His rooting and the $15 million cost of the movie were not able to produce a film that attracted large crowds, and it became one of the financial disasters of 1970. Heller thought that Catch-22 turned out "OK" despite his initial lack of expectations. He also believed that if the film "had been foreign, in black and white, without stars and based on an unknown novel, it would have been a major critical success. This is not a comment on the quality of the film but on the consistency of film reviewers."[16]

As it was, reviews ranged from Vincent Canby's "quite simply the best American film I have seen this year" to Stanley Kauffmann's opinion that the film broke most of the promises the opening sequence made and ended up "a disappointment." Canby put his finger on one of the problems when he said, "Great films are complete in themselves.

Catch-22 isn't, but enough remains so that the film becomes a series of brilliant mirror images of a Strobe-lit reality."[17]

Like Canby, the readers of Heller's novel could bring his words to the theater and merge the two cultural forms. Because they did not expect a war movie, the lack of combat did not disappoint them. Many other people probably came expecting to see aerial warfare, given the film's advertisements and publicity campaign, which had focused on Nichols's fleet of bombers. However beautiful they appeared taking off and in flight, audiences quickly discovered the planes had little to do with the story, which became a serious and reverent attempt to pictorialize the abstract, satiric, and sometimes philosophical ideas that Heller densely packed in his novel. The screen, in general, resists such efforts, and ironically, Nichols only complicated his task by visually stressing the war-film genre as the vehicle for conveying Heller's themes. Nothing becomes more central to a consideration of war than life and death. But with few exceptions, combat films have dealt with the subject in raw, basic terms—people fight and die.

Although *Catch-22* offered little to people who were seeking escapist entertainment, it impressed those opposed to the war in Vietnam. To them, Yossarian's paddling away to Sweden, to life, made sense. To them, combat or no combat, *Catch-22* contained a clear antiwar message. Nichols did "suppose" this was true, but he noted, "Nobody wants to make a pro-war film. And I don't know what an anti-war film is. It's like 'Fuck Hate.' Nobody likes war. It'd be like making an anti-evil film. Or a pro-good film."[18]

Hardly anyone likes war. But for a majority of the American people in 1970, heroes did not run away, either, even to live. Patton might harangue his men with the idea that "no bastard ever won a war by dying for his country." But death had always remained an unavoidable and noble part of Patton's life. The message proclaimed hundreds of times on the motion picture screen had always stressed the idea that a man can have no higher calling than to fight and die for his country. Yossarian's actions, his desire to stop flying, his escape to save his life would alienate the average moviegoer, just as James Garner's philosophy of cowardice in *The Americanization of Emily* had done six years before. Although 5 million people may have read *Catch-22* by 1970, the combination of readers and Americans opposed to the war in Vietnam did not comprise a large enough audience to make Nichols's film successful at the box office.[19]

In addition, *Catch-22* contained many flaws. Nichols attempted a serious inquiry into human survival and death. Yet his concept required him to undertake a hazardous journey, because Heller's novel encompassed too many ideas and levels of meaning to deal with visually in a brief time. Consequently, for most viewers, *Catch-22* failed intellectually, if not artistically and dramatically. Because it could not offer people Heller's ideas effectively, and because it did not attempt to depict the typical war film's action, it failed commercially. Nevertheless, *Catch-22* contains much beauty and even more meaning and remains a noble failure.

The same thing cannot be said of *Tora! Tora! Tora!*

In their hyperbole, the ad writers described *Tora! Tora! Tora!* as "The Most Spectacular Film Ever Made." The headline writer for Vincent Canby's review in the *New York Times* probably said it best: "Tora-ble, Tora-ble, Tora-ble."[20] Seldom had a studio spent so much money on a film—at least $25 million—and received so little visual and dramatic effect in return. Darryl Zanuck and Twentieth Century Fox adopted the style and scale of *The Longest Day* in an attempt to duplicate its box-office success. Using the same technique as in the earlier film and its imitators, *The Battle of the Bulge* and *The Bridge at*

Remagen, Tora! Tora! Tora! recreated a historical event, the sneak attack on Pearl Harbor, by crosscutting between the opposing forces as their actions led to confrontation. The attacking pilots used *Tora,* Japanese for *tiger,* as the code word to notify the carriers that they had achieved surprise and the raid could go forward as planned.

Done in a pseudo-documentary style with close attention to historical accuracy, the film fails to create any dramatic tension as events lead up to Sunday morning, December 7. Its characters seem to be marking time, waiting for the cinematic highlight of sweeping destruction, which the film portrays in vivid color designed to attract audiences. *The Longest Day* ultimately overcame the dramatic problem of a known outcome because it portrayed D-Day authentically, because it dramatized a glorious victory, and because its characters seemed believable. Despite four years of effort and at least $25 million, no one could instill the same illusions of reality into *Tora! Tora! Tora!* Even more important, no one could disguise the fact that the film depicted the Japanese killing Americans, sinking American ships, and destroying American planes, matériel, and facilities, with virtually no American response. Pearl Harbor remained a day of "Infamy."

Why would Americans want to be reminded of such a day? Before the film went before the cameras, Darryl Zanuck explained, "Audiences may not think they are waiting for *Tora! Tora! Tora!* but audiences never know what they want until it's put in front of them. *Tora! Tora! Tora!* will say something about today."[21]

When the film became embroiled in controversy during production, Zanuck took out full-page advertisements in the *New York Times* and the *Washington Post* to further justify portraying the defeat. He wrote that he hoped his film would serve "to arouse the American public to the necessity for preparedness in this acute missile age where a sneak attack could occur at any moment. You cannot arouse the public by showing films where Americans always win and where we are invincible. You can only remind the public by revealing to them how we once thought we were invincible but suffered a sneak attack in which practically half our fleet was lost." He claimed that *Tora! Tora! Tora!* was not "merely a movie but an accurate and dramatic slice of history that should never have occurred but did occur, and the purpose of producing this film is to remind the public of the tragedy that happened to us and to ensure that it will never happen again."[22]

While Zanuck was attempting to give significance to *Tora! Tora! Tora!* his son Richard, vice president in charge of production at Twentieth Century Fox, was expounding on the studio's philosophy in other terms: "We go for idea pictures which contain a lot of

The USS *Arizona* explodes during the re-creation of Pearl Harbor in *Tora! Tora! Tora!*

entertainment. We don't get involved with the message pictures or anything very preachy. We don't try to do anything terribly intellectual—that can be dangerous." For the most part, he said, Fox made "sheer entertainment pictures," compared to other studios.[23]

Elmo Williams, the producer of *Tora! Tora! Tora!* rebutted Darryl Zanuck's claims of social significance for his movie in blunter terms: "There is only one reason why studios make films and that is to make money. Nothing else." Nevertheless, he did suggest that filmmakers have social consciences: "[We] are concerned with telling stories fairly and presenting the truth as much as we can, especially in the case of films that require cooperation of a government agency."[24]

The failure of *Tora! Tora! Tora!* had nothing to do with its accuracy or truthfulness. Even though the film showed the U.S. military suffering its greatest defeat to that time, Williams said that no one in Washington asked him to distort the facts or "play anything down." The film's portrayal of Pearl Harbor adhered to the current historical interpretation of events that led up to December 7 and the reasons for the military's lack of preparedness for a surprise attack. The studio was to base the screenplay on two contemporary books about Pearl Harbor, Ladislas Farago's *The Broken Seal* and Gordon Prange's *Tora, Tora, Tora*. When Fox first circulated *The Broken Seal,* the story of the breaking of the Japanese code, throughout the studio, readers found the Pearl Harbor section of the book most exciting. However, the production received its primary impetus when Fox acquired Prange's best-selling book shortly after it was published in Japan in 1966.[25]

If developing a screenplay that portrayed both sides of the story fairly and yet did not "take years" to tell required great effort, turning the script into a movie seemed an insurmountable task. One producer to whom the studio initially offered the project turned it down, asking, "Do you want to bury me?" Elmo Williams finally received the job, largely because of his success in handling the production logistics on films such as *The Longest Day, The Blue Max,* and *Those Magnificent Men in Their Flying Machines.* At the same time, his early career as a film editor and his Academy Award for *High Noon* provided him the expertise necessary to supervise the editing of a long and complex movie. In fact, he had to edit two films into one integrated motion picture, one made in Japan portraying the Japanese story of the attack and one shot mostly in Hawaii, recreating the attack on December 7.

To bring order to a project of this scope, Williams explained that he took "a very simple approach . . . I used the Japanese point of view, the airman's point of view because it allowed me to use miniatures and to get around the problem of ships and planes that no longer existed, things we couldn't build." However important the "things" might become, the actual filming had to take place at Pearl Harbor if the re-creation of December 7 was to contain any sense of authenticity. Consequently, in July 1967 Williams and Richard Fleischer, the film's director, went to Hawaii with Defense Department approval to scout the necessary locations. They found that they could not use Hickman Field because it had become Honolulu's international airport. However, Ford Island and other airfields and military areas that had been involved in the Japanese attack could be utilized during filming.[26]

At the same time, Williams faced the problem of accumulating "things" with which to dress up his locations in Hawaii and Japan. He had to resort to miniatures for establishing shots of the Japanese fleet on the open sea and the American ships berthed at Pearl Harbor. But Williams did manage to create reasonable facsimiles of a few key ships on which to shoot on-board sequences. In Japan, the studio built full-size replicas of parts of the Japanese battleship *Nagato* and aircraft carrier *Akagi.* Constructed on dry land out of pine and bamboo, and seemingly held together with miles of wire, the "ships" were set on the

Comdr. Ed Stafford, the technical advisor, discusses the filming of the miniature sequences for *Tora! Tora! Tora!* with producer Elmo Williams and Fox's miniature expert. Note edge of painted backdrop.

shore so that they appeared to be at sea in the completed film. In Hawaii, Twentieth Century Fox built a replica of the aft half of the USS *Arizona* on two barges close to where the original *Arizona* had been moored on December 7. The mock-up also represented other battleships at Pearl Harbor that day and was constructed so that it could be "destroyed" during shooting. The cost of these and other replicas and miniatures came to $3.5 million.[27]

Williams had no choice but to use these re-creations for his two fleets. To restage the attack itself, however, he needed operable aircraft. Only a handful of airworthy Japanese planes, vintage 1941, still existed, and Williams needed an entire air force. Moreover, the existing aircraft lacked spare parts and the reliability to withstand the many hours of strenuous flying that the script demanded. Consequently, Williams ruled out using original Japanese planes and decided to remodel American planes to resemble the Japanese aircraft that had flown over Pearl Harbor.[28]

Although Hollywood had used the expediency of disguised American planes ever since *Air Force* and *Sahara,* Williams's goal of authenticity demanded that he do more than simply paint Japanese insignia on his aircraft. For example, filmmakers had always used American AT-6s to portray Zeroes, although they bore only a slight resemblance to the Japanese planes. However, the AT-6s (and the SNJs and Harvards, the Navy and Canadian counterparts) could also be rebuilt, with varying degrees of difficulty, to approximate Japanese Kate torpedo bombers and Val dive bombers. As a result, in *Tora! Tora! Tora!* AT-6s substituted for all three types of aircraft that had participated in the Pearl Harbor strike. Williams also had to come up with two flyable and two "taxiable" P-40s, five flyable B-17s, and one flyable PBY, as well as nonflyable derelicts and mock-ups of all three American planes (designated for destruction during the attack). The cost of the air operations came to $2.5 million.[29]

The studio also had to construct, locate, and recondition American warships and equipment, because the U.S. armed services had none dating from Pearl Harbor. Nevertheless, Twentieth Century Fox could not have made *Tora! Tora! Tora!* without Pentagon assistance. Williams secured approval to utilize facilities in Hawaii, subject to the usual requirements of safety and noninterference with regular activities. He also needed a few active and inactive ships in Pearl Harbor, men, and most important, access to an aircraft carrier to film the scenes of Japanese takeoffs and landings on December 7.

To ensure this assistance, Fox had kept the Defense Department informed of the progress of the project from its inception in September 1966. The Pentagon had provided research assistance in the form of information, stock footage, and comments on the several

Pearl Harbor burns following the Japanese attack in *Tora! Tora! Tora!*

versions of the script as it developed. In July 1967 Williams submitted a revised screenplay for approval. With only minor requests for changes relating to technical and historical accuracy, the Defense Department approved the script in mid-September and asked the studio to submit an up-to-date list of required assistance.[30]

Williams gave the military full credit for going along with the making of a film about its most humiliating defeat: "After all, what is a defeat? Sometimes you've got to lose a little battle to win a big one." According to director Richard Fleischer, the military's decision to assist showed its willingness to accept a necessary evil: "I think it was just one of these things where they had no choice because they're damned if they do and damned it they don't. I think they would have been more damned if they hadn't cooperated because then there would have been the accusation that they had something to hide and something to cover up."[31]

The military considered its decision to cooperate in more positive terms. J.M. Hession, the director of the Navy's Los Angeles Public Affairs Office, advised the chief of naval information that the service should cooperate because "the [July 1967] script is apparently an accurate document of the events leading up to the Japanese attack on Pearl Harbor. It is in the best interests of the Navy that this film be completed in order that it may impress the public with the importance of seapower and the necessity of maintaining a strong Navy."[32]

In October 1968, during the debate over whether to allow the filmmakers to stage takeoffs and landings on a carrier, R.M Koontz, the Navy's director of the Media Relations Division, wrote to the chief of information: "This film can and should be an accurate portrayal of a vital moment in our history. . . . Additionally, despite the fact that it was a Japanese Carrier Task Force, it will be a most effective and dramatic portrayal of a resoundingly successful carrier task force operation." Elmo Williams and Fleischer agreed that the positive image of a successful carrier raid figured in the Navy's decision to cooperate. Moreover, as Fleischer pointed out, the film showed the bravery of men at Pearl Harbor once the attack began. Yet he also conceded: "I don't know if there is any great positive value in the whole film for the Navy." In any case, *Tora! Tora! Tora!* presented a historically accurate account of events leading up to December 7 and of the attack itself, and as Fleischer suggested, the Navy probably had no real choice but to cooperate.[33]

The Pentagon had approved the revised script in September 1967, but it did not formally agree to cooperate on the film until it received the final corrected screenplay in February 1968. Mindful of the legacy of Arthur Sylvester, who had left office in early 1967, the military carefully analyzed all of Fox's requirements lists as the studio submitted them. In his 1967 memo to the chief of information, Captain Hession had suggested stipulating to the studio that the Navy would assist "only on those sequences portraying

American Navy forces, and then only within reasonable limits for sequences requiring the utilization of ships and aircraft, so that operational efficiency will not be impaired." Moreover, throughout the production, both the studio and the Pentagon tried to avoid any hint of impropriety that might trigger controversy like the one that occurred during the filming of *The Longest Day*. Ultimately, the General Accounting Office ruled that all military cooperation on the film had followed the guidelines set forth in Sylvester's 1964 regulations and that the studio had paid all the costs it had incurred.[34]

The only significant problem that arose between the studio and the Pentagon during the entire production related to using an aircraft carrier to stage the takeoffs and landings of the Japanese attack force with the reconstructed American planes. In formally approving cooperation on February 2, 1968, Daniel Henkin, deputy assistant secretary of defense for public affairs, advised the studio that the issue of landing the studio aircraft remained under advisement. As a result, he suggested that "it would be best to consider an alternate plan."[35]

With filming finally scheduled to begin in late 1968, Fox requested in August that it be allowed to use the carrier USS *Valley Forge*. In response, the Defense Department advised Ellen McDonnell, the studio's Washington representative, that although the request had received "every consideration," it had "determined that such use of an operational carrier cannot be authorized under the provisions of current Department of Defense Instruction." Since the carrier would represent a Japanese ship, assistance would have to be on a courtesy basis rather than part of the normal cooperation. According to the Pentagon, this assistance would involve "improper utilization of manpower and equipment" even if the studio could afford the cost of a carrier and crew for the period needed. In fact, the issue of safety remained at the heart of the matter: "Flight deck crews perform demanding and hazardous duties under the best conditions, and to require them to work with old equipment with which they are unfamiliar would add unacceptable risks for them and the pilots." Nevertheless, the Navy advised that the rejection did not preclude filming nonflying sequences aboard an available carrier on a noninterference, no-special-arrangement basis.[36]

Though Elmo Williams had a mock aircraft carrier in Japan, to create an authentic ambience in portraying the preparations aboard ship for the attack, he still needed a carrier as a camera platform for filming the launch and return of his reconstructed planes. Consequently, he went to Washington on September 5 to present his case to Daniel Henkin and to formally request reconsideration of the decision. This led to almost two months of spirited debate within the Pentagon. The Navy wanted to allow Fox to stage its landings and takeoffs, whereas the Defense Department Public Affairs Office expressed strong concern about the dangers of the action and the uproar that would result if a Navy man were killed or injured during filming.[37]

Acting on Williams's request for reconsideration of its decision, the Public Affairs Office again asked the Navy to comment on its ability to supply a carrier on which to film takeoffs and landings. Navy commands at all levels stated that the request was "feasible." As a result, on October 11, the chief of information advised Phil Goulding, the assistant secretary of defense for public affairs, that the Navy "strongly recommended" that it be permitted to provide a carrier for the studio's needs.[38]

Goulding's main concern remained the possible danger of the operations to the carrier's crew. Having spent some time on carriers as a journalist and as a government official, Goulding had found them "really terrifyingly dangerous places. The idea of crews, who were accustomed to dealing with jets taking off and landing, being put in a situation where they would be dealing with propeller-driven planes I thought was scary." Not only did he feel this constituted an unnecessary risk, but he also believed "very, very strongly" that men did not join the Navy to take part in Hollywood films. He did not see how the government could "explain to the family of the kid who backed into a propeller and lost his head what he was doing in the service of his country." Goulding's staff reinforced his concern when they advised him that "cooperation would be difficult to defend from a noninterference standpoint or if there should be an accident involving injury or death."[39]

Captain Koontz, director of the Navy's Media Relations Division, had anticipated this continued resistance and provided the Navy with answers to potential Defense Department objections. Koontz said that since the carrier was involved in a "precedent-setting way," he expected Goulding's office "to say no and base it on safety considerations determined by non-professional, non-aviation, and non-Navy personnel." He rejected the argument about the propriety of a U.S. carrier representing an enemy carrier, citing the many instances in which American men and equipment had depicted enemy forces, including John Wayne's recently released film *The Green Berets*. Koontz also expressed concern that a refusal to provide a carrier for *Tora! Tora! Tora!* would establish a precedent for disapproving cooperation on a film about the Battle of Midway, a glorious Navy victory, then in the early stages of development.[40]

The intra-Pentagon debate became more complicated when Jack Valenti, a former top aide to Lyndon Johnson and now president of the Motion Picture Association of America, brought to bear the weight of the film industry. Acting on a request for help from Darryl Zanuck, Valenti wrote letters on October 3 to both Goulding and Clark Clifford, secretary of defense, in support of Fox's request. Citing a possible "slight hang-up-resistance of some kind" to the use of a carrier, he asked Goulding to assist in "making sure that this request is granted." In his letter to Clifford, Valenti said he was writing for "his personal knowledge and because it may be that I may need your help." Mentioning "some minor resistance" to the Fox request, Valenti explained that he "just wanted you to know this in case this request gets to your level."[41]

On October 23 Valenti followed up a phone conversation with Clifford by responding to the Public Affairs Office's objections against a U.S. carrier portraying an enemy ship and to the safety issue. Valenti's strongest argument remained the long-established precedent that under certain circumstances, the armed services had permitted American military personnel and equipment to represent enemy men and armaments. He cited John Wayne's *The Green Berets* as the most recent example of this practice. He then recounted the measures Fox was taking to ensure the safety of the flying sequences. As an "incidental issue," he mentioned that the studio had already spent $5 million on the project and anticipated a total expenditure of more than $20 million on the film. He added, "I need not point out the catastrophic consequence to a major motion picture from the denial by the Defense Department in this instance."[42]

Valenti's arguments did not sway the Public Affairs Office. In a long memo to Clifford on October 24, Phil Goulding reiterated his position against approving the Fox request. He rejected the Navy's stated reasons for cooperating on the film—that it would help recruiting, serve as a historical document, evoke a patriotic response, and be a reminder of the need for strong armed forces to deter or defend against unexpected military attack. He wrote, "I have yet to see a reason why a U. S. carrier steaming at taxpayers' expense should represent a Japanese ship." Goulding also advised Clifford that Elmo Williams had informally sacrificed the need for carrier landings, "which represent the greatest danger," and had expressed his willingness to settle for filming only takeoffs. However, he rejected the compromise, arguing that no possible benefit to the military justified the risk involved. He continued to recommend disapproval of Fox's request for the carrier, while reiterating his support for cooperation on other aspects of the film.[43]

Clifford, of course, had more important things on his mind, including the management of the Vietnam War, and he turned over the matter to his deputy, Paul Nitze. Nitze, a former secretary of the Navy, quickly decided in favor of the Navy. He noted that the present secretary of the Navy approved of the film because he thought the service should continue to cooperate with Hollywood. Nitze himself believed the film would provide benefit to the Navy: "I thought we would be better off with the film being made than not being made even though there were risks involved." He acknowledged Goulding's concern for the danger, saying the issue "was whether or not to accept these risks, whether the benefits would be greater than the risks. I felt the benefits would be greater." To him, Pearl Harbor was part of U.S. history: "You have victory and you have defeat."[44]

Fox and the Navy did not, however, win a complete victory in their confrontation with the Defense Department. Clark Clifford accepted Nitze's decision but specifically ruled out any landings aboard the carrier. Even with this limitation, Elmo Williams and Richard Fleischer were able to obtain the footage they needed. At the end of November, thirty carrier-qualified naval aviators on authorized leave or inactive duty convened at El Toro Marine Base south of Los Angeles to familiarize themselves with the reconstructed aircraft and to practice Japanese-type formation flying. On December 1 the Navy loaded thirty pseudo-Japanese planes aboard the USS *Yorktown* docked at the Naval Air Station in San Diego, and the carrier departed on a regularly scheduled training exercise off the California coast.[45]

During the first two days aboard, the filmmakers and the pilots rehearsed the takeoffs, and Capt. George Watkins, the Navy's technical advisor for the carrier operation, recreated the landing of Air Group Commander Fuishida's Zero aboard a Japanese carrier. Since the studio planes could not actually land, the director first filmed Watkins flying the Zero off the carrier and then making a touch-and-go landing. Elmo Williams later created the illusion of the actual landing in the editing room. On December 4, under the supervision of Comdr. Ed Stafford, the overall technical advisor, and Watkins, the other twenty-nine planes took off in the dawn light, went into their formations, and did a flyby of the carrier as Japanese planes had done in 1941. Despite the Defense Department concerns, everything went smoothly during this phase of the filming, which provided Fleischer and Williams with all the carrier shots they needed.[46]

Thanks to this assistance, the carrier sequences conveyed an authentic feeling for the excitement of the moment when the Japanese launched their attack and for the beauty and grace of planes taking off from a carrier into the morning light. Likewise, the flying scenes later shot in Hawaii and over Pearl Harbor recreated the

Japanese planes take off at dawn for their attack on Pearl Harbor. Originally filmed for *Tora! Tora! Tora!*, the sequence appeared several times in *Midway* (1976).

shock of the sudden appearance of the Japanese planes as they began their bomb and torpedo runs. In particular, the film came alive during the sequence in which Japanese aircraft momentarily surround a civilian biplane out for an early-morning flight. The scene combines humor with the foreboding of events to come, and as long as the movie follows the planes over Hawaii and into Pearl Harbor, *Tora! Tora! Tora!* maintains a strong sense of reality.

Likewise, the studio carefully constructed the full-size mock-ups of the Japanese ships as well as of the USS *Arizona,* and they provided visual realism. In fact, some of the leased Navy ships looked less believable than the mock-up of the *Arizona* because of their post-1941 vintage. In at least one shot, the angle-deck of the *Yorktown* becomes visible during the carrier sequence. The staged explosions at Pearl Harbor appeared realistic because Fox used actual locales and original buildings—the filmmakers even blew up an old hangar that the Navy had scheduled for demolition. The destruction of the *Arizona,* which took over thirty seconds and became the visual climax of the movie, also provided more realism than most cinematic explosions. However, when the filmmakers cut from live action to the special-effects shots and miniatures photographed in the lake on the Fox Ranch near Los Angeles, the illusion of reality collapses. The miniatures and the painted backdrops look like miniatures and painted backdrops, and viewers cannot easily pretend otherwise and so suspend their disbelief.

Elmo Williams and Twentieth Century Fox cannot be faulted for their effort. The studio spent millions of dollars building the miniatures, which were as accurate as the art and special-effects departments could make them. The filmmakers simply faced an impossible task in matching the stunning live aerial shots over Pearl Harbor with the miniatures. The explosions of the miniatures and the destruction in Hawaii of the P-40 mock-ups look like what they were—special-effects explosions and disintegrating fiberglass models.

Since the filmmakers intended that the scenes of havoc provide the core of the film's visual impact, their shortcomings vitiated the success of the flying sequences and the destruction of the *Arizona.* However, the film's impotent drama, not its visual failures, remained at the heart of its artistic problems. In *The Longest Day,* history and drama had ultimately merged. The actors became historical figures, real people with whom the audience could empathize. Through them, the film portrayed the human struggle to survive. But in *Tora! Tora! Tora!* people and their actions remained secondary to the event, to the exploding bombs, to the ships, planes, and other instruments of war, "toys" that the director moved around in front of his cameras.

As a result, the actors remain actors, wooden caricatures of people, simply reading their lines. Admiral Kimmel, the Navy's commander at Pearl Harbor, whom a bullet narrowly missed, remarks in the film: "It would have been merciful if it had killed me." However, the tragic implication of his comment fails to move audiences. If the explosions, mock-ups, miniatures, and actual ships and planes had become integrated on the screen, the lack of realistic characters might have passed with less notice. However, all the construction, special effects, and military assistance never meshed. Consequently, *Tora! Tora! Tora!* failed as drama and as entertainment, even as it recreated the history of Pearl Harbor with reasonable accuracy.

In doing so, the film could not, of course, exonerate the American military for its lack of preparedness or the government for its failure to alert Hawaii in time to meet the attack. As a pseudo-historical documentary, *Tora! Tora! Tora!* showed the ironies and errors that produced Pearl Harbor, the bureaucracy and blind tradition that amplified each mistake beyond calculation. It also explained the Japanese intentions and showed the attack for

Men at the beginning of the attack on
Pearl Harbor, in *Tora! Tora! Tora!*

what it remains, a skillful military mission, which skillful tacticians carefully planned—a far cry from the image of the Japanese in Hollywood films of the war years.

No single person emerges as the American scapegoat, and no heroes appear. Once the attack begins, however, the film portrays American bravery under fire and the can-do attitude that has typified the majority of American war movies. Moreover, though the film portrayed an American defeat, the audience knew that the U.S. military would redeem itself and ultimately win the war. Upon receiving word that the strike on Pearl Harbor had succeeded, Admiral Yamamoto, the attack's planner and commander, observed on screen, "I fear all we have done is to awaken a sleeping giant and fill him with a terrible resolve." The admiral had studied at Harvard and later served as Naval attache in Washington. Therefore, he appreciated the potential might of the United States and undoubtedly held such sentiments.

Tora! Tora! Tora! makes it clear that Yamamoto recognized the improbability of defeating America in a protracted war and simply hoped that by wiping out the fleet at Pearl Harbor, the United States might agree to allow Japan to carry out its Asian policy without interference. As the film's closing image, Yamamoto's comment does convey America's resolve, the determination to fight back, and to ultimately overcome the momentary adversity. And given the acknowledged accuracy of *Tora! Tora! Tora!* to that point, audiences would naturally assume the film was drawing the quote from the historical record. In reality, no evidence exists that the admiral ever spoke the words which the film provided to his character.

From where then did the quote come? Richard Fleischer wrote to the *Los Angeles Times* in 2001 to deny that the words "were an invention." He said, "I wish we could take credit for that line, but those words are Yamamoto's." His source? He recalled that "everyone seems to be a little bit right about it. I was told, as I remember Elmo Williams telling me, that they were Yamamoto's words, but he never actually spoke them. They are from his diary." On his part, the producer explained that in 1943, Yamamoto wrote a letter containing the quote to the Admiralty in Tokyo from the South Pacific, where he was conducting a tour of Japanese bases. Williams said that during research in Japan for *Tora! Tora! Tora!* screenwriter Larry Forrester found the letter in a file of Yamamoto's memoirs which he borrowed.[47]

Historian Donald Goldstein, one of Gordon Prange's associates, questions both posited sources. He points out that Yamamoto never kept a diary and says that none of the Japanese naval officers Dr. Prange had interviewed during more than thirty years of research had ever heard of the quote or any letter containing such a comment. With no success, Prange had tried to persuade Fleischer and Williams not to have Yamamoto's character mouth the quote since it did not exist. Of course, even if the admiral had written the letter, the movie still would have been fabricating the quote since Williams acknowledged that Yamamoto had written the sentence in 1943, not spoken it in December 1941.[48]

The admiral's cinematic observation did provide a dramatic ending to *Tora! Tora! Tora!* However, the filmmakers could have avoided creating history without losing the drama by simply having the admiral stand up when he hears the news and, without speaking, walk out onto the ship's deck while a superimposed title states: "In early 1943, while on an inspection tour of Japanese bases in the Southwest Pacific, Yamamoto wrote a letter to the Admiralty in which he said, 'I fear all we have done is to awaken a sleeping giant and fill him with a terrible resolve.'" As rendered, however, the quote became a prime example of how Hollywood creates history, which then becomes validated through repeated recitation, rather than from respected historical research such as Prange and his associates conducted. Even if Yamamoto believed the sentiment his cinematic character mouthed and even if he wrote the words in one or another document as the filmmakers have represented, he did not speak them on December 7 (the 8th, Japanese date) 1941. Beyond that, the quote stands as a quintessential example of the danger of using motion pictures to teach history. While *Tora! Tora! Tora!* does get most of the story right, fabricating the ending compromises the credibility of what comes before.

In any event, given the situation in which the U.S. military found itself in Vietnam in 1970, even a portrayal of a glorious victory in World War II, presented in a better cinematic showcase than *Tora! Tora! Tora!* offered, would have had a difficult time helping the image of the U.S. armed services. Given the continuing quagmire in Southeast Asia and the reaction of reviewers to *Tora! Tora! Tora!* when Twentieth Century Fox released it in October 1970, the film's failure at the box office becomes readily explicable. Vincent Canby's review, which had inspired the "Tora-ble, Tora-ble, Tora-ble" headline, says it all: "From the moment you read the ads for *Tora! Tora! Tora!* ("The Most Spectacular Film Ever Made!"), you are aware that you're in the presence of a film possessed by a lack of imagination so singular that it amounts to a death wish. As it turns out, this poverty of fancy has gripped not only the advertising copywriters but just about everyone connected with the film, from the directors and writers and cameramen on down to the uncredited artists who painted some terrible Pearl Harbor backdrops, which, from time to time, are seen through office windows and look like old Orpheum circuit scenic drops against which jugglers used to perform."[49]

Ultimately, to Canby, *Tora! Tora! Tora!* fails because it adheres too strictly to its goal of recreating history, thereby eschewing "the prerogatives of fiction, or what it understands to be the prerogatives of fiction." He points out that movies of recreated history such as *A Night to Remember,* which told the story of the sinking of the *Titanic, Is Paris Burning?* and *Tora! Tora! Tora!* overlook "one elementary principle of film esthetics, that is, that every movie is fiction, whether it is a newsreel shot in Vietnam, a Stanley Kramer exploration of some contemporary gut-issue, or a cartoon by the Disney people. The very act of recording an event on film transforms the event into fiction, which has its own rules and its own reality." In the case of the re-creation of Pearl Harbor, Canby argues that despite the best of motives on the part of the producers, *Tora! Tora! Tora!* "purports to tell nothing but the truth" and yet "winds up as castrated fiction."[50]

In regard to the filmmaking itself, Canby pinpoints two crucial problems. To him, the characters seem very much like cartoon figures who never acquire life. Consequently, when an aide tells Admiral Kimmel that Admiral Halsey has arrived for a meeting, Canby observes that "the man who comes through the door is not Admiral Halsey, but James

Whitmore, actor, looking very waxy and foolish." Just as damaging, the reviewer noted that the Japanese and American components of the movie never become integrated. Consequently, audiences never have "any doubt they are two different movies."[51]

All the problems with illusion aside, in the end Canby suggests that the film's failure centers on its aspirations: "*Tora! Tora! Tora!* aspires to dramatize history in terms of event rather than people and it just may be that there is more of what Pearl Harbor was all about in fiction films such as Fred Zinnemann's *From Here to Eternity* and as the *Variety* review pointed out, Raoul Walsh's *The Revolt of Mamie Stover* than in all the extravagant posturing in this sort of historical mock-up."[52]

If *Tora! Tora! Tora!* failed dramatically and at the box office, it did succeed in one area, rekindling the controversy over military cooperation to the film industry, although both Twentieth Century Fox and the Defense Department had taken extensive precautions to avoid trouble. Apart from the problem of obtaining the aircraft carrier, the shooting of the film itself had gone so smoothly that Fleischer finished his location work in Hawaii eleven days ahead of schedule. Working with Comdr. Edward Stafford, the technical advisor and Defense Department liaison man, Fleischer had obtained just about everything he needed, sometimes on short notice. Stafford also had made sure that the Navy and other services satisfied Fleischer's requests at no cost to the taxpayer by billing the studio for all expenses.[53]

As with *The Longest Day*, however, the controversy surrounding *Tora! Tora! Tora!* grew out of media coverage of the production, which focused on the Pentagon's commitment of men, equipment, and facilities to Fox. Television's *Sixty Minutes*, acting on a tip from a serviceman, went to Hawaii ostensibly to do a feature on the film's re-creation of the attack on Pearl Harbor. In its May 13, 1969, broadcast, Mike Wallace raised questions about the decision to provide the carrier, about using the ship to transport the studio's planes to Hawaii after the launching sequence off San Diego, and about the Navy's assistance to the company at Pearl Harbor. He concluded by asking: "Should the taxpayer, and the serviceman, help to subsidize the undertaking?"[54]

Bill Brown, the producer of the "*Tora! Tora! Tora!*" segment of *Sixty Minutes*, later admitted that he had used "subterfuge" in his research in Hawaii, because both the military and Fox thought he was doing a feature on how the filmmakers were recreating history. More serious, he embarked on the project already convinced that the studio was taking advantage of the Navy and the American taxpayers. He refused to accept the Navy's explanations that the carrier, which transported the studio planes to Hawaii, had already been scheduled to go there on its way to recover an Apollo spacecraft, or that the studio had agreed beforehand to pay all costs: "But I didn't know that. They claimed they were doing that. I still am not convinced that was so."[55] In fact, even a minimum of research would have revealed that the Navy had assigned the *Yorktown* the Apollo mission before the service agreed to carry the planes and that the studio had ascertained that it could not arrange for suitable commercial transportation. Moreover, stories published the week the planes arrived in Hawaii reported that Fox was paying regular commercial freight rates for the carrier transportation.[56]

At the time of the broadcast, *Sixty Minutes* had not yet become an established network tradition, and the "*Tora!*" segment, because of the controversy it stirred up, helped make the program a continuing success. But the feature did so by playing loose with the facts, by refusing to give credence to the Navy's statements, and by selective editing to "prove" the broadcasters' case. Documentary evidence verifies that the Navy went out of its way to provide a full accounting of services rendered and that Twentieth Century Fox paid all bills presented. Ironically, a CBS-TV van containing television equipment to cover the Apollo landing was also hitching a ride aboard the *Yorktown*, something the network chose not to mention.[57]

None of this says that the Navy charged for every gallon of fuel used or every piece of material expended, something that has never happened during the history of the military–film industry relationship. Such an accounting would be virtually impossible. Without question, Fox was not eager to reimburse the military if it could avoid a charge. But the studio could not have made the film without assistance and so generally accepted the military's figures as appropriate. Furthermore, both congressional and General Accounting Office investigations concluded that the Navy's aid to Fox had followed Pentagon guidelines and that the studio had paid for all assistance it received outside normal military expenditures.[58]

Nevertheless, Congress has never been slow to recognize the political value in a controversy, the facts notwithstanding. Coming at a time when members of Congress and many in the press were attacking the armed services because of Vietnam, the *Sixty Minutes* program triggered a wave of congressional criticism that harked back to the uproar surrounding the making of *The Longest Day*. The renewed controversy raised filmmakers' fears of additional red tape and more congressional criticism of large-scale Pentagon assistance to other war movies. At the same time, the Defense Department became even more cautious in considering requests for assistance on productions that required a major expenditure of time and men. As a result of these issues, the financial failure of *Tora! Tora! Tora!* and the growing antimilitary sentiment in the country, Hollywood ended, at least temporarily, the cycle of films about World War II that it had begun more than twenty years earlier.

15 Changing Images

ALTHOUGH HOLLYWOOD TURNED AWAY FROM the production of "conventional" military movies after 1970, the American people did not lack visualizations of combat. Vintage war movies appeared regularly on late-night television, and the evening television news broadcasts continued to saturate the nation with combat footage from Vietnam until the final American withdrawal in 1973. Unlike Hollywood's re-creations, the network cameramen had no difficulty capturing on film all the authentic details of war—firefights, gunships spewing their rounds blindly into jungle foliage, body counts, medical helicopters evacuating wounded G.I.s, planes spreading agent orange over forests and fields, and children on fire fleeing napalm attacks. Less often, television newsmen even filmed soldiers, on cue, cutting the ears off a dead Vietnamese or torching bamboo huts with zippo lighters.

Hollywood had never matched the realism of these television images, all presented in living color. The power of these recurring pictures contributed significantly to the nation's revulsion against the Vietnam War and helped erode the respected image which the military had enjoyed throughout the nation's history. Given the country's growing antipathy to the war, the film industry concluded that, John Wayne and the success of *The Green Berets* notwithstanding, Vietnam offered no stories that audiences would pay to see, at least in the near future. Hollywood did not ignore the armed services completely during the early 1970s, but even those few films with a noncombat military setting that the motion picture industry did produce in the early 1970s met with resistance from high-ranking armed services information officers. The directors of the public affairs offices, usually older and more conservative officers, were likely to see anti-Vietnam statements implicit in every script that came to their attention.

At the same time, such movies as *The Last Detail* and *Cinderella Liberty* reflected the new realism that had developed in Hollywood with the breakdown of the Production Code in the 1960s. Swearing, drinking, and explicit sex scenes had become normal elements in American films; characters could even live happily ever after without benefit of marriage or fear of retribution. Fictional servicemen taking part in these activities on the screen undoubtedly better represented reality than the sanitized behavior of Hollywood's earlier fighting men. To the chiefs of information, however, portrayals of hard-drinking, swearing, and fornicating military men reflected liberal attacks on the Vietnam War and the military in general and would only further damage the services' already frail images.

In contrast to these beliefs, the lower-echelon public affairs officers in each service recognized the nation's changed perceptions of the armed services and the validity of these new portrayals of servicemen. If the stories did not benefit the military, the staffs believed it was still in the best interest of the services to discuss any and all military projects with producers and writers who came to the Pentagon for assistance. By working with them, the officers hoped to temper the extreme characterizations and produce more balanced images. Despite negotiating in good faith, however, filmmakers usually found that the senior officers would ultimately refuse to approve any agreements they had hammered out with the staffs on stories containing nontraditional portrayals of military life.[1]

The matter of cooperation aside, filmmakers had to deal with the impact of Vietnam on the American people in selecting their noncombat stories. Of necessity, television had given prominent coverage to the ground war, and the often unflattering stories about men in combat, including such occurrences as My Lai, did little to enhance the reputations of the Army and the Marines. The Air Force's saturation bombing had remained impersonal, unglamourous, and a symbol of the war's evilness. In contrast, although naval aviation had contributed to the destruction of Vietnam, its participation in the air war had produced less odious images. The riverboat patrols received television coverage, but Navy personnel did not usually get directly involved in ground combat. As a result, the service suffered less apparent damage to the aura of glamour generated at least in part by all the movies on which the service had provided assistance over the years.

Whatever the degree to which this entered into their considerations, filmmakers did first turn to the Navy as the subject for peacetime movies with a military setting. The service did not demonstrate any particular enthusiasm over this "honor," however, and adamantly refused to cooperate with the producers of *The Last Detail* and *Cinderella Liberty*. In each case, Vietnam contributed to the Navy's perception of the scripts and suspicion over the manner in which the filmmakers intended to portray the service. In fact, the films did convey the impression that military regulations counted for little, that sailors spent their time drinking and womanizing, and that their language consisted primarily of four-letter words.

Together the films created an image of the modern Navy that was strikingly different from portraits created in earlier peacetime films of the 1930s or in the innumerable musicals and comedies of the 1940s and 1950s. Moreover, these new films suggested that the discipline and patriotism shown in combat films such as *They Were Expendable, Task Force,* and *Tora! Tora! Tora!* had become obsolete. At the same time, both movies suggested that the Navy offered an interesting environment in which to spend a few years with unusual but friendly companions. These images may not have provided the services with informational value as stipulated in regulations on cooperation, but they would help, not hurt, recruiting, always a goal that the services saw in cinematic portrayals.

The Last Detail tells the story of two Navy MPs detailed to escort a young prisoner from the Norfolk, Virginia, naval base to the Navy prison in Portsmouth, New Hampshire. The filmmakers portray the youth, about to serve eight years for attempting to steal forty dollars from a charity box, as a big, pitiful slob. Along the way, the MPs initiate him into manhood through a series of drinking bouts and a sexual encounter. The movie establishes much of the texture and tone of its claim to military realism in its first three minutes, when the audience hears a string of obscenities uttered with dazzling speed. Jack Nicholson expresses extreme pride in his nickname, "Badass," while Otis Young and Randy Quaid trade lines throughout the film such as "Tell the M.A. to go fuck himself," "I ain't going on no shit detail," and "You're a lucky son of a bitch." Only fifteen years earlier the Production Code Office would have banned the film because of its few "mild" words (by recent standards), such as *crap, bastard,* and *badass.*

The Navy's reaction to the script and to the efforts of the producer, Gerald Ayres, to obtain even limited military assistance illustrate the service's extreme sensitivity about its image during the early 1970s. After visiting the Norfolk base in 1972, Ayres called Don Baruch to discuss the project and the process of obtaining cooperation. In his cover letter accompanying the script, he explained that he had found that the way "the Navy has responded to a changing society is impressive and should be noted in the film." With revisions he intended to make in the screenplay as a result of this research trip, Ayres thought the film "will be a credit to the Navy." He requested minimal cooperation, since the movie would require only a few days of shooting on the naval base. Ayres said he could fake the Navy facilities if he did not receive assistance but noted, "Given the extraordinary showcase appearance of the Norfolk base, that would be a shame."[2]

In responding by phone, Baruch recommended that Ayres not submit the original screenplay to the Navy. He explained that the script created the wrong image by showing the prisoner participating in various escapades with his escorts. Nevertheless, in asking Baruch to forward the script to the Navy, Ayres expressed a willingness to delete some of the profanity and discuss correcting any inaccuracies. Following up the phone conversation, the producer wrote to Baruch, "I sincerely hope that the Navy understands that I am as anxious to cooperate with them as to receive their cooperation."[3]

Despite Ayres's willingness to negotiate and compromise, the Navy decided it could find "no benefit" from assisting on the film. Its Information Office felt that while Ayres had indicated he would "delete some of the profanity and correct some inaccuracies . . . no minor modification of the script can produce an acceptable film for the Navy." After failing to change the Navy's mind by phone, Ayres wrote to Bob Manning, the civilian motion picture officer in the Navy Office of Information, pointing out that he did not consider himself "irresponsible in the representation of reality nor in any way hostile to our armed forces."[4]

Ayres stressed that he was trying "to show a human drama with a Navy background" and wanted "cooperation, advice and support to make the script all the more accurate and, as a consequence, all the more effective." He reminded the Navy that he had offered "to make script changes in accordance with your advice. If you found portions of the screenplay unsympathetic or unreal with regard to the Navy, I wanted to come to discuss those portions with you." He expressed "shock" at the Navy's suggestion that he save his airplane fare by not bothering to come to Washington to discuss the script. He repeated his offer to be cooperative in return for assistance: "You seem to feel my script is so far from pleasing the Navy that I would, to use your words, 'have no plot left by the time you altered your script sufficiently to get our cooperation.' I would appreciate further explanation of this, if it is possible for you to set it down for me."[5]

Ayres acknowledged that his characters broke some Navy regulations, but he pointed out that most films which received military assistance contained some infractions: "We can both list them. This rule breaking is shown in a mostly humorous light. On the more serious side of our story, the petty officers strictly adhere to orders and turn over their prisoner as ordered. In the course of these actions, they show themselves first and foremost to be humane and compassionate." Although he recognized that Manning seemed to disagree with him, Ayres closed by saying he refused to believe that the Navy "would not want men in positions of leadership who are humane and compassionate. Our times are too much in need of such men."[6]

Jack Garrow, the Navy's director of the Production Services Division, rejected Ayres's arguments, writing to the producer that "it is very unlikely we could arrive at a mutually agreeable script without emasculating the premise of your story." Conceding that it would make an entertaining R-rated movie, Garrow repeated that the Navy did not consider the "action of the film in the best interests of the Navy, or for that matter a reasonable occurrence within today's Navy." He conceded that although the Navy found the escorts "sympathetic in their own fashion and somewhat enthusiastic about the Navy, they do not reflect the best of the service and in many cases perpetuate a false derogatory stereotype." The Navy felt that Ayres could not change the script sufficiently to satisfy the service; but Garrow did say he would be willing to discuss the project.[7]

Given the finality of the response, Ayres and his director, Hal Ashby, made the film without cooperation. Despite the Navy's position, the producer, Lester Persky, a Navy veteran, had thought the script "had the ring of truth." Ashby managed to reinforce this sense of authenticity by taking some shots of the entrance to the Norfolk Navy Base. He was so successful in creating the illusion of being on the base that he was able to fool even knowledgeable viewers. Adm. John Will, for one, the technical advisor for John Ford's 1930 submarine movie *Men without Women,* became furious after seeing *The Last Detail.* Accepting the word of a film critic he had trusted, Will had gone to see the movie. Although he had walked out after ten minutes when he "got sick to my stomach," he had concluded that the Navy had assisted in the making of the film "because I recognized shots at the Fifth Naval District." The apparent cooperation made him angry since he believed the film would hurt Navy recruiting: "Any mother who sees this picture would never allow a son of hers to join the Navy or have anything to do with it."[8]

To be sure, the movie did distort Navy procedures to such an extent that its story was implausible to anyone familiar with Navy regulations and activities. Nevertheless, as Gerald Ayres had reminded Bob Manning, the service had over the years assisted on even more implausible comedies, ones that totally disregarded Navy procedures and regulations and distorted life in the peacetime service. In any event, for the average viewer with no frame of reference, *The Last Detail* seemed to show the Navy as it currently existed. And given the humor and good-natured friendship that developed among the three main characters, the film probably did more good than harm to the Navy image.

Cinderella Liberty, which contained the same positive images of life in the peacetime Navy, experienced a similar fate at the hands of the Navy's Public Affairs Office as had *The Last Detail,* even though the producer-director, Mark Rydell, went to greater lengths to secure assistance than had Gerald Ayres. Like Ashby, Rydell used the Navy primarily as background, in this case for a love story between James Caan, as a sailor, and Marsha Mason, as a prostitute. Having set the story on a Navy base and aboard a ship, Rydell sought Navy assistance, making his initial contact through its Information Office in Los Angeles.

The script he brought with him depicted sailors whose thoughts and actions followed decidedly unmilitary directions. The love story left something to be desired from the Navy's viewpoint—a prostitute did not represent the ideal girlfriend for a sailor, particularly when she had a son from her black former lover. The screenplay also included inaccuracies in Navy procedures as well as a good deal of profanity. Finally, the ending, which showed James Caan deserting the Navy, would have been so repugnant to the service that it alone would have precluded cooperation. The plot had Caan switching places with an old sailor who had been mustered out of the Navy, a good sailor who knows his job and wants to get back into the service.

Ironically, however, the desertion did not become an issue during Rydell's initial discussions with the Navy in Los Angeles or with officials in Washington. Focusing on the script's other problems, Rydell and lower-level Navy officers revised the story until Don Baruch's office and the Navy's Public Affairs Office had given the producer-director tentative approval for limited cooperation. At that point, top Navy brass stepped into the picture and demanded further revisions that would have totally changed the character of the film. In the end, despite additional changes, the Navy chief of information refused to approve cooperation, believing the script contained an implicit antimilitary statement.[9]

Baruch himself thought the Navy had not acted in good faith with Rydell. He said that the revised script had contained significant improvements and that the completed production would not have become detrimental to the Navy, especially if a project officer had overseen the appearance and actions of the characters. Nevertheless, his only possible option would have been to ask the assistant secretary of defense for public affairs to order the Navy to cooperate—something that had never been done before. Besides, the Defense Department itself had no direct involvement in the project, since Rydell's needs were limited assistance from the Navy alone.[10]

Rydell felt that he had more than upheld his end of the negotiations and so had solid grounds for appealing the decision to higher Navy authority. With this in mind, he contacted Jack Valenti, president of the Motion Picture Association, who in turn called the Navy. Valenti, however, was not willing to dispute high-level feeling that the incorrect portrayal of the service and its men demanded further script revisions. Unlike his extensive efforts on behalf of Darryl Zanuck only a few years before during preproduction on *Tora! Tora! Tora!* Valenti suggested to Rydell that he forget about cooperation and find a commercial ship. Despite his refusal to intervene further, Valenti did believe the government should not base its decision to cooperate simply "on whether or not they liked the director or the star of the story. I think the government should cooperate on the making of a film if it is not a costly thing for the government [and is] not going to interrupt training." Rydell's limited requirements did fall into this framework, and Baruch felt Valenti could have reversed the decision if he had tried harder, because Rydell "had shown good faith, was led down the primrose path, and had wasted time and money doing what the Navy asked, only to be told that it was useless!"[11]

When his efforts failed, Rydell returned to his original script, obtained additional financial backing from Twentieth Century Fox, and made the film without Navy cooperation. Whether the earthy language, unconventional love story, and Caan's desertion projected a realistic or a negative image of the service, *Cinderella Liberty*, like *The Last Detail*, did not show the Navy as it would have liked the American people to see it. Moreover, since Hollywood was not releasing any positive-military-image films, the essentially irreverent images of life in the Navy in these two films furnished the only fictional picture of the service during the early 1970s.[12]

The closest the armed services came to presenting themselves positively in these years came in films that had nothing directly to do with the military, particularly in *Airport 1975* and *Towering Inferno*, both major disaster movies, the most popular genre of the '70s. The military agreed to cooperate on these films because they showed the services performing as they would in an actual disaster. As with combat films, the Defense Department demanded an accurate portrayal of the military. Before agreeing to assist on *Airport 1975*, for example, the Air Force conducted a test to determine whether one of its helicopters could actually fly as fast as a 747 jet under the conditions described in the film. Only after a stuntman demonstrated that a helicopter could actually lower a person to the "stricken" airliner did the Air Force approve use of its aircraft and personnel to simulate the rescue.[13]

In *Towering Inferno*, Navy helicopters answer a request to assist in rescuing people from a burning skyscraper. The Navy felt that its involvement in this plot would help inform the public that a military emergency assistance network existed to meet such situations, and for this reason the Pentagon asked the filmmakers to include lines in the script describing the network. The explanation did not get into the movie because the service did not make the request a mandatory requirement for providing assistance. However, the screen credits acknowledged the assistance from the Navy and the Defense Department.[14]

Not all filmmakers felt the need to seek assistance from the Pentagon even if their stories included military characters. While the 1936 disaster film *San Francisco* had used Marines to help recreate the scenes of chaos during the 1906 earthquake, Mark Robson, the director of *Earthquake* (1975) preferred to use actors and extras rather than to request assistance from the National Guard and undergo its red tape. The Guard would undoubtedly have been reluctant to help anyway, given the film's portrayal of a deranged guardsman. In general, however, during the early 1970s, the Defense Department remained willing to discuss with filmmakers screenplays—combat or otherwise—that might in some way benefit the armed services.[15]

Frank McCarthy, for one, had begun work on *MacArthur* in mid-1972, hoping to duplicate his success with *Patton*. He admitted that he had resisted the subject for a long time, fearing it might seem "self-imitative." A comment from Gen. Robert Eichelberger, who had fought under MacArthur but had not liked him very much, provided McCarthy's inspiration. Eichelberger said that in view of MacArthur's love of publicity and his ego and his great success, if Patton, instead of serving under the more modest Eisenhower, had served under MacArthur, then Patton would have emerged from World War II as an unknown officer.[16]

McCarthy decided that if *Patton* had become a good film because its subject had had those qualities, then a film about MacArthur could prove even better. The producer thought he would make an appealing screen hero because he had been "enormously successful" and had become the great hero of the conflict in the Pacific. Furthermore, "every woman was in love with him and eventually, when he was relieved in Korea for insubordination, which you ordinarily would think is a disgraceful thing, he came home and got the biggest hero's welcome that anybody ever had. This is fascinating, I think."[17]

McCarthy accomplished his first step of finding financial backers in September 1972, when he reached an agreement with Richard Zanuck and David Brown and their newly formed independent company to make the film in association with Universal Studios. In announcing the project, Zanuck (who had been in charge of production at Twentieth Century Fox when the studio made *Patton*), said that the film was a "long-range project," which he hoped to have under way within a year. By March 1974, however, McCarthy did not have a completed script, although he had made a decision do the exterior shooting in South Korea and the Philippines, where armies had World War II equipment. Ultimately, the cost of sending a film company to the Far East ended those plans, and the movie, much scaled down in scope, did not go before the cameras until August 1976.[18]

In the meantime, Walter Mirisch had begun work on *Midway*. The first major American victory of World War II, the Battle of Midway became the turning point in the Pacific Theater. Mirisch conceived of his project as a tribute to the American Bicentennial, with the story symbolizing the nation's spirit and will to triumph in the face of great odds. At Midway, American forces had faced a vastly superior Japanese task force but had sunk four enemy aircraft carriers and emerged victorious. From that point onward, U.S. strength continued to grow, while Japan was unable to mount another offensive equal to that of Midway.

From their respective standpoints, the Navy and the Defense Department anticipated no problems in working with Mirisch. Unlike *Tora! Tora! Tora! Midway* would reveal no skeletons of unprepared military leaders, no unchallenged attacks, no victorious enemy.

The film would show a successful carrier-based attack and a significant victory over the Japanese. In his initial reaction to the script in December 1974, the head of Navy Aviation Periodicals and History wrote to the Navy's chief of information that the film "could be useful in recruiting efforts as part of the Bicentennial and as an adjunct to the Sea-Air Operations Hall of the new Air and Space Museum which will focus on carriers." Subsequently, the Navy informed the assistant secretary of defense for public affairs that it believed "cooperation is both feasible and in the best interests of the service."[19]

Although the Pentagon found that both *MacArthur* and *Midway* merited its cooperation, actual assistance was necessarily limited, given the paucity of World War II equipment. Because *MacArthur* dealt with one man's career, primarily in command positions, Frank McCarthy did not have the problem of recreating large-scale battles that he had experienced with *Patton.* Ultimately he utilized some stock combat footage, a few small-scale recreated combat scenes, a couple of facsimile PT boats, a few rented planes, and some Navy ships to produce the illusion of a military atmosphere.

In contrast, Walter Mirisch had to show two major naval task forces on the screen. Fortunately for the producer, at Midway the Japanese and American fleets had never come within sight of each other—airplanes of each side waged the entire battle against the other's planes and ships. To recreate their air-to-sea and air-to-air battles, Mirisch resorted to several expediencies, primarily the use of Navy combat and gun-camera footage. Mirisch also acquired some sequences from *Thirty Seconds Over Tokyo,* the 1944 MGM recreation of Jimmy Doolittle's raid on Japan, used miniatures and mock-ups from *Tora! Tora! Tora!* and rented two World War II F4F planes. The only significant Navy assistance he received was the use of the USS *Lexington,* the one World War II aircraft carrier still on active duty. The film company spent several days shooting aboard the ship while it was dockside at Pensacola, Florida. Then fifty members of the cast and crew and the two planes spent a week aboard the carrier during one of its regular training cruises, filming exterior sequences and interior atmosphere shots.

Perhaps mindful of the controversy within the Pentagon about the decision to allow Twentieth Century Fox to film takeoffs for *Tora! Tora! Tora!* the Navy refused to permit Mirisch to fly his two planes off the *Lexington,* even though they had flown to Pensacola from Texas and Illinois. As a result, Jack Smight, the film's director, used the aircraft solely as props for the actors. With only two planes, he had to stage his shots carefully to create the illusion that the flight deck or hangar deck contained the full complement of planes. To do this, he had to restrict the vision of his camera and so could not capture the huge size of the *Lexington.* Under the circumstances, the film could not convey the visual au-

Facsimiles of Japanese Zeroes practicing in formation for *Tora! Tora! Tora!* and, later, *Midway* (1976).

thenticity as successfully as the filmmakers had hoped, despite the Navy cooperation. Considering the static nature of the scenes that featured the old planes, Smight might just as well have shot them on a soundstage as Mervyn LeRoy had done thirty years before while directing *Thirty Seconds Over Tokyo.*

The problem of duplicating life aboard the carrier during the Battle of Midway paled when compared with Mirisch's task of recreating the actual battle. The scarcity of World War II planes gave him no choice but to use footage from earlier Hollywood productions and Navy archives. The film's opening montage, Doolittle's raiders skimming over the waves and flying inland over a Japanese city (actually Long Beach, vintage 1943), came from *Thirty Seconds Over Tokyo.* Although Mirisch had the footage tinted to blend with the color of the rest of *Midway,* the sequence remains secondhand, easily recognized material. The crash of a B-17 returning to Midway after a mission against the Japanese fleet came from *Tora! Tora! Tora!* (The crash itself became an example of Hollywood's creativity. When the plane's landing gear malfunctioned during a training flight, the pilot informed Elmo Williams of his difficulty. In turn, the producer had the cameras ready when the plane landed on one wheel.) To show the Japanese planes taking off from their carriers in search of the American fleet, the director used outtakes from the same film.

To get the American planes off the carriers and into the air to recreate the Battle of Midway itself, Mirisch relied on Navy combat and gun-camera footage. Fortunately, the Navy had used color stock almost exclusively during World War II and had preserved and cataloged the processed film in archives. Without this footage, Mirisch would have had to resort to models and process shots. More positively, he saw "two great advantages" in using the Navy footage: "It gives you a feeling of validity that I find tremendously dramatic" and it made possible "real, full-size planes, not models."[20]

Although Mirisch used actual combat film from World War II, the

Capt. George Watkins recreated the landing of Air Group Commander Fuishida's Zero aboard a Japanese carrier in this reconstructed AT-6. The sequence later appeared several times in *Midway.*

footage did not enable *Midway* to create an authentic sense of aerial warfare. Ironically, this failure grew out of the use of the footage itself. In blowing up the 16mm standard-dimension film to 35mm Cinemascope proportions, the filmmakers, of necessity, cut off the bottom and top of the frame. Mirisch thought this produced "a much more exciting effect" by placing the viewer in the center of the picture and made the action "much more dramatic than it was originally." Even so, audiences immediately recognized the combat footage by its deep blue cast and grainy quality, which resulted from being blown up. Consequently, though the battle sequences impressively convey the scope of the fighting, the film loses its sense of realism because the viewer remains constantly aware of the old footage as the screen images switch from "live" action to studio re-creations.[21]

Furthermore, for anyone who had seen any of Hollywood's older films about the war in the Pacific or documentaries such as *Victory at Sea,* the recognition of the borrowed sequences would necessarily lessen the impact of the visual image. Rather than becoming absorbed in the action, some viewers undoubtedly spent their time recalling where they had previously seen the sequences. In fact, most of the Navy combat footage postdated the Battle of Midway and so contributed to the film's lessened authenticity.

One spectacular and often-used crash sequence, in which an F6F Hellcat returning to its carrier breaks in two while landing, actually occurred in October 1944, during the Battle of Leyte Gulf. Moreover, the plane did not even make its maiden flight until three weeks after the Battle of Midway. The film's climactic plane crash played far looser with aviation history. Although it takes a sharp eye to recognize it, a Korean War–vintage jet plane, not a World War II dive bomber, slams onto the carrier deck. Admitting he simply needed one more spectacular crash, the film editor acknowledged that he did not realize the plane's identity.[22]

For the most part, only aviation enthusiasts, military historians, and World War II veterans could pick up these flaws or notice the repeated use of the same shot, which the filmmakers attempted to disguise by reversing the frame from left to right. Much of the box-office success the movie enjoyed resulted from people who went to see the battle sequences irrespective of their chronological accuracy. In particular, young viewers either had not seen the original dramatic footage and combat documentaries from which the battle scenes had been borrowed or had found them unimpressive on their television small screen. In addition, use of the Sensurround sound system gave a new dimension to the images even if the sound track did not always synchronize with the action.

Like most war movies, however, Mirisch had intended for *Midway* to become more than a series of World War II combat clips enhanced with technological gimmicks. The producer had aspired to create a dramatic story within the framework of a major historical event as a way of reminding the American people of "a most prideful" event in American history. And the film did succeed as history as well as any Hollywood theatrical release had ever done. Nevertheless, as with *Tora! Tora! Tora!* before it, *Midway* failed as drama.

The two films suffer the same basic problem. The historical figures fail for the most part to become living people with whom the audience can empathize. Only Henry Fonda, who plays Admiral Nimitz, successfully captures the essence of the man: a commander who has grown accustomed to the isolation that comes with the responsibility of four stars on his collar. The other Americans remain indistinguishable, all rumpled, informal, and skilled in the art of war. The Japanese, led by Toshiro Mifune as Admiral Yamamoto, appear more formal and stoic. This proved a wise casting decision, since Mirisch elected to dub their lines into English rather than use subtitles as was done in *The Longest Day* and *Tora! Tora! Tora!* The filmmakers treat both sides with an evenhandedness that refuses to explore the abilities and decisions of the combatants. Even though the Americans win and the Japanese lose, the film attributes the difference to luck. No one makes a major mistake or even voices serious fears about the outcome of the battle. This lack of emotionalism dissipates the drama inherent in the developing confrontation.

Recognizing the problems of creating a dramatic film within the framework of historical events, Mirisch chose to graft a fictional character onto the factual story. Capt. Matt Garth, played by Charlton Heston in his bigger-than-life style, finds himself at the center of events throughout the film. If, as Vincent Canby observed in the *New York Times*, Garth's character might "have been stolen from some terrible movie made shortly after World War II," his role served as the device through which the filmmakers introduced dramatic complications, in the form of a love interest, into the film. In the best tradition of a soap opera, Garth's son, also a Navy flier, informs his father that he has fallen in love with a Japanese-American girl, interned in Hawaii with her family.[23]

The Romeo and Juliet story suffers from some of the most ludicrous dialogue to appear in any Hollywood movie. Son: "Dad, I've fallen in love with a Japanese girl. I want to marry her. Dad, I need your help." Garth: "I damn well guess you do, Tiger." The romance draws on every cliché found in a Hollywood war movie. The girl is willing to give up her man for the good of his career and his country. Nevertheless, she waits for him as any good serviceman's woman does; and in the end, she welcomes him home, eager to love him despite the terrible burns he has suffered in the battle.

Garth the elder stands around looking grim about both the romance and the impending battle. Heston never makes his character into a believable person or any less wooden than the historical figures with whom he mingles. His role, intended to provide human drama in *Midway,* simply accentuates the film's lifelessness in everything except the Navy's combat footage. In the end, Garth dies after leading the final attack on the Japanese fleet—perhaps because Mirisch had one more fiery crash left in the editing room—and few people cared.

The filmmakers do not limit the script's ineptitude to the American historical and fictional characters. When an aide informs Admiral Yamamoto of Doolittle's raid on Japan, he adds: "This raid is a blessing in disguise. The Americans have done us an invaluable service. They have proven you correct. Our homeland is not invulnerable to attack. After today there will be no more foot dragging by the general staff." Such dialogue, combined with the badly matched battle sequences that cut from combat footage to miniatures to exploding mock-ups, made *Midway* little more than a competent, dull, and occasionally confusing history lesson. Nevertheless, the film became one of the major box-office successes of 1976.

Why? Why did a movie containing two-dimensional characters and purloined visual images, telling a story about a distant battle, attract such interest at a time when the armed services were still recovering from the trauma of Vietnam? While acknowledging that his film did not succeed completely from a creative standpoint, Mirisch thought that *Midway* rode the wave of nostalgia then in evidence in the United States. He said that World War II was becoming romanticized, and the generation that had grown up during conflict wanted to relive the earlier period in which a united country had fought a so-called good war with clearly defined issues. The producer did not see the desire to recall a victorious past as an attempt to forget the controversies of Vietnam, saying there was no connection between the war and his movie. To him, *Midway* simply helped young people learn about World War II and the major turning point in the war against Japan and provided a reminder of a most prideful period in American history.[24]

MacArthur offered the same opportunity to remind Americans about the triumphs of World War II. In addition, as historical biography, the film did not lack a strong central character around whom to create a dramatic story. In deciding to make

Midway burns, thanks to footage provided from *Tora! Tora! Tora!*

the movie, Frank McCarthy had concluded that Gen. Douglas MacArthur had at least as many facets to his personality and was probably more controversial than George Patton. Unfortunately, the completed movie only hinted at the ambiguities and controversies that surrounded MacArthur. As Richard Schickel observed in his *Time* review, the filmmakers "tiptoed up to the most fascinating enigma of his character, and then quietly backed away from it." Consequently, the film is at best a bland, official biography, at worst, a dull, unconvincing, often confusing story about one of America's greatest generals.[25]

General MacArthur was a consummate egomaniac. He regularly had his staff send films of his exploits back to the United States for exhibition in the nation's theaters. Like James Garner's admiral in *The Americanization of Emily,* who wanted to make a movie about the first dead man on Omaha Beach, MacArthur always wanted to give the impression that he became the first American on every beach. In one instance, the Army Signal Corps submitted to the Office of War Information, for possible release to commercial theaters, a thirty-minute film portraying the invasion of New Guinea. An OWI official recalled: "Though a full-length shot of MacArthur was not shown wading ashore, his figure in profile or his hat or pipe appeared in all three landings," which supposedly had taken place simultaneously. The official speculated that perhaps the film was meant to suggest MacArthur had been "there in 'spirit' if not in person." In any case, the footage arrived six or eight months after the invasion and its length made it unsuitable for theatrical release.[26]

When MacArthur landed in the Philippines, the cameramen and sound equipment were carefully placed to record his "I have returned," not "We have returned," even though an American fleet and landing force surrounded him. In the movie, however, MacArthur's public relations efforts seem more the product of an eccentric than an egotist. But if this and other aspects of MacArthur's personality lacked development or insight, the screenwriters' failure is perhaps explicable. The general's Army career spanned fifty-two years, the longest in American Army annals. According to Hal Barwood, he and his cowriter, Matthew Robbins, "faced an enormous task in narrowing his life to the confines of a feature film."[27]

By deciding to open the movie with MacArthur's departure from Corregidor under Japanese fire in 1942 and end it with his dismissal by President Truman in 1951, the writers focused on the most significant period of his career. Although they tried to "show the light and dark" in MacArthur's life, this approach precluded any real efforts to probe into the origins of his personality or trace its development. Robbins observed that the general's decisions "were frequently brilliant, but the way he carried then out was often ludicrous. He had a great capacity for self-delusion." The authors also attempted to illustrate that after the "grandeur" of ruling a conquered Japan and setting it on the road to spectacular recovery, MacArthur felt "he should be making the decisions instead of a former artillery captain who happened to be president."[28]

Portraying even the nine years from the ignominy of MacArthur's retreat on a PT boat to his removal from the Supreme Pacific Command still presented the writers with a huge task. *Patton* focused on less than three years of Patton's career, and so the film could explore the ambiguities in the general's personality at some length. In contrast, Barwood and Robbins could only suggest the complexities in MacArthur's personality. Perhaps an actor with George C. Scott's ability could have added his reading of MacArthur's life to the script to provide a complex picture of the general. In contrast, Gregory Peck simply did not get inside MacArthur. He spoke his lines rather than lived them. Just as important, whereas Scott became Patton both mentally and physically, Peck could not merge himself with MacArthur.

MacArthur himself created part of the problem. Many people remembered MacArthur. He had been visible for a longer time than had Patton, had generated more publicity, had had a longer career, had appeared on television, and had died only thirteen years before McCarthy filmed his biography. More important, Peck could not or would not completely submerge his own acting mannerisms or seem to age visually as MacArthur aged chronologically. Director Joseph Sargent vividly recalled that Peck simply refused to have himself made up to look like the eighty-two-year-old MacArthur coming to West Point for the last time in 1962.[29]

The filmmakers intended to use his address to the Cadets in an attempt to duplicate the power of Patton's opening monologue and to set the stage for everything that came after. According to the director, the crew had assembled in the Grand Hall "to shoot that very moving, very delicate, very vulnerable good-bye speech that his 82-year-old monarch was delivering with great fragility." In came Peck "with a little bit of shadowing here and there, and none of the make-up that we had discussed back at the studio that would transform this very healthy, robust, gorgeous-looking leading man into a reasonably-close to 80-year-old fallen warrior." Peck explained, "After I tried on rubber nose No. 1, rubber nose No. 2, rubber nose No. 3 and all the rubber jowls, I said, 'Fellows, I just can't do it. I feel unnatural; I feel like a ham.'" Peck later claimed that the filmmakers "were somewhat relieved by his decision." However Sargent recalled that without the makeup, Peck "had none of the pathos and none of the vulnerability and none of the fragility of the man that I had just watched with fascination in hundreds of feet of newsreel film." Faced with another creative disagreement with Peck, Sargent decided that "rather than make an ugly scene in front of 4,000 cadets, I chose to wing it through on a sheer hope and a prayer and chalk it up to some more Hollywood compromising. And that's what it was.[30]

Whatever the reason for Peck's decision, audiences found it difficult to forget that they were watching Gregory Peck play Douglas MacArthur, particularly since the director admitted that he had trouble getting the actor to look fifty, let alone more than eighty. On the other hand, Sargent acknowledged that a movie does not always become "the ultimate realization of a director's vision and a director's dream. A film sometimes is the coming together of many diverse elements that the director tries desperately to put into some cohesive form that comes close to his own sense of values and taste." In the case of dealing with an actor of Peck's stature, Sargent recalled Stanislavsky's observation that if an actor can have two honest moments in any given three-act play, he is doing very well: "It's an

Gregory Peck, as Douglas MacArthur, addresses cadets at the U.S. Military Academy, sans aging makeup, during filming of *MacArthur*, Frank McCarthy's attempt to duplicate his success with *Patton*.

Gregory Peck, as MacArthur on his final visit to West Point, looks his own age rather than MacArthur's.

unfortunate kind of rationale to have to face when you are thinking in terms of film and the kind of magnificent creative possibilities and control that you have as a director, when you are then faced with the loss of that control."[31]

To Sargent, the loss of that control over his work "hurts and it nettles and it stings a lot and you find yourself coming up with a lot of rationale that you normally wouldn't resort to, to say why I gave in, why I backed off. You like to pretend that you didn't." With Peck, however, Sargent had little choice but to give in because of the leverage that a star of his magnitude had and because of the demands of the production schedule. In the actor's defense, however, the film would also have worked better if McCarthy and his director had supported Peck with better visual surroundings.[32]

Despite the original hope of shooting the film on location, budgetary problems forced McCarthy to shoot *MacArthur* in the United States on a limited scale. For all practical purposes, this meant that the film became an interior, dialogue movie rather than an exterior, action war film on the grand scale of *Patton*. The few staged combat sequences resemble the battles Hollywood waged on its back lots for such early World War II films as *Bataan, Wake Island, Fighting Seabees,* and *Marine Raiders.* Because Sargent did not have

Joseph Sargent (with megaphone) directs Gregory Peck, as Douglas MacArthur, in the Japanese surrender scene in *MacArthur,* filmed at the actual location aboard the USS *Missouri,* then moored at Bremerton, Washington.

Filming on the USS *Missouri* helped give *MacArthur* a feeling of authenticity.

the resources to create any illusion of reality in these scenes, the actual combat footage used (supplied in large part by the Marine Corps) becomes even more obvious than in *Midway*.

When the director was able to use actual locations, he was relatively successful in giving actual events and meetings between MacArthur and historical figures a feel of authenticity. Peck's youth aside, MacArthur's farewell address at West Point, with cooperation from the Army, and the Japanese surrender aboard the USS *Missouri*, filmed on the battleship at Bremerton, Washington, where it was then mothballed, have an almost documentary ambience. In MacArthur's meetings with Presidents Roosevelt and Truman, dramatic license facilitates the sharp confrontations and clarifies personalities and issues, and the scenes come alive through the interactions of Peck, Dan O'Herlihy (Roosevelt), and Ed Flanders (Truman).

The dramatic highlight of the film is MacArthur's reunions with the survivors of the Bataan Death March, including Gen. Jonathan Wainwright. Sargent makes the meetings believable and even moving. Nevertheless, because the filmmakers failed to develop MacArthur's character, even these sequences create ambiguities. Early in the movie, MacArthur had refused to recommend Wainwright for the Medal of Honor because he had surrendered Corregidor rather than holding out to the last man. Yet when he meets the now-frail general after his liberation, MacArthur treats Wainwright with apparent affection and later arranges for him to be part of the surrender ceremony.

As played, viewers have a difficult time deciding whether MacArthur regretted his early denouncement of Wainwright or whether he was acting hypocritically. Sargent attributed the dramatic ambiguity to the complexity of MacArthur's character itself. He said that MacArthur probably had been happy to see Wainwright again, but he also "knew he had to make a performance for the rest of the men around him. We all do that. And that's essentially what it came to." Consequently, the director had to convince Peck that he was not acting hypocritically, a task made more difficult because it was the first scene actually shot and because Peck had already made it clear to the director that he wanted to avoid showing MacArthur's warts. The actor later said the opposite, "There was never any attempt to glorify him. I wanted the warts and the foibles and the vanities. That's part of him." However, Sargent recalled the actor "was beginning to get a little nervous about whether he would appear to be hypocritical. And, he didn't want the blemish to appear too much. And, I had to convince him that, yes, there was a certain amount of hypocrisy since he had worked so hard to relieve the good general of his Medal of Honor."[33]

In fact, MacArthur had become furious at Wainwright for surrendering and had wanted him drummed out of the Army. However, Sargent said he explained to Peck that these were "the emotions of a man who was not used to functioning in twentieth century warfare as much as he was in nineteenth century warfare and nineteenth century code of behavior and honor." According to the director, Peck had to play a man who was "flushed with victory, flushed with the generosity of amnesty. Both emotions existed: he was being both somewhat hypocritical and honestly glad to see his old friend." If both emotions existed within MacArthur, however, Peck only conveyed a sense of ambiguity that did not give audiences sufficient insights to understand the conflicting sentiments the general may have held.[34]

Beyond that, *MacArthur* suffers from some structural and historical defects. MacArthur's years as ruler of occupied Japan represent his greatest and most enduring success. Yet both historically and in the movie, the Japanese surrender marked the high point of MacArthur's life. Everything that followed necessarily became anticlimactic. The general could never achieve a greater role than as orchestrator of the American victory in the Pacific, and the film had to treat his years in Japan and as United Nations commander in Korea in a series of vignettes. This episodic treatment precluded a buildup of dramatic tensions leading to the film's conclusion. The filmmakers intensified their dramatic problems by using the general's farewell speech at West Point as their starting point and then flashing back to Corregidor as the true beginning of the biography. Although they returned to the farewell speech to close the movie, it seems more the ending of a circular journey than a meaningful dramatic climax.

Such problems aside, the filmmakers worked diligently to produce a historically accurate and evenhanded biography. Nevertheless, errors and misstatements crept in. MacArthur and his party left Corregidor aboard four PT boats, not two as shown in the film—probably because of budget problems, but a historical inaccuracy nevertheless. He arrived in Australia in March wearing a winter coat even though he would never have needed such apparel on Corregidor or during the down-under fall. He returned to the Philippines on Leyte Beach, not Luzon as portrayed on the screen. MacArthur probably did not answer President Osmena's comment, "Suppose people learn I can't swim?" with "Suppose they learn that I can't walk on water?" as the two men prepared to disembark. Although MacArthur actually shunned visits to wounded servicemen in hospitals and while on Corregidor received the sobriquet of "Dugout Doug," in the film he visited the wounded in the tunnel hospital on Corregidor. He did not come to Buna during the fight for the island, again contrary to the film. And Truman lived at Blair House when he decided to remove MacArthur from his Korean command, not in the White House as shown, because it was then in the process of being renovated.[35]

In the end, however, the failure of *MacArthur* as a dramatic, insightful, and moving film results not from the historical errors or even poorly recreated battle sequences. As a movie biography, *MacArthur* could only be as successful as the actor in the title role. Whatever Peck's acting talents, which he clearly manifested in films such as *Twelve O'Clock High* and *To Kill A Mockingbird,* he suffered an inevitable comparison with George C. Scott. Scott brought out all of Patton's ambiguities, his abilities and his weaknesses. Although he bore no physical resemblance to his character and did not try to imitate Patton's high-pitched voice, Scott simply became Patton to most people, even to those who had known the general. In contrast, Peck could not make people suspend their disbelief and see him as the aging general rather than a vigorous actor. As a result, he simply could not capture the grand MacArthur style and so could not convey why he became the center of so much controversy.

According to Richard Schickel in *Time,* MacArthur deserved a "robust life made of him: something that really attacked its subject, taking a strong point of view about him—whether for or against would not have mattered. The Great Commander never operated in a climate of caution, and there is no good reason why this movie should. Something of the spirit of *Patton* is what is required." Sargent did not agree with the judgment, but MacArthur biographer Robert Sherrod supports Schickel's observation more succinctly: "MacArthur was a better actor than Peck."[36]

Regardless of their dramatic shortcomings, both *Midway* and *MacArthur* presented the American military at its best, fighting and winning battles and emerging with its reputation unblemished. As far as the U.S. Army was concerned, Operation Market Garden, detailed in Cornelius Ryan's *A Bridge Too Far,* also became a military success. In that operation, which took place in September 1944, American forces captured all of their objectives and held them. For the British and Polish troops, however, the enterprise degenerated into a tragic fiasco. Of the ten thousand men of the British First Airborne Division who landed near the "Bridge Too Far" in the Dutch city of Arnhem, fewer than two thousand made their way back to Allied lines. More men died in the operation than on the Normandy beaches. Most important, the combined Allied effort failed to open the road to Germany in the fall of 1944, and the war dragged on until the following May. As a result, Operation Market Garden remained a little-known operation until Joseph E. Levine bought Ryan's best-seller and spent $27 million to create *A Bridge Too Far* (1977).

The spectacular epic focuses far more on the British efforts to capture the Arnhem Bridge than on the American role in the battle. Although the United States no longer had any World War II equipment, the Army did cooperate on the production, vetting the script, providing historical and technical information, and allowing the participation of some troops during the filming in the actual Dutch locales where the battles occurred. In the tradition of *The Longest Day, Tora! Tora! Tora!* and *Midway,* the film followed the battle from its inception through its implementation to its conclusion. Like its predecessors, *A Bridge Too Far* used two dozen or so leading German, British, and American actors, mostly in cameo roles. Several received huge salaries, including Robert Redford, to whom Levine reportedly paid $2 million for ten minutes of screen time. Whether the expenditure of such amounts of money for actors helps or hinders a film remains open to debate. Instead of getting caught up in the action, audiences tend to look for their favorite stars, who cannot, in any case, develop their characterizations, because of their brief time on the screen.

To be sure, the actors gave credible performances. However, many critics thought Levine miscast Ryan O'Neal as Gen. James Gavin. Richard Schickel suggested that the actor "looks as if he is about to inquire, 'Tennis, anyone?' like a summer-stock juvenile." General Gavin himself acknowledged that O'Neal "tried very hard, could not have been more serious in trying to carry out the role in which he was cast, and I admired his effort . . . [but he was] perceived as a matinee idol, and it may have been very difficult for him to carry out the role that I had."[37]

O'Neal had not received instruction in military procedures, and that created part of the problem. Gavin noted that the actor "carried a rifle like a broomstick over his right shoulder, the butt well to the rear behind him and holding the rifle by the metal part, near the muzzle." As a result, the general said O'Neal showed a total lack of readiness for action, although Gavin recalled that "being engaged by fire as soon as we landed, we all carried our rifles in a very ready position, knowing that we would need them."[38]

In the context of the film, this remained a small matter that would bother only people who came to the theater with a knowledge of military procedure. Most viewers saw only an extremely well made and reasonably accurate historical epic. Levine spent his money well in recreating the combat sequences. Despite his difficulty in acquiring World War II planes and tanks, the battle scenes became remarkably realistic and horrific without using any World War II footage. The William Goldman script clearly explains the origins of Operation Market Garden, the planning, the military risks, the expectations of success.

The film does carefully delineate the mistakes in planning and errors in judgment that doomed the attack before it began. However, it could have emphasized more General Montgomery's failure to heed intelligence reports that showed a German buildup at the precise point where the British intended to land their gliders and paratroopers. As a result, the troops landed in full view of German General Student's window, where he happened to be standing at that exact moment. And the screenplay could have been more explicit in explaining that Montgomery disregarded the reports, hoping that Operation Market Garden would enable him to beat Patton to Berlin.[39]

The film's real problems begin once the battle is launched. As a feature film, rather than a documentary, which could slap maps on the screen every few minutes, *A Bridge Too Far* lacked the means to easily keep the audience adequately informed of what was happening, where, and when. Events happen too quickly over too broad an area for director Richard Attenborough to handle effectively. Confusion reigned in 1944 Holland, and it reigns again in the movie. Military men and historians, as well as readers of Ryan's book, admitted to bewilderment during the film trying to follow the action even though they knew the story.[40]

At the same time, though the script attempts to humanize the struggle by following individuals as they try to survive the bloodbath, the scope of the actions often overwhelmed the effort of individual actors to develop their characters. In trying to follow the course of events while watching the stars go through their paces, the viewer has little time to consider the possible meaning of the images on the screen. Attenborough had thought *A Bridge Too Far* would become a "very moving" film that would "prove to be one of the greatest antiwar pictures ever made" by using the "war is hell" theme. Relaxing between takes of one of the more ambitious combat scenes, he observed, "The marvelous thing in this film is that the facts shout for themselves."[41]

What seemed an antiwar "shout" to the director during production seldom appears that way in the completed product. In part, *A Bridge Too Far* failed to make its statement because, filmed in color, it often seems too pretty, too much like a typical Hollywood combat epic and not enough like a portrayal of a tragic debacle. Consequently, the blood and gore fail to adequately create a repulsion during the scenes of death and destruction, particularly at the Arnhem bridge, where a few British soldiers at one end hold off a concerted German counteract for four days before finally surrendering.

The individual episodes too often ended up conveying a sense of excitement, adventure, and humor rather than the terror of being under constant attack. Paddling across the Waal River in a canvas boat at Nijmegen under heavy fire obviously shows the dangers of combat and the courage of the American soldiers. But performed by Robert Redford, as Maj. Julian Cook, who mumbles "Hail Mary, full of grace" all the way across, the sequence becomes almost comic, because the film fails to explain that he shortened the prayer to provide cadence to the oarsmen. Building a temporary bridge in a few hours so that the advance can continue becomes a tension-filled operation when hundreds of lives remain in the balance. However, the drama of the sequence when recreated on the screen dissipates because of Elliot Gould's performance, which has the aura of a Dean Martin comedy routine on a television special. Elements of high tragedy clearly exist in a Polish general's concern for the success of his assignment, the safety of his men, and his anguish over needless losses. Gene Hackman reduces the general to a Polish joke.[42]

Apart from the issue of whether the visualization of violence can create antiwar sentiment, the unintentional comedic and sometimes surrealistic portrayals of men in life and death circumstances effectively weaken the film's pacifistic message. As a result, most people probably left the theater remembering only the visual images of exciting combat, courage, and camaraderie among the troops. With that said, *A Bridge Too Far* remains a strangely haunting portrayal of a tragic episode in the history of war. The music, sounds, and dialogue reinforce the drama, the suffering, and the bravery of men on both sides who did their jobs under the worst possible conditions.

On another level, the film raises significant questions about the limits of dramatic license in films purporting to portray actual events. It may not matter that the bridge Levine used at Deventer had a windmill at the far end even though no windmill had existed at the Arnhem bridge. Unlike the bridge used in *The Bridge at Remagen,* the Deventer bridge looked like a twin of the "Bridge Too Far" since the Dutch apparently used the same blueprints for many of their river crossings. Of course, windmills are ubiquitous in Holland, and the smoke of the cinematic battle often rendered the windmill invisible anyway.

A more serious question about accuracy occurs in the portrayal of Major Cook's crossing of the Rhine and his capture of the high road bridge at Nijmegen. Cook and his men did paddle across the river in an action as bloody and courageous as any assault in World War II, whether at Tarawa, Iwo Jima, or Omaha Beach. In the following minutes, however, historical accuracy comes into conflict with individual recollections of events and the cinematic need to create a coherent story. Once ashore, the surviving Americans had proceeded to first capture the railroad bridge, which Attenborough did not portray. Cook and his men then moved toward the high road bridge a mile to the east, where they seized the north end as four British Sherman tanks began crossing from Nijmegen, not knowing whether the Germans would set off the explosives clearly visible underneath the deck. In the movie, Cook/Redford actually moved onto the bridge alone, firing on German snipers in the superstructure, and then greets the British tanks.

British soldiers and historians were to claim they had captured the bridge before the Americans and expressed their unhappiness at the director's rendering of history. In contrast, Cook later told Cornelius Ryan, "Oh yes, and if the

German tanks break through British defenses at the Arnhem Bridge during filming of *A Bridge Too Far,* using a similar bridge in Deventer, Holland.

British try to claim that they captured the Nijmegen Bridge, don't believe it, [my unit] was there first!" In fact, the actual link-up between the tanks and the American paratroopers occurred some two hundred yards beyond the bridge. Does this dramatic license matter? Winston Ramsey, editor-in-chief of *After the Battle,* a British journal devoted to the study of World War II, observed, "So who can claim capture of the bridge, the British who assaulted first and actually rolled across, or the Americans who reached the northern approach first? It was a shared victory." As for Redford's foray onto the bridge, Ramsey acknowledged: "Attenborough bent history to the advantage of the Americans. He should have had Redford waiting at the northern end of the bridge, perhaps watching the tanks roll across, and shown the link-up not *on* the bridge but just across it. Also, remember that in actual fact, Cook was not himself present at the link-up."[43]

Of course, Redford had to earn his $2 million, his character had led his soldiers courageously, and his men, if not he personally, had linked up with the British much as shown in the movie. From his perspective, screenwriter Goldman believed *A Bridge Too Far* "was terribly, terribly accurate, but acknowledged that "there were things that were not true . . . but those were things you amalgamate and try to get on with the story as quickly as possible. But nothing that was spectacular didn't happen." What about the tale of two bridges? Goldman explained: "There were so many bridges." Worse, except at Grave, each crossing had both a highway and a railroad bridge in tandem, and the plan for Market Garden required that attacking forces had to capture all of them. In contrast, the filmmakers felt that "if we dealt with all the bridges, we would bewilder an audience to the point of madness." Consequently, they decided "basically to just use the road bridges and ignore the existence of the railroad bridges."[44]

In light of the strategic importance of the two Nijmegen bridges, perhaps Attenborough should have given due credit to the attacking forces. But then, Levine wanted his money's worth from Redford's appearance and the road bridge offered a more dramatic vista than a lowly railroad crossing. Placing such visual concerns ahead of historical accuracy raises even more questions in the film's portrayal of the decision to withdraw the remaining British and Polish troops from the Arnhem side of the Rhine. Three British officers, Generals Browning and Horrocks, and Colonel Vandeleur, American General Gavin, and Polish General Sosabowski stand atop a tall church spire and look out over the battlefield toward Arnhem discussing the situation. In fact, two British generals and the Polish general had ascended a small church steeple to get an idea of the situation across the river. However, no tall church spire existed near Arnhem in September 1944, and the decision to withdraw the surviving soldiers took place twelve miles away near Nijmegen.

Does this matter? From the filmmaker's perspective, the impressive spire, actually in Deventer, provided a stunning visual locale from which to summarize for audiences what had gone wrong with Operation Market Garden. The generals' explanations accurately addressed the reasons Montgomery's fearless plan had failed: the bad weather which prevented the dropping of supplies and reinforcements, delays resulting from rebuilding one of the bridges the Germans managed to blow, the two-lane exposed highway to Arnhem, and the reality that Montgomery tried to go "a bridge too far." A room in Nijmegen certainly would not have served as well cinematically. Whether using the steeple as the podium to explain the failure to the audience exceeded the limits of dramatic and historic license remains open to debate.[45]

Just as important, do these and other changes of fact render *A Bridge Too Far* unsuitable for explaining the history of Operation Market Garden? After all, the Allies did reach within a mile or two of Arnhem and did hold their positions. The film left unsaid the fact that the Allies inflicted more damage on the city in their subsequent shelling than had taken place during the failed British assault and German counterattack or the fact that the Germans later blew up the bridge to keep it from falling into Allied hands. Nevertheless, *A Bridge Too Far* probably did capture the essence of the battle as well as could be expected from any three-hour movie. If audiences left the theater confused about the actual sequence of events and locales, the film did have the power to stimulate more interest in the epic struggle. As a result, many people may have read Ryan's book or, better yet, walked the battlefields and watched the documentary in the Arnhem Museum.

In any event, viewers can only respect Levine and Attenborough for attempting to recreate Market Garden on such a broad scale so many years after the event. Despite its real problems, its confusing portrayals of time and place, the dramatic license taken, and some of the acting, the film should have received a far better judgment than reviewers gave it, and it deserves a place among the most significant war movies ever made. As an antiwar statement, however, *A Bridge Too Far* probably failed, because people recognized the necessity for World War II, and in their minds it remained a successful, a necessary, and perhaps even a good war. Field Marshall Montgomery's grand plan may have become a disaster, but thanks in large measure to the film, people now remember the battle for the bravery and fortitude of the soldiers who fought and died trying to go a bridge too far.

The men who survived the aborted trip to Arnhem and the war returned home to receive the respect and appreciation of their nations. The Americans who fought in Vietnam found no such rewards, and even individual acts of heroism seemed to make little if any difference in the course of the conflict. Worse, when they returned home, they met with indifference, open hostility, and even condemnation.

For the first time, the United States had lost a war, and to a small, peasant nation at that. This made it difficult for Hollywood to use Vietnam as the setting for action-adventure movies that conveyed the excitement of combat and the glory of victory. However, the military and political failures in Vietnam and the resulting trauma that the American people suffered would provide filmmakers with an abundance of material from which to make antiwar and antimilitary statements—once Hollywood decided that moviegoers would pay to be reminded about the damage the war had inflicted on those who had done the fighting and on those who had watched from afar.

16 The Home Front, Vietnam, and the Victims of War

THE LAST DETAIL AND *CINDERELLA LIBERTY* had demonstrated that Hollywood was going to have a hard time obtaining assistance from the Pentagon if it wanted to portray the contemporary peacetime military. Filmmakers would find even more difficulty making a movie about the war in Vietnam or showing the impact the conflict had had on the American people. Col. Arthur Brill, head of the Information Branch at Marine Headquarters, put it most succinctly when he acknowledged that his office would have had difficulty providing help to any filmmaker except Walt Disney during the 1970s. Nevertheless, the armed services continued to have the same general appeal to screenwriters as they always had: different, exciting, often exotic settings in which to tell their stories.[1]

The issue of cooperation aside, the film industry faced an immense challenge in portraying the military after the United States pulled out of Vietnam in April 1973. During the 1970s, the nation's wounds from the war in Southeast Asia healed very slowly as the stigma of apparent defeat continued to confront all elements of the society. No one could offer a justification for the fifty-eight thousand American combat deaths. As a result, people came to see them as futile sacrifices, and maimed veterans as stark reminders of the war's continuing price. Reflecting the nation, Hollywood could not come to terms with the trauma the war had inflicted on the American people and so could not figure out how to turn an apparent defeat into popular entertainment.

Once the trauma of the withdrawal and the subsequent collapse of the South Vietnamese government began to recede, military people, past and present, would come to reject the contention that they had ever lost on the battlefields of Vietnam. To rationalize why they had not obtained great victories, many in the armed services argued that Washington had forced them to fight the war with their hands tied as a result of political considerations. They found convenient scapegoats in the media and politicians, whom they blamed for creating antiwar sentiment during the fighting and then for perpetuating the "myth" that the nation's military had suffered a considerable defeat. As might be expected, Gen. William Westmoreland, the commander in Vietnam from 1964 to 1968 and Army chief of staff from 1968 to 1972, became the foremost proponent of this thesis.

He pointed out that journalists had reported that the Vietcong attack on the American embassy during the 1968 North Vietnamese Tet Offensive had succeeded, even though he "knew it had not." In his autobiography, Westmoreland wrote: "That attitude on the part of the American reporters undoubtedly contributed to the psychological victory the enemy achieved in the United States. . . . Had the level of credibility and the art of reporting sunk to such a low?" He claimed that reporters "made little apparent effort to check facts, while basking in the praise of their home offices for their speed in beating the opposition." Referring to Chet Huntley's report on the NBC *Evening News* that placed the Vietcong inside the Chancery, which he denied had happened, Westmoreland wrote, "Was the long, costly American effort in Vietnam to be sacrificed to the idols of sensation and competition?"[2]

Westmoreland discovered the degree to which this was happening less than two months after Tet. In a meeting on March 24, 1968, Gen. Earl Wheeler, the chairman of the Joint Chiefs of Staff, told Westmoreland that the war had become a political issue, "with the prospect that the enemy might win in Washington as he had in Paris in 1954." Westmoreland recalled that Wheeler explained to him that press and television reporting on the Tet offensive had convinced many the United States had lost the war or that it could not bring the conflict to a satisfactory conclusion.[3]

Whatever the validity of these perceptions and arguments that Westmoreland, Wheeler, and other soldiers advanced to explain their failure in Vietnam, their contentions sounded very much like the "Stab in the Back" thesis of the German Army and later, Hitler, in the years after World War I. To be sure, the soldiers and officers in the field usually fought bravely and in no way deserved the animus they received from many sectors of the population upon their return. My Lai remained an aberration. The use of alcohol and drugs may have become only a matter of degree more extensive than in earlier wars. Racial tensions only reflected conditions on the streets of most large cities throughout the United States. Initially, and at least through the Tet offensive in January 1968, the average American, the politician in Washington, and the media did support the war effort completely and even enthusiastically. Nevertheless, things change, and the reality remains that soldiers seldom win or lose wars only on the battlefields.

If members of Congress, growing numbers of the media, and ultimately, the American people became disenchanted with Vietnam, they did so only in reaction to the way the military was conducting the war in Southeast Asia. The armed forces would argue that the political leadership in Washington had put strictures on the conduct of the war. However, as Truman demonstrated to MacArthur, in the United States, civilians ultimately dictate the scope of any conflict—for better or worse. The politicians may have dictated the military strategy in Vietnam and set the limits on engagement, but the question remains whether the military fought the best war it could have within these limits.

Patton aptly noted that Americans love a winner and will not tolerate a loser. But he did not prescribe the degree of success a person or army must attain to deserve the label "winner." A boxer wins whether by decision or knockout. A basketball team wins whether by one point or thirty points. A sprinter wins by a one-hundredth of a second or a tenth of a second.

General Westmoreland and some military scholars continue to claim that the Tet offensive became a disastrous failure for the North Vietnamese and the Vietcong. Nevertheless, on their television sets, Americans saw their embassy in the hands of the enemy. The evening news showed soldiers bravely taking Hamburger Hill and then saw them retreating from the summit much as other American soldiers had given back Pork Chop Hill to the North Koreans. The United States may have left South Vietnam in an orderly withdrawal in 1973. But the fall of Saigon two years later provided the American people with more memorable images—of South Vietnamese citizens desperately clinging to American helicopters taking off from the roof of the U.S. embassy and of Navy personnel pushing the aircraft off a carrier to make room for later arrivals with still more evacuees. Sen. Claude Aiken of Vermont came to argue that the United States should simply declare the war won and withdraw. However, it may be argued that the Pentagon and the Military Assistance Command, Vietnam (MACV), in Saigon did not provide the leadership and direction needed to ensure even that appearance of victory. Such a victory would have allowed the American people to believe they had enjoyed a semblance of success to compensate for the men and resources the war consumed. Declaring "victory" might have even saved some face in the eyes of the world.

The military's criticisms aside, the majority of the journalists who came to Vietnam may ultimately have emphasized the negative aspects of the war. But, as many of the writers, including Pulitzer Prize–winning Neil Sheean, have made clear, they arrived in Southeast Asia believing they would be covering a necessary and winnable war and trusting the military. Only after spending time in the field did their opinions begin to change, and their stories simply described the events that had influenced them. They could not report great victories or even measurable progress. Instead, they told of a steadily deteriorating situation in the South Vietnam government, a failure to win hearts and minds, and an effort in the field that could not stem the advances of a determined, totally committed enemy.

In fact, the media was describing a tragedy in the making. The United States needed at least twenty years and a victory over a petty tyrant in the Gulf War to come to terms with the ramifications of that tragedy. Explaining all of the war's complexities will continue to give scholars work for years to come. As *Tora! Tora! Tora! Midway, MacArthur,* and *A Bridge Too Far* demonstrated, the film industry may sometimes see itself as a military historian. But World War II presented few challenges in interpretation. The United States had fought a necessary war against evil enemies. With God's help, the right side won. In contrast, Vietnam posed a challenge that Hollywood has found difficult to solve.

Despite the box-office success of *The Green Berets,* no filmmaker had followed John Wayne's example and tried to portray combat while the war was still going on. Instead, as the U.S. presence in Southeast Asia began to wind down, Hollywood made its first halting comments about Vietnam by using the war only as a starting point, as the villain that scarred individuals and so the nation. This home front "victim of war" approach in portraying the horrors of combat has had an honored place in Hollywood filmmaking beginning with *The Big Parade.* People saw both world wars as necessary wars that might require sacrifices of their participants and the nation. Nevertheless, in the years after the end of World War II, the film industry devoted considerable attention to the returning veteran in ways that suggested the negative side of combat.

In *Pride of the Marines* (1945), Delmar Daves portrayed a blinded Marine's adjustment to civilian life. In William Wyler's *Best Years of Our Lives* (1946), one disabled veteran (played by an actual disabled veteran) had to come to terms with having lost both hands in battle; two other returning servicemen faced psychological and personal problems in readjusting to civilian life. Since the characters in both films put their lives back in order, the endings muted the otherwise negative images of the impact the war had had on its participants.

Fred Zinnemann's *The Men* (1950) also ended with the hero apparently coming to terms with his disability. But the paralyzed veteran, played by Marlon Brando in his first movie appearance, and the audience both know that he can expect no miraculous return to normalcy, that he will never walk again and will never function sexually. Despite this statement about the impact of war, the Army and the Veterans Administration provided producer Stanley Kramer with full cooperation because they saw the film as a means of informing the American people of the government's efforts to rehabilitate wounded soldiers. The images Zinnemann created suggested another message: war is destructive to human beings and many of the returning soldiers will never recover from their wounds.[4]

If the Army recognized the antiwar statement inherent in *The Men,* the service accepted it in return for the informational value the film provided. In contrast, the Air Force was quick to recognize the significance of the "victim" approach when they saw the script of *Limbo* in 1972. The film told the story of POW wives waiting for their husbands to return from North Vietnam or for word that they had died in combat. According to director Mark Robson, *Limbo* contained a powerful antiwar message because it showed the suffering of the women without any of the excitement or adventure usually found in a war movie.[5]

Initially, the Air Force provided assistance to Joan Silver and Linda Gottlieb, who went to the Defense Department while doing research for a book on prisoner-of-war wives. According to Gottlieb, who later produced the film, she and Silver, who coauthored the screenplay, "were fascinated with the theme, fascinated with the theme of women and what they did in that situation." She said they felt that "women had very rarely been portrayed honestly" and that the story offered a chance for them to do so. The producer explained that the POW wives had found that they were no longer married to heroes: "You may think he is a hero, but a lot of other people don't. And you waste your life. You wait. What are you faithful to, yourself or some social ideal about marriage?" Gottlieb thought it was a complex and "quite an interesting theme . . . that's what got us interested in it."[6]

Neither woman thought *Limbo* was a war movie, although "it touched on the Pentagon's dealings and of course the Pentagon's attitudes toward women. The Pentagon believes basically that women are unnecessary baggage, that they have to be dealt with in some fashion." Given their perspective, the script portrayed the POW wives as being shunted aside by a seemingly unfeeling Air Force, while caught up in their own desires. Each of the three wives featured in the film served as a stereotype with whom large segments of the audience could identify. Sandy (Kate Jackson) is a bright-eyed cheerleader type who married her husband only two weeks before he went overseas and disappeared on a mission over North Vietnam. She has received no news and has returned to college. Mary Kaye (Kathleen Nolan), a devout Catholic, works hard to raise her four children, buoyed by letters from her husband, who has been a prisoner for five years. Sharon (Katherine Justice), a rich southern belle, refuses to accept the evidence that her husband died when his plane received a direct hit and remains a strong supporter of the war. Mary Kaye and Sharon keep all potential suitors at arms length, but Sandy falls in love with a gas station attendant, an out-of-work space engineer, and begins a torrid affair.[7]

The Defense Department had given Silver and Gottlieb information about the POW wives and their various activities in behalf of the prisoners. The Pentagon also put the writers in contact with wives who were involved in various of the activities, such as the letter-writing and bumper-sticker campaigns. According to the Air Force officer who handled prisoner-of-war and missing-in-action matters in the DoD Directorate of Plans and Programs, the military helped "a hell of a lot in the preparation of the material. We held nothing back." But when the completed book came into the Pentagon, the officer found that it "overplayed the promiscuity, the unfaithfulness, of the wives, without trying to compensate to show that most of the wives were more level-headed, even more loving, more devoted, but were terribly frustrated."[8]

Ultimately, the dramatic requirements of making a movie that would appeal to general audiences produced a screenplay focused even more on Sandy's unfaithfulness. As a result, the Defense Department felt it had no choice but to turn down the filmmakers' request for assistance. The Air Force officer who worked with POW wives did not deny that some of them had been unfaithful. As the Defense Department saw the problem, the script lacked balance. However, the officer acknowledged that even if *Limbo* had presented a more objective picture of the wives, the military would have refused to give official cooperation.[9]

The Pentagon also expressed the concern that the completed picture would in some manner quickly reach the American prisoners in Hanoi, and the North Vietnamese would say in effect: "Look, this is official cooperation of the Defense Department and the Defense Department wouldn't cooperate if it weren't true. This is what your wives are doing." According to the Air Force officer, the Pentagon "figured the guys had enough of a burden as it was without having to worry about that."[10]

The DoD Public Affairs Office also recognized that the POW wives often had no one to turn to except the armed services. They had to trust that the Pentagon was doing all it could to help them. The officer explained that if the Defense Department had agreed to cooperate on *Limbo*, the wives would have had grounds to wonder about the military's true concern: "When we looked at the script, we did feel that it was not a balanced portrayal. We were defending ourselves against the charge that their husbands were war criminals. So we were sensitive to charges."[11]

Finally the Public Affairs Office felt that to provide assistance on the film "would destroy the morale of the women. If anything, we needed to uphold them and encourage them because they had so little to go on and some of them were trying awfully hard, they really were. They had heard nothing for years and were trying to raise the kids and make all those decisions and live this life of limbo. (It was a great name for the film, incidentally.) We just had to be very careful that we didn't do anything that would help to push some of them over the edge. Some of them were close. Some had been under psychiatric care."[12]

Bernard Donnenfeld, the president of the production company producing *Limbo* in conjunction with Universal Pictures, said he could "well understand" the Pentagon's concern about the film: "They may not have wanted to get involved in a very emotional picture that *Limbo* was. It showed the conflicts between the wives. Some were very pro-Administration on the war and some were not, as it was in real life. It was a very volatile subject at the time." Donnenfeld did think the script had taken "a very even-handed approach so that we could show all the women and their different approaches" toward their situations.[13]

Linda Gottlieb did not dispute the right of the Pentagon to refuse to assist on any film: "I think that indeed it's perfectly within their prerogative to refuse cooperation. After all, if anybody made a film that was a complete lampoon or satire of the Pentagon, why should they cooperate?" At the same time, the producer did think the Public Affairs Office was "insidious" for trying to influence the content of *Limbo* by suggesting changes in the first submitted script in return for cooperation. Consequently, when the Defense Department turned down the second script even with revisions, Gottlieb said she was "relieved." She explained it was worth the extra money that the lack of military assistance cost not to have a technical advisor on the set watching what Robson was filming.[14]

Gottlieb did not blame the Pentagon for refusing to cooperate on *Limbo* because of its subject matter: "I think they would have been fools to do it, quite realistically, quite honestly." Nevertheless, she labeled "absurd" the Pentagon's claim that a print of *Limbo* would reach the POWs in Hanoi. In fact, the pirating of motion pictures has become epidemic in recent years, with some new movies becoming available on video tape before they even reach first-run theaters. If the Pentagon had assumed correctly that North Vietnam would have obtained and showed *Limbo* to the POWs, it would undoubtedly have had a profoundly disturbing effect. And when the POWs did return to the United States in 1973, Pentagon officials warned them not to see the movie.[15]

Without Pentagon assistance, the film company had to spend an extra seven thousand to nine thousand dollars to rent a jet passenger plane to stage the sequence in which Sandy's husband returns home. The money remained the least of the problems the lack of cooperation caused, according to the producer. Gottlieb explained that it ultimately "took an incredible effort to get permission to land on an airfield we could shoot in." In addition, the filmmakers faced technical problems in ascertaining correct military outfits. Even on films that do not receive cooperation, the services will usually answer questions unofficially about uniforms and procedures. But in a display of overzealousness, Air Force people in the field followed the Pentagon directive about cooperation to the letter and refused to provide information about costumes.[16]

The completed movie proved not worthy of the concerns of the military or the efforts of the filmmakers; becoming little more than a glorified soap opera. Although *Limbo* did present both pro- and anti-Vietnam statements through the mouths of the several wives featured in the story, the arguments lacked any originality, insights, or passion. The hawkish views that Sharon, the southern belle, expressed became so cliché that they might have seemed laughable if the war itself had not been so deadly serious. Moreover, to create sympathy for the wives and so make an anti-Vietnam statement, the film ignored the POWs themselves. In the room Mary Kaye is offering to rent to Sandy, two posters proclaim that the POWs did not have a nice day today. However, as the scene is filmed, the audience sees only "POWs never have a n . . ." To have revealed the whole sign would have reminded people that while Sandy may be lonely, confused, and frustrated, her husband was not enjoying himself very much either.

In *Limbo*, Sandy and the other wives have become victims of war, the filmmakers' agents for conveying their anti-Vietnam statement through the images of suffering women forced to wait in limbo for their men. Sharon refuses to accept all evidence that her husband died when his plane crashed. Mary Kaye ultimately receives word that her husband has died in the POW camp. And Sandy becomes torn between her lover and her commitment to a husband whom she married after a brief courtship.

Sandy's situation, based on actual stories, had potential for a powerful dramatic climax when her husband is unexpectedly released and returns home. But as Kate Jackson renders the character, Sandy generates little sympathy, especially when she elects to remain with her lover even after she learns her husband is alive. As a result, their reunion, with the boyfriend watching in the waiting crowd, offers little hope of any lasting marital happiness. Nevertheless, the film's unlamented demise at the box office had as much to do with the timing of its release within weeks of the POW repatriation as with its dramatic and message shortcomings.

Ironically, *Limbo* made a direct visual connection to the next Vietnam film to appear. *Limbo* ends in a freeze frame of Sandy reaching toward her husband as he descends the airplane stairs. *Rolling Thunder*, appearing in the fall of 1977, begins with an Air Force officer returning home after seven years as a POW. His wife's policeman lover watches the couple's reunion and hears the officer's remarks to the welcoming crowd at the airport and then drives them home. Played by William Devane, Maj. Charles Rane becomes a symbol for the destructive impact which the war had on individuals and the nation.

Unlike *Limbo*, *Rolling Thunder* created powerful images of the POW and his wife as victims of the war. The film also captured the ambience of the changes that were taking place in society in the late 1960s and early 1970s, side by side with the war. During Rane's first night home, his wife tells him that she has a job and so has not used his pay and that her bralessness and miniskirts have become the norm. Then, with only a slight pause, she breaks the news that she has "been with another man." Showing no emotion, Rane answers, "I knew. We all knew. It couldn't have been any other way." In response to his wife's request for a divorce, Rane says without emotion that he has had enough for one night and they will work things out.

The film explains Rane's apparent lack of reaction to his wife's confession and his continued lack of emotion by juxtaposing almost subliminal scenes of North Vietnamese torture sessions with a demonstration he gives to his wife's lover of how the torture worked. He explains that he survived by learning "to love the rope. That's how you beat them. They don't know you're beating them." He later tells the girl who wore his POW bracelet while he was in prison that he has died emotionally, that his captors have pulled all feelings out of him.

The director, John Flynn, illustrates the impact of Rane's captivity more intensely when a gang of Mexican-Americans arrive in search of two thousand dollars in silver dollars that local citizens gave Rane after his return home. The film intercuts his silence in the face of the present beating and torture—which includes having his hand put in a garbage disposal in a final effort to make him talk—with scenes of his silence during torture sessions in Vietnam. When the gang kills Rane's wife and his son, who has become his only reason for living, the killers become the enemy he was not able to fight in Vietnam, an enemy against whom he can vent his pent-up rage for inflicting eight years of torture and deprivation and for, at least indirectly, causing his wife's unfaithfulness.

Once Rane recovers from his wounds, he sets out for vengeance against "the men who killed my son." He sharpens the hook that has replaced his right hand into a weapon, saws the barrel off a shotgun, practices loading a pistol with the hook, and enlists Linda, the bracelet-wearing POW groupie, to travel with him. After several bloody encounters, Rane tracks down the gang in a brothel and, with the help of a sergeant friend who flew home with him, proceeds to kill each of his tormentors in a shoot-out. In the best tradition of Sam Peckinpah, Flynn combined carefully choreographed and tightly edited images of violence with a sound track that emphasized the dramatic tensions of the climax to create a powerful, if bloody, visual impact.

The Air Force flatly rejected the producer's request for limited assistance, and the Defense Department advised him: "There are no known cases of Air Force officers becoming schizophrenic as happens . . . in the story. Yes, there are cases of returnees coming home to marital problems, but there is nothing beneficial for the Department of Defense in the dramatization of this situation." Whatever symptoms of mental derangement Air Force officials may have seen in the submitted script, however, Devane did not portray Major Rane as a "schizophrenic." Throughout the film, Rane shows that he is dealing with reality, not suffering from some psychosis. In light of what happened to him upon his return home, his actions are understandable, if not "normal."[17]

In the Air Force's eyes, Rane may not have acted sanely in allowing the gang to torture him and mutilate his hand in the garbage disposal rather than reveal the hiding place of the silver dollars. But given his short time home and the stresses to which he was again being subjected, the mental connection he makes between his torturers and his POW captors does not seem implausible. In reality, his refusal to reveal more than his name, rank, and serial number to his torturers stands in the highest tradition of the military and is not an indication of insanity.

Moreover, Rane's resort to extreme violence should not, in and by itself, have served as sufficient grounds for the military's refusal to cooperate on the production. The Army did provide limited assistance to the makers of *Good Guys Wear Black* (1978), another film that

The activities of Chuck Norris and his elite commando unit, charged with rescuing POWs from behind enemy lines in the Vietnam War, serve as the starting point for *Good Guys Wear Black* (1978), an action film set for the most part in the years following the end of hostilities.

touches on the Vietnam War. In it, Chuck Norris played a retired special-forces officer whose unit had been sent into North Vietnam to be wiped out as part of the agreement for settling the war. The State Department negotiator, now secretary of state–designate, orders the survivors of the unit to be killed to protect his reputation. To remain alive and ultimately eliminate the diplomat, Norris performs all manner of violence on his pursuers.

In any case, Rane's anguished and vengeful actions once he recovers from his wounds clearly reflect his war experiences. He had become hardened to the brutality he experienced in the POW camps. People had died and life had become cheap. As a result, Rane had lost a sense of human value. Perhaps he had overgeneralized from his experiences and so is still operating under the rules of war, not those of civilians in Texas. In fact, he wears his Air Force uniform when he confronts the gang in the final shoot-out—a gang that did not operate under the restraints of society either.

Newspapers, magazines, and television continue to tell stories of Vietnam veterans committing violent acts directly traceable to their Vietnam experiences. The film gives Rane much more justification for resorting to violent acts than most of the men whose actions reach the media. That Rane did not erupt against his wife or her lover provides further evidence that he remains in control of his mental faculties. In any event, Rane's actions do resemble not those of a schizophrenic, but rather those of a man whom war has brutalized. As with *Limbo,* however, the Air Force refused to assist on *Rolling Thunder* not because of Rane's mental condition or even because of his actions, but because it did not find any benefit in a film showing the adverse impact of the war on its officers.

Ironically, the Defense Department did acknowledge that "there are some positive elements in the portrayal of Major Rane's reactions to the brutal assaults by T-Bird and Texan and his stoic behavior as a POW." Moreover, the film portrays Rane as a loyal and dedicated officer. He tells the welcoming audience, "It's good to be back. We knew all along that everyone back home from the President on down was behind us 100 percent. It was God and faith in our families that kept us going. Speaking for myself, I would like to say that the whole experience has made a better man, a better officer, and a better American of me." The Air Force itself also comes across as performing exceptionally in dealing with Rane. It shows sympathy for his marital problems, his desire to keep his son, and his rehabilitation. Overall, the image of the military in *Rolling Thunder* was probably more positive than in any other Vietnam movie of the 1970s.[18]

At the same time, *Rolling Thunder* did set the pattern for the subsequent movies about America's Vietnam veterans. All return from the war scarred mentally or physically by their experiences. Rane's sergeant friend tells him he has found it hard to get used to home life again, being with his wife again. Rane tells Linda that he is dead, that he feels nothing. One of his torturers tells the gang that "this dude's crazy." But another of the gang "was right there in Nam . . . except that I was laying face down in the mud while you cats were flying over." His torture of Rane becomes his way of venting his own Vietnam frustrations just as Rane's subsequent actions become his catharsis.

William Devane's performance and John Flynn's insightful direction enabled *Rolling Thunder* to examine the problems of the returning veterans with a sensitivity usually not found in low-budget melodramas. Nevertheless, the graphic portrayals of violence did have a continuing impact on the fate of the film. Flynn recalled that, at the movie's preview in San Jose in April 1977, more than half the people walked out of the theater in reaction to graphic portrayals of violence. The director cited, in particular, the scenes in which the gang mangles Devane's hand in the garbage disposal; in which Devane drives his hook into the hand of a man from whom he is seeking information about the gang; and finally in which he thrusts the hook into the groin of a man who is threatening his groupie companion. Flynn said that he and the studio executives had to sneak out of the theater and into their limos to avoid irate customers. The next day, Twentieth Century Fox sold the distribution rights to the film to American International Pictures, citing "creative differences" with producer Lawrence Gordon over the editing. AIP proceeded to edit out a small portion of the garbage-disposal sequence and other of the more graphic scenes. Despite the changes, the film acquired a reputation as one of the most violent movies ever made.[19]

Reviewers in trade publications did not seem to have trouble with the violence, praising Devane's performance and Flynn's direction. *Boxoffice* thought that "good writing, directing and acting place this AIP release a cut or two above others of the genre in which the protagonist kills his enemies in vengeance." The writer said that Devane had the ability to develop "great emotional intensity just by the look in his eyes and the grim, inflexible set of his jaw. He draws heavily on the technique to create a highly believable character." The *Hollywood Reporter* described *Rolling Thunder* as "an above average hell-bent-for-revenge exploitation picture that combines an interesting story idea with plenty of violent action" and thought that Flynn's direction "serves the script very well." *The Motion Picture Product Digest* observed that the story had "a real feeling for nuances of character—the way experience shapes people and causes them to act the way they do." The reviewer believed that Flynn "respects this serious approach" and that when it came "time for the violence, he gets it over with quickly—but no less effectively than other directors who like to linger over the blood-letting and sometimes strive to make it seem 'poetic.'"[20]

Despite these positive reviews, the quality of the film itself and its social commentary became lost in the controversy over the intensity of the violence. However valid its use in developing the story and the characterizations, many writers responded only to the violence. Typically, *McCalls* observed, "The 'point,' I suppose, is that Vietnam brutalized the men we sent to serve us there. But the real point is to exploit audience lust for violence. Not for children or anyone."[21]

Such reviews and the film's reputation deterred audiences, and *Rolling Thunder* quickly disappeared from theaters. Whether the violence itself bore full responsibility for its failure remains open to question. Other Hollywood movies that had appeared in the previous few years had contained as much if not more bloody, violent scenes. *Clockwork Orange, Bonnie and Clyde, Straw Dogs, The Wild Bunch,* and *Death Wish* all received exceptional critical praise for their directors' creative depiction of the violence man often perpetrates on man. The negative reaction that *Rolling Thunder* engendered may well have resulted as much from its subject matter as from Flynn's portrayal of Devane's bloody pursuit of justice.

At least in 1977, American audiences had not yet become ready for films to remind them of the severity of the impact the war had had on many of those who had fought it. However, audiences may have had less interest in the film because the 1974 *Death Wish* had told a similar story. Not unlike Devane, Charles Bronson played a revenge-seeking husband pursuing his wife's killers and other criminals with deliberate violence. In any case, if *Rolling Thunder* passed quickly from sight, it undoubtedly deserved a better fate. Visually impressive, with a sound track that helped to create an authentic ambience of the time and place, it had a sparsely written script that contained telling insights into the changes the Vietnam War made in its participants and in American society as a whole.

Heroes, also released in late 1977, used the same veteran-as-victim thesis to convey an antiwar statement. However, in contrast to *Rolling Thunder,* it enjoyed good success, which was due not to its subject but to its comedic approach and the presence of TV's the Fonz, playing a demented Vietnam veteran who roams the country trying to find himself. Henry Winkler explained that he portrayed "a guy back from Vietnam who's a little touched." On the surface, the film was simply an offbeat love story and a typical Hollywood "road" movie in the genre of Clark Gable's *It Happened One Night.* On another level, however, *Heroes* attempted to convey the idea that Winkler's craziness grew directly from his Vietnam experiences.[22]

Unlike Major Rane, Winkler's Jack Dunne clearly lacks touch with reality. In the film's opening sequence, Jack wanders into the Army Recruitment Center in Times Square and insanely tries to drag potential enlistees from the grasp of the recruiting sergeant, who has been telling the youths that they will find parachute jumping "better than sex." As the police haul him away, Jack manages to yell one last warning: "Go home! You'll be safer!" Back in the VA hospital for the fourth time, he is told by the psychiatrist that he should stop pretending: "If you would accept reality and not butt your head against walls, you wouldn't be here in the first place."

Despite such actions, the Army did not see Jack's behavior as resulting from his tour of duty in Vietnam. Instead, the service considered that he had probably been a little mixed up before the war and so allowed the filmmakers to shoot Jack's confrontation with the recruiting sergeant in the Times Square Center. Nevertheless, the Army did request revisions in the portrayal of the sergeant, which served to make him "more sympathetic and place him in a defensive position" and made Jack "the aggressor and unstable to boot."[23]

Jack does not stay confined very long, managing to sneak out of the hospital and head to California, where he expects to start a worm farm with an Army buddy, Monroe. Despite this promising beginning, *Heroes* quickly degenerated into a romantic comedy filled with Winkler's TV antics and efforts to woo Sally Field, whom he picks up early in his odyssey. Only in the film's closing sequence does the cause of Winkler's derangement become visualized. Arriving at Monroe's home, Jack joyfully tells the parents that he and his wartime buddy are going into the worm business. Responding first with disbelief and then with deep bitterness at Jack's apparent jest, they scream that their son died in Vietnam.

Denying the news, which he has obviously been suppressing since Monroe died trying to save him, Jack tears out of the house yelling wildly and then crazily runs through the town, which becomes transformed into a Vietnamese village. In a brief but extremely well done firefight, created without military assistance, the filmmakers stage the moment of Monroe's death, the cause of Jack's insanity. Having made the connection between the terrible effect the war had on its participants and their subsequent behavior, *Heroes* then mutes the message with a happy ending as Sally Fields comforts Jack by telling him, "It's all over. . . . You're alive."

If audiences could miss the antiwar statement because of the upbeat vision of a happy future that *Heroes* offered, viewers had a harder time ignoring the thrust of *Who'll Stop the Rain?* (1978). An adaptation of Robert Stone's novel *Dog Soldiers,* the film told the story of a drug deal gone awry and the subsequent cross-country chase. Like *Heroes, Who'll Stop the Rain* contained a brief and effective combat sequence to establish the experiences which influenced the characters. Nevertheless, the film had a largely metaphoric connection with the war, and although the director, Karel Reitz, succeeds in transmitting a strong sense of the Vietnam era to the film, the story focuses more on the war's aftermath than on the impact the conflict had on those involved in it.

With the release of *Coming Home* the same year, however, Hollywood finally indicated a willingness to deal directly with the ramifications of America's experiences in a losing war. Focusing on the same subject as Fred Zinnemann's *The Men,* Hal Ashby told the story of the process by which a paralyzed combat veteran adjusts to his disability. As Marlon Brando had done, Jon Voight, playing Luke Martin, a Marine sergeant wounded in Vietnam, initially refuses all assistance, lashing out at the world in his frustration. Like Brando's character, Voight is a football hero who cannot accept his changed physical condition. As in *The Men,* a woman, Jane Fonda in the role of Sally Hyde, the wife of a Marine captain, provides the motivation for the veteran's rehabilitation. Unlike Zinnemann, however, Ashby could not or would not let a single story convey the antiwar message inherent in Luke's paralysis.

Perhaps reflecting Jane Fonda's intention to make an antiwar statement, perhaps reflecting the problems of making a film that evolved from several writers' efforts, *Coming Home* tries to tell too much. The original idea for the story came from Fonda's involvement with Vietnam Veterans Against the War in the early 1970s. Fonda commissioned Nancy Dowd to help her and an associate to write a screenplay about paralyzed veterans. When it proved "unworkable," the actress approached Waldo Salt, because she liked his film work and political views.[24]

Although the story's concept "fascinated him," he refused to rewrite someone else's script. At Salt's suggestion, Jerome Hellman joined the project as producer, and Salt proceeded to write his own script, which he and Hellman then revised and used as the basis for arranging financing with United Artists. When Ashby was brought into the project, the three men began another revision in preparation for filming. With only forty-five pages completed and production scheduled to begin, Salt became ill and Ashby brought his film editor into the writing.[25]

After only two days of shooting, however, the director saw how Voight was developing his character, discarded the screenplay being used, and began writing a new script as the film progressed. As a result of the constant revising of the story, Ashby reached a point where he realized he couldn't shoot Salt's original ending, which he liked, because he "didn't know how in the hell to do it after that much film" without having too much "stuff to explain all of a sudden."[26]

The problem Ashby faced in creating an ending resulted from having to resolve two intertwining stories. Instead of focusing on how Voight found the strength to accept his situation, as *The Men* did with Brando's character, *Coming Home* also followed the degeneration of Sally's husband, Bob, played by Bruce Dern. Although Luke remains the central character gaining strength and understanding, the film coincidently traces Bob's loss of his sense of identity and purpose. His story reiterates the film's message that "there is a choice to be made here," that war can destroy people in many ways, but it becomes redundant and so distracting.

In fact, Bob's transformation from a gung ho officer who could not wait to go to Vietnam into a mentally unstable casualty of the war probably says more about the nature of combat than Luke's physical destruction. Luke's wound came from without and might have been anticipated as one of the risks of battle in any war. In contrast, Bob is destroyed from within, unexpectedly, through his own lack of awareness of the world that he himself made. The process by which each man copes with the war became the framework within which Fonda, the writers, and the director made their statements about the war.

The opening scene in the film, a rap session among disabled veterans, provides a forum to convey through the mouths of the actors the filmmakers' own feelings about the war. One man justifies having gone to Vietnam because of "curiosity." Another explains his willingness to fight because of a moral obligation to defend the Vietnamese's right to determine their own future. A black voices disbelief that anyone would be willing to go back especially in light of what has happened to them. Another explains the willingness: "Some of us need to justify to ourselves what the fuck we did there. So if we come back and say if what we did was a waste, what happened to us was a waste, some of us couldn't live with it." He says that some veterans have found it necessary to lie to themselves continuously so that they might believe they had done right in order to be able to live with their wounds, to justify having killed people. But he wonders how many can live with reality and say, "What I did was wrong" and still live with themselves the rest of their lives.

Coming Home shows how Luke learns to do that, but the film begins its story with Bob and his preparation for war. It contrasts the opening images of the paralyzed veterans with Bob's doing road work on the Marine base and then his discussion with a fellow Marine about their impending tour of duty in Vietnam, "in combat city." He says he doesn't think "Sally understands it all, but she accepts it." Later he explains, "I've waited a long time for an opportunity like this. . . . That's where I belong. I am a Marine." In contrast, his relationship with Sally shows little understanding of her needs. She describes her relationships to Bob and the Marines as being the hole in a donut and voices the cliché line that if the Corps wanted a man to have a wife, it would have issued him one.

After Bob leaves for Vietnam, Sally becomes friends with Vi, whose boyfriend has also just left for Vietnam. Vi works in the local Veteran's Administration hospital so that she can be close to her brother, whom the Army sent home from Vietnam after only two weeks because of an unexplained mental breakdown. Vi explains that he no longer has "his ignition." In one of the film's needless and cluttering subplots, the brother wanders through several scenes in a daze, an extreme Jack Dunne. Through Vi's urging, Sally volunteers to work in the hospital, where, on the first day, Luke literally crashes into her with his bed. From the minute his urine bottle breaks in her hands, the two seem destined to develop a relationship.

Gradually, as Sally draws Luke out of his shell, they fall in love, and she becomes politicized. The change is visualized by having her curl her hair and buy a Porsche. The film reinforces the distance she has come from her passive, Marine wife days by showing her trying and failing to convince the women who run the "base gossip sheet" to do a story on the paralyzed veterans in order to recruit needed volunteers. Even here, however the film cannot understate the contrast. Instead, it chooses to hit the audience over the head by having the women on the paper discuss an article about Little League baseball.

The romance pauses temporarily when Sally receives her "marching orders" to fly to Hong Kong to visit Bob on R & R. Ashby uses the sequence to show how far Bob has deteriorated during his few months in combat. He describes how his "second lieutenant, this fucking Camp Lejune wiz kid" comes up to him and asks, "Do you think it would be okay if we put the heads on the pole. It really scares the shit out of the VC." He continues sullenly to describe how his "men were chopping heads off. That's what they were into." Clearly, the gung ho Marine had not expected this kind of war and he cannot adjust to the reality he has found.

In contrast, when Sally returns home, her relationship with Luke reaches its climax, literally. When Vi's brother commits suicide, Luke chains himself to the gate of the Marine base so that he can voice his frustration and pain to the world. He tells the television cameras, "This is a kind of a funeral service. I'm here because I'm trying to tell people, man, if we want to commit suicide, we have plenty of reasons to do it right here at home. We don't have to go to Vietnam to find reasons for us to kill ourselves. I don't think we should be over there."

His antiwar tirade, which Sally watches on television, serves to break her final link to the past, to her traditional views of love and faithfulness. She bails Luke out of jail, takes him back to his apartment, and goes to bed with him for the first time. In a sequence that many unaware people think shows them making love normally, Sally has her first orgasm. Subsequently, the relationship deepens, setting up the inevitable confrontation when Bob returns from Vietnam a certified hero who, in reality, had accidentally wounded himself. This irony coupled with the information about Sally's affair with Luke, received from the FBI, which has had him under surveillance following Luke's protest, pushes Bob over the edge.

With a bayoneted rifle in hand, he confronts Sally with a rambling and sometimes incoherent discourse about their relationship and his feelings of failure. Describing as "bullshit" her explanation that her friendship with Luke happened because she was lonely, he explodes: "Bullshit . . . don't bullshit me . . . Goddamn it, it's bullshit! Everybody needs somebody for Christ's sake." He screams in anguish, "I don't belong in this house. And they're saying that I don't belong over there . . . the people who make the decisions about the fucking war."

But Sally doesn't want to talk about the war. He asks, "What do you want to talk about, the fucking marriage?" He says he doesn't deserve to be married to her just as he doesn't deserve the medal he is to get: "How can they give you a medal for a war they don't even want you to fight?" When Luke arrives to try to explain where he is coming from and what has happened, Bob mumbles that he "just gotta figure for myself what happened and how I'm gonna deal with it." When Sally tries to reach out to him, he explodes with a stream of abuse against both of them and threatens them with the gun. Luke responds, "I'm not the enemy. Maybe the enemy is the fucking war. But you don't want to kill anybody here. You have enough ghosts to carry around." That seems to defuse the situation, and with weariness, Bob moans, "I'm fucked . . . I just want to be a hero, that's all. I just want to be a fucking hero! One day in my life, one moment, I want to go out a hero. That way, I will have done something that was mine."

But he chooses to go out a failure. Having attended his medal awards ceremony, in which another officer's heroism under fire was described at length, Bob returns to the house on the beach, carefully takes off his Marine dress uniform, walks into the surf, and slowly swims out to sea. Although the strong antiwar message inherent in Bob's self-destruction remains powerful, its impact on audiences becomes muted because of the manner in which Ashby portrays it. The suicide itself seems trite and almost comical in its parody of the ending of *A Star Is Born,* an ending that in itself has long since become a cliché. More seriously, by intercutting scenes of Bob's ritual-like death with Luke's antiwar monologue delivered to a group of high school students, the director diminished the power of both sequences.

Luke's appearance side-by-side with a Marine recruiting sergeant marks his final adjustment to his fate and allows the filmmakers the opportunity to collect all their antiwar thoughts in one place. After the sergeant closes his comments by saying, "The Marine Corps builds body, mind, and spirits," Luke wheels himself to the microphone "with a different perspective," a perspective sounding very much like Ron Kovic's *Born on the Fourth of July,* Frederick Down's *The Killing Zone,* and other first-person recollections of how the reality of war differed from the image with which a person had grown up.

He tells the students that he had wanted to go out and "be patriotic" and "get your licks in for the U.S. of A." But it is a different situation, he explains: "You grow up real quick . . . all you are seeing is a lot of death." He concedes that some of his audience will look at the uniforms and "remember all the films and you're going to think about the glory of other wars and think about some vague patriotic feeling and go off and fight this turkey too . . . I'm telling you, it ain't like it is in the movies, that's all I want to tell you." Luke says that he didn't have a choice, "because when I was your age, all I got was some guy standing up like that, man, giving me a lot of bullshit, man, which I caught . . . I was the captain of the football team and I wanted to be a war hero, man, and I wanted to go out and kill for my country." Now, Luke says he does not feel good having killed for his country "because there's not enough reason, man, . . . I'm here to tell you it's a lousy thing, man. I don't see any reason for it." Breaking down in tears, he tells the silent students: "There's a lot of shit I did over there that I find fucking hard to live with and I don't want to see people like you men coming back and having to face the rest of your lives with that kind of shit. It's as simple as that. I don't feel sorry for myself. I'm a lot fucking smarter now than when I went. And I'm just telling you, there's a choice to be made here."

In large measure the virtuosity of Voight's performance overcame the distractions of the cutting between him and Dern's slow-motion suicide and a music background that added nothing to the buildup of dramatic tensions. (Throughout the film, the music is out of sync with the action, serving only to establish the time period, unlike the music in *Rolling Thunder,* which helped create the ambience of the locales and reinforced the actions.) As a result, Luke's denunciation of the war conveyed the frustrations of the Vietnam veterans who had become the victims of the war through their disabilities.

The Marines would naturally find little to benefit the Corps or the Defense Department in a script containing such perspectives. Nevertheless, the producer did approach the Marines for assistance "in the interest of authenticity." Commenting on the request, the service's Office of Information said it found the story "interesting and will undoubtedly result in an entertaining and controversial film." However, it felt that *Coming Home* would "reflect unfavorably on the image of the Marine Corps." In particular, the service objected to the script's portrayal of the widespread use of drugs by officers and men as well as Hyde's description of how his men cut heads off enemy bodies in Vietnam. As a result of such images, the chief of information recommended that the Pentagon refuse to assist the production.[27]

Although the film company made an inquiry about the rejection, it did not pursue the matter further with the Marines. At the same time, the producer did seek assistance from the Veterans Administration. However, after initially cooperating with Waldo Salt in his research, the VA's communications with the production turned "vitriolic" when the agency concluded that the script exploited paralyzed veterans and was "very offensive" to them. In responding to the second script submitted, Dr. John Chase, the VA's chief medical director, observed that the story "incorrectly and unfairly portrays veterans as weak and purposeless, with no admirable qualities, embittered against their country, addicted to alcohol and marijuana, and as unbelievably foul-mouthed and devoid of conventional morality in sexual matters."[28]

Bruce Dern's unMarine-like haircut in *Coming Home* contributed to the Marine Corps' change of policy in negotiating for assistance on movies portraying the Marines in war and peace.

The completed film proved to be less offensive to the VA than the submitted script had suggested. Dr. Chase later observed that he would have probably agreed to assist the producer if the screenplay had reflected the movie's final form. And Max Cleland, who became head of the VA in 1977, loved *Coming Home* because he felt it provided hope for disabled veterans. Likewise, the Marine Corps found that the images in the movie had more balance than those in the script and began to reevaluate its policies on dealing with filmmakers in the post-Vietnam era, a period in which the military in general was learning to cope with a less favorable public opinion.[29]

Although *Coming Home* and particularly Luke's adjustment to his wounds made a significant antiwar statement, the filmmakers managed to dilute its impact along the way. Most obviously, the message came at least ten years too late. No one in the country, even those who most strongly had protested the war, really cared about the conflict in 1978, at least as a "cause." Therefore, *Coming Home* stands not only as an antiwar proclamation but as the vehicle by which Fonda and the liberal Hollywood establishment could vent their guilt over not protesting the war on film when it might have made a difference.

Even as an antiwar film, using the "victim" theme to create its message, *Coming Home* does not succeed in conveying the full reality that the veterans' injuries remain irrevocable and must be accepted, that they will never walk again and never be able to perform sexually. Instead, the filmmakers tried to have their cake and eat it, suggesting from the way they shot the scene that Luke and Sally were actually making love. Producer Jerome Hellman later acknowledged that he was, in fact, trying to have it both ways. He wanted Luke's paralysis to make an antiwar statement while having audiences believe Luke and Sally would live happily ever after with a normal sex life. As a result, some viewers missed the harsh reality that Luke would remain impotent, perhaps expecting him to jump out of his wheelchair at some point like Dr. Strangelove and yell, "Sally, I can walk! I can make *real* love."[30]

Ultimately, *Coming Home* does convey the destructive effect that the Vietnam War had on its participants both physically and mentally. But the filmmakers did not trust the images they created to speak for themselves, choosing instead to underline them to excess visually, musically, and verbally. They also chose to mute the harsh realities by turning the film into a slick Hollywood love story with a possible happy ending instead of leaving the audience to ponder over the continuing adjustments the veterans of Vietnam will always have to make.

To the degree that *Coming Home* failed, the explanation may lie in its makers' trying too hard to create their antiwar statement. Jerome Hellman claimed he did not make movies to make money but rather to convey a message, citing his Oscar for Best Picture for *Midnight Cowboy*. As a result, *Coming Home* wore its antiwar, anti-Vietnam statement in plain sight. Whether or not viewers might agree with it, by 1978 they had already rendered judgment on the war and Jane Fonda's opposition to it. Consequently, most people probably went to the movie to see Fonda and Voight in a rather unconventional love story rather than to be lectured on the evils of the Vietnam War.[31]

In a far more unpretentious way, *Same Time Next Year* addressed the same issue of the impact of the war on average people, in this case on mainstream Americans. Perhaps the portrayal made its statement so well because the story seemed to have nothing to do with the Vietnam War or the relationship between the film industry and the armed services. Transformed almost without change from the Broadway stage, the movie told in a series of vignettes how a chance meeting between Alan Alda, an accountant, and Ellen Burstyn, an initially unfulfilled housewife, evolves into a sometimes funny, sometimes tragic, always sentimental, twenty-five-year affair. The two gradually aging, gradually changing lovers meet one weekend a year, during which time they catch up on their lives and become revitalized by the thrill of their secret assignation.

One year, Burstyn arrives at their motel room dressed in her current guise, as an antiwar hippie, to find Alda dressed in a most severe business suit, gulping a drink. Despite having such a short time together, Alda fails to respond to Burstyn's enthusiastic greeting, "Wanna fuck?" and rebuffs her efforts to lure him into bed. Whereas Burstyn has entered college and begun to question the war, Alda has become an outspoken Hawk, admits he voted for Goldwater, and says the United States should use the atomic bomb in Vietnam to "wipe the sons of bitches off the face of the earth." In anger, she demands to know what is going on, how he could have become so stuffy and "so 40." When he says, "I grew up," she responds, "Well, as far as I'm concerned, you didn't turn out too hot." Despite his efforts to end the discussion, she calls him a Fascist and says, "You used to believe exactly like me." He answers, "I've changed." "But why?" He blurts out, "Because Michael was killed."

The shock silences Burstyn. Finally, sobbing, she asks how. Without apparent emotion, he explains, "He was helping a wounded man into a Red Cross helicopter and a sniper killed him." He says he thought he would feel the pain later: "I never did. I never shed a tear. All I have ever been able to feel is blind anger. I never shed a tear. He was my son. I loved him. And for the life of me, I can't seem to cry for him." As Burstyn holds Alda, he admits that he has "been a bit on edge lately" and suddenly breaks down completely, sobbing uncontrollably. The suddenness of Alda's revelation has a devastating impact even though viewers knew he was repressing something terrible.

Alda's portrayal of an establishment man turned grieving father, juxtaposed with Burstyn's antiwar garb and antiestablishment comments, reminded people how Vietnam had affected the entire nation, not just the combatants. To the fictional Luke and his real counterpart, Ron Kovic, the pain of never being able to walk or make love again would remain as a permanent reminder of the war. Unlike a physical loss, the anguish of personal loss does recede over time. Nevertheless, Alda would always carry with him the pain of his son's death, just as have the actual parents of all those men and women who died in Vietnam.

Walter Mirisch, the producer of *Same Time Next Year*, saw the tragedy of the Vietnam episode as making a comment on the war and "the very moving, high point in the material." At the same time, although the film needed to address the war, he said it should be obvious that *Same Time Next Year* did not focus on Vietnam. Instead, the episode added a dimension to the lovers' relationship, and according to Mirisch, it spoke "very well to the overall attempt to weave into the film the fabric of the history of the whole period" over which their rendezvous took place.[32]

In fact, few movies set in the Vietnam War period could avoid having the war in some way intrude upon their characters even if they did not suffer direct physical or personal loss. Such losses, like those which the characters experienced in *Limbo, Rolling Thunder, Coming Home,* and *Same Time Next Year,* became that much more tragic because of the nature of the war, because of its futility, and because the United States had lost in Vietnam, however one might define the scope of that loss. As Patton noted, "Americans love a winner and will not tolerate a loser."

17 Apocalypse When?

BY FOCUSING ON THE HOME FRONT, filmmakers were able to comment on the impact that Vietnam had on the American people while avoiding the blood and gore of combat. However, movies about physical and personal loss did lack the excitement inherent in all stories about men in war, regardless of their setting. Even after American participation in the war had officially ended, the film industry questioned whether people would pay money to see a reprise of combat which television had so long brought into homes in living color on the evening news. Nevertheless, Hollywood took its first halting steps toward recreating the Vietnam War within two years of the final American withdrawal from South Vietnam. The man who led the way had no experience with combat, and his only cinematic connection with things military consisted of his writing the original screenplay for *Patton.* Nevertheless, as he had demonstrated in directing *The Godfather* and *The Godfather Part II,* Francis Ford Coppola had a great faculty for portraying violence.

This ability to create scenes of intense bloodiness served Coppola well as he set about to transfer Joseph Conrad's novella *Heart of Darkness* into the first movie about the American combat experience in Vietnam. In fact, if the United States had waged war in Vietnam in the manner that Coppola and other filmmakers would portray the fighting, the Vietcong and North Vietnamese might well have driven American forces into the South China Sea within a few weeks of the 1965 escalation of U.S. involvement in Vietnam. With very few exceptions, filmmakers chose to show the conduct of the war, both by the command and in the field, in the worst light, real and imagined. The portrayals contained little balance and only superficial concern for the accuracy of military procedures or the history of the war.

Having completed his second *Godfather* film, Francis Ford Coppola told an interviewer in early 1975 that his next movie would deal with Vietnam, "although it won't necessarily be political—it will be about war and the human soul. But it's dangerous, because I'll be venturing into an area that is laden with so many implications that if I select some aspects and ignore others, I may be doing something irresponsible. So I'll be thinking hard about it." He told another interviewer that his planned film would be "frightening, horrible—with even more violence than *The Godfather.*"[1]

As the vehicle for his expedition, Coppola had selected a six-year-old script by John Milius, which shifted *Heart of Darkness* from the jungles of Africa to Southeast Asia. Milius's screenplay transferred Conrad's theme of civilization's submission to the brutality of human nature to the story of a Green Beret officer who defects and sets up his own army across the Cambodian border, where he fights both American and Vietcong forces. Working with "Agency" representatives, the U.S. Army orders an officer to find and "terminate" the renegade and eliminate his band of deserters.[2]

Throughout the production, Coppola shifted his intended focus from an antiwar to an action adventure film and back again. At one point, he characterized his film as "not anti-military. It is not anti U.S. It is pro U.S. It is pro-human." While filming in the

Captain Willard sets out in his search for Colonel Kurtz in *Apocalypse Now* (1978).

Philippines, he described the movie as "an anti-lie, not an antiwar film. I am interested in the contradictions of the human condition." With his intellectual attraction to the contradictions in man, to the good and evil that are inherent in all humans, Coppola said that he was trying to make a war movie that would somehow rise above conventional images of valor and cowardice. When asked why he was attempting to show this in a film set in Vietnam, he responded that it was "more unusual that I am the only one making a picture about Vietnam."[3]

Coppola made his first contact with the Department of Defense to discuss his film when his producer, Fred Roos called the Public Affairs Office on May 23, 1975, to say that he and the director wanted to come to Washington to discuss possible military assistance. In briefing him for the meeting, Norman T. Hatch, chief of the Audio Video Division, advised Assistant Secretary of Defense for Public Affairs Joseph Laitin that he and Don Baruch would first talk with Coppola, Roos, and their art director, Dean Tavoularis, to get "a better fix on their needs and expectations and we will also be able to present them with the facts of life on how to deal with us."[4]

Laitin recalled that a director's visiting the Pentagon to discuss a project so early was "highly unusual." In the meeting on the twenty-ninth, Coppola provided the Pentagon with a copy of Milius's script, which he described as a "surrealistic" interpretation of the issues surrounding the war in Vietnam. He told Laitin, "I don't know whether it is worth reading it because it is undergoing so many revisions that I don't know what of it will wind up in the final film." He explained that it still needed considerable changes and said that he would personally work on the final portion of the screenplay, particularly the last twenty pages or so.[5]

Coppola also stated that he wanted to work with the Pentagon as closely as possible to obtain background information, stock footage for study purposes, and possible physical assistance during actual filming. But he also admitted he had yet to decide where he would shoot the film or whether he would formally request military assistance. He also acknowledged, "I'll understand if the military doesn't want to give me cooperation. But, that's all right. Even if you don't, it isn't all that pressing. I can fake it, the helicopters, the tanks, all that."[6]

Although an assistant secretary for public affairs usually did not get directly involved with filmmakers, Laitin later recalled that Hatch thought he should attend the meeting because Coppola's project could become very controversial. Since Laitin had spent ten years in Hollywood, he thought Hatch was also "being polite" to include him in the meeting. In any case, the secretary considered the conversation "very pleasant" and low pressure. Although the director later changed his attitude on the need for cooperation, Laitin thought that initially Coppola acted very reasonably and did not try to put any pressure on the Pentagon to promise assistance.[7]

For several years, public affairs officials had believed the Vietnam War would make an attractive setting for a good action-adventure movie that focused on soldiers doing their assigned jobs professionally. They hoped that such a film would avoid the political issues of the Vietnam conflict, but they also recognized the inevitability that any film about the war would present negative as well as positive aspects. With this in mind, Baruch sent the script Coppola had left to the Army Office of Information, acknowledging "that there will be many things that the Army will not like in the script." Nevertheless, he advised the service that it had the opportunity "to present factual corrections and recommendations to put the story in proper perspective." Since Coppola had indicated he would make the film under any circumstances, Baruch suggested that the Army work with him "towards preparing a final script that will be an honest presentation," whether the Pentagon ultimately agreed to provide assistance or not.[8]

Laitin recalled that when he next met with the Army chief of information, Gen. Gordon Hill, the general told him that the service had no intention of cooperating with Coppola. Laitin expressed some irritation to Hill because he thought that he was supposed to make the final decision. Nevertheless, he recognized that since the military apparently felt so strongly about the story, he would have had a hard time overruling the service, "the myth about civilian control of the military notwithstanding."[9]

General Hill later said the script contained "simply a series of some of the worst things, real and imagined, that happened or could have happened during the Vietnam War." In the Army's formal response to Baruch's memo, Hill informed the Public Affairs Office that the service found little basis for discussing assistance: "In view of the sick humor or satirical philosophy of the film, it may be useless to point out individual shortcomings, but there are a number of particularly objectionable episodes which present the Army in an unrealistic and unacceptable bad light." These included scenes showing U.S. soldiers scalping the enemy, a surfing display in the midst of combat, an officer obtaining sexual favors for his men and later smoking marijuana with them, and the Army sacrificing troops so the command could say that they were keeping a particular road open. Hill paid special attention to the air cavalry attack on a Vietnamese village and the commander's organizing a surfing display, which he considered "ridiculous and in effect shows another Army officer as a madman." He found the officer's leaving playing cards on Vietcong bodies to be "repellent and uncivilized."[10]

The Army and the Defense Department probably would have been able to live with at least some of these negative incidents—in the proper context. But from the initial script onward, the military strongly objected to the main plot situation in which Colonel Kurtz (Marlon Brando) sets up his independent operation in Cambodia and the Army sends Captain Willard (Martin Sheen) to "terminate" him. In his response to Milius's script, Hill said Kurtz's apparent insanity, the taking of drugs, the committing of "various savageries and cannibalism and engaging in sexual license can only be viewed as a parody on the sickness and brutality of war."[11]

Both in Hill's letter and in subsequent comments, military men asserted that an officer would desert only if he had become mentally unbalanced. In such a situation, officials insisted that the Army would attempt to bring the officer back for medical treatment rather than order another officer to "terminate" him. Moreover, they explained that the military itself would handle any such problem with no help from a civilian "Agency" as the script described. Consequently, Hill argued that "to assist in any way in the production would imply agreement with either the fact or the philosophy of the film." In this light, Hill concluded: "If some fast-buck artist wants to try to make a bundle with this type of garbage, so be it. But he will do it without the slightest assistance from the Army."[12]

Clearly, most people would not call Francis Ford Coppola, a four-time Oscar winner, a "fast-buck artist." Hill later acknowledged that he intended that description "as a general statement about that particular script. I was not pointing to him." In fact, Hill said he was commenting on the worth of the script: "I was referring to the script, not the man. In my terms, the script could have come from anyone." However, given the reputation of the man from whom it did come, Don Baruch called General Hill as soon as he received the memo on June 17, to ask if he would talk with the director about the areas of the script that most concerned the Army. Hill later said he had no interest in discussing the problems, since he considered it "so bad that a few little, minor changes were not going to make it good enough to get any cooperation."[13]

Making it clear that the service felt that a "few little technical changes here and there" would not change the thrust of the movie, Hill and the Army effectively washed their hands of the project. In response to Baruch's request, however, Gen. Wynant Sidle, the deputy assistant secretary of defense for public affairs, did agree to talk to the filmmakers if they came back to the Pentagon. Baruch then called Gray Frederickson, Roos's coproducer, to advise him of the Army's position, particularly about the problems with the plot's springboard, and to invite the filmmakers to come back to Washington to discuss the script. Although Coppola did not follow up on the offer, in the next several months DoD public affairs officials attempted to keep communications open with Coppola, as he had hoped they would. In fact, given the significance and anticipated controversy the film would create, the Pentagon remained willing to seek some accommodation with the director. Very likely, if he had changed "terminate" to "investigate and take appropriate action," the Army would have extended at least some limited assistance.[14]

In any event, on July 9, Frederickson did call the DoD Public Affairs Office to arrange a research trip to Fort Bragg to look at a simulated Vietnamese village used in training. Baruch arranged for John Milius to visit the Green Berets training center and advised Frederickson again that the Army felt the basis for the film was not factual. Although General Hill still refused to meet with the producers, Baruch again suggested that the filmmakers stop in Washington for discussions with General Sidle and other DoD officials, which might help produce a more acceptable script. Milius never appeared at Fort Bragg or in Washington, and Coppola never returned to the Pentagon.[15]

Instead, the director headed to the Far East in search of suitable locations and military assistance. Going first to Australia, Coppola showed a lack of knowledge of American arms sales when he asked the government for use of B-52 bombers, which the United States has never sold abroad and for which the Australians would have no strategic needs. After he also requested the use of ten thousand troops and four hundred helicopters, the government turned him down cold, saying its army was "not a film-extra agency." Coppola then turned to the Philippines, where he reached an agreement with the government in December 1975 for suitable filming locations and use of its army and equipment.[16]

During his trip, Coppola also visited a U.S. naval base in the Philippines, where he inquired about the use of planes, helicopters, and men. The Navy advised him that the service "could not cooperate in any way in this venture" unless he first obtained Defense Department approval. In response, he indicated that he planned to discuss some "low level" cooperation with the Pentagon. After the Public Affairs Office received the Navy's report of Coppola's visit and read accounts of it, Norm Hatch wrote to Coppola repeating what he had told Roos, that "there was little or no possibility of Defense Department assistance being provided based upon a review of the script you presented to us informally." Hatch also said if Coppola felt "the latest script merits a further review," the office would be willing to read it and discuss a formal request for assistance based on an acceptable revision.[17]

On December 30 Fred Roos did submit a revised script to Hatch, saying that Coppola would "continue to work on it up until shooting." Nevertheless, he "honestly" doubted the new script would change the military's stance regarding formal assistance. Still, Roos told officials he wanted "to keep the communication between us open. Any constructive advice or suggestions you wish to give us unofficially will be welcome and considered." Since the revision differed little from the original script, Hatch's office saw no reason to comment on it in writing. However, the Pentagon advised Roos by phone to visit the Information Office of the Commander-in-Chief, Pacific, if he planned any military contact of a research nature.[18]

Apart from Coppola's reluctance to modify his script in any way to accommodate the Pentagon's concerns, the director had his own creative problems in trying to come up with a suitable ending for the movie. At one point, while still working in San Francisco on the screenplay, he commanded that Roos read the section then undergoing still one more revision. When Roos responded, "Francis, I'm having a hard time following it," Coppola grabbed the script from the producer's hands. Upset, he tried to explain his meaning: "These last five pages are crucial. The jungle will look psychedelic, fluorescent blues, yellows, and greens. I mean the war is essentially a Los Angeles export, like acid rock. Like in *Heart of Darkness*, Kurtz has gone savage, but there's this greatness in him. We are all as much products of this primitive earth as a tree or a native whooping around. The horror that Kurtz talks about is never resolved. As Willard goes deeper into the jungle, he realizes that the civilization that has sent him is more savage in ways than the jungle. I mean, we created that war."[19]

The United States did do that, and many of those who fought in Vietnam did remember the experience in surrealistic terms. But not everyone. In any case, the surrealism that existed in Vietnam did not result from drug-induced stupors imported from Hollywood or come from the minds of filmmakers. It grew out of the juxtaposition of conflicting realities in the conduct of the war. At the height of the U.S. involvement, MACV had five hundred thousand men and women in Vietnam. No more than ninety thousand carried out combat operations. Most of the others lived in air conditioned quarters in compounds that boasted swimming pools, tennis courts, and baseball diamonds. Even those men who went out on patrol would spend considerable time in the rear in relative comfort. But whether in enclaves or in the remote jungles, all service personnel received American radio and television programming from the Armed Forces Vietnam Network. On occasion, Marines within sight of the Demilitarized Zone would watch their favorite television programs from the comfort of their foxholes. And when a tour of duty ended, soldiers would board a jet plane and be home within twenty-four hours. The paradoxes inherent in fighting a war in this manner, in fighting a war that might provide entirely different experiences to soldiers thirty miles apart, six weeks earlier or later in time, created the surrealism that characterized Vietnam.

Coppola's attempt to render surrealistic the actual surrealism inherent in the day-today existence of the American forces in Vietnam may explain his failure to resolve his search for a coherent ending to his movie. Instead, he went off to the jungles of the Philippines, much like Willard went upriver looking for Kurtz, perhaps hoping that the chaos of making a movie under adverse conditions would produce an approximation of the American experience in Vietnam. However, despite all their preparations, Coppola and his coproducers failed to ensure that they would have the needed equipment to fulfill their script requirements. As a result, in early April 1976, with filming under way, the director discovered that the Philippine Army could not supply him with all the needed helicopters and jets.

Faced with this reality, Roos wrote to the new assistant secretary of defense for public affairs, William Greener, on April 9, describing the continued refusal of the Pentagon to provide assistance to *Apocalypse Now*. Saying that Coppola had "re-written the script yet again," he officially submitted it for Defense Department "approval, advice and perhaps even co-operation." In fact, Coppola had still not rewritten his ending, and Roos asked Greener to secure the December 1975 script from Norm Hatch. Since filming was under way, Roos asked for a early response.[20]

In addition to Roos's letter, Coppola proceeded to enlist support for his needs from within the film industry. On March 27 George Stevens Jr., director of the American Film Institute, sent a dispatch from the Philippines, where he had a small role in *Apocalypse Now,* to Secretary of Defense Donald Rumsfeld complaining that local U.S. military commanders had forbidden off-duty service personnel from working as extras in the movie. Stevens acknowledged that he understood the reasons for the Pentagon's refusing to give Coppola assistance "in view of subject matter," but he suggested that the secretary review the local order, "which has appearance of harassment" of Coppola: "My own view is that while withholding support is not unreasonable, the specific prohibition of the opportunity for off duty personnel to work as extras is inconsistent with precedent and causes unnecessary difficulties to Coppola. Suggest DOD revoke directive which will have added virtue of deflecting potential public relations problems."[21]

On April 9 Jack Valenti, president of the Motion Picture Association of America, sent a virtually identical letter to Rumsfeld. Acknowledging that the Pentagon could choose whether or not to cooperate on movies depending on their content, he asked, "But, don't you agree that prohibiting servicemen to work on the film in their off-duty hours, is not reasonable?" In response, Norm Hatch called Valenti on the twelfth to advise him that the problem did not result from military restrictions but from a Philippine government law that prohibited U.S. personnel from working in the Philippine economy. Consequently, the commanders in the Philippines had had to advise their men that they would be breaking the law if they worked for Coppola. Hatch said that if Coppola could get the law changed, commanders would allow their men to serve as extras during their off hours.[22]

The explanation satisfied Valenti. Whether or not it did the same for Coppola, he finally made an official request for cooperation to Secretary Rumsfeld in a four-page mailgram dated April 22, 1976, which reached the DoD Public Affairs Office on April 26. After a brief comment about his "incomplete" communications with the Pentagon, he introduced himself with all due humility: "My name is Francis Coppola. I am a film director, producer and writer." After citing his major credits, he concluded: "I am considered a major director of entertainment motion pictures and am not associated with any political movement or with any form of didactic political film." He then presented a detailed account of his plight, including the claim that he had asked for "cooperation from the military, along the lines of other films" and expressed the belief that he "might be permitted to pay rental for military hardware, especially helicopters and other weaponry. We particularly wanted the weapons and aircraft that were used in the Vietnam War."[23]

Acknowledging that the Pentagon had told him that "it was very unlikely that we could receive any form of military cooperation unless considerable changes were made," he said he had worked further on the script and "made certain changes." Although the Public Affairs Office had called Roos after receiving the script, Coppola told Rumsfeld, "We heard nothing." As a result, he said he tried to make arrangements to make the movie in Australia, but the military had turned him down: "It was rumored, though not confirmed, that this was the result of American military men contacting certain colleagues in the Australian military."[24]

Coppola then addressed the issue of why "a serious film-maker" such as himself would make a movie about Vietnam: "I think this is a very amazing question to me." He said he might ask why he was the only filmmaker making a movie about Vietnam. He then explained his project: "My film is not an attempt to mock, criticize or condemn those who participated in the war. My film is merely an attempt to use the theatrical, dramatic form to examine the issues of this war, which certainly must be among the important events in our history."[25]

In regard to the Philippine government's prohibition on U.S. servicemen working off base, Coppola claimed he had received a sanction allowing him to hire off-duty personnel but that the command had not changed its position. He then asked for limited cooperation in the form of helicopters, arguing that if the Pentagon denied it, he would have to assume that "the military uses its control of these aircraft as a means of dictating which films can be made and which films cannot be made." At the same time, he persisted in ignoring the DoD regulations governing cooperation, including the requirement that any screenplay had to be approved before the military could formally discuss assistance. Nor did he even consider the possibility that his script might not qualify for help under DoD guidelines, simply stating: "This film is not anti-military. It is not anti-U.S. It is pro U.S. It is pro human, and it tries to shed light on what I believe to be important and the truthful views on this war. It is not a morality play. It is a serious examination of the issues of Vietnam."[26]

Responding to the message on April 29, Rumsfeld advised Coppola that the same problems existed with the latest screenplay that had caused the Army to turn down the original script: "There are parts that are not factual and not in the best interest of the Department of Defense. At that time, we suggested that you come here for story conference rather than risk misunderstanding by correspondence." He repeated the invitation but with the understanding that Coppola would be able to eliminate certain objectionable scenes, including the sending of one officer to "terminate with prejudice" another officer. Rumsfeld suggested changing the film's springboard to that of an officer who is "investigating and bringing those guilty of wrongful action back for a courtmartial or medical/psychiatric treatment." He felt these changes "would be of mutual benefit by making the film more logical and factual." Finally, he warned that even if the script received approval for assistance, the needed military hardware might not be available in the Philippines when Coppola needed it.[27]

The dialogue continued when Coppola responded on May 3 with an offer to undertake several changes in the script, including making "it an unspecified civilian who sends Willard on this assignment, rather than an Army officer, and I will present the situation in such a way that it will be obvious that there is no alternative but to terminate Kurtz if he does not comply." He also said he would make it clear that the "desire to secure a surfing beach is secondary to some bona fide military mission." In regard to Kurtz's using drugs, Coppola offered to "make this character much less surreal and much more sympathetic.... A man only intent on implementing his country's oft-stated policies." Finally, the director expressed the concern that no one in the Pentagon "understands the style in which I am making this film and that the D.O.D. misinterprets the scenes and the intentions of the scenes." In closing, he said he hoped his "willingness to cooperate with the military on certain script changes" would lead to some assistance for the film.[28]

After reviewing Coppola's offer to make script changes, the DoD Public Affairs Office concluded that only the proposed new version of the surfing episode met prior objections. In responding on May 11, the office told the director that the other three revisions "do not correct our objections." Moreover, the office pointed out that the four revisions requested in its April 29 letter did not represent the sum total of the Pentagon's problems with the film. The office also indicated that even if Coppola were to make the requested revisions, the U.S. forces in the Philippines did not have the type of helicopters he needed. Nevertheless, the office said that it remained willing to reach some accommodation and recommended that if Coppola anticipated further require-ments, he should send someone "com-pletely knowledgeable of the project and its problems" to the Pentagon to discuss the script.[29]

Captain Willard and his crew steal Kilgore's surf board.

Fred Roos answered for Coppola on May 17, repeating the request for a he-licopter, but said it would be very diffi-cult for anyone to go to Washington for script discussions and asked if the Pen-tagon could send a representative to the Philippines. In determining how to an-swer Roos, Norm Hatch confirmed that neither the Navy nor the Air Force in the Philippines had the necessary heli-copter available. In regard to sending a representative to talk with Coppola, he concluded that his office considered "it pointless to have the meeting without some prior indication from Coppola that he will make some significant changes in the script." He advised Assistant Secretary Greener that the only possible assistance the military could lend would be the use of four Phantom jets for two days at company expense, but he did not know whether the director would think the planes were worth the requested revisions.[30]

Hatch then raised the question of whether the Pentagon would give assistance even if Coppola finally agreed to making script changes. He asked this because strong Army objections remained to the overall concept of the story, and General Hill still refused to talk with the company. Hatch also cited a "strong public outcry against our providing assistance" to Coppola resulting from a *Parade Magazine* article about the film the previ-ous July: "When I say strong, I refer to about 140 letters and congressional interest. That is not a lot compared to other major problem complaints but it is extremely high for a film not yet made and described in only a paragraph or two." However, Hatch did recommend that if Coppola would agree to the Pentagon changes, "we provide such assistance, as we are able," on a no-interference, no-cost basis.[31]

In his response to Coppola on May 25, Greener explained that the military could not provide a suitable helicopter. Indicating that it would consider the request for the Phantom jets, the secretary said the director would have to agree to five specific script changes: Willard must be sent to "investigate" with no reference to "terminating command with prejudice," Willard must not be shown smoking or encouraging the smoking of pot, the military command must have some other reason for the daily rebuilding of the bridge apart from "just not wanting to admit being surrounded," there must be some explanation as to why members of his Green Beret team continued to stay with Kurtz, and revisions must be made in the final sequences to dovetail with Willard's new mission. Furthermore, Greener suggested that in the screen titles Coppola include a statement "honoring those who served in Vietnam." He closed, "If you concur in principle to these revisions, detailed script changes can probably be negotiated. Pending these agreements, regret we cannot justify DoD support."[32]

During the spring sparring with the Pentagon, Coppola must have sometimes wondered if he would even need the planes or any other assistance. On April 16 the director fired Harvey Keitel, his Willard, in a contract dispute after the actor expressed concern that the director might shut down the production all summer to accommodate Marlon Brando, who did not want to work while his children were on their school vacation. Keitel had been working under a long-term contract with Coppola, but the delay in completing the film would have kept him from appearing in another movie that fall. Before casting Keitel, Coppola had considered Steve McQueen and Clint Eastwood for the part. He balked at McQueen's demand of $3 million first to play the lead and then for the part Brando was to play. Eastwood said he turned down Willard's role "because the story didn't make sense to me. And anyhow, who wants to spend a year and a half in the jungle making a movie?" Now, faced with no star, Coppola took a week to select Martin Sheen, whose recently completed role in *Cassandra Crossing* had precluded his being cast originally as Willard, according to Coppola's spokesmen.[33]

If his actors and the Pentagon did not cause him enough problems, nature added her obstructions to the production. The last week in May, a major typhoon hit the Philippines and inflicted heavy damage to the *Apocalypse Now* production, and Roos and Frederickson reported that the storm had destroyed 40 to 80 percent of the sets. At one point, one hundred members of the cast and crew were stranded for three days before they were rescued. Always an opportunist, Coppola began filming the storm as soon as the worst of

Martin Sheen as
Francis Ford Coppola's
Capt. Benjamin L. Willard.

the winds had passed, with the expectation that he would find a way to include the footage in the production.[34]

The typhoon also interrupted the long-distance sparring with the Pentagon, which resumed on June 1, when Fred Roos sent a long response to Greener's May 25 message. Because of the damage to the sets and the consequent delay in filming, the producer suggested that the time was right for a meeting between Coppola and a Pentagon representative, particularly since the director was using the break "to do considerable re-writing on the screenplay." Acknowledging the difficulty in communicating by telex, Roos wrote, "We feel a face to face discussion could be most beneficial to Defense as well as us. I am sure that Francis would welcome the Defense Department's input even if the end-result proved to be that co-operation was impossible."[35]

He assured Greener that because they wanted the widest possible audience, "we certainly cannot be aiming to make an anti-American film." Repeating the need for a helicopter, he explained that he had neglected to explain that the patrol boat that required lifting in the movie was only a mock-up that would not exceed the capacity of an available U.S. helicopter. In any event, Roos said that the cooperation itself aside, the film company was "also trying to defuse what appears to be an aggressive attitude of hostility and persona non grata directed toward us from every military office and person that we encounter in the Philippines." Although laying the blame on the Pentagon, Roos maintained that if the secretary of defense or his representative could meet with Coppola, "the Department's fears would diminish and we might get to some new understandings and treatment." He hoped this could occur before Coppola "begins writing his final draft."[36]

Don Baruch advised Greener that Roos had "ignored" his specific request for certain changes in the script and concluded that "it would be a waste of time and money to send someone to the Philippines . . . unless they concur" with the May 25 requests. As a result, Greener informed Roos on June 9 that he "would welcome a meeting with Mr. Coppola in Washington to discuss all aspects of possible DoD support of your production. Alternatively a meeting of my designated representative with Mr. Coppola in the Philippines might be productive if there was some affirmative indication that the suggested script modifications are being considered positively and constructively." He thought if Coppola agreed to the "general thrust of the suggested modifications," an agreement could be reached under these terms "without detracting from the overall impact of your production."[37]

Coppola did not respond to Greener's telegram, perhaps because filming had progressed too far for him to modify the basic story line or perhaps because of the chaos following the typhoon. Finally, in February 1977, Coppola again turned to the American government for assistance in the final stage of production for *Apocalypse Now*. Claiming that the film was "honest, mythical, prohuman, and therefore pro-American," Coppola telegraphed President Carter requesting "some modicum of cooperation or entire government will appear ridiculous to American and world public." He explained to the new president that "because of misunderstanding original script which was only starting point for me," the Pentagon "has done everything to stop" the production of the first major Hollywood film about Vietnam since the end of the war.[38]

Coppola asked Carter for use of one Chinook helicopter for one day, citing the assistance John Wayne received on *The Green Berets* as justification for his request. He also said he needed "immediate approval" to purchase ten cases of smoke markers, which the Pentagon had denied along with all other requests for assistance. In closing, Coppola told

Carter that his movie "tries its best to put Vietnam behind us, which we must do so we can go to a positive future."[39]

From the perspective of the Defense Department, nothing had changed in the nine months since Coppola's last efforts to obtain assistance. By February 1977 the director had completed most of the shooting and would not have been able to change the portions of the script to which the Army had objected. Therefore, the Pentagon had no basis on which to answer the telegram or give even a "modicum" of cooperation. Nor would the government be open to changing its position simply because Coppola made the implied threat that the "entire government will appear ridiculous to American and world public" if he did not receive Pentagon assistance.[40]

Despite Coppola's continuing claims to the contrary, the documentary evidence clearly shows that the Pentagon did not do "everything to stop" *Apocalypse Now*. Except for the Army's initial intransigence regarding the original script, Pentagon officials continued to communicate openly with Coppola and his staff, hoping to agree on a script that would qualify for assistance. In contrast to the Navy's sensitivity about its image in *The Last Detail* and *Cinderella Liberty*, both the Army and the Defense Department recognized that any film about Vietnam would necessarily contain elements that would not reflect favorably on the military's experience in Southeast Asia. Nevertheless, the Pentagon remained willing to assist—within the limits of its regulations—on scripts that contained reasonably accurate, balanced portrayals of the actions of the armed services.

The interdepartmental memos written during the exchanges between Coppola and the Defense Department from April to June 1976 show that officials were willing to take an extra step to avoid confrontation. In one memo on May 10, discussing how to respond to Coppola's latest message, Don Baruch indicated that the Public Affairs Office believed that "if we could come to a mutual agreement to changes, even if only to the opening sequence (springboard of the story) and to the closing episode at the Green Beret camp, it would be a worthwhile bargain to grant assistance by making four aircraft available on the basis of non-interference and no-additional-cost-to-the-government." Because of the problems of negotiating by correspondence, Baruch urged that a meeting be set up in the Pentagon with Coppola or his representative. In Hatch's memo on May 20, when he raised the question of availability of equipment even if an agreement was reached, he had recommended that the Pentagon should "provide such assistance, as we are able, in consideration of no cost to the government, no interference with missions, and all safety factors taken into account."[41]

Just as the Pentagon had not closed the avenue to assistance during the first half of 1976, it had not "denied" Coppola's request to purchase smoke markers or use a helicopter in February 1977—as he charged in his telegram to President Carter. At the time he made his accusation, the Pentagon was in the process of considering the request. Its subsequent decision to do nothing about it resulted from Coppola's own failure to negotiate in good faith and because the military could provide no assistance until the script had received official approval.[42]

Although Coppola did not follow up his telegram to President Carter, in June 1977 a San Francisco attorney wrote to the Pentagon seeking to obtain for an unnamed client "certain soundtracks or recordings" to use for a motion picture. Since Coppola had his headquarters in San Francisco and the attorney was requesting sounds of rifle fire, rocket launchers, jet fighters, and Chinese ordnance, the Pentagon did not have a difficult time figuring out the identity of the client. When the attorney called the Public Affairs Office,

Don Baruch advised him that the sound effects were available from any number of commercial sources, including Radio Shack. The lawyer later sent a thank-you note saying the technical people were "pleased with the cooperation they received."[43]

Coppola's difficulties with *Apocalypse Now* multiplied. Like the American intervention in Vietnam, which had bogged down in a quagmire, Coppola's project seemed to slowly sink beneath the weight of its problems and a budget that escalated from an original estimate of about $10 million to a figure approaching $30 million by 1978. First scheduled for release in April of 1977, the premiere was postponed until November and then finally delayed a full year to November 1978.

With a virtual blackout on information about the film and with Coppola continuing to reshoot exterior combat scenes even after his return from the Philippines in February 1977, including sequences in the Napa Valley in July 1977, expectations grew about the final form of the film. While in the Philippines, Coppola had said: "I can allow the film to be violent because I don't consider it an antiviolence movie. If you want to make an antiviolence film, it cannot be violent. Showing the horrors of war with people being cut up and saying it will prevent violence is a lie. Violence breeds violence. If you put a lot of it on the screen, it makes people lust for violence."[44]

Francis Ford Coppola became the first American filmmaker to undertake a film about the Vietnam War since John Wayne made *The Green Berets* in 1968. Like the war, the production of *Apocalypse Now* seemed to have no end.

Coppola's earlier films all showed his propensity for satisfying people's lust for violence. *Patton,* for which he wrote the original screenplay, contained broad scenes of bloody slaughter. *The Rain People,* ostensibly a cross-country odyssey, contained in it the threat of impending violence, a threat Coppola ultimately delivered. *The Conversation,* as well as the two *Godfather* films, utilized violence as a major theme, and Coppola splattered the screen with blood in them. And all reports that continued to filter out during the postproduction phase indicated that he intended to outdo himself in *Apocalypse Now.*

Of course, Vietnam provided Coppola with all the examples he might want. To duplicate its carnage, he went to great lengths to ensure visual authenticity. To create a village devastation scene, Coppola hired dozens of South Vietnamese refugees, and a crew member recalled, "We literally stacked them up like logs, dangled a few arms and legs around, and poured gallons of blood over them." Another crew member said, "It will make *The Godfather* look like a kid's story." One of Coppola's spokesmen claimed, however, that the director had "no intention or interest in making *Apocalypse Now* grisly or gory," and he attributed the stories to personnel who were "unqualified to assess the film's eventual tone and content."[45]

Precisely what tone Coppola would ultimately decide on remained perhaps the longest-running battle during the production of *Apocalypse Now.* Marlon Brando's stand-in (Brando showed up in the Philippines weighing 285 pounds, so Coppola decided to make

Colonel Kurtz six feet, five inches, and use a double for Brando's body shots) suggested, "What Francis is trying to say is that the military people were not second-class citizens and idiots. They were good hometown boys, but the war changed them. The whole military image is going to be changed after this." The special-effects chief observed that the "whole movie is special effects. You got three stars but the action's gonna keep the audience on the edge of their seats. It's a war movie." The production designer said, "This movie's about how wrong it was for Americans to go against their nature."[46]

Coppola himself refused to publicly discuss the film once he completed principal shooting in the Philippines. He expressed his only thoughts about the end result of his effort in his telegram to President Carter and in a memo to his staff in which he said on April 30, 1976, that in his "personal opinion . . . *Apocalypse Now* is going to be a very fine film, possibly even a great film. I have never worked on a film before that truly had that possibility." Nevertheless, the obvious fascination with violence that he had manifested in his earlier movies, the reports that filtered back from the Philippines, and his statements during production all suggested that Coppola was using images of violence in *Apocalypse Now* to create a catharsis in the viewer and so purge Vietnam from the American psyche. He himself answered the question as to why he wanted to "scratch old wounds" by saying, "I'm cauterizing old wounds, trying to let people put the war behind them. You can never do that by forgetting it."[47]

Whether repeated scenes of blood and guts and massive destruction would "help America put Vietnam behind us, which we must do so we can go on to a positive future," as he told President Carter, remained to be seen once he finally completed the film. Yet as Coppola himself observed, rather than repulse them, the portrayal of violence usually makes people lust for violence. Moreover, it remains doubtful that re-creating in living color Vietnam's horrors can be considered "pro-human and therefore pro-American." However much Coppola was to rework Milius's original script, it was difficult to see how the depiction of the fighting in Vietnam, whether in *Apocalypse Now* or any other movie, could significantly change the image created by ten years' television coverage of the war. It definitely could not improve the image the armed forces had been attempting to develop since 1973, as an aid in recruiting for the all-volunteer military.[48]

In any event, although *Apocalypse Now* had become the first film portraying combat in Vietnam to go into production after the American pullout in 1973, Coppola's seemingly endless struggle to complete the film ensured that it would not be the first feature film about the war since *The Green Berets* to reach the screen. Before that happened, several movies, which Coppola's production had spawned, appeared using the Vietnam War as their starting point, either to tell stories about returning veterans or simply to serve as a new locale for combat stories.

Max Youngstein, the consultant to the producer of *The Boys in Company C,* believed that by 1978 the American public was willing to "take a look back at what happened in Vietnam, warts and all." His film showed the warts by concentrating on a unit of young American Marines. On the surface, *The Boys in Company C,* which appeared in early 1978, could have been portraying any American war. It traced the rites of passage of a typical group of American boys from their arrival at the San Diego Marine Recruit Depot through their training to their maturity and the deaths of some of them under fire. *The Boys in Company C* followed the traditions of most war movies, not only in its story but also in its primary purpose, to make money. Unlike *Coming Home,* which Jane Fonda produced because of her desire to make an anti–Vietnam War statement, *The Boys in Company C* went

Marines prepare to repulse an attack in *The Boys in Company C.*

into production only after the filmmakers carefully considered its potential to return a profit. At the same time, however, the producers saw the film as an attempt to comment on the absurdity of war in general and one conflict in particular, the Vietnam War.[49]

According to Max Youngstein, the producer of *Fail Safe* and the American consultant to Golden Harvest Films, a Hong Kong–based production company, the project faced a basic question: "did the American public want to hear about Vietnam—in any form? Forget about what position you took, whether it was a good thing to do or a bad thing to do or a miserable thing to do—did they want to see anything about it and be reminded of something that turned out to be probably the only losing war that America has ever been involved in? Plus all the sociological and human aspects of 50,000 young men killed in the prime of their lives, with the quarter of a million that nobody talks about being anything from quadriplegics to maimed to where they are totally dependent on somebody else for their life."[50]

Up to 1976, the answer had remained "no." Like other Vietnam stories, the script for *The Boys in Company C,* which had been floating around Hollywood for a long time, had been turned down by both studios and independent production companies. When Raymond Chow, owner-president of Golden Harvest, took the story under consideration, he faced the very difficult decision of whether to take a chance with the story, because the United States constituted about 50 percent of the film's potential market. Chow did not feel qualified to judge the American pulse on the subject and so gave Youngstein the deciding vote. The consultant described the decision as a "judgment call," one that remained hard "to analyze because there are certain people who, to this day, don't want to talk about the Vietnam War. . . . It's like something they would like to blot out, put into oblivion somewhere and not talk about it."[51]

Personally, Youngstein felt the United States should not have become involved in Vietnam except to provide supplies "to the side that we believe in." In no case did he believe the United States should have committed "a single human being" to the struggle. He considered Vietnam "totally an internal war which we had no business even trying to guess at because we had shown no ability, certainly during my lifetime, to accurately evaluate what the hell the situation is, and we invariably wind up being on the wrong side." As a result, Youngstein hoped that by showing the "absurdities" that took place in Vietnam, *The Boys in Company C* would show that the war had been wrong. He believed that by early 1976 "the American people had really begun to take a hard look at the Vietnam War and would respond in enough quantities to make the picture a good commercial risk" at the cost for which Golden Harvest could make the picture. He therefore advised Chow to make the movie.[52]

Apart from financial considerations and his own feelings about Vietnam, Youngstein felt that *The Boys in Company C* had an "overriding objective to show that war in itself is the ultimate obscenity. . . . Any war is the ultimate obscenity . . . it's the constant proof that man has not yet evolved to maturity." He believed that it was possible to show violence in making an antiwar statement "because the violence itself proves in a very, almost perverted way . . . that man is capable still of killing and at the same time, saying that he is killing to prevent killing. And if that isn't Catch 22 then I don't know what the hell is. . . . It's like the neutron bomb . . . let's save the buildings but let's kill the people."[53]

The Boys in Company C did show the Vietnam War being fought absurdly. It portrayed foul-mouthed Marine drill instructors browbeating recruits, manhandling them, wrestling them to the ground by their balls, and generally humiliating them while at the same time seeking advice from some of them. It showed self-serving officers as incompetents. Like *M*A*S*H*, *The Boys in Company C* ends not on the battlefield but on a playing field, this time with the Marine commander ordering his men to lose a soccer game to a Vietnamese unit with a withdrawal from combat as their reward. All this absurdity inspired the advertising writers to imitate *Catch-22* in their sales pitch: "To keep their sanity in an insane war, they had to be crazy."

Realizing that the Marines would have no interest in assisting on a film containing such images, Youngstein told Golden Harvest not even to contact the Pentagon: "Don't waste your time. Don't even spend the ten cents for the phone call." Instead, Sidney Furie shot the movie in the Philippines with assistance from its military, ending up with a story that Marine officials maintain bore little resemblance to their training procedures, activities, or experiences in Vietnam. In fact, if the United States had fought the war as portrayed in *The Boys in Company C,* the Marines probably would not have made it off the beaches or out of their airplanes.

To be sure, in Vietnam the armed forces unfortunately had their normal share of incompetent officers, deserters, shirkers. However, *The Boys in Company C* raised the questions that must be asked about all the combat films Hollywood has released about the war. To make a fair statement against the Vietnam conflict, can filmmakers change history to satisfy the needs of their messages? Can they deliberately create false images and metaphors? Can they distort reality to show only incompetence and dereliction of duty and cowardice? Can they ignore the reality that most officers and men did their jobs as ordered and did them as best they could under adverse circumstances? Can they legitimately suggest that Vietnam was the only war in which men have complained about the military or have broken down in combat?

To Youngstein, the idea of the film "was to get across a certain point of view with

Had the United States fought the war as portrayed in *The Boys in Company C,* the Marines probably would not have made it off the beaches.

respect to the war, with respect to not only that war, but war generally." As a result, distorting Marine basic training or showing only incompetent officers in an effort to criticize the military "didn't bother" Youngstein at all. He contended, "While those specific incidents never happened, knowing what basic training was like, and during World War II, having been connected with films about basic training and everything else and having been able to observe basic training, the specifics were no more than dramatic license that a novelist would take or a painter would take or anybody else would take."[54]

Despite Youngstein's desire to make a statement against war, he acknowledged that *The Boys in Company C* was "far from being an in-depth statement," one that therefore "left open, by a large margin" room for more serious film statements about Vietnam. In contrast to the superficiality of the Golden Harvest production, *Go Tell the Spartans*, also released in 1978, made a serious effort to look at the American combat experience in Vietnam. Set in the early 1960s, the film focused on the role of U.S. military advisors working with the South Vietnamese army at a time when few Americans were giving Southeast Asia much thought.[55]

Based on Daniel Ford's novel *Incident at Muc Wa*, Wendall Mayes's tightly focused screenplay told a story that undoubtedly happened hundreds of times during America's ten years in Vietnam. From higher headquarters comes the order to move a detachment of troops into the abandoned outpost at Muc Wa. The American officer in charge, Maj. Asa Barker, objects to thinning out his ranks to occupy a hamlet that has no strategic importance, but the command prevails. When the unit, which comprises five Americans and twelve Vietnamese soldiers, arrives at Muc Wa, it immediately becomes a magnet for the Vietcong, who attack regularly in increasing numbers. In contrast to the American military reaction to a similar situation in *The Green Berets*, headquarters sends in a helicopter to evacuate Barker and his men, abandoning to their fate the Vietnamese soldiers and civilians who had accompanied them.

Barker's need to bribe a South Vietnamese politician to obtain support troops for his mission and the orders to leave the Vietnamese behind, as opposed to the idealized portrayal in Wayne's movie, provide a microcosm of the American role in Vietnam and its relationship to the people it was supposedly defending. When the time comes to get on the helicopter, however, one of Barker's men defies orders and elects to remain with the people he has gotten to know. As if to finally acknowledge the callousness and selfishness of the system and the American position in Vietnam, the major also stays, in the hope of leading the Vietnamese to safety. But in the ensuing firefight, Barker discovers that the civilians have sided with the Vietcong, as his interpreter had warned. Mortally wounded, the major can only mumble, "Oh, shit," as he sinks slowly into a ditch. The next morning, the corporal who had elected to remain and is now the only survivor of the fight stumbles from the battlefield and spots an old, one-eyed Vietnamese who aims a rife at him but does not shoot. As he heads away, the American yells back, "I'm going home, Charley." Mockingly, the closing title appears: "1964."

Despite such images, Don Baruch found the screenplay "unusual . . . as it basically shows U.S. 'advisors' heroically carrying out their assignment." In his memo of July 6, 1977, accompanying the script, he asked the Army for its opinion on the possibility of providing assistance to the production. He did acknowledge that "there may be some passages that you would prefer having revised and some others requiring changes for authenticity" and asked that the Public Affairs Office "expedite" its comments.[56]

In its response on July 26, the Army indicated it could provide assistance "only if the producers will make substantive changes to the script. The changes will involve the characterization of the individuals appearing in the script, the story detail involving Barker's failure to get promoted, and numerous historical details." The service explained that American advisors in Vietnam in 1964 were "virtually all outstanding individuals, hand-picked for their jobs, and quite experienced" and pointed out that the script, "in presenting an off-hand collection of losers, is totally unrealistic of the Army in VN in that period."[57]

The service said that such an inaccuracy "alone would preclude DA assistance because of the AR 360-5 provision that the production under consideration must present the Army realistically." In order for *Go Tell the Spartans* to qualify for cooperation, the Army said that "all the characters in the script would have to appear as outstanding soldiers; no drug use, no "LT Fuzz" characters, and no draftees. Barker would have to be cleaned up extensively, especially his language and drinking; the NCO should not commit suicide; no General Officer would be presented as a tactically inept egomaniac."[58]

Given Baruch's initial response to the script and the positive interest in it by some officers in the Army's Public Affairs Office, the service's objections to factual inaccuracies could probably have been resolved through negotiations between the producer, Allan Bodoh, and Pentagon officials. But as an independent producer with no knowledge of the Hollywood-military relationship, Bodoh did not follow up the Defense Department's turn-down directly. Instead, he tried to work with the Army's Los Angeles Public Affairs Office, whose primary function is to provide technical advice to filmmakers, not to make decisions for the Defense Department on whether to extend assistance. When Bodoh and Mayes found resistance to the script from the director of that office, who claimed that soldiers did not regularly use four-letter words in Vietnam, the filmmakers simply walked out of the office and made the film without any military cooperation.[59]

With *Go Tell the Spartans,* the Army and the filmmakers might have resolved the technical and even historical problems, because Bodoh and Mayes did want assistance and were prepared to revise the script to meet major objections. Moreover, the Army's problems, with one exception, focused on matters of procedure and fact, not on content or the thrust of the story—which had created the service's antipathy to *Apocalypse Now.* Even with the central "flaw" in the story, negotiations should have been able to resolve the objection if the filmmakers had returned to the Pentagon.[60]

The Army had stated that it could simply not accept the characterization of the movie's central figure, Burt Lancaster's character, Major Barker. Apart from objections to Barker's language and drinking, on which both sides could have compromised, the Army pointed out that a man of Barker's age and years in the military (a veteran of World War II and Korea) would not have the rank of major. The Army would have promoted him by then or he would have had to retire. Mayes agreed with the validity of the criticism and acknowledged that the Army had justification for refusing to assist on a film having such a factually implausible central character. At the same time, the screenwriter explained that he and the producer refused to consider changing the essence of the role to obtain assistance because they liked the way Barker described the reasons he had remained a major.[61]

Talking to his executive officer over a bottle of liquor in their jungle headquarters, Barker recounts in great detail and with much humor his misfortune of having been discovered making love with his general's wife in the gazebo of an embassy: "She sat with her back to the door while I remained standing, keeping a sharp look out all around, whereupon she proceeded to make love to me—orally. Well, as you well know, there comes a time in the sexual encounter when a fella is apt to lose interest in the surroundings which is precisely what I was guilty of doing." He explains that the general's wife did not notice that her husband, the ambassador's wife, and the president of the United States were standing in the entrance to the gazebo and so "had not ceased operations. And that is why, after all these years, I'm still a major." In response to his executive's question as to what he did when confronted, Barker says, "I did the only thing I've ever been trained to do, I saluted."

Mayes said that the major's explanation was worth the price of not obtaining assistance. Although conceding that the Army would have summarily thrown Barker out of the service if he had actually been caught in such a compromising situation, the screenwriter pointed out that he wrote the story and Lancaster ultimately rendered it tongue in cheek. He therefore believed that if the Army had entered into serious discussions with the filmmakers, they would have been able to explain the nature of the recitation and how Lancaster would play it, thereby alleviating the service's concerns. To make the story even more acceptable, the writer could have also given Lancaster an additional line (after a suitable pause): "And, if you believe that, I can sell you the Brooklyn Bridge." Mayes could also

Ted Post talks to Burt Lancaster during filming of *Go Tell the Spartans* (1978), one of the first combat movies about Vietnam to reach American audiences.

have proposed adding an explanation, drawn from the novel, that Barker had received a battlefield promotion to lieutenant in Korea and so most likely would have ended his career as a major, regardless of his age or years in service.[62]

While the filmmakers did not have the opportunity to make such a case, the script and the filmmakers had found a supporter in the person of the deputy head of the Army's Los Angeles Public Affairs Office. The day after his visit to the office, Bodoh called Maj. John Markanton to ask if he would become the technical advisor during the shooting. Markanton, who thought the script was the best thing he had read on the Vietnam War, immediately agreed and took a thirty-day leave to work on the film, providing director Ted Post the assistance he needed to give *Go Tell the Spartans* the authentic military ambience of the advisory period in Vietnam. As a result, despite the apparent implausibility of Barker's persona and some dramatic license in the portrayal of the men in his unit, *Go Tell the Spartans* did in large measure create a positive image of the Army's advisors in the early days of the war.[63]

Given the limited scope and equipment requirements of the story, the director probably needed Markanton's advice more than any material assistance the Army might have been able to provide if it had approved the script. Moreover, because of the film's small budget and short shooting schedule, going to the Philippines for the scenery and available

U.S. military hardware never became a viable option. Post shot *Go Tell the Spartans* north of the Magic Mountain amusement park in the San Fernando Valley, where he built a Vietnamese village and military compound.

The producers rented an old Marine helicopter from commercial sources and dozens of Vietnamese refugees from the Los Angeles area to play the required soldiers, peasants, and Vietcong. Many of the men had served as soldiers in the war and so were able to contribute their advice on technical details as well as perform realistically in the battle scenes. Some American equipment, a few soldiers, and one or two Huey helicopters like those actually in use in Vietnam at the time in which the story takes place might have enabled Post to create more authentic combat sequences and film them in daylight rather than at night, which he did to hide the deficiencies. Nevertheless, *Go Tell the Spartans* does not obtain its power from its combat sequences but rather from portraying the experiences of a small group of American advisors, their working relationship with their Vietnamese counterparts, and what happens when they meet the enemy in battle. Their "moment of truth" comes in a minor skirmish of the type that characterized much of the fighting in Vietnam, a battle fought with grenades and small arms, and finally in hand-to-hand combat.[64]

In some measure, *Go Tell the Spartans* contained little that audiences had not seen in countless World War II movies about small-unit action in the jungles of the South Pacific. If it becomes a traditional war film in that sense, its setting and the results of the climactic battle set it apart from a typical Hollywood war movie that offered a victorious ending. Major Barker's fate stands as an ominous omen that Vietnam would not offer similar conclusions for the U.S. military. Barker perhaps puts it best when he tells an arriving soldier, "Too bad we couldn't show you a better war."

In the end, Lancaster's portrayal of "a crusty officer who has been through too many wars to be a hero, but not too many to remember his duty to his men" became crucial to the power of the film. Although 65 years old when he played Major Barker, the actor looked almost believable as a 45-50-year-old soldier in fighting trim, in contrast to John Wayne, who looked every day of his 60 years as the overweight Lt. Col. Kirby in *The Green Berets.* Lancaster himself rejected the critics' claim that he was doing a disservice to the parents of American boys who had died in Vietnam: "People have to sit back and reflect on their lives at some point. You have to bring yourself up to date and take stock. You can't avoid things, and anyway, history eventually examines everything. I think this is the time to take a good hard look at what we were doing in Vietnam."[65]

Ted Post directing Burt Lancaster during making of *Go Tell the Spartans.*

In providing one window through which to take that look, Lancaster played Major Barker unsentimentally but with a warmth and believability that might have caused even a war resister to follow him into battle. The actor admitted that he once wanted to play Patton but had changed his mind because "I felt that to play Patton would have been to glorify him, which I didn't want to do. . . . My Major Barker is a very different man from Patton. He's an old pro, a reasonably intelligent man, a field soldier who really cares about his troops." As a result, despite the Army's rejection of his characterization in the script, Lancaster created in Major Barker an officer in whom the Army should have taken great pride.[66]

The whole production presented a balanced portrayal of the early days of American involvement in Vietnam. Ted Post felt that after Watergate the American people were "open to disillusion. It's now safe to cope with the issues the war raised." The producers believed the concept of surrounding Lancaster with young, little-known actors "coincides with the American consciousness of those early years in Vietnam, when we knew little more than what the president or the generals told us and the battle lines were being manned by the anonymous volunteers of our special combat forces."[67]

Major Barker's competence more than made up for his commander's mediocrity. Although some of his men used drugs or acted strangely, the majority did their jobs well in the face of a situation for which no training manual then existed—fighting a war in which even the civilians you helped might become your enemy. The combat itself, especially the climactic firefight, had the feel of a actual battle, unlike the major Vietcong attack in *The Green Berets*, which looked like a John Wayne western shoot-out with the Indians storming the walls.

Only occasionally do the ironies in *Go Tell the Spartans* seem pat and heavy-handed, such as when the "1964" closing title follows "I'm going home, Charley" or when the gung ho southern lieutenant observes, "We won't lose because we're Americans." For the most part, however, the film remains understated, and without the overt antiwar message in *Coming Home*. Nevertheless, Post and Mayes captured the essence of what the war was like probably better than any other movie about America's combat experience in Vietnam, before or since. It conveyed the war's complexities, the irrelevance of the United States' presence in Southeast Asia, the corruption that its presence created, and the cruelties and waste of the war. Perhaps because it so well portrayed the American experience in the war, *Go Tell the Spartans* failed to attract a large audience and passed from view almost as quickly as *Rolling Thunder*. Nevertheless, it received wide praise from critics and remains one of the two or three best Vietnam War combat movies.

18 The Deer Hunter, Hair, and Finally Apocalypse Now

NOT UNTIL THE RELEASE OF *THE DEER HUNTER* in early 1979, following its one-week screening in December 1978 to qualify it for the Academy Awards, did Vietnam become a financially rewarding subject for filmmakers. The two men who developed the original story had a much more limited goal—simply to come up with a marketable screenplay. They did not even plan, at first, to set their film within the context of the American experience in Vietnam. Quinn Redeker recalls that the initial concept came to him one night in 1971, while sitting with his wife looking for a hook on which to hang a screenplay. As one possibility, he tossed out the idea of a man who played Russian roulette for a living.[1]

Redeker recalled that the inspiration came from a *Life* magazine article he had read about a man with a .38-caliber breach-break revolver who played Russian roulette for the camera. The man had tied a towel around his face lengthwise as if he had a toothache, spun the cylinder, and pulled the trigger. He had survived the demonstration and seemed very happy. Redeker envisioned his own story juxtaposing jeopardy and personal dynamics. However, despite the dramatic possibilities, he did not pursue the idea until the fall of 1974.

At that time he telephoned his mentor, writer Lou Garfinkle, with the suggestion that they write a screenplay together. Garfinkle had just returned from New York, where he had been working on a project with a collaborator who had died unexpectedly, and he had no desire to begin a new writing partnership immediately. However, to his "consternation," Redeker insisted upon reading him a list of script ideas, including the concept for a story about a man who plays Russian roulette for a living.

Continuing to disavow interest, Garfinkle hung up. However, as he recalled, the one-line concept for a script about playing Russian roulette buried in the middle of the proposals grabbed his attention. Becoming excited, he immediately called Redeker back and asked him to come over to talk about the idea. Although Redeker had first set the story in the Bahamas, Garfinkle recalled that he quickly saw the game "as a perfect metaphor for the war in Vietnam." He wasn't sure they should locate the story in Vietnam, though: "I thought maybe it had to be that the guy had come home."

To resolve the issue, the writers searched for different ways to handle the story, setting it on Catalina Island and in the South Dakota cattle country during a blizzard, among other places. Ultimately, Garfinkle told Redeker, "No. The war in Vietnam is current. Nobody is touching it. It seems to me that we can develop something that will perfectly delineate the problem Americans have living with a gun at their heads. That is a condition man should not have to live with."

With the matter settled, the men began to work through this approach. Usually, Redeker would type up some pages and bring them back to Garfinkle for discussion. After twenty-two drafts, "The Man Who Came to Play" emerged, focusing on two American POWs who meet in a Cambodian prison camp. Redeker explained that by selecting this locale, they could "justify" the Russian roulette. Their two characters, Merle, a grunt who had fought on the ground, and Keys, an Air Force major who flew overhead in relative comfort, are simply trying to stay alive.

Merle arrived at the camp suffering a head wound and has become almost totally dependent on the leadership and intellect of Keys. The officer has become Merle's apparent protector very much in the literary and Hollywood tradition of George and Lennie in John Steinbeck's *Of Mice and Men* and, more recently, of Charlie and Raymond in Barry Levinson's *The Rain Man.* Garfinkle saw the story as a "typical Hollywood adventure melodrama" about the loyalty between the two men, the typical buddy film Hollywood regularly turns out, especially about soldiers in war.

Clear differences existed, however. Merle has become the "thing" of Keys, and Garfinkle admitted that the loyalty existed only in Merle's mind. Keys exploits that trust by "managing" Merle in ongoing games of Russian roulette for their captors' edification and as a game on which they can gamble. To protect his investment, Keys has managed to doctor the revolver; and when the ploy is about to be exposed, he orchestrates the men's escape, taking along the winnings he has stashed away over the months.

After making their way to Saigon, however, Keys tricks Merle into believing he has killed himself playing a game of Russian roulette, while trying to increase their stake. Still suffering lingering effects of his head wound and guilt-stricken over Keys's apparent death, Merle becomes a professional Russian roulette player in Saigon. Garfinkle explained that the script delineated "a highly sophisticated kind of game of death in which there were different kinds of games of Russian roulette. The weapons themselves were specialized."

In populating this world with stereotypical Orientals and devious Europeans, the writers drew up the images of their film-viewing youth. In particular, Garfinkle cited *Shanghai Express* (1932) and *The General Died at Dawn* (1936) as having influenced him in developing the original idea for "The Man Who Came to Play" into the final script. He did admit, however, that the portrayal of the Vietnamese forcing prisoners to play the Russian roulette and later gambling reinforced the negative images and worst fears that most Americans have of Orientals.

In this fantasy environment, Merle becomes the best, or perhaps more accurately, the luckiest Russian roulette competitor in Saigon. Or, as Keys used to tell him in the POW camp, mind can triumph over matter. Ultimately, Merle climaxes his career with a game of "stationary progression." In this version, the first contestant spins the cylinder and pulls the trigger. All subsequent rotations occur only by the revolver's mechanism until "determination." When his opponent confronts the loaded sixth cylinder and cannot pull the trigger, Merle wins the contest by "forfeiture." The triumph also completes his mental recovery: "The Victor. Indomitable. Almost omniscient, omnipotent. Coolly Oriental and inscrutable. Yet still very American—direct and guileless when he wants to be. He sits taking in the crowd but not really hearing. There is something in his eyes, the look of the Veteran, having borne all the pains that facing death can bring."[2]

Having ended that chapter in his life, Merle takes his accumulated wealth and flies to Los Angeles, where he seeks out Keys's "widow," expecting to share his winnings with her. Now divorced, she quickly recognizes her ex-husband's duplicity and directs Merle to Keys's van sales operation. After an initial bloody, violent confrontation, Keys tries to con Merle one more time. However, he is addressing a different man, one who has become the manipulator, one who is determined to extract revenge for his betrayed trust. Keys does not accept his fate quietly, drawing on all his cunning in a desperate attempt to turn the contest in his favor. Merle responds in kind. Ultimately, the two men return to Saigon and confront each other across the table in Merle's old Russian roulette gaming palace, playing for their lives and $2 million.

Garfinkle saw the story saying that the extent to which some men will exploit the mortality of others for their own advantage, for their own survival, can override loyalty and become monstrous. Some people who read the script told Garfinkle that they thought "The Man Who Came to Play" would have made a richer film than the one into which it ultimately evolved under the direction of Michael Cimino. The writer disagreed: "I frankly don't believe that. I think *The Deer Hunter* was one of those lucky things that comes together by accident in which the melodramatic idea of the Russian roulette paired with Deric Washburn's and Michael's concerns about mainstream America suddenly came together and added up to something bigger than we had certainly envisioned. And more than Michael may have felt."

Due to the nature of the Hollywood creative process, Redeker and Garfinkle never had the opportunity to find out whether their script could have stood alone. Having completed it in February 1975, they took it to their friend Herm Saunders, a producer at Jack Webb's Mark VII Productions, who thought "it was a fascinating piece." Saunders did ask the writers if they had based the Russian roulette on fact. Although they admitted that they had no evidence that it had occurred, they told him they felt it easily could have happened. In that light, Saunders said that the portrayal didn't bother him: "It didn't seem to strain the credulity to the filmgoer. I think that worse things probably occurred."[3]

As a producer, however, Saunders recognized that he could not develop "The Man Who Came to Play" for television, the medium in which he was then working. As a result, he took the script to an agent friend, Robert Littman. Agreeing with Saunders on the merits of the script, Littman began seeking a film company willing to produce the story. The Russian roulette became the problem in making a deal. One instance stood out in Redeker's mind. He recalled a meeting he and Littman had with producers Robert Chartoff and Irwin Winkler, trying to interest them in the screenplay. Redeker said that Chartoff liked the story, but "it scared the shit out of Winkler. He literally ran out of the room and slammed the door."[4]

Ultimately, Littman took the script to Barry Spikings and Michael Deeley, the heads of British Lion, who bought it with the idea it would become a moderately budgeted movie costing perhaps $2 million. During the process of coming up with the money, however, the British production company EMI took over British Lion. Saunders recalled that this "changed the entire complexion of the production because EMI had big bucks." In any case, Spikings and Deeley needed about a year to put a deal together to make "The Man Who Came to Play" and find someone to direct the film.[5]

Redeker said that EMI finally hired Cimino in November 1976, because it could not get anyone else: "People were afraid of it. The Russian roulette scared the hell out of them." Ironically, Cimino did not like or understand the Russian roulette centerpiece of "The Man Who Came to Play" and tried to get rid of it. On the day EMI hired him, Spikings and Deeley arranged for him to meet with Redeker and Garfinkle to discuss their screenplay. Redeker remembers sitting on his knees trying to explain the story to the director, who kept asking, "Why would he play Russian roulette?" The writers responded by explaining that the Russian roulette created the player's jeopardy, which became the hook to capture the audience, to have it feel: "My God, what is he going to do next?" Redeker considered this the heart of the story: "That he didn't understand that, really shook me up. When we walked out, we thought that it was all over: This guy just doesn't understand anything."[6]

Cimino had little apparent interest in the Russian roulette and "The Man Who Came to Play" because he arrived on the scene with his own ideas for a film focusing on the American experience in Vietnam. Consequently, if Deeley and Spikings thought they had hired a director to simply shoot their script, they quickly found that Cimino was developing an entirely different screenplay. In fact, he was to claim that EMI hired him on the basis of a story he had sold to Deeley and Spikings. The production notes in the film's press kit quoted Cimino saying, "I sat down with them for about two hours and told them the story and they said, 'Go make it.'" In a 1978 interview with the *New York Times,* he told the reporter he was so stunned by the approval that he asked, "What do you mean by O.K.?"[7]

Deeley later called Cimino a liar for peddling this story. The producers said they had hired Cimino because they liked his writing and directing of *Thunderbolt and Lightfoot* and thought he might be able to figure out a way to deal with the violence in their script. They quickly discovered that Cimino intended to do not only a different story than EMI had hired him to make but also a different kind of Vietnam movie than other filmmakers then had in production. He told a reporter that he planned to focus on a group of blue-collar workers in a Pittsburgh steel mill, on their work in the furnaces, and on their hunting weekends in the hills. He would take them to Vietnam, bring them back, and tell what happens to them. The director saw this story as the basis for a positive film, not positive about the war but about the human condition. He said he had three images in mind, the din and abrasiveness of the mill but also its warmth and human solidarity, the peace of the Allegheny hills and the delicacy of nature, and the place of a great disaster in men's lives. Cimino claimed he was portraying "a voyage to the heart of darkness, but it comes back. It's not nihilistic. The disaster of war is secondary to the attitude of men to each other."[8]

To help write this story, which he titled "The Deer Hunter," Cimino brought in his friend Deric Washburn. At the same time, however, EMI insisted on keeping the Russian roulette in the screenplay, which meant that the writers had to weld two disparate stories together. In doing this, they reduced the Russian roulette to a rudimentary form but left the original metaphor intact. However, if merging the two images was to create a film of epic proportions, not everyone liked the results.

Redeker recalled that when Barry Spikings read the new version, he "hated it, didn't like it at all." Nevertheless, he said, "What the hell," and told Cimino to go ahead. His partner, Michael Deeley, later told Redeker that he thought combining the two stories created the film's power. To Deeley, the steelworker story culminating in the huge Russian Orthodox wedding set up the audience emotionally. The sudden cut to Vietnam destroys the innocence and accounts for the emotional impact that the film engendered. Redeker himself felt that *The Deer Hunter* might have become "the heaviest movie ever made," noting that within two years of its release, at least twenty-seven children had killed themselves playing Russian roulette after seeing it.[9]

By its very size and the sweep of events it portrayed, *The Deer Hunter* would have commanded attention. Perhaps impressed by the effort its filmmakers had put forth, perhaps equating excellent acting performances and camera work with meaningful insights, reviewers rushed to acclaim the movie. Jack Kroll, in *Newsweek,* called the film one "of great courage and overwhelming emotional power. A fiercely loving embrace of life in a death-ridden time." Arthur Knight opened his *Hollywood Reporter* review unequivocally:

"No point in beating around the bush. For me, *The Deer Hunter* is *the* great American film of 1978." He said he "can't imagine anything more timely, more important, more uncompromising than this Universal-EMI production." Although recognizing that the film would "probably estrange both conservatives and liberals," Joy Boyum in the *Wall Street Journal* concluded that *The Deer Hunter* "cannot be ignored. It is one of the boldest and most brilliant American films in recent years. It confronts and illuminates what at this time and in this place is surely our most pressing concern: our toleration of—no!—our attraction to violence."[10]

The Deer Hunter may have contained the power and substance to elicit such responses. But Cimino considered it "a very personal film," one that did not originate from "intellectual notions." Instead, he attributed the source of his inspiration to his military career in a Green Beret medical unit: "My characters are portraits of people whom I knew. During the years of controversy over the war, the people who fought the war, whose lives were immediately affected and damaged and changed by the war, they were disparaged and isolated by the press. But they were common people who had an uncommon amount of courage." In telling their story, Cimino claimed that the "specific details of the war are unimportant. Because this is not a film of the intellect, it's a film of the heart—I hope."[11]

In his efforts to fulfill this hope, Cimino used the Vietnam conflict as a setting in which to attempt an American "war and peace" epic. He first focused on people at home, living in the shadow of the war, responding to the call to arms. He then created an image of men caught up in the morass of the war. Finally, he integrated the war and the home front into a single statement of how Vietnam had changed America. Without question, in doing all this, Cimino created a powerful and impressive film. It also had little to do with the American experience in Vietnam.

Cimino made no claim that his film dealt with the Vietnam War, either the politics that caused it or the nature of the combat within it. He emphasized to one writer, "My film has nothing to do with whether the war should or should not have been." Nor did he have any concern over the historical truthfulness of his portrayal: "Look, the film is not realistic—it's surrealistic. Even the landscape is surreal. . . . And time is compressed. In trying to compress the experience of the war into a film, even as long as this one, I had to deal with it in a non-literal way. . . . I used events from '68 [My Lai] and '75 [the fall of Saigon] as reference points rather than as fact. But if you attack the film on its facts, then you're fighting a phantom, because literal accuracy was never intended." Cimino even denied that he had set the film in Vietnam: "It could be any war. The film is really about the nature of courage and friendship."[12]

Filmmakers have always used dramatic license and often hidden behind it to justify their factual inaccuracies. If Cimino was portraying a generic war such as Ingmar Bergman did in *Shame*, then his argument might have credibility. In the case of *The Deer Hunter*, however, audiences and critics did perceive that in addition to attempting a portrayal of blue-collar life and pastoral retreat, the film was making a comment not on war but on the Vietnam War. Consequently, to the extent that Cimino ignored the historical and factual aspects of the conflict to suit his dramatic purposes, his "reference points" lost their ability to guide thought and feelings.

It does not matter that Clairton exists only as an illusionary steel town created out of eight towns in four states. It may not matter that Cimino has placed a ten-thousand-foot snow-capped mountain in the heart of the Alleghenies. Audiences may not even become confused or bothered when they see that the sequence of events does not adhere to the history of the U.S. involvement in Vietnam. To some it may not matter, as it did to the Army, that the film shows the United States withdrawing from Vietnam in "a Dunkirk-type bug-out" that was "associated with the fall of the South VN government" even though the United States had completed its troop withdrawal two years before the fall of Saigon.[13]

Those who did know the history, however, would find it difficult to suspend their disbelief and be drawn into the desperate search Robert De Niro undertakes for Christopher Walken, knowing that no American soldiers returned to Vietnam in the last days of the Saigon regime. Far more important, Cimino misses the point when he says, "I don't dispute the accounts of My Lai 4, but I think that anyone who is a student of the war or anyone who was there, would agree that anything you could imagine happening probably happened." Atrocities do happen in war, and the Vietcong undoubtedly committed massacres of the type Cimino portrayed in *The Deer Hunter.* But My Lai became so crucial to the American perception of Vietnam because U.S. soldiers committed the atrocities.[14]

Ultimately, however, Cimino's film failed to capture the essence of the American tragedy in Vietnam not only because it distorted or ignored history, but also because its central metaphor, the recurring game of Russian roulette, portrayed a fiction. It had simply grown out of the minds of Quinn Redeker and Lou Garfinkle as a representation of risks to life man takes during combat. Despite his early antipathy to the image, Cimino had visualized it with great skill and cunning. Nevertheless, it had no connection to anything American fighting men experienced during the war.

Initially, audiences and reviewers accepted the authenticity of the game. According to one critic, it apparently "was played in Saigon and other parts of Southeast Asia as well. It was a parlor sport of some sort." Jack Kroll went to some length to connect the ordeal that Robert De Niro, Christopher Walken, and John Savage go through playing Russian roulette as prisoners of the Vietnamese with the final game, which De Niro plays with Walken in his "casino of death" in Saigon. He observed that "the image of the Americans holding a gun to their temples is a gut-wrenching symbol of a society committing moral suicide" and said that the episode in the POW compound "is the ritual of death that stands against the rituals of life with which Cimino has structured his film."[15]

In fact, no evidence exists that any POWs ever played any form of Russian roulette while in captivity. Nor did such a betting game exist in Vietnam. Does this matter? When Peter Arnett, a reporter who won a Pulitzer Prize in 1966 for his coverage of the Vietnam War, first saw *The Deer Hunter,* the Vietcong torture of the American prisoners of war and the Russian roulette "personally troubled" him. Nevertheless, he acknowledged that "the sheer power of the film's photographic imagery, particularly the agonizing torture scenes, stunned me into mute acceptance of the divine right of the Hollywood dream-machine operators to drench us in fictional nightmares if they wish."[16]

Very quickly, however, Arnett became disturbed that "audiences and critics seem to have found much more historical truth and significance than there really was in the saga of the three Pennsylvania steelworkers going off to war." He realized that people were not viewing the film simply "as the spectacularly fevered product of an ambitious film director well-schooled in the cinematic arts of bloodletting." Arnett concluded that although neither Cimino, nor anyone on his production staff had ever served in Vietnam, audiences were "interpreting his film as a deep historical truth."[17]

In reaction, he tried to set the record straight: "I have found that enthusiasts are genuinely surprised and hurt when I tell them that while Vietnam had all manners of violence, including self-immolating Buddhist monks, fire bombings, rape, deception and massacres like My Lai in its 20 years of war, there was not a single recorded case of Russian roulette, not in the voluminous files of the Associated Press anyway, nor in my experience either. The central metaphor of the movie is simply a bloody lie. *The Deer Hunter* is no more an historically valid comment on the American experience in Vietnam than was *The Godfather* an accurate history of the typical Italian immigrant family in the United States."[18]

As a literary device to convey an implied comparison, a metaphor acquires meaning through the skill of its creator. It can portray a lie or a fiction, but in the strict sense, it cannot be "a bloody lie." Definitions aside, a metaphor can retain its power to inform and move only as long as people trust the validity of the comparisons it tries to make. Once audiences begin to question the validity of *The Deer Hunter*'s central image of the Russian roulette as the metaphor for the horrors of war and the random risk of dying, they cannot readily accept the validity of the people in the film.

Yet, Cimino claimed that his only hope for the finished film was that audiences "really love" his characters, "nothing deeper than that. I want people to feel they would like to go on knowing these characters. I guess I want them to believe in the validity of these people." The extent to which audiences did empathize with them resulted in part from the quality of the actors' performances. But reaction to them also comes from the situations they have experienced during the movie. If these situations have little or no basis in fact, then it becomes more difficult for audiences to believe in the portrayals. And as critics of the film began to express themselves, the images it contained became subject of growing controversy.[19]

Responding to Cimino's defense of his creative rights to use whatever representations of war he chose, Arnett argued: "Even more preposterous than using Russian roulette as his metaphor is the morally irresponsible way that Cimino casually telescopes the 20 years of the Vietnam conflict into a convenient backdrop for his bizarre macho heroics. So is history laundered. Absent are the disillusion at home, the bitterness of those who served, the destruction of a country and any other factors that might lessen his epic theme."[20]

To the extent that Arnett's comments have validity, they helped highlight the ambiguities inherent in *The Deer Hunter*. More important, Arnett's experiences in Vietnam and his credibility as a journalist ensured that his critique of the film would not go unnoticed. Outside the Los Angeles Music Center the night of the Academy Award presentation, April 9, 1979, Vietnam Veterans Against the War and other groups picketed the film's interpretation of history. One placard proclaimed: "No Oscar for Racism—*The Deer Hunter*'s a bloody lie." A Vietnamese demonstrator told a reporter, "The movie depicts us as barbarians and savages. It endangers the understanding for Americans of our people." A member of the Hell No, We Won't Go Away Committee said, "The movie distorts history. It doesn't show American atrocities. It conveys the message that war is hell for American white boys but not for yellow Asian boys."[21]

Inside the auditorium, a sense of embarrassment appeared when the film received the Oscar for best picture of 1978. One journalist familiar with industry nuances observed, "Early on, we all thought the film was powerful but flawed. Now I think there have been a lot of second thoughts that emphasize the flaws. When the picture's name was read, it was as if you had proposed to a girl and were horrified she had accepted. I had the peculiar feeling that—if the ballots had gone out one week later—*The Deer Hunter* wouldn't have won."[22]

In response to several articles that attacked the film as a lie and bad history, Edward Kaufman, a professor of cinema at the University of Southern California, observed, "All artists lie. Artists have always manipulated history. "Richard III" is history falsified by Shakespeare in order to justify Queen Elizabeth's claim to the throne." Ned Tanen, president of Universal Pictures, the distributor of the film, also defended Cimino's use of Russian roulette as the central metaphor for the absurdity of war: "Of course, that specific incident didn't happen. It's a film, and films use metaphors. I'm proud of the movie. It makes me feel good that people will sit through something that isn't intended as pure entertainment. And I know Cimino didn't intend the movie to be racist. His thrust was to make a film about comradeship among the people who volunteer to fight our wars. The men in the film were not drafted. They were second-generation Americans from the coal mines of West Virginia, the steel mills of Ohio, whose heritage is to offer to fight."[23]

To be sure, Cimino may be conceded his focus on "the ordinary people of this country who journeyed from their homes to the heart of darkness and back." The questions he asked about this journey remain valid: "How do they survive that? If they're lucky enough to survive, how do they return home? And after they return home, how do they go on without committing suicide, having seen and been through what they've seen and been through? And how do they go on with some sense of hope, with their spirits intact? And still believe in something? How?" The American people have been trying to answer these questions since the end of the Vietnam War. Probably the only answer in the film, and perhaps the only valid antiwar statement in *The Deer Hunter,* came from a Green Beret who wandered into the wedding. In answer to the inquiry of what Vietnam was like, he finally said: "Fuck it! Fuck it!"[24]

The Army undoubtedly appreciated Cimino's reversing the roles in the My Lai massacre. If asked, it also would have probably expressed pleasure that the final version of the movie did not contain a scene in the screenplay that showed De Niro overpowering an officer at a debarkation point, taking his uniform and credentials, and stealing a plane ride back to Saigon. Though that scene would have supplied viewers with an explanation, albeit historically inaccurate, of how De Niro ended up back in Vietnam, the Army would not have wanted people to think anyone might manage to stow away aboard a military plane.

Regardless, the service could find no benefit in cooperating in any way on a script that contained the Green Beret's comment about the war or that had so many technical and historical errors. Perhaps aware of this, perhaps because the combat sequences formed such a small part of the story, Cimino did not approach the Pentagon for armed forces assistance for the scenes he shot in Thailand. However, the Army did receive an opportunity to comment on the script when the Ohio Film Bureau contacted the DoD Public Affairs Office asking for permission to use Air Force Reservists and their equipment for a scene Cimino was to shoot at the Youngstown, Ohio, airport.

Although the service found technical errors in the screenplay, it recommended that the DoD refuse assistance "based on the absence of any benefit to the Army in the script." Referring to the one combat scene, which called for a force of helicopters landing an American unit without explanation, the service considered it "rather unlikely that the VC could successfully ambush two successive US units in the same place. This makes the Army look pretty stupid. So does the napalming of the village right after the ambush." The Army recommended that "the producer employ a researcher who either knows or is willing to learn something about the VN war."[25]

Of course, if Redeker, Garfinkle, and Cimino had been making a factual film about the American experience in Vietnam, they could not have used the Russian roulette metaphor. To the original writers, however, it became the raison d'être of the story, the message that in war, chance dictates who will live and who will die. And EMI gave Cimino no choice about using the image. The device does provide a powerful dramatic impact, but by the time Cimino repeated the game, audiences either had become immune to the blood and shock or simply closed their eyes.

The director further muted its impact with his final portrayal of the game. In "The Man Who Came to Play," Merle conquers Keys psychologically. In the final scene, the former grunt forces Keys to play a round of two-weapon Russian roulette, with each man's gun containing five bullets, for supremacy and for $2 million: "Merle puts the gun to his head. Keys, crumbling, finally manages to get it cocked and up to his head. Merle PULLS THE TRIGGER. The gun 'CLICKS.' And the gallery 'OOHS.' Keys collapses, dropping the gun, unable to pull the trigger, face down on the table in blubbering terror."[26]

In contrast, in *The Deer Hunter*, Robert De Niro returns to Saigon in an attempt to rescue Christopher Walken, who, unlike Merle, has retreated from reality. When De Niro cannot reason with Walken, he joins his friend in a game of Russian roulette in one last desperate effort to bring him back to his senses. De Niro spins the cylinder, tells Walken, "I love you," and pulls the trigger on an empty chamber. Walken seemingly smiles in recognition, spins the cylinder, pulls the trigger, and blows a hole in his scalp. If De Niro, the central figure in every relationship in the film, had died and the screen had gone red, Cimino would have left the audience with a far more powerful image of life as nothing but a game of chance.

In fact, the director had two movies to wrap up, "The Man Who Came to Play" and his own story of three steelworkers who went off to war. So he must end the film not with death but with life, with Walken's friends sitting around a table singing "God Bless America." The screenplay does not provide motivation: "They all seem caught up in the intensity of the moment, but whether in joy, relief, or for some other reason, we cannot tell." Some viewers saw the restrained singing as confirming the friends's love of the country; others considered it as an ironic antiwar statement. If he could not decide the reason when he wrote the script, with hindsight, Cimino explained that the singing only demonstrated a sincere expression of faith in America, an ode to "what we once were and will be again." In truth, the film's climax becomes only one more ambiguity in a movie filled with distorted history, stereotyped characterizations, and conflicting images of the meaning of war and the American experience in Southeast Asia.[27]

Like *The Deer Hunter*, *Hair*, released in the spring of 1979, ends with a song following an odyssey in which friends search for a friend. A group of young people travel from New York to an Army base in Nevada to visit John Savage, whom they had befriended before he joined the service. When they cannot get into the base, Treat Williams impersonates a sergeant to gain entry, finds Savage, and changes places with him so that he can leave the base to say good-bye to his other friends. While he is gone, the unit receives its orders to enplane immediately for Vietnam, and Williams marches into the darkened bowels of the huge transport and to his death in a war in which he had refused to fight. At his grave, the friends sing a song, not of resignation but of hope: "Let the Sun Shine In." They sing not to mourn the past or their lost friend, not to support the nation, right or wrong, but with a throng of other young people who magically appear and surge to the fence of the White House, to sing of a better future, a future based on the knowledge of past failures.

Although the film recreated the antiwar atmosphere of the late 1960s, it proclaimed the joys of life rather than any overt antimilitary message. Those antimilitary images that *Hair* conveyed, it presented with gentleness and humor. Only the most sensitive military man could take offense at a group of gay officers sitting on a draft induction panel singing about the virtues of white boys versus those of black boys. Only the most conservative, thin-skinned public affairs officer could mind the comedic scene of a withered general trying to address a formation of soldiers about the joys of battle as music suddenly blares from a public-address system that a burst of rifle fire ultimately silences. In fact, the training sequence shows recruits being subjected only to the normal demands of their drill instructors, fairly and without the physical and verbal abuse that characterized *The Boys in Company C* or would characterize *Full Metal Jacket*.

Although Williams's switch of identities with Savage and the Army's failure to detect the change strain plausibility, the armed forces has had a long history of providing assistance to musicals and comedies, which by their very nature have presented the military unrealistically and even surrealistically. In refusing to even discuss cooperation, however, the Army and later the Air Force were clearly not responding to the inaccurate portrayal of their procedures or even to the script itself, but rather to the antiwar images and themes that the original stage version had generated.

Producer Lester Persky said he experienced "an enormous prejudice" against the project, which continued throughout the negotiations for assistance. He recalled: "The military had a hard on against 'Hair.' They hated everything it represented. And that even spilled over into the people who had the same attitude in the small towns. They didn't want to see the movie even though the critics said this isn't the same thing." In contrast, Persky thought he was "making a love statement about Vietnam, not a hate statement. The passions were cooling, but we wanted to remind people of the way it was and the way people could live today and in the future."[28]

Despite the absolute opposition from the Army, Persky felt he had to have military assistance to facilitate telling the story. Consequently, unlike the producers of other films about the Vietnam experience who accepted Pentagon refusals, he and his staff diligently pursued negotiations with the Pentagon. In writing to Don Baruch on April 15, 1977, associate producer Robert Greenhut briefly explained the status of the production and sent the pages of an early version of the script containing the portion that would require military assistance. He said that given the "scope of the physical requirements, it is hard for me to imagine how they could be accomplished successfully without army or air force cooperation."[29]

Without waiting for the completed script or a meeting with the filmmakers, the Army's Public Affairs Office responded on April 26: "DA declines to assist in subject production. No benefit to the Army is apparent in the script fragment attached and the Army is not presented realistically. Recommend that no assistance be rendered." The Army did not even suggest that the producer obtain a technical advisor to deal with the perceived problems, as it had for *The Deer Hunter*.[30]

In conveying the Army's decision to Greenhut, Don Baruch wrote on May 10, 1977, that the Pentagon "can appreciate the fact that 'Hair' was a reflection of a youthful segment of the time and considered by some of the public as a modern 'classic.'" Nevertheless, he explained that Army assistance could not be "justified" under DoD regulations. He suggested that the production could obtain necessary airplanes from civilian sources and find military equipment at some Hollywood studio. He also cited the regulation that allowed a film company to hire off-duty military personnel if their location shooting took place near an active military installation.[31]

To be sure, the script for *Hair* did not present the military "realistically." Film musicals, by their very nature, become surrealistic, if not pure fantasy, and *Hair* did intend to appeal to audiences through its music and innovative dancing. Nevertheless, the movie does make the same comment about the human condition that Michael Cimino sought to convey with far more pretentiousness in *The Deer Hunter*. Without drenching the audience in blood, pieces of brain, overly long scenes of weddings or deer hunts, and with no self-indulgent metaphors, *Hair* shows friends taking care of each other as friends do.

More effectively than *The Deer Hunter*, *Hair* thereby conveys the idea that in war, chance dictates who will live and who will die. To create this message, the filmmakers intended to juxtapose the musical, surrealistic, antiwar story of a group of hippies in New York City of the late 1960s with the grim realism of the Army boot camp training. To do this, Persky and his company felt they "really needed not just paper mache, but we needed tanks, we needed to have those facilities. And the only place we thought we could get them was the U.S. Army. We wanted to do it on a grand scale which was not available anywhere else." Consequently, they refused to take the service's rejection as a final answer.[32]

In mid-June, Greenhut met with Army officials to discuss the script, and during the summer, they sought and received stock footage of Army trainees going through an obstacle course. The company also made a research trip to Fort Bragg to ascertain what assistance it might actually need if it could change the Army's mind. In making his request for the visit, Greenhut wrote on August 11 that the company intended "to accommodate as much realism as is feasible with the military sequences, while still holding true to the classic music and story structure of 'Hair' and the conventions of musical theater." Assuming negotiations with the Army succeeded, the producer indicated he would like to choose a base on which to do the shooting and resolve the logistical problems. However, he acknowledged that "the practical aspects are perhaps much easier to resolve than the creative ones, but I am hopeful and certain that working together, they both will be resolved."[33]

In his letter to Greenhut on August 22, Baruch explained that the production company might not be able to secure use of the full complement of soldiers that it desired. However, Baruch said Greenhut could discuss "various possibilities of filming parade/ exercises and making arrangements for men to participate voluntarily on their own time" when he was at Fort Bragg. Nevertheless, after Greenhut sent in a revised script in the fall, the Army had an even shorter answer, on October 6, than the original turndown of April 26: "The Department of the Army declines to support the filmscript "Hair."[34]

The Army's failure to give any reasons for its decision and the brevity of its memo prompted Baruch to immediately request that he "be furnished background information/ explanation for your declination to support" the film. He noted that neither the producer nor the Public Affairs Officer were able to "interpret your statement." To clarify the response, Baruch asked: "Do you intend to convey that 1) the Army is unable to offer the assistance desired by the company, 2) considers the revision of the Army sequences, recommended by your office about June 15 in meeting with company representatives, still to be unsatisfactory, 3) regardlessly reestablish the overall turn-down expressed by our letter of May 10,, 1977." He reminded the Army that since it had discussed the changes with the company, the producer "naturally believed that he could anticipate consideration of his requirements for assistance, providing the revisions overcame the objections. Likewise your attention is invited to the fact that the greater part of the script does not deal with the military and also indicates that the film will be done in a more circumspect manner than the stage presentation."[35]

On October 11, 1977, the Army Public Affairs Office responded: "The attached memo of 6 Oct 77 remains valid." The office did add that the chief of public information had also advised Greenhut of this. In turn, Assistant Secretary of Defense for Public Affairs Thomas Ross recognized the potential for controversy because of the Army's refusal to even discuss cooperation, despite the company's efforts to satisfy the Army's objections to the script. Consequently, he requested an opinion on the script from Norm Hatch, chief of the Audio Visual Division of the DoD Public Affairs Office, and Donald Baruch's immediate superior.[36]

Responding on October 19, Hatch advised Ross that he found the screenplay "quite tame according to today's standards" in regard to four-letter words and sexual references and explained that the effect on audiences of the antiestablishment "put downs" would depend "a great deal on how well they are acted out." In any case, Hatch said the film's message "that comes through is love and peace and even in the ending, one man willing to give up his life for another exemplifies the best of religious doctrine." Although Hatch could understand the "Army's adamant refusal to assist" the production, he was "not sure it was the best position considering all the circumstances. The producers have made considerable changes improving the military part of the script in collaboration with the Army."[37]

At the same time, Hatch acknowledged that the Pentagon would receive "a certain negative public reaction" if it did provide assistance. As a result, he concluded that the Public Affairs Office would be "safe" in declining to cooperate on the grounds that current policies did require a film to provide some benefit to the Department of Defense to qualify for assistance. However, he suggested that as "an escape clause," the office could recommend that the Air National Guard provide several planes to the producer "for ground use only at normal rental fees. He can always pick up military personnel, in uniform, while on their own time."[38]

In fact, this option coincided with a suggestion that Greenhut put forth in a mailgram to Don Baruch on October 20. He acknowledged that the Army's refusal to provide assistance at Fort Benning had "terribly disappointed" the company. He said the disappointment became "even more significant since it comes after your complete cooperation and permission to go ahead with a survey in Georgia and North Carolina where much effort and hope was expended working details, and after Milos Forman revised our screenplay, motivated only by the Army's suggestion that the project might then become acceptable." Nevertheless, he asked it he could explore the possibility of utilizing some National Guard unit that would be willing to assist the film company, if the Pentagon would approve this type of cooperation. In closing, he repeated the company's belief that "*Hair* remains a classic American musical entertainment that we are trying to produce in the most noble manner. I wish the Army could respect this."[39]

The Army Public Affairs Office never did accept this view. However, recognizing the potential for controversy, Secretary of the Army Clifford Alexander agreed with Tom Ross that approving National Guard assistance would provide an acceptable compromise. Nevertheless, before the Defense Department could work out an agreement, both the Army and the Air Force repeated their objections to the project. On November 2, Hatch advised Ross: "Neither service sees any benefits to be gained by our participation even if the military portions of the script are rewritten to provide a more accurate portrayal of military activities. Though the military portion of the story is minor to the total script, it is the story of 'Hair' that so heavily influences this collective negative position." Given this stance, Hatch said that Ross would have to order the services to comply with the production demands, which he did not feel should be done "on this particular production."[40]

After further discussion, Army secretary Alexander sent a telegram to California governor Jerry Brown on December 7, advising him that the service "would find it appropriate if the California National Guard chose to cooperate with the filming of *Hair*." With the governor's approval, the Guard did provide three hundred men in full battle dress to participate in the filming during February 1978. The State National Guard commander, Maj. Gen. Frank Schober Jr., admitted he "was not too anxious to participate because the script is not exactly pro-military. But had we said no, it would have amounted to a form of censorship because we have helped other film companies in the past." He also expressed the opinion that cooperation would serve the best interest of the armed forces because the film might have been even more antimilitary if the Pentagon had not found a way to provide assistance.[41]

In the end, however, the help simply lent an air of authenticity to the training sequences and to Williams's foreboding march into the bowels of the huge transport. With or without the assistance, the antiwar message would have differed little. Milos Forman had wanted to turn the stage play into a movie from the first time he saw it at the very first off-Broadway public preview in 1967. He had talked with the producers at least once a year about the movie rights, and so, according to Forman, he had the benefit "of once a year reviewing how 'Hair' should be done." He had found that for him "it was as revealing as only one other musical, *West Side Story*."[42]

The screenwriter, Michael Weller, saw the play and so his script as about more than Vietnam: "I was just one of those people who just naturally thought that Vietnam was a mistake. The protest movement was not just an anti-war movement but it was a movement against institutions in general and against a certain repressive regimentation and that kind of thing. In that way, the Army and its involvement in Vietnam represented a whole aspect of experience about which the film was really making a statement." Although he acknowledged that the war created the framework for the film, he saw the basic training sequence more as making "a statement about repression" than as about Vietnam.[43]

In fact, he and Forman had included a sequence set in Vietnam showing Claude in combat and the atrocity of the war. However, they decided that "it was much more subtle and much more universal to show the basic training and then leave your imagination to work on these people disappearing into the airplane." Like Persky, Weller saw the importance of juxtaposing the surrealism of hippie life and the realism of actual military training. "He explained that the film "has been very liberating and very colorful and very exultant and then suddenly you are showing grim, regimented, gray and sort of horrible repressive behavior that's being imposed on Claude and then you move in on his face and you get a sense of what he is experiencing."[44]

As a result of Forman's long considerations on the nature of the play and Weller's views of the time and place in which it was set, *Hair* became much more than a recycled Broadway musical brought to the screen. It may have ceased to be a musical altogether. Writing for the *Chronicle Review*, Paula Cizmar concluded, "Rather, it is a filmic, surreal poem—each image linked, each stanza woven seamlessly into the whole to form one unified metaphor—a metaphor for America's passage into a less innocent age."[45]

To the extent that *Hair* does this, it stands independent of the Broadway play, becoming a film of the 1970s rather than a nostalgic look backward to the 1960s. Still, like *The Deer Hunter*, it asks questions about the people it portrays, who experienced the Vietnam War and survived it: Why did they become rebels? What did they learn about themselves? What will they do to make the future better than the past? As important as these questions remain, and whether or not the film provided answers, *Hair* helped make a comment about the war's impact on the United States. At the same time, however, audiences could respond to the movie as a musical, perhaps one of the very best Hollywood has ever made. Yet, despite critical acclaim and a positive, unambiguous message of love and peace, *Hair* did not become a box-office success.

Perhaps *The Deer Hunter,* in general release at the same time, satisfied people's needs for a comment about the Vietnam War. Perhaps, like the Army, people believed that *Hair* was simply the stage play transferred unchanged to the screen with the same 1960s anti-war statement. Perhaps people were not yet ready to confront the trauma of Vietnam, at least in the guise of a musical. Perhaps they were still waiting patiently for the arrival of Coppola's *Apocalypse Now.* In any case, however powerful its comment about the American experience in Vietnam, *Hair* failed to attract wide attention and quickly passed from view, leaving the way clear for the movie that most people expected would make a definitive cinematic statement about the war in Southeast Asia. Nevertheless, *Hair* captured the American experience in Vietnam, the pain and suffering the war created, and the hope for the future better than *The Deer Hunter* had done.

Whether or not *Apocalypse Now* would be able to accomplish the same thing, it may well have become the most widely awaited movie of all time when it finally arrived, first as "a work in progress" at the Cannes Film Festival in May 1979, and then in the United States in August. Delays had followed delays. Most reviewers seemed to approach the film by trying to answer the question whether the time and money spent had made the wait worth while. The *UCLA Daily Bruin* answered simply: "It was." *Time* required a few more words: "The answer, it turns out, is not nearly so mysterious as one might suppose. Coppola delayed the completion of his Viet Nam film for the simple reason that he could not bring off the grand work he so badly wanted to make. He tinkered right to the end—long after a lesser director would have cut his losses—but the movie remains a collection of footage. While much of the footage is breathtaking, *Apocalypse Now* is emotionally obtuse and intellectually empty. It is not so much an epic account of a grueling war as an incongruous, extravagant monument to artistic self-defeat."[46]

In truth, the film contains much beauty, many moments of great filmmaking, and maybe even some insights into the war itself. The air cavalry attack on a Vietnamese village will remain a battle scene against which to judge all others. The integration of music and sound and visual images on the screen approaches the level of artistry that Stanley Kubrick attained in *2001.* Many men who fought in Vietnam claimed that the film, and particularly that sequence, captured the surrealism that distinguished the war from all others. To the degree that it did these things, *Apocalypse Now* makes a comment on the American experience in Vietnam.

Others who fought in Southeast Asia, however, found that *Apocalypse Now* bore no resemblance to their experiences in Vietnam. One soldier's experiences in Vietnam might be entirely different from another soldier's experi-

Robert Duvall and Francis Ford Coppola during filming of *Apocalypse Now.*

ences thirty miles away or a day, a week, or a month sooner or later. Some would argue that this reality alone gave Vietnam its surrealistic quality. The war certainly had many realistic aspects that varied little from the jungle warfare of World War II. Nevertheless, as helicopters became the metaphor for the American experience in Vietnam, *surrealistic* remains the one word that best describes the war. But just as a director does not have to make a boring movie to make a statement about boredom, Coppola did not have to make a surrealistic movie to create the surrealism of the war. Moreover, to try to stuff all the disparate experiences, real and imagined, into one movie did not ensure that it would make the definitive statement about Vietnam.

As the *Time* review suggested, Coppola may have tried too hard to succeed. The length of time it finally took him to complete the movie may have created too many expectations for it to support. Most likely, Coppola failed to make a definitive statement about the Vietnam War because he did not understand war in general and the war he was trying to portray in particular. As a result, he could not come to terms with what he wanted to say, and without a thesis he had no way of locating his ending in the heart of darkness.

The most telling explanation of this failure did not come from the many interviews Coppola gave during the production and while promoting the film, or from the plethora of articles and reviews that appeared before and after the film finally appeared. Rather, it came from the writers of NBC's *Saturday Night Live*, which parodied the making of *Apocalypse Now* shortly after the film opened. Although playing for laughs, the sketch drew upon many of the accounts about the problems Coppola had had in making the movie: the star's heart attack, Marlon Brando's obesity, the director's continued rewriting of the script, his improvising on the set, and his propensity for spending huge sums of money to build sets and shoot vast amounts of film. In addition to containing much truth, the sketch acquired considerable credibility because Martin Sheen, the movie's star, hosted the program and played the featured character, a studio representative, sent to the Philippines to "pull the plug with extreme prejudice" on Coppola's production because he had gone "over budget."

Following very closely the structure of the movie itself, studio executives, rather than a CIA operative, brief Sheen on the situation with the production. They show him a tape of Coppola's rambling appearance on the 1979 Academy Award ceremony presentations, during which the director made a pitch for new technology. Sheen observes: "As I listened to his rambling incoherent speech, it all became clear, Coppola was quite completely insane." Sheen's journey to the Philippines to end the madness imitated his Captain Willard's cinematic journey of discovery up the river to find Kurtz/Brando in *Apocalypse Now*.

When he finally arrives, he discovers a Coppola look-alike, with all the director's mannerisms, trying to figure out a way to get a grossly overweight Brando out of his trailer and shoot his next scene. After Coppola concludes, "Well, wouldn't it be less trouble to shoot it every way and then to decide later?" Sheen steps in to advise the director: "I'm afraid you won't be doing any more shooting, Mr. Coppola. I represent United Artists and I am authorized to terminate your production immediately." Shocked, Coppola answers, "But it's not finished." When an aide says they have enough footage to put together several different versions of the movie, Coppola addresses the crux of the matter: "But I have no ending. I don't know what the film is yet. How am I supposed to conceptualize my ending when I don't know what the film is?" Sheen tells the director that he doesn't have any choice, that to prevent the company from incurring any more debts, he has ordered a B-52 strike on the set. An aide brightens: "Francis! That's not bad. We never thought of blowing up this set. We ought to get this on film." He agrees: "Yeah. A B-52 strike." He pauses, thinks, and then explodes with exhilaration: "That's it. That's it! My ending!!! One of my endings!!" Told the strike will take place in ten seconds, the director urges his crew to roll cameras, and as the bombs begin to fall, he yells, "Incoming! Incoming!" much like Slim Pickens as he rode his bomb downward in *Dr. Strangelove.* The sketch ends as did Kubrick's movie, with mass explosions from one of the two endings of *Apocalypse Now.*

Did it happen this way? Maybe not exactly. But the sketch comes close to explaining why Coppola took so long to complete his movie, why the final confrontation between Sheen and Brando contains the same contradictions the director expounded upon during the making of the film, and why *Apocalypse Now* had at least two endings. Coppola ended the 70mm version of *Apocalypse Now* by having the screen go to black, with no credits. He ended the 35mm version (used in the general release and on cable) with the credits rolling over explosions enveloping Brando's jungle fortress.

Did Coppola include the explosions in the latter version simply to make use of some very expensive footage? Were the explosions in some way connected to the film's last scene, in which Willard slowly sails away from the compound after hacking Brando to death? Or do the two endings stand as proof of Coppola's own continued indecision? However one explains the contradictions and ambiguities, it remains doubtful that *Apocalypse Now* or any other movie about Vietnam can help the American image, be "pro-human and therefore pro-American," as the director claimed during production.

No film about Vietnam can delineate events that occurred there in black and white terms of American good versus enemy evil as Hollywood could do in its films about earlier American wars. Vietnam remains a war that the United States lost, perhaps not on the battlefield, as military men have continued to assert, but certainly in the political arena. As films about Vietnam up to that time had shown, Hollywood would have a difficult time finding upbeat endings for a losing effort. Only John Wayne could end a movie about the war by walking off in triumph into the setting sun, albeit a sun setting in the wrong direction.

Coppola did make a film that contains magnificent scenes of the evils that man perpetrates on his fellow man during war. But in creating his images, the director essentially visualized all the worst incidents, real and imagined, that he associated with Vietnam rather than providing any significant insights into the total American experience in the war. Ultimately, the unrelenting violence and destruction that Captain Willard encounters during his jour-

Robert Duvall as Lieutenant Colonel Kilgore in *Apocalypse Now.*

ney to find Colonel Kurtz numbed the audience in much the same way that the images of the Russian roulette aftermath numbed the audience watching *The Deer Hunter.*

Coppola provided no balance to his portrayals. Colonel Kilgore's attack on a village in order to stage a surfing exhibition creates impact from its surrealism. Robert Duvall's character's love of the smell of napalm differs little from George Scott's Patton's love of war. The slaughter of innocent peasants aboard a sampan shocks because it creates a recognition of truth. Leaderless black G.I.s firing randomly into the night while the Vietcong blow up a bridge convey an Alice-in-Wonderland aura to the war. But if the United States had actually fought the war as Coppola depicts it, the Vietcong and the North Vietnamese would have won a military victory as well as the political one. Because his film contains only evil, Coppola fails to create any dramatic tensions in the ultimate confrontation between Willard and Kurtz. As a result, *Apocalypse Now* lacks a meaningful climax or the significant comment Coppola had hoped to make about the American experience in Vietnam.

In contrast, an otherwise rather forgettable 1977 disaster movie, *Cassandra Crossing,* did make at least a tentative observation about the impact of the war. Burt Lancaster, as an Army Colonel, has to destroy a plague-ridden train by routing it over a condemned bridge. Even after a doctor discovers that the disease has been contained, Lancaster proceeds with his mission because he must destroy not only the virus but the "very idea" that it existed. In response to the doctor's repulsion at his actions, he tells her, "I know you must see me as some sort of monster . . . I realize it is no longer fashionable to be a military man. But it's my job and I do it well."

Among its other legacies, as the nation entered a new decade, the Vietnam War made it necessary for the American armed services to justify their competence and ability to do their jobs, something people had previously taken for granted. The military establishment, of course, recognized the ability of motion pictures to portray the armed services for good or evil without its assistance. By the end of the 1970s, therefore, each of the services in its own way was seeking to reestablish good relations with Hollywood, although recognizing that the product of the relationship probably would on occasion contain some warts. The films that began to appear did help to rehabilitate the military image that Vietnam had so tarnished.

19 The Marines Search for a New Identity

WHATEVER ITS ULTIMATE FLAWS OR VIRTUES, *Apocalypse Now* had initiated Hollywood's interest in portraying the American experience in Vietnam. Along with *The Deer Hunter* and *Hair,* released earlier in 1979, Coppola's film legitimized the war in Southeast Asia as a cinematic subject. But no portrayal of the war could offer a happy ending with the United States attaining a victory over the North Vietnamese and Viet Cong. The evil foe of government propaganda had won the war, if not on the battle field, then in the political arena. By the end of the decade, Americans were beginning to see the North Vietnamese and the Vietcong as the good guys winning over an evil Goliath. Ultimately, the military itself would embrace this interpretation—by 1992 the Marine Corps Command and Staff College presented an explanation of the Vietnam War with which any antiwar activist would have agreed.[1]

Even after *Apocalypse Now,* however, Hollywood continued to question whether stories portraying Americans as villains would prove too painful to serve as entertainment. Consequently, although filmmakers regularly explored the impact of Vietnam on the United States in feature films and on television during the next twenty years, they showed more interest in using the armed services as subjects for peacetime dramas and comedies that ignored the war. Unlike the bitter, antimilitary portrayals of the American experience in Southeast Asia, even the combat movies that appeared after *Apocalypse Now* generally contained a more balanced, if less reverent treatment of the armed services.

In responding to requests for assistance on these films, the Pentagon recognized that Vietnam had forever changed the way Hollywood would treat the armed services. As a result, despite occasional reluctance to provide assistance, and despite continued trepidation, the Defense Department demonstrated a willingness to discuss all projects that came to the Public Affairs Office. The individual services accepted the reality that filmmakers would make their movies with or without assistance, and in either case, the stories were going to contain less flattering portrayals than in the movies made before Vietnam. At the same time, if the new generation of films with a military setting showed some warts and presented the armed services with more realism than the movies of the 1940s and 1950s, they also began the process of rehabilitating the image of the American fighting man.

Discussing the requests for assistance on these movies often proved easier than actually agreeing to cooperate. The individual services and the Defense Department recognized the need to avoid future controversies of the type that had surrounded Coppola's film. Nevertheless, ensuring that any films that received assistance would contain positive portrayals became an ongoing concern. However inaccurate the portrayals, viewers were likely to remember only Hollywood's Vietnam, whether Bruce Dern's long hair or Willard's mission to "terminate" Colonel Kurtz. In light of its experience with *Coming Home,* the Marine Corps Office of Information took the lead among the services in reevaluating its policies on dealing with the film industry.

For the Marine Corps, concerned with preserving its separate identity as a service, images of a few good men doing their required duties remained the primary goal when considering support for motion pictures. After their experiences with *Coming Home*, Lt. Col. Art Brill, head of the Information Branch, and Capt. Pat Coulter, the officer responsible for actually handling the requests for assistance in Marine Headquarters, realized that filmmakers could make their movies without assistance. Consequently, they had undertaken to convince their superiors that the service should negotiate with any filmmaker submitting a script and asking for help. Ironically, one of the first projects to test the new approach turned out to be an instant replay of *Coming Home*, the film that had prompted the rethinking of the Marines' policies. Along with *The Great Santini*, then undergoing preliminary consideration, and *Rumor of War*, *Born on the Fourth of July* initiated an internal debate on Marine Corps policies governing cooperation with filmmakers.[2]

Based on Ron Kovic's 1976 autobiography *Born on the Fourth of July*, the screenplay, written by a still unknown Vietnam veteran, Oliver Stone, arrived in Don Baruch's office on March 3, 1978. During the next four months, the in-house discussions over whether to support the project provided a forum for competing philosophies on how the service should respond to Hollywood in the foreseeable future. On one hand, some Marines argued that the Corps should provide help only to movies that in some way benefited its mission. Others maintained that by agreeing to cooperate, the service would obtain leverage to secure a more accurate portrayal of its procedures and activities. In the process of reconciling the different opinions, the Marines created a new policy toward the film industry, one that served it well in the coming years.

The screenplay itself followed Kovic's account of how he grew up wanting to be a Marine, how he fought and suffered a paralyzing wound in Vietnam, how the horrors he experienced in the VA hospitals after his return affected him, and how he set about to tell the world his story. Capt. Art Webber Jr., the Marine officer who reviewed *Born on the Fourth of July* for *Marine Gazette*, described the work as "a hard hitting book that does not exactly extol the virtues of the Marine Corps in Vietnam but is painfully honest."[3]

Webber, a childhood friend of Kovic, said the book "could be the mirror image of many of us that served in Vietnam, that were products of the 1950s and 1960s. Many Vietnam Veterans, that try to figure out why they served in Vietnam will find some answers in Ron's work. . . . I can personally attest to his agony, pain, and disillusionment." Webber acknowledged that many of Kovic's actions, which the experiences he had in VA hospitals motivated him to undertake, would not find support among his fellow Marines. Nevertheless, the reviewer argued that the "ultimate tragedy about Ron Kovic that underlies his writing is that he was guided and influenced by all the 'Right Things' while growing up that pointed the way for him to enter the Marine Corps and fight in Vietnam. He had more or less made a compact with a World of illusion, a World many of us saw the same way."[4]

In Kovic's case, however, Webber noted, he "quickly discovered the illusions as mists of fantasy that faded into the harsh reality of war with its innate destructiveness of friends and innocents. His painful transition through these make believe and real Worlds has forged a strong, warm and compassionate human being." According to the reviewer, as Kovic's new self emerged, he felt "particularly betrayed by the inhuman treatment he received from the VA and that they had not kept their end of the bargain to take care of him after he fought for his country." When Kovic visited Webber, he expressed continuing bitterness at the war, the government, and the VA hospitals. But he stressed that he held no bitterness toward the Marines, whom he still considered his friends.[5]

Nonetheless, any script based on Kovic's experiences and conveying his views on the war and his treatment would pose real problems for the Marine Corps, however truthful his account. In fact, the more truthful the script, the more difficulty the service would have in agreeing to assist on its production. Unlike *Coming Home,* Kovic's story had balance. He loved the Marines and had done his job in a satisfactory manner while serving two tours in Vietnam. No one could justify the subsequent medical treatment he received under any circumstances, and his political protests remained explicable and perhaps even necessary. Nevertheless, any portrayal of his life was bound to make antiwar, antigovernment statements with which the Marines would have a very difficult time associating. As Webber's observations made clear, however, Kovic remained a Marine in the best sense of the word, which would explain why many Marines would see no reason for the Corps to object to the script.

In submitting the screenplay to the Pentagon, Burtt Harris, the associate producer of the project for Artists Entertainment Complex, and himself a former Marine, described Kovic as "a very dedicated Marine." Harris explained that he felt it necessary to actually shoot the training sequences at Parris Island because "its reality and authenticity are requisite in truly depicting the energies necessary to the molding of the Marines of Ron's experiences." Harris expressed no concern that the Marines would have a problem with the story, commenting, "As a former Marine, I personally regard the script's Parris Island sequence with a strong, realistic pride. Nothing about combat training was ever easy, but the results certainly support the methods."[6]

After critiquing the script, Lt. Penny Williamson advised Col. Margaret Brewer, then deputy director of the Marines' Public Affairs Office, that although she found it "very moving," she did not think the service would benefit from supporting the movie: "Its treatment of the USMC is not overtly negative, however, it does make a strong statement against the U.S.—and consequently the military's—participation in the Vietnam war." She described the theme as showing that Kovic "was used through his patriotism and duped into giving two thirds of his body (he was paralyzed from the breast down) for an immoral war. And that those who stayed behind were the smart ones who got rich off the war, but resented Ron because he reminded them of the war's immorality." Nevertheless, Williamson acknowledged that Kovic's Marine training provided him with the strength to survive his severe handicap.[7]

Focusing on particular problems with the script, she wrote, "The scenes of Marine Corps recruit training are unacceptable as written—verbal and physical abuse and hazing are represented as part of normal training." She cited a scene set in Vietnam that suggested that Marine officers "frequently" covered up incidents of accidental shootings of fellow Marines. In regard to the manner in which the script handled Kovic's life in a VA hospital, Williamson described the scenes as "very negative—presenting the hospitals as filthy and the staff as incompetent and generally abusive." Finally, she thought many people "would find the language throughout the screenplay and several of those scenes with sexual overtones to be offensive." Consequently, she recommended that the Marines "do *not* support" the script.[8]

Incorporating this view into a formal response to the producer's request for assistance on the production, Williamson stated in her initial draft that the best interests of the Marines precluded support to a film "based on the present screenplay." However, Gen. V.T. Blaz, the Marine Corps director of information, advised the lieutenant that he "would appreciate something stronger or more definitive. Present memo implies that revisions might make screenplay acceptable." If the Marines did not in fact have any interest in cooperating on the film, he asked that the revised memo provide a reason, "i.e., not in the best interest—counter-productive for recruiting—negative actions overshadow any positive."[9]

As a result, in turning down the script, the Marines advised Don Baruch that they did not want to become involved with the production, explaining that the script was "found not to be accurately representative of the Marine Corps; in particular, that portion of the script about the Marines undergoing recruit training is disturbing. In addition, the overall tenor of the script is negative and would tend to be counterproductive to the recruiting effort in the all volunteer environment. Consequently, we feel it would not be in the best interests of the Marine Corps to support the production of this motion picture."[10]

Unlike the producers of *Go Tell the Spartans* and Francis Coppola, whose projects the Pentagon rejected, Artists Entertainment wanted military assistance badly enough to enter into negotiations with the Marines. To this end, the company's lobbyist, Charles Russhon, met with General Blaz, Colonel Brewer, and other staff members on March 22, 1978. Russhon indicated that the company was willing to review the script "with a view toward allaying" the Marines' concerns. However, in advising Don Baruch of the meeting, Colonel Brewer said that the Marines still "cannot support this motion picture at this time because of two overriding reasons: the portrayal of Marine Corps recruit training and the general anti-military tenor of the script." She explained that the service "takes pride in the toughness and discipline of its recruit training, but that firmness is temporized with fairness and dignity." She argued, "The verbal and physical abuse and hazing depicted in the script are not consistent with Marine Corps policy relative to recruit training."[11]

Colonel Brewer noted that whenever the Marine Corps had discovered such abuse, it had taken immediate action to correct the situation: "There is a continuing effort to closely supervise and improve recruit training and any occurrence such as the one where Ron Kovic is punched by four drill instructors would never be tolerated." Brewer did not deny Kovic's account of what had happened to him during his training. Instead, she wrote: "To support the filming of such a scene would give an erroneous impression of Marine Corps recruit training in 1978."[12]

Having indicated that the service could not support the movie because of the training sequence, Brewer did recommend that the filmmakers change it "to reflect the above considerations." Although acknowledging that the scenes "could be rewritten into acceptable form," she did not address the reality that revising the script would make the scene historically inaccurate if the drill instructors had punched Kovic as he described. In any case, without the leverage of offering assistance, the Marines had no way to ensure that the change would be made.

In regard to the screenplay's "pervasive anti-military tenor," Brewer tied the problem to the new environment of the U.S. military's all-volunteer force and the effect the story would have on recruitment. She explained that the motivation for young men's willingness to enlist "must derive from an innate patriotism, a faith in the basic values of this country and a belief in the military service as an honorable profession."[13]

Putting aside the issue of American involvement in Vietnam or Kovic's injury, Brewer observed that he "came to reject the beliefs that led him to join the Marine Corps in the first place. Yet these same values and beliefs, that continue to motivate young men and women to join the Marine Corps today—are, in fact, interwoven into the traditions of the Corps." Consequently, Brewer argued that providing assistance to *Born on the Fourth of July*, with its antimilitary tenor, "would alienate today's men and women who still believe in the honor of the military service. It would also alienate the disabled veterans and their families and the families of Marines who died in combat who still believe their service honorable, their sacrifices worth the price."[14]

Having voiced the concerns of the Public Information Office and the Corps's opposition to cooperation with the production, Brewer hedged on the turndown. She acknowledged that the script suggested that Kovic's "physical strength and moral courage to come to terms with his severe handicap are due in part to his training as a U.S. Marine. The impression is also given that Kovic's disillusionment after his injury did not lie with the Corps but with the country's attitude toward the U.S. involvement in the Vietnam War." She suggested that the filmmakers could strengthen these positive elements by having Ron "overtly state that he is proud to be a Marine and that he still believes in the ideas of the Corps." Nevertheless, she stated that the Marines did not believe the Pentagon should support the film "as written."[15]

Responding to Don Baruch's letter of April 6, informing Artists Entertainment Complex of the Marine position, Burtt Harris sent the Audio Visual Branch a new script on April 14, with revised training sequences, and explained that he had made arrangements through the Georgia Film Office to film the training scenes at Fort Stewart, an Army base in Georgia. Since Harris had assured the public information officer there that he would coordinate arrangements with the Pentagon, he expressed the hope that the military would approve the filming.[16]

Baruch forwarded the revised script to the Marines on April 20 and then on May 8 sent a second revision, which contained an additional change that Hatch and Baruch had requested. In his cover letter accompanying the second script, Baruch asked if the Marines would approve authorization for filming at Fort Stewart and indicated that the company would probably hire Marines as extras for the basic training sequence. He also noted that the company had made no request for assistance in filming the combat sequences and advised the service that despite the portrayal of the manner in which the VA had treated Kovic, it was allowing the filmmakers to shoot at one of its hospitals.[17]

The Marines required three weeks to formulate a response to Baruch's memo. Finally, on June 2, Brewer, the new director of information and now a general, sent to the chief of staff of the Marine Corps a detailed memo about *Born on the Fourth of July*. In an informal accompanying note, Brewer explained that the memo went into considerable detail because "either support or non-support of the film would undoubtedly be somewhat controversial. In addition, our recommendation that the Marine Corps interpose no objection to filming the recruit training scenes at Parris Island while simultaneously declining to 'support' the film per se is a deviation from long-standing policy which essentially has been 'full support' or 'no support.'" Brewer anticipated that both the Defense Department's Public Affairs Office and the film producer would accept the recommendation. She also advised the chief of staff that the Public Affairs Office had given some consideration to the "feasibility/desirability of changing the current guidelines for film support in such a way that would essentially eliminate the script review process."[18]

In the formal memo, General Brewer first provided a brief synopsis of the script and explained why the Marines had found the original version unacceptable. In addition to the concerns about the training scenes and the antimilitary, anti-Vietnam tenor, she pointed out that the Public Affairs Office did not know what rating the film would receive from the Motion Picture Association. Turning to the crux of the matter, Brewer said that her office had spent the past several weeks negotiating with the producers on their request to film the training sequences at Parris Island. Neither the informal nor the formal memos state why the Corps had begun talking with the company after its turndown of the script in early April. However, since the talks began shortly after the filmmakers made arrangements to shoot on an Army base, that decision may well have convinced the Marines that their best interest required them to portray themselves on their own facilities. In any case, the negotiations produced "substantial changes in the script in return for permission to film at Parris Island." According to Brewer, the scenes of recruit training "have been drastically rewritten to reflect more accurately the philosophy of recruit training as it is in 1978 although the recruit training scenes are set in the 1960s."[19]

The changes included the removal of the use of profanity by the drill instructors, the elimination of instances of "extreme hazing," and the toning down of scenes of excessive physical-fitness drills. Most important, Brewer said that the climactic scene at Parris Island in which several D.I.s punch Kovic in the stomach to test his mettle "has been toned down to such an extent that the punches have been removed, although the sense that Kovic has become 'a man' by becoming a Marine not only remains, but is strengthened." Nowhere in the memo does Brewer acknowledge that the changes render the script inaccurate historically since it no longer describes the actual experiences Kovic went through in basic training.[20]

In the Marine Corps of 1978, D.I.s may have had instructions to avoid profanity and the Public Affairs Office may have liked to believe they followed orders. In practice, however, a presumption exists that an occasional four-letter word may well have crossed the lips of a renegade D.I. Furthermore, in the Marine Corps of the mid-1960s, D.I.s preparing recruits for Vietnam used such language as an integral part of their normal training routine. Cinematically, in *Sands of Iwo Jima,* John Wayne did not use four-letter words. Nor did James Whitmore in *Battle Cry* or Jack Webb in *The D.I.* But in the 1940s and 1950s, when these film appeared, the Motion Picture Production Code forbade any profanity or risque language, including such words as *virgin* and *seduce.* In the changed film industry of the 1970s, four-letter words and worse had become routine, and to have portrayed a Marine D.I. eschewing *fuck* and *shit* would have made the movie unbelievable for most viewers, particularly those who had read the book, gone through basic training, or ever listened to conversations of young males.

The elimination of the punching scene raised similar questions of tampering with reality. Marine regulations have always stipulated that no D.I. ever touch a recruit and that any deviations from these instructions required swift punishment. Over the years, however, newspapers and magazines have detailed the failure of the Corps to eliminate physical abuse from recruit training. More to the point, the Marines never denied that D.I.s punched Kovic as he had described in his book and as the original script chronicled. Nor did the incident probably stand as an aberration as the Corps would maintain it to be, even if they were to concede it had happened, particularly during the 1960s, when Kovic went through basic training at Parris Island.

Beyond that, the Marines themselves had created precedent that would have allowed for the portrayal of the sequence. After the matter had gone all the way up the chain of command to the commandant in 1949 during actual filming at Camp Pendleton, the Marines had allowed John Wayne to hit one of his men with a rifle butt, given the context of the action, and *Sands of Iwo Jima* had still become the paradigm Marine movie. In the peacetime Corps of the 1970s, the situation vis-à-vis physical and verbal abuse had changed, but undoubtedly some physical contact still occurred, and a D.I. might let slip an occasional four-letter word. Whether the Marines liked it or not, truth be told, such aberrations may never have disappeared from the Corps. In any case, *Born on the Fourth of July* was portraying events of an earlier period, and to eliminate the sequence would have put the Marines in the position of trying to rewrite history.

Not only did this render the movie unrealistic, but also, paradoxically, it should have disqualified the movie from receiving assistance. DoD regulations have always required that scripts must be historically and factually accurate, as the Army had explained in refusing to consider assistance for *Go Tell the Spartans* and *The Deer Hunter*. The filmmakers' willingness to go along with the requested changes because of their desire to film at Parris Island rendered such stipulation moot. Nevertheless, the compromise still failed to win official cooperation.

In her memo to the Marine Corps chief of staff, General Brewer indicated that the Public Affairs Office still considered "it undesirable for the Marine Corps to 'support' a film which is basically anti-military in nature" and repeated her concern that the film "could alienate today's men and women who still believe in the honor of military service. It could also alienate disabled veterans and their families, and the families of Marines who died in combat who still believe their service honorable and their sacrifices worth the price."[21]

Brewer then voiced the conundrum the Marines faced and which Pat Coulter and Art Brill had been addressing for several months: "Past policy regarding the rendering of assistance to motion picture productions has been that no assistance is given unless the film presents the Marine Corps and the military in a very positive light. However, this policy in the past has meant that the Marine Corps is unable to influence the script and portrayal of Marines in those movies deemed inappropriate for assistance. Yet, with or without our assistance, these films are made, often with negative effects on our public image."[22]

Brewer then suggested that movies like *Coming Home* and *The Boys in Company C* had the potential "for as much an adverse affect on recruiting as the *Sands of Iwo Jima* boosted recruiting during the early 1960s." How to solve the dilemma? Brewer recommended that the Marines "decline to 'support' the film per se; however, in an effort to help ensure a more positive depiction of recruit training as reflected in the revised script, it is recommended that the Marine Corps grant permission for the revised recruit training scenes to be filmed on location at MCRD, Parris Island on a noninterference basis with operational and training requirements."[23]

At the same time, she said the producers should understand that such assistance "not be construed as Marine Corps' 'endorsement' or 'approval' of the film as a whole or the tenor of the film." Moreover, the Marines should receive no credit on the film. Noting that the producers had liked the original script's portrayal of the training sequences, she warned that if the chief of staff and the commandant did not approve the recommendation, "it is reasonable for us to assume that they will use the original script if they do not film at Parris Island."[24]

After reading the memo, the chief of staff bucked the matter directly to the commandant on June 5, with a request for "concurrence or other guidance" to his recommendation that the company be allowed to film at Parris Island. In preparing for the meeting the commandant requested, General Brewer compiled a list of things to emphasize, starting with the fact that the Marines were not supporting the production, only allowing the filming to take place at Parris Island. She would acknowledge that the recruit training scenes would "reflect 1978, where Marines are treated with fairness and dignity. No punches. No profanity. No hazing. *But* if we disapprove the old scenes could conceivably be put back in." Although the Marines would receive no credit, she was going to advise the producers to give the Corps a disclaimer at the end. And she was going to stress that if the film was made using the old script, it would "have a *negative* affect on our image."[25]

After the meeting, at which the commandant agreed to the recommendation that the Marines allow filming at Parris Island, General Brewer sent a copy of the script to the deputy chief of staff for operations and training on June 9, with a request that he inform her office if he had any additional areas of concern to discuss with the producers. On June 20 she sent the chief of staff a draft of the answer to Don Baruch's memo of May 8, which the Marine Public Affairs Office had prepared containing the recommendation that filming be allowed. He approved it the next day with only minor revisions.[26]

On June 28, however, the deputy for operations and training advised General Brewer that he believed the Marines should not support *Born on the Fourth of July*. He wondered "how permission can be granted for the recruit training scenes to be filmed at MCRDep, Parris Island without implying Marine Corps endorsement of the finished film." Despite the changes in the script that resulted in a less damaging portrayal, he said this "does not alter the fact that viewers of the film are likely to interpret that the training KOVIC received in the Corps was/is at least partially responsible for his later actions."[27]

Addressing the problem of using 1970s procedures to represent Kovic's personal experience, the deputy suggested, "It would be more appropriate to keep the film historical and autobiographical in perspective, reflecting KOVIC's life of the 1960's, rather than a mix of before and after scenes/incidents." Given the "anti-society" tone of film, the deputy for operations and training concluded that this would "draw the Marine Corps into its poor light." As a result, his department "objects to the use of MCRDep, Parris Island as a location for this photography. In my judgment, other than to meet the requirements of public law, participation in the film is not in the best interest of the Marine Corps or the Department of Defense."[28]

Despite this objection, General Brewer sent the approved memo to Don Baruch on June 30, 1978. Reaffirming her memo of March 31, 1978, she stated that "it does not appear to be in the best interests of the Marine Corps or DoD to support this motion picture." Nevertheless, although the Marines did not "approve, endorse, or support" the movie, they were willing to allow filming at Parris Island because the producers had revised the training sequences. The conditions she included reflected prior internal agreement within the Corps that the approved script be used, that filming be at no cost to the government, that assistance be provided on a noninterference basis, that actors "adhere to Marine Corps grooming standards," that a technical advisor supervise all scenes involving Marines, and that no credit for Marine assistance be given or acknowledged.[29]

After phoning the film company with news of the Marines' agreement to allow filming at Parris Island, Don Baruch confirmed the information in a letter on July 11, 1978. However, the news came too late to save the production. On July 26, the *New York Post* reported that Al Pacino, who had been scheduled to play Ron Kovic, had withdrawn from the film because of the delays beginning shooting and his commitment to begin work on *And Justice for All*. Without a bankable star and with questions still remaining within the film industry over the viability of Vietnam as a box-office attraction, the project went into limbo for ten years. Then, having established his reputation as a director, Oliver Stone would be able to resurrect his script and go into production. Not having gone to the Pentagon for assistance, Stone could return to the original, unsanitized version of the screenplay, and with Tom Cruise now portraying Kovic, the director had the opportunity to repeat the box-office success of his Oscar-winning *Platoon*.[30]

The Marine Corps probably had its best interest served when *Born on the Fourth of July* did not go into production. The completed film might have shown the abilities, leadership, and courage of a Marine. However, even with the revisions the Public Affairs Office had obtained from the producers, Ron Kovic's life offered little benefit to the service in terms of recruitment or the conveying of any positive image. Moreover, the deletion of the four-letter words and the rewriting of history would likely have brought claims of censorship against the service and new questions about cooperation between Hollywood and the Pentagon. At the same time, the Marines had not wasted their effort seeking an appropriate response to the request for assistance on *Born on the Fourth of July*. Out of the debate came a new policy to deal with screenplays containing less than favorable portrayals of Marines in war and peace, a policy that better reflected the realities of the nation's perception of the armed services in the post-Vietnam period.

With its new philosophy in place, the Marine Corps began to seek out filmmakers undertaking any project in which its men appeared, on the theory that the final product would become better as a result of the support. In developing their new approach on cooperation, the Marine Corps retained as its primary goal the portrayal of "a few good men" doing their required duties. To the extent that they succeeded in their objective, the revitalized images helped the Corps in the effort to preserve its identity as an autonomous military service.

Having helped to develop the new policy toward cooperation during his tour of duty at Marine Headquarters, Pat Coulter immediately set out to implement the new approach when he took charge of the Los Angeles Public Affairs Office in September 1978. Coulter later explained that he considered it his job "to keep an ear to the industry. We read all the trades. We knew all the productions that were in the works. We sought out opportunities. I had enough contacts out in the infra-structure that I even heard if any Marine uniforms were being checked out of Western Costume. I would then start checking and find out the production and go to offer assistance."[31]

Coulter made it clear that he did not expect a producer to make major changes after a film was shot: "All we ask is that we be allowed to say we want a credit at the end or we don't want a credit at the end. The producer can just as easily say, 'The movie is shot. The hell with you guys.'" According to Coulter, how well the process worked depended on the relationship between the technical advisor and the production company: "Therein lies the key. I found that when you go out with the production company and you become so integral with their staff and so close to the producer and the director, everybody else is aside. The way I see the chain of command is the executive producer, the producer, director, and then all the other branch heads down there. And, a dotted line out to the side, technical advisor."[32]

Coulter was to need all his expertise as a negotiator and technical advisor while working on the 1980 CBS television miniseries *Rumor of War*, based on Philip Caputo's memoir of his experiences in Vietnam as a young second lieutenant. When compared to the story the filmmakers proposed to tell in the script they sent to Don Baruch on April 30, 1979, the Marines might well look back on the negotiations for *Born on the Fourth of July* with fond memories. Yet, Coulter's willingness to discuss the project with Charles Fries demonstrated how well the new regulations were working.[33]

If Caputo's book described the Marines' My Lai, albeit on a far smaller scale than the Army's much-publicized atrocity, the filmmakers gave no indication that they thought the story might cause the Corps any problems. They simply asked for assistance in the form of "equipment, helicopters, and weapons, personnel to operate, and a U.S. Marine training base, perhaps Camp Le June. Also, we would require a technical advisor." They did offer to reimburse any costs, "subject to review." In turn, Baruch advised the Marine Public Affairs Office that in his opinion, "the producer will not be receptive to make all the changes, we believe, you will desire. Nevertheless, the attempt should be made and the final outcome evaluated."[34]

In her analysis of the script, Lt. Penny Williamson summarized how Caputo's experiences during his tour "take their toll" on him and how the death of his best friend puts him "over the edge." In an effort to find "a real enemy—one that he can make pay, not only for the death of his friend, but for his own disillusionment" with the war, Caputo convinces himself that there are Vietcong in a village. As a result, he and two of his men attack the village, killing two civilians, whose innocence "remains questionable." Although the Marines court-martial Caputo and his men, the service drops the charges for lack of evidence. Williamson observed that in writing the book, Caputo was attempting to acquit himself of the charges.[35]

Overall, Williamson described the script as "heavy, with lots of symbolism. Caputo is a typical modern anti-hero—not a sterling character, but human and sympathetic. The movie is not anti–Marine Corps or even anti-establishment, but it is definitely anti-war. The villain is the war and the audience is asked to rage with Caputo at the waste and hopelessness of it all." She then pinpointed some areas that would cause the Marines particular problems. In a scene shortly after Caputo arrives in Vietnam, he sees Marines coming in from a patrol with Vietcong ears on a radio antenna and is shocked by his first exposure to the bestiality of war. Given the scene's importance to the story, Williamson concluded, "It may be difficult to get it out for this reason—it has dramatic impact." Commenting on a scene in which an officer tells Caputo: "If he's dead and Vietnamese, he's VC," Williamson concluded, "This is a minor line that is not good, but we can live with it."[36]

Noting that Don Baruch did not like a captain telling Caputo's unit to "bring back a body count," Williamson admitted that "it is pretty common knowledge that American troops were frequently told to 'bring back a body count' before they went on patrol. We might have difficulty justifying a request that the producers take it out—'body count' was a part of Viet Nam." In regard to a scene in which Americans accidentally shell South Vietnamese troops and then try to cover it up, she observed that the "accidental shelling is acceptable, as those things do happen, the cover-up is not. Not essential to the storyline, so this could come out." She also thought that the script needed some balance in the portrayal of officers, especially in the higher ranks, where it now had only unfavorable portrayals above the rank of lieutenant.[37]

Williamson also described a "black humor scene" in which three Vietcong bodies are unburied, buried, and then unburied: "This scene is very satirical, but might be offensive to some. It is one of the strongest scenes leading up to Caputo's breakdown; so it could be difficult to have taken out, if we decided to do so." Other problems included a corporal helping Caputo draft a false medal for a general; a chaplain telling him, "I hope none of these boys are getting killed because some officer wants a promotion"; and a captain offering extra beer to any Marine who gets a confirmed kill. Regarding this scene, Williamson noted, "Not good, but according to my informal survey of those who were there, it did happen. Not absolutely essential to the story line."[38]

Throughout the discussions, however, the most serious problem to the Marines remained the "scene that is also most important to the script." Williamson explained, "Caputo loses touch with reality and without authorization attacks a Vietnamese village and brutally questions a Vietnamese woman. He comes close to killing her." At the same time, his men kill two Vietnamese civilians as they try to escape. Despite the negative portrayal, Williamson made it clear that the Marines could do little about the scene even if they decided to support the film: "This scene is the crux of the story and the climax of the movie—it is the source of Caputo's guilt and the reason why the book as a catharsis was written. Therefore it cannot be eliminated." She pointed out, however, that the script did show how the Corps quickly investigated the incident and brought charges against Caputo. In addition to making it clear that the Marines would not tolerate such actions, the script also included a scene in which one of Caputo's men tells him that he did what he did because he could not 'cut it' as a Marine lieutenant."[39]

Although such comments did mitigate some of Caputo's actions, Williamson concluded that the Marines "would be better off if this movie was never made. I don't see how in this day and age we could ever win in a movie about the Vietnam War. It's a fact of life that the taint and smell of that war rubbed off on the men who fought it, regardless of the service." But since CBS was undoubtedly going to produce the miniseries, Williamson concluded that by assisting, the Marines "might be able to mitigate some of the worse parts; but I doubt we could turn it around as positively as we did Santini."[40]

In forwarding her comments to the Marine Corps director of information, Art Brill concurred with Williamson's conclusions: "It's the same old story . . . the movie will be made and we have more to gain by assisting than not. The anticipated huge TV audience won't know if we cooperated or not." Since he believed the filmmakers would use the original script if the Marines refused to cooperate, Brill concluded that the Corps's image would "be hurt more than if we compromised." Consequently, he recommended meeting with the producer: "This is not a Santini type script but it will have a definite effect on the image. Anything we can do to insure the Marine Corps is portrayed as it really was vice Caputo's warped image will be beneficial in my view."[41]

Ultimately, after considerable negotiations, the Marines did reach an accommodation on the script with Charles Fries and agreed to support the production. As with *Born on the Fourth of July* and *The Great Santini*, the Corps accepted that it could only exercise some control on how the filmmakers portrayed its men and actions if it involved itself in the production. Lt. Williamson reminded Art Brill of that on December 14, 1979, when she reported that the producers were considering hiring Sterling Hayden to play the incompetent general. She advised that he had a mustache and goatee, which he refused to shave off. Moreover, she added, "He's pretty old, too." She left unsaid the possible concern that Hayden might reprise his General Ripper role from *Dr. Strangelove* if left to his own devices.[42]

In advising Don Baruch of the Marines' decision to support *Rumor of War*, General Brewer acknowledged that although the screenplay's final version "cannot be considered totally balanced toward the military, we do believe that it deals more fairly with Marines and the Vietnam veteran in general." Consequently, she felt it was in the best interests of the Marines and the Pentagon "to provide limited assistance" to the production. However, to avoid the possible conclusion that such support conveyed endorsement of the portrayal, Brewer told Baruch the Corps was acting with the understanding that it would receive no credit or acknowledgment in the titles. She also said the company must agree to accept a technical advisor.[43]

The last requirement proved crucial to the manner in which the filmmakers transferred the Marine image from the script to the television screen. Given the deep concerns the Corps had about *Rumor of War*, Pat Coulter himself assumed the job of technical advisor for the same reasons as he had served in a similar capacity for *The Great Santini* shortly after coming to the Marines' Los Angeles office. As he had done during that project, Coulter devoted his full attention to *Rumor of War*, not only when filming took place on Marine facilities, but also when the company went on location in Mexico.

He later recalled that he drove to and from the set, an hour and forty-five minutes each way, every single day, for ten or eleven weeks, with the producer and director: "Every day, on the way out in the morning, we talked about what was going to happen. On the way back every night, we talked about what happened and what we could do to make it better. Every single day. Not the wardrobe guys. Not the prop guys. Not the assistant directors. Not the actors. The executive staff." As a result of the relationship that developed, Coulter said that when it came down to the time to cut certain scenes out of the film that the Marines had been unable to negotiate out of the original script back in Washington, he was now able to get the filmmakers to either cut them out or severely shorten them: "Seriously. I was able to have that good a relationship with them."[44]

Did these changes to Caputo's story constitute censorship, reordering of actual events, or whitewashing the Marine Corps's image? To what extent did the changes the Marines had previously requested in *Born on the Fourth of July* and *The Great Santini* become self-serving manipulation of historical reality or creative fiction? The fact remains that the armed services have never forced a producer to come to them to request assistance. Both Don Baruch and the individual services have stressed that if filmmakers do not wish to accede to any requested changes, they always has the option of making the movie without military help. Of course, such a claim becomes disingenuous if a filmmaker needs an aircraft carrier, a nuclear submarine, aircraft, or any esoteric equipment that is available only from the U.S. military. In any case, Baruch maintained that the armed services have never prevented any movie about the military from being made, however negative or inaccurate the portrayal.[45]

Since *Rumor of War* had its basis in Caputo's own account of his experiences in Vietnam, Coulter acknowledged that a different situation existed, particularly in the beating sequence: "It's in the book. The guy swears it happened. We have no reason to believe it didn't happen. Our hands are really tied when we try to get that scene out of the film. We don't like it. We certainly don't like it. We don't like to see a Marine officer beating a young lady. But we really don't have much to argue with. If we do knock it out, then we are making a major change in the film and in the story line."[46]

Instead of forcing the issue directly, Coulter enlisted the help of Brad Davis, who was portraying Caputo, to soften the scene. The night before Davis was to recreate the action, Coulter took the actor aside and told him that he was portraying a "professional" Marine officer: "There is no need for you to lose such complete control of yourself that you get to the point of beating this girl. You can show the tremendous frustration that you feel by just being able to check yourself before you actually do that. You can go right up to that point." Davis agreed and the next morning during rehearsal, he played the scene as Coulter had suggested. Taken aback by the deviation from the script, the director called Davis over to ask why he had changed his lines. The actor responded, "I am a professional Marine officer . . ." How did Coulter justify his deviousness? "It was a tremendously important scene to us."[47]

The issue of censorship or whitewashing aside, Coulter said that "if it is a good movie and if they got the bucks, they are going to make it with or without us. So if there is anything we can do to get in there and support that thing or at least influence it, then we are going to be able to turn it around." In the case of *Rumor of War*, Coulter said this meant "taking a very negative story . . . which was our My Lai, it was pretty close to the real version of My Lai for the Marine Corps, and taking that film and turning it around and making it maybe a little more authentic and accurate in its depiction of how it was for young snuffies out there in the field." According to Coulter, reviewers saw the movie this way: "It was not reviewed as a story about a Marine lieutenant who stepped on it and caused all these problems. It was reviewed as a film that was probably the most accurate depiction of what it was really like for those youngsters out there on the ground in Vietnam."[48]

Supporting Coulter's claim, the *Los Angeles Times* television critic Cecil Smith described *Rumor of War* as "a compelling work of television, particularly in the jungle scenes." At least part of the success the film had in creating an authentic ambience of Vietnam came from the thirty Marines detailed from Camp Pendleton to work on the production in Mexico. Apart from looking like real Marines in front of the camera, the men helped Brad Davis become a "professional" Marine: "They drank and chased women all night and after a couple of hours of sleep went back to work. As long as I was supposed to be a Marine, I did as they did. Damned near killed me." To the extent that the real and pseudo-Marines succeeded in their acting efforts, they enabled the film to capture "the hopelessness, the deadly monotony of the war and the utter callousness of those who fought it," at least to the television critic.[49]

Not all reviewers agreed. Tom Shales, the *Washington Post* television critic, found the miniseries both "morose and glib." He felt that the screenwriter, John Sacret Young, had turned Caputo's "firsthand account into hearsay and a graphic chronicle into a whining bill of particulars." Noting that Young and director Richard Heffron had complained that CBS had meddled with the completed film, Shales nevertheless concluded that this might be "a case where commercial compromise would be preferable to didactic self-righteousness."[50]

Nor did the critic think much of Davis's portrayal, saying he played Caputo "with the same blank, hangdog mope already overexposed to the breaking point in *Midnight Express*. He is a monotonously uninteresting actor, unimposing to the point of invisibility and awfully short, it would seem, to be a Marine lieutenant in the first place." Overall, Shales concluded: "The film lacks the dimensions of tragedy or the authenticity of journalism. Although it is true that TV dramas have not so far dealt in substantial, revealing ways with the Vietnam war from the soldier's point of view, *Rumors* does not comprise an overdue examination. It veers more toward sermonette, although the voice-over narration aspires to a self-pitying and yet self-glorifying pulp-poetry."[51]

In contrast, fellow *Washington Post* writer and former combat Marine in Vietnam Henry Allen began a companion review: "This time they got it right." He found the movie "about as true as a movie is going to get." Despite being shot in Mexico, Allen thought the film looked right: "It looks so much like I Corps, South Vietnam that it's eerie—all that soggy green . . . a green so green it was brown, a thick, dead tropical green going on and on, and then a bunch of palm trees booming up under a sky so hot it seems like no color at all, and this raggedy strip of asphalt with phone poles, called Route One, running through it all. . . . They got that." Allen also confirmed Coulter's claim of authenticity for *Rumor of War*, writing that it did "our effort in Vietnam the courtesy, if not the honor, of showing it the way it was, more than anything I've seen so far."[52]

How did the movie do this for Allen? He explained, "They made the lieutenants look like guys just out of college, which is what they were, not the grim-eyed, grizzled John Wayne types we've had to put up with for years. They made the smart guys the staff sergeants, and it's about time. Then they left it alone." To him, then, the movie "did about as good a job as we're apt to get of showing what Caputo wrote about. It's a nasty story, is all it is. It shows the war with no more moral or meaning to it than there is to an earthquake or lung cancer. It's about time."[53]

To the degree that reviewers saw *Rumor of War* making a comment about the Vietnam War rather than about any negative actions by Marines, Pat Coulter succeeded in his job. At the same time, given his concern for "authenticity and accuracy," he had ensured that the portrayal of the Marines and their activities conveyed a feel of reality, of what Marines had actually experienced in Vietnam. Philip Caputo's story might show that the war had no moral or meaning, but by supporting the production, the Corps was at least able to obtain a relatively balanced account of its activities.[54]

This more positive representation demonstrated the validity of the Marines' new policy on providing assistance to motion pictures, even ones about which the Marines had serious reservations and ones that offered no apparent benefit to the service. Moreover, by turning the negative focus of Caputo's book away from the Marines and onto the conduct of the war as a whole, the film contributed to the Corps's ongoing efforts to explain to the American people that in Vietnam, the military command had used the Marines in ways that ran counter to the mission for which they had trained. At the same time, *Rumor of War* served another purpose. To the degree that the final version avoided criticism of the Marine experience in Vietnam, the Corps avoided possible damage to its continuing campaign to survive as a separate service. Consequently, despite concerns about the original script, the decision to assist in the making of *Rumor of War* was probably in the best interests of the Corps.

Although no one would ever mistake the film for a John Wayne/*Sands of Iwo Jima* cinematic recruiting poster, it did continue the tradition that Marine films tell stories about men trying to survive in combat. Their bravery became the foundation of the Corps's recruiting campaigns: "The first to fight" and "The Marines are looking for a few good men."

20 The Search Continued: Two Non-Vietnam Case Studies

IN REALITY, *BORN ON THE FOURTH OF JULY* and *Rumor of War* shared credit with *The Great Santini* in forcing the Marines to reconsider their policies on how to portray its few good men. When it arrived in Marine Headquarters, Kovic's story became an immediate catalyst in moving the Public Affairs Office to develop new and more appropriate guidelines on dealing with Hollywood. However, the Marines had already been wrestling with the matter in a more leisurely way for two years before Oliver Stone's screenplay came into the Pentagon. On March 9, 1976, the director of information had received a letter from Talent Associates with a copy of the galleys of Pat Conroy's novel *The Great Santini*. The company indicated that it was considering making a movie based on the book and asked the Marines to review the manuscript as to its suitability for support.[1]

The Public Affairs staff found the story of Lt. Col. "Bull" Meechum, a highly decorated Marine Corps jet pilot, "very interesting." The novel, set in the early 1960s, followed one year in the life of Meechum, better known as "the Great Santini," a fictional character based on the life of Col. Donald Conroy, the father of the author. According to the senior Conroy, 60 to 70 percent of the story had a basis in fact. The author compiled the rest from some of the best "sea stories" Marines have ever tried to pass off on each other and unknowing civilians. Meechum comes across as a warrior soldier in the mold of George Patton, a man to whom a nation turns in time of war but who has no place in peacetime. A veteran of both World War II and Korea, Meechum might well have said, as Patton did, that he should have died with the last bullet of the last war. Instead, the Great Santini remains a maverick, a flamboyant, fun-loving, hard-drinking officer, relegated to flying jets in mock combat.

He loves his country, the Marine Corps, and his family, pretty much in that order; and despite his transgressions as a Marine, he is a better officer than a husband and father. As the story progresses, told from the perspective of his eighteen-year-old son, readers see Bull as a man with magnificent flaws that coexist with magnificent gifts. The book ran the full range of human emotions, beginning with the thrills and excitement of an aerial dogfight and the camaraderie that exists among fliers who work, train, fight, and live life to the fullest. However, Meechum has difficulty separating his military life from his family life. He accepts and obeys orders from higher authority and expects his family to likewise accept his orders.

Given his personality, Meechum was bound to find himself in perpetual conflict with his wife and children. Lillian remains the force that binds the family together, and she tries to act as the buffer between Bull and his children. Sometimes she even succeeds, helping them learn how to read the signals he gives. One daughter observes that recognizing them was not difficult because "he always gives off the signals of a psychopathic killer." Ultimately, on a routine night-training flight, Bull's jet runs into trouble and he rides it into the ground rather than ejecting over the city. In summarizing the story, Pat Coulter, who served as technical advisor on the production, observed, "As we have lived life to the fullest with Bull—we have flown with him, played with him, loved with him, hated him and just begun to understand him—a part of us dies with him."[2]

Clearly, the Great Santini did not resemble a typical Marine lieutenant colonel or even a typical Marine aviator, at least as the Corps perceived its own. Many of the things he does would cause any leatherneck to wince and feel embarrassment. Therefore, any script based on Conroy's book was bound to cause the Marine Corps Public Affairs Office problems. Initially, however, the office was able to avoid having to deal with the story by advising Talent Associates that it could comment only on a completed script and a request for actual support. In his letter, Gen. W.R. Maloney, the Marine director of information, did note that any assistance would come on a no-cost-to-the-government, noninterference basis and that any actor portraying a Marine "would be expected to conform to Marine Corps dress and appearance standards."[3]

The next day, General Maloney sent a memo to the Marine Corps chief of staff in which he described the novel as "an 'earthy' story which I believe will be turned into a very popular, modern movie rated R." He also admitted that he did not know where the autobiography ended and the fiction began. In his more detailed memo for the record, Maloney described the book as "highly authentic in detail, probably sited at Beaufort. There are several racist incidents described. The book is very upbeat towards USMC, ambivalent towards Lt Col Meecham. Some other specifics include examples of wife beating and derogatory statements concerning the USN and USNA. There is reference to PISC [Parris Island, South Carolina] as Biddle Is., where a fake shooting incident with D.I.s takes place. Meecham takes his son to the Depot on the latter's eighteenth birthday and they witness a DI shoot another with a blank .45 and throw his 'body' in the dumpster." (Actually, a D.I. shoots a recruit.) Although the director of information noted that the Marines had not committed themselves to the film, he thought the Defense Department was "likely" to do so, "in which case it will be in our interest to provide support."[4]

In sending the galleys to Don Baruch, the deputy director of information, C.W. Hoffner, said that the Marines had reviewed the book and had "no objection to it at this point." In fact, given the description of the book's contents in Maloney's memo, any script would have to leave out things that would cause Marines to "wince and feel embarrassment," such as a D.I. shooting a recruit even as a joke. However, the Public Affairs Office did not have to consider such things for another ten months, when Bing Crosby Productions wrote to Don Baruch informing him that the company had taken an option on the book. The company described Meechum as "a gargantuan, unforgettable and sometimes loveable, but always respected, giant of a man."[5]

Despite this characterization, *The Great Santini* concerned itself very little with the Marine Corps and with flying. Unlike virtually all other Hollywood movies about the armed forces, the novel probed life inside a military family, with few punches pulled, with no sugar coating designed to please the military. Recognizing this, the filmmakers wrote that the script would provide "a highly sympathetic portrait of a military family. The plot will concentrate on the interrelationships of this remarkable and loveable family and their reactions to events during this time period." The company expressed the hope that the completed film would be "valuable for stimulating Marine Corps recruiting." With this in mind, it assured the Marines that "the rough language of the novel will be severely toneddown" and that it intended "to dramatize Marine Corps personalities involved in a favorable connotation."[6]

Responding to Baruch's request for comments on the book, General Maloney wrote that the Marines found it "both entertaining and scandalous." He said the story was "upbeat toward the Corps but, in view of the recent incidents involving recruit training, it could ill serve the Marine Corps efforts at telling the story of 'firmness, fairness and dignity' in recruit training. Specifically, we refer to the fake shooting incident where the 'recruit' is 'shot' by his Drill Instructor." Maloney also cited other areas of concern, including Meechum's beating of his wife, abusing his children, and making negative references to the Navy and the Naval Academy. As a result of these issues, he advised Baruch that "Marine Corps support of a motion picture based on this book, as written, would be inappropriate and not in the best interest of the Corps at this time."[7]

Although the director of information had shown reluctance to become involved with the production, he had not closed the door, suggesting that the Marines might consider a formal request for assistance depending on how the final script turned out. The film company recognized the subtle phrasing, and on February 16 Charles Pratt, the president of BCP, sent Don Baruch a letter he had received from Pat Conroy in which the author set forth his own thoughts about the story and the direction the movie should take. Pratt said he concurred with Conroy's views and repeated the company's intention "to soften the character of BULL MEECHAM somewhat from the individual described in the novel. It is mandatory that BULL MEECHAM is a likeable, although flamboyant, person; otherwise, the audience will not feel a sense of loss at his demise." In closing, Pratt cited his military experience in World War II and belief in military discipline and the need for a strong military establishment: "I want to assure you that BCP expects to make a movie which will be a credit to the Corps and boost recruiting of the right sort of men."[8]

In his letter, Pat Conroy explained that he wrote the book "as a celebration of military life in America, a celebration of the military family, a celebration of one single military family—my own. But I meant the Meechum family to be a microcosm for all American military families. I wanted to tell a story that has not been told before. The military family is an unknown factor in American life. It has never been studied in American literature or film. It is an unknown, unpraised, undefined subculture." Conroy said that as a child he often wondered about the children of military heroes whose lives he saw portrayed on the screen: "How did their children cope with the powerful mythologies presented by their fathers? Like me, did they have trouble finding their identities through the blazing myth of heroes and warriors?" On the screen, he saw the soldier in battle but not at home, "at rest, unarmed beneath the gaze of wife and children, far from the eyes of enemies." Consequently, in *The Great Santini*, Conroy said he wanted to show how the life of a military man interweaves with the separate lives of his family: "I tried to show that the life of Bull Meecham is filled with extraordinary pressure and that this pressure affects each member of his family. But that the family also has uncommon experience which directly affects the pilot."[9]

Conroy saw Meechum, and indirectly, of course, his father, as "a supremely American hero." To be sure, the author recognized that he was "a profane, insensitive Ulysses who loves his vocation passionately and who loves his family just as much but inarticulately and in strange, unspoken ways." Meechum had more skill in the arts of war than in the arts of being a husband or a father, and Conroy said this "provides the tension the book develops as it should provide the tension in the film." Speaking directly to the nature of Meechum's character, the author observed: "He is a man of action not of introspection. He is a warrior never quite comfortable in the milieu of peace or in the milieu of his own home. He is motivated by the powerful mythology of the Marine aviator. This mythology should be emphasized."[10]

According to author Pat Conroy, Bull Meechum "is a man who sometimes confuses the difference between corporals and children."

The Marines would obviously find this portrayal beneficial. However, Meechum carried his military demeanor home with him at night, and his behavior there did create the image of a man out of control, a threat to his family, a bull in a china store. Conroy explained this side of Meechum's behavior as the result of his being a military man who "demands the best from the soldiers who serve him and the family whose duty it is to love him. He takes love and duty for granted. He himself receives orders from high authorities and he instinctively obeys them. He gives orders to his marines and his family and expects them to be obeyed. Bull Meecham brings the military home to his family. He runs his family like he runs his squadron. He is a man who sometimes confuses the difference between corporals and children, top sergeants and wives. Conflict with his children is inevitable."[11]

Unfortunately for the Marines who would consider a request for assistance in the making of *The Great Santini,* the "inevitable" conflict with wife and children manifested itself in spousal and child abuse. Apart from the problems that Meechum's on-duty behavior created for those considering a request for support, Bull's treatment of his family would become a sticking point in any discussion of a script that closely followed Conroy's narrative. And the author believed the film should be told from the perspective of Meechum's eighteen-year-old son Ben, whom he tests "constantly, challenges him, exhorts him to be better than Ben can possibly be, and goads Ben into being even better than he, Bull Meecham, is." According to Conroy, Ben and his siblings become what they are because Meechum is their father: "He has loved them, trained them, shaped them and formed them according to his belief in challenge, discipline and himself."[12]

During the year in which the story takes place, Ben moves toward becoming a man worthy of his father. In so doing, he clashes even more strongly with his father and, thereby, elicits Meechum's love and respect. When Meechum leaves his post to help his son, Conroy acknowledges that "the rules of the Marine Corps break down. . . . The Marine, above all, is a father." A noble sentiment, to be sure, but one that the Marine Corps would have a difficult time having portrayed on the screen. A Marine remains committed to duty first

Bull Meechum's treatment of his family would become a sticking point for *The Great Santini.*

and parenthood second. Still, Conroy himself did not see Bull's behavior causing problems with the Marines: "I would like this film to be based on a simple concept: *The Great Santini* is an American epic, grand in scene and character, made as an absolute celebration of the American military life. The film should say that being raised in a military environment can be both good and bad, with its own special glories and flaws, with its own failures and triumphs. . . . It should be a study of a complex family with an incredible network of conflicting emotions. But, finally, it should demonstrate unequivocally that this family is bound with a passionate love for each other. When Santini dies, a great life-force has passed out of their existence, a force that shaped them, a force they loved. The film of *The Great Santini* should not only be a celebration. It should be an honoring."[13]

Whatever Conroy believed, a novel and a film exist as two separate entities. A book reaches a relatively limited audience, and a reader can always stop reading if he or she does not like the material. Movies seek out wider audiences and convey their images to many more people. In addition, unlike the pre-Vietnam, pre–video recorder period, in which a film would come and go quickly, in the contemporary world, popular movies remain readily accessible. Consequently, in looking at the request for cooperation on *The Great Santini*, the Marines worried that if the filmmakers transferred the book to the screen relatively unchanged, an unacceptable image of Bull Meechum might continue to haunt them for a long time.[14]

If Conroy's letter did not in itself provide all the assurances the Marines needed about the focus of the movie, Charles Pratt did what he could to allay their fears. In forwarding the letter to the Marines on March 3, Don Baruch advised Pat Coulter that Pratt had told him that he was anxious to discuss the development of the screenplay in order to overcome Marine objections and obtain support for the movie. Coulter sent a note to his boss, Art Brill, saying that from reading Conroy's letter, he concluded that "there appears to be plenty of room for negotiation. I believe we can both come out winners in this venture." In sending the memo to the deputy director of information, Brill added, "I agree. Let's talk w/them."[15]

As writer Lew Carlino worked on the script, he kept in touch regularly with Pat Coulter, who continued his efforts to ensure that the final screenplay would satisfy the Marines. On June 28, 1977, Coulter informed Art Brill that the shooting scene at the recruit depot "has been cleaned up considerably; however, the producers may be wanting to put it back in. Haven't won this one yet." However, his efforts did result in significant changes to Santini's character from that in the novel. When John Pommer, the company's vice president for production, finally submitted the script to Don Baruch on October 5, 1977, he wrote, "You will note that the screenplay has altered the character of BULL MEECHAM from the autocrat depicted in the novel to a commanding officer more in tune with the Marine Corps and the Marine Corps family of today." He requested assistance on the production at the Marine Corps Air Station, South Carolina, because, as written, the story used that facility and nearby Beaufort as its setting. Included in the list of requirements, the filmmakers requested use of an aircraft carrier "moored to a dock in a location, preferably on the West Coast, where no land would be visible in one direction and where takeoffs would be feasible." Having revealed his ignorance of aerial mechanics—an aircraft carrier must be underway in order to launch its jet planes—Pommer showed the good sense to ask for a technical advisor once the company had made its selection of a location for its shooting.[16]

Don Baruch wrote on October 14 to the Marine Public Affairs Office, which had received a copy of the script directly from its Los Angeles Branch, saying that its "comments and position will be appreciated at the earliest date." Recognizing that *The Great Santini* remained "strictly" a Marine story, Baruch said his office "defers to your judgement on the overall beneficial effect that the picture might have for the Corps." Nevertheless, he said that DoD Public Affairs did question whether certain sequences served the best interest of the Corps. In particular, he cited a scene in which Meechum, using a can of mushroom soup to create the effect, pretended to vomit in front of Navy officers and their wives and then had his fellow Marines spoon up and eat the apparent mess. He also mentioned a meeting between Meecham and a fellow officer in which the two men wrestle to the ground, and the D.I. shooting scene. In closing, Baruch said he had sent a copy of the screenplay to the Navy chief of information in support of the request to use an aircraft carrier during production.[17]

During the review of the screenplay, which took two months, the Marines found themselves also having to deal with the Navy's reaction to the project because of the company's request for use of an aircraft carrier. On December 19, 1977, Adm. David Cooney, the Navy chief of information, advised Don Baruch that he found the "portrayal of Navy/Marine Corps personnel is highly inaccurate and derogatory." Consequently, he said the script did not meet the criteria of the DoD regulations governing cooperation with the film industry, and so he recommended that assistance be denied.[18]

The next day, Gen. V.T. Blaz, the new Marine Corps director of information, sent a memo to the Marines' chief of staff advising him of the status of the *Santini* project now that his office had completed its review of the script. Blaz explained that the producers had indicated a willingness to delete the recruit-shooting incident, but he said other sequences still reflected negatively on the Navy–Marine Corps team concept and Marine aviators. He also informed the chief of staff of the Navy's refusal to support the film.[19]

In reviewing the story, Blaz acknowledged that *Santini* contained "an interesting study in human behavior and has the potential to be a major motion picture." Since he believed the film company would make the movie with or without support from the Marines, Blaz said that the service's refusal to assist the production would "essentially preclude any ability to influence the production." However, he then conceded that even working with the filmmakers, as Pat Coulter had been doing, did not assure that the company would accede to the Marines' requests for script changes. Instead, he advised the chief of staff that though the screenplay now differed from the book, it "continues to portray a negative image of Marine officers and is derogatory to the Corps." Consequently, he concluded that since the Marines could not stop the negative portrayal, "it does not have to put what would be perceived as a 'stamp of approval' on the film by actively supporting production." He therefore requested permission to release a memo declining to support the movie.[20]

In a memo of December 30, Blaz advised Baruch that the Marines had no reason to change the opinion first stated on February 11, 1977, when commenting on the book. His office still felt "it would not be in the best interest of the Marine Corps to support the production of this movie based on the present script." As with the several rejections of the *Born on the Fourth of July* script, the memo did not end the discussions or the company's efforts to obtain assistance. Instead, the company asked Baruch not to formally respond to its request for support until after they visited the Beaufort area to see how important the setting would be to the film. Pat Coulter explained that the company would then have an idea "of just how far they will be willing to go to get DoD support . . . that is, just how much of the script they would be willing to change to be able to use the facilities at MCAS Beaufort."[21]

Marine Headquarters considered the project in limbo until the middle of May, when

Maj. H.J. Collins, in its Los Angeles office, advised the director of information that the film company had signed Robert Duvall to play Bull Meechum and that Lew Carlino would direct his own script. Just as important, John Palmer, the company's vice president for production, was planning to visit South Carolina at the beginning of June in order to select a filming location. Collins wrote that the company would then decide whether to make another request for support: "Mr. Palmer recognizes that certain segments of *The Great Santini* will have to be changed if service support is considered. However, the motion picture will be made, with or without service support."[22]

On May 17, Collins called Pat Coulter to say he was contacting the commanding officer of the Marine Corps Air Station at Beaufort to advise him that the filmmakers were going to visit. He also said he had been talking with the commanding officer on and off about the project. On his part, Art Brill recommended to the director of information that Major Collins continue to work with the company in hopes of resolving some of the problems with the script, again pinpointing the problem areas. In regard to the mushroom soup scene, he acknowledged that it might be "offensive to some," particularly the Navy, but argued that "it could be a funny episode if handled right." He reported that Collins had advised him that although he might get the company to tone down the scene, the filmmakers were "reluctant" to omit it completely.[23]

In light of the opening sequence, in which Marine pilots beat Navy fliers in a mock dogfight, Brill thought the Navy might refuse to cooperate. If so, the company would not have access to an aircraft carrier. At the same time, while the company was committed to making the movie, Brill noted that it had "already shown willingness to cooperate by dropping the boot camp sequence. But as a big scene, it may be returned to the script if we withhold support. Moreover, the script, taken as a whole, is favorable to the Corps." In this light and because Brill considered the film "a touching story based on the book that reflects an aspect of military family life," he recommended that the office advise Major Collins "to tell the producers that the Marine Corps will *recommend* support to DoD provided the changes are made. He will have to make it clear that we do not speak for the Navy."[24]

Five members of the film company did visit Beaufort from June 5 to 7, including an informal visit to the Marine Air Station on June 5. Before leaving, they told the commanding officer that they intended to film local scenes in Beaufort and hoped to win DoD approval of the script so that they could shoot on the Air Station. He reported that they had stated their willingness to make reasonable script changes. The commanding officer responded that he and base personnel "are enthusiastic about participating in this film. It is my opinion that the film will better represent the Marine Corps with our participation."[25]

After their visit to South Carolina, the producers advised Baruch that they were willing to do "whatever" the Marines wanted in order to receive permission to shoot at Beaufort. To this end, they requested a meeting in Washington with the Marine Corps Public Affairs staff to discuss the changes that the service would like to see in the script. When he asked the Marines for a tentative date for the meeting, Baruch also suggested they contact the Navy Public Affairs Office to see if that service was willing to negotiate on problems it had with the script, so that all interested parties could get together. In any case, the company's request galvanized the Marines to delineate exactly what position they would take on the script, whether or not the Public Affairs Office would compromise. If so, the filmmakers wanted to know precisely what the service wanted changed. The Marines, of course, had the option of not supporting *The Great Santini,* but allowing the company to film at Beaufort.[26]

In deciding on any approach, the Marines faced the ultimate question of how much influence they wanted to have on the film. The Navy's involvement in the negotiations because of the request for use of an aircraft carrier now complicated the process. As a result, the Marines' answer to the request for assistance now depended to a significant degree on the Navy's position vis-à-vis the Corps's new approach to assist on, but not necessarily support, a film and on whether the Marine Corps would, in fact, defer to its sister service's wishes.[27]

The Navy's interest or lack of interest in *The Great Santini* was quickly becoming an important issue with wide ramifications to both services. Although the Marine Corps considered itself a virtually autonomous military branch, in statutory terms it remained a part of the Navy Department and so under the authority of the secretary of the Navy. In the chain of command, the Marine director of information and the Navy chief of information had the same organizational rank. However, the chief of information also served as public affairs officer for the secretary of the Navy, and in that capacity he did outrank and so commanded the Marine director of information. Consequently, at least in theory, if the chief of information decided he did not want the Marines to cooperate on *The Great Santini* or any other movie, he could impose his decision, the Corps's wishes notwithstanding.

As Admiral Cooney had written Baruch in December 1977, he apparently wanted to do just that with *Santini*, because he believed that the film contained negative references to the Navy. In fact, despite the unresolved problems with the script, the Marines had no intention of letting Cooney shoot down their support of the movie. Pat Coulter said that the Public Affairs Office saw the story "as the first realistic film about Marine aviation since *Flying Leathernecks*," and the Corps wanted *Santini* made. When Cooney indicated that he would take the matter to the secretary of the Navy, the Marines in turn said they would ask the commandant himself to intercede with the secretary, since he liked the story.[28]

The situation came close to that when one of the officers in Cooney's office called Art Brill on June 14, 1978, to advise him that the chief of information was "dead against supporting the film primarily because of the language used." He also objected to the toilet scene in which Meechum reaches under a stall, thinking his friend is occupying it, only to discover he has grabbed an enlisted man. The Navy officer said that the matter had reached a point where the "underlings" had become "powerless" to influence Cooney's position, and he recommended that General Brewer discuss the situation directly with the admiral.[29]

In conveying this to Brewer, Brill said that until the call, the Marine public affairs people had the "impression" from the Navy people "THAT SANTINI *IS* A MARINE PROBLEM." He further said that he had gotten the feeling from the call that if the filmmakers deleted the Navy scenes from the script or reduced them, the project would be "our baby." Consequently, Brill thought that the office could "convince the producers to eliminate the Navy entirely or modify the two Navy scenes in question that affect the Navy. With this done, it's a Marine Corps film entirely." In fact, he noted that the film could be made without the Navy even being mentioned: "We do not want our sister service to look bad and I'm sure the producers will agree to modify the script accordingly."[30]

In regard to Admiral Cooney's efforts to impose his will on the Marines, Brill recommended, "We should not knuckle under to Admiral Cooney in this matter. The Marine Corps has too much to lose if we do not influence the script. The recruit training scene alone is enough to send CMC up the wall, particularly if he discovered we could have negotiated it out of the film entirely. CMC does not appreciate interference from the Navy and with the Navy scenes reduced or modified, this is interference. I think CMC would go to SecNav personally on this and he would WIN. Obviously, we don't want it to go that far."[31]

To prevent this from happening, Brill recommended that Brewer call Admiral Cooney to pave the way for a meeting later in the week between the Marine and Navy public affairs staffs and provided several talking points. He suggested that she stress that the Marines wanted to avoid future films such as *Coming Home*, which detracted from the image of the Corps and its recruiting effort. He said to emphasize that the recent commandant decision to support *Born on the Fourth of July* represented a major change in Marine policy: "Though we should take each film on a case by case basis, this decision should be interpreted as a precedent to the degree that cooperation doesn't mean condone and that the bottom line is preservation of the Marine image." Brill suggested that Brewer note that the film would be made with or without cooperation and that one way or another, it "will reflect the Marine image in the lean recruiting years of the 1980s and well beyond on television."[32]

In regard to the script itself, he said the director of information should tell Cooney that the office had already secured the elimination of the recruit training scene and believed that through negotiation, it could resolve most of the other disputed scenes and tone down the character. Further, the office intended to assign a technical advisor who would assure compliance. Finally, Brill suggested that Brewer make clear that the film showed Marine aviation for the first time in years and at a time when the Corps was justifying its mission, stressing the air-ground team and the need for the AV8B jet fighter.[33]

In a cover memo, Brill observed that the situation was "getting Hot." He also added one other selling point to those he had included in the formal memo, which he thought Brewer should mention to Admiral Cooney: "The City of Beaufort will realize about $50,000 per day for six to eight weeks from the film company. This is Strom Thurmond country and there could be political pressure if we resist. That's something to consider at any rate." In fact, on June 20, Pat Coulter, who had predicted Thurmond's interest in the project, advised Brill that the senator's office had called to say that he wanted the $3–5 million dollars the film company would bring to his area. Coulter also observed, "Will not be easy to say *no* to this cat."[34]

Meanwhile, the Marine Corps had been making plans for its meeting with the filmmakers. In his formal memo to General Brewer on June 14, Brill had recommended that the director of information meet with the filmmakers "for introductions and general discussion" prior to an already scheduled negotiating session with Brill and his staff the following week "to work out the details similar to the procedure used in the Kovic film." In preparation for the meeting, he said the office was "reviewing the script in detail to determine areas where we can humanize the Bull Meecham character."[35]

In the meeting on June 21, the writer-director, Lew Carlino; Charles Pratt; Brill; Coulter; and Lieutenant Williamson went over the screenplay page by page, scene by scene. At the end of the session, the filmmakers went back to their hotel, where they spent the night rewriting much of the script, which they brought back to the Marines the next day. As a result of the negotiations, the company agreed to eliminate the recruit training sequence with the shooting of the recruit. The company considerably toned down or eliminated several scenes of wife-beating and child abuse. In one instance where a drunk Meechum knocks down his wife and children in frustration over not being able to convey his feelings toward them, he simply shakes his wife "to calm her" and does not touch the children. The filmmakers agreed to eliminate Meechum's comment that the Navy thinks of the Marines as "some kind of anal fungus" and change his criticism of his squadron for "flying like squids" to "flying like pansies." They also eliminated three references Meechum makes to the Marines as being "killers" and a comment one of Ben's sisters makes when she predicts he will enlist in the Corps like his father and "slowly, all that's good in you will begin to dissolve."[36]

The filmmakers added a scene in which Meechum reports to his new assignment and his commander tells him that he will no longer tolerate his behavior, his rowdiness and drunkenness. He also says that although Meechum may be a good fighter pilot, this does not necessarily make him a good Marine, and his career will not survive if he continues his unprofessional behavior. The company did refuse to change the vomit scene, but said it would add a line later on showing that the Marines considered this behavior unacceptable and unprofessional. Likewise, the filmmakers refused to remove the scene in the men's room. But, they toned down the mock-dogfight sequence which opened the movie so that the Navy did not emerge humiliated.[37]

Did these changes constitute censorship? Pat Coulter said the filmmakers considered the revised script to be better. When they returned to Los Angeles, Charles Pratt wrote to Art Brill saying that he and Carlino "were most pleased with the outcome of our meeting with you. . . . We appreciate the forthright way you approached our script and are pleased with the revised version which was the result of our common effort." In his letter thanking General Brewer for the Marine cooperation, he noted that Brill "represented the Marines' position very clearly and firmly yet at the same time made every effort to be helpful." He added that the matter "is now in the hands of Admiral Cooney, who was very gracious to us in our meeting last Friday, June 23rd. The Admiral has promised to address himself to our problem promptly and we are hopeful the matter will be resolved shortly."[38]

Given the situation still existing between the Marines and the Navy, General Brewer followed up the June 21 meeting with a detailed memo to the commandant of the Marine Corps on July 7, summarizing the status of *The Great Santini*. She acknowledged that even after the recent negotiating session with the filmmakers, the Marines had not been able to have all the questionable scenes eliminated. Consequently, she expected some criticism for having provided any assistance to the production. Nevertheless, she felt that the benefits the Marines "will gain in improved image from the revisions made in the original script, which was very detrimental to the Marine Corps image, will outweigh any individual criticism that might result."[39]

Brewer then raised the issue of Admiral Cooney's objections to the film, stressing that since it remained primarily a Marine movie, the Corps "has the most to lose if we cannot continue to influence the film." She said that Cooney had indicated he already had discussed the film with the secretary of the Navy but that he had not yet taken a final position vis-à-vis approval of the script. Brewer thought that if the Navy would support the Marines' position, however, it might be possible to secure even further influence on the script and "tone-down" even more of the "objectionable aspects of 'Bull's' personality." In this context, she asked the commandant to recommend to DoD that the Marines provide limited assistance as distinguished from "support." Among other things, this included a limited shooting schedule at Beaufort, the assigning of a technical advisor, and no Marine credits. Subject to the final decision by the Navy, both the Marine chief of staff and the commandant approved Brewer's recommendations.[40]

Ultimately, after review of the final revised script, the Marines approved it on August 10, with the stipulation that the company meet the conditions listed in General Brewer's memo to the commandant. Despite his antipathy toward the project, Admiral Cooney also gave his approval on August 17, with the recommendation "that no Department of

Defense screen credits be requested or authorized." With these approvals in hand, Don Baruch notified Charles Pratt on August 17, 1978, that the Defense Department had given final approval for assistance to the production. Pat Coulter, who took over command of the Marines Corps Los Angeles Office shortly after helping wrap up negotiations, received the assignment as technical advisor on the film when shooting began at the end of September.[41]

After all the travails the Marines went through to reach an agreement on a script, making *The Great Santini* became almost anticlimactic. Director Carlino filmed the aerial sequences during the preproduction (before the actors arrived) phase of the location shooting at Beaufort from September 25 to 29. The Marine Fighter-Attack Squadron 312, the Checkerboard squadron, became Meechum's Werewolf squadron. Since the Navy's role in the film had shrunk to virtual noninvolvement, the Marine Thunderbolt squadron, also stationed at Beaufort, played the role of the Navy in the opening mock-dogfight sequence. To "costume" the planes, Coulter used masking tape to cover over the word *Marines* on the side of the jets and then painted the word *Navy* in its place. All other markings, including the distinctive bright orange "Thunderbolt," remained on the aircraft, but Coulter believed that only an aircraft expert would have caught the masquerade. The final night flight was shot during the day with special night filters on the camera.[42]

As with the use of the planes, some literary license was taken with the uniforms, since the company found it impossible to supply the extras with the 1962–63 styles. In a more blatant uniform error, Meechum traveled to his new assignment at Beaufort wearing a forbidden outfit, as the novel had described it. All Marines would immediately recognize the mistake. But according to Coulter, the senior Conroy told him during a brief visit to the set that he had actually traveled that way. To soften the impact, the technical advisor had Meechum not wear his rank insignia and wings during the trip. These are minor points that military advisors can live with in the context of dramatic license.[43]

In light of the Marine Corps's worry over Santini's character, Pat Coulter concerned himself primarily with ensuring that Meechum ultimately came across as a good Marine who would not embarrass the service. Robert Duvall brought to his role as Santini the reputation in the film business as a chameleon because of his ability to "become" the character he portrayed. He had recently completed roles as Dwight Eisenhower for the ABC-TV miniseries *Ike* and the surfing lieutenant colonel in *Apocalypse Now*. But he had never played a Marine, and he began his metamorphosis from a five-star general to a Marine flier as soon as he arrived at Beaufort. Coulter reported that the actor met with the commander of the air station, sat in on briefings and debriefings, attended social functions, and even got hosed down with a fire extinguisher at the fighter bar during happy hour. He visited flight lines and went through flight simulator rides. Finally, he spent a day with Marine recruits to better understand how the Corps turns civilians into leathernecks.[44]

Serving as technical advisor, Pat Coulter adjusts Robert Duval's uniform during filming of *The Great Santini*.

First of all, of course, Duvall was playing a hotshot jet pilot, and from Lt. Col. D.J. Kiely, who flew Santini's missions for the cameras, the actor learned to become a Marine pilot. Coulter noted that Kiely "even got him to speak with his hands like all good pilots do." The technical advisor said that Kiely had many of the positive attributes of Bull Meechum: "He is rugged and distinguished in appearance, flamboyant and authoritative, always in charge and highly respected and admired by all who know him." As a result, Coulter said that the way Duvall played his role "is a reflection of how he imagined Kiely would react in the same situation. What a team they made. It was a unique experience to see teacher and student, actor and coach, pilot and protege together."[45]

Duvall's efforts to become one with Santini carried over to the entire company. Coulter received full backing from the filmmakers to ensure that the finished product looked and felt authentic. Honoring his commitment to the Navy that the service would not look bad in the movie, the technical advisor rejected the first two actors proposed to play the officer who tries to quiet Meechum down in Spain just before the mushroom soup scene. Coulter said the first actor was too fat and the second refused to cut his hair. Instead, he found an actor who looked as good as any of the Marines. He went to even greater lengths to ensure the indoctrination of the cast to the need to do things according to Marine standards and perhaps succeeded too well. In the bedroom scene, the night Meechum returns from the Mediterranean, all nonessential crew members left the set to afford Duvall and Blythe Danner, as his wife, some privacy after they doffed their robes. As Danner was getting into bed, she turned to Coulter, who had remained in his role of technical advisor, and asked, "Pat, are you here to make sure we do this the Marine Corps way?"[46]

Perhaps not in bed, but certainly in the important scenes, Coulter ensured that the film had the right look, not only to benefit the Corps, but also to benefit the production. This becomes most evident not in the mushroom soup scene, which remains gross and unflattering to the Marines, however toned down it had evolved from the original script, but in the re-creation of Meechum's military funeral. Shot in Beaufort on one of the two days it rained during the company's stay in South Carolina, the sequence became one of the finest examples of a full-honors military funeral that Hollywood has ever committed to film. Here, Marines take care of their own, bidding farewell to a fallen comrade. As the final notes of taps sound, the whine of the F-4 Phantom jets grows louder, and the planes skim over the treetops and break through the clouds. Meechum's youngest son turns to his brother Ben and says, "There's one missing." Ben answers, "That's where Papa should be." As the planes disappear into the mist, the camera turns to a flag flying at half mast over the national cemetery. Only the most cynical viewer could leave the theater without having shed a tear.

Filming the burial of Bull Meechum for *The Great Santini.*

In the end, then, *The Great Santini* succeeded in the way Pat Conroy had hoped. If Bull Meechum did not fit the role model the Marines would have liked to convey, the image Robert Duvall created of the man may well have done as much good for the Corps as had John Wayne's Sergeant Stryker. Wayne/Stryker had become a man of mythic proportions, a godlike figure, just out of reach. In Vietnam, soldiers quickly found that war bore little resemblance to Wayne's *Sands of Iwo Jima* or *The Green Berets* and so became disillusioned and bitter. Although the men who fought the war discovered this reality, too many public affairs officers had no desire to permit a more realistic portrayal of life in the military or even admit that soldiers, sailors, and Marines used four-letter words, sometimes behaved grossly, sometimes even abused their wives and children.

The Bull Meechum who reached the screen had undergone considerable change from Conroy's character, but he still remained far more believable to audiences than previous portrayals of Marines. To the extent that viewers of both sexes could empathize with the man, with his virtues and his flaws, the image would have at least as much value for the Marines in the future as Wayne's Stryker had had in the past. Pat Coulter, for one, had little doubt that the film benefited the Corps, asking how the service could top the toast Meechum offers to his men: "Hogs! To the Corps elite. To that special breed of sky devil known and feared throughout the world: the Marine dogfighter. To the bravest fighting men that ever lived. There is not a force that can defeat us in battle, deny us victory or interrupt our destiny—Marines!!!!"

Despite ongoing concerns within the Corps about the possible negative reaction to Bull Meechum, in the end most Marines found the portrayal well worth the effort. After the review screening for the Marines in Washington on July 16, 1979, Don Baruch wrote to Charles Pratt on the twenty-fifth to confirm the "approbative remarks" that the Marines in attendance had made. He believed that the results on the screen "are evidence that by working with the Marines Corps, Department of Defense assistance was of mutual advantage."[47]

Ironically, the project that seemed to offer so much more potential benefit for the Marines and the Department of Defense than had *The Great Santini* was to cause the military in general and the Marine Corps in particular great embarrassment and, at least in the short term, set back the Pentagon's efforts to rehabilitate its image. The script, tentatively titled "Inchon," which arrived on February 3, 1978, provided no hint of the turmoil and controversies that were to develop around the project. In requesting "the fullest extent of cooperation" in making his film, Mitsuharu Ishii wrote to the Defense Department that the motion picture would have Gen. Douglas MacArthur's Inchon landing operation as its main theme. He explained that "the most important emphasis will be placed on the significance" of the amphibious assault. To the Japanese businessman turned film producer, "the free world was dependent on the success of this operation and all would have been lost if Inchon had been lost."[48]

In critiquing the script for the Marine Corps Public Information Office, Penny Williamson found that all mention of the Marines was "either neutral or *very* favorable. The Marines are portrayed as saving the day, hard fighting heroes and generally nice to have around when the fighting got tough." She noted that all the main characters were either Navy or Army: "In fact all the services are portrayed very favorably and the American/ROK characters come across as heroic." Although the script only portrayed the Marines launching the actual assault at Inchon, Williamson said that the Corps, as the heroes, helped save the free world. Consequently, she saw no reason the service should not support the production.[49]

To the other services, and particularly the Marines considering Ishii's request for assistance, the portrayal in the "Inchon" script stood in stark contrast to the antimilitary content of the first cycle of Vietnam movies and the scripts for *Born on the Fourth of July* and *The Great Santini*, which the Marines were then subjecting to critical evaluation. If the Korean War had not produced a great victory, most people attributed the ultimate stalemate to political decisions rather than any military shortcomings. Moreover, a screenplay that glorified General MacArthur and showed that "the good guys triumph" and "the free world is saved" offered particular appeal to the armed forces, then being savaged by Hollywood. Given the subject matter, the Defense Department concerned itself exclusively with the content of the script, its historical and technical accuracy, and the benefit it offered to the armed services in terms of informational value and as a recruitment tool.

Following the recommendations of the individual services, the Defense Department approved the original script submitted in February 1978 and a revised version in January 1979. The historical branch of each service found only minor errors of fact and military procedure that required correction. Both screenplays depicted the film's hero as a Navy officer modeled in part on the lieutenant who had kindled the lamp in the lighthouse that provided the beacon for the invasion armada as it entered Inchon's harbor under cover of night. When the film company could not obtain a release from the retired officer because the script portrayed him as having an affair with a Korean girl, the character underwent a metamorphosis, becoming instead a fictional Marine officer.[50]

When Pat Coulter in the Marine Information Office in Los Angeles discovered the change in the leading character's service in March 1979, he sent a memo to the Corps's director of information in Washington advising that the approved script was "not now to be used." Because of increasing Marine involvement in the story, Coulter said that "the Marine Corps needs to re-read the current script for any suggestions or changes that may be necessary." He said he had already pointed this out to the producers and they were planning to send him the new version as soon as they had it typed. Coulter concluded his memo with the suggestion that because of the "increasing USMC involvement" in *Inchon*, "it becomes more evident that a full-time technical advisor from WestPac will have to be assigned to the production."[51]

The director of information did not act on the memo, and the Defense Department Public Affairs Office did not learn about the revised script until articles about the film's production began appearing during the summer. Irrespective of the change in the leading character's service, neither the Defense Department nor the Marines considered appointing an on-duty officer to act as technical advisor and liaison man between the Pentagon and the film company. Both Don Baruch in the DoD Public Affairs Office and General Brewer acknowledged that by the late 1970s, the services had less concern with technical accuracy in stories about World War II and Korea than they did in contemporary films. Moreover, any active-duty officers who might have taken part in events being recreated from either war would have become too senior in rank to have the time or inclination to serve as technical advisors.[52]

Under these circumstances, neither the Defense Department nor the Marines had any objection when One-Way Productions hired retired four-star general Samuel Jaskilka to serve as its technical advisor. Jaskilka, who had led a Marine rifle company during the Inchon landing, had only recently left the Corps after serving as assistant commandant. But with no official ties to the Pentagon, he received no briefing on the role that technical advisors are supposed to perform to ensure adherence to approved scripts. Nor did the Public Affairs Office provide him with a copy of the screenplay before he left for Korea in late June 1979. Consequently, Jaskilka had no way of knowing that the Defense Department had not approved the script the filmmakers were shooting.[53]

In his position, working for One-Way Productions, Jaskilka found himself spending most of his time helping arrange for support in shooting the combat sequence from the Korean military and from American forces stationed in Korea, primarily in the form of off-duty troops. He readily accepted Terence Young's explanation that as director, he was concerning himself primarily with making an exciting, entertainment film rather than a historically accurate documentary of the Inchon landing. In any event, General Jaskilka lacked the leverage to insist upon adherence to an approved script, under threat of stopping assistance, which active duty advisors have always had.[54]

By the time the Pentagon received a copy of the revised, final script, Young had completed most of the location shooting in Korea requiring DoD support, and the Marines did not have time to dispatch an official technical advisor to the Far East to ensure that the film would portray the service accurately. In any case, as late as September 1979, the Marines found the screenplay acceptable for further assistance; One-Way Productions, Ishii's company, had also agreed to include in the titles a disclaimer concerning variances with the historical record. On its part, the Navy refused to allow use of the cruiser *Albany* as MacArthur's command post until assured that the script contained reference to the real Navy man to differentiate him from the movie's fictional hero.[55]

Ultimately, the changes in the script "disappointed" Col. Herb Hart, the new Marine Corps director of public affairs, when he previewed *Inchon* with other Pentagon officials on February 20, 1981. Among other things, the film portrayed a fictionalized Marine lieutenant general, whom the Marine public information director described as coming "across as an irrelevant participant in the planning" and so "does an injustice to the significant and positive influence" of the actual Marine general who did contribute to the preparation for the Inchon landing. Consequently, the information director observed, "As this is the only time a Marine general speaks in the film, this shoddy treatment reflects poorly on the whole Marine Corps and its generals." In fact, after the screening for Pentagon officials in February, the DoD Public Affairs Office advised General Jaskilka that the Defense Department had no objections to the release of One Way Production's motion picture *Inchon* as long as it contained a disclaimer to the effect that although the film was based on historical fact, "certain sequences are fictionalized for dramatic purposes."[56]

By the time One-Way Productions staged the world premiere in Washington, however, military and historical accuracy was no longer an issue. After more than nine months of rumor and denial by Ishii and One-Way Productions, the producer finally acknowledged that he had received much of the financial backing for *Inchon* from Rev. Sun Myung Moon and his Unification Church. Because of the controversies surrounding the self-proclaimed evangelist and his church, a wave of protest focused attention on the Pentagon's involvement with One-Way Productions.

During the almost seventy years that the armed forces had been providing men, facilities, and equipment to filmmakers, the military had never raised questions about where producers obtained the financial backing for their projects. Although a foreigner was making a movie about a great American hero and one of his greatest victories, no one in the Pentagon questioned Ishii's background or resources. With the $18 million to $20 million budget for *Inchon* reportedly coming from his own interests in newspapers and hotels and from wealthy friends, Ishii had claimed he was making the movie as a result of a "spiritual experience" while visiting Seoul in 1972.[57]

Originally, Ishii told Robin Moore, the film's screenwriter, that he had wanted to make a movie about the life of Christ. When he approached Japanese movie producers, however, they told him to start with something else and work his way up. According to Ishii, the spiritual experience caused him to cry "without reason" for seven days, stopping only after he saw a Korean movie about the war. As a result, he decided he "wanted to make a film about the Korean War, but on an international basis."[58]

Ultimately, Ishii settled on the story of MacArthur's amphibious landing that halted the North Korean invasion into the South as the focus of his film. Ishii claimed he intended only to make "an entertaining action film." At the same time, he said he was "very interested in depicting MacArthur as a human being and I want the world to know how miserable the war was for the Korean people." In setting out his requirements for the film to the screenwriter, he told Moore he wanted to show General MacArthur's spiritualism and his belief in divine destiny, divine guidance, and divine inspiration. He also wanted three love stories in the movie, one between two Americans, one between two Koreans, and one between an American and a Korean. Moore said "the love stories were supposed to tell the story of the tragedy of Korea, the tragedy of the Korean War." At the same time, Ishii told the screenwriter he did not want the film to become an anti-Communist tract.[59]

Ishii's professed intent notwithstanding, North Korea promptly saw the project as a propaganda vehicle, even before Moore had completed an acceptable screenplay. According to the producer, the North Koreans worked through Japanese labor unions to pressure Toho Studio not to make *Inchon*. As a result, the studio pulled out of the project. In their protests, the labor unions claimed that the Korean CIA and Rev. Sun Myung Moon's Unification Church were behind the project in an attempt to glorify war and justify the government of the South Korean president, Park Hung Chee. On his part, Ishii continued to periodically deny any propaganda motives for *Inchon* and any financial involvement of Rev. Moon or the Unification Church in the production.[60]

Receiving over $5 million in salaries, the leading stars of the production, Laurence Olivier, Ben Gazzara, Jacqueline Bisset, and Richard Roundtree, said they were never told they were signing up for a movie that Sun Myung Moon was financing. Gazzara, who portrayed the central character as the protector of a lighthouse whose beacon would be indispensable for the night deployment of troops from the armada, told the *Boston Globe,* in an article appearing in its June 8, 1982 edition: "Up until the eighth week of filming neither the director, Terence Young, nor the cast knew we were in the employ of the Rev. Moon." Several crew members said they would not have worked on *Inchon* had they known Moon's involvement from the onset of the project, a fact about which they claimed Ishii personally misled them by repeatedly denying the backing of Moon or the Unification Church. Psychic Jeanne Dixon, one of Ishii's "spiritual advisers," said she also asked Ishii directly about Moon's involvement in the production shortly after the project was initiated in early 1978. In a telephone interview, Dixon said, "Ishii swore to me that there was not one dollar of Moon money in that film. It was represented to me as being *all* Ishii's money. I guess he lied to me, didn't he?" The director was also very bitter about the sloppy and biased editing of his film, complaining that "the producers have turned *Inchon* into a Korean propaganda movie."[61]

During preparations for the world premiere in Washington, D.C., Ishii finally acknowledged to General Jaskilka that he had turned to the Japanese Unification Church for financial support when the movie began to go over budget. Ultimately, *Inchon* was to cost a reported $46 million, more than such budget-busting movies as *Cleopatra* ($44 million), *Star Trek* ($42 million), and *Heaven's Gate* ($36.5 million). In any case, despite all the denials, Rev.

Laurence Olivier, as Gen. Douglas MacArthur, talks with Richard Roundtree, playing a Marine sergeant, during a break in the filming of *Inchon!*

Moon's connection to the project dated from the inception of the production, whether directly or indirectly.[62]

Ishii himself admitted to membership in the Japanese branch of the Unification Church but claimed he was a member, "just like a Catholic is a member of the Catholic Church and I believe Rev. Moon is very sincere about doing the Lord's work." Ishii had become more than a churchgoer, however, serving as president of Rev. Moon's paper, the *World Daily News*. Moreover, the name for his film company, One-Way Productions, came from Moon's doctrine of one way to God. Additional ties existed between the film and Rev. Moon. The film's associate producer, Robert Standard, for one, had become a leading American disciple of Rev. Moon.

Inchon featured the Little Angels, a Korean singing group that Moon had founded. Several of the Korean and Japanese crew members on the production acknowledged that they were Unification Church members. Moon himself became heavily involved, according to Ishii, in suggesting, editing, and reshooting changes in the script. The auditor of the production, Robert F. Kocourek, stated that the Moonie influence was "very definitely there on the making of the picture. The Japanese and Korean Unification Churches supplied lots of free labor and extras for background scenes."[63]

By the time the film had its world premiere at the Kennedy Center in Washington in May 1981, Rev. Moon's involvement with *Inchon* had become a matter of public record. The screen credits acknowledged him as "Special Advisor on Korean Matters." More than that, the press kit made clear Moon's influence on the film, with one of the releases entitled "The Korean War and Revelations." The release began with the story of how a B-29 bomber pilot flying a mission over North Korea took a photograph of "the face of Jesus Christ" appearing "amidst the bombers." The tract then observed, "While some called the occurrence a coincidence, many others agreed that it was only one of many incidences of God's guidance throughout General Douglas MacArthur's life."[64]

The essay continued in the same vein: "Jesus Christ has appeared at significant times throughout the 2,000 years of Christianity. It is common for Generals and those with the opportunity to change history, to receive guidance through revelation." The essay then cited examples throughout history of military leaders from Constantine through Lincoln and Churchill who received revelations and noted that General MacArthur had written in his *Reminiscences* that a revelation had initiated the Inchon operation. The tract claimed that MacArthur's "attempt to overcome communism was particularly significant, because the General embodied three qualities: love for God; love for mankind; and hatred for Communism."[65]

The release also described how MacArthur's image appeared in a photograph the movie's art director had taken of the door to the general's office in his Tokyo headquarters. According to the tract, MacArthur then came "in spirit" to a Korean psychic who had seen the photo. MacArthur told the psychic that he "was very happy to see this picture being made because it will express my heart during the Korean War." (It should be noted that General MacArthur had been dead almost fifteen years at the time of this conversation.) As a result, the general told the psychic, "I will make more than 100 percent effort to support the movie."[66]

As the man to play MacArthur in *Inchon*, Ishii selected Laurence Olivier. Unlike Gregory Peck, who played the general in *MacArthur* (1977), Olivier did at least look the age, and according to one reviewer, his portrayal became "excruciating yet morbidly fascinating." However, his characterization bears little resemblance to one of the most self-confident, egotistic military leaders of all time. Instead, reflecting the image Ishii and the Unification Church wanted to create, Olivier's MacArthur becomes a man who sits on his wife's bed confessing that he cannot sleep because of his concern over his age and ability to lead the United Nations forces. To find the strength to carry out his assignment, the general retreats to his own room and prays for God's divine guidance.[67]

Although this scene appeared in the original version, screened at the world premiere in Washington, it had not appeared in the print shown for Pentagon officials in February. Nor had Robin Moore written a bedroom scene into the screenplay that the Defense Department approved in January 1979. According to General Jaskilka, Terrence Young shot the sequences most overtly depicting MacArthur's spirituality in Ireland, where Olivier made his home, long after the principal shooting had been completed in Korea, Japan, and Italy.[68]

Acting performances aside, critics had a field day citing the technical gaffs in the film. In one scene, an editor spliced in footage of a digital watch not invented until twenty-five years after the Korean war. The filmmakers used cut-out cardboard aircraft in the key battle scenes, and according to critic Rex Reed, the viewer could "almost see the threads from which they were dangling." In his *Washington Post* review, Gary Arnold described Ben Gazzara as a Marine who was "meandering about" so much that "it's impossible to figure out what sort of Marine" he was.[69]

For the American military, and particularly the Marines, the problems with the film related less to the portrayal of MacArthur, the absurdities of the fictionalized story, the cliché-ridden dialogue, and the countless references to the power of God than to the matter of historical accuracy. The original script told its story within a framework that generally followed actual events, but the completed film bears only a loose connection to history. As they used dramatic license to change an individual's identity and actions, the filmmakers used historical license to rewrite events to serve their needs. In addition to the metamorphosed Marine hero and the reluctant Marine lieutenant general, the film gave the South Koreans a role in the assault on Inchon that the ROK Army did not have. As the Marine Corps public affairs director noted, this was "contrary to historical fact and also was not in the script seen at this headquarters." Consequently, he refused to permit any credit or acknowledgment of Marine assistance to *Inchon* and "strongly" recommended that the Pentagon do the same.[70]

Because the world premiere benefited the Carl Vinson Home for military widows and retired officers, the Marine Corps did ultimately permit its Drum and Bugle Corps to perform before the screening. But the Marine commandant and chief of naval operations did not attend the black-tie event because of the involvement of the Unification Church. The growing controversy also caused the Defense Department to decide to have reference to its cooperation removed from the titles. It advised One-Way Productions that "to avoid further misunderstandings on credits or DOD's relationship with the Unification Church, it is requested that screen credits for DOD and military assistance be deleted. We wish to reiterate the understanding that the public release of the film will not be used directly for fund-raising or church propaganda."[71]

The military did not stand alone in wanting to put distance between itself and the completed film. Senator Alphonse D'Amato (R-N.Y.), the listed chairman of the benefit, decided not to show up for the premiere after the New York newspapers played up the film's connection with the Unification Church. At first, he denied having known about the connection, but after the premiere, he told the *Washington Star* he had known about Rev. Moon's involvement all along. In addition, of the twelve members of Congress who allowed their names to be used as honorary members of the benefit committee and forty-eight other congressmen who accepted tickets for the screening, no more than fifteen or sixteen were willing to brave the pickets outside the Kennedy Center protesting the Unification Church and its involvement with the movie.[72]

The controversies aside, the Pentagon received very little for its support of the film. Like *The Great Santini*, which had more to do with a family than with the Marine Corps, *Inchon* had little to do with the Korean War, using it only as a framework in which to tell stories about people trying to survive in a hostile atmosphere. Perhaps the most accurate description of the film appeared in the disclaimer that opened the film: "This is not a documentary of the war in Korea, but a dramatized story of the effect of war on a group of people. All persons other than those whose real names are used in this film are fictitious and any similarity between them and any persons living or dead is purely coincidental. Where dramatic license has been deemed necessary, the authors have taken advantage of this license to dramatize the subject."

Fortunately for the Pentagon and the services that cooperated on *Inchon*, the cinematic people had little to recommend them. Their actions often became incomprehensible, and what combat the film portrayed lacked any believability or authenticity. As a result, the movie met with almost unanimous critical disdain. Even the reviewer in the Rev. Moon–owned *Washington Times* could find nothing nice to say about *Inchon:* "Puerile dialogue, perfunctory acting and haphazard construction doom from the start this visually impressive would-be epic about love and dead Reds in wartime Korea." The writer described Olivier's performance as the "nadir of his career" and said the script "is pure twaddle—a cross between *South Pacific* and *The Green Berets*."[73]

Faced with such adverse criticism and then the death of David Jansen, who had played a reporter covering the war, One Way Productions cut out the actor's role entirely and shorted the film by more than forty-five minutes. Nothing helped, not even General MacArthur's posthumous promise to promote the film, and few people ever saw *Inchon*. Given the film's distortions of military history and its absurd story, the U.S. armed services undoubtedly benefited from its unlamented disappearance. In any case, the Marines ended up with only one hit in its first four attempts to use its new negotiating approach to the film industry. Even *The Great Santini* required considerable patience before it reached the public. Despite critical acclaim, few people went to see the film in its initial release. Ultimately, BCP re-released the film the same month as it appeared on Home Box Office. With the captive audience of cable and good word of mouth, the film finally found receptive viewers and the Marines achieved their goal, a good story about the Corps, one that would help their recruiting. Perhaps more important, *The Great Santini* humanized the Marines and so helped the rebuilding of the service's image, which the Vietnam War had so savaged.

21 | The Navy's Search for Normalcy

UNLIKE THE MARINE CORPS AND THE ARMY, the Navy had not broken its relationship with the film industry during the Vietnam War. Instead, as it had done throughout the Cold War, the service continued to use motion pictures in its ongoing competition with the Air Force for appropriations to acquire nuclear weapons delivery systems. In contrast to long-range bombers and intercontinental ballistic missiles, which its sister service sought, the Navy wanted to acquire nuclear aircraft carriers and submarines. To this end, the service wanted to assist movies that portrayed the efficacy of its military hardware in order to sell its ships and planes to Congress and the nation. The service therefore saw cooperation with Hollywood as inexpensive lobbying, which regulations forbade them to pursue in traditional ways.

Filmmakers found the hardware visually impressive and the Navy more receptive to equipment-driven stories than people-oriented films, as it had demonstrated in refusing to cooperate with *The Last Detail, Cinderella Liberty,* and *The Great Santini.* After all, no record existed of a ship or plane leading a mutiny, deserting its post, or vomiting in front of officers' wives. In fact, the quality of the story or the completed movie counted for very little to the Navy if the filmmakers portrayed its ships or planes doing their jobs, as the poorly written, poorly acted *Midway* so well illustrated. The Navy did not even require live heroes celebrating their successful missions at fadeout. Both Charlton Heston and William Holden die in the closing frames, one in a fiery crash into a carrier and the other face down in a muddy ditch. If such images convey the downside of combat, *Midway* and *Bridges at Toko-Ri* did show aircraft carriers extending the range of the fleet. Although the service certainly appreciated the glorious victory that *Midway* provided, *Tora! Tora! Tora!* illustrated that it did not even matter to the Navy whose aircraft carriers had launched a successful airborne strike as long as the film demonstrated the value of carrier warfare.

As Darryl Zanuck had explained in comparing his *Wing and a Prayer* to *Destination Tokyo,* however, Hollywood found more drama inherent in submarine stories. Nevertheless, to create that suspense, filmmakers had to portray a failure of Navy systems and procedures, something the service would naturally not want to appear on the screen. As a result, the Public Affairs Office and most particularly submariners found problems in virtually all undersea stories filmmakers submitted to the Pentagon for assistance. With the original screenplay for the 1968 *Ice Station Zebra,* the service initially objected to some of the portrayals of characters, believing they provided an "unfair distortion of military life" and would "damage the reputation of the Navy and its personnel." This included the showing of a pornographic film aboard the submarine at sea. When the producer did not receive a response to his revised screenplay, MGM asked its Washington representative to inform the Navy that it intended to proceed with or without cooperation, ominously observing, "Without any assistance from the military, then naturally, anything can happen."[1]

Of course, nothing bad did happen. The Navy ultimately obtained a script with which it could live and provided a nuclear submarine and technical advice during production. The filmmakers shot for four days at the submarine base and aboard a nuclear submarine in San Diego. The director, John Sturgis, even mounted a camera on the USS *Ronquil* to obtain some underwater footage for the Cold War story about the race between the United States and the Soviet Union to recover secret spy satellite photographs from a Russian capsule that has landed near an Arctic research laboratory. Or something like that.[2]

On one hand, despite the virtually incomprehensible plot and resolution, the *Variety* reviewer, an old Navy man, thought the film contained "some excellent submarine interior footage, and good shots—if a bit repetitious in the end—of diving, surfacing and maneuvering under an ice field." He also found that "the procedural business and nomenclature rang true: not so stilted and artificial (and usually incorrect), as in many pix." He did find the potentially dramatic near-sinking of the submarine by a saboteur had "little feeling of disaster engendered; the depth indicator simply displays the increasing descent." In part, the problem lay with the dialogue itself, which included a sailor shouting, "She's slowing fast." On the other hand, the Navy received a documentary-like portrayal of nuclear submarine operations, a visual reminder of the dangers submariners face when they venture beneath the sea, and the positive image of Rock Hudson in the guise of a stalwart, competent captain.[3]

In the end, however, *Ice Station Zebra* never became more than a mundane Cold War film more reflective of the 1950s and early 1960s than the period in which it appeared, serenely oblivious of the real war being fought in Vietnam. Likewise, the screenplay "Event 1000," based on David Lavalle's novel of the same name, ignored the war. Nevertheless, the Navy looked on the story with very mixed feelings when it first arrived in the Navy Public Affairs Office in 1971. Like most peacetime submarine stories, beginning with *Submarine* and *Men without Women*, the drama came from an accident that sent the undersea craft to the bottom, where the survivors waited as rescuers raced against time to reach the men before the oxygen ran out. Despite such horrific images, the submarine service could also see the project as a perfect vehicle to feature its new rescue hardware developed since the sinking of the nuclear subs *Thresher* and *Scorpion* in the 1960s.

Reality suggested that an actual disaster might well take place in waters so deep that a submarine would be crushed before it hit bottom. However, if the Navy was going to recruit sailors for the all-volunteer submarine service, it had to show the men and their families that it had the means to rescue the crews before they asphyxiated, as the Navy had demonstrated with the McCann diving bell in *Submarine D-1*. Although this remained the rational for developing the Deep Submergible Rescue Vehicle (DSRV), post–Cold War researchers discovered another reason for the new hardware—using the minisubs to help tap Soviet undersea phone lines. Movies that showed the DSRVs as rescue craft would help mask the intended espionage use of the technology.[4]

In any case, the difficulties in transferring the story from the novel to the screen came not only from the Navy but also from the several filmmakers who waged their own war over the rights to, and then credit for, the final script. Beginning in the fall of 1971, Frank Rosenberg (then at Avco Embassy Pictures) and ABC Pictures made inquiries to the Pentagon about the prospects of the story's receiving Navy assistance. Although the service early on agreed to provide both research help and even a cruise aboard a nuclear submarine, the project was to follow a tortuous path before it received final approval and went into production.

The original scenario portrayed the plight of a U.S. nuclear submarine colliding with a foreign freighter off the eastern U.S. coast and sinking to a depth somewhat below the limits for the rescue equipment the Navy then had available. According to Bing Crosby Productions, which acquired the rights to the novel in early 1973 and hired Rosenberg to write and produce the film, the plot was to focus on "the actions and reactions of the survivors below and the rescue force above—with special emphasis on the commander of the rescue operation. We intend to depict the modern Navy, weaving into the film many of the recent innovations in the field of human relations and would hope that the finished product will be an incentive for naval recruiting."[5]

Not likely, given the images proposed. Not surprisingly, after some initial discussions, Rosenberg ran into a wall of silence from the submarine service in San Diego. After investigating the problem, Don Baruch discovered that the refusal to provide assistance "was just another way that the Sub people were making it difficult because the Admiral doesn't like the story." Ultimately, however, the writer-producer did complete and finally submit a script to Baruch's office on July 10, 1973. Although Baruch had requested a response from the Navy within two weeks, the submarine service did not answer until mid-August, when the service's Information Office discussed with Baruch the proposed memo that the chief of information was planning to send to Baruch's office.[6]

In the memo, the Navy said it could not recommend Pentagon assistance "based on the script as presently written." Nevertheless, it thought that with major modifications, the filmmakers might come up with a story that benefited the service: "The film could show the public the immense effort the Navy has expended in equipping submarines and in planning and developing rescue systems and salvage assets for a disabled submarine event. Further, the film should depict the tremendous reaction and marshaling of assets such a disaster would generate. It is believed this could be done without reducing the suspense or impact of the story." The memo then went on to enumerate the "inaccuracies and innuendoes which obviously would not enhance recruitment for the Navy and especially for the submarine service."[7]

Among other things, the service objected to the script's painting a picture of a Navy unprepared for such an emergency and apparently lacking much concern about the trapped men, resulting in the slow pace of the rescue effort. In addition, the script failed to show all the rescue and survival aids available to the submarine and to depict the massive search effort that the Navy would mount. Central to its unhappiness with the script was the portrayal of the trapped sailors: "The detail of the crew's plight inside the submarine may be designed to make the film interesting and perhaps macabrely fascinating to the audience. However, the psychological effect on many viewers could well be detrimental to submarine recruiting efforts." In particular, the Navy complained that the script contained a scene in which one of the submersible rescue crafts found in its floodlights the body of the captain, who had been trapped on the bridge; that nineteen men were to die in a fire after having been trapped on the bottom for a period of time; and that several men were to die of pulmonary problems. In the last instance, the Navy suggested that the "men's plight can be depicted without so many of them dying."[8]

When Don Baruch advised Rosenberg of the Navy's problems with the script, he agreed to make changes and scheduled a meeting with the Navy on August 21, 1973. Following the discussion in the Pentagon, Rosenberg sent the service a letter of understanding about the revisions he would make. Nevertheless, on September 18 the Navy advised Baruch that it did not recommend assistance to the production: "After extensive review of the script and subsequent memoranda, as well as taking into account the great amount of military assistance which would apparently be required, it has been determined that providing cooperation would not significantly benefit the Department of Defense as delineated [in the DoD instruction governing cooperation]." By then, however, Rosenberg had advised Baruch that BCP had decided to make the film without cooperation. In relaying the Navy's decision to the producer, Baruch acknowledged that he had "no obligation now to consider any of our story recommendations." Nevertheless, he did hope that Rosenberg would "retain the legend about the present day capability of the Navy to rescue personnel from submarines."[9]

In reality, given the need for the Navy's expertise and equipment to give the production authenticity and accuracy, Rosenberg had little chance to make the film without Pentagon support. He acknowledged as much when he wrote to Baruch in November 1974 to advise that BCP remained very much interested in "Event 1000" and asked that the Pentagon review the matter of cooperation. To encourage a reconsideration, Rosenberg "agreed to make reasonable changes in the screenplay in order to obtain the necessary assistance." He attempted to strengthen his case by saying that "Event 1000" could ultimately "be not only a fine motion picture but one that would be beneficial to the Navy."[10]

The producer-writer then listed seven reasons why the film would achieve this goal, including giving the Navy a "more visible profile and, thereby, give our citizens—and especially the new Congress—a sympathetic look at a modern Navy that many people are aware of in only the vaguest way." More specifically, the producer said the film would show "that at enormous cost, the Navy had developed a deep-water submergence vehicle that is capable of rescuing men at almost any depth." As a result, Rosenberg believed the completed movie would "encourage men to join a proud Navy and have pride in themselves as well."[11]

Despite such claims and the suggestion from Norm Hatch to the service that Rosenberg "should be given the opportunity to discuss with the Navy possible changes which could make the screenplay acceptable," the Navy remained unimpressed. In responding, the Office of Information advised Baruch: "The positive objectives that Mr. Rosenberg outlined in his letter do not alter the very thorough review given to this project by cognizant offices of the Navy upon which the Navy position was developed." Accordingly, the office said it remained reluctant to encourage the producer in any way "because we do not believe that the scope of revision required would be satisfactory to Mr. Rosenberg." Moreover, the Navy advised Baruch that since it could not "identify any basis for reconsideration at this time it is recommended that no further action be taken unless there is some new and substantial proposal" that would warrant further discussion. As a result of such intransigence, Baruch wrote the producer, "It is regrettable that a workable solution for continuing discussions has not materialized. It is apparent that the Navy feels most negatively about the story of 'Event 1000.'"[12]

Accepting reality, Rosenberg turned his full attention to a film biography of Gen. Richard Stillwell on which he had been working. However, refusing to die, "Event 1000" reappeared eleven months later when director Robert Aldrich submitted a script entitled "Gray Lady Down" to the Pentagon and requested assistance in its production. He admitted, "Neither the author, nor anyone in this company, pretends to know the technical nuances and procedures involved in our film. Because of this, we would welcome any and all suggestions and/or changes that relate to the practical feasibility of making an operation such as we envision more credible, more factual and more believable."[13]

In regard to the story, Aldrich observed, "There is inherent in this project an area of psychological and emotional conflict between a civilian and the Navy. Should the language used in the specific dramatization of these differences be considered too abrasive, we certainly would undertake revision of all such specific situations as pointed out to us, if such an effort on our part made the difference between winning Defense Department approval and/or having our project rejected." Nevertheless, the director candidly said that if the Navy demanded that the conflict between the men "be reduced to a point where it is not dramatically viable, we could not, in good conscience, undertake the manufacture of this material, because in our opinion a great deal of the excitement and motivation would have been reduced below an acceptable level." At the same time, he assured Baruch, "I will meet as many compromises of your Department, the Navy, and the Submarines as possible, as long as we all recognize there is a point beyond which those concerned can 'compromise' a movie out of being meaningful, entertaining and exciting."[14]

Despite a new title and minor changes, the Navy's response to *Gray Lady Down* differed little from its reaction to "Event 1000." In particular, the Navy Operations Office advised the Public Information Office that it objected to the technical quality of the script, which it found "extremely poor. . . . There is a total lack of understanding of how submarines and deep submergence vehicles operate, basic laws of physics, maritime law, chain of command and government structure. In addition to a lack of basic research by which the writer could have avoided myriad errors and misconceptions, the basic story is flawed to a point where filming it would be next to impossible." Given these shortcomings, the Navy felt that if the story ever reached the public, it "wouldn't do our recruiting effort any good. Incompetent reactions, ineffectual officers, bleating enlisted men and imagined 'dangers' such as gravity slides and the effects of a thermal layer are not required elements for a good submarine drama."[15]

Observing that submariners faced enough real dangers without manufacturing false ones, the memo's author expressed the concern that any submarine movie, "no matter how grim, seems to stimulate interest in the mystique of submarines." If such a portrayal created an audience for the film, the officer said they would see a story that "does not portray the Navy in a very favorable light. Our leadership may not always be characterized as enlightened, but the whole organization isn't quite that ineffectual and petty." Consequently, the Navy recommended that the project receive no military assistance.[16]

Don Baruch had another problem with the script, advising the Navy chief of information that the screenplay for *Gray Lady Down* appeared "virtually identical" to Rosenberg's "Event 1000." As a result, he said he anticipated that the Navy would "recommend unfavorable consideration" to the new script. Nevertheless, if the service felt the script had "some redeeming qualities," he said that his office believed it had "a moral obligation" to Rosenberg to give him another chance to develop a revised script "which might meet with your approval." Baruch informed the Navy that he had advised both Aldrich and Rosenberg of the apparent plagiarism and reported that the director said he would look into the similarities in the stories.[17]

The Pentagon, of course, had no interest in how Aldrich had come into possession of a script so similar to Rosenberg's "Event 1000." The principals in the matter would ultimately resolve the question among themselves during the production of the motion picture. From the Navy's perspective, only the contents of the screenplay itself figured in its decision whether to support the film. In that regard, the service advised Don Baruch on December 9, 1975, that it was recommending that the Pentagon provide no assistance to Aldrich because of the many inaccuracies in the portrayal of Navy procedures and operation of its equipment.[18]

Perhaps most important, the Navy pointed out that the script incorrectly claimed that its Deep Submersible Rescue Vehicle (DSRV) could not effect the rescue because the stricken submarine had come to rest at too great an angle. In fact, the Navy said it had tested the DSRV at a steeper angle. In any case, even if the filmmakers revised the script so that the angle actually did make the rescue impossible, the Navy still opposed the scenario: "A large amount of taxpayers' money has been devoted to developing rescue systems for submarines, and development is continuing. The Navy is opposed to supporting the production of a motion picture which emphasizes what the Navy *cannot* do, rather than what it can do."[19]

The Navy also found a number of other aspects of the script objectionable. These included the characterization of the submarine captain "as a parochial militarist, antagonistic towards civilians in general and the press in particular; drinking aboard the submarine; and firing across the bow of the civilian yacht." In addition, the service advised Baruch that it did not find it "feasible" to provide a complete listing of errors in the screenplay because of their very number.[20]

The Navy's reaction to the script, whatever its title or genesis, ended Aldrich's interest in making the film. But the story surfaced one more time a month later when Walter and Marvin Mirisch acquired the screenplay for their Mirisch Company, headquartered at Universal Studios. According to Marvin Mirisch, the William Morris Agency had brought in the script and, liking the basic story, the company had bought it from the writer through the agency.[21]

The Mirisch acquisition of the property immeasurably improved the prospects of its being made. The two brothers had a long relationship with the Department of Defense, going back to the early 1950s, when they had produced *Flat Top* and *The Annapolis Story*. More recently, they had made *Thousand Plane Raid* in 1969 and were then in the process of completing *Midway*. Working out of Universal Studios gave them additional leverage and credibility with the Pentagon, in contrast to Frank Rosenberg and particularly to Robert Aldrich, whose work included such antimilitary films as *Attack!* (1956), *The Dirty Dozen* (1967), and the anti-Vietnam *Twilight's Last Gleaming*, then in production.[22]

Recognizing that the script did contain inaccuracies and aspects that did not reflect Navy procedures, the Mirisches immediately requested through Universal's Washington representative, John Horton, the Navy's comments on the previous script. Consequently, on January 16, 1976, Baruch forwarded to Marshall Green, the Universal executive production manager, the Navy's December 1975 review of *Gray Lady Down*. However, he advised Green that he had informed both Aldrich and Rosenberg that if the Navy decided that an acceptable screenplay could be developed from the existing script, his office "considered there was a moral obligation" to give Rosenberg "the option of trying another approach to 'Event 1000' since the properties are so similar."[23]

Meanwhile, in Los Angeles, Marvin Mirisch had talked with Comdr. Bill Graves in the Navy's Information Office about getting together to discuss how to make the script technically correct and acceptable to the Navy. Graves, who had worked on the earlier versions of the script, concluded that "if anyone will make a submarine picture acceptable to the Navy, it will be Mirisch." However, when Baruch heard about the scheduled meeting, he called the Navy's Information Office to report what was happening, and the office agreed to advise Graves to cancel the conference. From Baruch's perspective, a "meeting with producer suggesting changes would be tacit indication the revised script would be approved."[24]

Despite Baruch's concern, Graves did meet with Mirisch on January 23, and he informed the producer that the Navy would not cooperate with the script as it stood. He suggested that the Mirisches look for another vehicle if they wanted to do a movie on submarines or deep-sea rescue. Nevertheless, Mirisch persisted, saying the company wanted to produce *Gray Lady Down*. In turn, without encouraging the producer, Graves offered to keep his door open if they needed technical information during the rewriting of the script. Marvin Mirisch later said that the company then set out to revise the script on the basis of the Navy's comments and its own judgment that some of the script contained too much melodrama. Among other changes, Jim Whittaker, the company's new screenwriter, took out the military-civilian clash and the involvement of a Soviet nuclear submarine in the rescue operation.[25]

The Mirisch Company's acquisition of the script and the company's clear intention to produce a script that would meet Navy objections had an immediate impact on the prospects for the service's providing support to the production. On January 28, John Horton advised Don Baruch that the Navy's Information Office was now saying that the service would not rule out accepting a feature film project in which a nuclear submarine has an accident. In his memo for the record, Baruch observed: "This is contrary to the 'party line' I had been told earlier." In confirming the change the next day, Baruch learned that the Navy had advised Universal it would review a revised script if the filmmakers would delete such objectionable items, including the Russian participation in the rescue and the loss of the submarine's captain. In turn, Baruch called Frank Rosenberg to advise him of the Navy's new position and affirm that the Pentagon would consider a rewrite of his screenplay "if he wanted to cut out those same elements in his project." Although the producer no longer expressed an interest in the project, Baruch told him and Universal that neither one would have an exclusive right to a story about the nuclear submarine disaster.[26]

Although Rosenberg had given up on making his submarine film, he did begin legal action seeking remedies for the loss of his story. Ultimately, he received suitable remuneration and a screen credit for his adaptation of the novel. Before this came to pass, the Mirisches had to face a Navy that remained unenthusiastic about the project. In fact, when the company sent Whittaker's first effort to the Navy in April 1976, it met the same fate as had Rosenberg's and Aldrich's scripts.

After reading the new version, the office found that it remained "essentially the same script" that the Navy had turned down in December 1975. Consequently, the reviewing officer advised Adm. David Cooney, the new chief of information, that the screenplay "must be disapproved. The only decision we have to make is whether or not to encourage another major rewrite. (I recommend against any further encouragement.) It is a compelling drama, but I have searched in vain for any justification for cooperation. I can find nothing positive about the Navy throughout this script." Beyond that, the officer observed that despite technical advice of a submariner, the writer "continues to show a complete lack of understanding of submarines. He continues all previous errors in terminology, ship types, and other details covered by the numerous and specific notations we made in the first draft."[27]

Meanwhile, back in California, the filmmakers continued their research. Bill Gray, assigned to the project as production manager after his work on *Midway*, advised Bill Graves that the Mirisches were having second thoughts about making the movie. In addition to the concern Universal had about the amount of money needed to do the film right, the studio worried about the possibility of an expensive settlement with Rosenberg. These potential problems would become moot if the Mirisches could not persuade the Navy to change its position on the story, and Admiral Cooney's letter to Walter Mirisch on May 25 did not paint a positive picture.[28]

In writing to the producer, Cooney said he was "disappointed to find that the basis of many of the Navy's original objections still exists in the script." He dissected the story's springboard, pointing out that "there is no logical reason for the submarine to surface in the middle of the night so far out to sea, and the circumstances surrounding the actual collision are most unlikely. These events are a preamble to further scenes in the script which either give a false impression of some aspect of naval service or highlight possible hazards of serving in a submarine." In regard to the manner in which the script made rescue "nearly impossible" and the use of an explosive charge to upright the submarine, Cooney observed that the portrayal remained "so unrealistic that it does nothing to counteract, in the minds of the audience, the hazard of an impossible rescue situation. The possibility of a sinking with no chance of escape will seem realistic to the audience, but the final escape sequence of events will not."[29]

He also objected to other parts of the script, "which will do harm to the Navy. The bickering between the two key naval officers throughout the rescue attempt certainly does the Navy no good, and it is totally unrealistic. Nor does having whiskey aboard the submarine, which is also unrealistic." In addition, Cooney cited the script's many technical inconsistencies and concluded that "there is much that must be done to the basic script before the Navy can lend its assistance in production." Although he said that his staff would continue to provide technical advice, he expressed the concern that "a basic rewrite will not solve the problem."[30]

Cooney's letter apparently inspired the company. On June 15 Bill Graves wrote to the chief of information: "'Gray Lady' is giving one last try. A very significant rewrite of the entire story will be in your office by Thursday." He also reported that he had been working on a daily basis with Marvin Mirisch and the screenwriter, and that their work had included calls to submariners to obtain technical advice. As a result of the combined efforts, Graves said the new story would have no incompetence or failures by Navy personnel, no Navy equipment failure, and no accidental loss of life or injury to the submarine's crew as a result of the sinking. He also promised, "No panic, no fires, no illegal liquor, no sailors stumbling over each other, no yelling, no crying—just officers and men reacting as they have been trained." The filmmakers had also agreed to delete the use of explosives to right

To help obtain Navy cooperation for *Gray Lady Down,* the filmmakers agreed to highlight the capabilities of the Navy's DSRV.

the submarine, tone down the conflict between the two officers, and most important, demonstrate the unique capabilities of the DSRV.[31]

Graves now believed that the point of drastic change by the company had passed: "However, I think we have a workable script, assuming the basic premise of the sunken submarine and the problems encountered in its rescue are not on automatic stop." In any case, Graves concluded that many "sunken submarine stories" were making the rounds in Hollywood and that sooner or later, someone would make one: "If there is to be such a submarine story, I would certainly rather do it with Mirisch and Universal than anyone else in Hollywood. They are known entities, with whom I have some influence."[32]

Finally, on July 2, John Horton forwarded to Don Baruch a copy of the revised script for *Gray Lady Down*. After reading it, the assistant deputy chief of naval operations (submarine warfare) wrote to Admiral Cooney, "The script overall is very pro-Navy." He did note that some technical inaccuracies remained, which he did not consider significant but which he felt detracted from "the realistic flavor that the author attempts to portray." In addition to offering suggested corrections, he noted, "Despite the many improbabilities, am sure my kids would enjoy the show and OP-02 sees no reason why the Navy shouldn't support."[33]

In helping the Mirisches reach this point, Bill Graves had acted in much the way the Marines had done in their negotiations on *Born on the Fourth of July, The Great Santini,* and *Rumor of War.* If Hollywood was going to make a movie about a submarine disaster, the Navy had more to gain by supporting the production than by ignoring it, even though the service might have serious reservations about the nature of the portrayal. In any event, with the submarine service's opinion in hand, the Navy completed its review of the script, and on July 16 Admiral Cooney advised Don Baruch that the service would agree to cooperate with Walter Mirisch and Universal Pictures in the making of *Gray Lady Down,* provided the filmmakers would accept additional revisions to the June 15 script and agree that "any differences encountered in portraying the U.S. Navy will be resolved by the on-scene technical advisor or Navy Information Office representative."[34]

In return for agreeing to make the requested changes in the script and agreeing to a technical advisor's overseeing the production, the Mirisch Company received use of a nuclear submarine, a submersible, Navy rescue ships, other equipment, and sailors to serve as extras. Without such help, no filmmaker could have created a submarine movie with the authentic ambience that filled *Gray Lady Down.* Nevertheless, the question remains whether the effort expended to obtain a screenplay that satisfied both parties to the relationship, in the end, created a film that benefited either side.

From the Navy's perspective, any deviation from the norm aboard a submarine—a collision or a sinking, a personality conflict among the officers that interferes with operations, the launch of a nuclear strike—is an aberration. In an ideal world, of course, the Navy would prefer that any movie about its nuclear submarine fleet detail only a typical uneventful six-month cruise. The dearth of such movies suggests the almost insurmountable challenge to a screenwriter trying to create drama out of the mundane. In actually attempting to come up with just such a story for a made-for-television movie, producer Peter Greenberg went to Hawaii with his screenwriter in June 1983 to research life aboard a submarine. Saying he did not want to make the typical disaster story, he suggested to Mel Sundin, a Navy public affairs officer at Pearl Harbor, that he make the ship's captain a pacifist or the executive officer a homosexual, or both. The filmmakers got a ride aboard a nuclear sub, but they never did make their movie.[35]

In contrast, the producers of *The Fifth Missile,* based on the novel *The Gold Crew,* were able to sell the far-fetched melodrama to NBC television. The film told a story of strange happenings aboard a Trident-class submarine: a toxin contained in the paint used in a refit of the ship causes an adverse reaction among the crew and almost triggers a nuclear strike. David Soul, who played the submarine's captain, said his character's strength became his weakness during the crisis: "Therein was his frailty. When the going got tough on this ship, his malleability, his humanness was tested and he cracked. He's sort of like Capt. Queeg." Suffice it to say that the Navy turned down the request for cooperation, and the producers had to make a reproduction of the topside of a Trident and use an Italian navy base at Taranto as a setting.[36]

Clearly, the images in *Gray Lady Down* validated the early concerns the Navy had expressed about supporting a submarine disaster movie. Although the film did give the Navy the opportunity to demonstrate its submarine rescue equipment, the service could not avoid the reality that it had to call upon the DSRV and the supporting flotilla because one of its ships was resting on the ocean bottom. All the creative finessing of dialogue and actions could not disguise the fact that a U.S. submarine had collided with another ship on the open sea. Collisions do happen, and ships do sink or run aground despite having the most technologically advanced guidance systems. Ironically, as Charles Champlin observed in his review of *Gray Lady Down*, the disaster may have resulted from the failure to use such systems: "One sharp-eyed science major in the crowd noted with alarm that the navigator was calculating the position with a *slide rule*. Everyone knows that slide rule companies are going bankrupt right and left, left behind by the new pocket calculators of which every schoolchild has one. (The year of the accident is not clear; maybe it was BC.)"[37]

Whatever the reason, of course, accidents by their very definition occur for inexplicable reasons. But assisting on a movie that used such an event as the springboard to the story could not provide benefit or serve the best interest of the Navy. The Mirisches undoubtedly empathized with the Navy's position, but they faced the same situation with which Max Youngstein had had to deal in negotiating with the Air Force for assistance to make *Fail Safe*. If he accepted the service's contention that the U.S. Fail Safe system remained infallible, then he had no movie. Likewise, the Mirisches could not make a disaster movie without a disaster. However much the Navy tried to limit the visualization of the death of its men, the graphically depicted drowning of the submarine's executive officer and the loss of most of the crew, despite heroic rescue efforts, remained essential to the drama and so to any box-office success the film might enjoy.

Moreover, despite his best efforts, Bill Graves, who served as the technical consultant to *Gray Lady Down* during the actual filming, could not tone down the dramatic conflict

Graphic loss of life remained essential to the drama and box-office success of *Gray Lady Down*.

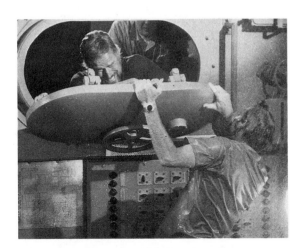

between the submarine's captain and his executive officer, the portrayal to which the Navy had always objected. Script changes notwithstanding, the film also visualized the bitter disagreement between the senior officers conducting the rescue operation. Worse, the argument took place in full view of the crew aboard one of the rescue ships. Differences of opinion do occur between honorable people, especially during times of crisis. But to the Navy, officers should not disagree in public, in front of enlisted men, and certainly not on a motion picture screen.[38]

In the end, the Navy's ultimate decision to support *Gray Lady Down,* which explicitly traced the grim disaster from crisis to crisis, probably provided no benefit to the service. Supporting the production may not even have served its best interest. If the film did show the Navy's ability to rescue its men from a disaster in which it had some culpability, *Gray Lady Down* did little to improve the submarine service's image so carefully burnished in such World War II classics as *Destination Tokyo* and *Run Silent, Run Deep.*

At the same time, from a cinematic perspective, *Gray Lady Down* itself added little to the submarine film genre or its cousin, the underwater exploration and rescue genre. In fact, the plot differed little from that of *Airport 77,* which the Navy also supported in a further effort to demonstrate its underwater rescue equipment. In this instance, however, the implausibility of the rescue of passengers aboard a 747 jetliner, which somehow managed to remain intact after crashing into the ocean, probably negated whatever value the Navy hoped to gain.

A race against time to save trapped people, whether in a coal mine cave-in, in a space ship marooned in orbit, atop a burning skyscraper, in a capsized ocean liner, or in a nuclear submarine, has drama inherent in its denouement. Whether that drama becomes gripping or merely diverting when brought to the screen depends on the quality of the screenplay and the ability of the director and the actors to create a buildup of tension within the audience. Director David Greene did impart "a crisp professionalism" to *Gray Lady Down.* Nevertheless, the story remains so predictable that if the film moved the audience in any way, it probably only caused them to move their lips to predict the next bit of action or mouth the next line.[39]

Certainly, a sunken submarine provided a more authentic setting than a submerged 747 jetliner in which to feature the Navy's underwater hardware. Unfortunately, the actor crew of the disintegrating submarine craft seemed to take its cue from the film's star, Charlton Heston, who impersonated the ship's captain with the same "agreeable stalwartness" he had brought to the officer role in *Midway.* As a result, although they were facing a horrible death, the sailors seemed to have a "job-oriented" air about them throughout the rescue operation. Richard Schickel, for one, wrote in his *Time* review, the film's "only queasy moments occur when, for dramatic punctuation, someone is required to crack under pressure. For the most part, however, a tight rein is kept on emotion and lips are kept well stiffened against adversity."[40]

This lack of dramatic tensions inspired *Washington Post* reviewer Gary Arnold to observe: "*Gray Lady Down* is by no stretch of the imagination an exemplary suspense thriller, submarine division. At best it's a tolerable exercise in stalwart hokum, a cliche snack that won't provide much nourishment but won't back up on you either. Presentably negligible may be the best term for it." Such praise does little to stimulate the interest of people to see a film. As a result, *Gray Lady Down* probably did little to further one of the Navy's goals in providing assistance to filmmakers, the encouragement of its men to reenlist. Arnold further observed: "Far be it from the landlubber like me to point out the obvious, but if any movie provokes merriment among U.S. Navy personnel, it is likely to be *Gray Lady Down*."[41]

No one in Hollywood starts a movie project with the expectation that it will receive such negative comments. If filmmakers could judge the quality of their completed work from a screenplay, the motion picture industry would probably have fewer box-office failures. Likewise, the public affairs officers of the individual services have no way of telling how a movie will turn out from the script they approve. Certainly the Navy had little to gain from supporting a movie that might cause laughter among its own men and disinterest from moviegoers. However, the Pentagon does not include dramatic quality or audience appeal among its criteria for determining whether a screenplay qualifies for support. Neither do the services usually allow a bad experience with Hollywood to influence decisions on subsequent requests for assistance from studios or independent producers. Each project that comes into the Pentagon receives the same scrutiny in an effort to answer the one relevant question: will the proposed film in some way benefit the services providing assistance?

Using this guideline, Don Baruch concluded, after reading the initial script of *Raise the Titanic*, which arrived in the Pentagon in June 1977, that the Navy did not have anything to gain from supporting the production: "Gives Navy a repeat on *Airport '77*—entertaining clap trap of no great significance!! Questionable value, personally see no reason for Navy wanting to do it. . . ." Bob Manning, Baruch's counterpart in the Navy's Office of Information, agreed and recommended to the chief of information that the service provide no assistance. Their judgments might well have ended the Pentagon's consideration of the project if the script had recounted the raising of a "generic" ship or if Robert Ballard had already made his discovery of the *Titanic*. But, just as the *Titanic* has developed a mythic personality, *Raise the Titanic* acquired a life of its own, which enabled the production to survive a change in directors, at least $15 million in preproduction costs, the need to find a ship to double for the *Titanic*, reservations by the Navy, and strong objections from the State Department before filming finally began in October 1979.[42]

Ballard's 1986 location of the *Titanic* resting in pieces on the ocean floor made any stories about raising the ocean liner implausible in the same way that Apollo 11 rendered obsolete all prior fictional accounts of the first landing on the moon. However, at the time Clive Cussler's *Raise the Titanic* appeared in 1976, people could still suspend their disbelief sufficiently to make the novel a best-seller. Its success prompted two filmmakers from Marble Arch Productions, Martin Starger and his partner Lord Lew Grade, to purchase the film rights for $450,000. And despite Manning's recommendation, the Navy saw the production as offering still another chance to show the capabilities of its underwater exploration and rescue equipment.

During the two years it took four writers to fashion a final screenplay, Marble Arch regularly sent the Navy each new version of the script. The service responded with its comments, intended to produce an acceptable story. On October 12, 1978, Bill Graves advised Marble Arch that Admiral Cooney had found "a large number of technical inaccuracies" in the script that depicted the service in ways that "are not consistent with current or even possible Navy operations and missions. For Navy cooperation, the story must portray Navy operations as they are currently executed or would be executed should the requirement exist." The message from Graves advised the company that the Navy would deny a request for support, as the screenplay was currently written.[43]

The next May, Admiral Cooney met with Jerry Jameson, who had replaced Stanley

Kramer as the film's director, and discussed two "very substantive changes" that the Navy said Marble Arch *must* make before the service would consider supporting the project. Afterward, the Office of Information informed Don Baruch: "The Navy cannot assist unless the script is changed to remove that portion that indicates the U.S. Navy might have a high seas involvement with the Soviet Navy, and second, that section where the Navy officer is trespassing on Soviet soil without the knowledge of the Russian Government." In addition to obtaining an agreement from Jameson to have those sections rewritten, the office said that Cooney had made "numerous minor comments and requests for change," and Bill Graves was working on them with the production company.[44]

The company incorporated this effort into the August 27, 1979, script that Marble Arch submitted to the Navy for approval. In asking the service, on October 2, for its position on the new version, Don Baruch advised the Office of Information that his office and the Department of State were also reviewing the screenplay. In response, the Navy advised Baruch on October 15 that it "interposes no objection to the subject screenplay as presently written" and so was undertaking efforts to provide the assistance that the company had requested.[45]

Two days later, however, George Bader, the deputy director of European and NATO affairs in the office of the Defense Department's International Security Affairs, writing for the assistant secretary of defense for international security affairs, James Siena, informed Baruch that his office supported the State Department's "concern about the 'Cold War' aspects of the screenplay." He felt that it neither met "the established criteria or is the type of motion picture which the Defense Department should be supporting. While our relationship with the Soviet Union does have aspects of confrontation, as well as cooperation, we find nothing to be gained by highlighting these on the public screen, in fictional circumstances, with the full support of the Defense Department." Moreover, Bader said the story "has no relationship to any true historical event, and we find it far-fetched and unrealistic." In particular, the secretary objected to the U.S. trespassing on Soviet soil and an American agent shooting a Soviet soldier carrying out his duty, the portrayal of which would "play into the hands of current Soviet propaganda that it is US policies which are provocative and 'militaristic,' while Soviet policies are 'peaceloving' and truly supportive of detente."[46]

In sending the memorandum to the Navy on October 19, Baruch informed the Office of Information that the State Department had advised him verbally that it believed the showing of official participation in Cold War activities would be counterproductive to the best interests of the United States. Consequently, he asked the Navy to comment on Siena's memo and to indicate whether it would cause the service to require additional script revisions before *Raise the Titanic* could receive Pentagon support. In responding on October 22, the Navy advised Baruch that Admiral Cooney had offered the film company solutions to the problem areas that the State Department and the Defense Department had cited but that Marble Arch had not incorporated them into the final screenplay. Nevertheless, the service repeated its October 15 position that it had "no objections to the screenplay. This position was not intended to be construed as embracing aspects of the screenplay which are beyond Navy purview and over which other departments might have objection." At the same time, the Navy stated that it had made clear to Marble Arch that Navy acceptance of the script did not represent final Pentagon approval, that some additional changes might be necessary to make the screenplay acceptable to the Defense and State Departments.[47]

The next day, Baruch asked the State Department's Bureau of Public Affairs to put in writing "as expeditiously as possible" its earlier phone comments about *Raise the Titanic.*

He also reported that John Horton, on behalf of Marble Arch, had indicated that the company might make some changes in the early sequences of the movie, which involved American agents trespassing on Russian soil. Nevertheless, Baruch stated that Horton did not believe the filmmakers would consider altering the friction or the clash between the Russians and the Americans on board the *Titanic* after it had been raised.[48]

On October 24 Paul Auerswald, the director of the State Department's Office of Public Communication, sent Baruch the reaction of the department's Bureau of European Affairs to the *Raise the Titanic* script. Auerswald stressed that the "strictly advisory opinion should not be used to portray the State Department as obstructing DOD cooperation." Nevertheless, he proceeded to obfuscate the State Department's position in order to avoid becoming a party to the Pentagon's ultimate decision: "If, as we understand, production has already begun and substantial sums have been spent in anticipation of DOD cooperation, then clearly it is up to the Defense Department to determine the nature and extent of its own commitments and to decide whether this script, as written or amended as the producers propose, can satisfy your own criteria for cooperation." He suggested that Baruch contact the Pentagon's Internal Security Affairs Office if he had "any further questions about the foreign policy implications of the script," and that office could then contact the State Department "if they believe it is necessary." Auerswald concluded with the recommendation that Baruch follow this procedure "for all scripts you receive in the future, well in advance of production."[49]

The Bureau of European Affairs offered its judgment that "there are aspects of the film which could have an adverse affect on US-Soviet relations, if the Department of Defense made its resources available to support the filming, due to the manner in which the US-Soviet confrontation is depicted in the film." Stating that the Pentagon "must make" the decision whether to support the production, the bureau acknowledged, "We believe any adverse consequences given DOD cooperation in the present circumstances would in no way be serious enough to permanently damage our national interests or the US-Soviet bilateral relationship." The bureau closed with the gratuitous advice that "the film as projected seems to meet none of the DOD policy requirements" for assistance as spelled out in Pentagon guidelines. To the State Department, this reality "strikes us as being more important in the consideration of DOD support than concern about the 'Cold War' aspects of the film."[50]

After reading this correspondence, George Bader advised Baruch on October 29 that the International Security Affairs Office continued "to believe that, as written, the film is not particularly helpful to our national interest." However, he said his office would defer to the State Department's conclusion that the film would do no permanent damage to U.S. national interests or U.S.-Soviet bilateral relations. Noting that Marble Arch had agreed to accept changes in the most objectionable scene in the film, the shooting of a Russian soldier by an American agent, Bader further requested that Cold War confrontational aspects be held to a minimum and that "neither side actually be shown to bring weapons to bear." He then left it up to the Public Affairs Office "to determine whether the film meets the established DoD criteria for authenticity and dignity and whether previous DoD commitments and recruitment and publicity benefits to the Navy warrant Defense Department Assistance."[51]

Responding to the Navy's memos of October 15 and 22, as well as Bader's memo, Baruch called the Navy Office of Information on the twenty-ninth and followed that conversation up with a formal memo on the thirty-first, to inform the service that his office would approve the *Raise the Titanic* screenplay containing the changes that Marble Arch had promised to make. He asked the Navy to advise him on the actual assistance it would be able to render so that he could officially notify the company of the decision. He also asked the Navy to provide him with "supportive statements" to confirm its stated belief that it considered the project beneficial "by showing positive action, characters and displaying modern equipment in a realistic way in a fictional situation" and that "the film indirectly will benefit recruiting." Complying with the request the same day, the Navy recommended that DoD approve cooperation: "The Navy position is that providing assistance is warranted and will aid in recruiting efforts by showing the public the sophisticated equipment used by the Navy to explore the ocean depths and give some insight on expertise required for undersea salvage work."[52]

In fact, Marble Arch still did not have a done deal with the Defense Department or the Navy. Responding to the list of assistance the Navy planned to give to *Raise the Titanic*, Baruch advised the service on November 13 that authorization was granted only for filming two scenes in Washington. He explained that the film company had not yet incorporated all the requested changes into the script. Consequently, he said that unless the final version "made it clear that the so-called island 'Off Russia' is one that is under international dispute and therefore no nation has sovereignty over it, further assistance will not be approved." He also cited other "mandatory" changes, including the addition of dialogue to explain that the Soviet soldier whom an American civilian shoots has no right to be on the disputed island as a military policeman.[53]

Without full Navy support, including a flotilla of salvage vessels and a submersible, Marble Arch had no way to make *Raise the Titanic*. Consequently, on November 16 the company delivered to the Pentagon virtually all the script changes Baruch's office had demanded, and on the nineteenth Baruch called John Horton to advise him that the Defense Department had approved the script for assistance. He specifically reminded Horton that the Navy was giving support "on a non-interference and no-additional cost to the government basis." He also reiterated the DoD requirement "which you are familiar with" that the company give a screening of the completed film in Washington to Navy and Public Affairs representatives. In addition, Baruch informed Horton that neither the Defense Department nor the Navy desired an acknowledgment of military assistance "in this instance" but did not object to giving a screen credit to the Navy technical advisor if Marble Arch wished to include it.[54]

Despite the long and delicate negotiations that led to the script approval and the Navy's wide-ranging support, the completed movie became a $35 million disaster for Marble Arch and another disappointment to the service. Although the project started with an exciting novel, which culminated in the raising of the *Titanic*, the completed motion picture managed to wring out all dramatic tensions existing in the story. Becoming enamored with the naval hardware and the special-effects miniatures, the filmmakers failed to develop the characters. Instead, they became cardboard figures, mouthing comic book dialogue, while playing second fiddle to the *Titanic*. A potentially interesting love triangle among the civilian scientist, the retired Navy intelligence officer heading the salvage operation, and a beautiful journalist disappeared on the cutting-room floor. Only when the scientist disdainfully observes, after the ship has come to the surface, "We are on a ship that never learned how to do anything but sink," does the dialogue emit a semblance of wit. As a result, the visualization of the underwater salvage efforts cannot sustain the excitement inherent in the story, and the film becomes a pseudo-documentary study of naval salvage techniques. Only the actual raising of the luxury liner, created using a model and reinforced with a haunting musical theme, is artistically stimulating.

Ironically, by focusing on the hardware, *Raise the Titanic* diminished the human and political elements—particularly the confrontations between the United States and the Soviet Union that had concerned the Navy and the State Department. The race in the original script between the superpowers to recover a rare mineral needed to create a Star Wars–like defense or the most powerful bomb ever built became incidental to the underseas salvage operation. However, with the Cold War aspect of the story diminished, the film's climax accentuated the idea that the United States might well intend to use the mineral to built a bomb, not a defense system, and Admiral Cooney believed the Navy should not support a project that suggested duplicity on the part of the government.

From the service's perspective, *Raise the Titanic* did show its considerable underwater salvage equipment to full advantage, and the scenes of the flotilla at work provided strong visual images of the service's men and capabilities. However, any benefit that the film provided the Navy diminished in its eyes when Marble Arch failed to honor its apparent commitment to use the ending Admiral Cooney had written in hopes of eliminating the negative implication about the morality of the U.S. government. Although such agreements have no legal weight, producers have usually honored promises they make on the contents of scripts reached through negotiations with the armed forces. The Pentagon has little leverage to enforce agreements except to threaten the withdrawal of support if the film is still in production or possibly withholding assistance on a future project. However, on those few occasions when filmmakers have incorporated unapproved revisions into their completed movies, they have had sufficient resources to ignore adverse military reactions.[55]

With *Raise the Titanic,* Admiral Cooney, the chief of information, had had problems with the ending throughout the long negotiations. Instead of finding the rare mineral needed to fuel a nationwide missile defense system, the American salvage crew discover once the liner surfaces that the crates in the hold contain only gravel. Jason Robards, as the retired admiral in charge of the whole operation, tries to alleviate the disappointment of the scientist by telling him, "Look, if it will make you feel any better, I'll tell you something I didn't want to admit even to myself. If we had found the Byzanium, I'm not sure we could have hung onto it. I don't think we could have tagged it for defense only and made it stick." In response to the scientist's rejoinder that they had the president's assurance, Robards says, "That's right. But, presidents don't stay in office forever. And even if they did, circumstances change."

The scientist still does not comprehend. Robards continues, "If a government falls in the Middle East somewhere or if they start bombing Pakistan or somewhere else, it affects all of us. . . . I am just saying that somewhere in the world, in some think tank, right now, they're figuring out a way to build a Byzanium bomb." Explaining why he would go along with the whole operation believing that, Robards rationalizes, "I believed in what we were trying to do. And if it didn't work defensively, if somebody *was* going to make a Byzanium bomb, I wanted it to be us." He then walks away, leaving the scientist self-righteously to claim that he would not have started the project in the first place.

In the original script, as in the book, the intelligence officer figures out where the Byzanium had actually been hidden, and the heroes track down the mineral to a seaside English cemetery. There, the scientist finally acknowledges the intelligence officer's cynicism that the bad guys "have us outnumbered" and, by implication, that the American government cannot be trusted to use the mineral only for defensive purposes. United in their disillusionment, the two men walk away from the grave site in agreement to keep their discovery from the world.

To Cooney, who had liked the book and Cussler's ending, in which the United States does build an antimissile shield, the cinematic conclusion cast aspersions on military integrity and U.S. leadership and so would negate any benefit the film might offer in portraying the service's underwater capabilities. As a result of discussions with the chief of information, the movie's producers agreed, at least as far as Cooney was concerned, to use the ending that he had written. In it, the heroes find that the crash of a World War II German bomber had obliterated the cemetery, which the town had replaced with a playground and a memorial plaque.[56]

The producer did not take the completed movie to the Pentagon for the required prerelease screening. As a result, the Navy chief of information discovered that the filmmakers had not used his ending only when he requested a preview while in Los Angeles on other business. No Marble Arch representative attended the showing, and Cooney did not learn that the producer had had no intention of shooting the revised conclusion until the company responded to Don Baruch's inquiry after the film had premiered. Then Richard O'Connor, Marble Arch's executive in charge of production, explained that the company had understood that Cooney's revisions "were to be taken as suggestions." He said that the admiral's ending "was seriously taken into consideration even to the extent of writing the scene to the Admiral's specifications." Beyond that, when the scene was sent to Baruch's office, O'Connor said that it was "the intended ending to our picture."[57]

The filmmaker said, however, that during production "it was decided that the ending as originally written by Adam Kennedy was creatively the better ending, and that was the scene eventually filmed." O'Connor acknowledged that it was "unfortunate that [producer] Bill Frye apparently neglected to notify Admiral Cooney and you of this change but because of his many responsibilities during filming, I can understand this oversight." Likewise, he said that he was "not aware" of any request for a Pentagon screening prior to the release of the film. In reality, given the clearly stated requirement and Don Baruch's reminder to John Horton, a veteran film company liaison with the Pentagon, the professed ignorance has little credibility and suggests that the filmmakers knew they would have a serious problem if they screened the movie in the Pentagon before its premiere.[58]

In any case, Admiral Cooney need not have worried about the possible impact that the ending of *Raise the Titanic* might have had on audiences, since few people went to see it. Made at a cost of at least $35 million, the movie returned only $6.8 million to Universal Studios. Clive Cussler, for one, observed, "The movie was so poor, it boggles the mind." According to *Daily Variety,* which bends over backward to support Hollywood's product, *Raise the Titanic* "hits new depths hitherto unexplored by the worst of Lew Grade's overloaded Ark melodramas. This one wastes a potentially intriguing premise with dull scripting, a lackluster cast, laughably phony trick works, and clunky direction that makes *Voyage of the Damned* seem inspired by comparison." In a similar vein, Judy Maslin, in the *New York Times,* answered her own question: "Take the adventure out of an adventure movie, and what have you got? A lot of hearty he-men, barking commands or insults and offering terse congratulations on a job well done." Unfortunately for Marble Arch, she concluded that it had not done *Raise the Titanic* very well: "The glistening, quivering air bubbles that burst out of the ship should be readily familiar to anyone who's ever broken a thermometer. They look just like globs of mercury, and there's no mistaking the miniature TITANIC for anything truly ship-sized. Nor will anyone imagine, in the process shots near the film's ending, that a real, rusting ocean liner has actually made its appearance in New York harbor."[59]

People will accept movie magic when they can suspend their disbelief and empathize with the characters involved in telling a plausible story. Before Robert Ballard found the *Titanic,* people just might have accepted the idea that the almost mythical ocean liner might someday reappear if the men doing the raising seemed real. But believable or not, the model and the derelict ship together impersonating the *Titanic,* not the men trying to raise her, became the central character of the movie. The film's producer, William Frye, probably said it best, pointing at the old freighter transformed into the raised liner: "There is the 'star' of our movie, with my apologies to the human ones. It will probably go down as the eighth wonder of the world, and upstage everyone at the same time." It did not, notwithstanding the money spent on the effort, and all the Navy's support went for naught.

The film's quick demise at the box office and the company's failure to honor its promise to Admiral Cooney did not discourage the Navy from continuing to talk with filmmakers about any script that offered the potential for showing off its hardware to good advantage. In fact, once *Midway* had rekindled Hollywood's interest in the Navy as a subject, the service's Office of Information usually had several major projects in various stages of development simultaneously. Despite its encouragement, however, the process of shepherding an original script from an initial Navy reaction through negotiations to completion usually took several years. More often than not, the exigencies of the film industry, rather than objections from the Navy, slowed progress, and by the time a movie reached the screen, both the production company and the story had usually undergone many transformations.

The service even remained ready and willing to ignore the implausibility of a story about a nuclear aircraft carrier being transported back in time. After all, as written, "The Last Countdown" would star one of the Navy's most prized ships. In their script submitted in June 1975, writers Peter Powell and Thomas Hunter used a Bermuda Triangle–type phenomenon as the means of locomotion to deposit the aircraft carrier in question off the coast of Serbia just before the assassination of Archduke Ferdinand and the outbreak of World War I. According to Hunter, the "science fiction approach in telling our story serves only as a broad canvas of a larger picture of man and his continual fight to save himself from destruction. Thus, the script is more allegorical than science fiction." At the same time, he acknowledged that during the writing, "the aircraft carrier has evolved in our eyes, into the main character, the star of the film." Recognizing the need for Navy cooperation, Hunter presented the story as one that "can put the Navy's way of life over in a very credible and exciting way. By giving the film entertainment value in addition to technical expertise, we would hope to reach the largest possible audience in America. That includes prospective Navy volunteers and particularly men who are now serving in the Armed Forces—men who would like to see a film about what they really do and how they also really do it without the negating edge of propaganda."[60]

Although the Navy had some problems with elements in the script, it advised Baruch that the Information Office "has no objection to the story-concept of subject script." Baruch informed Capt. C.D. Griffin, the retired Navy officer representing the writers, of the Navy's reaction and said the Navy would "be glad to discuss any story points with you whenever you wish." In submitting a revised script to Baruch's office the next May, Griffin noted that the new version "reflects the suggestions made by the Office of Naval Information." He said the writers believed the proposed movie "will be a first-rate adventure film which will project a very positive image of today's Navy, its capability, and the vital need to maintain control of the seas."[61]

The Navy agreed, and on June 1 Admiral Cooney advised Don Baruch that he "considered that Navy cooperation in the production of the film would be in the best interests of the Navy." Informing Griffin of the decision, Baruch said that the service would be able to work out support for the production and concluded, "The Navy and ourselves are looking forward to working on the production and its release bringing to the public in an intriguing way a better understanding of carrier operations." The Navy may have acted quickly for this reason. However, despite Griffin's report in August that things were moving along, the English company holding the rights to the screenplay failed to get the project off the ground.[62]

In the course of events, Peter Douglas, the twenty-two-year-old son of Kirk Douglas, received a copy of "The Last Countdown" and took an immediate interest in the story, "because it used a carrier and it brought up the possibility of filming on a carrier. I'm a pilot and the fantasy of flying a civilian plane is not closing your eyes, but envisioning the sound or the roar of jet engines and the thrust of your afterburners. The thought of one day being able to ride in a Navy jet and watch those planes take off and land on a carrier excited me." Consequently, the fledgling producer took an option on the screenplay in early 1977 and set out to try "to make the story work" for him.[63]

To that end, he shifted the story from the original script's time and setting, explaining that he didn't like the Bermuda Triangle: "I don't really believe in it. I also think that World War I is such a non-specific war. There is no one single incident. I don't think today's generation would even know Ferdinand unless they happened to be particularly well-educated in history. So, it was a question of what we could use as a catalyst and certainly Pearl Harbor was promising. Everyone knows it. Even today when you mention Pearl Harbor the immediate reaction is not the naval base in the mid-Pacific, but the disastrous sneak attack by the Japanese during WWII." With this idea in mind, the producer brought in screenwriters David Ambrose and Gerry Davis to redo the Hunter-Powell story.[64]

Believing the screenplay to be a "positive story from the onset," the producer sent an early draft to the Pentagon to get a sense of the Navy's willingness to provide assistance, particularly an aircraft carrier, that he would need if he were to make the film. Douglas recalled that the script "had certain aspects which we didn't like and which they didn't like, such as an executive officer who goes crazy." However, since the human roles were of secondary importance to the story, the producer had "little interest" in the character as written and therefore had no "severe problem" in creatively revising the portrayal to give the proper depiction of an officer.

Although not entirely enthused by the science fiction aspect of the story, the Navy and the Pentagon made no attempt to change that element of the production. The screenplay lacked any semblance of believability, but the service's Information Office "considered that production of this film will benefit our recruiting effort, and it will be of great assistance in familiarizing the public with the professionalism of Navy personnel." If the Navy did not concern itself with the story, Douglas found that the service remained a "stickler for details," correcting such things as changing "no" to "negative" and focusing on how an aircraft carrier captain would have performed when confronted with a series of hypothetical situations for which he had no frame of reference. To make sure that the film would contain an accurate portrayal of these matters, the Navy assisted Douglas in locating the retiring captain of the USS *Ranger*, Doug McCrimmons, to serve as the technical advisor about life aboard an aircraft carrier. Douglas found him to be "extremely knowledgeable and helpful and more specifically savvy to the needs of our industry. We used him to get the input for accuracy—what goes on a carrier."[65]

While Douglas and his writers were completing the script, the executive officer of the *Nimitz* heard through the grapevine that Douglas's production company was looking for a ship to feature in their film. Douglas recalled that the officer thought that if the ship served as the location for the movie, its use would build crew morale as well as serving the Navy as a recruitment and retention vehicle. Consequently the officer contacted the producer directly and invited him to come aboard the *Nimitz* to see the ship itself and meet the captain.

Once the *Nimitz* expressed its willingness to allow the filmmakers to come aboard for an extended stay, support for the project grew within the Navy Office of Information. In particular, Douglas recalled that the service was interested in creating "a more glamorous environment" and saw the movie as "a positive thrusting sword for the Navy and carrier aviation." Douglas explained that the Navy was very, very aware of the retention problems, particularly the retention problems . . . over and above recruitment" because they were spending millions of dollars on training, and if they couldn't keep the men, they weren't getting the value of their investment.

Douglas made his contribution to the authenticity of the film, not to mention fulfilling his own fantasy, by spending much of the six months from February through August of 1979 on board the *Nimitz*. While there, he researched the script, brought out screenwriters, and incorporated the "very complex" carrier flight schedule into a filming schedule. The film crew itself boarded the *Nimitz* for two months of shooting during that summer. According to the producer, the motion picture people "learned very quickly what these guys had to go through." The already collaborative art of film required "the dangerous collaboration of two totally alien environments," the cinema and the Navy worlds coming together.

Douglas praised the crew of the *Nimitz* for doing "everything they could, legally within their power, to cooperate." In addition to giving recommendations and suggestions, the sailors spent off-duty hours helping to make the picture technically accurate. Ultimately, the assistance the Navy provided over and above the

The *Nimitz,* not the actors, was the true star of *The Final Countdown.*

filming of normal shipboard operations cost Douglas about $2 million. Unfortunately for the producer, the money could not give *The Final Countdown* box-office appeal or bring it critical acclaim, and Douglas later admitted that he did not create a high-quality film, probably as a result of his inexperience. Nevertheless, though the movie's ad campaign in the United States did not highlight the Navy's hardware as a selling point, the service apparently received the benefit for which it had hoped. According to Douglas, the retention rate went up 23 or 24 percent above the norm following the release of *The Final Countdown*. Moreover, whatever problems the film had commercially, the producer felt that in the end it had captured the Navy's love of its ships: "The star of the picture was truly the *Nimitz*."

The science fiction fantasy provided moviegoers with a guided tour of the nuclear carrier. In fact, the *New York Times* reviewer thought the ship became "the only thing of interest in the movie. She's the principal character, but a chilly one." The two months that Douglas's film crew spent aboard the ship did enable them to capture the essence of the *Nimitz*, her men performing their assigned duties and her planes demonstrating their firepower, albeit directed against World War II Japanese Zeroes. The carrier's F-14s helped create dramatic, wide-screen aerial combat sequences with the pseudo-Zeroes, the same SNJ Navy trainers, rebuilt to masquerade as Japanese fighters for *Tora! Tora! Tora!* and now rented from the Confederate Air Force, which had bought them from Twentieth Century Fox. Like too many Hollywood stars, however, the *Nimitz* found herself having to perform in a vehicle unworthy of her stature.[66]

By their very nature, time-travel films require an extra modicum of suspension of disbelief. In fact, the audience knows the climax of the story before entering the theater. If the Nimitz, now transported through a huge storm back to December 7, the morning of the sneak attack on Pearl Harbor, had launched her planes to engage the Japanese aerial armada, they would have changed history and would have ceased to exist. Both the filmmakers and the Navy, of course, had no choice but to ignore this conundrum or they would have had no story. But like a festering sore, it remained at the heart of the movie, dissipating any dramatic tension before it could even develop.

Despite this reality, David Ansen in *Newsweek* concluded that although *The Final Countdown* "is clunky, square filmmaking . . . it's rarely boring, and the screenwriters come up with a final mysterious twist that saves the movie at the last moment from a disastrously anti-climactic turn of events. The twist, when it comes, doesn't really explain anything that precedes it, nor does it make the least

The crew of the USS *Nimitz* face the dilemma of whether or not to change history.

bit of sense. But after the tedium of a *Raise the Titanic!* even one crude sleight of hand can begin to look like art." Still, the *New York Times* perhaps said it best: "*The Final Countdown . . .* looks like a "Twilight Zone" episode produced as a Navy recruiting film." The Navy's impact on the story resulting from its assistance caused the reviewer to observe that the ship's crew "are so proper, so gung-ho, so perfectly integrated racially and so all-around sunny-natured, they seem more like members of a gigantic choir than seasoned sailors. You know it would never be necessary to show these men a training film on the perils of venereal disease."[67]

Whatever the success or lack of success that *The Final Countdown* enjoyed at the box office, any film in the post-Vietnam era that showed well-adjusted, happy military men would satisfy the Defense Department's fondest hopes. More important, it fulfilled the Navy's goal of advertising its hardware and showing its ships and planes well manned. Nevertheless, as presented in *The Final Countdown*, the sailors differed little from automatons, functioning just as predictably as the ships and planes, causing no problems and no controversy. If the Navy demonstrated a willingness to show off its equipment and "perfect" sailors, it did not seem to matter that the equipment and men sometimes failed to function as expected, as with *Tora! Tora! Tora!* or *Gray Lady Down.* At the same time, however, the service did continue to have difficulty providing assistance to a script that focused on "flawed" people, who drank, lusted after women, or simply did not conform to the Navy's ideal officer or enlisted man.

22 | New Images Despite Themselves

IF THE PUBLIC AFFAIRS OFFICERS OF EACH of the military services ultimately resigned themselves to Hollywood's revamped images of the military, they did not abdicate their authority to determine which films would receive support. More important, even in the changed climate of the early 1980s, the services still worked to ensure that as few warts as possible would appear on the nation's movie or television screens. What constituted a wart, however, often became a matter of dispute. A portrayal that one service found offensive, another service might accept routinely. Even the same service might approve it later on. In particular, before Vietnam, the Army had a history of providing assistance on a less discriminating basis than the other services.

A priori, the Army lacked the glamour, romance, and elitism that the Navy, the Marines, and the Air Force usually managed to convey in cinematic appearances. The life of the foot soldier simply did not provide filmmakers with such visual opportunities as carrier landings and takeoffs, sweeping aerial combat sequences, midair refueling, or underwater derring-do. One of the gang members torturing William Devane in *Rolling Thunder* probably said it best: "I was right there in Nam . . . except that I was laying face down in the mud while you cats were flying over." To be sure, Marines often found themselves lying in the same mud, especially in Vietnam. But at least in pre-Vietnam-era Hollywood movies, they seemed do it with more élan and with more flare than their Army counterparts; and their amphibious assaults on some remote tropical beach seemed more exciting and daring than the Army's massive landing at Normandy.

Such representations only reflected the reality that the Army had to face vis-à-vis the other services. Unlike them, the Army and the Marines had to rely on draftees, rather than volunteers, to fill their ranks until the end of the Vietnam War. As a result, the Army had welcomed most filmmakers seeking assistance, regardless of the nature of the project, simply to ensure that it would have some visual appearance before the American people. On at least one occasion, the service had even supported a story on which the Marine Corps had refused to cooperate. The filmmakers simply changed the uniforms and location of the original script for the 1953 *Take the High Ground,* but not the elements to which the Marines had objected.

With the creation of the all-volunteer military after Vietnam, however, the Army found itself having to compete with the other services for recruits. As a result, the Army's public affairs offices in Washington and Los Angeles set out to create a better cinematic image in much the same way as the Marines and the Navy had been doing. Apart from the unflattering comparisons with the other services, the Army had an additional burden to overcome. In Vietnam the Army had fielded the greatest number of men and therefore had received the most coverage in the print and visual media. As a consequence, the service had experienced more than its share, quantitatively, of negative reportage. Although the Marine Corps suffered with its Lieutenant Caputos and its Khe Sanhs, more often than not the Army's My Lais and Hamburger Hills came to represent the nation's frustrations in Vietnam. Even more important, the Army's less-than-heroic images became not only military tragedies but also the Army's particular public affairs disasters.

The service's refusal to support *Go Tell the Spartans, Apocalypse Now, Hair,* and *The Deer Hunter* clearly reflected the Army's concern over the manner in which filmmakers chose to portray its actions and men in Vietnam. Just as often, however, the Army's responses to requests for assistance in portraying its peacetime activities demonstrated a continuing distrust of Hollywood's intentions and proposed portrayals. As a result, even as the harshest images of Vietnam began to recede from the psyche of the civilian population by the late 1970s, the Army was still expressing reluctance to become involved in productions that contained any negative elements. In turn, Hollywood came to see the Army as obstructionist, even when its objections had validity. Filmmakers therefore showed less interest in developing positive stories about either the Army in Vietnam or its subsequent peacetime activities, especially in the first few years after the American withdrawal from Southeast Asia. Consequently, the Army fell even farther behind the other services in using film to promote itself and its current activities.

Ultimately, as happened with the Navy, World War II served as the setting in which the Army saw the beginning of the rehabilitation of its image. Unlike *Midway,* however, the film that became the instrument of change offered characters with whom audiences could empathize and whom they could root on to final victory. Yet, if *The Big Red One* resembled nothing so much as a traditional Army war film of the 1950s on which the Pentagon gave pro forma approval, the Army had virtually nothing to do with its production. Instead, the project came to fruition because of the obsession of one man, the director-screenwriter, Sam Fuller.

More honored and respected abroad as a film auteur than in the United States, where people saw him as simply a director of B grade action movies, Fuller had dreamed of making a movie about his World War II experiences for more than thirty years. Yet he readily acknowledged his own responsibility for not making the movie sooner: "It's my fault. I stalled and stalled until I started to fool around with the idea for the book. I wrote 30 or 40 pages, then I got into a picture, then another picture, and it went on year after year. I knew I'd eventually finish it." However, his reputation as the director of low-budget movies inspired little enthusiasm in Hollywood to back his proposed war epic, particularly in the years after the American withdrawal from Vietnam.[1]

Ultimately, in 1976, film critic turned director Peter Bogdanovich, with whom he had first discussed the movie in 1965, urged Fuller to "stop fooling around with lousy scripts. Why don't you write that good one, the one you really ought to do, *The Big Red One?*" Initially, Bogdanovich agreed to produce the film and even play the "Fuller" role. But by the time Fuller had completed the script, Bogdanovich had committed himself to directing a movie, and he arranged for Gene Corman to take over the film. Together, Fuller and Corman sought locations, raised money, cast the actors, and shot the film.[2]

The story Fuller wrote and set out to make became a traditional 1950s Hollywood World War II film. Originating in Fuller's own wartime experiences, *The Big Red One* traced the odyssey of Lee Marvin's rifle squad across Africa, through Sicily, to the Normandy invasion, culminating with the liberation of a concentration camp in Czechoslovakia and final victory in Europe. Fuller used one of the squad as his surrogate narrator and Marvin's sergeant as the glue holding the story together. With so much time and territory to cover in slightly less than two hours, the director resorted to a series of episodic pictures of the soldier's-eye view of World War II. Both Marvin and his men occasionally offer pithy observations on the futility of war, but to the extent the movie makes a statement, it says that man must fight for his country out of necessity, not for the love of combat.

The Army and the Pentagon would have had no problem with such a portrayal if a filmmaker had requested assistance on such a story during the 1950s or early 1960s, and certainly not in the post-Vietnam period, given the bitter nature of most cinematic renderings of the war in Southeast Asia. By the time Fuller finally found backers and put the project into motion, however, the U.S. military establishment had virtually nothing in the way of World War II equipment to offer the producers. Moreover, to make *The Big Red One,* which needed a diversity of locations, in the United States would have required a huge budget. Consequently, after scouting locations throughout Europe, Fuller and Corman turned to Israel, both for the ability of its military to provide needed men and equipment and for its land to serve as suitable doubles for the actual locations. According to Corman, the country also offered very low filming costs and "technicians so good we only had to bring a skeleton crew."[3]

In the end, Fuller made a film that stands as an anachronism among the movies about the U.S. armed services that began to appear in the years following the American withdrawal from Vietnam. Audiences could cheer in all the right places as Lee Marvin and his group of four survivors triumphed over the Nazi threat. To be sure, Fuller was dealing in terms of black and white, not shades of gray. His men were fighting in a necessary war and performed bravely. They gave food to children, delivered a baby, and as Marvin stressed, they killed, not murdered, their enemy, only out of necessity. Compared to the portrayals of the service in Vietnam, such images could only benefit the contemporary Army.

Fuller did not, of course, make *The Big Red One* to rehabilitate the military, but rather to memorialize his own World War II experiences. His film did more than that, however. Perhaps the long incubation period added a dimension to the director's vision. Perhaps the very nature of the positive portrayal of the Army added to the visual impact. Perhaps just the sight of the U.S. military winning again on the movie screen created a strong reaction among viewers. Whatever the reason, the film elicited great praise from the critics and helped give new life to the war film genre.

David Ansen, in *Newsweek,* believed that *The Big Red One* knew "exactly what it's after, in which every shot and every scene build toward a clearly sighted objective." As a result, the critic thought that Fuller had "resurrected" the World War II movie with "swift, bold strokes," and his film had "restored one's faith in Hollywood professionalism." Ansen saw no point in trying to label Fuller's movie as prowar or antiwar: "His theme is survival and his method is to put us in the shoes of a squad of teen-age soldiers and their sergeant. . . . This is war, as Fuller tells us. This is how men die and how they survive. Period. There is no strategic overview, no psychologizing, no patriotic speeches." Although Ansen acknowledged that the characters remained "purely functional" and the film had no plot, he felt it had "a relentless forward thrust, an emotional momentum that deepens as it progresses. Fuller is no more ashamed of macho sentimentality than he is of the crudest GI survival humor, but what his film lacks in subtlety, it makes up in brute force."[4]

Likewise, the *Time* reviewer described *The Big Red One* as "fine, fully justifying Fuller's faith in himself and his great subject." As a result, the writer felt that Fuller was able to capture the true nature of combat: "Wars are periods of anxious boredom, mitigated by soldierly camaraderie and punctuated by moments of sheer terror, bloody farce and amazing grace which, because they are so intense, have the capacity to shape the lives and spirits of the uniformed youths who fight them." Despite such images, both the *Time* writer and Vincent Canby in the *New York Times* concluded that the film had a "mellow" quality to it, in contrast to Fuller's earlier work. The *Time* reviewer observed: "Fuller's dream movie has about it a mellowness that contrasts sharply with the brutal force of his earlier films, which often derived their power from the simple act of upending generic conventions—having the hero actually pull the trigger at the moment when normally he might be expected to holster his gun, or even fall into hysterics just when he was supposed to be most tightly controlled. Fuller is still doing this in *Big Red,* but in a much more benign way." Still, Canby said that the director was able to "show us a kind of war not often seen on the screen, that is, a war reduced to what can be seen from the point of view of the foot soldier who has no connections to headquarters or to decision-making."[5]

However positive this portrayal of the Army, the images that *The Big Red One* contained would not move very many young men and women to enlist in the all-volunteer military of the 1980s. Thanks to Fuller's own experiences and directorial ability, his story made it clear that even when it may become necessary, war still had few socially redeeming qualities. In contrast, another Army story, *Private Benjamin,* set in the contemporary world, suggested that a military career offered adventure, fun, an opportunity to see the world, and the chance to become a better person. Ironically, even though such images would benefit the service's recruiting efforts and further the rehabilitation process, the Army would have nothing to do with the project.

Instead, in much the same way as the Marines had initially reacted to the scripts of *Born on the Fourth of July* and *The Great Santini,* the Army found that the script for *Private Benjamin* (1980) contained decidedly unflattering portrayals of its procedures and officers. Its Public Affairs Office failed to see how a film which showed that the contemporary Army could turn even a Jewish American princess into a "man" could serve the Army well as a recruiting vehicle. To be sure, Edward Morey, vice president and executive production manager at Warner Brothers, admitted to Don Baruch by phone and in a letter on July 31, 1979, that *Private Benjamin* "is an outrageous comedy and I hope no one will take offense." He said the studio "certainly can use your help on this picture, and I hope your people can see their way clear to give us an okay." He asked that any changes the Army might suggest should be sent to him and he would transmit them directly to the producer of the film.[6]

Despite the implied willingness to work with the service to create an acceptable script, Baruch advised Morey on August 20 that although the film "undoubtedly will be a funny picture, especially with Goldie Hawn playing Benjamin," the script "contains many negative aspects for the Army, e.g., the exaggerated or false recruiting pitch, unrealistic sequences in basic training and the portrayal of the General with his 'Private Army' and his advances to the ladies." According to Baruch, the Pentagon believed Warner Brothers could make the film without Army assistance. Consequently, he rhetorically suggested that "the producer undoubtedly, would not want to make extensive script changes necessary to qualify it for approval." In any case, he said that the producers should "not hesitate" to call the Army's Los Angeles Public Affairs Office if they needed "technical information."[7]

Given such a reaction, the filmmakers made no further effort to secure assistance during production, although they did seek and receive technical advice for the military sequences. In fact, the cinematic Army merely served as the instrument for turning a spoiled Jewish princess into an independent person; or, as the slogan claims, the service became the place where a person can "be all you can be, in the Army." In the case of Judy Benjamin, the Army provided "a good place to start." The heart of the Army's objection to the script was the manner in which Judy chose to embark upon her military career. As written and produced, a less-than-honest Army recruiter entices the previously divorced and suddenly widowed Judy Benjamin to meet him after speaking to her over the radio during a late-night talk show. In his sales pitch, the recruiter fails to correct Judy's verbalized images of the "new" army, when she likens the barracks and yacht basin at Fort Ord to "condos" and a Club Med.

Once signed up and rudely introduced to basic training, Judy's troubles begin in earnest. Princesses do not have to wake up before dawn, make their own beds, or obey orders from drill sergeants or abrasive, sarcastic female captains. Played with suitable spite by Ellen Burstyn, the sexually frustrated officer embarks on a personal vendetta with the sole purpose of drumming Judy out of the Army. She rags Judy mercilessly, and at the appropriate moment calls Judy's parents to come to the base, expecting that Judy will agree to depart with them.

Responding to her father's familiar attempts to subjugate her and her mother's continued acquiescence, Benjamin does the only thing she has so far learned from the Army. Not unlike Burt Lancaster, discovered with his pants down in the gazebo, Judy salutes her parents and her superior, and, leaving them stunned, beats a retreat from the ward room to the security of her unit. Having made her choice, Judy begins to evolve from a subservient child to an independent woman. Acquiring confidence in herself and her abilities, she becomes the informal leader of her unit. During "war games," her patrol captures the opposing commander, in flagrante delicto, with one of his "prisoners of war."

Private Benjamin faces her first parachute jump during advanced individual training.

Despite this success, her military education does not always progress smoothly. When faced with making her first parachute jump during advanced individual training, Judy freezes and begs her commanding officer not to make her follow her comrades out of the plane. Posthaste, he offers her an alternative and begins to take down his pants with a leer in his eye. No longer the compliant female, however, she decides that a leap into space is better than sexual harassment at ten thousand feet and jumps out the door. Having completed her basic training, Private Benjamin uses the incident to garner a dream assignment at Supreme Headquarters Allied Europe (SHAPE) in Brussels.

The last third of the film contains fewer negative images of the military, except for the female captain, who reappears, this time with a lesbian lover in tow. In fact, Benjamin's military career seems to confirm that the Army has created a new person and given her a chance to finally make something of herself. But until the last few seconds of the film, feminists in the audience would have fears that Judy has not learned to transfer her professional competence to her personal life. She accepts a marriage proposal from her Jewish-French physician lover, signs a prenuptial agreement presented to her shortly before her wedding, albeit with some reluctance, dyes her hair to satisfy her fiancé's demands, and spends her off-duty hours shopping. In the end, however, the Army's efforts succeed. She refuses to acquiesce to her husband-to-be's efforts to dominate her, slugs him in the jaw, and walks out of her wedding. She succeeds in breaking the bonds of male dominance through the strength she acquired from her Army training and seemingly embarks on a new life, unlike Elaine in *The Graduate,* who had to rely on the help of a man to break her ties to her parents.

Director Howard Zieff said he became "fascinated by the concept of an upper middle class girl being thrown into a totally different milieu such as the Army. It's an intelligent idea for a film. It's a portrait of a girl coming of age." Producer-writer Nancy Meyers said she never became comfortable with the Marjorie Morningstar image of Jewish girls: "I love Jewish girls. I wanted to do a movie about the good things about them, and I wanted to show why so many are the way they are. Jewish girls are raised to be nothing, to belong to someone else. And then to try to make herself something causes a big response from her family. It was, I think, an interesting idea."[8]

In truth, the film has an abundance of cardboard characters and military gags that every filmgoer over ten had seen before in countless military comedies of the post–World War II period. Nonetheless, *Private Benjamin* does contain a fine scene late in the film in which Goldie Hawn's commander at NATO Headquarters encourages her to deliver an important briefing because he recognizes her ability to present the information better than

he could. More important, the film makes it perfectly clear that the Army provides the impetus for Judy Benjamin's personal war against submissiveness and dependence in much the same way that the Marines ac-knowledged that Kovic survived his ordeals because of the discipline he had received dur-ing basic training.

Though the Army's initial reaction to the script dissuaded the filmmakers from enter-ing into negotiations for assistance, the service's office in Los Angeles did provide some technical advice to the production, and to the embarrassment of the service, two of its officers received a film credit. The studio arranged to have most of the Army sequences shot at Fort MacArthur, now an inactive in-stallation, which Hollywood was regularly using to provide an authentic military ambi-

Most of the Army sequences for *Private Benjamin* were shot at Fort MacArthur.

ence, and at Newhall Ranch, where the production company constructed an obstacle training course specifically for the film. The producers also hired moonlighting soldiers, Marines, and airmen to serve as extras during the filming of the training sequences. Nevertheless, *Private Benjamin* had little to do with military procedures or life in the contemporary Army, and the filmmakers felt little need to create a documentary on the recruitment or training of a woman soldier in this man's Army. In fact, given the liberties which the writers and the director took with the Army's "Standard Operating Procedures," one re-viewer even wondered out loud what the Army technical advisors did in return for their screen credit.[9]

Ultimately, of course, *Private Benjamin* would succeed or fail not for its portrayal of life within the Army but as a comedy and a feminist statement. It did become a box-office smash and even fostered a short-lived television series, but the film opened to mixed reviews. Although most critics appreciated the physical comedy that Goldie Hawn displayed, not unlike her popular "Laugh-In" routines on 1960s television, the verbal humor did not always draw praise. In particular, reviewers objected to the self-deprecating, Jewish American princess jokes concerning shopping, Jewish fathers, and so forth. The *Village Voice*'s Andrew Sarris expressed surprise that *Private Benjamin* had become so "ferociously anti-male," observing: "Almost every critic quoted a Goldie Hawn line to the effect that she would have married Alan Bates in a second if she had been Jill Clayburgh in *An Unmarried Woman*. The implication of this line is that Hawn's character is a refreshingly antifeminist rebuke to the Jill Clayburgh character."[10]

Sarris noted that with the exception of Hawn's boss at NATO headquarters, all the males in the film act in an overbearing, deceitful, unloving, uncaring, and thoroughly contemptible manner. Hawn develops rapport only with a few of her lower-class female buddies in the Army. Sarris pointed out that the men in Benjamin's life become "progressively disastrous to the point that she winds up at the altar socking her third-husband-to-be out of her life forever." In contrast, in *An Unmarried Woman*, Jill Clayburgh remains "far more solicitous of the men in her life."[11]

Charles Champlin, in the *Los Angeles Times*, had a more broad-based range of criticisms of *Private Benjamin*, saying in the first sentence of his review that he found it "a movie you don't salute, you courtmartial." Putting aside its portrayal of the military, Champlin opined that the film "raises holy hob with the laws of film making, the first of which is that you start with a good script." He concluded that since the three credited producers also received credit for the screenplay, the possibility existed "that there was no one around empowered to say that the script needed work." Believing that Goldie Hawn represented "the sole surviving asset of the patchwork comedy," as well as serving as the executive producer, Champlin speculated that the actress "saw the project only as a collection of individual scenes she felt she could play well, rather than as a coherent and consistent comedic whole, which it certainly isn't."[12]

Charles Champlin, onetime movie critic of the *Los Angeles Times*.

Instead, he saw the film "as one of those actor's composites: rustic pose, glamour pose, natural, youthful, mature. Or, in the present instance, slapstick foil, madcap heiress, battered wife, liberated woman." To Champlin, the film's range of material "is negatively astonishing, from the sexual lines and scenes that would have gone better in, say *Carnal Knowledge*," to Army "barracks cut-ups that would have been rejected as too broad for *Abbott & Costello Join the WACs*." Ultimately, he concludes that having already ended and restarted with a new story, *Private Benjamin* "reaches a painful creative chaos in which some of the performers from the first half of the film show up again like unemployed actors looking for work."[13]

Worse, he believed that Goldie Hawn, as Private Benjamin, had not given audiences "a character to comprehend, care about or even be particularly amused by." As far as the Army standing "as a fertile parade ground for satire in any season," Champlin observed that "the authors seem to have confined their researches to a handful of World War II comedies, with a trace more coeducational activity than I remember as the norm at Camp Croft. The point, of course, is not that anything is inaccurate, just unfunny, and very weary." However, Champlin objected most not to the film's failure to "amuse" or that it might "find some takers for its simple-minded slapstick and its mild interweavings of sex," but that "wastage is always hard to watch, the ill-deployment of talent and opportunity even more than money."[14]

Not all critics saw the film in such negative terms. Vincent Canby, in the *New York Times*, saw *Private Benjamin* as "an old friend brought up to date in this woman's Army." Moreover, he felt that the director demonstrated "great skill in keeping the gags aloft and in finding new ways by which to free the laughs trapped inside old routines about latrine duty, war games, forced marches and calisthenics." He also found the film "funny, and every now and then, like Judy Benjamin, possessed of unexpected common sense. Judy is ultimately most appealing because she's no dope." Further demonstrating the extreme differences in the manner reviewers often perceive movies, Canby considered Benjamin's comment "I really didn't get the point of *An Unmarried Woman*. I would have been Mrs. Alan Bates so fast" not as Andrew Sarris did as a "refreshingly antifeminist rebuke," but as a demonstration of her intelligence: "She could also be a movie critic."[15]

The film itself also demonstrated that reviewers often count for little in determining whether a movie will succeed in the marketplace, becoming one of the smash hits of 1980. As a result, it also introduced large numbers of young people to life in the peacetime Army. If *Private Benjamin* did not provide an accurate portrayal of the service's activities, it probably did not stray any farther from reality than countless Hollywood comedies that had used the military as a setting for high jinks of all sorts. Consequently, despite the Army's refusal to become involved in the project, the service undoubtedly derived the same benefit as it had from the adventures of Francis the Talking Mule in the Army, from Dean Martin and Jerry Lewis in the Army, and from Abbott and Costello in the Army, or any number of other military comedies. Whether young males discovered, as Judy Benjamin had done, that Army life consisted of more than fun and games, many of those who had joined the military did so because life in the service did seem like a lot of fun in the movies. *Private Benjamin* maintained that tradition and so provided the Army with a free recruiting vehicle, according to the *UCLA Daily Bruin*. To the collegiate reviewer, it did this by doing a "beautiful job of showing . . . today's armed forces." In fact, for women of the eighties, the movie leaves the impression that the services "are probably leading the nation in granting women equal opportunity."[16]

As Don Baruch had suggested, the producers of *Private Benjamin* probably made no effort to follow up on their initial request for Army cooperation because they had correctly determined that they could make the film without assistance from the service. In contrast, Dan Goldberg, the producer of *Stripes*, requested Pentagon assistance from the beginning of the research and development phase of the project in August 1979. Goldberg's first letter to Don Baruch, following up on a phone conversation, reflected the naïveté of those involved: "I would like to join the army (along with my writing partner) for four to five weeks this September, and go through basic training, experiencing army life firsthand." He also requested a meeting in Washington within the next week or two "to get more information about today's army."[17]

In memorializing the visit, Goldberg asked permission to visit basic training posts and installations: "We feel that in developing this story, it would be tremendously helpful for us to be able to view army life firsthand." The producer reiterated that the story he hoped "to develop is a warm humorous look at Army life." In regard to the regulations concerning cooperation, he said he would "find no problem whatsoever in complying with these guidelines." Despite these good intentions and visits to Army facilities, which Baruch did arrange for later that fall, the script that Goldberg took almost a year to complete proved less than satisfactory to the Army.[18]

The plot for *Stripes*, in fact, became a male counterpart to *Private Benjamin*. John Winger (portrayed by television comedian Bill Murray) loses his job, his car, his apartment, and his girl—all in one day. In a state of passing depression, Winger persuades his amiable sidekick Russell to enlist with him in the "new" U.S. Army. Borrowing from numerous earlier military comedies, the pals wind up in a unit of misfits, who suffer through their drill instructor's standard litany of verbal and mental abuse, ultimately emerging as newly minted privates. Like Judy Benjamin, Winger and his friends end up in Europe, but not in the comfortable setting of NATO headquarters. This time around, the wayward soldiers survive "misunderstandings with the third world; a little trouble with the Czechs; and a major conflict with the Russians."[19]

Although the script might have seemed harmless enough to Goldberg and his team of writers when the producer delivered it to the Army's Los Angeles Public Affairs Office on August 15, 1980, Lt. Col. Dennis R. Foley had an entirely different perspective when he read it. Worse, from the filmmakers' point of view, Foley advised them when he met with them a couple of days later that they could obtain "virtually every Army item" through commercial sources. He did acknowledge that Goldberg would have to approach the Air Force for the aircraft that the script required. Unlike Pat Coulter, who was operating across the hall on the assumption that the Marines should keep close watch on any production portraying the Corps, Foley noted in his memorandum for the record that he had explained to Goldberg "that there was no need for the production company to think that we were the total source of props, locations and equipment."[20]

Suddenly faced with having to add the rental of military equipment to his budget, Goldberg told the Army officer that he had visited Fort Knox and felt that it was essential to his story that he actually use a portion of that installation in his production. At that point, Foley advised him to submit his screenplay directly to the Department of Defense with a request for full cooperation. Nevertheless, Foley had serious reservations about the script itself because of many objectionable aspects of the story. He felt that it "grossly misrepresents the Army in its entire presentation. Admittedly, it is intended to be a comedy, but it is replete with inappropriate and exaggerated presence and acceptance of sex, drugs, and misconduct. There does not appear to be one redeeming character in the entire script. The bottom line: There's nothing in it for us." Nor did Foley believe that the producers actually needed Army assistance to make the film. In the memo, which he sent on to the Army in Washington, Foley concluded by suggesting that the service respond to Goldberg along the lines he had already discussed with the producer: he could make the movie without Army assistance; to make it acceptable would take too much time and destroy the comedy; he could find a suitable location and make the film with only courtesy assistance; and the Army would help without committing taxpayers' assets.[21]

With Foley's comments in hand, Lt. Col. Richard Griffitts, the chief of the Policy and Plans Division of the Army Public Affairs Office in the Pentagon, informed Don Baruch that the script it had received resembled a 1950s service comedy "clothed in the 1970–80's milieu of sex, drugs, disregard for authority, and crass language. Admittedly, it is intended to be a comedy; however, it blatantly misrepresents the Army today." Noting that the filmmakers would have to undertake an "extensive" rewrite to create an acceptable script, Griffitts said this "would probably destroy the comedic intent." Among other problems, he cited scenes of never-ending supplies of drugs in the barracks, the D.I.'s harassment of the recruits, and sexism. As a result, he concluded, "Unless an acceptable version of the script can be developed, the Army must decline support."[22]

When Goldberg received this negative assessment from Baruch, he immediately flew to Washington to meet with the Army to discuss its objections to the script. The next day, he sent Baruch the list of changes he had agreed to make during the meeting "in order for the Department of Defense to give us full cooperation in the shooting of this film." In making virtually every revision the service had demanded, the producer demonstrated the extent to which he was willing to go to satisfy the Army. He further demonstrated his anxiousness to curry the Army's favor when he wrote to Baruch on the tenth that, if he had not made it clear in his September 5 letter, he wanted to assure the Pentagon "that our intention in producing *Stripes* is to make a comedy film with patriotic overtones that would hopefully have a positive effect on Army recruiting. Although there will be a certain amount of humor and parody in the film, the overall intent is not to portray the Army as a collection of aberrant personalities."[23]

Despite Goldberg's anxious and even zealous efforts to please the Pentagon, the producer had undoubtedly overreacted to the Army's requests for changes in the screenplay. The movie he intended to make "about how a platoon of misfits are transformed into a platoon of Army heroes" differed little from both serious and comic stories Hollywood had regularly produced before the Vietnam War. The crew of the B-17 "Leper Colony" in *Twelve O'Clock High*, and the men in *The Devil's Brigade* and *The Dirty Dozen* became model fighting men as a result of their transformations. In a lighter vein, the Bud Abbotts and Lou Costellos, the Dean Martins and Jerry Louises, and the Goldie Hawns showed audiences that the military could become a place of personal growth as well as a place to find romance and humor. By its very nature, however, a military comedy does not generally provide a documentary, realistic portrayal of a typical soldier's life in the Army. Simply put, daily military routine offers little in the way of excitement or adventure to recommend it.

At the same time, even if *Stripes* could not "realistically" portray the Army, as Goldberg claimed his film would do, the Army had little real reason to decline support to the film, since military comedies usually create positive, albeit less than accurate, images of service life. Moreover, given the producer's willingness to make all the changes in the script that the service requested in the guise of ensuring accuracy, approval of support for *Stripes* became a pro forma exercise. In fact, in the name of "balance" and the comedic approach, Baruch said the Army agreed to allow the filmmakers to keep in the story one "screwy character. That was the captain, who had toy trains in his office and wanted to watch a girl taking a shower. We didn't think it was doing any harm."[24]

Ultimately, on October 30, by phone and then in a formal letter, Baruch advised Goldberg that the Army would cooperate with his production. He made it clear that some of the requested equipment might not be available at Fort Knox, where Goldberg planned to film most of the military sequences. However, he anticipated that the National Guard could provide the hardware elsewhere without any problem. Finally, he thanked the producer for his "expediency and cooperation in making all the changes discussed."[25]

The Army's decision to support *Stripes* after showing no interest in *Private Benjamin* only a few months earlier, of course, reflects Goldberg's abject willingness to readily accept requests for changes in the script. Having worked with the producer from day one, the service recognized that it had the power to virtually dictate the content and tone of the finished film. More important, even the initial script had not contained the type of negative portrayals of two important "Army" characters in *Private Benjamin,* the recruiter and the basic training post commander. Both characters were crucial to the development of the story, and the filmmakers would have ended up with a innocuous movie without them.

Goldberg, in contrast, had apparently decided to work with the Army every step of the way because he felt that assistance was crucial for budgetary reasons and to provide the authentic ambience in which to fashion his lighthearted parody of Army life. From the Pentagon's perspective, Don Baruch explained, "The Army was very pleased with it and the generals have said they were delighted to have cooperated on it, and so are we. It was an opportunity to reach an audience we had not been reaching, younger people. The only thing we missed out on was a card saying 'This picture made possible through the sense of humor of the Army.'"[26]

The actual filming in Kentucky, primarily at Fort Knox, during November and December 1980, went uneventfully for all parties concerned. Capt. Barry Sprouse, the chief of the Public Information Branch on the post and technical advisor during the filming, had particular praise for the filmmakers: "Their work touched virtually every directorate in the Armor Center. I have yet to receive a major complaint against Columbia from anyone here." He noted that the company followed the script closely during shooting on the post, but later filming at the Jim Beam Distillery did deviate slightly from the approved story. Nevertheless, he concluded, "The general theme of the movie was not changed, however, and I did not consider the script alterations an issue." Columbia reimbursed both the Army and the Kentucky National Guard for all costs to the military, and according to Sprouse, the production brought $4 million to $6 million into the state's economy.[27]

Whether the Army equally benefited from its eighteen months of working on *Stripes* is another matter. *Newsweek* acknowledged that Bill Murray remained "a funny, original presence" but questioned whether it was possible "to build a movie around a protagonist whose strongest quality is flip disengagement." Instead, the reviewer found the film "another variant of slob humor—platoon of misfits makes good—but the humor is so tepid, the point of view so wishy-washy (it vacillates between anti-establishment insolence and flag-waving platitudes) that the most it offers is a few tolerant chuckles. Could it be that Murray himself doesn't give a damn that he's diddling away his talents on mediocrity? *Stripes* reeks of halfheartedness."[28]

Very likely, Goldberg's requirements and willingness to satisfy the Army's demands in order to get their help caused the filmmakers to bleach out any satire or wit that might offend the Pentagon. In contrast to the novelty of a Judy Benjamin joining the Army, the *New York Times* observed, "there's nothing particularly fresh in the idea of a layabout like Mr. Murray joining up, though." Why then did the film enjoy the success it did? *Time* Magazine offered as good an explanation as any: "Director Ivan Reitman is a canny merchant. He knows that the easy laughs are the surest, that teen-agers love to watch goofballs shape up without losing their shambling style, and that it doesn't hurt business to insert a sorority shower scene or nude mud-wrestling match every half-hour or so. *Stripes* will keep potential felons off the streets for two hours. Few people seem to be asking, these days, that movies do more."[29]

Images of Bill Murray lazing his way through a career in the Army and almost starting World War III may not have helped the Army's recruiting campaign. But they would not hurt the service's efforts to sell life in the all-volunteer Army to young people with nothing better to do with their time. In contrast, *Taps*, to which the National Guard provided assistance, could only damage the military's effort to rehabilitate its image, in light of the film's portrayal of the extremes to which a military education can lead.

Set in a military school, *Taps* concerns itself with the ramifications of the decision of the board of trustees to close the 140-year-old academy to allow development of a condominium complex. The students, who have no input into the decision and naturally oppose the shutdown, stage an armed takeover of the school. Equipped with weaponry from the school armory, which the academy's late superintendent has stockpiled with automatic weapons and mortars in case of an emergency, the students soon prove more than a match for the state police, who call in the National Guard to assist them. After a series of accidents, the students finally decide to surrender. However, as the students are about to give up, one disturbed senior classman opens fire on the Guard colonel commanding the troops and police SWAT teams. The colonel reluctantly orders his troops onto the campus, returning fire *only* to the one room from which the cadet is firing with an M-60. The Guard recaptures the school with the loss of the senior who started the shooting and the star of the film, the cadet major, who tries to stop him.

Not surprisingly, when the National Guard Bureau, the Pentagon's coordinator of all National Guard activities, read the original script in April 1980, it did not want to be associated with the production in any way. In a memo to Tom Ross, the assistant secretary of defense for public affairs, Don Baruch explained that the Guard thought the film could have a "feeling of a Kent State. They feel the story is false, not factual, as now written. The Pennsylvania National Guard does not want to become involved, regardless, because of training exercises and the added requirements brought about by the Cuban refugees in the State." Baruch also reported that Stanley Jaffe, the producer, became "incensed" when he called to advise him of the Guard's position. After apologizing, however, the producer agreed to wait until he received the Guard's comments in writing before "trying to change our position."[30]

Jaffe explained to Baruch that he had become so upset because he felt the Guard did not understand his needs: "Very simply, we are doing a story about a military academy which is taken over by the cadets as a *positive* form of protest. The cadets are demonstrating against the decision to close the school so that the property can be turned into another

A group of military academy teens stage an armed takeover of their school in *Taps*.

suburban development. The school represents a home that the boys have come to love." In regard to the portrayal of the National Guard, Jaffe said it was acting "in the most compassionate of ways. Instead of being portrayed as war-mongering or bloodthirsty soldiers, we have portrayed them as intelligent, sympathetic members of society. They do what is necessary to try to intimidate the boys into surrender and later on when compelled to go into action, there are no lives lost. It is a very compassionate statement of what the National Guard stands for."[31]

Jaffe may have seen his script, then titled "Father Sky," in these terms and so expressed a lack of understanding on how "a picture that reflects positively on the National Guard might be denied assistance." He might also have "assumed there would be no major stumbling blocks" to cooperation based on "certain assurances" from conversations with the Pennsylvania National Guard. In fact, the National Guard Bureau, the Pentagon's administrative umbrella agency for the Air and Army National Guards, and the Pennsylvania National Guard, had significant problems with the project. As a consequence, the bureau informed Don Baruch on May 19 that after consultation with the Pennsylvania Guard, both organizations fully agreed that support of the project "would be counterproductive to the best interests of the National Guard and the Department of Defense and we therefore decline to support this particular production."[32]

The bureau's Office of Public Affairs then detailed the Guard's problems with the script: "The general theme of the work can only serve to reawaken public enmity for the National Guard as an enemy of young students and an invader of campuses. We have tried over the last ten years to put the incident at Kent State into the proper context. 'Father Sky' would depict the National Guard as preparing to crush young children with overwhelming military might. This is not the image we wish to project." The office also noted that the level of Guard response depicted in the story "is grossly out of proportion to the threat presented and while we realize this is done for dramatic impact we cannot approve of it." After citing numerous technical inaccuracies, the office suggested that the producers secure commercially available equipment to depict the action sequences on which they had wanted the Guard to assist.[33]

On May 29, answering Jaffe's letter of May 14, Don Baruch quoted extensively from the National Guard Bureau's memo to him. He advised the producer that the Defense Department "does not feel that there is any basis for not supporting that position" and suggested that Jaffe rent needed equipment from commercial sources. At the same time, he did not close the door completely on the project, indicating that if a revised script put "the National Guard in proper perspective by showing them in the supporting role that they actually would play in such situations, the use of state 'armored' vehicles would be most appropriate."[34]

Like Dan Goldberg, Jaffe recognized that he had not received a flat-out rejection and set out to revise the screenplay, now titled *Taps.* When he sent the new script to Baruch on July 3, he said it reflected efforts to meet the objections and concerns of the National Guard. He expressed the belief that the new version "is now accurate in the manner in which the National Guard would be used and as important, I believe that the National Guard, especially as personified in the character of [Colonel] Kirby is shown to be a voice of reason and intellect, of logic, and of humanity." Responding to the Guard's concern that the film would evoke images of Kent State, the producer observed: "Kent State, unfortunately, is a reality and as a result of it people came away with negative feelings about the National Guard. I believe the way to counteract these feelings is to portray the National Guard as an organization manned by intelligent humane members of society whose objective is to preserve the peace. I believe that 'TAPS' does just this. I believe 'TAPS' rather than hurting the National Guard will prove to be a wonderful public relations tool for it."[35]

Since the movie would be made, Jaffe said that he had "attempted to make it more accurate in its portrayal of the Guard and the way in which it would be utilized." He assured Baruch that "TAPS" would become a first-class motion picture "in which there are no easy solutions to the problems presented." He expressed the hope that the Pentagon would now look favorably on the project, saying the country needed a motion picture about integrity, loyalty, courage, and honor and stated his belief that *Taps* made a comment about these values.[36]

Baruch forwarded the revised script to the National Guard Bureau on July 8, requesting that an "expeditious review be undertaken" and asking that he be advised if the new version "could be considered acceptable with a few additional changes or whether you still believe that original comments basically remain substantiated." He also advised Jaffe that things seemed positive. The producer apparently took that literally and wrote to Baruch that he was "thrilled" with the news. Nevertheless, he was still facing "rather extensive negotiations" and an actors strike before the Defense Department finally authorized assistance on April 2, 1981.[37]

For the National Guard, the long effort to assure itself of a positive image in *Taps* proved worthwhile. In an information paper detailing the bureau's involvement in the project, after the film's release, Joe Hanley of the Public Affairs Office described the original script as "probably the most negative piece on the Guard that I have ever reviewed." In contrast, he said that in the final version, "the Guard fares very well," with the senior guardsman portrayed "as an intelligent, compassionate human being who wants to avoid armed confrontation with the students at all costs. He is depicted as a no nonsense leader of troops—trim and with a fine military appearance. Without doubt, he is the *only* one in the film without a character flaw and is the sole voice of reason in the conflict."[38]

Perhaps reflecting the reality that the movie focused on the military academy students, not the National Guard, Jaffe had answered virtually all the National Guard Bureau's objections to the original script. Hanley noted that instead of being depicted "as bloodthirsty murderers," *Taps* portrayed the guardsmen "as competent professionals doing their jobs." More important, the film did not show any guardsmen actually firing at a student, and the final scene, in which the two students were killed, "was purposely left vague at our insistence so that it would not be determined definitively whether the lethal shots were fired by the Guard or police SWAT teams, both of whom are shown earlier." As a result of the negotiations and the resulting changes, Hanley felt that the film depicted the Guard "as a professional military force who are performing a task they want to end without any bloodshed." To Hanley, this revised portrayal would produce a "favorable" image in the average moviegoer.[39]

If *Taps* told a story about the National Guard, then the film could be judged on that basis. In fact, as Jaffe had written to Don Baruch, he saw the movie as making comments about the value of integrity, loyalty, courage, and honor as learned in a military academy. Consequently, the National Guard concern about its portrayal aside, the question remains as to how well *Taps* addressed the issues the filmmakers were purporting to illuminate. And did the film even answer the question Rex Reed thought it was raising: "Do we need military schools anymore?" He thought *Taps* was simply pretending "to examine a clash between the military, which gets its idealism from Patton and the Pentagon, and the new society, which gets its idealism from computers, home economists, real estate developers, and Erma Bombek." Instead, Reed thought the film "all but bludgeoned to death" the issue of military education "in the crossfire of confused motives. Rarely have I seen a movie

There was too much motivational dialogue in *Taps*.

so at odds with its own purposes. You go away saddened and depressed without even knowing what it is you're supposed to be depressed about. What begins as food for thought ends up a big mess on the floor and you don't know how to clean it up."[40]

Vincent Canby answered Reed's question by describing *Taps* as "a solemn, ponderously silly film about the dangers of a military education." Having his own trouble deciding what *Taps* had intended to do, the *New York Times* reviewer concluded that he supposed the film "means to be the terrible last word on the military mind run amok, and on the sort of thinking that led the United States into Vietnam not long ago." While acknowledging that the writers and the director had serious intentions in making the movie, he said that *Taps* had turned out "less serious than absurd, though without ever being funny." Worse, as far as the Pentagon involvement in the film was concerned, Canby thought the National Guard officer laid out the antimilitary position "with such unconvincing high-mindedness" that he longed for the reappearance of the "staunchly nutty" military school superintendent who had disappeared a third of the way through the film.[41]

Instead of dealing with producer Jaffe's values of integrity, loyalty, courage, and honor, *Taps* ultimately spent too much of its time on ceremonies and motivational dialogue and, in the end, provided empty rhetoric rather than reaching any conclusions about the value and dangers of a military education. Nevertheless, both *Stripes* and *Taps* demonstrated that filmmakers could once again negotiate successfully to receive cooperation from the armed services. They also confirmed the reality that the military could no longer expect only positive images from the films on which they did assist. Just as important, however, movies about the services in war and peace were again appearing in screens on a regular basis.

The Army's particular search for absolution from its sins in Vietnam bore more positive fruits with *Tank*, which became the vehicle that completed the process of making the Army once again a respectable subject for family entertainment. Given the lack of knowledge of military procedures and language of most writers, the project's initial screenplay, not surprisingly, met with some objections, once again from Joe Hanley in the National Guard Bureau's Office of Public Affairs. Writing to the Army's Office of Public Relations, Hanley argued, "The entire tenor of the production does not enhance the public's perception of the Army. While, admittedly, crude and offensive language is a reality of life, the glorification of it in this production does not enhance the professional image of the NCO and officer Corps. The depiction of the relationship between the different command levels is also not, I feel in the best interest of the Army." More to the point, he found that the story's "hook," the hero's private ownership of a fully operational World War II Sherman tank, "casts serious doubt on the capability of the Army to maintain adequate ammunition security and accountability as well as a countenancing of a violation of federal firearms regulations."[42]

The tank in question has become a cherished possession of Sgt. Maj. Zack Carey, who has refurbished it in much the same way as a collector of classic automobiles and hauls it from base to base with his family. Nevertheless, Hanley pointed out that when Carey, whom James Garner played with his usual woodenness, uses the tank to rescue his son from jail, he is taking justice in his own hands. Despite the fact that the local sheriff has framed the boy on a trumped-up drug charge, Hanley wrote, "The flagrant disregard of accepted 'due process' approaches to redressing a legal grievance gives an erroneous impression that military members are above the law, and the actions of the commanding general in the final scenes only reinforce this impression." As a result, he saw "no compelling reason" for the Pentagon to support the production on this ground and because he believed the producers "are obviously not interested in increasing the public's understanding and acceptance of the Department of the Army."[43]

Following a meeting with the Army in the Pentagon on January 18, 1983, John Horton, Lorimar's liaison to the Pentagon, submitted a new script revised "to reflect the discussions." He also advised Baruch that the producer wanted to photograph "the modern Army background to the fullest extent possible with the scenes depicted in establishing Zack as a Sergeant Major of outstanding quality. The importance of this background is key to the quality of the film and benefits accruing to the Army in creating empathy of the audience with the Army personnel portrayed."[44]

Hanley's overall criticisms notwithstanding, the Army found the new script immediately acceptable for cooperation. Maj. Gen. Lyle Barker Jr., the Army's chief of public affairs, concluded: "*Tank* will provide an excellent opportunity to show the modern Army, as it provides the shooting background for approximately 30% of the film. Further, the primary military characters are depicted as highly motivated, honest and dedicated soldiers." The completed film did show this, and unlike Meechum in *The Great Santini, Tank* also portrayed Zack Carey not only as a good military man but also as an excellent father. Whether such a palatably mediocre movie as *Tank* provided the Army the proper vehicle to convey these images remains debatable.[45]

Despite its initial enthusiasm, the Army found the completed film disappointing because it did not contain more scenes showing the service's training and modern equipment interwoven into the narrative. Nevertheless, Baruch informed Horton that the Pentagon believed the end results of the cooperation had proven "beneficial for the Army and the producer" and hoped that the audience reactions would be "favorable" for the service. Reviewers, however, demonstrated far less graciousness in assessing the movie. Rita Kempley, in the *Washington Post Weekend,* described *Tank* as "a trite vehicle that lumbers along like its namesake. Clankety-clank." Vincent Canby, in the *New York Times,* showed even less charity, writing that the screenplay "wobbles uncertainly between sadistic melodrama and populist farce" and concluding that *Tank* became "implausible all the way round."[46]

Despite such harsh words and little success at the box office, *Tank* did provide totally positive images of the Army and its men, something that had happened only occasionally in Hollywood movies since the beginning of the escalation of the Vietnam conflict in 1965. Filmmakers were to shortly embark upon a new cycle of Vietnam movies that would again remind the nation of the horrors of the American experience in Vietnam, and the military would again suffer from the negative images of its experiences in the conflict. Nevertheless, *Tank* would go a long way toward completing the rehabilitation of the image of the armed services, making patriotism once again acceptable, and so stand in opposition to the negative portrayals that the Vietnam films were bound to contain.

23 | The Air Force Seeks a Better Image

IN THE DECADE AFTER THE END of the Vietnam War, the Air Force was to contribute little to this rehabilitation. In Vietnam, the Air Force had dropped more bombs on a tiny agricultural land than all the tonnage the United States had dropped on Germany and Japan during all of World War II. To some extent, the impersonality and detachment with which the service carried out its mission muted the reality of the destructiveness of its military actions in Vietnam. Air Force personnel usually had little contact with the war on the ground. Unless a flier was shot down, he could do his full tour of duty without ever seeing a single Vietnamese, friend or enemy. Bomber crews, in particular, flying overhead at more than thirty thousand feet, often did not even see the countryside they were destroying. For them, flights to Vietnam from Guam, Thailand, and Okinawa resembled training missions they might have been carrying out from bases in the United States.

To be sure, particularly late in the war, Surface to Air Missiles (SAMs) posed a real danger to planes flying over North Vietnam. To the fliers, however, the anti-aircraft missiles may well have simply lent a sense of adventure to what otherwise might have become only another routine day at the office. Most Americans likely associated the Air Force actions in Vietnam with the sudden swooping attacks of jet fighters, which left brilliant splotches of fire erupting across fields or forests, or the ethereal beauty of massive B-52s lumbering across the sky, loosing their bombs on unseen targets. Except for an occasional image of a child on fire fleeing from a napalm attack or scenes of the rubble left from B-52 bombs, the Air Force managed to avoid the worst images from Vietnam that tarred the Army and Marines: the dead Vietnamese civilians, the soldiers burning peasant villages with Zippo lighters, or the young American boys dying in full color on the evening news.

Even the scenes of massive destruction that the bombers wrought lacked the immediacy of ground combat that sometimes reached television within hours of a battle. Moreover, rubble in the South Bronx or burned-out buildings in Watts or the H Street corridor in Washington looked very little different from rubble in Hanoi. Of course, the Air Force had created the rubble which Jane Fonda and other peace activists used as background for their attacks on the U.S. government's Vietnam policy and their support of North Vietnam. In effect, however, their posturing trivialized the destruction. After all, how serious could a war be when a delegation from the hated enemy's country could sit on anti-aircraft guns as they waited the arrival of the next attackers. In any case, the Air Force emerged from the war less disgraced and less damaged than the Army or the Marines and with the public still perceiving the Air Force as the primary deterrent to Soviet nuclear attack.

Such images provided filmmakers with few story lines that they could develop into positive productions. Instead, Hollywood returned to the negative aspects of nuclear weapons in an attempt to create visual drama. On its surface, Robert Aldrich's 1977 *Twilight's Last Gleaming* seemed to draw its inspiration from *Fail Safe* and *Dr. Strangelove*. Unlike the rabid anti-Communism of Stanley Kubrick's Generals Ripper and Turgidson, however, Gen. Lawrence Dell has opposed the Vietnam War and finds himself framed for murder as a result of his convictions. Breaking out of prison with three other inmates, Dell, played with a self-righteous fervor by Burt Lancaster, seizes a SAC missile silo and threatens to start World War III unless the president agrees to read to the American people a secret memo that details the reasons the United States became involved in Vietnam.

Twilight's Last Gleaming moves so rapidly that audiences can easily ignore its structural flaws and implausibilities. As a result, the buildup of tensions seems to grow naturally as Dell aborts a missile launch at the last moment and then meets the president in the climactic confrontation. In fact, *Twilight's Last Gleaming* cannot stand up to a close inspection. Dramatically, the film contains so many implausibilities that viewers ultimately find it impossible to suspend disbelief. Given Dell's background as a high-ranking Air Force officer and his knowledge of SAC procedures, the seizure of the mis-

Because of financial concerns and negative implications about the military in *Twilight's Last Gleaming*, Aldrich decided to film in Germany rather than ask the Pentagon for assistance.

sile complex seems credible, if not probable. However, once Dell has secured the silo, he does not seem to realize that he has painted himself into a corner with no way out. The missiles constitute his only leverage, albeit a powerful one, over the government. Yet, given his character and stated intention of trying to make the government more responsive to the people, audiences have great difficulty believing that Dell would actually destroy the world simply to reveal a single document.

Ironically, the document Dell wants revealed to the American people contains nothing of great surprise or importance to anyone who had read the "Pentagon Papers." Therefore, the president's shock when he reads the document and the general's extreme efforts to make the document public do not ring true to the audience. As a result, the movie's centerpiece message of the government's duplicity in getting the United States involved in Vietnam lacks the power to anger the American people, as the filmmakers apparently assumed it would. Moreover, Dell's expectation that the very government he is trying to expose would actually allow him to carry out his mission and escape show his naïveté. Consequently, the general comes across as a somewhat crazed victim of the Vietnam War rather than a hero trying to alert the nation to the wrongs its government has perpetrated on it.

In his defense, Aldrich was attempting to make a serious statement about the impact of the Vietnam War on the United States and a government run by men so amoral that they would shoot the president rather than reveal their complicity in involving the nation in Southeast Asia. Initially, however, Aldrich had found *Twilight's Last Gleaming* "only a middling action script. Nothing you haven't seen before. One of those unlikely-but-possible things. It had the usual paraphernalia, the tests and bluffs, for any ransom-hijack-jeopardy story." In fact, the original script lacked a motivation to explain why the crazy general hijacks a missile silo. Then Aldrich remembered seeing on television a returning

Navy POW captain who bent down and kissed the ground: "At the time, I thought it was a very showboat thing to do."[1]

Later, while visiting a Navy base in Norfolk, Virginia, Aldrich found himself at the same party with the officer, now an admiral. The director overheard the man telling a friend about his terrible mental conflicts, and according to the director, the anguish left an indelible impression on him. When he reread the original script for *Twilight's Last Gleaming* several years later, he remembered the admiral: "This admiral obviously wasn't going to go out and bomb Pearl Harbor the next day, but he was certainly going to have some kind of breakdown eventually. He just couldn't reconcile the radical views he held with the uniform he wore." With this vision in mind, Aldrich decided "to dramatically project the character of that admiral onto the general in this story." He spent eight weeks working with new screenwriters to make "a silk purse out of the sow's ear" and then convinced Lancaster to play General Dell, although he had turned down the original script.[2]

Lancaster's general became a Daniel Ellsberg in uniform, using missiles instead of a Xerox machine to pry the Vietnam story out of the Pentagon's top-secret files. Clearly missiles are sexier crowbars than copiers to the financial people who back motion pictures. In any case, the actor and the director shared a liberal view of American politics and so attempted to put their beliefs on the screen. To Aldrich, the U.S. intervention in Vietnam resembled the German intervention in the Spanish Civil War: "In 1957 two books came out, one by Gen. Maxwell Taylor, one by Prof. Henry Kissinger. Each had to do with the necessity of being ready to wage limited wars, in order to avoid having to wage nuclear war. Our going into Vietnam demonstrated our willingness to go to war, and it allowed us to do it in a limited way."[3]

This, then, became the contents of the secret memo that General Dell tried to blackmail the government into revealing in *Twilight's Last Gleaming*. Having appeared in several "political" films, including *Executive Action* and *Seven Days in May* as well as *Go Tell the Spartans*, Lancaster had no problem with message films: "They can be entertainment pictures, as long as they have some point of view about something. These days, political pictures can achieve fairly substantial grosses because there's so much controversy about government operations." Lancaster thought that in the mid-1970s, people "have a despairing picture of democratic life in America. Some people will take *Twilight's Last Gleaming* as entertainment, others will come away saying there's an element of truth there. The world changes slowly. But you have to keep making an effort. Societies have to. Otherwise there's no change."[4]

If *Twilight's Last Gleaming* had appeared while the United States was still fighting in Vietnam, Aldrich's message might well have had an impact on people's perceptions of the war, and the film might have contributed to shortening the nation's involvement in Southeast Asia. However, like *Go Tell the Spartans* and *Coming Home*, *Twilight's Last Gleaming* arrived too late, leaving Aldrich with a stale message trying to invigorate an action, adventure movie that the director had not wanted to make. Moreover, the many other problems with the script vitiated the excitement and suspense inherent in the plot. Richard Schickel, for one, thought the film unraveled "mostly because of an ill-considered attempt to make a statement about contemporary issues." In fact, the reviewer observed that nothing in the "infamous" documents was "worth picking up a picket sign to protest, let alone knocking over a missile base. In short, the movie's not inconsiderable possibilities for innocent entertainment are undercut by the feckless desire of small minds to make a big statement."[5]

A big statement or not, from the Pentagon's perspective, *Twilight's Last Gleaming* contained no saving graces. The immortality of the military establishment and the government officials surrounding the president would have disqualified the screenplay for assistance a priori. After all, who would want to be associated with a movie in which the secretaries of state and defense agree that the president can be shot as part of the effort to kill a renegade general? Moreover, how could the Air Force cooperate on a film that demonstrates how an outsider could penetrate the security of a missile complex, seize control of the facility, and hold it for ransom?

Perhaps worst of all, the film posited that Vietnam had destroyed General Dell, as it had altered the admiral whom Aldrich used as his model for Lancaster's character. If the war made Dell unreliable, then it might be argued that other top military officers still on duty might be suffering from post-traumatic stress syndrome and so might also act irrationally. The military simply could not support a story that contained such a suggestion. Well aware of the problems such images would cause the Pentagon, Aldrich never approached the military to even discuss possible assistance. Instead, having obtained three-quarters of the film's $5.5 million budget from a group of German investors, Aldrich went to Germany to make *Twilight's Last Gleaming*.

In the end, Aldrich gambled not only on the story but also on the manner in which he told it, on occasion splitting the screen up to six times to create a fragmented narrative of different actions occurring simultaneously. The director thought his gamble might pay off: "I have the feeling that audiences have a larger attention span than pictures usually call upon them to use. I think that if you split the screen up into panels, you can direct the audience's attention to one or the other by varying the clarity or level of the sound." For his efforts, Aldrich created a visually interesting movie. If *Twilight's Last Gleaming* did not also contain the powerful warning the director and star had hoped to make, they did produce a serious, sometimes stimulating movie that reflected the nation's paranoia in the post-Vietnam, post-Watergate period. However, it clearly did nothing to improve the image of the Air Force or the other armed services.[6]

Firefox did not even pay lip service to a meaningful comment on the military's place in American life. Instead, it attempted to hide an absurd story, horrendous acting, and imitative special effects behind Clint Eastwood's box-office appeal and implausible, unrelieved melodrama. Nevertheless, Eastwood remained a favorite with the military, who saw *Firefox* simply as "his science-fiction derring-do." Such a film, devoid of any intellectual pretensions, would have considerable appeal since it substituted action and adventure for any serious questioning of the armed services. Beyond that, a film that showed an American flier and Vietnam POW hijacking a state-of-the-art Soviet stealth fighter offered a rare chance for the Air Force to project a positive image of itself and its men.[7]

In this context, *Firefox* seemed to offer the perfect vehicle to erase any continuing negative images of the service in Vietnam. After all, it provided a testament to the skills of Air Force fighter pilots and the visual excitement of another aerial dogfight reminiscent of countless Hollywood war-in-the-air movies as well as of the war-in-space combat of *Star Wars* and *The Last Star Fighter*. Certainly the Pentagon saw the film that way when Warner Brothers made its initial inquiries to the military in January 1980. According to John Horton, the studio's Washington representative, the Air Force and the Navy had "favorable reactions" to the production and recommended pushing through a request for assistance in the near future. Horton also noted that the current diplomatic situation between the USSR and the United States following the Russian invasion of Afghanistan "would alleviate the State Department or International Security Agency (DoD) reticence about approving any film critical of the Soviets." As a result, he recommended that although the studio's production plans remained indefinite, "we should pursue DOD approval on providing assistance on a tentative start date basis."[8]

Following through on Horton's suggestion, the studio wrote to the Pentagon describing the project and requesting an overall approval of the script even though the filmmakers did not yet know whether they would need any more than some Air Force stock footage and technical advice. Nevertheless, the producer expressed his willingness to make "the necessary modifications [of the script] in the interests of technical accuracy or to facilitate Department of Defense support. In our view, this film might help contribute to a better public understanding of the Soviet strides in advanced technology while underscoring American ingenuity." Acknowledging that the company wanted to make a highly entertaining and profitable movie, he stressed that they wanted "to positively represent the U.S., its military personnel and the Defense Department."[9]

After reading the script, the Air Force Public Affairs Office in Los Angeles advised its Pentagon headquarters, "This script does not negatively portray the USAF but it can provide some positive benefits in that the lead character, Mitchell Gant, is an ex-AF pilot—one of the best who's ever flown." The office felt that the relatively minor changes to the script it was suggesting to the filmmakers would further strengthen Gant's character. More important, it stated: "Policy-wise, we believe this movie, even though it's dramatic entertainment, would help inform the American public about Soviet strides in weapons development." Consequently, the Los Angeles office recommended concept/policy approval of the project.[10]

After further Air Force and Navy reviews, Don Baruch advised the producer on March 21, 1980, that the Defense Department approved the basic concept of the screenplay and said that he was looking forward to reading the revised screenplay that contained the requested changes. He did request that the new script "tone down some of the language in the Navy sequence as it is the only time that 'earthy' dialogue is utilized. Actually, it is not that customary with Navy personnel. Also, it is requested that Gant does not kill the Soviet agent in the subway sequence." He concluded by stating that as soon as the Defense Department approved the revised script, the services would work out arrangements for whatever assistance the filmmakers would actually need.[11]

Despite the military's willingness to support the script from its initial arrival in the Pentagon, the film did not go into production until the summer of 1981, after Eastwood's own company, Malpaso Productions, took over the project. However, at least to the military, the end result made the wait seem worthwhile. When the company screened the film in the Pentagon, Don Baruch wrote to the producer that the services' reaction to *Firefox* "was most favorable. There were no objections from those representing the Navy, the Air Force, and others we required for coordination." He confirmed the approval for screen credits acknowledging the support of each of the armed services and reported that people with whom he had spoken had reported that "they felt it was suspenseful, exciting and proof that it is of mutual advantage to the producer and DoD to work together. Also, you will be pleased to know that reports from the field have been most complimentary of Malpaso Productions, especially Clint Eastwood and yourself for following guidance and requirements for assistance."[12]

Eastwood told people at the world premiere of *Firefox* the next month in Washington that "he made the movie for the entertainment value." Despite his warning to the audience to "fasten your seatbelts because no one is allowed out of the theater the last ten minutes," some viewers emerged from the screening to report they "were exhausted from the intense action." To be sure, the climactic dogfight contained visually thrilling sequences, albeit created with special effects that looked as if they had been lifted from the closing scenes of the original *Star Wars*. Nevertheless, any excitement which the dogfight between the two identical MiG fighters may have engendered became immediately tempered by the reality that audiences were only watching the skills of special-effects artists, not actual pilots manning jet planes cartwheeling across the sky.[13]

More important, however impressive the futuristic aerial duel might appear to viewers, it could not hide the cliché-ridden story and the implausibility of its premise. Eastwood's mountain-climbing part-time-secret-agent professor from *The Eiger Sanction* or a James Bond might work his way into a highly secret Soviet Air Force test facility and steal the most advanced fighter plane ever built. But Eastwood's detached, slightly confused, slow-to-react fighter pilot never acquired a believability that might persuade audiences to suspend their disbelief. Consequently, most viewers had a hard time accepting that Eastwood could masquerade as a Russian, walk into the Soviet base, and fly away, let alone regain his flying skills sufficiently to pilot a strange aircraft in a dogfight to end all dogfights. Worse, the audience probably didn't care by then anyway, given the sorry dialogue, crude efforts to insert anti-Soviet, Cold War rhetoric, and plain sloppy filmmaking. The sun's setting into the East China Sea at the end of John Wayne's *Green Berets* had symbolized that anti-Communist movie's confused nature. In the same way, the actors' switching from English to Russian and back again without rhyme or reason epitomized the filmmakers' disinterest in infusing even a modicum of intelligence into *Firefox*.

Of course, the Pentagon did not concern itself with the film's production values or dramatic quality in determining the script's suitability for assistance. But even in the way in which the film portrayed Air Force men and actions, the service's primary interest, *Firefox* did not provide a uniformly positive picture. The opening sequence quickly established the connection between the Air Force actions in Vietnam and its postwar mission. The film begins with an Air Force helicopter flying across the Alaskan wilderness toward Eastwood's home, to which he has retreated from society, suffering from combat fatigue in Vietnam. The noisy arrival of the helicopter triggers a post-traumatic stress disorder (PTSD) flashback in which Eastwood's character relives his being shot down in Vietnam while on a ground support mission. The Vietnamese capture him and parade him in a cage through the countryside, where he witnesses an Air Force napalm attack which incinerates a young

A scene from the film *Firefox*, with Clint Eastwood starring as a Vietnam veteran suffering from post-traumatic stress disorder.

Vietnamese girl. Back in Alaska, the uninvited visitors find Eastwood huddling in a corner in a PTSD-induced stupor, clutching a hunting rifle, effectively reminding the audience of the effect that the war had on its combatants.

Despite this explicit reference to Vietnam and the film's absurdity, implausibility, and dullness, the Air Force and the Pentagon still saw *Firefox* as creating a positive image of the military's contemporary efforts to maintain world peace through strength and sophisticated intelligence. In fact, the filmmakers resorted to the entire file cabinet of Cold War Soviet stereotypes to create a justification for international theft. Nevertheless, director Eastwood demonstrated an inability to decide how to best make his statement and provide the American people with a great victory over its implacable Cold War foe.

During the final seconds of the dogfight, the Russian pilot, who has pursued Eastwood in an identical Russian stealth fighter, refuses to avail himself of an easy kill opportunity, reminiscent of gentlemanly World War I aerial encounters. Eastwood promptly reciprocates by blasting the Russian out of the sky with rear-firing rockets. Except for the obvious dramatic necessity to end the film with a spectacular explosion, the story would have made more sense if the Russian pilot had defected and joined Eastwood in a flight to freedom, with everyone living happily ever after.

Whatever else might be said about *Firefox,* the Air Force and the armed services as a whole probably benefited from the portrayal of the military establishment aggressively defending the security of the United States. In contrast, *Wargames* took the image of the Air Force in Hollywood movies to its absolute nadir. Aside from the total implausibility of the story itself, the film's representations of Air Force men and procedures bore virtually no resemblance to the manner in which the service carried out its mission of protecting the nation from nuclear attack. Instead, the film suggested, in much the same way *Dr. Strangelove* and *Fail Safe* had savaged the service almost twenty years earlier, that the Air Force could not control its weapons of destruction.

The Air Force Los Angeles Public Affairs Office had actually provided screenwriters Walter Parkes and Larry Lasker with a research trip to the North American Air Defense Command (NORAD) on Cheyenne Mountain, in Colorado Springs, Colorado. There, on September 15, 1980, the writers supposedly talked at length with Lt. Gen. James Hartinger, NORAD's commander in chief, sketching out the premise of their story. Although they had not yet clearly formulated their ideas, they explained that the theme of the movie would focus on the need for human control rather than computer control of the nation's nuclear strike force.[14]

In the MGM/US *Wargames* press kit, Lasker reported that when the general heard that the writers intended to come down on the human side of control as opposed to turning things over to computers, "he just fell in love with us." According to the writer, the general told him and Parkes that defense contractors and technology experts were trying to get humans out of the decision-making process over the objections of the Air Force. Whether or not Lasker correctly represented the general's concerns on the matter, the Air Force had a somewhat different recollection of the writers' visit. Lt. Col. Al Alderfer, a NORAD public affairs officer at the time *Wargames* opened, denied the studio's story: "Hartinger didn't talk to them and he certainly didn't sit around and B.S. with them. He never addressed them directly except maybe only to answer questions in a Q&A session."[15]

Whatever the truth about their visit and their claim to being in agreement with the commander of NORAD, Lasker and Parkes's completed screenplay bore little relationship to actual Air Force operations. Of course, if the writers had portrayed NORAD, the Strategic Air Command, and the military-civilian control of the nuclear arsenal correctly, they would have had no story. In any case, given distortions and inaccuracies in the script, the Air Force would have had no basis on which to consider assistance to the production if the filmmakers had ever made a formal request for support.

Universal Studios, which then had the rights to the screenplay, did submit a script to the Air Force's Los Angeles Office for comments in June 1981 but received a negative reaction. Universal then asked John Horton, its Washington representative, to discuss the military's objections to the project with the Pentagon. In writing to Baruch on June 21, Horton described in some detail the writers' meeting with General Hartinger at NORAD and advised that "substantial changes are being made in the story, including an explanation of the 'fluke,' largely due to telephone wire crossovers of the origin of the computer exchange." After stressing that the theme of the story is human control rather than computer failure, Horton explained that the filmmakers' "judgment on changes can be enhanced considerably with specific knowledge of objections to scenes, characters, portrayals, dialogue, etc. We are interested in alleviating the elements in our script which may be considered objectionable by the Department of Defense, but without any information from you, the effort may not be meaningful." However, during the meeting to discuss the request, Baruch advised Horton that the script contained a false premise, and later, on the bottom of Horton's letter, he noted, "John said he didn't want answer turning down in writing."[16]

In the summer of 1982, after MGM/UA had acquired the rights to the screenplay, the Air Force offered to discuss the project with the new producers, but the filmmakers "refused to even consider any modifications." As with *Fail Safe*, if they had accepted the service's criticisms and had rewritten the script to bring it in line with actual procedures, they would have had no movie. On their part, Lasker and Parkes saw no reason to make any changes, since they had not written a documentary about the Air Force's procedures but a story they hoped would make people think about the threat of nuclear war. As a result, the Air Force and the Pentagon found themselves virtually powerless to influence the production.[17]

In fact, the film continued the tradition of *Fail Safe* and *Dr. Strangelove* in attempting to warn the American people about the possibility of accidental nuclear holocaust. Like the 1970 *Colossus*, which also did not request cooperation, *Wargames* posits a computer's total control over the nation's nuclear arsenal, not the malfunction of a single computer part as in *Fail Safe*, which brings the world to the brink of destruction. Lasker and Parkes said they wanted audiences to come out of the theater with the message that no nation can win a nuclear war: "That is a message of the film. That is probably the first one people come out of the theaters with, because it is the last one we leave them with." At the same time, the writers thought *Wargames* also addressed the need for humans to take responsibility for their own technology.[18]

Unlike the earlier antibomb films, the story in which Lasker and Parkes placed their message had an appeal beyond its serious purpose. Instead of Stanley Kubrick's mad Gen. Jack Ripper ordering the B-52 attack to get the Commies or *Fail Safe's* grim Air Force officers desperately trying to save the world, *Wargames* had as its protagonist a winsome teenager, Matthew Broderick, as David, an underachieving computer whiz. Broderick and Ally Sheedy, as his girlfriend Jennifer and comrade in adventure, gave the film the added dimension of believable adolescents whom the audience, particularly the teenage market, could identify with and cheer on in their struggles with unthinking adults and an out-of-control computer.

David Lightman (Matthew Broderick) assists his girlfriend (Ally Sheedy) in changing her grades by infiltrating the school's computer system.

While demonstrating his skills with his home computer to Jennifer, David goes from changing their school grades to accidentally plugging into a NORAD computer, recently installed to replace man in the nuclear launch decision-making process. Believing that he has simply entered an unidentified computer system that has new computer games to challenge him, David begins playing Global Thermonuclear War with WOPR, short for War Operations Plan Response. In fact, he has challenged the Defense Department's computer to a war game that will lead to the launch of the nation's nuclear strike force, since its creator has programmed WOPR not only to learn from its mistakes but also to play out every strategy and option to the end. In the penultimate moment, David, with the help of WOPR's creator, manages to overload the computer's circuitry and save the world.

To audiences caught up in the hectic pace of a well-crafted, visually exciting movie and the adventures of two charming teenagers, the story's dramatic implausibilities, inaccurate depictions of the military, and criminal actions might tend to pass unnoticed. Consequently, they might not have been bothered that David could so readily avoid going to school or that his parents did nothing after the FBI arrested him and whisked him off to NORAD headquarters. Viewers might not even show incredulity that the film portrayed the FBI as a bunch of idiots who actually seemed to believe they had caught a dangerous spy in the guise of a seventeen-year-old boy instead of immediately realizing that they had apprehended a computer hack who had gotten unlucky in one of his forays into computer networks. They might not even think about the reality that David had changed both his and Jennifer's grades, had broken into WOPR thinking he had reached a software company's computer from which he could steal computerized games, had cheated the telephone company, and had entered into an airline's ticket computer. Worst of all, they might even have applauded David for averting a nuclear holocaust, irrespective of his having initiated the threat through his illegal actions.

Only an occasional viewer was moved to see below the surface of *Wargames*. One who wrote to the *Los Angeles Times* perhaps best put the film's reality into proper perspective: "I do not remember ever having seen crime so winningly portrayed. If this is the attitude we expect our children to have to the large social institutions that serve us, we are in trouble that is almost as deep as thermonuclear war." Nevertheless, this sort of criticism remained in the minority. To the extent that most people had any opinion about *Wargames* beyond their visceral reaction to the entertainment value of the movie, they found it "just a big, flashy, exciting and noisy vehicle for a timely if over-used message about nuclear war: 'The only winning strategy is not to play.'" Most Air Force and military people would undoubtedly agree with that assessment. Lieutenant Colonel Alderfer, for one, acknowledged that *Wargames* was "highly entertaining" but quickly added that it remained "a complete fantasy."[19]

To Lasker and Parkes, the film served only as the medium to cause people to think about the issue of nuclear war: "We hope the thinking public's response to the movie would be to look at the various issues which are freely dramatized and fictionalized, and become curious about them, and look into the actual details." They claimed a difference existed between "being real and being realistic" and argued that they had responsibility to be real: "It may not be specifically realistic that missile commanders are removed from their silos. It is an obvious fictionalization. However, hopefully, the dramatization of that scene points up a real issue, i.e., that human beings, as we found in our research, [missile commanders] sometimes, when asked to do the ultimate inhuman act which amounts to perhaps the senseless killing of four to five million people by the turning of a single key, . . . when given that task, human beings may buckle at it, for moral or ethical or psychological reasons. That is a real issue." Consequently, the writers felt they had "a greater responsibility to dramatize the reality of that issue, than to go through the specific steps realistically." They then made a leap of faith and argued that since they presented *Wargames* as "a piece of fiction, a piece of popular entertainment, that the motion picture audience hopefully is sophisticated enough to read it as such."[20]

Perhaps. But just as likely, filmgoers believe that what they see on the screen represents reality and would base their knowledge of the Air Force nuclear launch procedures on the portrayal in *Wargames*. And what they saw, from the opening sequence, in which an Air Force missile launch officer refused to turn his key, bore no resemblance to reality. The refusal of the officer and 22 percent of his comrades to turn the key in a test simulation became the springboard for the film. If so many Air Force officers would not turn the key, the service would have no recourse but to replace humans in the loop with a foolproof computer that would act on the basis of inputs, not emotions. Although the writers and the Air Force might disagree over the actual number of officers who would refuse to act, even Lasker and Parkes agreed that the figure would be far lower than 22 percent. In any case, Lt. Col. Duncan Wilmore, the Air Force public affairs officer in Los Angeles, who had arranged the writers' trip to NORAD, acknowledged that the service would have no choice but to turn down any script containing such a misrepresentation of the actual situation among officers in the missile silos.[21]

Ironically, once Wilmore had retired from the Air Force, he took a different perspective on the story, given his new job as technical advisor on the production. To be sure, he still admitted that few officers in missile silos would actually refuse to turn the key to launch a nuclear missile. Nevertheless, Wilmore now suggested that if 22 percent of Air Forces officers, in a simulated crisis situation, would not turn their keys if they received orders to do so, then the defense establishment, as posited in *Wargames*, would have a valid reason to replace humans with computers in the launch process. Given this hypothesis, Wilmore explained that he could suspend his disbelief and agree to work on the film, despite his Air Force training and public affairs orientation. In fact, before he began his job, he did ascertain from Lt. Col. Donald Gilleland, his replacement in the Los Angeles office, that his involvement with *Wargames* would not preclude his later working on films that received Air Force cooperation, and he did work on such movies as *The Right Stuff*. In any event, Wilmore's job on *Wargames* consisted primarily of ensuring that the military aspects of the film looked and sounded correct rather than trying to change any substantive aspects of the story.[22]

In the end, *Wargames* may have looked reasonably authentic. Coming during the height of the nuclear freeze movement, its message readily fitted into the antibomb sentiment of a large portion of the nation's population. Nevertheless, the film used inaccurate representations of Air Force procedures and caricatures of its officers to create its message. As far as the Air Force was concerned, the events as portrayed in the film simply could not happen. No WOPR or any computer like it existed, and the Air Force had no plans to replace men in the decision-making process in any way resembling what happened in the film. In total contrast to what *Wargames* portrayed, NORAD had as its sole responsibility the identifying, monitoring, and reporting of unidentified objects that might be an attacking enemy force. It had no responsibility or control over the Strategic Air Command; only the president had the authority to order any retaliatory attack, based on information that NORAD and other agencies might provide him. Simply told, the commanding general of NORAD could not order a nuclear launch as he almost did in the film.

The cinematic commanding general of NORAD became another Hollywood stereotypical rendering of Gen. Curtis LeMay, down to his long cigar. Although he ultimately decided that WOPR had malfunctioned and tried to countermand the computer's efforts to launch a nuclear strike, he had allowed the situation to escalate by not having recognized much earlier all the signs indicating that he had a runaway computer. Any alert military man, especially one who has become a commanding general of such a key military facility, would have made immediate inquiries about the state of the world and any crises suddenly developing between the superpowers that might have triggered WOPR's actions. Instead, he ignored the warning signs that the computer had serious problems and allowed it to continue its countdown instead of shutting it down while his men still had the chance to do so. Of course, if the film had portrayed Air Force personnel operating as they actually do, *Wargames* would not have had a beginning, a middle, or an end.

In broader terms, however, the filmmakers misrepresented the nation's defense efforts and the role of the computer in them. NORAD had, in fact, experienced false alarms over the years. But the men operating the system had caught and solved the problems in minutes, not hours, as portrayed in *Wargames*. However, this counted for little to Lasker and Parkes, since they approached their story in much the same way that Max Youngstein had approached *Fail Safe*. If no absolute exists, then the Air Force's fail safe procedure could not become absolutely infallible, and so a nuclear-attack accident became possible.

Likewise, Lasker and Parkes approached their story with the apparent presumption that if NORAD has experienced false alarms, and if computer hackers have entered sensitive computer networks, then someday, someone would actually compromise the most secret defense computers and launch a nuclear war. Why bother with the fact that opera-

A computer-savvy teenager (Matthew Broderick) prevents the outbreak of nuclear war by overloading the computer's circuitry at the crucial moment.

tional computers such as a theoretical WOPR would have no connection to any computer network and more especially to normal telephone lines, which David used to access the NORAD supercomputer. In essence, they simply argued that if a hacker can penetrate existing computer networks, then any computer can be penetrated, even the most carefully guarded one. They then used this fallacious premise as the basis for a warning to the American people of the dangers of relying on computers and technology rather than on human beings.[23]

Whether the importance of the message justified the inaccurate portrayal of the Air Force's control of the nation's nuclear strike force, Lasker, Parkes, and director John Badham did create an exciting motion picture. *Wargames* deserved its widespread appeal, drawing audiences into the adventures of David and Jennifer with just the right combination of tension and humor as it builds up to the final climax. Most viewers probably were able to suspend their disbelief at the plot's many implausibilities, at least up to the final special-effects light show, a computer simulation of massive global destruction, which effectively destroyed any illusion of authenticity that the filmmakers had managed to create.

From the Air Force perspective, that came too late. For the service, *Wargames* lacked any redeeming qualities, and its public relations efforts to inform people that the film did not accurately portray its procedures apparently had little impact. Fortunately for the Air Force, although audiences apparently enjoyed the movie as pure entertainment, they did not take its rendering of the military seriously. In writing to the *Los Angeles Times*, Jeffrey Cotton observed: "Let's face it. If any of us really believed that the *Wargames* scenario could really happen, we wouldn't be sitting in movie theaters cheering for some egghead brat and his Valley-Girl sidekick, we'd be out in the backyard digging holes." Likewise, Bob Kerstein wrote, "Few of my friends who have seen the movie harbored any misconceptions that the *real* thing was being depicted. I think most moviegoers are able to differentiate between the fantasy of a motion picture and the reality of our country's defense organization." He argued that none of the advertising for the movie claimed that *Wargames* was a faithful portrayal of NORAD and suggested that the military's concern about the film's inaccuracies illustrated its "penchant for paranoia."[24]

Rather than paranoia, the Air Force's concern about its portrayal in *Wargames* reflected its congressional mandate and own need to inform the American people about its mission and procedures so that they would better understand how the military is protecting the nation and, not incidentally, spending its tax dollars. Each of the armed services had considered motion pictures as a valid conduit for efficiently conveying this information. To be sure, filmmakers usually had a different agenda in using the military as a setting for their stories. Consequently, differences of opinion were bound to occur over what constituted a valid, that is, "accurate" rendering of a service's personnel, procedures, and equipment.

People looking at the Air Force's refusal to provide support to *Wargames* without sufficient knowledge of DoD regulations governing military cooperation to Hollywood or filmmakers' own penchant for creative freedom might well have a difficult time appreciating why the Pentagon could not assist on the production. One writer to the *Los Angeles Times* observed: "With all due respect, I think the armed forces should put up or shut up. How can they accuse the film of being inaccurate 'hogwash' if they refused to cooperate with the producers or writers of the film? If the military is so worried about the public getting the right idea of what goes on at NORAD, then why didn't they cooperate?"[25]

Wargames provided a perfect illustration of how filmmakers themselves often created barriers to obtaining military assistance by their refusal to even discuss script revisions.

The armed services, however, remained committed to working with any producer willing to enter into give-and-take negotiations. In fact, *Wargames* remained an aberration in Hollywood's return to more positive portrayals of the armed services, at least in non-Vietnam films, that had begun in the late 1970s. The two-hour television pilot *Call to Glory*, broadcast in August 1984, immediately following the Olympics, and the subsequent weekly series based on it went a long way to completing the rehabilitation of the postwar military's image in movies and on television and made patriotism once again acceptable.

Call to Glory focused on Air Force fliers and their families during the period from the Cuban Missile Crisis to the assassination of President John F. Kennedy. It had its origins in 1981, when Duncan Wilmore, in his capacity as chief of the Air Force's Public Affairs Office in Los Angeles, discussed with producers Jonathan Avnet and Steve Tisch the idea of creating a television series featuring the Air Force. Neither Avnet nor Tisch had any military background, but the suggestion came at the time when Tom Wolfe's *The Right Stuff* had stimulated an interest in military flying and *The Great Santini* was becoming a hit in its second release. Consequently, Wilmore's suggestion struck the producers as both a commercially attractive enterprise and, according to Tisch, "an opportunity to be exposed to the military life style."[26]

CBS television turned down the proposed project, but Jordan Kerner, head of dramatic development at ABC television, became excited about the concept and gave the producers the go-ahead. Avnet and Tisch felt that focusing the story on the period of the Cuban Missile Crisis not only offered the advantage of being "an interesting, difficult, and exciting" time in American history but also gave them an opportunity to return to the formative period of their lives. In his formal pitch for military assistance on his production in December 1982, Avnet wrote to the Air Force's Los Angeles Office: "We have a wonderful script which can become an equally wonderful movie describing the courage and professionalism which led members of our armed service to successfully help the President of our country with a most serious threat to our security. We place great emphasis on the role of his family in making him a superior serviceman."[27]

No longer fearing the antipathy of U.S. audiences to military subjects, Avnet stated that by exploiting values that are rarely experienced on television, "namely—patriotism, sacrifice, and service for one's country," he could make a show that would be "quite unique and very commercially successful." The producer clearly recognized that the Pentagon only provided assistance when a project in some way benefited a service or seemed in their best interest and so suggested that his production, originally titled *Air Force* and intended as a TV pilot, would "be of enormous benefit to the Department of Defense by creating an image of the Air Force that is both positive and one worthy of emulation." Acknowledging the long eclipse of military subjects since Vietnam, Avnet reminded the Air Force that "a show of this kind is quite visibly lacking from the primetime network arena and has been for a number of years. This show is therefore a most unique opportunity for both of us."[28]

The Air Force had recently cooperated on Paramount's TV miniseries *The Enola Gay*, the story of Col. Paul Tibbets and the dropping of the two atomic bombs on Japan. Given the developing Nuclear Freeze Movement and the dramatic limitations of television docudrama, the production did little to promote the service and its current mission. In contrast, the Air Force quickly recognized the benefits that *Call to Glory* offered the service and the entire military establishment. According to Lt. Col. Donald Gilleland, Wilmore's replacement in the Air Force Public Affairs Office in Los Angeles, his office had no great interest in making movies: "We want to only make certain Air Force people are depicted as accurately as possible carrying out their professional assignments in the manner that officers and men actually perform. We have a public trust to defend the nation and if filmmakers are going to depict us in that role, we want to be shown as accurately as possible." To that end, Gilleland worked closely with the producers and their writers to help mold the concept and the script in order to avoid technical problems.[29]

Once the writers had completed the initial script, Gilleland forwarded it to Brig. Gen. Richard Abel, the Air Force director of public affairs in Washington. He advised his boss that the project "offers the best opportunity we have ever had to showcase the Air Force way of life before millions of American viewers every week. It is a family-oriented show, depicting Air Force people as dedicated professionals who love their work and their families. It has the lure of flying, with a sense of doing something patriotic that is also personally rewarding and emotionally satisfying to the airman and his family." Noting that the producer had "agreed to make whatever reasonable script or location modifications are necessary to accommodate Air Force operational considerations," Gilleland urged the Air Force and the Pentagon to "approve Air Force support to this excellent film effort."[30]

In light of the close working relationship between the producers, the writers, and the Air Force Los Angeles Office, the completed script had no problem meeting the Pentagon's criteria of plausibility, accurate portrayal of procedures, and positive image. Only a few minor technical errors had crept into the script, such as designating Air Force officers as "commanding officers" (the Army term) instead of "commanders" (the Air Force term) and describing jet plane fuel as high-octane fuel instead of kerosene. The script reviewers did have a few substantive objections, most significantly about the opening sequence, in which a visiting three-star general receives an escort to an Air Force base from a tight formation of jet fighters. Although Gilleland acknowledged that such a display would be taboo, *Call to Glory* did open with such an aerial greeting, which he justified as "legitimate dramatic license."[31]

Don Baruch's only concern with the project focused on the need for the Air Force to avoid becoming "involved in a soap opera." In approving assistance, Baruch reminded the service that cooperation was to be at no cost to the government and that Air Force personnel who performed as extras would do so "on a voluntary basis and in most cases on their own time." M. Sgt. Rick Racquer, who served as a liaison with the production in the Air Force Public Affairs Office, felt that *Call to Glory* reflected "the current attitude of Americans toward the military that began to shift in a more positive direction following the Iranian hostage rescue attempt which showed to the American people the armed forces working in unison making a concerted effort to help fellow citizens."[32]

To Don Baruch, the completed two-hour pilot "lived up to the promises which Avnet had made to produce a positive, interesting, and exciting television feature which would give the public a better understanding of the Air Force in action during a significant period in United States history." After he and other Pentagon officials had screened the television film, Baruch expressed the hope that *Call to Glory* could gain popular acceptance without resorting to the melodrama of the other recent military series, including *For Love and Honor* and *Emerald Point*.[33]

Gilleland found the product of his two years of work with the producers "satisfying" because his efforts had helped produce "one of the best depictions of the Air Force audiences have seen in years and in particular, the best portrayal of an Air Force wing commander and his family that has ever been done." Gilleland's wife described the program as "the only film she has seen that has presented an accurate view of an Air Force wife's perspective." And coproducer Steve Tisch felt that *Call to Glory* provided "a great example of working in harmony with the government." Of the production itself, Tisch concluded, "I'm going to use the word *patriotism*. People are going to respond to this series the way they responded to the Olympics. They'll be entertained, and they'll be proud."[34]

Even before the producer had the opportunity to test his prediction, ABC executives who screened the pilot immediately made a commitment to produce thirteen additional episodes. They also changed the broadcast date from February 1984 to the night after the Los Angeles Olympics, using their coverage of the sporting event to plug the program in patriotic terms at every opportunity. In truth, the two-hour pilot and subsequent episodes remained little more than standard television fare exploiting the flying sequences for their intrinsic visual excitement. Whatever success the series enjoyed came not only from the patriotism and sense of national pride that the Olympics had engendered but also from the nostalgia emanating from the Kennedy years, the last time the United States had stood unchallenged militarily and politically before the escalation of the war in Vietnam.

24 Vietnam: A More Moderate Approach

BY THE TIME *CALL TO GLORY* WAS MAKING patriotism an acceptable emotion, Vietnam was beginning to appear regularly on theater screens, either explicitly or by implication. How to create appropriate images of the war remained unclear to filmmakers. Although *The Deer Hunter* and *Apocalypse Now* had enjoyed box-office success, the epic scope of each movie had provided the unique appeal to audiences. Moreover, as the culmination of the first cycle of Vietnam movies that began with *Limbo,* the two films had, at least temporarily, seemed to sate people's interest in epic re-creations of the American experience in Vietnam. Hollywood had no way of forecasting whether or when people would again want to see combat movies, large or small in scope, that depicted a small peasant nation defeating the U.S. military, in full color, with all the warts.

Furthermore, the armed services perceived that they could gain little or no benefit from any film attempting to make a comment about the American experience in Vietnam. Worse, in light of Hollywood's initial portrayals of the war, the Pentagon could reasonably expect that any future movie about Vietnam would likely do great harm to the positive image of the contemporary military that the services had been diligently encouraging in such postwar, peacetime motion pictures as *The Final Countdown* and *The Great Santini.* Nevertheless, the controversial nature of the war, the excitement inherent in combat movies, and the "messages" that individual filmmakers wanted to send ensured that Hollywood would use Vietnam as a subject throughout the decade.

In creating the platform from which to make their statements, however, the motion picture industry faced the fact that *The Green Berets* remained the only combat movie about the war that had received full assistance from the Pentagon. Given the continuing intransigence that the armed services had demonstrated in their rejection of stories about Vietnam, producers had an understandable reluctance to even approach the Pentagon with their scripts. Moreover, producers were finding that they could readily make their movies in the Philippines or Thailand without U.S. military assistance. Since these countries offered a more realistic ambience of Vietnam than Fort Benning provided for *The Green Berets,* filmmakers most often chose not even to bother asking the Pentagon for assistance. On their part, the armed services had less and less Vietnam-vintage equipment to provide Hollywood. Worse, they had a hard time dealing with filmmakers, who usually considered any military requests for changes in their scripts an affront to their creative prerogatives irrespective of whether the revisions simply addressed accuracies of procedure, equipment, and history.

Filmmakers wanting to comment on Vietnam but lacking the budgets of Michael Cimino or Francis Coppola thus had several options. They could set their discussion of Vietnam in a noncombat setting, as in *Twilight's Last Gleaming,* or limit the portrayal of combat, as in *Who'll Stop the Rain?* or *More American Graffiti.* They could make their comments allegorically in what might best be described as non-Vietnam Vietnam films or tell stories about the war's impact at home. *Breaker Morant,* an Australian production set in South Africa during the Boer War but aimed at American audiences, and *Southern Comfort*, set in the bayous of Louisiana, both clearly intended to make comments about the American experience in Vietnam, as did *Gardens of Stone* and *Running on Empty*.

In the 1978 *Who'll Stop the Rain?* Karel Reisz used brief glimpses of combat in Vietnam as the springboard to his story exploring the impact that the war had on individuals and the nation as a whole. Based on Robert Stone's *Dog Soldiers*, which had won the 1973 National Book Award for fiction, the film used heroin as the metaphor for the destructiveness that Vietnam inflicted on the American people. The story, which Stone and Judith Rascoe adapted from the novel, followed the descent into hell of Michael Moriarty, playing an ex-Marine turned combat correspondent; Nick Nolte in the role of Moriarty's buddy from his days in the Corps; and Tuesday Weld, as Moriarty's wife.

Moriarty's experiences covering the war have turned him into a shell-shocked, walking casualty. In the film's opening sequence, he witnesses troops stampeding elephants that are supposedly carrying supplies for the Vietcong and he comes under attack from American jets which miss their targets and hit the forward fire base that he is visiting. As a form of protest for such absurdities, he agrees to serve as the conduit for the delivery of two kilos of heroin to the United States. In a letter to his wife, he explains, "You see, in a world where elephants are pursued by flying men, people are just naturally going to want to get high." To aid and abet this, Moriarty recruits Nolte to smuggle the drugs into the country and deliver the shipment to his wife, herself a prescription-drug doper.

The plans collapse almost immediately when Nolte encounters a corrupt narcotics agent and his two sadistic goons who attempt to appropriate the drugs for themselves. Not knowing who is actually pursuing him, Nolte and Weld take off, with the apparent bad guys following close behind, with Moriarty in tow. The chase covers much of the southwestern United States, which Reisz visualizes entirely as a wasteland. In the process, the director creates a succession of classic crime-story-genre confrontations culminating in a shoot-out at a hippie commune in the mountains of New Mexico.

Although the movie functions reasonably well on this level, Reisz is using the chase as the instrument to explore the nature of American life in the chaotic early 1970s. The drug scene had lost its glamour, and the antiwar movement had only replaced Lyndon Johnson with Richard Nixon, who seemed perfectly willing to keep American troops in Vietnam. The hallucinogenic nightmare the director creates to represent this period envelops his characters, and they become so disengaged from society that they have no place to go but down. Moreover, in portraying the drug scene as "a world of uncontrollable moral squalor," Reisz provides an implicit portrayal of the Vietnamization of the United States.[1]

The very nature of such images would create problems for the Pentagon in considering even limited assistance to *Who'll Stop the Rain?* After reviewing the script, Capt. Ralph Blanchard, Navy assistant chief of information, advised Don Baruch on February 18, 1977, that "Department of Defense assistance be denied as a matter of propriety and because the script does not qualify" for support under DoD regulations. Meanwhile, Baruch's office had received two requests that the Pentagon provide assistance to the film. The head of the Louisiana State film department informed Baruch that the state intended to assist on the production and that his office "would consider it a great courtesy" if the Pentagon would approve use of Navy facilities along the Mississippi to represent a docking area in Vietnam. Likewise, Congressman Richard Tonry of Louisiana requested that the military give the filmmakers' request for assistance "early approval if it is in order."[2]

Faced with these inquiries, Baruch's office asked the Navy for a more detailed explanation of its reaction to the script. On March 2 Blanchard answered: "The film treatment reflects unfavorably on the Marine Corps and its personnel. The script does not benefit the Department of the Navy or the Department of Defense, in any way, nor is the production in the national interest." Consequently, he wrote that the screenplay "does not appear to qualify for assistance" and recommended that military assistance be disapproved.[3]

In a note to Admiral Cooney on March 10, Maj. Gen. Guy Hairston Jr., the deputy assistant secretary of defense for public affairs, observed, "I don't see that we have anything to lose in this case. 'Ex-Marines' are in the film, and the story is not entirely absurd. We're not really in the moralizing/script editing business." Concluding that limited cooperation would satisfy all parties, he noted that the film was "really an anti-drug piece." Cooney saw the screenplay far differently, writing to Don Baruch, "I have again reviewed the script, 'Dog Soldiers.' My first impressions remain unchanged. The film is void of all social value, and it holds law enforcement up to ridicule." Nevertheless, he advised Baruch that if he determined that "overriding considerations to provide limited assistance" existed, the Navy would support the decision. However, he recommended that no credits or mention of Defense Department assistance be made in the film.[4]

Despite the continued antipathy to the script from the Navy as well as from the Marines, the Pentagon ultimately decided to provide the production with courtesy assistance in the form of permission to shoot scenes on naval facilities on the West Coast. Such limited cooperation in no way represented an approval of the film's subject matter, and certainly the armed services in no way benefited from associating themselves with *Who'll Stop the Rain?* To be sure, the film did not make the military the villain of the piece. That honor went to the drugs that were corrupting America. However, the drugs themselves came from Vietnam and so become the metaphor for the damage the war had inflicted on the United States.

Given this portrayal, the film's dense texture, and its unrelenting negative rendering of American society during the Vietnam war, the film attracted more critical attention than box-office success. Ironically, the Czech-born, English-raised Reisz himself claimed to see his film in a less profound light: "What tempted me to make it in a sense was that it was a genre story—a thriller, which is the way the best of American cinema operates. I didn't want it to be a 'problem' picture, with the problem neatly resolved at the end, but a rip-roaring adventure yarn, with plenty of fights, chases and all the pure action that American movies are so good at." At the same time, he saw *Who'll Stop the Rain?* as "a highly serious movie, even 'moralistic' in tone: It has a paradoxical premise: We're for the 'bad guys,' because they're the best their culture has to offer. They're survivors, and Hicks [Nolte's character] really is a heroic figure, a soldier with a soldier's code but without an honorable war to fight in. He'd like to be a loving man, too, but above all he'd like to be a conformist—even a Marine—if his society gave him a chance."[5]

Instead, Nolte ends up outside society, fighting to save a friend but dying needlessly, just as some fifty-eight thousand young men and women died in Vietnam with nothing to show for their sacrifices. Whatever else might be said about the film, it did make an effort to explain just that. If *Who'll Stop the Rain?* did not prove to be an important film in the effort to create *the* Vietnam movie, it did contain much to stimulate the mind. In contrast, *More American Graffiti* seemed to have no more purpose in being made than to exploit the popularity of the 1973 box-office smash *American Graffiti*. The scenes set in Vietnam become almost gratuitous because of their banality and serve only as a setting in which to place one of the film's characters.

Yet, *More American Graffiti* does draw on the war to help create the ambience in which its characters exist, and Vietnam does shape their actions. In anticipation of obtaining stock footage for the obligatory helicopter and battle scenes, John Horton's office sent Don Baruch an outline of the story in April 1978, saying that the writers would complete the script by early May. As Horton's assistant described it, the Vietnam segment constituted one of the four interwoven stories that would make up the movie. According to the outline, one of the characters from the original film has become a helicopter copilot "involved with medical rescues. He is searching for a way to get out of Vietnam, just as this country was searching for a way out." While not an image that the Army would like, the outline described the tone of the segment as "similar to a *M*A*S*H*-like comedy. It is centered around the helicopter base where our co-pilot becomes a hero to his men when his helicopter is shot down and he pulls off a daring rescue."[6]

M*A*S*H, of course, did not receive Pentagon assistance, but by 1978 times were changing, and the script might well have satisfied the Army's requirements for approving cooperation, particularly for what seemed like limited support. Nevertheless, as late as June 15, Baruch noted on the routing sheet that he had not heard anything further from Horton or Universal Studios. In fact, the filmmakers apparently had thought so little about the need to create an authentic Vietnam that they did not actually ask the Army for support until they were well into the shooting schedule.

Then, in late July, the producers went into the Army's Los Angeles Office with the script and a request for immediate assistance. According to Lt. Col. Dennis Foley, who met with the filmmakers, their shooting schedule "was so close that even if we immediately loved the script, we couldn't help them in the mechanical time frame involved." Everything else being equal, the Army might have rounded up some trucks, jeeps, and other equipment on short notice. However, the producers needed something more important to ensure instant recognition of the location of their story. Michael Cimino used helicopters to open his Vietnam sequence and to create dramatic tension in the rescue of Michael, Nicky, and Stephen after their escape from their Vietnamese captors. Francis Coppola used helicopters to open *Apocalypse Now,* and Robert Duvall's helicopter assault on a Vietnamese village became the enduring visual highlight of the movie, if not the quintessential image of the Vietnam War film genre. Likewise, the makers of *More American Graffiti* intended to open the film with a flight of helicopters in battle formation to create the same visual credibility and then use the helicopter as a recurring image to provide continuity to the Vietnam segments of the film.[7]

Therein lay the initial problem for the Army in considering the request for cooperation. Foley explained, "You can just about ask the Army for anything you want until you mention the word helicopter and then you come into so many problems of who is going to fly it and the safety aspects involved. It is not like loaning them a five-ton truck. It really is a dangerous, dangerous article, for which very few people want to take the responsibility of saying, 'Yes, I will fly in and around this production.' . . . When you get helicopters around motion picture companies, you got problems." As a result, when the producers arrived at the office with their requirements of helicopters and other equipment to give their Vietnam set an authentic ambience, Foley asked to look at the script, see what they wanted, and then subtract from the list what they could obtain from commercial sources, since the Army could not compete with private enterprise.[8]

Foley recalled, "They didn't want to hear that. What they wanted was everything they wanted, when they wanted it." In fact, he said that even if everything "had been wonderful, which it wasn't, it would probably have taken several weeks to several months" to arrange for all the assistance. Consequently, he told them it was "virtually impossible. No, you can't even count on getting the thing done. Plus, we have some heartburn with the script." Foley stressed that these remained two separate issues and that even if the Army had had no problem with the story, he would probably not have been able to provide the requested support.[9]

In fact, Foley and the Army found the script "grossly misleading." Consequently, Foley suggested that the filmmakers should rewrite the story to give it accuracy or turn it into a comedy. In any case, he told them not to "make it half-way believable." He simply didn't see any virtue in another "incestuous repeated Hollywood rewrite of the same script . . . in which all the privates are trying to screw off on all the NCOs; all the NCOs are trying to pull the wool over all the officers' eyes; all the officers are sitting in the officers club getting drunk and trying to figure out how to court Congressmen. It has been rewritten a thousand times. Over and over and over again." Foley said that the *More American Graffiti* script contained things like that as well as "major improprieties."[10]

Nevertheless, Foley emphasized that his office would not sit down with a producer and say, "We don't like your script. Go away." Instead, he would offer the filmmaker solutions that might help improve the script and make it acceptable for cooperation. Foley said the decision had nothing to do with whether or not the script contained comedy: "What we want to do is give them the facts and let them make their own decision." In the end, *More American Graffiti* became the only script Foley had to turn down because it "so grossly misrepresented" the Army. He said the producers were simply reluctant to change the script. But even if they had been willing to revise it, he did not know whether the Army would have been able to give assistance, because they could not stop production while he brought together the requested equipment: "They had shot everything else and for us to provide the things they needed, they would have had to stop production and start up again. This would have been a disaster for production costs."[11]

In any case, Foley said he proposed to the producers: "We need to do two things. We need to adjust either the amount of things you want or the time you want them, because mechanically, I don't think we can get it done. Secondly, this script is not going to fly in its present form. Here are some of the changes that need to be made." According to Foley, the filmmakers told him: "We are not going to change the script. And we are not going to change the schedule." In turn, he told them, "Then, you are not going to get our help." They answered: "We'll see about that."[12]

Believing that Foley did not represent the final word, the filmmakers promptly sent the script to John Horton, who submitted it to the Pentagon on July 31, 1978, for Pentagon review and comments in response to its request for assistance. Among other things, the filmmakers wanted four Huey Assault Helicopters, three to five artillery pieces, and two or three jeeps, vintage 1965. Perhaps reflecting Foley's warning about the time it would take to arrange for material assistance, Horton said that the shooting schedule called for use of the equipment and operating crews for approximately two weeks beginning in mid-October.[13]

The filmmakers then flew John Horton out to Hollywood for meetings on August 11 and 15, to try to convince the Army to change its position. Foley said the effort "was a complete and total failure." Although his boss advised representatives of Universal Studios that the Army remained willing to negotiate acceptable script changes, the filmmakers responded that they "could not accommodate the major script revisions we would require." As a result, the service informed Don Baruch that it could see "no benefit in providing assistance to this production in its present form. Even with liberal license for satire and humor, we can not support a script which consistently emphasizes the portrayal of Army personnel and members of Congress as buffoons and subjects of ridicule." Under the circumstances, the Army declined to assist on the film unless the producers made "significant script revisions." In advising John Horton of the decision on August 18, Baruch made it clear that the Army had taken into consideration that some of the demeaning scenes "were to be done humorously."[14]

Despite the formal turndown of the request for support, Foley stressed that no hard feelings existed between his office and the filmmakers: "We tried to help, but it was a totally insupportable script, time-wise, equipment-wise, and story-wise." He had talked with the producers for hours, "trying to figure out alternatives that would be creative for them, but that wouldn't give us knee-jerk." When the effort proved fruitless, however, the Army office did provide courtesy assistance in the form of technical advice on how things would look and procedures that were followed.[15]

The courtesy input gave the Vietnam sequences an authentic ambience that the film would not otherwise have had. Nevertheless, *More American Graffiti* suffered from the segmented stories that never intertwine; and worse, even though the characters were living in the Vietnam period, even though they served in Vietnam or protested the war, none seemed touched by their experiences. The heart of the problem remained the motives of the filmmakers themselves. They had not intended to create a statement about the war. Instead, they simply wanted to capitalize on the success of the original movie. Consequently, *More American Graffiti* had few socially redeeming moments and little real awareness of the impact that the war had on the United States.

Ironically, an Australian-made movie probably best explained the nature of the Vietnam War to the American people. Of course, *Breaker Morant* ostensibly focused on another war, in another time, in a different setting. On the surface, Australian director Bruce Beresford told the story of an Australian officer fighting in South Africa during the Boer War. A court-martial finds Morant and a fellow officer guilty of committing atrocities, sentences them to death, and executes them. As Beresford created the narrative, Morant's guilt or innocence becomes relatively unimportant. Instead, the issue becomes his attorney's contention that the nature of the Boer War itself forced its participants to do things they would not have done under normal combat circumstances.

The arguments he presents sound virtually identical to the ones Lt. William Calley's lawyers advanced at his court-martial for his role in the My Lai massacre. In part, the pointed similarities result from the director's acknowledged belief that *Breaker Morant* had a relationship to the American involvement in Vietnam: "One of the reasons [the producer] and I were interested in the project was the modern parallels." Given this belief, Beresford would naturally be predisposed to selecting his material in such a way as to support his views. In reality, he did not have to take liberties with history, because the two wars were so similar in nature.[16]

In each case, a large, powerful, imperial nation was attempting to impose its will on a relatively small group of insurgents conducting a guerrilla war in their own countryside. Women and children fight alongside the men and use every means at their disposal, thereby increasing the normal cruelties of war. To the Boers, as to the Vietcong, the conventional rules of combat meant nothing. Both groups were fighting for their homeland and had far more to lose than did the regular army forces transported thousands of miles to fight in a strange land.

In both the Boer War and the Vietnam War, the civilian soldiers had a far stronger commitment to their cause than either the soldiers of the British Empire or of the United States, who were simply performing their duties until they could go home. Moreover, in each conflict the military command usually operated from headquarters insulated from the gritty realities of the war. At the same time, the commanders in chief had to attune themselves to domestic and international political considerations rather than the immediate reality of day-to-day combat. In turn, the lower-ranking officers and soldiers doing the actual fighting often felt that they lacked the support of their respective nations and headquarters and so experienced increasing frustration at the conditions of warfare under which they labored.

In such situations, the atrocities of which Breaker Morant and William Calley stood convicted did occur more often than the respective military establishments might wish to acknowledge. However, what the military commands and civilians back home might consider illegal, immoral acts, the guilty men and their supporters would argue happened as a result of the nature of war in general and the character of counterinsurgency war in particular. If, then, the message in *Breaker Morant* sounds like a comment about Vietnam, it resulted from the dilemma the combatants faced in each conflict, "Kill or be killed." As Beresford observed, "Yes, the three did kill the Boers. But as the defense speech proposes, you would have done the same thing if you had been in their place."[17]

At the same time, the director denied that he was making an apology for war crimes, claiming he only wanted audiences to "reconsider their viewpoint of someone like Morant—or Calley—in this situation. If you're stuck with a charge of atrocity, it's not so simple; it's not just a case of being a madman with a gun in your hand. The film says that in this kind of situation, you can't simply turn around and condemn the people who've done the deed." Recognizing that people might interpret this message as providing an excuse for such actions, Beresford explained, "That's not what I intended. I tried to make it balanced. The same thing came up in Nuremberg—the dreadful following of orders. What's truly horrific about war is that it puts normal people into circumstances where they have to cope with pressures that no one should ever have to confront. They're too awful."[18]

In graphically portraying this situation in the context of the Boer War, *Breaker Morant* visualized to the American people the philosophical dilemmas which the Vietnam War had created. However, it did it in a less emotion-laden context than occurred in movies actually showing American fighting men in action. As a result, viewers could focus exclusively on the issue of how the war impacted the combatants themselves without the intrusion of the visual images of the conflict.

If *Breaker Morant* supplied insights into the Vietnam war through comparisons with a similar nationalist rebellion against foreign intervention, people could also choose to view the film simply as another courtroom drama, not unlike those Hollywood regularly turns out. In the same way, audiences, including the National Guard, might well see Walter Hill's 1981 *Southern Comfort* as simply another action, adventure melodrama. Combining the 1934 British classic *The Lost Patrol* with the more contemporary *Deliverance,* the director follows the disasters that befall a small National Guard unit that goes into the Louisiana bayous on a routine weekend training exercise. Adhering to Hollywood tradition, the group represents a cross section of southern society, rich and poor, smart and dumb, knowledgeable and inept.

Early on, the men take some Cajun flatboats to get across a lake. The owners become riled at this unauthorized appropriation and further angered when the weekend soldiers fire blanks at them. What started as a war game suddenly becomes a deadly struggle to survive after the one professional soldier, a sergeant who fought in Vietnam, becomes the first victim of the natives. The remaining guardsmen have no real chance against the locals, who manifest all manner of cruelty, cunning, and ultimate knowledge of their soggy country. In the end, only two of the men reach the apparent safety of a Cajun village, where they are finally rescued after one more confrontation with death.

Like the other armed services, the National Guard had a desire to support films that increased public understanding of its activities and showed its men in a good light. Joseph Hanley, at that time in the National Guard Bureau's Pentagon Public Affairs Office, acknowledged that the Guard would provide assistance to a movie that did not show the organization positively, if the story portrayed a historical event, such as the Kent State shootings. In the case of *Southern Comfort*, however, Hanley recalled that it had "probably one of the most uncomplimentary scripts we had ever seen regarding the types of people in the National Guard and what happened to them in a training activity." Even more important, since the story had no basis in fact and plausibility, the Public Affairs Office could find no way to "fix the story to make it plausible or acceptable" for the Guard.[19]

As with *Fail Safe* or *Wargames*, if the filmmakers had agreed to remove the implausibilities inherent in the script, such as having the guardsmen carrying live ammunition, they would not have had a movie. In a historically accurate story, according to Hanley, "what would have happened on that day, if they were out and were ambushed by some crazed men, they would have all probably been killed immediately because they would have had no ammunition." In any event, given the script with its factual problems and depiction of the Guard as "less than professional and really as a bunch of crazed rednecks," Hanley said his office had "no interest whatsoever" in supporting the production.[20]

The National Guard and the Defense Department might have also objected to the script on the grounds that it contained an allegorical message about Vietnam. Hanley recalled that he did not connect the story to the war in Southeast Asia. However, he did see "probably a reflection of some hostility that may have been generated by the public's perception of the Guard's non-participation in Vietnam." In other words, people did not consider the Guard "a professional force that would be capable of dealing with what basically amounts to a low level threat" that the men faced in *Southern Comfort*. Hanley accepted the story literally, but Vincent Canby, in his review in the *New York Times*, expressed the deep fear that the movie might actually be "meant to be the last word on the United States involvement in Vietnam." Perhaps not the last word, but *Southern Comfort* can be easily viewed as trying to make a definite statement about the war. If nothing else, the film put into cinematic terms David Halberstam's seminal work on the American involvement in Southeast Asia, *The Making of a Quagmire* (1964).[21]

Keith Carradine, one of the film's stars, thought the director clearly had the connection with Vietnam in mind. While the actor acknowledged that not all viewers might view *Southern Comfort* as an allegory for the American experience in Vietnam, Carradine claimed that the filmmakers had deliberately conceived the story as a Vietnam allegory: "They were trying to find a way to do a film about Vietnam without doing a film about Vietnam. At the time they were putting the thing together that subject was taboo at the major studios." If they did make a comment on the war, Carradine said, the filmmakers were also commenting on the entire military experience: "There's the guy who's by-the-book; there's the guy who has the real experience; there's the guy who's the complete idiot; there's the guy who's kind of a wimp. I imagine that being in the Army is like that on a much larger scale."[22]

Whatever the filmmakers' actual intentions, many reviewers did see *Southern Comfort*

A group of National Guardsmen trudging through the Louisiana Bayou in the film *Southern Comfort.*

using the Louisiana bayous to make a comment about the American experience in Vietnam and the National Guardsmen as a surrogate for the failure of the nation's military establishment. The reviewer for the *UCLA Daily Bruin,* for one, emphasized the parallels: "Here is a group of young Americans, poorly trained and commanded, trapped in a hostile territory for no real military goal beyond survival itself. They are fighting an unseen enemy, one which speaks a foreign language, on terrain familiar to their opponents but not to themselves. And all they can really hope for is to find a highway, a sort of light at the end of the proverbial tunnel." The reviewer concluded that the filmmakers' "point of view seems to be one of sympathy for both the Guardsmen and the Cajuns (each forced by their own values to fight the other), but one of scorn for the institution of the National Guard, (which provoked the battle in the first place)."[23]

The *Playboy* reviewer saw the manner in which the director developed his story once the guardsmen began to die as helping to create, at least to some viewers, the comparison to Vietnam: "Half the time it's insidious psychological warfare, and there may be meaningful resonance here that ambitious critics connect to Vietnam about U.S. innocents abroad, as dangerous to themselves as they are to the hidden foe whose turf they violate. But I don't think Hill intends to be that pretentious, and his cryptic, pungent script . . . speaks for itself eloquently in such lines as one redneck's dogged assertion: 'There comes a time when you have to abandon principles and do what's right.'"[24]

In Vietnam, doing the right thing, at the expense of morality, often meant the difference between death and survival. In any case, the *Newsweek* critic also saw the relationship of *Southern Comfort* to Vietnam, observing that a viewer will quickly recognize the intended metaphor, that "this Louisiana swamp is a microcosmic parallel of Vietnam, that the behavior of these frightened, arrogant Americans toward their Cajun foe mirrors the military chaos that transpired in the jungles of Southeast Asia. This, and the related implications *Southern Comfort* draws about our military system and the internal breakdown of the social fabric, are interesting to contemplate, but they neither make nor break the movie." Instead, he saw the director's use of action, out of which any comments about Vietnam might arise, as his primary concern as well as his forte.[25]

Audiences can find considerable satisfaction in the intensity of the action, which builds up unrelieved tension as the guardsmen wage their losing battle to survive. And if that is all the director intended, he did succeed, at least in the opinion of *New York* magazine: "Brilliantly made, exciting, yet terribly limited, *Southern Comfort* is both a celebration and a satire of macho prowess. See it if you long for action." Nevertheless, the analogy to Vietnam remains too strong to ignore.[26]

Reviewer Michael Sragow felt the guardsmen in *Southern Comfort* proved as "ill-equipped to handle these backwater Cajuns as the regular troops were with the Viet Cong."

In his *Rolling Stone* review, Michael Sragow observed that in *Southern Comfort*, the director "created a terrifying mood piece—a blood-and-guts tale that's also a parody of the military sensibility, a metaphor for the Vietnam War and a study of gracelessness under pressure.... These men aren't hapless vacationers like the heroes of *Deliverance*, hoping to find some special masculine consummation in the wilderness. They're weekend soldiers playing out commando daydreams or just trying to get through their senseless maneuvers without breaking an arm or a leg." The reviewer points out that the guardsmen prove as "ill-equipped to handle these backwater Cajuns as the regular troops were with the Viet Cong. Not long into *Southern Comfort*, you begin to feel as if you're watching scenes from Vietnam relived in a twilight zone."[27]

Sragow felt that by taking a Vietnam-like situation out of its confused political context, the filmmakers were able to "clarify how such disasters and atrocities occur." In making the comparison between the Cajuns and the Vietnamese, both "the masters of their terrain," *Southern Comfort* illustrated the problems that the United States faced in Vietnam. Sragow concluded: "It may antagonize those who'd prefer the cracker soldiers to be either heroized or more harshly judged. And because the Cajuns are Americans, and, at first, the victims, the emotional effect of the combat is even more devastating than if they were Cong. We see the enemy, and it is us."[28]

Virtually every movie about the American experience in Vietnam appearing subsequent to *The Green Berets* had contained this message in one form or another. According to Paul Hensler, who had served in Vietnam and later as a technical advisor on *The Boys in Company C* and *Apocalypse Now*, all filmmakers "want to make an anti-Vietnam film and not an anti-war film." Having no interest in balanced or accurate portrayals of what happened in Vietnam, they used the worst images they could imagine or draw from historical events to create their statements.[29]

Col. Donald Gilleland, who had commanded the Air Force Public Affairs Office in Los Angeles in the early 1980s, believed that Hollywood was "really not very good at depicting reality." At least he said he had not seen a good film about Vietnam: "Instead of depicting dedicated American men and women doing the best they could under extremely difficult and thankless conditions, which is how most Americans served, Hollywood producers cram every alleged atrocity into a two hour film, focusing on horrors, and claim their story accurately represents the Vietnam experience. In most of these films, there isn't a sane or reasonably responsible human being in the movie."[30]

Not until the completion of *Don't Cry, It's Only Thunder* did a story acknowledge that in Vietnam at least some men's "feelings and humanity just spoke every single day." Hensler said all Vietnam war films up to that time had lacked this understanding: "There were a lot of cracked people. But there were a lot of cracked people in the First World War and the Second World War. War does that to you. But there was also a great deal of humanitarians." Consequently, in *Don't Cry, It's Only Thunder,* based on his own experiences in Vietnam, Hensler tried to show that not every American who served in Vietnam became a crazed killer, a befogged drug user, or an incompetent officer. Writing the screenplay at the urging of Francis Coppola, for whom he had worked during the production of *Apocalypse Now,* Hensler told the story of Brian, a young soldier who fulfills a promise to a dying buddy that he will assume the role of benefactor to a Catholic orphanage in Saigon.[31]

In both a visual and a literal sense, the film becomes the direct link to the message that John Wayne put into *The Green Berets* to explain to the American people why the United States had become involved in Vietnam. Standing on a beach watching the sun set into the South China Sea, Wayne's Colonel Kirby tells the Vietnamese waif: "You're what this is all about." Of course, by 1982, when *Don't Cry, It's Only Thunder* had its premiere, most people knew full well what had happened when the U.S. military establishment had attempted to use its full weight to win Vietnamese hearts and minds.

The orphanage, which Hensler's alter ego keeps supplied with food and other necessities, would not exist except for the destruction that the war has wrought. Focusing as it did on the victims of the war, Hensler believed that *Don't Cry, It's Only Thunder* contained an antiwar statement. Nevertheless, for the first time, a motion picture about the war portrayed a relatively normal American soldier trying to help, not kill, Vietnamese. As a result, while acknowledging that he was talking about his own actions, Hensler saw Brian as "the first hero of Vietnam" that Hollywood had portrayed.[32]

The film actually created conflicting images of war. By concentrating on the victims of the war, *Don't Cry, It's Only Thunder* made an antiwar statement. But it also showed Brian undergoing the rite of passage from an immature teenager to a concerned, feeling adult as a result of his wartime experiences. Since American culture and society glorifies a male's coming of age, *Don't Cry, It's Only Thunder* suggested that positive benefits accrue from war while also condemning the war.

Hensler thought Brian's coming of age as a result of his wartime experiences differed little from anyone growing up or learning from the environment in which he finds himself. In his/Brian's case, Vietnam rather than the Peace Corps or college or some adversity became the instrument for change: "If you think you learn only from your priest or from your counselor or your psychologist or psychiatrist, then you are denying you are alive. Brian, in the movie, is being bombarded with life and death and then forced into life and death in the mortuary to the point, where to make it, to understand, he's got to make decisions."[33]

More important to the screenwriter, Brian's becoming the benefactor to the orphanage stood as a metaphor for the typical American reaction in any war when confronted with innocent children caught in battle: "The Americans would move into a position of protecting them because they are human beings. They're not Koreans or Vietnamese. They're human beings." Consequently, Hensler felt that *Don't Cry, It's Only Thunder* provided a response to earlier Hollywood movies about Vietnam which had contained almost universally negative portrayals of the U.S. military: "I think Brian shows the American people what they knew all the time. The American was in Vietnam." In any case, whatever the paradoxes inherent in the film, it did contain a balanced portrayal of the American involvement in Southeast Asia, something lacking in most Hollywood screenplays up to that time.[34]

As such, it provided the Pentagon with a story about the war that it could support. Hensler recalled that the services had "not one problem" with the script. In reality, most likely unbeknownst to Hensler, not every military man felt that the script benefited the armed services. Duncan Wilmore, then serving as director of the Air Force's Los Angeles Public Affairs Office, saw the story as degrading the Army in many ways: "I thought it was an awful movie about the American military in the sense that institutionally, it showed the military as being very corrupt, ridden by graft, black marketeerism, etc. But it also showed that a guy could care about children and could ultimately devote his life to save children. So, I was ambivalent about it. The only reason he was able to support those orphans was because there was enough graft in the Army in Vietnam to provide him with the where-withal to do it."[35]

Fortunately for the producers, Dennis Foley, in the Army's Los Angeles Public Affairs Office "loved the script," even though Brian massages the system, philosophizes against war while doing autopsies as an Army mortician, and even carries on a discourse with a young soldier who has committed suicide. Less than five years before, the Army had cited the suicide in *Go Tell the Spartans* as one of the reasons for not supporting the film; and concurrently, the Navy was objecting to the suicide in the script of *An Officer and a Gentleman*. However, Hensler said that none of the services objected to the scene in *Don't Cry, It's Only Thunder* because of the way he had approached the matter. He noted that *Go Tell the Spartans*, unlike his story, had portrayed the suicide "as drug-crazed" and that the film-makers were preaching that this "was the mentality of an awful lot of people at that time in the war." By the time the Army received the script for *Don't Cry, It's Only Thunder*, however, Hensler said the service had come to terms with the fact that men had committed suicide in Vietnam. Hensler's screenplay did not explain the cause of the suicide, and he admitted that circumstances had changed: "They felt that the picture and the script were very, very close to reality of the situation in Vietnam as well as in any war. And, I didn't say suicide 300 times."[36]

Ironically, despite the Army's approval of the story because of its positive aspects, the service could not give assistance to the film because it had no bases in the Philippines. Nevertheless, Foley was able to arrange for the Air Force to provide locations at Clarke Air Force Base for exterior shooting, a few helicopters, and off-duty airmen to serve as extras. Notwithstanding the authentic ambience that the Philippine locations created for the film and a sentimental story about orphans in wartime, which had usually guaranteed money in the bank, *Don't Cry, Its Only Thunder* failed mightily at the box office. Despite generally good reviews, it produced lackluster ticket sales in its initial opening in Los Angeles, and Sanrio Communications, the foreign-based production company, folded. Walter DeFaria, the film's producer, had no explanation for the film's failure: "It's a shame. We received such great reviews in the U.S. The problem was we couldn't get the people in to see it. We had such high hopes for this film. We thought it was going to be our turning point."[37]

Reviewers did generally like *Don't Cry, It's Only Thunder*. In the *New York Times*, Janet Maslin concluded that it was a very good, overlooked Vietnam movie that took "an unexpectedly homespun approach to its subject." Although she found that it contained "an element of sentimentality . . . it isn't overstated, and it's easily offset by the abundance of gallows humor." She did not think the director carried the jokes about life in the morgue to a *M*A*S*H*-like extreme, "but he goes far enough to illustrate how hardened the soldiers' nerves have become." More important, she thought the film "manages to become genuinely heart-warming even without the romantic element that is tacked on in Paul Hensler's screenplay." Noting that *Don't Cry, It's Only Thunder* was scheduled for only a brief run, she concluded that "it's as worthy as plenty of other new movies enjoying longer engagements around town. Its inspirational qualities don't deprive it of backbone, and they don't set it on an utterly predictable course. As wartime dramas go, this one isn't a whitewash or a fairy tale. It's just an effort to tell the story on a very small, very human scale."[38]

Also acknowledging that the picture contained sentimentality, the *Daily Variety* reviewer did not think the filmmakers had overloaded the emotional content: "*Don't Cry, It's Only Thunder* is an accomplished proclamation that individual virtue can still surface in a swamp of human cruelty." He described it as a throwback to World War II pictures, "concerned as it is with the plight of innocent orphans in Vietnam. Unfortunately, it does not share the earlier films' conviction that all wrong is the fault of the enemy and all right will return with victory." Although the reviewer did not consider it a political film, he thought that "the American presence in the troubled country is certainly a villain in the background." He concluded that it was to the director's credit, "but maybe the picture's commercial weakness, that he never gives in to a simple solution. For a moment, a happy ending does loom, only to turn tragic again before coming to rest on a thin glimmer of hope. For the kids of Vietnam, clearly the American cavalry never came to the rescue. The best that *Thunder* says is a few were swooped out of the path before the hordes ran over them."[39]

As much as anything, that probably best explains why *Don't Cry, It's Only Thunder* failed to attract an audience of any sort. People still apparently had no interest in a small, personal story about Vietnam. Even if the film did portray a good American doing good deeds, he remained an aberration in a hellish world which his fellow soldiers had created. Brian remained no more than a lone figure with his finger in the dike. Moreover, he could not even keep tragedy from entering into his small world. The mortar attack that kills the little girl he is trying to adopt symbolizes Brian's failure and gives lie to John Wayne's promise to protect the orphans of Vietnam.

To be sure, other factors contributed to the almost immediate withdrawal of the film from theaters. *Don't Cry, It's Only Thunder* lacked the production values of a major film, and as a small subsidiary of a foreign-based communications company, Sanrio did not have the resources required to successfully promote the film to the nation's moviegoers. Although it did reach the American public when it appeared on cable television, its lack of commercial success doomed it to a quick oblivion. Consequently, its message that at least some Americans in Vietnam acted in a praiseworthy manner reached few people. Nevertheless, *Don't Cry, It's Only Thunder* became the first film set entirely in the combat zone since *The Green Berets* to receive full Defense Department cooperation. More important, it became the first movie about the war after the American withdrawal from Southeast Asia that attempted to show the Vietnamese as real people rather than as shadowy figures in the jungle or deceitful guerrillas masquerading as friendly civilians who sprang to the attack in the final reel.

Without balanced portrayals of the American forces who fought the war or three-dimensional Vietnamese instead of Hollywood's stereotypical image of Orientals, movies about the war would contain only the screenwriters' and directors' own perceptions. As a result, the films lacked the ability to provide meaningful insights into the nature of the American experience in Vietnam or to explain why the United States had such a difficult time fighting a war against a small peasant nation. Ironically, the motion picture that best showed the Communist enemy perhaps made the best argument why the United States should have persevered even longer in Southeast Asia. Like *Don't Cry, It's Only Thunder,* *The Killing Fields* had its origins in a true story, the friendship between Sydney Schanberg, a *New York Times* reporter in Cambodia, and Dith Pran, his Cambodian photographer.

Refusing to leave Phnom Penh during the triumphant advance of the Khmer Rouge,

Pran becomes separated from Schanberg and disappears into the depths of Cambodia during the Communist effort to relocate virtually the entire population to the countryside and reeducate them. Based on Schanberg's article about his efforts to find Pran and the photographer's own story of his escape from Cambodia, *The Killing Fields* vividly portrays Pran's survival and ultimate escape to Thailand, where he reunites with Schanberg. In detailing the horrors that the Khmer Rouge inflicted upon Cambodia and its people, the film provides a bitter denunciation of the Communists, whose devastation of their own country was far worse than the destruction the United States wreaked in Indochina. Using Schanberg's friendship with Pran as the framework in which to portray the carnage, the film manages to make a powerful antiwar statement. Like *Southern Comfort,* the message gains strength because *The Killing Fields* at least nominally stands above the political issues and lets the visual images of slaughter speak for themselves.

The Killing Fields originated from the true story of the friendship between Sydney Schanberg, a *New York Times* journalist in Cambodia, and Dith Pran, his Cambodian photographer.

To recreate Cambodia, director Roland Joffe went to Thailand, obtaining the limited amount of military equipment he needed from the Thai government. Only after he had completed the principal photography did the producers realize that the Thai military did not have the helicopters needed to replicate the evacuation of the U.S. embassy personnel and other civilians from Cambodia in April 1975. As a result, John Horton, representing ENIGMA Ltd., wrote to Don Baruch on August 26, 1983, requesting the use of six Marine helicopters at either Camp Pendleton or El Toro at the end of October. To expedite the review process, Horton advised Baruch that the associate producer, Iain Smith, would come to Washington the first week of September to meet with Pentagon officials.[40]

Following the meeting on September 6, Smith wrote to Baruch to confirm details of the discussion. Describing *The Killing Fields* as "a story of human dignity and survival set against the backdrop of war," Smith said the producers had "taken the utmost care in ensuring that as much research and consultation as possible has gone into those characters represented in the film which could be held to be based on actual persons." In particular, he said that the fictionalized ambassador to Cambodia in the movie "could quite reasonably be recognized" as John Gunther Dean, who had served as ambassador in Phnom Penh in 1975. Consequently, the producer said the filmmakers had consulted with Dean, now the U.S. ambassador to Thailand, to ensure "the accuracy of our reconstruction of historical events." Smith explained that he wanted to use the Marine Sikorsky Sea Stallions to recreate the U.S. embassy's departure from the Cambodian capital: "In the context of film this event forms the background to a scene of sadness and immense pathos during which Dith Pran encourages his wife and family to evacuate from Cambodia, whilst he himself elects to stay behind with Schanberg." Citing the cooperation the filmmakers had received from many international relief agencies, Smith said that *The*

Killing Fields "concerns the human tragedy of refugees and fugitives from war" and that gala charity premieres throughout the world would benefit many aid organizations.[41]

Baruch submitted the script to the director of the East Asia and Pacific Region in Office of the Assistant Secretary of Defense for International Security Affairs and to the Marine Corps Public Affairs Office for their reactions. In his letter to the Marines, Baruch wrote that he believed Marine support "affords an opportunity to portray the sequences factually." In response, the ISA Office posed no objections to DoD cooperation. However, after meeting with the producer in Los Angeles and helping him select a site for the filming at Camp Pendleton, Pat Coulter voiced some reservations about providing assistance to the movie.[42]

In his letter to Marine Headquarters, Coulter said he had heard that the Americans in Thailand who had taken the role of Marines had created an appearance "in accordance with the high standards we demand of film projects before we give them support." Nevertheless, he had not yet received photographs of the "Marines" and so was not able to verify the report. Consequently, Coulter counseled care in deciding to support *The Killing Fields:* "Since this film, depicting a major chapter in Marine Corps history, was made without our knowledge and support, and because they have come to us at this late date, I recommend caution in granting approval." He noted that some British filmmakers in the past had not demonstrated concern for accuracy or authenticity in their depiction of American servicemen. Coulter then said that the movie had excellent prospects for success and so asked whether the Corps wanted to be "rushed into supporting a film depicting Marines in a manner we have no knowledge of or in which we were not permitted to participate or exert influence."[43]

Once he had screened for the Marines portions of *The Killing Fields* shot in Thailand, however, Smith satisfied any doubts the service had about supporting the production, and the filming at Camp Pendleton took place without a hitch. On October 28 the producer wrote to Baruch to express his appreciation for the Pentagon's help in arranging for cooperation. He also reported that Coulter had assured the filmmakers that they had left Camp Pendleton in good order. To John Horton, Smith became even more effusive: "I must tell you that we received maximum co-operation and assistance from the U.S. Marine Corps, in particular Major Pat Coulter and Captain A.L. Hanson, who truly worked like Trojans on our behalf. The helicopters arrived on time and performed marvelously for the cameras." Horton also expressed his appreciation for the military's help and said he expected the film "will achieve pinnacles in both content and reception. It should be superb."[44]

Most reviewers were to agree with that assessment. Writing in the *Washington Post,* Paul Attanasio began: "Of all the movies made about America's experience in Indochina, *The Killing Fields* is the simplest and most serious and, because the truths of war tend to be simple and serious, the best." The reviewer did complain about the inclination of the British filmmakers "to add a discordant dram of moralism: this journey into the lower depths ends with the namby-pamby fatuity of John Lennon's 'Imagine.' That's not what this story is about at all—after watching a people whom Americans had devastated finally throw the foreigners out, only to set about murdering each other, these reedy maunderings about 'no country,' 'no possessions' and 'no religion' seem perversely idiotic (indeed, Pran's Buddhism and his patriotism were the keys to his personality, and his survival). You don't leave the theater humming along, but with your head humming, as the painful images of the waste of war refuse to go away."[45]

The film's feel of authenticity and its power might draw praise from reviewers, but *The Killing Fields* provided a too intense and depressing story to become a box-office smash.

Paul Attamasio, writing in the *Washington Post*, called *The Killing Fields* the "simplest and most serious of all the film portrayals of America's activity in Indochina."

Moreover, it gave the lie to the nation's antiwar liberals who in their opposition to the government intervention in Vietnam had rushed to embrace the Communist enemies in Southeast Asia. The American destruction might have become unpalatable, but *The Killing Fields* suggested that neither side deserved support. In agreeing to cooperate on a film that contained this message, the Pentagon demonstrated a growing awareness that a full accounting of the American involvement in Southeast Asia could benefit the military establishment, not hurt it. Instead of continuing to deny such incidents as a B-52 attack on a friendly village at Neak Luong in Cambodia, which the movie portrayed in gruesome detail, the Pentagon's support of the production indicated a tacit acknowledgment of the accidental bombing. It also suggested that the military might have come to the realization that the saturation bombing of the countryside had radicalized opposition to the U.S.-backed Lon Nol regime and so paved the way for the rise of the xenophobic Khmer Rouge. Only by reevaluating its actions in Southeast Asia could the armed services themselves begin to look at their involvement in the war objectively rather than defensively.

To the degree that *The Killing Fields* did enjoy commercial success despite its unrelenting portrayal of the horrors of war, it would also encourage filmmakers to turn to the Vietnam War as a subject not only to portray combat itself but also to depict the impact that the war had on the veterans and on the civilians who learned about the war from afar. Like *Heroes,* which it closely resembled, *Cease Fire* used a flashback to a Vietnam veteran's combat experience to illuminate the source of the demons that continue to haunt him. The soon-to-be-famous Don Johnson played Tim Murphy, an unemployed veteran suffering from post-traumatic shock syndrome who wages a desperate struggle to adjust to civilian life. Given its limited budget and few pretensions, *Cease Fire* did a surprisingly good job of probing the depth of Murphy's problems, which conspire to alienate him from his wife and children and keep him on the edge of a complete breakdown.

Director David Nutter's film did lack one thing—originality. If George Fernandez, who adapted the screenplay from his play *Vietnam Trilogy,* did not steal his story from *Heroes,* he clearly drew his inspiration from the same "veteran in search of himself" theme of the 1977 Henry Winkler vehicle. In *Cease Fire,* death also triggers the flashbacks that reveal the source of Tim Murphy's ongoing nightmares and set him on the road to recovery. Returning home from watching the police remove the body of his fellow Vietnam vet who had suddenly committed suicide, Murphy acts out a flashback to one of his combat experiences.

In a scene virtually identical to the climax of *Heroes,* Murphy's wife, Paula, tries to comfort him without understanding the depth of his pain: "I want to help you, but I don't know how." Rejecting her offer of sympathy, Murphy crawls on the ground, preparing for an imagined enemy mortar attack. Holding on to him for dear life, Paula finally wrestles

Tim back to reality, telling him: "Stop it! Stop it! Stop it! You're not going to do this to me. I'm not going to let you do this to my family. You're not in this by yourself. I'm here. Listen to me. I love you." Here *Cease Fire* departs from *Heroes*, because love brings only a momentary calm. It takes Luke's funeral to provide the impetus for Murphy to reveal to his counselor at the Vietnam drop-in center, and so to himself, the secret horror that has so traumatized him.

Going no farther than the jungles of South Florida and without Pentagon assistance, the director well endowed the film's single combat scene with the abject terror that only men in combat experience. During a sweep of a Vietnamese village, Murphy's unit discovers in a well the rotting, rat-infested body of an American soldier. At almost the same instant, the men come under attack from an unseen enemy and retreat in disarray to their landing zone, where a helicopter picks them up. Although Murphy pleads with the crew to wait for his best friend, the helicopter begins its ascent to safety in a hail of fire. As it does, Murphy's friend stumbles out of the jungle just ahead of the pursuing enemy, raising his hands in supplication to his departing unit, in a scene that Oliver Stone was to replicate for his own purposes in *Platoon*.[46]

With the vision of the American soldier's decaying body as a reminder of what happens when the Vietcong capture a U.S. serviceman, Murphy tries to persuade the helicopter crew to go back: "I saw the well. Please don't let him die." But as the aircraft continues to rise, Murphy grabs the machine gun and cuts down his friend, crying, "Forgive me. Forgive me." As the soldier slumps down in tears, Nutter dissolves to Murphy crying in the arms of his counselor and other veterans, who provide him with the support he needs to finally return to society. Perhaps overstating the obvious, however, the filmmakers tack on a scene at the Vietnam Memorial, using the Wall for the first time as a cinematic icon. Nevertheless, as Murphy touches the name of his friend and receives a "Welcome home" from a fellow veteran, *Cease Fire* does convey the distance some soldiers had to travel to expunge the memories of Vietnam.

To the degree that the film explains the problems some veterans had coming to terms with their experiences in Vietnam, it does a service to all those who fought and died in the war. Without all the rhetoric of *Coming Home* or the *Rambo* and *Missing in Action* movies, it also made a strong antiwar and anti-Vietnam statement, using the "veterans as victims" rather than the "war as hell" approach. However, by focusing exclusively on those soldiers who did not make a smooth reentry to civilian life, *Cease Fire* does an equal disservice to the vast majority of Americans who fought in Vietnam. As the movie so well showed, the soldiers in country were simply trying to survive in a hostile environment the best way they could. If Vietnam became an evil manifestation of U.S. foreign policy, it did not follow logically that the men who fought the war became evil.

Nor did it follow that their combat experiences, however wrong the war, should affect them any differently than World War II impacted those who fought in it. In fact, most American soldiers returned home from Vietnam relatively unscathed by the war, went to college, got jobs, married, had children, and went on with their lives like most of their fellow citizens. Of course, normality has never sold many tickets. Moreover, it was still true that most people perceived that the United States had lost in Vietnam and, rightly or wrongly, chose to blame the military. Consequently, whereas fighting men returned from World War II as heroes of a necessary war, Hollywood chose, in its infinite wisdom or infinite greed, to create images of Vietnam veterans as drug addicts, misfits, suicide-prone individuals, or violent killers. As a result, while *Cease Fire* deserved a wider audience for the quality of its exploration of the impact Vietnam had on at least some of its combatants, it still contributed to the misperceptions that movies about veterans helped to create.

Whether such views helped form or simply reflected the views of a significant segment of the population, the question remained as to whether in mid-1985 people were willing to watch the postwar suffering of the Vietnam veterans. Concluding that *Cease Fire* "dramatically treated" the problems of the returned soldiers, *Variety* nonetheless observed that its chances of box-office success "will depend on the public's willingness to check out a very serious approach to a subject recently and successfully giving rise to the comic-strip heroics of *Rambo*." In the *Los Angeles Times,* Kevin Thomas also contrasted films of that ilk with *Cease Fire*, which "brings home the reality of the war as a lingering nightmare for the men who fought it." He described the film as "a work of determined simplicity, unswerving in focus and purpose. Don't be surprised if you find your eyes misting over at its finish."[47]

Whatever its dramatic impact, when Nutter completed *Cease Fire* in 1983, distributors apparently thought the viewing public had no desire to respond in that manner to a Vietnam movie. As a result, *Cease Fire* did not reach audiences until 1985, and then only because *Miami Vice* became such a television sensation. Even so, despite praise of Don Johnson's performance as Tim Murphy (outtakes from the movie had helped him win the role in the TV series), the film failed to attract audiences and quickly entered the home video market. Dale Chute, in his *Los Angeles Herald-Examiner* review, provided as good an explanation as any for the film's failure. Having criticized the story and the film's quality, he acknowledged that "strong emotion manages to seep through" and concluded "that there is still a strong, nasty, honest film in this material—exactly the kind of gritty movie nobody wants to make these days."[48]

Of course, as a small, independently made film, with a first-time director, *Cease Fire* might well have enjoyed only limited success whatever the box-office climate. Whether noncombat stories about Vietnam could provide an appealing subject for Hollywood would remain unanswered until a major director explored the war's impact on the American people at home. Francis Ford Coppola certainly had all the credentials necessary to make such a large-budget movie. Nevertheless, his track record on military subjects and his use of violence to move his stories along might seem to disqualify him from exploring, at least in a sensitive manner, how Vietnam affected the soldiers and the civilians who were experiencing the war from afar.

Although some people might find an antiwar statement in Coppola's contribution to the screenplay of *Patton,* to most viewers, including Richard Nixon, the film seemed to glorify war as an instrument for achieving national goals. Whatever it might have said about Vietnam and the military, *Apocalypse Now* had alienated the Defense Department from the moment Coppola had come into the Pentagon in May 1975. Moreover, the completed film had continued to irritate most men who had fought in the southeast Asia, however accurately they found it captured the surrealistic ambience of the conflict. Just as important, *Apocalypse Now* and Coppola's two *Godfather* films had demonstrated how well the director understood the emotional impact that graphic violence had on audiences.

In this context, few people could ignore the irony of Coppola's going to the Pentagon for assistance on *Gardens of Stone.* Nevertheless, the director had no other choice if he was going to make a film about the Old Guard, the Army's elite ceremonial unit. Stationed at Fort Myer, the Old Guard performs at concerts, serves as presidential escorts, takes part in state visits and Fourth of July activities, and handles burial duties at Arlington National

Cemetery. The Philippines or Thailand might pass admirably for Vietnam. Filmmakers could rent equipment, use off-duty soldiers as extras, and train actors to give reasonable performances as U.S. fighting men. However, Arlington remains a unique shrine that no art director could ever reproduce. Equally important, even if Coppola used some other military cemetery as a locale, he would have no hope whatsoever of creating a reasonable facsimile of the Old Guard, whose ceremonial rituals have evolved over many years and countless hours of practice.

In 1968 the Old Guard was doing a brisk business among the gardens of stone that spread over the rolling hills across the Potomac from Washington. Coppola wanted to use this setting as the framework in which to develop several relationships that revolve around James Caan, playing Sgt. Clell Hazard, a dedicated but frustrated senior NCO in the Old Guard. A more culturally sophisticated and socially aware soldier than most Hollywood senior NCOs, Hazard has fought in World War II and Korea and has served two tours in Vietnam. Although a career soldier of the old school, he likes good food and good books, has become an expert in fine Oriental rugs, and does not need to read *Cosmopolitan* to have sensitivity to the contemporary woman.

Despite his opposition to the way the United States is waging the war in Vietnam, Hazard loves the Army and does not easily accept his choice assignment with the Old Guard. Instead, he wants a transfer to Fort Benning, where he can impart his well-earned knowledge of combat to a new generation of soldiers. While his superiors continue to frustrate his efforts to transfer out of the Old Guard, Hazard becomes a surrogate father to Jackie Willow, the son of a man with whom he fought in World War II and Korea. In a story laden with implausibilities, Willow also has no use for his cushy tour of duty and looks for a way to get to Vietnam. While Hazard falls in love with "Sam," an antiwar *Washington Post* journalist, Willow courts and ultimately marries Rachel, the daughter of an Army colonel who opposes the relationship because of Willow's lowly rank. Following the honeymoon, he goes to Officer Candidate School and gets his wish to go to Vietnam. There he ultimately becomes disillusioned with the Army and dies less than three weeks before the end of his tour of duty. After Hazard eulogizes him, the Old Guard does its duty and "plants" him with full military honors.

Gardens of Stone clearly had a different tone and view of the Army than did *Apocalypse Now*. None of the images Coppola had created in his surrealistic war epic conveyed as strong a sense of the wastefulness of Vietnam as did his portrayal of the daily round of burials of soldiers who had fought and died in Southeast Asia. Robert Duvall's ode to the virtues of napalm notwithstanding, Caan's Hazard better expresses the absurdity of the U.S. war effort when he tells Willow that Vietnam has "no front. It's not even a war. There's nothing to win, and no way to win it." Yet he remains powerless to dissuade Willow from going off to Vietnam, much as the antiwar movement proved helpless to stop the war through their protests. Unlike John Wayne's parenting of his men and his necessary death, however, Caan's efforts to teach Willow how to survive fail, and the son dies, rather than the father figure.

Coppola, however, professed not to see the message which the story clearly delivered, claiming that he had not intended *Gardens of Stone* to convey an antiwar or anti-Vietnam statement. To him, the movie focused on the critical importance of family ties, ritual, honor, tradition, and loyalty: "Obviously, there is a message there, that we are sworn to protect our children and we keep putting them in situations that make that impossible, that you want to save your kids but you end up burying them, all dressed up in ritual."

Moreover, he didn't associate *Gardens of Stone* with his earlier film: "*Apocalypse* was big and sort of mystical and incorporated the dark themes of Joseph Conrad's *Heart of Darkness.*" He thought his new movie, in contrast, told a "small story," centering on the Hazard-Willow relationship and its connection to the larger Army family.[49]

Having gone to military school, Coppola claimed he had always had a fascination with "the role of ritual in the military, particularly the code of honor." He said he had an even greater interest in the chance to depict the Army in an unconventional light, not simply as a team of military men but as a specialized family whose members shared tradition, loyalty, and affection. Moreover, he found in Nicholas Proffitt's novel *Gardens of Stone* the story that gave him the opportunity to portray soldiers, especially NCOs, as complex individuals rather than cliché figures.[50]

To do that, however, Coppola needed full Defense Department assistance in order to film on location at Fort Myer and in Arlington National Cemetery and to use the Old Guard performing their ceremonial duties. Despite the problems the Defense Department had had with Coppola and *Apocalypse Now,* the Army was bound to find the story appealing. Even with its obvious antiwar images and dialogue, *Gardens of Stone* offered the service a unique opportunity to have its most prized unit featured in a major Hollywood movie. In fact, the Pentagon voiced only the most routine criticisms of the scripts from the initial submission, which John Horton delivered on March 19, 1986, never once raising a question about the manner in which Coppola commented on the war.[51]

Responding to the first screenplay, the Pentagon's Force Management and Personnel Office advised Don Baruch that from a policy standpoint, "we pose no objections as written. We believe the script presents a realistic portrayal of personal life within the military and is technically accurate." The Army Public Affairs Office had essentially the same reaction to the screenplay, writing to Baruch on April 4 that the service recommended "its approval for full DOD cooperation," subject to the correction of the problems it had noted. For the most part, the comments the officer offered focused primarily on matters of procedure, historical accuracy, and correct language.[52]

As had occurred with *Go Tell the Spartans* and was then taking place in negotiations on Clint Eastwood's *Heartbreak Ridge,* the Army did object to the "excessive profanity in this script, which is both gratuitous and unrealistic." Acknowledging the real world, however, the service asked only that the amount of profanity "be reduced." The office said it could not allow the filmmakers to shoot an "assault" on the Guard Quarters of the Tomb of the Unknown Soldier at Arlington National Cemetery. However, it suggested the ammunition dump at Fort Myer as an alternative location. In any event, most of the Army's requested changes dealt with technical inaccuracies, which it said a technical advisor assigned to the film could correct.[53]

Coppola made every effort to avoid the mistakes he had committed while trying to obtain cooperation for *Apocalypse Now.* On April 9 he and his producer, Michael Levy, went into the Pentagon to meet with the Army's chief of public affairs, Maj. Gen. Charles Bussey, taking with them a revised script of *Gardens of Stone.* In a cover letter dated April 7, the director explained that the screenplay included his first contribution to the project. More than that, the letter demonstrated an almost slavish desire to please the Army in order to ensure the service's support. The director explained that the rewrite reflected "primarily an attempt to intensify the dramaturgy of the story through the addition of some minor pieces dramatizing the fact that Clell is a father without a son and Jackie a son without a father." Describing *Gardens of Stone* as a tragedy, he explained: "Some of the devices used in the first act—the profanity, the sacrilegious humor, are meant to heighten the events of the third act—the tragic death of Jackie and the grieving of Clell. Were it not for some of the grittiness, the humor and language of the first and second acts it might not be possible to achieve the deep solemnity of the ending."[54]

Attempting to defuse any Pentagon attempts to change the script, Coppola suggested that he felt it "very important that we try to always consider the screenplay as a whole rather than finding objections on a piece by piece basis." He then discussed the specific concerns of the Army, first trying to justify the profane language and apparent irreverent comments by members of the Old Guard during burials. He addressed the service's strong objection to a scene in which a widow attends her husband's funeral in a drunken state: "I felt that by preparing the audience that the widow was drunk in order to dramatize her grief and fear would make her behavior during the burial more moving and understandable, especially her line 'at least now I know where you're spending your nights' more understandable. The main point is that Clell, as representative of the Army quickly turns this around to a chivalrous moment as he tenderly leads the widow on with the proceedings." After explaining other scenes that might cause problems for the Army, Coppola closed: "I will enjoy working shoulder to shoulder with representatives and advisors from the Army to insure that the total film and the effect it has on its audiences will be precisely what the Army hopes. . . . [The filmmakers] want to make a major American tragedy, and a beautiful film."[55]

The Army had no way of judging whether Coppola was making a sincere representation or simply saying what he thought he should say to secure support for his film. Most likely, the service did not care about the director's veracity as long as it had input into the manner he put the images onto the screen. In fact, the Army found only technical problems with the revised script and advised Baruch on April 15 that it recommended approval of support for the project. Informing John Horton, the film company's Washington representative, of the Pentagon's approval, Baruch wrote on April 17 that "there is no question now" that the Defense Department and Army would provide assistance. He said that only the matter of working out specific details and scheduling shooting at certain locations remained to be done. Briefing Assistant Secretary of Defense for Public Affairs Robert Sims of the movie's status on May 12, Baruch explained that the filmmakers had made changes in the original script to eliminate "some unacceptable language and action." In any case, he said that he and General Bussey felt that *Gardens of Stone* "will be a good, patriotic film for the Army and should appeal to general audiences. There is colorful background action, human characters, romance, drama, tragedy and touch of sentimentality."[56]

Reflecting the Pentagon's and Coppola's desire to make a movie that would benefit both parties, the filming of *Gardens of Stone* at Fort Myer, which began on May 23, experienced "very few problems." However, life almost immediately became as tragic as the story Coppola was creating, when his son Gian Carlo died on Memorial Day in a widely publicized boating accident on Chesapeake Bay. Much in the way that Hazard tried to educate Willow in hopes that he would survive Vietnam, Coppola had been teaching his son the cinematic craft. Consequently, Gian Carlo's death and the memorial service at the Fort Myer chapel cast a pall over the production and may well have contributed to the somber ambience of the completed movie. The director himself acknowledged the impact of the tragedy on *Gardens of Stone,* observing: "In a way, the movie paralleled my own life."[57]

From the producer's perspective, working with the Army had proved "gratifying and successful in all aspects." Writing to General Bussey on August 4, the day after Coppola completed filming in Washington, Levy said he and the director were "confident that the results on film will provide you with the feeling of accomplishment and pride that we all share from the collective efforts of so many." He emphasized that a major objective of *Gardens of Stone* "was to present the Army life during the Viet Nam period in a true to life manner through personal experiences of believable human beings." At the same time, the filmmakers had wanted to "convey the tradition, ceremonies, military character and professionalism typifying the Army. We sincerely believe we have achieved these goals and that the motion picture which has resulted will be a credit to the Army and a source of entertainment that will be both informative and emotionally appealing to the public."[58]

Despite such confident hopes, *Gardens of Stone* became less than the sum of its parts. The Army's full cooperation, a great director, a heartrending story, and real-life pain could not infuse the film with a story worth long remembering. Perhaps Coppola himself could not find a way to bridge the gap between his portrayal of the Army in *Apocalypse Now* and the one that Levy said the filmmakers were trying to present in *Gardens of Stone*. Undoubtedly, James Caan's Clell Hazard stands as a more realistic representative of the American soldier who fought in Vietnam than any of the characters in *Apocalypse Now*. Nevertheless, audiences always knew that Robert Duvall's Lieutenant Colonel Kilgore, if he ever did exist, was only an aberration. Consequently, viewers could suspend their disbelief and enjoy his bloodthirsty joy of

Director Francis Coppola and his director of photography, Jordan Crovenweth, on the set of *Gardens of Stone.*

killing without much emotional involvement. In contrast, although audiences could understand Hazard's frustrations and pain, his very normality did not engender any deep empathy or leave the viewer with any new insights about life or the American experience in Vietnam.

The Army found that the completed film did not quite measure up to expectations. After the required screening in Washington on November 25, General Bussey advised Levy that the service "found the motion picture to be acceptable." However, he offered several suggestions for changes. Saying that the Army still had concern about "the excessive and gratuitous use of profanity," he wrote, "We urge you to eliminate as much of the profanity as possible." In addition, he provided a series of comments and suggestions, which, in fact, primarily addressed creative matters rather than strictly technical issues.[59]

In the accompanying document, the Army suggested that the film should have a subtitle in the beginning to establish the time frame of the story. More importantly, the service reminded the filmmakers that the original script showed Hazard as "a cultured, sensitive man," whereas the film "does not clearly convey this. We recommend that portions of those scenes from the script be reinstated in the film. Those attributes set Hazard apart from other non-commissioned officers and make him a more sympathetic character." The Army suggested that *Gardens of Stone* "does not flow as well in the last half of the film as it does in the first. Continuity suffers particularly in the OCS sequences, 'Jackie's' death, and the final funeral scene." To solve the problem, the service recommended inserting "voice overs" if footage did not exist to correct the problem.[60]

The Army noted that in the version of the film it had seen, the audience might not realize for "some 30 minutes" that the Old Guard is a unique unit. The service recommended "that for dramatic impact and to establish the necessary ambience, the pomp and ceremony of the unit be shown early-on." Of more concern historically and image-wise, the Army pointed out that in one scene a television news program showed the famous scene of General Loan summarily executing a Vietcong. It observed: "This is an unnecessary cliche, frequently used to demonstrate the 'immorality' of the Vietnam War. It is also out of context in regard to the time it actually occurred and where it is placed in the film's time-frame." Consequently, the Army recommended that the filmmakers insert another Vietnam sequence on the TV screen.[61]

Of course, the execution sequence had only become a cliché after the fact. When broadcast, it had served as a vehicle to change opinions about the war, even though General Loan's action remained a legitimate use of force in a time of martial law during the Tet Offensive. It may well have become an overused visual comment on the immorality of the Vietnam War only to a sensitive military man. In fact, the graphic newsreel footage perhaps better serves as a continuing reminder of the inhumanity that man demonstrates to his fellow man during any war. In any case, Coppola's decision to use the news report in *Gardens of Stone* and his refusal to replace it did impinge needlessly on the credibility and integrity of the film. Technically, Coppola could probably not have changed the visual image on the television screen. However, the picture was sufficiently indistinct that Coppola could easily have substituted a new voice-over news report without anyone's being aware that the picture and narration did not match.

Assistant Secretary Sims did not push the matter in his letter to Levy on December 12. Rather, he expressed his awareness that the producer and director were making "conscientious efforts to rectify problem areas" that Bussey had cited as well as those he had discussed with Levy after the screening. He did repeat his particular concern "about the profanity in some of the opening scenes." Nevertheless, he thought that with a few minor revisions, *Gardens of Stone* would become "an excellent film—one in which the Defense Department, the Army, and especially your production company, can take great pride." In closing, he expressed his sincere appreciation of the filmmakers' "excellent spirit of cooperation in this endeavor" and said he looked forward to viewing the final product.[62]

Coppola did make some changes in the final version of *Gardens of Stone*. The film acquired an opening title to set the time frame, included some dialogue to better establish the elite nature of the Old Guard, and better established Hazard's interest in good books, Oriental rugs, and fine wines. Somewhere in the evolution from original script to the completed film, the drunken widow and the technical inaccuracies disappeared. Lt. Col. John Myers, the service's principal liaison officer on *Gardens of Stone*, expressed his satisfaction: "From the Army's standpoint, the film's depiction of the military is beyond reproach." Coppola said the Army had demanded and received a right to censor the script. However, he conceded that the Pentagon did not place many obstacles in his way, except for wanting to limit the amount of foul language that the characters used, taking pains to assure that "the Army's leadership appeared honorable and competent," and ensuring that the military scenes were technically accurate.[63]

The Pentagon's efforts to remove profanity from films remains, of course, a denial of reality and a rejection of its own policies requiring accurate portrayals of its personnel. Virtually all military men swear regularly and proficiently while on and off duty, except perhaps within the corridors and offices of the Pentagon building. But whether the services' requests to delete or limit spoken obscenities constitute censorship remains open to debate. By definition, censorship results in the prevention of a work from appearing at all. No record exists that the Pentagon ever stopped a motion picture from being made. Instead, the degree to which the military services have been able to impose their wishes on filmmakers reflects the resolve that individual producers, screenwriters, and directors manifest in asserting their creative freedom through give-and-take negotiations. Moreover, the demands of the Motion Picture Association's rating system probably have a greater influence on filmmakers' choice of dialogue than do requests from the Pentagon. Although *Gardens of Stone* ultimately contained less profanity than the original script and more than the Army liked, the completed film failed to enjoy wide success not because of the number of four-letter words, but rather as a result of its dramatic deficiencies.

Hal Hinson, in the *Washington Post*, may have given the best brief judgment about the film when he wrote, "*Gardens of Stone* can't in any way be counted a success, but it's not a disaster either." Agreeing with the Army's assessment, the reviewer observed that "about half-way through the whole thing collapses in a heap. But, for a while at least, it's eminently watchable." Noting that Coppola "has always been good at weddings and funerals," Hinson wrote, "In *Gardens*, the rituals of burial—the rolling drums, the folding of the flag, the playing of 'Taps'—are stately and somber, with a theatrical crispness. They're choreographed, like dance routines, in grim, metronomically slow motion. It's a death dance in dirge time."[64]

The Army rather than Coppola provided these images. However, Hinson acknowledged that in setting out the early interaction of the characters, the director had done some of his best work since the *Godfather* films. He then suggested that they remained only "remnants of a once-great director" and thought that Coppola "seems to be trying to remember what it's like to build a movie on a human scale, to deal with the basics of character and story and emotion. But it's a bit like watching a gifted athlete learn to walk again after a serious injury. The moves are somewhere in his head, if only he can get them." As a result, Hinson concluded that Coppola "doesn't seem to know where he wants his movie to go: It's like a pleasant Sunday drive with somebody who's hopelessly lost."[65]

Given this lack of direction, Hinson thought *Gardens of Stone* felt more like a little brother to *Platoon* than a companion to *Apocalypse Now*. More than that, however, because it focused on the grave rather than the details of combat, the reviewer thought the film made an antiwar rather than an anti-Vietnam statement: "Still, there's a curious ambiguity in Coppola's feelings about the soldiers and their life. As a pacifist work, it's cockeyed—an antiwar movie that condemns war but embraces the military." Consequently, Hinson felt that Coppola had not resolved his thoughts about the military: "He separates the warriors from the war, and it throws the movie out of wack."[66]

Voicing similar sentiments, Vincent Canby, in the *New York Times*, found "an emotional resonance" in the early scenes of the film that disappears quickly: "Though a seriously conceived film about the American experience in Vietnam, *Gardens of Stone* has somehow wound up having the consistency and the kick of melted vanilla ice cream." Canby concluded that the problem lay in the reality that the men in the Old Guard, "though decent, aren't very interesting as described by the film. Their world is small and arid. There's no sense of contrast between what they do in what they call 'the garden,' and the hopeless war being fought overseas. When they talk, it's mostly in the sentimental-obscene language of service-comedy palship."[67]

Canby thought that James Caan's portrayal of Clell Hazard resulted in the only fully realized character, but he concluded that the actor had wasted his performance on *Gardens of Stone*, "about which it would be praise to say that it has too many things on its mind. In fact, it's simply unfocused and clumsily composed. There's occasional poignancy but too often, what are supposed to be dramatic confrontations are just exchanges of plot information." Given Coppola's proven talents as a screenwriter, the reviewer wondered how he came to direct a screenplay that remains "alternately lame and utterly confusing. Possibly he tried to improve things, but the movie builds to no point. It unravels." Canby concluded: "The most important missing ingredient is Mr. Coppola."[68]

Its quality as a work of art aside, *Gardens of Stone* does remain the paradigm of an antiwar movie. Without combat or blood-drenched bodies cluttering the screen, the film shows the true victims of war, the nation's young, being "planted" in assembly-line fashion, however much ceremony and pomp the Old Guard can give to the funeral ritual. Some viewers might find the gallows humor which members of the burial detail verbalize during the ceremonies disrespectful and out of place. The attempt at levity, however, only emphasizes the film's antiwar message. The effort to mitigate the solemnity of the moment, a moment repeated many times during each week of their tour of duty, becomes a necessity to the burial detail. Without the forced irreverence, the members of the unit would undoubtedly break down under the weight of the knowledge that they are burying their comrades in arms, their friends, the next generation, before they have had a chance to live, let alone make their mark. In this context, the refrain "Ashes to ashes, dust to dust, let's bury this guy and get on the bus" becomes a cry of pain, not a sacrilegious ditty.

At the same time, the drawn out, carefully orchestrated burial ceremony seems at first glance like cruel and inhuman torture to the grieving families of the dead soldier. One wonders how the friends and relatives avoid breaking down. The three rifle volleys that render the military honors jolt the bodies as much as if bullets actually hit home. "Taps" pierces the silence and closes the ritual with the finality of death. But if the ceremony inflicts its own pain, it also serves as a catharsis for the loss of loved ones.

In recording the burial ritual, *Gardens of Stone* creates a more powerful antiwar statement than any other movie about the armed services set in the Vietnam era. Its images of death and lost potential pervade the psyche far more powerfully than the surrealistic images Coppola himself produced in *Apocalypse Now* or that Oliver Stone sought to produce out of the blood, gore, and chaos he was to put on the screen in *Platoon*. In closing his eulogy to Jackie Willow, Clell's promise, "I know him. I won't forget," stands as a poignant reminder to the nation not to forget those who died in Vietnam. But most Americans were trying hard to forget the war and get on with their lives. Only those few people who still carried the war within themselves, most obviously the disabled veterans and the grieving relatives, remained trapped in a limbo they could not or would not change.

Another, much less visible, group of Americans also failed to find peace with the end of the Vietnam War. Despite their efforts to change the nation's policies in Southeast Asia, those antiwar radicals who still cannot or will not return home, literally or figuratively, continue to bear the effect of their opposition to Vietnam. Only when an individual "revolutionary" emerges from the underground to surrender after years of flight are most Americans reminded of the extreme measures that some antiwar protesters were willing to undertake to stop the war. If these radicals have been forgotten for the most part, they remain victims of the war as much as any other Americans.

Few people would equate their suffering with the physical loss of paralyzed or otherwise disabled veterans. Nor do their lost opportunities seem as significant as the mental anguish of those who once fought in the jungles and now still fight the war in their minds. Moreover, few people would suggest that they deserve the same sympathy as the parents, wives, and friends who lost loved ones in the war. Still, those who chose to protest the war with violent acts rather than peaceful rhetoric often lost more than just their innocence. To a significant degree, these people stand as a metaphor for what Vietnam did to the United States as a whole.

Hollywood had, of course, portrayed the more violent aspects of the antiwar movement in such movies as *Medium Cool, The Strawberry Statement, Between the Lines,* and *More American Graffiti.* By the time of *Gardens of Stone,* however, Coppola could even pair off a dedicated soldier with an antiwar activist and make the relationship almost believable. In reality, by the late 1980s, most people had come to accept the conventional wisdom that the antiwar protesters had seen the light and become Yuppies or, worse, conservative parents, just like their fathers and mothers.

Such movies as *Return of the Seacacus Seven* and *The Big Chill* only reinforced this image. Yet, some people who opposed the war had done more than make one or two pilgrimages to Washington to demonstrate, and not all antiwar activists came in out of the cold and joined the establishment. But until Sidney Lumet's *Running on Empty* appeared in the summer of 1988, Hollywood ignored those radicals who remained at war with themselves as with the nation. Nevertheless, in following the travails of Annie and Arthur Pope, Lumet and writer-producer Naomi Foner perhaps best addressed the key question of the Vietnam era: what did the U.S. involvement in the war ultimately cost the American people?

Even as other Hollywood films continued to seek answers on the battlefield and in the plight of the returned veterans, *Running on Empty* attempted to explain the nature of the American experience in Vietnam by looking solely at how the war dislocated one family of noncombatants. In choosing this approach, Lumet and Foner avoided the pitfalls of trying to use the horror of combat, with its inherent visual excitement, to make an antiwar, anti-Vietnam statement. Drawing on many of the incidents and polemic arguments from the protest movement and the underground subculture, Foner fashioned an "after" story that allowed her and the director to probe the depths of the damage the war did within American society as a whole, not just among the soldiers, sailors, Marines, and fliers who did the actual fighting.

To be sure, neither of the Popes represent everyman who opposed the Vietnam conflict. After all, not everyone blew up a napalm factory to protest the war and then spent the next sixteen years in flight from the FBI. Based in some measure on the bombing of a University of Wisconsin laboratory, the Popes' attack left a janitor maimed. In their almost constant movement from job to job, city to city, they have managed to avoid arrest while raising two relatively well-adjusted children. But they have paid a high price for making their violent gesture to protest the war. They have lost virtually all contact with their families, have had promising careers destroyed, have endured relative poverty, and have had to deny their children any semblance of a normal life. As a result, the odyssey of the Popes becomes a metaphor of how the Vietnam War very nearly destroyed the fabric of the nation's life and even its raison d'être.

Lumet saw two themes in *Running on Empty:* "I would hardly deny it's a political movie. Everything that propels them into this situation is political, but fundamentally it's about something a bit longer-lasting—the parent-child relationship." The director recalled that Foner moved him with the observation that the parent-child relationship remains the only love affair in which, going in, you know it has to break up. Even though the success of the love affair can be measured by how easy breaking up becomes, Lumet acknowledged that children are going to leave under any circumstances, and as Foner created the story, he said the leaving is also "fraught with other agonies."[69]

In *Running on Empty*, the catalyst for change in the Popes' lives comes when seventeen-year-old Danny falls in love and wants to go to college. Initially, Arthur adamantly opposes any breaking up of the family, since it would mean the end of any contact with his son so long as he and Annie remain underground. Danny's growing independence, which his girlfriend aids and abets, steals much of the film's attention and forces Arthur to balance his needs with those of his son and the entire family. Nevertheless, the ongoing ramifications of blowing up the napalm factory continue to define the nature of the relationship between Arthur and Annie and ultimately force the denouement. To Lumet, the toll that a radical act takes on innocent bystanders became the focus of his film: "When you lead an impassioned, committed life, you'll pay for it to a degree, but others pay for it too. The cost spreads out, like a stone in the pond; the ripples go on. Her parents pay for it, his parents pay for it, and now their children are paying for it. The circles of consequence are greater than their own lives."[70]

In writing the screenplay, Foner approached the story with the belief that people very rarely have total control over the consequences of their actions. In regard to the Popes, she acknowledged that they had done something against the law to stop a war they considered immoral and dangerous: "But, I think they acted with integrity about something they cared about as opposed to just sitting back, as the generation in the present tense does and watching the world go by and doing nothing about it." Herein lies the conundrum of the film and by extension, of the American involvement in Vietnam. Sometimes to do good deeds, people use violent means, with unforeseen results. Does blowing up the napalm factory to protest the war accomplish its goals if a janitor becomes maimed and Annie and Arthur spend the next sixteen years as fugitives? Does burning a village to save it win hearts and minds? Do the military reasons for taking Hamburger Hill help the American war effort if the media and politicians cite the losses as a symbol of the futility of the war?[71]

Foner acknowledged that like all young people, the Popes may well have not thought about the negative ramifications of their political gesture. At the same time, she saw her characters as knowing "what they were doing in terms of what was going on in the war. They were clearly very up on why they were doing what they were doing at the moment they were doing it. I don't think they probably saw the consequences of their actions." Nevertheless, she did not consider Arthur and Annie victims of the war, because they had acted consciously rather than being acted upon. Furthermore, given the nature of the war they were opposing, Foner had clear ambivalence about the efficacy of their action to oppose the war. In fact, she had drawn her characters from radicals she had known who had gone underground: "To some degree, I admired that they put their money where their mouths were. I opposed the violence. But there was a certain admiration for people who were willing to give up everything for the cause."[72]

According to Amy Robinson, one of the coproducers, the filmmakers "were dealing with people with whom we had an affinity." As a result, she said that as the producers developed the material, they decided they were going to do everything they could "to portray these people sympathetically." To do this, the Popes' bomb only maimed the janitor, rather than killing him as happened with the researcher in the University of Wisconsin bombing. The film did not make the Popes members of the Weather Underground or some similar group. And to contrast the Popes' essentially nonviolent approach to revolution, the filmmakers created a gun-toting, bank-robbing radical who visits his old friends, giving Arthur the opportunity to tell his sons that he and Annie never believed they could attain their political goals with guns.[73]

In fact, Foner created in the Popes the stereotypical 1960s antiwar radicals, easily recognizable to anyone who had lived through the protest movement. Nevertheless, however well she did her homework and remembered her friends, the screenwriter and most viewers may well not understand the characters and true natures of Annie and Arthur and their real-life counterparts. In almost all cases, the radicals were simply playing at revolution. The protest movement, for them, remained only a game that offered excitement, a diversion from the real world, the chance to weave conspiracies, and a sense of apparent or actual danger, all in the name of doing good deeds. Most of the radicals had no idea what it meant to become a revolutionary. Opposing the war does not equate with developing a philosophic battle plan to overthrow the old order and replace it with something better.

Neither the Popes nor their long-lost radical friend ever espouse an alternative to the society in which they lived. The war seems to have been their only point of contention with the government. To be sure, Annie and Arthur have given up everything as a result of their actions. But the results of their violent protest took the possibility of living normal lives from them; they did not consciously give up the creature comforts. In that sense, they surely become victims of the war, even as Foner defines the term. Nothing in the text of the film suggested that they would not have moved to suburbia and lived happily ever after if only the janitor had not happened to be in the wrong place at the wrong time. Foner may believe that the Popes knew what they were doing and why. Nevertheless, they show no recognition anywhere in the movie that they have any real comprehension of what revolutionaries must do to succeed in their chosen profession. In fact, their actions before and after the bombing suggest just the opposite.

Vladimir Ilich Ulyanov, the model of a successful twentieth-century revolutionary, and his wife understood full well that if they embarked upon careers as professional revolutionaries, children would have no place in their lives. So, although Lenin clearly loved children, he and Krupskaya did not become parents. Moreover, they went into exile in order to have the freedom to expound their views and spread them. In contrast, Annie and Arthur already have Danny before they bomb the napalm factory, and later on, six years into their fugitive lives, they have a second son. Their revolutionary activity consists of some behind-the-scenes union organizing. Annie does question, at one point, whether they should have brought Harry into their world. A true revolutionary would never have had to ask the question.

Whatever the degree to which Annie and Arthur may have become victims of the war, their actions have clearly made Danny and Harry quintessential victims. They are suffering their fugitive lifestyle because of their parents' actions, not their own. Trying one more time to stop him from leaving, Danny's girlfriend reminds him of the obvious: "You can't keep running away from something you had nothing to do with. You deserve your own chance." To her question of why he has "to carry the burden of someone else's life," Danny can only answer, "He's my father."

Annie and Arthur have done nothing to extricate themselves from the situation in which they live, in order to give Danny and Harry a more normal childhood. Worse, throughout the movie, Arthur adamantly refuses, for his own selfish reasons, to allow Danny to make a better life for himself. Even when Annie finally pleads with him to let his son go, Arthur will only answer, "That is unacceptable to me." Ironically, Arthur's very commitment to fatherhood shows how far he and Annie have evolved from their radical days. In the midst of semipoverty and separation from family, whatever idealistic goals and commitment to changing the system the Popes ever had have disappeared. Instead, the Popes have become traditional parents, and their children are their only reason for being.

In capturing an "after" of the radical antiwar protest movement, *Running on Empty* made a profound comment on how much Vietnam dislocated all of American society. Two scenes in particular presented as well as any Hollywood film has ever done the manner in which Vietnam alienated the generations from each other and a whole generation from society itself. Seeing a picture of his grandmother in the paper while auditioning for admission to Juilliard to study piano, Danny goes to her apartment, masquerading as a pizza delivery boy. Not being able to reveal his identity, Danny confronts his grandmother for the first time, barely able to control himself. She senses that his discomfort has deeper origins than what to do with an unordered pizza but cannot allow herself to imagine the truth. They stare at each other, not able to bridge the gap of time and lost opportunities.

"The restaurant scene," as it quickly became known in film lore, provided an even more descriptive moment. As cinema, it drew almost universal praise from critics. Charles Champlin wrote that "for overwhelming emotional force [it] may be as moving as anything you'll see all year." More than that, the scene becomes perhaps the most insightful cinematic rendering of the impact that Vietnam had on the American people.[74]

Having finally resolved to break the island of isolation surrounding the family, Annie arranges to meet with her father to ask him to take in Danny so that he can enter Juilliard. Initially, the father hides behind his icy demeanor, berating Annie for having thrown away everything to make an empty gesture, and accuses Arthur of leading her into radical action. In a telling retort about the quality of her marriage, Annie responds, "It was my idea. I'm living with the consequences of my own choice." More important still, she has revealed to herself very possibly for the first time the reality of her relationship with Arthur and the emptiness of their lives together. As she tells him about the grandchildren, however, the father's control begins to evaporate, and they try to reach out for each other in the few minutes they have.

Ultimately, her father agrees to take in his grandson, but Annie cannot follow. As Danny explains to his girlfriend, Arthur could not survive without his family and Annie cannot yet inflict that pain on him. In the end, Arthur himself gives Danny his freedom, although the war continues to exert its influence, still splitting families asunder. Saying good-bye to her father, Annie can only tell him, "I love you dad," leaving him alone sobbing deeply. When Arthur, Annie, and Harry take flight one more time, they leave Danny standing at the side of the road, now alone and now free.

Despite its power and exploration of the fundamental issues that Vietnam raised about the relationship of a government to its opponents, *Running on Empty* remained a relatively obscure film despite rave reviews and acknowledgment of its clear insights. In his review, Champlin focused on its serious intentions, citing first its portrayal of the disruption of family relationships that became a "grim penalty of life in the '60s." More than that, however, he said the film showed "the long after-effects of the flamboyant gesture, the slow cost of commitment. There is a terrible poignancy in the prices the parents have had to pay for what they believed in, and they aren't yet through paying even if, in a clever piece of story-structuring, the last feeling is of satisfaction and relief. What Lumet and Foner have proved is that a film can be about something, and also be suspenseful, engrossing, romantic, moving, funny and truthful. You can only wish there were more like it."[75]

Still, some reviewers noted that the film contained many ambiguities and implausibilities. To be sure, the FBI might well have caught the Popes many times over the years if the agency had given top priority to their apprehension. Without question, some school administrator would have become sufficiently concerned about the lack of Danny's and Harry's school records to alert authorities. Although Annie had had a promising musical career before she went into the underground, she would have had a difficult time providing Danny sufficient instruction to enable him to gain admission to Juilliard. After all, supporters of the underground remnants would not give high priority to furnishing each of the Pope's temporary homes with a piano; and Danny's traveling practice keyboard, which he always managed to rescue, would prove a poor substitute for the real thing.

At the heart of the film's lack of success, however, was the very seriousness Champlin had so praised. As a serious film, *Running on Empty* had the same problem as *Gardens of Stone*. Most people by the end of the 1980s had seen enough of that side of the war and did not feel a need to be reminded one more time of what Vietnam had done to the nation or to individuals. Moreover, although the combat movies, the non-Vietnam Vietnam films, and the home front stories may have presented a more balanced portrait of the war, they did not do much to rehabilitate the still-stained image of the American military. Three peacetime movies that had virtually nothing to do with Vietnam were to accomplish that feat.

25 Rehabilitation Completed

AN OFFICER AND A GENTLEMAN CONVINCED Hollywood that audiences were ready for peacetime military stories of the old kind. Like the pre-Vietnam Navy films, it created a setting for romance and adventure. It made it clear that the armed services remained necessary for the security of the nation. It also showed how the military was training its now gender-integrated officer Corps to become consummate professionals. These new cinematic warriors may have suffered from identity problems, self-doubts, and even rebelliousness. But they did not harbor the hatreds or ambivalences toward their nation or their service that their counterparts in the Vietnam combat movies had regularly manifested. Instead, they had chosen military careers out of love of their country and desire to use their talents to help ensure the survival of the United States. To them, the Vietnam War served as an ongoing reminder of past failures and as a motivation to make sure that their watch would not fail. To that extent, Hollywood would seem to suggest that the war became a benign influence on these men and on the military as much as the war might ever contribute positively to the nation's well-being.

Once again, however, the Navy demonstrated its difficulty in providing assistance to a story that focused on "flawed" people, who drank, lusted after women, or simply did not conform to the image of the Navy's ideal officer or enlisted man. Like Jack Nicholson in *The Last Detail,* James Caan in *Cinderella Liberty,* and Robert Duvall in *The Great Santini,* Richard Gere, as Zack Mayo in *An Officer and a Gentleman,* did not have the background and presence the Navy expected in its officers. Worse, the script contained graphic sex and portrayals of its training that the service found inaccurate. The illegitimate son of an Navy enlisted man, Zack grows up on the fringes of the sordid world of U.S. sailors stationed in the Philippines, graduates from college, and decides to enter the Naval Flight Officer program, despite his tattoo and motorcycle.

During the course of his training, he meets Debra Winger, playing a local blue-collar factory worker, who frequents the Navy base dances looking for an officer and a husband. Coincidentally with the unexceptional boy-meets-girl, boy-loses-girl, boy-wins-girl love story, Zack struggles to become a naval officer under the watchful and always demanding eye of his drill instructor, Sergeant Foley. In a role that Hollywood had turned into a cliché, Lou Gossett Jr. imparts a believability worthy of Jack Webb's classic portrayal in *The D.I.* or Lee Ermey's vintage performance in *The Boys in Company C.* In fact, despite the torrid love scenes between Gere and Winger, Gossett becomes the focus of the movie, ultimately turning Gere into an officer worthy of his salute.

To the service, it did not matter that *An Officer and a Gentleman* combined the traditional coming-of-age story of an outsider rising above his background with a military love story set at a typical naval training facility, not unlike the 1930s *Shipmates* and *Shipmates Forever.* Instead, the Office of Information saw a story of a drill instructor's physical and verbal abuse of a group of naval officer candidates, the explicit depiction of sexual encounters, and the suicide of an officer candidate who drops out of the program. As a result, from the initial submission of the script to the Navy's Los Angeles Office of Information, the service voiced strong objections to the project.

Capt. Dale Patterson, the head of the office at the time, explained that he reacted so negatively "because, to be brutally honest, I didn't think it was much of a story, rather trashy, a lot of violence, sex and filthy language in it. And the characters in the script were not characteristic of Navy men." Following two months of informal discussions about the screenplay and a formal request for Navy assistance, the office advised producer Marty Elfand that "prior to Navy consideration for assistance the script would need re-writing or major revision." In a memorandum for the record on July 16, 1980, Patterson cited "a multitude of problem areas" just in the first twenty pages of the script. These included inaccuracies in the status of Zack's sailor father, a Philippine gang attack on sailors, which "is not an accurate portrayal of the Philipine [*sic*] community and their relationship with American sailors," "atrocious" language, harassment of female officer candidates, which is "not tolerated in any phase of training or in the Navy as a whole," "offensive and most inaccurate" Jody calls, and reference "to Mobile Debs offensive to City of Mobile and not accurate."[1]

When this memo reached Washington, the Navy Office of Information proposed to Don Baruch that the service send the list of objections to the producer as the answer to his request for guidance in dealing with the Navy's objections to the script. Don Baruch did not concur, advising Bob Manning, his civilian counterpart in the Navy Office of Information, that the service needed to provide a more detailed explanation than a simple list of problem areas. Moreover, he noted that even if the filmmakers corrected the cited problems, the chief of information might still object to the project.[2]

Instead, following up his phone conversation, Baruch, on August 7, offered a more detailed recommendation. He agreed that the Navy's comments were "well taken," but he repeated his concern that even if the filmmakers corrected the listed objections, the Navy still might not approve the script. As an alternative, he suggested that the Navy "endeavor to develop a version that could be considered acceptable, especially as the story of pilot training has not been on the screen for sometime and because this is considered to be a major theatrical release." He also advised the Office of Information that, at his suggestion, producer Marty Elfand was coming to Washington to visit him and the Navy the next week, "both for further clarification on objections and developing something more satisfactory."[3]

Following the meeting, Elfand spent the next several months working to revise the script. Nevertheless, after reading the second version, which the Los Angeles office received in early December, the Navy found that it differed little from the original script, which it had considered "profane and morally objectionable." According to the reviewer, the new screenplay remained "sordid, emphasizing the seamy side of life and featuring numerous sexually explicit scenes. Production assistance offers no benefit to the service, rather, the portrayal would be damaging to the Navy and to the recruiting effort." Consequently, with the concurrence of the Los Angeles office, the Office of Information recommended that the Navy deny the filmmakers' request for assistance on the grounds that the "Navy would suffer by association with the production . . . which features numerous sexually explicit scenes and other objectionable material."[4]

Still not willing to take the turndown as a final answer, associate producer Bob Williams went to Washington and met with Baruch and Navy representatives on January 13, 1981. According to Baruch, the Office of Information "gave him chapter and verse" as to why it still found the story inaccurate. Among other things, the Navy indicated that the script did not present a factual account of naval aviator training and suggested that since the story did not involve any flying, the filmmakers should consider making it a movie about the Navy's OCS in Newport. More important, Baruch noted that the role of the D.I. "needs clarification as to his duties." The office also advised Williams that he would have to delete the opening montage of the film, which shows Zack, as an eleven-year-old, coming to the Philippines to live with his father after his mother commits suicide. Baruch noted, "This shows seamy-side of life there which we probably would not want to approve as it would be negative for govt.-to-govt. relations." He also complained that the script had too much sex and concluded that Williams "would let us know if producer will rewrite this considerably or make pix on his own."[5]

As a follow-up to the meeting, the Navy Office of Information authorized a research visit to the Pensacola Naval Air Station for the filmmakers, "to give them an overview of the aviation program. Familiarization visit would enable them to rewrite script to more accurately reflect various aspects of basic flight training contemplated for the screenplay." Accounts of what happened next vary depending on which party to the negotiations is recalling the events.[6]

Pat Coulter, in Los Angeles, advised the Marine Corps Public Affairs Office at Headquarters on February 20 that he had learned that Elfand had been working with the Navy for more than a year on the project and had "hit an impasse in the negotiation process." However, as late as March 20, Coulter found that the Navy Office of Information in Los Angeles was still "talking to the producers and maintaining the lines of communications." Nonetheless, in describing the situation to Headquarters, he also said that "the 'official' Navy response to a request for assistance, appears to be negative. As I understand it, that has never been conveyed by letter from either DOD or CHINFO to Paramount. It has all been verbal to date."[7]

Marine Headquarters had additional information. In an undated memo to the director of public affairs commenting on Coulter's request for permission to provide substantive assistance to the filmmakers, Lt. J.L. Schilling said that the Navy "has indicated they don't intend to support the film—'not only NO, but "Hell NO!"' As the Navy has supported films in the past, it doesn't appear to be a matter of *not* providing support to any films. I therefore feel their position is legitimate and firm."[8]

Don Baruch thought the failure to reach an agreement occurred because Marty Elfand "felt that the Navy requirements for making the script acceptable would take the guts out of the picture and therefore decided to go ahead without cooperation." Elfand apparently saw things differently. Shortly after *An Officer and a Gentleman* opened in the summer of 1982, Coulter reported to the Marine Combat Correspondents Convention that Elfand had told him that when the Navy turned down the film, "they were really adamant about it." Worse, the producer said that the service "did not keep the door open." Coulter observed that filmmakers are professionals who know how to negotiate with actors about salaries and with people about facilities and recalled that Elfand had told him: "God damn it, they cut me off before I had a chance to hit my final point. I would have given the things they were concerned about. I would give them the language. I would give them the suicide. I'll give them the sex. God damn, I need the facilities. It's costing me millions." Whatever the truth, communications clearly had broken down. Don Baruch later concluded, "Personnaly [*sic*], I believe the Navy was overly restrictive in dealing with the producer."[9]

In any event, Coulter first became involved in the project in February 1981, when Comdr. Chris Bauman from across the hall in the Navy's Los Angeles Office of Information brought him the information that the Navy was about to turn down the request for cooperation on *An Officer and a Gentleman*. Bauman thought Coulter should "be aware" of the situation because of the Marine D.I. character. He gave Coulter a copy of the script with the admonition: "Don't tell anyone I gave you the script." Coulter explained that Elfand had not submitted the screenplay to the Marines: "He probably wasn't knowledgeable enough to know that he should have touched base with both services."[10]

After reading the script that night, Coulter concluded that the film would appeal to young people, and so he had special concern that the Marines should do what they could to protect the image of the Corps. Consequently, when he took the script back to the Navy office, he told Bauman: "You're right. This has got the potential to be a dynamite story. The Marine Corps needs to be involved, especially if you guys are going to turn it down, we need to play a key role in this thing." After calling General Brewer, still the Marine director of information, to get permission to approach the film company, Coulter contacted Bob Williams on February 19. In doing so, he wanted to "begin deliberations on what could be done to portray the Marines in the most authentic, accurate and positive manner as possible." In addition, assuming the Navy would not change its position, he wanted to push the idea of turning the story into a Marine film.[11]

After Coulter discussed the situation over the phone with him, Williams wrote to Coulter that afternoon to say that the company was "most anxious to meet with you to incorporate any changes or ideas that you might have regarding this project." He added that if the script met with Marine approval, the filmmakers would like to arrange "for an immediate survey trip to Quantico. It is anticipated that production would begin sometime in April, so you can see time is of the essence." In fact, Elfand was working under the threat of a directors' strike, and he had to complete the film before the stoppage, since the backers had told the producer that they were not going to leave their money tied up for an extended period.[12]

Given the objection the Navy had had to the suicide, Elfand, in his first meeting with Coulter, asked whether the Marines would have a problem with the incident if he changed the film to a Marine officer candidate story. Coulter said he told the producer, "Anybody who can't be a Marine has every right in the world and every reason in the world to commit suicide." Even though Coulter later said he made the comment "tongue in cheek," the comment helped break the ice: "They liked that. You know, as Marines, we can get away with being a little more colorful. We have an image that we are very proud of, one that has taken 206 years to create. We have a certain constituency we are responsible for. We aren't concerned about the propriety of a lot of things that the other services are."[13]

Likewise, Coulter said that the sex, per se, did not bother the Marines as it had the Navy, particularly after it became clear that because of the time constraints, Elfand was not going to be able to transform *An Officer and a Gentleman* into a Marine story. However, Coulter expressed concern to the producer about the problems he faced, telling him: "You're the one who's going for the hard 'R' rating. You've got to maintain a modicum of decorum. It cannot come across as it does in the script." At the same time, Coulter suggested that some of the problems the Navy had with the sex resulted from the service's failure to realize that the company could not afford to lose the R rating and so would have had to tone down the explicit sex that the script described.[14]

In fact, the Marines focused their primary attention on the characterization of the D.I. in order to ensure that the scenes depicting Sergeant Foley's verbal and physical harassment of the officer trainees would not adversely affect the Corps's image. At the very time the Marines were considering whether to become involved in the film, two major recruit-abuse incidents had occurred: one with Pugi sticks at the Recruit Depot in San Diego, and one as the result of a D.I. shooting a recruit at Parris Island. Coulter recalled that the Marines were "in the papers every time we turned around because we were getting these drill instructors doing these things." As a result, Coulter said that the Marine commandant had changed the philosophy to where "there was absolutely no question that recruit abuse was absolutely verboten. You did not do it. Of course, our job was to try to drive home the message that we don't do that."[15]

Given this reality, Coulter's primary job in working with producer Elfand and director Taylor Hackford in the making of *An Officer and a Gentleman* centered on toning down the characterization of the Foley persona. The original script called for the D.I. to appear as a "rough character." From his perspective, Coulter could not have the drill instructor "be a Neanderthal, knuckle dragging, son of a bitch," which was the stereotype Gossett had initially envisioned as his character. As part of his effort to change his perception, Coulter told the actor that the Marines wanted him to visit the Recruit Depot in order to see for himself how the D.I.s operated in the contemporary world. Coulter said that during Gossett's two days there, on April 13 and 14, the actor "became aware of the DIs' role as teacher and coach, and the meaning of the words 'firmness, fairness and dignity' in the DI/ recruit relationship."[16]

Gossett later claimed that he had actually "hung with the DIs" for ten days at drill instructor school at Camp Pendleton, north of San Diego. He said he had run seven miles each morning and had gone through intensive physical and survival training, karate and hand-to-hand combat, and close order drill. He also described how the Marines had allowed him to practice on actual recruits and said he found that the D.I.s "do anything they can think of to approximate life and death. They embarrass you, insult you, strip all the stuff that you come there with, especially your ego. Strip away everything but your spirit, and then they build you back up. And if you make it, you say thank you and you carry it with you the rest of your life." Gossett recalled that "the hardest part was learning the cadences. Trying to stop 35 people on a dime is very difficult."[17]

The Marine records indicate that Gossett spent only the two days at the Recruit Depot, and the director of the Corps's Public Affairs Office at the time the film premiered suggested that either Gossett "exaggerated his itinerary there or the reporters misunderstood" what he told them. In any case, his visit, whatever its length, did provide Gossett with "insight into the philosophy, motivation and techniques of today's Marine drill instructor." The actor explained that in developing his role, he modeled Foley on the chief drill instructor at Camp Pendleton, William Stoner: "I was never quite as tough as he was.

Lou Gossett Jr. attempting to turn Richard Gere into an officer and a gentleman.

Jack Webb provided the quintessential portrayal of a Marine drill instructor in *The D.I.*

Even the DI's were scared of him." In addition, Gossett said he also obtained bits and pieces of his character from Gunnery Sgt. W.P. "Buck" Welcher, the off-duty Marine D.I. who worked as technical advisor on the film while on leave from his assignment at Pensacola. Finally, he drew upon his own drill instructor from his days as a paratrooper at Fort Benning and from watching Jack Webb in *The D.I.*[18]

Once actual filming began at Port Townsend, Washington, which became the stand-in for Pensacola because of the Navy's denial of assistance, Welcher helped ensure the accurate portrayal of how D.I.s train the aviation officer candidates. The Marine recalled that his "first task was to show them how to march. Overall, the actors were very professional and they learned quickly." Coulter worked on the film in an unofficial capacity because the Marines were providing only courtesy assistance. Even then, he had had to obtain permission from headquarters to continue his informal liaison during the actual production. In this capacity he traveled back and forth four or five times from Los Angeles to the Washington location, at the production company's expense. In addition to making sure that Gossett assumed the proper characterization, probably Coulter's greatest contribution to the authentic ambience of the completed film was his arranging for off-duty Marines from local facilities to work on the set as extras.[19]

Director Hackford helped add authenticity to the portrayals by ordering Gossett to live in a condo twenty miles away from the rest of the cast because of his concern that the actor's good-natured personality off the set would affect his interaction with the actor/officer candidates on camera. Gossett acknowledged that the arrangement "made it difficult and lonely, but it worked. Taylor figured I am too nice a guy and that when I screamed and yelled at somebody they would probably giggle." Hackford agreed: "I wanted him literally to be a pariah. I wanted to create an aura around him; I wanted an intimidation factor about him." As a result, he felt that the same lack of familiarity worked in the interaction between Gossett and Gere to the benefit of the film: "I think Richard got to the point where he was thinking about Lou, 'Maybe he is a little strange. Maybe he is a little screwy.' These are things you utilize." The director said Gossett was able to maintain this intensity by the things he did to Gere as the drill instructor, such as squirting water on him with a hose and making him do pushups in the mud: "Richard's exhaustion from the scenes was horrendous, and the humiliation of what was being done to him was horrendous, and that helped keep the intensity up."[20]

The authenticity Gossett imparted to his role won him an Academy Award for best supporting actor. His performance also stole the movie from the Gere-Winger fairy-tale

490

love story, despite the explicitness of their sexual encounters. Perhaps never before or since in a movie have lovers worried about who should get up to get a towel after having made love. In the end, however, the development of the love story has a predictable climax when Gere, in his white graduation uniform, whisks away his lady to Hollywood-variety bliss as a Navy flier's wife. Far more interesting, *An Officer and a Gentleman* details the process through which Gossett turns Gere from an selfish loner, distrustful of anyone, into an officer and a gentleman. Hackford captures the change exquisitely during a scene in which Gere's unit makes a run over an obstacle course. Sergeant Foley watches from the finish line as Gere, instead of going for a record, returns to help a female classmate overcome a physical and mental wall to complete her run. With a subtle look of satisfaction, Gossett's expression gives meaning to the movie and crowns Pat Coulter's efforts: Marine drill instructors create naval officers and gentlemen.

To be sure, the love story may have sold *An Officer and a Gentleman.* Gossett, looking back on the movie, probably explained its appeal best: "It ain't got no special effects, ain't no spaceships. There are people looking into each other's eyes and dealing with relationships. It's got an ending that people seem to want, especially women, who come out of there crying. Women love the hell out of this movie. It's left up to the actors, the director and the cinematographer. No special effects at all. It's real, it's today."[21]

However powerful the film's ending, the Marines had other issues with which to concern themselves about the completed work. When they went to a preview screening of the film in Washington in July 1982, Marine Corps representatives had few problems with *An Officer and a Gentleman.* They found that Gossett portrayed "a reasonably accurate image of a trim, fit, strict D.I. whose mission is to weed out unfit aviation officer candidates." They saw only minor negative aspects of the D.I.'s image, including a "slightly non-regulation mustache; excessive profanity; the D.I.'s deliberate attempt to cause a candidate to 'D.O.R.'; and a fight with the candidate." Nevertheless, if Coulter's efforts to tone down Foley's character satisfied the Marines, the resulting portrayal produced negative reactions from some viewers. Several actually found the film so authentic that they criticized the Marines for having such brutal training methods.[22]

In her syndicated article, Judy Klemesrud began with a recitation of Foley's excesses: "He is foulmouthed, abusive, insulting, and calls his young recruits 'queers' and 'eggheads' and 'dummys.' He even carries a swagger stick, on which he has carved a notch for each naval aviation officer candidate who has D.O.R.'d (dropped out on request) from the 13 weeks of intensive training that he administers." Nevertheless, she says that underneath Foley's "fastidious Marine Corps exterior . . . there beats a paternal, caring heart. By the end of the training, Sergeant Foley has become a father figure to the young officer candidates who have survived the grueling 13 weeks."[23]

Not everyone, however, saw both sides of the coin—that turning civilians into officers requires discipline to weed out those who simply do not have the ability to lead. Columnist Richard Cohen liked *An Officer and a Gentleman,* suggesting that if an Oscar existed for Best Kissing in a movie, Gere and Winger "are going to walk off with it—that is if they can still walk." But he objected to the movie's message that brutality has value in turning a punk into a man: "In *Officer,* it's not the Army that does the trick but the Navy's boot camp for potential pilots. Ex-GI's will be relieved to know that the Navy has mud, too." What disturbed Cohen as much as the message was the fact that a movie with this message "is a big, big hit—second only to *E.T.*—and that audiences that should be laughing are instead eating it up."[24]

Some people took an even more direct approach in expressing their unhappiness with the movie. Richard Bell Jr., of Brooklyn, New York, complained directly to Pres. Ronald Reagan that he was shocked at "being subject to the most revolting display of filthy language I have ever heard. The filth came out of the mouth of a U.S. Marine in his official duty as a drill instructor. I am incensed to find that such filth is the official language used by our country to train gentlemen and officers." Mr. Bell said that he had not experienced such "atrocious gutter talk" during his World War II training as an air cadet. Consequently, he argued: "No bible believing christian [*sic*] should ever be subjected to such obscene training methods and I demand that it be eliminated at once from the entire Marine Corps. . . . Please insist Mr. President that the morons who speak that way do not lead or train our soldiers. It is an abomination in the sight of God."[25]

Ultimately, with its serious concern about its representations on the screen in the post-Vietnam era, the military's judgment of *An Officer and a Gentleman* remained the important one. Although believing that all the objectionable scenes and portrayals "could have been brought into total compliance with current regulations and policy" if the Navy and the Marines had given full cooperation, Pat Coulter still thought the film "is considerably more positive and reflects more favorably on the Marine Corps THAN IT EVER WOULD HAVE had we not become involved." Don Baruch concluded: "The picture has many positive elements and should reflect favorably on the Navy and especially the Marine Corps through the portrayal of the D.I." In an ironic twist, Baruch reported that the Navy "appears pleased and surprised by the results," although they remained "satisfied that they are not officially identified with it."[26]

Fortunately for the Navy, most people believed the service had cooperated with *An Officer and a Gentleman* because of the authenticity that Pat Coulter and retired Navy public affairs officer Bill Graves helped give the film. In the end, however, as the failures of *Gray Lady Down, Raise the Titanic,* and *The Final Countdown* demonstrated, hardware and accuracy do not count as much as a good story about characters with whom people can empathize. *An Officer and a Gentleman* had these elements; and despite the Navy's concern about language, sex, and physical abuse, the movie most likely gave the service its biggest cinematic boost of any film since the end of the Vietnam War.

As a result, the Navy came to accept the reality that Pat Coulter had taught the Marines—more often than not, Hollywood was going to make a movie with or without cooperation, and the end result would become better for the service if it decided to support the production. Just as important, all the armed services were coming to realize that movies about the military in the post–Vietnam War period would no longer contain only positive images of their men, equipment, and actions. Moreover, audiences accepted these portrayals as more honest, more authentic representations of the services than those in the essentially sanitized stories that Hollywood generally produced before Vietnam.

Still, the services, and particularly the Navy, did not rush to cooperate on every project that arrived in the Public Affairs Office, even when the story seemed to differ little from one on which it had only recently provided assistance. Like *The Final Countdown, The Philadelphia Experiment* had as its premise that a Navy ship moved through time, in this instance, forward from World War II rather than backward. Nevertheless, the service refused to even consider helping the filmmakers. The movie had its origins in a 1977 book of the same name by William L. Moore in consultation with Charles Berlitz, the author of *The Bermuda Triangle.* The full title, *The Philadelphia Experiment: Project Invisibility, an Account of a Search for a Secret Navy Wartime Project That May Have Succeeded—Too Well,* describes the author's approach and bias perfectly. Moore simply wove together all previous accounts of an alleged experiment that the Navy conducted in the Philadelphia Navy Yard in 1943, which apparently got out of hand and transported a destroyer to Norfolk, Virginia, and back in a matter of a minute or two.

The resulting book had as much credibility as Berlitz's account of the Bermuda Triangle or any of the narratives proving the existence of flying saucers. Nevertheless, starting with this myth, the screenwriters concocted a science fiction time-travel story with the same level of plausibility as *The Final Countdown*, in which the USS *Nimitz* and its crew went back in time. Here, two sailors taking part in a World War II experiment designed to make ships invisible to German radar find themselves transported from the Philadelphia Navy Ship Yard in 1943 to the Utah desert in 1984. The film's portrayal of the "experiment" and the efforts to reverse its disastrous consequences remain incomprehensible. The sailors' efforts to understand the future in which they find themselves, however badly rendered on the screen, provide the movie's only saving grace.

In asking the Navy to allow the filmmakers to shoot the opening and closing scenes at the Philadelphia Navy Yard, Michele Casale, director of the Pennsylvania Bureau of Motion Picture and Television Development, recognized the "Navy's stance concerning the title and content of a book by the same name." While assuring the service that the screenplay "does not in any way follow the book," she acknowledged that "the idea does emanate from it." The producer, Doug Curtis, claimed when he sent the script to the Navy: "We decided long ago that the so-called 'Philadelphia Experiment' never happened. However, the basic idea that it could have happened provided us with what we think is a great premise for a *fictional* motion picture."[27]

After reading the script, Dale Patterson, then the Navy's acting chief of information, advised Don Baruch on August 22, 1983, that the Navy "does not desire to provide assistance. The position of the Navy has been that the 'Philadelphia Experiment' is a mythical event based on a fabricated story. Even though the planned film would imply the fictional character of the experiment, references are made to real-life people, places and facilities connected with the project." Without leaving the door open to further discussions as usually happened when the Navy or any other service found an initial script unacceptable, Patterson tersely concluded: "We feel that a movie of this nature would perpetuate the myth of the Philadelphia Experiment, and the role of the Navy in it. Participation or cooperation of the Navy in this project would not appear to be in its interest."[28]

Baruch advised the producer of the Navy's decision on August 26, 1983, writing that he had reviewed the screenplay and agreed with the service's position. He repeated the Navy's view that the film "probably would perpetuate the myth about such an experiment during the WW II era and the Navy's role in it. Strictly as fiction, the screenplay does not portray anything that can be considered positive or in the best interest of the Department of Defense (DoD) to qualify for approval under the criteria of the enclosed DOD Instruction."[29]

Even in the post-Vietnam period, with the military still wary of Hollywood's intentions, such an absolute refusal to assist on a production was an aberration. In truth, the filmmakers themselves provided the Navy with the basis for its decision. Curtis had stated that the "Philadelphia Experiment" had never happened. However, he then immediately acknowledged that "the basic idea that it could have happened provided us with what we think is a great premise for a *fictional* motion picture."[30]

As long as science fiction stories remained pure fantasy, the services would usually provide the kind of limited assistance that the filmmakers were requesting for *The Phila-*

delphia Experiment. In fact, the Air Force had refused to assist Steven Spielberg on *Close Encounters of the Third Kind*, released in 1977, on similar grounds, that the director was attempting to create reality, not fantasy. The service had pointed out that it had repeatedly denied the existence of flying saucers since the early 1950s. In contrast, it said that the proposed film "leaves the distinct impression that UFO's, in fact, do exist." Moreover, the Air Force said the story portrays "the government and military in a big cover up of the existence of UFOs." Consequently the service concluded that these "two points are counter to Air Force and DOD policy and make support to the production inappropriate."[31]

Clearly, the Navy found itself in the same situation in dealing with the request for assistance on *The Philadelphia Experiment*. Since 1955, when Morris Jessup mentioned in his *Case for UFO's* an alleged secret naval experiment that the Navy had conducted in Philadelphia in 1943, the service had been regularly denying that any such research had ever occurred. Therefore, unlike the time travel in *The Final Countdown*, which the Navy always saw as fantasy, the service would clearly have a problem providing assistance to a production that even suggested such an event could have happened.[32]

Faced with such opposition, the filmmakers made no effort to negotiate with the Navy. Instead, they used the aircraft carrier USS *Yorktown*, the *Fighting Lady* of World War II, the destroyer *Laffey*, and the submarine *Clamagore*, all berthed at the Maritime Museum in Charleston Harbor, to recreate the Philadelphia Navy Yard and to film shipboard scenes. Even with this limited visual authenticity, *The Philadelphia Experiment* lacked any believability. Still, the sailor hero of the movie provided a positive image of a Navy enlisted man, which at least in some small way contributed to the post-Vietnam rehabilitation of the military that had begun with *Midway*.

An old-fashioned, peacetime Navy story, the top box-office hit of 1986 became the instrument that completed the rehabilitation not only of the Navy but of all the armed services. Even though the film had virtually nothing to do with Vietnam, its story had its origins in the American experience in Southeast Asia and showed how the war was still having an impact on the contemporary military. In the Navy's case, it had created the Navy Fighter Weapons School as a response to the mediocre performance of its pilots during the escalation of fighting in Vietnam. In contrast to a kill ratio of 15 to 1 in World War II and 17 to 1 in Korea, early on in Vietnam, naval fliers shot down three enemy planes for every one American plane destroyed. Once it became aware of the deteriorating skills, the service conducted a study which concluded that American pilots no longer knew how to dogfight. As a result, the Navy gathered together a few crackerjack fighter instructors at its Air Station in Miramar, California, and started a program to train the top 1 percent of carrier pilots in aerial combat techniques. Mimicking the pilots' own use of nicknames, the school soon became known as "Top Gun" from an annual aerial combat competition that the armed services had held in the 1940s and 1950s.[33]

In May 1983, while reading *California Magazine*, film producer Jerry Bruckheimer chanced upon an article by Israeli writer Ehud Yonay that captured the excitement of the "Top Gun" school. He and his partner, Don Simpson, immediately saw that the school could become an "arena" for a movie which featured daring young men sweeping across the sky in aerial dogfights. The producers thought a film with such images might become another *Star Wars*, this time on earth, with jet planes replacing space ships and the cream of naval aviators assuming the roles of the cute robots and providing the love interest.[34]

Simpson recalled that they both wanted to make a movie as soon as they saw the title: "It was such a strong, unique concept, a look at the inside world of these top pilots who are really the modern equivalent of the gunslingers of the old, wild West. It was irresistible, so we immediately optioned the story and then sat down to figure out how the hell we could make the picture." The producers stressed, however, that they had no intention of making a recruiting poster for the Navy. They saw themselves solely as tellers of stories about people: "We set them in particular environments because that is necessary to tell a story. The 'Top Gun' school was a wonderfully bright and hot venue, against which to push a character. The truth of the matter is that we could quite easily make a movie that deals with the military and goes the opposite way because it is full of human beings."[35]

Nevertheless, they said that at the heart of their story remained "an exceedingly rebellious character who learns the value of winning through team effort. It was supposed to be a movie about a guy who came from the outside and learned how to play on the inside and did it for all the right reasons." Despite perceptions from the military and the public, Simpson and Bruckheimer believed that *Top Gun* "really did not have a lot to do with the Navy, per se. It had a lot more to do with a contemporary American rebel, who was not tamed, but got better through understanding that when he teamed up and played within the structure, not necessarily within the rules, he won in even a bigger way."[36]

Simpson and Bruckheimer may not have seen their movie as being about the Navy. Nevertheless, the setting dictated that the producers must go to the Pentagon for assistance, since, unlike *An Officer and a Gentleman*, *Top Gun* would need an aircraft carrier and jet planes. Fortunately, they approached the Pentagon while the Navy was still ruing its failure to assist on *An Officer and a Gentleman*. Moreover, Secretary of the Navy John Lehman was actively encouraging his public affairs officers to find a suitable project to support, one that would provide direct benefit to the service.[37]

The producers had another advantage when they went to Washington, apart from the positive, rite-of-passage story they wanted to tell. Simpson had brought the screenplay for *An Officer and a Gentleman* with him when he had become head of production at Paramount Studios. In that capacity, he had overseen the progress of the project and had gained insights on negotiating with the Pentagon from the failure of the producers to obtain assistance from the Navy. He had concluded that the filmmakers had gone to the Pentagon too far along in the production process. To be sure, he disagreed with the Navy's turndown of *An Officer and a Gentleman*: "Hey guys, are you trying to tell me that people in the Navy don't fuck, drink, and swear? Of course they do."[38]

The very success of the film had helped change the Navy's outlook, however. Keeping in mind the problems the producers of *An Officer and a Gentleman* had experienced with the service, Simpson and Bruckheimer decided to visit Navy headquarters in Washington before they even started work on a screenplay. In fact, the producers did not intend to tell the Navy any story when they arrived at the Pentagon in early June 1983: "It was just to be a basic chat." Unfortunately, their plans immediately came apart. Adm. Jack Garrow, Navy chief of information, said, "Great. Tell us the movie you are going to make." The producers looked at each other and, using their years of experience spinning stories to potential backers, responded, "Okay, here's sort of the story we are going to do." Although they didn't create the exact story, the plot they told essentially became *Top Gun*. Even in oral form, the Navy loved the story, and the producers left Washington "extremely enthusiastic" about the project and with the Navy "100 per cent receptive" to their plans.[39]

To ensure that no hitches would develop, John Horton, representing the Paramount Pictures Corporation, followed up the producers' initial Pentagon meeting with a letter to Don Baruch on June 10, 1983. Summarizing the discussion, he wrote that the producers intended "to develop this project in close coordination with the Department of Defense and U.S. Navy to insure mutuality of interest pending the request for assistance in production." In that light, the company hoped to begin research at the Fighter Weapons School at Miramar upon the chief information officer's approval for the producers and writers to visit the installation in early July 1983. In closing, Horton emphasized that the producers and the studio were "extremely enthused about the prospects of developing and producing" the film.[40]

Less than two years after the fiasco of *An Officer and a Gentleman*, the Navy found itself in a position "to regain some of the ground on the public relations front that it had lost." It had a production that would feature a Navy hero, an unidentified enemy, and no scenes of an unpopular war. Apart from the raison d'être for the school, the only mention of Vietnam came in the description of the hero's father as an ace pilot who died during the war under mysterious conditions that the government was unwilling to explain. More important, the filmmakers were modeling their characters on the Navy's best, the top 1 percent of Navy pilots who received the coveted assignments to the Top Gun school, professional military men all, devoted to the service and its traditional lifestyle. If the hero began the film as a rebel, he did undergo a metamorphosis, emerging as a team player. While *Top Gun* had an obligatory love interest that caused the Navy some initial discomfort, the sex remained relatively restrained. More important, the Tom Cruise–Kelly McGillis relationship never became the focus of the film except to the romantics in the audience—certainly not to the Navy, which had eyes only for the $37 million F-14 Tomcat jets, the aircraft carriers, and the flying sequences.

In any case, despite the success of the initial contacts, writers Jim Cash and Jack Epps Jr. required more than a year to produce the initial screenplay. In the November, 15, 1984, cover letter accompanying the script, Horton advised Don Baruch that the producers desired "to present a positive patriotic film about the Navy" and requested "review and comments from the Department of the Defense and Navy for any elements to be considered in the script revisions." The service needed less than two weeks to complete the initial review of the screenplay, and on the November 29 Horton went into the Pentagon to discuss the Navy's comments.[41]

Writing to Bruckheimer later in the day, he characterized the reception of the screenplay as "positive with the belief that produced with care and interpretation as a positive patriotic film that you have stated you desire, the film could be beneficial to the Navy." Horton said that the Navy's primary concern centered on the producers' decision to change the female lead from a civilian to a naval officer, "because of the inordinate sensitivity to the relationships in the service between male and female personnel." He did acknowledge that "romances—and marriages between male and female officers in the Navy [exist] but how the relationship is handled in a motion picture supported fully by The Navy puts them in the position of condoning the specific scenes." Horton also advised Bruckheimer of the Navy's concern about "the portrayal of the aviators with any sophomoric characteristics—particularly with respect to hard drinking. Fighter pilots are a breed in themselves with certain traits that are identifiable. These characteristics can be captured—and are in the script—but the full dimension should be portrayed within the artistic license necessary for entertainment."[42]

The Navy did not stand alone in its desire to have its officers and men shown as teetotalers and even sexually chaste. The history of the negotiations between filmmakers and each of the services is replete with arguments back and forth on how to portray military men off hours in a realistic manner without offending the sensibilities of overly zealous public affairs officers or generals' wives. In any event, during the next five months, the writers changed the female love interest to a civilian astrophysicist at the school and made other requested revisions. The new script met with a more favorable response, and on May 8, 1985, Baruch notified Horton that the Navy had approved the revised March 28, 1985, script for assistance if the filmmakers deleted a scene "showing our aircraft flying after MIGs over land of the fictional foreign country." Characterizing the negotiations to date as "friendly, cooperative," and smooth, Baruch closed by thanking the producers "for their sincere and enthusiastic interest in bringing *Top Gun* to fruition."[43]

Top Gun actually differed little from Hollywood's peacetime Navy movies of the 1930s, 1940s, and 1950s, which used the service as a backdrop to a love story. Boy meets girl; girl flirts with boy; boy experiences emotional crisis, temporarily losing his grip; girl helps boy regain his confidence and wins boy in the end. The producers, however, did not see it quite that way. They saw Tom Cruise's Maverick as a skilled F-14 pilot who learns to function not only in combat situations but also in peacetime, unlike General Patton and the Great Santini: "You really want him in wartime. This is a guy who can kick ass and take names. That's his brilliance. But, we tried to take him through the emotional curves in the movie. He started out 80/20. We tried to move him to a place where he was civilized enough to where he could walk around."[44]

At the same time, Simpson and Bruckheimer saw Maverick as "emblematic of the best of the best, truly because of his abilities, his physical ability, his emotional characteristics, and his intellectual ability—this guy is an all-star." In contrast, they considered Richard Gere's character in *An Officer and A Gentleman* as a kid from the wrong side of the tracks "who fundamentally doesn't have any skills." Unlike Maverick, the producers described Gere's Zack Mayo as "street scum. He has his ass kicked by a black D.I. and had to learn how to straighten up and tie his tie. The movie's about a guy who quite simply just grows up." To Simpson and Bruckheimer, Gere would take a decade to reach the point from which Cruise was starting. More than that, however, the producers created a character they wanted the audience to see as "a real warrior of the heart."[45]

The producers did not see this image as fostering militarism, maintaining that they "understand the need for defense. It has nothing to do with being right wing, left wing, or center." Instead, they believed in the need for "eternal vigilance" and so found it "fun for us to invent a character who's not ashamed to be in the service of his country." Despite having created an idealized military man, the producers felt that because of the continuing impact of Vietnam, "the military is probably never going to be safe for Hollywood again. Vietnam was a major fuck up. So the military is never going to be safe, not as long as people who lived during Vietnam are alive and are making movies."[46]

For them, however, *Top Gun* always remained a story about a guy, never about the military in which he served: "The military is a metaphor, it's true. But it's real clear that the movie is not about war. It doesn't take a position on whether war is good or bad. It's bad. We don't want to be at war. It only takes a position regarding a particular character in his growth and frankly about ethics and commitment and about heart and about courage and teamwork. In a very major way, it is about teamwork and understanding what it takes to get a job done." Even more than that, the producers thought the movie dealt with "professionalism, professionalism in any capacity, whether as a writer, moviemaker, car wash guy. It's about understanding—being a pro is at the end of it."[47]

Simpson and Bruckheimer may well have wanted to impart to *Top Gun* some social significance, and the film undoubtedly can provide material to support their perception of its messages. Nevertheless, audiences did not flock to theaters to philosophize about its contents. The producers admitted as much in offering their explanation of the success of the movie: "It is because a great majority of the audience found the picture to be totally accessible. It created an environment where they were transported, where they, for 97 minutes, got to enter into a world that is not only real but is exciting and one to which they had never been exposed and to which they never will be exposed." In a sense, therefore, they said they were "in the transportation business. We want to transport you. That's what we like to do."[48]

Director Tony Scott and Tom Cruise on the flight line. Cruise thought *Top Gun* should be viewed as a "joy ride" instead of being over philosophized.

For the most part, reviewers thought very little of the particular vehicle. *Commonweal* concluded, "*Top Gun* melds *Rambo* and *An Officer and a Gentleman*. It lacks the former's wild sincerity and the latter's raw treatment of genuine emotional needs. It also has the defects of both films, echoing the first's jingoism and the second's already familiar passage of young male hero through love and the death of a friend to greater emotional maturity. Nevertheless, it has a kind of style, in part laughable and in part visceral. The macho strutting is absurd. The casting of sultry McGillis as a flight instructor is beyond credibility. But some powerful opening and closing action sequences catapult the viewer into flight (and a kind of exhilarated vertigo) like nothing before. Sadly, the cinematic and aerial skills involved at the end serve some bad politics: combat between Navy fighters and Soviet MIGs, breezily passed over as an event of little note."[49]

David Ansen, in *Newsweek*, decided, "For all its reliance on old macho cliches, *Top Gun* is devoid of a strong dramatic line. It's a disjointed movie about flying school bracketed by two arbitrary action sequences." Ansen saw Tom Cruise as "simply miscast—he's not the dangerous guy everyone's talking about, but the boy next door. Nor, for all the erotic posing, is there any real spark between him and the more sophisticated McGillis. Cruise seems to think that if he stares at her hard enough chemistry will result." The reviewer attributed the problem to the director and producers, who "have only myth-making on their minds. Yet the effortless flyboy glamour of *Only Angels Have Wings* or *The Right Stuff* eludes them. They don't realize the importance of laconic understatement in any good macho fantasy. They're so busy inflating their characters there's no flesh and blood left to grab on to. *Top Gun* isn't boring, but it's solemnly silly. This movie has taken too many hormone shots."[50]

In the *Village Voice*, J. Hoberman not only carried the male-sexuality-in-combat thesis to hitherto unexplored depths in a review entitled "Phallus in Wonderland" but also turned *Top Gun* into a pseudo-Vietnam movie. In the process, he denigrated the film in particularly virulent terms: "Sleek, fragmentary, and expertly fetishized, *Top Gun* is state of the art war-nography. It's the sort of suave, go-go propaganda you'd expect to be shown to kamikaze pilots. This teenage dating film may be devoid of 'ideas,' but it's still a conceptual leap. *Top Gun* doesn't posit sex as aggression, it reformulates aggression as sex." Despite its "masterful packaging job—all chrome and close-ups," Hoberman found the movie an "ultimately depressing fly-boy saga" and Tom Cruise "almost ferally avid" to prove his rebelliousness. Calling Simpson and Bruckheimer's earlier box-office hit *Flashdance* and *Top Gun* "teenage trance-outs," the reviewer said they gave "a new meaning to 'go with the flow'" and their "spectacle of narcissistic performance (whether flash dancing or dive bombing) is underscored by a back-beat of nonstop rock'n'roll."[51]

Hoberman thought the sound track gave the movie "a kind of amoral insistence and subliminal history" by establishing a direct link to Vietnam. To support his interpretation, he cited Herman Rapaport's thesis, in *The 60s without Apology,* that Vietnam became the first rock 'n' roll war: "Introjected into the technology, the libidinal impulses of rock became the lure by which some men killed with pleasure . . . putting the weapon on 'automatic fire' was called putting it on 'rock and roll.'" Hoberman then argued that by recycling the music of Vietnam, *Top Gun* used rock "for militaristic ends, to evoke an utterly specious nostalgia." To him, this illustrated the cynicism of the movie and of the producers, who had claimed they were not making a military story. In particular, he cited a comment Simpson had given to an interviewer during shooting of the film: "I'm not the sort of person you'd find in the military. I got out of the military on purpose. I wrecked a motorcycle and shall we say, I managed to stay out of the military, even though I had a lot of guns around my house."[52]

Hoberman further tried to make *Top Gun* into a Vietnam movie by arguing that throughout its course, the film "practices a relentless displacement, both political and sexual. Maverick's father disappeared during the early stages of the Vietnam war, his F-4 bomber shot down under classified circumstances over some unspecified border. He's a heroic Viet victim unscarred by defeat and washed clean of our war crimes; still his image is tainted in the eyes of an ungrateful nation. It's up to Mav to redeem Dad's memory—lucky for him that war is such a thrill." Here, however, Hoberman equates the thrill of war with the thrill of sexual conquest, and he launches into a psychosexual interpretation of *Top Gun* as "blatantly homoerotic," concluding: "Of course, as Freud is supposed to have said, sometimes a cigar is just a cigar. Still, there are moments in this movie when the screen is so packed with streamlined planes and heat-seeking missiles, wagging forefingers and upright thumbs that, had Freud lived to see it, he might be excused for thinking *Top Gun* an avant-garde representation of Saturday night at the St. Marks Bath."[53]

Of course, sometimes escapist entertainment remains purely escapist entertainment. Neither Hoberman's interpretation and deprecation of *Top Gun* nor the other less-than-enthusiastic reviews dissuaded people from making it the nation's top-grossing movie of 1986. To a significant extent, this success resulted from the pure visual excitement of the film's aerial sequences, not very different from the space dogfights in *Star Wars* in form and execution, but live, thanks to the Navy's assistance. In addition to allowing director Tony Scott and his crew access to the *Enterprise* and the *Ranger,* the service made available technical advisors, twenty or so fighter pilots, Miramar Naval Air Station, and a small fleet of $37 million F-14 jets, charging only for the fuel. Ultimately, Paramount paid the Navy $1.1 million for the assistance, of which $886,000 covered the cost of flight time for five types of airplanes.[54]

Such assistance enabled the filmmakers to create in *Top Gun* some of the most dra-

"MAVERICK"

Tom Cruise, Anthony Edwards, and the F-14 Tomcat starred in *Top Gun,* the film that completed the rehabilitation of the U.S. armed services after Vietnam and won support from the American people for the Gulf War.

matic scenes of jet fighters in action that Hollywood was ever to put on the screen. The images represent the culmination of military cooperation on flying movies, begun when the Army lent virtually its entire complement of aircraft in the making of *Wings* in 1927. To many viewers, then and in 1986, such assistance produced recruiting posters for the supporting military service and patriotic jingoism for the nation.

Tom Cruise recognized that "some people felt that *Top Gun* was a right-wing film to promote the Navy. And a lot of kids loved it." Nevertheless, the actor felt compelled to distance himself from the images he helped create: "But I want the kids to know that that's not the way war is—that *Top Gun* was just an amusementpark [*sic*] ride, a fun film with a PG-13 rating that was not supposed to be reality. That's why I didn't go on and make *Top Gun II* and *III, IV,* and *V.* That *would* have been irresponsible." In fact, he saw the film only as "a joy ride and shouldn't be looked at beyond that. *Top Gun* should be looked at as going on Space Mountain—it's like a simple fairy tale."[55]

Whether as a fairy tale or a transporter of people to an exotic location, as the producers saw *Top Gun,* the film succeeded despite the negative reviews because it offered many different appeals for viewers. In explaining how this worked in selling the movie, Barry London, head of distribution for Paramount, observed that the story worked at all levels and provided many different market segments toward which to direct advertising: "You could make it look like an action movie. You could make it look like a love story. You could make it look like a real beefcake movie with young males. And it was a relationship picture as well as a war movie. Any kind of variation from those things."[56]

Beyond this, however, London attributed the success of the film to changes within the country itself, particularly the move toward a more conservative outlook: "It got more patriotic. It became the right thing to do to wave the flag. It became a supportive issue of supporting the armed forces overseas because of the deteriorating position of the United States in the eyes of the rest of the world." At the same time, of course, the film had a more mundane appeal. According to London, *Top Gun* told the story of an underdog and had "some terrific looking people, with some terrific music, all set in a terrifically structured movie." Whatever the reasons or combination of reasons, the film earned great amounts of money for its backers, the studio, and Bruckheimer and Simpson.[57]

Its popularity also justified the assistance the Navy gave the production. Although the producers may deny that they made a Navy recruiting movie, *Top Gun* did have that effect. The service's West Coast coordinator of recruiting observed: "It is a definite plus for the Navy. The feeling that we have here in recruiting is that the movie has mostly increased awareness. It is hard to put any numbers on what exactly *Top Gun* has done for the Navy, but it sure has helped." Capt. Mike Sherman, then spokesman for Secretary of the Navy John Lehman and later director of the Navy's Los Angeles Public Affairs Office, felt that the movie gave the Navy "a high profile, and it gives us a competitive edge with the other services." Moreover, the success of the film generated the kind of media attention the service would not otherwise have received. The CBS *Evening News,* for one, did a series about Navy pilots, which a Navy public affairs officer thought resulted solely from the interest the movie created: "There is no way we could have paid any amount of money and gotten that kind of story done."[58]

Unfortunately for the Navy, *Top Gun* apparently also had an unforeseen, less positive impact. When the Pentagon's report on the Tailhook scandal appeared in April 1992, it contained accusations from senior Navy officers that "many young officers had been influenced by the image of naval aviators portrayed in the movie *Top Gun,*" and this had contributed to their "rowdy behavior" at the 1991 Tailhook convention in Las Vegas. According to the investigators, senior officers believed that "the movie fueled misconceptions on the part of junior officers as to what was expected of them and also served to increase the general awareness of naval aviation and glorify naval pilots in the eyes of many young women." Donald Mancuso, the director of the Defense Criminal Investigation Service, which produced the report, said the senior officers had volunteered their perceptions that the younger aviators had "an impression of themselves which was built partially on the Tom Cruise image."[59]

Whatever the validity of the accusations, other factors, of course, contributed to the behavior of the Marine and Navy jet pilots at the Tailhook convention in Las Vegas in 1991. One female Navy commander suggested that the "heightened emotions from the Gulf War were also enhanced with the forthcoming . . . downsizing of the military, so that you had people feeling very threatened for their job security and to more than just their jobs, their lifestyle. . . . You had people that had been to the Gulf War. You had alcohol. You had a convention that had a lot of ingredients for any emotional whirlwind of controversy." The officer also felt that the congressional inquiries regarding women in combat had created "an animosity in this Tailhook that existed that was telling the women that 'We don't have any respect for you now as humans.'" She believed male fliers saw women threatening their lifestyle: "This was the woman that wanted to take your spot in that combat aircraft."[60]

Ascertaining the actual influence of *Top Gun* on either younger viewers or jet pilots lies beyond the abilities of a historian. However, any film that attracts the huge audiences that *Top Gun* did contains powerful visual and sound images. Tom Cruise in no way became a John Wayne figure. Yet, his swagger and his casual challenging of death conveyed the arrogance and self-confidence that carrier pilots must have if they are to practice their profession. In any event, whatever deleterious impact the film may have had on the aviators attending Tailhook, *Top Gun* certainly had a more beneficial influence on the nation's perceptions of its military and its ability to once again defend the country from any threat.

Before Vietnam, the American people believed their armed services had become invincible. The post–World War II Hollywood movies made a significant contribution to the creation of that belief. To be sure, as their model for portrayals of an all-conquering military, the filmmakers were drawing on the reality that the United States had defeated Germany and Japan with only a little help from its allies. Ultimately, the images and realities had merged into a singular perception. As a result, the American people had no reason to question the military leadership who promised a quick victory in Vietnam against a small peasant nation. The North Vietnamese regular army gave the lie to such arrogant predictions, and the ultimate withdrawal of American forces in defeat traumatized the nation. The manner in which the media and, most particularly, filmmakers subsequently portrayed the war and the returning soldiers effectively completed the destruction of the nation's unsullied perception of its military establishment.

Beginning with *Midway* and culminating with *Top Gun,* Hollywood's treatment of the Navy in war and peace made a significant contribution to the rehabilitation of the military image. Consequently, when the crisis in the Gulf began in August 1990, the American people once again believed its fighting men could successfully meet any challenge and so made it possible for President Bush to take the nation into battle again. Ironically, the military leaders hung back and demanded a buildup of forces beyond anything needed to defeat the paper tiger in Iraq before willingly committing their men to combat. Instead of responding to the images of Tom Cruise shooting down MiG fighters, they were still remembering the opprobrium that the nation had heaped on the armed forces for losing in Vietnam.

In any case, *Top Gun* completed the process of rehabilitating for most Americans the military image that the war had so savaged. It also provided Hollywood with easier access to the Pentagon. There, the services again maintained an open door and a willingness to at least consider, on a case-by-case basis, all requests for cooperation, whether the projects portrayed Vietnam or the peacetime military. Not all the scripts contained positive portrayals, but the public affairs officers usually tried to negotiate the best possible image rather than turn filmmakers away, as had happened well into the 1980s. As a result, Hollywood began to use the military as a setting for all manner of stories—combat, peacetime drama, and comedy.

ing: "It's very sinister because it creeps into the national consciousness. People start to think of war as not so bad. War becomes a function of hand/eye coordination. You push a computer button and blow up a Russian MIG. It's like a video game. There is no reality to it."[6]

Stone, in contrast, was approaching *Platoon* with the fervor of a true believer: "I had to make it. I mean, if we didn't make that story, I felt we wouldn't be telling the truth, we would be denying history. America would be a trasher of history, blind to its past. That's what bothered me. And when those films came along, the *Apocalypses* and the *Deer Hunters,* which I liked a lot, but they didn't really fundamentally deal with the reality that I saw over there as an infantryman." To Stone, this reality had nothing to do with the politics of the war: "It's really dealing—if anything, it's more religion than politics in the foxholes. I think that the film sets out to show what the average infantryman went through." Dye hoped that "when veterans, whether they were in Vietnam or not, the guys who have served our country in uniform, take a look at this, they'll get that little chill up the back of their neck that says, 'Aha, that's the way it was. I remember that.'"[7]

In Stone's mind, the film that provoked such feelings made an antiwar, not an antimilitary statement: "I'm not out to trash the military. I think there is a purpose and place for a strong military. I think I'm out to trash the mythologies." To do that, the writer-director drew upon his fifteen months of duty in Vietnam from September 1967 to November 1968, fighting with the Twenty-fifth Infantry Division. The story he created became little more than a series of vignettes about his unit's efforts to survive. It contains virtually no reference to how the platoon fits into the larger picture of the war or any explanation of why the soldiers in Stone's unit manifest none of the camaraderie usually associated with men in combat. The audience can only assume that the abusive behavior that the members of the unit manifest to each other became one of the ways in which the director chose to "trash the mythologies" of Hollywood war movies.[8]

Whatever the intent, *Platoon* depicted war from the perspective of the individual soldier, whom Stone would have the audience believe suffered through his tour of duty confused and disoriented from beginning to end. Without the occasional voice-over narrative from letters to his grandmother, which Chris Taylor, Stone's film persona, provides, the plot would become even more confused and disjointed. As it stands, Stone has created a typical good-versus-evil confrontation between Willem Dafoe's Sergeant Elias and Tom Berenger's Sergeant Barnes. Their personal animosity and the efforts of each to win the loyalties of their men convey the hell of Vietnam. Arriving in country as a naive grunt, Charlie Sheen's Taylor experiences his rite of passage and emerges with an understanding of Vietnam and of war: "I think now, looking back, we did not fight the enemy, we fought ourselves. And the enemy was in us. The war is over for me now, but it will always be there, for the rest of my days, as I'm sure Elias will be, fighting with Barnes for 'possession of my soul.' There are times since then I've felt like a child born of those two fathers."

Tom Berenger as Sergeant Barnes and William Dafoe as Sergeant Elias in *Platoon.*

Physically, Stone recreated the world in which Taylor became a man in the Philippines, in fifty-four days of shooting, with a budget of $6 million, using Philippine military equipment and men. Backing came from Hemdale Productions, a British company, after Dino De Laurentis decided he would not be able to distribute the film. Visually, the writer-director produced the images of men in combat from his own recollections of his fifteen months in Vietnam. According to Stone, he received the inspiration to put the memories into a story while watching the Tall Ships in New York harbor on July 4, 1976: "I finally sat and dealt with the war as I had known it realistically. It took me eight years to get to that screenplay, because I couldn't deal with it before. I needed the distance."[9]

Whether the distance gave Stone the ability to accurately and fairly portray his own experiences or those of the 3 million or so other Americans who fought in Vietnam became a matter of considerable debate. Reflecting on the completion of shooting in the Philippines, the writer-director wrote: "I know that although I finished the film, a part of it will never be there, any more than the faces of the gawky boys we left behind in the dust. As close as I came to Charlie Sheen, he would never be me and *Platoon* would never be what I saw in my mind when I wrote it and which was just a fragment, really, of what happened years ago. That, too, is gone. And we move on."[10]

Yet, Stone claimed that he was portraying the reality of the war in a way no one else had done. After all, he became the first Vietnam veteran to write and direct a movie about his combat experiences. As such, he had assumed a certain responsibility to his fellow comrades-in-arms: "I wrote it with all my heart. I'll sell it flagrantly. Otherwise, nobody will go see it—it has no stars. . . . But it's wearying to always talk about myself. I mean, I'm basically standing in for 4 million men. That's not such an easy thing to do." In his mind, at least, Stone did the job very well, showing Vietnam as it existed, not as it might have been, should have been, or as earlier filmmakers had imagined it to be: "I wanted to set the record straight. I wanted to do it before my memory faded about the war."[11]

His cinematic effort produced a series of depictions of men pushed to their limits, fighting real and imagined enemies everywhere in country: the weather, the jungle, women, children, old men, simple villagers, the Vietcong, and North Vietnamese Army regulars, all of whom conspired against the American soldier. He believed the realism of his screenplay prevented it from being made for the ten years following its writing. To him, the very lack of such realism in the first two cycles of Vietnam films made them more attractive to audiences: "The first cycle was the sort of larger-than-life, mythic, surreal Vietnam of *Apocalypse Now* (1979), and *The Deer Hunter* (1978), which showed the American state of mind and wanted to embrace larger issues." In contrast, he thought the second wave of movies, including the two *Rambo* films (1982 and 1985), the two Chuck Norris *Missing in Action* films (1984 and 1985), and *Uncommon Valor* (1983), "was the more down-to-earth, we-won-the-war revisionism." Stone considered *Platoon* as starting the third cycle of movies: *Platoon*, along with

In Stone's depictions of Vietnam, everyone and everything was a possible threat.

Hamburger Hill, The Hanoi Hilton, and *Full Metal Jacket,* would be a "more realistic wave. . . . This I hope sets the record straight."[12]

The degree to which *Platoon* successfully fulfilled Stone's hope depends on the viewer's perspective and how he or she defines reality and accuracy. To Dale Dye, the story rang true: "We've had comments from the guys who lived it that it is precisely a slice of life. They felt the heat. They felt the bugs. They were back in it. So, in that regard, it is fair." Nevertheless, he acknowledged that the movie's portrayal of Americans murdering and raping Vietnamese did not happen to everyone: "It is not fair to say that every infantryman experienced those things and that every infantry platoon carried those things out. And we hastened to point that out. But it is certainly fair to say those things happened. They're on the record and if you want to deny the record, then go do *Rambo*."[13]

Dye himself may have missed the point of the Pentagon's objections to *Platoon.* No one in the military, except perhaps William Westmoreland, denied that atrocities had taken place. The good general denied that some American soldiers had murdered and raped Vietnamese civilians, had used dope, or had objected to fighting the war. The Pentagon, however, had simply maintained that a screenplay which showed only the negative side of the American involvement lacked balance and so did not convey the reality of the war. Without question, Vietnam became so surrealistic because the norm at one time and place might differ radically from a place thirty miles away, six months earlier or later, or even contemporaneously. Nevertheless, even in Vietnam, a nominal reality existed that encompassed the way the United States conducted the war.

In that broadly based reality, most soldiers carried out their assigned missions in a disciplined manner. The portrayal of the command structure in *The Boys in Company C* notwithstanding, orders did flow down the chain of command, and the men in the field obeyed their superiors' directives with little or no question. Soldiers did count their days in country very carefully, in much the way Stone described it to journalists and portrayed it in *Platoon.* The truth be told, however, the one-year tour of duty, instead of a tour for the duration or for the length of enlistment, contributed as much as any other factor to the United States' lack of military success on the battlefields of Vietnam.

If some soldiers did smoke dope and drink during their off-duty hours, most went into combat with reasonably clear heads because they recognized that they needed all their senses fully operating if they were going to survive combat. Likewise, soldiers of all rank disagreed, often hated and mistrusted, and even came to blows, but seldom did personal differences get in the way of combat. Finally, although Stone claimed on his *20/20* appearance that officers did not know what was going on among their men, most field officers maintained lines of communications through their NCOs to the enlisted men under their command to ensure their own survival in battle.

In any case, when Stone acknowledges, "I'm not saying this is the definitive Vietnam film," he is simply recognizing that Vietnam is too complex for any one film or one book to make a definitive statement. When he says his film contains "one reality," he is actually saying that *Platoon* portrays his reality or, more accurately, his own experiences. In fact, the experiences Stone includes in the film are only the ones he has chosen to remember and to portray. Consequently, *Platoon* requires that audiences accept uncritically the director's representation that he experienced only the worst things, real and imagined, during his fifteen months in Vietnam and did none of the normal things soldiers in combat have done in all wars.

Despite the questionable portrayals of social and military life, the technical magnificence of the combat sequences does make it easy for viewers to suspend their disbelief about Stone's vision of Vietnam. Although Dale Dye's work as technical advisor contributed to this, he admitted that his mandate covered only actual battlefield matters: "I suppose I offer a certain latitude. I offer to not interfere with the director's creative vision." As a result, Stone had no restraint on the way he chose to portray his experiences. In taking dramatic license to convey the essence of his tour of duty, however, he ended up making a movie that more satisfied the need to purge his Vietnam demons than "to set the record straight" as he claimed.

The heart of the story focuses on the conflict between Elias and Barnes for the soul of their unit and the respect of Taylor. As such, the two sergeants represent the two poles of Stone's Vietnam experience. Elias, who considers everything about the war bullshit, presides over an unofficial club in a bunker where everyone smokes dope to forget his troubles. Barnes, the warrior, hard-boiled and unsentimental, has survived so many wounds that his men think he can never die. To Taylor, both men become awesome giants, as they did to Stone himself: "I knew the originals of Elias and Barnes in Vietnam. I saw them as mythic people, as warriors. I wondered, what if these two guys, who I knew in different units, had been in the same unit? How would they co-exist? Could they co-exist? That's where the backbone of the story comes from—that, and the young man who comes of age."[14]

Experiencing his rite of passage in combat like his cinematic representation, Stone returned home with a view of the war that he ultimately imparted to *Platoon:* "When I came back from Vietnam, the one association I was always making was between what we were doing there and Homer's *Iliad*—the endless length of the war, the purposelessness, the moral breakdown, the infighting among allies." The very act of answering his questions about Barnes and Elias, as well as couching his portrayal of Vietnam in epic terms, required Stone to move away from his professed desire of infusing his film with the reality of the war. Nowhere does this become more apparent than in the way he depicts the chain of command, the officer–enlisted man relationship, the socializing of the troops, and perhaps most important, the manner in which Barnes and Elias work out their antipathy toward each other.[15]

The decision to play off the two men immediately removes *Platoon* from a re-creation of Stone's actual experiences and into a fictional dramatization. However powerful the emotional impact, the tampering with the facts reduces the credibility of Stone's claim to portraying reality. In his defense, all creative writers regularly rearrange events and actions to suit their purposes. That Harold Abrahams and Eric Liddell never raced each other as depicted in *Chariots of Fire* does not weaken the emotional impact of the story. Nevertheless, unlike that film's director and screenwriter, Stone did claim that *Platoon* represented an advancement over earlier cycles of Vietnam movies since it showed the reality of the war in such a way as to explain to the American people its impact on the men who fought its battles.

Does Stone's fictionalizing the conflict of Barnes and Elias truly matter? Most viewers might well answer that the story remains the thing, not the historical accuracy. According to two Marine officers who looked at *Platoon* from the perspective of its portrayal of legal and leadership issues, Stone dramatized far more than a relationship between two men. Capt. Michael Decker and Col. James Jeffries III argued that the only similarity between history and *Platoon* is that the film's Twenty-fifth Division and the actual Twenty-fifth Division both operated along the Cambodian border. The heart of their criticism focused on Stone's portrayal of the men in his/Taylor's company: "Stone divides the members of his fictitious company into four groups: incompetent, uncaring officers; bloodthirsty lifers; indifferent background characters who are trying to stay alive; and last, but not least, the drug-using 'good guys.'"[16]

Why did Stone populate his film with such stock characters, ignoring the traditional Hollywood heterogenous unit? What happened to the Brooklyn Jew or the Texas cowboy, staples of virtually every military film? Decker and Jeffries had a rather cynical answer: "These categories represent the liberal media's stereotypes of choice when depicting the 'real war' in Vietnam, and Stone leaped upon what he knew would sell. Most reviewers have picked up on these categories and have turned their reviews into essays on an allegedly universal Vietnam experience where patriotic servicemen became either disillusioned participants or sadistic killers, or both; where officers cared only for their careers; and where the only men to occupy the moral high ground were those who turned to drugs upon discovering the horror of modern war. Stone's depiction of the pharmaceutical crowd as the white hats is suspect both from a common-sense analysis and because of Stone's own publicly described narcotics involvement."[17]

Having brought into question Stone's professed purpose in making *Platoon*, the Marine officers summarized the "tired plot" in order to pinpoint specific scenes that they believed did injustice to the American military in Vietnam. To them, the way Stone portrayed the killing of civilians "is unfortunate, since viewers may easily be led to believe that this happened often during the war. A more evenhanded approach would have been to show that while this type of behavior occurred and was sometimes overlooked, it was often investigated and punished."[18]

They reported that during the war, courts-martial convicted ninety-five soldiers and twenty-seven Marines of murdering Vietnamese civilians and found a proportionately larger number guilty of lesser war-crime offenses. Noting that the portrayal of American soldiers burning enemy villages "has always played well in the media," the Marines conceded that *Platoon* plays on that "sympathetic nerve." However, they then pointed out that the film fails "to distinguish between legitimate military necessity and wanton destruction. In *Platoon* the soldiers relocate the villagers and destroy a village that is clearly an enemy stronghold and supply point. On reflection, it is the enemy who has stripped the civilians of their immunity and put them at military risk."[19]

Of course, the officers were looking at the film in terms of law-of-war issues and how military instructors could use Stone's portrayal to train soldiers. But even those officers who looked at the film in broader terms had problems with the way Stone represented the war. Marine general Leonard Fribourg, a veteran of World War II, Korea, and Vietnam as well as the technical advisor to *Sands of Iwo Jima*, said that *Platoon* contained the best portrayal of small-unit combat he had ever seen in a movie. Nevertheless, he thought it misrepresented the overall American experience in Vietnam, particularly the "NCOs permitting use of drugs in a combat situation or in any situation" and the deprecation of the officers.[20]

To be sure, most ranking officers considered the war in terms of what should have occurred, not what actually transpired. The reality of Vietnam remained that American involvement grew like Topsy; the ideal never came into being because traditional military procedures did not work, could not work in the environment in which the U.S. military found itself in Southeast Asia. Stone may well have experienced all the situations he depicted in *Platoon*, or, like most storytellers, he may have simply provided a composite of many incidents and situations that he saw or heard about while in country. In the end, whether Stone portrayed the reality of Vietnam or one reality of the war probably does not matter. Stone and his financial backers had only two concerns. Were American audiences now ready to relive Vietnam in full color with all the warts? And if so, would they be willing to suspend their disbelief and accept the images on the screen as valid representations that had the capacity to stir emotions?

The initial reaction suggested that Stone had done his job as a filmmaker, if not necessarily as a historian of the war. Released in December 1986 in New York and Los Angeles in order to qualify for the 1986 Academy Awards, *Platoon* met with instant acclaim from reviewers. Vincent Canby, in the *New York Times*, said that none of Stone's previous work as a screenwriter or director was "preparation for the singular achievement of his latest film *Platoon*, which is probably the best work of any kind about the Vietnam War since Michael Herr's vigorous and hallucinatory book *Dispatches*." He wrote that Stone's film did not resemble "any other Vietnam film that's yet been made—certainly not like those revisionist comic strips *Rambo* and *Missing in Action*." Nor did Canby think it had much in common with *Apocalypse Now*, which he thought "ultimately turns into a romantic meditation on a mythical war" or with *The Deer Hunter*, which he considered "more about the mind of the America that fought the war than the Vietnam War itself."[21]

Canby described *Platoon* as a "vivid, terse, exceptionally moving" film that dealt with "the immediate experience of the fighting—that is, with the life of the infantryman, endured at ground level, in heat and muck, with fatigue and ants and with fear as a constant, even during the druggy hours back in the comparative safety of the base." Meaning it as praise, the reviewer observed that the movie "appears to express itself with the same sort of economy that used to be employed in old, studio-made action movies—B-pictures in which characters are largely defined through what they do rather than what they say." Nevertheless, he said this remained only the impression, since the soldiers in *Platoon* "do talk quite a lot, though for the most part, they don't get too literary, nor do they explain too much. They are so exceedingly ordinary that they sometimes jump off the screen as if they were the originals for all the cliched types that have accumulated in all earlier war movies."[22]

Commenting on the central conflict in *Platoon* between Elias and Barnes, Canby observed, "It's a measure of how well both roles are written and played that one comes to understand even the astonishing cruelty of Barnes and the almost saintly goodness of Elias. Each has gone over the edge." He also measured Stone's success by the way the writer-director created "narrative order in a film that, at heart, is a dramatization of mental, physical and moral chaos." Although *Platoon* itself initially seemed to lack focus, Canby suggested that this becomes only the first impression: "Yet the tension builds and never lets up (until the anti-climactic final moments). Somewhere in the second half of the film, there's a sequence of astonishing, harrowing impact that sort of ambles into a contemplation of how a My Lai massacre could have happened. It's not easy to sit through, not only because it's grisly but also because, all things considered, it's so inevitable."[23]

Canby concluded that Stone managed to create this feeling because of the control he had over his own screenplay. As a result, he said that "*Platoon* seems to slide into and out of crucial scenes without ever losing its distant cool. He doesn't telegraph emotions, nor does he stomp on them. The movie is a succession of found moments. It's less like a work that's been written than one that has been discovered, though, as we all probably know, screenplays aren't delivered by storks. This one is a major piece of work, as full of passion as it is of redeeming, scary irony." As such, Canby concluded that *Platoon* "honors its uneasy, complex, still haunted subject."[24]

In the same vein, Paul Attanasio, in the *Washington Post*, called *Platoon* a triumph for Stone, saying that the director's "visceral approach to violence, which has always set him apart, is balanced by classical symmetries and a kind of elegiac distance. This is not the Vietnam of op-ed writers, rabble-rousers or esthetic visionaries, not Vietnam-as-metaphor or Vietnam-the-way-it-should-have-been. It is a movie about Vietnam as it was, alive with authenticity, seen through the eyes of a master filmmaker who lost his innocence there." As a result, Attanasio considered *Platoon* "the first serious youth movie in ages, for at its heart, the war is treated as a rite of passage in its most intense form."[25]

The reviewer thought the filmmaker had "beautifully written" the movie, constructing it "with strong, clean lines, immaculately paced and regularly surprising. Stone uses dialogue to evoke social class and a bygone era, or to add humor—the talk is street-smart and wittily profane. And when Stone writes a speech, he writes a *speech*—he's a one-man antidote to the sterile, laconic naturalism that has dominated screen writing for years." Likewise, Attanasio praised the director for having "brilliantly cast against type" in choosing Dafoe as the "humanist" Elias and Berenger as "a monster with scars crawling across his face. By turning Dafoe, a classic villain, into a saint, Stone gives you a sense of the anguish

of sainthood—you get a sense that Dafoe's Elias has battled back his own dark side." At the same time, the reviewer observes that Berenger's Barnes "seems less like a cardboard Satan than a kind of ruined man—you see the high school football hero he once was."[26]

According to Attanasio, Stone has created "a sense of brooding ominousness, an atmosphere teeming with danger" in which the two sergeants wage their war for Taylor's soul. At the same time, the director shows the "soldier's boredom, the endless hikes and ditch-digging, without boring the audience." In doing this, Stone convinced at least the *Post* reviewer that he had captured the real Vietnam: "*Platoon* is a marvelously tactile movie, in which you feel the heat, the rain, the bugs and snakebites. But mostly, Stone, himself a Vietnam veteran, shows you the fear

One reviewer described Sergeant Barnes as "a monster with scars crawling across his face" and "a ruined man."

and confusion of war, the sleeplessness, and the terror when you finally fall asleep and invite an ambush; the odd sort of scorekeeping after the ambush when you count how many you 'got' and discover that one of your own had his chest blown apart." While acknowledging that *Platoon* did have obvious flaws, such as the hero's voice-over narration, Attanasio concluded that it had "the most brilliantly realistic war footage of any Vietnam movie yet, startling, chaotic battles without an overlay of esthetics or ballet."[27]

In his *Time* magazine review, Richard Corliss also acknowledged some of the film's problems, noting that Stone "is a muckraker disguised as a moviemaker" who "concocts films . . . whose blood vessels burst with holy indignation." The reviewer wrote that with Vietnam, "Stone means the drama, the carnage, the horror, the horror to be so white-hot they will cauterize and heal the wounds of war, and singe everyone's soul in the process. Well, not quite, but *Platoon* is still the most impressive movie to deal with the fighting in Vietnam. *Apocalypse Now* was, by comparison, all machismo and mysticism; Stone's film is a document written in blood that after almost 20 years, refuses to dry."[28]

At the same time, Corliss believed that Stone sometimes gets too close to his material: "Much of *Platoon* is strong meat, indifferently prepared. His script is over-wrought—fine, the material virtually demands excess and excrescence—but it is also overwritten, with too much narration that spells out what has already been so eloquently shown." The problem, according to Corliss, results from Stone's still lacking the craft "to match or mediate his passion. His film works in spurts: a scene that sputters with bombast will be followed by some wrenching fire storm of death in combat." To Corliss, Vietnam itself separates *Platoon* from other works with the same problem because its spurts "prove that someone out there, working from the mind and gut, is willing to put both aggressively onscreen. So *Platoon* is different. It matters."[29]

Not all reviewers saw the film in those terms, choosing instead to criticize both Stone's work as a filmmaker and his message about the war. *Daily Variety* observed that *Platoon* became "an intense but artistically distanced study of infantry life during the Vietnam War." Saying that Stone had sought "to totally immerse the audience in the nightmare of the United States' misguided adventure, and manages to do so in a number of very effective scenes," the reviewer argued that "his set of dual impulses—to stun the viewer with a brutal immediacy on the one hand, and to assert a reflective sense of artistic hindsight on the other—dilutes whatever the film was meant to say, and takes the edge off its power." Concluding that Stone "implicitly suggests that the U.S. lost the war because of divisions within its own ranks and an unwillingness to go all the way," the reviewer said the film leaves audiences "with the tragic result that all the suffering and trauma was for nothing. Unfortunately, the analysis here goes no further than that; better if Stone had stuck to combat basic."[30]

No Vietnam film is complete without the helicopter.

The criticism from the conservative media proved even more bitter. John Simon found it "amazing" that Oliver Stone, with fifteen months' experience fighting in Vietnam, "managed to make a film scarcely different from the soap operas written by hacks who never got closer to the VC than their VCRs." He asked, "Can you trust a movie that is finally going to tell you The Truth about the Vietnam War if it contains a smiling, ruddy-faced soldier passing around the picture of his girl with whom he will live happily ever after, only to be killed in the next reel? Can you swallow a film whose soundtrack, at a crucial moment of terror, erupts into an amplified heartbeat? Would you buy a used car from a filmmaker whose autobiographical hero, Chris Taylor, begins as a raw volunteer ('Why should just poor kids go to war and the rich kids get away with it?'), only to emerge as not only a wily, wise veteran, but also the supreme justicer?"[31]

Simon found Stone's message insidious: "The implications of *Platoon* are that if we had had a few more Oliver Stones, we might not have lost the war; but because we had at least one, we did not wholly lose our honor; Barnes got fragged by gallant Chris, as he deserved to be, and you should just hear the movie audience applaud." The reviewer saved his strongest venom for the director: "*Platoon* is the film of a wild man who wants to be also a philosopher and a poet. Alas, Stone thinks in cliches and writes in tie-dyed prose, but as a wild man he is authentic enough." Despite his dropping out of Yale, teaching in Vietnam, serving in the merchant marine, fighting in Vietnam, and returning a "bona-fide druggie," Simon says Stone still had not become a writer and so had two choices, "either God or something equally hospitable to universal dropouts: film school."[32]

Simon conceded that *Platoon* had "some real, albeit, submerged merits" in its ability to evoke "the full spectrum of horrors, from infestation with red ants and marching on ballooningly blistered feet to undergoing or inflicting the most appalling deaths." However, Simon suggested that the unsparing detail and visualized chaos of the film cuts two ways: "The effect, on the one hand, is to make horror more horrible by its very inscrutability; on the other, to make it more impersonal and abstract." Admitting that *Platoon* has some gripping scenes, Simon said, however, that he found "few moments that grabbed me by anything other than sheer brutality or pandemonium." In the end, he argued that although "*Platoon* may enlighten those who still harbor delusions about Vietnam, and serve the very young as an effective anti-recruiting poster, it is poster art. Even its most belabored point, that our defeat was caused by dissension, is not made compelling enough."[33]

As might be expected, the farther right the reviewer, the most strident the criticism of *Platoon* as a film and of Stone as a commentator on the war. In the ultraconservative *Washington Times Insight* magazine, John Podhoretz acknowledged that *Platoon* seemed to carry a special authority because of Stone's status as a Vietnam veteran. He also conceded his creative talent: "Stone is a distinctive writer; there is a ferocity about his work that gives it a kinetic charge. But this energy is rather like a hyperactive child's: It is nonstop, diffuse, exhausting to watch and finally destructive." Seeing Stone as a self-promoter, seeking greatness, Podhoretz suggested that the writer-director hoped to "win over the critics by denouncing the war experience while at the same time making violent goo of everybody on the screen." According to the reviewer, the end result of this effort "is nothing if not vivid, nothing if not painful, nothing if not an exposition of brutality. But all this is in the service of a plot that is, at root, an adolescent revenge fantasy."[34]

The heart of Podhoretz's complaints focused on Stone's portrayal of Taylor's tour of duty "as a representative Vietnam experience, one duplicated by all platoons in all companies in all the U.S. Army. Given the appalling behavior not only of Barnes but of the platoon in general, Stone's effort to use his sleazy little story as a metaphor for the American experience in Southeast Asia blackens the name and belittles the sacrifice of every man and woman who served the United States in the Vietnam War (including Stone)." The reviewer found Stone's dedication of the movie to those "who fought and died in the Vietnam War" even more galling: "Needless to say, there are many people who actually think this movie is a tribute to those Americans who died in Vietnam. Needless to say, people who think so never knew anybody who went anywhere near Vietnam—Canada, yes, and Sweden, but not Vietnam." But Podhoretz saved his strongest criticism till the end: "It is a mark of how far we really are from a realistic and sober appraisal of our defeat in Vietnam that *Platoon* has garnered praise for its 'realism,' 'intensity' and 'honesty.' In fact, this is one of the most repellent movies ever made in this country."[35]

Not likely. Any film containing the multiplicity of images found in *Platoon*, telling a story about an event of such surmounting complexity and controversy as Vietnam would engender its own controversies and debate. Truth became the first casualty in the U.S. military effort in South Vietnam. In the aptly titled *A Bright Shining Lie,* Neil Sheehan describes in great detail how the U.S. military chose to represent a devastating South

Vietnamese defeat at Ap Bac on January 2, 1963, as a great victory. Nor have historians and the military completely resolved the conflicting stories about what happened in the Tonkin Gulf in August 1964. Given the diversity of perceptions about the war from its earliest days, reviewers and audiences have probably asked too much of all the cinematic recreations of Vietnam.[36]

The reaction to Podhoretz's castigation of *Platoon* illustrates the difficulty of coming to any consensus on a film, let alone the war itself. On one hand, a reader agreed "whole-heartedly" with the review, saying that three of his close friends had died in Vietnam: "None of them were drug users or brutally violent. Stone's movie depicts U.S. soldiers as either demented killers or heavy drug users. It is a disgrace to the memories of those who fought and died there, and most of all, a disgrace to those who returned home to a country that did not honor them or care for their sacrifice." On the other hand, a veteran wrote that the review "almost gagged me. . . . I found the movie to be a masterpiece of detail and in many ways a mirror image of my experience there. A horrific nightmarish trip back in time. Sullied by the film? No, I feel honored by it. Oliver Stone has given the Vietnam veteran something that no one else in film has given us before: the simple truth."[37]

Soldiers' views of the film probably carry the most weight in any discussion about the veracity of Stone's representation of the war. As the ongoing debates among those who had fought in Vietnam illustrated, no simple truth existed either about the nature of the war or about *Platoon,* the first movie in the wave of "realistic" portrayals of the war. Among other newspapers, the *Los Angeles Times* provided a forum for a discussion about the film in its "Calendar" section on January 25, 1987. In it, critics, movie stars, soldiers, and even Vietnam refugees, who gave *Platoon* good reviews, had an opportunity to express their views.

Jane Fonda said she wept after seeing the movie and told an interviewer: "A movie like this helps to insure that it [another Vietnam] will never happened again." She reported that while she was crying, several veterans joined her and "we wept together." Explaining that she had "been so close to guys who have been devastated by the war," she opined, "What *Platoon* does—better than I've ever seen before—is show what it was like *being* there. What those men went through." In contrast, although agreeing that the cinematography and performances were superb, Chuck Norris wondered whatever happened to heroics. The actor said the film did not convince him that it delivered a true depiction of what went on in Vietnam: "Maybe it happened. But I don't believe it worth a damn. If I was a Vietnam vet who'd put my life on the line over there, and then went to see *Platoon*—with those scenes of G.I.s tormenting villagers and raping young girls—I'd be furious." Remembering his younger brother who died in Vietnam in 1970, Norris recalled: "In his letters he wrote about brotherhood and camaraderie. There wasn't anything about the kind of stuff that went on in *Platoon*."[38]

Of course, some of that stuff had actually taken place, and Norris knew that. But some soldiers also performed heroically, perhaps not as heroically as Norris's characters in *Good Guys Wear Black* or in the *Missing in Action* series, but heroically in the best tradition of the American fighting men. And people who read Norris's remarks quickly let the actor know what they thought of his perceptions of the war. One writer observed: "How dare someone who has only experienced war via props, lighting and special effects deny what another man's real war experience was or is to be. War is obviously not the romantic we-always-win-despite-the-odds occurrence he (and his buddy Stallone) would have young people believe. I shouldn't be surprised to find that a movie about what war is really like would be too 'realistic' and 'depressing' to a man who makes dangerously unrealistic and depressingly bad war movies." Another suggested: "There is a murky sea of gray matter that Norris refuses to acknowledge in regard to the Vietnam War. The truth sometimes hurts, and hurt *Platoon* does. Films like *Platoon* do not diminish our patriotism, as Norris suggests. Nor do they diminish the memory of the men and women who died. They simply present another layer of a complex and often painful story. I mean, jeez Chuck, wake up and smell the napalm."[39]

Perhaps the best retort, however, came from a veteran of Vietnam who acknowledged: "*Platoon* was not a pleasant movie, nor was it a pleasant war." But, in contrast to Norris's *Missing in Action*, which did not portray reality, he found that *Platoon* made the bullets, the torn bodies and minds, and the body bags seem "real." He felt that Stone's film portrayed his experiences "about 99% accurately. While the company I was in did not rape and pillage, the drugs, the violence, the heroes and the cowards were right on the button. No, Mr. Norris, we did not win this war. We never lost a battle, but we lost the war. The politicians in Washington saw to that. Not the press, not Jane Fonda, not Abbie Hoffman. Try Johnson, Nixon, Kissinger. So you just go on with your 'causes' and be a hero and make your millions. But please remember your younger brother who died in Vietnam. He gave this country something you cannot—his life."[40]

In the end, the Pentagon's reaction to the original screenplay for *Platoon* may have provided the best explanation for the great diversity of views on the film: "In our opinion, the script basically creates an unbalanced portrayal by stereotyping black soldiers, showing rampant drug abuse, illiteracy, and concentrating action on brutality." Without balance, whatever its power to movie audiences, the film still opened itself to criticism. Even Stone had to concede that his portrayal of black soldiers left something to be desired: "I can see it being interpreted that way. . . . Perhaps I didn't think it out enough and say, 'Maybe I ought to give a black character something heroic to do.' There were a lot of white guys who weren't so heroic."[41]

With that said, and despite all the controversy it created, *Platoon* remains an overpowering film, one with which all other movies about Vietnam must be compared. At its core, Stone's film differs little in its portrayal of small-unit action from countless other stories of Americans in combat, whether of World Wars I and II, Korea, or even Vietnam. However, the language, the violence, Taylor's rite of passage, and the classic clash of good and evil between Elias and Barnes all combine to give *Platoon* a unique ambience. Whether it provided only one man's perspective on the American experience in Vietnam or recreated reality for the majority of soldiers who fought in Southeast Asia, *Platoon* convinced most viewers that they had seen Vietnam as never before and should never see again. In any case, the skill with which Stone made his film won the hearts and minds of the Motion Picture Academy, which recognized *Platoon* as the best movie of 1986. It also brought the filmmaker an Oscar as best director of the year. Whether its huge financial return opened the door to box-office success for other soon-to-be-released movies about Vietnam remained to be seen. But it did make the war a subject for renewed debate and an arena in which other filmmakers no longer feared to tread.

Three other movies about Vietnam were nearing release as *Platoon* was garnering its Oscars. Like Stone's film, each portrayed Vietnam in graphic detail, which undoubtedly contributed to the problems in finding financial backing and lengthened the time from initial concept to theater screens. With its focus on American prisoners of war, mostly confined to their cells, *The Hanoi Hilton* did not even offer the excitement of combat or the sleazy off-duty sexual escapades that lightened the documentary realism of *Full Metal Jacket* and *Hamburger Hill*.

When first submitted to the Pentagon in 1975, *The Hanoi Hilton* told the story of a single POW, Navy flier John McCain, juxtaposed with the failed raid in 1970 to liberate Americans thought to be held at the Son Tay prison in North Vietnam. In response to a conversation with the producer in 1976, Don Baruch questioned the connection between the two stories but said his office deferred "to your dramatic judgment on this point." He did point out, however, that the Pentagon had received a copy of a book about the Son Tay raid that was to serve as the basis of a screenplay. As a result, he said the Defense Department felt it should not grant "any exclusivity on this subject matter. We therefore will be free to consider assistance on both projects, if and when they materialize."[42]

By the time the producer visited the Air Force Public Affairs Office in Los Angeles on October 3, 1978, to discuss the project, it had become a three-hour special on ABC-TV, scheduled for broadcast, without commercials, at the end of 1978. In his memo for the record, Col. Donald Burggrabe, the director of the office, described Lionel Chetwynd, who was writing the script, as "a Canadian ex-military type." Noting that the producer expected to submit a script for review by mid-December, Burggrabe wrote that the filmmakers had eliminated the Son Tay raid from the story and expanded the cast to include eleven major and minor characters, with an even mix of Air Force and Navy personnel. He did see one potential problem with the screenplay, however, saying that it would include the story of the POWs, albeit with disguised names, who had collaborated with their captors. In addition, the filmmakers planned to include the visits of Jane Fonda and Ramsey Clark to North Vietnam and the assistance they provided to North Vietnam's propaganda program.[43]

Responding to the producer's letter of November 2, confirming his many discussions with his office, Burggrabe wrote: "It can be a truly marvelous production which will help tell the story of the many heroic men who suffered so many years in North Vietnam POW camps. I personally pledge you our very best professional advice and assistance in the development of the script." The script seemed to reward such ongoing help when it arrived in January 1979, along with a request for limited support when production began that spring. Burggrabe recommended to the Air Force Public Information Office in Washington that it and the Defense Department approve cooperation.[44]

All the services reviewed the script and had the same recommendation. The Air Force advised Don Baruch that it had no objection to the script but suggested that "to insure the desired accurate portrayal of the POW/MIA subject, we recommend ex-POWs be given the opportunity to review the script." The Public Information Division also recommended that ex-POWs serve as technical advisors during filming. Penny Williamson, who reviewed the script for the Marines, found it accurate and "definitely pro-American. The men are all portrayed as heroes. The anti-Vietnam [war] visitors (a la Jane Fonda) come across as fools at best; traitors at worst." Although the only Marine portrayed "is not the *most* heroic of the film; he is still a positive character—especially at the beginning. We can live with it." Likewise, the Navy gave its approval, with a request for only minor revisions.[45]

Col. Frederick Kiley in the Secretary of Defense History Office pointed out only minor technical errors. Overall, he advised Baruch that "the scriptwriter and producer have made a great effort to create a serious, accurate, uncompromising movie. Frankly, it is far better than what I expected, and so far superior to any other film already out which deals with the POWs that comparison is useless." To the historian, the script captured the reality of the POW experience: "The elements of captivity—terror, illness, despair, torture, extortion, extreme cruelty, communication, leadership under terrible pressure, illness, collaboration, interrogation, isolation—they are all here. It is an amazing piece of work in that respect because the captivity is not like the cliche captivity in most American war films. There is a special kind of accuracy—not that of a specific individual at a specific time but that of a general and common truth in the experience which is at work here. It is an impressive recreation of the atmosphere, the sense of what it was." In conclusion, Kiley advised Baruch that he thought "it extremely important that it be presented with as little interruption as possible. I hope they can sell it to someone who will agree to that sort of a presentation."[46]

With the responses in hand, Baruch advised the producer that the "consensus of opinion is that it is an unusually fine script and should make a gripping television feature that will benefit DoD by presenting a realistic resume, in a fictional manner, of the ordeal endured by our POWs at the Hanoi Hilton." He provided the recommendations that the services and the History Office had made, noting that Colonel Kiley "considers that you and the scriptwriter have made a great effort to create a serious, accurate and uncompromising film." As a result, Baruch said the Pentagon would consider any request for cooperation. Despite such a favorable reaction and the military's desire to see *The Hanoi Hilton* made, the screenplay went into limbo for six years.[47]

In the course of events, ABC decided not to pursue the project, and Chetwynd began seeking another option, but without success: "When I first started trying to sell *The Hanoi Hilton*, in script form, the very script that I eventually shot, I was laughed out of the place. Every producer in Hollywood turned me down twice, the more important ones three times. I more than once found myself in a meeting to which I had been attracted on the basis that we'd talk about *The Hanoi Hilton*, but they wanted to talk about something else. They knew they could get me anywhere anytime to talk about this film."[48]

Ultimately, Chetwynd believed the successful release of the *Rambo* movies and the other action-adventure films such as *Uncommon Valor* and the *Missing in Action* series helped him obtain backing. In contrast to *Apocalypse Now*, which he saw as "in the mythic mode," the later films were "basically very broad and bright strokes. The combination of the two in a curious way kind of took a lot of the political steam out of the question of the Vietnam war film." More important, he thought that Stallone's and Norris's films "were positioned so far to the right, in effect, in their cartoon simplicity that suddenly a film like *The Hanoi Hilton* became very thoughtful."[49]

The writer's own determination to make his movie on his terms contributed to Chetwynd's inability to find backing: "I had the opportunities to make the film over the years—this is different than Oliver Stone's experience—but what was requested in order to make it were things that went to the very integrity of the piece, compromises I wasn't willing to make." While recognizing the need to make some changes, Chetwynd said that he was not prepared to remove the sequence in which the anti–Vietnam war activities visited the POWs, "because many American civilians, some of renown and significance, did go to Vietnam and allow themselves to be taken into a closed society. It's naive to believe you can go into a closed society and see anything except what they wish you to see and do anything except what they wish you to do. I never wanted to give that up because that was terribly important."[50]

Nor was the writer willing to turn *The Hanoi Hilton* into a star vehicle: "I can't tell you how many times someone said, 'Well, if you'd like to restructure it and maybe blend these three characters and we'll get you Bobby or Al or Dusty,' and they'd be prepared to let me make the film. I had always seen this as an ensemble piece." In the end, however, Chetwynd found a producer in Cannon Films, ironically the company that had made Chuck Norris's

Missing in Action movies. The writer explained: "Hollywood has an unerring instinct for the commercial, so it was inevitable than sooner or later they'd see they couldn't go on making *Rambo*. The only way to really make money out of it was to slip into something a little more authentic. We benefitted from that."[51]

Chetwynd, who assumed the role of director, also enjoyed the artistic freedom that Menahem Golan, the president of Cannon Films, gave him, saying, "Make it your way and I will not interfere." The writer-director recalled that Golan adhered to his word. Nor did he ever talk about *Platoon* appearing before *The Hanoi Hilton:* "It was an independent judgment by him that this was a film worth making and a film Americans really ought to see and know about."[52]

To that end, as soon as Cannon Films had acquired rights to the project, its production manager, James Herbert, advised Don Baruch of the new arrangements. He described the screenplay he had enclosed as "essentially the same" as the one on which Orion Pictures had received approval in 1985. Although citing some minor additions and deletions, he characterized the script as one that "maintains the integrity of the original piece, and should meet with your approval." The company requested limited assistance in the form of a location site, the 146th Tactical Airlift Wing at Van Nuys Air National Guard Base, for filming. Although he did not anticipate involving other services in the production, Herbert said he was forwarding them copies of the screenplay. He closed by saying he felt fortunate "to be associated with this project, as it seems to be an accurate and patriotic portrayal of the tremendous hardships endured by the American prisoners of war during the Vietnam conflict."[53]

As both Cannon Films and the Pentagon had anticipated, *The Hanoi Hilton* required relatively minor military assistance during its production in and around Los Angeles. Instead, Chetwynd relied primarily on information from the couple of dozen former POWs who visited the set during production and from Col. Leo Thorsness, who served as the actual technical advisor. Sounding like Dale Dye, Thorsness, who had spent six years in the Hanoi Hilton, observed during the filming that Chetwynd's prison "looks the way it was. It's not identical, obviously, that would be impossible." To him, the important thing remained the director's determination "not to strike a false note." Chetwynd said this effort grew out of his memory of a kindness an American G.I. showed him when he was a four-year-old evacuee, living in the English countryside. He felt he owed his being a free man to the soldier who died on D-Day and saw a connection between him and the fifty-eight thousand Americans who died in Vietnam. To him, they "gave us no less a gift. Now, finally, I've been given the chance to make a film showing what some of them were like."[54]

Hanoi Hilton director Lionel Chetwynd, technical advisor and former Hanoi Hilton captive Col. Leo Thorsness, and Everette Alvarez, the first POW at the prison.

In contrast to the ten years he needed to find backing, Chetwynd took only six months to shoot, edit, and prepare *The Hanoi Hilton* for release. Following its required showing to the Defense Department on March 4, 1987, Don Baruch advised Cannon Films that everyone "felt the picture was most interesting and will bring the all important story of the ordeal our POWs endured in Viet Nam to a wide public audience." While not intending to slight the other actors, Baruch said the audience felt it "only fitting to congratulate Michael Moriarty on his superb performance." Likewise, he wanted "to commend Lionel Chetwynd on his perseverance over the years in arranging this production. We trust his determination will result in great success for *Hanoi Hilton*."[55]

Similar praise came from a most unlikely source. In *Playboy*, Bruce Williamson described *The Hanoi Hilton* as a "dynamic drama, a kind of angst-laden epilog to *Platoon*." At the same time, the reviewer pinpointed the problem that the film would have finding an audience: "Applauding Oliver Stone's definitive battle epic was easy for antiwar activists and liberals, who may feel stiffly challenged by writer-director Lionel Chetwynd's poignant homage to U.S. prisoners of war." Nevertheless, Williamson thought the cinematographer had devised "an unnerving essay on claustrophobia" and that Michael Moriarty had achieved brilliance "at portraying stubborn courage corroded by fear." He did acknowledge that because of a "technical snag," the POWs "appear surprisingly able-bodied after years of abuse on a starvation diet." Nevertheless, he wrote that their performances "express progressive decay and despair." Saying that the film "lobs over-the-shoulder pot shots at some targets likely to stir debate," such as the visit of a Fonda-clone movie star, Williamson concluded: "Whatever one's opinion of its politics, *Hanoi Hilton* is inarguably an important picture."[56]

Director Lionel Chetwynd works on a scene in which the North Vietnamese try to get a POW to talk in exchange for the fruit on the table.

After seeing the initial cut of the film, Menahem Golan, the chairman of Cannon Films and producer of *The Hanoi Hilton*, offered Chetwynd the same estimate: "This is a powerful, incredible film. It's antiwar and pro-American.... I'm very proud of this. I'm so desperately proud we got involved in this. Hurry up and get it finished." However, he also had the same perceptions as Williamson about the reception it would receive: "But understand, you're going to be very deeply hurt when this film goes out there. As powerful as this film is, as powerful is the rejection you're going to get." Seeing that he had not made himself clear to Chetwynd, Golan explained, "You don't understand. You have made a film that touches on political beliefs, and as far as the media will be concerned, they're the wrong kind. It's going to be perceived as a right-wing film."[57]

Unfortunately for Chetwynd, both Williamson and Golan correctly perceived the reaction *The Hanoi Hilton* was to engender among most reviewers. Their criticisms left no aspect of the production untouched, reflecting their antipathy to the writer-director's politics—as well as their own views on how to make a movie about Vietnam War POWs—as much as they related to the actual quality of the movie. Richard Schickel, in *Time*, provided one of the more generous commentaries about *The Hanoi Hilton*, observing: "It is as an earnest attempt to redress a festering grievance, not as film art, that *Hanoi Hilton* deserves attention." He suggested that as presented, the film did not offer "the stuff of compelling drama. There is not enough filth in the corners, not enough ambiguity when the movie shows prisoners resisting the pressure to confess to 'war crimes.'" Schickel concluded that Chetwynd "generates only a distant compassion for his subjects. The kind of vivid identification that a film like *Midnight Express* created eludes him." Nevertheless, he conceded that if the POWs "deserve in the end a higher art than Chetwynd commands, they are at least entitled to the respect he accords their heroism."[58]

Likewise, Tom Matthews, in *Boxoffice*, mused that *The Hanoi Hilton* should have provided Cannon Films with a box-office success, seeing it as the "perfect sidebar to *Platoon*, showing us that while it was Hell up at the front, it was a Hell of a different kind for those Americans who spent years hidden away in Vietnamese prison camps. But *Hanoi Hilton* misses the mark by quite a distance. It's not really a bad film, but it's simply not as powerful as it should be and consequently it fails." Recognizing that not much happens in prison for long periods of time, Matthews pinpointed that reality as the film's main problem: "It's a structureless story that meanders lazily through the years, and writer-director Lionel Chetwynd has simply not written enough good material to keep our interest. When you're devoting more than two hours to a film in which men basically stay in small rooms and talk, you'd better give them awfully interesting things to say. Chetwynd doesn't." Because the characters became so boring, the reviewer says any emotion inherent in the dramatization of their ultimate release "falls flat." Instead, he concludes that the audience never comes to care about the men, which "is unfortunate, both for Cannon and for the viewers who were hungry for a look at this side of the Vietnam experience."[59]

From here, the reviews took a turn for the worse. Using the identical adjective as Richard Schickel, Vincent Canby in the *New York Times* described *The Hanoi Hilton* as "an earnest but clumsy tribute" to the American POWs during the Vietnam War. Writing that the film focused on "a big, tough, sorrowful subject," Canby observed that "Mr. Chetwynd finds no way to dramatize its singularity." He acknowledged that in contrast to *Platoon*, which left the Vietnamese "vague and unseen," Chetwynd did try to give character to the enemy in *The Hanoi Hilton*. However, Canby suggested that the director came forth only with "secondhand stereotypes." In fact, the reviewer admitted that the director did "no more justice to the characters of the prisoners than those of the Vietnamese." In the end, Canby decided that although the film contained "scarcely any action and though it's as sincere as a pledge of allegiance to the flag, its point of view is no less narrow than that of *Rambo*."[60]

Stanley Kauffmann, in the *New Republic*, also saw a connection between *Rambo* and *The Hanoi Hilton*. But his vitriolic criticism of Chetwynd's film escalated the attack to a level seldom seen in any movie review: "*The Hanoi Hilton* is filth. It exploits the sufferings—and deaths of American POWs in North Vietnam in order to promote a distortion of history: that the peace movement in the United States and elsewhere prolonged the imprisonment of those men by impeding American victory. More realistically than *Rambo*, and therefore more dangerously, it clearly implies the *Rambo* stab-in-the-back idea." That interpretation of *Rambo* undoubtedly gives too much credit to the intellectual pretensions of the filmmakers. In fact, Kauffmann's effort to force a conservative message onto *The Hanoi Hilton* led him to conclude that the movie "implies that if it hadn't been for the anti-war protesters, the United States and its allies would have swept north and opened the prison gates."[61]

Kauffmann's argument did have validity. Most of the antiwar protesters probably did not understand the dilemma inherent in their movement. The insidious nature of the war required protest. However, that protest undoubtedly convinced the North Vietnamese, who did not understand democracy and the place of opposition to government policies within the constitutional system, to interpret the protest as a sign of weakness. So they remained willing to continue the war despite the huge losses in men and resources that the American military inflicted upon the peasant nation. Nevertheless, without the protest movement, Lyndon Johnson and his advisors would have been able to pursue victory unfettered. Yet that "victory" would have besmirched the very concept of democracy and the moral authority it provided for the nation. So, protesters had no alternative to protesting, even if their opposition to the war prolonged it. A clear Joseph Heller Catch-22.

Chetwynd offered his own rejoinder to the review: "You see, that is not anything that the film is about. We never show what is going on on the home front. All that is shown is what our POWs were told was going on: that the Vietnamese wanted to use them as propaganda pieces because the real war was not being fought in the Delta [but] in the newspapers in the United States. That's what they were told. I didn't invent that." Nor did he invent the visit of Jane Fonda to Hanoi, the portrayal of which heightened the criticism of *The Hanoi Hilton*. In *People*, Ralph Novak observed: "Even Jane Fonda's hardest critics would cringe at the doltish behavior of the actress character (played by Gloria Carlin) who visits the Hanoi prison camp to sweet-talk the POWs into confessing guilt." Likewise, in *New York*, David Denby, who described *The Hanoi Hilton* as "a tedious movie about men in a prison camp" called the portrayal a "completely unsympathetic caricature of Jane Fonda's misguided trip to Hanoi."[62]

Chetwynd denied that he was trying to damage Fonda's reputation by his re-creation: "My character doesn't sit in an enemy gun site and pretend to take aim at American planes, and say, 'I wish I had one of those murderers in my sight'; my character doesn't go on [prison] camp radio and broadcast live; my character doesn't call [POWs] 'liars and hypocrites and murderers'; my character doesn't report back to the Vietnamese things that were said by the POWs; my character doesn't persecute these men on their return." If anything, the writer-director treated Fonda and her visit to North Vietnam with kid gloves, and he observed that this prompted the one criticism of the film from POWs: "They wonder why the character is allowed to play with so much sympathy, why I did not tell the truth about what she and other so-called peace delegates did, and how many men were tortured and beaten because of them." He explained that he did not show the whole story because "that isn't what the film is about. What I'm trying to show is what happens when you go from an open society into a closed society. You will not see or hear or learn anything but what that closed society wants you to see, hear and learn. And if Jane Fonda and Joan Baez and Cora Weiss and Tom Hayden and Ramsey Clark—and the list is endless—made any mistakes, it was believing that they were seeing the truth."[63]

Kauffmann apparently wanted to watch a different movie, one that would have simply shown that the United States "ought not to have been involved" in the war: "Nowhere does this cynical film state or imply what is now a widely accepted belief: anti-war demonstrations or not, there was no way for South Vietnam, the United States, and their allies to win, short of nuclear blasting. Nowhere in the film is there an attempt to place the real blame for the sufferings of those American prisoners. It is fixed in far higher places than the streets and campuses of America where the protesters marched." Paradoxically, after complaining because the film did not address the political issues, Kauffmann reversed himself and criticized Chetwynd for including comments such as Michael Moriarty's explanation that he is obeying orders and wants to help bring freedom to the Vietnamese. Wondering aloud how the speech "sounds to Vietnam vets," the reviewer concluded that if the writer-director is really "trying to tell us that *Platoon* misrepresents the grunts by omitting their political convictions, then *The Hanoi Hilton* is as stupid as it is vicious."[64]

During the production and even more following the severe criticism of Chetwynd and his film, the POWs made it clear that they thought *The Hanoi Hilton* fairly represented their experiences and their feelings about the peace activists who visited North Vietnam. Leo Thorsness, one of the technical advisors to Chetwynd, later commented: "Everything in the film happened. I never knew that truth could be political." Another former POW, Capt. Richard Statton, thought the criticism of the film resulted from the continuing friendship of the North Vietnamese government with the antiwar activists: "To say the peace movement was naive is as understated as the portrayal of the film's actress character." To him, those who visited Hanoi "and returned to parrot the Communist Party line exacerbated our maltreatment, prolonged our imprisonment and are in the same league as Tokyo Rose and the Rosenbergs, Walkers and Pollards." Nevertheless, he differentiated between them and the majority of Americans who opposed the war: "Those in the peace movement who protested at home, within the Constitution and out of deep humanistic concern, are quiet heroes of a different kind whose rights we fight (and die) to protect even while disagreeing."[65]

Chetwynd simply maintained that he had no intention of grappling with the rights and wrongs of the war, believing that if the critics "are so sensitive, the reason is—and I say this to Stanley Kauffman and all of these other people—they are very insecure in their credentials for having opposed the war. The man's curiosity has disappeared, like the entire generation's. You can't get a good discussion out of my generation."[66]

All praise or criticism aside, the contents of the film virtually assured its failure at the box office. *The Hanoi Hilton* in no way resembled *A Bridge on the River Kwai* or *The Great Escape* or *Stalag 17*. The men in the Hanoi Hilton had little hope of escape or expectation of an early end to the war. Their lives centered almost entirely on their cells, and they lacked the ongoing contacts with their fellow prisoners that made life bearable to the majority of the downed fliers or even the bridge-builders in World War II. So, although the film did convey the patriotism, fortitude, and bravery of the POWs, it also conveyed the despair and depression the men faced. Such images lacked any appeal for filmgoers, particularly after the savaging the film received from reviewers. And when combined with the bottom line that the United States had lost in Vietnam, few people had any reason to spend money to be reminded of such realities.

In fact, *The Hanoi Hilton* made one of the strongest antiwar statements to appear in any American war movie. It showed the POWs as victims of the war, suffering far more than the grieving, frustrated wives in *Limbo* or even the veterans who came home with continuing mental or physical problems. For the POWs, life had simply stopped and the

Filming inside the set of the Hanoi Hilton.

years they spent in the Hanoi Hilton became lost. All the postwar rehabilitation and successful careers within the military or private life, whether as educators or as politicians, could not compensate for the wasted years in Hanoi, however bravely they had survived.

Ironically, the film could have made an even more powerful statement against the war if it had taken a more evenhanded approach to the North Vietnamese captors. No one questions that the jailers treated their prisoners severely, that their use of torture violated agreements on the treatment of prisoners, that they showed little if any compassion to their wards. For the most part, the North Vietnamese in *The Hanoi Hilton* resembled Hollywood's stereotypical Oriental enemy: cruel, evil, and vicious, lacking any of the humane characteristics of Western man. Worse, with the exception of only a few sentences scattered throughout the film, the director does not attempt to explain why the North Vietnamese might have so little feeling for their captives.

If Chetwynd had included some significant reference to the destruction that the U.S. Navy and Air Force were wreaking on North Vietnam, then the film would have portrayed how the war rent asunder both sides in the conflict. It would also have conveyed an appreciation of how dearly the North Vietnamese held their beliefs that they would endure the massive bombing inflicted upon them for so long. In acknowledging the deficiency, Chetwynd admitted: "I made a lot of suppositions that people understood this reality. They didn't understand it. There should have been more of that in the film. . . . That was the mistake in presenting the film. I believe that the case for the ultimate nobility of the POWs, in the way they behaved one to another, would not have in any way been diminished by showing what was going on. If I had to do it again, that is the thing we would change." If these images had appeared in the film, then its antiwar statement might have compensated for its lack of dramatic appeal and might well have rendered moot all criticism engendered on the basis of politics. But even without a more explicit explanation of how the North was suffering from the war, *The Hanoi Hilton* did show the reality of the war that many, many Americans still had a difficult time acknowledging.[67]

In contrast, *Full Metal Jacket* had no serious pretensions of presenting the war realistically. Any images about the nature of the American experience in Vietnam resulted almost coincidentally from the virtuosity of Stanley Kubrick's filmmaking skills in transferring Gustav Hasford's 1979 novel *The Short-Timers* to the screen. According to Kubrick, he did not even set out to make a Vietnam movie after he completed *The Shining* in 1980. Instead, he had simply begun a search for a new subject that would allow him to tell a good story: "There are certain things about a war story that lend itself to filming, but only if the story's good. There's something about every kind of story. There's something about a love story, or an animal story. . . . I would say it's the story, not the subject." In beginning his literary reconnaissance, Kubrick compared himself to a lion looking for a meal: "I'm always looking."[68]

The novel he found in 1982 told a story of how boot camp molded young Marine recruits into fighting men and how combat then changed them. Kubrick recalled that the book had an immediate emotional impact on him: "The sense of the story the first time you read it is the absolutely critical yardstick. I remember what I felt about the book, I remember what I felt in writing the script, and then I try to keep that alive in the very inappropriate circumstances that exist on a film set where you've got a hundred people standing around and nothing but particular problems, still trying to sustain a subjective sense of what it is emotionally—as well as what it is that pleases you." Whether Kubrick's efforts to film the story would succeed became another matter: "This book was written in a very, very, almost poetically spare way. There was tremendous economy of statement, and

Hasford left out all the 'mandatory' war scenes that are put in to make sure you understand the characters and make you wish he would get on with the story. . . . I tried to retain this approach in the film. I think as a result, the film moves along at an alarming—hopefully an alarming—pace."[69]

To give substance to that pace, Kubrick had to undertake a crash course on the Vietnam War. Unlike the earlier cinematic chroniclers of the conflict, he lacked one important ingredient—proximity. Having lived in England since the early 1960s, and having not even visited the United States since 1968, Kubrick had not experienced the war on a day-to-day basis on television or in print as had most Americans. To make up for this shortcoming, he set about to learn everything he could about Vietnam through books, newspapers, feature films, and documentaries. Even while immersing himself in the war, he began collaborating on the screenplay for *Full Metal Jacket* with Hasford, who had served as a Marine combat correspondent, and with Michael Herr, the author of *Dispatches* and one of Francis Coppola's advisors on *Apocalypse Now*.[70]

The director even turned to the Marines, writing to *Leatherneck Magazine* to place an ad for a technical advisor for his film. The editor wrote back to advise Kubrick that an ad would not serve as the best means of securing an advisor. Instead, he recommended that the director get in touch with Fred Peck, head of the Marine Corps Public Affairs Office in Los Angeles. When the editor informed Peck that he might be receiving a letter from Kubrick, the public affairs officer took the initiative and wrote the director a letter in which he suggested two candidates for the job. Ultimately, Kubrick hired Lee Ermey, one of the men Peck had recommended. In the course of events, the retired Marine drill instructor, Vietnam veteran, and technical advisor on *The Boys in Company C* and *Apocalypse Now* convinced Kubrick that he should also have the key role as the D.I., Sergeant Hartman.[71]

Like Hasford and Herr, Ermey had gone to England to work for Kubrick because of the director's reluctance to leave the security that his small world of country estate and film studio afforded him. Not even the obvious physical requirements of *Full Metal Jacket* caused Kubrick to change his lifestyle. Instead, he attempted to bring Vietnam to him rather than traveling to the look-alike locations of Thailand, the Philippines, or even Fort Benning, Georgia. After searching sites throughout England, he settled on a British Territorial Army base as a stand-in for the Marine boot camp at Parris Island, South Carolina. For Vietnam, and particularly for Hue during the 1968 Tet Offensive, Kubrick found what he considered the perfect spot, an abandoned gasworks, already scheduled for demolition, at Beckton, on the Thames, southeast of London. According to the director, the architecture of the site closely resembled certain neighborhoods in Hue, including the industrial functionalism style of the 1930s.[72]

To prepare the "Hue" site for shooting, Kubrick sent in a demolition team for a week to blow up the buildings and then dispatched the art director and a wrecking crew for six weeks to knock holes in the corners of buildings and generally create a sense of the destructiveness of battle. He thought the effort provided him with "interesting ruins—which no amount of money would have allowed you to build." He finished off his re-creation with grillwork and other architectural touches, two hundred palm trees from Spain, and thousands of plastic plants from Hong Kong. To the director, the indigenous grass and weeds, "which look the same all over the world," provided the final elements needed to create his Vietnam. To fill the scenery, he acquired six M-47 tanks courtesy of a Belgian army colonel who liked the director's work and leased helicopters and weapons from arms dealers. Naturally, Kubrick thought the result looked "absolutely perfect, I think. There might be some other place in the world like it, but I'd hate to have to look for it. I think even if we had gone to Hue, we couldn't have created that look. I know we couldn't have."[73]

Not surprisingly, some veterans of the fighting in Hue during Tet found Kubrick's re-creation authentic, given the infinite variety of Vietnam experiences and the way the participants remembered the events. In fact, the director and his staff created a strangely sterile and surrealistic landscape. To be sure, Vietnam became surrealistic to most of those who fought in the war. But that surrealism grew out of the nature of the conflict itself, not the physical environment, and certainly not representations that Kubrick believed recreated the "look" of Vietnam.

Full Metal Jacket had a second, probably more serious, deficiency. Kubrick actually was telling two, only vaguely related short stories. However well done, the first third, in which he detailed the recruit training of the Marines bound for Vietnam, never became more than a stale rehash of countless boot-camp films. Like *The Boys in Company C*, on which Lee Ermey had served as a technical advisor, *Full Metal Jacket* distinguished itself from such movies as *The D.I.* and *Battle Cry* only by its greater reliance on profanity for its claim to authenticity. The sudden, if not really unexpected, murder-suicide climax to the training portion offers a visual jolt but does not provide the meaningful transition to Vietnam that Kubrick apparently expected. Instead, the audience simply finds itself in a different world.

Kubrick was marching to his own creative drummer, however, and chose not to listen to those who pointed out the disharmony between the two disparate parts of the movie or the dramatic problems caused by having to take valuable time to give flesh to new characters. Consequently, *Full Metal Jacket* became a strangely detached and uneven movie, but one that was bound to stir much discussion and critical analysis. Given the director's reputation, most film critics chose to first analyze *Full Metal Jacket* in the context of Kubrick's body of work and only then to comment on its relationship with *Platoon* and the way it explored the American experience in Vietnam.[74]

Vincent Canby, for one, began his *New York Times* review by observing: "More than any other major American film maker, Stanley Kubrick keeps to his own ways, paying little attention to the fashions of the moment, creating fantastic visions that, in one way and other, are dislocated extensions of the world we know but would prefer not to recognize." As a result, he wrote that the best of his films "are always somewhat off-putting when first seen. They're never what one has expected. No Kubrick film ever immediately evokes the one that preceded it. Yet it's so distinctive that it can't be confused with the work of any other director." Canby says this can be "infuriating" to a serious student of film "who wants to be able to read a film maker's accumulated body of work as if it were a road map leading to some predetermined destination. As movie follows movie, the Kubrick terrain never becomes familiar. You drive at your own risk, confident only that the director has been there before you."[75]

As this related to the director's view of Vietnam, Canby called *Full Metal Jacket* a "harrowing, beautiful and characteristically eccentric" movie that "is going to puzzle, anger and (I hope) fascinate audiences as much as any film he has made to date." Although audiences will compare it to *Platoon*, Canby warned that "its narrative is far less neat and cohesive—and far more antagonistic—than Mr. Stone's film." Of course, Kubrick was not trying to make a realistic movie about something he knew or had experienced firsthand. Rather, the story that had enthralled him just happened to contain Marines who end up fighting in Vietnam. As Canby points out, *Full Metal Jacket* actually more resembles *Apoca-*

lypse Now, "even if it has none of the mystical romanticism of the Coppola film in either its text or physical production."[76]

Neither director had fought in Vietnam and had to rely on secondhand advice on how to recreate the war. As a result their films lacked the emotional, gut-wrenching impact that only a participant in the war could instill in the visual images. Their renditions of combat came from their imaginations, and they never strayed far from their cameras. If Coppola actually drifted across the screen impersonating a TV newsman covering Robert Duvall's helicopter assault on the Vietnamese village, Canby saw a similar apparition in *Full Metal Jacket:* ". . . lurking just off-screen, there's always the presence of Mr. Kubrick, a benign, ever mysterious Kurtz, who has come to know that the only thing worse than disorder in the universe is not to recognize it—which is, after all, the first step toward understanding and possibly accommodation." Whether or not *Full Metal Jacket* offered that understanding of Vietnam, Canby did feel that the film had "immense and very rare imagination."[77]

As a consummate filmmaker, Kubrick had the ability to infuse that imagination onto the motion picture screen, compensating to some degree for his lack of firsthand experience in Vietnam. In his *Los Angeles Weekly* review, John Powers concluded that the finished picture portrayed "the limits of *Platoon*'s vaunted realism. (Kubrick has cinematic skills that Oliver Stone can only dream of)." At the same time, he thought that Kubrick had tried to make too much of a virtue out of what his movie was not: "Even as he strips away the conventions of the war movie, he doesn't replace them with enough fresh, strong material to move an audience sated with 'Nam lore; there are still too many unredeemed cliches in this movie—and not enough ideas." Nor did Powers believe Kubrick replaced the cliches with raw emotions: "One doesn't feel of Kubrick as one felt of Stone, that here is a guy who really cares passionately about the Vietnam War and the men who fought it."[78]

Without that passion, *Full Metal Jacket* became less a comment on Vietnam than an exercise in filmmaking. Peter Rainer, in the *Los Angeles Herald Examiner,* saw *Full Metal Jacket* as a cinematic happening: "Stanley Kubrick has a visionary genius rep that transforms each of his movies into an event." Nevertheless, Rainer warned that if audiences expected some sort "of grand summing-up from the *2001* guy," they might well feel short-changed: "Whatever else *Full Metal Jacket* may be, it's not the ultimate Vietnam movie. And the fact that Kubrick couldn't pull it off—may not have wanted to—is perhaps the 'statement' that some people have been looking for in vain. The movie's limitations seem not only Kubrick's; they seem to belong to the Vietnam experience itself, to our inability to come to terms with what it was all about. The only grand-scale emotion that arises from the film, as from most Vietnam movies and journals, is a furious nihilism."[79]

If *Full Metal Jacket* ultimately failed to break new ground or become *the* Vietnam movie, it still contained much to praise. Whether it also lived up to the standards by which most people judged Kubrick's body of work remained a matter of some debate. In *Time,* Richard Corliss wrote that with the "splendid first 45 minutes" of the movie, the director "reenters the real world." To the reviewer, for the past twenty-five years, Kubrick had been hitting "the cerebral fantasy button" in such movies as *Dr. Strangelove* and *2001.* With *Full Metal Jacket,* Corliss believed that the director had not made "a realistic film—it is horror-comic superrealism, from God's eye view—but it should fully engage the ordinary movie grunt."[80]

If it did so, Kubrick succeeded in spite of the film's ill-matched parts. In fact, Corliss believed that *Full Metal Jacket* "never quite survives its bravura beginning." Moreover, because Kubrick shot the film in England, it lacked "the lush tropical colors" of the Vietnam

Matthew Modine in *Full Metal Jacket*.

movies shot in the Philippines or Thailand. With its "desaturated green-gray of a war zone as it would appear on the 6 o'clock news," Corliss felt that Hue looked little different from Pittsburgh: "Here, only death looks luscious; gunfire makes a gutted warehouse flare into brilliant orange, and the blood of strafed civilians waters the countryside, turning it into poppy fields."[81]

Worse, Corliss says, having also "desaturated" the drama, the director gave the Marines "no ideas to defend, just their asses." As a result, he thought that in the Vietnam half "the movie becomes a notebook of anecdotes, always compelling, but rarely propelling the story toward its climax." In the end, Corliss concluded, like Peter Rainer, that *Full Metal Jacket* had not made the definitive statement about Vietnam: "Unlike Oliver Stone's *Platoon*, with which it will unfortunately be compared, Kubrick's film does not want to say every last word about Viet Nam. It wants to isolate a time, a place and a disease."[82]

To some extent, the problem may well have lain within Kubrick's personality and the evolution of his career. Corliss notes that in returning "to the movie mainstream, he also waters down his material with a Hollywood ending." After following Hasford's novel until the penultimate sequence, the director cops out: "Now—we will say no more—Kubrick pretties up the climax with a bogus moral dilemma and some attenuated anguish. A viewer is finally left to savor earlier delights: the dialogue's wild, desperate wit; the daring in choosing a desultory skirmish to make a point about war's pointlessness; the fine, large performances of almost every actor . . . most important, the Olympian elegance and precision of Kubrick's filmmaking." Nevertheless, Corliss argues: "By normal movie standards, with whatever reservations one may entertain, the film is a technical knockout."[83]

Perhaps. But impressive filmmaking alone, without meaningful insights, cannot give substance to the images. Reviewing *Full Metal Jacket* in *Movieline,* F.X. Feeney suggested that the film "gives us the illusion of a documentary" and "comes the closest of any Vietnam picture yet made to capturing the war *exactly* as it looked on television. There's a brute reason for this which has nothing to do with Kubrick—news cameras almost never went into the jungle." Other Vietnam films had "the power of revelation on their side: they offer mythic excursions into the world of terror beyond what most Americans could imagine first-hand in those years; as a result, inevitably, these movies treat Vietnam as a rite-of-passage, a journey out to a place of transformation and even healing." In contrast, he maintained that Kubrick offered no such comfort in *Full Metal Jacket,* choosing instead to make "an assault on consciousness, a meditation in which 40 centuries stare down from the pyramids at the American Waterloo."[84]

If Vietnam itself assaulted the American consciousness and exposed the paradox of the nation's love of war while claiming to be peaceloving, many people thought *Full Metal Jacket* should also do more to show the pointlessness of war. Sam Fuller, for one, wanted Kubrick to say something else, to ask, "What are we doing here?" The director of *The Big Red One* thought Kubrick's ending the movie with the death of the girl sniper remained the best thing in the film: "I don't know how he got that wonderful expression of contempt on her dying face. It was beautiful. It was war." But as Richard Corliss noted, the ending also contained "a bogus moral dilemma": Should the Marines answer the girl's pleas for death and shoot the Vietcong sniper or should they leave her to die slowly and painfully?[85]

In *Dr. Strangelove* and *2001*, the ambiguities grew out of the images themselves. Not this time, however. Kubrick created a cold and distant movie, a set piece in which he sought, purely through his skills as a filmmaker, to manipulate audiences' emotions to suit his fancy. In deciding to transfer Hasford's novel to the screen, the director may have become enthralled with the story. Nevertheless, his self-imposed isolation from the United States perhaps caused Kubrick to forget that *The Short-Timers* dealt with a very specific war, at a very specific time in American history. Instead, Kubrick let the material itself guide him. He liked the boot camp, liked the way Lee Ermey created his D.I. persona, and so let his camera run too long. Worse, as Cimino did with his Russian Orthodox wedding, Kubrick put away his editing block too soon. The resulting portrayal of Marines preparing for war may have taken its place in the galaxy of Hollywood's greatest military basic training movies. But it added little to the understanding of America's involvement in Vietnam.

In fact, the success or failure of *Full Metal Jacket* ultimately depended on viewers' reactions to the images of Vietnam that Kubrick created. Unfortunately, the director brought these images to the screen second or third hand, without even the benefit of having been inundated with the Vietnam of the nightly television news reports, which most Americans had experienced whether or not they liked it. All his reading of books, newspapers, and magazines and all his screening of feature movies and documentaries could not compensate for his distance, mentally and physically, from the United States during the years when the war so profoundly impacted on the fabric of American society and culture. Consequently, *Full Metal Jacket* became a movie with little scope, with few insights about the American involvement in Vietnam and any broader issues about the nature of war. Kubrick's film had an even greater problem in trying to attract audiences already overwhelmed by *Platoon* or moved by *The Hanoi Hilton*. It contained little if any of the passion for the subject that Oliver Stone or Lionel Chetwynd had imparted to their stories.

If *Full Metal Jacket* had a plastic, surrealistic, sterile aura about it, the fourth Vietnam story to appear in less than a year almost reeked of the smells of combat and death. Nevertheless, the belated appearance of *Hamburger Hill* created an immediate, almost insurmountable obstacle to potential success at the box office, whatever its quality. Moreover, its story offered no uplifting ending, rite of passage, or even sense of military accomplishment. As such, it remains the simplest, most straightforward of Hollywood's movies about the Vietnam conflict and one of the least seen and discussed.

Like *Platoon* and *Full Metal Jacket*, *Hamburger Hill* looked at Vietnam through the eyes of the average soldier.

Like *Platoon* and *Full Metal Jacket*, *Hamburger Hill* looked at Vietnam through the eyes of the average soldier. According to the writer and coproducer, Jim Carabatsos, himself a Vietnam War veteran, that remained the only common thread in the three combat stories: "They're drastically different movies." He argued that *Hamburger Hill* became the first film to accurately portray the war as the ordinary G.I. experienced it. The writer believed that *Platoon* and *Full Metal Jacket* were "political movies in that their soldiers just seem to be used as metaphors for the very strong beliefs of the people involved in making those films. . . . I think the purpose of the story was to present the political views of the filmmakers." In contrast, he claimed that none of the people involved in the production of *Hamburger Hill* "had an interest in that. We all said this is a movie about soldiers, and I wasn't going to sacrifice a 19-year-old soldier to present my political views."[86]

To Carabatsos, Oliver Stone and Stanley Kubrick gravely misrepresented the ordinary soldiers who fought in Vietnam by portraying them as "idiots." In particular, two key scenes in *Platoon* bothered him and damaged the reputation of U.S. soldiers: "If you say it's typical that in an American infantry platoon or squad a platoon sergeant kills his squad leader and a new guy kills the platoon sergeant . . . (then) I'd say we should can the Army and close our borders." More to the point, he expressed the concern that audiences might not understand that Stone and Kubrick were using their characters and situations to illuminate their own antiwar beliefs rather than accurately depict how soldiers behaved in combat: "Metaphors are dangerous." As Carabatsos saw it, the danger resulted from viewers' believing that the images represented reality: "The portrayal of the soldiers as incompetent, as not part of our society, I think is dangerous, because when you hear people talking today about going to, say, the Middle East or South America, they'll say, 'Well, we're going to do it better this time. We saw those movies, and we know that the soldiers in Vietnam were a bunch of idiots and this time we'll send better soldiers.'"[87]

Although he criticized the message of *Platoon*, Carabatsos believed that Stone's film performed a valuable service, because it forced Americans to look at their feelings about the war for the first time: "It opened the dialogue and now we're presenting another point of view to further that dialogue." To become part of that dialogue, Carabatsos needed the same length of time as Oliver Stone had required to bring *Platoon* to the screen. He had returned home from Vietnam with the same idea of wanting "to write about what happened over there." Initially, however, he wrote *Heroes* for Henry Winkler, an autobiographical account of what happened when he returned home: "Maybe at the time, that was easier to write about."[88]

Not until producer Marcia Nasastir asked him almost ten years later what sort of script he would most like to write did Carabatsos have the opportunity to return to his wartime experience. When he told her his idea, she agreed to listen to his story because she had had a son in Vietnam. Once he had completed the script, however, Carabatsos and Nasastir required five years to put the project into production, because of money problems, scheduling problems, and the very nature of the subject matter. The story he chose to tell focused on a savage ten-day battle in the Ashau Valley, originally named Operation Apache Snow. Beginning on May 10, 1969, the Third Brigade of the Army's 101st Airborne Division undertook eleven bloody assaults on Hill 937. The fight for the insignificant position produced such carnage that the participants called it the battle of Hamburger Hill. Nevertheless, having suffered 70 percent casualties in the process of securing the hill and destroying the enemy bunkers, they abandoned the territory, receiving only a Presidential Unit Citation for their troubles.[89]

Although in country during the battle, Carabatsos had not taken part in it. He chose to memorialize it, however, because "it seemed to be the perfect stage," explaining that from a screenwriter's perspective, it offered everything: "an isolated area, bravery and dedication." The writer claimed he was not making a political statement about war or the

Vietnam war but rather telling a story about young men who go to war and the effects of one battle on a squad of draftees. Carabatsos believed that most of the other Vietnam films did not "have a damn to do with what happened over there." To him, they said to the families of Vietnam veterans: "Hey, your son or husband or father is a real maniac, a psychopath, because this is what we have to believe."[90]

The writer said that no one had yet said "that the guys who were in Vietnam are no different from the guys who were at Iwo Jima or at the Chosin Reservoir—just as brave, just as courageous." Consequently, Carabatsos wanted to make *Hamburger Hill* to set the record straight: "It's for the guys who were there, for their families. I'm hoping maybe some wife (of a veteran) will understand her husband a little better, or some kid will understand his father a little better." Nasastir believed the script had a link to her recent hit *The Big Chill:* "It seeks to show what young American infantrymen in Vietnam actually experienced in the war." In the early 1980s, however, such stories still did not interest studio executives or many directors. Therefore, having agreed to coproduce the completed script, Carabatsos and Nasastir faced two hurdles to get the film in production. They had to find a director who would put their message on the screen in the way they envisioned it, and they needed to obtain financial backing.[91]

Locating the right person proved the easy part. During lunch with British director John Irvin in 1982, Nasastir discovered that he had spent three months in Vietnam in 1969, making a documentary on the war for the BBC and had been "so shocked by what I saw in Vietnam that I stopped making documentaries." After telling him about Carabatsos's script, Nasastir said she would like his reaction to the story. Irvin recalled that he "wept all the way through it," and despite warnings from friends that the project would not help his career, he called the producer the next day to tell her he wanted to direct the film: "I will do everything and anything in my power to get this film made." Irwin said the script impressed him because he "recognized so many of the characters in the story. When I was in Vietnam, what impressed me most was how young the soldiers were. They were mere kids."[92]

A pause in the fighting for Hill 937 in *Hamburger Hill*, one of the few Vietnam movies to receive full Pentagon assistance.

Coming up with the financial backing for the project took much longer; not until 1986 did the filmmakers finally convince RKO pictures to back the project. Irvin said that the studio finally agreed to back the film because "they were impressed with my passion for the project." Perhaps as important, the studio had ascertained by then that the Pentagon would give favorable consideration to providing assistance to the production.[93]

On August 1, 1985, Mark Seiler, the president of RKO Pictures, had met in Washington with Don Baruch to discuss the project and give him the screenplay of *Hamburger Hill* for Pentagon and Army review. After reading the script, the Army advised Baruch that if the filmmakers corrected problems with language, portrayals of men, and inaccurate procedures, the service "would have no objection to the script." Among other things, the Army thought that the "number of scenes involving the soldiers with prostitutes and visits to whore houses is excessive. In particular, the discussion . . . dealing with a general allegedly operating a whore house is not factual and should be deleted. It lends nothing to the advancement of the story line." The Army also noted that having a sergeant major "arrive to give a reenlistment talk during a combat operation stretches credibility beyond its limits." Perhaps most telling, the service suggested that the sign posted on the hill "implies that the efforts of the soldiers were in vain. This is a very 'down' ending and we recommend that the line 'WAS IT WORTH IT' be deleted."[94]

In his letter advising Seiler of the Army's response, Baruch said that if the filmmakers undertook the requested revisions, the Defense Department would be able to approve the script for official support during filming in the United States. He noted that the Army did not have any real presence in the Philippines, where the filmmakers planned to do their shooting. Baruch then carefully pointed out that the company was "under no obligations to make any revisions if you make satisfactory arrangements for the overseas filming, but we trust you will consider them to make the picture more accurate. If the writer knows the scene to be factual covering the reenlistment promises, perhaps it could be resolved with the Army as we discussed."[95]

At the same time, Baruch said the Pentagon would "like to be able to work with you on the production as we believe it will dramatically and positively show audiences how, especially the uninitiated carried-out the Army mission in Vietnam, commendably in the best way they knew how. That courage and those sacrifices deserve the understanding *Hamburger Hill* could bring to the public." Consequently, Baruch suggested that the film company reconsider "the possibilities of Army support for filming in this country, in areas where equipment is available and looks like parts of Vietnam. It is understood that certain places in the South also have Vietnamese/oriental types."[96]

Despite this suggestion and the real lack of available American support in the Philippines, in June 1986 the production company officially requested DoD support during filming that fall. In particular, the company wanted to use training facilities in Clark Air Base or Subic Bay, where the Department of Defense could provide a two- to three-week boot camp for the actors, Chinook helicopters for a minimum of six days, air strikes by Phantom jets, and thirty days' availability of a Huey helicopter. The Hamburger Hill Company also included a revised script and advised the Army that Retired Col. Joseph B Conmy, the actual brigade commander during the battle of Hamburger Hill, was representing the producers in Washington.[97]

In forwarding the letter to Baruch on July 2, the Army advised him: "With some minor exceptions, the script has been changed to accommodate our recommendations of August 1985." The service followed up the memo on the July 8 with a detailed reaction to the script in which it suggested changes for "historical and technical accuracy." These included revising the portrayal of the processing of newly arrived soldiers, which "overemphasizes the mindlessness of the inprocessing activities and fails to explain why the inprocessing activities seemed mindless," and pointing out that smoking in a helicopter "in flight with the doors open is a near physical impossibility." The Army said that once the filmmakers corrected the inaccuracies, it would have no objections to the script, which it considered "a good one." But although recommending support for the production, it reiterated that Army support would of necessity be limited because of the company's decision to film in the Philippines.[98]

The decision to film *Hamburger Hill* in the Philippines limited the Army's ability to provide assistance.

Ultimately, Baruch's office worked with the services there to procure requested equipment and off-duty personal as extras during the filming, which took place without incident. Fulfilling its obligation, RKO provided a rough cut of *Hamburger Hill* for screening on May 15, 1987, in the Pentagon. Afterward, Maj. Gen. C.D. Bussey, the Army's chief of public affairs, recommended that the Department of Defense approve the movie. He did so "fully aware that this film is generally a realistic and moving, yet an often brutal, portrayal of Americans at war." He did "urge the producers to make two changes. First, the foul language is excessive, often unnecessary, and needs to be toned down. Second, the scene in the steam bath should be cut. The scene's explicit sexual foreplay far overshadows the thrust of the dialogue." Ironically, Bussey was not objecting to the message, but that the nudity and sexual foreplay would detract from the plot development and the sergeants' complaints that the South Vietnamese are not interested in fighting the war.[99]

In addition to his own comments, Bussey included both positive and negative reactions from enlisted soldiers who had also viewed the rough cut and suggested that the filmmakers read them carefully. With virtual unanimity, the men praised the film's technical achievements, especially the sound of the incoming artillery. One man wrote, "In comparison with the movie *Platoon*, *Hamburger Hill* presents a more realistic view of the struggles of combat soldiers in Vietnam. I was particularly pleased with the authenticity of the dialogue." Another observed, "For those Americans who were anti-Vietnam, the movie should make them feel guilty. For the young, that know nothing about Vietnam, this movie displays combat and war without centering around one character to make it his story. It seems more objective. Most importantly, this movie should make those who fought in the Vietnam war proud of what they did do, in spite of the political side of war. The men that are shown in this movie are realistic, human as well as courageous . . . they are dedicated. I left the theater feeling very sad for the soldiers that served in Vietnam although with a renewed respect."[100]

If such comments suggest that Carabatsos and Irvin succeeded in making the movie they had hoped to do, *Hamburger Hill* nevertheless did not engender the same reaction or even controversy that marked the release of *Platoon* and *Full Metal Jacket*. In part, Vietnam was quickly becoming too common a subject, with *Hamburger Hill* the fourth major production about the war in the field to appear in eight months. Whatever the quality of the films that followed *Platoon*, familiarity was bound to create disinterest.

The filmmakers, of course, realized they had to live with the situation and had prepared to answer the inevitable questions. Irvin admitted, "Obviously, I like to be first. I'd be dishonest if I said I didn't. On the other hand, when I was at school running the 400 meters, I was quite often laughed off the blocks, but I frequently won." He had read Stone's screenplay and felt that "the spirit of *Hamburger Hill* was very different from that of *Platoon*" and hoped that the earlier movies would only serve to prepare audiences for his film. More important, he believed he had taken a different focus on the war: "There were things I wanted to remind the audience too. I wanted to show them that the soldiers there were mere kids. They were asked to do unspeakable things in the most appalling battlefield conditions, and yet they retained their humanity. I spent one of the funniest evenings of my life listening to Marines swap jokes as they were waiting for human-wave attacks. What no Vietnam film has shown is that it was virtually a teen-age army there. That was the pathos of it. So, I think *Hamburger Hill* is a celebration of the simple humanity and the simple heroism of these kids in the face of the most horrific conditions." He believed the power of this portrayal came from Carabatsos's firsthand experiences in Vietnam, which he was able to reinforce from his own visit to the war zone: "I'm sure I was asked to do the film because I had been in Vietnam. That didn't entitle me to make the film. Just qualified me to do it."[101]

His experiences enabled Irvin to impart an authenticity to *Hamburger Hill* that neither Francis Coppola nor Stanley Kubrick managed to convey despite their renowned directorial skills. Nevertheless, reviewers did not rush to heap praise on Irvin's story. Vincent Canby, in the *New York Times,* called it "a well-made Vietnam War film that narrows its attention to the men of a single platoon in a specific operation" in much the manner of *Platoon.* Unlike its predecessor, however, he wrote that *Hamburger Hill* "refuses to put its characters and events into any larger frame. It could have been made a week after the conclusion of the operation it recalls, which is both its strength and weakness, depending on how you look at it." Furthermore, he noted that the straightforward, pseudo-documentary style did not comment on whether or not the taking of the hill was worth the high price paid for it. By not taking a position, he suggested that *Hamburger Hill* "may be read in such a way as to seem hawkish."[102]

Canby acknowledged, however, that such a view would "oversimplify the movie to fit one's own politics." He pointed out that the writer and director make "some discomforting points about the antiwar movement at home, which, while directed at the war and political leaders, and not at the men fighting it, did result in ugly experiences for soldiers whose only aim was to survive to come home." Furthermore, the critic observed that none of the soldiers in the film questioned what he is doing in Vietnam: "He's there. That's the only reality that matters. In fear, fatigue and desperation, the men psyche themselves up by repeating, in a kind of auto-brainwashing chorus: 'It don't mean a thing. It don't mean a thing!' The film leaves it up to the audience to decide if the war was, from the start, disastrous and futile, or if it was sabotaged by those same bleeding-heart liberals who figure so prominently in the oeuvre of Sylvester Stallone."[103]

Like Canby, Kevin Thomas in the *Los Angeles Times* saw *Hamburger Hill* as possibly containing a hawkish attack on the anti-Vietnam War movement that ultimately distracted from its antiwar images. He acknowledged that the film "pays heartfelt richly deserved tribute to the young American soldiers who fought so valiantly there." Nevertheless, he complained that the director and writer should have remained "content to honor these men who were prepared to risk their lives in what had become a singularly unpopular war. But they don't trust the soldiers' brave actions to speak for themselves and instead give them a series of preachy, rabble-rousing speeches that add up to a diatribe against the antiwar movement at home rather than an attack on U.S. involvement in the war in the first place." He believed that the problem lay with the filmmakers' unwillingness to "distinguish between cause and effect as those Americans who have simply-mindedly blamed Vietnam on our veterans. A little subtlety would have greatly enhanced *Hamburger Hill's* potential for tragic irony, but the film makers are rigorously dedicated to the proposition that it's impossible to underestimate the intelligence of moviegoers."[104]

The review engendered an immediate reaction from a reader who described the film as "a shocking, vivid portrayal of the bloody assault by American airborne troops on Hill 937" and so "a welcome departure from the long series of blatantly propagandistic films we have been exposed to on the subject of that war." The writer thought the filmmakers were simply telling the story of a battle and of the bitterness of the men who fought it, knowing they were being undercut by vocal elements back home. From this perspective, he criticized Thomas's view that the movie criticized the antiwar movement rather than the war itself: "What a revealing comment on the liberal mind-set then and now! Has he really forgotten who the rabble-rousers were? I sincerely hope that this fine tribute to the American fighting man will find a large audience, so that overdue recognition will come both to the Vietnam veterans and to those who betrayed them."[105]

In fact, to see *Hamburger Hill* as anything but an antiwar statement would require a viewer to ignore virtually everything on the screen, either stated or implicit in the action. The soldiers themselves talk about the futility of the war and of the battle they undertake. The soldiers are counting the days until their tours of duty end. The medic complains about the impersonality of death and impossibility of identifying a G.I. without his dogtags and his face. The filmmakers even include a scene straight out of *Woodstock* with soldiers bathing in a pond along with Vietnamese girls to the music of Country Joe McDonald's "I-Feel-Like-I'm-Fixin'-to-Die Rag." All these images serve only to reinforce the overriding statement of the movie, the absurdity of having to take a meaningless hill at a huge price, only to immediately give it up. Any movie that shows this or any book that describes this must inevitably convey an antiwar statement.

In the Korean War, the U.S. Army took Pork Chop Hill during the final days of the conflict only to prove to the Chinese that the nation was prepared to continue fighting unless they finally agreed to a negotiated settlement. Sy Bartlett, a decorated World War II flier and a producer of several military films, made *Pork Chop Hill* as an antiwar statement. The Army loved the movie because it showed soldiers doing their job in the face of adversity. The Navy loved *Bridges at Toko-Ri* despite the shot of William Holden dead in a ditch because the film demonstrated the power of Navy aircraft carriers. That *Hamburger Hill* became the first major Hollywood production about combat in Vietnam to receive full assistance despite the weight of the antiwar messages remains perhaps the most significant thing about the movie.

It gives the lie to the claim of Oliver Stone and Dale Dye that *Platoon* would have lost its power if the filmmaker had negotiated with the Pentagon for cooperation. The images of combat in *Hamburger Hill* conveyed every bit of the horror of war that Stone infused in his film. The script probably had just as many *fucks* and *shits* as did *Platoon's*. The difference between the two films comes down to one word, balance. In *Hamburger Hill* the soldiers do their jobs in the best way they can. They recognize that if they try to fight in a drunken or drug-induced haze, they will not have the alertness needed to survive in the jungles. To be sure, some of the officers demonstrate an incompetence or disinterest in their men and the job at hand. But—unlike the portrayal presented in *Platoon*—other officers provide the leadership necessary to carry out the job at hand. If the Army did not like the portrayal of the whorehouses and the soldiers' consorting with prostitutes, at least the service recognized that sex existed in the theater of operations as a normal part of life and did not interfere with the job at hand.

Just as important, the Army and the Defense Department had come to recognize that Hollywood was now going to make Vietnam movies and that supporting them would give the military leverage in creating more accurate portrayals. Filmmakers had come to the realization that if they needed assistance, they would have to provide some balance in their stories. However, the reality remained that no combat story about Vietnam could portray the military in a positive light and that no movie about the war could benefit the military. *Hamburger Hill* also had a message for Hollywood: too much of a good thing could quickly dull the interest in Vietnam. *Platoon* had become such a success because it tapped an audience waiting for a realistic Vietnam movie and because reviewers more often than not touted the film as the first great movie about the war. By the time *Hamburger Hill* reached the theaters eight months later, people needed a respite from the war, whatever the quality of the film. Whether subsequent stories would attract audiences on their merit remained to be seen.

27 Vietnam: Balanced Portrayals

COULD A COMEDY SET IN THE WAR ZONE make a comment about the American experience in Vietnam? By the late 1980s, had enough time passed for people to be willing or able to find humor in the midst of death and destruction? Should filmmakers even consider injecting laughter into war. To be sure, as *Gardens of Stone* showed, gallows humor became necessary for the survival of members of the burial units at Arlington National Cemetery. However, *Good Morning, Vietnam* took an entirely different approach to the war: the filmmakers intended to use Vietnam simply as a stage on which Robin Williams could do his thing—make people laugh.

Members of the production team did try to impart a serious component to their endeavor. Producer Larry Brezner claimed: "From the very inception of the project, the dream was to make *Good Morning, Vietnam* as a metaphor for the war. In early 1965, no one was

taking the Vietnam situation very seriously, but by the end of the year, the number of troops had increased by the thousands. 1965 was the year that Jekyll became Hyde." Director Barry Levinson said he had no intention of making a movie about the war itself: "We've already seen the combat stuff in *Platoon* and *Full Metal Jacket*. So I wanted to give a sense of what it was like in 1965. This movie is on the train tracks heading for the wreck. We're still at a point where we're seeing the scenery along the way." In observing the countryside, the director said, "I was interested in showing soldiers in the city when the escalation was taking place and to be able to show the Vietnamese not as just those that we fought or those that were just the victims, but as just people in a normal environment."[1]

Director Barry Levinson wanted *Good Morning, Vietnam* to show soldiers in the city during escalation and the Vietnamese as more than just the enemy or just victims.

Certainly the filmmakers had noble intentions. To fully appreciate the impact of the war on the Vietnamese people required images of the civilians "in a normal environment." Gen. Edwin Simmons, director of Marine history and museums and a veteran of the war, thought *Good Morning, Vietnam* "captured Vietnam much better than *Platoon.*" But that may be faint praise at best. Vietnam had precious little normality before or after American forces arrived. More to the point, the vehicle Brezner and Levinson used to create their metaphor had virtually no basis in the reality or even the surrealism of Vietnam. To be sure, the film had at its center a real person, Adrian Cronauer. A disk jockey of some notoriety on Armed Forces Vietnam Network (AFVN), Cronauer had written a story about his experiences, which became the starting point for the screenplay. Nevertheless, in the end, *Good Morning, Vietnam* became only the stage on which Robin Williams performed one of his extended comedy routines.[2]

On that level, *Time* called the movie "the best military comedy since *M*A*S*H* disbanded." Richard Schickel explained that the film "is not afraid to work the extremes. Sometimes it is on the edge of hysteria. At others it can approach the fringe of sentiment. But wherever it stands, it is sure-footed and strong-minded—no easy laughs, no easy tears." According to the reviewer, Williams makes the whole thing work because of his "confidence" with the role. Throughout, he creates monologues on the nature of the escalating war, turning reality into comic relief. Ultimately, "compassion and panic invade his routines," according to Schickel, who commended Levinson for his ability to wire "comic asides to a delay fuse." He says that all of *Good Morning, Vietnam* works on this principle: "You may be out on the sidewalk before you realize that these are not just broadcasts. They represent the confused voices of all America registering shock as solid-seeming ground turns to quagmire. You may be all the way home before you realize you may have seen not just the comedy (and the comic performance) of the year, but just possibly the most insinuatingly truthful movie yet about Viet Nam."[3]

Vietnam, of course, contained an infinite variety of truths. *Good Morning, Vietnam* may provide an approximation of the truth for some people. Nevertheless, whatever judgment audiences might render on the quality of the comedy and Williams's performance, truthfulness and historical accuracy will never be considered the strong points of *Good Morning, Vietnam*. The film does not in any way portray how Armed Forces Radio and Television Service operated in Vietnam. Likewise, its representation of the military command-and-control structure bears about as much resemblance to reality as the portrayal of the chain of command in *The Boys in Company C*. Cronauer himself later observed that the film did not represent anything he had done on AFVN radio during his full tour of duty in Saigon from May 1965 to April 1966. Moreover, only in the vaguest way did the movie depict any of his other experiences in Vietnam: "Robin did a great job, too. Am I that funny? No way! He doesn't sound like me. He doesn't talk like me. I wouldn't even try to do that stuff." When asked why the filmmakers even bothered to use his name, Cronauer could only answer, "It beats me."[4]

Insights about Vietnam, of course, can come from comedy just as well as from more serious-minded films. But if *Good Morning, Vietnam* has anything to say about the nature of the American experience in Vietnam, it does so very subtly and from some inner truth rather than the historical record. Most likely, any comment about the war that audiences found in the movie had arrived by chance rather than from the filmmakers' research about Vietnam or Armed Forces Radio and Television. More precisely, any message about the war resulted from the joint creativity of Levinson and Williams and particularly from the actor's ad-libbing talents. According to coproducer Mark Johnson, Cronauer's character provided Williams with "the perfect role." He explained: "Nobody else works with the inventiveness, the quickness and the zaniness of Robin Williams. When he sat down in

Playing disc jockey Adrian Cronauer, comedian Robin Williams ad-libbed something new on virtually every take.

the control booth to do the scenes involving Cronauer's broadcasts, we just let the cameras roll. He managed to create something new for every single take."⁵

Audiences came to see that inventiveness, not to receive a lesson about the nature of the Vietnam War. As a result, despite a fine supporting cast, *Good Morning, Vietnam* remained little more than a one-man tour de force. That fact further served to limit the ability of the movie to provide insights into the war. *Daily Variety* observed: "Although the film is set in Vietnam in 1965, at the very moment when the 'police action' is about to explode into a full-fledged war, the fighting seems to take a backseat to Williams' joking. Instead of the disk jockey being the eyes and ears of the events around him, a barometer of the changes about to happen, Williams is a totally self-contained character, and despite numerous topical references, his comedy turns in on itself rather than opening on the scene outside."⁶

If *Good Morning, Vietnam* failed to look outward to the reality of what was happening in Saigon in 1965, its box-office success did contribute to Hollywood's renewed interest in the war as a suitable subject. However, like *Platoon, Good Morning, Vietnam* did not help to ensure that the subsequent films about the war, whatever their dramatic quality, would return a profit to their backers. Yet, the movies that continued to appear provided more complex images of the nature of the Vietnam experience and so became better able to probe the war's enduring impact on the American people.

A real person also inspired *Bat-21*. In this case, Lt. Col. Iceal Hambleton, an Air Force navigator shot down on a reconnaissance mission over South Vietnam on April 2, 1972, and the lone survivor of the electronic jamming aircraft's six-man crew, became the object of the largest rescue operation in U.S. military history. Based on Lt. Col. William Anderson's 1980 book of the same name, the film almost completely fictionalized Hambleton's odyssey through the Vietnam countryside. Nor did it convey the full scope of the rescue effort in which eleven men actually died or explain that the rescue itself had as much to do with the way Americans fight their wars as it did with the fate of one man.⁷

Instead, *Bat-21* portrayed only Gene Hackman in his typical aging hero performance as an out-of-shape intelligence officer who gets shot down while on a busman's holiday from his office. He has experienced the war only from thirty thousand feet, from maps, and from recon photos, and has never seen the results of the missions he has flown or plotted. Now, with only six months until retirement, he comes face to face with the enemy and the realities of the destructiveness of the American military might in Vietnam and of war itself. At the expense of accuracy, the filmmakers portray Hambleton as a top military strategist too valuable to fall into the enemy's hands and so make him the subject of a massive rescue effort. In fact, the real Hambleton differed in no way from other downed fliers, nether more nor less valuable than any other American. By this time, however, rescuing their comrades had become the *de facto* primary mission for the Air Force, Marine, and Navy aircrews still fighting in Southeast Asia. This reality drove the huge effort to rescue Hambleton and two other downed fliers whom the movie does not mention.

During his trek through the Vietnamese countryside to safety, Hambleton receives support by radio from Birddog, a spotter pilot, who early on swears to rescue the downed flier. Actually a composite of several of the colonel's would-be rescuers, Danny Glover's black captain character, who serves as Hambleton's unseen friend, has become bitter at being passed over for promotion, suspecting his color as the cause. In fact, Birddog has always marched to his own drummer, surviving in the military as long as he has because of his competence, which he now uses to the fullest as he flies over South Vietnam, leading Hambleton to safety. In the course of his trek, the colonel becomes a party to an ill-fated rescue attempt in which American fighter-bombers destroy a village. Wanting to avoid further killing, he sets out for safety alone with only a voice from the sky to encourage his progress. Along the way, however, he kills a Vietnamese peasant in self-defense because he cannot communicate his desire to avoid a confrontation. Ultimately, Birddog steals a helicopter and effects Hamilton's rescue.

Given the story, the Air Force quickly embraced the script when it first arrived in the Pentagon, in February 1984. The service advised Don Baruch on March 5 that the screenplay "is an excellent, dramatic account of a true incident that occurred in Vietnam. *Bat-21* is a fine depiction of the sincere concern Air Force people have for a fellow blue suiter in need and the dedication and professionalism employed to give assistance." Consequently, the Public Affairs Office recommended that the Pentagon give support once the filmmakers provided a detailed list of needs. Baruch informed Hanna Productions that his office would approve the script, "providing the racial comments are deleted from the hospital sequence. . . . In our opinion, these lines are gratuitous, having no plot significance." He said the Pentagon believed the picture would benefit the military and hoped that the public would find it "exciting and intriguing."[8]

Nevertheless, the road from approved script to approved movie contained many obstacles. By 1987, when the project was close to shooting, the Air Force found unacceptable changes in the script. In particular, the service expressed concern "about the scenes surrounding the bombing of the civilian village. We feel changing the target to a military one is appropriate." As a result, the Air Force recommended that "overall approval be withheld contingent on the production company's willingness to accept the proposed changes," although approving release of stock footage.[9]

Ultimately, the Air Force did assist in the production after the filmmakers agreed to make the changes. However, when the service's Public Affairs Office in Los Angeles screened a rough cut of *Bat-21* in January 1988, it found problems. Acknowledging that it was "a powerful, dramatic film containing all the elements which we hope lead to a large commercial success," the office advised the producer that three scenes would cause problems when he screened the movie in the Pentagon. These included showing Birddog drinking beer shortly before taking off, the destruction of the peasant village, and the use of F-16 footage (the fighter did not go into service until 1978). Although the filmmakers eliminated the F-16 scene, they could not or would not remove the other two areas of contention, and the Air Force declined the producer's offer to give the service a screen credit.[10]

In fact, *Bat-21* did contain an exciting story that reflected well on the Air Force. Colonel Hambleton's experiences on the ground certainly made an antiwar statement. Nevertheless, such things happened, and his response to the events showed him as a compassionate, concerned officer, someone in whom the Air Force could take pride. However, despite its balanced portrayal and good reviews, audiences ignored the film. Rita Kempley, in the *Washington Post*, put her finger on the problem: "Though well made, *Bat-21* is no *Platoon*. It doesn't pack a wallop, though it does have something to say in its old-fashioned, rather wishy-washy way—War is heck."[11]

And it had a long reach all the way back to America, as *Heroes, Coming Home, Cease Fire*, and *Gardens of Stone* had illustrated. Although seemingly a detective story with only a limited military connection, *The Presidio* was to also show how a distant war, a long time ago, still reverberated on America. Except for a climactic, Vietnam-movie-like, bloody shoot-out that provides the denouement of the mystery, the film used the Army only as a framework in which to tell its story. The high speed car chases and steamy, intense sexual couplings serve to create the ambience in which the hero tries to solve an on-base murder. Even though *The Presidio* drew its title from the Army base sited in the shadow of the Golden Gate Bridge, the location mattered little in the development of the tale and said even less about the service or the two-hundred-year-old installation. The filmmakers used the locale only to give authenticity to the stage on which *The Presidio* unfolds. The Army ceremonies, the Presidio's museum, administrative buildings, cemetery, roads and grounds, as well as its uniformed personnel acting as extras all help to transport audiences to a place they would otherwise probably not have seen, even on a visit to San Francisco. In the end, however, as *Variety* observed in its review, the film "is even less about the Presidio than *The Big Easy* was about New Orleans."[12]

Nevertheless, the producers took their story to the Pentagon and received full cooperation from the Army. To demonstrate their desire to receive assistance, they showed up en masse in Don Baruch's office. He later recalled that the six or eight people constituted the largest studio delegation ever to visit the Defense Department to discuss a project. However, even though he wanted to film on the Presidio, director Peter Hyams did not in any way consider that he was making a movie about the Army. Nor did he have any intention of creating an Army recruiting poster or glamorizing the military. Instead, he saw the base as simply providing an exotic, scenic environment for an action-adventure detective story with a requisite love story to complicate matters. Furthermore he thought viewers would be "stretching" things to see *The Presidio* as having a connection with the Vietnam War.[13]

Despite the director's disclaimer, *The Presidio* did have explicit connections to the Vietnam War and its impact on the American people. Sean Connery, as the provost marshal of the Presidio, and Jack Warden, as a retired sergeant major, reminisce on several occasions about the war and how it has affected them. The bad guys established their friendship there, and the film clearly suggests that the war created in them their propensity for illicit behavior. The *Variety* re-

The Presidio, located near the Gold Gate Bridge, served merely as a backdrop for the film of the same name.

viewer thought the concluding shoot-out in a water bottling plant became "as hairy as the swamps of 'Nam.'" And Michael Wilmington, the *Los Angeles Times* reviewer, described *The Presidio* as a "would-be moral fable interspersed with profanity and gun-fights, a post-Vietnam conciliation saga."[14]

In any event, *The Presidio* never rises above its genre and contains no overt message about the war or the military. Still, the producers' desire to use the Presidio suggested that Hollywood had returned to the good old days when filmmakers regularly used military installations to provide the framework for their stories. The Army's willingness to support a film in which both a high-ranking officer and a retired sergeant major take part in a smuggling ring illustrated that the service had come to the point of acknowledging that such things did happen. Better than anything else, that recognition demonstrated how much the wounds of Vietnam had healed.

However, not until sixteen years after the United States withdrew from Vietnam did Hollywood finally provide a graphic portrayal of the true hell that the American military imparted to the Vietnamese civilians. Based on an actual 1966 incident and Daniel Lang's short 1969 book of the same name, *Casualties of War* detailed how a five-man Army reconnaissance patrol abduct, rape, and murder a Vietnamese peasant girl. One soldier, given the pseudonym Sven Eriksson in the book and movie, refuses to join in the gang rape and reports his comrades' criminal actions to his superiors. When they choose not to follow up his report, Eriksson tells his story to a chaplain, who goes to the Army's Criminal Investigations Division. The resulting probe leads to a court-martial in March 1967 and the conviction of the four soldiers. The men ultimately have their sentences reduced or dismissed, whereas Eriksson, still fearing retribution, lives under an assumed name somewhere in the Midwest.

Director Brian De Palma recalled that he wanted to make a movie about the incident from the time he read Lang's story, when it first appeared in the October 18, 1969, *New Yorker*. Initially, another filmmaker had optioned the story but succeeded only in getting a script written. In 1979 playwright David Rabe suggested that De Palma resurrect the project and told the director he would like to write the script. But it was not until Vietnam became a viable subject after the release of *Platoon* and De Palma had made the 1987 critically acclaimed box-office success *The Untouchables* that the director was able to undertake *Casualties of War*.[15]

To De Palma, the story had "all the elements of a classical tragedy, and that's what makes it exciting and unique." More than that, the director believed that *Casualties of War* "encapsules our involvement in Vietnam in a simple, dramatic story." In regard to the American intervention itself, De Palma felt that the story "showed that we were over there basically fighting ourselves instead of the enemy." Perhaps more to the point, the film contains the singular metaphor for the inferno that the United States inflicted on Vietnam, one far more truthful and powerful than the Russian roulette in *The Deer Hunter*. Just as the four soldiers raped and murdered the innocent peasant girl, American forces in Vietnam ravished the countryside and killed its people, both friends and enemies. Similarly, Eriksson's decision to oppose the actions of his comrades and ultimately report their crimes symbolizes the dilemma that Americans faced in deciding whether or not to support their government's actions in Vietnam.

In any case, *Casualties of War* uses a historical event to make its comment about man in war and particularly what combat in Vietnam did to the soldiers forced to fight in a conflict that seemed to have no meaning. In so doing, the film raised the question of whether the Vietnam War differed from other wars in which Americans had fought. U.S. soldiers

Sean Penn and Michael J. Fox in *Casualties of War.*

have, unfortunately, raped women abroad during and after other wars. Hollywood has even portrayed such actions in *Town Without Pity* and *The Dirty Dozen,* among other movies. However, *Casualties of War* conveys the message that somehow Vietnam put an additional stress on the Americans who fought there. Otherwise, how does one explain Sean Penn's Sergeant Meserve suddenly becoming a rapist so close to his departure from the combat zone?

For the most part, however, De Palma allows the story to unfold without sermonizing. At its heart, the film captures the dilemma that Ericksson faces. If he tries to intercede in the kidnapping and rape, the other members of the squad might well kill him. Ultimately, Eriksson has only one recourse if he wants to save the girl—kill his comrades. Does this represent a viable option? Is one peasant girl's life worth four American lives? Whatever his feelings toward the girl and his desperate desire to save her, Eriksson obviously did not think so, or at the least, he could not act. Nevertheless, unlike the hippie veteran in *Kinflicks,* who also did not choose to pull "a John Wayne," Eriksson did not join in the rape. But did his refusal to bend to peer pressure and his exposure of the atrocity absolve him from guilt? After all, what reason did the United States have to intervene in Vietnam if not to protect the lives of all the innocent civilians?

In a most direct way, then, *Casualties of War* raised questions about the nature of the American intervention in Vietnam, its impact on the people, and the value of individual lives. More than that, through the violation and murder of one peasant girl, De Palma reminded his audiences of the ultimate irony of the American experience in Vietnam. To carry out the government's professed goal of saving Vietnam from Communist domination, the U.S. military wrought untold destruction on the small peasant nation. Eriksson's failure to stop the rape and murder also symbolized the inability of the antiwar movement to stop the conflict in a timely fashion. Unlike the heavy-handed Russian roulette metaphor Michael Cimino used in *The Deer Hunter* to make his statement, De Palma's use of an actual incident to comment on the war gave *Casualties of War* that much more power. The peasant girl had died, her would-be protector lived, still in fear for his own life, and her killers walked free, whatever guilt they still might feel.

For the stage on which to create his morality play, De Palma took his cast and crew to Thailand, which looked like Vietnam and came cheaply. Once there, the technical advisors, retired Army major Art Smith Jr. and Michael Stokey, a former Marine correspondent in Vietnam, put the actors through basic training to familiarize them with the weapons, the rations, and the uniforms. However, Smith said he intended to do more than make the actors look like soldiers: "Within this miniature basic training structure, we emphasized leadership, because *Casualties of War* is about leadership. And out of this shared experience came a bonding process between each of the two squads we had set up, mirroring the relationship in the movie." Michael J. Fox agreed, saying that apart from learning how to act like soldiers, the training was to "knock me down a peg and teach me how to be a private. I became Private Eriksson. It helped enforce that feeling of being part of a group, of having a certain designation in terms of rank. And that's something that you really can't prepare yourself for as an actor."[16]

The basic training and the Vietnam-like ambience enabled De Palma to elicit from Sean Penn and Michael J. Fox realistic performances as soldiers experiencing hell on earth. Of course, the Army would have preferred that this particular hell not appear on movie screens. However, the service did not have the opportunity to ameliorate the images because the filmmakers went to Thailand and never sought assistance. Yet, to a significant degree, *Casualties of War* contained a balanced portrayal. Four of the soldiers took part in an abominable atrocity, but the fifth acted responsibly in an impossible situation. He did not shoot his fellow soldiers, but he did report the crime at considerable risk to himself. Yet his actions and their portrayal did not please everyone.

John Wheeler, chairman of the committee that built the Vietnam Memorial, believed that "every dollar spent to see this film is a knife in the heart of some vet, his kids or others who love him." He told reporters at a press conference he called on August 23, 1989, that the film "depicts vets as morally insensitive, barely competent soldiers with cynical and cowardly officers." Wheeler claimed that *Casualties of War* "is a lie about what we were really like in Vietnam. By focusing on a rape, De Palma declines to tell the greater truth, that in Vietnam the overwhelming number of us were decent, (and) built orphanages, roads, hospitals and schools."[17]

At the same news conference, Marc Leepson, speaking on behalf of the Vietnam Veterans of America, observed that recently Hollywood movies and television shows had been "depicting the war more realistically, less sensationally, and showing vets who are not just cartoon characters and cliched stereotypes." However, Leepson said that in De Palma's film "the cinematic image of those who fought in Vietnam has taken a giant step backward. The unspoken message of *Casualties of War* is that the norm in Vietnam was rape and murder and that only a brave handful of GIs acted humanely. That message is 180 degrees from the truth."[18]

Wheeler and Leepson might want people to believe their view of reality. Like the Pentagon, they undoubtedly wished they could erase from the historical record what William Calley and his men did at My Lai. They would also have wanted to deny that an American special-forces team had summarily executed, "terminated with extreme prejudice," in the official jargon, a suspected Vietcong spy. However, in *Casualties of War,* De Palma was portraying an actual historical event, and he had intended to make an antiwar film, not an anti-American polemic. As he pointed out, he did not actually portray the rape: "I could have had a highly [commercial] movie. I could have had the vengeance scene—Eriksson shooting down the entire patrol after the rape. That's what the audience wants at that moment."[19]

In contrast, David Halberstam, author of *The Best and the Brightest,* said that despite De Palma's reputation for gratuitous violence in such films as *The Untouchables, Casualties of War* contained rather understated images of what had happened. In spite of that, he found the film "exceptionally faithful" to Lang's story: "The liberties De Palma takes with the essential facts of the case . . . are completely within the bounds of cinematic license. If anything, he has worked hard to rein in his tendency to be graphic." The director explained, "I wanted, if at all possible, to make it simple. The Lang piece is really in the best sense a short story and I love its terseness. I did not want to make a war movie in the conventional sense. The danger is in overdoing it."[20]

To De Palma, Vietnam remained "the scar which refuses to heal. It's like an abused child—the damage from the abuse never goes away and years later the child is still damaged and yet he can't explain why he's damaged." The director said he had wanted to make a film based on Lang's book for a long time because he thought it contained all "the craziness that made the war so different." More than that, he saw it "not so much as a Vietnam film as a movie about a larger moral issue: "The dilemma is there the moment you look at it—what would I have done in this situation? Would I have had the moral courage to act as Eriksson did? Would I be the person I like to think I am? Who knows what the pulls and loyalties are in a situation like that. I challenge anyone to be confident

Casualties of War forced viewers to ask the question, "What would I have done?"

of what he would do in that situation. But it is about morality—even in something like Vietnam, there is a moment where you can't blame the war for your actions, you have to accept responsibility for your behavior. That's what the movie is all about. That's why I jumped at the chance to do it."[21]

Halberstam thought the country had "badly needed" films like *Casualties of War:* "Now, slowly, we are coming to terms with the Vietnam War, and this movie is an important benchmark. We do not, in general, live any longer in a country where there is a boy next door, but if we did, he could be Michael J. Fox, who in *Casualties,* takes us through this particular American agony." He thought the film "tells what Vietnam did to some

of the young men who fought there, and what it does to the thin membrane which in any society separates decency from indecency." In the end, he thought that of all the Vietnamese who died in the war, "the senseless killing of one, a young woman, a noncombatant stolen one morning from her home, and raped and murdered—can there be anything more terrible?—is, 23 years later, recalled as an act of witness for us all."[22]

If that rape became the metaphor for what the United States did to Vietnam, then the wound that paralyzed Ron Kovic may well stand as the ultimate metaphor for what the Vietnam War did to the American people. In portraying that impact on one symbolic person, *Born on the Fourth of July* made an enduring cinematic statement about the American experience in Vietnam. Oliver Stone's script, which received Marine approval for cooperation in 1979 and then disappeared for ten years, finally became a movie in 1989. In it, Stone managed to incorporate both combat and the home front into one unified, if flawed, whole. We see Kovic growing up enamored of John Wayne and the Marines, accepting John Kennedy's call for service to the country, enthusiastically going off to Vietnam, receiving an irreparable wound, returning home to a nation torn apart by the war, and finding official disinterest in his physical and mental condition. How Kovic adjusts to his condition becomes the core of Stone's story.

Filming Oliver Stone's
Born on the Fourth of July.

Tom Cruise, who became one with his character, portrayed Kovic as the ultimate survivor, finding as much peace as anyone in his situation could, taking on the system and trying to make it more responsive to its citizens. The original screenplay differed little in substance from the completed movie, albeit with less attention to the military aspects of Kovic's life, ironically deleting the training sequence at Parris Island that had caused the Marines and General Brewer so much concern. Similar portrayals in *The Boys in Company C, An Officer and a Gentleman,* and *Full Metal Jacket* had simply rendered Kovic's introduction to the Marines redundant. Instead, Stone explained, "I tried to put that same spirit in the wrestling coach scenes, that there was the competitive aspects of American society in sports as well as the Marine Corps."[23]

Stone did not consider going to the Pentagon for help to create the film's two combat sequences: "Our experiences were so negative on *Platoon* that it never occurred to me to even bother. DoD had sent me a letter criticizing the script and describing to me all the changes that would have had to be made. I realized how unrealistic that was. It was totally foreign to my experience—what they were saying." In any case, *Born on the Fourth of July* focused on what happened to the wounded Kovic once he returned home. There, he found a government that showed little apparent sympathy for his physical and mental plight. How he responded to the disinterest, or perhaps normal bureaucratic incompetency, becomes the heart of the film. As Stone tells the story, the war does not change Kovic. The peace does.[24]

At the time he began writing the screenplay for *Born on the Fourth of July* in Paris during the summer of 1977, based on his first meeting with Kovic rather than on the book, Stone remained a virtually unknown Vietnam vet, trying to find himself like so many of his comrades in arms. *Midnight Express,* for which he wrote the Oscar-winning screenplay, had not yet appeared, and he had had no success in selling the screenplay for *Platoon.* Stone's name never appeared in any of the correspondence between the producers of the *Born on the Fourth of July* project and the Pentagon when they submitted their request for Marine support in the spring of 1978. Stone himself recalled that he knew nothing about the subsequent negotiations: "I was simply screenplay-writing which means I tried to avoid all the production problems that were going on all around me." Moreover, neither producer Martin Bregman nor any of the other people involved with the project had told him that any changes in the script resulted from Marine requests.[25]

Stone later on expressed surprise that the Marines had objected so strongly to the training sequence: "Really. That's their major issue! It's a minor point. I'm amazed at their opacity." Instead, he said he would have thought they would have objected to the scene in which Kovic reported to his commanding officer that he had accidentally killed one of his own men and the major told him to forget about it. As Stone saw it, the officer was instituting a cover up: "That would obviously be a huge point of much more importance to the story." He also thought the Marines and the Pentagon would have objected to the script "on overall atmospheric grounds, that it would not make the military look good because the military, in fact, did not function as well as it should have in Vietnam. The fact is, we lost the war. Who wants to make a film about losing the war? That would be their major point I would think."[26]

Of course, at that time, the Marines had begun the process of reevaluating their position on cooperation with Hollywood, and apparently unbeknownst to Stone, they had agreed to allow the filmmakers to shoot the training sequence at Parris Island only a few days before the financing package for the film fell apart. On his part, Stone had developed "a very close attachment to the material in so far as I had been in Vietnam" both as a civilian and as a soldier, and he "totally empathized with Ron Kovic" and his story. Once he had read the book, the writer followed its format of weaving in and out of time, beginning and ending with Kovic's paralyzing wound. But when Stone returned to Paris to work on the screenplay with William Friedkin, the project's original director, he agreed to put the story in chronological order, beginning with Kovic's early life. The writer said he loved the early sequence: "It's about growing up in a small town in America. What it's like to believe in everything you believe in and go off to fight a war and the war destroys him in part and he comes back to the same America and it's no longer the same America."[27]

Stone realized the town has changed; the people have changed; the friends have changed; and most important, the United States has changed: "The story is about what happens. It's a bit like *Best Years of Our Lives* at that point. And then it's about the boy's resurrection, the boy's redemption, the boy's ability to come back from the depth's of despair. That was the approach we took. It's a corny saga, I suppose. But it's good corn." Perhaps. But, at least on the surface, it resembled *Coming Home,* then in production and scheduled to appear before *Born on the Fourth of July* would even go before the camera.[28]

According to Stone, he had written his script before he read a script of *Coming Home* and expressed his concern to the producer that the two stories resembled each other. Bregman discounted the similarities and convinced Stone that his story would not only make "a greater film," but would be made. However, while the project was still in preproduction, the producer, Stone, and Al Pacino, who was slated to play Kovic, saw *Coming Home;* and Stone immediately realized that Fonda's film had hurt the chances for producing *Born on the Fourth of July* at that time. His fears proved correct when studio executives told Bregman that they didn't want to make another film on the same subject, particularly when *Coming Home* did not rack up great profits during its initial release.[29]

Given the plethora of Vietnam stories that began to appear, Kovic's story remained in limbo for almost ten years. Then, Stone's success directing *Platoon* and the interest that Tom Cruise manifested in the project following his success in *Top Gun* provided the impetus for restarting production. Cruise thought Stone had produced "one of the most powerful scripts I have ever read. I knew I wanted to do it ten pages into it. . . . It's as true a story as ever told about the effects of the Vietnam War on America—and on the times America lived through." He did not, however, want audiences to consider it as simply another Vietnam movie: "It's a film which tells us that we just can't blindly trust the leaders of this country, that we ourselves must search and find out where we stand and what we believe in. It's not easy finding the truth about *anything*."[30]

In contrast to *Top Gun*, which Cruise called a "joyride" and a "simple fairy tale," he thought *Born on the Fourth of July* "portrayed real people and real events" and was "a movie that *had* to be made." He felt that "Ron Kovic could have been me. I was interested in the fact that I didn't understand a lot of this—the whole thing of confusing the war with the

Oliver Stone directing Tom Cruise and Ivan Kane in *Born on the Fourth of July*.

soldier. It's innocence lost and true courage found." He said he had talked with many people who lived during the war who had "had a sense of commitment to our community, country, the Pledge of Allegiance. It was a time of blind commitment to our Government. It was very innocent and naive. It was easy to manipulate people into committing to something like Vietnam." He saw Kovic making that sort of commitment: "Oliver went to Vietnam to be John Wayne. . . . he was going to be a hero. Kovic was too." Instead, Cruise said he and his comrades found Vietnam "a brutal, ugly, confusing experience. It was not *Top Gun*. It was none of that." To compound the problem, those who came home found only "contempt."[31]

Cruise also saw the film as focusing on more than just coming back from the war: "It's also a personal struggle with his body and his manhood, his penis and his balls. That's what Vietnam was. It took away our power. The country became impotent and embarrassed." As a result, the actor thought the United States had become a greater nation through its defeat. Likewise, he saw Kovic having to "re-evaluate what it is to be a man" when he can no longer have an erection: "The whole notion now is that a man is a man because of his penis or because of the size of his penis or how many girls he can lay. For any man, the thought of losing his penis is frightening on so many levels. Having children, having pleasures, having what it is that defines the male."[32]

Born on the Fourth of July, then, became a story of Ron Kovic's search for answers. How well it accomplished its goals would depend on how well Stone transferred his script to the motion picture screen and how well the performance he elicited from Cruise created a believable and sympathetic Kovic. Those who had not read the book or who knew nothing about the real Kovic and his life undoubtedly found in the movie a powerful and moving story of a man who loved his country and suffered immensely in return for his unquestioning patriotism. If Stone had been telling a fictional story that combined some combat, some anti-Vietnam protest, and some returning but damaged veterans, his film might well have provided the final word about what the war did to the American people. In fact, the messages Cruise saw in *Born on the Fourth of July* would have perhaps been better served by a fictional story, like *Coming Home*, that allowed the tragedy of a paralyzed veteran to stand on its own merits.

Unfortunately, Oliver Stone's bent for seeking the dramatic and ignoring the balance, for rewriting history to create controversy in order to promote his work, may well have distracted from the very real tragedy inherent in Kovic's story. Stone acknowledged that how far a writer can deviate from history and still maintain credibility remains "a delicate question and there is no simple answer to that. I would say that the overall objective would not be to violate the spirit of the time." He argued that writers "have to take dramatic licence in terms of condensing or compositing characters or events. But I think the key is not to violate the spirit of the time." In response to the accusations that he had added things to and subtracted things from *Born on the Fourth of July*, Stone did not think that "overall I violated the spirit of the coming home experience."[33]

Most writers and even critics have maintained that capturing the essence of an event

Oliver Stone in a "Vietnamese jungle" in Mexico during the filming of *Born on the Fourth of July.*

usually is more important than portraying the factual history. Nevertheless, in *Born on the Fourth of July,* Stone clearly exceeded the limits of dramatic license, apparently assuming audiences would not know or care. In his book, Kovic makes much of the impact that the death of President Kennedy had on him when he was seventeen. Do viewers know or care, or does it even matter if Stone uses the 1961 inauguration at the impetus for Kovic's patriotism and love of his country? Perhaps not. And people may not even notice that the actor who plays Kovic as a ten-year-old baseball player in 1956 appears in the next scene as the fifteen-year-old Kovic, who runs across the lawn on a bright, sunny, fall day into his house to watch President Kennedy's inauguration. Perhaps not. However, some people might remember that the 1961 swearing in ceremony in Washington took place on one of the coldest inauguration days ever. If they did not remember, they certainly could see the cold breath rising from President Kennedy's mouth in the newsreel footage Stone inserted onto the TV screen. At best, viewers might conclude that Stone had simply not wanted to hire an older actor and match the cinematic season with the historic reality. At worst, the sequence showed that the director did not care about what he put on the screen. And if audiences think this, they might choose to believe that the director had no commitment to recreating even a semblance of Kovic's life, however dramatic it might appear on the screen.

In truth, Stone showed about as much concern with accurately portraying Kovic's post-Vietnam experiences as he had had with Kovic's age, the calender, and the weather. The distortions, misrepresentations, and outright fabrications that constitute the dramatic core of Kovic's story may well render the message invalid. In his book, Kovic does not describe any meeting with the family of the Marine that he may have accidentally killed. The original script does contain a meeting with the parents at their home in Venus, Georgia, but Kovic does not tell them he did the killing or even that it resulted from friendly fire. However, in the movie, the confession becomes the pivotal event in Kovic's rehabilitation. Stone explained, "I think it was necessary for Ron Kovic to clarify his private demons, to exorcize himself from his private demons for him to operate in the political arena. He could not go on to being a public figure without having dealt with his private life. He had to exorcize his personal demons."[34]

Without question, the meeting provided a dramatic catharsis for the cinematic Kovic. However, it never happened. Venus, Georgia, does not exist, and Kovic later admitted that the pilgrimage depicted in the movie only dramatized a recurring nightmare he had experienced over the years. Moreover, the historic Kovic clearly survived and entered the public realm without the confession Stone put in his mouth. In addition, showing Kovic putting his personal need to cleanse himself before the probable pain of the "mythic" parents places the real and cinematic Kovic in a very bad light.[35]

Stone acknowledged that the scene portrayed Kovic acting selfishly: "But I think that the movie tries to show that he was in such pain that he had no choice, that he knew what he was doing would hurt them. But it was hurting him more. It is a case of do you tell the truth or do you not tell the truth." He explained that the parents "after a period of time" will return to their belief that their son died patriotically for his country in a war despite what Kovic tells them. Consequently, Stone argues, "So I think that ultimately Ron did the right thing because he couldn't bear it anymore personally. He could not bear it. He could not function." In fact, Kovic had not visited the parents. Like the metaphor of the Russian roulette in *The Deer Hunter*, which had no basis in fact and so lost its power to make a comment about the human condition, the portrayal of Kovic's "confession" lacked the ability to even convey the "spirit" of the event. In fabricating the meeting, Stone far exceeded the limits of dramatic license, and his justification for rewriting Kovic's autobiography served only as a rationalization for his own creative decision.[36]

Perhaps not as significant dramatically, Stone, with some help from his cowriter Kovic, also distorted the birth of Kovic's political radicalism. In his book, Kovic claims that the Kent State shootings caused him to go to a "huge" rally in Washington in May 1970. No such rally took place there at that time protesting Kent State or Cambodia. In *Born on the Fourth of July*, Stone has Kovic visit an hometown girlfriend (who does not appear in his book) at Syracuse University, where he attends an antiwar rally that the police break up.[37]

It never happened. A state senator who did attend the protest recalled: "There was no use of force. The police understood the significance of the demonstration, and their right to demonstrate." A Syracuse policeman stated that the university never called the police to come onto the campus. When informed of the historical reality, a spokesperson for the film claimed that Stone had not meant to depict any specific clash. However, the senator observed: "I don't think maligning a particular police department and misrepresenting a real incident is acceptable in artistic license. The irony is that in showing with sensitivity the injustices suffered by Vietnam War veterans, it is equally insensitive in stereotyping police officers."[38]

By stretching, if not breaking the limits of artistic license, Stone undoubtedly weakened the impact of his images, of Kovic's loss of manhood, of his radicalization, of his efforts to improve his situation and that of his fellow disabled veterans. If the director and his subject had not consciously or unconsciously infused their stories with errors of fact and narrative, *Born on the Fourth of July* would have engendered less controversy and more attention to the very real and important messages Tom Cruise had found in the screenplay. Very likely a fictional movie inspired by Kovic's book rather than one purporting to portray his life would have much better spoken to the issues that he and Stone hoped to raise.

Nevertheless, despite its many errors of fact and distortions of history within its almost two and a half hours, *Born on the Fourth of July* incorporated virtually the entire American experience in Vietnam better than any other film about the war that had appeared up to that time. It revealed the naive patriotism that contributed to America's easy entry into the quagmire of Southeast Asia. Albeit briefly, its combat sequences captured the impossible situation the military faced in fighting a guerrilla war in a distant, agricultural environment. Most importantly, it combined the trauma which the Vietnam War produced for both its participants and the home front in the persona of Tom Cruise's Ron Kovic.

In the end, Cruise's performance became the film's raison d'être and his character the vehicle for conveying the pain and suffering Kovic experienced and overcame. In *Cosmopolitan*, Guy Flatley said Cruise's "depiction of Ron Kovic is an astonishing, seamless achievement. Whoever says they don't make movies about heroes anymore hasn't seen *Born on the Fourth of July*." The *Newsday* reviewer called the film "an extraordinary moving experience. Tom Cruise's portrayal is a shattering piece of work, one of the strongest performances of the year. No movie this year has shaken me or moved me as much as *Born on the Fourth of*

July." And Vincent Canby wrote in the *New York Times:* "Stunning. A film of enormous visceral power with a performance by Tom Cruise that defines everything that is best about the movie. Watching the evolution of his Ron Kovic is both harrowing and inspiring. *Born on the Fourth of July* connects the war of arms abroad with the war of conscience at home."[39]

Born on the Fourth of July thus rendered a valuable service, encapsulating in one film the issues that continue to resonate in any discussion of the American experience in Vietnam. *Flight of the Intruder* had no such intention or pretension. Instead, John Milius used Vietnam simply as the setting for a straightforward movie about naval aviators, little different in tone or focus from the several aircraft carrier movies portraying World War II aerial combat. The film does contain a brief comment about the way the politicians back home were controlling the conduct of the Vietnam War. Nevertheless, it portrays the American fighting man as brave, dedicated, and resourceful. Vietnam becomes just the arena in which the characters perform their duties, not the controversial war that divided the nation. Producer Mace Neufeld claimed it was "not a Vietnam movie, but it takes place during the Vietnam War." The fliers could just as easily have been doing their fighting in World War II or Korea.[40]

Neufeld said he became interested in the story when he read Stephen Coonts's *Flight of the Intruder* and in it "found the best, the most vivid description of bomber flying that I had ever read." In addition, he thought the novel contained "an interesting story, with a great hook, a man unraveling and then going against the Navy code, jeopardizing his own men, and then redeeming himself." Finally, the book, only the second novel that the Naval Institute Press, a publisher of military histories, had released, simply "appealed" to him as a pilot of thirty-five years. He stressed, though, that his film "is totally apolitical. My feeling is that we have been able to distance ourselves from the issues of the Vietnam War."[41]

Flight of the Intruder does not deal with the issues of whether the United States should have become involved in Southeast Asia. Instead, it simply acknowledges that the war was tearing the United States apart and then focuses on the story of men in combat in much the same way as did *Men of the Fighting Lady* and *Bridges at Toko-Ri.* From the Navy's perspective, the film differed not at all from any one of the stories about carrier warfare on which the service had regularly assisted for almost fifty years before the Vietnam war brought a temporary end to Hollywood's relationship with the Navy.

Sending the script to Don Baruch in April 1989, John Horton asked for "review and comment" from the Pentagon and the Navy in anticipation of Paramount's request for assistance in producing the story of naval aviators flying against Vietnam in late 1971. He explained: "The missions are vividly dramatized, the characters realistically portrayed, in a story destined to create extraordinary empathy and involvement of the audiences who will ultimately view the final motion picture film." He claimed that the "enormous appeal" that *Top Gun* engendered "should be recaptured in this stirring Viet Nam drama," which would "contribute positive understanding of the basic tenets of military service. The entire film should provide substantial benefits in the National interest as well as bringing gripping entertainment to the motion picture audiences worldwide."[42]

Any film doing all this certainly would find a favorable response within the Pentagon and the Navy. As expected, the service did find technical and historic inaccuracies with the script, which Mike Sherman compiled at the Navy's Los Angeles Office of Information and sent back to the chief of information on May 2. Among the minor problems, he noted that the dialogue "You're too high" should be changed to "Work it down" or "Fly it down." He also pointed out that the Officers' Club at the Naval Air Station, Cubi Point, in the

Philippines did not have a swimming pool, only a small wading pool for the "touch and goes." More serious, he noted that a conversation about body counts "is not only historically inaccurate for 1972, but would be impossible today as well. First, body count was a feature of the VN war in the South, not of the air war in the North. Second, we did not then and do not now, have the capability to count bodies immediately following an air attack conducted deep inside enemy territory in the daytime or at night." He indicated that instead, the filmmakers would have to use some other more realistic damage assessment, such as the number of buildings or trucks destroyed.[43]

After four pages of similar observations, Sherman reported that the filmmakers were doing an extensive rewrite of the script, which would be done within ten days, and he suggested that the Navy wait to discuss the project "to see what the future holds." Paramount, however, requested that the Navy use the February screenplay to approve assistance, with the understanding that any subsequent versions would incorporate the service's suggestions.

After a review of the problems the Navy had found with the script, Sherman said that Paramount intended to "pull out the stops" in making *Flight of the Intruder* "in an attempt to create another blockbuster 'ala' *Top Gun*." Stating the obvious, he noted that the A-6 Intruder "community can hardly wait to assist, and is avidly supporting this one."[44]

If the Navy agreed to assist on the production, Sherman suggested that Puerto Rico serve as a stand-in for Vietnam, with the service flying in A-6 bombers specifically for the filmmakers. He also recommended that shooting in port and at sea aboard a carrier be done pier side and out of San Diego. He said the studio understood "that this will be wildly expensive and is prepared to foot the bill." He further explained that Paramount had agreed to hire a former Navy pilot with Vietnam combat experience as technical advisor. Given the willingness of the studio to accede to the Navy's requests, Sherman recommended that the Navy approve cooperation and inform Baruch's office of the decision.[45]

At the request of Adm. J.B. Finkelstein, the Navy's chief of information, and with Sherman's memo in hand, the assistant chief of naval operations for air warfare reviewed the script again and offered additional suggestions. In particular, he offered "*the strongest possible objection . . . to the use of marijuana by the hero.* The casual use of an illegal drug by a Navy pilot sends a negative signal throughout the Navy (where it smacks of hypocrisy within the officer Corps), as well as throughout a society which expects its military officer Corps to maintain high standards of personal conduct." He also complained that the "vulgarity of the language used throughout the story is a bit overdone, even considering the environment and conditions of the time." Nevertheless, he wrote that his office "would like to remain actively involved in the movie."[46]

Acting on the memos from Sherman and naval aviation, Admiral Finkelstein advised Phil Strub, who had just replaced Baruch as the Pentagon's liaison with the film industry, that the Navy approved cooperation on *Flight of the Intruder,* on the assumption that the filmmakers would make the suggested changes. Once Strub concurred with the service's chief of information, Sherman informed the producers of the decision and indicated that his office was now assuming coordination of the cooperation. Neufeld praised Paramount for committing itself to finance the film, saying it was "a very courageous decision at the time. Whether it was a wise decision when the movie comes out, we don't know. It is an expensive film. We got the green light on this about three weeks after *Casualties of War* came out and failed." He thought that to go ahead with another Vietnam movie under the circumstances was "an extraordinary move."[47]

Whatever the reasons for the studio's decision, both Neufeld and director John Milius saw the film primarily as an action-adventure movie about men in war, not about the nature of the Vietnam War. The producer said the story "could have happened in several wars," whereas the director thought the film became "a celebration of valor and it is also a celebration of people having loyalties and honor and doing much for each other that they wouldn't necessarily in other situations." In contrast to *Casualties of War*, which rubbed audiences' faces "in this terrible crime that is committed by American soldiers," Milius said that *Flight of the Intruder* "sympathizes with the American soldier and shows him as an honorable person."[48]

Whether the Navy liked the image or simply the opportunity to show the Intruder in action, it proceeded to provide more extensive cooperation than any other movie about naval aviation had received. As the first order of business, the service selected four A-6 Intruders from Whidbey Island Naval Air Station in Washington State to appear in the film's flying sequences and began modifying them to resemble the 1972 version of the attack bomber used in Vietnam. Because of political instability in the Philippines and the threat of hurricanes in Puerto Rico, Paramount chose sites in Georgia and in Hawaii to recreate North Vietnam for the overland flying sequences. On September 25, the three A-6s that had completed their modifications flew east, where they began flying simulated missions over predesignated areas south of Savannah, completing as many as six sorties a day. The four air crews that made the trip rotated among the two planes that flew in front of the cameras at any one time.[49]

When Milius had completed his filming in Georgia, the planes, air crews, and support forces returned to Washington briefly before all four modified A-6s flew to Kauai, Hawaii. There, the director, the cast, and the crew spent a month shooting additional aerial sequences and low-level flights over rice paddies as the hero's A-6 heads to Hanoi for the climactic air strike. Milius also filmed on the island the rescue operation after the A-6 has crashed, for which the Navy also provided helicopters stationed at Barking Sands Naval Air Station. However, since the Navy had retired the prop-driven Skyraiders twenty-one years before, private owners supplied the two A-1 aircraft that provided covering fire for the downed pilots waiting rescue. With the filming completed, the A-6s flew back to Washington on November 13, to prepare for the final phase of their participation in the film, flying on and off the USS *Independence*.

Since the Navy no longer flew the Vietnam-era planes, Milius faced the problem of creating an authentic looking background for the scenes aboard the carrier. The service came to the rescue by hoisting aboard the carrier in San Diego vintage fighters and bombers painted in period colors, some in flying condition and others non-carrier operational. On November 27, the Intruders flew from Washington State to the Miramar Naval Air Station in San Diego and then out to the carrier, 120 miles off the southern California coast. There, Paramount's 108–man crew filmed on a "not-to-interfere" basis during an eight-day cruise while the *Independence* carried out its training operations.

Fortunately, all the Intruder cinematic missions except the final one took place at

Director John Milius receives advice
during filming of *Flight of the Intruder*
aboard the USS *Independence.*

night, enabling the Navy to use the deck during the day and allowing Milius to shoot
without interruption at night. The second-unit crew filmed during the day to capture
flight deck operations. Although Milius could have shot some of the sequences dockside
on a soundstage, he considered the cost and effort of going to sea justified: "Being on the
ship puts everybody in the right mood." Moreover, it helped the director obtain the right
lighting. In one case, to match footage taken two days earlier, the captain reversed the
carrier's direction 180 degrees, causing Milius to exclaim: "If I need backlighting, they just
turn the ship around!"

Some things the Navy refused to do, such as flying their planes trailing smoke, firing
missiles, or dropping bombs over dry land, and obviously having their fliers eject or crash
their aircraft. As a result, the studio had to build and fly scale models of the Intruder and
other planes in order to create those events in the film. In particular, one of the models
attacked the scale model of Hanoi, which became the visual special-effects high point of
the movie. In addition, once Milius discovered that Navy pilots have the option of ejecting
through the canopy, he had the model designers change plans so that he could film full-
sized dummies being ejected through a full-size canopy.

Did such special effects and the Navy's almost unlimited assistance give Paramount a
fair return on its $30 million, including $1.2 million to the service for the cost of its
cooperation? In truth, Paramount obtained a movie that differed little from other naval
aviation stories about World War II or Korea. The hero, Brad Johnson, as Jake Grafton,
the A-6 Squadron's leading pilot, complains about fighting a meaningless war, loses his
original navigator-bombardier, and carries out an unauthorized bombing of People's Resistance Park in downtown Hanoi with his new crewman, William Dafoe, as Virgil Cole.
The clearly mutinous mission disrupts the Paris peace talks, but when President Nixon
orders the military to resume bombing Hanoi, Danny Glover, as squadron commander
Frank Camparelli, informs his rebels that their mission never happened.

Grounded and denied the chance to take part in the daylight attack on Hanoi's air
defenses in the opening gambit of Operation Linebacker 2, Grafton and Cole listen as
Camparelli crash-lands his damaged plane while leading the squadron. Striding onto the
deck like hired guns, the fliers commandeer an Intruder, albeit with the apparent acquiescence of the carrier's commander of flight operations, who only sees "a strike preparing to
launch," and set off to provide air cover for Camparelli, who awaits rescue. Arriving on
station implausibly fast, their plane immediately receives fatal ground fire and the fliers eject.

Grafton lands near Camparelli, but Cole falls a distance away and suffers a mortal
wound in a confrontation with a North Vietnamese soldier. Surrounded, he calls down
bombs on his position, thereby giving a helicopter time to effect the rescue of Grafton and
Camparelli. Like Brubaker's death in *Bridges at Toko-Ri,* however, Cole's sacrifice does not

help ensure victory any more than did the fliers' one-plane raid on Hanoi. In truth, Cole understood this reality, having told the board of inquiry, "I think we're going to lose this one, but I do love the work." Nor can the rescue of Grafton and Camparelli and their upbeat conversation back aboard the carrier provide a happy ending to the film.

From its perspective, the Navy did receive exciting images of its bombers in action as well as one more positive portrayal of carrier operations. To make sure no one would miss the film's intention of giving Intruder crews their due recognition, Grafton answers a fighter pilot's deprecation of his plane: "Fighter pukes make movies. Bomber pilots make history." Unfortunately, the images and words did not provide the service the benefit it had expected from the degree of assistance it provided. Despite the efforts of all parties, *Flight of the Intruder* remained just another aviation movie with little new to offer viewers. The reviewer in *Daily Variety* put it most succinctly, writing that the film enjoyed "the dubious distinction of being the most boring Vietnam War picture since *The Green Berets* but lacks the benefit of the latter's political outrageousness to spark a little interest and humor." Moreover, the review concluded that any message which Milius still might have on the Vietnam War "is lost here amid a flotilla of banalities and cliches straight out of bloated 1950s service dramas." Just as bad, perhaps, he described Grafton's brief romantic interlude with a young American war widow "as possibly unprecedented in its feebleness."[50]

Despite Milius's claim that he was making an apolitical war movie, reviewers still chose to offer their anti–Vietnam War commentaries. Desmond Ryan, for one, in the *Long Beach Press-Telegram*, described the film as "a misguided missile. To pinpoint what went wrong with this picture before the cameras even started rolling, you have only to recall one of the most famous photographs taken during the Vietnam War. It showed a naked child fleeing in terror from an eruption of napalm in an image that was to be etched into the conscience of the world. In making a movie about the men who dropped the bombs, John Milius at least explains why the great Vietnam combat pictures have stayed close to the ground."[51]

Ryan acknowledged that "there is no escaping the status of the bomber as the chief symbol of the high tech, indiscriminate savagery of modern warfare." He also noted: "Whenever the Intruder bombers touch down on their home carrier, they land on a flight deck jammed with so many war movie cliches there is scarcely room to park the planes." The reviewer observed that the film only came to life in the clash between Grafton and his superiors: "It is deepened by the understandable feeling among the airmen that the war is meaningless and that their peril is increased by the reluctance of the politicians back home to use all available military power to prosecute it."[52]

Given the time in which the film appeared, Ryan concluded, "It's hard to imagine a more unfortunate moment for a movie depicting a sky filled with bombs—whatever the scruples of the pilots dropping them." In contrast, Peter Rainer, in the *Los Angeles Times*, considered *Flight of the Intruder* mediocre, but felt that "it comes at a time when audiences may be in the mood to see even a sub-par film about American bomber and fighter pilots braving the odds and strutting their codes of honor." As a result, he thought the film may have found "its commercial salvation. It certainly won't find salvation in its mundane script, direction, performances."[53]

Rainer felt that Milius had tried for the war-movie effect of John Ford in *They Were Expendable,* but he concluded that the director had failed, because Ford's film "was considerably darker and more complex than this straight-arrow tub-thumper. Milius attempts to recapture our feelings for the rousingly patriotic war movies of 50 years ago, but the kind of traditional, true-blue sentiments he's parading seem out of place in this Vietnam set-ting. That war, and our feelings about it, are far more complicated than this film allows for. Its banalities don't do justice to the war or the Americans who served in it."[54]

Unfortunately for the Navy and the filmmakers, Ryan rather than Rainer proved more accurate. Paramount released *Flight of the Intruder* within days of the outbreak of the Gulf War, in January 1991. Beaming flights of Intruders and smart bombs hitting their targets twenty-four hours a day, television brought the air war almost live into the nation's living rooms. Worried about the impact the war might have on appeal of the film, and needing the money to promote *Godfather III,* Paramount let *Flight of the Intruder* quickly disappear from theater screens, much to the Navy's regret. As a result, the real war, not Milius's rather unexceptional drama, confirmed for the American people that the images of *Top Gun* represented the reality of the post-Vietnam Navy.[55]

28 | The Cold War Ends on the Motion Picture Screen

FLIGHT OF THE INTRUDER PROVIDED THE ONLY significant images of the Vietnam War during the 1990s. The few other films that contained any portrayals of the American involvement in Southeast Asia used the war only as the springboard for the advancement of their stories. The end of the Vietnam war movies also marked the conclusion of the fifty-year cinematic confrontation between Capitalism and Communism. Except for combat in the Korean and Vietnam war films, that confrontation had rarely turned hot, and then only in some brief firefight such as Clint Eastwood's *Firefox,* or the climactic apocalypses in *Dr. Strangelove, Fail Safe,* and *The Bedford Incident.*

With Hollywood at least temporarily eschewing full-scale combat, the armed services became receptive to stories about their peacetime activities. From the perspective of the public affairs officers, any motion pictures showing their men and equipment, whether as the centerpieces of the story or as a subordinate element in a non-military film, provided at least some benefit by informing the American people of how the Pentagon was using their tax dollars. At the same time, even when these stories contained only a relatively brief military appearance, the public affairs offices remained solicitous of the images the film-makers were creating of the services.

When John Horton delivered the script for *Star Trek IV: The Voyage Home* to the Pentagon on behalf of Harve Bennett and Paramount Pictures, the Navy requested several changes. To satisfy the service's objection to the line "You're not one of those creeps from the military trying to teach whales to plant mines," producer-writer Bennett modified it to read "You're not one of those military types are you, trying to teach whales to retrieve torpedoes?"[1]

Bennett also wanted to assure the Navy that the entry to a base building "will not constitute a breach of Naval security. No fences will be cut, no guards overpowered. Uhura and Chekov will instead by [*sic*] 'beamed in' to within the center of the room they wish to enter, utilizing the internationally famous trademark of *Star Trek.* Clearly, this use of *Star Trek* 'magic' is something both funny and unique, and obviously no one else but our show can do it." He explained that the lead shield of the room in which Uhura and Chekov find themselves prevents them from being beamed out. Consequently, Bennett pointed out that contrary to the Navy's concerns about the film showing a lapse in Navy security, "it is getting *out,* not getting in, that becomes the drama."[2]

In regard to the assistance he needed during the production, Bennett told Horton that the studio would like to use facilities at the Naval Air Station at Long Beach. In addition, if the Navy's schedule permitted, he said he would like to have a second unit film Chekov and Uhura seeing the USS *Enterprise* docked at Alameda in Oakland. According to the writer-producer, the *Star Trek* characters seeing "the carrier of today which bears the name of their Starship of the future . . . would enhance a rich tradition of public relations which has been carried on in the past between these two *Enterprises.*"[3]

The Navy advised Don Baruch that it approved cooperation, with additional changes already discussed with Bennett. The service did say that the filmmakers would have to create a different means for Uhura's escape from the carrier: "We have recommended a scenario which would not allow her to walk off the ship during a nuclear reactor incursion alert. As written, her escape would leave the audience with the impression that naval security of nuclear reactions is lax." In addition, the Navy required that an FBI agent rather than a naval intelligence officer interrogate Chekov: "As the character . . . would be in civilian custody in a situation like that portrayed, we have also asked that the Shore Patrol portrayed in the hospital scenes be replaced by civilian policemen."[4]

When the namesake of the starship *Enterprise* proved unavailable, Bennett and Paramount settled for the use of the USS *Ranger*, the carrier that had served as a set for *Top Gun* only six months before. The shooting itself required three days at North Island Naval Base, San Diego, beginning on February 25, 1986, with the filmmakers taking both interior and external sequences, using both sailors and Marines as extras aboard the ship. Although the scenes created aboard the carrier did not show the Navy treating the space-time travelers particularly well, the service did get images of its huge nuclear carrier before the American people with its crew doing its job correctly.[5]

Whatever benefit the Navy received from its assistance to the film probably resulted from association with an American cultural icon, rather than the images of the service's men and equipment. In contrast, the Pentagon and the Navy could receive no benefit from becoming involved with *No Way Out*. The film's script contained such an adverse portrayal of the Pentagon leadership that producer Mace Neufeld did not even bother to

Producer Harve Bennett aboard the USS *Ranger* during the filming of *Star Trek IV: The Voyage Home*. The production was not able to use the USS *Enterprise*, which was at sea.

submit a script to the Defense Department. After all, how could the Pentagon assist on a movie that has the secretary of defense maintaining a mistress whom he ultimately murders in a jealous rage? Worse, his homosexual top aide leads the cover-up by trying to frame the decorated Navy hero assigned to solving the crime. In most instances, having Kevin Costner in the starring role would ensure a benefit to the service. However, in this case, the climax of the film reveals that Costner was spying for the Soviet Union as a deep Communist mole.[6]

Although the filmmakers did not seek Defense Department assistance, they could not create the one prop that would give their production an air of authenticity, the Pentagon itself. Consequently, exercising their rights as citizens, the producers requested permission from the General Services Administration, which provides facilities management for the Pentagon building, to shoot a scene on the public concourse. After approving the request, however, the GSA changed its policies because of concerns over security and withdrew permission.

The filmmakers then complained that they had already made their plans and the change would drastically affect their production. As a result, the GSA reversed itself and approved shooting on the concourse after hours and with security guards in attendance. However, as their predecessors had done in finessing Navy personnel to provide unapproved assistance to the original *King Kong* and *Seven Days in May*, the producers of *No Way Out* talked the guards into letting the filmmakers into the innermost A-Ring, NATO corridor of the Pentagon. As a result, visually, the movie looks authentic because the actors are going where private civilians tread only on guided tours or escorted visits.[7]

In fact, the Pentagon building imparted virtually the only physical and geographic realism to the movie. Otherwise, the filmmakers used the Baltimore subway as a stand-in for the Washington Metro, put a station in Georgetown, something not even the subway builders had been able to accomplish, and created a story so filled with holes that only the speed of the action masked the implausibilities. Moreover, given its intellectual barrenness, audiences might well come away from *No Way Out* without much thought to the way the film portrayed the duplicity of the Pentagon leadership, particularly after the revelations of Watergate and the Contra scandals. Only its ironic plot twist in the last few frames, exposing the Navy hero as a Soviet spy, provided *No Way Out* with any uniqueness. Despite the movie's visual references to the Pentagon and the job descriptions of its principal characters, it remains a traditional action-romance Cold War film, rather than a story about the military.[8]

Despite this negative portrayal, all the services were actively seeking projects that might enhance their peacetime preparedness images. For the Army, the opportunity came in the guise of a contemporary John Wayne. As one of Hollywood's true superstars, Clint Eastwood's image had come to pervade society in much the same way as had Wayne's persona. His "Make my day" remark to a wounded bank robber became every bit as famous as Wayne's "Saddle up" order to his Marines. To the extent that a difference existed, it resulted from Eastwood's greater versatility as an actor and a director. Whereas John Wayne always played John Wayne, Eastwood could become a Dirty Harry, a cowboy, a bare-knuckle fighter, and even a vulnerable disk jockey pursued by a jilted lover. If Eastwood seemed more human than Wayne, even occasionally out of control, he nevertheless proved up to any challenge. Consequently, when he approached the Army in late March 1985, through his producer Fritz Manes, with a story focusing on Ronald Reagan's Cold War Grenada incursion, the service had every reason to expect that any assistance they extended would provide ample returns.

After talking with Baruch, Manes followed up with a letter and a draft copy of the screenplay for *Heartbreak Ridge*. He stressed that Malpaso Productions, Eastwood's production company, was still "at a very early stage" with the project and so didn't know what support it would ultimately require. In any case, he said that Eastwood wanted to shoot on location at the home of the Army's Eighty-second Airborne Division at Fort Bragg, "using the practical sets rather than building them" for most of the exterior sequences and "obviously" needed personnel and equipment on the base. In closing, he confirmed that once the Army had had a chance to read the script, he and Eastwood would be coming to Washington to discuss the production in person.[9]

In preparation for the meeting, Baruch sent a memo to the assistant secretary of defense for public affairs, Michael Burch, advising him that the screenplay had generated "unfavorable reactions." Baruch wrote that "the story is not in our best interest and it is questionable if it can be fixed without a complete rewrite and with a new story line." Nevertheless, he said his office and the Army "will do what we can to encourage sending the writer to the field to see Airborne training and to meet with selected members for research and possible personal stories."[10]

As Baruch summarized the story, *Heartbreak Ridge* followed the waning career of Tom Highway, a member of the Army Airborne since Korea, where he received the Medal of Honor. Eastwood would be playing Highway as "a hard drinker and divorced from his wife. He often gets into trouble with the police and is put in charge of a goof-off group of Airborne troops" after his latest bout with the bottle. He gains the respect of the men and turns them into a fine unit, which fights well in the U.S. invasion of Grenada. As for the dramatic conflict, Baruch explained that "there is his C.O., a Captain, who doesn't care about anything except to look good in training exercises even if he has to cheat."[11]

As the script then portrayed him, Highway did not convey the image of the contemporary Army the service believed it had become. In his defense, as Eastwood reforms his unit, he reforms himself, and he even reconciles with his ex-wife. In terms of the public's perspective of Eastwood, Baruch advised Burch that the *New York Times Magazine* had recently featured the actor in an article that described "his great appeal throughout the world and used an excellent picture on the cover." Not only had many countries honored him and run film retrospectives of his work, but Baruch also noted that Eastwood served as a member of a White House committee on the arts and would be attending a luncheon with President Reagan the next month.[12]

Eastwood demonstrated his appeal during his visit to the Pentagon on April 24, when dozens of fans crowded the corridors to catch a glimpse of the star. He did not have quite the same effect on Burch during their meeting, however. Burch acknowledged afterward that he had some problems with the script, as had the Army, but said, "We would be interested in a film with Clint Eastwood in uniform. That would be great."[13]

Despite the personal visit, such visible interest, and Eastwood's many political connections, when the revised script of *Heartbreak Ridge* arrived in the Pentagon, it contained all the problems to which the Army had objected initially. In its memo to Baruch on December 16, 1985, the service advised him that it could not recommend approval for support. According to the Public Affairs Office, the screenplay presented "the Army, especially the Airborne community, in a highly unfavorable and inaccurate light. The writers have taken a number of Hollywood stereotypes of military personnel from the World War II era and portrayed modern soldiers according to these stereotypes. The general conditions which might have existed in World War II and the Korean War no longer prevail in today's Army."[14]

The Public Affairs Office found the screenplay rife with historical and factual mistakes as well as erroneous portrayals. Among other things, it pointed out that personnel management policies would not allow a Korean War–era sergeant, albeit a Medal of Honor recipient, to remain on active duty thirty years later. Just as important, the office noted that the "title of the script is of Korean War vintage and is misleading, since the story is about the Army of the 1980s." The battle for Heartbreak Ridge occurred during the Korean War, whereas Eastwood's script focused on Highway's efforts to bring a ragtag platoon to full readiness and then lead them into combat when the United States invaded Grenada in 1983.[15]

Just as the Marines and the Navy objected to the obscene language in the original screenplays of *Born on the Fourth of July* and *An Officer and a Gentleman,* the Army also found the excessive profanity reinforced an unwarranted stereotype of the service: "There is vulgar language used in the Army and in the civilian populace; but, nothing as obscene as that offered in this script exists in either group. The obscene language in the script verges on the ludicrous and does nothing to enhance the story. It detracts, in fact, from the true qualities of the soldiers portrayed. It must be toned down and a great deal of it eliminated to accurately portray the language of today's soldiers."[16]

The Army also addressed the changes in gender makeup of the peacetime military. Paying homage to the women who now accounted for 10 percent of the soldiers and officers, the Army stated that the scriptwriters had "chosen to ignore this fact of life and have incorrectly attributed to the Airborne a derogatory attitude about women." Similarly, the Public Affairs Office noted that the screenwriters had not taken into account the changed living arrangements of soldiers in an all-volunteer military: "The 'squad bay' scenes of the platoon, if they are found anywhere in today's Army—and that is doubtful—would be found only in basic training units. With many soldiers married and not living in the barracks—a fact which the writers either ignored or were not aware of—and the others released after duty requirements are fulfilled (unless on alert), the barracks scenes are totally unrealistic." Therefore, the script's portrayal of a soldier "sneaking out to be with his family is ludicrous. He would be authorized to live off-post and would receive a housing allowance. The entire story line, to include stealing field rations to feed his family, must be deleted from the script."[17]

Given the screenplay's many problems, the Army advised Baruch that it could not approve the script for cooperation. Nevertheless, the service said it "would like to continue working with the writers and producer to try to develop a more accurate and interesting script about the 82d Airborne Division and/or other elements of today's Army." It also expressed the concern that if the producer decided to make the movie without Army involvement, it "would result in considerable damage to the Army and disservice to the soldiers and the public whom they serve."[18]

By the time Baruch received the Army's memo, Fritz Manes had discussed the service's objections with the chief of public affairs, Maj. Gen. Charles Bussey, and had advised Eastwood of the Army's reaction to the script. Not unlike Francis Coppola, Eastwood took umbrage that the service would object to any portrayal of the Army he might care to render and immediately expressed his unhappiness to General Bussey. He suggested that the service had missed the crux of the script, "that Sergeant Highway is a throwback to the *old* Army, completely out of step with 'today's' Army to the point where it has affected his personal as well as his military life, and he does have trouble adapting to the new Army." Eastwood explained that "although the new Army is probably superior to the old Army, there must be *some* virtues in the old Army, and with all respect for the men who served and gave their lives in two world wars—Korea and Vietnam—I don't think that memory shouldbe discarded."[19]

Eastwood further reminded the Army that he was making a movie and not a training film, "and at present day the only image of the military out there for the general public is Rambo. This film will be a terribly patriotic film touching on America's involvement and conflicts of the present time—we would have it no other way." In regard to the Army's complaints, he noted that Marty Elfand, the producer of *An Officer and a Gentleman,* had told him that "the Navy's objections and eventual turn-down of his film were the exact comments we are receiving today. As you know, the Navy was very chagrined in hindsight for not supporting the picture and enlistments in that particular branch of the Navy were up considerably after that film." In closing, Eastwood did not sound very different from Francis Coppola in his telegraph to President Carter virtually threatening to make the United States look "ridiculous" if he did not receive cooperation on *Apocalypse Now:* "It would be a shame for Sergeant Highway not to be in the service of the U.S. Army and the 82nd Airborne Division who participated in the rescue mission in Grenada."[20]

As with Coppola, the Army did not seem too impressed with Eastwood's veiled threat. Answering for General Bussey, Brig. Gen. Richard Griffitts, the acting chief of public affairs, wrote that the service could "appreciate your view that we're missing the point about Sergeant Highway being 'a throwback to the *old* Army.' Believe me, we understand that. We also agree that the old Army had 'some virtues'—many, in fact. Like you, we want to preserve the memory and properly honor those who served and gave their lives in our Nation's wars. And there's no question that we'd like to see you make a film that does this." Although the Army also accepted *Heartbreak Ridge* on its own terms as "neither a recruiting nor a training film," Griffitts maintained that "parts of the script are hard to accept." Nevertheless, he said that the service thought the differences "can be resolved to our mutual satisfaction. We certainly want to try."[21]

Eastwood, however, no longer wanted to try. Instead, he and Fritz Manes began working with Lt. Col. Fred Peck, Pat Coulter's replacement as director of the Marines' Los Angeles Office, to turn *Heartbreak Ridge* into a Marine story. After Peck had sent the revised screenplay to Marine Headquarters, Don Baruch heard about the change "inadvertently," and only then did he discuss the company's new tack with Manes. Once Peck had received "assurances that the project is one which the Marine Corps wishes to support," the producer advised Baruch that he wanted to come to Washington to visit Navy and Marine officials and meet with Robert Sims, the new assistant secretary of defense for public affairs.[22]

In briefing Sims for Manes's March 24 courtesy call, Baruch advised him that Eastwood would now play a Marine reconnaissance sergeant and that Malpaso Productions planned to release the film during the Christmas season. In contrast to the Army's objections, Baruch offered his opinion that "the Marine Corps might make allowances for some things not acceptable to the Army. Therefore, that part of the story should be left to the Marine Corps as long as no overall DoD policy is violated." Under those circumstances, he said he would recommend Pentagon approval.[23]

Despite the "assurances" and Peck's continued work with Manes and the screenwriter to develop "a mutually acceptable script," Brig. Gen. D.E.P. Miller, Marine director of public affairs, found that the revised script still contained "much objectionable language." Nevertheless, he thought the project "otherwise benefits the image of the U.S. Armed Forces, particularly the final climactic scene in Grenada." As a result, he advised Baruch, "The Marine Corps poses no objection to supporting this film on a noninterference, reimbursable basis."[24]

When Don Baruch completed his own

Clint Eastwood directing a scene for *Heartbreak Ridge,* which began life as an Army film but became a Marine story.

review of the reworked script, however, he informed Sims that he "found it leaving much to be desired." Nevertheless, he advised the assistant secretary that he believed "the Marine Corps image is something they should be responsible for and we should be concerned where and how overall DOD policy and criticism of DOD might be concerned." As a result, he had solicited comments from other DoD offices about the effect the film might have on personnel and training. At the same time, he asked the Marines' chief of information to review the script again and asked the Marine historian to do a historical review. In addition, he had called Manes to alert him about the continuing problems he saw with the script.[25]

Baruch reported to Sims that Manes "immediately became defensively offensive. He feels he has followed guidance from the Marines and has not taken anything away from the Army and given it to the Marine Corps such as rescuing the students." Baruch said that Manes had repeated Eastwood's contention that since he were not making a documentary, people should not worry about historical accuracy. In addition, he said the producer had reminded him that after Peck had briefed Sims about the Marines' position during the March 24 meeting, the assistant secretary had told Manes he would approve assistance if the Marine Public Affairs Office approved the script. Consequently, Baruch asked Sims for guidance on what to tell Manes when he called back.[26]

The agencies to which Baruch had sent the script shared his concerns. The Navy Office of Information expressed its suspicion about the story's historical accuracy. Moreover, it found that the language used in the script "is the worst encountered in any previous scripts submitted to this office." The director of training policy in the DoD Office of Force Management also objected to the "coarse and vulgar" language, saying he would be reluctant to have the Pentagon "appear to sponsor such language," particularly because it seemed so "gratuitous." Moreover, he felt that Baruch should ask the Marines "to verify that the training practices portrayed are within established guidelines. If they are not, then Departmental sponsorship would be inappropriate." Finally, the office suggested that the film should have shown that Highway's superiors had recognized and done something about his serious drinking problem.[27]

Regardless of such ongoing concerns, the commandant of the Marine Corps approved assistance to *Heartbreak Ridge,* dependent on DOD approval of the script. The Public Affairs Office saw the production "as a fictional action entertainment film, not as an historical documentary. While the writers have taken considerable dramatic license in some areas, particularly in the Grenada sequence, the Marine Corps is portrayed positively. A technical advisor will be assigned to continue to work with the producer to tone down some of the objectionable portions of the script."[28]

Despite the expectation that a technical advisor would mitigate the problems, the responses to Baruch's request for comments from DoD agencies continued to focus on areas of concern. The Force Management and Personnel Office counseled that the Pentagon should have several scenes changed or eliminated, including the film's opening sequence in a jail cell: "Highway's dialogue is in poor taste and demeaning to women. The language is excessively crude." In regard to a scene in which Highway rips the earring off the recruit and abuses him, the office noted: "These acts connote excessive brutality of a noncommissioned officer towards a trainee and do not reflect the training environment dictated by Departmental policy." In regard to Highway's drinking problem, the office noted that Pentagon policy provided for dealing with the man "for both his own benefit and that of the Service."[29]

Brig. Gen. Edwin Simmons, director of Marine Corps history and museums, found that the *Heartbreak Ridge* screenplay generally portrayed Marines and Marine combat training "in a realistic manner, given the nature of this fictional, dramatized account." He pointed out, however, that the screenplay contained an inaccurate account of the rescue of American medical students on Grenada: "While Marines both evacuated students by helicopter, and located and evacuated student 'stragglers' in various locations on the island, Marine units were not involved in a building to building search for students at Saint George University." Despite this variance from the historical record, Simmons accepted the way Hollywood operated: "Given the considerable theatrical license evident in contemporary action, entertainment films, *Heartbreak Ridge*'s central theme of Marine dedication to Corps and country, along with the ever-present need for vigilance in readiness and training, is effectively presented." Morever, Simmons said that his office had been helping the Marine technical advisor in Los Angeles during his work on the script, and it remained "ready to provide any further assistance in the area of historical accuracy."[30]

With these inputs in hand, Sims advised General Miller on May 5 that he would approve the script, providing Malpaso made several revisions. He wanted the language toned down and the opening lines "specifically must be deleted. We do not mean to take away from earthy expressions that may be fairly common in certain segments of the Marine Corps, but we do want to avoid the impression that all Marines talk so crudely." He felt that the filmmakers could serve the best interest of all parties if they made the story "entirely fictional with the action taking place on a fictional island in the Caribbean." Eastwood could use Cubans as the antagonists, but "the time frame should be divorced from Beirut and the Recon forces being ordered to Lebanon."[31]

To solve the problem of Highway's apparent longevity in the Marines, Sims wanted the script to make it clear he had been in and out of the Marines because of his drinking and arrest problems. In addition, he insisted that the filmmakers eliminate undue violence such as the earring scene, using virtually the same language as the force management and personnel office. Sims insisted that the credit card story "must not be used" in the script, because it had not actually occurred. He also objected to the characters as stereotypes dating from World War II and advised Miller to again look at the impressions of the officers and noncommissioned officers in the script: "We believe audiences will leave theatres with one impression that the noncommissioned officers make the Marine Corps. As Lt. Col. Hastings states in the script, they '. . . motivate, counsel, challenge, and most of all lead.'" Once the filmmakers had incorporated the requested changes into the script, Sims said he would authorize the needed requirements.[32]

Sims's mandate emphasized the Pentagon's continuing problems with *Heartbreak Ridge*, which had now been going on for more than a year since Fritz Manes's initial contact with Don Baruch. Despite Eastwood's attempts to satisfy first the Army and then the Marines, the same basic disagreements remained unresolved. In fact, the Pentagon had seldom before attempted to dictate such sweeping revisions to a story. Either a service and DoD Public Affairs would approve a script after suitable negotiations, or the filmmakers would find the military's requests unacceptable and go away. In this case, the Pentagon had been working with Manes and Eastwood on an incremental basis both in the development of an acceptable script and more recently in allowing the movie company to film scheduled training exercises.

In giving what amounted to courtesy assistance, Baruch had made it clear that this did not constitute formal support: "There is no objection interposed to Malpaso Productions filming newsfilm type coverage for stock footage. This is applicable for coverage of any training exercises scheduled within the next couple weeks. However, the cast is not approved until such time as script approval and assistance authorization." He also gave the filmmakers permission to shoot footage from a Marine helicopter as long as they used the aircraft only as a camera platform, it was flying on a scheduled exercise, and the company carried insurance to protect the government against liability in case of accident or damage.[33]

Given such ongoing involvement in the production, Eastwood had come to assume that at some point he would receive formal approval for all needed assistance. Nevertheless, with his ego and reputation, the actor-director clearly did not feel that the Pentagon had any right to impose its vision, historical as well as military, on his creative work. However, by the time Sims mandated his requirements for giving formal approval to the production, Eastwood no longer had the option of finding an alternative source of material support for his project. Whatever the validity of his requests for changes in the script, Sims had come to see his stipulations as necessary for the good of the Marines, the Defense Department, and ultimately the nation.[34]

Having received word of Sims's memo, Eastwood called the assistant secretary on May 8 to discuss the secretary's continued unhappiness with the project, in an attempt to reach some sort of an accommodation. In his follow-up letter to Sims on May 9, he repeated telephoned assurances that he fully intended "on working closely with the Marine Corps in establishing as accurate a history as possible on the Grenada intervention, thus resolving your concerns." He told Sims that it "assuredly is to our advantage to stay away from stereotypes—something that certainly does not apply to the Marines." He said he would "look for alternatives to the credit card call and review language and undue violence." Finally, he assured Sims "that within this character study of a career non-commissioned officer we intend to make this an extremely patriotic film—one in which the Marine Corps and the Department of Defense can take great pride." He closed by thanking the assistant secretary for his "cooperation and flexibility."[35]

Sims wrote back to Eastwood on May 12, 1986, informing him that he had discussed *Heartbreak Ridge* with Secretary of Defense Casper Weinberger and Marine Corps Commandant Paul Kelley and that all three "hope for a result in which the Department can take great pride, and we appreciate your assurances on that score." He advised Eastwood that the "the Marine Corps has already received Defense Department approval for cooperation on this project, subject to its being able to resolve with you the concerns we have about historical accuracy, language, undue violence, etc."[36]

To that end, Don Baruch sent a memo to Sims on May 16 stating the "need to establish on-the-record action taken by telephone conversations that cooperation is now authorized" for *Heartbreak Ridge*. He explained, "I believe it also is important to have a record reiterating that we hold the Marine Corps responsible for accomplishing changes including specific points on the Grenada action. I feel certain that the Army would complain if the Marines are shown freeing the students." He provided Sims with a memo for his signature for him to send to the Marines to accomplish that suggestion.[37]

Sims then sent the memo to the Marines' director of public affairs, advising him that he had "no objections now about dramatizing the Marine Corps action during the Grenada operations." At the same time, he reiterated that his approval of support to the film remained subject to the Marines' "being able to resolve my listed concerns. Specifically in regard to accuracy, Marines are not to be shown doing something factually and publicly credited to other Services, nor being shot at and killed on the ground, contrary to established Marine losses."[38]

As revised, the script portrayed Highway as a grizzled Marine gunnery sergeant whom the Marine Corps had reassigned to a supply unit as punishment for brawling and insubordination. Nearing the mandatory retirement age, he was given one more chance: he must whip a group of hopeless prima donnas into fighting shape, very much as Sergeant Stryker did in *Sands of Iwo Jima* and General Savage did in *Twelve O'Clock High*. Simultaneously, he must do battle with the civilian world and with the "new" Marine Corps. Despite the Army's complaints about the original screenplay and the Marines' ongoing concerns, the plot distinguished itself by its lack of any significant story. The Grenada incursion is the only unique aspect of the film, which otherwise duplicates countless other Marine stories that devote a significant portion to illustrating how the Corps prepares its men to fight. Moreover, despite the Pentagon's ongoing efforts, the Marines ultimately failed to get Eastwood to accurately portray their role during the U.S. incursion into Grenada.

Two months after Sims thought he had received a commitment from Eastwood to provide a more faithful portrayal of the Marines in the Grenada operation, the problem continued to haunt the Corps. Brig. Gen. Walter E. Boomer, the new director of Marine Corps Public Affairs, found that he was still struggling with the filmmakers to produce a mutually acceptable revised script. On July 21 he learned from one of his staff that Eastwood had not made all the changes the Marines and the Pentagon had requested. He confirmed the information with Fred Peck, who had assumed the duty of on-site technical advisor.

Peck told the general that Eastwood had filmed some of the scenes in the screenplay that the Marines had found most objectionable in their original form and he would not make any changes. In particular, he indicated that the film still showed Marines rescuing the American students, a Marine dying during the battle, and Highway striking an enlisted man, and the language remained very profane.[39]

Clint Eastwood looks on during filming of *Heartbreak Ridge*.

General Boomer then informed Sims and the commandant of the situation. With their concurrence, the general instructed Peck on July 23 to advise the actor-director that unless he complied with the provisions for cooperation, the Pentagon would withdraw support. Eastwood immediately put through a call to the White House asking to talk with the president. Boomer then called Eastwood to discuss the Marine Corps's concerns about the production. During the conversation, he became convinced that the problems resulted from "misunderstandings" between the two parties, and he told Eastwood that he would discuss the matter with the commandant. He also told the actor-director that he hoped further discussions would resolve the differences. In response, Eastwood told the general he would call the White House back and ask that his earlier call be disregarded.[40]

In his memo to Sims, Boomer reported that he had had a "very professional" conversation with the filmmaker. He said that Eastwood "stated emphatically that he had never agreed to make all of the changes, but that he had promised to do the best he could, and he felt that he had done that." The filmmaker cited specific changes he had made to tone down the language and violence and told General Boomer that he believed dramatic license enabled him to depict the Marines picking up the students, using the credit card, and a Marine being killed "because the story itself was fiction." Boomer also reported that Eastwood had repeated his earlier assertion that he believed *Heartbreak Ridge* told a very patriotic story and viewers would receive it well.[41]

Boomer advised Sims that Eastwood had somewhat alleviated his concerns "in that I do not believe he has deliberately misled us, or has manipulated DoD to his own benefit. My concern still remains that there will be some scenes in the film that we will find objectionable." The general also reported that Eastwood had again said he intended to bring the film to Washington for a screening prior to final cutting. As a consequence, and since only two days of filming remained, Boomer explained that it had "seemed pointless to withhold Marine Corps support. The ill will that would have been generated, probably would have harmed DoD and Malpaso Productions in the long run." Boomer told Sims that the commandant had agreed with his judgment. To avoid such problems in the future, the general recommended that a written agreement should be made between filmmakers and the Marines concerning specific changes expected before the Corps would approve a script for support. Nevertheless, he told Sims that the Marines have always believed that *Heartbreak Ridge* "was worth supporting. We still feel that way, it just makes us a 'little nervous.'"[42]

In the meantime, on another front, Commandant Kelley had written to Eastwood on behalf of Korean Army veterans who had been vehemently opposing the use of the title of the film and the Marine story. In a series of letters to military officials, they had stressed that the battle for Heartbreak Ridge had been exclusively an Army action and one that had produced severe casualties. Kelley told Eastwood that he shared the soldiers' concern about the title: "Had a motion picture about Army operations been entitled *Mt. Suribachi* (site of the Iwo Jima flag raising), the reaction among Marine Veterans would have been at least as vocal." He stated his belief that "the film's title is grossly misleading. . . . I am convinced that the title is a disservice to the Army veterans who fought there so valiantly." Consequently, in asking Eastwood to change the title, Kelley expressed the hope "that you will recognize the sincerity and depth of this request."[43]

With the matter not resolved and concern about how Eastwood would handle the Pentagon's requests for changes, Don Baruch wrote to Manes on September 5, reminding him that the Marine and Defense Department officials expected to review the film "at the earliest stage possible, and especially before titles were incorporated." A week later, Sims asked that the Marines prepare an after-action report detailing the charges the government was billing to Malpaso. He also asked for information about how Eastwood had dealt with his specific requests for changes made in May and how the filmmaker had responded to Kelley's request to change the title of his movie.[44]

In answering Sim's request, Fred Peck provided a detailed accounting of the charges the company had accrued during filming at Camp Pendleton and at Vieques, where Eastwood shot some of the action sequences. Peck was less successful in giving an appraisal of how the actor-director had responded to Sims's mandate for revisions, saying, "I simply do not know yet, what the overall tone will be." Peck pointed out that Eastwood let the actors ad lib in most of the scenes. Complicating the problem, as had become the case with most R-rated movies, the filmmakers shot both a theatrical and a television–in-flight version. In any case, the technical advisor described how Eastwood had handled the prob-

Marines assisting Clint Eastwood during production of *Heartbreak Ridge*.

lem scenes during filming and said the actor-director continued to promise that he would screen *Heartbreak Ridge* for the Marines as soon as possible.[45]

When that finally happened, on November 14, the Marines and the Defense Department found that their concerns and "nervous" feelings had not prepared them for what they saw. In his letter to Manes, Sims expressed his regret that "little was done to incorporate the requisite changes into the final shooting script." Worse, he discovered a scene in which Highway shot an enemy soldier twice in the back after he had already been wounded. Pointing out that Highway would be subject to court-martial for such an act, he urged Manes to "consider deleting the few seconds of footage in which this action occurs." In any case, because the objections he had raised remained in the completed film, Sims advised the producer that any acknowledgment of military assistance "would be inappropriate."[46]

In his letter to Eastwood on November 18, Sims expressed his "disappointment that you did not consider our requested revisions to be in the best interest of the film, as well as that of the Department." He explained that he had authorized assistance because of Eastwood's need to begin production in order to deliver the finished movie for the holiday season, with the full expectation that the filmmakers would accede to the Pentagon's request for changes. He closed by advising Eastwood that if he sought Defense Department assistance in the future, "it will be necessary to have a final script approved, or at least a more binding commitment than we had in this case, before any cooperation will be authorized."[47]

In some measure, the Pentagon and the Marines must accept responsibility for the failure to secure an acceptable end product. Sims cannot hide behind his rationalization that he finally authorized assistance out of a recognition of Eastwood's production schedule problems. As assistant secretary of defense for public affairs, Sims's responsibility was to the military establishment, not to a filmmaker. Moreover, his particular sensitivity to the film's profanity ignored the reality that Marines do swear, very likely as much as Highway did. In any case, if the problems with violence and historical inaccuracies bothered him and other Pentagon officials, he had a simple recourse: refuse to authorize Marine support.

The Marines probably received the film they deserved. The Corps so much wanted its own *Top Gun* that it began working with Eastwood even though it knew the Army had objected to the initial screenplay and then did not insist on a binding commitment from Eastwood to make the requested changes they felt necessary. Even if Highway's character did not reflect the contemporary image of the Marines the Corps was trying to create, Eastwood's hard-drinking, foul-mouthed NCO undoubtedly did little harm to the service's recruiting campaign. In fact, Highway did not differ very much from John Wayne's classic

Sergeant Stryker, who also drank far too much, who also had a problem establishing a meaningful relationship with his wife, who also manifested a streak of brutality toward his men. In regard to Eastwood's portraying the death of a Marine on Grenada, which the Marine Corps said did not happen historically, the filmmaker had a perfect rejoinder. Apart from the fact that three Marines did die in a helicopter crash, Eastwood could have pointed out that although no Marines actually died during the flag-raising on Mount Suribachi, John Wayne died in *Sands of Iwo Jima* as the flag went up, with no complaint from the Marines.

Beyond that, as technical advisor, Fred Peck did not have a problem with the way Highway dispatched a downed enemy soldier on Grenada. Peck said that the script had included a scene in which Highway shoots three Cuban soldiers during a firefight but did not have him administrating a coup de grâce. The technical advisor explained that during the setup for the scene, Eastwood simply choreographed how he would do the shooting. As things worked out, he shot one in the chest, the second in the back, and the third as he ran away. Afterward, Eastwood told Peck that John Wayne would never have shot a man in the back. He noted, however, that Wayne never said "fuck" in a movie either, although in private he used "fuck" in every other sentence. In any case, as the director shot the sequence, Peck considered it to be realistic.[48]

As the action played itself out, after shooting the three Cubans with an M-16, Eastwood goes up to one lying face down, shoots him twice more, turns him over, takes a cigar out of the dead man's pocket, and remarks that it was a Cuban. Peck said the scene had not bothered him because the man was already dead and a Marine in combat might well do that. Whatever the truth, the sequence caused a problem for the Marines because of the way Eastwood added sound to the action during the editing process. As seen and heard, the Cuban was rasping as if he were still alive. Peck, of course, had not known that the scene would end up on the screen that way. Consequently, when he received a call from Washington after the screening to complain about Eastwood's shooting prisoners, Peck asked what prisoners, since he had not yet seen the movie. He said, however, that he would not have objected to the scene even if he had known during the filming how it would be done. He pointed out that with three M-16 slugs in the downed soldier, he was going to die soon enough, and Highway's action became a kindness.[49]

With his film completed, Eastwood showed no such kindness to the Pentagon or the Marines. In responding to Sims's letter of November 18, he denied that he had not considered the military's requests for revisions. He said he had toned down the "overall language" and removed all references to Beirut, "even though we thought it was a rather silly request to ignore a fact of history." To solve the problem of Highway's service in Korea and the Army veterans' concern about the film's title, Eastwood advised Sims that he had made his alter ego a soldier during that war and a Marine subsequently. At the same time, he wondered why if the credit-card call remained pure fiction, "how does it all of a sudden belong to the DOD?"[50]

Eastwood also wrote that he found the Pentagon's "obsession" with the new volunteer military "an indirect putdown of the military who served in World War I, World War II, Korea, and Vietnam—the same military that produced Sergeant York, Audie Murphy, and many other great American citizens who fought and died for their country either on a volunteer or draft basis." Nevertheless, he was sure the Marines who had assisted him "will enjoy this film because they are intelligent enough to know it is just a movie. It is a crime you have forbidden us to give them credit where credit is due on this project." Saving his strongest criticism of Sims to the end, he wrote: "Your threat to close down this film during progress via General Boomer was less than noble indeed. And, as to the last paragraph of your letter about seeking DOD cooperation in the future, please be advised that this will not happen as long as you are the Assistant Secretary."[51]

Given the dramatic and artistic deficiencies of *Firefox* and *Heartbreak Ridge,* Eastwood might well have been showing common sense in wanting to avoid the military as a future arena for his macho posturing. In fact, Highway differed little from Eastwood's film persona. He had typically played a loner, fighting the system, even when nominally a part of the system, as in his Dirty Harry roles. In contrast, the military demanded that the individual suppress his singularity in favor of the team. Like Patton, the Great Santini, and Tom Cruise's Maverick, Eastwood's Highway did not easily exist within the confines of the peacetime military. As much as anything else in the script, the Pentagon may having been reacting to the problem Highway symbolized: how to find a place for a warrior in the new armed services, where self-improvement and technology counted more than old fashioned soldiering. Eastwood himself did not help matters, even if he did not deliberately mislead the Marines into believing he would reshape, during filming, the problems about which Sims and the Corps had objected. Like John Wayne, Eastwood played Eastwood on and off the screen. Consequently, any challenge to his opus, however valid, became a challenge to him personally. Moreover, as a filmmaker, he considered the Pentagon's, and more particularly's Sims's, demands for changes in his story a challenge to his artistic creativity, and so he had no choice but to resist. With the lines so joined, the resulting misunderstandings became inevitable as well as irreconcilable.

The controversies over the film continued when the Marines refused to allow Eastwood to stage the world premiere of *Heartbreak Ridge* as a benefit at Camp Pendleton, where the company had done most of its location filming. Although the action served to give even more publicity to the film, nothing could help make it a box-office success on the order of most of Eastwood's productions. Whatever the Marines might think of the film and however much Eastwood might believe its patriotic images benefited the Corps and the nation, if truth be told, *Heartbreak Ridge* does not stand as a shining example of the military genre.

Vincent Canby put his finger at the heart of the film's problem: "*Heartbreak Ridge,* a movie at war with itself, has the same effect on the viewer. It requires a certain crazy vision to transform the American invasion of Grenada into the equivalent of Iwo Jima." Nevertheless, he thought Eastwood's performance as the "gritty, raspy-voiced" Highway became "one of the richest he's ever given. It's funny, laid back, seemingly effortless, the sort that separates actors who are run-of-the-mill from those who have earned the right to be identified as stars." In the end, however, Canby observed: "Even the dimmest moviegover is likely to find that the aircraft carrier transporting the marines to their objective looks bigger than Grenada itself, which diminishes both the suspense and valor factors." If he did not find the film as "aggressively muddle-headed" as *Rambo,* perhaps due to the low body count, Canby concluded that *Heartbreak Ridge* proved "almost wistful. Though it may not realize it, it seems as sadly out-of-date as its aging Cosmo-reading Sergeant Highway."[52]

The Pentagon's failure to have a significant influence on the way *Heartbreak Ridge* portrayed the Marine Corps and the actions of its men during the Grenada incursion again demonstrated how little leverage the Defense Department and the individual services actually had in dealing with filmmakers. They could, of course, turn down a script if it offered no benefit or was not in the best interest of a service or the military establishment. Or a service could open up its doors if it liked a script, as occurred with *Top Gun.* But unless the filmmakers needed an aircraft carrier or some hardware unobtainable in the private sector, the Pentagon could do little but request changes and hope the producers, in the name of accuracy, would revise the script. In the case of *Heartbreak Ridge,* the Marines, unlike the Army, began giving away the store before they had established a fair rate of exchange, and Eastwood burned them.

In contrast, the Navy saw significant benefit in cooperating on *The Hunt for Red October,* and the images the service received more than justified the effort. Beyond that, if viewers allowed their suspension of disbelief free rein, they could see in the film the end of the Cold War and the beginning of the Soviet Union's disintegration. In the double-talk vernacular of the Cold War, the film's opening disclaimer, "According to repeated statements by both Soviet and American governments . . . nothing of what you are about to see . . . ever happened," might actually be stating that something approximating what will appear on the screen truly did happen. Director John McTiernan pointed out that this message "tells the audience that these events took place before Gorbachev came to power. Also, we added a few lines in which we gently tried to hint that this incident, or some incident like it might have been part of what shocked the Soviet hierarchy into changing."[53]

McTiernan believed that audiences picked up on the suggestion that the defection of Ramius, the Soviet submarine captain, contributed to the end of the Cold War. Furthermore, he noted that at the beginning of the film, as the submarine embarked on its cruise, Ramius warns, "It's time." The director saw this comment meaning "It's time for a change, time to take a desperate chance for peace." McTiernan believed that audiences understood what the film was suggesting: "Can they get where they're going on time? Can they meet somebody who will trust them? Will somebody take a chance for peace?" He admitted that it sounded "sloppy, but those questions always enter into what's happening in the film."[54]

In fact, apparently something like what appeared on the screen did occur in November 1975, aboard the Russian antisubmarine frigate *Storozhevoy* (Sentry), which gives a modicum of plausibility to *The Hunt for Red October.* Shortly before the film appeared in 1990, *Izvestia* confirmed reports that Valeri Sablin, a captain third rank in the Soviet navy, and a dozen accomplices had put to sea from their base in Riga, Latvia, in an attempt to reach Sweden. Soviet aerial bombing stopped their defection fifty miles from Swedish waters and forced the ship to return to base. The military prosecutor's office found Sablin guilty of betraying the homeland and sentenced him to death by firing squad while his accomplices received various prison terms.[55]

Tom Clancy, the author of *The Hunt for Red October,* said he first read about the incident in a 1976 *Washington Post* article. He then obtained more details in 1982 from a master's thesis written by a student at the Naval Academy. The novelist explained that he learned from an *Izvestia* reporter that the imminent release of the movie gave the Soviet government a reason to acknowledge that "the incident really did take place." Consequently, although admitting he had taken considerable license with events, Clancy said, "My book has a historical foundation. But it is a work of fiction." It also became far more complex than the reality.[56]

In the novel, instead of undertaking a shakedown cruise, Ramius heads to the West with the *Red October* after informing his superiors by letter of his intention to defect. With his senior officers joining him, Ramius plans to turn over to the United States the secret, silent-running, first-strike vessel. The Soviet navy gives chase, but the U.S. Navy and Jack Ryan, a CIA consultant, join forces to intervene, enabling the submarine to elude its pursuers. In the film, the *Red October* makes it safely to the Maine coast, where Alec Baldwin, as Ryan, tells Sean Connery, portraying Ramius, "There will be hell to pay in Moscow when the dust settles from all this." The submarine captain responds, "Perhaps some good will come of it."

Connery later said he insisted *The Hunt for Red October* "be dated pre-Gorbachev and pre-glasnost" as a condition for his accepting the role. He explained that he "wanted the film not to be a film about the Cold War, but about an individual who would go to such an extreme to secure peace and what would make him tick." To ensure that his views prevailed, he brought in writer-director John Milius to rewrite his dialogue and better focus Ramius's motivation for his actions. Connery said, "When I read the script, I wanted it to be clearer why the captain was defecting—it couldn't just be anger toward his country. [Milius] resolved and simplified quite a few things and events and made it easier to understand." Connery also remained adamant that the film must in no way undermine Gorbachev's reform efforts: "Gorbachev is undoubtedly the man of the decade, and I don't think even he could have anticipated the rapidity of the changes sweeping throughout that country." Saying he admired Gorbachev for what he had done, Connery did not "want *Red October* to be construed as negative in any way."[57]

In truth, in *The Hunt for Red October,* Clancy did not provide a clear-cut explanation for Ramius's decision to defect beyond his anger over his wife's death during childbirth. In his final screenplay, Larry Ferguson created the idea that the Soviets had built the *Red October* as an offensive, first-strike weapon, which Ramius found unacceptable. However, Milius said the writer had not developed this "real strongly," and thanks to Connery's request he made the motivation clearer. Producer Mace Neufeld said the completed film showed that Ramius had defected "to prevent the use of a first strike weapon to start a war. I can think that almost everybody can identify with that, Russians and Americans alike. That motivation was not in the book." As a result, Neufeld saw Ramius as becoming a "good" Russian, not a traitor.[58]

Nevertheless, all the script-doctoring that Milius and others undertook could not change the reality that Ramius's actions did make him a traitor to the Soviet Union. No one loves, let alone trusts, a traitor. While recognizing this, Milius still believed that mitigating circumstances existed, because Ramius "is trying to stop this weapon from being used." Nevertheless, he thought that Neufeld was stretching things to see Ramius as a man of all countries: "He is a traitor, but he has made a moral choice."[59]

To convey the nature of this choice, *The Hunt for Red October* needed to create within the submarine captain's persona a plausible, selfless hero, a man who transcends national borders and takes a chance that might leave the world better off than he found it. The film ultimately fulfills this imperative, despite some of the actions Ramius must undertake along the way, such as killing a KGB political officer aboard the submarine and, of course,

Sean Connery, as captain of the *Red October,* and his second in command Sam Neill (left), as they try to bring the secret Soviet submarine to the United States in the last Cold War and first post–Cold War movie.

collaborating with the enemy. Moreover, the filmmakers do spare him from destroying a pursuing Soviet submarine and its crew, as he did in the novel. Instead, the captain of the pursuing boat, one of Ramius's progenies, torpedoes his own submarine in his obsessive effort to sink the *Red October*. In the end, therefore, Ramius comes to symbolize the new world order, and his defection becomes a lone man's effort to save the world rather than a traitorous act. Moreover, when he tells Ryan, once the *Red October* has reached safety, "Perhaps some good will come of it," the audience may make the connection between an event that never "happened" and the changes that had been occurring in the Soviet Union.

In any case, the filmmakers found it easier to define the intent of *The Hunt for Red October* than to come up with a suitable script. McTiernan explained that turning the lengthy, highly technical novel into a film became a difficult and time-consuming process. He explained that the "basic secret we found is that underneath everything, it's a sea story, and all sea stories are in essence the same: A boy goes down to the sea in ships, and he's swept off into a weird and alien world full of colorful characters, and he eventually learns to stand up and be a man among these wild characters, and he comes home forever changed. It's the same as *Kidnapped* or *Treasure Island*."[60]

In addition to finding the right approach to take with *The Hunt for Red October*, the director and producers Mace Neufeld and Jerry Sherlock also faced the problem of keeping up with the rapidly changing international political landscape. When they acquired the rights to the best-selling novel in 1985, the Soviet Union remained the implacable enemy of the United States. During the time the filmmakers needed to develop a suitable script and put the production before the cameras, however, the evil empire began its disintegration. Consequently, the producers had to ensure that events did not outrun the completed film.

Sherlock and Neufeld had actually begun negotiating for the rights before the book became a best-seller. Sherlock noted that praise for the story from President Reagan, Lee Iacocca, and others whetted the producers' interest in the sea tale of a Soviet navy captain who attempts to defect to the United States with Russia's most sophisticated nuclear missile submarine. Neufeld had observed: "The interesting thing about the book is that the Americans come out looking very good in it. It's a patriotic thriller and it's making the rounds in the government establishment." Apart from the president's calling it "a perfect yarn," Neufeld thought the story had two great leading man parts—the Russian submarine captain and the American CIA investigator: "They're both strong characters."[61]

Despite the obvious interest in capitalizing on the success of the novel, Sherlock said after obtaining the rights that actual production would not begin for at least a year, since the producers had not yet selected a screenwriter. Nor had they found a studio willing to finance the production. Initially, Neufeld had "thought it would be an easy movie." However, he later explained that despite the success of the novel, he needed fourteen months to secure backing, because studio executives who approve projects do not read books, relying instead on reports from readers.[62]

Compounding the problem, according to Neufeld, *The Hunt for Red October* did not "synopsize well in three or four pages. It becomes very complicated." At one point, MGM stunned the producer when it rejected the project, calling the book "just another submarine story." Only after he gave the novel to Ned Tanen, a friend and the production head of Paramount, to read during a thirteen-hour flight to England could Neufeld finally get a studio to consider the project. However, even though he felt the book would "make a terrific movie," Tanen required Neufeld to secure Navy cooperation and come up with a reasonable budget before Paramount would give final approval to the production.[63]

In fact, the development of the script itself took longer than Sherlock had expected. Three different writers worked on the adaptation of the novel, beginning with Donald Stewart, Oscar winner for *Missing*, who received inputs from Tom Clancy on the initial version. Nevertheless, Stewart recalled that *The Hunt for Red October* remained "a tough book to crack—there's a lot of gadgetry to it, the technology is an important part of the intrigue. And there's a lot, including characters, to boil down into two hours. Paramount's trying to get the best screenplay it can, and if it takes more than one writer to do it, that's the nature of screenwriting."[64]

Finally, on February 19, 1987, John Horton, Paramount's Washington representative, sent to Don Baruch Stewart's first screenplay. Although Horton said the studio could not yet submit any detailed requirements, the producers contemplated that they would build the interiors of two Russian and one U.S. submarine on soundstages. However, they anticipated requiring access to a Kennedy-class aircraft carrier for both interior and exterior photography as well as the use of other Navy combat and support ships. Horton indicated that production would begin within six months, during which time, he said, the studio would be able to coordinate the requirements with the Navy.[65]

Ultimately, work continued on a final shooting script for almost two more years due to Paramount's unhappiness with Stewart's effort, a writers' strike, as well as problems of rights between the Naval Institute Press and Clancy's new publisher, Putnam. Consequently, not until November 23, 1988, did Horton submit Larry Ferguson's final script, dated November 17, 1988, to Don Baruch's office. Horton advised him that "the requirements for assistance will be extensive" but promised to produce "a motion picture that should certainly provide substantial benefits for the U.S. Navy, particularly, the Submarine Service."[66]

To accomplish this, the producers would have to obtain Navy approval of the script. The huge success of *Top Gun* would normally have given Neufeld and Sherlock every reason to expect an immediate positive reaction to their request for assistance. The submarine service itself had reason to affirmatively respond. "Frankly, we learned something from *Top Gun*," said retired Navy Captain J.H. Patton Jr., technical consultant for *Red October*. With *Top Gun* proving a recruiting bonanza for the carrier branch, Patton said the submarine service "had to get in this movie game for recruiting sake." Perhaps more accurately, submariners needed a more positive portrayal than in their last appearance on the motion picture screen in *Gray Lady Down*.[67]

In fact, Neufeld did have some concern about how the Navy would react to his request for assistance. While in Washington shooting *No Way Out*, soon after he obtained rights to *The Hunt for Red October*, the producer had gone to the Pentagon to discuss the project. He recalled that "in the back of my mind I thought, well, if I can get permission, will they object later when they see *No Way Out* and then withdraw it. After all, we portray Costner as a spy and the Secretary of Defense as a murderer." Despite this concern, Neufeld pursued all avenues of assistance, including an effort to obtain access to two nuclear submarines the United States was dismantling as part of the Salt II Treaty. The producer thought that filming the subs would "absolutely" enhance the film. Although nothing came of his letter to the White House, the producers had better luck reaching an agreement with the Navy for the necessary assistance.[68]

After reading the November 17, 1988, script, Adm. J.B. Finkelstein, the Navy's chief of information, advised Don Baruch on December 12, 1988, that the service had completed its review of *The Hunt for Red October* and was providing a list of changes, which "are strongly recommended to enhance the motion picture." However, he made clear the

Navy was providing the comments "for guidance and should not be interpreted as mandated changes to the script which the Navy requires prior to cooperation and support." Instead, the service was voicing its concern that the script "is shallow. Paramount is obviously relying heavily on visuals to carry the picture. The script does not do justice to the detailed character and plot development of Tom Clancy's novel." Nevertheless, the chief of information said that the Navy remained ready to support the film and waited for Paramount's requirements list.[69]

Most of the Navy's comments dealt with technical matters, such as pointing out that the captain of the *Red October* would not address a member of his crew, "Hey you!" and noting that an aircraft carrier does not "bob like a cork." More serious, the service suggested that the banter between Jonesy, the sonar operator, and the chief of the boat "must be kept very light and deferential. Remember he is the senior CPO [chief petty officer] on the ship and is treated with great respect. Pay close attention to this dialogue." Documenting Finkelstein's concern about the shallowness of the script, the Navy observed that it contained "insufficient explanation . . . to explain or justify the Soviet defection." Moreover, the service said it found "insufficient development of the tremendous professional respect and admiration between Mancuso, the captain of the U.S. submarine *Dallas*, and Ramius. This could be easily developed by a little dialogue." Most important, the Navy felt that the film's closing scene "regarding reason for Ramius' defection is vague and confusing."[70]

Capt. Mike Sherman, director of the Navy's Los Angeles Office of Information, had a more positive view of the script, considering it "an exciting representation of Clancy's novel that presents the U.S. Navy in a professional and realistic environment." In a memorandum to the commands that would be providing assistance, Sherman said that the filmmakers were requesting extensive assistance, including "top of the line Navy assets." Nevertheless, he said the service expected that the finished film would "provide the first contemporary public look at the capabilities and professionalism of our modern Navy in years. Thus it is important, within the boundaries of security and feasibility, that the public be able to see the high tech, professional quality of our personnel and equipment." However, while the film would provide a wealth of opportunities for the Navy to demonstrate its hardware, Sherman acknowledged that "no one said it was going to be easy."[71]

Doing his best to at least make it easier, McTiernan wrote to Sherman on December 20, confirming their conversation on how he intended to satisfy Admiral Finkelstein and the Navy's concerns. In several instances, he said he understood he was taking dramatic license, such as in using Navy blue dress "because it is more impressive looking," but he said he would correct any inaccuracies. In regard to the bobbing aircraft carrier, he apologized for "the exuberance of Mr. Ferguson's description," explaining that he "was trying to say that it was stormy." He explained that the tone of banter between the sonar man and his superior "is perhaps misleading. What is intended here is that Jonesy and the COB are the closest of friends and that this dialogue is part of a long running and basically affectionate game between them. If Jonesy has overstepped here we'll try and pull it back. There is no intention for this scene to be in poor taste. The 'god damn' remark from the COB will be removed."[72]

In regard to the Navy's concerns about the insufficiencies of the script, the director answered, "The most candid thing I can say is that *we agree with you and share your concerns.*" He explained that the filmmakers were working to clarify the points the service had raised: "Specifically, with respect to explaining the defection, we are going to attempt to place the story in the past—prior to Gorbachev's ascension." He said they would "strive to improve the relationship between Mancuso and Ramius in terms of their mutual professional respect and admiration for each other." Instead of being the reason for Ramius's defection, the director said his wife's death would serve merely as "a release which made defection possible." Finally, he assured the Navy that the filmmakers would revise the closing dialogue to better explain why Ramius actually defected.[73]

With McTiernan's letter in hand, Sherman sent a memorandum to the chief of information on December 20, advising, "I am confident that each suggestion will be acted upon and that the script will be to our satisfaction." As a result, he recommended that the Navy approve the script and agree to assist on the production. Don Baruch then met with Admiral Finkelstein on December 24, to discuss McTiernan's letter and Sherman's memorandum. On December 27 Baruch advised the chief of information that since the director had answered all of the Navy's concerns, his office was formally approving the screenplay and assistance.[74]

The Navy did not, of course, really have a Soviet submarine secreted away up a Maine river. Nor had the evil empire yet been reduced to renting out its men and equipment. Since the producers had only Tom Clancy's description of the *Red October* with which to work, budgetary constraints provided the only limits the producers faced in creating the Soviet underseas craft. For the exterior shots of the submarine running on the surface, the studio built a five-hundred-foot fiberglass mock-up of the *Red October,* capable of submerging and surfacing, rather than the easier and far less costly expedient of using a model. As a result, the giant missile boat actually seems authentic and manages to convey the huge size of the submarine, which the script describes as the size of a World War II aircraft carrier, three football fields in length. As such, it seems to fulfill James Thach's wartime prediction in his comments on the original script of *Task Force* of "undersea carriers, avoiding detection."[75]

As with all submarine films, the producers had to shoot the interiors of the *Red October,* its Soviet pursuer, and the USS *Dallas* on soundstages at Paramount Studios. There, the filmmakers built portions of each ship on hydraulically operated fifty-by-fifty-foot platforms that provided a plus-or-minus twenty-five-degree pitch and roll, lending additional credibility on the screen. Not concerned with security considerations, the filmmakers created a control room for the *Red October* filled with electronic monitors and gadgets that resembled a *Star Trek* bridge. In contrast, although the Navy helped McTiernan give the control room of the *Dallas* an accurate ambience, he said shortly before filming began that the service had "a concern that it not be too accurate. They've told us why they'd prefer that certain things not be depicted in the movie, and they help us get around those things."[76]

For the most part, however, the Navy went out of its way to give *The Hunt for Red October* as much visual and technical authenticity as possible. The service allowed the director to film a submarine in dry dock, which it had never done before. In addition the

The control room of *Red October,* designed to appear ultra-modern.

Hunt for Red October producer Mace Neufeld aboard the USS *Enterprise* during filming of the Tom Clancy novel.

Navy gave the producers, director, and Alec Baldwin tours of the submarine base at New London. Neufeld, Stewart, and all the principal actors, with one exception, also took trips aboard one or another nuclear submarine. Ironically, Sean Connery, who joined the cast late in preproduction, never went to sea. Most important, beginning in late April the Navy provided the filmmakers, at several West Coast facilities, frigates, helicopters, three submarines, and the USS *Enterprise,* as well as off-duty personnel as extras aboard the submarines. Producer Neufeld reported that "it got to the point that rather than try to coach a crew of actors how to be like submariners, we just started using Navy instead of actors whenever possible. They were used to constantly drilling and, consequently, picked up direction better."[77]

The assistance came with a price, however. As it had done on countless other films, the Navy remained solicitous of its image. Originally, the script called for the hoist line to break as a helicopter lowered Jack Ryan onto the *Dallas.* For obvious reasons, the Navy would not want audiences to see a failure in a piece of its equipment. Consequently, in the completed film, Ryan releases the line rather than be hauled back aboard the helicopter. Mike Sherman, who had worked long hours on the script, thought that from "a story point of view it works a lot better." As played, the scene shows Ryan's determination to reach the *Dallas,* and of course, hoist lines seldom do break. More important, as Sherman pointed out, in a previous scene a jet crashes aboard the *Enterprise,* which "doesn't make naval aviation look too safe" if combined with the broken hoist line.[78]

In any case, cooperation clearly benefited both sides. When *The Hunt for Red October* opened during the first week of March 1990, it "pulverized the competition" by bringing in more than a third of all the money spent nationwide at the box office during its first weekend. Like *Top Gun,* however, the film received lukewarm reviews. In *Newsweek,* David Ansen observed that Clancy's book, the cast, and the director all had primed the audience "for an old-fashioned white-knuckle night at the movies. All we ask is to be kept on the edge of our seats; anything else the movie might offer—wit, interesting characters, great acting turns—will be so much gravy. But it's at the gut level that *Red October* disappoints. This smooth, impressively mounted machine is curiously ungripping. Like an overfilled kettle, it takes far too long to come to a boil."[79]

Hal Hinson, in the *Washington Post,* described *The Hunt for Red October* as "a leviathan relic of an age that no longer exists. It's also a leviathan bore, big, clunky and ponderously overplotted. And that it lurches into view as a Cold War anachronism is, in fact, the picture's most fascinating feature. It makes it irrelevant in an astonishingly up-to-date way." While saying that Connery could not fail completely at this stage in his career, the reviewer thought the actor's work in the film "consists entirely of the eyebrow thing—there's eyebrow up . . . and eyebrow down." Worse, he considered *Red October* "in its own peculiar way, a disaster movie . . . though not perhaps in the way the filmmakers intended. After spending about an hour with it, you begin to feel the walls of the theater closing in. You long for wide open spaces, or even just a room with a view. Most of all, what you want is to open the hatch and escape."[80]

Not everyone reacted so negatively. Vincent Canby, in the *New York Times,* found the film "most peculiar, but it's not without its entertaining moments." Recognizing that *Red October* had become "an elegy for those dear, dark, terrible days of the cold war," Canby considered it "the kind of movie in which the characters, like the lethal hardware, are simply functions of the plot, which in this case seems to be a lot more complex than it really is. Because everybody knows that the terrible things that might happen can't (or the movie would betray its genre), the only question is how they will be averted." In any event, he concluded that the "movie is never very convincing. Even the special effects aren't great."[81]

Perhaps not, but *The Hunt for Red October* became a huge box-office success, despite the naysaying critics, in part because the novel had presold the film. Of course, Neufeld thought it succeeded "because it is a terrific movie." Beyond such self-praise, the producer believed the time "was right for a submarine story, an American submarine adventure," as well as the importance of Connery as the film's star. Most of all, Neufeld thought the film benefited from "one of the most brilliant marketing and distribution campaigns I have ever been involved with." He explained that Paramount decided that instead of releasing the film at Christmas, it would open it in March "where you normally don't open big films like this," but then did "an incredible campaign to get audience awareness out." Nevertheless, he pointed out that if *Red October* had not delivered, people would have stopped coming.[82]

The Navy, of course, benefited from the fact that people kept coming and so saw the service's hardware, manned by highly competent officers and men. Most especially, they saw the professionalism of Jonesy, the young sonar expert, who skillfully recognizes that he is tracking something more esoteric than a whale. Hip to music, computers, and his sonar screen, he alone on the submarine distrusts the "40 million dollar computer" and uses his own faculties to solve the mystery of the missing submarine. More important for the Navy, audiences saw in Jonesy's character how enlisted men could achieve their full potential by going to sea.

Likewise, people found in Admiral Greer, the director of the CIA's naval intelligence, played by James Earl Jones with his comfortable majesty, the example of how anyone, regardless of race, could rise through the officer Corps on ability. Idealized or not, the portrayal of such competent people in *The Hunt for Red October* provided reassurance to audiences that the Navy was continuing to perform its mission in an exemplary manner. To be sure, black admirals might remain rare commodities in the real world. McTiernan acknowledged that "Admiral Greer is not black in the book," but he claimed he was not seeking to paint an idealized portrait of the service. Instead, he maintained that he used

James Earl Jones as Admiral Greer in *The Hunt for Red October.*

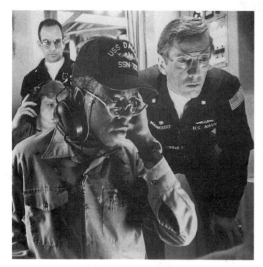

Frank Mancuso, chairman of Paramount Pictures, originally suggested the writers change the name of Tom Clancy's USS *Dallas* captain.

Jones because he conveyed Greer's "combination of sternness, rectitude and warmth." In any case, the Navy would certainly appreciate Hollywood's cinematic image rather than the reality. And Jonesy, Greer, Mancuso, and Ryan did help Ramius reach a safe haven in the new world and so contribute to the end of the Cold War, at least on the silver screen.[83]

McTiernan considered *The Hunt for Red October* more than just a sea yarn. Having a black admiral and a black sonar operator reinforced his belief that "in a way, the film is about immigration and integration. It's about a group of people trying to get to America." He said that when Mancuso, the captain of the *Dallas* and "obviously the descendant of immigrants," reaches the *Red October*, he becomes the first person of authority Ramius meets. Although Frank Mancuso, chairman of Paramount Pictures, wanted McTiernan to change the captain's name, the director said he persuaded the executive to keep it, not just because 5 million people had read the name in the book, "but that it said something."[84]

Whatever it said, *The Hunt for Red October* was to share the final images of the Cold War with *The Fourth War*, which appeared two weeks later. The title came from an observation Albert Einstein had made that a Third World War would be fought with nuclear weapons, and the Fourth World War would be fought with stones. In a Cold War parable showing how World War III might have begun and how warriors would have fought the next conflict, Roy Scheider plays a hardline American colonel, Jack Knowles, confronting Jurgen Prochnow, his Russian counterpart, Colonel Valachev. One became a decorated hero in Vietnam, the other in Afghanistan. Both combine the best and worst characteristics of Patton and the Great Santini. Their countries need their patriotism and combat skills during wartime but do not know what to do with their inborn belligerence during peacetime.

Despite regular run-ins with his superiors, Scheider has remained in the Army and in 1988 finds himself along the Czechoslovak border, under the command of a long-time friend who regularly tries to rein in his hawkishness. After helplessly witnessing the Soviets killing a defector only feet from freedom, Scheider launches a one-man war against Prochnow, who manifests the same frustrations of the ongoing Cold War confrontation. Each man spends the rest of the movie sneaking back and forth across the border fighting his own private war, which none of his fellow officers can halt. Ultimately, the two men face off in an icy pond, with armed troops from both sides watching the hand-to-hand combat, which ends in a standoff with both men exhausted but unbowed. Director John Frankenheimer made it clear that he was creating a film that could play in Moscow, saying that "the Russians certainly don't come off in this thing as heavies."[85]

From the Army's perspective, however, the image of an out-of-control renegade and a commander who implausibly did not remove him from the ranks would have made it difficult for the service to approve assistance to the production if it had received a request from the producers. Not needing any significant amount of equipment or men and undoubtedly aware of the reception their script would have received, the filmmakers went north to Alberta, Canada, which more than adequately substituted for the German-Czech locale. Visual authenticity was irrelevant, however. Instead, the film condensed the entire

Cold War confrontation to two men, who appear unsympathetic on the surface but are patriots who well represent and carry out their nation's Cold War policies. In this light, the film captured the essential nature of the Cold War and suggested how close the East-West confrontation came to turning hot.[86]

In the *New York Times,* Janet Maslin observed: "Giving equal emphasis to the unwavering dedication of these seasoned soldiers and the essential childishness that underlies their tenacity, *The Fourth War* takes some unusual risks. "It attempts to understand the heroism of a man like Knowles by casting him in an extremely foolish light and the result is an idiosyncratic portrait." Although Hal Hinson, in the *Washington Post,* called the premise "surrealistically improbable," the film did provide a cinematic end to the Cold War and an implied warning that the world should not go down the same path again. During production, director John Frankenheimer observed: "These guys are dinosaurs. In the age of glasnost, you don't need them. They're yesterday's business. . . . What we're trying to show without hitting people on the head—boom, boom, boom—is that war is an unthinkable alternative."[87]

The last word on the subject came in the 1990 HBO cable movie *By Dawn's Early Light,* which essentially began where *Fail Safe* had ended. Terrorists fire a nuclear-tipped rocket from Turkey at the Soviet Union, which launches a retaliatory strike against the United States before ascertaining the rocket's source. Both sides then frantically seek ways to prevent escalation to the global destruction that had occurred in *Dr. Strangelove* and was barely averted in *Fail Safe.* The Soviet president tells his American counterpart that he has three choices—accept the American losses, including Washington; reply in kind, which the Soviet Union will accept; or go for all-out retaliation. In the end, trust and common sense barely prevail. By the time the film appeared, however, events had overtaken the message. The Berlin Wall had come down and the evil empire was disintegrating, leaving both Hollywood and the armed services seeking new enemies to confront.[88]

29 | The Search for New Enemies

FOLLOWING THE REHABILITATION OF THE MILITARY with *Top Gun*, the end of the Cold War, and the overwhelming victory in the Gulf War, Hollywood produced a plethora of movies during the 1990s about the armed services or which used their personnel or facilities as incidental locales. Although the relationship between Hollywood and the Pentagon again assumed a comfortable normality, the Pentagon no longer easily approved cooperation as it had before Vietnam and not all films which received assistance contained completely positive images. Non-military dramas requiring only a brief presence by one or another of the services, which previously had obtained almost routine approval, now received greater scrutiny. Even in the case of military comedies, long a Hollywood staple, the individual services sometimes found sufficient problems with the scripts to turn down requests for assistance.

The producers of John Sayles's 1996 *Lone Star*, a quirky murder mystery set in a small western town, sought the use of a military base on which to film a few scenes. Col. Mitchell Marovitz, in the Army's Los Angeles office, spent long hours on the phone with the filmmakers answering technical questions about procedures and regulations. Ultimately, when he thought the script contained an accurate portrayal of the service, he asked the producers to sign the standard DoD form permitting him to be present during the filming of the Army sequences to check on the correctness of uniforms, props, and set dressing. Marovitz explained that he also wanted to verify that Sayles in fact shot the scenes portraying the service the way he had agreed . However, the officer recalled that the producers informed him that Sayles would not allow any outsider to remain on the set during filming. The Army then denied the filmmakers permission to use its facilities, and Marovitz pointed out that a colonel appeared in the film with his insignia upside down. Nevertheless, Marovitz considered that he had provided courtesy assistance which improved the authenticity of the service's image even without material help.[1]

Likewise, the Navy provided very limited, but significant, assistance to the 1993 comedy *Dave* and the 1999 drama *Random Hearts*. For obvious reasons, the Marines could not allow the filmmakers to use the real Marine One to recreate the arrival of the president on the White House lawn. However, the Navy did let director Ivan Reitman shoot the arrival of the stricken president at the Bethesda Naval Hospital. Although most people might not have noticed or cared whether the filmmakers had used the real Navy facility, the scene did acquire an authentic ambience from the actual locale. Similarly, the brief sequence in Sydney Pollack's *Random Hearts* in which a Navy rescue team responds to the crash of an airliner near the Pawtucket Navy facility acquires a sense of reality since the audience sees the service's men and women performing their jobs professionally and well.

The hugely successful 1994 *Forrest Gump* portrayed Forrest Gump as a brave soldier doing his job well, rescuing his comrades from certain death on the battlefield, and receiving the Medal of Honor for his efforts. What more could the Army want from a story showing one of its men as patriotic and courageous and the service itself helping him to become all he can be despite being, in the current vernacular, mentally challenged? As it turned out, the service wanted much more and ultimately decided it could not provide assistance to a film that most people would consider contained a highly positive portrayal.

In submitting the script to Phil Strub on June 21, 1993, John Horton wrote, "This delightful, heartwarming story of Forrest Gump, through whose eyes and experiences we witness an [sic] unique perspective of key happenings of American History of the last thirty years, has a number of scenes involving the military service during the Viet Nam war." In May, members of the production company had scouted the Marine Corps Recruit Depot at Parris Island, South Carolina, and Horton now informed Strub that the filmmakers would like to use Parris Island, "which though a Marine Base could provide a 'generic' basic training facility that could play as Army." If this proved not feasible, Horton suggested Fort Jackson in South Carolina as an alternative. In any case, the filmmakers would also require some military equipment of the Vietnam period "typical for firebases with flyovers of Air Force tactical air support. Forrest Gump arrives in the combat area in a Chinook Helicopter and leaves in a Med Evac helicopter."[2]

After reading the script, Colonel Marovitz, from Los Angeles, advised Strub that the Army could not recommend cooperation for several reasons. He cited "harsh" language throughout the script and a depiction of the military in the 1960s that "is inaccurate, stereotypical and implausible." More specifically, he observed, "The generalized impression that the Army of the 1960's was staffed by the guileless, or soldiers of minimal intelligence, is neither accurate nor beneficial to the Army. I cannot substantiate the notion that the Army ever attempted, 'an experiment to put together a group of dumbos and halfwits who wouldn't question orders.'" In addition, Marovitz stated: "The improbable behavior of uniformed personnel and the portrayal of active and ex-servicemembers is dyslogistic. The 'mooning' of a President by a uniformed soldier is not acceptable cinematic license." He also noted that the sexual content of the script "is excessive and gratuitous."[3]

Strub then wrote to Charles Newirth, the production manager for *Forrest Gump* at Paramount pictures, detailing the Army's problems with the script. He first cited the Pentagon's current criteria for cooperating on motion pictures: "For us to provide assistance, the military depictions must be historically accurate or feasible, of information value to the public, and of benefit to recruiting and retention." He then stated that the script "doesn't meet these criteria. The principal problem is one of inaccuracy, in that Forest [sic] Gump appears to have been recruited and trained to serve in a special unit comprised solely of others like him, then led into combat in Vietnam by an inexperienced officer as a kind of inhumanly senseless, doomed experiment." Strub acknowledged that the depiction of combat and the Medal of Honor Award ceremony served "a dramatic purpose and that the use of irony furthers both comedy and pathos. Apart from our earlier observation, we do not intend to debate the accuracy or realism of those scenes. Rather, we simply point out that they offer no compelling reasons for us to provide military assistance." Strub closed by saying the Defense Department and the Army remained willing to discuss their "fundamental concerns."[4]

Secretary of Defense Robert McNamara had in fact created the "100,000 Project" with the purpose of bringing mentally challenged young men into the military. However, the program intended to integrate recruits into regular units, not segregate them on a basis of IQ, as the original script had depicted. In responding to this misrepresentation, the filmmakers did change the screenplay so that it portrayed Gump undergoing basic training with normal recruits and fighting in Vietnam as a regular soldier. Both Strub and Marovitz felt that this correction alone significantly improved the image of the Army and justified the time they spent working on the project. In any event, the producers accepted Strub's willingness to continue discussions and attempted to respond to all the inaccuracies he had listed. In submitting the new screenplay on July 15, Newirth said the filmmakers had reshaped "the screenplay so that it addresses all the concerns you raised with us. I feel that the new draft is also very helpful on its own."[5]

Marovitz continued to work with the producers, providing them with research help to get the dialogue correct, making sure the uniforms and sets looked right, recreating a hospital in Vietnam accurately, and obtaining Armed Forces Vietnam Network tapes and logo. He also obtained permission for two of the actors to visit Parris Island to gain a sense of what took place during basic training. Nevertheless, the filmmakers never could correct the most significant portrayals that the Army considered inaccurate, and so the service did not provide formal assistance during production. In particular, Marovitz cited two problems that "caused us ultimately to say no to full support for them," even though he had found it "rewarding to work with them."[6]

He said that the filmmakers were unwilling to remove or change the scene in which Gump moons President Johnson during the Medal of Honor award ceremony. Although the writers may well have been imitating Johnson's display of the surgical scar from his gall bladder operation to the entire world, Marovitz and the Army felt that Gump's action showed disrespect for the presidency. In any case, Gump's attendance in uniform at the antiwar rally on the steps of the Lincoln Memorial itself, not his subsequent address to the rally, was bound to cause the Army significant problems.[7]

In the initial script, Gump expresses his ambivalence about the war to the throngs. However, what he says did not figure in the Army's decision, because the filmmakers ultimately chose to have the words go unheard, knowing the service's unhappiness with the dialogue. Instead, Marovitz explained that the service objected to Gump's appearance: "He didn't belong there and his being there in uniform was a violation of military regulations, not to participate in political events, activities, in uniform. You can do it out of uniform. If he had been out of uniform, it would not have been an issue. But he was in uniform wearing his Medal of Honor, appearing at the anti-war rally. And the film company knew that was a problem of mine from the beginning. His presence in uniform was the problem, not his presence, but his presence in uniform." Marovitz cited the Army's regulations and Code of Ethics, explaining: "I had a real hard time with him being there." Despite his concerns, of course, he did not have the final decision on whether or not to provide assistance. Instead of Colonel Marovitz making the decision, the Army's director of public affairs in Washington decided against providing assistance based on the recommendation from Los Angeles.[8]

With that said, Marovitz's particular concern over Gump's appearance in uniform at the anti-Vietnam rally remains explicable only if the story had hinged on issues relating to adherence to military policy and regulations, such as occurred with *The Caine Mutiny* and other military court-martial films. Given Gump's mental capacity, it could be argued that he simply had not absorbed or had forgotten the dress regulations. Moreover, over the years, all the services have shown a willingness to extend the dramatic license in deciding whether to provide assistance to comedies and fantasies since they do not intend to make a serious comment about the military establishment.

Forrest Gump was not making an explicit anti-war, anti-military, or anti-Vietnam statement. Gump himself clearly benefitted from his time in the Army. He fought bravely and returned home without any apparent damage, unlike most of Hollywood's Vietnam veterans. His mooning President Johnson, however well deserved it might be, would have become disrespectful only if Gump had acted out of disrespect and the director had created the scene with that intention. In reality, Gump was only being Gump.

Perhaps more to the point, the film portrayed the Army positively in the way it treated Gump, not as an idiot or stupid, but as a soldier who obeyed orders, did his job, and acted bravely. If the Army had failed to recognize Gump's courage in rescuing his comrades, if it had somehow turned him into a fool, then the service might have had grounds for refusing to provide the limited assistance the filmmakers required. Yes, Gump did appear in full uniform, proudly displaying his Medal of Honor at the anti-war rally. But as portrayed, he does not in any way discredit the Army, his comrades in arms, or his country. If anything, Gump's demeanor and dress at the rally stands as a reminder that most soldiers in Vietnam did their jobs well and returned home with few if any problems.

In any case, apart from the technical matters which led to the formal turndown, other factors contributed to Marovitz's recommendation to Washington. He explained that while he was providing informational assistance to the *Forrest Gump* company, two other projects were competing "very closely" for his time. He said they ultimately won out because they both were ready to begin shooting before *Forrest Gump* and "needed immediate attention." In fact, Marovitz felt that he might have been able to resolve the problems he had with the script if he had had the time to negotiate with the producer and if he had had the resources to assist on three movies simultaneously.[9]

While quality of a script has seldom figured into the military's ultimate decision on whether to provide assistance, the uniqueness of the Forrest Gump story and its portrayal of the Army perhaps should have caused Marovitz to solicit the means necessary to support the film. Whether *Forrest Gump* deserved its Oscar as best film of 1994, it certainly offered more entertainment value, and so bigger audiences, than either *In the Army Now* or *Renaissance Man,* the two projects on which Marovitz chose to cooperate. Regardless, if the denial of formal approval did prevent the filmmakers from shooting their basic training sequence on an Army base, Marovitz said the filmmakers were not disappointed with the courtesy assistance they received because it enabled them to infuse the military portion of the movie with visual authenticity. People assumed this came courtesy of the Army, and Marovitz felt the service received benefit from the film because his inputs into the production made the military portrayal more accurate than in the original script.[10]

The University of Alabama's concern about *Forrest Gump* probably had more legitimacy than the Army's. The film showed a young man with only borderline normal intelligence graduating from the school only because of his athletic ability. An aide to the university's president complained: "The indication is if you play football, even a slow-witted person could graduate. That has never been the case." People could only hope this claim had validity. The university took no chances, however, refusing to allow the filmmakers to shoot the football scenes at its stadium.[11]

Given the realistic combat sequences and the seemingly positive images of the Army, most viewers probably thought the service had provided more than informal technical advice to *Forrest Gump.* And given the extraordinary success of the film, people came out of the theater feeling good about the Army. In contrast, Nicholas Hassitt, vice president of Daniel Petrie and Company and the executive producer of *In the Army Now,* recognized immediately the problems he would have obtaining assistance in the making of his film, which ultimately appeared the month after *Forrest Gump:* "The first thing we had to do was convince the Army that we could make an outrageous Pauly Shore comedy without at the same time making the Army look stupid."[12]

By its very nature, a comedy creates its humor by making fun of people and institutions. Understanding this, the armed services have usually given comic screenplays wide latitude, both as to their content and as to their distortions of fact and procedure. For every *Private Benjamin* that did not receive assistance because it sometimes came too close to reality, the Army probably had cooperated on ten comedies whose contents no one took seriously, including the service. In the case of *In the Army Now,* the Army and DoD technical advisor Maj. Thomas McCollum explained why the service decided to cooperate on the film: "We look for two main things in deciding whether we will provide the cooperation requested from a film company. One, will the movie enhance our recruiting and retention programs, and two, does the movie enhance the public's understanding of the Armed Forces and the Department of Defense?"[13]

The initial screenplay that Hassitt brought to the Army's Los Angeles Pubic Affairs Office in October 1993 with a request for assistance did not meet those criteria. Marovitz "identified numerous unrealistic and unflattering stereotyping of military officers, noncommissioned officers and soldiers, outdated concepts of military life and training methodology, and a general misunderstanding of today's Army." Marovitz and his office proceeded to establish a line of communication with the filmmakers, which resulted in a more realistic approach to script development, and arranged for the company to survey locales suitable for filming the story. This effort created a script that satisfied both of the Army's requirements for assistance. McCollum said that the completed movie "shows that the military has the capability of teaching an irresponsible individual responsibility for his actions and the ability to help others."[14]

Phil Strub accepted Colonel Marovitz's recommendation of February 22, 1994, that the Army should agree to support the film. He acknowledged "the substantial changes that the producers have made to the script to date" and said he considered "that the latest version meets the criteria for support, particularly in its potential benefit to recruiting." Hollywood Pictures then signed the Production Assistance Agreement between the studio and the Pentagon, which delineated how the relationship between Hollywood and the armed services was to operate during productions. It put the filmmakers on notice that the agreement "is subject to immediate revocation due to non-compliance with the terms herein, with the possible consequence of the temporary suspension or permanent withdrawal of the use of some or all of the above military resources identified to assist this project." It then incorporated all aspects of the cooperation process stated in earlier DoD regulations on the subject, dating back to the ones that Don Baruch's office had issued. At the heart of the agreement, as always, remained the expectation that assistance would be "in the best interest" of the Defense Department.[15]

Once the Army ascertained that the completed movie would do this, it went all out to help the director make his movie. He shot the basic training sequences at Fort Sill in Oklahoma, where the stars of the film went through the ordeal of basic training for four days. During the shooting, the Fort allowed the director use of the barracks facilities, provided live firing of howitzers, and lent a company of soldiers for a full day of shooting. The Arizona National Guard provided Apache and Blackhawk helicopters for flyover filming by five cameras, and the Army allowed the company to shoot at the recruiting

Pauly Shore (left) and Andy Dick (center) join the Army Reserve in *In the Army Now*, a traditional Army comedy.

office in Hawthorne, California. Producer Hassitt said the Army "totally supported" the production: "Their cooperation was invaluable. The Army was impressed with us, probably because our planning and strategy were not unlike a military operation."[16]

Nevertheless, the effort did not produce a very good film or one that provided the benefits that the screenplay had seemed to offer, perhaps because of the less than five months the company took to shoot and release *In the Army Now*. Desson Howe, in the August 12, 1994, *Washington Post*, observed that Pauly Shore, "the tousled dude from Glendale is rarely allowed to be all that he can be. Enlisting for the formulaic potboiler about impromptu combat duty in the Sahara, Shore is too caught up in military maneuvers to—you know—be funny." Like Private Benjamin before him, Shore joins the Army as a way to escape his current woes, in this instance of having just been fired. He tells his buddy: "It's like joining a health spa, only they pay us." Unfortunately, he ends up being sent to the African desert as part of a deployment to counter a threat from Libya to blow up a collection of Army bases. The reviewer concluded that every promising situation for comedy in the film "suffers immediate creative fatigue. You wait for the big laugh but—apart from minor Shoreisms—it never really comes."[17]

To be sure, the Army did not judge the success of its cooperation by the number of laughs a film would receive. *In the Army Now* did portray how the contemporary Army trained its recruits and demonstrated its desert warfare operations, which justified the service's efforts. Whether people came away with an awareness of the Army's ability to transform an irresponsible individual into a responsible person, as Major McCollum said the film did, is debatable. In contrast, *Renaissance Man* left no doubt about its message that young men could learn to be all they could be in the modern Army, thanks to the teaching of Danny DeVito. Very much like Pauly Shore, DeVito's character is slowly sliding downhill after he is fired from his advertising job in Detroit. The unemployment office finds him a civilian job teaching thinking skills to Army recruits during basic training. Feeling his way in a totally unstructured environment, DeVito finally hooks his students by describing *Hamlet* in *National Enquirer* terms: incest, murder, intrigue.

The Army would clearly have no problem with such positive images and had only a few problems with the script, primarily because the writers were drawing on stereotypical images of previous Hollywood basic training movies. Producer Sara Colleton explained that drill sergeants in the contemporary Army differ significantly from the older generation: "It's no longer about tearing recruits down until they're nothing and then building them back up. It's all about accessing each soldier, and trying to find what they have that can be used as a basis to build up. There is a great deal of respect and love for what they do as drill sergeants." Director Penny Marshall said that the original script had "a lot of cursing from drill sergeants, but we found that in the real volunteer Army they aren't allowed to curse at the recruits, or else they'll get fired. Who knew?"[18]

Once the writers had updated the portrayal, the Army approved the script and gave

Danny DeVito attempts an Army maneuver in the comedy *Renaissance Man,* which received full Pentagon assistance.

permission to Marshall and the production company for six weeks of filming at Fort Jackson, near Columbia, South Carolina. One of only three functioning induction centers in the country, the installation has become the world's largest and busiest basic training facility. There, Maj. David Georgi served as technical advisor to the production, arranging for support that included everything from tanks to platoons of basic trainees. He saw his job as making sure the actors wore the correct uniforms, used the right military terminology in their dialogue, and operated the vehicles in the proper manner. Greorgi explained, "Accuracy improves the production."[19]

To that end, the Army subjected the eight actors who portrayed DeVito's students to a short course of basic training that compressed the eight weeks of recruit indoctrination into ten days. The producer observed, "Once our actors donned the uniform of the United States Army and while they were at the Fort, they were expected to obey all the rules and regulations that every soldier wearing that uniform would have to obey." She acknowledged that initially the playing of soldiers "was quite trying for the actors, but they rose to the challenge. It's grueling to be forced to get up at 0400 hours! It's a shock to the system when you're not used to it." One of the Army drill sergeants responsible for the training said, "There's not much difference between training actors or people right off the street. During that 10-day period, they learned how to march, how to wear the uniform and how to fire a weapon." Another instructor added, "The difference is that with regular recruits we have time to go into detail on everything. For the actors, we skipped over a lot and only taught them what they needed to know."[20]

The filmmakers learned the same lessons that the *In the Army Now* company had learned. On location, cast and crew operate the same way as the Army. Colleton observed, "It's all about scheduling and organizing. By the time filming was completed there was a great deal of respect and admiration on both sides." The effort and the mutual admiration notwithstanding, each party to the relationship had its own agenda. The Army received a reasonably accurate portrayal of how it trained its recruits in the contemporary, all-voluntary military environment. Whether or not a potential enlistee really wanted to learn Shakespeare, he or she might well come away from the movie recognizing that a tour of duty could prove beneficial even with early wake-up calls and long days of drilling.[21]

For helping to create these positive images, the director and the producer received a very inexpensive locale, the use of free extras, and a stage for DeVito to portray a man who goes through his own, albeit late, rite of passage along with his student recruits. The resulting film also became probably the kindest portrait of the U.S. Army since the Vietnam War. Nevertheless, its feel-good ambience did not satisfy reviewers. Hal Hinson, in the *Washington Post,* complained: "*Renaissance Man,* Penny Marshall's intellectually ambitious new comedy, is an extravagant and all-too-familiar Hollywood contradiction—a movie that celebrates the life of the mind and the uniqueness of the individual but does so in glib slogans and is, itself, a sort of knockoff." Hinson wrote that once DeVito uses *Hamlet* to inspire his students, "the movie loses all contact with reality. The rest of the picture is spent reducing Shakespeare to the literary equivalent of fast food, while at the same time demonstrating how being smart builds character." To add insult to injury, the reviewer concluded, "'Hamlet' may be the most indestructible of Shakespeare's plays, but *Renaissance Man* pounds it into politically correct dust."[22]

Roger Ebert complained that teaching Shakespeare had nothing to do with the Army. He pointed out that the lead drill sergeant, played by Gregory Hines, thought DeVito was simply wasting the time of his recruits. Worse, he noted that the writers had crossed *Dead Poets Society* with *Private Benjamin* to create *Renaissance Man.* Although acknowledging that both films also drew their inspiration from earlier stories, he claimed that they seemed "less labored" than *Renaissance Man.* At the heart of the film's problem, according to Ebert, "is its gloominess"; he said it "seems strangely thoughtful and morose for a comedy." Perhaps, but the Army's only concern remained how it portrayed its men and procedures, and the film did that well, within the limits of the comic genre.[23]

In contrast, the service would have nothing to do with the 1996 *Sergeant Bilko,* inspired by the 1950s sitcom featuring Phil Silvers as a conniving but lovable sergeant. Director Jonathan Lynn himself probably best explained the Army's disinterest in providing assistance: "For some reason, the Army chose to not to support the film, simply because the Commanding Officer is a dope and Fort Baxter is run as a country club for the benefit of a corrupt motor pool sergeant. We couldn't understand why." Nevertheless, Brian Glazer, the producer, claimed: "Nonetheless, we consider this film very supportive of the armed services, since, after all, Bilko is living up to the very Army ideal—being all he can be. I mean, if any soldier has reached his full potential, it's Ernie Bilko."[24]

By that logic, of course, *Babe* also served as a promotion film for the Army since Babe, the pig, became all he could be. In fact, the cinematic Bilko has no interest in becoming a recruiting-poster NCO. In charge of the Fort Baxter motor pool, he has never looked under the hood of a car. According to the press kit, Bilko's "skills simply lie elsewhere, such as being able to smell money hidden in the brim of a cap at a 100 paces. If he has discovered that renting out Army Humvee vehicles is a far more profitable use of one's time, who's to say he's wrong?"[25]

Reviewers answered that question, at least implicitly, by uniformly finding the film terrible. *Daily Variety,* never known for its harsh criticisms, commented: "Though [Steve] Martin and a solid supporting cast produce a few scattered moments of near-hilarity, for the most part the terrain here is as flat as it gets, and pic seems destined to run out of B.O. firepower quickly." The *Hollywood Reporter,* the other major industry trade paper, described *Sergeant Bilko* as being "as padded and bloated as a Defense Department budget." And Anthony Lane wrote in the *New Yorker* that he went into the screening asking why he should bother and came out "without having come close to an answer." Kenneth Turan, in the *Los Angeles Times,* said, "*Sgt. Bilko* is one of those joyless comedies that have lately become so prevalent, a halfheartedly amusing film that avoids originality while relying on old and tired material. Places where laughter is expected are always clearly indicated, but more often than not there is no reason to actually laugh."[26]

Apart from the positive but often implausible portrayals and the failure of military humor to actually produce laughs, the problem with comedies for the Pentagon remains the absence of serious enemies against whom the military can deploy its personnel and high-priced weapons. Moreover, without a credible foe, any combat lacks the dramatic tension that exists on battlefields. Science fiction films, however, by their very nature, contain real challenges to the armed forces, whether in the form of giant gorillas, mutant grasshoppers or ants, aliens, or meteors plunging toward earth. More often than not, the individual branches of the military have agreed to cooperate on these stories except where the portrayals ran counter to official government policy—as happened with *Close Encounters of the Third Kind* and *The Philadelphia Experiment.* The Marines, for one, gladly provided director Tobe Hooper full assistance on the 1986 *Invaders from Mars,* a remake of the 1953 classic.

Maj. Fred Peck, who had replaced Pat Coulter as director of the Los Angeles Public Affairs Office, explained, "Marines have no qualms about killing Martians." Hooper liked the comment so much he put it into the film. Peck and his deputy, Chief Warrant Officer Chas. Henry, helped Hooper visualize how the Marines might actually react in a confrontation with alien invaders. They also helped the director identify Marine reservists to constitute the cinematic leatherneck unit and recruited a retired Marine public affairs officer, Capt. Dale Dye, to serve as the paid technical advisor to prepare the off-duty extras to battle the Martians. The job started Dye on a highly visible career as an actor and a civilian technical advisor, and the film portrayed the Marines living up to their motto of being the first to fight in any crisis.[27]

In contrast, the Marines and their fellow services had serious reservations about the filmmakers' request for military assistance in the making of the 1996 *Independence Day.* In his critique of the original script that the Army Public Affairs Office in Los Angeles had received, Tom McCollum found that "there is very little depiction of us and therefore nothing in it for us." Moreover, he felt that the "military's depiction on a whole is not realistic." He said that "in order to get the cooperation of all the services, since all are depicted, many points must be addressed. He noted that the script does not make it clear whether General Grey headed the U.S. Space Command or served as chairman of the Joint Chiefs. McCollum also raised questions about the script's portrayal of military command and control, saying the president "does not have the capability to watch individual attacks, nor should he be doing this. He should be concerned with the strategic operations, not the tactical operations."[28]

McCollum objected to having the president lead the final attack on the aliens: "He is the President and there is more to leading the country than acting like a 'king leading the charge'" Instead, he suggested that the filmmakers should make General Grey a Vietnam-era fighter pilot and have him lead the strike. He also provided a long list of technical and procedural inaccuracies, including stationing tanks outside the White House, the use of military personnel to direct traffic rather than the highway patrol, and the use of the wrong type of helicopters. In regard to Will Smith's key role as the black Marine fighter pilot, McCollum cited several problems, among them having his rank change, having him dating a stripper, and having him steal a helicopter.[29]

In preparing for a meeting with the producers to discuss the initial script submitted to the Marines' Los Angeles Public Affairs Office, director Maj. Nancy LaLuntas cited essentially the same concerns in a memo she faxed to Phil Strub on April 24, 1995. She noted that as written, "the screenplay had no true military heroes. Military appears impotent and/or inept; All advances in stopping aliens are result of actions by civilians." She found the portrayals of the secretary of defense and the chairman of the Joint Chiefs of Staff "both negative" and the military chain of command inaccurate. Describing the Roswell alien landing as a "myth," LaLuntas said the Pentagon "would not want to support a film which perpetuates myth; DoD cannot hide info from president (i.e. aliens and ship in custody)." She objected to the film's suggestion that anyone could fly a high-tech aircraft and to having the president lead the aerial attack against the aliens. She also pointed out that all the action takes place in three days, which would not provide enough time for the National Guard or active military units to mobilize in order to meet the alien onslaught.[30]

Following the meeting with the services in Los Angeles, screenwriter Dean Devlin revised the script and sent it to Strub on May 8. He cited changes, including "some of the chain-of-command issues" and turning the chairman of the Joint Chiefs character into the head of the U.S. Space Command. He suggested that by clarifying the "proper channels of the military we hope this adds to the public understanding of how the military operates." Whether a simple alien-versus-earth science fiction movie had any informational value, particularly showing how the armed services operated, remains debatable and of less concern to the military than the myth of alien landings, which it had been denying for almost fifty years. Recognizing this, Devlin wrote that he had removed the "Roswell incident" and "Area 51" from the "domain of the military. Both incidents, now in the script, are part of a fictional government agency called the National Information Agency." The writer claimed "that by altering these things we've put the military in a better and more realistic light."[31]

Devlin then suggested that the changes in the script had enhanced recruiting and retention values for the military. He pointed out that the head of the Space Command had served in the Gulf War with the president and had become "a stronger and more effective character." He said he had given the "scientist nerd" character a military background in the National Guard, and so he had "some insight into the satellite signal he discovers." He explained that as a former fighter pilot, the president "believes he must get back to what made him a leader in the first place—the things he developed in the military. This is why he chooses to lead his men into battle at the end of the movie (like a King leading the charge)." Devlin said that the filmmakers believed that "by strengthening the military aspect of these characters, we'll portray the military experience in a more positive and alluring portrait. The military is now much more effective."[32]

In regard to the flying sequences, Devlin claimed, "We're going to make Star Wars and Top Gun look like paper airplanes! Just wait, there has never been any aerial footage like this before. If this doesn't make every boy in the country want to fly a fighter jet, I'll eat this script." After responding to some other concerns that the services had expressed during their meeting with the filmmakers, the writer acknowledged that he had had to work quickly. Consequently, he asked Strub to "remember that this is still very much a work in progress and will continue to change. Some of the changes we discussed did not work and I could not use them, some of the changes I may have simply over-looked. So please do not feel this draft is written in stone."[33]

Perhaps in the minds of Devlin and director Roland Emmerich, but not to the Pentagon. Despite the Hollywood rhetoric, neither the DoD nor the services would accept such claims, each responding to the new script in memos to Strub in much the same manner. The Navy, for one, did not think the project would ever qualify for assistance: "There's nothing in the script so far that we won't get automatically if they make the film without us." The service complained that the plot remained "the same tired story of nasty aliens ruthlessly brushing aside the pathetically desperate, inappropriate and completely futile attempts by the military to counterattack." The Navy pointed out that, as in all films of the genre, "earth's ultimate and totally unbelievable victory is the result of a last-minute, heroic, fortuitous assault by a tiny number of extraordinary civilians." The memo dismissed the contribution of the black Marine flier because he "is not really military, he's the stereotypical loner/soldier of fortune type." The service suggested that the Pentagon should ask if it wanted to become involved with the project before going any farther, pointing out that the other military portrayals, "whether they be people, missions, facilities, or weapons systems are at best mildly unrealistic and at worst completely ridiculous."[34]

If the Pentagon wanted to proceed, the Navy felt that "there's a huge amount of work ahead of us to increase the realism and positive military portrayals" and wondered if the filmmakers were willing to make the necessary changes to obtain assistance. Phil Strub thought that before the development of computer graphics, the producers would have had to agree to script changes because of their need for actual planes and military equipment. To him, *Independence Day* became a key film in the relationship between the military and Hollywood, since technology had reached a point where studios could create their planes and actions in the computer and so no longer absolutely needed to come hat in hand to the Pentagon for assistance. In any case, the Navy said that the "big ticket items" in the initial script that had caused the services immediate problems remained unchanged in the new screenplay. In particular, the office cited the portrayal of the Marine pilot as immature, the relationship with a stripper, and the destruction of B-2 bombers and other prized military hardware.[35]

On May 15 the Marine Corps Public Affairs Office in Los Angeles forwarded to producer Bill Fay a slightly updated version of the Army's April 10 "Points of Concern." Writing for the two services, Lt. Dustin Salem said that although Devlin had made some changes to the script, the services felt that "there are still many concerns about the revised script which would preclude Department of Defense assistance. In order to create an accurate and favorable portrayal of the military, all these problem areas will need to be addressed. The script as it stands is not supportable." Fay then listed some of the services' continuing concerns, including the portrayal of the aliens decimating military bases and aircraft and civilians ultimately saving the world. In regard to Roswell and Area 51, Fay suggested eliminating "any government connection" to the locales and having a "grass roots civilian group . . . protecting the alien ship on an abandoned base."[36]

Although claiming to want Pentagon assistance, the filmmakers showed no real willingness to address the military's concerns and made no serious effort to resolve the problems. In response to an inquiry from *Inside Edition* in December 1995, when *Independence Day* was in postproduction, Twentieth Century Fox suggested that while studios sought assistance, particularly for big-budget productions, they "rarely" obtained it: "The government and/or military, perhaps Hollywood's toughest critics, usually set forth an extremely detailed and strict of [*sic*] criteria that must be met before such cooperation is granted." The studio maintained that the producers of *Independence Day* had "made every effort to meet these government requirements," and the government "in turn, was impressed by the story's patriotic themes and heroic portrayals of the country's fictional leaders, including the President."[37]

In the end, however, the studio said the government "requested only one change—but it proved to be a deal breaker: All references, said Uncle Sam, to 'Area 51,' thought by many to be the home of a top secret alien study project, must be deleted." The studio explained its refusal: "Since Area 51 was critical to the film's themes of our world being visited by a non-terrestrial force of incredible magnitude, the filmmakers, as much as they desired the military's cooperation, could not comply. Filming proceeded—without government help."[38]

Clearly self-serving, the press release at the least showed no understanding of the Pentagon's policy on cooperation and at worst distorted the truth beyond recognition. Regulations had not changed much in the thirty years or so since Arthur Sylvester had stirred up controversy and issued new guidelines. Even before *Top Gun* had completed the rehabilitation of the armed services in 1986, the Pentagon had been providing assistance to filmmakers on both large and small productions, and during the 1990s the number of projects receiving assistance was increasing significantly. More to the point, the refusal of the Pentagon to cooperate with *Independence Day* did not result from one particular "deal breaker." The military had no problem fighting "fictional" aliens on the screen as the Marines had done in *Invaders from Mars*. In contrast, *Close Encounters of the Third Kind, The Philadelphia Experiment*, and *Independence Day* represented explicitly that their stories had some connection to actual events that the military had officially labeled as myths.

Since the armed services had regularly stated that they could not provide assistance to projects which ran counter to official policy, the Pentagon had no leeway in dealing with a story that posited an alien landing in Roswell, New Mexico, or the existence of real aliens and flying saucers in Area 51, whose very existence the government denied. The *Independence Day* producers simply were refusing to create a generic locale along the lines the services had proposed. At the same time, other issues remained unresolved that would also preclude military assistance to the production. By their very nature, science fiction villains, either earthly mutants or alien invaders, have unique power or they would not have much dramatic value. Consequently, whether the enemy came in the guise of irradiated grasshoppers in *The Beginning of the End*, giant ants in *Them*, or aliens from as close as Mars or as far as a different galaxy, mere humans would have a difficult time defeating the nonhuman threats.

Sometimes, after suffering significant cinematic defeats, the armed services receive help from unexpected sources such as microbes, as in *War of the Worlds*. More often, the military itself ultimately triumphs, by luring the grasshoppers into Lake Michigan or by using overwhelming firepower in *King Kong, Godzilla*, and *Invaders from Mars*. In *Independence Day*, however, the armed services suffer continuing defeats and show no ability to stop the alien invasion. Ultimately, a nerdy computer expert, not the military, delivers the fatal blow. Only then do the armed services, with the president in the lead, mop up the aliens. When combined with negative portrayals of the military command structure and leaders, the Pentagon could simply find no benefit in approving cooperation.[39]

Without military assistance, the producers turned to the Israeli Defense Forces, who lent the studio training and promotional films from the army, the aircraft industry, and an arms manufacturer to assist the studio and director in developing ideas for staging the movie's combat sequences. The film company also created special effects "in-camera" and used "20-inch store bought models of F-18 fighter jets" for the scenes of aerial destruction. Commenting on the use of models, Devlin explained: "Digital technology, especially for computer-generated animation, is a fantastic tool, but it's not for everything. There's a tendency to latch on to whatever new toy has been invented, but sometimes you need a good old-fashioned model on a string." However, the writer acknowledged that on occasion the production needed something more elaborate: "There were times when we'd look at an action sequence and say, 'Yeah, it's good, but wouldn't it be great if this whole thing blew up and then he flew underneath it?'" In fact, according to Devlin, the special effects "went from the highest level of high-tech, state-of-the-art digital animation to a simple model on a string in front of a photo."[40]

Of course, special effects drove *Independence Day,* and scenes of mass destruction of the White House and other landmarks helped the film draw huge audiences. Nevertheless, the story itself, recycled from any number of earth-versus-the-aliens movies, remained trite and utterly predictable. After all, no filmmaker would have the courage to portray the truth that any alien invasion would logically lead to the destruction of the planet or, at a minimum, the subjugation of mankind. If aliens had advanced enough to develop the technology to travel across space to earth, the U.S. armed services would simply not have the resources to stop any invasion force, whether or not the Pentagon would acknowledge the truth. The only hope for humans rests in Gene Roddenbury's thesis that to reach beyond its own planet, any life form would have first conquered its warrior instincts and would arrive at earth offering friendship, as the alien in *The Day the Earth Stood Still* attempted to do. Of course, in this instance, the United States immediately mobilized its military and launched a futile attack, a pattern Hollywood has regularly followed in such science fiction movies as *Starman.* In the 1984 John Carpenter fantasy, what seems like the entire defense establishment attempts to capture the alien during a cross-country chase, and for obvious reasons, the producers did not even submit a request for assistance.

Despite the concerns of the armed services, *Independence Day* did not contain such negative images. Most viewers would ignore the early futility of the military's response to the alien attack and would leave the theater remembering only the ultimate victory that the president had led from the front, not the rear. Of course, audiences also came away from the movie with inaccurate portrayals of the Pentagon's command-and-control operations, of its personnel, its procedures, and its potential ability to stop an alien invasion. As the military also feared, at least some people came away from the movie probably believing in the myths of Roswell, Area 51, preserved aliens, and space ships, as well as a government conspiracy to keep the secret from the American people.

Like the pre–World War II military preparedness films, *Independence Day* may also have created a false sense of security in people, since American armed services once again vanquished the aliens at the penultimate moment. For most people, however, *Independence Day* remained another science fiction fantasy that simply entertained audiences. In contrast, evidence of actual dangers from outer space existed in meteor craters and exhibits of meteors themselves in museums, theories about the death of dinosaurs from some cataclysmic event, and regular stories in the media about falling space stations and satellites, as well as predictions of potential encounters with asteroids. To be sure, the odds against an actual destructive collision with some sort of space debris, comets, or moon-size rocks remains statistically improbable.

This reality did not stop Hollywood from turning out during the 1990s three virtually indistinguishable disaster movies about natural threats from outer space. *Asteroid* appeared as a television miniseries in February 1997. *Deep Impact* arrived in theaters in May of the next year. *Armageddon* followed almost immediately in June. The two feature movies became box-office hits despite their similarities, the proximity of their releases, and poor reviews. All three sought and received assistance from the Pentagon, although in each film the armed services had a subordinate role, carrying out the maintenance of order and rescue assignments, which they would have done in any natural disaster resulting from flooding, earthquakes, hurricanes, or forest fires.

The original script for *Deep Impact* that Dreamworks submitted to the Army's Los Angeles Public Affairs Office in September 1997 contained several scenes depicting the service and the National Guard "engaged in disaster relief activities, supplementing law enforcement agencies, and assisting in the construction and staffing of a massive shelter." Maj. Ben Frazier, chief of the office, recommended to Phil Strub that the Pentagon approve assistance to the film, since he had "determined that supporting this project will benefit the Army and DOD. This production depicts a feasible interpretation of military operations and policies, and additionally will enhance U.S. Army recruiting and retention programs." Despite the endorsement, the Defense Department did not act, and the filmmakers continued to work on their story, ultimately submitting a revised script dated July 15, 1997.[41]

By then, director Mimi Leder had begun filming on location on the East Coast, and Kathy Ross, deputy chief of the Army's Los Angeles office, wrote to the production company suggesting that the service might be able to provide a "presence in the background. And if you are shooting any scenes with military members in it, we could arrange for someone to be on site to check uniforms." Nevertheless, the Pentagon had not yet given official approval to the film, and Ross enclosed the comments that she and Strub had made on the latest script. The two officials found the depictions of the Army "greatly improved," but they said the script "has very narrowly portrayed the military's role in a true national emergency by limiting the services' participation to law enforcement functions." They pointed out that the armed services "would be heavily involved in disaster preparedness especially since any existing civil defense system would be overwhelmed. Consequently, the depiction of the Army could and should be more multifaceted and less a depiction of heavy-handed, heavily armed dragoons."[42]

The Pentagon then provided specific comments, mostly on technical matters that would give the portrayals more authenticity. Ross pointed out that the president would say he is federalizing the National Guard and placing all the armed services on full alert, not just the Army as called for in the script. She noted that the scene in which one of the astronauts tells his sons he probably would not be coming back "runs contrary to the optimism and reserve that real soldiers use with families when discussing their future missions. Keeny should just tell his sons that 'this one looks tougher than most.' These young soldiers will know what he means." Ross did have one strong objection, saying the "depiction of the lieutenant *MUST* be changed. He can be polite and sympathetic and still get the job done." She explained that in checking the list of people who were going to an underground bunker, he would not use physical force: ". . . doesn't sound as if the situation is so dire that he can't behave more appropriately. He is, after all, in command and doesn't want to look panicked in front of his men."[43]

After meeting with Ross to discuss the military's comments, Richard Zanuck, head of the Zanuck Company and producer of *Deep Impact*, wrote to the Army on September 9 to answer the concerns that had been raised. He said he had talked with the film editor about changing some of the president's dialogue and assured Ross that the president would no longer say that anyone caught looting would be shot on sight. Zanuck said the director had agreed to make the lieutenant's "character more sympathetic but still stern enough to get the job done." The producer confirmed that M.Sgt. Thomas Field, from the Army's Los Angeles office, "should be in attendance when we shoot this scene as well as other scenes in our schedule whenever the Army or other military forces are depicted in the script." Ultimately, on October 9, Phil Strub wrote to Zanuck saying the Pentagon had approved assistance on *Deep Impact*. By that time, the help consisted only of filming a missile launch at Vandenberg Air Force Base, California, and the use for a few days of Army National Guard trucks, helicopters, and tactical and armored vehicles.[44]

Despite his presence on the set, Sergeant Field expressed to the filmmakers, in a letter

Richard Zanuck and David Brown, longtime partners on such movies as *MacArthur* and *Deep Impact*.

of December 12, his concerns about the portrayal of military personnel in *Deep Impact*. In response, the production supervisor, Peter Tobyansen, pointed out that the company had not yet made a final cut version of the movie. He explained, "The actual scenes that include the Military may not require any adjustments as noted in your letter." But he said he was distributing Field's letter to the editors, "and where it is possible, we will try to make adjustments required if necessary."[45]

Tobyansen pointed out that because Field and other service representatives had observed the filming of the scenes in which the military had appeared, the producers had presumed "that all the scenes were within acceptable boundaries of depiction for the Military. It is troubling for us to receive notice at this date that some scenes may not reach the standards you were to address during shooting." He noted that if Field had discussed the problems immediately, "a cost effective measure to do a reshoot would have been possible. The filming of the sequences with you and your advisors on the set was intended to prevent this very problem." Nevertheless, Tobyansen assured Field that the company would "make every effort to avoid using any scenes at length that may not reach your standards."[46]

To the extent that the Army would have had a problem with its portrayal, the service would have had to accept responsibility for the images, since the filmmakers had clearly made the effort to address the Pentagon's concerns. Fortunately, when Field viewed the final version of *Deep Impact*, he found that it did "conform to our agreements, and that the Army's portrayal in the film is accurate and reflects positively on the role it plays in disaster relief operations." In fact, Field acknowledged that the film contained a "minimal" depiction of the Army, and so the Pentagon waived the normal screening, though asking for a credit acknowledging the military assistance.[47]

However positive the images of the military in *Asteroid*, *Deep Impact*, and *Armageddon*, the services themselves had done nothing to save the world from the threats from outer space. Moreover, opposing aliens or meteors remained outside the normal realm of combat for which the armed services prepared. Hollywood and the Defense Department faced the same problem—finding credible enemies to confront. Deprived of the Soviet Union as a worthy enemy, the Pentagon sought new missions to justify its maintaining the world's largest and most powerful military establishment. Hollywood had returned to the armed services as worthy subjects, but filmmakers too needed meaningful enemies to challenge the United States in cinematic combat.

From where would they come? Tom Cruise had provided one answer in *Top Gun* when he engaged and shot down jet fighters from an unnamed Middle Eastern country. At first glance, Saddam Hussein and other Third World petty despots did appear ready to take their places as viable enemies, even though reality suggested that their armed services offered no real threat to the United States. Terrorists, hijacking and attacking American civilians, military personnel, and facilities, would continue to pose low-level challenges during the 1990s. Likewise, Russian nationalists from within the old Soviet Union and drug cartels might create limited dangers to the security of the United States. In one form or another, each would provide the grist for screenwriters to create stories in which the government ordered one or another of the armed services to take appropriate but small-scale actions against these new enemies. Within some of these stories, filmmakers were to place the most insidious enemy of all, a rogue officer or enlisted man who for one reason or another dishonors his service, his profession, and so his nation.

Who would actually fight these battles? Officers and military lawyers would attempt to root out the malcontents and traitors. In combat situations, Army special forces units provided the government with one option. The Navy Seals offered a second option. The top secret special forces organization was a direct descendant from the World War II Underwater Demolition Teams, which Hollywood had first introduced to the American people in *Frogmen*. However, over the years, with the very minor exception of *Underwater Warrior* in 1958, the service has remained reluctant to expose the group to much publicity for obvious reasons.

That very secrecy, of course, made the Seals an appealing subject. It also made the screenwriter's job somewhat easier. If the Navy would not reveal much about the organization, filmmakers could create whatever story they pleased, with little worry that the service would publicly dispute its accuracy. At the same time, of course, because of the Navy's protectiveness of its special forces, a producer would have little hope of obtaining extensive assistance to make a movie about the Seals. Consequently, when Orion Pictures submitted the script for *Navy Seals* in May 1989, the company probably had little expectation of receiving a favorable response.

Mike Sherman, the director of the Navy's Los Angeles Office of Information, read the script and informed Admiral Finkelstein, the chief of information, that he could not recommend approval for full cooperation. Although the filmmakers had made several changes in their story from the one submitted months before, Sherman said that "it still remains a flamboyant representation of the SEALs." He also questioned the authenticity of the final mission. Worse, he observed: "The SEALs' hallmarks, teamwork and professionalism are depicted only marginally in this script. . . . In short, this is not close to an accurate portrayal of the SEALs or their mission."[48]

Sherman enclosed for Admiral Finkelstein's signature a letter to Orion Pictures, informing the film's producing company that the service could not provide assistance to *Navy Seals*. He noted that the letter did not address the issue of limited cooperation. Sherman then reminded Admiral Finkelstein that Sen. John Warner (R-Va.), a former secretary of the Navy, and Virginia governor Gerald Baliles had shown an "inordinately high attention" to the script. He also reported that Michael Medavoy, the executive vice president of Orion Pictures, who had contacts with Governor Baliles through the Virginia Film Commission, had called the Navy's Los Angeles Public Affairs Office several times asking about the status of the script and the Navy's willingness to cooperate on it.[49]

Sherman also said he understood that Orion had prepared itself for a rejection and was seeking assistance abroad in making the film, most likely from Spain. Consequently, he recommended that the Navy advise its commanders there "to watch for end-runs for support" on the production. Nevertheless, he suggested, "*We should also look very hard at providing limited cooperation, if that's possible, as damage control.*" In an effort to do that, Sherman recommended that the Navy include in its letter to Orion his office's comments on the inaccuracies in the script.[50]

Most of the observations focused on technical matters such as terminology and procedures. The Navy pointed out that a Navy helicopter had a crew of two pilots and two enlisted men, not seven as in the script. In another place, the service pointed out that SEALs "would not fire 'make sure' rounds into each of the bodies . . . that is murder. They would not hurt or kill anyone unless 'deadly force' were authorized." The office noted that there "is no room for discussion in the Navy. When the officer in charge gives an order, that's it, ESPECIALLY in a combat situation." Interestingly, the service acknowledged that the SEALs "are not this nation's 'most secret combat unit,'" without identifying the actual unit, and then suggested the filmmakers refer to the organization as the Navy's "elite special operating forces."[51]

Admiral Finkelstein agreed with Sherman's recommendation and advised Phil Strub that although "the script is exciting and well-written, we cannot recommend Navy or Department of Defense production support of a film which depicts Navy sailors on covert operations in the Middle East killing with abandon. Further, the frequent unprofessional and undisciplined conduct of the characters does not reflect the tactics or esprit of Navy SEALS." In turn, Strub advised Finkelstein, "We concur with your recommendation not to support the subject film. The script contains fundamental and irresolvable inaccuracies regarding the mission and character of Navy SEALS." On June 27 Sherman informed Orion Pictures that the Navy, with the full agreement of the Defense Department Public Affairs Office, could not assist in the production of the film.[52]

As often happens, the Pentagon's decision did not end the matter. Although the production company shot most of the action scenes in Spain, after returning to the United States it wrote to Mike Sherman's office, asking permission to project footage from the Navy film *Be Someone Special* on television monitors. When Phil Strub received the request, he advised the Navy's Office of Information that he would not approve it, having previously concurred with the service's refusal to assist on the production. However, he did say that he would take action if the "the Navy would like to reconsider its position regarding the production."[53]

In response, the Navy did modify its position, and Strub approved use of the requested footage. The service also agreed to provide limited cooperation to the filmmakers, "only in the form of exterior location filming at the Norfolk Naval Base. Use of Navy equipment, personnel support, technical advice and locations other than those designated . . . will not be authorized. Access to any Navy SEAL compounds or working areas is not permitted." Even this limited assistance, when combined with a script by a retired Seal, Chuck Pfarrer, and his subsequent technical advice during the production, provided *Navy Seals* with an aura of authenticity. In particular, the film very well portrayed the rigors of the Seals' training regime, but not its weaponry or manner of actual deployment.[54]

The limited assistance and Pfarrer's firsthand experiences could not make *Navy Seals* different from any of Chuck Norris's special-forces movies. The heroes did a lot of shooting and killing and some romancing, a few died, but most lived. Ultimately, the violence became so gratuitous and random and the plot so implausible that the Seals lost little of their secret identity to the empty theater seats.

Peter Rainer, in the *Los Angeles Times*, described the film as "essentially a mechanical shoot-'em-up about a bunch of hell-raising heroes." The headline for the review in the *Chicago Sun-Times* tersely summarized the whole review: "Idiotic *Navy SEALs* Earns Disapproval." In the *New York Times*, Caryn James asked, "What Will Teen-Age Mutant Ninja Turtles Be When They Grow Up? On the evidence of *Navy Seals*, they are perfectly suited to be members of an elite Navy commando team. The men who fight Middle East-ern terrorists in this new action film are a mere step away from the adolescent Turtles in maturity and complexity of character, though they are not likely to come near them in box-office grosses." Not surprisingly, then, the film quickly disappeared to cable channels, perhaps because audiences did not find the enemies credible.[55]

Nuclear thieves and military turncoats were to prove a more serious threat in *Under Siege,* and the Navy image fared far better on a film that received very little courtesy assis-tance. In fact, it became a bad news–good news film for the Navy. Given its springboard, the Navy could see little benefit in assisting in its production. After all, what good could the service derive from helping make a movie in which terrorists, with the help of a high-ranking Navy officer, kidnap its most famous battleship, the USS *Missouri?* In truth, un-like other "kidnap" movies, *Under Siege* offers a story with at least a modicum of plausibility, at least until its closing scenes, which occur with such speed that they almost mask the inaccurate if not absurd resolution.

For the Navy's purposes, the portrayal of the magnificent ship at sea should have triggered excitement in the public affairs offices. Unfortunately, no benefit could accrue to the service from such images, since the *Missouri* was returning to its home in Bremerton, Washington, and most assuredly entering its final retirement from active service. More-over, the service could certainly not benefit from a film that showed hijackers, including the ship's executive officer, easily overcoming the battleship's officers and men.

Even having Steven Seagal play the good guy could not completely appease the Navy, since the hero, a demoted Navy Seal, is serving out his career in relative disgrace and obscurity as a chef aboard the battleship. However, he becomes the only person able to defeat Tommy Lee Jones, a deranged ex–Special Forces commander, and Gary Busey, the corrupt naval commander, who launch a plot to steal nuclear weapons and rockets from the *Missouri.* With his usual mixture of martial arts and modern weaponry, Seagal ulti-mately succeeds, although perhaps not in the traditional heroic image the Navy would have preferred. Still, *Under Siege* does contain some magnificent shots of the *Missouri* under full steam, which provide a fitting tribute to the ship.

In contrast, the Navy had reason to like the way *A Few Good Men* portrayed its offic-ers. Nonetheless, the Marine Corps had been expecting with trepidation a request for assistance on a film based on the 1989 stage play about the court-martial of two Marines accused of murdering a fellow Marine at Guantanamo Bay. When the script finally arrived in 1991, the Marine Public Affairs Office found its worst fears confirmed. Consequently, in a paper he prepared for a meeting with the producers of the movie, the Marine Corps chief of public affairs, Brig. Gen. Tom Draude, could only ask rhetorically, "Where are the 'few good men'?"[56]

Unfortunately for the Marine image, Draude found that the screenplay portrayed the service filled with "anything but good men. The officers are self-serving, ambitious, hol-low, weak-willed, abusive liars." He felt that only the Marine prosecuting attorneys re-ceived positive portrayals from the filmmakers. The enlisted men suffered as well as the officers. Draude described them as "robots who blindly follow a 'code' which flies in the face of the 'band of brothers' relationship among Marines—especially those in an infantry unit preparing for combat." Perhaps as bad, the Navy provided the few good people who prevented a miscarriage of justice. In this case, the Navy hero, in the guise of Tom Cruise, slays evil incarnate, Jack Nicholson, playing a highly decorated Marine officer who drips venom at every opportunity.[57]

In complaining about the absence of a few good Marines, General Draude acknowledged that the Marines did have some problems with their units and even their officers. However, he argued that those were aberrations and quickly discovered. In the case of *A Few Good Men,* all the Marine officers had severe flaws: "Col Jessep and Lt Kendrick, the bad officers, become worse. Jessep lies under oath, abuses the Judge, cracks under Kaffee's questioning, and physically attacks him. Kendrick continues to act like a supercilious ass and lies under oath repeatedly." Given such portrayals, Draude concluded: "In essence, the depiction of Marines is *totally* negative and, in my opinion, *totally* false."[58]

Draude concluded that the screenplay "seriously violated" the requirements of the DoD instruction governing cooperation with the film industry. Even if the filmmakers would change the script, the general thought they would only alter "this morality play's tension of 'good versus evil' into 'good versus real'—still with tragic results. In other words, unless there are strong, principled Marine characters to offset the other caricatures of Marines, the image portrayed of us is inaccurate and disturbingly unflattering."[59]

Although the Navy had felt the script on which General Draude was commenting deserved cooperation, its Los Angeles Public Affairs Office recognized the problems the story would cause its sister service. In a memo to the producer, Mike Sherman observed that the story did not contain "a strong Marine character to serve as a counter-point to all the dirt bags" in the script. He suggested that one of the Navy lawyers, Lt. (jg) Weinberg, become a Marine so that "he becomes a touchstone for the audience to see what a good Marine is. It also provides much better rationalization for his ire later on when he responds so negatively to the two enlisted men. *Believe me when I say this would be well received by the Marine Corps, the Defense Department and the lawyers.*"[60]

Despite this strong suggestion, at a meeting with the Marines on September 17, 1991, the filmmakers showed little understanding of the service's concerns with the portrayal of its officers. General Draude said that Rob Reiner, the film's director, saw Colonel Jessep as a solid officer who had simply made a mistake, in contrast to the Marines' view of him "as lacking the character and moral fibre expected of a Marine Corps colonel." In any case, Reiner indicated he was making the judge, the prosecuting attorneys, and the point defense attorney Marines and giving the judge a brief monologue in which he inveighs against Colonel Jessep, the principal villain. However, General Draude considered this simply as an effort to placate the service.[61]

More to the point, he recognized the difficulty of changing the script to make Tom Cruise into a Marine. In contrast to his Navy persona as a relaxed wise-ass, Cruise, as a Marine, would have had to assume a more serious, no-nonsense demeanor. In addition,

Tom Cruise works to uncover the truth in *A Few Good Men.*

Draude noted that if Cruise had become a Marine, the story would have lost the tension inherent in the rivalry between a Marine prosecuting attorney and a Navy defense attorney.[62]

In any case, after the meeting the general concluded: "At this point we're at an impasse. Reiner is obviously very passionate about this film and wants our help, but he does not appear willing to make the types of substantial revisions we would require in order to give it official support." He did note that the filmmakers actually needed relatively little assistance, which they could do without if necessary. From the Marines' perspective, however, if the service provided official support, it would be formally sanctioning the project. Draude felt that without major changes in the script, the Marines should "avoid the public's perception of Marine Corps endorsement."[63]

Likewise, Phil Strub concluded, "It became apparent that neither side was willing or able to compromise its position." In particular, Strub noted that the filmmakers refused to consider the Marines' proposal that Colonel Jessep's executive officer become "forceful" and "positive." He wrote that the director argued that this would change the plot and characterization "in an unacceptable way in terms of the drama, conflict, and thematic structure of the film overall."[64]

Despite the impasse, with a relatively modest revision of the script, the filmmakers might have found a basis for resolving their differences with the Marines and receiving cooperation. As written and portrayed, the climax of *A Few Good Men* comes when Tom Cruise as Navy Lieutenant Kaffee, the lead defense attorney, demands to know whether Jack Nicholson, the venial Colonel Jessep, ordered the Code Red that led to the death of a Marine enlisted man. In a scenery-eating response, Nicholson expounds on how his leadership has made the world safe for people like Cruise: "Son, we live in a world that has walls and those walls have to be guarded by people with guns. . . . I have a greater responsibility than you can possibly fathom."

Jessep maintains that the death of the Marine, "while tragic probably saved lives. And my existence, while grotesque and incomprehensible to you, saves lives. . . . You want me on that wall, you need me on that wall. We use words like 'honor,' 'code,' 'loyalty.' We use these words as the backbone of a life spent defending something. You use them as a punch line." However, he has not convinced Cruise, who demands, "Did you order the Code Red?" Not satisfied with the answer "I did the job," Cruise repeats his question, to which Nicholson shouts: "You're goddamn right I did!"

If the script had then had Jessep stop, realize what he had done, as Captain Queeg had done in *The Caine Mutiny,* and then acknowledge the truth by silence, the Marines may well have been satisfied that the film vindicated the Corps. Instead, Nicholson continues to maintain that he had done no wrong: "What the hell is this?. . . . I did my job. I'd do it again. . . . What the hell is this? I'm being charged with a crime? Is that what this is? I'm being charged with a crime? This is funny. That's what this is." He then lunges out of control and tries to get at Cruise, shouting: "I'm going to rip the eyes out of your head and piss in your dead skull. You fucked with the wrong Marine! Fucking people! You have no idea how to defend a nation. All you did was weaken a nation today, Kaffe."

Clearly, the Marines could not accept a portrayal in which one of their officers admitted lying, justified the killing of one of his men, and then in public threatened in the vilest terms to kill a fellow officer. On their part, the filmmakers would have been reluctant to part with the drama of Nicholson's breakdown, whatever its implausibility in light of his brilliant military career as well as his strength and control over every aspect of his life to that moment. Moreover, the lack of Marine assistance did not particularly hinder director

Reiner's efforts to create a realistic military ambience in *A Few Good Men*. Like all courtroom dramas, it remained a talking head film, albeit with very attractive heads, mostly set indoors.

Conveying the Pentagon's ultimate decision not to cooperate on the film, Strub wrote to the producer: "Simply put, it is the portrayals of the principal Marine Corps characters that we find to be inaccurate and consistently negative. Our regulations preclude providing assistance under these circumstances." While it did not expect every character to be a role model or recruiting advertisement, he said that the military was "convinced that a balance of positive and negative characteristics among the principal Marines would be more realistic, therefore more credible and involving to an audience, and potentially more dramatic as well." To Strub, all the Marines in charge of the barracks were "negatively portrayed, individually and collectively. Further, we have concluded that the current script reinforces the conclusion that not only is criminal harassment a commonplace and accepted practice within the Marine Corps, but that it requires a sister military service to uncover the wrongdoings and bring the perpetrators to justice. As presented in the script, the guilty Marines never even understand that they have done anything wrong."[65]

Still, Strub and the Marines did recognize that the filmmakers had "made a sincere effort in trying to reach an accommodation with us. We noted the substantive changes you made, such as changing some of the lawyers from Navy to Marine officers, placing a disclaimer at the beginning of the film, and making the military judge a Marine colonel rather than a Navy captain." As a result, the Navy agreed to provide courtesy assistance by letting the filmmakers use the Naval Air Station at Point Magu California as a stand-in for Guantanamo Bay.[66]

In the end, of course, artists should have the final say in how they present their work. As long as the filmmakers were willing and able to create their film without Marine assistance, their failure to reach an agreement with the service had little impact on the final product. In the case of *A Few Good Men*, Rob Reiner was able to make a dramatic, exciting film. Nevertheless, from the military's perspective, it did fail to fulfill the director's promise to the Marines to portray the military justice system accurately. In an actual military court-martial, Tom Cruise's decorum and demeanor as the lead defense lawyer would undoubtedly have caused the judge to reprimand him and the members of the court to become alienated by his actions. Furthermore, in a military court, sentencing would not have followed immediately after the rendering of the verdict. Nor does the "conduct unbecoming" verdict against the two enlisted men exist in the uniform code of military justice.

A Few Good Men owed more to Perry Mason, *The Caine Mutiny*, and other fictional courtroom dramas than to actual judicial process, civil or military. The lawyers' preparation and the trial itself followed the traditional formula in which tension builds to the final resolution when the good-guy lawyer traps the villain into admitting his transgression. In reality, any lawyer, civilian or military, who wants a long and successful career would not base his or her hope of winning a case on the slim chance of breaking a hostile witness on the stand. Although Colonel Jessep's explosion provides a pleasing dramatic impact, it lacks any plausibility. Nothing in his portrayal to that point suggests that he would lose control and admit that he had lied, particularly when no sufficient evidence existed to reveal the lie.[67]

Ironically, in *A Few Good Men*, Jessep's acknowledging that he had ordered the Code Red does not fully save the innocent victims of his actions. Although he finds them innocent of murder, the judge sentences the two enlisted Marines to dishonorable discharges for their involvement in the episode. To most Marines, and especially to the two Marines in the film, discharge from the Corps is far worse than a prison sentence.[68]

Such inaccuracies and implausibilities did not affect the dramatic impact of *A Few Good Men*. Nor did the actions and characterizations of Colonel Jessep or his subordinate officers or the fact that the few good persons proved to be Navy officers probably do the Marines much harm. Colonel Jessep differed only in degree from General Patton and the Great Santini in his commitment to the military and in his self-perceived role as savior of the nation. Although the implementation of his orders proved tragic, audiences could find truth in the need for warriors to man the wall to defend the nation, even if they found Jessep himself "grotesque." In fact, with Tom Cruise again playing a successful military hero, the film undoubtedly benefited the Marines, the Navy, and the military as a whole simply by showing that the services could attract the best and the brightest to honorable duty for their nation.

The Marines fared much better in *True Lies,* albeit in a minor role, helping Arnold Schwarzenegger combat nuclear terrorists. After first discussing possible cooperation with Maj. Jerry Broeckert, in the Corps's Los Angeles Public Affairs Office, producer Stephanie Austin wrote to Phil Strub on May 20, 1993, indicating the company's desire to use three Harrier jets and related support. As currently envisioned, Austin exclaimed that the "Harriers will be showcased in the grand finale and will, together with Marine Corps pilots and Mr. Schwarzenegger, play a pivotal role in the film's action-packed climax. Given the high visibility of this film, the intended use of this equipment and the heroic depiction of the Marine pilots, we believe that this film would well serve what Major Broeckert has described as the Marines' twin goals of educating the public as to the Marine Corps' operations and capabilities and generally enhancing the Marines' profile among Mr. Schwarzenegger's many young fans."[69]

The Marines were not about to refuse a proposal containing so many positive elements, and they had few problems with the script that Strub forwarded to Gen. J.M. Shotwell, the director of public affairs. In response, Shotwell imposed "no objections in principle" to assisting the production, subject to the normal requirements of no cost to the government and that assistance would be on a noninterference basis. He did stipulate that Harrier landing-site supervisors "must be available to supervise all flight operations during filming." He also "strongly" suggested in his memo to Strub two minor adjustments in the script "to make the Marine Corps element of the scenario more plausible." In one scene, as written, Schwarzenegger's character Harry Tasker climbs into the Harrier cockpit and starts the engine while the Marine pilot stands by idly. General Shotwell pointed out: "In all likelihood, a real pilot would object strenuously and would attempt to physically restrain a civilian from hijacking his plane." To solve the problem, Shotwell suggested having the pilot stand too far away to intercede or having another character restrain the pilot from trying to stop Harry. The general also recommended that the same character tell the pilot that Harry "is a former Marine Corps Harrier pilot." This would give plausibility to Harry's action, according to the general, who pointed out that the

Arnold Schwarzenegger, in a mock up of a Marine Harrier, prepares to rout terrorists in *True Lies.*

Harrier "is a unique and highly complex aircraft to fly; having a pilot who is unfamiliar with the Harrier immediately take off in the aircraft is too much of a strain on credulity."[70]

When he notified Austin of the approval of assistance to the production, Strub cited Shotwell's requests. And in the end, *True Lies* did portray Harriers in action accurately up to the point where Schwarzenegger takes the Harrier and flies away to Miami for his final confrontation with the terrorists. In a studio mock-up, Harry performs feats that the Marine plane simply could not do. Nevertheless, most people could not determine where reality turned into cinematic magic. Instead, even though the Harrier and the Marines made only a minor contribution to the story, they created a positive image of the Corps's men and weapons helping stop terrorists.[71]

The Marine appearance in *True Lies,* apart from the very positive association with Arnold Schwarzenegger and the huge success of the film, served another and more important purpose. In his column "Scramble over Roles and Missions," in the October 14, 1994, *Washington Post,* Stephen Rosenfeld wrote that the Marines "had scored a public relations coup by getting a Hollywood star into a plane that exemplifies and advertises their real-world effort to move to the cutting edge of technology and post–Cold War relevance." Rosenfeld put the cooperation that produced this result in the context of the defense debate "that is increasingly consuming military Washington." Citing the continuing tensions in the Persian Gulf, which Saddam Hussein was stirring up at that moment, the columnist observed: "Any battle that may yet engage U.S. forces in Iraq, Haiti or wherever is not nearly so likely to touch the core interests of our separate services as the battle now developing in Washington over the future roles and missions of the American military."[72]

This competition helps to explain why the services worked so hard to ensure that Hollywood would present them in the best possible light. Nevertheless, during the 1990s, filmmakers found many ways to circumvent the Pentagon and make their movies without Defense Department assistance. As a result, negative images of individual officers and men vied with positive portrayals on television and theater screens. Even mythic military figures such as Generals Eisenhower, Patton, and MacArthur had begun to receive exposé-like portrayals. The 1978 TV miniseries *Ike: The War Years* had presented in full color Eisenhower's relationship with Kay Summersby. The 1986 TV movie *The Last Days of Patton* revealed Patton's intimate relationship with his niece by marriage, which the Patton family had tried to keep hidden.[73]

Less salaciously, the 1995 cable TV movie *In Pursuit of Honor* posited that Gen. Douglas MacArthur, as Army chief of staff in the mid-1930s, had ordered the slaughter of hundreds of cavalry horses. Supposedly based on a true story, the movie depicts MacArthur arguing that he has a choice—either feed the horses, which no longer have a place in twentieth-century warfare, or buy tanks in anticipation of the next war. As portrayed, MacArthur callously refuses to consider simply giving away the horses to Indians or letting them run free. Believing that a cavalryman owes his first obligation to his horses and that regulations specifically forbid endangering their lives outside of enemy engagements, five soldiers ultimately take matters into their own hands.

Don Johnson, playing a senior sergeant and Medal of Honor recipient, refuses to march against the Bonus Expeditionary Force in 1932. His small mutiny gets him and three of his buddies from the good old days of the Mexican incursion and World War I exiled to a godforsaken cavalry station on the Texas–Mexico border. Craig Sheffer, portraying a brilliant but outspoken West Point graduate, also ends up at the outpost after hitting a fellow officer who was abusing his horse. When the outpost commander gives the order to shoot most of the now expendable cavalry mounts, Sheffer, who admits to having a problem with authority, requests to see the directive, arguing that only written orders have legal authority. The colonel, a petty despot in his own right, threatens to court-martial Sheffer unless he carries out the order. After watching the first group of horses machine-gunned and if necessary dispatched with rifle fire, Sheffer, Johnson, and Johnson's fellow cavalry soldiers kidnap the remaining mounts and herd them toward a safe haven in Canada with half the U.S. Army in pursuit. Their actions to save the horses, though clearly mutinous, more than balanced the negative portrayal of MacArthur's leadership and the Army's apparent inflexibility.[74]

The Rock, Broken Arrow, and The General's Daughter all contained even less flattering images of officers who become the enemies of their own services and so the nation. Very much in the style and tone of Twilight's Last Gleaming, the 1996 The Rock featured Ed Harris as General Hummel, a retired Marine and Medal of Honor recipient who seizes Alcatraz, takes eighty-one tourists as hostages, and demands a $100 million ransom as restitution to families of soldiers who died in covert operations and consequently were denied compensation. To back up his claims, Hummel threatens to launch at San Francisco nerve-gas-tipped rockets that he and his small group of renegade former Marine commandos seized from a naval base before their assault on the former federal prison. Like Twilight's Last Gleaming, The Rock requires audiences to suspend their disbelief and accept the implausible premise that a successful general would occupy a site that offers him no means of retreat. Viewers are also expected to believe that a general with such good intentions would actually be willing to kill thousands of people.

From the perspective of the Marines and the Pentagon, a noble goal would in no way balance the image of a rogue general stealing highly lethal weapons, taking hostages, and threatening to kill hundreds of thousands, if not millions, of people. Nevertheless, producers Jerry Bruckheimer and Don Simpson, perhaps hoping to draw upon the goodwill they had created with Top Gun, approached the Pentagon seeking military assistance. Although the Defense Department declined to help, they did suggest that if the producers would transform Harris and his men into a civilian militia, the services might cooperate. Bruckheimer and Simpson refused, saying that they did not want to give up the concept of Harris's character as a man whose "intentions were honorable." Be that as it may, the Pentagon saw no benefit to helping make a movie about military men turned terrorists, a movie that at the minimum suggested that generals lacked mental stability and sound tactical judgment.[75]

To be sure, General Hummel was not acting out of greed or evilness. In contrast, John Travolta, in Broken Arrow, played a villainous psycho who steals two nuclear warheads from his stealth bomber purely for monetary gain. Worse yet, the ease with which the traitorous pilot absconded with the atomic weapons ran counter to all the representations that the Air Force and the Defense Department have made for more than fifty years about the safeguards placed on the nation's nuclear arsenal. Even though Christian Slater, Travolta's copilot and friend, ultimately foils the plot after one bomb goes off, the story contained no possible benefit for the Air Force, and no record exists that the filmmakers even considered going to the Pentagon for assistance.

If possible, The General's Daughter, the 1999 generic murder mystery, offered an even bleaker portrayal of senior military men as villains. In a role reversal, Travolta becomes one of only two Army personnel with any redeeming features. Along with his former lover and fellow Criminal Investigation Division warrant officer, played by Madeleine Stowe, Travolta tries to unravel the bizarre murder of a highly decorated general's daughter found spread-eagled, bound, half naked, and strangled in the urban warfare range of her father's Georgia Army base.

In the course of the investigation, Travolta and Stowe discover that the daughter, a respected Army Psych-Operations officer, has apparently slept with most of the officers on base. As portrayed, her gang rape by fellow classmates during her third year at West Point has caused her deviant behavior. During the first of her two brief meetings with Travolta, she tells him that she teaches soldiers to mess with people's minds. In fact, she is messing with her father's mind in retribution for his insistence that she not file charges against the rapists since the resulting scandal would destroy his career. The denouement of the murder mystery reveals that the daughter's death resulted from one more effort on her part to get inside her father's head, as he is retiring and being considered as a vice-presidential candidate.

To create an authentic military ambience in which to play out the murder mystery, producer Mace Neufeld claimed to have "spent a lot of time" and hired Jared Chandler, a career reserve officer, to serve as technical advisor. He explained that he tried to surround the actors with the military culture, recruiting active-duty soldiers to serve as extras on their own time. He said that even though he provided the actors with "a foundation of understanding, you can't get everything from reading a book or just hearing about an exercise, you've got to experience it for yourself. Having so many military personnel about creates an environment for the actors; if they're playing an officer, everybody treats them like an officer. I think of it as a mini-boot camp."[76]

From the Army's perspective, an accurate military ambience would have remained beside the point if the filmmakers had approached the service for assistance, which they did not. To be sure, Travolta did not salute or show the general's daughter even the basic respect to which she was entitled during their brief meetings. More than that, he was clearly trying to hit upon her even though the military forbids fraternization between officers and enlisted personnel, although some interaction might ultimately have occurred given her sexual predilections. Instead, the very portrayals of rampant sexuality, the suppression of the gang rape, and, worst of all, the general's egocentricity by putting his career ahead of his own daughter's well-being would have produced a quick refusal to any request for assistance.

Of course, from the filmmaker's point of view, the Army base became only a locale in which to set the murder mystery. They could have used any service or academia or the financial world as the stage on which to play out their story. Most people went to the movie to watch how the two detectives tried to explain why a beautiful, brilliant young woman had died, not to learn how the Army actually investigated murders or trained its forces for urban warfare. Moreover, since *The General's Daughter* relied on sex, not hardware, to drive its story, the Army did not have to worry about inaccurate portrayals of stolen weapons to besmirch its image. As a result, the service and the Pentagon did not suffer irreparable harm to their images from the film.

From the motion picture industry's perspective, however, the few individuals who served as enemies to the services in *The Rock*, *Broken Arrow*, and *The General's Daughter* did not constitute high-level threats to the security of the nation, the element in any military film that provided the dramatic tensions at the heart of the story. In their continuing search for enemies capable of providing meaningful opposition, filmmakers turned to external opponents, whether drug dealers as in *Fire Birds* and *Clear and Present Danger* or Russian nationalists in *Crimson Tide* and *Air Force One* or Middle Eastern despots or terrorists in *Courage under Fire* and *The Siege*. Still, though showing the military in combat situations, filmmakers continued to include individual officers and men who posed real internal threats to their comrades in arms and so to the nation.

On the surface, *Crimson Tide* appeared to be simply another submarine genre Navy film. A nuclear missile submarine, a boomer in the contemporary vernacular, receives orders to put to sea to provide a possible response to Russian nationalists who have seized a missile site and are threatening to launch nuclear weapons against the United States and Japan. Such a story would seem to provide a positive portrayal of the power of the nation's submarine fleet and the competence of its officers and men in meeting an external threat to the security of the country. Moreover, prospects for obtaining Navy cooperation on the first post–Cold War underwater epic would have appeared favorable, since the producers of *Top Gun*, Don Simpson and Jerry Bruckheimer, and the director of the film, Tony Scott, would again be combining their talents.

In reality, the possibility of support may well have been doomed even before Schiffer traveled to Washington, given his original premise "to do something like *Fail Safe*" set in a submarine. There, he revealed to the Navy that he intended to create a mutiny aboard the submarine. After the visit, he worked with story consultant Richard Henrick, trying to develop a treatment which would interest Hollywood Pictures, a subsidiary of Disney Pictures. However, Schiffer described his first efforts as "bogus. We had a captain who was going to launch incorrectly and the only way you could postulate that he was going to launch incorrectly would be to make him a madman." The writer said that he would then have had to go down the path of another *Caine Mutiny*, with the captain "rolling steel balls in his hand," which did not add up. As a result, he "begged" the Navy's Los Angeles office to allow him to go the Bangor submarine base to do the necessary research to come up with a plausible story.[77]

In confirming the approval for the trip, Comdr. Gary Shrout, the director of the office, reminded Schiffer that it "is a preliminary research opportunity to help you obtain a clear picture of the roles and mission of the Navy's submarine force and its hardworking professionals." Nevertheless, he stressed the visit "in no way implies a commitment from the Department of Defense or Navy to formally assist with the production of 'Crimson Tide.' That decision will not be made until the studio formally submits a script to this office along with a letter requesting production support."[78]

After his two-day visit, Schiffer said he decided to stay in the area to do additional research, including interviews with submarine officers and enlisted men, asking specific questions. In the course of his work, he came up with the truth of the launch procedures and at "a real way that a launch message could be interrupted and could create confusion." With this concept, Schiffer said he no longer had to show the submarine captain as a madman: "By the research that I did, I found out that there really was a potential problem that could crop up and then I had a movie because I said, 'Well, if there is a message in hand, orders in hand, and a second message gets interrupted, you won't know what that second message is.' Every captain I spoke to on this issue said, 'If you have orders in hand and the second message got interrupted, you would launch. You *would* launch.'"[79]

Schiffer said that every civilian to whom he talked argued, "Of course, you can't launch. You would never launch under those conditions." In contrast, he recalled that "every single captain, every single officer I spoke to said you would launch." He explained that in the scenario he created for the movie, a Russian submarine was tailing the American boat, which it had damaged. As a result, the American submarine could not surface to confirm the launch message without getting blown out of the water. Schiffer said that under the

circumstances he had created, submarine captains "unanimously said they would launch. And, suddenly I had a movie in which men of principle could disagree. The executive officer, on principle, believes the submarine shouldn't launch. The captain, on principle, believes he should."[80]

Although Schiffer put the disagreement in terms of principle, to the Navy principle had nothing to do with whether or not a submarine would launch nuclear missiles. The service was to look at the story simply in terms of how accurately it portrayed launch procedures. In contrast, the screenwriter maintained that his story's central concern focused on the fact that at times the Geneva Convention holds that officers are entitled to disagree with unlawful commands. As a result, Schiffer saw at the core of the movie the issue of principle, whether orders are legal or illegal, and when is an officer required to step up and act.[81]

To the Navy, the decision of whether or not to launch had nothing to do with principle and everything to do with procedure.

When the screenplay arrived in his office in April 1994, Shrout found the script "extremely well written." However, in his memo to Phil Strub via the chief of Navy information, he recommended that the Pentagon not cooperate since the story did not depict a "favorable interpretation of Navy operations and policies," which Department of Defense instructions governing support required. Shrout explained that the screenplay "depicts a mutinous situation" between the captain and the executive officer of the USS *Alabama* after it has received "a legitimate national command authority message order to launch strategic missiles" against rebellious Russian nationalists.[82]

Shrout then explained that before the *Alabama* can move into position to carry out the orders, a Russian submarine attacks the sub, interrupting the reception of a second message. After sinking the enemy sub, the captain decides to continue the missile launch. At that point, the executive officer objects and requests that the *Alabama* attempt to obtain the balance of the new message before carrying out the original orders. Logic would, of course, suggest that the second message had to contain an abort order—nothing in the script explains the need for a second launch order. However, according to Schiffer, the captain believes that the window of time for a launch is elapsing and so he refuses to halt or delay the launch until he can obtain the second message. He then tries to relieve his executive officer, who in turns relieves the captain and confines him to his quarters. Shrout acknowledged Hollywood's need for dramatic conflict, but argued that "the reality of the submarine service is in direct opposition to this scene. In reality, the entire sequence of command and control is designed to allow for any non-concurrence to block the launch of strategic nuclear weapons."[83]

Ironically, Shrout pointed out that the script did include the executive officer's argument that the Navy had "redundancy in strategic systems so that if one platform (i.e. the *Alabama* cannot carry out the mission, others will." Given this reality, about which the captain had to know, Shrout maintained that a decision not to launch would in no way endanger the United States. Schiffer disagreed, saying that the *Alabama* was the point submarine in the area and that if it was to launch a preemptive strike to stop an enemy launch against the United States and Japan, then time was very much of the essence. Consequently, he said he went through all scenarios and felt strongly that the launch was justified.[84]

In any case, Shrout noted: "In order to launch, there must be complete agreement among the numerous designated individuals. The screenplay's portrayal of part of the crew rallying behind the CO to launch anyway when the XO does not concur is simply and completely wrong and does a disservice to the professionalism of the submarine community. In reality, at the point where the XO does not concur with the launch, everything would stop until such time as the XO did concur." Shrout went on to say that the crew would not "tolerate" an attempt by the captain to relieve the executive officer for non-concurrence with the launch and to find a "compliant officer."[85]

In this instance, the public affairs officer had the procedures wrong. Concurrence applies only to validating the launch order. Once the executive officer agrees that the submarine has received a valid order, only the captain can decide not to launch. Schiffer might have had a more interesting story if the captain had decided not to launch until he received the second message. In fact, Schiffer said that many submarine captains told him that at the point an executive officer tried to stop a launch, they would have shot him. Moreover the writer said that most of the crew would have supported the captain as they had been trained to do. Schiffer also pointed out that the interrupted message could have been a dummy message, and without the authorization codes the message had no validity. Consequently, Schiffer maintained that with a validated order in hand, the captain had no choice but to launch.[86]

On his part, Shrout next discussed the manner in which the screenplay tried to create a plausible scenario by showing that Navy procedures could cause a submarine to "inadvertently launch strategic nuclear weapons even when the national command authority is recalling their authorization. Given the professionalism of the submarine force, the probability of an inadvertent launch is less than getting kidnapped by Martians." Of course, the Navy and the Air Force believed in the infallibility of their command and control over nuclear weapons and wanted people to also believe that this control remained "fail safe." Consequently, in the Pentagon's view, any movie portraying a contrary scenario would provide an inaccurate portrayal of procedures, which would automatically disqualify the production for support under DoD regulations.[87]

Shrout had other problems with the screenplay, although obviously not as serious in nature. He said that the script contained more than eighty instances of profanity: "While profanity is not unknown in the military, this script's use of profanity is continuous to the point of being gratuitous. In addition to being unrealistic in today's Navy, this pervasive profanity conveys an incorrect and negative stereotype of the Navy that runs counter to Navy core values and the current emphasis on human values in the workplace." The public affairs officer also questioned Schiffer's portrayal of the captain as being "off base for the submarine community," explaining that officers maintained a quiet demeanor aboard ship rather than shouting as written in the script.[88]

In any event, the considerable research assistance which Michael Schiffer received during his two visits to the Bangor Submarine Base and on a ride aboard the *Florida* did help the screenwriter produce a high-quality screenplay. However, the Navy saw their help as having simply put the nuts and bolts in the right places while telling a story the service maintained did not accurately portray the service's personnel and procedures. Schiff disagreed, saying that at the film's core was the moral dilemma that men face if the system screws up, which he believed could happen since a good system was not necessarily infallible. And to the writer, resolving the dilemma made for interesting drama.[89]

Whatever the differences of opinion, Shrout considered it "unfortunate" that the Navy

The Pentagon bristled at the plan to depict an armed mutiny aboard an American ballistic missile submarine.

could not cooperate in the production: "There is a sense in this script that a determined effort is being made to put the Navy in the most positive light possible. While not evidenced in the current script, virtually all of the entertainment industry personnel connected with this film have stated that they wanted to portray the conflict between the CO and the XO as that of a disagreement between reasonable people." However, the script showed what amounted to a mutiny with officers and men using M-16 rifles to assert control of a ballistic missile submarine. As a result, Shrout could only hope that the studio would be "willing to be flexible on the creative content" so that "there might be a middle ground on which all could agree."[90]

Shrout then offered alternative scenarios which "might open the door to Navy support." However, he acknowledged that his suggestions "would certainly change the nature of the film from an action film to a more intellectual thriller." In any event, he stressed that Bruckheimer and Disney Studios would make the film with or without the Navy's help and had already begun construction of the sets. Why then would the producers be willing to change the portrayal? To obtain, according to Shrout, the same sorts of things for which Hollywood had been coming to the armed services for more almost ninety years: "What the studio would obtain from Navy cooperation is an extra degree of realism through the use of authentic establishing shots not otherwise obtainable, an important shot of a Trident boat [a boomer] submerging in Hood Sound and active duty technical expertise."[91]

The studio recognized this and Jeff Katzenberg, president of Disney Studios, traveled to Washington to talk with the secretary of the Navy concerning the service's refusal to cooperate on the production. In his memo to Strub recommending that the Pentagon not provide assistance, Adm. Kendel Pease, the chief of information, reported that at the meeting he told Katzenberg that the main reasons the service would not help "is the portrayal of an armed mutiny by the crew and senior officers of the fictitious ballistic missile submarine, as well as the characterization of their behavior, decisions and performance in general and during the missile launching sequences." He advised Strub that the Navy did not consider a "significant rewrite likely at this time." Despite the research trips, including one by director Tony Scott, Pease said that the Navy would insist that the film credits contain no reference to DoD or the Navy and no implied cooperation or support.[92]

Strub then advised the filmmakers, on July 8, that the Pentagon had determined that it could not provide support "due to the unrealistic portrayal of the Navy personnel assigned to the fictional ballistic missile submarine." Strub acknowledged that toning down the story "might dilute the drama." Nevertheless, he explained that "the fundamental premise of an armed mutiny, with its attendant depictions of the crewmembers' behavior, decision, and performance, is unacceptably unrealistic." He pointed out that the submarine-based nuclear deterrence mission "is predicated in large measure on the conviction that even during the gravest of crises, the crew would behave rationally, reasonably, and responsibly." Strub then stressed that adequate redundancies existed "in systems and safeguards in procedures to further obviate the breakdown in command authority and crisis in nuclear strike capability as depicted in the script."[93]

Simpson and Bruckheimer could not change the script and still make the film Schiffer had envisioned. As a result, they produced *Crimson Tide* without the Navy's assistance, telling an exciting story to people whether or not they knew anything about submarines and nuclear launch procedures. According to Schiffer, this included Navy people who told him they loved the movie. However, while audiences might enjoy *Crimson Tide* on a visceral level, the completed film contained most of the elements to which the Navy had objected in the script.[94]

Gene Hackman's somewhat overage captain is explicable, given Hollywood's need to cast bankable stars in high-cost productions. The shouting match between Hackman and Denzel Washington remains another matter. Schiffer believed that in stressful circumstances even highly disciplined men might yell at each other. Shrout had acknowledged in his critique of the script that "screamers" have served in leadership positions in the Navy. Nevertheless, he pointed out that "it is a particular point of pride with submariners to accomplish the mission in a low key and quiet manner." Moreover, the military has always objected to scenarios that portray officers disagreeing in public in front of enlisted personnel.[95]

Gene Hackman as a submarine skipper seemed a bit overage to some Navy filmgoers.

In the case of the submarine service, the Navy trains its officers to act with one mind. Consequently, the personality clash between Hackman and Washington, however dramatic, never would have occurred in front of the crew or even in private, the matter of a launch order aside. Given such significant problems, most viewers may not have noticed or even cared that several of the crew members were egregiously overweight, one sailor even dying of a heart attack during an early crisis. In the end, the film simply drew on the drama inherent in any submarine story, that when a sub submerges, it might not come up. However, since most nuclear submarines do reappear, the filmmakers had no choice but to hype the story, resulting in a movie which contained a portrayal of life under the sea that stretched the limits of dramatic license and provided no real benefit to the Navy.

As might be expected, the screenwriter and the technical advisor, Capt. Malcolm Wright, a former commander of the real *Alabama*, disagreed with such criticisms. Schiffer acknowledged that Hackman may have looked too old to portray the submarine captain, but explained that apart from the exigencies of the film industry, only his "towering performance" mattered. In this case, Hackman received $4 million for his appearance and Washington received a salary of $7 million. The actors, of course, gave the film star power of the first magnitude, and Washington's appearance provided diversity and a positive image for Navy recruiters. Nevertheless, Hackman created a character that offered the Navy no benefit and one that might well create concerns among viewers about the competency and mental stability of the men commanding boomers, even with the Cold War a fading memory. The dog, which director Tony Scott insisted upon putting aboard the submarine despite the objections from Schiffer and Wright, did little to improve the image of Hackman's captain.[96]

Naturally, the matter of the mutiny remained at the heart of the Navy's concerns, just as it had throughout the negotiations for assistance in making *The Caine Mutiny*. Whether the Navy's claim that no mutiny has ever occurred aboard ship has validity, it is true that no mutiny has ever occurred aboard a ballistic missile submarine. However, the confrontation between Hackman's captain and Washington's executive officer went far beyond a simple disagreement on principle. With each man threatening the other with physical violence, the cinematic *Alabama* clearly experienced a full-blown mutiny. If Schiffer had accepted one submarine captain's solution to the situation, the standoff would have ended almost before it began. Schiffer asked a submarine captain what he would have done if his executive officer had gotten into his face, as Washington did to Hackman's character. In response, the officer said, "I would put a bullet in his head right there. There would be no discussion. There would be no mutiny." Americans can only hope that the captain was speaking facetiously.[97]

To show that "reality," Schiffer would have had a very short submarine movie and perhaps a nuclear war movie. Likewise, if he had accepted the Navy's version of launch procedures with its requirement of concurrence by the captain and executive officer only to validate the launch order, he would have had no movie. Instead, he created a story that the Navy found stretched the limits of dramatic license beyond the breaking point. This did not matter to Michael Eisner, who had replaced Katzenberg as president of Disney. He believed that "it's a good story—and it's only a movie. I happen to have read the script, so I know about it. It is a very good script." Gary Shrout had acknowledged the accuracy of that claim. However, Phil Strub put the issue in perspective: "There is no question this armed mutiny is not going to make it in the Navy."[98]

Agreeing with Eisner, Captain Wright felt that Schiffer had kept the dramatic license within "acceptable limits. Let's face it, almost every movie about the Armed Forces has some measure of licence, exaggeration or fanciful thinking to enhance the dramatic impact of the story." In particular, he cited *The Hunt for Red October* as being "widely regarded as a 'good' movie because it's a good story, for one thing, and because it reflects favorably on the Navy. As good as it is, however, the film contains several artificialities that would make it 'unrealistic' to a determined critic." For example, Wright asked whether it was realistic "to expect a Russian submarine to be commanded by an aging, bearded Scots-speaking Captain?" As with the casting of Hackman as the *Alabama* captain, Wright noted that it helped "the story, because Connery has star power and he's such a magnetic personality." In any event, Wright said that submariners to whom he had talked thought *Crimson Tide* had captured their experiences aboard ship. Whether accurate or not and whether that included mutinies, Wright observed most succinctly: "I'll say it again and again: *Crimson Tide* is just a movie, Folks!! Lighten up."[99]

That may be true. And like *The Hunt for Red October*, *Crimson Tide* told a good story well. Does its apparent inaccuracies matter? Captain Wright said he grew weary of the "carping criticism of the movie, usually centered on the film being 'unrealistic' by some of my Navy colleagues." He thought that "critics seem to pick out minor details to illustrate their point." Although he acknowledged that "there were technical details that were incorrect," he thought they "were relatively few in number." However, he said that some of the supposed errors "are not outside the realm of possibility." Wright said that he had "witnessed 'screamers' and their conduct is not too different from that observed in Hackman's character." He recognized that "it is not likely that a submarine skipper would be as old as Hackman, but it is not unrealistic to see one who looks as old as Hackman!" He pointed out that the submarine service had had overweight sailors and officers, "given the high-calorie diet and the relatively restricted exercise facilities" aboard ship.[100]

Denzel Washington and director Tony Scott on the set of *Crimson Tide*.

Of course, these remain things the Navy could have lived with if Washington's non-concurrence to the launch had not escalated to mutiny. The technical advisor rightly pointed out that because of the non-concurrence, no launch took place, saying that "the portrayal of those actions necessary to launch missiles, were excruciatingly accurate. The words used by the actors are 'right out of the book.'" With Wright's help, Schiffer had that right. Instead, the service's criticism focused on what happened after Washington refused to go along with the launch, apart from the reality that the executive officer did not have the authority to non-concur at that point. As portrayed, Washington's refusal to concur escalated to armed mutiny, and that, as Phil Strub had written to Disney, "is not going to make it in the Navy."[101]

As often happens, however, the service probably did not suffer any long-term harm from *Crimson Tide*. Unlike many peacetime submarine movies, no submarines sank, the only death came from a heart attack, and the officers reconciled at the fade out. In contrast to Jack Nicholson's colonel in *A Few Good Men*, Hackman's captain recognized his errors in judgment and action. The film cannot leave it at that. Reality be damned. At Hackman's recommendation, Washington receives command of the *Alabama* and his career continues. Unfortunately, the Navy does not do things that way. What happened aboard ship would have automatically ended Washington's career whether by court-martial or formal reprimand. The service simply does not forgive transgressions or failures of command, large or small, and leading a mutiny does not look any better on a personnel record than it did in the script for *Crimson Tide* that came into the Navy's Public Affairs Office.

Schiffer acknowledged that the producers opted for a "feel good" ending by giving Washington command of the *Alabama*. He recognized that in the real world, the Navy would undoubtedly have court-martialed the executive officer. However, he suggested that Washington might not have been found guilty, given the issues of morality and principle the incident raised. In fact, Schiffer believed that the court-martial could have become the subject of a second film, one which the Navy probably would have avoided. Nevertheless, the writer maintained, "This movie does respect the profession of military men," and he said, "I am deeply grateful to the Navy for allowing me to research the story so that I could write an honorable screenplay."[102]

Ironically, although it remains equally implausible as the mutiny, neither the Navy nor the Department of Defense cited the launch order as a problem in *Crimson Tide*. The scenario asked people to suspend their disbelief and accept the premise that the U.S. government would order a nuclear strike against another country in peacetime. The makers of *Above and Beyond* had justified their inaccurate portrayal of Paul Tibbets's manifesting doubts about dropping the atomic bomb on Hiroshima on the grounds that no movie could show an American flier "killing eighty thousand Asiatics in a flash, and expressing no feelings of conscience about this, without seriously playing into the propaganda hands of the Kremlin." By the time *Crimson Tide* appeared, the Cold War had ended. Nevertheless, the same argument could be made about showing the United States ordering a nuclear attack against another nation and the captain of a ballistic missile submarine trying to carry out the order despite the possible existence of an abort order. Moreover, *Crimson Tide* itself provided the most plausible ending to the crisis—the Russian military eliminated the threat to the United States and Japan without recourse to nuclear weapons, theirs or ours.[103]

To be sure, most moviegoers do not think in geopolitical terms. Nor did many people who saw *Crimson Tide* concern themselves with issues of concurrence or non-concurrence or even whether Gene Hackman looked too old to captain a ballistic missile submarine. They simply wanted the film to entertain them, and if the cinematic mutiny appeared plausible and created dramatic tensions, so much the better. But not for the Navy, which maintained that it had never experienced a mutiny and that a mutiny like the one portrayed in the movie could never occur.

In contrast, the Army acknowledged that a mutiny in some form "is not completely impossible but highly improbable." Nevertheless, the service would take almost seven months to decide whether it would agree to assist in the production of *Courage under Fire,* which used a mutiny as its springboard. Writer Patrick Duncan came up with the idea as a result of his interest in the Medal of Honor and his direction of a cable series on the subject. With Akira Kurosawa's 1950 *Rashomon* as his model, Duncan created the story of Lt. Col. Nathaniel Serling's efforts to validate the nomination of Capt. Karen Walden to receive the Medal of Honor posthumously for actions during the Gulf War.[104]

Despite the locale and the nature of the war, Saddam Hussein does not emerge as the cinematic villain in the morality play as the plot unfolds. Instead, Serling quickly discovers that Walden's death does not have a simple explanation, irrespective of her courage under fire. Worse, she may have died not from Iraqi bullets but from an enemy within. To ascertain the truth and so find the actual killer, Serling must sort through the accounts of the four soldiers at the scene, each told from a different perspective. He also must labor under political pressure from the White House and the Army, since Walden would become the first woman to receive the Medal of Honor, which would provide a bonanza of good publicity for the Pentagon and the president.

While working on the story, Duncan requested and received permission from the Army for a research trip to Fort Hood in Texas, which he visited in July 1994. At the end of March 1995, producer Stratton Leopold submitted a script to the Army's Los Angeles office as part of his request for assistance in making *Courage under Fire.* Despite its research help, the service found a multitude of problems with the script, some more significant than others. Many went unresolved despite ongoing discussions. In its "Points of Concern," which the Army sent to Leopold on April 7, the service began, "With work, this script can become supportable by the DOD." However, noting that the script "raises a number of serious issues relating to negative portrayals and military authenticity," the Army told the filmmakers it wanted to meet with them "to see if we can reach an accommodation that will allow us to provide DoD support."[105]

The portrayal of the mutiny was to remain one of the Army's two primary concerns. To be sure, the confrontation did not have the potential to start World War III. Instead, it began as a disagreement between an officer who happened to be a woman giving orders to a man who rebelled against accepting them. The confrontation then escalated into violence, with matters made worse by an Iraqi attack. From its perspective, the Army explained: "The problems are multiple. Walden's crew is prepared to mutiny, astonishing behavior for the all-volunteer, post-Vietnam Army. Yet she does not seem surprised as she tries to confiscate their weapons. Worse, she is subsequently murdered by Monfriez, and her crew accepts her murder, abandons her to the enemy, and successfully covers up their crimes. Apart from Walden, the soldiers are all very negative."[106]

Of almost equal importance, the service expressed concerns about the portrayal of a friendly-fire incident in which Serling's tank destroys another one in his unit during a night battle in the desert. The Army noted the implausibility of Serling's receiving the assignment to investigate Walden's nomination while he himself remained under investigation. In a technical matter, the service pointed out that Walden's medivac helicopter, under the Geneva Convention, could not be armed as described in the script, since that would constitute a war crime. Instead, the Army suggested that Walden be flying a logistics mission.[107]

After submitting the comments to the filmmakers, representatives from the Army's Los Angeles office and Phil Strub, visiting from Washington, met on May 23 to discuss the script with the film's production company, including Leopold, director Ed Zwick, and Fox 2000 executives. Since it had not received a new version of the script, the Army repeated its concerns and explained the criteria for supporting a production. On his part, Zwick revealed his intention to incorporate into the portrayal of Serling's friendly-fire incident an attempted Army cover-up, based on a newly released Government Accounting Office report about an actual incident that occurred during the Gulf War.[108]

Although the Army had initially believed that it could correct or improve most of the technical problems through negotiations, it never was able to resolve its two major concerns with the story, the mutiny against Walden's command and the service's attempt to cover up Sterling's friendly-fire incident, which evolved into a significant aspect of the story. When the revised script, dated June 15, 1995, arrived in the Los Angeles office, the Army found that the major points of concern in the original screenplay, particularly the mutiny, "had not been addressed, and therefore they remain the same at this point." The office also found the new problem, the portrayal of the Army "trying to cover up Serling's fratricide incident." In regard to the script's suggesting that the Medal of Honor was being awarded for political purposes, the service explained: "The impression was that the Army was willing to award the Medal of Honor to Walden, regardless of the out-come of the investigation, just to satisfy the White House." However, Zwick had agreed verbally to tone down the portrayal. Nevertheless, the third script, dated July 27, contained many of the same problems and some new ones, all of which the Army discussed with Zwick in a meeting in early August.[109]

After receiving a fourth script, dated August 28, the Army met on August 30 with the producer and Rory Aylward, a civilian technical advisor whom the production had hired, and then with Zwick on September 1. Zwick indicated that he was rewriting the mutiny scene to depict the confrontation as the actions only of Monfriez, and "the depiction became muddled" when Walden tried to disarm one of the other soldiers. The director verbally agreed to the Army's suggestion that Monfriez's actions "could be left ambiguous if it appeared that he did not mean to shoot Walden." But Zwick refused to change the portrayal of a cover-up of Serling's friendly-fire incident despite the Army's suggestion "that the dialogue be changed to reflect that Serling could not tell the parents the whole story about their son's death because it was under investigation." The director's insistence on retaining the cover-up became one of the Army's reasons "for our inability to support this production."[110]

When the fifth script, dated September 11, 1995, arrived on September 12, the Army found that it still contained the same concerns and concluded that "without the corrections, support looked doubtful." In fact, Zwick verbally agreed to stage the mutiny "so that it is unclear whether Monfriez shot Walden on purpose or not." However, the director refused to change the depiction of Serling lying about the fratricide to the parents of the dead soldier. Given the service's regulations governing support, the Los Angeles office concluded that it could not recommend that the Army assist in the production: "There are too many unresolved issues that do not lead to an accurate portrayal of the Army to the general public."[111]

Despite the unresolved problems, the filmmakers still submitted to the Army a list of equipment and locations they were asking to use during production. Kathy Ross, then acting chief of the Los Angeles office, forwarded the requirements on September 15 to appropriate facilities, asking if they had the requested assets available. Still hoping to find common ground with the producers, she described the screenplay as depicting the Army "fairly and accurately," and thought the film "could be considered damage control in light of the GAO's investigation and reported attempted cover-up" of a friendly-fire incident during the Gulf War: "This production shows that the Army investigates its own problems, that we do not attempt to cover them up and that we move to correct them ourselves. Additionally, this motion picture shows true leadership, the abilities of female soldiers, and the human side of soldiers." However, she did not mention the portrayal of the mutiny as the center of the movie.[112]

On September 25, Judith Johnston, director of programs in the Army's Public Communications Division, advised General Fred Gordon, the Army's chief of public affairs, of the current status of the script. She reported that Leopold had met with the undersecretary of the Army in early September to discuss the disagreements between the studio and the service, and she said that by September 8, the production company "had made changes to the script that improved chances of gaining Army support. The friendly fire incident is now presented in a more positive light, and both the pressure from the White House and the mutiny are toned down." The Army's Los Angeles office had then advised Leopold on the twentieth about additional changes that still must be made before the Army could approve support. In turn, the office assured Johnston that all the requested revisions "have been agreed to verbally by the production company, except for the coverup of the friendly fire incident. On that matter, the Army continued to insist that "the impression of a coverup be removed."[113]

Ed Zwick would not concede the point to the service, and on October 5 the Army office in Los Angeles recommended to the chief of information and Phil Strub that "full support not be provided" to *Courage under Fire*. Lt. Col. Al Lott, the new head of the office, said that despite changes, the mutiny scene remained a major concern: "As currently written, the audience will leave the theater believing that a mutiny during combat operations is not only possible but highly probable." Among other continuing problems, he reported that Serling still states that the Army told him to lie to the parents of the soldier who died in the friendly-fire attack: "This gives the impression that the Army is attempting to cover up the fratricide." Although the script now depicted Captain Walden as a search and rescue helicopter pilot, Lott explained that the change did not solve the problem of her assignment, pointing out: "Women were not assigned to such units or missions during Desert Storm. Additionally, a UH-1H armed with only one machine gun would not be used for such a mission."[114]

Lott then noted that Zwick had informed the office that he no longer had enough time to address any of the outstanding issues, since he was to start filming on October 16. In a separate, handwritten memo to the Public Affairs Office, Lott reported that the director's conversation with his deputy "was friendly and cordial from beginning to end."

He also said that Zwick asked if he could continue to call the office for technical advice and was told he could. Lott followed up his deputy's conversation with a personal call and confirmed his demeanor as "cordial."[115]

The Army chief of information approved Lott's recommendation on October 11. General Gordon agreed that courtesy assistance was "in the best interests of the Army and the Department of Defense," since the producers had indicated they wanted it: "We believe the ability to acquaint producers, directors, and cast with Army personnel, equipment and facilities, and with Army customs, courtesies, language, uniforms and procedures will enhance overall the accurate portrayal of the Army in the film." On October 19, Strub concurred with the decisions, and on the twenty-sixth Lott wrote to Leopold confirming their prior conversation: that the Army could not provide "full support" but would extend courtesy assistance by answering questions and providing information "regarding scenes which depict the U.S. Army."[116]

Despite his apparent cordiality over the phone, courtesy assistance did not satisfy Zwick. Shortly before *Courage under Fire* opened in June 1996, the director complained: "How can the military be asked to be the arbiters of which films should be given assistance? To some degree our tax dollars are being spent on noncontroversial films." From the Army's perspective, the portrayal of the cover-up, which became more prominent as the script evolved, had become the main obstacle to providing cooperation. General Gordon repeated his belief that a cover-up "was absolutely implausible in terms of what would really happen in our Army." Zwick disagreed, claiming that the script reflected new information about friendly fire during the Gulf War, including the GAO investigation, which listed thirty-five soldiers who died from friendly fire during Desert Storm.[117]

Of course, cover-ups at the highest level of government have occurred, and no absolutes exist, except perhaps the Navy's fail safe procedures. Moreover, General Gordon's claim that *Courage under Fire* did not "reflect how our forces performed in the Persian Gulf War" perhaps misses the point. The film did not purport to repeat CNN's coverage of the one hundred hours of combat that the armed services took to reveal Saddam Hussein's feet of clay. Instead, Zwick was telling a story about people, some of whom acted bravely and at least one who mutinied. Things happen, and at least as presented, they did not seem to exceed the limits of dramatic license. Nor did the mutiny, as rendered on the screen, suggest that it occurred regularly, Lott's claim notwithstanding. Even General Gordon admitted that he understood the appeal the film had: "If I were simply reading the script as a private citizen, not responsible for the institutional image of the Army, I would say 'Gee, this is probably the kind of film to come see.'" More to the point, despite the Army's concerns, people who went to see *Courage under Fire* most likely did not leave the theater with a negative image of the Army or the way it fought during Desert Storm. They did see a mutiny of sorts, but certainly not one having the possible ramifications of the one that occurred aboard the *Alabama*.[118]

In *Courage under Fire*, Monfriez did challenge Walden's orders and authority to command. However, as ultimately portrayed, after all the discussions and rewrites, the confrontation became believable. Many officers and men in all branches of the armed services vehemently oppose women in the military. Who can predict how apparently stable men with such views would react to orders from a female superior, particularly if they found themselves under the sort of stress Walden's crew was experiencing on the battlefield? In any case, as played by Meg Ryan, Captain Walden portrays a competence and bravery that provided a positive image for the Army and certainly justified the awarding of the Medal of Honor for courage under fire. Nevertheless, the film did not contain an enemy that threatened the national security of the United States and so did not provide Hollywood with the kind of drama inherent in good, old-fashioned combat between powerful foes.

Whether or not the Pentagon offered full military assistance to a production would not solve the problem for filmmakers if they could not create a viable battlefield on which to show tanks and planes waging battle. Yes, terrorists can kill thousands of people, but as Israel's continuing confrontation with Palestinian civilians and terrorist bombers has demonstrated, military hardware has only limited value. Ed Zwick's 1998 *Siege* very well illustrated the problem and even the dangers of the Army's becoming involved in trying to stop terrorists in an urban environment. Given the image of an out-of-control general leading forces into the heart of New York City, the Pentagon once again refused to assist Zwick, much to his disgust.

For the most part, however, whether facing Russian nationalists, Middle Eastern terrorists, or in-house enemies of the people, confrontations remained small-scale and the military's role limited to small-unit operations, as in *Executive Decision,* which received assistance from the Pentagon, and the misnamed *G.I. Jane,* which did not. Ironically, Hollywood found its most unsavory enemy within the Pentagon itself. In perhaps the most damning portrayal of the U.S. armed services ever produced, the made-for-cable 1998 *Pentagon Wars* contained a devastating look at Army procurement procedures. Although played for laughs, with Kelsey Grammar as the general leading the charge, the film reveals the deceit and stupidity within the Army as it tries to build and test the Bradley Fighting Vehicle. Based on the account of Air Force Lt. Col. John Burton, who was assigned to evaluate the usefulness of the new weapons system, *Pentagon Wars* portrayed out-of-control Army officers interested only in promotions. In the end, the Army gets its new, if flawed, hardware, Grammar's general gets his promotion, and Burton's career ends because he tried to blow the whistle on a poorly designed vehicle's huge cost overruns.

Where, then, was Hollywood to find suitable enemies to challenge the U.S. military on the battlefield? Reverse the process that began in 1943 and unrehabilitate the most evil enemies that had ever threatened the nation, Nazi Germany and Imperial Japan. Robert Ludlum showed the way in using unreconstructed Nazis as villains in his novels at a time when the Soviet Union's feet of clay were becoming visible and so lessening the danger of Russian expansion. The 1996 miniseries *The Apocalypse Watch,* based on Ludlum's novel of the same name, portrayed real Nazis and their descendants, not neo-Nazis or skinheads. The old-line fascists have a charismatic leader espousing the end of democracy and hoping to carry out Hitler's goal of world domination.

When the would-be führer dies after his plans barely fail, the old Nazi general behind the plot observes sadly to his colleague and granddaughter, "So close this time. So close." She answers, "Don't despair, grandfather. We're not finished yet. We still have a strong following in every country in Europe. And somewhere out there is a new leader. We just have to find him."

Hollywood could live with that. Very soon, filmmakers returned to the bad old days of G.I. Joe versus Hitler and Hirohito. Unfortunately, the Pentagon had little to gain from this renewed interest in World War II, since the armed services no longer had any vintage weapons and no active-duty officers to serve as technical advisors. Nevertheless, if the war films that Stephen Spielberg, Terrence Malick, and Jonathan Mostow were to create showed the American armed forces positively, then the nation and the military would benefit from the images of soldiers, sailors, Marines, and fliers saving the world from implacable foes.

30 World War II: One More Time

HOLLYWOOD HAD NOT FORGOTTEN ABOUT World War II even during the height of the negative portrayals of the military following the end of the Vietnam War. *Midway* had become a major box-office success in 1976, and *The Big Red One* had enjoyed critical acclaim in 1980, with audiences cheering in all the right places. Although not a film about combat, *The Last Days of Patton* in 1986 presented Patton as a great war hero and created sympathy for the man after his automobile accident and painful death. Nominally set in World War II, *Day One* and *Fat Man and Little Boy* had a different agenda. Each presented the United States as a villain for using the atomic bomb against Japan and so played down the reasons we had built the atomic bombs. As a result, Japan becomes a victim of an evil weapon that we should not have used.

In the sixteenth century, Francis Bacon observed that histories "make men wise." From that follows the converse that bad history, trivialized history, history distorted, history sensationalized can make men ignorant. Both movies tried to make men wise, but in the end they lost their power to inform because of their inaccurate portrayals of events and people. In the language of the computer age, garbage in, garbage out.

Based on Peter Wyden's book of the same name, *Day One* focused on the scientists and how they ultimately regretted working on the Manhattan Project. The 1989 made-for-television movie conveniently ignored the fact that the scientists had willingly joined the bomb-building endeavor, at least in part because the Manhattan Project gave them the resources to do research that would have otherwise been impossible. Only when they realized they had succeeded did some, such as Leo Szilard, begin to have second thoughts. Though the movie is set in scientific laboratories and at Los Alamos, the filmmakers did ask the Army for some stock footage.

After reading the script, Dr. Alfred Goldberg, the historian of the Office of the Secretary of Defense, advised Don Baruch that Wyden's book itself contained "a large number of errors in the text and end notes. These consist of inaccurate renderings of quotations and occasionally of paraphrases, incorrect page references, and citation of sources that have no relation to the text." In addition, he observed: "Wyden sometimes contrives dialogue that does not exist in his sources or expands dialogue from the existing sources." Not surprisingly given the problems with the original book and the screenwriters' penchant for dramatizing events, Goldberg found the script "far more flawed than Wyden in dealing with dialogue, containing many inaccuracies, even in quoting Wyden's quotations."[1]

In regard to historical accuracy, Goldberg said that "the greatest transgression is the contrivance of dialogue (and probably scenes also) that does not exist in the sources, the imaginative and inventive elaboration of dialogue derived from sources, and changes in timing, scene, and circumstances." The historian acknowledged, "This may be justified in terms of literary license and the need for dramatic effect, but there are instances when the changes are inappropriate or prejudicial." Consequently, he concluded that the script "has obviously taken liberties with its sources and with the facts." If the Pentagon decided to provide assistance, he recommended that "some form of disclaimer be required of the producer before the Department of Defense lends official assistance and, by implication, official sanction to this production."[2]

This did not become necessary, since Baruch's office advised Aaron Spelling Productions that the script's historical inaccuracies prevented the military's involvement with the project. In turn, David Rintels, the writer and executive producer, advised Baruch on November 10 that the company was withdrawing its request for stock footage. He then launched into a bitter attack against Goldberg's vetting of his screenplay, claiming he had done considerable research apart from using Wyden's book. He cited his own knowledge of historical method and accuracy, having graduated from Harvard magna cum laude. Rintels offered to provide his sources and resented that Baruch had sent Goldberg's "inaccurate memorandum" and denial of cooperation to his colleagues. He then pointed out that Goldberg had not cited any of the sources on which he had based his letter, which Rintels found "less than professional."[3]

The writer then objected to Baruch's comment in the current issue of *Emmy* magazine in which the Pentagon official had said, "If you want to make a picture that puts us in a bad light, you may as well not even come to us. We're not in the business of making ourselves look bad. But we will look everything over. Then, if the producer is willing to talk to us about making some changes, we may be able to do business." Rintels claimed that nothing in the picture would make the Defense Department look bad and found "the standard you choose for yourself a poor substitute for the standards of truth and fairness I have tried to apply." Saying the experience he had had working with military, historical, and scientific consultants that the company had hired to ensure accuracy in the production had been "completely professional," he concluded: "I am sorry that I cannot say the same of my experience with the Department of Defense."[4]

Aaron Spelling, CEO of the production company, launched his own diatribe against Baruch the next week, saying that the Pentagon had "terribly impugned Mr. Rintels' integrity as a writer and as one of the foremost historians in our industry." He expressed dismay that Goldberg had not cited specific inaccuracies in the screenplay and maintained that Rintels would have willingly made corrections as he had done with the advice from the hired consultants. He closed: "I'm afraid that I speak for many members of our Entertainment Industry who are disappointed with the treatment we have received from your office."[5]

Goldberg, of course, recognized that errors in both books and movies "are inevitable." In responding to the criticisms from Rintels and Spelling, Goldberg also acknowledged that the script "does bear evidence of extensive and thoughtful research, much more so than any of the movie and TV scripts I have reviewed over the years." He said that many of the errors "are minor or not of sufficient factual consequence to alter the general accuracy and thrust of the story line," but some became significant "because they give a misleading impression or are in bad taste." Appreciating that the Pentagon was dealing with the entertainment industry, Goldberg observed: "Obviously, a certain amount of literary license for dramatic effect is permissible and even necessary in scripts for this purpose." Getting to the heart of the problem, Goldberg wrote that although "the thrust of the script is accurate . . . the tone is sometimes intensified or manipulated. The sharpness of character delineation—particularly Groves, Oppenheimer, and Szilard—once again for dramatic effect, does not always do the protagonists justice."[6]

To buttress Baruch's decision not to approve assistance to *Day One*, he then provided a limited sampling of the sources he had used in analyzing the script, including K.D. Nichols's *The Road to Trinity*, Leslie Groves's *Now It Can Be Told*, and Atomic Energy Commission historians Richard Hewlett and Oscar Anderson's *The New World, 1939–1946*. He then cited more than thirty errors of fact that he had found in the screenplay. Among others, he pointed out that Alexander Sachs had met with Roosevelt on consecutive days in October 1939 to sell the president on the idea of developing an atomic bomb, not one time as in the script. He said that Rintels made Groves "look even more high-handed and brusque than he was." Goldberg also pointed out that in the portrayal of a key meeting about the use of the bomb, some of the people appearing in the scene had not actually attended, whereas others who had attended did not appear in the scene.[7]

Of course, a filmmaker must sometimes compress actual reality to avoid redundancy. Patton had made two similar speeches to his troops before D-Day, which Coppola combined. Likewise, the general apologized twice for slapping soldiers, and the film showed it only once. In *A Bridge Too Far*, William Goldman showed only the five road bridges to avoid confusing the audience. Nevertheless, a writer or director has less flexibility in portraying facts than in creating a fictional story. By representing that a movie is informing viewers about actual events, especially in regard to something as significant as the development of the atomic bomb, the filmmaker raises the bar on how far he can extend the limits of dramatic license. Although capturing the essence of the Manhattan Project, *Day One* played loose with the facts and so supported Goldberg's judgment that it lacked the historical accuracy to meet the requirement of DoD regulations governing assistance. Not having access to the historical record, however, most viewers came away from their television sets believing they now knew how the United States had built and decided to deliver the atomic bombs to Japan, including the perpetuation of the myth that Tibbets's copilot had actually uttered the words "My God, what have we done?"

Fat Man and Little Boy, appearing later in 1989, visited the same territory, this time on the big screen. Whereas *Day One* showed some respect for history, as Dr. Goldberg had indicated, director Roland Joffe cared less about the facts than the message he intended to make the raison d'être of his film. He therefore far exceeded the limits of dramatic license in a work purportedly portraying historical events. Playing a very slimmed-down Gen. Leslie Groves, Paul Newman observed that although the film aspires to entertain, it also addresses "a terrible moral question that needs to be asked: should the bomb have been dropped?"[8]

Joffe sought to answer in the negative at every point in the story, even when faced with resistance from others working on the production: "It was inevitable that the bomb should have been built, but my own view is that it would have been much more courageous not to have dropped it." He saw the bomb as "a product of particular times, pressures and social and moral views. It was made by human beings and therefore it can be unmade by human beings. If enough people care, if enough people feel that their values are offended by spending an enormous amount of time creating weapons of mass destruction, we'll take that step and stop them."[9]

At the time Joffe was making his

Models of "Little Boy" and "Fat Man," the bombs dropped on Hiroshima and Nagasaki.

film, the Cold War was winding down and people had come to appreciate all the ramifications of the bomb. However, *Fat Man and Little Boy* portrayed events at a different time and a different place. Americans and Japanese were fighting and dying. The week before the *Enola Gay* and *Bock's Car* dropped their bombs, more than six hundred U.S. servicemen had died in combat although no major battles were taking place. On July 29, a Japanese submarine sank the USS *Indianapolis* after it had delivered the uranium components of the Hiroshima bomb to Tinian; more than eight hundred men died either from the attack itself or from sharks in the water, a tragedy that inspired *Jaws* and the 1991 television movie *Mission of the Shark*. Even after the Navy received orders to cease offensive operations on August 15, Japanese planes attempted to attack an American task force off the coast of Japan.

To portray that reality would, of course, weaken Joffe's message, and so it received no mention in his movie. Worse, to support his arguments, the director and his co-screenwriter, Bruce Robinson, revised history to serve their purposes. Ironically, Newman claimed, "If you know something about history, you are not tempted to repeat it. If the young people manage to get a history lesson out of this at the same time, in a comfortable and entertaining way, that will be useful." To avoid repeating history, however, the account has to portray events accurately. To create or perpetuate myths does a disservice to anyone trying to understand what really happened in something so complicated as the building and use of the atomic bomb.[10]

Dwight Schultz, who played J. Robert Oppenheimer, expressed his concerns about the accuracy of the portrayal: "I hope that no one comes to this thinking that it is an accurate representation of reality. If the film is successful, it will not dictate an answer. It should spur you to go into the library and get your book out and see what is real." Most people accept what they see on the screen as real and so have no motivation to go to the library. Joffe himself had no worries about his cinematic revisionism: "I think the facts will shine through quite clearly. I mean, where we have made stuff up is quite clear. I think we have done our research very well and been very serious about all of the facts."[11]

Hardly. To demonstrate the insidiousness of radiation and the callous disregard for human life by the Manhattan Project leaders, Joffe included a scene that suggested that scientists had injected people with radioactive material at Oak Ridge during the war to measure the effect of radiation on humans. When one of the scientists serving as a technical advisor pointed out that polonium, the material being injected, would not produce the physical effects being portrayed, Joffe simply changed the material to plutonium. Never happened. Apart from the reality that plutonium was available only in very limited amounts almost up to the moment of the Trinity test, scientists knew perfectly well the deadly impact the element would have on humans. Equally inaccurate, Joffe portrayed a fatal experiment of one of the scientists at Los Alamos that did not, in fact, occur until after the war had ended.[12]

In considering the efficacy of Joffe's approach to history, two issues stand out. First, even "poetic truth" is merely a handy justification for historical fabrication if it derives from a deliberate disregard for facts. Second, given the power of film and television to inform or manipulate, creators of visual images can misinform audiences without their knowledge. Historian Wilhelm Dilthey, for one, believed that man can know himself only in his history. If so, the distortion of the past, particularly for motives of profit, or in the case of Roland Joffe, for a political goal, becomes a matter for serious meditation. Joffe maintained that although *Fat Man and Little Boy* remains a work of fiction, it arrives at an "internal truth" about the building of the atomic bomb. He claimed that the film "recreates in an impressionistic way, but with great warmth and heart, what really happened."

Moreover, he said it contains "more truth to what actually happened than any documentary will ever be."[13]

Either Joffe had not seen the award-winning *Day after Trinity* or he had chosen to ignore the 1980 documentary, which combined archival footage and interviews with Oppenheimer and many of his colleagues, detailing the building of the atomic bomb. Like all documentaries, of course, the director is putting images of reality on the screen. In this case, however, Jon Else allows the scientists themselves to tell their stories, not actors mouthing words put there by screenwriters for their own purposes. In contrast to this approach, Joffe took considerable effort to get the basic details correct and then intermingled them with fictionalizations of actions and ideas, the method of all good propaganda. In addition to the bogus human experimentation and the misdated fatal laboratory accident, Joffe invents a scene in which Groves's train stops in the desert so that a courier can deliver to the general crucial information about the German nuclear program. Another fabricated and ludicrous scene shows Groves offering Oppenheimer the directorship of the Los Alamos laboratory while sitting in the cockpit of a plane in a hanger, with the engines revved up to ostensibly drown out their conversation. Groves had no experience flying airplanes, and the event took place on a train traveling from Chicago to Detroit. Dramatic, perhaps, but inaccurate in every respect.

Do such images simply constitute dramatic license, which allows the filmmakers to get at an "internal truth" as Joffe contends, or do they cause harm by allowing people to believe they know the truth when they actually have seen fabrications and distortions? The director would maintain: "The purpose of a movie is to try to find that interior truth that lies behind the often surface and superficial facts." To him, the reality focused on the scientists' abandonment of their moral responsibility by giving up not only control over their discoveries but also knowledge about the uses to which the government would put their discoveries. According to the director, even such a trivial scene as the stopping of Groves's train shows the deeper reality of the frenetic life that Groves lived while directing the Manhattan Project, a life that left little time for him to reflect seriously on the moral ramifications of the atomic bomb.[14]

In this case, the truth remains far more interesting than Joffe's "internal truth." If he had simply portrayed Groves and his deputy, then-colonel K.D. Nichols, crisscrossing the country for three years and Oppenheimer and his scientific team working nonstop to develop the bomb, as the 1982 BBC miniseries *Oppenheimer* showed, Joffe would have come far closer to the truth than he did. Of course, if he had done that, he would not have had the movie he intended to make. Neither Groves nor anyone else in the military connected with the Manhattan Project had the slightest moral qualm about building and using the atomic bomb. Groves could have sat on a beach contemplating for ten years and still not have changed his opinion. Given his complex nature, Oppenheimer certainly understood the ramifications of dropping the atomic bomb, but he never hesitated to recommend its use. Some of his scientists may have ultimately offered statements of regret for helping to build the bomb, but no one had held a gun against their heads to force them to work in the Manhattan Project. More to the point, however, these are issues that reasonable people can discuss—but only if they have accurate information, not an "internal truth."[15]

Joffe and his colleagues and Paramount Pictures certainly understood that the Pentagon would never provide assistance to a film that so misrepresented one of the defining events of World War II, and no request for support was ever made. In contrast, producers Catherine Wyler and David Putnam went to the Air Force seeking help to make *The*

Memphis Belle. Unlike *Fat Man and Little Boy*, the film did not question the weapons of war or contain any philosophic musing on the nature of combat. Instead, it intended to glorify the men who fought the war in the air. Putnam explained that while he admired *Top Gun*, it had made him angry: "I felt that it trivialized courage and turned war into an arcade game. Wyler's documentary showed what people actually went through. It wasn't plastic courage; it wasn't guys zipping through the air with whoops of glee. It was real courage, the kind you needed if you were an ordinary person in an extremely slow-moving and vulnerable aircraft knowing that it wasn't *whether* the flak would hit you but where it would hit." Mirroring that sentiment, the film's credit read: "This film is dedicated to all the brave young men, whatever their nationality, who flew and fought in history's greatest airborne confrontation."[16]

In requesting assistance, Catherine Wyler explained to Chuck Davis, chief of the TV/ Motion Picture Liaison, in the Air Force Public Affairs Office in Los Angeles, that the film "is inspired by the story of the twenty-fifth mission of the B-17 named Memphis Belle," which her father, the famed director William Wyler, had immortalized in his 1944 documentary. She said the film's aim "is to delineate the ordeal of a B-17 crew of the

The actual crew and plane featured in William Wyler's documentary *The Memphis Belle,* which later inspired the director's daughter to produce the fictionalized *Memphis Belle* almost fifty years later.

Eighth Air Force on a single mission over Germany in the spring of 1943. It will vividly portray the courage, heroism and interdependence of these young men and give contemporary audiences a 'you-are-there' awareness of what it was like to be in the front ranks of the air war during this awesome moment in history." To help carry out this goal, Wyler asked to view and duplicate aerial footage to see if its quality was sufficient to allow the filmmakers to integrate it with the sequences they would be creating.[17]

When Davis forwarded the request to the Air Force Public Affairs Office in Washington, he expressed some concern about the "informal use of first names and lack of acknowledgment of ranks" between officers and enlisted personnel. However, he had "major difficulty" with the depiction of the plane's navigator "as being extremely intoxicated shortly before this important bombing mission." He suggested that the Air Force history office might "be of assistance in determining the accuracy of the event." Davis then cited other concerns, including a scene where a rookie pilot is "sniffling" prior to a mission, the tail gunner falling asleep aboard the B-17 just prior to the mission, and a fight between the navigator and the bombardier.[18]

The Air Force then conferred with Capt. Susan Hankey, Don Baruch's assistant, about how to decline Wyler's request. The DoD did not want to act, because Baruch's office had never received a formal, written request for assistance. Hankey also wanted to know whether the producers would agree to making changes in the script, noting that if the Pentagon could support *Disaster at Silo 7,* a TV film about a fire in a missile silo, then it "certainly ought to look at doing what we can to support this one. This one is a much stronger storyline and is therefore a better springboard, and far more worthy of assistance." In response, Davis advised Hankey that he would contact Wyler to find out if she would be amenable to script changes. Nevertheless, Hankey told him that they remained willing to become "the heavy" in refusing to approve support, because Baruch recognized that Davis "needs to maintain positive relationships with the industry and in some cases it's better for 'the Pentagon' to decline support." However, Baruch felt that if the Air Force did not want to support a project, the "no" should come from it.[19]

Ultimately, on December 2, Davis wrote to Wyler: "I was informed yesterday that the Department of Defense will be unable to support your request as the screenplay does not conform to their policy which requires fictionalized stories to depict a feasible interpretation of military life, operations, and policies." He then cited the problems the Air Force and Defense Department reviewers had with the script, including the informality and lack of respect for rank, the intoxicated navigator, the "sniffling" pilot, an officer's acknowledgment of his men's hangovers, the tail gunner falling asleep, and the fight between the navigator and the bombardier in flight. Davis recognized that while some of the objections "may seem trivial, we are concerned about the negative, unprofessional depiction of the crew and how that would affect the public's view of the crew of the real Memphis Belle. Not to correct the inaccuracies would imply a factual portrayal of events and real people which would be a disservice to the crew, the Air Force and the American public." He concluded with the offer to reevaluate a revised script.[20]

Instead, Wyler and Warner Brothers brought the rejection to the attention of Sen. Pete Wilson (R-Calif.), who wrote to the secretary of the Air Force on February 1, 1989, requesting that he look into the matter and sort out the problems "that the producers have apparently encountered." He also said that if the service finds that it "remains unable to accommodate the film-makers' request, I would like to have a full explanation of the reasons for such a decision." Recognizing the implication inherent in the inquiry, the Air Force drafted its response very carefully, finally sending a letter to the senator on March 22, 1989, in which the service said it had, in fact, "cooperated fully" with Wyler about her request to obtain stock footage: "To this point, we have not provided the footage because the screenplay presents an inaccurate and unrealistic account of the historic mission of the actual aircraft called Memphis Belle." The Air Force also noted that DoD policy "requires fictionalized stories to depict a feasible interpretation of military life, operations and policies" and said that it had told Wyler it would reevaluate its decision if it received a revised screenplay portraying "a more realistic depiction of actual events." To date, the letter said, the service had received no response.[21]

By then, however, Wyler had written to Davis renewing her request for combat footage and saying that the filmmakers had changed the title to "Southern Belle." In the letter of February 16, she said that a new script "is nearing completion and will be sent to you within the next two weeks. You'll see that we've taken your comments seriously and corrected the inadvertent inaccuracies." Nevertheless, she pointed out that since this "is a dramatic feature film and not a documentary, it is sometimes necessary for the audience's understanding of the action, to take some liberties." She explained, "The characterizations of the crew members have been refined since the version you read. . . . While some of the characterizations have been altered in the process of rewriting the script, others have not, and it is the opinion of those friends and advisors of the production that the characterizations are true to life, honest depictions of officers and enlisted men in the stressful situations engendered by war."[22]

The letter and script did not persuade Davis or the Air Force that the filmmakers had the rendering correct. Davis wrote to the Air Force Public Affairs Office in Washington on March 21, saying that other than the title change and "a few minor adjustments, the screenplay appears to remain unsuitable for Air Force support. Although it could be considered a fictional portrayal now that the title has been changed, the similarities to the actual Memphis Belle mission are very close." He also found that the story had "little informational value and does not reflect a realistic depiction of military life, operations and policies." Davis said that his major concern was still "the portrayal of the navigator as being extremely intoxicated just prior to the mission and the subsequent concealment of his condition, by the co-pilot and bombardier, which puts members of the crew and the aircraft in serious jeopardy." He attached specific comments and asked for the opinion of the service and Baruch's office as soon as possible."[23]

In vetting the script, the Air Force Public Affairs Office contacted, in England, Roger Freeman, one of Wyler's advisors, an Eighth Air Force flier, for his impression of the second script. He told the service he had not seen the second script and had not approved it as Wyler had implied in her letter to Davis. In any case, Freeman agreed with the Air Force's concerns about the drunk navigator and the other crew members' collaboration to keep him part of the mission. The Air Force memo for the record reported that Freeman also cited as a problem the lack of professionalism by the fliers: "The whole crew acts like a high school football team—nothing but childish pranks and shenanigans . . . showing no professionalism." He also told the Public Affairs Office that the screenwriter had portrayed the fliers not as young men in the mid-1940s: "Their behavior reflects 1980s standards, language . . . WWII flyers were indeed very professional, and this is not shown in the script."[24]

Freeman had other areas of concern, saying that the screenplay's love scene, which takes place in the nose of the B-17, "would not have been possible as each aircraft was, in fact, under guard." He objected to the copilot's leaving his position to go to the rear of the plane and noted that his reaction to the loss of another B-17 "was wholly contrived and unrealistic (e.g., he just realized it wasn't fun & games.) Anyone who had flown 24 prior missions could not possibly have viewed war as fun and games." Finally, Freeman noted the technical flaw in the portrayal of a radio operator listening to a conversation from another plane. He said that only a pilot had ship-to-ship ability. Therefore, the entire dramatic scene where Danny listens to cries from a sister ship radio operator as the plane is going down is technically impossible.[25]

With this reaction in hand, M.Sgt. Mary Stowe wrote in the Air Force's public affairs "Daily Updates" for April 10, 1989, that "it is unlikely we'll be able to assist as the production company has been unwilling to make several changes we have recommended which might qualify the project for support." Phil Strub concurred with this decision, and on May 19, 1989, the Air Force Public Affairs Office advised Wyler that the service had found the new script "basically unchanged, the similarities to the actual Memphis Belle mission are very close. The story does not reflect a realistic depiction or feasible interpretation of military life, operations and policies." He cited Davis's concerns about the drunken navigator and the concealment of his condition by the copilot and the bombardier: "This conspiracy puts members of the crew, the aircraft and the mission itself in serious jeopardy." He also mentioned the negative portrayals of the crew, which "would affect the public's view of the World War II crew force." The office attached five pages of specific comments and said unless the filmmakers resolved these considerations, "it would be inappropriate to provide support for this production."[26]

Wyler and coproducer Putnam did not respond to the letter. Instead, they made the film in England, using B-17s from the Royal Air Force Museum at Duxford for their flying sequences. In large part, filmmakers did not seriously negotiate with the Air Force, because the service had virtually nothing to offer the production company in the way of men or equipment. Although Wyler had requested Air Force combat footage, the company had no problem securing film from other sources. And without having to make revisions to suit the service, Wyler and Putnam could put on the screen whatever images they chose, including a positive reference in the dedication to the German Luftwaffe pilots whom the real *Memphis Belle* had faced in the air over Germany.

Wyler said that her father's wartime documentary had inspired her to make the theatrical film, but her film did as much disservice to the plane's crew as the original movie had paid homage to its bravery and accomplishments. With the film again titled *The Memphis Belle,* most viewers would think they were seeing a true story when, in fact, it bore little resemblance to what the fliers experienced in the air war over occupied Europe, with two exceptions. Unlike the earlier World War II flying movies, most particularly *Command Decision, Fighter Squadron,* and *Twelve O'Clock High, The Memphis Belle* used young actors of the same relative age as the actual fliers. And the film used actual combat footage, which did create an authentic ambience of the war in the air.

With that said, the film went wrong right from the beginning. A mortally wounded B-17 returning home explodes on landing as if it were fully loaded with fuel and bombs. Yes, fumes in the fuel tanks might burn if a plane crash-landed. However, aircraft had very little gas left when they reached base after a long mission, and even if they had not dropped their bombs during the mission, they would have jettisoned them before trying to land. In any case, the film's veracity goes downhill from there, containing virtually all the inaccurate portrayals to which the Air Force had objected.

Within these images, perhaps the most egregious misrepresentation of life in the midst of war came in the staging of a huge party on base in which officers and enlisted men mixed socially with women in sight of the flight line, with one of the crew from the *Memphis Belle* retiring to the plane with his girlfriend. Equally absurd, two of the plane's crew members get into a fistfight while the plane is flying over Germany on its last mission. Wyler and Putnam may well have recognized that they could not match the dramatic impact of the real war in the air during World War II as captured in William Wyler's 1944 documentary. As a result, they decided to create a fictional drama that showed fliers playing at war rather than performing as professional warriors against an implacable foe whom they could defeat only through devotion to their fellow crew members and their fellow comrades, a necessity that *Twelve O'Clock High* had portrayed so well forty years before.[27]

In contrast, *Saving Private Ryan* did not show soldiers enjoying childish pranks and shenanigans or playing at war. To be sure, Steven Spielberg had played war games as a young boy and had listened with rapt attention to his father's experiences aboard a B-25 bomber stationed in Burma during World War II. He watched all the war movies that appeared during the 1940s and 1950s, which provided him his knowledge of men in combat. And he even made home movies portraying him and his friends as soldiers in mortal combat. Likewise, Spielberg's 1998 re-creation of the D-Day landing on Omaha Beach focused on the serious side of men in combat, the violence, the deaths, the dismemberments, the reality that luck often determines whether men live or die.[28]

In the initial rush to judgment, critics heaped praise on *Saving Private Ryan*. Most called it the greatest war movie ever made. Reviewers, veterans, and the average filmgoer accepted Spielberg's claim that the unrelenting violence of torn bodies, blood, gore, and vomit, particularly in the opening twenty-four-minute sequence on Omaha Beach perfectly captured the reality of combat. And without question, Spielberg made brilliant use of his handheld cameras to create images of men in battle trying to survive in a hostile environment. Whether images of extreme violence alone produce the reality of combat becomes the crucial issue in judging the place of *Saving Private Ryan* in the galaxy of great war movies.

Steven Spielberg and Tom Hanks during filming of the Omaha Beach landing.

On the NBC *Today Show,* the director himself argued that he was "trying to show something the war film really hadn't dared to show" at a time when people have become "desensitized to mindless cinematic violence," which he admitted he had helped to create. Instead, he wanted to show that "war is immediate; it's chaotic; it's abrupt, and it's without mercy." To accomplish this, he explained that he wanted "to recreate the Omaha Beach landing the way the veterans experienced it, not the way Hollywood producers and directors have imagined it." He used the violence to put audiences "in the physical experience of being inside the combat zone." Nevertheless, in touting *Private Ryan,* Spielberg prided himself on warning people to stay away from the theater if violence bothered them, even though he claimed this would cost him millions of dollars at the box office.[29]

For the first time in more than sixteen years, Spielberg went on tour to promote one of his films, explaining, "The reason I'm going across the country on this one is to warn parents and young people that this film may not be their cup of tea. I have a real responsibility to do that, especially because of the first 24 minutes of this film." Given the graphic violence, many people within the industry thought that *Saving Private Ryan* received an R rating rather than an NC-17 only because of Spielberg's station within the Hollywood establishment. He admitted, "I sell a lot of tickets, and I understand what that means to parents. I want people to know that the R rating has

Spielberg's repeated warnings about the intense violence in the first twenty-four minutes of *Saving Private Ryan* may have attracted more viewers than it turned away.

a very important warning attached, to let them know what is there. But I believe in this film, and I am very passionate about it." Consequently, he said that if it had received an NC-17, "I would have worn that like a Purple Heart, with pride and dignity."[30]

Of course, the more he talked about the violence and warned people to stay away, the more most people would want to see the film. After all, as Patton once said, "All real Americans love the sting of battle." More to the point, Spielberg had the audacity to claim that in making his film "honest and truthful and realistic," he was showing 'what war really is.'" How did this differ from earlier war movies? He explained, "You know, in this age of disclosure, it would have been irresponsible for me to undercut the truth of what that was like." He then observed, "There have been 84 World War II films that showed something else. This would have been the 85th slap in the face to the men who died knowing the truth."[31]

Ironically, Spielberg's only knowledge of war came from watching the very movies he was now denigrating; and despite his claim that he had created a unique portrayal of combat, if the truth be told, the director had appropriated virtually every scene in *Saving Private Ryan* from other films. The blowing up of the tank barrier on Omaha Beach and the accidental shooting of German prisoners exactly replicates the same two scenes in *The Longest Day*. The cross-country trek of Captain Miller and his rescuers appeared in countless infantry movies, probably most famously in *A Walk in the Sun*. The last-second arrival of the airplanes and infantry at the end of *Saving Private Ryan* mimics the cavalry to the rescue in scores of Hollywood Westerns as well as Patton's more contemporary arrival in the nick of time at the Battle of the Bulge. The confrontation between Miller's men and German soldiers after the wall of a building collapses, their yelling and screaming and then the shooting, resembles nothing so much as the fight at the water hole in *2001* between the educated and uneducated apes.

This reality aside, where the director came up with the figure 84 remains a mystery. Hollywood had made more than 200 pure combat World War II movies before Spielberg began production on *Saving Private Ryan*. Of these, only a handful even remotely portrayed the U.S. armed services in less than a positive manner. *Attack!* does show an enlisted man shooting an officer, but he does that not for evil reasons. Even in *The Americanization of Emily*, James Garner's cowardly officer metamorphoses into a hero. Of the four movies focusing on D-Day itself, none contains any portrayal that might be considered slapping

Overlooking the beach in Ireland that stood in for Omaha Beach in the D-Day sequences of *Saving Private Ryan*, Dale Dye, military advisor for the film, uses radios to stage an action sequence.

the American military in the face. And *The Longest Day* shows the Army probably in the most positive light Hollywood filmmakers have ever created.[32]

Of course, only the men who actually landed on Omaha Beach could judge whether Spielberg's twenty-four minutes of "almost virtual reality" filmmaking even approximated the reality of D-Day. Nevertheless, the director's pretentiousness in believing he alone had captured the verisimilitude of combat and the way he promoted his film did not sound all that different from Oliver Stone, who has regularly created controversy simply to get people into theaters. Once there, however, the question remains as to whether audiences needed the extreme violence that Spielberg created in order to gain a better understanding of the nature of war than previous films had provided. Andy Rooney, who took part in D-Day, once said that the Normandy invasion constituted the most unselfish act that one nation ever did for another. That judgment, rather than dismembered bodies, rotting corpses, and unrelenting violence, may best explain the significance of the Longest Day.[33]

From a different perspective, Fred Zinnemann was once asked whether he would have preferred to make *From Here to Eternity* in the 1970s, when he could have used four-letter words and graphic sex, rather than under the Motion Picture Code restrictions of the early 1950s. The director acknowledged that the film might have better captured the time in which the story took place without the censorship and the changes in the story the Army demanded in return for military assistance. Nevertheless, Zinnemann said he still felt the film he made captured the essence of James Jones's novel and well reflected the time in which he had made it.[34]

Spielberg himself acknowledged that his use of violence simply reflects the time in which he created *Saving Private Ryan* as much as the reality of Omaha Beach. By the late 1990s, audiences expected and even demanded blood and gore in their movies. Consequently, for Spielberg to make a movie that differed from the gratuitous violence then dripping from theater screens, he had no choice but to outdo his fellow filmmakers. So he simply threw more arms, legs, heads, guts, and vomit all over the screen and then justified the images as necessary to capture the realism of battle, in much the same way Robert Altman used blood and raw flesh in *M*A*S*H*.

In fact, the graphic violence Spielberg created did not really differ all that much from the "necessary" violence of many of the classic Hollywood movies of recent years. Certainly, Bonnie and Clyde's dance of death leaves nothing to the imagination. In both of Francis Coppola's Godfather epics, blood and violent killings abounded. The choreographed murders of the Godfather's rivals, particularly the shot through the eyeglasses, may not have occurred on a battlefield, but they had the visual power to shock audiences of the 1970s every bit as much as anything in *Private Ryan*. And then there is *Jaws*.

Of course, Spielberg was making a war movie in which death does become a part of life. However, he may have conveniently forgotten that Hollywood has always used battlefield stories as a socially acceptable means of circumventing the Production Code to put graphic violence on motion picture screens. The U.S. military had to eliminate the evil Nazis and slant-eyed Nips for the good of the nation and the democratic way of life. Consequently, the Production Code Office always allowed filmmakers more leeway in portraying violence to do in the bad guys than in other movie genres.

However, violence or nudity does not have to permeate the screen to create a perception of reality. A woman in a sheer negligee or a man in a skimpy bathing suit may sometimes become more titillating than the bare essentials. Even the soft-core porn of late-night cable TV has power to turn people on in much the same way as *Deep Throat* or *The Devil in Miss Jones.* Too much of a good thing may be too much of a good thing. Spielberg himself acknowledged this on the *CBS Evening News* three years after the release of *Saving Private Ryan:* "I don't know anything more terrifying than off-screen violence."[35]

In any event, most Hollywood war movies made with military assistance have, of course, contained a high degree of realism in portraying men trying to survive in the hostile environment of the battlefield, even without the graphic violence of *Saving Private Ryan.* Gen. David Shoup did such a good job of helping the filmmakers recreate the landing on Tarawa for use in *The Sands of Iwo Jima* that he could not watch the actual filming. Yet powerful images of the terrible ordeal the Marines experienced, dying in place, bunched up and pinned down at the sea wall, did not rely on graphic violence and bodies flying about. Moreover, although John Wayne dies at the movie's end from a single bullet in the back without a drop of blood darkening his uniform, his death has the same impact as if he were blown apart.

Retreat, Hell!—arguably the best portrayal of the American experience in Korea— followed the Marines on their retreat from the Yalu River through bitter, subzero cold in what became the first defeat of American imperialism. The director did not show blood or gore or frostbitten feet or hands. Yet, audiences felt the Marines' terrible suffering.

Ultimately, however, the authenticity and realism of any war movie must be judged against the standard that Darryl Zanuck set in *The Longest Day.* Certainly the black and white photography does not lend itself to portraying blood in the waves, on the sand, or oozing out of people as Spielberg was able to show. Nor would the Production Code Office permit Zanuck and his directors the luxury of using "casual profanity" or tearing bodies apart to create their vision of Normandy. Nevertheless, despite the docudrama exposition, the use of high-profile actors, the errors of history that crept onto the screen, and the trite and misguided ending, *The Longest Day* worked at the time and still provides a visual and emotional impact of the first order.

Why? The confusion and chaos in making the movie impacted on Zanuck and his directors, who then conveyed that sense of confusion and chaos to the screen and so captured the ambience of D-Day. *The Longest Day* had one other thing going for it that *Private Ryan* did not. For the most part, Zanuck portrayed real people doing real things. When Army Rangers and the actors climbed Pointe du Hoc for Zanuck's cameras, audiences knew that soldiers had actually climbed the same cliff in the face of withering German fire. Although audiences recognized Red Buttons, the actor, snagged on a church steeple, they also knew that a real paratrooper had landed on that steeple and a German soldier had actually shot him. They also knew that although French stuntmen recreated

The impact of *The Longest Day* can still be seen in St. Mere Engles, where the town has hung a dummy from the church steeple where Pvt. John Steele hung after parachuting into the town.

Steven Spielberg on the set of *Saving Private Ryan.*

the parachute jump into the village and mannequins blew up in a burning building, on June 6, 1944, real soldiers had fallen into the burning building and actually died.

In contrast, while most of the things Spielberg put on the screen may have happened at one or another time and place during and after the Normandy invasion, what he shows remains fiction. The audience knows it is seeing actors who got up at the end of the filming, took off their costumes, and went back to their hotel rooms. More to the point, viewers consciously or unconsciously knew that Spielberg was manipulating their emotions and sensibilities. Who was going to live or die? Spielberg already knew. Thanks to his directorial ability, audiences may not guess the ending until it happens. At the same time, nothing on the screen had actually happened, despite the violence, blood, and gore.

Most people probably do not understand that filmmakers are only creating images and telling stories as they choose to tell them. A critic might want to say that Spielberg lost his nerve and should have killed Private Ryan while allowing Tom Hanks's Captain Miller to live with his demons. This might well have become a far more powerful, far more jolting ending, one which truly proclaimed that war never rises above the level of hell. However, a reviewer must only judge whether the director succeeded in what he intended to do.

If people have reservations about Spielberg's use of violence or his claim that he needed extreme violence to create "virtual reality," no one can question the power of the images the director has created. Nevertheless, a historian has an obligation to point out that *Private Ryan* remains only one man's creation of events that occurred more than fifty years ago. Worse, the film often strains and even far exceeds the limits of dramatic license. Or, to put it perhaps more kindly, Spielberg too often retreats from serious filmmaking and returns to his Hollywood roots.

However powerful the opening Omaha Beach sequence is and however close it comes to recreating the experiences of men in combat, the truth remains that the film's high point has feet of clay. A close examination of the twenty-four minutes, with the sound off, reveals that Spielberg used virtually every cliché in the genre in a way that seems fresh only because of the camera work and editing. Blood flows from bodies shot underwater. A soldier removes his helmet to marvel at his close escape and is immediately shot in the head. A flamethrower soldier blows up in a mass of flames. Soldiers cower behind barriers before their officers force them from the water's edge, up the beach. In the end, however, a disconnect exists between the noise, the dismemberments, the heroism, on the one hand, and the events that follow, on the other. Spielberg's virtuosity in the first twenty-four minutes has nothing to do with the story that the director is going to tell, except to introduce the audience to Tom Hanks's Captain Miller. For most people, the strength of the Omaha Beach sequences probably carried the narrative to the climax.

For military historians, for those who landed on the Normandy beaches, and for those who may simply recognize implausibilities and contrived drama or careless filmmaking, *Saving Private Ryan* contained a story filled with errors and a lack of believability. Although Spielberg had little need for assistance from the Pentagon, and the Army had no World War II hardware to offer, the director sent a script to the Army's Los Angeles office, soliciting technical advice. The service responded with four full pages of comments, mostly dealing with military procedures and terminology. The review began with the observation that "the Miller character is performing the duties of two people. If you do not want to introduce another character, as a minimum his rank should be reduced to a First Lieutenant. It would also make it much more plausible to make him part of the 101st instead of a Ranger since Private Ryan is with the 101st."[36]

The problems with the portrayal of Miller did not stop there. Spielberg had Tom Hanks play an overage captain for the same reason Gene Hackman and Sean Connery played overaged submarine commanders: producers need bankable stars to obtain funding for major productions. Of more relevance, many military people pointed out that the Army would not have detached a highly trained Ranger for the type of mission on which he is sent. The Army reviewer noted that Miller would be carrying an M-1 carbine rifle, not a Thompson machine gun. Military experts, including retired Chairman of the Joint Chiefs of Staff Gen. Colin Powell, were to question Miller's abilities as a tactician because of his decision to fight a holding action against German tanks in the film's climactic battle. In regard to procedural matters, the reviewer explained that Miller could request fire support through channels but would not be able to radio a ship directly. The service also advised that Miller could request that Upham, the Army journalist, be assigned to him, but he had no authority to make the reassignment himself.[37]

Small matters, perhaps, but Spielberg and world-renowned historian Stephen Ambrose, the director's historical consultant, were to proclaim that *Saving Private Ryan* stood alone as the most accurate movie ever made about men in war. An accumulation of such mistakes can erode credibility, at least for the men who had lived through D-Day and fought across France. Novelist Max Evans, who landed on D-Day plus one, became disillusioned with the very first image of Captain Miller aboard the landing craft. From all the publicity surrounding *Saving Private Ryan,* Evans went into the theater expecting to see a film that mirrored his combat experience accurately and well. Instead, he saw Miller wearing his

Seeing the captain's bars still visible on Tom Hanks's helmet during the Omaha landing caused a number of veterans to question Speilberg's claims of accuracy.

captain's insignia on his helmet, visible to any German rifleman, and recalled that he immediately lost all confidence in Spielberg's claims of accuracy. Although regulations may have required an officer to have his rank visible, Evans said that all intelligent officers he saw had covered their insignias to avoid becoming targets. Spielberg knew this, because he created a scene in which a soldier stops Upham from saluting Miller for that reason, even though Miller continues to wear his captain's bars throughout the film.[38]

Most veterans who were there have attested that Spielberg captured the essence of the D-Day on Omaha Beach, but not all soldiers experienced the same degree of German opposition to their landing or witnessed the historical events in the manner the film recreated them. Noel Dube, for one, had walked ashore without resistance and later blew up the concrete tank barrier under circumstances far different from the way *The Longest Day* showed the event. Stephen Ambrose knew the truth, having cited in his 1994 article in the *Historical Journal of Film, Radio, and Television* the error in Zanuck's portrayal of the event. Nevertheless, *Saving Private Ryan* virtually duplicated the scene during the twenty-four-minute assault on Omaha Beach, which suggests that Spielberg had no more concern with historical veracity than Zanuck had had in *The Longest Day*. Perhaps worse, Ambrose had no problem praising Spielberg's commitment to accuracy, despite having written only three years earlier about Zanuck's destruction of the tank barrier: "Unfortunately, nothing remotely like it ever happened on D-Day."[39]

Likewise, only with a significant suspension of disbelief can audiences accept that anything in *Saving Private Ryan* actually happened. Spielberg so far exceeds the limits of dramatic license in the film's opening sequence, prior to the beach landing, and in the springboard of the story that he renders the term meaningless. Both montages have absolutely no plausibility and so illustrate the director's arrogant disregard for historical reality, cinematic believability, and the intelligence of his audience. As a result, the plot cannot sustain serious scrutiny and so severely weakens the credibility of the director's portrayal of men in combat.

The opening minutes of the film, as the veteran slowly walks through the rows of graves in the military cemetery at Normandy, does convey a deep sense of loss which he and the nation had suffered on D-Day. When the old man falls to his knees in front of a grave marker, viewers do feel his pain. However, the problems with the film begin as soon as Spielberg moves his camera in tightly on the man's face, the cinematic device for announcing a flashback, in this case back in time to a landing craft headed to Omaha Beach on June 6, 1944. To put it bluntly, the veteran's journey simply could not have taken place.

Spielberg does not identify the old soldier and only in the film's last moments does the audience learn they had watched Private Ryan, not Captain Miller, at the cemetery and that Ryan had served as the director's magic carpet to D-Day. However, he could not have carried out that assignment. As a paratrooper in the 101st Airborne division, Ryan parachuted inland during the early hours of June 6 to help capture the causeways leading off the beaches and so would have had no first-hand knowledge of Omaha Beach. Consequently, the twenty-four minute assault which Spielberg created becomes a pure fabrication which he perpetrates on the audience. While the director may argue he was entitled to such dramatic license, the reality remains that he could have just as easily created a generic flashback by moving away from Ryan at Miller's grave, slowly panning out to the English Channel, and then retreating in time to Miller in the landing craft. As created, however, Spielberg has fraudulently persuaded the audience that they have watched the veteran's flashback, a deceit which becomes obvious when the director returns to the cemetery at the end of the film.

Nor could the springboard that Spielberg uses to drive his story ever have happened. From bloody water washing over bodies drifting on Omaha Beach, one with the name Ryan stenciled on his pack, the director cuts to the Pentagon on D-Day plus two. There a bank of typists are writing letters of regret to families of soldiers killed in action. The audience sees a single typist suddenly discovering she has written three letters to a Mrs. Ryan. On D-Day, one son died on Omaha Beach and a second son on Utah Beach, and a third son had died on New Guinea the week before. When informed of their deaths and that a fourth brother has parachuted with the 101st Airborne behind German lines on D-Day, Army Chief of Staff George C. Marshall orders a rescue mission to save the surviving son. Captain Miller receives the assignment on D-Day plus three, and the odyssey begins. The Pentagon montage combined with a scene of Mrs. Ryan receiving the three letters the same day creates a poignant and dramatic beginning to the story Spielberg intends to tell.

Matt Damon as Private Ryan.

Unfortunately, the sequence has absolutely no plausibility. The reports of the deaths of Private Ryan's two brothers on D-Day simply could not have reached the Pentagon in two days. Official casualty lists took many weeks to be processed and returned from the theaters of operation. Given the chaos of D-Day, it undoubtedly took even longer for the names of the dead and wounded to be collected and notifications to be typed. Bedford, Virginia, which lost more than thirty men on D-Day, began receiving the news six weeks later.[40]

The Army advised Spielberg of the implausibility of his springboard as well as the reality that few military clerks worked in the Pentagon in 1944. With no loss of dramatic impact, the brothers could easily have died in the Italian campaign two or three weeks prior to Normandy and the battery of typists could have been working in any generic building. Apparently Spielberg hoped the power of Omaha Beach landings would sweep up audiences and people would ignore the inaccuracy of the Pentagon sequence and the coincidence that one typist would have written the letters about all three brothers. Or perhaps he hoped people would assume that E-mail and faxes existed in 1944.[41]

Just as bad, although he wanted to show the reality of war and not slap the soldiers in the face again, Spielberg does a great disservice to the very men he is trying to memorialize in his film. All the soldiers who rode the thin-hulled landing craft to the beaches had trained for at least nine months for the landing. The Rangers whom Captain Miller commanded were the Army's elite troops, and many, like Miller, had landed in North Africa or Italy, or both. They knew what to expect and knew they had a good chance of dying on the beaches. They had already made their peace with God and went forth understanding why they were assaulting the beaches and cliffs. Instead, Spielberg shows the men vomiting, crying, and lacking discipline. Some soldiers undoubtedly vomited on their way to the beaches, but mostly because they were simply seasick from bouncing around in tiny landing craft for several hours, not out of fear. When they reached the beaches, they performed admirably in the almost untenable position in which they found themselves.[42]

Although loudly proclaiming that he wanted to portray men in combat accurately and bravely, Spielberg does not honor his commitment once he sends Miller and his men out across the fields of France. No hedgerows, the major obstacle the troops faced once they moved off the beaches, appear. Instead, the soldiers move out across open fields carrying on a philosophical conversation about the validity of a mission that risks the lives of eight men to save one. Filmmakers have always had to portray men in combat closer to each other than they would be on an actual battlefield, but Miller's men do not even approximate normal operating procedures. Instead of moving rapidly, quietly, and under cover as much as possible, they provide the Germans an easy target of opportunity. Conveniently, no Germans show up to interrupt the dialogue. And when the unit finally comes across an enemy machine-gun nest, Miller ignores his orders to save Private Ryan. Instead, he wastes valuable time, ammunition, and one of his men by engaging the enemy in a brief firefight. Exciting, perhaps. But the portrayal remains a Hollywood set piece, not an accurate portrayal of what followed after the Allies secured the Normandy beachhead and moved inland.

In any event, the lack of any reference to the nature of the war and the brutality of the enemy becomes the greatest flaw in *Saving Private Ryan*. Yes, the men themselves bonded with their comrades and would say they fought for their own survival and that of their buddies. But they were fighting for something even more important, the defeat of Nazi Germany. Certainly, no war should be labeled "good," but some wars remain absolutely necessary. The failure to put the war on the screen into historical context becomes even more ironic in light of Spielberg's having made *Schindler's List*.

Given the images he had created in his Holocaust movie, viewers can only wonder why Spielberg portrayed the Americans and the Germans as equals. In truth, the Americans even act worse than the enemy because they shoot Germans who are trying to surrender during the initial assault on Omaha Beach. Nowhere does Spielberg include even a single sentence to remind viewers why the Allies had to defeat Hitler. To be sure, World War II might have been avoided if wise men had acted wisely and bravely during the 1920s and 1930s. But after December 7, 1941, the United States had no choice but to fight Hitler's Germany.

Most of the soldiers either knew this intellectually or had learned it from government propaganda, most particularly from Frank Capra's *Why We Fight* series, which the armed services showed to all men during training. Whether the soldiers or even the nation fully comprehended the genocide against the Jews, Communists, Gypsies, or homosexuals is beside the point. Strong, persuasive reasons existed to defeat Hitler apart from the Holocaust itself. Unfortunately, *Saving Private Ryan* contains only the vaguest hint of this when an American soldier taunts German prisoners with his Star of David and his yelling "Juden, Juden!" Consequently, apart from setting the opening sequence on Omaha Beach, *Private Ryan* is only a generic war movie about a generic war, not at all different from Igmar Bergman's 1968 *Shame*, a story set in a nameless civil war on a nameless island.

Perhaps the many less serious flaws may be considered only nitpicking. However, since Spielberg claims so much for *Saving Private Ryan*, the film demands a higher level of judgment from viewers. Unfortunately, the technical and historical errors within the film as well as its implausibilities suggest that the director has not completely risen above his Hollywood roots. The "wrong Ryan" scene may seem funny, but it goes on far too long and adds nothing to the odyssey of Captain Miller and his unit. The confrontation between German and

American soldiers after a building wall collapses is ludicrous, because both sides would have started shooting immediately rather than yelling at each other.

Likewise, the sequence following the capture of a German soldier guarding a radar site becomes Hollywood melodrama. D-Day veterans had two words to describe what Miller should have done with the soldier: "Shoot him!" When Miller prepares to do just that, one of his men objects and a philosophical debate rages in the middle of hostile territory. It quickly escalates into a mutiny on a minor scale, one that is as implausible as the rebellions in *Crimson Tide* and *Courage under Fire*. Miller had picked seven of his best men. The unit had already bonded. The confrontation and denouement, with Miller finally revealing his personal background, does not provide the positive portrayal of American soldiers that Spielberg claimed he was making. It might even have become the eighty-fifth slap in the face that the director said he was avoiding.[43]

Ignoring common sense and reality, Miller lets the German soldier go, telling him to surrender to the first American unit he finds. In one of cinema's hoariest clichés, the soldier reappears to contribute mightily to the film's bloody and implausible climax. For it, Spielberg created a set piece battle for a tiny bridge in a destroyed village, in which Private Ryan and his unit have established a defensive position. The director has presented Captain Miller as a highly skilled battlefield tactician. Given the situation Miller finds at the bridge, particularly the lack of tank-stopping weapons and ammunition, he should have pulled the men back over the bridge, blown it when the first German tank rolled onto it, and returned with Ryan to American lines as ordered. The argument that the Americans would need the bridge for the advance inland has no merit, since the engineer troops could readily have constructed a new span over the very narrow ribbon of water whenever they arrived. After all, the engineers were able to quickly put a pontoon bridge over the wide, rapidly flowing Rhine at Remagen.

Ignoring reality and his orders to save Private Ryan, Miller develops a tactical plan to stop the German advance. With no heavy weapons that can stop tanks and limited resources, the plan has virtually no chance of success and exposes Ryan to great risk. In the one-sided battle that follows, Miller loses most of his combined force of Rangers and paratroopers, does not stop the German tanks, and fails to blow up the bridge. During the skirmish, the released German soldier materializes, surprises the Jewish soldier in his gun position, and in a fight to the death slowly slides the G.I.'s own knife into his body, whispering, "Sh, sh." Spielberg juxtaposed the gratuitous violence with shots of Upham, rifle in hand, cowering on the stairs leading up to the room. However horrific the montage may become, the director immediately destroyed the impact by having the German come out of the room, look at Upham for a few seconds, and then walk by him and back into the battle.

Not having the German immediately shoot the petrified G.I. is even more implausible than Spielberg's allowing the German to walk away after his capture. Predictably, he has the German fire the shot that kills Miller and then has Upham redeem himself by coming out of his trance, capturing the German, and then shooting him in cold blood. At the penultimate moment, when Spielberg might have shown a modicum of creativity and made a definitive statement about the futility of war, he opts for the traditional Hollywood ending. Rather than having the Germans taking the bridge, or having Private Ryan die and Captain Miller live, the cavalry shows up in true cinematic tradition in the form of P-51 Mustangs in the air and hundreds of soldiers on the ground. Even though six of Miller's eight-man patrol die, Ryan lives, as he might have done anyway.[44]

Yes, war is hell. But audiences knew that anyway. And the men who did the fighting knew that. In fact, soldiers may have feared death, but probably not the actual form of death. After all, a soldier is dead whether his head is blown off or he is shot in the back like John Wayne. More likely, the training through which a soldier went ensured that he would charge off the landing craft when the ramps went down, truly expecting that the bullets raining down would hit the man next to him, not him.

With this said, what about *Saving Private Ryan*? Tom Hanks recounted that Gen. Colin Powell told him that the opening twenty-four minutes "was really right. I've been there." However, the retired chairman of the Joint Chiefs of Staff then asked the actor: "But why didn't you just blow the bridge at the end?" In response, Hanks told him: "It isn't a documentary! It's a movie." Powell agreed: "Historical accuracy is desirable, but entertainment value and using the visual power of film to make a point usually comes first. I don't expect perfect or even close historical accuracy. The written word and documentaries do that best."[45]

True. However, with *Saving Private Ryan*, Spielberg claimed to have attained a higher level of reality, thanks to his use of violence and serious commitment to his subject. In hyping *Saving Private Ryan*, the director explicitly stated that he was not making another "movie," but rather *the* American war movie. Consequently, *Saving Private Ryan* cannot simply be viewed as a work of fiction that permits all manner of dramatic license. All combat films contain some implausibilities, distortions of fact, historical inaccuracies, and errors of military procedure or regulations in order to create a dramatic impact. In this, *Private Ryan* remains no more or less a traditional war movie, differing only in the amount of graphic violence Spielberg put on the screen. It probably does not matter whether he believed he needed the violence to create his message or was simply using violence to market the film. Instead, the director too often painted by the numbers and recycled the clichés from the countless war movies he had watched over the years, rather than allowing his creative juices to lead him.

Steven Spielberg, Tom Hanks, and others on the set of *Saving Private Ryan*.

Despite such deficiencies, Spielberg clearly produced a significant film with *Saving Private Ryan*. Yes, he may even have made one of the great war movies, certainly the most violent and noisy film about men in combat up to that time. Nevertheless, its greatest emotional impact came not from the violence that ultimately overwhelms the senses, but rather from the brief opening and closing sequences in the military cemetery overlooking the English Channel. The identity of the veteran walking down the rows of markers makes no difference. The audience cannot help but be moved to tears as the man and his family move slowly past the crosses and Stars of David.

Some critics described the cemetery sequences as maudlin and thought that Spielberg was simply playing on the audience's emotions. Still, everything people need to know about the horrors of war they can learn from watching the veteran sink to his knees in grief and remembrance. In returning to the veteran's pilgrimage at the film's climax, Spielberg reinforces the sense of loss that he created in the opening sequence. It does not matter that Private Ryan rather than Captain Miller has survived. After all, survival remains the goal of each man who enters the field of combat. Better than any of the violence Spielberg thought he needed, the quiet thanks that Ryan offers at Miller's burial spot serves as the film's raison d'être.[46]

Regardless of how a person perceived *Saving Private Ryan*, no one could question that Spielberg intended to make a serious comment about the nature of soldiers' experiences in combat. Only with great difficulty could anyone say the same thing about Terrance Malick's *The Thin Red Line*, which appeared later in 1998. The second film to be based on James Jones's novel *The Thin Red Line*, it ostensibly portrays the final days of the 1942 battle for Guadalcanal following the Army's relief of the Marines who had landed on the island on August 7, 1942, in the first American amphibious assault since 1898. Andrew Marton's 1964 production, made in Spain with no U.S. military assistance, captured the essence of the book in a philosophical rather than an epic war movie.

Marton believed the title referred to "a non-existent line, an imaginary line. It is a line that separated the insane from the sane people." Sounding not very different from Joseph Heller's Yossarian, the director explained that the basis thesis in Jones's book "is that today's warfare with fragmentation bombs and phosphorous bombs and machine guns and land mines is such a hell that you have to be insane to stay in there. If you were sane, you would say—'To hell with all this, I'm going home.' You have to be insane during the battle, but then the question is, When the battle is over, can you step back across the line of insanity? This is always a difficult moment. *The Thin Red Line* is the story of one G.I. who couldn't easily, and almost goes completely bananas." Jones appreciated the 1964 rendering of his thesis and story, writing to the director: "Very rarely can a writer sit down and write a letter to someone who directed a story of his and tell him that he came as close to the intention of the writer's ideas as any human being can."[47]

Jones himself had acknowledged that he had fictionalized many of the locales in his book. Consequently, it remains an impressionistic rendering of the combat that the author himself had experienced, not a story about the actual battle for Guadalcanal. Perhaps trying to transfer this approach to the screen, Malick created no more than a bloated art film, a three-hour kaleidoscope of images of soldiers, natives, animals, and vegetation that said almost nothing about war. In Malick's *Thin Red Line*, combat serves only as an instrument of death. The director, returning to Hollywood after a twenty-one-year absence, knew even less about the reality of men in war than did Spielberg, and only one of his five technical advisors had ever served in the armed forces. The lead advisor said this probably had little impact on the on-screen images, since Malick paid only lip service to the accuracy of his portrayals of men in battle. Ultimately, the slow pace and lack of intellectual focus leaves only an image of confusion. Consequently, the film makes only a limited comment on man's efforts to survive in the hostile atmosphere of the battlefield.[48]

The producers did send the script to Phil Strub on October 29, 1996, requesting information about arranging for cooperation during filming in Australia. They hoped to use any Navy ships that happened to be in the area the next June: "Period or modern day? Can modern ships be modified to pass as WWII for filming purposes?" They wanted to know if the Pentagon could help them obtain any World War II equipment, including machine guns, mortars, and rifles. They also asked if the Pentagon could "supply us with technical advice on the U.S. confrontation with the Japanese on Guadalcanal."[49]

Initially, Strub advised producer John Roberdeau that the script seemed worthy of support. Roberdeau followed up the conversation with a letter in which he explained that the filmmakers' goal "is to recreate an army which is 'antique' in contrast with today's modern, all-volunteer force." Apparently unaware of Jones's reaction to the original production, the producer claimed that the author "was extremely critical of what he called 'phony war films,' and we hope by all means to respect the historical accuracy of *The Thin Red Line*." To that end, he requested that Maj. Thomas McCollum, formerly in the Army's Los Angeles Public Affairs Office, and Walter Bradford, a historian in the service's Center for Military History, be assigned as technical advisors to the production.[50]

Clearly, the filmmakers had little appreciation of the reality that the Army and the Navy no longer maintained a store of World War II equipment or ships. Nor had Roberdeau apparently read *The Thin Red Line*, since he seemed to believe that the book contained an accurate account of the battle for Guadalcanal. Beyond that, he undoubtedly misinterpreted the reaction to the script by Strub and Al Lott in the Army's Los Angeles office. In March, Lott sent Strub a memo in which he explained that he had told the producer in October that "the story was adequate, but the Army depiction needed a lot of work." In fact, Lott told Strub that the Army "cannot consider supporting this project without a major rewrite of the screenplay." He then listed reasons why it would not benefit the service to support the film.[51]

Lott explained that the screenplay "does not portray soldiers in an authentic manner. There are numerous instances of cowardice by the soldiers, cowardice by the leadership, callous leadership, alcohol abuse on the battle field, war crimes including murder and a total lack of esprit de Corps. Additionally, the language is exceptionally vulgar." Under the circumstances, Lott pointed out that the movie would provide "no informational value that would assist the public's understanding of the Army or DoD because our soldiers are portrayed as mutineers, drunkards and cowards. Additionally, they are portrayed as being very disrespectful to authority." Finally, he observed that the screenplay showed officers as "men who overlook war crimes including murder, condone alcohol abuse [in] a combat zone and put personal accomplishments above the welfare of their soldiers." He said that American soldiers in World War II "fought honorably. This screenplay depicts them as selfish cowards who only care about staying alive."[52]

If the filmmakers had actually needed support that the Pentagon could provide, they might have been willing to revise the script in order to obtain help. However, neither the Army nor the Navy had any World War II assets remaining. Moreover, Malick was going to shoot the film in Australia and on Guadalcanal, far from bases where the service could provide off-duty service personnel who might have lent the production an air of authenticity. In any case, the director was marching to his own drumbeat and had little interest in accurately portraying the Army in combat. As a result, he produced an overlong film that said virtually nothing about war or men in combat or the battle for Guadalcanal.

In contrast, Jonathan Mostow very much wanted to convey the experience of World War II submarine warfare for a new generation of filmgoers. As his vehicle, he wrote and directed *U-571*, which returned to the classic Battle of the Atlantic conflict between submarine and destroyer, only with a twist. To create his story, Mostow drew upon the account of the May 1941 British capture of the top-secret Enigma decoder from the German U-110, one of the pivotal events of World War II, as well as the account of the 1944 American capture of the U-505. In reinventing history, the writer-director extended plausibility beyond the limits of dramatic license. He also created the most exciting submarine movie Hollywood has ever produced.[5]

Mostow did his most egregious tampering with history in the springboard of his story. To propel the plot, he transformed the British destroyer *Bulldog,* which actually captured the cipher machine, into an obsolete American S-Class submarine disguised to look like a German submersible. He then sent the American submarine to seize the Enigma machine from a crippled U-boat, now named the U-571. Do the changes matter? One viewer responded, "If I want truth, I'll watch PBS." A History Channel poll supported that reaction: 14.2 percent of the people said films should be as captivating as possible, and 52.2 percent said that fictionalizing history was "fine" if the films interested people in history.[54]

The British saw it differently. While the film was still in production, survivors of the original engagement complained about the liberties Mostow was taking with an event that King George VI described as the most important single action in the war. Lt. Comdr. David Balme, who had actually carried the Enigma machine out of the U-110, expressed outrage at the American usurpation of a heroic British feat. In an effort to assuage the criticisms, the filmmakers promised Balme to put full credits at the end of the movie setting forth the actual history.

Matthew McConaughey, Thomas Guiry, William Estes, and T.C. Carson portray members of a World War II submarine crew in *U-571.*

The crew of an American submarine sets out to capture the top secret Enigma decoding device from a disabled German submarine in *U-571.*

Satisfied with the response, Balme reported that the filmmakers "were very sorry that they had upset the British and are trying to put it right."[55]

Universal Pictures clearly knew how to handle the retired officer. While filming was still going on, the studio flew Balme to Malta to meet with the cast and describe the actual operation. Later on, during postproduction in Los Angeles, Universal brought Balme to the United States, filmed interviews with him, and screened the work print for him. Not unexpectedly, his perspective changed. After the film had become a box-office hit, Balme told an interviewer on the ABC *Evening News* that he "absolutely loves it" and pointed out, "They spent $75 million making this film, so there's got to be American action to get their money back."[56]

Mostow had similar success in handling a member of Parliament. Paul Truswell wrote to Universal Pictures in late 1999, saying the historical transformation was "a source of great concern" to his constituents, whose contributions had paid for one of the ships that had forced the U-110 to the surface. He expressed the hope the filmmakers would understand that the people "are angry at what they regard as a re-writing of the history that they helped to make." In response to Truswell's request to give credit to the "real facts of the engagement," Mostow wrote on November 18, explaining his purpose in making *U-571.* He claimed that he had no intention "of stealing credit from the courageous men" who

Jonathan Mostow,
director/co-screenwriter
of *U-571*.

captured the Enigma machine. Instead, he explained, "Our film is a fictional account of World War II American submarine sailors." He said the inspiration for the story he had written came from two sources: Operation Drumbeat, Hitler's devastating U-boat attacks on shipping along the East Coast of the United States in 1942, and the U.S. Navy's capture of the U-505 in 1944.[57]

Beyond that, the director explained that he wanted to "show as realistically as possible the psychological and physical effects of submarine combat on the men who served. Our film imagines what might have happened had American submariners discovered that a German U-boat was lying disabled in the middle of the Atlantic." Mostow stressed that his film "is *not* about code-breaking, nor does it address in any detail the Enigma itself." Instead, he saw *U-571* as simply "an action-adventure movie. It follows a long tradition of fictional sea tales set against the backdrop of history. I wrote and directed it with the primary objective of showing modern audiences the unique challenges of WWII submarining. The Enigma is but one element in the film." Nevertheless, he informed the MP that he was including a specific tribute to the British capture of Enigma materials.[58]

Mostow recognized that he had "a moral responsibility not to rewrite history. I believe that I am fulfilling that obligation. It is my sincere hope that *U-571* will focus public attention on aspects of the Battle of the Atlantic that would otherwise risk slipping into the footnotes of history. I hope that young people particularly will see this fictional movie and be motivated to study about the real-life heroes who fought to preserve world freedom."[59]

Why tell a World War II story at the start of the new millennium? Mostow felt that the Vietnam War had made it "impolitic to make a movie that celebrated old-fashioned heroism in war." He thought that by now the American people had digested the Vietnam experience, so that filmmakers could talk about heroic aspects of war in general and World War II in particular.[60] He perceived that now "people are willing to feel proud and patriotic about the men who fought in that conflict." Moreover, he believed, "If it's possible to call a war a 'good war,' that label would have to apply to World War II. Never before in our history was there such a clear-cut case of good versus evil." The director saw "no moral ambiguity" in the nation's rising up to defeat Hitler: "I believe that accomplishment deserves recognition and celebration which is what *U-571* does. I am proud as a filmmaker to celebrate World War II submarining and the brave men who fought on those boats."[61]

Fictional films can certainly educate people about historical events, and they can inspire people of all ages to learn more about what they have seen on the motion picture screen. However, stressing that audiences should understand that *U-571* remains just an action-adventure movie carries Mostow only so far. For most people, what they see on the screen becomes their reality. They have no other frame of reference. They cannot separate fact from fiction, and contrary to Mostow's hope, not many people run to the library to transplant what they have seen on the screen into the framework of actual events.

With *U-571*, the fictional images bear no resemblance to the reality of history. American and British destroyers fought the Battle of the Atlantic against German submarines. No American submariners ever commandeered a German submarine. With the exception of a single, short-lived, small-scale excursion by American submarines to the coast of France early in World War II, the United States conducted all its submarine operations in the far Pacific against Japanese shipping. Although Mostow did accurately portray life aboard a decrepit S-class submarine, the mission he created can in no way inform or educate viewers. If he truly wanted to show "as realistically as possible the psychological and physical effects of submarine combat on the men who served," he should have set his story in the Pacific Theater. Many American submariners there experienced action every bit as exciting and dramatic as the fictional events in *U-571*.

Historical accuracy aside, whatever the nationality of the submarine being portrayed or the makeup of the crew, the question remains whether Mostow has provided a unique or authentic portrayal of life aboard a World War II submarine beyond some leaking pipes and fittings and exploding depth charges. Reviewers and audiences compared *U-571* to the classic 1981 German submarine film *Das Boot* (released in the United States in 1982). In contrast to all World War II Hollywood submarine movies, with their sanitized portrayals of shipboard life, director Wolfgang Petersen's film very well captured the hardships that U-boat crews, and by implication all submariners, faced. The problem with *Das Boot* remains its purpose in being made and the images it contains.

Capt. Hans-Joachim Krug, German Navy (retired), a U-boat executive officer and later an officer in the German Republic Navy, the technical advisor on the film, explained that Petersen had the point of view that the U-boat should become the star and that the movie's "victims are not the enemy, but the crew." The myth-making begins with the opening sequence, set in the fall of 1941, in which a drunken officer verbally attacks Hitler. Krug claims that the submarine service had greater freedom of expression than the other military branches. In reality, at that time Germany still appeared to be winning the war, and few if any officers in Hitler's military harbored such traitorous thoughts. More likely, if any submarine officer had spoken out like the one in the movie, the Gestapo would have had him shot immediately, if he was so lucky.[62]

Petersen then made explicit his theme that the German submariners rather than the enemy have become the victims of war in the montage that begins with the U-boat attacking several British ships and then suffering a horrific depth-charge attack. When the submarine finally surfaces, the captain launches one more torpedo at a burning tanker, forcing its crew to abandon ship into the flaming sea. As filmed, however, the depth-charging the Germans have had to endure has indeed made them the victims and the British seaman simply the distant enemy.

Petersen then completed his polemic by creating an antiwar statement in the closing sequence. After safely returning to port, the star of the movie is destroyed and the brave captain killed in an Allied attack. With such antiwar images, the director was consciously trying to convince the world of the 1980s that the Germans had become peace-loving people who could be trusted. Few people would question that truth. However, *Das Boot* became so insidious because Petersen attempted to connect the present to the historical past and convey the idea that good Germans existed during World War II and even became the victims instead of the evil enemy.

In any case, only in the operational scenes aboard the U-571 does *U-571* convey a sense of what life was like aboard a German submarine. This resulted from the work of

Captain Krug, who served as one of the German consultants to Mostow, and two members of the technical staff, who had worked in the production staff on *Das Boot*. According to Krug, *U-571* gained its visual accuracy because the set in Rome and the submarine mock-up off Malta were "more or less exact copies of what we had in *Das Boot*."[63]

Nonetheless, Krug "found the story rather unrealistic and overblown, typical of the Hollywood super action thrillers of to-day." He said he had hoped he would be able to rectify procedures and environment. Instead, he "found that Jonathan Mostow showed very little interest in these matters and historical correctness." Krug said his suggestions for correcting errors in uniform and other matters were not accepted. In particular, he noted that the German destroyer "looked the plump tugboat that it was. No mariner would mistake her for a sleek two-stack destroyer. At least a dummy could have been added for a second stack." Here, too, Krug said Mostow had ignored his technical advice.[64]

In light of his experiences working on the production, Krug concluded that Mostow's claim that submarines had always fascinated him "sounds rather superficial to me. Irrespective of historical correctness (not always relevant for a screen play) the plot is to me rather unrealistic." He thought that Mostow "had little idea of the realities of submarine warfare or didn't even want to know. As usual for many war movies, action, suspense, and sensation had more appeal to him than concern for naval and submarine environment."[65]

When questioned about such matters, Mostow repeated his previous comments: "My primary goal was to create for the audience the visceral experience of being aboard a World War II submarine. The best way I could make the audience appreciate the kinds of things these submariners went through was to recreate as well as I could, the experience of being aboard one of these antiquated vessels." Yet he often stretched plausibility to the breaking point, if not beyond. Why did he portray a German fighter plane several hundred miles west of England? Why not use a float plane? The director acknowledged it was "a stretch" to have a long range recon plane out there, "but here's where I must rely on the disclaimer that it's only a fictional movie. The plane sequence served several dramatic purposes in the movie, which is why I included it."[66]

Likewise, since the Germans had no destroyers in the mid-Atlantic, logic would have suggested that Mostow use a raider or a supply ship as the opponent of the almost-powerless "U-571." The director had a similar answer: "Again, it's a movie folks. A German destroyer simply looks more threatening than a raider." Furthermore, Mostow disagreed with naval historians who said that the Germans had no long-range destroyers in the Atlantic: "I could never find firm evidence that the Germans did not operate the occasional destroyer in the Atlantic. To the contrary, I had several indications that they did."[67]

The three torpedo incidents at the heart of the story all raise serious questions about plausibility. Just as the S-33 has completed its heist of the Enigma machine and the away crew is about to return to the ship, a torpedo, apparently from the U-boat sent to help the U-571, blows up the American submarine. Given the weather and the darkness, audiences might well wonder how the German captain could possibly see what was happening and decide which submarine to sink.

Worse, after the American boarding party returns to the U-571 and it gets underway, its new crew wages an undersea battle with the German rescue submarine. The torpedoes from the German U-boat miss while those from the U-571 score a direct hit. Submariners maintain that before the development of homing torpedoes later in the war, it was virtually impossible for one submerged submarine to hit another submerged submarine, since there was no way to accurately know the depth or precise direction of the enemy.

Then, after the appearance of a German destroyer, the U-571 wages war both on the surface and under the sea against its new enemy. Having suffered the longest and loudest depth-charging in cinematic history, the U-571 sinks the destroyer with a one-torpedo, "down the throat" bow shot. Yes, an American submariner did "perfect" that technique, but he used three torpedoes with a very narrow spread centered on the target. Although he enjoyed initial success, the captain and his boat did not return from a subsequent patrol.

In response to such facts, Mostow argued: "Again, dramatic license prevails. In movies, as Hitchcock once explained, what matters is what's possible, not necessarily what's most plausible. However, the fact remains that such a firing solution is possible—indeed, under the circumstances, firing the torpedoes head on with zero gyro was their best option. . . . Were they likely to hit their target? No. Was it possible to hit the target? Yes. And that's precisely why the sequence is suspenseful."[68]

In the end, what does a scholar or a submarine buff say about a film that relies on such chance for its believability? Director Mostow certainly ameliorates some of the factual and historical criticism by his claim of simply making a fictional action, adventure movie. However, the closer a film adheres to reality and plausibility, the better its ambience and believability. In *Greed*, Erich von Stroheim had his actors wear silk underwear, not because the audience would ever know, but because the apparel helped the players submerge themselves into their roles.

It is not enough for Mostow or supporters of *U-571* to say that most people do not know the difference between reality and imagination: that a German single-engine, land-based fighter plane could not reach into the middle of the Atlantic Ocean, that German destroyers never ventured into the North Atlantic, that German destroyers had only one stack. But even if only a minority of the audience knew the history of the Battle of the Atlantic, a greater adherence to actual events, procedures, equipment, and plausibility would most likely have produced a better sense of believability than what audiences saw on the screen in *U-571*, and without affecting the excitement Mostow so well created.

The Germans contributed to this excitement as a believable enemy, albeit in the role of the pursuer rather than the prey. Likewise, in *Saving Private Ryan* and, to a lesser extent, in *The Memphis Belle* and *The Thin Red Line*, Germans and Japanese once again served as credible enemies in motion pictures. They provided a viable threat to the security of the United States that drug dealers, Russian nationalists, terrorists, and even Saddam Hussein were not able to become in such movies as *Courage under Fire*, *Crimson Tide*, and *Air Force One*. Nevertheless, filmmakers will have difficulty making movies about the last necessary war without equipment, and even uniforms. Spielberg could rent the Irish Army to stage his Omaha landing. Wyler could find a couple of old B-17 bombers. Mostow could build the interior of a submarine on a soundstage. In any case, Hollywood has told the stories many times over and will need to find new approaches and new insights if it is to continue attracting audiences.

The return to the good old World War II enemies offered the U.S. armed services relatively little benefit. They had virtually nothing except some historical and technical information to provide *U-571* and *Saving Private Ryan*, despite the positive images of the American fighting man that those films contained. As *The Memphis Belle* and *The Thin Red Line* illustrated, without the leverage of possible assistance, filmmakers had no reason to sacrifice their creative freedom by revising their scripts to suit the Pentagon requirement that it receive some benefit in return for its assistance.

Moreover, portrayals of World War II American soldiers, sailors, Marines, and fliers defeating Germany and Japan offered little informational value to the services at the beginning of a new millennium. The military did not need B-17 bombers, Mustang fighters, diesel submarines, or M-1 carbines. To convince Congress to appropriate funds for nuclear submarines, cruisers, and aircraft carriers, and even night vision goggles, the military would need to show their use in contemporary cinematic combat. Consequently, both the Pentagon and Hollywood would need to find suitable enemies who could provide a credible threat and so sustain the symbiotic relationship. Only if filmmakers found viable contemporary enemies would they be able to sustain an interest in military stories in the twenty-first century. To a significant extent, the answer would depend on the real enemies the U.S. armed services would face, the equipment they would use, and the battlefields on which they would fight, whether under the sea, on the ground, in the air, or even in outer space. In the short term, however, Hollywood had several historical wars in which to set military stories.

31 | Pearl Harbor: Bombed Again

DURING THE 1990S, HOLLYWOOD HAD FOCUSED its attention on finding new enemies and revisiting World War II. Having examined Vietnam so thoroughly during the 1970s and 1980s, filmmakers showed less interest in the war in the 1990s, especially after *Flight of the Intruder* failed at the box office. *Forrest Gump* used combat in Vietnam, but only to propel Gump's life forward, not to make a comment about the war. The 1995 *Operation Dumbo Drop* provided one of the few positive portrayals of the American military in the war, with soldiers bringing an elephant—rather than candy—to a Vietnam village whose own elephant the Vietcong had killed. However, with filming done in Thailand, the producers did not need or request Pentagon assistance.

A Bright Shining Lie, a 1998 HBO movie, provided the only full-length exploration of the war during the decade, and while John Paul Vann had fought and worked in Vietnam for much of the 1960s, the Pentagon provided no assistance to the production. Like the Neil Sheehan book on which it was based, the film had great difficulty deciding whether it was discussing the war and Vann's efforts to win hearts and minds or titillating audiences with Vann's sexual predilections for young girls. While in Vietnam and later in the Pentagon, Vann argued for a policy that would provide reforms for the South Vietnamese people and so win their allegiance. When he failed to win support within the armed services, he resigned and returned to Vietnam as an Agency for International Development (AID) worker and, if the film is to be believed, came to command U.S. military forces as the Pentagon drew down the number of troops in country.

Ultimately, he seemed to change his views on military strategy and support the use of aerial bombing to defeat the North Vietnamese. As portrayed, he wins a battle with the use of carpet bombing, only to die in a helicopter crash on his way back to the front. Some students of the war have suggested that if the military had accepted Vann's proposals, the United States might have won in Vietnam. However, such a victory might well have been worse than the defeat, whether military or political, which the nation suffered. In any case, *A Bright Shining Lie* moved back and forth between Vann's military career and his life as a pedophile and bigamist, which he becomes when he marries his young pregnant Vietnamese girlfriend even though his wife has not yet divorced him.

Oliver Stone's *Heaven and Earth,* the third film in his Vietnam trilogy, moves from Vietnam to the post-war United States, and Vietnamese-born, American filmmaker Tony Bui's *Three Seasons* and *The Green Dragon,* also set in the post-war period, looked primarily at the impact which the war had on the Vietnamese people. Each in its own way portrayed the transition from war to peace. Only *The Green Dragon,* which partly takes place in a refugee center for Vietnamese who escaped to the United States after the fall of Saigon, received cooperation, in the form of location shooting for several months at the Marine Corps base at Camp Pendleton.

Like *Forrest Gump, Rules of Engagement* used Vietnam (as well as the Middle East) only as a locale to propel the story. In Vietnam during a brief firefight which civilian technical advisor Dale Dye stages well, Samuel L. Jackson rescues a badly wounded Tommy Lee Jones. Some thirty years later, leading a Marine expeditionary force to rescue the cowering ambassador from an angry crowd besieging a Middle Eastern embassy, Jackson orders his men to return fire from snipers and the crowd, killing eighty-three Arabs and fomenting an international incident. The "transparently evil" national security adviser demands that the Marines court-martial Jackson for giving illegal orders to murder unarmed civilians, hoping to take responsibility for the action away from the U.S. government.[1]

Jackson turns to Jones, who had remained in the Marines after his nearly fatal wounds and became a Marine Corps attorney, until his retirement two years earlier. Although claiming, "I'm a weak lawyer," Jones takes the case out of friendship for Jackson, who tells him: "If I'm guilty of this, I'm guilty of everything I've done in combat for the last thirty years." Of course, the government has stacked the deck, with the national security adviser

Samuel L. Jackson and director William Friedkin during filming of *Rules of Engagement*.

destroying a videotape which clearly shows that the Marines on the embassy roof were taking hostile fire from the mob. The trial itself focuses on a crucial issue facing the U.S. military in a world filled with anti-American sentiment and missions for which the armed services had only recently begun training—when does the use of force become acceptable and necessary? Ultimately, the court finds Jackson guilty of only the least serious of the three charges.

Given the images inherent in the story, Dye had told producer Richard Zanuck and director William Friedkin not to bother approaching the Marines for cooperation. Apart from the portrayal of Americans firing on civilians, the script contained a scene in which Jackson kills a captured Vietnamese soldier and threatens to kill an officer, in order to get the enemy to cease fire. Shortly before the film was to begin shooting in Morocco, Dye approached the Marine Corps Public Affairs Office in Los Angeles for some technical information and gave Capt. Matt Morgan the script. When Friedkin called the office for some additional information, Morgan advised the filmmakers that, with some revisions, the Marines would be able to support the production.[2]

Friedkin was about to leave for Morocco to begin shooting, but after "extensive negotiations," Phil Strub "considered it appropriate that we provide a modest degree of production assistance." In addition to technical advice on how the Marines would conduct a rescue operation, this assistance was to include use of a Marine helicopter for the scene of the rescue force taking off from a Marine amphibious assault ship for the besieged embassy. Due to the limited assistance, the gunship metamorphs into a Moroccan helicopter for the rescue sequence.[3]

In the end, *Rules of Engagement* simply becomes another military courtroom drama, in this case filled with implausibilities. Of course, if the national security adviser had looked at the videotape when he received it, Friedkin would not have had a movie since it clearly showed the Marines were taking hostile fire from the crowd.

Instead, as Morgan later observed, the film did not specifically address the question of where a commander's "obligation" begins and ends, and what is "necessary action" in the given situation. The public affairs officer believed this subject was "infinitely more dramatic and realistic than the silly Bad-Politician-and-His-Scapegoat story that the picture turned into." Nor did it explore the issue of shooting a prisoner during combat to obtain information that could save lives, although in the movie the North Vietnamese colonel whose radio operator Jackson shot acknowledges during the trial that he would have done the same thing.[4]

In contrast to the few combat sequences in *Rules of Engagement* and its focus on serious questions about military conduct, *Three Kings,* only the second major film set in the Gulf War, told its story in the guise of a fiery, action-comedy. George Clooney, as a Special Forces major, recruits Mark Wahlberg, Ice Cube, and Spike Jonze, three gung-ho soldiers who missed the short-lived war, to help him find and keep millions of dollars in gold bullion that Iraqi soldiers had stolen from Kuwait. When the men run across Iraqi soldiers slaughtering anti-Saddam civilians, Clooney and his men face the moral dilemma of either helping people whom the United States had told to rise up against Hussein or following their plan of becoming men of leisure back home.

Perhaps because the film had so many targets—the lampooning of a zealous Christiane Amanpour clone, the Bush administration, and the military—or just because of its quirkiness, it failed to find a large audience. Twentieth Century Fox did send a script to Phil Strub, but the filmmakers went to Mexico for their location shooting and did not ask for assistance. Nevertheless, *Three Kings* did ultimately contain a positive image of the U.S. Army since Clooney and his men put the welfare of innocent civilians before their own prosperity.

Men of Honor had all the ingredients of a feel-good, positive portrayal of the Navy and one man's victory over racism and personal adversity. In this case, Carl Brashear, the son of black sharecroppers, joins the Navy in 1948 to better himself just after President Truman has ordered the military to integrate. Brashear finds that the order is honored more in theory than in practice. Nevertheless, he ultimately decides to become a Navy diver, succeeding

(Below) Cuba Gooding Jr. and Robert DeNiro prepare to confront each other during filming of *Men of Honor,* which told the story of the first black Navy master diver. (Right) Carl Brashear with his alter ego on the set.

despite the efforts of the mentally unbalanced head of the diving school and of his instructor, Robert DeNiro, playing Master Chief diver Billy Sunday, a fictional, composite character. Having won over Sunday and married a doctor, Brashear loses a leg in an accident aboard ship, but remains on active duty after demonstrating he can still carry out his work.

Beyond this inspirational story, however, the film contains decidedly negative images of life in the Navy for a man of color. The portrayal of a senile officer commanding the Navy's dive school also raises questions about the service's personnel policies. And the way in which the Navy treated Brashear during his efforts to return to active duty suggests a real lack of compassion. Despite such images and the appearance of a fictional Russian submarine that threatens to kill Brashear as he is trying to locate a lost nuclear bomb off the coast of Spain, the Navy provided some limited technical and informational assistance. Lt. Comdr. Darren Morton, then director of the Navy's public affairs office in Los Angeles, explained, "I thought a film about Carl Brashear would be fascinating. It's a very inspirational story, one that transcends race." While the script had several sensitive scenes, Morton said he "was never offended either as a Naval officer or as an African-American. In the end, an ethnic member of the Navy achieved his dream at a time when society at large often failed its minorities."[5]

Although it remained primarily a political drama, *Thirteen Days* reminded Americans how the nation came to the brink of war during the Cuban Missile Crisis and, in a small way, showed how the military was prepared to go to war. At the same time, of course, the crisis was to initiate the process of limiting the nuclear arsenals of both superpowers. However, the film contained little action and no gratifying slaughter of an evil enemy. For that, Hollywood returned to World War II for the first time in the new millennium. The immediate subject, the Japanese attack on Pearl Harbor, would seem to lack any originality. After all, beginning with John Ford's documentary *December 7,* filmmakers had revisited the date that will live in infamy several times, beginning with Howard Hawks' 1943 *Air Force.* Each of the feature films, until the 1970 *Tora! Tora! Tora!,* had only used Pearl Harbor as one aspect of a broader story, such as the climactic event in the 1953 *From Here to Eternity* or the opening sequence in Otto Preminger's 1965 *In Harm's Way.*

In 1970, *Tora! Tora! Tora!* had presented an objective, reasonably accurate account of the attack from both sides, even if Admiral Yamamoto never said that the attack on Pearl Harbor would only "awaken a sleeping giant and fill him with a terrible resolve." However, in doing so, the filmmakers forgot the cardinal rule that Hollywood movies must entertain if they are to earn money, the primary and secondary goals of every feature motion picture. Consequently, despite the value of *Tora! Tora! Tora!* as history, its characters remained two-dimensional cardboard figures and the film failed to attract audiences.

What else could a feature film say about the event that changed the United States forever? Director Michael Bay attempted to answer that question before he began location shooting for *Pearl Harbor* in April 2000. He predicted, "You will see what happened at Pearl Harbor like you have never seen it in any other movie. Our goal is to stage the event with utmost realism." He said that he wanted it "to be the movie about Pearl Harbor by which all other such films are measured." He dismissed *Tora! Tora! Tora!* as being "more of a documentary. And all of these other (Pearl Harbor) films glorified war; there were no characters to latch onto."[6]

Producer Jerry Bruckheimer agreed with Bay's sentiments: "In contrast to *Tora! Tora! Tora!,* we felt that by adding a love story, we could bring in customers." Nevertheless, after a memorial service aboard the USS *Arizona* on April 2, 2000, the day before shooting

The USS *Arizona* in
Tora! Tora! Tora! (top)
and *Pearl Harbor* (bottom).

began in and around Pearl Harbor, Bruckheimer told a press conference that the fictional story would be interwoven with actual events: "We've done enormous amounts of research. It will be very accurate. We're trying to tow a very strict line." He later conceded that "as far as accuracy of the film, the film captures the essence of it. You have to understand that it is not a history lesson." To do that, he said it "would take six hours to tell the story of what really happened." Instead he explained: "We had to combine characters. We had to speed up the drama. We are not making a documentary. We always say that to the press. We got the essence of it."[7]

"Essence" remains a very subjective term that may conceal a plethora of sins, and long before *Pearl Harbor* appeared in May 2001, questions arose as to whether the filmmakers' crash course on December 7 would be enough to infuse their movie with even a reasonable portrayal of what occurred one Sunday morning, a long time ago and far away. Ultimately, one of the trailers for the movie perhaps described it more accurately than either the director or producer: "*Pearl Harbor* is a fictional tale crafted from a kaleidoscope of real life personal experiences of those living through this terrifying tragedy." The operative word remains "fictional."

If the film had retained its original pre-production title "Tennessee," Bay and Bruckheimer could have legitimately claimed they were simply using the Japanese attack on Hawaii as the stage for a love story. However, the very title *Pearl Harbor* implied that audiences would be viewing a reasonably accurate account of what happened on December 7, 1941. As a result, the film became fair game for historians, media critics, and Pearl Harbor survivors who found its almost three hours surfeited with historical and factual errors, inaccurate portrayals of military men, procedures, regulations, and combat, as well as implausible and even impossible actions by its characters both real and fictional.

The project itself had begun with discussions Bay had with *Braveheart* writer Randall Wallace and Joe Roth, then head of production at Disney Studio, while seeking a suitable subject for the director's next project following his successes with *Armageddon* and *The Rock.* Ultimately, one of Bay's friends asked if he had considered doing a movie about Pearl Harbor. Initially, the director wondered whether anyone "would ever be crazy enough to do a movie on Pearl Harbor of that size and magnitude."[8]

After hearing that Bruckheimer, who had produced Bay's last two films, had also developed an interest in doing a story about the events surrounding December 7, the director made a research trip to Hawaii. Upon arriving there, he said he "was really surprised how period the stuff was." He also found that the military bases were "some of the prettiest he had ever seen." At that point, he said, "Okay, it's starting to really seem interesting. How can I create this war?" An answer came when he discovered the inactive fleet which he could use as props: "I'm a director who likes to use real stuff to blow up, stuff to inter-cut with digital effects."[9]

Bay then met with Bruckheimer and Wallace to brainstorm ideas for a story set within the framework of Pearl Harbor. Subsequently, the director and writer spoke with eighty Pearl Harbor survivors, after which Bay said that "the movie started to come together." Ultimately, Wallace produced a script that attempted to solve the problem of having interesting characters by creating a love triangle in which two lifelong friends fall in love with the same nurse. Bay explained that without the love story in *Titanic*, it's "just a boat sinking," and without his two-guys-and-a-girl story, *Pearl Harbor* would have become a documentary about December 7. Still, he acknowledged that he probably would not have been interested in making the love story if the Japanese attack had occurred too far in the background. Likewise, Bruckheimer conceded that the Japanese attack, not the love story, "brought in the audience." To help insure that, the producer said the "explosive nature of the teaser trailer" whetted the audience's expectation that the director would be providing a "spectacular."[10]

In the original script, one of two fighter pilot friends, Ben Affleck, as Rafe, goes off to England to join the RAF Eagle Squadron, composed of American volunteers. During

Director Michael Bay during filming of *Pearl Harbor.*

aerial combat with German bombers over the English Channel, enemy fighters shoot him down and Rafe is presumed dead. His friend Josh Harnett, as Danny, and Kate Beckinsale, as Evelyn the nurse, first comfort each other and then fall passionately in love. On the evening of December 6, as Evelyn is completing her work at the hospital, Rafe returns from the dead, expecting to take up the relationship. He does not understand Evelyn's hesitation to embrace him until Danny emerges from the darkness. A night of drinking, recriminations, and brawling leaves the two friends asleep on the beach as the attack begins on Pearl Harbor. Ultimately, Rafe and Danny find two P-40s, manage to take off, and shoot down seven Japanese planes.

As written, the script graphically portrayed the attack, the sinking of the battleships, and the death and destruction that occurred. Despite the title and the destruction, the filmmakers chose not to end with downbeat images or even President Roosevelt's clarion call to avenge the day of infamy. Instead, then Lt. Col. Jimmy Doolittle summons the friends to Florida to take part in the raid on Japan in April 1942. Before they depart, Evelyn tells Rafe she is pregnant with Danny's baby. At the end, Danny dies after telling Rafe to become the baby's father.

To bring this story to the screen, Bruce Hendricks, vice president of motion picture production at Walt Disney Pictures, which was bankrolling the film, visited the Los Angeles armed services public affairs offices on June 18, 1999, to discuss the infant project. Later in the day, he wrote to Phil Strub saying that the officers "were very excited over the idea" even though the company had no script or even an outline of the story. Nevertheless, he indicated Disney would like to use a naval facility to "double for" Pearl Harbor, over which to fly vintage planes that would drop dummy torpedoes and bombs. He asked if the filmmakers could perhaps use Pearl Harbor itself and indicated that the company would like to use an aircraft carrier to launch B-25 bombers, as well as military airfields, World War II ships, and ground facilities in Hawaii or southern California.[11]

Then on October 7 executive producer Jim Van Wyck, on behalf of Bruckheimer, Bay, and Disney Pictures, submitted Wallace's initial script, titled "Tennessee," to Strub. Van Wyck wrote that the film "manifests America's desire to make a difference in the war, the violation and the end of American innocence as a result of the attack on Pearl Harbor, and the heroism, pride and volunteer spirit of the Doolittle raid." He also included Disney's preliminary request for assistance, explaining that the company was looking at filming locations in Hawaii, and asked for permission "to try to recreate 'Battleship Row,' using ships from the Reserve Fleet at Pearl Harbor. We would like your assistance in moving and anchoring approximately eight ships—first to an area where we could construct set pieces on board and do refurbishment and then to specific placement in 'Battleship Row' for filming." The company also wanted to film on board the USS *Missouri*, which had only recently arrived in Pearl Harbor to become a museum.[12]

On their part, the Los Angeles public affairs offices immediately began discussions with Disney's production people about the projected assistance in anticipation of a research trip to Hawaii later in the month. Navy lieutenant Melissa Schuermann, who would become the DoD's project officer during the filming of *Pearl Harbor* the next year, sent a memo to other Navy officers and Strub on October 13, stating that Disney "realizes their initial requests are ambitious, but would like to determine the feasibility of a project of this magnitude." She suggested that the earlier the service identified and addressed its concerns, the easier the production company would find it "to shape and streamline some of their very large creative thoughts into a smaller request package." In particular, she noted that the filmmakers' primary areas of interest concerned the use of the Naval Reserve Fleet and Ford Island.[13]

At the same time, the public affairs offices began to vet the initial script. On October 26, Kathy Ross, the civilian chief of Army public affairs in Los Angeles, wrote to Strub with concerns and questions. She pointed out that Adm. Husband Kimmel witnessed the first attack from his house, not while playing golf as the script described. She questioned the portrayal of the nurses: "Boobs—why use such low-class terminology; nurses were generally well-educated and raised to be respectable. Women applicants for the military were much more scrutinized for their character and manners than men ever were." Ross asked why Rafe and Evelyn would steal a New York City police boat to visit the Queen Mary instead of finding a private fishing boat and pointed out that Danny's use of a P-40 fighter to fly Evelyn over Pearl Harbor "seems unlikely to have occurred. These weren't the pilot's private property, after all."[14]

The Navy, which understood it would "be providing support on a grand scale" if DoD approved cooperation, accumulated a more extensive list of concerns in its memorandum of December 7, 1999. Like Ross, the director of the service's office of information complained about the portrayal of the nurses and stated concern about the appearance of their breasts in their uniforms. He objected to the portrayal of mess attendant and later hero Dorie Miller "as a bow-to, unintelligent, Black male. . . . Please no stereotypical black colloquiums [*sic*]." He pointed out that Evelyn "seems a bit loose. First she jumps into a relationship with Rafe, then when she suspects he might be dead she jumps into the cockpit with Danny." The public affairs officer questioned why Danny would say that the Japanese attack had started World War II. Finally, he wrote that "Danny's death scene seems to be overdone. He crash lands his plane and is near death from that, then he is beaten by the Japanese and then finally shot after trying to protect Rafe. He dies though only after Rafe tells him he's going to be a father. But he doesn't die yet before he squeaks out 'No you are,' then he dies, I think."[15]

For the most part, the filmmakers chose not to address such concerns during the script's several rewrites. Nevertheless, Bruce Hendricks did claim that the final draft of the script, now titled *Pearl Harbor*, which he submitted to Strub and the services on December 22, 1999, contained changes the services had recommended. In fact, the DoD list of "Essential Problems to be Resolved" in the December 20 script had grown considerably from the initial concerns. Among other issues, the Notes again criticized the introduction of the Navy nurses "in a fashion that is anachronistic and also a bit crudely, fixated on how their breasts will appear. Recommend having them stress the importance of having not only good uniforms, but, more significantly, alluring party dresses and bathing suits." More seriously, the Notes complained about the manner in which the script portrayed Jimmy Doolittle, saying it should substitute "another name for Colonel Doolittle's anachronistic 'pussies.'" The critique also focused on the continuing inaccurate representation that the War Department had not wanted him to fly the mission and the manner in which Doolittle ridicules his co-pilot's praying before take off from the Hornet.[16]

In his January 10, 2000, letter to Bruckheimer containing the Notes, Strub advised the producer that, while the Pentagon had "concerns regarding some of the military depictions, we don't believe that any will be impossible to resolve." Consequently, he indicated that the military was determining the feasibility of providing the degree of help which the company was requesting. Despite the problems with the latest script, Strub closed, "We look forward to continuing to work with you on this exciting and inspiring motion picture."[17]

In a letter to Secretary of Defense William Cohen, which Strub prepared for Deputy Assistant Secretary of Defense for Public Affairs James Desler on January 12, Desler advised Cohen that Bruckheimer, Bay, and Hendricks would be visiting the Pentagon on January 20. He said that the filmmakers would be "delighted" to meet with the secretary and show him a short animated rendering of the attack on Battleship Row. While explaining that it is only a preliminary research tool, he said the "video is quite striking nonetheless." Desler then described *Pearl Harbor* as "reminiscent of the patriotic, romance and action oriented genre films of the 40's and early 50's." He also explained that while the Pentagon had not yet approved cooperation, the military was "confident that we will reach accommodation on all areas of concern in the script."[18]

[handwritten margin note: Like old films]

In fact, from the initial script onward, the services (particularly the Navy) had many concerns about the accuracy of the history in the several versions of the screenplay. On January 19, Capt. Kevin Wensing, the senior Pacific fleet public affairs officer, sent a memo to several Navy officers and to Strub about one of the most sensitive issues, the portrayal of Japanese-Americans. Wensing reported that while Strub had said the film would not state that Japanese-Americans were involved in any spying or sabotage, the script still "has a scene with a Japanese looking person . . . perhaps a 'tourist' taking photos. This leaves an impression that the Japanese had good intelligence as they planned their attack while not directly suggesting a member of the local population." Likewise, Wensing worried about the film's account of Doolittle's bombing of Tokyo "since Japan is our number one ally in the Pacific today" and he would "hate to see any demonstrations outside Disneyland Tokyo." He reported that Disney had been asked to discuss the matter with the Japanese government and Bruckheimer responded that the studio had received a go-ahead from Japan.[19]

Although the services had not yet resolved all such problems, the filmmakers did visit Secretary Cohen on January 20 to discuss their project and show him the animated video attack on Pearl Harbor. Four days later, Hendricks wrote to the secretary thanking him for his hospitality in meeting with the filmmakers. He assured Cohen that *Pearl Harbor* "will be a project that we can all be proud of and in some small way pay honor to the service men and women who sacrificed so much during World War II." He then acknowledged that without DoD assistance "we would not be able to make a film of this magnitude and bring to it the authenticity and realism it deserves." He also expressed his gratitude for the secretary's "support and confidence as we undertake this ambitious project."[20]

On January 31, Bruckheimer wrote as well, thanking Cohen for "chiseling out time . . . to accommodate us." He hoped that the secretary learned that the filmmakers "are candidly passionate about our project, PEARL HARBOR. We would be honored and extremely grateful for any guidance and support you could offer us." Inviting Cohen and his wife to dinner on their next visit to Los Angeles, the producer said he hoped to talk with the secretary again soon.

The courting of Secretary of Defense William Cohen by Bruce Hendricks, vice president of motion picture production at Disney (left), producer Jerry Bruckheimer (center), and director Michael Bay (right) may have greased the wheels for easier military assistance for *Pearl Harbor.*

Cohen wrote back on February 9, saying, "It was great seeing you and having a chance to talk with you about your PEARL HARBOR project. Please don't hesitate to let me know if I can be of assistance."[21]

No record exists of any other secretary of defense meeting with filmmakers to discuss a project, and rarely has an assistant secretary of defense for public affairs or a secretary for one of the armed services become directly involved with a production. Did the meeting have any effect on the Pentagon's decision to approve cooperation for *Pearl Harbor*? Given the extensive DoD assistance *Tora! Tora! Tora!* had received, the filmmakers did not need to overcome military reluctance to have the disaster on December 7, 1941, portrayed one more time. Nor did the very magnitude of the assistance being requested become an issue. The Pentagon had been providing large-scale assistance to such projects as *Top Gun, Heartbreak Ridge,* and *The Hunt for Red October* since the mid-1980s and, with the collapse of the Soviet Union and the victory in the Gulf War, the military had no overriding demands on its men, locales, or equipment.[22]

The very size of the project, Disney's bankrolling of the film, and the box-office successes of the producer and director gave credibility to the formal request for assistance. In any case, the filmmakers' meeting with Cohen did not have any visible influence on the approval process. Instead, Phil Strub and the services followed standard operating procedures in handling Disney's request for assistance. On February 2, the Army chief of public affairs sent a memo to Strub recommending DoD approval of "this entertainment project," describing the story as "a very patriotic portrayal of the . . . historic events." On the third, the Navy chief of information followed suit, advising Strub that its Los Angeles office had been working with the filmmakers "on correcting Navy portrayals. The latest version of the script reflects that effort. The story line is patriotic, inspirational and romantic." As a result, the chief of information recommended support for the project. Likewise, the Air Force informed Strub on February 7 that it approved assistance, saying it "would be beneficial to the service and entertaining to the American public."[23]

With these approvals in hand, Strub advised Bruckheimer on February 15 that the Pentagon had agreed to support the making of *Pearl Harbor.* He acknowledged that the task of satisfying the environmental and historical requirements "has been daunting for filmmakers and for the military. However, we believe these efforts will ultimately result in our being able to participate to the maximum extent possible in the production of this historic and patriotic landmark motion picture." Nevertheless, on February 17, Strub wrote to the producer that the military had found several small problems in the January 25 version of the script "that were inadvertently overlooked in the rewrite. We consider them to be important, but so easy to resolve that I didn't let them stand in the way of approving military assistance." He asked that the filmmakers incorporate the "few" corrections into the next version of the script "or at least before principal photography begins in Hawaii."[24]

Strub included a list of the four problems the Pentagon wanted resolved. He asked the filmmakers to "please delete the 'stick jabbing you' gag, it's a bit anachronistic and vulgar." He requested that the "'f' word" be deleted for the same reason. On a more serious level, he asked that the filmmakers change the scene in the *Hornet's* briefing room in which Jimmy Doolittle seemingly flaunts War Department orders not to fly the mission. Strub explained, "We understand the dramatic effect, but believe that it's historically too much of a reach and damning to his reputation." Finally, he said to substitute "crap" for "shit" in Doolittle's line to his co-pilot before the Raiders' take off for Japan.[25]

During the weeks before production began in April in Hawaii, the services provided additional comments on various technical and historical problems in subsequent versions of the screenplay, some of more significance than others. The Air Force office in Los Angeles, for one, cited more than forty areas of concern in the March 3 script. It pointed out that, although the story shows Rafe and Evelyn visiting the Queen Mary in New York harbor on the purloined police boat, the liner did not visit the city in 1941. The office recommended that, since the pre-war Army Air Corps forbid any reference to "boobs" or "nipples," a line be inserted, "Gooz, you know you guys *can't* paint those on there." Far more important than breasts on airplanes or the portrayal of gambling aboard ships—which regulations also forbid—the office noted that the script had the date of the Pearl Harbor attack wrong on the calendar appearing aboard the aircraft carrier *Akagi*. For the Japanese, the attack took place on December 8. Worse, it showed Admiral Yamamoto aboard the carrier when he actually remained in port aboard his flagship *Nagato,* on the Inland Sea of Japan.[26]

While Bay ultimately made some minor changes to the screenplay, particularly in the portrayal of Jimmy Doolittle, most of the errors of fact, history, and procedure in the several versions of the script made it through to the completed movie. Why? Like scores of filmmakers before him, Bay argued he was only creating a dramatic story, not an historical documentary. He explained, "There are people who will come out and say this is not right, that is not right, this isn't right. But, if you were to do the accurate movie of Pearl Harbor, it would take nine hours." Consequently, to help compress the action, Bay said that the script did include some composite characters, including Dan Aykroyd, the cryptologist, who was actually playing seven different people "to help the audience understand."[27]

The director also acknowledged he had delayed Kimmel's receipt of the November 27 message from the Navy Department which stated: "This dispatch is to be considered a war warning" until after the Japanese attack had ended on December 7. He admitted, "That's not historically accurate, but it's more drama." Bay also understood that people might have problems with some of the dramatic license in the film, such as placing the battleships fifty yards apart, instead of showing them tied together as they actually were on December 7. He explained that "what I tried to go after were the essences of what happened at Pearl Harbor. And, I think we got that right."[28]

Screenwriter Randall Wallace had a much more cynical view of historical accuracy, as he had demonstrated in writing *Braveheart*. In an interview for the History Channel's *The Making of* Braveheart, Wallace said, "I make it a policy never to let the facts interfere with the truth." He amplified his philosophy after completing the script for *Pearl Harbor:* "I would always argue for the broader truth and I would also say that the great thing about a drama is that it stimulates people to read the actual history." In seeing the movie, he felt people would want to "find out exactly who Franklin Roosevelt was, who Jimmy Doolittle was, exactly what happened." Recognizing that some people wanted to get the story exactly right, he hoped that people would judge the final product, not the details: "I don't think the audience will leave the theater with a bad view of Jimmy Doolittle or of any of the Americans who fought." More important, he thought that the film would honor those who fought at Pearl Harbor or with Doolittle, which would not be the case if it had not been made.[29]

Given the inaccuracies of fact and history in his script, Wallace probably should have visited his local bookstore and bought one of the many good histories about December 7 before he put a word onto paper. Except for the fact that the Japanese did bomb Pearl Harbor, his account of events bears little resemblance to what actually happened before, during, and after the date that will live in infamy. Nor did he get much right about the

Doolittle raid or its aftermath. For the film's closing voice over, Wallace originally wrote: "The early headlines were wrong. Five fliers died, five more were taken prisoner and held 'til the end of the war." If he had taken the time to read any account of the attack, he would have known that three fliers died at the end of the raid, the Japanese captured eight more men, three of whom they executed, and one died in prison.

Ironically, Wallace would have gotten at least closer to the truth about Pearl Harbor by simply watching *Tora! Tora! Tora!* And he could have acquired an accurate account of Doolittle and his raid on Japan from retired Air Force colonel C.V. Glines, Doolittle's biographer and historian of the attack. However, the screenwriter never took advantage of Glines's willingness to advise him about the Tokyo Raid portion of the film after Bay's office had tried to arrange a meeting soon after Wallace started working on the script. As a result, after Bruce Hendricks sent Glines the script in May 2000, the historian advised Lieutenant Schuermann: "The errors are extremely gross and the script is an injustice to the very brave men who flew the mission. The scriptwriter obviously did no research for this portion of the script." And he later told a reporter, "Oh, I'm sure it will be extremely spectacular. I know they said they laid a fictional story on top of it. It's just that some of what they portray as history is just ridiculous. I think they've done a disservice to the men who flew on the Doolittle raid. These men are national heroes."[30]

In a letter to Hendricks on June 6, Glines explained: "I am greatly concerned about the characterization of General Doolittle and the errors of fact concerning the Tokyo Raid." He expressed his disappointment at the preface to Wallace's original script in which the writer stated that he had "made every effort to capture the truth of what happened, drawing not only from the best historical works, but from the personal accounts of many who saw these events through their own eyes, and shaped them with their courage." Glines maintained, "The script shows that he could not possibly have consulted my books about Doolittle's life or the facts about the Tokyo Raid. Further, none of Doolittle's Raiders, whom I know very well, were contacted before he submitted it." Glines's criticisms focused primarily on Wallace's characterizing Doolittle "as a profane individual," which he said did the flier "a great disservice," observing that he had never heard Doolittle "utter any profanity at any time." He further reported that Doolittle once told him that "profanity was the sign of a weak vocabulary."[31]

Glines pointed out that the script implied Doolittle did not know the purpose of a slide rule even though he had actually earned a Doctor of Science degree in Aeronautical Sciences from MIT. Moreover, he said that the dialogue "shows him to be nearly illiterate and a leader who would open the mail of one of his men and eat his brownies." He also objected to Doolittle's insulting comment to his co-pilot who was crossing himself just before the take off from the *Hornet,* which Glines said "would be profoundly resented by the Doolittle family and the co-pilot who lives here in Texas." In fact, the scene came only from Wallace's imagination since Doolittle's co-pilot, Richard Cole, was not even Catholic.[32]

Glines expressed his anguish about the "fabrications and twisting of facts" and wondered how Disney could not have checked the historical record. He said the script "demeans" the Doolittle raiders by portraying an "absurd selection process" of men who flew the mission. The heart of his concern focused on the distortion of history: "The younger Americans who know little about World War II and its heroic moments will get a completely false impression about this epic event and its leader which will have a lasting effect and do the real heroes a grave injustice. The falsehoods will be accepted as facts because the film was made by Walt Disney Pictures."[33]

Does this matter? Would Bay and Bruckheimer have been willing to make changes in the historical aspects of the script so that the film bore at least a reasonable approximation of what actually happened? Why did the Defense Department and the individual services not insist on a more accurate portrayal of Pearl Harbor and the Doolittle raid? Truth matters only to the extent that truth matters. Filmmakers have always maintained they are in the business of entertaining audiences, not educating them. They argue that they have to fictionalize events for the sake of drama, without considering the reality that truth might well provide more excitement than fiction. They have sold audiences and most likely themselves that in bringing history to the screen, they must not only create composite characters, but rearrange and even fabricate events for the sake of drama, even if that means sacrificing truth and accuracy. At the same time, directors would likely see any challenge to their vision of history, however false or inaccurate, as a challenge to their very artistic creativity.

In the case of Michael Bay, Jack Green observed that the director had "a very strong and detailed vision" of what he wanted in *Pearl Harbor*. How did this play out in regard to accurately portraying history? Green explained: "In those cases where the historic details fit this vision, he enthusiastically put them in. In those cases where they did not, he, like most directors, used dramatic license." Moreover, as far as his own duties as DoD historical advisor, Green said he was not serving in any way as a historical accuracy policeman: "The filmmakers are ultimately responsible for what is in this movie."[34]

Could the Pentagon have done more to ensure that *Pearl Harbor* told an accurate story? The bottom line in all decisions regarding assistance has seldom had anything to do with historical accuracy or the plausibility of the storyline. Instead, the armed services have always asked the same question: does cooperation benefit the military or, in the alternative, does support serve the best interest of the military. *From Here to Eternity* could provide little benefit to the Army, given the officer's attempt to force an enlisted man to box, the images of brutality in the stockade, the relationship between an officer's wife and an enlisted man, and the overall portrayal of Army life in pre–Pearl Harbor Hawaii. On the other hand, it clearly was in the best interest of the service to provide assistance, since it allowed the Army to ameliorate some of the worst elements in James Jones's original novel. In the case of *Pearl Harbor*, regardless of all the factual and historical errors, the script would clearly remind the American people of the bravery and fortitude of those who responded to the attack on Pearl Harbor, as well as the fliers who volunteered for what most considered a suicide mission against the Japanese homeland.

With that said, a strong case can be made that the Defense Department provided its assistance too readily and with too little concern for the accuracy of the portrayals Bay and Bruckheimer would be creating with the men, ships, and locales to which they would have access in Hawaii. The filmmakers stated unequivocally that they would not have made *Pearl Harbor* without the ability to film the Japanese attack on location in Pearl Harbor. The Pentagon recognized that reality after reading the preliminary list of requirements Disney submitted, and which Bruce Hendricks acknowledged in his letter of January 24, 2000, after he, Bay, and Bruckheimer met with Secretary Cohen on January 20. Why then did the Pentagon not use this leverage?[35]

The "Cohen" factor was clearly part of their decision to cooperate. While no evidence exists to suggest that Cohen consciously influenced either the services or Phil Strub to approve assistance so easily, the secretary had made it clear in his meeting with the filmmakers that he supported the project. On February 7, Strub drafted a letter for Cohen's signature to the commander-in-chief of the Pacific fleet with copies sent to other commands informing them that DoD had approved cooperation for *Pearl Harbor*. The letter explained, "The script for this patriotic, epic period motion picture depicts positive, reasonably accurate portrayals of military men and women, and is anticipated to be of considerable public affairs, recruiting, and retention benefit." Then on February 9, Cohen told the producer in a letter not to "hesitate to let me know if I can be of assistance."[36]

On the same day he informed Bruckheimer that the Pentagon had approved support for *Pearl Harbor*, Strub sent a message to Adm. Thomas Fargo, commander of the Pacific fleet, thanking him for his help in working with the filmmakers on their research trips to Hawaii. He said that Secretary Cohen "is very interested in this project. He'll find it quite gratifying that we have successfully passed this crucial milestone. We look forward with great anticipation to what we expect to be a landmark picture that portrays American service members at their best. We know it would be entirely impossible to produce without your support."[37]

Cohen's office made no effort to hide the secretary's interest in *Pearl Harbor*. On March 2, the in-house newsletter *Inside the Pentagon* carried a story about the decision to approve assistance, citing the military's recruiting woes as the reason the secretary "has been schmoozing with the likes of Bruckheimer and other Tinsel Town big shots to promote movies and other projects that portray the military in a positive light, as was done in *Top Gun*." The article said that Cohen's "blessings and the strong support the Navy is showing for *Pearl Harbor* indicate the Pentagon hopes the movie will replicate the success of *Top Gun*." It also cited a statement from the Naval Sea Systems Command that the "DoD and Navy leadership see the feature film as a superb opportunity to pay tribute to the American heroes of Pearl Harbor and to all veterans of World War II."[38]

The article then claimed that Cohen had read the script, and it quoted from the February 7 letter that Strub had drafted for the secretary, that *Pearl Harbor* would be a "patriotic, epic period motion picture." Cohen later stated that he had not "read the script itself." Nevertheless, the article created the perception that Cohen had become friends with the filmmakers (seduced by might be a better description) and fully supported the production. Under the circumstances, Strub would have had little leverage to demand substantive changes in the script so that it more accurately presented the history of Pearl Harbor. Likewise, having read the *Inside the Pentagon* article, Jack Green felt that he and Melissa Schuermann could only offer suggestions to Bay on how to improve the historical verisimilitude of *Pearl Harbor*, not insist upon changes.[39]

In any case, the Pentagon's approval of assistance to *Pearl Harbor* did not end negotiations between the military and the filmmakers to correct historical inaccuracies in the script. Jack Green later observed that efforts to obtain changes created "a massive amount of work." In addition to the portrayals of Doolittle and Kimmel, the Pentagon continued to challenge the suggestion that Japanese-Americans spied on Pearl Harbor. It also pointed out the inaccuracy of having Rafe flying for the Eagle Squadron while in his American uniform. In fact, Americans volunteering to fly for the British formally joined the RAF. Bruckheimer rejected Green's suggestion that Rafe be shown serving as an observer and flying unofficially because he considered it was too complicated for audiences to understand.[40]

Beyond the implicit limitations on what he could accomplish, Green later explained that the Pentagon had to deal with two conflicting concerns. On one hand, the military saw *Pearl Harbor* appealing to young people and so serving as a recruiting tool. As a result, it wanted to help make the film as entertaining and dramatic as possible. On the other hand, the controversies surrounding the *Enola Gay* exhibit at the Smithsonian Institution in 1995 had sensitized veterans groups, who felt empowered to have their legacy presented accurately. Consequently, Green and Schuermann worked long hours to reconcile the differences between the filmmakers' desire for drama and the veterans' insistence upon accurate portrayals of what they had experienced at Pearl Harbor and during the Doolittle raid on Japan.[41]

The Pentagon representatives faced the reality that they could not influence a key element of the story which had the two fighter pilot friends taking part in the attack on Japan. Green acknowledged: "If I was making this movie, I would not have them go with the Doolittle Raiders. There is too much of a historical 'stretch' in this for my tastes." In reality, Doolittle recruited his crews from the only B-25 Group in existence at the beginning of the war. The all-volunteer crews had trained together, each member knew the bomber inside and out, and Doolittle never invited any fighter pilot to join the mission. While the surviving raiders did not comment to the filmmakers about the heroes joining the raid, several laughed when they learned this constituted a significant part of the storyline. On his part, Green was "willing to compromise on this point as long as the characterization of Doolittle was acceptable."[42]

Nor did the military advisors object strenuously to such inaccuracies in the script as having broomsticks, masquerading as tail guns, installed moments before the takeoff from the *Hornet*. In fact the broomsticks had actually been put into the bombers during training at Eglin Field before they flew to the West Coast. However, Green and Schuermann did not consider this a major inaccuracy, recognizing the drama the scene would create for the audience as the B-25s prepared to take off on short notice. Instead, they focused their primary attention on insuring that the film would accurately portray Doolittle: "Both Mel and I agreed that the

Doolittle biographer C.V. Glines and Alec Baldwin, who played Jimmy Doolittle in *Pearl Harbor*, aboard the USS *Lexington*.

characterization of Doolittle was the most important point that we would 'go to the mat for.' Rafe and Danny being on the raid can be dismissed as 'Hollywood BS,' but the original unflattering portrayal of Doolittle, in a DOD supported movie, was totally unacceptable."[43]

In addition to having portrayed Doolittle as profane and ignorant of the use of a slide rule, the initial script made Doolittle into a liar. Aboard the *Hornet* on its way toward Japan, one of the fliers asks him if a B-25 bomber had ever taken off from the deck of a carrier. To create tension about whether the planes could actually get airborne, Doolittle replies, "No." In reality, to confirm that a B-25 could launch from a carrier, the Navy had taken two bombers aboard the *Hornet* and off the coast of Norfolk, Virginia, on February 1, Air Corps pilots successfully flew off the deck with no difficulty. Doolittle would have, of course, known about the test.[44]

After finally meeting with the director during filming of takeoffs of four vintage B-25s and facsimiles of Japanese aircraft on board the USS *Lexington* in July, C.V. Glines offered Bay suggestions to correct the distortions of fact and characterization. How much advice Bay accepted would not be known for almost a year. The director himself later said he changed Doolittle's character "very little" apart from taking out that he swore. At the same time, he recalled that the surviving raiders who watched the bombers take off from the *Lexington* did provide him with information that he then incorporated into the story. Nevertheless, the director maintained that historians themselves "contradict each other. Survivors will even contradict what historians say. . . . It's like everyone is an expert on Pearl Harbor and that's part of the problem with this movie."[45]

While all memories may be created equal, some remain more equal and more accurate than others. Until the movie opened, the questions remained as to which memories the director would choose and whether the love triangle would help or hinder the story telling. Despite the stated focus on the characters, which the filmmakers claimed would separate *Pearl Harbor* from *Tora! Tora! Tora!*, the huge mural on the side of a building in Los Angeles promoting the film only showed the Japanese planes swarming into Pearl Harbor and their date with infamy.

Pearl Harbor did get a few things right. The Japanese did bomb Pearl Harbor Sunday morning, December 7/8, 1941. The computer graphics people did accurately replicate one of the Japanese aircraft carriers with its island on the port side of the ship, and during the cinematic launch the unique structure clearly appears on the left side of the flight deck as one of the attacking airplanes takes off. The film also captures the chaos the Japanese planes created during the first minutes of the surprise attack. And, Jimmy Doolittle did lead sixteen B-25 bombers against the Japanese homeland on April 18, 1942.

Beyond these few truths, however, *Pearl Harbor* fails to provide even a reasonable historical account of the attack on Hawaii and the American retaliatory raid on Japan. Given the choice between dramatization or reality, the filmmakers too often chose to create a cinematic vision that lacked plausibility or any resemblance to the history of the sneak attack. Despite the efforts of Green and Schuermann, the film's representations of historical events differed little from Wallace's original script. Nor did Bay show any interest in accurately portraying the events leading up to December 7, military procedures or regulations, the Doolittle raid on Japan, or the character of the man who led the first attack on the Japanese homeland.

Wallace erroneously placed Admiral Yamamoto aboard the Japanese task force and had the planner of the Pearl Harbor attack utter the first half of the infamous sentence that the attack would only "awaken a sleeping giant." Bay kept these inaccuracies in the completed film, but changed Wallace's voice-over ending, ignoring the fate of the captured fliers, a reality Bay apparently felt should be left unstated.

However, in fairness to the filmmakers, Green said they always listened to and sometimes accepted the suggestions from him, Schuermann, and C.V. Glines. Alec Baldwin's Doolittle still erroneously commands a fighter base on Long Island before the war. But in the film, he becomes a strong character and a far less profane person than in the original script. In particular, he makes a powerful statement that he would crash his damaged plane into a target of opportunity rather than bail out and be captured, one of the very few comments Doolittle actually made.[46]

Likewise, the filmmakers corrected the script's portrayal of the Eagle Squadron. In response to Green's explanation that the unit was comprised of Americans who had volunteered to fly in the RAF, Bay has Rafe tell Danny that he had been ordered to England. However, he later explains to Evelyn that he had volunteered and had made up the story so that Danny would not have tried to come along. Moreover, while the script indicated that Rafe wore his American uniform in England, in the movie his flight jacket covers up whatever uniform he was actually wearing when he arrived at the squadron base.

Despite such revisions, *Pearl Harbor* ultimately provides only a superficial account of the Japanese attack on Hawaii and the American response five months later. More important, history usually comes in a poor second to dramatic license. To be sure, neither Bay nor Bruckheimer ever claimed they were making a documentary or even a docudrama. Instead, they said they were telling a fictional story using Pearl Harbor as a stage on which to set a love triangle. If the film had borne the original title of "Tennessee," a code name used to hide the subject of the project in its early days of development, then their representations might have carried more weight.

However, the very name of the film implies that audiences would be witnessing a historical event, accurately rendered. Therefore, viewers must ask whether *Pearl Harbor* exceeds the limits of dramatic license and falsely gives audiences the impression that they know why the Japanese attacked on December 7, 1941, and how the Japanese carried out the attack. And do they really learn anything about the planning for and execution of Doolittle's raid on Japan. Of course, any critic bears the heavy responsibility of exposing elephants instead of ants. Does it matter, for example, that not one character smokes in the film, even Roosevelt who often appeared with a cigarette during his presidency? What about the paucity of native Hawaiians in a movie set in part in Hawaii? At the same time, the film never mentions that most of the civilian deaths and injuries came from friendly fire—spent rounds from the anti-aircraft guns.[47]

Some people complained about the implausibility of a woman hanging clothes as a Japanese plane flies by before the attack began at 7:50 in the morning. In this instance, Bay intended that image and the next scene of young boys on a ball field watching the attacking planes stream past to represent the sudden loss of innocence, rather than any literal portrayal of life in Hawaii on the morning of December 7. The montage does that very well, just as the opening of *Patton*, with the general in full uniform and wearing four stars, a rank he had not yet achieved, became the defining image of the man and the film. In *Patton*, the license taken did not affect the subsequent accuracy with which the film portrayed Patton's actions or character. In contrast, while the scenes ushering in the attack may provide legitimate symbolism, *Pearl Harbor* contains more than enough factual errors and distortions of reality to pique any historian or layperson without having to resort to picking on reasonable cinematic license.

Perhaps most relevant to any historical film, few portrayals in *Pearl Harbor* provide an accurate or even plausible account of the events leading up to Pearl Harbor or the attack itself. Does anyone really care? Too many people in the United States today, as was the case on the mainland in December 1941, probably have no idea of Pearl Harbor's location or historical importance. After seeing the film, most viewers will at least know where the Japanese attacked and will have some idea of the destruction that took place there. However, they will know precious little of why Japan undertook the enterprise, how its Navy successfully carried out the sneak attack, or even the impact which Doolittle's raid had on the course of the war.

The film's closing voice-over does say that before the April attack on Japan, the United States had known only defeat, and afterward only victory. But why? How, for instance, did the Doolittle raid affect the outcome of the battle of Midway? Nor does the film make any mention of Doolittle's great contribution to the victory in the air over Europe. Does it also matter that the *Pearl Harbor* filmmakers would have the audience believe that the peacetime Army Air Corps, with its strict requirements, would accept Rafe into the service even though he has dyslexia and cannot read an eye chart? (To be sure, after going to England,

Rafe manages to write beautiful, poetic letters to Evelyn and read her answers.) And would the Air Corps have actually accepted Red, who has a terrible stutter, as a pilot?

Despite the military's on-going concerns with the script's handling of the nurses, Wallace's original portrayal ended up in the movie almost unchanged. Although Navy nurses would never provide routine medical exams to Army personnel in peacetime, as occurred in *Pearl Harbor*, Bay refused to transform them into Army nurses simply because he wanted to have Navy nurses in the film. Then there is nineteen-year-old nurse Betty, the object of Red's affection whenever he can get the words out. In fact, all pre-war military nurses were actually highly educated, professional women, not teenagers who had left home to join the service. Moreover, having the nurses behave like today's women looking for a good time rather than adhering to the morality of the time in which they were living does a disservice to the military nurses of 1941. Furthermore, Bay cared so little about historical reality that he usually had the nurses wearing civilian clothes instead of their military uniforms, contrary to the regulations of the time. Of course, he also killed off Betty during the Japanese attack, although no military nurses had actually died, and then compounded the inaccuracy by having the other nurses all receive purple hearts at the end of the movie for no apparent reason.[48]

The fictional characters aside, *Pearl Harbor* shows little concern for either geographical or military reality or a valid historical time line. On Long Island, where the audience first meets the adult Rafe and Danny, a tall hill provides the background to Mitchel field (spelled with two *l*s on the hangar in the movie). Likewise, the same protrusion appears as the background for Eglin Field in the Florida panhandle, where Doolittle's pilots flew over the flat countryside. When Rafe returns from the dead after being shot down by a German fighter during the Battle of Britain, he describes being rescued from the ocean by a French fisherman, although the warring air forces met over the English Channel, close to the white cliffs of Dover, which do appear as the setting for the aerial combat. And the hill-encircled, rock-filled bay where Rafe sat burning Evelyn's love letters looks more like a California seashore than the wide, sandy Florida beaches near Doolittle's training base.

Despite the questions raised about the script's having Danny fly his single-seat P-40 fighter over Pearl Harbor with Evelyn aboard for a joy ride, the scene ended up in *Pearl Harbor*. Yes, during the war, in a very few instances, American pilots did land in occupied Europe to snatch fellow fliers from pursuing German soldiers, and manage to take off despite the crowded cockpit. However, the rescues took place in a wartime situation, not during peacetime. Jack Green suggested that Danny could rent a private plane, but Bay rejected the suggestion. However, instead of making love on the concrete tarmac as in the script, Danny and Evelyn found their way into the parachute loft, which at least provided a modicum of privacy and comfort.

The film's raison d'être, the forty-minute cinematic Japanese attack, never rises above the level of a generic computer video war game, despite Michael Bay's description of himself as "a director who likes to use real stuff to blow up." In essence, the montage remains only a series of set-piece explosions, real and computer generated graphics, planes flying in all directions, and men being strafed on land, in the water, and in the air—the sort of action for which the director is justifiably known. But do any of the visual images have a real connection to what happened during the actual attack?

Bay begins by blowing up the *Arizona* almost immediately with a bomb the audience follows down, through the decks, where its mechanism continues to whir for a few seconds before exploding. The truth be told, the Japanese planes hit the *West Virginia* and then the

Oklahoma in the first minute or so of the attack, and the *Arizona* did not receive its mortal wound until twenty minutes or so after the attack began. The bomb's hokey cinematic journey into the ship does provide a unique perspective, but historians have never established for sure exactly how the *Arizona* suffered its mortal blow. In any case, ignoring the historic time line, Bay continues his recreation of the destruction at Pearl Harbor and surrounding facilities without a pause, although the Japanese actually sent two separate waves of planes to Oahu.

To heighten the drama of the attack, as promised, the director separated the battleships so that the attacking Japanese planes could fly between the two rows. While it may have given "a little more visual flare" to the action, the fabrication produced a problem in the portrayal of Dorie Miller, the first black man to receive the Navy Cross. Some critics of the original script pointed out that no record existed to show that Miller shot down any Japanese planes during the actual attack. In fact, with the smoke, the cacophony of anti-aircraft firing, and the general chaos, no one could accurately determine which man could claim responsibility for any of the few attackers shot down by ground fire. In the cinematic recreation, however, Miller fires repeatedly at the Japanese planes as they swoop down to deck level between the two rows of battleships. His machine guns clearly point directly at the battleships fifty yards away. Regardless of whether Miller hits any planes, he surely hits his own ships.

Cuba Gooding Jr. mans a machine gun during the attack on Battleship Row in *Pearl Harbor*.

Far more serious, Bay actually revised the interpretation of blame for the failure to better defend Pearl Harbor when he manipulated the time at which Admiral Kimmel received the November 27 war message from Chief of Naval Operations Harold Stark. If the director had presented history accurately, audiences might well have concluded that Kimmel failed to take proper precautions against a surprise attack. However, by showing the admiral receiving the telegram after the attack, Bay effectively switched the blame to Stark and the government in Washington, and even President Roosevelt. In fact, the director portrays FDR as reacting with genuine surprise to word of the attack, albeit in a White House hallway rather than in his study, where he was playing with his stamp collection.[49]

Bay may create irony in showing Admiral Kimmel receiving the warning while inspecting the destruction the Japanese attack had wrought, and he does capture the initial shock and subsequent chaos which the military men and women experienced. However, he has produced only a generic portrayal of surprise and confusion, far less dramatic that the few minutes of terror which Fred Zinnemann provided in *From Here to Eternity*. Likewise, while the hospital scenes convey the horrific suffering of the casualties, they do not differ from portrayals of front-line military hospitals in other combat films such as *M*A*S*H* and *A Bridge Too Far*.

In any case, any semblance of historical accuracy virtually disappears once Bay embarks upon his account of Doolittle's raid. He follows Wallace's script with its inaccuracies and distortions virtually unchanged. Following the attack on Pearl Harbor, President Roosevelt berates Army Chief of Staff George Marshall and CNO Stark for failing to come up with a plan to retaliate against Japan for Pearl Harbor. In response, the senior officers whine and argue that the United States cannot launch a direct attack. The president glares at them and lashes out: "I was strong, and proud, and arrogant. Now I wonder, every hour of my life, why God put me into this chair. But when I see defeat in the eyes of my countrymen—in your eyes, right now!—I start to think that maybe he brought me down for times like these, when we all need to be reminded who we truly are. That we will not give up—or give in."

The president then rises unaided from his wheel chair as Wallace had written it: "With inhuman physical effort, his neck veins bulging and sweat popping on his face, Roosevelt stands on his withered legs." He says, "Do not tell me . . . it can't be done." Although not strictly a military scene, Green noted that the president, as commander-in-chief, would not have treated the service heads as portrayed. During a sneak preview in Denver in early March, a member of the audience described the scene as "overly dramatic." Nevertheless, it remained in the film even though Jon Voight, who played Roosevelt, acknowledged that the president "had no legs." In reality, of course, FDR could not stand without help.[50]

Such heroics quickly led to the introduction of one of the few real people in the movie. Capt. Francis Low, the Navy officer who suggested in early January the idea of flying Army bombers off an aircraft carrier to attack Japan. Accuracy and plausibility immediately disappear. Low took the idea to his boss, Adm. Ernest King, the new chief of naval operations, in early January. In the movie, King then takes Low to the White House to brief the president, which never happened. Continuing to ignore the historical time line or even common sense, Bay immediately returns to Hawaii to a scene of flag-draped coffins of the Pearl Harbor victims stretching across a hangar floor and onto the outside tarmac.

Jack Green explained that the director wanted to replicate images he had watched on television of American military dead, arriving at Dover, Delaware. Even though the film does not provide the actual date on which Low came to King with his proposal for the raid, most viewers would understand that a considerable amount of time had passed since December 7, especially since the film has included a montage of American mobilization of industry to wage war. Apart from Hawaii's tropical climate, the armed services had had no time for ceremony following the attack and had buried its dead within a day or two, not weeks after the attack.

In any event, during the coffin scene, Rafe and Danny receive orders to report to now-Colonel Doolittle for a secret mission. Despite his claim of changing very little of Wallace's characterization, Bay does create in Alec Baldwin's Doolittle a more positive figure than in the original script. However, once aboard the cinematic *Hornet* on its way to Japan, the director still has Doolittle subvert the truth when he tells one of the fliers that no bomber had ever taken off from an aircraft carrier, clearly intending to heighten the drama for audiences when the cinematic launch takes place. Nor did Bay satisfy the Pentagon's concern that the film might show Doolittle violating orders by going on the raid. He still tells his men that some people in the War Department did not want him to fly the mission, which was true. However, he then says he could not stand and watch them go without him and so he will be leading them. This still sounds very much as if Doolittle is ignoring orders, since he does not explain to the men that he had managed to get permission from

Arnold to lead the attack. Consequently, Doolittle's motivational speech remains only a cinematic fabrication.

Things go downhill, accuracy-wise, from there. Twelve hours before the task force reaches the planned launch point, Japanese picket boats at a distance of twelve miles discover the flotilla Wallace used the figure of four thousand yards in his script. Bay translated it to four hundred yards and then a mile in the film's account. *Pearl Harbor* then portrays Doolittle deciding to launch, when in fact Admiral Halsey aboard the *Enterprise* gave the order. While Bay eschewed some of the script's dramatic, last-minute efforts to lighten the planes, he still included the removal of machine guns and their replacement with the broomstick handles. In fact, the weight-reduction configuration of the bombers had taken place during training in Florida. Nor would the crews have had time to do anything except man their planes—Doolittle's plane left the carrier deck a half hour after sighting the first Japanese patrol boats and the whole launch effort took only one hour.

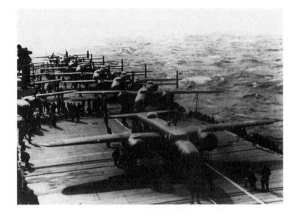

Ultimately, all sixteen B-25s did launch successfully. In contrast to the portrayal in *Pearl Harbor,* in which Doolittle's plane sinks toward the ocean after taking off, his and fourteen of the other the bombers actually climbed immediately from the deck. Only the plane of Ted Lawson, the author of *Thirty Seconds Over Tokyo,* initially dipped toward the water due to an incorrect control setting. In any case, despite the voiced concerns over fuel when the planes have to take off prematurely, the film shows all the bombers rendezvousing over the task force before setting out for Japan in formation. In the actual event, the early launch and the need to conserve fuel for the now longer flight dictated that each plane would immediately set out on its own course to Japan and one of the five selected cities. As a result, only two or three bombers ever spotted other planes in the distance.[51]

Doolittle's raiders just before takeoff in 1942 (top) and B-25s aboard the USS *Lexington* during filming of *Pearl Harbor* (bottom).

In the cinematic attack, however, the planes arrive together and bomb in formation. Some pilots are shown ordering, "Bombs away," although the bombardier actually calls out that information after releasing his bombs, which anyone having seen any of the many Hollywood air combat movies would have known. Again, Bay demonstrates his ability to film spectacular explosions, although the ordinance sometimes appears to explode before the planes arrive over their targets. At the same time, Bay's need for drama and blood required that he show Danny's plane receiving significant damage from anti-aircraft fire, which kills one of his crew. In reality, the attack caught Japan by surprise, even though the picket ships had radioed back word of the task force. Using their own experience in such matters, the Japanese assumed the carriers would have to get within three hundred miles of the mainland to launch their single-engine planes. Not expecting the bombers to arrive so soon, Japanese gunners and fighters had not yet deployed. None of the B-25s received any significant damage, and so none of the bomb crews were wounded or died as Bay portrayed.

Such factual and historical errors pale to the egregious fabrication of Evelyn's efforts to monitor the raid. Both in the script and on the screen, Evelyn intimidates an officer into admitting her to a secure communications center that is tracking the course of the attack. Never happened. Could not have happened. Not even the military commanders in Hawaii knew about Doolittle's mission, and Roosevelt himself did not receive a detailed briefing until a few days before the scheduled launch. The world learned about the attack only when Japanese radio broadcasted the news.

Even if a command post did exist, Evelyn could not have known of the secret raid, since none of the fliers knew where they were going until the *Hornet* put to sea from the Alameda, California, Naval Air Station. At best, from their training, some of the fliers might have concluded they would be delivering their planes to some forward base in the Pacific. Moreover, even if Evelyn somehow learned of the plans and could have talked her way into the phantom facility, she could not have listened to any dialogue once inside.

The planes, of course, were flying under radio silence and intercom conversations did not reach the air waves. More to the point, Doolittle had had the long-range radios removed from the bombers to save weight. And even if any of the planes had somehow managed to keep its radio, the technology of the time was incapable of transmitting dialogue from near Japan all the way to Hawaii. All this ignores the reality that Doolittle had to launch twelve hours ahead of schedule when Japanese picket ships discovered the task force. So Evelyn actually arrived in the cinematic communications center after Doolittle's raiders had dropped their bombs. Green did offer Bay a solution, suggesting that the American military attaché in China send a message back to Hawaii after the mission ended, which the director rejected undoubtedly because of the drama inherent in the sequence.[52]

In any event, the inaccuracies, implausibilities, and simple carelessness continue unabated once the bombers reach the Chinese coast with fuel-starved engines sputtering. Rafe calls out to Danny to land in a rice paddy, which proves to be a cornfield when Rafe's bomber crash-lands and bursts into flame, despite having run out of fuel. When the crew comes under attack by a Japanese patrol, Danny manages to find a few more ounces of gas and strafes the attackers. He then crashes in the next field and manages to crawl out of the burning plane, where Rafe finds him as grievously wounded as in Wallace's script. The Japanese immediately surround and capture the surviving crew members and proceed to truss Danny Christ-like to a yoke. Rafe conveniently finds a loaded handgun and shoots two of the Japanese soldiers, turning the tide of battle. However, having been shot along the way, Danny dies after anointing Rafe to become the father of Evelyn's baby.

The Japanese did capture eight of the raiders, but not immediately, and without any of the histrionics which Bay creates. *Pearl Harbor* omits any mention of the real drama of how Doolittle and most of his men returned to the United States. Instead, after Chinese soldiers rescue Rafe and surviving crews, Bay dissolves to a scene of some of the fliers returning to an unidentified air base (incorrectly set in Hawaii in the original script) bearing Danny's coffin. In fact, the ashes of the seven dead fliers only returned to America after the war.

Jon Voight, as President Roosevelt, prepares to decorate Ben Affleck, as Rafe McCawley, for his participation in Doolittle's raid on Japan in *Pearl Harbor*. The scene, with Gen. George Marshall looking on, never happened. The president presented the Medal of Honor to Doolittle, but met with none of the other raiders.

Ultimately then, the film's Doolittle sequence contains virtually no accuracy and, worse, fails to convey the courage of the men who actually attacked Japan in what most of them and the planners recognized would probably be a suicide mission. Moreover, only in the vaguest terms did the film acknowledge that Doolittle's raid inflicted little material damage on the Japanese war machine, with the loss of all sixteen planes and the death of seven fliers. Nor did Bay even recognize Doolittle's leadership or acknowledge that he received the Medal of Honor from President Roosevelt following his return from China. Instead, the film shows the president pinning the Distinguished Flying Cross on Rafe, something no president would ever have done—Rafe would have received it at a much lower echelon.[53]

A rewritten voice-over then offers a few words intended to explain the importance of the raid, while omitting any mention of the seven fliers who died during or after the attack. After all, Hollywood creates movies only to make money, and financial expediency dictated that the truth might result in a smaller box-office return in Japan. Faced with that reality, Disney deleted a few words out of sensitivity "to international audiences," including removal of "dirty" from one character's outburst against the Japanese.[54]

During the world premiere in Hawaii, a CNN reporter asked Bruckheimer if he thought *Pearl Harbor* might have portrayed the Japanese as heavy-handed or if it sugar-coated the attack. He responded, "Not really, because it's all about perspective. They (Japan) have a certain point of view and we (the United States) have a certain point of view. We've tried to show their point of view versus our point of view. We were strangling them because we'd cut off their oil and their iron." Ignoring the reasons why the United States had acted, the producer explained that the Japanese "had to do something." Like launching a sneak attack. Given Bruckheimer's interpretation of events and the manner in which Bay recreated on the screen one of the great victories in military history, *Pearl Harbor* naturally enjoyed considerable success in Japan.[55]

Of course, the filmmakers claimed they were only telling a love story, not creating a documentary of men at war or a history of December 7. Unfortunately, the pursuit of Evelyn by Rafe and Danny never rose above the level of trite soap opera. It did not have the power to mask the deficiencies in the portrayal of actual events in the way that the love story in *Titanic* made the film more than a documentary about a sinking ship.

Perhaps if Rafe and Danny had come home to Evelyn from the Doolittle raid and all three had settled down together in the hills of Tennessee to raise the love child, the drama might have justified the huge cost of the film. Instead, A.O. Scott, in his *New York Times* review of *Pearl Harbor,* may have said it best: "The Japanese sneak attack on Pearl Harbor that brought the United States into World War II has inspired a splendid movie, full of vivid performances and unforgettable scenes, a movie that uses the coming of war as a backdrop for individual stories of love, ambition, heroism and betrayal. The name of that movie is *From Here to Eternity.*"[56]

If not good history and not good drama, what then did $140 million provide to American audiences? Lt. Col. Bruce Gillman, the director of the Air Force's Public Affairs Office in Los Angeles felt that *Pearl Harbor* showed the "lethality of air power," both from an Allied and Axis perspective. He saw the film as an aviation picture because the heroes were fliers and the "audiences will take away an impression of W.W.II aviation. From a recruiting perspective, if one can use those words, it certainly pays more than lip service to the excitement of flying a military aircraft." On a personal level, Gillman said that he had "enjoyed the film and as a military member I marveled at the sacrifices my predecessors made . . . it made me proud to wear our country's uniform."[57]

Beyond that, *Pearl Harbor* did provide a reminder to Americans of the bravery of the men and women who withstood the unprovoked attack on December 7 and who then embarked upon the long road to victory. Perhaps that alone justified the assistance which the Pentagon and the Navy provided and the cost of making the film, regardless of how much it rewrote history. *Pearl Harbor* may have offered one other benefit. It reminded younger viewers that on a quiet Sunday morning long ago and far away, those friendly people who sell Play Stations, video recorders, cameras, and cars to the United States once launched a sneak attack on American territory and its people, who then believed they were at peace with the world.

Epilogue

THE ARMED FORCES HAD FAILED TO PREVENT the attack on Pearl Harbor despite the promises contained in the Hollywood preparedness movies from 1939 to 1941. However, working together, the armed services and filmmakers immediately began to repair the damage, to show how the nation would fight back from adversity and defeat its vile enemies. Films like *Wake Island, Bataan, Air Force, Destination Tokyo, Guadalcanal Diary,* and *Thirty Seconds Over Tokyo* all conveyed the message that President Roosevelt had delivered to the nation on December 8, 1941: "No matter how long it may take us to overcome this premeditated invasion, the American people will in their righteous might win through to absolute victory."

The terrorist attacks on September 11, 2001, produced the same trauma among the American people as had the Japanese attack on December 7, 1941, and the nation responded with the same patriotic fervor that followed Pearl Harbor. More than that, much as *Top Gun* served to complete the rehabilitation of the military's image which the Vietnam War had so savaged, the attacks on the World Trade Center and the Pentagon most likely completed the reunification of the nation and its people, which the war in Southeast Asia had rent asunder. As victims ourselves, we could also finally gain at least a modicum of empathy for the Vietnamese people, who had suffered so grievously from their long war against France and then the United States.

Unlike the motion picture industry after Pearl Harbor, however, Hollywood seemed unable to come to terms with September 11. Although government officials came to Los Angeles seeking help in the war on terrorism, times had changed from the early days of World War II when studios could turn out war effort movies very quickly. Now, under the best of circumstances, filmmakers need close to two years to develop a project, put it before the camera, edit the footage, promote the movie, and put it into theaters. More to the point, what kind of films could the industry create that would stiffen the resolve of the American people any more than the images of the collapsing World Trade Center towers or the gaping hole in the side of the Pentagon or the smoking crater in the Pennsylvania countryside had already done?[1]

Hollywood could also point out that in some measure the terrorists were actually imitating art in their attacks and threats of attack on the United States. *Executive Decision* and *Air Force One* had portrayed terrorist takeovers of an airliner and of the president's own plane. Chuck Norris had almost single-handedly defeated a Russian terrorist plot to take over the entire country in *Invasion USA.* Steven Seagal had thwarted the kidnaping of the USS *Missouri* and a threatened missile attack on Honolulu in *Under Siege.* Sean Connery and Nicholas Cage had saved San Francisco from Ed Harris's disaffected Marine Corps general, with chemical-tipped rockets aimed at the city in *The Rock.* Terrorists threatening nuclear attacks, biological attacks, and chemical attacks had appeared on theater screens regularly during the 1980s and 1990s. Arabs had even tried to take over New York City in *The Siege,* although the more serious threat to the country and the Constitution seemed to come from Bruce Willis, playing an American general who wants to impose martial law to ensure the safety of the city. Having been there and done that, what more could filmmakers say that would help the government fight terrorism?

Worse, studios could not even decide what to do with combat movies ready to be released or in final post-production on September 11. Ultimately, hoping that the patriotic fervor welling up across the country would help the box office, Twentieth Century Fox moved up the release of *Behind Enemy Lines* from 2002 to November 17, 2001. A routine, fictional, missing-in-action flier story inspired by but not about the rescue of Air Force pilot Scott O'Grady, shot down over Bosnia, received limited assistance from the Navy and the Marines, particularly for scenes aboard an aircraft carrier. Its box office success, due in large measure to its action sequences, opened the door for the other military films in waiting.

Black Hawk Down, which appeared at the end of the year, documents an American military operation in Somalia in 1993 in which Rangers and Special Forces lost eighteen soldiers. Based on Mark Bowden's best-selling history of the same name, Ridley Scott created a movie of unrelenting, uninterrupted combat for almost its entire 144 minutes, a synthesis of *Zulu, Starship Troopers,* and the first twenty-four minutes of *Saving Private Ryan.* The film offers the best portrayal of men under siege since *Zulu* and, like the 1964 British classic, some might see *Black Hawk Down* as racist, since white soldiers comprised most of the force that went into Mogadishu and killed black Somalis. Others saw the movie as portraying the failure of a noble, humanitarian effort to feed starving people or the defeat of elite American forces by a ragtag native population.

The Pentagon saw *Black Hawk Down* as a tactical victory and "an important opportunity to help depict both the distinctive valor of our soldiers during the Somalia operation, as well as the challenges of conducting operations in ambiguous situations that our forces may encounter in today's uncertain security environment worldwide." After negotiations which eliminated the original script's rivalry between the Rangers and the Special Forces, the Army provided Scott eight helicopters and one hundred soldiers during filming in Morocco, at a cost of $3 million dollars. Although lacking significant character development, *Black Hawk Down* became a huge box office success due to the quality and realism of its combat sequences. In fact, it probably recreated combat operations as accurately as any Hollywood war film has ever portrayed a historical event.[2]

We Were Soldiers also portrayed a true story of a badly outnumbered American force which comes under siege, this time early in the Vietnam war. In contrast to *Black Hawk Down,* the film spends time fleshing out the characters of some of the men who will be doing the fighting, the sons and husbands and lovers before they leave for Southeast Asia,

The filmmakers paid the U.S. Army $3 million for the use of one hundred soldiers and eight helicopters in making *Black Hawk Down.*

where, in 1965, they engage in the first major American battle of the war. Screenwriter/ director Randall Wallace took his story from the best-selling *We Were Soldiers Once . . . and Young* in which Joe Galloway and Gen. Harold Moore recounted minute by minute the November 1965 battle in the Ia Drang valley which changed the course of the conflict. In bringing to the screen the confrontation between an American airborne unit and for the first time regular North Vietnamese units, Wallace focused on the fight in and around only one of the two actual landing zones, and for the first time a major Vietnam movie presented the enemy as equals, as three-dimensional people.

Mel Gibson, who plays Col. Harold Moore in *We Were Soldiers,* and retired Sgt. Maj. Basil Plumley, who fought at Ia Drang in 1965.

The writer/director did omit one element of the book's narrative, the Vietnamese's killing of wounded American soldiers on the battlefield, perhaps because the two countries have established diplomatic and economic ties. In any event, the Americans left the battlefield bloodied but unbowed, having demonstrated the efficacy of helicopter assaults as the means of defeating the enemy in the jungles of Vietnam. On the other hand, Senior General Vo Nguyen Giap, head of the North Vietnamese Army, later observed: "After the Ia Drang battle we concluded that we could fight and win against the Cavalry troops. We learned lessons from this battle and disseminated the information to all our soldiers. These were instructions on how to organize to fight the helicopters."[3]

From the perspective of the Pentagon, however, *We Were Soldiers* would show a significant tactical victory by heroic soldiers. As a result, the Army provided full cooperation to the filmmakers at Fort Benning, Georgia, where the service put Mel Gibson and the other actors through an abbreviated basic training routine and then provided helicopters, men, and equipment during shooting on the actual locations where the homefront story had taken place. The service then helped Wallace stage the combat sequences at Fort Hunter-Liggett in California. Although Francis Coppola had tried to muscle in on the new interest in war films by re-releasing the surrealistic *Apocalypse Now Redux* in August 2001, with only limited success, *We Were Soldiers* portrayed Vietnam as the veterans remembered it. If the film made no effort to explain why the United States was committing its young men to combat twelve thousand miles from home, it did present a balanced portrayal of the soldiers who believed in their country and were willing to die for it, in contrast to the images in the initial Vietnam movies such as *Go Tell the* Spartans, *Coming Home, The Deer Hunter,* and *Platoon,* to which the Pentagon had refused to provide assistance.

Although Vietnam had become a bankable subject, Hollywood also returned to World War II one more time, first with *Hart's War,* which reprised every POW film from *Stalag*

Filming on the set of *Windtalkers*, which received full cooperation from the Marines.

17 to *The Great Escape*. Combat reached the screen in June with *Windtalkers*, originally scheduled to open in November 2001 but delayed by September 11. A Marine drama set in the South Pacific, the film tells the story of the Navaho Indians who relayed messages in their native language, which the Japanese could not decipher. Filmed in Hawaii with full Marine cooperation, the production provided Hollywood the comfort of showing Americans winning a necessary war against a clearly defined enemy. But where does the motion picture industry go from here?

Early in the new Millennium, filmmakers demonstrated their willingness to make combat stories, whether in a necessary war, a losing war, a war against genocide, or a failed humanitarian effort. However, World War II has become ancient history for most Americans, *Pearl Harbor, Hart's War,* and *Windtalkers* notwithstanding. Despite the positive images which *We Were Soldiers* contained, Vietnam will never provide a happy ending, except on the purely tactical level. And as Patton so eloquently orated, Americans love a winner and will not tolerate a loser. Of course, winning and losing remain relative terms. The Marines may be simply advancing in another direction. The Japanese may have destroyed much of the Pacific fleet, but only awakened a sleeping giant. The Army may have lost eighteen soldiers in Somalia, but they did not leave any men behind, completed the assigned mission, and when it became necessary, executed the contingency plan successfully.

What then really matters in war films and why their continued popularity? Why have filmmakers created images of men in combat from the earliest days of the industry, even before Hollywood existed? With few interruptions, the American people have demonstrated their willingness to pay to see action-adventure war stories on the screen. Neither the visual quality nor the historical accuracy of any particular cinematic battle nor even the

As shown by *Black Hawk Down,* Americans will pay to see action-adventure war stories on the screen, regardless of whether the United States wins or loses.

outcome of the war being portrayed seem to determine whether people will go to see a combat film. Jerry Bruckheimer and Disney Studios made money with *Pearl Harbor* despite generic explosions, obviously computer-generated graphics, egregiously flawed history, and mostly terrible reviews. Otto Preminger's excruciating *In Harm's Way* and John Wayne's *The Green Berets* made money, however much the critics panned each film.

Combat movies offer something more important than artistic merit. They portray heroes triumphing over evil. Even when the film portrays a defeat, the audience knows that Robert Taylor does not die in vain in *Bataan* and the Marines in *Wake Island* will be avenged. William Holden may have died in a ditch at the end of *Bridges at Toko Ri*, but he died a hero carrying out the nation's will. Even in a war in which the United States suffered defeat at the hands of a small peasant nation, most people consider it a political setback, not a loss on the battlefield. John Wayne can still walk off into the sunset, albeit in the eastern sky, a hero to young males. For the most part then, war movies allow audiences to leave the theater with a sense of pride in their military men and their country. After September 11, the cinematic images in *Behind Enemy Lines, Black Hawk Down,* and *We Were Soldiers,* however much blood flowed and however many men died, had the power to reinforce the patriotism that swept the United States.

That very blood, dying soldiers, and violence that men wreak on their fellow men probably provide the more significant explanation for the continuing popularity of war movies. Despite their protestations to the contrary, most Americans like to watch violence, at least in the safety of a darkened theater or from their sofas in the TV room. More than the violence itself, most Americans seem to enjoy watching other people challenge death, whether at a stock car race, in a boxing ring, or in a downhill ski race. Most especially, people seem to find cinematic killing particularly satisfying.

In the old-time Western, the bad guys, particularly the Indians, die in great numbers. In the gangster movies the criminals die in bunches. But even in the modern incarnations of these genres, in *The Wild Bunch,* in *Butch Cassidy and the Sundance Kid,* in *Bonnie and Clyde,* in *The Godfather* movies, in *The Unforgiven,* the violence and the killing remain on a relatively small scale. Only the violence inherent in war movies offers slaughter on a scale to satisfy most people's needs. If these portrayals show the U.S. armed services in a reasonably good light, doing their jobs, protecting the nation, and the killing serves a socially redeeming purpose, the Pentagon will continue to provide assistance to filmmakers. Hollywood will gladly take that all the way to the bank.

Appendix A
Films Cited

Note: References to the Air Force include films featuring the Army Air Corps, which was a branch of the Army until 1947.

Title	Date	Service	Cooperation	Studio	War	Director
Above and Beyond	1952	Air Force	FC	MGM	WWII	Melvin Frank & Norman Panama
Action in the North Atlantic	1943	Navy	LC	WB	WWII	Lloyd Bacon
Air Force	1943	Air Force	FC	WB	WWII	Howard Hawks
Air Force One	1997	Air Force	FC	Sony	Terror	Wolfgang Petersen
Airport 1975	1974	Air Force	LC	Univ	Peace	Jack Smight
Airport 1977	1977	Navy	FC	Univ	Peace	Jerry Jameson
America	1924	Army	FC	UA	Revol	D.W. Griffith
The Americanization of Emily	1964	Navy	NR	MGM	WWII	Arthur Hiller
Annapolis Farewell	1935	Navy	FC	Para	Peace	Alexander Hall
Apocalypse Now	1979	Army	D	UA	Vietnam	Francis Coppola
Attack!	1956	Army	D	UA	WWII	Robert Aldrich
Bat-21	1988	Air Force	FC	TriStar	Vietnam	Peter Markle
Bataan	1943	Army	LC	MGM	WWII	Tay Garnett
Battle Cry	1955	Marines	FC	WB	WWII	Raoul Walsh
Battleground	1949	Army	FC	MGM	WWII	William Wellman
The Battle of San Pietro (doc)	1945	Army	NR	USAPS	WWII	John Huston
The Battle of the Bulge	1965	Army	NR	WB	WWII	Ken Annaki
Beachhead	1954	Marines	D	UA	WWII	Stuart Heisler
Beach Red	1967	Marines	CC	UA	WWII	Cornel Wilde
The Bedford Incident	1965	Navy	D	Col	CW	James Harris
Beginning of the End	1957	Army	LC	Rep	CW	Bert Gordon
The Beginning or the End	1947	Air Force	FC	MGM	WWII	Norman Taurog
Behind Enemy Lines	2001	Navy/Marines	FC	20th	Bosnia	John Moore
The Big Lift	1950	Air Force	FC	20th	CW	George Seaton
The Big Parade	1925	Army	FC	MGM	WWI	King Vidor
The Big Red One	1980	Army	NR	UA	WWII	Samuel Fuller
Birth of a Nation	1915	Army	LC	Epoch	Civil	D.W. Griffith
Black Hawk Down	2002	Army	FC	Rev	Somalia	Ridley Scott
Blue Thunder	1983	Army	D	Col	Vietnam	John Badham
Bombers B-52	1957	Air Force	F	WB	CW	Gordon Douglas
Born on the Fourth of July	1989	Marines	NR	Univ	Vietnam	Oliver Stone
The Boys in Company C	1978	Marines	NR	Col	Vietnam	Sidney Furie
Breaker Morant	1979	N/A	NR	NWQ	Boer (Viet)	Bruce Beresford
The Bridge at Remagen	1969	Army	NR	UA	WWII	John Gullermin
Bridges at Toko-Ri	1954	Navy	FC	Para	Korea	Mark Robson
A Bridge Too Far	1977	Army	FC	Levine	WWII	Richard Attenborough
A Bright Shining Lie (cable)	1998	Army	NR	HBO	Vietnam	Terry George
The Caine Mutiny	1954	Navy	FC	Col	WWII	Edward Dmytryk
Cassandra Crossing	1977	Army	NR	Avco	CW	George Casmatos
Casualties of War	1989	Army	NR	Col	Vietnam	Brian De Palma
Catch-22	1970	Air Force	NR	Para	WWII	Mike Nichols

674

Appendix A

Title	Date	Service	Cooperation	Studio	War	Director
Cease Fire	1985	Army	NR	Cineworld	Vietnam	David Nutter
Cinderella Liberty	1973	Navy	D	20th	Peace	Mark Rydell
Clear and Present Danger	1994	Navy/Army	FC	Para	Peace	Philip Noyce
Close Encounters of the Third Kind	1977	Air Force	D	Col	Peace	Steven Spielberg
Coming Home	1978	Marines	D	UA	Vietnam	Hal Ashby
Command Decision	1948	Air Force	FC	MGM	WWII	Sam Wood
Courage under Fire	1996	Army	D	20th	Gulf	Edward Zwick
Crash Dive	1943	Navy	FC	20th	WWII	Archie Mayo
Crimson Tide	1995	Navy	D	Disney	Peace	Tony Scott
Dave	1993	Navy	CC	WB	Peace	Ivan Reitman
Day One (tv)	1989	Army	D	SpelEnt	WWII	Joseph Sargent
The Day the Earth Stood Still	1951	Army	LC	20th	SciFi	Robert Wise
D-Day, the Sixth of June	1956	Army	LC	20th	WWII	Henry Koster
Deep Impact	1998	Army	FC	WB	SciFi	Mimi Leder
The Deer Hunter	1978	Army	D	UA	Vietnam	Michael Cimino
Destination Tokyo	1943	Navy	FC	WB	WWII	Delmer Daves
Devil Dogs of the Air	1935	Marines/Navy	FC	WB	Peace	Lloyd Bacon
The Devil's Brigade	1968	Army	FC	UA	WWII	Andrew McLaglen
The Devil's Playground	1937	Navy	FC	Col	Peace	Eric Kenton
The D.I.	1957	Marines	FC	WB	Peace	Jack Webb
The Dirty Dozen	1967	Army	NR	MGM	WWII	Robert Aldrich
Disaster at Silo 7	1980	Air Force	FC	Car	CW	Larry Elikann
Dive Bomber	1941	Navy	FC	WB	Peace	Michael Curtiz
Don't Cry, It's Only Thunder	1982	Army	FC	Sanrio	Vietnam	Peter Werner
Dress Parade	1927	Army	FC	Pathe	Peace	Donald Crisp
Dr. Strangelove	1964	Air Force	NR	Col	CW	Stanley Kubrick
The Enemy Below	1957	Navy	FC	20th	WWII	Dick Powell
Executive Decision	1996	Army	FC	WB	Terror	Stuart Baird
Fail Safe	1964	Air Force	D	Col	CW	Sidney Lumet
Fat Man and Little Boy	1989	Army	D	Para	WWII	Roland Joffe
A Few Good Men	1992	Marines/Navy	LC	Castle	Peace	Rob Reiner
Fifth Missile (tv)	1986	Navy	D	NBC	CW	Larry Peerce
Fighter Squadron	1948	Air Force	FC	WB	WWII	Raoul Walsh
The Fighting Seabees	1944	Navy	FC	Rep	WWII	Edward Ludwig
The Final Countdown	1980	Navy	FC	UA	ScFi	Don Taylor
Fire Birds	1990	Army/Air Force	FC	Touch	Peace	David Green
Firefox	1982	Air Force	FC	WB	CW	Clint Eastwood
Flight	1929	Marines	FC	Col	Peace	Frank Capra
Flight of the Intruder	1991	Navy	FC	Para	Vietnam	John Millius
Flirtation Walk	1934	Army	FC	WB	Peace	Frank Borzage
Flying Leathernecks	1951	Marines	FC	RKO	WWII	Nicholas Ray
Forrest Gump	1994	Army	CC	Univ	Vietnam	Robert Zemeckis
The Fourth War	1990	Army	NR	Kodiak	CW	John Frankenheimer
The Frogmen	1951	Navy	FC	20th	WWII	Lloyd Bacon
From Here to Eternity	1953	Army	FC	Col	Peace	Fred Zinnemann
Full Metal Jacket	1987	Marines	NR	WB	Vietnam	Stanley Kubrick
The Gallant Hours	1960	Navy	LC	UA	WWII	Robert Montgomery
Gardens of Stone	1987	Army	FC	TriStar	Vietnam	Francis Coppola
A Gathering of Eagles	1963	Air Force	FC	Univ	CW	Delbert Mann
The General's Daughter	1999	Army	NR	Para	Peace	Simon West
G.I. Jane	1997	Navy	D	Disney	Terror	Ridley Scott
Good Guys Wear Black	1978	Army	FC	Cannon	Vietnam	Ted Post
Good Morning, Vietnam	1987	Army	NR	BV	Vietnam	Barry Levinson
Go Tell the Spartans	1978	Army	D	Avco	Vietnam	Ted Post

Title	Date	Service	Cooperation	Studio	War	Director
Gray Lady Down	1978	Navy	FC	Univ	Peace	David Greene
The Great Santini	1979	Marines	FC	BCP	Peace	John Carlino
The Green Berets	1968	Army	FC	WB	Vietnam	John Wayne & Ray Kellogg
The Green Dragon	2001	Marines	FC	Franchise	Vietnam	Timothy Linh Bui
Guadalcanal Diary	1943	Marines/Navy	FC	20th	WWII	Lewis Seiler
Hair	1979	Army	FC	UA	Vietnam	Milos Forman
Halls of Montezuma	1950	Marines	FC	20th	WWII	Lewis Milestone
Hamburger Hill	1987	Army	FC	Para	Vietnam	John Irvin
The Hanoi Hilton	1987	Air Force/Navy	FC	Cannon	Vietnam	Lionel Chetwynd
Heartbreak Ridge	1986	Marines	FC	WB	Grenada	Clint Eastwood
Heaven and Earth	1993	Marines	NR	WB	Vietnam	Oliver Stone
Hell Below	1933	Navy	FC	MGM	Peace	John Conway
Heroes	1977	Army	LC	Univ	Vietnam	Paul Kagan
Hiroshima (cable)	1995	Army/Air Force	NR	Showtime	WWII	Roger Spottiswoode
Hold Back the Night	1956	Marines	FC	AA	Korea	Allan Dwan
The Hunt for Red October	1990	Navy	FC	Para	CW	John McTiernan
I Aim at the Stars	1960	Army	FC	Col	WWII/CW	J. Lee Thompson
Ice Station Zebra	1968	Navy	FC	MGM	CW	John Sturges
Inchon	1981	Marines/Navy	FC	One Way	Korea	Terence Young
Independence Day	1996	Army/Air Force/Marines	D	20th	SciFi	Roland Emmerich
In Harm's Way	1965	Navy/Marines	FC	Para	WWII	Otto Preminger
In Pursuit of Honor (cable)	1995	Army	NR	HBO	Peace	Ken Olin
In the Army Now	1994	Army	FC	Disney	Peace	Daniel Petrie Jr.
Invaders from Mars	1986	Marines	FC	Cannon	SciFi	Tobe Hooper
Invasion, USA	1985	Army	FC	Cannon	CW	Joseph Zito
The Killing Fields	1984	Marines	FC	Enigma	Vietnam	Roland Joffe
King Kong	1933	Navy	D	RKO	SciFi	Mehan Cooper
The Last Days of Patton (tv)	1986	Army	LC	CBS	WWII	Delbert Mann
The Last Detail	1973	Navy	D	Col	Peace	Hal Ashby
Limbo	1972	Navy/Air Force	D	Univ	Vietnam	Mark Robson
Lone Star	1996	Army	D	Sony	Peace	John Sayles
The Longest Day	1962	Army/Navy/Marines	FC	20th	WWII	Andrew Marton & Ken Annakin
MacArthur	1977	Army/ Mar	FC	Univ	WWII	Joseph Sargent
The Madame Butterfly	1915	Navy	D	FPL	Peace	Sydney Olcott
Marine Raiders	1944	Marines	FC	RKO	WWII	Harold Schuster
*M*A*S*H*	1970	Army	NR	20th	Korea	Robert Altman
Memphis Belle (doc)	1944	Air Force	NR	USAAC	WWII	William Wyler
Memphis Belle	1990	Air Force	D	WB	WWII	Michael C. Jones
The Men	1950	Army	FC	UA	WWII	Fred Zinnemann
*Men of Honor**	2000	Navy	FC	20th	Peace	George Tillman Jr.
Men of the Fighting Lady	1954	Navy	FC	MGM	Korea	Andrew Marton
Men without Women	1930	Navy	FC	Fox	Peace	John Ford
Midshipman	1925	Navy	FC	MGM	Peace	Christy Cabanne
Midshipman Jack	1933	Navy	FC	MGM	Peace	Christy Cabanne
Midway	1976	Navy	FC	Univ	WWII	Jack Smight
Military Air Scout	1911	Air Force	FC	Vita	Peace	William Humphrey
More American Graffiti	1979	Marines	NR	Univ	Vietnam	B.W.L. Norton
Navy Seals	1990	Navy	CC	Orion	Terror	Lewis Teague
No Man Is an Island	1962	Navy	FC	Univ	WWII	John Monks Jr.
No Way Out	1987	Navy	NR	Univ	CW	Roger Donaldson
An Officer and a Gentleman	1982	Navy/Marines	D/FC	Para	Peace	Taylor Hackford
One Minute to Zero	1952	Army	FC	RKO	Korea	Tay Garnett
On the Beach	1959	Navy	CC	UA	CW	Stanley Kramer

Title	Date	Service	Cooperation	Studio	War	Director Operation
Dumbo Drop	1995	Army	NR	BV	Vietnam	Simon Wincer
The Outsider	1961	Marines	FC	Univ	WWII	Delbert Mann
The Patent Leather Kid	1927	Army	FC	FN	WWI	Alfred Santell
Patton	1970	Army	FC	20th	WWII	Franklin Schaffner
Pearl Harbor	2001	Navy	FC	Disney	WWII	Michael Bay
Pentagon Wars (cable)	1998	Army	NR	HBO	Peace	Richard Benjamin
The Philadelphia Experiment	1985	Navy	D	New World	WWII	Stewart Raffill
Platoon	1986	Army	D	Orion	Vietnam	Oliver Stone
The Presidio	1988	Army	FC	Para	Peace	Peter Hyams
Pride of the Marines	1945	Marines	FC	WB	WWII	Delmer Daves
Private Benjamin	1980	Army	D	WB	Peace	Howard Zieff
PT-109	1963	Navy	FC	WB	WWII	Leslie Martinson
The Purple Heart	1944	Air Force	NR	20th	WWII	Lewis Milestone
Purple Hearts	1984	Navy/Marines	FC	WB	Vietnam	Sidney Furie
Raise the Titanic	1980	Navy	FC	MA	CW	Jerry Jameson
Renaissance Man	1994	Army	FC	Disney	Peace	Penny Marshall
Retreat, Hell!	1952	Marines	FC	WB	Korea	Joseph Lewis
The Rock	1996	Marines/Air Force	NR	HP	Terror	Michael Bay
Rolling Thunder	1977	Air Force	D	AI	Vietnam	John Flynn
Rules of Engagement	1900	Marines/Navy	FC	Para	Vietnam	William Friedkin
Rumor of War (tv)	1981	Marines	FC	Fries	Vietnam	Richard Heffron
Running on Empty	1988	N/A	NR	WB	Vietnam	Sidney Lumet
Run Silent, Run Deep	1958	Navy	FC	UA	WWII	Robert Wise
Sahara	1943	Army	FC	Col	WWII	Zolton Korda
Same Time Next Year	1978	N/A	NR	Univ	Vietnam	Robert Mulligan
Sands of Iwo Jima	1949	Marines	FC	Rep	WWII	Allan Dwan
Saving Private Ryan	1998	Army	NR	DW	WWII	Steven Spielberg
Sergeant Bilko	1996	Army	D	Univ	Peace	Jonathan Lynn
Sergeant York	1941	Army	LC	WB	WWI	Howard Hawks
Seven Days in May	1964	Marines/Navy	D	Para	CW	John Frankenheim
Shipmates	1931	Navy	FC	MGM	Peace	Harry Pollard
Shipmates Forever	1935	Navy	FC	FN	Peace	Frank Borzage
The Siege	1998	Army	NR	20th	Terror	Edward Zwich
Southern Comfort	1981	Army	FC	EMI	Vietnam	Walter Hill
Star Spangled Banner	1917	Marines	FC	Edison	Peace	Edward Griffith
Star Trek IV: The Voyage Home	1986	Navy	FC	Para	SciFi	Leonard Nemoy
The Story of G.I. Joe	1945	Army	FC	UA	WWII	William Wellman
Strategic Air Command	1955	Air Force	FC	Para	CW	Anthony Mann
Stripes	1981	Army	FC	Col	Peace	Ivan Reitman
Submarine	1928	Navy	FC	Col	Peace	Frank Capra
Submarine D-1	1937	Navy	FC	WB	Peace	Lloyd Bacon
A Submarine Pirate	1915	Navy	FC	Triangle	Peace	Sidney Chaplin
The Sullivans	1944	Navy	FC	20th	WWII	Lloyd Bacon
Tank	1984	Army	FC	Univ	Peace	Marvin Chomsky
Taps	1981	Army	FC	20th	Peace	Harold Becker
Task Force	1949	Navy	FC	WB	WWII	Delmer Daves
Them	1954	Army	NR	WB	ScFi	Gordon Douglas
They Were Expendable	1945	Navy	FC	MGM	WWII	John Ford
The Thin Red Line	1964	Army	NR	AA	WWII	Andrew Marton
The Thin Red Line	1998	Army	D	Sony	WWII	Terrence Malick
Thirty Seconds over Tokyo	1944	Air Force/Navy	FC	MGM	WWII	Mervyn LeRoy
Three Kings	1999	Army	NR	WB	Gulf	David Russell
Top Gun	1986	Navy	FC	Para	Peace	Tony Scott
Tora! Tora! Tora!	1970	Navy/Air Force	FC	20th	WWII	Richard Fleischer
To the Shores of Tripoli	1942	Marines	FC	20th	WWII	Bruce Humberstone

Title	Date	Service	Cooperation	Studio	War	Director
Towering Inferno	1974	Navy	LC	20th/WB	Peace	John Guillermin
Town without Pity	1961	Army	NR	UA	Peace	Gottfried Reinhardt
True Lies	1994	Marines	FC	20th	Peace	James Cameron
Twelve O'Clock High	1949	Air Force	FC	20th	WWII	Henry King
Twilight's Last Gleaming	1977	Air Force	NR	AA	Vietnam	Robert Aldrich
U-571	2000	Navy	CC	Univ	WWII	Jonathan Mostow
The Unbeliever	1918	Marines	FC	Edison	WWI	Alan Crosland
Under Siege	1992	Navy	CC	WB	Terror	Andrew Davis
Via Wireless	1915	Navy	FC	Pathe	WWI	George Fitzmaurice
The Victors	1963	Army	NR	Col	WWII	Carl Foreman
Wake Island	1942	Marines	FC	Para	WII	John Farrow
A Walk in the Sun	1945	Army	FC	20th	WWII	Lewis Milestone
Wargames	1983	Air Force	D	MGM	CW	John Badham
War Hunt	1962	Army	D	UA	Korea	Denis Sanders
We Were Soldiers	2002	Army	FC	Para	Vietnam	Randall Wallace
What Price Glory?	1926	Marines	LC	Fox	WWI	Raoul Walsh
Who'll Stop the Rain?	1978	Army	LC	UA	Vietnam	Karel Reisz
Windtalkers	2002	Marines	FC	MGM	WWII	John Woo
A Wing and a Prayer	1944	Navy	FC	20th	WII	Henry Hathaway
Wings	1927	Air Force	FC	Para	WWI	William Wellman
Young Lions	1958	Army	FC	20th	WWII	Edward Dmytryk

Types of Cooperation

D	Request Denied
FC	Full Cooperation: Men, equipment, locales, technical advice
LC	Limited: Locales, few personnel, technical advice
CC	Courtesy Cooperation: Technical advice, combat footage
NR	Not Requested or Not Required

Wars

CW – Cold War; Bosnia – Bosnia; Gulf – Gulf War; Korea – Korean War; Peace – Peacetime; SciFi – Science Fiction; Somalia – Somalia; Terror – Terrorism; Vietnam – Vietnam; WWI – World War I; WWII – World War II

Studios

AA – Allied Artists; AI – American International; Avco – Avco Embassy; BCP – Bing Crosby Productions; BV – Buena Vista Pictures; Car – Mark Carliner Productions; CBS – CBS Television; Cannon – Cannon Films; Col – Columbia Pictures; Disney – Disney Pictures; DW – DreamWorks SKG; Edison – Thomas A. Edison Inc.; EMI – EMI Films Ltd.; Enigma – Enigma (First Casualty) Ltd.; Epoch – Epoch Production Corporation; FN – First National; Fox – Fox Film Corporation; FPL – Famous Players Lasky; Franchise – Franchise Pictures Fries – Charles Fries Productions; HBO – Home Box Office; HP – Hollywood Pictures; Kodiak – Kodiak Films; Levine – Levine Productions; MA – Marble Arch Productions; MGM – Metro-Goldwyn-Mayer; NBC – NBC Television; New World – New World Productions; NWQ – New World-Quartet; Orion – Orion Pictures; Para – Paramount Pictures; Pathe – Pathe News; Rep – Republic Pictures; Rev – Revolution Pictures; RKO – RKO Radio Pictures, Inc.; Sanrio – Sanrio Communications; Showtime – Showtime; Sony – Sony Pictures; SpelEnt – Spelling Entertainment; Touch – Touchstone Pictures; Triangle – Triangle Film Corporation; TriStar – TriStar Pictures; 20th – Twentieth Century Fox; UA – United Artists; Univ – Universal Studios; USAAC – U.S. Army Air Corps; USAPS – U.S. Army Pictorial Services; Vita – Vitagraph Studios; WB – Warner Brothers

★ Appendix B
Interviews

Note: This list of interviews includes those cited in the endnotes and those interviews which provided background information in the writing of the narrative. Where I conducted additional interviews with a person beyond those listed, I have added an asterisk next to the dates. In particular, I conducted more than twenty formal interviews with Donald Baruch. The finding aids in the Suid Collection at Georgetown University list each interview by date. Where a person answered E-mail questions, I have used "E-mail" and the year rather than a date. Each person has a file which includes the E-mails.

Person	Area of Interest	Date(s)
Aldrich, Robert	Director	Mar. 14, 1974
Altieri, James	Army Public Affairs	Aug. 23, 1975
Andrews, Robert	Screenwriter	Aug. 19, 1975
Annakin, Ken	Director	Feb. 18, 2000
Arnold, Bruce	Son of Gen. Hap Arnold	Mar. 13, 1977
Arthur, Robert	Producer	Mar. 7 & 29, 1974
Austin, Adm. Bernard	Director, Navy Public Affairs	May 29, 1974
Austin, Stephanie	Producer	Mar. 1, 2001
Aylward, Rory	Civilian Technical Advisor	Mar. 29, 2000
Bartlett, Sy	Screenwriter, Producer	Feb. 9, 1974; July 9, 1975
Baruch, Donald	DoD Liaison to Motion Picture Industry	Mar. 22, 1973*
Bassett, Joseph	Author of *In Harm's Way*	July 16, 1975
Bauman, Chris	Navy Public Affairs, Los Angeles	Aug. 24–25, 1988*
Bay, Michael	Director	Feb. 28, 2001
Beach, Edward	Author of *Run Silent, Run Deep*	May 30, 1974
Beebe, Marshall	Navy Technical Advisor	Mar. 20, 1974
Begg, Charles	Air Force Technical Advisor	Aug. 28, 1975
Bell, Raymond	Film Industry Representative	Apr. 8, 1975
Bellamy, Ralph	Actor	July 18, 1978
Benjamin, Robert	Film Industry Executive	May 24, 1974
Bennett, Harve	Producer	July 17, 1978
Benson, Roy	Navy Technical Advisor	Jan. 8, 1978
Berman, Henry	Producer	June, 28, 1975
Berry, Robert	Navy Technical Advisor	Aug. 17, 1975
Bialka, Charles	Air Force Technical Advisor	June 17, 1975
Blankfort, Michael	Screenwriter	July 19, 1975
Blaustein, Julian	Producer	Mar. 28, 1974
Bodoh, Allan	Producer	Apr. 5, 1978
Booth, Blake	Navy Technical Advisor	Aug. 16, 1974
Bradlee, Benjamin	Editor, *The Washington Post*	Apr. 1, 1975
Brewer, Gen. Margaret	Marine Corps Public Affairs Director	Apr. 4, 8, 1981
Brill, Arthur	Marine Public Affairs	Apr. 4, 1978; Jan. 8–9, 1979
Brown, Alan	Navy Public Affairs, Washington	Mar. 27, 1974
Brown, Bill	TV Producer, *60 Minutes*	Jan. 9, 1976
Brown, David	Producer	Apr. 11, 1974
Bruckheimer, Jerry	Producer	Feb. 6, 1989; Feb. 26, 2001
Bumstead, Henry	Art Director	Apr. 3, 1974
Bunting, Josiah	Soldier, Author of *The Lionheads*	Dec. 23, 1974
Burch, Gerald	Army Public Affairs, Los Angeles	Aug. 7, 1981
Byrnes, William	Army Technical Advisor	June 25, 1975

Person	Area of Interest	Date(s)
Call, William	Army Technical Advisor	Jan. 13, 1976
Calley, John	Producer	Aug. 21, 1975
Canby, Vincent	Film Critic	Jan. 12, 1976
Capra, Frank	Director	Sept. 11, 1982
Carabatsos, James	Screenwriter	Dec. 14, 1989
Champlin, Charles	Film Critic	Mar. 14, 1990
Chappell, Adm. Lucian	Navy Technical Advisor	Aug. 7, 1975
Chayefsky, Paddy	Screenwriter	May 28, 1974
Chetwynd, Lionel	Screenwriter, Director	Feb. 3, 1989; Mar. 7, 1990
Clark, Kenneth	Motion Picture Association Executive	Dec. 17, 1973, Apr. 3, 1975
Cleland, Max	Soldier	May 9, 1978
Coffey, Alan	Army Public Affairs	Mar. 26, 1980; Sept. 19, 1980
Coghlan, Frank	Navy Public Affairs	Mar. 23, 1974
Collier, William	Army Technical Advisor	Jan. 18, 1977
Conmy, Joseph	Army Technical Advisor	Dec. 5, 1975
Cooney, Adm. David	Director, Navy Public Affairs	Mar. 21, 1978; Jan. 10, 1984*
Coulter, Pat	Marine Public Affairs	Apr. 4, 1978; Aug. 8, 1981*
Cronauer, Adrian	Armed Forces Radio & TV, Vietnam Network	Mar. 4, 1988
Crowe, James	Marine Technical Advisor	Dec. 11, 1977
Cutter, Slade	Navy Public Affairs	June 21, 1975
D'Amato, Paul	Actor	May 2, 1979
Daves, Delmer	Screenwriter, Director	Jan. 31,1974; Feb. 2, 1974
Davis, Chuck	Air Force Public Affairs, Los Angeles	Mar. 8, 1990; Mar. 27, 2000
Davis, Richard	Air Force Historical Advisor	Apr. 12, 2001
Deeley, Michael	Producer	Sept. 2, 1989
Donnenfeld, Bernard	Producer	Mar. 13, 1974
Doolittle, Gen. James	Commander, Raid on Japan	June, 30, 1975
Dorn, Gen. Frank	Director, Army Public Affairs	Jan. 7, 1976
Douglas, Gordon	Director	Apr. 2, 1974
Douglas, Melvyn	Actor	Oct. 27, 1975
Douglas, Peter	Producer	Aug. 3, 1981
Dove, Ralph	Air Force Technical Advisor	Aug. 25, 1975
Draude, Gen. Tom	Director, Marine Public Affairs	May 18, 1993
Dube, Noel	D-Day Veteran	Oct. 31, 2001
Dye, Dale	Civilian Technical Advisor	July 18, 1987
Edelman, Louis	Producer	Mar. 11, 1974
Eisenhower, John	Army Officer, Son of President	Jan. 8, 1976
Eller, Adm. E.M.	Navy Public Affairs	May 29, 1974
Ermey, Lee	Marine Technical Advisor, Actor	Jan. 4, 1989
Espenoza, Pablo	Civilian Technical Advisor	Mar. 27, 2000
Evans, Max	D-Day Veteran	Apr. 17, 2000
Ferguson, J.D.	Navy Technical Advisor	Apr. 5, 1975
Ferguson, Larry	Screenwriter	Mar. 6, 1990
Findley, Raymond	Marine Officer	Mar. 8, 1976
Fleischer, Richard	Director	June 26, 1975
Flynn, John	Director	Aug. 3, 1981
Foley, Denis	Army Public Affairs	Aug. 5, 1981
Foner, Naomi	Producer, Screenwriter	Feb. 8, 1989
Foreman, Carl	Screenwriter, Producer, Director	Aug. 3, 1978
Foy, Brian, Jr.	Producer	Aug. 5, 1975
Fribourg, Leonard	Marine Technical Advisor	Aug. 17, 1975
Fritchey, Clayton	Director, Office of Public Information, DoD	Dec. 18, 1974
Fuller, Samuel	Director, Screenwriter	July 12, 1975
Galloway, Joseph	Author of *We Were Solders Once . . . and Young*	Aug. 29, 2001
Garfinkle, Lou	Screenwriter	Jan. 18, 1989
Garnett, Tay	Director	July 13, 1975
Garrow, Adm. Jack	Director, Navy Public Affairs	Apr. 18, 1990
Gavin, Gen. James	Army Officer	Mar. 30, 1977

Appendix B

Person	Area of Interest	Date(s)
Gillespie, Buddy	Art Director	July 14, 1975
Gilmer, Dan	Army Technical Advisor	Aug. 9, 1975
Glines, C.V.	Historian, Biographer	E-mails, 2001–2002
Goldman, William	Screenwriter	Mar. 15, 1979
Goldstein, Donald	Historian	E-mail, 2001
Gottlieb Linda	Producer	June 15, 1973
Goulding, Phil	Assist. Sec. of Defense, Public Affairs	Apr. 4, 1975
Grainger, Edmund	Producer	July 30, 1975; Aug. 1, 1978
Graves, William	Navy Public Affairs, Los Angeles	July 19, 1978
Green, Jack	DoD Historical Advisor	Feb. 2, 2001; E-mail, 2001
Gruchey, Ron	Air Force Public Affairs, Los Angeles	July 25, 1975
Hackford, Taylor	Director	Aug. 7, 1981
Halberstam, David	Author of *The Best and the Brightest*	Mar. 29, 1975
Hamill, Peter	Writer	Nov. 23, 1977
Hanley, Joseph	National Guard Public Affairs	Aug. 25, 1989
Harding, William	Navy Public Affairs	Apr. 11, 1974
Harkins, Gen. Paul	Army Technical Advisor	Aug. 18, 1980
Harris, James	Director	Feb. 25, 1974
Hart, Herb	Marine Public Affairs	Mar. 24, 1981
Hatch, Norman T.	Chief, Audio/Visual Division, OASD (PA), DoD	Apr. 7, 1975*
Haines, William	Screenwriter	Mar. 15, 1974
Hechler, Kenneth	Military Historian, Author	May 30, 1975
Hellman, Jerome	Producer	Sept. 17, 1982
Hendricks, Bill	Studio Executive	Mar. 25, 1974
Hensler, Paul	Screenwriter	Aug. 8, 1981
Hetu, Herbert	Navy Public Affairs, Technical Advisor	Apr. 3, 1975
Hickey, Robert	Navy Public Affairs	Mar. 19, 1974
Hill, Gen. H. Gordon	Director, Army Public Affairs	May 19, 1977
Hiller, Arthur	Director	Mar. 14, 1974
Horton, John	Film Industry Representative	Dec. 18, 1973; Apr. 8, 1975*
Hough, Stan	Producer, Studio Executive	July 1, 1975
Hunter, James	Air Force Technical Advisor	July 15 & 31, 1975
Hunter, Tab	Actor	Feb. 16, 1978
Huston, John	Director	Mar. 27, 1974
Hyams, Peter	Director	Feb. 2, 1989
Irvine, Gen. William	Army Air Corps Technical Advisor	July 1, 1975
Jaffe, Leo	Film Executive	Dec. 21, 1973
James, D. Clayton	Historical Advisor	Jan. 12, 1980
Jaskilka, Gen. Samuel	Marine Technical Advisor	June 10, 1981
Jones, James	Author of *From Here to Eternity, A Thin Red Line*	Dec. 30, 1974
Jones, Phil	Journalist	Sept. 12, 1976
Just, Ward	Author	Aug. 12, 1974
Kael, Paulline	Movie Critic	Aug. 17, 1990
Kalisch, Bertram	DoD Public Affairs	Apr. 7–8, 1975
Kauffmann, Stanley	Movie Critic	Dec. 21, 1973
Kellogg, Ray	Director	July 3, 1975
King, Henry	Director	July 2, 1975
Kinnard, Gen. H.W.O.	Army Technical Advisor	June 15, 1974
Kneble, Fletcher	Author of *Seven Days in May*	Aug. 28, 1974
Koch, Howard W.	Producer	July 23, 1975; Jan. 5, 1989
Koch, Howard	Screenwriter	Aug. 11, 1974; Sept. 27, 1981
Koster, Henry	Director	July 17, 1975
Kramer, Stanley	Director, Producer	Feb. 8, 1974
Krulak, Gen. Victor	Marine Corps Public Affairs	May 26, 1983; Apr. 15, 2000
Ladd, Fred	Army Technical Advisor	Apr. 2, 1975
Laitin, Joseph	Assist. Sec. of Defense, Public Affairs	Sept. 6, 1979
Lange, Harry	Art Director	Mar. 24, 1987

Person	Area of Interest	Date(s)
Lasker, Larry	Screenwriter	Aug. 4, 1983
Lay, Beirne, Jr.	Screenwriter	Aug. 5, 1975
Lazarino, Tony	Producer	Dec. 26, 1974
Leacock, Philip	Director	June 28, 1975
LeMay, Gen. Curtis	Air Force General	Aug. 17, 1975
LeRoy, Mervyn	Director	July 22, 1975
Lesser, Sol	Producer	Apr. 8, 1974
Leuhman, Gen. Arno	Air Force General	July 1, 1975
Lewis, Joseph	Director	Apr. 4, 1974
Lifton, Robert	Author of *Home From the War*	June 8, 1976
Logan, Joshua	Producer, Director	May 25, 1974
Lomell, Bud	D-Day Veteran	Feb. 6, 2001
London, Barry	Studio Executive	Feb. 1, 1989
Lott, Al	Army Public Affairs, Los Angeles	Nov. 19, 1999
Lubin, Arthur	Director	Feb. 9, 1974
Mackenzie, C.J.	Navy Technical Advisor	Aug. 28, 1994
Malden, Karl	Actor	Aug. 9, 1975
Maltz, Albert	Screenwriter	July 25, 1975
Mancuso, Donald	Office of Inspector General, DoD	July 20, 1994
Mann, Delbert	Director	Mar. 13, 1975; Sept. 25, 1982
Manning, Bob	Navy Public Affairs	Mar. 10, 1978; Aug. 24, 1989
Markanton, John	Army Technical Advisor	Aug. 6, 1981
Marovitz, Mitchell	Army Public Affairs, Los Angeles	Aug. 4, 2000
Marshall, S.L.A.	Author of *Pork Chop Hill*	Jan. 26, 1974
Martinson, Leslie	Director	July 10, 1975
Marton, Andrew	Director	July 21 & 31, 1975
Matthews, Tom	Army Technical Advisor	February 19, 2002
Mayes, Wendell	Screenwriter	Mar. 6, 1974; Aug. 4, 1981*
McAuliffe, Gen. Anthony	Army General	May 31, 1974
McCarthy, Don	D-Day Veteran	Feb. 7, 2001
McCarthy, Frank	Producer	Mar. 4, 1974; July 31, 1975*
McGregor, Rob Roy	Navy Technical Advisor	Aug. 15, 1975
Milestone, Lewis	Director	Feb. 7, 1974
Milius, John	Screenwriter, Director	Mar. 14, 1990
Miller, Harold	Navy Public Affairs	Aug. 27, 1974
Mirisch, Marvin	Producer	Mar. 22, 1978
Mirisch, Walter	Producer	Jan. 6, 1989
Mitchell, S.G.	Navy Technical Advisor	April 5, 1975
Moore, Robin	Author of *The Green Berets*	Dec. 22, 1974; June 23, 1981
Morgan, Byron	Government Public Affairs	Apr. 4, 1975
Morgan, Matt	Marine Public Affairs	Mar. 1, 2000
Morgan, Robert	Air Force Pilot of the *Memphis Belle*	Apr. 25, 2000
Mostow, Jonathan	Director	Apr. 14, 2000
Murphy, George	Actor	July 14, 1977
Murphy, Richard	Screenwriter	Aug. 13 & 15, 1975
Nankin, Rick	Screenwriter	Dec. 14, 1988
Nebenzal, Harold	Marine Technical Advisor	Feb. 25, 2001
Neufeld, Mace	Producer	Mar. 14, 1990
Nichols, Mrs. K.D.	Wife of Manhattan Project District Engineer	Apr. 16, 1982
Nitze, Paul	Sec. of the Navy	Apr. 8, 1975
Nolan, Lloyd	Actor	July 1, 1975
Norstad, Gen. Lauris	Commander of NATO, Army General	June 11, 1975
North, Edmund	Screenwriter	Mar. 10, 1974; Aug. 14, 1987*
Nuckles, William	Air Force Technical Advisor	Oct. 6, 1975
O'Connor, Richard	Producer	Aug. 7, 1981
Ostlind, Ben	Air Force Technical Advisor	Aug. 21, 1975
Panama, Norman	Producer, Director, Screenwriter	July 20, 1975
Parks, Adm. Lewis	Director, Navy Public Affairs	Dec. 21, 1974

Appendix B

Person	Area of Interest	Date(s)
Parks, Walter	Screenwriter	Aug. 4, 1983
Peck, Fred	Marine Public Affairs	Aug. 16, 1988; Aug. 22, 1989
Persky, Lester	Producer	May 21, 1981
Pforzheimer, Walter	CIA Agent	Oct. 24, 1977
Pirosh, Robert	Screenwriter, Producer	Mar. 5, 1974
Poe, James	Screenwriter	Aug. 4, 1975
Post, Ted	Director	Aug. 5, 1981
Preminger, Otto	Director	Aug. 16, 1973
Ransohoff, Martin	Producer	Mar. 1, 1974
Redeker, Quinn	Screenwriter	Jan. 7, 1989
Reynolds, William	Film Editor	July 5, 1975
Robson, Mark	Director	July 2, 1975
Roeder, Harold	Navy Public Affairs	Dec. 15, 1977
Rosenberg, Frank	Producer, Screenwriter	July 12, 1978
Ross, Kathy	Army Public Affairs, Los Angeles	Feb. 22, 2000
Ross, Thomas	DoD Public Affairs	June 2, 1978
Rydell, Mark	Director	Sept. 3, 1975
Salinger, Pierre	White House Press Secretary	Oct. 16, 1979
Sanders, Russ	Director	July 30, 1975
Sanders, Terry	Screenwriter	Aug. 17, 1975
Sargent, Joseph	Director	Aug. 3, 1978
Saunders, Herm	Producer	Feb. 2, 1989
Schary, Dore	Producer, Studio Executive	Dec. 20, 1973; Mar. 3, 1975
Scheuer, Philip	*Los Angeles Times* Film Critic	Mar. 2, 1974
Schieffer, Bob	TV Correspondent	Aug. 6, 1977
Schiffer, Michael	Screenwriter	Mar. 6, 2000
Schilling, Joanne	Marine Corps Public Affairs	Sept. 22, 1980
Seaton, George	Writer, Director	Mar. 4, 1974
Shavelson, Melville	Screenwriter	Aug. 1, 1978
Shaw, Adm. James	Navy Technical Advisor	Aug. 17, 1974
Sherdeman, Ted	Screenwriter	Mar. 7, 1974
Sherman, Michael	Navy Public Affairs, Los Angeles	Mar. 7, 1990; Aug. 30, 1993
Shoup, Gen. David	Marine Corps Commandant	Apr. 2, 1975
Shrout, Gary	Navy Public Affairs	Feb. 18, 2001
Sidey, Hugh	Journalist	Nov. 29, 1976
Sidle, Gen. Wynant	Director, Army Public Affairs	Aug. 5, 1989
Siegel, Don	Director	July 8, 1975
Simmons, Gen. Edwin	Director, Marine History and Museums	Apr. 22, 1977; Nov. 11, 1977
Simpson, Don	Producer	Feb. 6, 1989
Sims, Robert	Assist. Sec. of Defense, Public Affairs	Feb. 11, 1990
Smith, Ray	Army Public Affairs	Mar. 24, 1978
Sperling, Milton	Producer	Mar. 25, 1974
Spikings, Barry	Producer	July 19, 1989
Stadler, Clement	Army Technical Advisor	July 7, 1975
Stafford, Ed	Navy Technical Advisor	Apr. 7, 1975
Stern, Stewart	Screenwriter	Mar. 14, 1974
Stevens, George, Jr.	Producer	Dec. 18, 1973
Stone, Oliver	Director	Aug. 3, 1981; Mar. 8, 1990
Strub, Phil	DoD Liaison to Film Industry	On-going Q&A
Stuart, William	Producer	Apr. 10, 2001
Swink, Robert	Film Editor	July 25, 1978
Sylvester, Arthur	Assist. Sec. of Defense, Public Affairs	Aug. 16, 1973; Dec. 23, 1974
Tallman, Frank	Motion Picture Aviation Consultant and Pilot	Aug. 21, 1975
Taradash, Daniel	Screenwriter	Mar. 27, 1974
Taurog, Norman	Director	July 15, 1975
Taylor, Ted	Navy Public Affairs	Mar. 15, 1974
Tibbets, Gen. Paul	Air Force General	July 7, 1976
Towne, Clair	Army Public Affairs	Aug. 15, 1975

Person	Area of Interest	Date(s)
Trammell, Charles	Army Technical Advisor	Jan. 5, 1976
Triffy, Sam	Army Air Corps Technical Advisor	Jan. 5, 1976
Trumbo, Dalton	Screenwriter	Apr. 10, 1974
Uris, Leon	Author, Screenwriter	June 18, 1975
Valenti, Jack	President, Motion Picture Association	Nov. 11, 1977; Oct. 1, 1979*
Vidor, King	Director	July 28, 1975
Warner, Jack, Jr.	Studio Executive	Apr. 4, 1974
Watkins, George	Navy Technical Advisor	Dec. 10, 1977
Wayne, John	Actor, Director	Feb. 7, 1974
Wayne, Michael	Producer	Aug. 5, 1975
Webb, James	Screenwriter	Feb. 15, 1974
Weller, Michael	Screenwriter	Mar. 7, 1984
Wellman, William	Director	June 23, 1975
Wendkos, Paul	Director	Aug. 4, 1975
Whitcomb, Darrel	Author of *The Rescue of Bat-21*	Jan. 26, 2001
Whitmore, James	Actor	Oct. 2, 1985
Whitmore, Stuart	Screenwriter	Mar. 20, 1974
Wilde, Cornell	Actor, Director, Producer	Aug. 15, 1975
Will, Adm. John	Navy Technical Advisor	May 22, 1974
Williams, Elmo	Producer	Mar. 18, 1974; July 11, 1975
Wilmore, Duncan	Air Force Public Affairs, Technical Advisor	July 20, 1983
Wilson, Gen. Samuel	Army Technical Advisor	Jan. 5, 1976
Winston, Gen. John	Marine Aviator	Sept. 20, 1977
Wise, Robert	Director	Apr. 10, 1974
Wolper, David	Producer	July 21, 1975
Wright, Malcolm	Navy Technical Advisor	Email, 2001
Young, R.W.	Screenwriter	Aug. 18, 1975
Young, Terrence	Director	Sept. 22, 1986
Youngstein, Max	Producer	Apr. 5, 1974; July 19, 1978
Zanuck, Richard	Producer	May 17, 2001
Zinnemann, Fred	Director	Mar. 5, 1974

Note on Sources

IN THE STRICTEST SENSE OF THE TERM, I do not have a bibliography for *Guts & Glory* since I wrote it mainly from primary documents and oral interviews. The citations to printed sources, newspapers, magazines, and books, mostly biographies or autobiographies, are found in the endnotes. I have used these secondary sources only to the extent they supply general information on some aspect of the subject or contain first-person quotes. I have used the film reviews only as documents to support my own observations about a movie, not for their artistic judgments. Although I have copied many of the *New York Times* and *Variety* reviews and included them in my files, the two papers have published entire sets of their reviews which are available in most large libraries.

I have placed all of the material which I have collected over the years in the Georgetown University Library, Special Collections Divisions, in the Lawrence H. Suid Collection. In the footnotes, I have cited the Collection as the repository for all the documents cited in the individual film files even if the original material came from other sources on the theory that researchers will find it easier to travel to one repository rather than to several different locales, even in the same metropolitan area. The documents from the National Archives, the presidential libraries, and most other repositories do have their original location, box numbers, file numbers, etc. cited.

The National Archives holds the files relating to cooperation between the film industry and the individual services from the 1920s, 1930s, and 1940s. For the early periods, the individual documents about any film project are usually mixed in with material relating to all aspects of a service's public affairs operations. Beginning with World War II, each major film received its own file. When I first met Donald Baruch in March 1973, he informed me that the records for the first four years of his office had disappeared. Quite by accident, I discovered them on a shelf deep in the downtown National Archives building. His records for the nine years between 1953 and 1961 also found their way to the National Archives and, thanks to the loan of a copy machine by the Marine Corps, I was able to duplicate all relevant material for this twelve-year period. All these files are now in the new College Park National Archives building.

After I moved to Washington in 1976, Mr. Baruch gave me access, under the Freedom of Information Act, to records beginning with *The Longest Day* in 1962 and I was able to copy much of the relevant material for my own files. Phil Strub continued this access after he replaced Mr. Baruch in 1989. In all cases, use of the material came with the proviso that I would submit to them copies of anything I wrote to ensure that I was not violating the confidentiality of corporate information or the creative work of the individual filmmakers. However, at no time did either man refuse me permission to use the information in the files, and more important, neither tried to impose his ideas on my work.

Over the years, individuals including Ed Stafford, the technical advisor to *Tora! Tora! Tora!*, and Clair Towne, Baruch's assistant in the early 1950s, would provide me with documents they had preserved. After duplicating the material, I would return the originals. The Motion Picture Association also proved a particularly valuable set of documents covering the period during which Arthur Sylvester was changing the regulations on military assistance to the film industry. The repositories in which I have done research over the years include:

The Academy of Motion Picture Arts and Sciences Library, Beverly Hills, Calif.
The Library of Congress Film Section, Washington, D.C.
The Dwight D. Eisenhower Library, Abilene, Kans.
The John F. Kennedy Library, Boston, Mass.
The Lyndon Johnson Library, Austin, Texas
The George C. Marshall Library, Lexington, Va.
The National Archives, Washington, D.C., and College Park, Md.
The Stanford University Special Collections Library, Palo Alto, Calif.
The Harry Truman Library, Independence, Mo.
The USC Cinema-Television Library, Los Angeles, Calif.
The UCLA Film Studies Library, Los Angeles, Calif.
The University of Wyoming Library, Division of Rare Books and Special Collections, Laramie, Wyo.

However, without the material in the Department of Defense records, I would not have been able to write the original edition of Guts & Glory, my Ph.D dissertation, Sailing on the Silver Screen, or this revised, expanded edition. I therefore remain eternally grateful to both Mr. Baruch and Mr. Strub.

I would also like to acknowledge the approximately four hundred people I interviewed whose information has enriched this book beyond what most of them could have imagined.

"It's a good thing you called today because I'll probably be dead tomorrow." How does a historian respond to such news? If you are conducting oral history interviews for a study of the relationship between the film industry and the armed services and the person co-directed *The Green Berets* and worked on *Tora! Tora! Tora!*, you pick up your tape recorder and run out the door. Being practical, I had Ray Kellogg sign my standard release form then rather than following my usual procedure of including it when I sent the completed transcript. In fact, Kellogg lived another three months, which he undoubtedly would have attributed to his use of laetrile.

A similar situation occurred when I tried to contact Dalton Trumbo, the screenwriter for *Thirty Seconds Over Tokyo*. My first two letters brought no response. I tried one more time the week before I was leaving Los Angeles. Mr. Trumbo called to explain he had not answered my letters because he was recovering from a heart attack and removal of a cancerous lung. I assured him that these were good reasons. He then said he would see me the next day. While the interview lasted less than an hour, it became one of my most valuable, both for the information about the film itself and for how Hollywood operated under the studio system.

However, times have changed since I first traveled to Los Angeles in January 1974 to begin research for my Ph.D. and ended up first writing *Guts & Glory*. Perhaps because I had approached filmmakers as a struggling graduate student or because most of the people from whom I requested interviews had retired and wanted to memorialize their experiences, I was able to obtain more than two hundred interviews on my first visit and a second one the following summer.

In 1981 and 1988, when I came to Los Angeles to do research for the later Vietnam and post-Vietnam military films, I was still able to conduct many significant interviews, including one with Don Simpson and Jerry Bruckheimer, the producers of *Top Gun,* which I was able to schedule with one phone call and do the next day. Likewise, in 1993, when doing research for *Sailing on the Silver Screen,* I was able to contact and interview many of the relevant filmmakers. By 2000, when I headed west to complete research on the recent movies for this book, I found it difficult to reach many of the active producers, directors, and screenwriters.

Although I had not been able to obtain an interview in 1993 with Rob Reiner, the director of *A Few Good Men,* I tried again. His secretary answered immediately: "Unfortunately, his schedule is extremely full, and he will be unable to participate." On the off-hand chance that he might respond after reading a draft discussion of the film, I sent the manuscript to him, indicating I could submit written questions if that was the only way to secure the information. The secretary responded with an even curter refusal. And so it went.

The assistant to Simon West, the director of *The General's Daughter,* demanded to know whom I had interviewed on my current visit, which was then only two weeks old. She did not care that I had previously interviewed Frank Capra, John Wayne, Oliver Stone, and Fred Zinnemann, among others. Perhaps I am not being fair since three of the four are dead and most people do not recognize Zinnemann as the director of *High Noon, From Here to Eternity,* and *A Man for All Seasons.*

In any case, virtually all of my letters remained unanswered. Phone calls produced much the same response. In part, this may have reflected the reality that I was now trying to interview working directors and screenwriters, rather than the retired people I had met on my earlier research trips. Moreover, most filmmakers today seem to have bigger egos and agents who act as gatekeepers, whether on orders or because of their own perceptions that their clients should only talk to the media to promote a current film or project. As a result, few of the films of the past eleven years included in this volume benefit from information obtained from interviews with the people from the industry side of the story.

Three exceptions must be noted. I was able to conduct a phone interview with writer/director Jonathan Mostow the evening his *U-571* opened. I then transcribed the interview from my notes and e-mailed it to him the next night after I started back east. He responded with a corrected version two nights later and subsequently answered several additional questions while I was writing an article about the film. I never heard back after he read it, which should be understandable to anyone who has read my discussion of the film in the article or in this book. Nevertheless, I remain most appreciative that he took time to answer my questions.

I was also able to conduct an interview with Michael Schiffer, the screenwriter of *Crimson Tide.* As with *U-571,* I had some very pointed questions, this time about the accuracy of the portrayal of nuclear launch procedures in the movie. Mr. Schiffer answered all of them, explaining the lengths to which he had gone to make the story plausible and accurate. He also provided me with the name of one of his technical advisors, Capt. Malcolm Wright, who regularly answered questions about procedures portrayed in the film. After I had completed the draft of the discussion of the film, I sent it to Mr. Schiffer in lieu of the transcript of our interview. He called and spent a half hour or so responding to my narrative. While I did not accept all his suggestions for changes, I would like to think that the final version of my *Crimson Tide* critique accurately reflects his views about the movie and justified the time he and Captain Wright spent providing me information.

On a follow-up trip to Los Angeles in February 2001 to research the forthcoming *Pearl Harbor,* I was able to obtain interviews with producer Jerry Bruckheimer and director Michael Bay, despite the significant demands on their time since the film was in the final stages of post-production. This time, however, my requests for interviews went through the Navy's Public Affairs Office in Los Angeles and Melissa Schuermann, who had served as technical advisor and the Navy's liaison to the production. Recognizing that I was only one of many people seeking audiences to both men, I kept the interviews short and to the point.

The interview with Mr. Bay came with a bonus. I did it in the editing studio, and before and after our conversation I was able to watch the sequence in which Rafe is shot down, which gave me a better appreciation of how the technology of film editing has changed from the days when an editor generally sat alone in front of a moviola. Now, several editors sit in front of computer screens adjusting the sound, cutting or adding frames, with the director overseeing the operation, except when he is interrupted to talk with a writer. I only regret that I did not have nicer things to say about *Pearl Harbor.*

Whereas the filmmakers generally remained aloof during these two research trips, active duty and retired military people have continued to provide much valuable information about their involvement in the making of military movies. In fact, technical advisors, like Tom Matthews, who participated in the mission in Somalia and later worked on *Black Hawk Down* after he retired from the Army, usually had advised on only one production and so had vivid recollections of the unique experience. Consequently, even Admiral Will and General Irvine, who had worked on films in the late 1920s, could describe their activities in great detail.

Unlike on previous forays to Los Angeles, on-duty military people and civilian personnel in the four service offices in Los Angeles regularly now offered help and documents. In part, this probably resulted from my continuing contacts with the Pentagon Public Affairs Office, which included two contracts to update the Department of Defense database of motion pictures portraying the American military, and the positive receptions *Guts & Glory* and *Sailing on the Silver Screen* had received from military people. Nevertheless, the help came with the knowledge that I retained my objectivity and was not beholden to either side of the symbiotic Hollywood-military relationship. I made it clear that I would tell my story based on the documents and interviews I obtained, not out of any friendship or kindness shown.

I did benefit from one new source. Before Vietnam and even into the 1980s, each service would assign an active duty technical advisor to all major and most minor productions. If the project dealt with a World War II or Korean War subject, the service would provide names of retired officers who had served in those earlier conflicts. Now, however, the services do not always have the resources to assign project officers to serve as technical advisors even on films about the contemporary military. As a result, filmmakers often hire civilians, not always retired military people, to provide technical information that they hope will give authenticity to their projects.

Dale Dye, a retired Marine captain, began this trend when he served as technical advisor on Oliver Stone's *Platoon,* with which the Army had refused to cooperate. Dye, a veteran of twenty years of active duty with the Marines, had enlisted at age nineteen, served three tours as a public affairs officer in Vietnam, and retired in 1984, after a tour in Lebanon. Dye worked for two years as editor of *Soldier of Fortune* magazine before going to Los Angeles. Once there, he sold his services to Stone by arguing that earlier Vietnam movies had lacked visual authenticity. To change that, Dye would institute a short boot camp for the actors playing military roles so that they would look like soldiers or Marines, a practice active duty officers had been conducting for actors for many years.

Dye religiously promoted himself as the guru of the proper military image and acted in many of the films on which he worked, and his Warriors, Inc. became the model for other former military men offering their services to the growing number of military projects that Hollywood began to develop in the late 1990s. Whether filmmakers listened to or accepted all or just some of the suggestions which the civilian advisors offered is another matter. Unlike the active duty officers, who had the power to withdraw assistance if the filmmaker deviated from the agreed-upon screen portrayals, the civilian technical advisors had no leverage and could, of course, be fired if they objected too long or too loudly. In any case, I was able to interview several of these technical advisors, all of whom provided useful information, and Dale himself answered questions and loaned me several photographs while I was writing this book.

I do not know whether Dale Dye's e-mail responses and those of Jack Green, the DoD historical advisor on *Pearl Harbor,* and C.V. Glines, who would promptly respond to my questions about the Doolittle raid and the inaccuracies in the portrayal of Doolittle in *Pearl Harbor,* can be considered formal interviews. Nevertheless, I have created files for each person who answered my questions and placed their e-mails in them since they constitute a significant source of information.

In any case, in Appendix A, I have listed all the interviews used in writing this book. I have quoted directly only from those transcripts for which I have received approval from the interviewees or from interviewees who have approved their comments as they appeared in the narrative. However, I have cited, without direct quotes, the interviews of many of those involved with a particular production since the information itself provided the framework in which to tell my story. All the interviewee files are in the Suid Collection in the Georgetown library. They include the correspondence I had with the person, biographical material, and any notes I may have taken during the interview. All approved transcripts are also in the individual files. Most of the audio tapes have also been put on deposit.

I am fully aware that some historians still question the validity of oral interviews. They challenge the interviewee's veracity, memory, and self-serving recollections. For example, an interview I did with Theodore Sorensen was questioned on the ground that he was serving as gatekeeper for Camelot. In truth, Mr. Sorensen had initially refused to give me an interview to talk about President Kennedy's decision to send astronauts to the moon, claiming he knew nothing about space policy, although I had read Sorensen's handwritten drafts of Kennedy's speeches at Rice University and to Congress. However, after reading the draft of an article on the President's space program, he did talk with me. Afterward, I realized that in contrast to wanting to burnish Kennedy's image, he had been reluctant to give the interview because it still hurt to talk about the past.

Then there is the problem of a person retracting his or her comments after giving an interview. During my interview with George Stevens Jr., he described the search for a director for *PT-109.* While watching in the White House with Pierre Salinger a very bad Marine movie by one of the candidates, the president came into the screening room, sat down, and watched for ten minutes. He then got up and showed his judgment of the film by saying to Stevens that he could tell Jack Warner to "fuck himself" and left. Stevens deleted the expletive from the transcript. When I called to ask why, he explained that he did not want to have the president using four-letter words in print. However, years later while writing *Sailing on the Silver Screen,* I asked Stevens if he would change his mind since times had changed and the word served a legitimate purpose. He agreed.

In any case, I have treated the oral interviews as a historian should treat any primary document: with caution. I have always tried to use the information from the interviews in combination with other interviews, with primary sources, and with secondary sources. In those few instances where the interview stood alone, I have used my considered judgment as to the accuracy of the information. In the course of more than one thousand interviews for my various projects, I believe I have had only one person deliberately lie to me.

I knew beforehand that he would probably lie and knew why he was going to lie. He did lie, and when I told him I could not corroborate his information, he continued to claim he was telling the truth. I did not use the interview. On the contrary, when I wrote my history of Armed Forces Radio and Television Service, I had to put in a footnote explaining why I had failed to mention the person since most people in the organization had accepted his claims for more than forty years that he had helped create the first military radio station in Alaska.

For the most part, however, the interviews have provided me with valuable insights and information not otherwise obtainable. To be sure, questions must be asked carefully to avoid putting words in people's mouths while still stirring up old memories. Even then, information must always be reexamined in the light of new material. Adm. John Will, for example, told me that he had ruined a shot during the filming of *Men Without Women* because he blurted out in surprise at the realism which John Ford created during the sinking of the submarine. When I first screened the film at the Library of Congress, I found it had no sound track. Was Admiral Will padding the story? One book on Ford said that only silent versions of the film remained extant. At least that suggested a sound version had once existed and that Will might well have remembered correctly. In fact, the Museum of Modern Art did have a sound version copy of the movie, and a person can understand from watching *Men Without Women,* with or without the sound, why a submariner would act as Will did.

In any event, after researching and writing about the relationship between the film industry and the armed services for twenty-nine years, I still feel the trite comment "So much to do, so little time to do it" has real validity in describing each of my research trips to Los Angeles, however long my stay. Whether I was searching the major repository of film files from several studios at the University of Southern California or the Motion Picture Academy library files, I found more material than I could possibly use, and the lack of in-person interviews on my 2000 trip, while regrettable, had little negative impact on my ability to tell the full story of the making and remaking of the military's image in Hollywood motion pictures.

 **Notes**

1. Hollywood and War

1. This and subsequent quotations of Scott as Patton are from the soundtrack to *Patton,* Twentieth Century Fox, 1970.

2. Walter Mirisch, interview by author, Jan. 6, 1989.

3. Roger Copeland, "When Films 'Quote' Films, They Create a New Mythology," *New York Times,* Sept. 25, 1977, sec. 2, p. 1.

4. Otto Preminger, interview by author, Aug. 16, 1973.

5. In the author's more than four hundred interviews within the motion picture community, no filmmaker ever said he had glorified war.

6. Joseph Heller, interview, *Playboy,* June 1975, p. 6.

7. Peter Hammill, Washington television station WJLA, interview by author, Nov. 23, 1977.

8. Leon Trotsky, *My Life* (New York: Grosset and Dunlop, Universal Library, 1960), p. 233.

9. David Halberstam, interview by author, Mar. 29, 1975.

10. Navy memorandum, Apr. 14, 1933, RG 80, box 80, National Archives (hereafter abbreviated NA).

11. James Jones, "Phoney War Films," *Saturday Evening Post,* Mar. 30, 1963, p. 67.

12. Tay Garnett, interview by author, July 13, 1975.

13. Maxwell Taylor to author, Mar. 8, 1975.

14. David Shoup, interview by author, Apr. 2, 1975.

15. Paul Tibbets, interview by author, July 7, 1976.

16. Michael Herr, *Dispatches* (New York: Alfred A. Knopf, 1977), pp. 135–36.

2. Beginnings

1. The author is indebted to Dr. Frederick Harrod for the information on the Navy's use of film before the entry of the United States into World War I. In particular, see his "Managing the Medium: The Navy and Motion Pictures before World War I," in *The Velvet Light Trap* (spring 1993).

2. *Scientific American Supplement,* Dec. 3, 1904, pp. 24, 180.

3. Ibid.

4. Navy Department, *Regulations for the Government of the Navy, 1913* (Washington, D.C.: Government Printing Office, 1913); Navy Department, "Taking of Photographs, Passengers on Board Ships, Etc.," General Order 78, Feb. 25, 1914, Cooperation Regulations file, Georgetown.

5. Secretary of the Navy Josephus Daniels to International News Service, Dec. 24, 1914, General Correspondence, RG 24, 5287-1259, NA.

6. *"Via Wireless,"* Weekly Variety, Sept. 24, 1915.

7. W.S. Benson, acting secretary of the Navy, to Gaumont Company, July 16, 1915, General Correspondence, RG 24, 52878-865, NA.

8. Daniels to Daniel Frohman, Oct. 12, 1915, General Correspondence, RG 24, 5287-952, NA; *New York Times,* Nov. 8, 1915, p. 13.

9. Daniels to W.D. McGuire Jr., executive secretary, National Board of Censorship, Nov. 17, 1914, General Correspondence, GS 24, 5287-644, NA.

10. McGuire to Daniels, Jan. 7, 1915; Daniels to McGuire, Jan. 11, 1915; McGuire to Daniels, Jan. 21, 1915.

11. *Motography,* Nov. 27, 1915, p. 1111; Charles Chaplin, *My Autobiography* (New York: Simon and Schuster, 1964), p. 160.

12. *Motography,* Nov. 27, 1915, p. 1111.

13. Ibid.; *New York Times,* Nov. 15, 1915.

14. Franklin Roosevelt to Hearst Pathe News, June 6, 1917.

15. Bruce Arnold, interview by author, Mar. 13, 1977.

16. Lillian Gish, *The Movies, Mr. Griffith and Me* (Englewood Cliffs, N.J.: Prentice-Hall, 1969), p. 47. Lillian Gish to author, June 12, 1975.

17. Robert M. Henderson, *D.W. Griffith: His Life and Work* (New York: Oxford University Press, 1972), pp. 246–47. *New York Times,* Sept. 30, 1923, sec. 2, p. 3. "Chicago Industrial Solidarity, November 24, 1923," File "America," Museum of Modern Art, New York (hereafter abbreviated MOMA).

18. The quotation is from a film title.

19. Q.M. Sgt. Percy Webb, "Marines Fight Germans in New Movie," *Recruiters' Bulletin,* Nov. 1917.

20. Alan Crosland to L.W. McChesney, Nov. 10, 1917, box 57, Kleine Collection, Library of Congress. All subsequent correspondence cited in this chapter comes from the Kleine Collection.

21. McChesney to Crosland, Nov. 12, 1917.

22. Crosland to McChesney, Nov. 14, 1917.

23. *New York Times,* Feb. 12, 1918.

24. Louis Harrison, "*The Unbeliever,*" *Moving Picture World,* Mar. 2, 1918.

25. Joseph Steurle to the George Kleine System, Apr. 25, 1918.

26. H.E. Ellison to L.E. Schaeffer, June 14, 1918.

27. Ellison to George Kleine, June 10, 1918.

28. Capt. H.C. Daniels to the Edison Company, Feb. 20, 1918. See my discussion of *Retreat, Hell!* in chapter 9 of this volume.

29. Marine Corps Recruiting Publicity Bureau to the Edison Company, May 6, 1918. The George Kleine System, the distributor of the film, bought the entire rights to *The Unbeliever* from the Edison Company in May 1918. Edison Company to the Marine Corps Recruiting Publicity Bureau, May 9, 1918.

30. George Kleine System to the mayor, Fort Thomas, Kentucky, Oct. 15, 1918.

31. D.E. Waterston to the George Kleine System, Oct. 24, 1918.

32. James A. Davis to Hinton Clabaugh, n.d. [Mar. 1918].

33. Ibid.

34. Ibid.; "revolute" and "dassent" spelled as in text.

35. Ibid.

36. George Kleine to Hinton Clabaugh, Mar. 16, 1918.

37. Ibid.

38. Ibid.

39. Col. A.S. McLemore to Kleine, Oct. 24, 1918.

40. Kleine to McLemore, Dec. 28, 1918.

41. Marine Corps Recruiting Bureau to George Kleine System, Jan. 4, 1922.

3. A Standard for the Future

1. "A Talk with King Vidor," n.d [Oct. 1925], source not identified in MOMA file on *The Big Parade,* cited hereafter as Vidor/MOMA; interview condensed in *New York Times,* Nov. 8, 1925, sec. 8, p. 5.

2. Charles Higham, "Long Live Vidor, A Hollywood King," *New York Times,* Sept. 3, 1972, sec. 2, p. 1, cited hereafter as Higham, *NYT;* King Vidor, interview by author, July 28, 1975, cited hereafter as Vidor interview; King Vidor, *A Tree Is a Tree* (New York: Harcourt, Brace, 1952), p. 111

3. Vidor/MOMA; Vidor interview; Vidor, *A Tree Is a Tree,* pp.111–12.

4. Alistair Cooke, "Notes on *The Big Parade,* MOMA, 1941; Vidor interview; Vidor, *A Tree Is a Tree,* pp.112–14.

5 Ibid.

6. Ibid.

7. Vidor, *A Tree Is a Tree,* pp. 120–21.

8. Vidor interview; *New York Times,* Oct. 4, 1925, sec. 9, p. 5

9. Ibid.; Vidor, *A Tree Is a Tree,* p. 117

10. Ibid.

11. Vidor interview; *New York Times,* Feb. 21, 1926, sec. 2, p. 6

12. Ibid.

13. Vidor interview; Higham, *NYT,* Sept. 3, 1972, sec. 2, p. 1

14. Vidor/MOMA

15. Ibid. Vidor interview.

16. Vidor interview.

17. Quoted in *Literary Digest,* Mar. 6, 1926, p. 38.

18. Ibid.

19. *New York Times,* Nov. 20, 1925, p. 18.

20. Vidor, *A Tree Is a Tree*, pp. 114–15; Vidor/MOMA.

21. *New York Times*, Feb. 21, 1926, sec. 2, p. 4.

22. *Outlook*, Jan. 6, 1926, pp. 18–19.

23. Ibid.

24. Vidor, *A Tree Is a Tree*, pp. 124–25.

25. *New York Times*, Nov. 21, 1926, B; Raoul Walsh, *Each Man in His Time* (Farrar, Straus, and Giroux: New York, 1974), p. 186.

26. Capt. C.L. Arnold to commandant, Third Naval District, Sept. 20, 1924, "What Price Glory?" correspondence, RG 80, box 155, Secretary of the Navy general correspondence, 1916–1926, file 5012 (270) to (343), NA. All cited material in regard to the play is located in this file.

27. Inspector Peterkin Report, Sept. 20, 1924.

28. Ibid.

29. Ibid.

30. Ibid.

31. Commandant, New York Navy Yard, to secretary of the Navy, Sept. 25, 1924.

32. Office of the judge advocate general to the secretary of the Navy, Oct. 28, 1924.

33. Walsh, *Each Man*, pp. 185–86.

34. Ibid., pp. 186–87.

35. Eileen Bowser, *What Price Glory?* "Films from the Archives," MOMA, Department of Film, 1975.

36. Ibid.; *New York Times*, Apr. 14, 1974, sec. 2, p. 13.

37. *New York Times*, Apr. 14, 1974, sec. 2, p. 13.

38. Ibid.

39. Walsh, *Each Man*, pp. 189–91; *New York Times*, Oct. 3, 1926, A; Nov. 21, 1926. Gen. Edwin H. Simmons to author, Sept. 5, 1999.

40. Richard Watts Jr., *New York Herald-Tribune*, Nov. 28, 1926, sec. 6, p. 3; P.A. Webb, "Sea Soldiers of the Screen," *Leatherneck*, May 1935, p. 14.

41. Byron Morgan to Walter Wanger, Dec. 16, 1926, in *Wings* file. In his letter, Morgan was requesting payment for his contribution to the development of *Wings*.

42. Ibid.

43. Ibid.

44. Ibid.

45. Ibid.

46. John Monk Saunders, "The Government Cooperated to Make Wings Thrilling and True," *New York Times*, July 31, 1927, sec 7, p. 3.

47. Ibid.

48. Ibid.; John Monk Saunders, "Filming of an Epic," *Wings Theater Program*, reprinted in *Los Angeles Herald-Examiner*, Apr. 9, 1972. This is a longer version of the *New York Times* story of July 31, 1927.

49. William Wellman, *A Short Time for Insanity* (New York: Hawthorn Books, 1974), p. 163.

50. MOMA Release, n.d. [after 1974], *Wings* file in MOMA Film Studies Center.

51. Wellman, *Short Time for Insanity*, p. 163; *New Yorker*, Sept. 25, 1971, p. 104.

52. William Wellman, interview by author, June 23, 1975.

53. Wellman, *Short Time for Insanity*, pp. 163–65. Wellman interview.

54. Gen. Bill Irvine, interview by author, July 1, 1975.

55. *New York Times*, July 10, 1927, sec. 7, p. 3.

56. Wellman, *Short Time for Insanity*, pp. 170–74. Kevin Brownlow, *The Parade's Gone By . . .* (New York: Alfred A. Knopf, 1969), p. 202.

57. Wellman, *Short Time for Insanity*, p. 170.

58. Ibid., p. 170–71.

59. Ibid., p. 171–73.

60. Ibid., p. 173.

61. Ibid., p. 174; *Motion Picture World*, quoted in "Films from the Archives," MOMA, 1975. *Exceptional Photoplays*, Sept. 1972. *New York Times*, Aug. 21, 1972, sec. 7, p. 3.

62. *New Yorker*, Sept. 25, 1971, p. 106.

63. Wellman, *Short Time for Insanity*, p. 177–78.

64. Irvine interview.

65. A.L. Rockett to Lt. Harrison Johnson, Aug. 12, 1926, 000.7 Publicity Division, File July 1927 to December 1928, RG 111, box 3, Office of the Chief Signal Officer Correspondence, 1917–1940, NA. All documents cited for *Patent Leather Kid* come from this file.

66. Ibid., Maj. Gen. Charles Saltzman to the adjutant general, Aug. 21, 1926.

67. Johnson to Rockett, Aug. 14, 1926; Rockett to Saltzman, Aug. 10, 1926; Saltzman to adjutant general, Aug. 21, 1926.

68. Saltzman to adjutant general, Aug. 21, 1926; Saltzman to Rockett, Aug. 21, 1926.

69. Acting adjutant general to Rockett, Aug. 31, 1926; Rockett to Johnson, Dec. 28, 1926; Saltzman to adjutant general, Jan. 4, 1927; Rockett to Jack Connelly, Feb. 16, 1927; Robert Alexander to commanding general, Ninth Corps Area, The Presidio, San Francisco, Calif., "After Action Report: Participation of Troops in Filming 'The Patent Leather Kid,'" May 9, 1927.

70. Rockett to Connolly, Feb. 16, 1927; Connelly to Saltzman, Feb. 19, 1927; Saltzman to the adjutant general, Feb. 19, 1927; adjutant general to Saltzman, Feb. 21, 1927.

71. Adjutant general to Saltzman, Feb. 21, 1927.

72. Mordaunt Hall, "*Patent Leather Kid*," Aug. 16, 1927.

4. The Golden Age of Military Movies

1. See Harrod, "Managing the Medium," cited in chapter 2, note 1; author interviews with naval officers.

2. *Weekly Variety*, Oct. 14, 1925.

3. "An Alumnus" to *Army Navy Journal*, May 13, 1925, RG 24, box 1011, NA.

4. Arthur Barney to the secretary of the Navy, June 18, 1925; Barney to the editor of *Army Navy Journal*, June 18, 1925, RG 24, box 1011, NA.

5. Superintendent to CNO, June 5, 1933, RG 80, box 431, NA.

6. Ibid.

7. *New York Times*, Nov. 20, 1933, p. 18.

8. Frank Capra, interview by author, Sept. 11, 1982. Frank Capra, *The Name above the Title* (New York: Bantam Books, 1971), pp. 110–13.

9. Adm. John Will, interview by author, May 22, 1974.

10. Ibid.

11. Harry Cohn to the secretary of the Navy, July 28, 1936; Capt. H.A. Badt to the Navy Motion Picture Board, Aug. 4, 1936, RG 80, box 425, NA.

12. Badt to the Navy Motion Picture Board, Aug. 4, 1936, RG 80, box 425, NA.

13. Navy Motion Picture Board to the CNO, Aug. 12, 1936; CNO to Cohn, Aug. 12, 1936, RG 80, box 425, NA.

14. Badt to Adm. Sinclair Gannon, Aug. 28, 1936, RG 80, box 425, NA.

15. Ibid.

16. Ibid.

17. Ibid.

18. Capt. H.A. Jones to Gannon, Sept. 2, 1936, RG 80, box 425, NA.

19. Ibid.

20. Ibid.

21. Ibid.

22. Ibid.

23. Gannon to Badt, Sept. 4, 1936, RG 80, box 425, NA.

24. OPNAV to COMELEVEN, Sept. 8, 1936; OPNAV to CINCUS, Sept. 21, 1936; Lt. C. Young to Lt. Alfred Bolton, Sept. 25, 1936, Record Group 80, NA.

25. Ibid.

26. Ibid.

27. Ibid.

28. Adm. William Leahy, CNO, to Cohn, Feb. 27, 1937, RG 80, box 425, NA.

29. Leahy to Cohn, Mar. 18, 1937, RG 80, box 425, NA.

30. *New York Times*, Feb. 15, 1937; *Weekly Variety*, Feb. 17, 1937.

31. *Weekly Variety*, Feb. 17, 1937.

32. Jack Warner Jr., interview by author, Apr. 4, 1974; Delmer Daves, interview by author, Jan. 31, 1974.

33. Spig Wead to Navy Department, July 28, 1936, RG 80, box 426, NA.

34. Ibid.

35. Ibid.

36. Office of Naval Intelligence to Navy Motion Picture Board, Nov. 13, 1936; CNO to commanding officer, Naval Submarine Base, Dec. 11, 1936; CNO to chief of Bureau of Construction and Repair and chief of Bureau of Engineering, May 14, 1937, all in RG 80, box 425, NA.

37. "*Submarine D-1:* Hand Book of Useful Information," Warner Brothers, n.d. [1937].

38. Ibid.

39. Leahy to Warner Brothers, June 7, 1937, RG 80, box 425, NA.

40. CNO to Hal Wallis, Nov. 4, 1937, RG 80, box 425, NA.

41. Frank Janata to Sen. Hamilton Lewis, Dec. 29, 1937, RG 80, box 425, NA.

42. Navy Department to Lewis, Jan. 19, 1938, RG 80, box 425, NA.

43. RKO Studios to the Navy Department, Dec. 13, 1932, RG 80, box 431, NA.

44. Ibid.

45. CNO to Herb Hirst, Dec. 21, 1932, RG 80, box 431, NA.

46. Gen. John Winston, interview by author, Sept. 20, 1977.

47. Ibid.

48. Ibid.; Orville Goldner and George Turner, *The Making of King Kong* (New York: Ballantine Books, 1976), pp. 167–69.

49. Professional Pilots Association to CNO, Sept. 27, 1930; CNO to commanding officer, Eleventh Naval District, Oct. 2, 1930, box 432, RG 80, NA.

50. Capra, *Name above Title,* pp. 123–24.

51. In *Flying Leathernecks,* John Wayne's fighter squadron is ferried to Guadalcanal aboard an aircraft carrier, and the film includes a scene of planes taking off, engaging in a brief strafing mission, and landing on the island. However, the Marine planes then fly from the airfield with no mention of carrier-based operations.

52. Sen. Elbert Thomas to Secretary of the Navy Claude Swanson, Jan. 18, 1935; Swanson to Thomas, Jan. 28, 1935, RG 80, box 429, NA.

53. Swanson to Thomas, Jan. 28, 1935, RG 80, box 429, NA.

54. *Washington Herald,* Jan. 22, 1935.

55. Ibid.

56. *New York Times,* Feb. 7, 1935.

57. Unsigned memorandum, "Pictorial Publicity in the Army," Jan. 19, 1928, box 3, A46-484 062.2, OCSIGO, NA.

58. Author's conversations with Gen. K.D. Nichols during his work on the Manhattan Project district engineer's autobiography in the early 1980s.

59. William Orr to Secretary of War Dwight Davis, Jan. 20, 1927. Unless otherwise indicated, all correspondence cited subsequently in this chapter is in RG 11, Office of the Chief Signal Officer Correspondence, 1917–1940, box 3, file 000.7, Publicity, Photographic Division, Jan. to Oct. 1929.

60. Dwight Davis to William Orr, n.d. [Jan. 22, 1927].

61. M.B. Stewart to adjutant general, Jan. 28, Feb. 8, 14, 1927.

62. Maj. Walter Prosser to Adjutant General Livingston Watrous, Feb. 25, 1927; adjutant general to superintendent, U.S. Military Academy, Feb. 26, 1927.

63. Adjutant general to superintendent, U.S. Military Academy, Feb. 26, 1927.

64. Stewart to Maj. A.W. Chilton, Mar. 3, 1927; Chilton to Stewart, Mar. 5, 1927.

65. Stewart to adjutant general, Mar. 16, 1927.

66. Walter Prosser to adjutant general, Mar. 30, 1927.

67. Prosser to adjutant general, Mar. 26, 1927; adjutant general to superintendent, U.S. Military Academy, Mar. 26, 1927; Chilton to Prosser, June 3, 1927; Chilton to Stewart, June 4, 1927.

68. Stewart to adjutant general, June 6, 1927; Lt. Col. John Hemphill, Signal Corps executive officer, to adjutant general, June 15, 1927.

69. Hemphill to adjutant general, June 15, 1927.

70. Adjutant general to superintendent, U.S. Military Academy, June 17, 1927; Prosser to Hemphill, June 18, 1927.

71. C.M. Saltzman to adjutant general, June 23, 1927.

72. Ibid.

73. Adjutant general to superintendent, U.S. Military Academy, June 27, 1927; adjutant general to Grey Productions, June 27, 1927.

74. Acting adjutant general to Orr, June 28, 1927; acting adjutant general to superintendent, U.S. Military Academy, June 28, 1927.

75. Schuyler Grey to adjutant general, July 7, 1927; adjutant general to Grey, July 11, 1927; Grey to Office of the Chief Signal Officer, Aug. 13, 1927.

76. Grey to Prosser, Sept. 12, 1927.

77. *New York Times,* Oct. 31, 1927.

78. Ibid.; *Variety,* Nov. 2, 1927.

79. *New York Times*, Jan. 2, 1928, p. 28.

80. Daves interview, Jan. 31, 1974.

81. Louis Edelman, interview by author, Mar. 11, 1974.

82. Edelman interview.

83. E.C. Roworth to Secretary of the Navy Frank Knox, Aug. 21, 1941, RG 80, box 94, NA.

84. Arthur Keil to Knox, Dec. 1, 1941; Ens. Alan Brown to Roworth, Aug. 26, 1941, RG 80, box 94, NA.

85. Appendix to *Congressional Record,* 77th Cong., 1st sess., Aug. 4, 1941, p. A3736.

86. Hearings Before Subcommittees of the Committee on Interstate Commerce, United States Senate, 77th Congress, 1st Session, pp. 339–40.

87. Ibid.

88. Ibid.

5. World War II: Fantasy

1. *New York Times,* Sept. 2, 1942, p. 19.

2. Samuel Triffy, interview by author, Jan. 5, 1976.

3. *Air Force* was the first war movie the author ever saw, and the next day, he recounted the entire story scene by scene in his kindergarten class.

4. Triffy interview.

5. War Department memoranda, May 18, 19, 1942, RG 165, box 6, NA.

6. War Department to Jack Warner, May 22, 1942. War Department memo, June 6, 1942, RG 165, box 6, NA.

7. Triffy interview.

8. Ibid.; the plane that played the *Mary Ann* was later lost in combat in the South Pacific.

9. Ibid. Gen. Hewitt Wheless to author, June 23, 1977.

10. *New York Times,* Feb. 4, 1943, p. 17.

11. Dore Schary, interview by author, Dec. 20, 1973.

12. Ibid.

13. Ibid. War Department memo, Oct. 23, 1942, RG 165, box 7, NA.

14. War Department to Metro-Goldwyn-Mayer, Oct. 26, 1942, RG 165, box 7, NA.

15. Tay Garnett, *Light Your Torches* (New Rochelle, N.Y.: Arlington House, 1973), pp. 248, 256–57.

16. Ibid. Garnett interview, July 13, 1975.

17. *New York Times,* June 4, 1943, p. 17. *Time,* June 7, 1943, p. 94.

18. Garnett, *Light Your Torches,* p. 248. Garnett interview.

19. *New York Times,* Nov. 12, 1943, p. 25.

20. Ibid.

21. Gen. William Collier, interview by author, Jan. 18, 1977.

22. *New York Times,* Apr. 29, 1943.

23. Frank Wead to Comdr. H.R. Thurber, June 9, 1941, RG 80, box 95, NA.

24. Ens. Alan Brown to Louis Edelman, Feb. 6, 1942, RG 80, box 95, NA.

25. OWI, Los Angeles Overseas Bureau, Motion Picture Division, Progress Report, Oct. 28–Nov. 10, 1943, RG 208, box 3510, NA; teletype, Nov. 5, 1943, box 3509, RG 208, NA.

26. Atrocity Policy File, box 3509, RG 208, NA; John Flynn to Roy Disney, Nov. 9, 1943, in Suid Holocaust papers, Special Collections, Georgetown University, Washington, D.C.

27. Alexander Sachs, "Soviet Foreign Policy, Totalitarian Processes and Russo-Allied Rifts," Apr. 1943, box 116, Sachs papers, FDR Library, Hyde Park, N.Y.

28. Motion picture files, FDR Library.

6. World War II: Pseudo-Reality

1. *Destination Tokyo* script of May 13, 1943, Delmar Daves papers, Stanford University, Palo Alto, Calif.

2. Ibid.

3. Joseph Breen to Jack Warner, June 22, 1943, *Destination Tokyo* file in Warner Brothers Collection, University of Southern California Film Library, Los Angeles.

4. J.W. Coe, "Suggested Constructive Criticims of Temporary Script—*Destination Tokyo* (From a Submariner's standpoint)."

5. Stan Cohen, *Destination Tokyo* (Missoula, Mont.: Pictorial Histories Publishing Company, 1983), p. 3; James Doolittle with C.V. Glines, *I Could Never Be So Lucky Again* (New York: Bantam Books, 1991), pp. 230–75, contains Doolittle's account of the planning and execution of the raid.

6. Slade Cutter, interview by author, June 21, 1975, and follow-up discussion, Jan. 8, 2000. Captain Cutter was a great Navy hero who kicked a winning field goal against Army and tied for the second-largest number of Japanese ships sunk during World War II. He did enter Tokyo Bay, but he said it had no submarine nets guarding the entrance as portrayed in *Destination Tokyo*.

7. Daves memo, May 20, 1943, Delmer Daves papers. Daves interview, Jan. 31, 1974.

8. *New York Times*, Jan. 1, 1944, p. 9.

9. OWI memo, n.d. [after Feb. 23, 1944], RG 208, box 3524, NA.

10. Preface to script of *Thirty Seconds Over Tokyo*, June 18, 1943, RG 165, box 41, NA. War Department to Metro-Goldwyn-Mayer, Aug. 25, 1943, RG 165, box 41, NA.

11. Ibid.

12. Dalton Trumbo, interview by author, Apr. 10, 1974.

13. Ibid. Mervyn LeRoy, interview by author, July 22, 1975.

14. Ibid.

15. Writers, including Doolittle himself, have given several different figures for the distance Doolittle's raiders had to fly after Japanese picket boats discovered the task force. Col. C.V. Glines, the historian of the attack, noted: "The distance of the carrier from Japan really doesn't matter. The carrier was moving toward Japan at about 25 knots (25 nautical miles per hour). It took an hour for all to get off. No one really calculated the exact distance as far as I know. That's why Doolittle probably rounded off the approximate distance at 650 miles. And none of them state whether they mean statute or nautical miles or what part of Japan they were measuring from. So, it's no big deal. Your 624 miles is as good as anyone else's."

16. War Department to Metro-Goldwyn-Mayer, Aug. 25, 1943, RG 165, box 41, NA.

17. Ibid.

18. Ibid. LeRoy interview. MGM production notes, *Thirty Seconds Over Tokyo* file, Academy of Motion Pictures Arts and Sciences Library, Los Angeles, Calif.

19. LeRoy interview. Buddy Gillespie, interview by author, July 14, 1975.

20. *New York Times*, Nov. 16, 1944, p. 19.

21. Trumbo interview.

22. Ibid.

23. LeRoy interview.

24. *New York Times*, Nov. 16, 1944, p. 19.

25. *Wing and a Prayer* file, University of Southern California Film Studies Center.

26. Screenplay "Torpedo Squadron 8," Jan. 8, 1943, *Wing and a Prayer* file; *New York Times*, Feb. 6, 1944. Samuel Eliot Morison, *The Two-Ocean War* (Boston: Little, Brown, 1963), p. 156.

27. Jerry Cady, "Wing and a Prayer," Oct. 26, 1943, *Wing and a Prayer* file. *New York Times*, Feb. 6, 1944.

28. Minutes of Nov. 19, 1943, meeting, *Wing and a Prayer* file.

29. Ibid.

30. Minutes of Jan. 24, 1944, meeting, *Wing and a Prayer* file.

31. Ibid.

32. Morison, *Two-Ocean War*, pp. 139–47.

33. Lars-Erik Nelson, "Where Did Reagan Hear That One?" *Washington Post*, Jan. 1, 1984, p. H5.

34. *New York Times*, Aug. 31, 1944.

35. Ibid.

36. John Wayne, interview by author, Feb. 7, 1974.

37. Ibid.

38. Philip Hartung, "The Fighting Seabees," *Commonweal*, Feb. 25, 1944, p. 471.

39. John Wayne interview.

40. Lloyd Nolan, interview by author, July 1, 1975.

41. Wellman interview, June 23, 1975.

42. Wellman, *Short Time for Insanity*, p. 81.

43. War Department telegram, Sept. 6, 1943; Lester Cowan to War Department, Sept. 13, 1943; War Department memo, Sept. 22, 1943, RG 165, box 15, NA.

44. Since United Artists had no studio facilities, it simply provided financial backing to independent filmmakers, who then rented facilities at a major studio. United Artists to War Department, Oct. 8, 1943. Lester Cowan to War Department, Oct. 19, Nov. 17, 1943. War Department letter, Nov. 27, 1943, RG 165, box 15, NA.

45. Cowan to War Department, June 28, 1944, RG 165, box 15, NA.

46. Ibid.

47. Cowan to War Department, telegram, July 6, 1944, RG 165, box 15, NA.

48. War Department memo, Oct. 6, 1944, RG 165, box 15, NA.

49. Dudley Nichols, "Men in Battle: A Review of Three Current Pictures," *Hollywood Quarterly*, Oct. 1945, p. 35.
50. Wellman, *Short Time for Insanity*, pp. 81–82. Wellman interview.
51. Ibid.
52. Ibid., pp. 83–89.
53. Ibid.; War Department memo, Nov. 13, 1944, RG 165, box 15, NA; Wellman interview.
54. Ibid.
55. Wellman, *Short Time for Insanity*, pp. 233–34.
56. Ibid. Wellman interview.
57. *Time*, July 23, 1945, p. 96. *New York Times*, Oct. 6, 1945, p. 9.
58. Nichols, "Men in Battle," p. 35.
59. Ibid., pp. 35–36.
60. Col. Robert Morgan, interview by author, Apr. 25, 2000. Colonel Morgan was the pilot of the *Memphis Belle* during its twenty-five missions.
61. Wellman, *Short Time for Insanity*, p. 235.

7. World War II: First Reflections

1. Lt. Col. Gordon Swarthout to Taylor Mills, May 22, 1945, RG 208, entry 269, box 1488, "War Department" file, NA. No explanation of the ban on writers was offered. As was to become clear, however, the usually left-leaning writers might well have questioned the anti-Soviet bias that pervaded the messages given to the tour members.
2. Taylor Mills to Francis Harmon, May 23, 1947, RG 208, entry 269, box 1488, "War Department" file, NA.
3. Francis Harmon, "Western Europe in the Wake of World War II," manuscript report of film executive tour, 1945, Library of Congress Rare Book Room, cited hereafter as "Tour Report."
4. Ibid.
5. Ibid., notes 8, 9, p. 3.
6. Ibid., notes 15, 5.
7. Ibid., report no. 14.
8. Sol Lesser, interview by author, Apr. 8, 1974.
9. "Tour Report," note 5, p. 2.
10. Ibid., note 10.
11. Ibid.
12. Ibid.
13. Ibid., note 19, pp. 1–3.
14. Ibid.
15. Ibid., note 12, pp. 3–4.
16. Ibid.
17. Ibid., page 15; note 11, p. 1.
18. Navy Department memo, May 14, 1945, Daves papers. Delmer Daves, interviews by author, Jan. 31, Feb. 2, 1974.
19. Early script of *Task Force* (circa 1945), Daves papers.
20. Final script of *Task Force*, Oct. 22, 1948, p. 110, Daves papers.
21. *New York Times*, Sept. 4, 1949, p. 32. *Daily Variety*, Sept. 28, 1949, p. 3. Scripts in Daves papers and in Warner Brothers Collection, University of Wisconsin Center for Film and Theater Research, Madison, Wisc.
22. Daves interviews.
23. Dore Schary, interview by author, Mar. 25, 1975.
24. Ibid.
25. Ibid. Dore Schary to author, Apr. 21, 1977. Robert Pirosh, "Memo from a Man Who Never Had It So Good," *New York Times*, Oct. 23, 1949, sec. 2, p. 5. Robert Pirosh, interview by author, Mar. 5, 1974.
26. Pirosh, "Memo from a Man." Gen. Anthony McAuliffe, interview by author, May 31, 1974.
27. Schary interview; Schary to author, April 21, 1977.
28. Ibid.; Robert Pirosh Papers, University of Wyoming Library, Laramie, Wyo., box 1; Dore Schary, "I Remember Hughes," *New York Times Magazine*, May 2, 1977, pp. 42–43.
29. Schary interview, Mar. 3, 1975; Schary to author, April 21, 1977.
30. Schary, "I Remember Hughes," p. 43; Schary interview, Mar. 3, 1975; McAuliffe interview; *Daily Variety*, Oct. 6, 1948, p. 4; Dec. 28, 1948, p. 1.
31. Schary, "I Remember Hughes," p. 43; Wellman interview; Oscar Doob, interview by author, Jan. 23, 1974.
32. Wellman interview.
33. Schary interview, Dec. 20, 1973; George Murphy, interview by author, July 14, 1977; Jack Dunning, interview by author, Mar. 12, 1974.

34. Pirosh interview, Mar. 5, 1974; McAuliffe interview; Gen. H.W.O. Kinnard, interview by author, June 15, 1974; Wellman interview.

35. From script of *Battleground*, Metro-Goldwyn-Mayer, 1949.

36. Wellman interview.

37. Robert Pirosh to Dore Schary, memo, n.d., file "MGM Publicity Book," Pirosh papers.

38. Twentieth Century Fox memo, Apr. 16, 1947, Lyman Munson Papers, Harry S. Truman Library, Independence, Mo.

39. Twentieth Century Fox memo, July 21, 1947, Munson papers.

40. Twentieth Century Fox memos, Sept. 10, 11, 1947. Lyman Munson to Louis Lighton, Sept. 19, 1947, Munson papers.

41. Ibid.; Sy Bartlett, interview by author, Feb. 9, 1974; Beirne Lay Jr., interview by author, Aug. 5, 1975.

42. Twentieth Century Fox memo, Oct. 14, 1947, Munson papers.

43. Ibid. Air Force to Twentieth Century Fox, Nov. 17, 1947, RG 330, box 677, NA. Munson to Lighton, Oct. 28, 1947. Twentieth Century Fox memo, Jan. 22, 1948. Lighton to Munson, July 29, 1948, Munson papers.

44. Darryl Zanuck to Gen. Hoyt Vandenberg, Sept. 17, 1948, RG 330, box 677, NA.

45. Ibid. Vandenberg to Zanuck, Oct. 2, 1948. Stephen Leo to Zanuck, Oct. 13, 1948, RG 330, box 677, NA.

46. Air Force to Twentieth Century Fox, Nov. 17, 1948, RG 330, box 677, NA.

47. Bartlett interview.

48. Col. Frank Armstrong, whom Bartlett and Lay used as the model for Gen. Frank Savage, suffered no mental breakdown. However, according to Bartlett, individual fliers in the Eigth Air Force did on occasion go through the type of collapse portrayed in *Twelve O'Clock High*. See also Thomas Coffey, *Decision over Schweinfurt* (New York: David McKay, 1977). Air Force to Twentieth Century Fox, Nov. 17, 1948, RG 330, box 677, NA.

49. Air Force to Twentieth Century Fox, Nov. 17, 1948.

50. Twelve O'Clock High's *Exhibitors Campaign Book*, MOMA. Henry King, interview by author, July 2, 1975.

51. King interview. Don Dwiggins, *Hollywood Pilot* (Garden City, N.Y.: Doubleday, 1967), pp. 172–74; the author describes the crash as including a slide along the ground into the tents. In fact, the plane does not touch the ground until it hits the first tent.

52. Ibid. Frank Tallman, interview by author, Aug. 21, 1975.

53. *Twelve O'Clock High* was released at the end of 1949 to make it eligible for Oscar consideration.

8. The Image of the Marines and John Wayne

1. See, for example, Josiah Bunting, *The Lionheads* (New York: George Braziller, 1972); Robert Lifton, *Home from the War* (New York: Simon and Schuster, 1973); Phillip Caputo, *Rumor of War* (New York: Holt, Rinehart, and Winston, 1977); Ron Kovic, *Born on the Fourth of July* (New York: McGraw-Hill, 1976); Herr, *Dispatches*.

2. The first episode of *Baa, Baa, Black Sheep* was broadcast on NBC on Sept. 23, 1976.

3. Quigley Publication Annual Poll of Exhibitors, which lists the top ten money-making stars of each year, included John Wayne a record twenty-four times up to 1974. *Family Weekly*, a popular magazine in "middle America," rated Wayne as the most popular actor among its readers for three years in a row as recently as the early 1970s. *Product Digest*, May 22, 1974, pp. 101, 104. *Photoplay* announced on an NBC television special, June 17, 1977, that Wayne was its choice as its all-time movie star.

4. Harry Truman to Congressman McDonough, Aug. 29, 1950, quoted in *Washington News*, Sept. 5, 1950.

5. Norman Hatch to Victor Krulack, February 13, 1995; Victor Krulak to Norman Hatch, February 21, 1995; author interview with Victor Krulak, April 14, 2000; Victor Krulak to author, August 13, 2001; conversation with Norman Hatch, August 28, 2001.

6. Ibid.

7. Edmund Grainger, interview by author, July 30, 1975. Republic Pictures, "Production Notes on *Sands of Iwo Jima*," n.d.; *New York Times*, Aug. 7, 1949, sec. 2, p. 3.

8. Grainger interview. Shoup interview.

9. Grainger interview.

10. Gen. Leonard Fribourg, interview by author, Aug. 17, 1975.

11. Ibid.

12. John Wayne interview; John Wayne to author, June 15, 1977.

13. Grainger interview. John Wayne to author, June 15, 1977. Edmund Grainger to author, July 12, 1977. In his letter, Wayne questioned the judgment that his career was "on the downgrade" during the period. In answer to a question about Wayne's reaction, Grainger wrote, "With reference to your inquiry about Mr. Yates' statement, that was his opinion, right or wrong. I quoted the facts."

14. Fribourg interview.

15. Ibid.

16. Ibid.; John Wayne to author, 1977.
17. John Wayne to author; Wayne interview.
18. Shoup interview; Col. James Crowe, interview by author, Dec. 11, 1977.
19. Grainger interview.
20. *New York Times,* Dec. 21, 1949, p. 9; *New Yorker,* Jan. 14, 1950, p. 75.
21. Shoup interview. Col. Raymond Findley, interview by author, Mar. 8, 1976. Grainger interview. *Variety Annual,* Jan. 3, 1951, p. 55.
22. Col. R.R. Crist to the Marine Corps commandant, Oct. 2, 1953. Unless otherwise cited, all documents relating to *Battle Cry* are in the Warner Brothers Archives, University of Southern California, Los Angeles; Leon Uris, interview by author, June 18, 1975.
23. Leon Uris to Henry Blanke, Oct. 19, 1953; Uris interview.
24. Karl Malden, interview by author, Aug. 9, 1975.
25. Ibid.
26. Grainger interview.
27. Ibid.
28. Ibid.
29. Schary interviews, Dec. 20, 1973, and Mar. 25, 1975.
30. Frank McCarthy, interview by author, Mar. 4, 1974.
31. Howard W. Koch, interview by author, July 23, 1975; *Weekly Variety,* Aug. 19, 1953, pp. 7, 18.
32. Ibid.
33. Uris to Henry Blanke.
34. Ibid.
35. Ibid.
36. Ibid.
37. Claire Towne to George Dorsey, Oct. 16, 1953.
38. Ibid.
39. Crowe interview; Russ Sanders, interview by author, July 30, 1975; Uris interview.
40. Gen. Edwin Simmons, director of Marine Corps Museums and History, interview by author, Apr. 22, 1977; Norman T. Hatch, Marine combat correspondent on Tarawa and later director of the Audio Visual Division in the DoD Office of Public Affairs, interviews by author, Dec. 17, 1974, and many subsequent informal conversations; Uris interview; Crowe interview.
41. Finlay McDermid to Raoul Walsh, Mar. 15, 1954.
42. Walsh to Steve Trilling, Mar. 19, 1954.
43. Joseph Breen to Hal McCord, July 1, 1954.
44. Trilling to Sam Schneider [in Warner Brothers' New York office], Aug. 28, 1954.
45. Donald Baruch to George Dorsey, Nov. 19, 1954.
46. Walsh to Trilling, Nov. 23, 1954.
47. Gen. Lemuel Shepherd Jr. to Jack Warner, Dec. 9, 1954.
48. *Weekly Variety,* Feb. 2, 1955, p.6.
49. *American Movie Classics Magazine,* Sept. 1997.
50. *Newsweek,* Jan. 16, 1950, p. 78. John Wayne, interview by *Playboy,* May 1971, p. 80. *New York Times,* Dec. 31, 1951, p. 9.
51. Grainger interview. Shoup interview.
52. Jim Brown, *Out of Bounds* (New York: Zebra Books, 1989), p. 146.
53. Kovic, *Born on the Fourth of July,* p. 43.
54. "Richard Pryor, King of the Scene-Stealers," *New York Times,* Jan. 9, 1977, sec. 2, p. 11.
55. Script of *The Alamo,* United Artists, 1960.
56. Jimmy Carter Library, Audio-Visual Collection, "Inaugural Eve Gala Performance, A Special Entertainment Tribute to the Nation and to President-Elect Jimmy Carter and Vice-President-Elect Walter Mondale, Presented by James Lipton Productions in Association with Time-Life Television on the CBS Television Network, Wednesday, January 19, 1977, 9:00pm-11:30pm EST, Tape III."
57. *New York Times Magazine,* Jan. 27, 1974, p. 9. Author's personal inquiry, Apr. 15, 1976.
58. Michael Wayne, interview by author, Aug. 5, 1975.
59. Dore Schary, interview by author, Mar. 25, 1975.
60. Delbert Mann, interview by author, Mar. 13, 1974; "Owen Marshall" episode, Mar. 30, 1975.
61. R.W. Young to author, May 11, 1974.
62. Bunting, *Lionheads,* p. 162.
63. Alther, *Kinflicks* (New York: Signet Books, 1975), p. 447.

64. Ibid.

65. Ronald Glasser, *365 Days* (New York: George Braziller, 1971), p. 60.

66. Kovic, *Born on the Fourth of July*, p. 61. Caputo, *Rumor of War*, p. 6.

67. Bob Schieffer, interview by author, Aug. 6, 1977. Ward Just, interview by author, Aug. 12, 1974. *New York Times*, June 20, 1968, p. 49. Halberstam interview.

68. Gen. Samuel Wilson, interview by author, Jan. 5, 1976. Josiah Bunting, interview by author, Dec. 23, 1974.

69. Wayne interview.

70. Bunting interview.

71. R.W. Young, interview by author, Aug. 18, 1975.

72. Halberstam interview.

73. John Wayne, *Playboy*, p. 92. Wellman interview. *Time*, May 10, 1976, p. 58.

74. *Cleveland Plain Dealer*, Jan. 21, 1976. *New York Times*, Jan. 27, 1976, p. 33.

75. Frank McCarthy, interview by author, Mar. 4, 1974. Wayne interview.

76. Lifton, *Home from the War*, chap. 8. Robert Lifton, interview by author, June 8, 1976. Kovic, *Born on the Fourth of July*, p. 98.

77. *Life*, Jan. 28, 1972, p. 44.

78. Lifton interview.

79. John Wayne interview.

80. Ibid.

9. A Different Image

1. Donald Baruch, chief, Motion Picture Production Office, Directorate for Defense Information, Department of Defense, interviews by author, Mar. 1973 onward. Clayton Fritchey, interview by author, Dec. 18, 1974. Adm. Robert Berry, interview by author, Aug. 17, 1975. Regulations governing DoD cooperation. Department of Defense, *Fact Sheet* (Washington, D.C.: GPO, 1974).

2. Ibid.

3. Samuel Fuller, interview by author, July 12, 1975.

4. Garnett interview. Edmund Grainger, interview by author, July 13, 1975. Baruch interviews. Garnett, *Light Your Torches*, pp. 280–85.

5. No evidence exists to indicate that the filmmakers were aware that U.S. soldiers had shot civilians in an effort to stop North Korean infiltrators, much as the movie portrayed. Most likely, art and reality were simply moving on parallel tracks.

6. This is the Marines' version of General Smith's comment. Marine Director of Public Information to Clair Towne, August 31, 1951; *Time Magazine*, January 9, 1978, p. 72, gives a slightly different version in its obituary for General Smith. Marine Corps Oral Interview with Gen. Oliver Smith, June 11, 1969, p. 246, June 12, 1969, p. 304; Marine lore has another origin for the phrase: On June 5, 1918, as French soldiers were retreating in front of a German onslaught at Belleau Wood, they advised Marines to join them. Captain Lloyd Williams responded: "Retreat, Hell! We just got here."

7. Interview with Edwin Simmons, April 22, 1977, and subsequent letter to author, July 27, 2001.

8. George Dorsey to Clair Towne, December 7, 1950; Osgood Roberts to George Dorsey, n.d., [December 15–16, 1950]; Clair Towne to George Dorsey, December 15, 1950; George Dorsey to Clair Towne, December 20, 1950.

9. Milton Sperling, January 4, 1951; plot outline, n.d [before January 4, 1951]; George Dorsey to Clair Town, January 9, 1951.

10. Marine Director of Public Information to Clair Towne, August 9, 1951; List of Requirements, August 28, 1951.

11. Smith interview, June 12, 1969, p. 305.

12. Gen. Oliver Smith to Gen. Lemuel Shephard Jr., January 29, 1952.

13. Ibid., p. 304.

14. Ibid.; F. Clarke Newlon to George Dorsey, November 20, 1951; Donald Baruch, Memo for the Record, December 3, 1951.

15. Donald Baruch, Memo for the Record, June 23, 1953.

16. V.J. McCaul to DoD Public Affairs, June 24, 1953

17. Donald Baruch, Memo for Record, July 7, 1953; Clair Towne to Walter Mirisch, July 13, 1953; George Welch, Army Public Affairs, to Donald Baruch, August 12, 1953; Clair Towne to Allied Artists, August 13, 1953; Donald Baruch, Memo for Record, November 29, 1954; Donald Baruch, Memo for Record, December 10, 1954.

18. Donald Baruch to Allied Artists, December 15, 1954; Commandant of Marine Corps to Donald Baruch, December 23, 1954; Commandant of the Marine Corps to Commanding General, Camp Pendleton, March 21, 1955.

19. Smith interview, pp. June 12, 1969, 306–7.

20. See Lawrence H. Suid, *Sailing on the Silver Screen: Hollywood and the U.S. Navy* (Annapolis, Md.: Naval Institute Press, 1996), for an in-depth discussion of the Navy's assistance in the making of *Men of the Fighting Lady* and *Bridges at Toko Ri*.

21. Dialogue from *Bridges at Toko-Ri*, Paramount Pictures, 1955.

22. Julian Blaustein, interview by author, Mar. 28, 1974.

23. Raymond Bell, interview by author, Apr. 8. 1975.

24. Daniel Taradash, interview by author, Mar. 27, 1974.

25. Bell interview.

26. Daniel Taradash to author, June 10, 1976; Bell interview.

27. Bell interview.

28. Towne to Bell, Apr. 3, 1951, DoD files.

29. James Jones, interview by author, Dec. 30, 1974.

30. Herbert Mitgang, "Transmuting a Touchy Topical Tome," *New York Times*, June 14, 1953, sec. 2, p. 5.

31. Ibid.

32. Ibid.

33. Ibid.; Fred Zinnemann, interview by author, Mar. 5, 1974. ·

34. Taradash interview; Taradash to author, June 10, 1976.

35. Taradash interview.

36. Donald Baruch, memorandum for the record, Feb. 11, 1952. Memorandum to Clayton Fritchey, Feb. 14, 1952. *From Here to Eternity* files. Baruch interview, Mar. 22, 1975. Gen. Frank Dorn, interview by author, Jan. 7, 1976. Clair Towne, interview by author, Aug. 15, 1975.

37. Fritchey to Gen. Floyd Parks, Feb. 19, 1952, DoD files.

38. Baruch, memorandum for the record, Feb. 19, 1952, DoD files.

39. Taradash interview; Baruch, memorandum for the record, Feb. 20, 1952, DoD files.

40. Taradash interview; Zinnemann interview; Fred Zinnemann to author, Feb. 24, 1977.

41. Baruch, memoranda for the record, Sept. 9, 10, 11, 1952, DoD files.

42. Baruch interview, Mar. 22, 1973.

43. Taradash interview; Taradash to author, May 6, 1976.

44. Ibid.; Taradesh to author, June 10, 1976.

45. Zinnemann interview; Zinnemann to author, Feb. 24, 1977.

46. Diana S. Dreiman, "A Critical Analysis of the Films of Fred Zinnemann" (master's thesis, UCLA, 1971), pp. 146–47.

47. Zinnemann quoted in Dreiman, "Films of Fred Zinnemann." Taradash interview.

48. Taradash interview.

49. Zinnemann interview; Zinnemann to author, Feb. 24, 1977.

50. Taradash interview; Ray Bell to Towne, with attachment, Jan. 28, 1953, DoD files.

51. Army memo, July 10, 1953; Towne to Bell, July 10, 1953, DoD files.

52. Zinnemann interview.

53. Ibid.

54. *New York Times*, Aug. 6, 1953, p. 16.

55. James Jones interview.

56. *Los Angeles Times*, Oct. 1, 1953.

57. Towne to David Bingham, Dec. 11, 1953. Towne to Russ McFarland, Sept. 10, 1953, DoD files.

58. *Daily Variety*, Aug. 31, 1953, p. 3. Towne to author, Sept. 1975. Bell to author, Jan. 13, 1976.

59. Zinnemann interview.

60. Adm. Lewis Parks to Bell, n.d. [after Sept. 8, 1953], DoD files.

61. Towne to George Dorsey, Apr. 25, 1951.

62. Ibid.

63. Ibid.

64. Consensus of naval officers interviewed.

65. Adm. James Shaw to author, Mar. 28, 1977; Adm. James Shaw, interview by author, Aug. 17, 1974; Adm. Robert Hickey, interview by author, Mar. 19, 1974.

66. Shaw interview; Felix Riessenberg, *The Story of the Naval Academy* (New York: Random House, 1958), pp. 40–41; Leonard F. Guttridge, *Mutiny* (Annapolis, Md.: Naval Institute Press, 1992), pp. 87–116.

67. Ibid.

68. Col. Bill Call, interview by author, Jan. 13, 1976.

69. Hickey interview.

70. Stanley Kramer, interview by author, Feb. 8, 1974.

71. Kramer interview; Slade Cutter to author, June 13, 1974.

72. Cutter to author, June 13, 1974.

73. Ray Bell to author, Jan. 13, 1976.

74. Kramer interview.

75. Herman Wouk to author, undated, in reply to questions submitted Dec. 20, 1975; Kramer interview.

76. Slade Cutter to author, June 13, 1974.

77. Kramer interview.

78. Bell interview.

79. *Daily Variety*, Nov. 25, 1952; Kramer interview.

80. *Christian Science Monitor*, July 21, 1953, p. 4; *Daily Variety*, Nov. 26, 1952, pp. 1, 11; Cutter, letter to author; Cutter interview; Shaw interview.

81. Lewis Parks interview, Dec. 31, 1974; Kramer interview; *Daily Variety*, Dec. 2, 1952, pp. 1, 4; *Daily Variety*, Dec. 19, 1952, pp. 1, 8; Although Admiral Parks did not recall the meeting with Secretary of the Navy Kimball and Kramer, the producer remembers it in vivid detail and believes it was responsible for his obtaining cooperation.

82. Michael Blankfort, interview by author, July 19, 1975; Shaw interview; Shaw, a highly decorated officer during the war, had later worked with Samuel Eliot Morrison on the writing of the Navy's official history of World War II.

83. Kramer interview; Shaw interview.

84. Adm. Lewis Parks to Ray Bell, n.d. [after Sept. 1953].

85. *Daily Variety*, Jan. 21, 1954, p. 4.

86. Wouk letter to author.

87. Bunting interview.

88. Kramer interview; *Newsweek*, Oct. 17, 1960.

89. James Jones interview.

90. See Suid file on *Attack!* at Georgetown University.

91. Robert Wise, interview by author, Apr. 10, 1974. Capt. Edward Beach, interview by author, May 30, 1974. Cutter interview.

92. Bosley Crowther, "*Run Silent, Run Deep*," *New York Times*, Mar. 28, 1958, p. 29.

10. The Most Ambitious Undertaking

1. *12 O'Clock High* file, Suid Collection, Georgetown University; Edward Jablonski's *Flying Fortress* (Garden City, N.Y.: Doubleday, 1965), p. 103, contains a description of virtually the same incident as described in the novel.

2. Directorate of Public Affairs to Air Force Headquarters, Wiesbaden, Germany, Feb. 10, 1949; Stephen Leo to Lucius Clay, Feb. 10, 1949.

3. George Seaton to Leo, Apr. 1949.

4. *Los Angeles Times*, May 5, 1997, pp. 1, 3.

5. DoD Public Affairs handwritten notes, Dec. 14, 15, 1950; Army memorandum for record, Jan. 21, 1951; Gen. George C. Marshall to Darryl Zanuck, Feb. 6, 1951.

6. Harry Green to Eric Johnston, Feb. 4, 1951.

7. Ibid.

8. Thomas Brady, "Hollywood's Shifting Sympathies," *New York Times*, Feb. 25, 1951.

9. Ibid.

10. Winston Churchill, *The Grand Alliance* (Boston: Houghton Mifflin, 1950), p. 200.

11. Harry Green to Nunnally Johnson, Mar. 3, 1951; Sidney Orenstein to Harry Truman, Dec. 12, 1951.

12. Lt. Col. Clair Towne to Orenstein, Dec. 29, 1951.

13. The original script can be found in the *Enemy Below* file at the UCLA Special Collections Library.

14. Wendell Mayes, interview by author, Mar. 6, 1974.

15. Ibid.; Herb Hetu, interviews by author, Apr. 3, 1975; n.d., 1999.

16. Ibid.

17. Edward Dmytryk, interview by Linda Obalil, March 17, 1978, in Program Notes, March 27, 1978, for retrospective by Department of Radio/Television/Film at the University of Texas, in *The Young Lions* file, Suid Collection, Georgetown.

18. Ibid.

19. Irwin Shaw to author, Mar. 3, 1975.

20. Ibid.

21. Byron Morgan to author, Sept. 6, 1988.

22. Hazel Flynn, "Von Braun Film Poses Problems," *Beverly Hills Citizen,* July 8, 1959.

23. Ibid.

24. Kate Cameron, "Film Life Story of Rocket Inventor," *New York Sunday News,* Oct. 2, 1960, sec. 2, p. 1.

25. Donald Baruch to Charles Schneer, Dec. 4, 1958.

26. *Daily Variety,* Apr. 22, 1959.

27. *Los Angeles Times,* Nov. 25, 1960.

28. Philip Scheuer, "Patriot or Traitor; Idealist or Realist?" *Los Angeles Times,* Sept. 11, 1960.

29. *Congressional Record,* 86th Cong., 2d sess., Aug. 23, 1960.

30. Bosley Crowther, *New York Times,* Oct. 20, 1960.

31. Byron Morgan to author, Sept. 6, 1988.

32. After man first landed on the moon thanks to his Saturn rocket, von Braun said that man had now become immortal; he compared the event to the first time animals emerged from the sea and crawled on the land.

33. Mel Gussow, *Don't Say Yes until I Finish Talking* (New York: Doubleday, 1971), pp. 198–99.

34. Ibid., p. 199.

35. *Variety,* Dec. 7, 1960, p. 5; *New York Times,* Dec. 3, 1960, p. 19.

36. Elmo Williams, interview by author, July 11, 1975. Andrew Marton, interview by author, July 21, 1975. Henry Koster, interview by author, July 17, 1975. Col. Dan Gilmer, interview by author, Aug. 9, 1975. Arthur Hiller, interview by author, Mar. 14, 1974.

37. Leonard Mosley, *Battle of Britain* (New York: Ballantine Books, 1969), pp. 51–62.

38. See Martin Caidin, *Everything But the Flak* (New York: Duell, Sloan, and Pearce, 1964), and Don Dwiggins, *Hollywood Pilot* (Garden City, N.Y.: Doubleday, 1967), for accounts of how Hollywood recreated World War II in the air after the Air Force could no longer supply vintage aircraft.

39. Elmo Williams, interview by author, Mar. 18, 1974.

40. *Variety,* Dec. 7, 1960, p. 5; *New York Times,* Dec. 3, 1960, p. 19.

41. Ken Annakin to author, June 4, 1976; Ken Annakin, interview by author, Feb. 18, 2000.

42. *New York Times,* Sept. 30, 1962, sec. 2, p. 7.

43. James Jones, "Phoney War Films," *Saturday Evening Post,* Mar. 30, 1963, p. 67.

44. *Variety,* Dec. 7, 1960, p. 5; "Calendar," *Los Angeles Times,* Apr. 1, 1962, p. 6; *Film Daily,* Dec. 5, 1960, p. 4.

45. "Calendar," *Los Angeles Times,* Apr. 1, 1962, p. 6.

46. Gen. Lauris Norstad, interview by author, June 11, 1975. Darryl Zanuck to Eric Johnson, Oct. 5, 1962, author's file. *New York Times,* Oct. 2, 1962, p. 45. Richard Oulahan Jr., "The Longest Day," *Life,* Oct. 12, 1962, p. 114.

47. Ibid.

48. "Calendar," *Los Angeles Times,* Apr. 1, 1962, p. 6.

49. Ibid. Zanuck to Johnson, Oct. 5, 1962, author's file. Department of Defense Chronology for *The Longest Day,* n.d., DoD files.

50. Norstad to Arthur Sylvester, Feb. 1, 1961, DoD files.

51. Sylvester to Norstad, Feb. 8, 1961, DoD files. Arthur Sylvester, interview by author, Aug. 16, 1973.

52. Zanuck to Burke Wilkinson, public affairs advisor to General Norstad, Feb. 21, 1961, DoD files. Chronology for *The Longest Day.* Donald Baruch to Twentieth Century Fox, May 5, 1961, DoD files.

53. Elmo Williams, interview by author, Mar. 18, 1974. Gussow, *Don't Say Yes,* pp. 217–18. Treatments and screenplays may be found in *The Longest Day* files in the Georgetown University Special Collections Library and in the Cornelius Ryan papers in the Special Collections Library at Ohio University.

54. *Time,* Dec. 9, 1974, p. 107.

55. Ibid., p. 225.

56. Informal discussions with Edmund North, Oscar-winning screenwriter for *Patton;* Charles Champlin, arts editor of the *Los Angeles Times;* and Wendell Mayes, screenwriter for *The Enemy Below* and *Go Tell the Spartans* at the time of the controversy surrounding Oliver Stone's *Born on the Fourth of July.* Stone himself dismissed the factual errors in his film as irrelevant (see subsequent discussion of the film).

57. Richard Dyer MacCann, "Hollywood Letter," *New York Times,* n.d., 1960; Morison, *Two-Ocean War,* pp. 193–214.

58. Gussow, *Don't Say Yes,* pp. 224–25.

59. Cornelius Ryan, *The Longest Day,* 1st ed. (New York: Simon and Schuster, 1959), p. 67; *D-Day Then and Now,* vol. 2 (London: After the Battle, 1995), pp. 546–49; Stephen Ambrose, *D-Day June 6, 1944* (New York: Simon and Schuster, 1994), p. 554.

60. *D-Day Then and Now;* Annakin interview.

61. This discussion is based on documents in the Cornelius Ryan collection at Ohio University and on archivist Doug McCabe's analysis of the relevant papers, which the author gratefully acknowledges.

62. Gussow, *Don't Say Yes,* p. 221.

63. Williams interview, Mar. 18, 1974; Marton interview.

64. Gussow, *Don't Say Yes*, p. 224.

65. Ibid.

66. *New York Times*, May 21, 1961, sec. 2, p. 7; Sept. 30, 1962, sec. 2, p. 7. Oulahan, "The Longest Day," p. 114. *Newsweek*, Sept. 18, 1961, p. 104. *Time*, Sept. 8, 1961, p. 74.

67. "Calendar," *Los Angeles Times*, Apr. 1, 1962, p. 6; *New York Times*, Sept. 30, 1962, sec. 2, p. 7; May 21, 1961, sec. 2, p. 7; Oulahan, "The Longest Day," pp. 116–17.

68. *New York Times*, May 21, 1961, sec. 2, p. 7.

69. Oulahan, "The Longest Day," pp. 116–17.

70. Williams interview, Mar. 18, 1974.

71. Gussow, *Don't Say Yes*, p. 229. Marton interview. Williams interview, Mar. 18, 1974.

72. Oulahan, "The Longest Day," p. 117; *Newsweek*, Sept. 18, 1961, p. 104.

73. Ibid; Marton interview.

74. Ibid.; *New York Times*, Sept. 30, 1962, sec. 2, p. 7.

75. *New York Times*, Sept. 17, 1961, sec. 2, p. 9; Sept. 30, 1962, p. 7. Marton interview.

76. Marton interview. Ken Annakin to author, June 4, 1976. *Newsweek*, Sept. 18, 1961, p. 104. *New York Times*, Sept. 17, 1961, sec. 2, p. 9.

77. *Newsweek*, Sept. 18, 1961, p. 105.

78. *New York Times*, Sept. 30, 1962, sec. 2, p. 7; Marton interview.

79. Ibid.

80. *Variety*, Sept. 20, 1961, p. 7.

81. *Congressional Record*, 87th Congress, 1st Session, Sept. 8, 1961, pp. 18733–35.

82. Ibid., pp. 18733–36.

83. *Variety*, Sept. 20, 1961, p. 7.

84. *Variety*, Sept. 13, 1961, pp. 3, 30. Congressman Bob Wilson to Arthur Sylvester, Sept. 13, 1961, Bob Wilson Papers, San Diego State University. Sylvester to Wilson, Sept. 25, 1961, DoD files.

85. "Calendar," *Los Angeles Times*, Apr. 1, 1962, p. 6.

86. *Variety*, Oct. 4, 1961, pp. 5, 19; Oct. 18, 1961, p. 18. *New York Times*, Oct. 17, 1961, p. 3. Norstad interview.

87. *Variety*, Oct. 18, 1961, p. 18. *New York Times*, Oct. 21, 1961, p. 8. *Daily Variety*, Oct. 24, 1961, pp. 1–4. Norstad interview.

88. Darryl Zanuck to Eric Johnson, Oct. 5, 1962, author's files. "Calendar," *Los Angeles Times*, Apr. 1, 1962, p. 3.

89. Department of the Army message, Nov. 1961, DoD files. *New York Sunday News*, Nov. 12, 1961, p. 6.

90. *Variety*, Jan. 3, 1962, p. 18.

91. Donald Baruch to Twentieth Century Fox, Sept. 24, 1962, DoD files.

92. Zanuck to Department of Defense, Oct. 1, 1962, DoD files.

93. Baruch to Zanuck, Oct. 11, 1962, DoD files.

94. *New York Times*, Oct. 5, 1962, p. 28; *New York Times*, Oct. 7, 1962, sec. 2, p. 1.

95. Interview with Len Lomell, February 6, 2001; "History Versus Hollywood: *The Longest Day*," first broadcast August 7, 2001.

96. "History Versus Hollywood."

97. Interview with Noel Dube, Oct. 10, 2000; "History Versus Hollywood."

98. Ibid.

99. Elmo Williams to author, n.d. (Oct. 3, 2001).

11. A Marriage Ends

1. Arthur Sylvester, interviews by author, Aug. 16, 1973; Dec. 23, 1974. Baruch interviews. Department of Defense file on *No Man Is an Island; Daily Variety*, Jan. 30, 1962, pp. 1, 4, 15.

2. *Congressional Record*, 87th Congress, 2nd Session, Feb. 22, 1962, pp. 2817–18.

3. Sen. Humbert H. Humphrey to Arthur Sylvester, June 14, 1962; Sylvester to Humphrey, June 30, 1962; Cooperation File, 1960s, Suid Collection.

4. Sylvester to Humphrey, June 30, 1962.

5. Bartlett interview. Baruch interviews. Gen. Arno Leuhman, interview by author, July 1, 1975. Requirements list for *A Gathering of Eagles*, DoD files.

6. Gen. Curtis LeMay, interview by author, Aug. 17, 1975. Bartlett interview.

7. LeMay interview.

8. Air Force memo from Curtis LeMay to Arthur Sylvester, June 7, 1962, DoD files.

9. Bartlett interview. Mann interview. LeMay interview.

10. Leslie Martinson, interview by author, July 10, 1975. Brian Foy Jr., interview by author, Aug. 5, 1975. *Newsweek*, July 23, 1962, p. 72. Lewis Milestone was replaced as director shortly after he made these remarks.

11. Pierre Salinger to Secretary of the Navy Fred Korth, Jan. 6, 1962, *PT-109* file, Suid Collection; Jack Warner Jr. interview.

12. *Wall Street Journal*, July 12, 1962, p. 1. *Time*, July 13, 1962, p. 54.

13. Salinger to Korth, Jan. 6, 1962, Kennedy papers. Bill Davidson, "President Kennedy Casts a Movie," *Look*, Sept. 6. 1962, pp. 26–27.

14. Sylvester to Humphrey, June 30, 1962, Kennedy papers.

15. Kenneth Clark to Charles Boren, Aug. 8, 1962, author's file.

16. *New York Times*, Oct. 2, 1962, p. 45.

17. Eric Johnson to Darryl Zanuck, Oct. 11, 1962, author's file.

18. Sylvester interviews.

19. Stan Hough, interview by author, July 1, 1975. Memo from Stan Hough to Richard Zanuck, Feb. 4, 1964, author's file.

20. Otto Preminger, "Keeping out of Harm's Way," *Films and Filming*, Feb. 1965, p. 6; Preminger interview.

21. *Cleveland Plain Dealer*, June 2, 1965; Preminger interview.

22. Preminger interview.

23. *Life*, Mar. 5, 1965.

24. Capt. C.J. Mackenzie, interview by author, Aug. 28, 1994.

25. C.J. Mackenzie to author, Aug. 8, 1975; Capt. Blake Booth, interview by author, Aug. 16, 1974.

26. In fact, Preminger did more for Wayne than Wayne did for the Navy in the movie. When the director completed the production ahead of schedule, the actor had a chance to have a complete physical, which revealed that he had lung cancer. So Preminger claimed he had saved Wayne's life. Preminger interview; *Weekly Variety*, Mar. 31, 1965.

27. *Time*, Apr. 9, 1965, pp. 102–3; Philip Scheuer, *Los Angeles Times*, Apr. 9, 1965, p. 15.

28. Hough memo; John Horton, interview by author, Dec. 18, 1973; Kenneth Clark, interview by author, Dec. 17, 1973.

29. Annakin interview.

30. Robert Aldrich, interview by author, Mar. 14, 1974; Baruch interviews.

31. Aldrich interview.

32. Cited in "Hollywood Versus History."

33. Robert Hughes, editor, *Films of Peace and War* (New York: Grove Press, 1962), p. 183; script in Cornelius Ryan papers, Ohio University Library.

34. Marton caption to photograph of unused scene, n.d.; Gussow, *Don't Say Yes*, p. 234; in the screenplay, the soldier on the beach came immediately after Mitchum's scene that now ends the movie.

35. *The Longest Day*, p. 176; William McClintock file, box 18, folder 30, Cornelius Ryan collection.

36. "Calendar," *Los Angeles Times*, Aug. 17, 1975, p. 32.

37. Bartlett interview; Gen. S.L.A. Marshall, interview by author, Jan. 26, 1974.

38. Terry Sanders, interview by author, Aug. 17, 1975. Undated Sanders memo with list of Army objections, author's file.

39. Sanders interview.

40. Cornell Wilde, interview by author, Aug. 15, 1975.

41. Ibid.

42. Ibid. DoD file on *Beach Red*.

43. Cornel Wilde to author, Nov. 17, 1977.

44. *Chicago Daily News*, Oct. 9, 1967; *Boston Globe*, Aug. 31, 1967, p. 34; *Boston Herald Traveler*, Aug. 30, 1967, p. 22C.

45. John Huston, interview by author, Mar. 27, 1974. Huston claimed that he alone decided to eliminate some scenes. Other accounts suggest that he did so at the direction of the War Department.

46. Ibid.; John Huston interview with Robert Hughes, in Robert Hughes, ed., *Film, Book 2, Films of Peace and War* (New York: Grove Press, 1962). Baruch interviews.

47. Fred Zinnemann, interview by author, Mar. 5, 1974; Kramer interview.

48. Linda Gottlieb, interview by author, June 15, 1973.

49. *Hollywood Citizen-News*, Dec. 30, 1964.

50. Arthur Hiller, "Calendar," *Los Angeles Times*, Jan. 3, 1965.

51. *Newsweek*, Nov. 2, 1964, p. 96; Paddy Chayefsky, interview by author, May 28, 1974; Hiller interview.

52. Hiller, "Calendar," *Los Angeles Times*.

53. Ibid.

54. Ibid.

55. Ibid.

56. James Altieri, "Calendar," *Los Angeles Times,* Jan. 10, 1965.

57. Melvyn Douglas, interview by author, Oct. 27, 1975.

58. Martin Ransohoff, interview by author, Mar. 1, 1974; Drew Pearson column, *Washington Post,* Jan. 27, 1965, p. D15.

59. Douglas interview; Chayefsky interview; Hiller interview.

60. *New York Times,* Oct. 28, 1964, p. 51; *Daily Variety,* Oct. 28, 1964.

61. Hiller interview.

12. The Bomb as Friend and Enemy

1. MGM Press Book.

2. Carter Barron to Stuart Palmer, Aug. 14, 1945; Pictorial Branch to Liaison Branch, Nov. 3, 1945; Pictorial Branch to Bureau of Public Relations, Nov. 9, 1945.

3. MGM Press Kit; Barron to Lt. Col. Swarthout, Dec. 1, 1945; Barron to Swarthout, Apr. 17, 1946; Col. D.R. Kerr, chief, Pictorial Section, to Colonel Ginesburgh, memorandum, Nov. 6, 1946.

4. Barren to Swarthout, Apr. 17, 1946; MGM Press Book; Army Liaison Group, Chungking, China, to War Department, Feb. 14, 1946; Gen. K.D. Nichols, the Manhattan district engineer, interview by author, n.d. [1982]. The author worked with General Nichols on his autobiography, and he recalled that he had appeared in the film as a composite, fictional character even though he actually was one of the three people most responsible for the building of the bomb.

5. Gen. Leslie Groves to Barron, Apr. 15, 1946.

6. Ibid.; Groves to Barron, Apr. 16, 1946.

7. MGM Press Book; MGM list of requirements needed for filming, Apr. 16, 1946; Army Information Branch to chief, Pictorial Branch, Apr. 17, 1946; Barron to chief, Pictorial Branch, July 11, 1946; Barron to Charles Ross, Apr. 19, 1946; Army Public Relations to Pictorial Section, July 16, 1946; chief, Pictorial Section, to Barron, Jan. 7, 1947.

8. Groves to Gen. F.L. Parks, Public Relations Division, Jan. 3, 1947; chief, Pictorial Section, to Barron; William Parsons to Col. Walter Ott, Air Pictorial Division, U.S. Air Force, Dec. 14, 1951; MGM Press Book.

9. Gillespie interview.

10. The author worked with Gen. K.D. Nichols, the Manhattan Project district engineer, on his autobiography. General Nichols joined the project before Groves and became Groves's deputy.

11. Tibbets interview; Lay interview.

12. Mrs. K.D. Nichols, interview by author, 1982.

13. Tibbets interview; Lay interview.

14. Ibid.

15. Ibid.

16. Ibid.

17. Ibid.

18. Lay interview.

19. William Parsons to Department of the Air Force, Dec. 14, 1951; Paul Tibbets, *The Tibbets Story* (New York: Stein and Day, 1978), p. 265.

20. Tibbets, *The Tibbets Story,* p. 265.

21. Charles Begg, interview by author, Aug. 28, 1975.

22. Ibid.; the 1995 Showtime cable TV docudrama *Hiroshima* contains footage of two B-29 crashes on Tinian, one a landing in the water off the beach and one a wreck that becomes a blazing inferno.

23. Schary interview, Dec. 20, 1973; Tibbets interview.

24. Schary interview, Dec. 20, 1973.

25. Gordon Thomas and Max Morgan Witts, *The Enola Gay* (New York: Stein and Day, 1977), pp. 4–5.

26. Tibbets, *Tibbets Story,* p. 265.

27. Lay interview.

28. Thomas and Witts, *Enola Gay,* p. 217.

29. Perhaps the best expression of Tibbets's feeling that he was carrying out a necessary assignment and that he had no regrets over his actions appears in his statement released by the Airmen Memorial Museum on June 9, 1994, which is available on the Paul Tibbets Web site. See also his book *The Tibbets Story,* pp. 5–9.

30. Parsons to Air Force Public Affairs, Dec. 14 1951.

31. Norman Panama and Melvin Frank to Adm. William Parsons, Jan. 15, 1952.

32. Lay interview. Jimmy Stewart was the first movie star to enter the service for World War II, joining a year before Pearl Harbor was bombed. He was initially refused entry into the Air Force because he weighed five pounds less

than the required 148 pounds, but he talked the recruitment officer into ignoring the test. He eventually became a colonel, and earned the Air Medal, the Distinguished Flying Cross, the Croix de Guerre, and seven battle stars. In 1959 he served in the Air Force Reserve.

33. Ibid.

34. Ibid.

35. Ibid.

36. Ibid.; *New York Times*, Apr. 21, 1955, p. 33.

37. Malden interview.

38. Col. Charles Bialka, interview by author, June 17, 1975; Maj. Ben Ostlind, interview by author, Aug. 21, 1975; *New York Times*, Nov. 23, 1957.

39. Ostlind interview. During his work on the film, the pilot helped investigate his and a similar crash that was ultimately attributed to fuel leaking into the fuselage and being ignited by a piece of electronic equipment.

40. Donald Baruch, interview by author, April 7, 1975; Edmund North, interview by author, Mar. 10, 1974; Wise interview.

41. Stanley Kramer, "*On the Beach:* A Renewed Interest," in Danny Peary, ed., *Moni's Screen Flights/Screen Fantasies* (New York: Dolphin Books, 1984), p. 117; Nevil Shute, *On the Beach* (New York: William Morrow, 1957), pp. 67–71.

42. Rudolph Sternad to Donald Baruch, May 28, 1958.

43. Navy Office of Information to Baruch, June 9, 1958.

44. Director, Motion Picture Service, USIA, to Baruch, June 24, 1958.

45. Baruch to Sternad, July 1, 1958.

46. Sternad to Baruch, July 17, 1958; Wallace Marcey to Sternad, Aug. 5, 1958.

47. Bertam Kalisch, memo for the record, Aug. 27, 1958.

48. Ibid.

49. Ibid.; C.C. Kirkpatrick to Baruch, Oct. 20, 1958.

50. Kirkpatrick to Baruch, Oct. 29, 1958; Baruch to Stanley Kramer, Nov. 4, 1958.

51. Baruch to Kramer, Nov. 4, 1958.

52. Ibid.

53. U.S.G. Sharp, Office of Chief of Naval Operations, to chief of information, Dec. 5, 1958.

54. Ibid.

55. Baruch to DoD Office of Plans and Programs, Dec. 8, 1959.

56. Shute, *On the Beach*, p. 238.

57. Ironically, looking back, Kramer wondered if the closing statement "offered enough hope." Kramer, "*On the Beach*," p. 118.

58. One of the few changes that Kramer made in transferring the novel to the screen was having the lovers consummate their relationship. Although Shute complained, Kramer believed it was realistic: "Peck's memory of wife and children was not damaged: they were dead. It was sacrifice enough that Peck finally took the submarine home from Australia to satisfy his crew and left Gardner behind." Kramer, "*On the Beach*," p. 118.

59. Baruch to Myer Beck, Sept. 18, 1959.

60. Baruch to DoD Office of Plans and Programs, Dec. 8, 1959; *Chicago Tribune*, Feb. 4, 1959; Kramer interview.

61. *Newsweek*, Oct. 17, 1960.

62. Bartlett interview.

63. Barlett interview; Pirosh interview; LeMay interview; Delbert Mann, interview by author, Mar. 13, 1974; *Gathering of Eagles* file.

64. LeMay interview; Pirosh interview; Mann interview.

65. LeMay interview and two subsequent informal conversations.

66. *New York Times*, Apr. 21, 1963, sec. 2, p. 7; *Newsweek*, Feb. 3, 1964, pp. 79–80; *Variety*, Feb. 27, 1963, p. 11.

67. Ibid.; Baruch interview, Mar. 22, 1973.

68. Arthur Reagan, "Images of the Military as Portrayed in Three Novels Made into Screenplays since 1958" (master's thesis, Boston University, 1964).

69. *New York Times*, Feb. 5, 1964, p. 29.

70. Bosley Crowther, "*Dr. Strangelove,*" *New York Times*, Jan. 30, 1964, p. 24.

71. Bosley Crowther, "Hysterical Laughter, Further Thoughts on *Dr. Strangelove* and Its Jokes about the Bomb," *New York Times*, Feb. 16, 1964, sec. 2, p. 1.

72. Ibid.

73. Lewis Mumford to the editor, *New York Times*, Mar. 1, 1964, sec. 2, p. 8.

74. *Newsweek*, Feb. 3, 1964, p. 79.

75. Ibid.

76. Max Youngstein, interview by author, Apr. 5, 1974.

77. Ibid.

78. Eugene Burdick and Harvey Wheeler, *Fail Safe* (New York: McGraw-Hill, 1962).

79. Youngstein interview.

80. The 2000 live TV remake of the film, which Bernstein also wrote, so closely follows the original movie that all comments herein remain pertinent. More to the point, the passage of thirty-six years had essentially validated the Air Force's contention that Fail Safe had worked. Moreover, since the Cold War had ended, the TV version had little relevance to nuclear safeguards and so became simply a vehicle in which George Clooney could demonstrate his acting ability.

81. Youngstein interview.

82. Ibid.

83. Ibid.

84. Ibid.; Sidney Hook, *The Fail Safe Fallacy* (New York: Stein and Day, 1963). In this short book, Hook refutes the basis of the novel.

85. Youngstein interview.

86. Ibid.; Robert Aldrich claimed to have experienced a similar reluctance on the part of private organizations to provide him needed equipment for *Attack*. Aldrich interview.

87. Youngstein interview.

88. Ibid.

89. Ibid.

90. *New York Times*, Sept. 16, 1964, p. 36.

91. Hubert Humphrey to Bill Moyers, Sept. 28, 1964; Bill Moyers to Lyndon Johnson, Sept. 29, 1964.

92. *New York Times*, Sept. 16, 1964, p. 36; Youngstein interview.

93. Bell interview.

94. Ibid.

95. Ibid.

96. Ibid.

97. *Variety*, Oct. 17, 1962, p. 5.

98. Ted Sorensen, *Kennedy* (New York: Harper and Row, 1965), pp. 606–7; Gerald Pratley, *The Cinema of John Frankenheimer* (New York: A.S. Barnes, 1969), p. 114.

99. Pratley, *Cinema of John Frankenheimer*, p. 114.

100. Donald Baruch to the Motion Picture Association of America, Aug. 16, 1963.

101. Ibid.

102. Edward Lewis to author, Oct. 25, 1976.

103. Fletcher Knebel, "The White House Was Pleased, the Pentagon Was Irritated," *Look*, Nov. 19, 1963, p. 95.

104. James Harris, interview by author, Feb. 25, 1974; James Poe, interview by author, Aug. 4, 1975.

105. Department of Defense memo, June 14, 1964.

106. Ibid.,; *Daily Variety*, Aug. 3, 1964.

107. Ibid.; Harris interview; Capt. J.D. Ferguson, interview by author, April 5, 1975.

108. Ferguson interview; Harris interview.

109. Richard Widmark to author, Dec. 7, 1977.

110. Ferguson interview.

111. Ibid.

112. Ibid.

113. Ibid.; Harris interview.

114. Ibid.

115. Ibid.; Bell interview.

13. John Wayne, *The Green Berets*, and Other Heroes

1. John Wayne interview.

2. Herbert Hirschman to Army Office of Information, Los Angeles, Jan. 24, 1963; interoffice memo, Public Information Division, Dept. of Army, Feb. 4, 1963; chief, Army Public Information Division, to DoD Production Branch, Audio-Visual Division, memo, Feb. 14, 1963; Donald Baruch to Ray Bell, Dec. 20, 1965; June 23, 1966.

3. Robin Moore, interview by author, Dec. 22, 1974; *Daily Variety*, May 10, 1967.

4. David Wolper, interview by author, July 21, 1975.

5. John Wayne to Lyndon Johnson, Dec. 26, 1965.

6. Ibid.

7. Jack Valenti to Lyndon Johnson, Jan. 6, 1966; Norm Hatch, interview by author, June 4, 1975.

8. Michael Wayne to *Green Berets* file, memo, Mar. 1, 1966; Michael Wayne interview.

9. John Wayne to Bill Moyers, Feb. 18, 1966.

10. John Wayne to Donald Baruch, Apr. 18, 1966.

11. John Wayne to Moyers, Apr. 18, 1966; John Wayne to senators, Apr. 15, 1966.

12. *Time,* June 9, 1967, p. 67.

13. Michael Wayne to Baruch, May 27, June 30, 1967.

14. Michael Wayne to Baruch, Aug. 19, 1966.

15. Baruch, memorandum for the record, Sept. 1, 1966.

16. Army to DoD Public Affairs, Sept. 14, 1966.

17. James Barrett to Baruch, Sept. 24, 1966.

18. Michael Wayne interview; Baruch, memo for record, Sept. 29, 1966.

19. Michael Wayne interview.

20. James Barrett to Army Office of Information, Dec. 30, 1966.

21. Michael Wayne to Baruch, Feb. 2, 1967; Army comments on "Special Forces Movie Script," n.d., forwarded on Feb. 15, 1967, to Baruch.

22. Michael Wayne's copy of Army comments with handwritten approval of changes; Michael Wayne to Baruch, Mar. 1, 1967; Daniel Henkin to Michael Wayne, Mar. 30, 1967.

23. Enclosure to Henkin letter, "Requested Changes for Screenplay," *The Green Berets,* n.d.

24. Ibid.; Henkin letter.

25. Michael Wayne to Army Office of Information, Los Angeles, Apr. 10, 1967.

26. Michael Wayne interview; *New York Times,* Sept. 27, 1967, p. 41.

27. Baruch interviews, Mar. 31, 1975; *Daily Variety,* June 23, 1967, p. 1.

28. Ray Kellogg, interview by author, July 3, 1975; *Time,* June 9, 1967, p. 67; notations from meeting in Pentagon on May 12, 1967, between the filmmakers and Pentagon officials.

29. Kellogg interview; Michael Wayne to Baruch, June 1, 1967.

30. Army memorandum to DoD Public Affairs, June 8, 1967; Kellogg interview; Michael Wayne interview; Col. William Byrnes, interview by author, June 25, 1975.

31. Baruch interview, Mar. 31, 1975.

32. Michael Wayne interview; Kellogg interview; Byrnes interview; Joan Barthel, "John Wayne, Superhawk," *New York Times Magazine,* Dec. 24, 1967, pp. 4, 22.

33. *Hollywood Reporter,* June 26, 1969, p. 1; June 27, 1969, pp. 1, 4; *Motion Picture and Television Daily,* June 30, 1959, pp. 1–2; Michael Wayne interview.

34. Halberstam interview.

35. Michael Wayne interview; John Wayne interview, *Playboy,* May 1971, p. 88.

36. Renata Adler, *New York Times,* June 20, 1968, p. 49.

37. *Hollywood Reporter,* June 17, 1968, p. 3.

38. *Congressional Record,* June 28, 1968, 90th Congress, 2nd Session, pp. 18856–57.

39. *New Yorker,* June 29, 1968, pp. 24–27; Simmons interview.

40. Michael Wayne interview.

41. *Time* magazine, on June 5, 1964, p. 28–29, had not been able to find any easy way out of Vietnam even though the United States had less than ten thousand troops in country.

42. Warner Brothers to author, Apr. 7, 1997.

43. John Wayne, interview, *Playboy,* May 1971, p. 88.

44. Wolper interview. United Artists Trailer for *The Devil's Brigade,* 1968.

45. Ken Hechler, interview by author, May 30, 1975.

46. Col. Cecil Roberts to author, Sept. 30, 1976.

47. Ibid.

48. Hechler interview.

49. Wolper interview.

50. Ibid.

51. Ibid.; *Los Angeles Times,* Apr. 10, 1968, pt. 5, p. 20. *Congressional Record,* 91st Congress, 1st Session, June 30, 1969, pp. 17897–98.

52. Ibid.

53. David Wolper to author, Oct. 11, 1977.

54. Heckler interview; Wolper letter.

55. Gen. James Gavin to author, Nov. 9, 1977.

56. McCarthy interview. *Film and Television Daily,* Oct. 8, 1968, pp. 1–2.

57. DoD memorandum for record, Nov. 1, 1950; Clair Towne to Ray Bell, Nov. 1, 1950; DoD memorandum for record, Dec. 8, 1950.

58. Towne to George Dorsey, Oct. 1, 1953; interoffice Warner Brothers communication, W.L. Guthrie to Steve Trilling, Oct. 6, 1953.

59. Guthrie to Trilling, Oct. 6, 1953; Guthrie to Trilling, interoffice communications, Oct. 6, 9, 1953.

60. Guthrie to Trilling, Oct. 9, 1953.

61. Frank McCarthy to Paul Harkins, July 11, 1955; McCarthy to Tony Muto, Mar. 20, 1956; *San Francisco Sunday Examiner and Chronicle,* Apr. 11, 1970; A reading of the letters from the Patton family's lawyers to the Defense Department cites the slapping incident as well as other unnamed reasons for the family's opposition to any production. The TV movie *The Last Days of Patton* does reveal the relationship. The director, Delbert Mann, explained that he included the story because it appeared in Patton's diary, among other sources.

62. McCarthy interview.

63. Donald Baruch to Anthony Muto, Jan. 20, 1956.

64. McCarthy to Muto, Mar. 20, 1956; McCarthy to Buddy Adler, Mar. 14, 1957.

65. McCarthy to Adler, June 24, 1959.

66. McCarthy, memo for the record, June 25, 1959.

67. Baruch, memos for the record, Nov. 16, 18, 21, 1960, DoD files.

68. McCarthy interview.

69. Ibid.

70. Law firm of Luce, Forward, Hamilton, and Scripps to Spyros Skouras, president, Twentieth Century Fox, Sept. 11, 1961, DoD files.

71. Arthur Sylvester to Army chief of information, Sept. 14, 1961, DoD files.

72. Firm of Bingham, Dana, and Gould to Arthur Sylvester, Dec. 13, 1961; Feb. 26, 1962. McCarthy to Baruch, Feb. 5, 1962. Baruch to Twentieth Century Fox, June 18, 1963. Public Affairs Office to Twentieth Century Fox, July 30, 1963, DoD files.

73. *Hollywood Reporter,* Mar. 12, 1965, p. 1. *Daily Variety,* Mar. 12, 1965, p. 1.

74. Dwight Eisenhower, *At Ease* (Garden City, N.Y.: Doubleday, 1967), p. 261; McCarthy interview.

75. General Eisenhower to McCarthy, Jan. 6, 1966, Eisenhower Library, Abilene, Kans.

76. Ibid.

77. McCarthy to Eisenhower, Jan. 18, 1966, Eisenhower Library.

78. Baruch to Twentieth Century Fox, July 2, 1965, DoD files.

79. Bingham, Dana, and Gould to Secretary of Defense Robert McNamara, Aug. 10, 1965; Office of General Counsel, Department of Defense, to firm of Bingman, Dana, and Gould, Aug. 23, 1965, DoD files.

80. McCarthy to Richard Zanuck, July 30, 1965; *Daily Variety,* July 26, 1965, p. 1. *New York Times,* Apr. 21, 1971, p. 47.

81. Twentieth Century Fox to Baruch, June 1, Nov. 23, 1966, DoD files.

82. McCarthy interview. McCarthy to Zanuck, Aug. 17, 1962; Twentieth Century Fox to Baruch, Aug. 7, 1967; George C. Scott to author, Dec. 21, 1977.

83. Scott letter; *New York Times,* Mar. 29, 1970, sec. 2, p. 15; Apr. 21, 1971, p. 47.

84. *New York Times,* Apr. 21, 1971, p. 47.

85. Zinnemann interview, Mar. 5, 1974.

86. *New York Times,* Apr. 21, 1971, p. 47. McCarthy interview.

87. Edmund North, interview by author, Aug. 14, 1987. Edmund North to author, Sept. 27, Oct. 10, 1977. McCarthy interview.

88. Ibid.

89. North interview.

90. North to author, Sept. 27, 1977. Twentieth Century Fox to DoD Public Affairs Office, Dec. 23, 1968. Gen. Paul Harkins to author, n.d. McCarthy interview.

91. North interview, Mar. 10, 1974. North to author.

92. McCarthy interview.

93. *New York Times,* Apr. 21, 1971, p. 47. McCarthy interview.

94. George C. Scott to author, Dec. 21, 1977.

95. *Variety,* Mar. 10, 1971, pp. 1, 47. *New York Times,* Mar. 29, 1970, sec. 2, p. 15. "George C. Scott," *Playboy,* Apr. 1971, p. 140.

96. Ibid.

97. Ibid.

98. *Sunday London Times,* Apr. 13, 1969, p. 11.

99. Scott to author.

100. Ibid.

101. Ibid.

102. Ibid. Harkins to author, n.d.

103. *Film and Television Daily,* Oct. 8, 1968, p. 2.

104. McCarthy interview.

105. *Patton* Press Book, n.d. *Variety,* July 9, 1969, p. 19. *Dallas Morning News,* Aug. 31, 1969.

106. Ibid.; McCarthy interview.

107. *Los Angeles Herald Examiner,* June 18, 1969. McCarthy interview. Malden interview.

108. McCarthy interview.

109. "Calendar," *Los Angeles Times,* May 18, 1969, p. 18. *Patton* Production Notes, n.d.

110. North interview. North to author, Sept. 27, 1977.

111. Scott to author.

112. North to author, Sept. 27, 1977.

113. Ibid.

114. Ruth Patton Totten, "All I Could Hear Was George Patton's Body Lies a-Moulderin," *San Francisco Sunday Examiner and Chronicle,* Apr. 11, 1970.

115. Ibid.

116. *New York Times,* Feb. 5, 1970, p. 33.

117. Ibid.

118. *New Yorker,* Jan. 31, 1970, pp. 73–74.

119. Ibid.

120. Ibid.; *New York Times,* Feb. 5, 1970, p. 33.

121. Richard Nixon, interview by David Frost, Nov. 20, 1977.

122. Hugh Sidey, "The Presidency," *Life,* June 19, 1970, p. 23. Hugh Sidey, interview by author, Nov. 29, 1976.

123. Quoted in Sidey, "The Presidency."

14. Illusion and Reality of War

1. *Commentary,* Sept. 1970, p. 20. *New York Times,* Mar. 22, 1970, sec. 2, p. 19.

2. *Hollywood Citizen News,* Feb. 20, 1970, p. 20.

3. George C. Scott, interview, *Playboy,* Apr. 1971, p. 192.

4. Baruch interviews.

5. Richard Corliss, ed., *The Hollywood Screenwriters* (New York: Avon Books, 1970), pp. 142–43.

6. Robert Altman, interview, *Playboy,* Aug. 1975, p. 62.

7. *New York Times Magazine,* June 20, 1971, p. 47. *Sixty Minutes,* Jan. 22, 1977.

8. Joseph Heller, interview, *Playboy,* June 1975, p. 60.

9. Tallman interview. John Calley, interview by author, Aug. 21, 1975.

10. Marton interview; *Time,* June 15, 1970, p. 66.

11. *Time,* June 15, 1970, p. 66.

12. Mike Nichols, interview, in Joseph Gelmis, ed., *The Film Director as Superstar* (New York: Doubleday, 1970), pp. 268–69. Marton interview.

13. *Time,* June 15, 1970. Heller interview in *Playboy,* pp. 60–61.

14. Joseph Heller, *Catch-22* (New York: Simon and Schuster, 1961), p. 440.

15. Heller interview in *Playboy,* p. 72.

16. Ibid.

17. *New York Times,* June 25, 1970, p. 54. *New Republic,* July 4, 1970, p. 22.

18. Nichols interview in Gelmis, *Director as Superstar,* p. 268.

19. *Time,* June 15, 1970, p. 66.

20. *New York Times,* Oct. 4, 1970, sec. 2, p. 1.

21. Vincent Canby, "The Last Tycoon," *New York Times Magazine,* Mar. 17, 1968, p. 33.

22. *New York Times,* June 16, 1969, p. A-4. *Washington Post,* June 16, 1969, p. 10.

23. "Calendar," *Los Angeles Times,* June 15, 1969, p. 22.

24. Williams interview, Mar. 18, 1974.

25. Ibid.; *Tora! Tora! Tora!* originally appeared in *Reader's Digest* in a very condensed version. It was an early working of Prange's continuing research on Pearl Harbor. *At Dawn We Slept,* his first book in English, appeared in 1981, after his death.

26. Williams interview.

27. Ibid. "Final Information Guide," Twentieth Century Fox, n.d.

28. Ibid.

29. *Air Classics,* Feb. 1969, pp. 15, 20, 62, 66. George Watkins, interview by author, Dec. 10, 1977.

30. Williams interview. "Department of Defense Assistance to Twentieth Century Fox Film Corporation in the Production of *Tora! Tora! Tora!*" 1969.

31. Williams interview; Richard Fleischer, interview by author, June 26, 1975.

32. Navy memo, Aug. 9, 1967, DoD files.

33. Confidential Navy memo, Oct. 15, 1968, DoD files; Williams interview; Fleischer interview.

34. Navy memo, Aug. 9, 1967; "Review of Support Provided by the Department of Defense to the Twentieth Century Fox Film Corporation for the Film *Tora! Tora! Tora!*" by the comptroller general of the United States, Feb. 17, 1970.

35. Daniel Henkin to Twentieth Century Fox, Feb. 7, 1968, DoD files.

36. Twentieth Century Fox to the Department of Defense, Aug. 1, 1968. Department of Defense to Twentieth Century Fox, Aug. 27, 1968, DoD files.

37. Watkins interview. Phil Goulding, interview by author, Apr. 4, 1975.

38. Navy memo to Phil Goulding, Oct. 6, 1968, DoD files.

39. Goulding interview; interoffice memorandum to Goulding, Oct. 11, 1968, DoD files.

40. Confidential Navy memo, Oct. 15, 1968, DoD files.

41. Jack Valenti to Goulding and to Clark Clifford, Oct. 3, 1968, DoD files.

42. Valenti to Clifford, Oct. 23, 1968, DoD files. Jack Valenti, interview by author, Nov. 11, 1977.

43. Goulding to Clifford, Oct. 24, 1968, DoD files.

44. Paul Nitze, interview by author, Apr. 8, 1975. *Sixty Minutes,* May 13, 1969.

45. Department of Defense project officer's final report, July 1969, DoD files.

46. Watkins interview. Edward Stafford interview, Apr. 7, 1975. Fleischer interview. Williams interview.

47. Richard Fleischer to *Los Angeles Times,* June 2, 2001; Elmo Williams responses, n.d. [Oct. 3], 2001, to letter from author, Aug. 21, 2001.

48. Undated E-mails from Dr. Donald Goldstein to author during October 2001, saying that neither Prange, the foremost expert on Pearl Harbor, nor his associates had ever been able to locate Yamamoto's comment in any Japanese record. Williams said in October 2001 that he no longer had the letter and did not know where it was. Crosby Day, "Quote has awakened a gigantic argument," *Orlando Sentinel,* Oct. 19, 2001, sec E, p. 5. In fact, the producer told the author during an interview in March 1974 that when he could not get a tax credit for his papers, he destroyed them.

49. Vincent Canby, *New York Times,* Oct. 4, 1970, sec. 2, pp. 1, 7.

50. Ibid.

51. Ibid.

52. Ibid.

53. Stafford interview. Fleischer interview.

54. *Sixty Minutes,* May 13, 1969.

55. Ibid.

56. Goulding to Department of the Navy, Nov. 27, 1968. Twentieth Century Fox to Department of Defense, Nov. 29, 1968, DoD files. As part of its response to Bill Brown's request for research information in preparing his program (Bill Brown to Navy Department, Mar. 24, 1969), the Department of Defense Office of General Counsel ruled on Apr. 2, 1969, that the correspondence between Twentieth Century Fox and the military could be made available to CBS under the Freedom of Information Act. *Navy Times,* Oct. 7, 1970, p. 29. *Honolulu Star-Bulletin,* Dec. 13, 1968, p. B-1. *Navy Times,* Dec. 13, 1968.

57. Stafford interview. Baruch interviews. Department of Defense file on *Tora! Tora! Tora!*

58. GAO report of Feb. 17, 1970. Military Operations Sub-Committee staff memorandum of Committee on Government Operations, House of Representatives, Dec. 1969.

15. Changing Images

1. Baruch interview, Aug. 19, 1989.

2. Gerald Ayres to Donald Baruch, Aug. 17, 1972, DoD files.

3. Baruch memo for the record, Aug. 24, 1972, Defense Department memo to Navy, Aug. 25, 1972. Ayres to Baruch, n.d. [before Aug. 28, 1972], DoD files.

4. Navy memo to DoD Public Affairs Office, Sept. 7, 1972; Ayres to Navy Department, Oct. 2, 1972, *Last Detail* file.

5. Ayres to Navy Dept., Oct. 2., 1972.

6. Ibid.

7. Navy Department to Ayres, Oct. 19, 1972, DoD files.

8. Will interview. *New York Times,* Sept. 5, 1976, sec. 2, p. 9.

9. Lt. William Harding, interview by author, Apr. 11, 1974. Mark Rydell, interview by author, Sept. 3, 1975. Don Baruch, interview by author, Aug. 16, 1976.

10. Baruch interview.

11. Ibid. Jack Valenti, interview by author, Nov. 11, 1977.

12. Rydell interview.

13. Maj. Ron Gruchey, interview by author, July 25, 1975.

14. Baruch interview.

15. Mark Robson, interview by author, July 2, 1975.

16. McCarthy interview.

17. Ibid.

18. *Hollywood Reporter,* Sept. 7, 1972, p. 3. McCarthy interview.

19. Navy memo, Dec. 19, 30, 1974.

20. *Cleveland Plain Dealer,* Jan. 25, 1975, sec. 4, p. 2.

21. Ibid.

22. Robert Swink, interview by author, July 25, 1978.

23. *New York Times,* June 19, 1976, p. 11.

24. Mirisch interview.

25. *Time,* July 12, 1976, p. 49.

26. Taylor Mills to author, Nov. 11, 1977.

27. *Pacific Stars and Stripes,* Sept. 4, 1974, p. 14.

28. Ibid.

29. Joseph Sargent, interview by author, Aug. 3, 1978.

30. Ibid.

31. Ibid.

32. Ibid.

33. Ibid.

34. Ibid.

35. Robert Sherrod, memo to self, Aug. 13, 1977.

36. *Time,* July 4, 1977, p. 54; Sherrod memo to self.

37. *Time,* June 13, 1977; James Gavin to author, Nov. 9, 1977.

38. Gavin letter; James Gavin, interview by author, Mar. 30, 1977.

39. William Goldman, interview by author, Mar. 15, 1979; HBO documentary on the making of *A Bridge Too Far,* 1977; *After the Battle,* no. 17, 1977.

40. Gen. Edwin Simmons, interview by author, Nov. 11, 1977. (General Simmons is director emeritus of the Marine Corps History and Museums and author of published Marine Corps histories.) Walter Pforzheimer, interview by author, Oct. 24, 1977. (Mr. Pforzheimer was an intelligence officer during World War II, worked as an intelligence officer for the Central Intelligence Agency, knew Cornelius Ryan, had read *A Bridge Too Far,* and was personally familiar with the battlefields in the Netherlands.)

41. "Calendar," *Los Angeles Times,* Sept. 19, 1976, p. 40. *New York Times,* June 13, 1976, sec. 2, p. 1.

42. Cornelius Ryan, interview with Julian Cook, 1968, Cornelius Ryan Papers, Alden Library, Ohio University.

43. Ryan interview; Cornelius Ryan, *A Bridge Too Far* (New York: Simon and Schuster, 1974), pp. 472–77; Winston Ramsey email to author, n.d., 2000.

44. Goldman interview.

45. The author discussed the issue with a Dutch historian who had presented a paper titled "Who Owns History?" at a conference in Amsterdam in 1993, after his first visit to the Market Garden battle sites and before his second. The historian felt that the scene rendered the film useless as history. The author remains undecided.

16. The Home Front, Vietnam, and the Victims of War

1. Art Brill, interview by author, Jan. 8, 1979.

2. William Westmoreland, *A Soldier Reports* (New York: Doubleday, 1976), p. 396.

3. Westmoreland, *A Soldier Reports,* pp. 435–36.

4. Zinnemann interview; Kramer interview.

5. Robson interview.

6. Gottlieb interview.

7. Ibid.

8. Gen. H.J. Dalton, interview by author, May 8, 1980.

9. Ibid.

10. Ibid.

11. Ibid.

12. Ibid.

13. Bernard Donnenfeld, interview by author, Mar. 13, 1974.

14. Gottlieb interview.

15. Ibid.; interview with Jack Valenti, Oct. 1, 1979; Tom Philpott, "The Prisoner," *The New Yorker,* April 2, 2001.

16. Gottlieb interview.

17. DoD to Lawrence Gordon Productions, memo, Aug. 22, 1975.

18. Ibid.

19. John Flynn, interview by author, Aug. 3, 1981; *Daily Variety,* Apr. 25, Aug. 5, 1977.

20. *Boxoffice,* Oct. 17, 1977; *Hollywood Reporter,* Oct. 4, 1977; *Motion Picture Product Digest,* Oct. 19, 1977.

21. *McCalls,* Dec. 1977.

ug. 1977, p. 70.

y author, Mar. 24, 1978; Universal Studios to John Horton, Mar. 29,

merican Film, June 1978, pp. 34–35.

hor, Sept. 17, 1982.

nerican Film, May 1980, p. 55.

o Department of Defense, Sept. 8, 1978; Marine Corps to assistant

13, 1976.

w; Veteran's Administration, Los Angeles, to Mulvehill, Jan. 13,

9, 1978; Lt. Col. Arthur Brill, interview by author, Apr. 4, 1978.

. 4, p. 12; Francis Ford Coppola, interview by *Playboy,* July 1975, p.

on the Senses," *Cleveland Plain Dealer,* Sept. 12, 1975, Action sec.,

, 1990.

nse Donald Rumsfeld, Apr. 22, 1976; George McArthur, "Coppola

Storms Philippines for Re-creation of Viet War," Calendar," *Los Angeles Times,* June 6, 1976, pp. 37, 39.

4. Norm Hatch to Joseph Laitin, May 28, 1975.

5. Joseph Laitin, interview by author, Sept. 6, 1979; "DoD Background of Association with Francis Ford Coppola," n.d. [Aug. 1976]; Baruch interviews; Norm Hatch conversations.

6. Ibid.

7. Laitin interview.

8. Baruch interviews; DoD memo, June 2, 1975.

9. Laitin interview.

10. Gen. H. Gordon Hill, interview by author, May 19, 1977; Army memo to DoD Public Affairs Office, June 16, 1975.

11. Ibid.; Baruch interviews.

12. Army memo of May 19, 1977.

13. Hill interview; Ray Smith interview, Apr. 8, 1989.

14. Ibid.; DoD record of contacts with Coppola; Gen. Wynant Sidle, interview by author, Aug. 5, 1989.

15. DoD memo for the record, July 9, 1975; Baruch interviews; Sidle interview.

16. *Variety,* Sept. 3, 1975, p. 27; *Washington Star,* Sept. 13, 1975, p. A-2.

17. "Background of DoD Association with Francis Ford Coppola and *Apocalypse Now,*" n.d.; DoD to Fancis Ford Coppola, Nov. 18, 1975.

18. Fred Roos to DoD Public Affairs, Dec. 30, 1975; "Coppola and *Apocalypse Now.*"

19. Susan Braudy, "*Apocalypse Now,*" *Atlantic,* Aug. 1976, p. 68.

20. Roos to William Greener, Apr. 9, 1976.

21. George Stevens Jr. to Donald Rumsfeld, Mar. 27, 1976.

22. Jack Valenti to Rumsfeld, Apr. 9, 1976; Norm Hatch, intraoffice memorandum, Apr. 12, 1976.

23. Francis Ford Coppola to Rumsfeld, telegram, Apr. 22, 1976.

24. Ibid.

25. Ibid.

26. Ibid.

27. Rumsfeld to Coppola, telegram, Apr. 29, 1976.

28. Coppola, mailgram, May 3, 1976.

29. DoD Public Affairs to Copppla, May 11, 1976.

30. Fred Roos to DoD, telegram, May 17, 1976; Norm Hatch to William Greener, memo, May 20, 1976.

31. Hatch to Greener, May 20, 1976; *Parade Magazine,* July 13, 1975.

32. Greener to Coppola, May 25, 1976.

33. *Daily Variety,* Apr. 19, 27, 1976; Clint Eastwood, interview by *Cosmopolitan,* July 1980, p. 184.

34. *Daily Variety,* May 28, 1976, p. 4.

35. Roos to Greener, June 1, 1976.

36. Ibid.

37. Greener to Roos, June 9, 1976.

38. Francis Ford Coppola to Pres. Jimmy Carter, telegram, Feb. 12, 1977.

39. Ibid.

40. Ibid.

41. DoD memos, May 10, 20, 1976.

42. Baruch interviews.

43. William Hoffman to DoD, June 3, 1977; Donald Baruch to Hoffman, June 21, 1977; Hoffman to Baruch, June 24, 1977.

44. *Cleveland Plain Dealer,* July 9, 1976, clipping in *Apocalypse Now* file.

45. *Wall Street Journal,* May 25, 1977, p. 1; "Calendar," *Los Angeles Times,* Oct. 23, 1977, p. 32.

46. *Newsweek,* June 13, 1977, p. 63.

47. Coppola, memorandum to his staff, Apr. 30, 1976, published in *Esquire,* Nov. 1977, p. 196; *Wisconsin State Journal,* June 27, 1976, sec. 4, p. 12.

48. Milius himself claimed that the film's climactic scenes differed very little from his orignal screenplay. Milius interview.

49. *Wall Street Journal,* Nov. 1, 1977, p. 1; Max Youngstein, interview by author, July 19, 1978.

50. Youngstein interview.

51. Ibid.

52. Ibid.

53. Ibid.

54. Ibid.

55. Max Youngstein to author, Mar. 4, 1980.

56. Donald Baruch to Audio Visual Branch, OCPA, Dept. of the Army, July 6, 1977.

57. Army Office of Public Affairs to Baruch, July 28, 1977.

58. Ibid.

59. Allan Bodoh, interview by author, Apr. 5, 1978; Lt. Col. John Markanton, interview by author, Aug. 6, 1981; Maj. Ray Smith, interview by author, Mar. 24, 1978; over the years, many officers assigned to the Los Angeles Public Affairs Offices of each of the military services lost sight of their mission to provide technical and procedural information to filmmakers seeking help and guidance. Instead, they became star-struck and operated on the assumption that they had decision-making authority and final say on script approval and cooperation. In fact, Don Baruch's office and the Public Affairs Office in the headquarters of each service in Washington always retained final control over the decisions on whether to extend military assistance to a production.

60. Bodoh interview; Wendell Mayes, interview by author, Aug. 4, 1981; Baruch interviews.

61. Mayes interview; Army memo, July 28, 1977.

62. Mayes interview.

63. Markanton interview; Ted Post, interview by author, Aug. 5, 1981.

64. Post interview; Markanton interview; conversation with Daniel Ford, July 15, 2000.

65. *Go Tell the Spartans* production notes, Mar Vista Productions, 1977; *Boston Globe,* Sept. 27, 1978.

66. Ibid.

67. *Wisconsin State Journal,* June 27, 1976, sec. 4, p. 12; *Go Tell the Spartans,* production notes.

18. *The Deer Hunter, Hair,* and Finally *Apocalypse Now*

1. Quinn Redeker, interview by author, Jan. 7, 1989; Lou Garfinkle, interview by author, Jan. 18, 1989. The discussion of the writing of the original screenplay that follows comes from these two interviews.

2. From original script, "The Man Who Came to Play."

3. Redeker and Garfinkle interviews; Herm Saunders, interview by author, Feb. 2, 1989.

4. Redeker interview, Saunders interview.

5. Saunders interview; Barry Spikings, interview by author, July 19, 1989; Michael Deeley, interview by author, Sept. 2, 1989.

6. Redeker interview.

7. Production notes, Press Kit, n.d., 1978; Leticia Kent, "Ready for Vietnam? A Talk with Michael Cimino," *New York Times,* Dec. 10, 1978, sec. 2, pp. 15, 23.

8. Spikings interview; Deeley interview; Richard Eder, "The Deer Hunter," *New York Times,* Dec. 24, 1976.

9. Redeker interview; Deeley interview; Spikings interview; *Washington Post,* Mar. 21, 1980, p. A9; Peter Koper, "Can Movies Kill?" *American Film,* July–Aug. 1982.

10. Jack Kroll, *Newsweek,* Dec. 11, 1978, p. 113; *Hollywood Reporter,* Dec. l, 1978, p. 3; Joy Gould Boyum, *Wall Street Journal,* Dec. 15, 1978, p. 19.

11. Kent, "Ready for Vietnam?" p. 23.

12. Ibid.; Mark Carucci, "Stalking *The Deer Hunter:* An Interview with Michael Cimino," *Millimeter,* Mar. 1978, p. 34.

13. Army Public Affairs to DoD Public Affairs, memo, May 24, 1977.

14. Kent, "Ready for Vietnam?" p. 15.

15. *Weekly Variety,* Nov. 29, 1978, p. 24; Kroll, *Newsweek,* December 11, 1978.

16. Peter Arnett, "*The Deer Hunter,* Vietnam's Final Atrocity," *Los Angeles Times,* Apr. 8, 1979, pt. 6, page 1.

17. Ibid.

18. Ibid.

19. Roger Copeland, "A Vietnam Movie That Does Not Knock America," *New York Times,* Aug. 7, 1977, sec. 2, p. 19.

20. Arnett, p. 1.

21. Peter Grant, "War and Peace at the Awards," *Los Angeles Times,* Apr. 11, 1979.

22. Aljean Harmetz, *New York Times,* Apr. 26, 1979, p. C15, cited hereafter as Harmetz, "*The Deer Hunter.*"

23. Ibid.

24. Kent, "Ready for Vietnam," p. 23; Paul Dammed, interview by author, May 2, 1979. Dammed played the Green Beret.

25. Ohio Film Bureau to Donald Baruch, May 5, 1977; Army memo to Baruch, May 24, 1977.

26. In *Deer Hunter* file.

27. *Deer Hunter* script submitted to the Department of Defense; Harmetz, "*The Deer Hunter,*" p. C15.

28. Lester Persky, interview by author, May 21, 1981.

29. Robert Greenhut to Baruch, Apr. 15, 1977.

30. Army Public Affairs memo to DoD Public Affairs, Apr. 26, 1977.

31. Baruch to Greenhut, May 10,, 1977.

32. Persky interview.

33. DoD intraoffice memorandum, July 13, 1977; Greenhut to Baruch, Aug. 11, 1977; Baruch to Greenhut, Aug. 22, 1977.

34. Baruch to Greenhut, Aug. 22, 1977; Army Office of Information to Baruch, Oct. 6, 1977.

35. Baruch to the Army Public Affairs Office, Oct. 7, 1989.

36. Army to Baruch, Oct. 11, 1977; Norm Hatch to Thomas Ross, Oct. 19, 1977.

37. Hatch to Ross, Oct. 19, 1977.

38. Ibid.

39. Greenhut to Baruch, Oct. 20, 1977.

40. Ross to Hatch, Oct. 25, 1977; Hatch to Ross, Nov. 2, 1977.

41. UPI dispatch, Jan. 21, 1978.

42. Milos Forman, interview by Stephen Silverman, *New York Post,* Mar. 8, 1979, p. 33; Persky interview.

43. Michael Weller, interview by author, Mar. 7, 1984.

44. Ibid.

45. Paul Cizmar, *Chronicle Review,* Apr. 2, 1979, p. R21.

46. *UCLA Daily Bruin,* Aug. 23, 1979; *Time,* Aug. 27, 1979, p. 55.

19. The Marines Search for a New Identity

1. The Marine Corps lieutenant colonel coteaching the history of the Vietnam War with the author in 1992 delivered a lecture that any antiwar academician would have praised.

2. Brill interview, Apr. 4, 1978; Capt. Pat Coulter, interview by author, Apr. 4, 1978; Brill interview, Jan. 8–9, 1979; Capt. Pat Coulter, interview by author, Aug. 8, 1981.

3. Arthur Webber, Review of *Born on the Fourth of July, Marine Gazette,* Dec. 1977, pp. 14–15.

4. Ibid.

5. Ibid.

6. Burtt Harris to Don Baruch, Mar. 3, 1978.

7. Lt. Penny Williamson to Col. Margaret Brewer, n.d. [Mar. 4, 1978].

8. Ibid.

9. Draft memo, Mar. 15, 1978; Gen. V.T. Blaz to Williamson, Mar. 18, 1978.

10. Blaz to head, Audio Visual Branch, Mar. 20, 1978.

11. Brewer to head, Audio Visual Branch, Mar. 31, 1978.

12. Ibid.

13. Ibid.

14. Ibid.

15. Ibid.

16. Don Baruch to Artists Entertainment Complex, Apr. 6, 1978; Burtt Harris to Norm Hatch, Apr. 14, 1978; Harris to Baruch and Hatch, May 4, 1978.

17. Baruch to Marine Corps Information Branch, May 8, 1978.

18. Cover memo from Brewer to the chief of staff of the Marines, June 2, 1978; several weeks earlier, Tom Ross, the assistant secretary of defense for public affairs, had tossed out the idea of giving assistance to any filmmaker requesting it or stopping cooperation altogether, but nothing came of the proposed changes. Thomas Ross, interview by author, June 2, 1978.

19. Cover memo from Brewer to the chief of staff of the Marines, June 2, 1978.

20. Memo for the chief of staff, Marine Corps, June 2, 1978.

21. Director of information to Marine chief of staff, June 2, 1978.

22. Ibid.

23. Ibid.

24. Ibid.

25. Brewer to deputy head, Information Branch, June 7, 1978.

26. Brewer to the deputy chief of staff for operations and training, June 9, 1978; Brewer to Marine Corps chief of staff, June 20, 1978; Marine Corps chief of staff to Brewer, June 21, 1978.

27. Deputy chief of staff, operations and training, comment on *Born on the Fourth of July*, June 28, 1978.

28. Ibid.

29. Brewer to DoD Public Affairs, June 30, 1978.

30. Baruch to Charles Russhon, July 11, 1978; *New York Post*, July 26, 1978; Oliver Stone, interview by author, Aug. 6, 1981.

31. Pat Coulter, interview by author, Jan. 26, 1989.

32. Ibid.

33. Charles Fries Productions to Audio/Visual Branch, Department of Defense, Apr. 30, 1979. Although this narrative focuses on feature motion pictures, the author believes *Rumor of War* falls into the scope of this study given the nature of the negotiations that took place before the Marine Corps agreed to cooperate. Moreover, made-for-television movies have for all practical purposes replaced Hollywood's B films, and the distributor did release *Rumor of War* in Europe as a feature film.

34. Ibid.; Don Baruch to Head, Information Branch, U.S. Marine Corps, May 8, 1979.

35. Penny Williamson to Art Brill, undated memo [May 1979].

36. Ibid.

37. Ibid.

38. Ibid.

39. Ibid.

40. Ibid.; Coulter and the Marines had only recently wrapped up negotiations on *The Great Santini*.

41. Brill to General Brewer, n.d. [May 1979].

42. Williamson to Brill, Dec. 14, 1979.

43. Brewer to Baruch, Dec. 26, 1979.

44. Coulter interview, Aug. 8, 1981.

45. Ongoing Baruch conversations.

46. Coulter interview, Aug. 8, 1981.

47. Pat Coulter, in a speech to the Marine Combat Correspondents Convention, in Long Beach, Calif., Sept. 28, 1982.

48. Ibid.

49. Cecil Smith, "*Rumor of War* as Moment of Truth," *Los Angeles Times*, Sept. 23, 1980.

50. Tom Shales, "*A Rumor of War:* Self-Righteous Sermonette on CBS," *Washington Post*, Sept. 24, 1980.

51. Ibid.

52. Henry Allen, "Remembrance: A Salute from an Ex-Marine," *Washington Post*, Sept. 24, 1980.

53. Ibid.

54. Coulter interview.

20. The Search Continued: Two Non-Vietnam Case Studies

1. Talent Associates, Ltd., to director of information, Headquarters, Marine Corps, Mar. 9, 1976.

2. Lt. Col. Art Brill and Capt. Pat Coulter, interview by author, Apr. 4, 1978; Capt. Pat Coulter, "Stand by for a Fighter Pilot," *Marine Corps Gazette*, Feb. 1980, pp. 45–46.

3. Gen. W.R. Maloney to Talent Associates, Ltd., Mar. 23, 1976.

4. Maloney to Marine Corps chief of staff, Mar. 24, 1976; Gen. W.R. Maloney, memorandum for the record, Mar. 24, 1976.

5. Col. C.W. Hoffner to head, Audio-Visual, DoD, Mar. 29, 1976; Sean Fitzpatrick, vice president, BCP, to Donald Baruch, Jan. 12, 1977.

6. Fitzpatrick to Baruch, Jan. 12, 1977.

7. Maloney to Baruch, Feb. 11, 1977.

8. Charles Pratt to Baruch, Feb. 16, 1977.

9. Pat Conroy to Pratt, n.d. [Feb. 1977].

10. Ibid.

11. Ibid.

12. Ibid.

13. Ibid.

14. Brill and Coulter interview, Apr. 4, 1978; Brill, interview by author, Jan. 8–9, 1979.

15. Baruch to Coulter, Mar. 3, 1977; Coulter to Art Brill, Mar. 4, 1977.

16. Coulter to Brill, June 28, 1977; John Pommer to Baruch, Oct. 5, 1977.

17. Baruch to Marine Corps Public Affairs, Oct. 14, 1977.

18. Adm. David Cooney to DoD Public Affairs, Dec. 19, 1977.

19. V.T. Blaz to Marine chief of staff, Dec. 20, 1977.

20. Ibid.

21. V.T. Blaz to DoD Public Affairs, Dec. 30, 1977; Pat Coulter, memo for record, Feb. 15, 1978.

22. Maj. H.J. Collins to director of information, May 16, 1978.

23. Brill to director of information, n.d. [May 1978].

24. Ibid.

25. Paul Siegmund to commandant of the Marine Corps (Code PAI), June 9, 1978.

26. Lt. Penny Williamson to Brill, June 12, 1978.

27. Ibid.

28. Coulter interview, Aug. 8, 1981; Gen. Margaret Brewer, interview by author, Apr. 4, 1981.

29. Brill to Margaret Brewer, June 14, 1978.

30. Ibid.

31. Ibid.

32. Ibid.

33. Ibid.

34. Brill to Brewer, June 14, 1978; Coulter to Brill, memo, June 20, 1978.

35. Brill to Brewer, June 14, 1978.

36. "Results of Negotiations with the Producers of *The Great Santini*," June 21, 1978.

37. Ibid.

38. Coulter interview, Aug. 8, 1981; Charles Pratt to Brill, June 26, 1978; Pratt to Brewer, June 26, 1978.

39. Marine Corps director of information to the commandant of the Marine Corps, July 7, 1978.

40. Ibid.

41. Brewer to Baruch, Aug. 10, 1978; Adm. David Cooney to Baruch, Aug. 17, 1978; Baruch to Pratt, Aug. 17, 1978; Coulter interview, Aug. 8, 1981; Pat Coulter, "Stand By for a Fighter Pilot," *Marine Gazette*, Feb. 1980, p. 49, cited hereafter as Coulter, "Pilot."

42. Coulter interview, Aug. 8, 1978; Coulter, "Pilot," p. 50.

43. Ibid.

44. Ibid.

45. Ibid.

46. Coulter, "Pilot," p. 52.

47. Baruch to Pratt, July 27, 1979.

48. Mitsuharu Ishii to Norman Hatch, chief, Audio Visual Division, Department of Defense, Feb. 3, 1978.

49. Penny Williamson to Brill, Mar. l, 1978.

50. Gen. Samuel Jaskilka to Baruch, Sept. 24, 1979.

51. Coulter to director of information, Mar. 30, 1979.

52. Margaret Brewer, interview by author, Apr. 8, 1981; informal conversations with Donald Baruch.

53. Jaskilka to author, May 18, 1981; General Jaskilka, interview by author, June 10, 1981.

54. Ibid.

55. Brewer to assistant commandant, Aug. 29, 1979; Williamson to Brill, Sept. 4, 1979; Brewer to Baruch, Sept. 24, 1979; Cooney to Baruch; Sept. 11, 1979.

56. Col. Herb Hart to Baruch, Feb. 25, 1981; Baruch to Jaskilka, Feb. 27, 1981.

57. Baruch to Jaskilka, Apr. 21, 1981.

58. Robin Moore, interview by author, June 23, 1981.

59. Ibid.

60. Kevin Thomas, "Invasion of Korea for 'Inchon' Film," "Calendar," *Los Angeles Times,* July 29, 1979, pp. 25–26.

61. Dale Pollock, "*Inchon!*—Shooting for the Moonies," "Calendar," *Los Angeles Times,* May 16, 1982; *Boston Globe,* June 8, 1982; Terrence Young, interview by author, Sept. 22, 1986.

62. Jaskilka to Baruch, Apr. 17, 1981.

63. Pollock, "*Inchon,* shooting for the Moonies."

64. *Inchon* Press Kit.

65. Ibid.

66. Ibid.

67. Gary Arnold, *Washington Post,* Sept. 17, 1982, p. D-2.

68. Jaskilka to author, May 18, 1981.

69. Rex Read, *Boston Globe,* June 8, 1982; Arnold review.

70. Herb Hart to Baruch, Feb. 25, 1981.

71. Baruch to Robert Standard, May 8, 1981.

72. "'Inchon!': More Controversy," *Washington Star,* May 4, 1981, p. C-2; Robert Andrews, "Protesters Organize for 'Inchon' Premiere," *Washington Post,* May 5, 1981, p. B1; Henry Allen, "Pickets & Politics at the Second Battle of 'Inchon,'" *Washington Post,* May 5, 1981, pp. B1, B3; "Black Tie and Picket Signs at Premier of 'Inchon!,'" *Washington Star,* May 5, 1981, p. C1–2.

73. *Washington Times Magazine,* Sept. 17, 1982, p. 19. The *Washington Post* reported the next day that the *Times* had refused to run Scott Sublett's complete interview, Sept. 18, 1982, pp. C1, C4; instead the paper reprinted Vincent Candby's negative *New York* Times review, *Washington Times,* Sept. 21, 1982, p. 6A. The *Washington Post* ran a follow up article on Sept. 29, 1982, p. A22.

21. The Navy's Search for Normalcy

1. *Daily Variety,* Apr. 9, 1965, p. 2; Louella Parsons, "Zebra Has Navy Trouble," *Los Angeles Herald-Examiner,* Apr. 19, 1965; Howard Horton to Orville Crouch, June 2, 1965.

2. MGM "Facts Book for Editorial Reference," n.d. [1968].

3. *Variety,* Oct. 23, 1968.

4. PBS *Nova,* Jan. 25, 2000; Sherry Sontag and Christopher Drew, *Blind Man's Bluff* (New York: Harper Paperbacks, 1998), pp. 69, 76.

5. BCP to Donald Baruch, Feb. 12, 1973.

6. Baruch, memo for record, Mar. 15–16, 1973; Baruch, memo for record, July 25, 1973; Baruch, memo for record, Aug. 21, 1973.

7. Chief of information to Baruch, n.d. [mid-Aug. 1973].

8. Ibid.

9. Baruch, memo for record, Aug. 21, 1973; Frank Rosenberg to Navy Office of Information, Aug. 23, 1973; Navy chief of information to Baruch, Sept. 18, 1973; Baruch to Rosenberg, Sept. 20, 1973.

10. Rosenberg to Baruch, Nov. 7, 1974.

11. Ibid.

12. Norm Hatch to Navy, Nov. 12, 1974; Navy Office of Information to Baruch, Dec. 2, 1974; Baruch to Rosenberg, Dec. 4, 1974.

13. Bill Graves, interview by author, July 19, 1978; Robert Aldrich to Baruch, Nov. 4, 1975.

14. Aldrich to Baruch, Nov. 4, 1975.

15. Navy Operations Office to chief of information, Nov. 18, 1975.

16. Ibid.

17. Baruch to chief of information, Nov. 18, 1975.

18. Navy Office of Information to Baruch, Dec. 9, 1975.

19. Ibid.

20. Ibid.

21. Marvin Mirisch, telephone interview by author, Mar. 22, 1978.

22. Ibid.; John Horton to Baruch, Jan. 13, 1976.

23. Baruch to Marshall Green, Jan. 16, 1976.

24. Navy Office of Information, "Special News Items of Interest," Jan. 19, 1976; Baruch intraoffice memorandum, Jan. 20, 1976.

25. Navy memorandum for the record, Jan. 26, 1976; Marvin Mirisch interview.

26. Baruch, memos for the record, Jan. 28, 29, 1976.

27. Memorandum for the chief of information, May 10, 1976.

28. Navy memo for the chief of information, May 21, 1976.

29. David Cooney to Walter Mirisch, May 25, 1976.

30. Ibid.

31. Bill Graves to Cooney, June 15, 1976.

32. Ibid.

33. Assistant deputy chief of naval operations (Submarine Warfare) (OP-02B) to chief of information, July 15, 1976.

34. Cooney to Baruch, July 16, 1976.

35. Peter Greenberg conversation with Lt. Comdr. Mel Sundin and author at Pearl Harbor, June 15, 1983. Greenberg showed no interest in a story featuring an enlisted submariner in love with a female Navy officer, a plot on which the service might have reluctantly agreed to assist since such things did happen—certainly more often than the sinking of a nuclear submarine.

36. "TV Week," *Washington Post*, Mar. 1, 1986, p. 9.

37. Charles Champlin, "Delayed Horror in *Gray Lady*," Mar. 10, 1978.

38. Graves interview.

39. Richard Schickel, *Time*, Mar. 27, 1978, p. 81.

40. Ibid.

41. Gary Arnold, "*Gray Lady Down:* The Intrigue of Technology," *Washington Post*, Mar. 11, 1980, p. B8.

42. Don Baruch's comment on Adam Kennedy's *Raise the Titanic* screenplay, n.d. [June 1977]; Charles Schreger, "Preproduction: A Titanic Task," *Los Angeles Times*, Oct. 20, 1979, pt. 2, p. 6.

43. Bill Graves to Marble Arch Productions, Oct. 12, 1978.

44. Navy Office of Information to Baruch, May 16, 1979.

45. Baruch to Navy Office of Information, Oct. 2, 1979; Navy Office of Information to Baruch, Oct. 15, 1979.

46. George Bader for James Siena to Baruch, Oct. 17, 1979.

47. Baruch to Navy Office of Information, Oct. 19, 1979; Navy Office of Information to Baruch, Oct. 22, 1979.

48. Baruch to Department of State's Bureau of Public Affairs, Oct. 23, 1979.

49. State Department Office of Public Communication to Baruch, Oct. 24, 1979.

50. State Department Bureau of European Affairs to State Department Office of Public Communications, Oct. 24, 1979.

51. George Bader to Baruch, Oct. 29, 1979.

52. Baruch to Navy Office of Information, Oct. 31, 1979; Navy Office of Information to Baruch, Oct. 31, 1979.

53. Baruch to Navy Office of Information, Nov. 13, 1979.

54. Baruch to John Horton, Nov. 20, 1979.

55. Adm. David Cooney, interview by author, Apr. 2, 1981.

56. Ibid.

57. Richard O'Connor to Baruch, Aug. 20, 1980.

58. Ibid.; Richard O'Connor, interview by author, Aug. 7, 1981.

59. *Time*, Mar. 30, 1981, p. 71; *Daily Variety*, Aug. 1, 1980; Judy Maslin, *New York Times*, Aug. 1, 1980.

60. Baruch to Navy Office of Information, June 17, 1975; Thomas Hunter to Baruch, n.d. [summer 1975].

61. Navy Office of Information to Baruch, June 30, 1975; Baruch to Capt. C.D. Griffin, July 2, 1975; Griffin to Baruch, May 21, 1976.

62. Baruch to Griffin, June 3, 1976; Griffin to Baruch, Aug. 30, 1976.

63. Peter Douglas, interview by author, Aug. 3, 1981, Unless otherwise noted, all further information about Douglas's production of *The Final Countdown* comes from this interview. Although a small DoD file exists on "The Last Countdown," the Pentagon file on *The Final Countdown* was misplaced sometime after the release of the movie, probably during legal proceedings against the Navy technical advisor. The author did see the file and use it in writing about military cooperation with Hollywood in the post-Vietnam period.

64. Charles Champlin, "Launching a New Genre—Sea-Fi," *Los Angeles Times*, Aug. 1, 1980.

65. The author took this quote from the DoD *Final Countdown* file for a 1980 newspaper article, before the file disappeared.

66. *New York Times*, Aug. 4, 1980.

67. *Newsweek*, Aug. 18, 1980; *New York Times*, Aug. 4, 1980.

22. New Images Despite Themselves

1. Fuller interview; David Wilson, "The Best Known War Movie Never Made," "Calendar," *Los Angeles Times,* Jan. 22, 1978.

2. Ibid.; Joan Borsten, "*The Big Red One* in Israel," "Calendar," *Los Angeles Times,* Aug. 13, 1978.

3. Borsten, "*The Big Red One* in Israel."

4. David Ansen, *Newsweek,* July 28, 1980.

5. *Time,* July 21, 1980; Vincent Canby, "Three Years of War," *New York Times,* July 18, 1980.

6. Edward Morey to Don Baruch, July 31, 1979.

7. Baruch to Morey, Aug. 20, 1979.

8. Warner Brothers "Production Information" for *Private Benjamin,* n.d. [1980]; Wayne Warga, "Back to the Basics for Goldie Hawn," "Calendar," *Los Angeles Times,* Mar. 2, 1980, p. 30.

9. *Daily Variety,* Oct. 6, 1980.

10. Andrew Sarris, "Review," *Village Voice,* Nov. 5–11, 1980.

11. Ibid.

12. Charles Champlin, "The Script Went AWOL," *Los Angeles Times,* Oct. 10, 1980.

13. Ibid.

14. Ibid.

15. Vincent Canby, "Review," *New York Times,* Oct. 10, 1980.

16. *UCLA Daily Bruin,* Oct. 14, 1980, p. 15.

17. Dan Goldberg to Baruch, Aug. 14, 1979.

18. Goldberg to Baruch, Aug. 31, 1979.

19. Preliminary production information, Columbia Pictures, n.d. [1981].

20. Dennis Foley, memorandum for record, Aug. 15, 1980.

21. Ibid.

22. Richard Griffitts to Baruch, Aug. 28, 1980.

23. Dan Goldberg to Baruch, Sept. 5, 10, 1980.

24. Don Baruch, quoted in Joseph Gelmis, "The Movies and the Military," *Newsday,* June 8, 1986.

25. Baruch to Goldberg, Oct. 30, 1980.

26. Gelmis, "The Movies and the Military."

27. Capt. Barry Sprouse, "After Action Report," Jan. 22, 1981.

28. *Newsweek,* July 13, 1981.

29. Janet Maslin, "*Stripes,*" *New York Times,* June 26, 1981; *Time,* July 6, 1981.

30. Baruch to Tom Ross, May 16, 1980.

31. Stanley Jaffe to Baruch, May 14, 1980.

32. Ibid.; chief, Office of Public Affairs, National Guard Bureau, to Baruch, May 19, 1980.

33. Chief, Office of Public Affairs, National Guard Bureau, to Baruch, May 19, 1980.

34. Baruch to Jaffe, May 29, 1980.

35. Jaffe to Baruch, July 3, 1980.

36. Ibid.

37. Baruch to Office of Public Affairs, National Guard Bureau, July 8, 1980; Jaffe to Baruch, July 9, 1980; Joe Hanley, information paper on *Taps,* Dec. 15, 1981.

38. Joseph Hanley, information paper; Joseph Hanley, interview by author, Aug. 25, 1989.

39. Ibid.

40. Rex Reed, "*Taps* Loses the Battle—with Itself," *New York Post,* Dec. 1981, p. C23.

41. Vincent Canby, "Scott as General in Taps," *New York Times,* Dec. 9, 1981, sec. C, p. 28.

42. Joseph Hanley to the Army Office of Public Relations, Jan. 10, 1983.

43. Ibid.

44. John Horton to Baruch, Jan. 26, 1983.

45. Maj. Gen. Llyle Barker Jr. to Baruch, Feb. 8, 1983.

46. Baruch to Horton, Jan. 12, 1984; Rita Kempley, *Washington Post Weekend,* Mar. 16, 1984, p. 19; Vincent Canby, *New York Times,* Mar. 16, 1984.

23. The Air Force Seeks a Better Image

1. Bart Mills, "*Last Gleaming* of Admiral X—Overlay of a Crackup," "Calendar," *Los Angeles Times,* June 6, 1976, p. 36.

2. Ibid.

3. Ibid.

4. Ibid.

5. Richard Schickel, "Review," *Time*, Feb. 21, 1977.

6. Ibid.

7. Don Baruch, quoted in Gelmis, "The Movies and the Military."

8. John Horton to Warner Brothers, Jan. 22, 1980.

9. Robert Daley to DoD Public Affairs, Jan. 29, 1980.

10. AFAPA-West to SAF/PANB, Feb. 13, 1980.

11. Baruch to Daley, Mar. 21, 1980.

12. Baruch to Fritz Manes, May 21, 1982.

13. *Washington Times*, June 15, 1982, p. 2B.

14. Duncan Wilmore, interview by author, July 20, 1983; Horton to Baruch, June 22, 1981.

15. Horton to Baruch, June 22, 1981; "*Wargames*—Authenticity from the Source," MGM/UA Press Kit, 1983; Lee Grant, "*Wargames* Playground," "Calendar," *Los Angeles Times*, July 3, 1983, p. 14.

16. Horton to Baruch, June 22, 1981; Baruch's undated handwritten notes in DoD *Wargames* file [June 1983].

17. Baruch's undated handwritten notes in DoD *Wargames* file [June 1983].

18. Joint interview with Larry Lasker and Walter Parkes, Aug. 4, 1983.

19. Charles Mosmann to "Calendar," *Los Angeles Times*, July 17, 1983; Jeffrey Cotton to *Los Angeles Times*, July 10, 1983; Grant, "*Wargames* Playground."

20. Lasker-Parkes interview.

21. Wilmore interview.

22. Ibid.; Lt. Col. Donald Gilleland, interview by author, July 6, 1983.

23. Lasker-Parkes interview.

24. Letters to the Editor, "Calendar," *Los Angeles Times*, July 10, 1983.

25. Ibid., July 10, 17, 1983.

26. Wilmore interview; Lawrence Suid and Jack Curry, *USA Today*, Aug. 13, 1984, pp. D1–D2.

27. Ibid.; Jonathan Avnet to Donald Gilleland, Dec. 20, 1982, *Call to Glory* file.

28. Ibid.

29. Gilleland interview.

30. Lt. Col. Donald Gilleland to Brig. Gen. Richard Abel, Jan. 4, 1983.

31. Gilleland interview.

32. Baruch to the Air Force Public Affairs Office, June 2, 1983; M. Sgt. Rick Racquer, interview by author, Aug. 5, 1984.

33. Donald Baruch, interview by author, Aug. 5, 1984.

34. Gilleland interview; Suid and Curry, *USA Today*, Aug. 13, 1984, pp. D1–D2.

24. Vietnam: A More Moderate Approach

1. David Denby, "A Man of Honor," *New York*, Sept. 4, 1978, p. 88.

2. Ralph Blanchard to Donald Baruch, Feb. 18, 1977; Congressman Richard Tonry to Secretary of Defense Robert Brown, Feb. 10, 1977; Baruch to DoD director for management, Mar. 3, 1977.

3. Blanchard to Baruch, Mar. 2, 1977; Baruch to director for management, Mar. 3, 1977.

4. Maj. Gen. Guy Hairston Jr. to R. Adm. David Cooney, Mar. 10, 1977; Cooney to Baruch, Mar. 25, 1977.

5. Richard Freedman, "*Who'll Stop the Rain* Will Whet Appetites of Moviegoers," *Sunday Newark Star Ledger*, Aug. 27, 1978, p. 10.

6. Donna Morton to Baruch, Apr. 11, 1978; *More American Graffiti*, "Script Outline."

7. Lt. Col. Dennis Foley, interview by author, Aug. 5, 1981.

8. Ibid.

9. Ibid.

10. Ibid.

11. Ibid.

12. Ibid.

13. John Horton to Baruch, July 31, 1978.

14. Ibid.; Army Pubic Information Division to Baruch, Aug. 15, 1978; Baruch to Horton, Aug. 18, 1978.

15. Foley interview.

16. Annette Insdorf, "Issues of Moral Behavior in War," *New York Times*, Dec. 21, 1980, pp. 19–20

17. Ibid.

18. Ibid.

19. Joseph Hanley, interview by author, Aug. 25, 1989.

20. Ibid.

21. Ibid.; Vincent Canby, "Review," *New York Times*, Sept. 25, 1981, p. C20.

22. *Fullerton (Calif.) Daily News Tribune*, Oct. 23, 1981.

23. *UCLA Daily Bruin*, Sept. 29, 1981.

24. *Playboy*, Dec. 1981.

25. *Newsweek*, Oct. 5, 1981.

26. *New York*, Oct. 19, 1981.

27. Michael Sragow, "Review," *Rolling Stone*, Oct. 29, 1981.

28. Ibid.

29. Paul Hensler, interview by author, Aug. 8, 1981.

30. Donald Gilleland to author, Oct. 6, 1989.

31. Hensler interview.

32. Ibid.

33. Ibid.

34. Ibid.

35. Hensler interview; Wilmore interview.

36. Hensler interview.

37. Ibid.; Foley interview; Wilmore interview; Walt DeFaria, interview by author, Aug. 7, 1981; *Daily Variety*, Mar. 23, 1982.

38. Janet Maslin, *New York Times*, Dec. 3, 1982.

39. *Daily Variety*, Mar. 4, 1982, pp. 3, 6.

40. Horton to Baruch, Aug. 26, 1983.

41. Iain Smith to Baruch, Sept. 15, 1983.

42. Baruch to the director, East Asia and Pacific Region, Office of the Assistant Secretary of Defense for International Security Affairs, Sept. 21, 1983; Baruch to the Marine Corps Public Affairs Office, Oct. 4, 1983; DoD Office of Internal Security Affairs to Baruch, n.d. [Oct. 1983]; Pat Coulter to director of Marine Corps Public Affairs, Oct. 10, 1983.

43. Coulter to Marine Headquarters, Oct. 10, 1983.

44. Media Branch memo to director of Marine Corps Public Affairs, Oct. 12, 1983; Marine Corps routing sheet, Oct. 14, 1983; Smith to Baruch, Oct. 28, 1983; Horton to Baruch, Nov. 7, 1983.

45. Paul Attanasio, "The Powerful *Killing Fields*," *Washington Post*, Jan. 18, 1985, pp. C1, C6.

46. Oliver Stone, interview by author, Mar. 8, 1990. The director acknowledged that he had seen *Cease Fire* before filming *Platoon*.

47. *Variety*, July 8, 1985; Kevin Thomas, *Los Angeles Times*, Nov. 27, 1985, pt. 6, p. 6.

48. Dale Chute, *Los Angeles Herald-Examiner*, Dec. 4, 1985.

49. Robert Lindsey, "Coppola Returns to the Vietnam Era, Minus *Apocalypse*," *New York Times*, May 3, 1987, sec. 2, pp. 1, 34.

50. Ibid.

51. Horton to Baruch, May 21, 1986.

52. Department of Defense Force Management and Personnel Office to Baruch, Apr. 1, 1986; Army Office of Public Affairs to Baruch, Apr. 4, 1986.

53. Army Office of Public Affairs to Baruch, Apr. 4, 1986.

54. Francis Coppola to Maj. Gen. Charles Bussey, Apr. 7, 1986.

55. Ibid.

56. Army Public Affairs Office to Baruch, Apr. 15, 1986; Baruch to Horton, Apr. 17, 1986; Baruch to Robert Sims, May 12, 1986.

57. Lt. Col. John Meyers to Bussey; "*Gardens of Stone* After Action Report," n.d. [Aug. 1986]; Lindsey, "Coppola Returns to the Vietnam Era."

58. Michael Levy to Bussey, Aug. 4, 1986.

59. Bussey to Levy, Dec. 5, 1986.

60. "Comments/Suggestions," n.d. [Dec. 5, 1986].

61. Ibid.

62. Sims to Levy, Dec. 12, 1986.

63. Lindsey, "Coppola Returns to the Vietnam Era."

64. Hal Hinson, "*Gardens of Stone*: Rocky," *Washington Post*, May 8, 1987, pp. D1, D10.

65. Ibid., p. D10.

66. Ibid.

67. Vincent Canby, "*Gardens of Stone*," *New York Times*, May 8, 1987, p. 20.

68. Ibid.

69. *Hartford Courant,* Sept. 11, 1988.

70. Ibid.

71. Naomi Foner, interview by author, Feb. 8, 1989.

72. Ibid.; Peter Kerr, "Campus Radicals Count the Cost of Commitment," *New York Times,* Sept. 4, 1988, sec. 2, p. l.

73. Kerr, "Campus Radicals Count the Cost."

74. Charles Champlin, "The Fullness of *Running on Empty,*" *Los Angeles Times,* Sept. 29, 1988.

75. Ibid.

25. Rehabilitation Completed

1. Dennis Anstine, "Paramount Film Doesn't 'Reflect Navy's Mission,'" *Port Townsend (Washington) Leader,* Apr. 22, 1981, p. A-1; memorandum for the record, July 16, 1980.

2. Navy Office of Information to Don Baruch, July 18, 1980, and Baruch's undated handwritten notations on memo.

3. Baruch to chief, Production Services Division, CHINFO, memo, Aug. 7, 1980.

4. Navy Office of Information memo for deputy chief of information, Dec. 12, 1980; draft memo to Baruch, n.d. [Dec. 12, 1980].

5. Navy Office of Information to Baruch, memo, n.d. [Jan. 1981], on which Baruch recorded his recollection of meeting, n.d. [after Jan. 13, 1981].

6. Navy chief of information to Pensacola Naval Air Station, Jan. 29, 1981.

7. Pat Coulter to Marine Corps Public Affairs Office, Feb. 20, 1981; Coulter to Public Affairs Office, Mar. 21, 1981.

8. J.L. Schilling to director of Public Affairs, n.d. [after Mar. 21, 1981].

9. Baruch to Col. Robert O'Brien on *An Officer and a Gentleman,* July 30, 1982; Coulter, Combat Correspondents Convention, Sept. 28, 1982.

10. Chris Bauman, interview by author, Aug. 24, 1988; Coulter interview, Jan. 26, 1989.

11. Coulter interview, Jan. 26, 1989; Coulter to commandant of the Marines, July 27, 1982.

12. Bob Williams to Coulter, Feb. 19, 1981; Coulter interview, Jan. 26, 1989.

13. Coulter interview, Aug. 8, 1981; Coulter made virtually the same comment to the audience at the Marine Combat Correspondents Convention in 1982 (see note 8).

14. Coulter interview, Jan. 26, 1989.

15. Ibid.

16. Coulter interview, Aug. 8, 1981; Coulter to Marine Corps director of public affairs, July 22, 1981; Gen. H.T. Kerr, director of public affairs, to General Cooper, Apr. 27, 1981.

17. Judy Klemesrud, "Earning Sergeant's Stripes for a Movie Role," *New York Times,* July 25, 1982. David E. Early, "Lou Gossett Drills Reality into Acting," *New York Daily News,* Aug. 20, 1982, p. 91, syndicated in other newspapers in slightly revised form.

18. Ibid.; J.T. Hagen, director of Marine Corps public affairs, to commandant of the Marine Corps, June 27, 1982; Kerr to Cooper, Apr. 27, 1981.

19. Sgt. T.W. Lyman, "Marine's Expertise Creates Hit Movie," *Marine,* n.d. [1983], p. 26; Coulter interview, Jan. 26, 1989.

20. Early, "Lou Gossett Drills Reality"; Klemesrud, "Earning Sergeant's Stripes"; Taylor Hackford, interview by author, Aug. 7, 1981.

21. Early, "Lou Gossett Drills Reality."

22. Undated, unaddressed handwritten internal Marine memo, n.d. [after July 21, 1982].

23. Klemesrud, "Earning Sergeant's Stripes."

24. Richard Cohen, "Brutality Wrong Tool for Making a Man," *Los Angeles Times,* Sept. 8, 1982.

25. Richard Bell Jr. to Pres. Ronald Reagan, Aug. 17, 1982.

26. Coulter to Marine director of public affairs, July 22, 1982; Baruch to Col. Robert O'Brien, July 30, 1982.

27. Michele Casale, director, Pennsylvania Bureau of Motion Picture and Television Development, to Navy chief of information, June 20, 1983; Doug Curtis to Navy chief of information, June 27, 1983.

28. Dale Patterson to Baruch, Aug. 22, 1983.

29. Baruch to Curtis, Aug. 26, 1983.

30. Curtis to Navy chief of information, June 27, 1983.

31. Air Force Office of Information to Office of Public Affairs, National Guard Bureau, May 3, 1976.

32. Office of Naval Research, "Information Sheet, Philadelphia Experiment; UFO's [*sic*]," n.d.; the Naval Historical Center Library, in the Washington Navy Yard, has an extensive file on the "Philadelphia Experiment," which refutes the story that the Navy performed any experiments of the nature described in Moore's book.

33. Les Paul Robey, "Flying High with *Top Gun*," *American Cinematographer*, May 1986, p. 50; Ehud Yonay, "Top Guns," *California Magazine*, May 1983, p. 95.

34. Don Simpson and Jerry Bruckheimer, joint interview by author, Feb. 6, 1989. The men spoke as one voice unless otherwise indicated.

35. Ibid.; Iain Blair, "Team behind *Top Gun* Brings Back Creative Producing," *Chicago Tribune*, "Arts," May 11, 1986, sec. 13, p. 2.

36. Simpson-Bruckheimer interview.

37. Bauman interview, Aug. 24, 1988; Capt. Michael Sherman, interviews by author, Mar. 7, 1990; Aug. 30, 1993.

38. Ibid.

39. Simpson-Bruckheimer interview; ABC *20/20*, Mar. 26, 1987; Don Simpson and Jerry Bruckheimer to Baruch, June 14, 1983; Jack Garrow, interview by author, Apr. 18, 1990.

40. John Horton to Baruch, June 10, 1983.

41. Horton to Baruch, Nov. 15, 1984.

42. Horton to Bruckheimer, Nov. 29, 1984.

43. Baruch to Horton, May 8, 1985.

44. Simpson-Bruckheimer interview.

45. Ibid.

46. Ibid.

47. Ibid.

48. Ibid.

49. *Commonweal*, June 20, 1986.

50. David Ansen, "Macho Myth-Making," *Newsweek*, May 19, 1986.

51. J. Hoberman, "Phallus in Wonderland," *Village Voice*, May 27, 1986, p. 59.

52. Ibid.; Alexander Cockburn, "The Selling of the Pentagon," *American Film*, June 1986, p. 52.

53. Hoberman, "Phallus in Wonderland."

54. "*Top Gun*" Press Book, Paramount Pictures; Richard Halloran, "Guardians of the Screen Image," *New York Times*, Aug. 18, 1986, p. 12.

55. Interview in *Playboy*, Dec. 1989.

56. Barry London, interview by author, Feb. 1, 1989.

57. Ibid.

58. *Washington Post*, July 16, 1986.

59. "Tailhook 91 Report," Apr. 1992, pt. 2, X-2, in "Tailhook" file, Suid Collection; Donald Mancuso, interview by author, July 20, 1994.

60. "Tailhook 91 Report."

26. Vietnam: Full Color with All the Warts

1. Rick Nankin, interview by author, Dec. 14, 1988.

2. A. Kitman Ho to Donald Baruch, June 19, 1984.

3. Army Office of Public Affairs to Baruch, June 28, 1984.

4. Baruch to Ho, July 5, 1984.

5. ABC Television News, *20/20*, Mar. 26, 1987, cited hereafter as *20/20*. The author also appeared in the feature as a consultant about the Hollywood-military relationship.

6. Ibid.

7. ABC Television News, *Nightline*, Dec. 19, 1986.

8. *20/20*.

9. *Nightline*, Dec. 19, 1986; Peter Blauner, "*Platoon*," *Time Out*, Apr. 1, 1987.

10. In an article about *Platoon*, *Time* magazine gave a 2.7 million figure, whereas Stone used 4 million as the total number of Americans who went to Vietnam. Oliver Stone, *Oliver Stone's Platoon and Salvador: The Screenplays* (London: Ebury Press, 1985), p. 12.

11. Stephan Salisbury, "Stone Rode Realism to Crest of New Wave of Vietnam Films," *Long Beach Press Telegram*, Jan. 6, 1987.

12. Ibid.

13. *20/20*.

14. Roger Ebert, "Film Clip: Oliver Stone," *Roger Ebert's Movie Home Companion* (New York: Andrews, McBeel, and Parker, 1988), pp. 433–34.

15. Ibid.

16. Capt. Michael Decker and Col. James Jeffries, "*Platoon*—The Movie and Law of War Training," *Marine Corps Gazette,* Apr. 1987, p. 40.

17. Ibid.

18. Ibid.

19. Ibid.

20. Gen. Leonard Fribourg to author, Oct. 10, 1989.

21. Vincent Canby, "The Vietnam War in Stone's *Platoon,*" *New York Times,* Dec. 19, 1986.

22. Ibid.

23. Ibid.

24. Ibid.

25. Paul Attanasio, "*Platoon*'s Raw Mastery," *Washington Post,* Jan. 16, 1987.

26. Ibid.

27. Ibid.

28. Richard Corliss, "A Document Written in Blood," *Time,* Dec. 15, 1986, p. 83.

29. Ibid.

30. *Daily Variety,* Dec. 2, 1986, p. 3.

31. John Simon, "Found in the Mud," *National Review,* Mar. 13, 1987.

32. Ibid.

33. Ibid.

34. John Podhoretz, "*Platoon* Sullies Vietnam Veterans," *Washington Times Insight,* Jan. 19, 1987, p. 65.

35. Ibid.

36. Neil Sheehan, *A Bright Shining Lie* (New York: Random House, 1988), pp. 211–65, 269–83.

37. "Letters," *Washington Times Insight,* Feb. 16, 1987.

38. "Calendar," *Los Angeles Times,* Jan. 25, 1987.

39. "Letters Annex," "Calendar," *Los Angeles Times,* Feb. 2, 1987, p. 16.

40. Ibid.

41. *Cosmopolitan,* Dec. 1988, p. 132.

42. Baruch to Stephen Dart, Aug. 11, 1976; Dart to Baruch, Nov. 2, 1978.

43. Air Force memo for record, Oct. 3, 1978; Dart to Air Force Los Angeles Office of Information, Nov. 2, 1978.

44. Donald Burggrabe to Dart, Nov. 8, 1978; Dart to Burggrabe, Jan. 25, 1979; Burggrabe to Air Force Public Information Office, Jan. 29, 1979.

45. Air Force Office of Information to Baruch, Feb. 22, 1979; Penny Williamson to Art Brill, Feb. 26, 1979; David Cooney to Baruch, Apr. 17, 1979.

46. Col. Frederick Kiley to Baruch, Mar. 13, 1979.

47. Baruch to Dart, Apr. 30, 1979.

48. Martin Grove, "Hollywood Report," *Hollywood Reporter,* Mar. 13, 1987; Lionel Chetwynd, interviews by author, Feb. 3, 1989; Mar. 7, 1990.

49. Ibid.

50. Grove, "Hollywood Report."

51. Ibid.

52. Grove, "Hollywood Report."

53. James Herbert to Baruch, Sept. 12, 1986.

54. Roderick Mann, "The Vietnam Experience . . . Minus the *Rambos,*" "Calendar," *Los Angeles Times,* Nov. 9, 1986.

55. Baruch to Cannon Films, Mar. 17, 1987.

56. Bruce Williamson, "Movies," *Playboy,* June 1987, p. 17.

57. Diana West, "Unwelcome Chronicle of a Prison in Hanoi," *Insight,* June 8, 1987.

58. Richard Schickel, "Remembering Viet Nam," *Time,* Apr. 13, 1987, p. 78.

59. Tom Matthews, "*Hanoi Hilton,*" *Boxoffice,* July 1987, p. R-66.

60. Vincent Canby, "The Hanoi Hilton," *New York Times,* Mar. 27, 1987.

61. Stanley Kauffman, "Hanoi and Elsewhere," *New Republic,* Apr. 27, 1987.

62. West, "Unwelcome Chronicle," p. ll; Ralph Novak, "*The Hanoi Hilton,*" *People,* Apr. 20, 1987; David Denby, "Flea-bagged," *New York,* Apr. 13, 1987, p. 90.

63. West, "Unwelcome Chronicle."

64. Kauffmann, "Hanoi and Elsewhere."

65. West, "Unwelcome Chronicle"; "Letters," *Insight,* July 6, 1987, p. 4.

66. Kauffman, "Hanoi and Elsewhere"; West, "Unwelcome Chronicle."

67. Chetwynd interview, Feb. 3, 1989.

68. Lloyd Grove, "Stanley Kubrick, at a Distance," *Washington Post,* June 28, 1987, pp. F1, F5.

69. Francis X. Clines, "Stanley Kubrick's Vietnam," *New York Times,* June 21, 1987, sec. 2, p. 34; Grove, "Stanley Kubrick," F5.

70. Grove, "Stanley Kubrick."

71. Ibid.; Fred Peck, interview by author, Aug. 16, 1988; Lee Ermey, interview by author, Jan. 4, 1989.

72. Grove, "Stanley Kubrick."

73. Ibid.; "Tanks for the Memories," *Los Angeles Times,* Apr. 12, 1987.

74. Harry Lange, interview by author, Mar. 24, 1987.

75. Vincent Canby, "Kubrick's *Full Metal Jacket,*" *New York Times,* June 26, 1987, p. C3.

76. Ibid.

77. Ibid.

78. John Powers, *Los Angeles Weekly,* June 26, 1987.

79. Peter Rainer, "*Full Metal Jacket:* Apocalypse Then," *Los Angeles Herald-Examiner,* July 26, 1987, p. 6.

80. Richard Corliss, "Welcome to Viet Nam, the Movie: II," *Time,* June 29, 1987, p. 66.

81. Ibid.

82. Ibid.

83. Ibid.

84. F.X. Feeney, "Review," *Movieline,* July 10, 1987.

85. Corliss, "Welcome to Viet Nam, the Movie: II."

86. Soren Andeson, "Battle of *Hamburger Hill,*" *(Long Beach, Calif.) Press-Telegram,* Aug. 23, 1987, p. H-4.

87. Ibid.

88. Ibid.

89. Ibid.

90. Ibid.; Jay Sharbutt, "Proposed Vietnam Film: A Real Battle Written by a Veteran," *Los Angeles Times,* Feb. 9, 198 5, pt. 5, pp. 10–11.

91. Ibid.

92. Lawrence Van Gelder, "Remembering Vietnam," *New York Times,* Aug. 28, 1987, p. C6.

93. Ibid.; Susan King, "John Irwin Climbed Mountains to Do 'Hill,'" *L.A. Herald-Examiner,* Aug. 23, 1987.

94. Army to Baruch, Aug. 7, 1985.

95. Baruch to Mark Seiler, Aug. 22, 1985.

96. Ibid.

97. Larry De Waay to Department of the Army, June 25, 1986.

98. Army to Baruch, July 2, 8, 1986.

99. Gen. C.D. Bussey to Baruch, May 21, 1987.

100. Ibid.

101. Van Gelder, *New York Times,* Aug. 28, 1987, p. C6.; Bruce Cook, "Documentary Skills Helped Director Climb "Hamburger Hill," *L.A. Life,* Aug. 30, 1987, p. 29.

102. Vincent Canby, "*Hamburger Hill,*" *New York Times,* Aug. 28, 1987, p. C16.

103. Ibid.

104. Kevin Thomas, "*Hamburger Hill,*" *Los Angeles Times,* Aug. 28, 1987.

105. Letter in the *Los Angeles Times,* Sept. 5, 1987.

27. Vietnam: Balanced Portrayals

1. *Good Morning, Vietnam* Press Kit; *Newsweek,* Jan. 4, 1988, p. 50; Barry Levinson on "Saturday Night with Connie Chung," Nov. 11, 1989.

2. Gen. Edwin Simmons on "Saturday Night with Connie Chung," Nov. 11, 1989; Adrian Cronauer, interview by author, Mar. 4, 1988; *Hollywood Reporter,* Dec. 30, 1987.

3. Richard Schickel, "Motormouth in Saigon," *Time,* Dec. 28, 1987, p. 74.

4. The author has written a history of Armed Forces Radio and Television, in which he discusses at length the operation of AFVN; Lawrence Suid, *History of AFRTS: The First 50 Years* (Washington, D.C.: GPO, 1992), chapters 20 and 21; *Hollywood Reporter,* Dec. 30, 1987; Cronauer interview.

5. *Good Morning, Vietnam* Press Kit; no record exists to show that either the Pentagon or the American Forces Information Service received a script or a request for assistance.

6. *Daily Variety,* Dec. 15, 1987.

7. Lt. Col. William Anderson, "Selling a Military Picture to Hollywood," *Retired Officer,* Aug. 1988, pp. 46–48.

8. Air Force Public Affairs Office to Donald Baruch, Mar. 5, 1984; Baruch to Hanna Productions, n.d. [Mar. 1984].

9. Air Force Public Affairs Office to Baruch, June 7, 1987.

10. Air Force Los Angeles Public Affairs Office to Michael Balson, Jan. 15, 1988; Air Force Office of Public Affairs to Baruch, Mar. 29, 1988.

11. Rita Kempley, "*Bat 21:* Vietnam Brought Down to Earth," *Washington Post,* Oct. 2, 1988, pp. D1, D7.

12. *Daily Variety,* June 15, 1988.

13. Donald Baruch, interview by author, Dec. 18, 1989; Peter Hyams, interview by author, Feb. 2, 1989.

14. *Variety,* June 10, 1988; Michael Wilmington, "*The Presidio,*" *Los Angeles Times,* June 10, 1988, pt. 6, p. 31.

15. Bruce Weber, "Cool Head, Hot Images," *New York Times Magazine,* May 21, 1989, p. 117; Michael Norman, "Brian De Palma Explores Vietnam and Its Victims," *New York Times,* Aug. 13, 1989, sec. 2, p. 13.

16. Columbia Pictures Press Kit, n.d. [1989].

17. *Daily Variety,* Aug. 24, 1989; *New York Times,* Aug. 24, 1989.

18. Ibid.

19. Stanley Karnow, *Vietnam, a History* (New York: Viking Press, 1983), pp. 600–601; David Halberstam, "Law of the Jungle," *Elle,* Sept. 1983, p. 140.

20. Halberstam, "Law of the Jungle," p. 140.

21. Ibid.

22. Ibid., p. 142.

23. Oliver Stone, interview by author, Mar. 6, 1990; the actual wrestling coach did not appreciate the honor Stone intended to give him, refusing permission to use his name: "I'm not that type of person."

24. Ibid.; although the author had sent Stone the Pentagon's approval of cooperation on the 1979 script, the director refused to believe it: "I didn't know about that. They gave approval to the original version? They did. That is amazing." When told that had been his reaction in 1981, he laughed: "I still don't believe it!"

25. Oliver Stone, interviews by author, Aug. 3, 1981; Mar. 6, 1990.

26. Stone interview, Aug. 3, 1981.

27. Ibid.

28. Ibid.

29. Ibid.

30. Tom Cruise, interview by *Playboy,* Dec. 1989.

31. Ibid.

32. Ibid.

33. Stone interview, Mar. 6, 1990.

34. Ibid.

35. Kovic, *Born on the Fourth of July;* Diana West, "Does *Born on the Fourth of July* Lie?" *Washington Times,* Feb. 23, 1990, pp. E1, E-8, cited hereafter as West, *Washington Times.*

36. Stone interview, Mar. 6, 1990.

37. Ron Kovic, *Born on the Fourth of July,* pp. 120–21; West, "Does *Born on the Fourth of July* Lie?"

38. Nich Ravo, "*Fourth of July* Unfair to Syracuse Police, Some Residents Say," *New York Times,* Jan. 15, 1990.

39. Guy Flatley, *Cosmopolitan,* Dec. 1989; Mike McGrady, *Newsday,* Dec. 20, 1989; Vincent Canby, *New York Times,* Dec. 20, 1989, p. C15.

40. Mace Neufeld, interview by author, March 14, 1990.

41. Ibid.

42. John Horton to Baruch, Apr. 10, 1989.

43. Mike Sherman to Navy Office of Information, May 2, 1989.

44. Ibid.; Sherman to chief of information, May 16, 1989.

45. Sherman to chief of information, May 16, 1989.

46. Assistant chief of Naval Operations (Air Warfare) to chief of information, May 26, 1989.

47. J.B. Finkelstein to Phil Strub, June 22, 1989; Strub to chief of information, June 23, 1989; Sherman to Lance Young, June 27, 1989; Neufeld interview.

48. Neufeld interview; Milius interview.

49. Milius interview; James Farmer, "Making *Flight of the Intruder,*" *Air Classics,* Aug. 1990. In a lengthy article, Farmer details the filming of the aerial sequences in Georgia, Hawaii, and aboard the USS *Independence,* as well as at Paramount Studios. Other sources for the discussion of Navy cooperation include a memo from the chief of naval operations to various commands about the assistance being provided to the film, n.d. [after Sept. 2, 1989]; Penny Smith, "On Location: *Flight of the Intruder,*" *Hollywood Reporter,* 1989, Hawaii Special Report, Nov. 21, 1989, pp. S-8–S-9; Lt. Comdr. R.O. McHurg, *Hook,* summer 1990; Ralph Rugoff, "It's Not Just an Adventure, It's a Job," *Premiere,* Aug. 1990; *Daily Variety,* Nov. 6, 1989. Unless otherwise cited, the discussion is based on a synthesis of all these sources.

50. *Daily Variety,* Jan. 18, 1991.

51. Desmond Ryan, "Misguided Missile," *Long Beach Press-Telegram,* Jan. 18, 1991.

52. Ibid.

53. Ibid.; Peter Rainer, "*Flight of the Intruder* Takes to the Air at the Right Time," *Los Angeles Times,* Jan. 18, 1991, p. F12.

54. Rainer, "*Flight of the Intruder.*"

55. Sherman interview, Aug. 30, 1993.

28. The Cold War Ends on the Motion Picture Screen

1. John Horton to Donald Baruch, Dec. 2, 1985; Harve Bennett to Horton, Dec. 18, 1985.

2. Bennett to Horton, Dec. 18, 1985.

3. Ibid.

4. Director, Production Services Division, to Baruch, Feb. 7, 1986.

5. Bennett to Baruch, Feb. 14, 1986; "*Star Trek IV*" Press Kit.

6. Neufeld interview.

7. Baruch interview, Dec. 18, 1989; three or four short scenes, including two on the A Ring, or innermost, corridor, were clearly filmed in the Pentagon.

8. Neufeld explained that he had to use the Baltimore subway because Washington transit officials did not want "chases or anything resembling violence shown in its subway."

9. Fritz Manes to Baruch, Apr. 1, 1985.

10. Baruch to Michael Burch, Apr. 22, 1985.

11. Ibid.

12. Ibid.

13. *Los Angeles Times,* Apr. 25, 1985.

14. Army Public Affairs to Baruch, Dec. 16, 1985.

15. Ibid.

16. Ibid.

17. Ibid.

18. Ibid.

19. Clint Eastwood to Maj. Gen. Charles Bussey, Dec. 17, 1985.

20. Ibid.

21. Gen. Richard Griffitts to Eastwood, Dec. 23, 1985.

22. Baruch to assistant secretary of defense for public affairs, Apr. 23, 1986; Manes to Baruch, Mar. 14, 1986.

23. Baruch to Robert Sims, Mar. 21, 1986.

24. Brig. Gen. D.E.P. Miller to Baruch, Apr. 18, 1986.

25. Baruch to Sims, Apr. 23, 1986.

26. Ibid.

27. Navy Office of Information to Baruch, Apr. 24, 1986; DoD Office of Force Management and Personnel to Baruch, Apr. 28, 1986.

28. Headquarters Marine Corps routing sheet, Apr. 29, 1986.

29. Force Management and Personnel Policy Office to Baruch, Apr. 29, 1986.

30. Gen. Edwin Simmons to Marine Corps Public Affairs Office, forwarded to Baruch, Apr. 30, 1986.

31. Sims to Miller, May 5, 1986.

32. Ibid.

33. Marine Corps memorandum to Baruch, n.d. [Apr. 1986]; Baruch to Marine Corps Office of Public Affairs, Apr. 25, 1986.

34. Robert Sims, interview by author, Feb. 11, 1990.

35. Eastwood to Sims, May 9, 1989.

36. Sims to Eastwood, May 12, 1986.

37. Baruch to Sims, May 16, 1986.

38. Sims to Marine Corps director of public affairs, May 16, 1986.

39. Brig. Gen. W.E. Boomer to Sims, July 28, 1986.

40. Ibid.; Capt. Nancy Laluntas to ASD(PA), July 23, 1986.

41. Boomer to Sims, July 28, 1986.

42. Ibid.

43. Gen. P.X. Kelley to Eastwood, July 31, 1986.

44. Baruch to Manes, Sept. 5, 1986; Sims to director of Marine Corps public affairs, Sept. 12, 1986.

45. Fred Peck to director of Marine public affairs, Sept. 18, 1986.

46. Sims to Manes, n.d. [Nov. 17 or 18, 1986].

47. Sims to Eastwood, n.d. [Nov. 18, 1988].

48. Col. Fred Peck, interview by author, Aug. 22, 1988.

49. Ibid.

50. Eastwood to Sims, Nov. 18, 1986, with copies to Pres. Ronald Reagan and Secretary of Defense Casper Weinberger.

51. Ibid.

52. Vincent Canby, "Film: Clint Eastwood in *Heartbreak Ridge,*" *New York Times,* Dec. 5, 1986, p. C3.

53. William Honan, "Can the Cold War Be a Hot Topic for a Movie?" *New York Times,* Feb. 25, 1990, sec. 2, p. 15.

54. Ibid.

55. *Time,* Mar. 12, 1990, p. 81; *Washington Post,* Mar. 19, 1990, p. A28; *Parade,* June 24, 1990, p. 2.

56. Ibid.

57. *Village View,* Mar. 2–8, 1990, p. 19; Milius interview.

58. Larry Ferguson, interview by author, Mar. 6, 1990; Milius interview; Neufeld interview.

59. Milius interview.

60. *Washington Post,* Mar. 17, 1989, p. D7.

61. *Daily Variety,* May 29, 1985, pp. 1, 18; *Hollywood Reporter,* July 3, 1985, pp. 1, 12.

62. *Daily Variety,* May 29, 1985, p. 1; Neufeld interview; "Calendar," *Los Angeles Times,* Sept. 21, 1988, pt. 6, p. 1.

63. Neufeld interview; "Calendar," *Los Angeles Times,* Sept. 21, 1988, pt. 6, p. 1.

64. *Los Angeles Times,* Nov, 8, 1987.

65. Horton to Baruch, Feb. 19, 1987.

66. "Calendar," *Los Angeles Times,* Sept. 21, 1988, pt. 6, p. 1; Horton to Baruch, Nov. 23, 1988.

67. Jim Stewart, "Navy Goes Hollywood," *(Long Beach, Calif.) Press-Telegram,* Mar. 3, 1990.

68. Neufeld interview; *Los Angeles Times,* June l, 1986.

69. Chief of information to Baruch, Dec. 12, 1988.

70. Ibid.

71. Captain Sherman, memorandum for the record, Dec. 15, 1988.

72. John McTiernan to Mike Sherman, Dec. 20, 1988].

73. Ibid.

74. Sherman to the chief of information, after Dec. 20, 1988; Baruch to chief of information, Dec. 27, 1988; Sherman's letter is dated Dec. 12, 1988. However, he had not received McTiernan's letter until Dec. 20. Baruch gives a December 20 date in his memorandum, but Sherman's memorandum has a fax date of Dec. 22.

75. Patton, "The Making of *Hunt for Red October,*" *Naval Institute Proceedings,* Jan. 1990, pp. 10–11.

76. Ibid.; "The Shoot of *Red October,*" *Washington Post,* Mar. 17, 1989, p. D7.

77. Ibid.; Navy chief of information to CINCLANTFLT, Norfolk, Feb. 28, 1989; *(Long Beach, Calif.) Press-Telegram,* Mar. 3, 1990, p. C-3; Neufeld interview.

78. Cathryn Donohoe, "Navy Action Starring Real McCoy," *Insight,* Mar. 26, 1990, p. 55.

79. *Washington Post,* Mar. 9, 1990, p. D7 ; David Ansen, *Newsweek,* Mar. 5, 1990, p. 63.

80. Hal Hinson, "*Red October,* Full Speed Astern," *Washington Post,* Mar. 2, 1990, pp. Dl, D7.

81. Vincent Canby, *New York Times,* Mar. 2, 1990, p. C13.

82. Neufeld interview.

83. Honan, "Can the Cold War Be a Hot Topic for a Movie?" p. 18.

84. Ibid.

85. *Los Angeles Times,* Mar. 23, 1990, p. F-4.

86. No record exists of the filmmakers' requesting Army assistance on the production.

87. Janet Maslin, *New York Times,* Mar. 24, 1990, p. G16; Hal Hinson, *Washington Post,* Mar. 26, 1990, p. B2.

88. No record exists in DoD files to show that the filmmakers ever contacted the Air Force for assistance; the service undoubtedly would have refused to provide assistance for any film portraying the breakdown of the command-and-control system for nuclear weapons, just as it had refused to cooperate on *Wargames.*

29. The Search for New Enemies

1. Lt. Col. Mitch Marovitz, interviews by author, Aug. 4, 2000, and Dec. 18, 2000.

2. John Horton to Phil Strub, June 21, 1993; Lt. Col. Jerry Broeckert to commanding general, Marine Corps Recru it Depot, Parris Island, Aug. 5, 1993.

3. Mitchell Marovitz to Strub, June 29, 1993.

4. Strub to Charles Newirth, July 7, 1993.

5. Marovitz interview; undated discussion about film with Phil Strub; Charles Newirth to Strub, July 15, 1993.

6. Marovitz interviews, Aug. 4, 2000, and Dec. 18, 2000.

7. Ibid.

8. Ibid.

9. Marovitz interview, Dec. 18, 2000.

10. Ibid.

11. *People,* Aug. 22, 1994.

12. *In the Army* Press Kit, n.d. [Aug. 1994].

13. Ibid.

14. Ibid.; Thomas McCollum, "*In the Army,* After-Action Report," attached to memorandum for the Army chief of public affairs and Strub, Nov. 15, 1994.

15. Marovitz to chief of public affairs of the Army, Feb. 22, 1994; Strub to Marovitz, Feb. 23, 1994; Strub to Hollywood Pictures, Feb. 23, 1994; Production Assistance Agreement No. SAPA-LA 003-94, attachment to letter of Mar. 8, 1994 from Hollywood Pictures to Capt. Thomas McCollum.

16. Ibid.

17. Desson Howe, *Washington Post,* Aug. 12, 1994.

18. *Renaissance Man* Press Book, n.d. [June 1995].

19. Ibid.

20. Ibid.

21. Ibid.

22. Hall Hinson, *Washington Post,* June 3, 1994.

23. Roger Ebert, *Chicago Sun-Times,* June 3, 1994.

24. *Sergeant Bilko* Press Kit, n.d. [1996].

25. Ibid.

26. *Daily Variety,* Mar. 29, 1996; *Hollywood Reporter,* March 29, 1996; Anthony Lane, *New Yorker,* Apr. 8, 1996; Kenneth Turan, *Los Angeles Times,* Mar. 29, 1996.

27. Informal conversation with Chas. Henry, Nov. 16, 2000; Fred Peck to author, Nov. 16, 2000.

28. "Army Points of Concern," *Independence Day,* Apr. 10, 1995.

29. Ibid.

30. Nancy LaLuntas to Strub, Apr. 24, 1995.

31. Dean Devlin to Strub, May 8, 1995.

32. Ibid.

33. Ibid.

34. Undated, unsigned "Talking Points" on *Independence Day* script of May 5, 1995.

35. Ibid.; author's unrecorded conversation with Phil Strub, Jan. 2000, about the key films of the 1990s.

36. Dustin Salem to Bill Fay, May 15, 1995, with attachment of the same date.

37. Diana Romo, story coordinator, *Inside Edition,* to Maj. Mary Feltault, Air Force Public Affairs, Dec. 14, 1995, with undated Twentieth Century Fox statement.

38. Ibid.

39. Undated conversation with Phil Strub, who stressed that the primary problem from his perspective was the devastating defeats the military suffered.

40. *Daily Variety,* Aug. 15, 1995; "Summer Slate," *Hollywood Reporter,* May 31, 1996; Steve Pond, "Alien Nation," *Premiere,* Aug. 1996.

41. Benjamin Frazier to Strub, thru Army chief of public affairs, Sept. 17, 1996; Army and Department of Defense comments, July 22, 1997.

42. Army and Department of Defense comments, *Deep Impact,* July 22, 1997.

43. Ibid.

44. Richard Zanuck to Katherine Ross, Sept. 9, 1997; Strub to Zanuck, Oct. 6, 1997.

45. Peter Tobyansen to Thomas Field, Dec. 19, 1997.

46. Ibid.

47. Field to Joan Bradshaw, executive producer of *Deep Impact,* Apr. 15, 1998.

48. Mike Sherman to chief of information, May 30, 1989.

49. Ibid.

50. Ibid.

51. Ibid.

52. Adm. J.B. Finkelstein to Strub, June 20, 1989; Strub to Finkelstein, June 20, 1989; Sherman to Mike Medavoy, Orion Pictures, June 27, 1989.

53. Navy Seal Production to Navy Office of Information, Los Angeles, Sept. 1, 1989; Strub to Navy Office of Information, Sept. 19, 1989.

54. Navy chief of information to commander in chief, Atlantic Fleet, Norfolk, memo, Sept. 26, 1989; Strub to chief of information, Oct. 2, 1989; David Scheiderer, "This Screenwriter Trained the 'Navy SEALS' Way," *Los Angeles Times,* Aug. 6, 1990, p. F6.

55. Peter Rainer, "*Navy SEALS:* It's Dirty Dozen with Flippers," *Los Angeles Times,* July 20, 1990, p. F18; *Chicago Sun-Times,* July 20, 1990, p. 35; *New York Times,* July 20, 1990, p. C9.

56. Gen. T.V. Draude, memorandum for the record, n.d. [Sept. 17, 1991].

57. Ibid.

58. Ibid.

59. Ibid.

60. Draft letter of Capt. Mike Sherman to Jeff Stott, Sept. 6, 1991.

61. Draude, memorandum for the record, Sept. 17 1991; Strub, memorandum for record, Sept. 19, 1991.

62. Gen. Tom Draude, interview by author, May 18, 1993.

63. Draude, memorandum for the record, Sept. 18, 1991.

64. Strub, memorandum for the record, Sept. 19, 1991.

65. Strub to Jeff Stott, Oct. 2, 1991.

66. Ibid.

67. Maj. Lewis Bumbgardner, a Marine Corps attorney, interview by author, Feb. 15, 1993.

68. Ibid.

69. Stephanie Austin to Strub, May 20, 1993.

70. J.M. Shotwell to Strub, June 14, 1993.

71. Strub to Austin, June 15, 1993.

72. Stephen Rosenfeld, "Scramble over Roles and Missions," *Washington Post,* Oct. 14, 1994, p. A27.

73. The Defense Department provided full assistance to "Ike" and agreed to give limited help to *The Last Days of Patton,* although the filmmakers did not ultimately use it.

74. Although the film states that it is based on a true story, the Army's Center for Military History, which did provide some research assistance to the production, could find no record of any such event. Author conversation with William Bradford, who worked with the filmmakers.

75. Marilyn Beck and Stacy Smith, *Los Angeles Daily News,* June 1996.

76. *The General's Daughter* Press Kit.

77. Interview with Michael Schiffer, March 6, 2000; Schiffer later called the author to discuss the draft of the manuscript. His comments have been incorporated into the narrative. A copy of the text with Schiffer's comments is filed with his interview. Transcript of *Los Angeles Times* interview with Gary Shrout, June 22, 1994; Navy Memorandum, December 2, 1993.

78. Gary Shrout to Michael Schiffer, November 17, 1993.

79. Schiffer interview.

80. Ibid.

81. Ibid.

82. Comdr. Gary Shrout to Phil Strub via Chief of Navy Information, April 26, 1994.

83. Ibid.; Schiffer interview and comments. The writer said all submarine officers to whom he talked said they would launch under the circumstances.

84. Shrout to Strub, April 26, 1994; Schiffer comments.

85. Shrout to Strub, April 26, 1994.

86. Schiffer comments.

87. Ibid.

88. Ibid.

89. Shrout to Strub, April 26, 1994; Schiffer comments.

90. Shrout to Strub, April 26, 1994.

91. Ibid.

92. Kendell Pease to Phil Strub, July 5, 1994.

93. Ibid.; Phil Strub to the Walt Disney Company, July 8, 1994.

94. Schiffer comments.

95. Shrout to Navy Information and Phil Strub, April 26, 1994; Schiffer's comments; See discussion of public disagreements between officers in *Gray Lady Down.*

96. Schiffer interview; letter from Captain Malcolm Wright to author, April 1, 2000.

97. Schiffer interview.

98. Associated Press story in *The Virginia Pilot,* June 30, 1994, p. A8.

99. Wright to author.

100. Ibid.

101. Ibid.

102. Schiffer comments.

103. Norman Panama and Marvin Frank to William Parsons, January 15, 1952.

104. Memorandum from Maj. Gen. F.A. Gordon to director of the Army staff, Sept. 28, 1995; Hollywoodd@aol.com, *Courage under Fire* Web site.

105. Undated Fact Sheet, "Courage under Fire" [Oct. 1995]; "Points of Concern, "Courage under Fire, Apr. 7, 1994.

106. "Points of Concern, "Courage under Fire, Apr. 7, 1994.

107. Ibid.

108. Undated Fact Sheet, "Courage under Fire" [Oct. 1995].

109. Ibid.

110. Rory Aylward, interview by author, Mar. 29, 2000.

111. Fact Sheet, *Courage Under Fire,* n.d. [after Sept. 11, 1995].

112. Kathy Ross to Fort McPherson, Ga., Fort Monroe, Va., the Texas National Guard, and the Army Reserve Command, Atlanta, Ga., Sept. 15, 1995.

113. Judith Johnston to Army chief of public affairs, Sept. 21, 1995.

114. Al Lott to Strub and Army chief of public affairs, Oct. 5, 1995.

115. Ibid.; undated note to Army chief of public affairs [before Oct. 5, 1995].

116. F.A. Gordon to Strub, Oct. 11, 1995; Strub to Gordon, Oct. 19, 1995; Lott to Stratton Leopold, Oct. 26, 1995.

117. Kathleen Hughes, "What Do You Have to Do to Get a Deal on a Used Tank?" *Wall Street Journal,* May 21, 1996.

118. Ibid.

30. World War II: One More Time

1. Alfred Goldberg to Donald Baruch, Nov. 2, 1988.

2. Ibid.; the author also read the screenplay at the request of Don Baruch, because he had worked with Gen. K.D. Nichols, the Manhattan Project district engineer, on his autobiography and so had done considerable research on the subject. He advised Baruch of the errors in the script, in particular, the focus on the dangers of radiation, which Wyden claimed had been ignored during the building of the bomb and the decision to use it against Japan. This was simply untrue.

3. David Rintels to Baruch, Nov. 10, 1988.

4. Ibid.

5. Aaron Spelling to Baruch, Nov. 15, 1988.

6. Goldberg to Baruch, Nov. 22, 1988.

7. Ibid.

8. Larry Rohter, "The Road to Critical Mass," *New York Times,* Oct. 15, 1989, p. 15.

9. Ibid.

10. Ibid.

11. Ibid., p. 19.

12. Ibid.; Richard Bernstein, "Can Movies Teach History?" *New York Times,* Nov. 26, 1989, sec. 2, p. 18; Dr. Hymer Friedell, interview by author, Oct. 23, 1983; one of the senior doctors in the Manhattan Project, Friedell's specialty was radiation.

13. Bernstein, "Can Movies Teach History?" p. 18.

14. Ibid.

15. Lawrence Suid, "History by Television, Believe It or Not," *Washington Post,* June 27, 1982; Lawrence Suid, "Oppenheimer and Television History," *Air University Review,* Nov.–Dec. 1982; author's work with Gen. K.D. Nichols on *Road to Trinity.*

16. Benedict Nightingale, *New York Times,* Dec. 31, 1989.

17. Catherine Wyler to Chuck Davis, Oct. 4, 1988.

18. Charles Davis to M. Sgt. Kris Baker, Oct. 13, 1988.

19. Air Force memo for the record, Dec. 1, 1988.

20. Davis to Wyler, Dec. 2, 1988.

21. Pete Wilson to James McGovern, acting secretary of the Air Force, Feb. 1, 1989; Air Force to Pete Wilson, Mar. 22, 1989; undated drafts of letter to Pete Wilson.

22. Wyler to Davis, Feb. 16, 1989.

23. Davis to M. Sgt. Mary Stowe, Mar. 21, 1989.

24. Air Force public affairs memorandum for the record, Mar. 23, 1989.

25. Ibid., Col. Robert Morgan, the pilot of the *Memphis Belle* on its twenty-five missions, concurred with Freeman's criticisms. Morgan interview.

26. Air Force public affairs "Working Papers," Apr. 10, 1989; Phil Strub to Air Force Public Affairs Office, Apr. 26, 1989; Col. Arthur Dederick III, chief, Programs Division, Air Force Public Affairs, to Wyler, May 19, 1989.

27. Morgan interview. Colonel Morgan acknowledged that he had praised the completed film in *People* magazine on Oct. 29, 1990, only because he was standing between the director and the producers.

28. CNN, "Steven Spielberg," May 25, 2000.

29. *Today Show,* Matt Lauer interview with Steven Spielberg, July 23, 1998. The interview was broadcast over two days. Spielberg continued to justify his use of violence as the only way to capture the experience of men in combat.

30. Judith Brennan, "Rating the Big One," "Calendar," *Los Angeles Times,* July 15, 1998, pp. F1, F5.

31. *Today Show;* Brennan, "Rating the Big One," p. F5.

32. During the research for this volume, the author compiled a list of more than 700 American movies that portrayed the U.S. armed services in some manner in peace and in war. Of these, more than 200 films contained scenes of combat during World War II. There were at least another 30 comedy and musical films set during the war years. The Internet Movie Database listed 8 movies that contain even a minimal portrayal of combat in and around Normandy. Of these, only 4 show fighting on Normandy or Omaha beaches on D-Day.

33. David Horton, "Old WWII Films Were No 'Slap in the Face,'" *Los Angeles Times,* July 27, 1998; Andy Rooney, *My War* (New York: Public Affairs, 1995, 2000).

34. Zinnemann interview, March 5, 1974.

35. *CBS Evening News,* Oct. 19, 2001.

36. *"Saving Private Ryan"* comments, Feb. 24, 1997.

37. Ibid.

38. Max Evans, interview by author, Apr. 17, 2000. Dale Dye did research and found a few photos from the Normandy period that showed officers with their insignias on their helmets, although he found that most quickly scraped them off or covered them with mud. However, he bowed to the costume designers, who desperately wanted to be sure we could spot Miller in crowds (undated E-mail from Dale Dye to author in Dale Dye file, Georgetown); Noel Dube, interview by author, Oct. 31, 2000; Tracy Sugarman, *My War* (New York: Random House, 2000), p. 83.

39. Stephen Ambrose, *"The Longest Day* (1962) 'Blockbuster' History," *Historical Journal of Film, Radio and Television,* no. 4, 1994; Dube interview.

40. Neither Spielberg nor his office would answer questions about the flashback or the problems with the timing of notification of next of kin. According to Dale Dye, "It was a film short-cut we had to take" (Dye E-mail).

41. *"Saving Private Ryan"* comments, Feb. 24, 1997.

42. Sugarman, *"The Longest Day,"* p. 74. Sugarman was a Navy officer aboard a landing craft on D-Day and states that the vomiting resulted from sea sickness.

43. Evans interview.

44. Spielberg even has the planes wrong. The P-47 Thunderbolt, not the P-51 Mustang, was known as the "tank buster," as portrayed in *Fighter Squadron.* The director could have avoided the error, of course, by simply leaving out the description of the planes.

45. "Intelligence Report," *Parade,* July 13, 1999; Gen. Colin Powell to author, Apr. 13, 2000.

46. Conversation with Charles Champlin, then retired arts editor of *Los Angeles Times,* Mar. 2000.

47. Andrew Marton, interview by Joanne D'Antonio, in *Andrew Marton* (Metuchen, N.J.: Scarecrow Press, 1991), pp. 426–28.

48. James Jones, preface to *A Thin Red Line* (New York: Scribner's, 1962); Pablo Espinoza, interview by author, Mar. 27, 2000.

49. Edward Teets, senior vice president of physical production, to Strub, Oct. 29, 1996.

50. Walter Roberdeau to Strub, Jan. 30, 1997.

51. Al Lott to Strub, Mar. 4, 1997; Al Lott, interview by author, November 19, 1999.

52. Ibid.

53. Jonathan Mostow, interview by author, Apr. 14, 2000, with subsequent revisions and additions.

54. The actual U-571 sank in the North Atlantic on Jan. 28, 1944, during its eleventh tour, after fighting on the surface with an Australian Sunderland aircraft on a long-range search mission. The submarine had no connection with any of the British seizures of German decoders. Comment to author after a preview screening of the film, Apr. 13, 2000; poll on History Channel Web site, May 16, 2000.

55. *(London) Daily Telegram,* May 13, 1999.

56. Ibid.; Jonathan Mostow to Paul Truswell, M.P., Nov. 18, 1999; ABC *Evening News,* June 8, 2000; Balme's Los Angeles interview appears on the DVD version of *U-571.*

57. Truswell to Universal Pictures, n.d. [Oct.–Nov.], 1999; Mostow to Truswell, Nov. 18, 1999.

58. Mostow letter.

59. Ibid.

60. Mostow interview.

61. Ibid.

62. Capt. Hans-Joachim Krug, "Filming *Das Boot*," *Naval Proceedings*, June 1996; author conversation with Captain Krug, May 1997.

63. Capt. Hans-Joachim Krug to author, May 30, 2000.

64. Ibid.

65. Ibid.

66. Mostow interview; Mostow to author, May 23, 2000.

67. Ibid.

68. Ibid.

31. Pearl Harbor: Bombed Again

1. Capt. Matt Morgan, interview by author, March 1, 2000.

2. Ibid.

3. Ibid.; Phil Strub to Marine Corps Director of Public Affairs, June 15, 1999.

4. Morgan interview; Matt Morgan, e-mail to author, January 2002.

5. *Men of Honor* press kit.

6. Tim Ryan, "Helmer Bay's Epic to Rock Pearl Harbor," *Daily Variety*, September 7, 1999, p. 1. Unless otherwise indicated, all documents and printed sources cited are in *Pearl Harbor* files, Georgetown Library Special Collections.

7. Jerry Bruckheimer, interview by author, Feb. 26, 2001. All Bruckheimer citations which follow are to this interview; Mike Gordon, "*Pearl Harbor* movie filming begins," for Reuters wire service, April 2, 2000; Jack Green, informal conversation with author, December 20, 2001. Green attended the ceremony and press conference. Author's notes of informal conversations with Jack Green, as well as e-mail answer to author's questions in Jack Green's interview file, in the Suid Collection at Georgetown University

8. John Chadwell, "Randall Wallace: The Man Behind *Pearl Harbor*," Cinemenium website, n.d. [July 2000], cited hereafter as Chadwell; Michael Bay, interview by author, Feb. 28, 2001.

9. Bay interview.

10. Ibid.; Bruckheimer interview.

11. Bruce Hendricks to Phil Strub, June 18, 1999.

12. Jim Van Wyck to Philip Strub, Oct. 7, 1999.

13. Melissa Schuermann to Navy Public Affairs officers, with copy to Phil Strub, Oct. 13, 1999.

14. Kathy Ross to Phil Strub, Oct. 26, 1999.

15. Director, Navy Office of Information, L.A., to Navy Chief of Information Rear Adm. Thomas J. Jurkowsky, "Script Summary," Dec. 7, 1999.

16. DoD notes on "Pearl Harbor," Dec. 20, 1999, version of script

17. Phil Strub to Jerry Bruckheimer, Jan. 10, 2000.

18. Memorandum for the secretary of defense, prepared by Phil Strub for James Desler, Jan. 12, 2000.

19. Capt. Kevin Wensing to Navy Pubic Affairs officers and Phil Strub, Jan. 19, 2000.

20. Bruce Hendricks to William Cohen, Jan. 24, 2000.

21. Jerry Bruckheimer to William Cohen, Jan. 31, 2000; William Cohen to Jerry Bruckheimer, Feb. 9, 2000.

22. The author recognizes that "no record" is an absolute statement and understands the risk of making such a claim. Nevertheless, he has been researching the Hollywood relationship with the armed services for twenty-nine years as this book goes to press and has found no documents to counter the statement. He has further checked with Norm Hatch, who was Don Baruch's supervisor for more than thirty years, and he can recall no meeting of filmmakers with a secretary of defense. Francis Coppola did meet with the assistant secretary of defense for public affairs in May 1975, but only corresponded with the secretary of defense. Stanley Kramer did meet with the secretary of the Navy during his efforts to obtain cooperation for *The Caine Mutiny*, but not even Arthur Sylvester met with filmmakers during his efforts to rewrite DoD regulations on cooperation, and there is no evidence that he talked directly with Secretary of Defense McNamara about the change in policy on assisting filmmakers.

23. Office, Chief of Public Affairs, Dept. of the Army to Phil Strub, Feb. 2, 2000; Chief of Information Thomas Jurkowsky to Phil Strub Feb. 3, 2000; Air Force Public Affairs to Phil Strub, Feb. 7, 2000.

24. Phil Strub to Jerry Bruckheimer, Feb. 15, 2000; Phil Strub to Jerry Bruckheimer, Feb. 17, 2000.

25. DoD notes on "Pearl Harbor," Jan. 25, 2000, version of the script.

26. Air Force Comments, "Pearl Harbor," March 3, 2000, version.

27. Bay interview.

28. Ibid.

29. *The Making of* Braveheart, The History Channel; Chadwell interview.

30. C.V. Glines to Lt. Melissa Schuermann, May 18, 2001; Mark Lisheron, *American-Statesman*, Austin, Texas, Dec. 7, 2000; the author corresponded regularly by e-mail correspondence with Col. Glines, March to June 2001,

about the problems with the portrayal of General Doolittle and the raid, correspondence in C.V. Glines interview file, Georgetown Library, cited hereafter as Glines correspondence.

31. Glines to Hendricks, June 6, 2000.

32. Glines to author, Dec. 26, 2001 in Glines correspondence.

33. Glines to Hendricks, June 6, 2000.

34. John Chadwell, interview with Jack Green, on Pearl Harbor Film Internet site, n.d., May 2000; conversations with author.

35. Hendricks letter to William Cohen of Jan. 24, 2000; author interviews with Michael Bay and Jerry Bruckheimer.

36. Draft of letter from Secretary of Defense to Commander-in-Chief Pacific Fleet, Feb. 7, 2000; Cohen to Bruckheimer, Feb. 9, 2000.

37. Phil Strub to Adm. Thomas Fargo, Feb. 15, 2000.

38. "DoD Goes to Hollywood," *Inside the Pentagon,* March 2, 2000, p.25.

39. Ibid.; William Cohen to author, May 17, 2001; author's informal interviews with Jack Green.

40. Green interviews.

41. Green interviews.

42. Ibid.

43. Ibid.

44. "Pearl Harbor" script, *Pearl Harbor* file, DoD file, Georgetown Library.

45. Glines correspondence; Bay interview.

46. Glines correspondence.

47. The author ultimately compiled six pages of mistakes and implausibilities in the film. He is also indebted to those people who offered him additional flaws.

48. Conversations with Jack Green.

49. Jon Voight, who played Roosevelt, claimed he had seen a documentary in which a butler testified to having seen Roosevelt receive news of Pearl Harbor, and so the actor said he knew "what [FDR's] response was in words and emotion." If so, and if the actor was committed to portraying Roosevelt accurately, one can only ask why the scene was set in a hall rather than the study. Sound bite from press kit videotape, Suid *Pearl Harbor* file.

50. Ibid.

51. Glines correspondence.

52. Glines correspondence; Green correspondence.

53. Colonel Glines, in a brief interview in the press kit tape, told the story of Doolittle's receiving the Medal of Honor from President Roosevelt. So the filmmakers knew the truth and again ignored it.

54. CNN on the Internet, May 25, 2001.

55. Ibid.

56. A.O. Scott, "War Is Hell, but Very Pretty," *The New York Times,* May 25, 2001, "Weekend," p. 1.

57. Lt. Col. Bruce Gillman, e-mail to author, n.d. [June], 2001.

Epilogue

1. Andy Seiler, "Hollywood Now Facing a Different Kind of War," *USA Today,* October 10, 2001.

2. Secretary of Defense Memorandum, "Public Affairs Guidance for DOD Assistance to Motion Picture *Blackhawk Down,*" April 1, 2001; Thomas Matthews, interview by author, February 19, 2002.

3. Harold Moore and Joseph Galloway, *We Were Soldiers Once . . . and Young* (New York: Random House, 1992), p. 399.

Index

Note: Numbers in bold indicate photographs.

Index

Index

Index

Index